TREATMENTS OF PSYCHIATRIC DISORDERS

VOLUME 1

American Psychiatric Association Task Force on Treatments of Psychiatric Disorders

Chairperson

Toksoz Byram Karasu, M.D.

Executive Committee Members

Robert Cancro, M.D.
Fred H. Frankel, M.D.
Gerald L. Klerman, M.D.
John C. Nemiah, M.D.
Martin T. Orne, M.D.

Assembly Representatives

Erwin Smarr, M.D.
Abram Hostetter, M.D.

Joint Board/Assembly Ad Hoc Committee to Review the Report of the Task Force on Treatments of Psychiatric Disorders

Paul J. Fink, M.D.
Edward Hanin, M.D.
Thelissa Harris, M.D.
Lawrence Hartmann, M.D.
G. Thomas Pfaehler, M.D.

APA Staff

Harold Alan Pincus, M.D.
Sandy Ferris

TREATMENTS OF
PSYCHIATRIC DISORDERS

A Task Force Report of the
American Psychiatric Association

VOLUME 1

Published by the
American Psychiatric Association
1400 K Street, N.W.
Washington, DC 20005
1989

The findings, opinions, and conclusions of this report do not necessarily represent the views of the officers, trustees, or all members of the Association. Each report, however, does represent the thoughtful judgment and findings of the task force of experts who composed it. These reports are considered a substantive contribution to the ongoing analysis and evaluation of problems, programs, issues, and practices in a given area of concern.

First Edition

The paper used in this publication meets the minimum requirements of the American National Standard for Information Sciences—Permanence of Paper for Printed Library Materials ANSI Z39.48-1984.   ∞

Correspondence regarding copyright permissions should be directed to the Division of Publications and Marketing, American Psychiatric Association, 1400 K Street, N.W., Washington, DC 20005.

The correct citation for this book is:

American Psychiatric Association: Treatments of Psychiatric Disorders: A Task Force Report of the American Psychiatric Association. Washington, DC, American Psychiatric Association, 1989.

Library of Congress Cataloging-in-Publication Data
Treatments of psychiatric disorders.

   "American Psychiatric Association Task Force on Treatments of Psychiatric Disorders" —P. facing t.p.
   Includes bibliographies and indexes.
   1. Psychiatry. 1. American Psychiatric Association. Task Force on Treatments of Psychiatric Disorders. [DNLM: 1. Mental Disorders—therapy. WM 400 T7866]
RC454.T69   1989   616.89'1   89-248
ISBN 0-89042-201-X (set : alk. paper)

ISBN 0-89042-202-8   VOLUME 1
ISBN 0-89042-203-6   VOLUME 2
ISBN 0-89042-204-4   VOLUME 3
ISBN 0-89042-205-2   INDEXES

Contents

VOLUME 1

Section 1
Mental Retardation
C. Thomas Gualtieri, M.D., *Chairperson*

Pharmacotherapy

Psychological, Educational, Vocational, and Residential Services

Pervasive Developmental Disorders

Magda Campbell, M.D., *Co-Chairperson*
Eric Schopler, Ph.D., *Co-Chairperson*

SECTION 3

Specific Developmental Disorders

Theodore Shapiro, M.D., *Chairperson*

Introduction

Clinical Description

Evaluation and Intervention

SECTION 4
Attention-Deficit Hyperactivity Disorder and Conduct Disorder
Maureen Donnelly, M.D., *Chairperson*

SECTION 5
Anxiety Disorders of Childhood or Adolescence
John F. McDermott, Jr., M.D., *Chairperson*

SECTION 6
Eating Disorders
Katherine A. Halmi, M.D., *Chairperson*

Treatment of Anorexia Nervosa

SECTION 7
Paraphilias and Gender Identity Disorders
James L. Mathis, M.D., *Chairperson*

Section 8
Tic Disorders
Donald J. Cohen, M.D., *Co-Chairperson*
James F. Leckman, M.D., *Co-Chairperson*
Kenneth E. Towbin, M.D., *Co-Chairperson*

Section 9
Elimination Disorders
Mark A. Riddle, M.D., *Chairperson*

Section 10
Other Disorders of Infancy, Childhood, or Adolescence
Joseph M. Green, M.D., *Chairperson*

VOLUME 2

SECTION 11
Organic Mental Syndromes
Lissy F. Jarvik, M.D., Ph.D., *Chairperson*

SECTION 12
Psychoactive Substance Use Disorders (Alcohol)
Marc Galanter, M.D., *Chairperson*

Treatment of Alcoholism

Special Treatment Contexts

SECTION 14
Schizophrenia

Robert Cancro, M.D., *Chairperson*

SECTION 15

Delusional (Paranoid) Disorders

Sir Martin Roth, M.D., F.R.C.P., F.R.C.Psych., *Chairperson*

SECTION 16

Psychotic Disorders Not Elsewhere Classified

Allen J. Frances, M.D., *Chairperson*

VOLUME 3

SECTION 17

Mood Disorders

Gerald L. Klerman, M.D., *Chairperson*

SECTION 18
Anxiety Disorders
Martin T. Orne, M.D., Ph.D., *Co-Chairperson*
Fred H. Frankel, M.B.Ch.B., D.P.M., *Co-Chairperson*

SECTION 25

Adjustment Disorder

Joseph D. Noshpitz, M.D., *Co-Chairperson*
R. Dean Coddington, M.D., *Co-Chairperson*

SECTION 26
Personality Disorders
John G. Gunderson, M.D., *Chairperson*

Treatment Modalities

Treatment of Specific Disorders

INDEXES

List of Consultants

C. Alex Adsett, M.D.
W. Stewart Agras, M.D.
C. Knight Aldrich, M.D.
Arnold Allen, M.D.
Kenneth Z. Altshuler, M.D.
Wayne R. Anable, D.O.
Nancy C. Andreasen, M.D., Ph.D.
Paul A. Andrulonis, M.D.
Laurie Appelbaum, M.D.
Gary K. Arthur, M.D.
Stuart S. Asch, M.D.
Boris M. Astrachan, M.D.

Hrair M. Babikian, M.D.
Thomas H. Babor, Ph.D.
William E. Bakewell, Jr., M.D.
Cornelis B. Bakker, M.D.
Ross J. Baldessarini, M.D.
Gail M. Barton, M.D.
B. Lynn Beattie, M.D., F.R.C.P. (C)
Aaron T. Beck, M.D.
Alan S. Bellack, Ph.D.
Jules Bemporad, M.D.
Elissa P. Benedek, M.D.
R. Scott Benson, M.D.
Norman B. Bernstein, M.D.
Norman R. Bernstein, M.D.
Shashi K. Bhatia, M.D.
Subash C. Bhatia, M.D.
Raman Bhavsar, M.D.
Kay H. Blacker, M.D.
Barry Blackwell, M.D.
Barton J. Blinder, M.D., Ph.D.
Irvin Blose, M.D.
Daniel B. Borenstein, M.D.
Jonathan F. Borus, M.D.
Peter G. Bourne, M.D.
Malcolm B. Bowers, Jr., M.D.
David L. Braff, M.D.
Reed Brockbank, M.D.

Kirk Brower, M.D.
William E. Bunney, Jr., M.D.
Ann W. Burgess, R.N., D.N.Sc.
Ewald W. Busse, M.D.

Dennis P. Cantwell, M.D.
Bernard J. Carroll, M.D., Ph.D.
Stanley Cath, M.D.
Richard D. Chessick, M.D., Ph.D., P.C.
Eve S. Chevron, M.S.
James Claghorn, M.D.
Norman A. Clemens, M.D.
C. Robert Cloninger, M.D.
Raquel E. Cohen, M.D.
Calvin A. Colarusso, M.D.
Bernice E. Coleman, M.D.
Gregory B. Collins, M.D.
Liane Colsky, M.D.
Shirley M. Colthart, M.D.
Arnold M. Cooper, M.D.
Rex W. Cowdry, M.D.
Thomas J. Craig, M.D., M.P.H.
Miles K. Crowder, M.D.
Thomas J. Crowley, M.D.
Homer Curtis, M.D.
Thomas E. Curtis, M.D.

Amin N. Daghestani, M.D.
I. Deborah Dauphinais, M.D.
John M. Davis, M.D.
Jorge G. De La Torre, M.D.
Marian K. DeMyer, Ph.D.
Martha B. Denckla, M.D.
Bharati Desai, M.D.
Daniel A. Deutschman, M.D.
Robert De Vito, M.D.
William G. Dewhurst, M.D.
Leon Diamond, M.D.
Alberto Di Mascio, Ph.D.
David F. Dinges, Ph.D.

C. Wesley Dingman II, M.D.
Susan R. Donaldson, M.D.
John Donnelly, M.D.
Mina K. Dulcan, M.D.
David L. Dunner, M.D.
Jack Durell, M.D.
Maurice Dysken, M.D.

Felton Earls, M.D.
Marshall Edelson, M.D., Ph.D.
Irene Elkin, Ph.D.
Donald E. Engstrom, M.D.
Nathan B. Epstein, M.D.
Jack R. Ewalt, M.D.

Louis F. Fabre, Jr., M.D.
Peter J. Fagan, Ph.D.
Howard Farkas, B.A.
Beverly J. Fauman, M.D.
Ronald R. Fieve, M.D.
Stuart M. Finch, M.D.
Max Fink, M.D.
Paul J. Fink, M.D.
Joseph A. Flaherty, M.D.
Stephen Fleck, M.D.
Don E. Flinn, Jr., M.D.
Marc A. Forman, M.D.
Richard J. Frances, M.D.
Robert O. Friedel, M.D.

Warren J. Gadpaille, M.D.
Pierre N. Gagne, M.D.
Robert S. Garber, M.D.
Max Gardner, M.D.
Russell Gardner, Jr., M.D.
Joseph Gaspari, M.D.
Francine L. Gelfand, M.D.
Robert W. Gibson, M.D.
Stanley Gitlow, M.D.
Rachel Gittelman, Ph.D.
Alexander H. Glassman, M.D.
Ira D. Glick, M.D.
Richard L. Goldberg, M.D.
Charles Goldfarb, M.D.
Stuart J. Goldman, M.D.

Gerald Goldstein, M.D.
Michael J. Goldstein, Ph.D.
Donald Goodwin, M.D.
Tracy Gordy, M.D.
Fred Gottlieb, M.D.
Marvin E. Gottlieb, M.D.
Louis A. Gottschalk, M.D., Ph.D.
Paul Graffagnino, M.D.
Harry Grantham, M.D.
Wayne H. Green, M.D.
Harvey R. Greenberg, M.D.
Lester Grinspoon, M.D.
William N. Grosch, M.D.
Mortimer D. Gross, M.D., S.C.

Seymour Halleck, M.D.
Abraham L. Halpern, M.D.
James A. Hamilton, M.D.
Edward Hanin, M.D.
Richard K. Harding, M.D.
Saul I. Harrison, M.D.
Lawrence Hartmann, M.D.
Irwin N. Hassenfeld, M.D.
Leston Havens, M.D.
David R. Hawkins, M.D.
Robert G. Heath, M.D.
John E. Helzer, M.D.
Hugh C. Hendrie, M.B.Ch.B.
Marvin I. Herz, M.D.
David B. Herzog, M.D.
A. Lewis Hill, M.D.
Douglas P. Hobson, M.D.
James Hodge, M.D.
Charles J. Hodulik, M.D.
Charles C. Hogan, M.D., P.C.
Jimmie C.B. Holland, M.D.
Steven D. Hollon, Ph.D.
Harry C. Holloway, M.L.
Daniel W. Hommer, M.D.
Jeffrey L. Houpt, M.D.

David Israelstam, M.D., Ph.D.

Marc Jacobs, M.D.
Kay R. Jamison, Ph.D.

Michael S. Jellinek, M.D.
Keith H. Johansen, M.D.
Mary Ann Johnson, M.D.
Merlin H. Johnson, M.D.
Charles R. Joy, M.D.
Lewis L. Judd, M.D.
Nalini V. Juthani, M.D.

Nicholas Kanas, M.D.
Sylvia R. Karasu, M.D.
Jack L. Katz, M.D.
Edward Kaufman, M.D.
Jerald Kay, M.D.
David Kaye, M.D.
Alan E. Kazdin, Ph.D.
John F. Kelley, M.D.
Philippe J. Khouri, M.D.
Elizabeth Khuri, M.D.
Chase P. Kimball, M.D.
Donald F. Klein, M.D.
Arthur H. Kleinman, M.D.
Lawrence Y. Kline, M.D.
William Klykylo, M.D.
Peter T. Knoepfler, M.D.
Michael F. Koch, M.D.
Jonathan E. Kolb, M.D.
Lawrence C. Kolb, M.D.
Donald S. Kornfeld, M.D.
Douglas A. Kramer, M.D.
Peter D. Kramer, M.D.
Robert F. Kraus, M.D.
Daniel Kripke, M.D.
Markus Kruesi, M.D.
John W. Kuldau, M.D.

Yves Lamontagne, M.D., F.R.C.P.(C)
Ronald Langevin, Ph.D.
Donald G. Langsley, M.D.
Camille Laurin, M.D.
Ruth L. La Vietes, M.D.
Robert L. Leon, M.D.
Denis Lepage, M.D.
Joseph B. Leroy, M.D.
Stanley Lesse, M.D.
H.J. Leuchter, M.D.

Stephen B. Levine, M.D.
Peritz H. Levinson, M.D.
David J. Lewis, M.D., F.R.C.P.(C)
Robert Paul Liberman, M.D.
Paul Lieberman, M.D.
Rudolf W. Link, M.D.
Margaret W. Linn, Ph.D.
John R. Lion, M.D.
Marvin H. Lipkowitz, M.D.
Zbigniew J. Lipowski, M.D.
Melvin M. Lipsett, M.D.
James W. Lomax, M.D.
Catherine E. Lord, Ph.D.
Maria Lorenz, M.D.
Earl L. Loschen, M.D.
Reginald S. Lourie, M.D.
Eugene L. Lowenkopf, M.D.
Joseph F. Lupo, M.D.

K. Roy MacKenzie, M.D.
John A. MacLeod, M.D.
Leslie F. Major, M.D.
Michael J. Maloney, M.D.
David B. Marcotte, M.D.
John Markowitz, M.D.
Judd Marmor, M.D.
Ronald L. Martin, M.D.
Jules H. Masserman, M.D.
Thomas A. Mathews, M.D.
Kenneth L. Matthews, M.D.
Teresita McCarty, M.D.
Layton McCurdy, M.D.
John J. McGrath, M.D.
F. Patrick McKegney, Jr., M.D.
George N. McNeil, M.D.
Beverly T. Mead, M.D.
Herbert Y. Meltzer, M.D.
James R. Merikangas, M.D.
Harold Merskey, D.M.
Heino F. L. Meyer-Bahlburg, Dr.rer.nat.
Robert Michels, M.D.
Larry Michelson, Ph.D.
Ira Mintz, M.D.
Steven M. Mirin, M.D.
Arnold H. Modell, M.D.

Gordon L. Moore II, M.D.
Robert A. Moore, M.D.
Loren R. Mosher, M.D.
David A. Mrazek, M.D., M.R.C.Psych.
Frances J. Mulvihill, M.D.
Cecil Mushatt, M.D.

Carol C. Nadelson, M.D.
Theodore Nadelson, M.D.
Donald F. Naftulin, M.D.
Carlos Neu, M.D.
Theodore W. Neumann, Jr., M.D.
Robert G. Niven, M.D.
Grayson Norquist, M.D.
John I. Nurenberger, Jr., M.D.

Charles P. O'Brien, M.D., Ph.D.
William C. Offenkrantz, M.D.
Donald Oken, M.D.
Harold S. Orchow, M.D.
Emily Carota Orne, B.A.
Morris G. Oscherwitz, M.D.
Helen J. Ossofsky, M.D.

Lee C. Park, M.D.
Dean X. Parmalee, M.D., F.A.A.C.P.
Robert J. Pary, M.D.
Robert O. Pasnau, M.D.
William Patterson, M.D.
Chester A. Pearlman, Jr., M.D.
William S. Pearson, M.D.
Roger Peele, M.D.
William E. Pelham, Jr., Ph.D.
Irwin N. Perr, M.D.
Helen M. Pettinati, Ph.D.
Betty Pfefferbaum, M.D.
Irving Philips, M.D.
Edward Pinney, M.D.
William Pollin, M.D.
Harrison C. Pope, Jr., M.D.
Robert M. Post, M.D.
Harry Prosen, M.D.
Brigette Prusoff, Ph.D.
Joaquim Puig-Antich, M.D.
H. Paul Putman II, M.D.

Robert Racusin, M.D.
Judith L. Rapoport, M.D.
Allen Raskin, Ph.D.
Robert J. Reichler, M.D.
William H. Reid, M.D., M.P.H.
Karl Rickels, M.D.
Arthur Rifkin, M.D.
Louis Rittelmeyer, M.D.
Lee N. Robins, M.D.
Nicholas L. Rock, M.D.
Paul Rodenhauser, M.D.
Rita R. Rogers, M.D.
John Romano, M.D.
Howard P. Rome, M.D.
Patricia Rosebush, M.D.
Maj-Britt Rosenbaum, M.D.
Milton Rosenbaum, M.D.
Loren H. Roth, M.D.
Bruce Rounsaville, M.D.
Donald K. Routh, Ph.D.
Lester Rudy, M.D.

Benjamin Sadock, M.D.
Virginia Sadock, M.D.
Clifford J. Sager, M.D.
Watt T. Salmon, M.D.
Carl Salzman, M.D.
Alberto Santos, M.D.
Burhan Say, M.D.
Nina R. Schooler, Ph.D.
John Schowalter, M.D.
John J. Schwab, M.D.
Harvey J. Schwartz, M.D.
James H. Scully, M.D.
Peter M. Semkiw, M.D.
Mohammad Shaffii, M.D.
Charles Shagass, M.D.
Brian Shaw, M.D.
Kailie R. Shaw, M.D.
Michael H. Sheard, M.D.
David V. Sheehan, Ph.D.
Edwin Shneidman, Ph.D.
Miles Shore, M.D.
Michael Shostak, M.D.
Lorraine D. Siggins, M.D.

Peter M. Silberfarb, M.D.
Donald J. Silberman, M.D.
Archie A. Silver, M.D.
Joel J. Silverman, M.D.
Everett C. Simmons, M.D.
Bennett Simon, M.D.
George M. Simpson, M.D.
Margaret Singer, M.D.
Phillip R. Slavney, M.D.
William Sledge, M.D.
Gary W. Small, M.D.
Joyce G. Small, M.D.
Erwin R. Smarr, M.D.
Gail Solomon, M.D.
David Spiegel, M.D.
Robert L. Spitzer, M.D.
Daniel J. Sprehe, M.D.
Robert St. John, M.D.
Stephen M. Stahl, M.D., Ph.D.
Monica N. Starkman, M.D.
Dorothy A. Starr, M.D.
Roy Steinhouse, M.D.
Peter E. Stokes, M.D.
John S. Strauss, M.D.
Max Sugar, M.D.
David W. Swanson, M.D.

Zebulin C. Taintor, M.D.
John A. Talbott, M.D.
Allan Tasman, M.D.
Sam D. Taylor, M.D.
Lenore C. Terr, M.D.
Alexander Thomas, M.D.
Gary Tischler, M.D.
Arnold Tobin, M.D.
Garfield Tourney, M.D.
Darold A. Treffert, M.D.
Margaret Owen Tsaltas, M.D.
Gary J. Tucker, M.D.
William M. Tucker, M.D.
Ann R. Turkel, M.D.

Kathleen Bell Unger, M.D.
Yogendra Upadhyay, M.D.

George E. Vaillant, M.D.
Bessel Van der Kolk, M.D.
Christian D. Van der Velde, M.D.
Hugo Van Dooren, M.D.
Herman M. van Praag, M.D., Ph.D.
Ilza Veith, Ph.D., M.D.
Milton Viederman, M.D.

Thomas Wadden, Ph.D.
Raymond Waggoner, M.D.
Richard L. Weddige, M.D.
Walter Weintraub, M.D.
James M.A. Weiss, M.D.
Kenneth J. Weiss, M.D.
Sidney H. Weissman, M.D.
William D. Weitzel, M.D.
Elizabeth B. Weller, M.D.
Charles E. Wells, M.D.
Paul H. Wender, M.D.
Jack C. Westman, M.D.
Kerrin L. White, M.D.
Wayne Whitehouse, Ph.D.
Roy M. Whitman, M.D.
Jan N. Williams, M.D.
C. Philip Wilson, M.D.
G. Terence Wilson, Ph.D.
Ronald Wintrob, M.D.
Michael G. Wise, M.D.
Joseph Wolpe, M.D.
Edward A. Wolpert, M.D., Ph.D.
David R. Wood, M.D.
William M. Wood, M.D.
Sherwin M. Woods, M.D.
Henry H. Work, M.D.
Richard W. Worst, M.D.
Lyman C. Wynne, M.D., Ph.D.

Irvin D. Yalom, M.D.
Alayne Yates, M.D.

Robert G. Zadylak, M.D.
Leonard S. Zegans, M.D.
Norman Zinberg, M.D.
Charlotte M. Zitrin, M.D.
Joel P. Zrull, M.D.

Foreword

T. Byram Karasu and the hundreds of our colleagues who have contributed to this massive effort deserve our highest respect and admiration.

The sheer magnitude of the undertaking would have discouraged most, but the enormous complexity provided the challenge that Dr. Karasu and the APA Task Force on Treatments of Psychiatric Disorders needed to endure this seven-year process. The APA is particularly grateful to Dr. Karasu for his patience, thoughtfulness, and comprehensive intelligence about psychiatric therapies. The result is a work of unprecedented significance. Even though, in its present four volumes, it is by no means a definitive work, this report is a major contribution to the literature and a basis on which much more will be accomplished in the years to come.

Coming to fruition just at the end of my presidency of the American Psychiatric Association, the report advances two of my major interests and concerns. It is the first major attempt to clarify and specify the tools available to psychiatry. As such it will serve as the basis for our continuing effort to describe and define our profession within the world of medicine.

The eradication of stigma has been the theme of my presidency, and it is my hope that *Treatments of Psychiatric Disorders* can help us to demonstrate to the public the positive effective treatments in the psychiatric armamentarium. In its present form it serves to educate the profession, but I hope it will be refined and condensed into material for the general public so that there can be broader understanding of the effectiveness of psychiatric treatment.

Paul J. Fink, M.D.
President, American Psychiatric Association (1988–1989)

Introduction

Science provides only interim knowledge.

Psychiatric treatment, like the rest of medicine, is inherently a flexible and open system which will continuously be influenced by new knowledge. This report represents a description of clinically useful current approaches for the treatment of mental disorders with a balanced perspective. It is important to emphasize that a treatment plan inherently must be an open system. Thus, this report is a working document reflecting a combination of cumulative scientific knowledge and clinical judgment about the treatment of psychiatric patients.

Historical Background

This undertaking began with the establishment of a previous Commission on Psychiatric Therapies in 1977 by Jules Masserman, M.D., then the president of the American Psychiatric Association. The charge was to examine critically the somatic, dyadic, group/family, and social therapies in current use—and to recommend criteria for evaluating therapeutic approaches.

In its attempt to meet this difficult task, the Commission produced two publications, both published by the American Psychiatric Association. The first was a critical review of a large body of evaluation research, entitled *Psychotherapy Research: Methodological and Efficacy Issues* (American Psychiatric Association Commission on Psychiatric Therapies 1982). This work pointed to the complexity of the variables involved in defining both the nature of a psychotherapeutic treatment and its outcome. The second publication, *The Psychiatric Therapies* (American Psychiatric Association Commission on Psychiatric Therapies 1984), was a comprehensive compendium of the many psychosocial and somatic treatment modalities currently in use.

In continuation of the previous Commission, Daniel X. Freedman, M.D., then the president of the APA, established a Task Force on Treatment of Psychiatric Disorders in 1982 to produce a comprehensive document that would describe the state of the art for treatment of psychiatric disorders.

The Process of Development

Because of the multiplicity of psychiatric disorders and their related approaches, the Task Force designated Chairpersons for 26 Panels, each of whom would draw together a working group to review the treatment of a different disorder or group of disorders. Chairpersons and Panel members were chosen from among many well-qualified individuals on the basis of certain criteria: the publication of research or clinical reports concerned with the treatment of a specific category of mental illness; and nomination by peers based on acknowledged eminence in clinical practice, national reputation, past accomplishments, and broad perspective. In order to assist them in their task, each Panel was empowered to retain the specialized services of a wide variety of consultants and representatives of consultant organizations.

The consultants were selected so as to represent a breadth of disciplines and orientations, in appreciation of the diverse patient and treatment variables important in these fields. They encompass expertise in general psychiatry, child psychiatry, psychoanalysis, psychotherapy, pharmacotherapy, and biological and social psychiatry, as well as exposure to treatments in diverse settings. This method of selecting contributors and consultants, and the desire for integration and synthesis of divergent views, led to multiple responses and challenges. We believe this approach has had a salutary effect on the outcome of the report.

Panels were assigned psychiatric diagnostic groups for which they were to provide treatment considerations. They identified distinct categories within the given diagnostic groupings which deserved full narration and discussed the variation of treatment as applied to other categories. The Panels operated on the basis of the clinical model that assumes that, for an individual with specific characteristics who is suffering from a given disorder or combination of disorders, there are one or more preferred treatments and/or combinations as well as acceptable alternative and possibly adjunct treatments.

Once a draft was prepared by the contributors, that document marked the beginning of an elaborate review process, as follows: 1) it was sent to a number of consultants, chosen by the contributor(s) for comments; 2) Draft II was prepared by the contributor(s) on the basis of the consultants' suggestions; 3) the Task Force sent Draft II to five to ten consultants; 4) the comments and critiques of these individuals were sent to the original contributors(s) for preparation of Draft III; and 5) Draft III was then reviewed and finalized by the Task Force. This complex process of consultation and review produced sections that reflect the input and ideas of many experts. Although in some sections a single author, in others a group of authors, and in still others individual chapters are given credits depending upon the level of contribution, the completed product represents the original work of the primary author(s), views of the Chairperson and Consultants of each Panel, and the Members of the Task Force.

Format

As there was no precedent for us to use as a model, and also recognizing that the consideration of treatment for various disorders may require different approaches to their subjects, the Panels were given a relatively free rein as to the format, style, and length of their presentations.

The sections do not deal with the issues of diagnosis, but assume the reader's prior knowledge. Where there was a need for further elaboration of the *Diagnostic and Statistical Manual of Mental Disorders* in its utilization for treatment planning, these issues were discussed. The work progressed during the transitional stage from DSM-III to DSM-III-R. Whenever we were able, we tried to keep the pace.

Naturally, some topics were repeated to varying degrees in different chapters. This also helped to state some of the finer points between them. At times a clinical example was presented to clarify differential diagnostic issues.

In discussion of treatment of a condition from more than one perspective, an attempt was made to integrate multiple points of view within a single section. Wherever this was not feasible, multiple chapters are included from diverse perspectives. A clinician must be able to consider each clinical problem at several conceptual levels in designing the most appropriate treatment program. Often combined applications are included to describe complementary models that are in use. Wherever empirical data were available, they were cited. In newer fields there are detailed discussions of studies instead of conclusions, to allow a proper perspective on the data. Special references were added in the text for readers who may want to study the subject in greater depth.

Use of This Report

This report is a professional document designed to suggest useful treatments for psychiatric disorders as an aid for treatment planning. It is not intended to impose rigid methods. It aims to demonstrate the complexity of the treatment planning process and its application, the true nature of comprehensive diagnosis, and the depth and breadth of knowledge that is required to assess a patient's need for the provision of treatment.

Proper use of this document requires specialized training that provides both a body of knowledge and clinical skills. Furthermore, many specific factors will influence the treatment needs for a particular individual. The chapters in this report do not dictate an exclusive course of treatment or procedures to be followed and should not be construed as excluding other acceptable methods of practice. Therefore, it would be incorrect to assert that any single treatment in this book automatically fits any single patient. Sound use of this book requires a clinician's judgment based on knowledge of a patient and a valid background of training and practice in psychiatry. Ultimately, it is individual practitioners—based upon their clinical judgment, experience, and assessment of the scientific literature—who will determine the usefulness of various therapeutic approaches. Futhermore, the mental disorders discussed in this report do not encompass all of the conditions that a psychiatrist may legitimately treat.

Future Directions

It is also important to note that this report reflects current assessment from an evolving knowledge base. Psychiatry participates in the continual expansion of knowledge that is taking place in all areas of science and medicine. New psychotropic drugs and other somatic approaches are constantly being tested and evaluated. Similarly, new psychotherapeutic and psychosocial techniques are being developed and assessed. In addition, combinations of treatment which hold promise are being evaluated. The continual accrual of new information will need to be integrated into these formulations in an ongoing way.

An important implication of the attempt to systemize our knowledge is that as the Task Force proceeded with its work, both what is known as well as what needs to be known became more evident. In particular, there is a need for increasing refinement of significant variables toward a greater understanding of individual differences in response to different therapeutic approaches. Such refinement will depend upon ongoing research which must take into account specific interventions, specific disorders or patient subgroups of responders and nonresponders, specific dosages, specific durations, and specific combinations and sequences of the treatments—in short, the ultimate establishment of carefully delineated criteria for titrating the nature and timing of various therapies and their combinations to be utilized in a biopsycho-social approach to the treatment of psychiatric disorders (Karasu 1982).

Toksoz Byram Karasu, M.D.

References

American Psychiatric Association Commission on Psychiatric Therapies: Psychotherapy Research: Methodological and Efficacy Issues. Washington, DC, American Psychiatric Association, 1982

American Psychiatric Association Commission on Psychiatric Therapies: The Psychiatric Therapies. Volume 1 (Somatic Therapies) and Volume 2 (Psychosocial Therapies). Washington, DC, American Psychiatric Association, 1984

Karasu TB: Psychotherapy and pharmacotherapy: toward an integrative model. Am J Psychiatry 139:7, 1982

Acknowledgments

This work was accomplished with the generous help of many people. Both the size of this project as well as the spirit of cooperation by which it was undertaken are demonstrated by the large number of clinicians involved and cited as contributors and consultants. I am deeply indebted to all.

I would like to thank the Chairpersons of the Panels and all contributors who not only prepared scholarly documents, but also gracefully allowed their original works to be modified through the consultation process. I would also like to express my gratitude to the consultants for their productive criticism.

I am most thankful for the support of Daniel X. Freedman, M.D., founder President of the Task Force, and Paul J. Fink, M.D., who presided during the crucial stage of the project, as well as to Keith H. Brodie, M.D., George Tarjan, M.D., John A. Talbott, M.D., Carol C. Nadelson, M.D., Robert O. Pasnau, M.D., George H. Pollock, M.D., Herbert Pardes, M.D., who served as Presidents, and also Lawrence Hartmann, M.D., William R. Sorum, M.D., Harvey Bluestone, M.D., Fred Gottlieb, M.D., Roger Peele, M.D., Irvin M. Cohen, M.D., and John S. McIntyre, M.D., who served as Speakers of the Assembly during the lifetime of the Task Force.

My special thanks to Melvin Sabshin, M.D., Medical Director of the American Psychiatric Association, for his unfailing leadership and the wisdom which he provided with great generosity, and to Harold Alan Pincus, M.D., Director, Office of Research, who gave administrative direction to the project and who, jointly with Paul J. Fink, M.D., the chairman of the Joint Ad Hoc Review Committee, weathered the most complicated organizational issues and skillfully brought this project to a successful conclusion.

I want to express my gratitude to Sandy Ferris for her organizational ability; to Philomena Lee, who maintained the highly complicated correspondence with a large number of people and corrected final drafts with exemplary patience, good humor, and dedication; to Betty Meltzer for her elegant editorial assistance; and to Louise Notarangelo, Rita Segarra, and Shirley Kreitman, who assisted them with equal competence and generosity.

My sincere appreciation and gratitude to Ronald E. McMillen, General Manager of the American Psychiatric Press, Inc., Timothy R. Clancy, Editorial Director, and Richard E. Farkas, Production Manager, for their leadership, and to their dedicated staff, Christine Kalbacher, Project Coordinator, Karen E. Sardinas-Wyssling and Lindsay E. Edmunds, Principal Manuscript Editors; to Editorial Experts, Inc., specifically Mary Stoughton and the staff editors, Pat Caudill and the staff proofreaders, and June Morse and the staff indexers, and to Robert Elwood and Nancy Borza at Harper Graphics, Typesetter, and Tom Reed at R. R. Donnelley & Sons Company, Printer, whose expert labors have facilitated the transformation of the raw material into four carefully wrought and handsome volumes.

Toksoz Byram Karasu, M.D.

Cautionary Statement

This report does not represent the official policy of the American Psychiatric Association. It is an APA task force report, signifying that members of the APA have contributed to its development, but it has not been passed through those official channels required to make it an APA policy document.

THIS REPORT IS NOT INTENDED TO BE CONSTRUED AS OR TO SERVE AS A STANDARD FOR PSYCHIATRIC CARE.

SECTION 1

Mental Retardation

Chapter 1

Introduction

The roots of psychiatry are in the care of severely handicapped people: the chronically mentally ill and the mentally retarded. Until a generation ago, psychiatry continued to be the most significant profession in treatment and research in mental retardation. In the interval of the past generation, however, modern developments in psychiatry have been made in other areas of clinical concern, and the modern revolution in care for retarded people has been accomplished by advocates and professionals from a variety of different disciplines and points of view. The extraordinary new contributions of modern neuropsychiatry have only recently been directed to the care of retarded people. This rapprochement promises a new revolution in the care of our most severely handicapped citizens.

Just as psychiatrists are developing renewed interest in the care of the chronically mentally ill, they are developing new interest in the care of retarded people as well. They are discovering a vast population of retarded people whose need for modern neuropsychiatric treatment represents an important new frontier for the profession. They are finding success and gratification in tending to individuals whose psychological problems seemed to be, only a short time ago, remote and without much likelihood of change.

The field of mental retardation has grown up, in the past generation, largely apart from modern psychiatry. It has developed some extraordinary models for treatment and care, models that psychiatry would do well to study. Advocacy for the retarded has sprung from the richest of sources: the families of afflicted individuals. Deinstitutionalization and community care have been a success for most retarded citizens. Models for education, habilitation, and behavior management have been creative and effective, and continue to evolve in innovative directions.

Mental retardation represents a major area for applied neuroscience in the study of brain-behavior relationships, the etiopathogenesis of brain disorders, the structure of psychological sex differences, neuroimmunology, behavioral genetics, epileptology, and psychopharmacology. Neuropsychiatrists are concerned with severe brain-based disorders, which, in addition to mental retardation, include certain severe psychiatric disorders. The dementing conditions and the behavioral sequelae of epilepsy and of head injury are the proper concerns of modern neuropsychiatry. This new field utilizes treatment and evaluation technology from psychopharmacology, behavioral neurology, epileptology, behavioral psychology, and neuropsychology. It represents a new and promising synthesis in applied neuroscience.

This section of *Treatments of Psychiatric Disorders* is an introduction to the neuropsychiatric care of mentally retarded people. It is designed to complement current psychiatric nosology. Some important neurobehavioral syndromes known to occur in retarded people are not classified or even recognized by psychiatrists. On the other hand, many established psychiatric disorders may be hard to recognize in severely retarded individuals.

The primary focus is on specific neuropsychiatric treatment. However, since neither people nor brains function outside of a social context, the wider treatment world of the retarded person is given as much emphasis as are specific neuropsychiatric treatments. Economic, political, and professional elements that bear upon this world are given appropriate attention.

After a general introduction to issues of classification, prevalence, treatment, and psychopathology, this section is divided into subsections.

Subsection One describes the diagnosis and treatment of traditional psychiatric disorders in retarded people. Subsection Two describes the neurobehavioral syndromes associated with mental retardation (and largely unfamiliar to conventionally trained psychiatrists). This division can be defended on the grounds of clinical usage: although psychiatric disorders do occur in retarded people, a substantial number of the most severe problems that afflict this population are not classifiable within any current psychiatric framework. Subsection Three is concerned with the issue of pharmacotherapy in retarded people. The proper practice of this science must be modified considerably for retarded patients. Subsection Four addresses, albeit in the most general terms, psychoeducational treatments. Subsection Five considers certain factors that have a bearing on the mental health of retarded citizens.

Chapter 2

Psychopathology in the Mentally Retarded

Behavior problems and psychopathologic symptoms are much more likely to occur in a retarded person than in someone whose intelligence is normal. Research has affirmed that the full range of psychopathologic conditions is present in the population of retarded people (Jacobson 1982; Rutter et al. 1976). In fact, psychiatric disorders are four to six times more frequent in retarded people than in the general population (Jacobson 1982; Matson and Barret 1982; Rutter et al. 1976).

The frequency and severity of such conditions tend to increase in direct association with the severity of intellectual impairment, although traditional psychiatric diagnoses are much more difficult to apply to severely retarded individuals than to the mildly retarded. Indeed, traditional psychiatric concepts and terminology may well be irrelevant to the unique problems of severely retarded individuals.

In addition to the problems of frequency and severity, the prognosis for improvement or for medical control for retarded people with psychiatric disorders may be much lower. The behavior problems of retarded people tend to persist over many years; this is based on longitudinal studies by Reid (1980b) and by Koller et al. (1983). Prognosis for improvement may also be less favorable as the degree of mental handicap increases; thus the prognosis for psychiatric disorders in retarded people resembles that of autistic people and epileptics, for whom low IQ is also a poor prognosis indicator (Thurston et al. 1982).

There are three reasons why psychopathology is so prevalent and severe among the retarded and why they tend to be refractory to conventional treatments. The first reason is the neurological damage that initially caused the patient to be retarded. The diffuse cortical and subcortical injuries that impair cognition may naturally be expected to exercise diffuse effects on personality and coping style and specific effects on temporal, frontal, and limbic structures that subserve behavior and emotional response. Thus retarded people have behavior problems and psychopathology for the same reasons they may have seizures; there is a neuropathic substrate.

The second reason is no less important. The world of the retarded person relentlessly poses challenges and threats against an individual who is poorly equipped to respond and to cope. The occurrence of behavioral disorders in the retarded and their dim prognosis is, in large part, attributable to the life circumstances of the retarded person. The confusing, frightening nature of a world he or she cannot understand is often characterized by frustration in self-expression, loneliness of a mere day-to-day existence, and stigmas inflicted because of the handicap and the insensitivity of others. A substantial part of the behavior problems of retarded people may be explained by the burdens of having to live in a developmentally inappropriate environment or of having to conform to expectations that far exceed their comprehension and their limited capacities. Behavior problems may often be a consequence of boredom, frustration, and misery.

The third reason has to do with psychiatric care. For many retarded people, there is no such thing as psychiatric care. Few psychiatrists are trained to work with the retarded and fewer still choose to concentrate their careers in this field. Psychopharmacologic agents are most frequently prescribed to retarded patients by nonpsychiatrists, often in the most clumsy and inept fashion. Behavioral treatments may be ignored or applied in a perfunctory, dilatory fashion.

A psychotic or a depressed patient in an institution for retarded persons may never even be seen by a psychiatrist. It is not surprising that psychiatric disorders are rife in a group of people who seldom receive the benefit of medical attention or psychiatric care.

Although it is easy to exaggerate the frequency and the severity of psychiatric problems in this group of people, it is important to emphasize that not all retarded people have psychiatric problems and that the majority, even of the severely retarded, are reasonably content and well adjusted. The fact that their treatment prognosis may be less favorable, in the main, does not mean that all treatments are futile or that dramatic treatment effects are never to be seen. Nor does the fact that the world of the retarded may be hostile and destructive suggest that all of their behavioral difficulties are environmental in origin or that they will be alleviated by environmental change. The particular difficulties of retarded people are only in part attributable to environmental circumstance. The major element that gives rise to behavior disorders in severely retarded people is neuropathic. Behavior problems are the frequent and necessary consequence of the neuropathic changes that cause mental retardation, just as they are the frequent concomitant of brain injuries that occur later in life.

The proper understanding of behavior disorders in retarded people, and their proper treatment, requires an appreciation of the patient's environment and how it may elicit or sustain deviant behavior, as well as of pertinent neuropathic elements of the case. The former may be more amenable to study than the latter, although there is an extraordinary new interest in the relation between specific behavioral syndromes in retarded people and the etiologic and pathophysiologic matrix out of which they arise.

Psychopathology in the retarded is a difficult issue. Despite the enormity of the problem—more than a million Americans are both mentally ill and mentally retarded—there is very little research; we simply don't know very much about the problem. Everyone agrees that behavior and emotional problems are not uncommon in retarded people, and that they increase in frequency and severity with the degree of mental handicap. But no one seems to know exactly how frequent they are, or even how to define or measure them. Reliable and valid measures have not been developed or widely tested. Behavioral psychologists have contributed an exquisite technology for the objective description of behavior disorders, a technology that is advanced in periodicals like the *Journal of Applied Behavior Analysis* and the *Journal of Applied Research in Mental Retardation*. But it is a system that is too molecular for psychiatric nosology, concentrating as it does on individual target behaviors and abjuring any inference that clusters of such behaviors may represent a meaningful "disorder." Structured interviews and behavior checklists represent innovations in the study of behavior problems in the mentally retarded (e.g., Aman and Singh 1985; Kazdin et al. 1983). Such instruments are promising for nosologic research but they are essentially untested in the wide arena of clinical research.

The fact that many retarded people may not be able to report symptoms means that assessment must rely heavily on information provided by parents or health care technicians. Such informants are not, as a rule, trained in psychiatric observation or behavior analysis, and the information they impart may be unreliable. Behavior problems may be viewed quite differently by different members of an interdisciplinary team, depending on the nature of a professional's interaction with a retarded client or patient, education and professional orientation, inferences about the reason for a given behavior, and desire to see a certain type of intervention implemented. Psychiatrists who consult to such teams learn not only to try to understand the basis for a retarded patient's behavior, but also to understand the basis for the team's reports about the behavior, and the reasons why inconsistencies and disagreements arise among members of a team. To translate this kind of clinical intuition into a reliable research method is a formidable task.

In this area, developmental, behavioral, and ideological points of view tend to compete with the traditional medical-psychiatric approach (Reid 1980a). The competition is neither ardent nor is it heated, however, because there have been few attempts to introduce concepts of psychiatric diagnosis into the field. Nevertheless, there is now some consensus that recognized psychiatric categories are applicable, especially to patients who are mildly or moderately retarded, but less so to more severely handicapped individuals (Heaton-Ward 1977; Reid 1984). It is important to develop appropriate psychiatric diagnostic approaches to these patients because there are serious limitations to treatment approaches based exclusively on developmental, behavioral, or sociological perspectives, just as there are limitations to treatment approaches based exclusively on psychiatric concepts (Reid 1980a).

There are two major competing viewpoints: psychiatric and behavioral. The former holds that traditional psychopathologic categories are germane to the problems of the mentally retarded, and that such disorders are probably as prevalent, or more so, compared to the general population. Schizophrenia, affective illness, attention deficit disorder, and explosive disorder may be tricky to diagnose in a subverbal patient, but reliable and valid diagnosis is not impossible. Proponents identified with this view include Menolascino (1983b), Reid (1980a), Sovner and Hurley (1983b), and Matson and Barret (1982).

The competing view is represented by psychologists like Schroeder et al. (1981) and Baumeister and Rollings (1976), who adopted the behavioral perspective and maintain that psychiatric taxonomies are irrelevant to problems like self-injurious behavior, rumination, "digging," pica, hyperactivity, or aggression. Such theorists have little difficulty in pointing up the fallacy of "diagnosing" a "thought disorder" in someone whose IQ is no higher than 15 or 20.

The development of a rational and empirical taxonomy for mentally retarded patients with severe behavior problems should be an attainable goal, and it is not impossible to reconcile divergent views. To at least some degree, traditional psychiatric categories are relevant; to what degree is an empirical question. Schizophrenia and psychosis may be overdiagnosed in the retarded, but the disorder is certainly compatible with mental retardation. Affective disorders, phobias, anxiety syndromes, and panic disorders are almost certainly underdiagnosed in the retarded (Sovner and Hurley 1983). The occasional efficacy of lithium and of carbamazepine in controlling aggressive behavior suggests that "episodic dyscontrol" or explosive disorder may merit careful research (Gualtieri et al. 1983).

A new psychiatric taxonomy for retarded people, however, should incorporate the behavioral viewpoint as well, especially for the severe and profoundly retarded. Psychiatrists need to recognize the limits of present taxonomy and the importance of defining problem behaviors, in some instances, simply as behaviors, rather than disorders. Some variant of a two-tiered approach will probably be necessary for well-constructed taxonomic studies. Such research ought to be a high priority.

Instrument development is essential for psychopathologic studies of the retarded. Research into an appropriate diagnostic method with reliability and validity is essential. Studies of retarded people with positive family histories of schizophrenia or affective disorders might go a long way toward establishing the validity of diagnostic categories and a proper diagnostic method, as well as rational and specific treatments. Instrument development for psychopharmacologic studies in the retarded is another priority area. There is at least one behavior rating scale for the retarded (Aman and Singh 1985), but its sensitivity to drug treatment—or to behavioral interventions— has not been tested. Modern behavioral technology, including interval observations and frequency counts, is appropriate for psychopharmacologic investigations, but it is also very technical and very expensive and may be unwieldy for large-scale studies of drug effects.

A number of psychopathologic conditions have been described in retarded people, and proper identification and treatment has at least been addressed in the literature for major affective disorders (Matson 1982, 1983a; Sovner and Hurley 1983), schizophrenia (Menolascino 1983), hypochondriasis (Matson 1984), and phobias (Matson 1983b). Other traditional psychiatric categories that have not been well studied or described but that are commonly encountered in this population include hyperactivity, Tourette's syndrome, explosive disorder, and the wide range of anxiety disorders. The major problem here is not to prove that these disorders occur in retarded people, or to demonstrate that they can be treated effectively, but rather how to modify diagnostic criteria for use in retarded people, how to develop diagnostic instruments, and how to modify specific treatment approaches.

The problems of antisocial behavior, aggression, violent outbursts, and destructiveness are very real in retarded populations. There is ample opportunity for traditional psychiatric diagnosis here, but there are also real limitations. An adolescent with Prader-Willi syndrome, for example, may seem to be a real sociopath in attempts to steal food, but a psychiatric diagnosis is not really appropriate here. Nor does the diagnosis of explosive disorder fit retarded persons whose occasional explosions are their only mode of self-expression within an oppressive and frustrating environment.

A second class of psychopathologic conditions is more or less unique to retarded people, and so has escaped the careful scrutiny of psychiatric nosologists. These disorders include self-injurious behavior, stereotypy, rumination, pica, and autism. Here the problem of classification is intense; these problems may occur in patients who are not retarded, although they are far more frequent in retarded people than in any other group. Certain problems like stereotypy or self-injury may occur as symptoms of chronic mental illness. Autism is considered to be a psychiatric category distinct from mental retardation, but most autistic people are retarded, and autistic symptoms are extraordinarily common in the severe and profoundly retarded. There should be a separate classification for psychiatric disorders that occur most commonly in association with mental retardation.

A third class of psychopathologic conditions is easy to describe but impossible, under present circumstances, to classify. Many retarded people suffer, by dint of temperament or training, in social and interpersonal skills. They may have clear deficits in verbal or affective self-expression. They may appear rude or clumsy in social situations. If the occasion is unfamiliar and taxing, their behavior may be overweening and offensive, and it may be described to the psychiatric consultant as bizarre. A retarded person who is afflicted by a sudden memory or an improper impulse may simply act on it, no matter what the social situation demands. There may be no self-control mechanism to mitigate the person's action. There may be no reservoir of alternative behaviors to satisfy the requirement of a sudden, untoward impulse. The retarded person perhaps understands reactions of other people, but, in fact, does not understand that other people may indeed have a plausible reaction.

Some retarded people may compensate for a deficit in social skills by exhibiting an excess of certain inappropriate behaviors. An excitable child may stereotype wildly; a surly child may harbor a secret grievance until he or she finds the opportunity to lash out. A slight in the dinner line may be brooded over, amplified, and resolved only later in a fit of temper or aggression.

It is not sufficient to pretend that a "normalized" environment will alleviate all of the mischief that can arise out of deficits in social and interpersonal skills. It is essential to remember that severely retarded people may have difficult or outlandish behaviors simply as a consequence of their cognitive deficit. A developmentally appropriate environment may diminish the excesses of such behavior, but it may not eliminate them entirely. What is also required is a special tolerance for at least some manifestations of deviance. Not every eccentricity displayed by a retarded person deserves to be classified as pathologic or as a target behavior. The third class, therefore, is not psychiatric at all. It is a broad behavioral baseline that embraces an extraordinary range of peculiar responses against which the existence of true psychopathology has to be measured. A sympathetic understanding of this baseline is an essential measure of a psychiatrist's skill in helping retarded people.

Chapter 3

Introduction

People who are mentally retarded are not immune to the full range of psychopathology; there is probably no psychiatric condition that cannot arise in someone who is mentally retarded. In individuals whose cognitive handicap is only mild, or moderate, the traditional psychiatric method is usually quite adequate for purposes of diagnosis and treatment. In more severely handicapped individuals, the method is imperfect; the unique circumstances of the patient render diagnosis uncertain and treatment outcome unpredictable. Accurate diagnosis and proper treatment are no less important in this latter group, however, although intelligent clinical judgment must be guided more by experience and intuition than by any existing body of systematic research.

Although the disorders that are described in this subsection are dealt with in much greater detail in other parts of the book, it is appropriate to address aspects of diagnosis and treatment that are unique to retarded individuals. Intellectual deficit may confer no immunity to established psychiatric conditions, but it does introduce a degree of complexity to the diagnostic process that has to be dealt with in very special ways. The same is true, of course, for treatment. So much of psychiatric practice is based on verbal exchanges between the patient and the physician. When such intercourse is precluded, in a nonverbal patient, a vital dimension is lost. It can be replaced only by inference and surmise; the validity of surmise can be supported only by a broad and sympathetic conceptual base. The psychiatrist who attempts to care for the emotional and behavioral problems of a retarded person must be well versed in all of the contexts that frame these problems: the neuropathic substrate of mental retardation; the distinct neurobehavioral sequelae of certain mental retardation syndromes; the complexities of behavioral analysis and the profound ways that the ecology of retarded individuals influence their behavior; the social demands and depredations that afflict retarded people; and the severe pathologic consequences of a relatively minor condition that is left unattended for no less than a lifetime.

This subsection covers only four general conditions: affective disorders, anxiety disorders, antisocial behavior, and schizophrenia. Other psychiatric conditions may have been included as well; even the treatment of tobacco dependence in an institutionalized retarded person requires special techniques and sensitivity. But it is sufficient here to focus only on the most important psychiatric disorders for the sake of brevity and to avoid repeating too many times the injunction that "there is little research to guide clinical decisions on this issue." In the future world of psychiatric treatment, there will be a great deal of such research, and it will enlighten the practice of neuropsychiatrists who work with retarded people. It will also broaden the horizons of our whole field.

Chapter 4

Affective Disorders

The diagnosis and treatment of affective disorders in retarded people is not well advanced. Surveys of behavior problems or psychopathology among the retarded may not even list affective disorders as a discrete category (Koller et al. 1983; Philips and Williams 1975, 1977; Reid 1980b). Surveys of psychopharmacologic prescription for retarded patients invariably list antidepressants and lithium among the least frequently prescribed medications. There is virtually no literature on newer practices, like the use of imipramine or alprazolam for panic attacks. There are no current guidelines for the diagnosis of affective disorders. There has been only limited development of assessment methods. There is no solid body of treatment research.

On the other hand, there is no doubt that affective disorders occur in retarded people, that the frequency of occurrence is by no means inconsequential, and that even the severe and profoundly retarded may be afflicted. There is a literature spanning at least 62 years regarding the occurrence of all types of affective disorders in mentally retarded individuals. The literature may be compromised by a lack of systematic presentation but it is sufficient, by virtue of clear-cut cases, to conclude that the mentally retarded suffer from the full range of affective disorders (Sovner and Hurley 1983).

In two population-based studies of psychopathology in the mentally retarded, the prevalence of affective disorders was reported to be low to nonexistent. In the Camberwell study, applying ICD-8 criteria, only 22 (5.5 percent) of 402 subjects had current or previous episodes of unipolar or bipolar depression (Corbett 1979). In the Nebraska study of 115 retarded people referred for psychiatric evaluation, the frequency of affective disorders was nil; this survey used DSM-III (American Psychiatric Association 1980) criteria (Eaton and Menolascino 1982). Neither of these surveys can be said to measure the true incidence of affective disorders, however, because problems with assessment and referral bias are not taken into account. In contrast, Reiss (1982) reported that depression was diagnosed in nine (13.6 percent) of 66 referrals to an outpatient mental health program when a "broader" diagnostic system was applied.

It is impossible to describe the frequency of affective disorder in this population, and no one can say that depression is more or less prevalent in the retarded than in the population as a whole. It is certain, however, that cognitive handicap does not preclude the development of affective disorder, that the disorders are underdiagnosed, and that substantial numbers of retarded people with affective disorders are never treated appropriately.

There is evidence that the presence of mental retardation may prevent the attribution of a psychopathologic symptom to "mental illness." The phenomenon is called "diagnostic overshadowing" (Reiss et al. 1982). Intellectual subnormality is such a salient clinical feature that concomitant emotional disturbances may be obscured or overlooked in the presence of mental retardation. Emotional problems may be attributed to the patient's intellectual weakness; they may therefore not be regarded as discrete entities that require psychiatric referral, modern diagnosis, or specific treatment.

As the advances of modern neuropsychiatry gradually become available to retarded people, one may expect to see increased attention to the diagnosis and treatment of affective disorders. New assessment techniques will be developed and the usefulness of diagnostic tests like the dexamethasone suppression test will be measured. Modifications will probably be made in established diagnostic criteria. DSM-III criteria for affective disorders may be useful only for verbal and insightful mildly retarded people and will probably require considerable adjustment for the diagnosis of affective disorder in severely retarded people.

Diagnosis of Affective Disorders

There may be considerable differences in how affective symptoms are manifested in retarded individuals. Retarded people frequently lack the requisite verbal and conceptual skills necessary to communicate their feeling states. It has been observed, for example, that the retarded do not display classic manic euphoria and flight of ideas. They may display depressive affect only indirectly through aggressive behavior, withdrawal, or somatic complaints.

Symptoms of depression in mentally retarded people may include the following:

Mood: sadness, melancholy, crying and irritability
      angry outbursts and tantrums
      emotional lability, anhedonia
      anxiety, fearfulness, agitation
      somatic complaints, hypochondriasis
      suicidal thoughts or gestures
      morbid preoccupations

Behavioral symptoms: social withdrawal, isolation, hypoactivity
      aggression, destructiveness
        self-injurious behavior
        poor school/workshop performance
        inattention to task
      developmental regression

Vegetative symptoms: loss of appetite
                     anorexia, hyperphagia
                     anergia
                     constipation,
                     insomnia or hypersomnolence
                     weight loss

A clearly defined change in the patient based on the observations of care givers may be the central factor in differentiating between symptoms of affective disorder and the relatively nonspecific problems associated with severe retardation. On the other hand, depression may be persistent and staff may not be so observant of withdrawal symptoms as they are of "positive" symptoms, like hyperactivity or aggression. A retarded person who is anergic, sad, and isolated may not be referred for evaluation and treatment until long after the onset of problems. Thus an unequivocal onset history may not be elicited.

A retarded person with a "cyclic" pattern of behavioral or emotional difficulties may have a variant of bipolar disorder, or of recurrent unipolar depression, even if the symptoms that cycle are not unequivocally affective. There is danger here, however, because a history of behavioral cycles may be overstated or unreliable. Periodic events in the patient's environment, like home visits or staff changes, may cause transient, reactive behavior problems that are not really affective cycles.

Manic attacks may not be as classic in retarded patients as they often are in patients of normal intelligence, but they are not so dissimilar that diagnosis is impossible. The diagnosis is by no means easy, however, if the manic episode is characterized only by an increase in baseline levels of untoward behaviors: hyperactivity, chatter, screaming, aggression, destructiveness, or peculiar or obnoxious social interactions.

Other concomitants or variants of affective disorder—like catatonia, psychosis, schizoaffective disorder, phobias, panic attacks, and severe anxiety—have also been described in retarded people.

In some cases, a strong family history of affective disorders may be the diagnostic key. Prior treatment with medications that may cause depression—like certain antihypertensive agents, benzodiazepines, or anticonvulsants (e.g., clonazepam, ethosuccimide)—may be important clues.

Since patients with Down's syndrome are prone to the early development of Alzheimer's disease, the classic differential between dementia and depression must be made, but with a unique twist: how to assess the evolution of a dementing process in someone who has always been cognitively impaired, and how to differentiate such changes from the consequences of a clinical depression. A careful antidepressant trial may be the only way to settle the question.

Treatment of Affective Disorders

Since there is only a slim literature on this topic with respect to mentally retarded people, one has to rely on clinical experience. Standard psychiatric treatments have not been systematically tested, but are probably relevant to affective disorders in retarded patients. Appropriate modifications are obviously required for such a large group of individuals, varying widely as they do in age, medical status, and developmental level. The necessary first goal is to bring standard psychiatric treatments to bear on behalf of patients who have never enjoyed the benefits thereof. The second step will be for clinical researchers to study the modifications in standard treatment that will be required for retarded patients.

Two general issues are pertinent to treatment of retarded patients, especially nonverbal patients: the patients' unique vulnerability to the circumstances of their environment and the physician's difficulty in monitoring response to treatment in behavioral terms alone (i.e., the reports of observers and care givers).

Retarded people may inhabit a world they don't understand, living all too frequently among people who don't understand them. A severely retarded person may never experience an environment that is developmentally appropriate. In an institutional environment, physical surroundings may be ugly and oppressive, diversionary relief only occasional, and companions remote or overbearing. In a community environment, with caretakers that may be intolerant of behavioral or emotional instability, the retarded person's surroundings may be complex and terrifying. In any environment, the capacity of retarded people to develop recreation and leisure and to experience a reasonable range of emotional fulfillment is sharply limited. They may be isolated from their closest family. They may have no friends. Separations and losses may come without warning. They may be helpless to work on their world to any effective degree, to find ways of raising their spirits, or to win even slight alleviation from misery. A helpless person in a strange world may be expected to grow demoralized, alienated, embittered, or depressed.

A clinical depression may grow autonomous from the environmental stressors that led to its becoming, and it may require specific treatment as an entity in its own right. But the oppressive circumstances of a retarded person's small world require clinical attention, too. The character of living arrangements and companionship, access to appropriate schooling and work, contacts with loved ones, and opportunity for physical exercise and recreation are all important parts of a retarded person's world. A deficit in any of these elements may contribute to the development of an affective syndrome. Improving these elements may influence the success of treatment.

The second general treatment issue is the reliability of clinical methods for evaluating change in the patient. The mildly retarded person may report feeling states accurately, although idiosyncratically at times. But the severely retarded person may convey feeling states only indirectly, and behavioral observations by seasoned and sympathetic care givers are really the only clue to the patient's inner life.

Changes in obvious depressive symptoms like crying, withdrawal, and sleep disturbance are essential to monitor, although not easy to quantify. Changes in school or workshop performance (e.g., pieces completed per shift) are easier to quantify, but not quite so direct. It is never an easy or reliable job for one person to judge the happiness of another if words cannot be exchanged, but sometimes the most important clinical clues are the opinions of workers who care for the patient. In the most effective settings, behaviors for which treatment is prescribed are measured directly, or counted or timed, but such measurement may not always be appropriate to the analysis of depressive symptoms.

The appropriate treatment of affective disorders in retarded patients may be guided by principles that often operate in general psychiatry:

1. Relief from environmental circumstances that may aggravate or that may have caused the illness.
2. Counseling, when appropriate, for the patient or care givers.
3. Appropriate pharmacotherapy.

Proper attention to environmental stressors and appreciation for the stressful quality of a developmentally inappropriate or an emotionally oppressive environment require a sensitivity to the larger world of the retarded person. Making changes in the patient's world is not always an easy chore, but the most toxic stressors may be alleviated at the urging of a caring physician, even when families or program staff have no influence.

Chapter 5

Anxiety Disorders

Anxiety is a universal phenomenon, and one from which mentally retarded people are by no means exempt. The last several years have witnessed an explosion of interest in anxiety disorders, as evidenced by numerous journal articles and books, treatment advances, and diagnostic improvements. However, from this explosion, retarded people have been largely excluded. In short, despite significant advances in the understanding of anxiety and its related disorders, little attention has been paid to anxiety in the mentally retarded individual. This is especially unfortunate given the well-known relationships of anxiety with performance and self-esteem, two areas in which the intellectually disabled already have difficulties. For example, Menolascino (1983a) and Potter (1964, 1965) have noted that mentally retarded individuals are repeatedly subjected to situations of failure due to their cognitive and adaptive limitations. They postulate, therefore, that the presence of anxiety may be a particular problem in this intellectually impaired population, as these failures are viewed as a threat to their self-esteem. Furthermore, Levine (1985) and Levine and Langness (1983) have reported that anxiety may be such an important factor in the lives of mentally retarded persons as to virtually give rise to a different "world view" from their nonretarded peers, and that their "normalized" environment may paradoxically deny them the opportunity to strengthen self-esteem, while truly normal experiences are protective.

Clearly, then, anxiety plays an important role in the understanding and psychiatric care of the mentally retarded, and pathologic anxiety may seriously disrupt their already compromised intellectual and adaptive abilities.

Definitions

It is generally conceded that anxiety is comprised of two primary aspects, often referred to as psychic and somatic. The psychic component includes the subjective feelings of nervousness, worry, and fear, and usually requires a certain degree of introspection and verbal ability to allow accurate reporting of these feelings. Therefore, in some mentally retarded individuals, an accurate appraisal may be somewhat difficult. However, with proper accounting for verbal skills and developmental level, this should not pose a problem in the majority of situations. In addition, behavioral observations may often allow the subjective state to be inferred. The somatic component of anxiety is largely attributable to autonomic hyperarousal and includes such diverse symptoms as rapid breathing and shortness of breath, palpitations, sweating, distal parasthesias, and an urge to urinate. While these symptoms lend a degree of objectivity to the concept of anxiety, many of them, too, are dependent on subjective report. Nevertheless, it is frequently helpful to differentiate these two realms of symptomatology to assist in the diagnostic evaluations as well as in tailoring specific treatment programs. For example, in the nonverbal severely retarded patient, episodes of agitation and overactivity accompanied by an appearance of fear and autonomic arousal may be indicative of pathologic anxiety in an individual not otherwise able to report his or her subjective state. However, such a clinical picture always requires a complete evaluation.

Incidence

It must be stated at the outset that little can be said with confidence concerning the frequency of anxiety disorders among mentally retarded individuals beyond the observation that they do occur. In addition to the usual methodological difficulties found in surveys of psychopathology among the mentally retarded, earlier studies used diagnostic schemes sufficiently different from those used presently, for example, DSM-III (American Psychiatric Association 1980), as to make comparisons with more current investigations virtually impossible. For example, what we would now refer to as anxiety disorders were likely to be lumped among psychoneurotic disorders, neuroses, behavioral reactions, and personality disorders. Nevertheless, an impression does emerge from these studies that excessive anxiety may occur among the mentally retarded at a greater than expected frequency (Ollendick and Ollendick 1982).

On the other hand, Craft (1959), using DSM-I (American Psychiatric Association 1952) criteria, found no patient with an anxiety neurosis among 314 adult residents of an institution for the mentally retarded in England, although he did note that "several with personality disturbance had anxiety feelings."

Philips and Williams (1975), using DSM-II (American Psychiatric Association 1968) criteria, diagnosed neuroses (not otherwise specified) in 5 of 100 mentally retarded children referred to a psychiatric clinic, mostly in those with less severe intellectual impairment. However, they also noted "neurotic traits," consisting of phobias, obsessive-compulsive symptoms, mannerisms and preoccupations, and anxiety reactions in 23.8 percent of the 62 nonpsychotic patients and went on to point out that "anxiety reactions were considered a frequent concomitant of the disorder rather than a diagnostic category in themselves."

In a more recent study, Eaton and Menolascino (1982) indicated using DSM-III criteria in an examination of the types of mental illness seen among 114 patients with coexisting mental retardation. They noted only one with an anxiety disorder, and that occurring in a patient with borderline intellectual functioning. However, in a continuation of that investigation, which excluded the original 114 patients, Menolascino (1988) noted anxiety disorders in 20 of 543 "dually diagnosed" patients. Of these, there were nine with generalized anxiety disorder, 10 with posttraumatic stress disorder, and one with obsessive-compulsive disorder; no mention was made of the presence of panic or phobic disorders.

In a Swedish population study examining the frequency of psychiatric disorders among the mentally retarded and using DSM-III criteria, Gostason (1985) found seven cases of anxiety disorders, an incidence that did not differ from that of the control population. These consisted of one case of simple phobia, one of obsessive-compulsive disorder, and five of atypical anxiety disorder, with a larger number occurring among those less intellectually impaired. There were none with generalized anxiety disorder. However, the author pointed out the difficulties inherent in diagnosing symptoms of anxiety, particularly obsessions and phobias, in the severely mentally retarded patient. However, in another study, Richardson et al. (1979) found that problems with anxiety occurred more frequently in the mentally retarded and, within that group, more frequently among those with more severe degrees of mental retardation, although this study did not employ DSM-III criteria nor did it specifically examine anxiety disorders.

It would appear that the present situation with regard to our knowledge of the frequency of anxiety disorders among the mentally retarded is less than satisfactory, especially in this "age of anxiety." However, we may safely conclude that anxiety disorders do occur among those with mental retardation. Whether they are more or less common than among the general population cannot be clearly stated; whether the particular types differ in frequency from the general population and along the spectrum of intellectual impairment, likewise, cannot be stated with certainty. Although some of this uncertainty may be related to the very nature of anxiety (e.g., are the severely mentally retarded unable to develop anxiety because they lack some necessary capacity), much would appear to be related to issues of diagnosis and assessment.

Diagnosis

Clearly, the first issue confronting the clinician who is evaluating a mentally retarded patient in whom anxiety is prominent is that of diagnosis, particularly differential diagnosis. Anxiety may be a prominent symptom, or the most prominent symptom, in a variety of medical conditions. Anxiety is present in varying degrees in most psychiatric disorders. Therefore, a complete evaluation is always in order, with attention to the host of etiologies, so that appropriate and rational treatment may be instituted. As in the rest of medicine, correct diagnosis usually leads to correct treatment.

As most experienced clinicians are aware, a number of medical conditions may present with anxiety or may have anxiety as a prominent part of their clinical picture. These include hyperthyroidism, complex partial seizures, autonomic dysautonomia, and paroxysmal tachycardia, to name only a few. However, probably the most common category would be that related to medications. The administration of stimulant drugs, such as methylphenidate and pemoline, can cause anxiety, as can a variety of other medications, including cold preparations, theophylline derivatives, and anorectics, as well as caffeine-containing beverages. In addition, of course, withdrawal from central nervous system depressants may lead to symptoms of anxiety. Therefore, a careful medical evaluation and drug review is a mandatory component in the evaluation of the mentally retarded patient with symptoms of anxiety.

Anxiety may be a symptom of virtually every psychiatric disorder, and this distinction must be made to ensure appropriate treatment. Obvious considerations in this respect would include the psychotic anxiety of schizophrenia and the persistent worry and fear that may accompany depression. These disorders are reviewed in separate chapters.

With the above considerations in mind, one may consider the diagnosis of a primary anxiety disorder. In the verbal, mildly mentally retarded patient, such an evaluation may proceed essentially as one would with a nonretarded patient, with allowances made for some concreteness of thought. However, with increasing degrees of intellectual impairment, one is confronted with the difficulties implicit in diagnosing a subjective experience requiring a degree of introspection and insight in an individual whose cognitive abilities may limit his or her abilities to do just that. It is certainly no secret that the diagnosis of a primary anxiety disorder may be extremely difficult, or even impossible, in a nonverbal, severely or profoundly mentally retarded person; behavioral observations and the reports of care givers become critical sources of information.

DSM-III-R (American Psychiatric Association 1987) recognizes a number of anxiety disorders and provides clear diagnostic criteria. The appropriateness and applicability of these criteria to the full range of mental retardation is not yet clear, although there is no a priori reason to conclude that they cannot be used as at least general guidelines with even the more severely impaired patients. These anxiety disorders include generalized anxiety disorder, panic disorder, phobic disorders, obsessive-compulsive disorder, and posttraumatic stress disorder; in addition, the adjustment disorders include adjustment disorder with anxious mood, which may also be grouped phenomenologically with the anxiety disorders. These disorders will be examined briefly, with particular attention to their clinical presentation in mentally retarded individuals.

Generalized anxiety disorder is marked by persistent symptoms of anxiety, encompassing both somatic and psychic complaints. This may be recognized by continuous feelings of nervousness, worry, and tension accompanied by the variety of somatic symptoms or concerns; irritability, hypervigilance, and distractibility may also be prominent. In the mentally retarded patient, this may present as restlessness, fidgeting, and general motor overactivity.

Panic disorder is notable primarily by its unpredictable and discrete episodes of panic, with intense symptoms of anxiety. Virtually nothing is known about panic disorder among the mentally retarded, although one may hazard a guess that at least some of the episodic behavioral disturbances that occur may be panic attacks.

Phobic disorders include agoraphobia, social phobia, and simple phobia. They are distinguished by their circumscribed nature, with symptoms of anxiety related to a specific situation, activity, or object, resulting in a desire to avoid the phobic stimulus. That phobias occur among the mentally retarded can scarcely be questioned, and undoubtedly many behavioral psychologists "cut their teeth" by devising treatment strategies for particular phobic avoidance behaviors in this population. While behavioral avoidance should be fairly easy to recognize with careful observation, it may be somewhat more difficult to "tease out" a psychological understanding of the accompanying fear. One may anticipate a higher incidence of simple phobias in the developmentally delayed, as is the case in nonretarded children, and one may likewise anticipate a higher incidence of social phobias among the mildly mentally retarded with their anticipated failures subject to scrutiny by others and the accompanying threat to self-esteem, as already noted above. However, although intuitively appealing, these speculations have yet to be demonstrated using acceptable diagnostic criteria.

Obsessive-compulsive disorder requires the presence of recurrent and persistent thoughts that the individual finds repugnant (obsessions) and/or the presence of repetitive, seemingly purposeful and ritualized behaviors (compulsions). When the patient attempts to resist the performance of the compulsive behavior, as is usually the case initially, there is a mounting sense of tension, which is relieved by carrying out the activity, the performance of which serves no other purpose than the relief of this tension. Because self-report is critical, this anxiety disorder may be particularly difficult to diagnose in the mentally retarded patient in whom verbal skills may be limited and thinking concrete. In addition, the various stereotypies and mannerisms that are frequently observed among the more severely retarded may be extremely difficult to differentiate from compulsive behaviors, and errors in diagnosis are probably quite frequent (Hurley and Sovner 1984).

Posttraumatic stress disorder is characterized by symptoms of anxiety following a psychologically traumatic event, and includes a reexperiencing of the event and a numbing of ongoing responsiveness. The key here is that the etiologically related event is generally outside the range of usual human experience and would evoke significant symptoms of distress in almost everyone; such events include natural catastrophes, war, and rape. Certainly a degree of caution is in order when making this diagnosis in a mentally retarded individual, lest the degree of perceived trauma of a particular event be overemphasized; for example, moving to a group home is not necessarily a trauma of catastrophic proportions nor an event outside the range of usual human experience. Nevertheless, elements of the posttraumatic stress disorder have been reported in the mentally retarded (Varley 1984), and the full syndrome should be diagnosed when present.

Finally, anxiety may be the predominant feature in an adjustment disorder, which requires the presence of a maladaptive reaction to an identifiable psychosocial stressor. There is little doubt that mentally retarded individuals often face major changes in their living situations that may be followed by the development of such a clinical picture. However, adjustment disorders are self-limited, remitting when the stressor ceases or leading to a new level of adaptation if it persists.

Treatment

For such a diverse constellation of psychiatric disorders, it should come as no surprise that treatment approaches have been equally diverse. However, the mainstays have been the eclectic triad: psychotherapy, behavior therapy, and psychopharmacologic therapy. Psychotherapeutic approaches should generally remain supportive, reality-based, and educational, although in some individuals insight-oriented therapy may be appropriate. Issues to be addressed would include strengthening of self-esteem and teaching adaptive social skills with an eye to symptom reduction rather than understanding. A variety of behavior therapy techniques has been used successfully in the treatment of anxiety disorders in the mentally retarded and includes desensitization (usually in vivo), modeling, fading, and overcorrection. Clearly, these techniques are most appropriate for the more circumscribed anxiety disorders, such as phobias and compulsions. Finally, psychotropic agents are often quite helpful in the treatment of anxiety disorders and would include anxiolytics, antidepressants, and beta-blockers. These are dealt with in the appropriate chapters.

Conclusion

Suffice it to say that anxiety disorders do occur among the mentally retarded. Beyond this, little can be stated with certainty. While some investigators have proposed a variety of etiologic explanations for the development of anxiety disorders in the mentally retarded (see Ollendick and Ollendick 1982 for a review), the fact remains that to this point there are not even diagnostic criteria that are applicable to the full range of intellectual impairment. Studies of the incidence are rare and the available ones are quite disparate in their findings. It would appear that at least three possibilities present themselves regarding the relationship between anxiety and mental retardation. First, it may be that anxiety, as generally conceptualized and defined, is an increasingly irrelevant and inapplicable concept with increasing degrees of intellectual impairment; it may be that only with the development of a modicum of insight and self-awareness can we speak of the development of anxiety and its disorders. On the other hand, it may be that with decreasing abilities to understand and affect one's environment, the resulting confusion and frustration make anxiety an increasingly important factor. Finally, it may be that, in the final analysis, anxiety bears no relationship to intellectual abilities and that it represents an "independent" emotional or physiologic condition. We know so little about anxiety disorders in the mentally retarded that further research and clinical investigation is badly needed.

Over the past several years, we have witnessed a flurry of activity in the areas of schizophrenia and affective disorders; some of that has now "spilled over" to the mentally retarded. We are presently in the midst of another flurry of activity, this time surrounding the anxiety disorders, and we may hope that some of that, too, will spill over to the mentally retarded. However, we must also bear in mind that the investigation of anxiety and its disorders also deserves special attention in this population because of the probable relationships with adaptive abilities and performance, not to mention the simple need for appropriate diagnostic and therapeutic strategies.

In the meantime, the clinician is faced with a patient. Anxiety disorders must remain a diagnostic consideration regardless of intellectual level if the clinical picture is suggestive. Furthermore, following a complete evaluation, appropriate treatment frequently yields gratifying results.

Chapter 6

Antisocial Behavior, Aggression, and Delinquency

Problems of antisocial behavior, aggression, and delinquency include verbal and physical assault, fighting, destructive misuse of objects and property, stealing, lying, some forms of inappropriate sexual behavior, and severe disruptive or noncompliant behavior in the classroom, work, or residential environment. They are clearly differentiated from other severe behavior problems in people with mental retardation, like self-injury and stereotypy. They are usually instrumentally directed toward other people and have more obvious immediate reinforcing consequences. People with mental retardation and antisocial behavior are likely to be excluded from educational, vocational, or social programs and community placements (Lyon and Bland 1969; Sutter et al. 1980). Aggressive or antisocial behavior is a common cause for reinstitutionalization and failed community placement (Conroy 1977; Pagle and Whitling 1978).

For children, the broad category of conduct disorder represents the most frequent reason for referral to a mental health facility. Such children often present with additional problems like hyperactivity, attention deficit disorder, poor school performance, and social skill deficits. Aggressive conduct disorders have been reported in 3 to 4 percent of children in the general population (Rutter et al. 1976), but estimates of this behavior problem in children with mental retardation are higher. Special education programs are characterized by higher rates of conduct disorders than are regular education programs, and this is understandable; referral for special placement is often initiated by teachers in response to a child's pattern of behavior problems in the regular classroom (Forehand and Baumeister 1976; Russell and Forness 1985).

Jacobson (1982) analyzed information about problem behavior and psychiatric impairment in a population of more than 30,000 individuals receiving services in New York through the statewide developmental disabilities service network. Major antisocial behavior problems occurred in about 13.5 percent of the population across all ages and residential settings. Behavior problems were distributed differentially as a function of age, level of retardation, and residential setting. Children (0–12 years of age) tended to have more minor behavior problems and fewer cognitive and affective problems than older individuals. Teenagers and adults (13–59 years of age) had more major behavior problems than did children or the elderly (60 years of age or older). The greater the degree of retardation, the more likely were reported behavior problems. More restrictive residential settings were associated with an increased likelihood of behavior problems. Some specific categories such as assault, property destruction, tantrums, genital display, disrobing, wandering, fecal smearing, self-injury, and stereotypy increased in frequency as degree of retardation and setting restrictiveness increased. Coercive sexual behavior increased as setting restrictiveness increased.

Studies of residential facilities like community residences and developmental centers tend to report even higher rates of antisocial behavior. Ross (1972) reported that some form of antisocial behavior occurred at least monthly in 27 percent of people living in California developmental centers. Hill and Bruininks (1984) examined both community residential facilities (CRF) and public residential facilities (PRF) throughout the United States and reported that about 16 percent of the CRF residents and about 30 percent of the PRF residents exhibited behavior likely to injure others. In addition, antisocial behavior patterns were one and one-half to six times more prevalent in PRF new admissions and readmissions than in residents in CRFs, suggesting that antisocial behavior may have been an influential factor in the decision to seek a more restrictive residential placement.

Clearly, antisocial behavior represents a serious problem for families and professionals who desire greater community integration for children and adults with mental retardation. A large body of research relevant to antisocial behavior and its management presently exists. Practical treatment strategies can be derived from a careful review of this literature (Mulick et al. 1980b).

Etiology

Biologic Factors

There has been tremendous progress in work on the neurologic and biologic basis for agonistic behavior in research areas such as behavior genetics, behavioral endocrinology, neuropsychiatry, and behavioral neurology (Eleftheriou and Scott 1971; Gandelman 1984; Johnson 1972; Meyer-Bahlburg and Ehrhardt 1982; Moyer 1976). While most of this research has employed animal models, there is little doubt that human aggression is affected by many of the same elements that have been studied in other species. Brain injury and certain types of epilepsy are associated with the occurrence of extremely assaultive behavior and rage states in humans, and a combination of stereotaxic brain surgery and anticonvulsant medication has been reported to help patients who were intellectually normal or retarded (Mark and Ervin 1970; Narabayashi et al. 1963). However, seizure control via surgery or drugs may still leave environmentally maintained problem behavior unaltered.

Genetic factors are probably involved in the tendency to perform violent acts and possibly to acquire criminal patterns of behavior, but the relationship between genetics and antisocial behavior is a complex one involving many physical characteristics that interact opportunistically with elements of the environment during social development. A genetic anomaly in which males have an extra Y chromosome (XYY) has been reported by some to be associated with both mental subnormality and antisocial behavior (e.g., Jacobs et al. 1965). This research is sometimes flawed by biased sampling procedures involving the use of prison populations and other subgroups (Bandura 1973; Witkin et al. 1976). Men with the extra Y chromosome in the general population tend to show no marked tendency toward violence (Schiavi et al. 1984).

Behavioral Antecedents and Consequences

Among the most reliable methods to produce intra- and interspecies aggression in the laboratory, or attack behavior toward any available target, is to arrange for the delivery of noxious stimuli while blocking escape or avoidance. Hutchinson (1973) demonstrated that elicited aggression could be obtained in animals and humans following the onset of intense, noxious, painful, or negatively reinforcing stimuli and stimuli previously paired with such events; and by the withdrawal of positive reinforcement (Foster 1978; Frederiksen and Peterson 1977). These stimulus events include those subsumed under formulations emphasizing the relationship between frustration and aggression. Aggression generated under these antecedent conditions is associated with physiologic and facial responses in humans that suggest emotional arousal.

Physical illness resulting in pain and discomfort may be a major factor in the disruptive behavior of severely handicapped people, especially when behavioral episodes are sporadic or seemingly unrelated to external events in nonverbal patients. Emotional arousal, struggling, and attempts to escape are sometimes observed in response to care giving, teaching, and other intervention procedures and occasionally can be considered examples of elicited aggression. Further, given the time-locked activity schedules and rigid behavior requirements in many residential and daytime activity programs, it would not be surprising to discover that some aggressive behavior in this population can fairly be characterized as schedule-induced adjunctive behavior (Foster 1978). Indirect evidence from studies of changes in rates of aggressive acts in institutions as a function of alterations in scheduled meals supports this notion (Boe 1972; Cleland et al. 1976; Talkington and Riley 1971).

Operant consequences influence the learning and performance of all classes of behavior. Aggressive behavior may be shaped and maintained by positive reinforcement such as adult or peer attention (Burchard and Tyler 1965), attention from the victim (Martin and Foxx 1973), successful territorial defense (Paluck and Esser 1971), and material gain (Patterson et al. 1967); and by negative reinforcement such as avoiding a feared situation or the loss of a material reinforcer (Patterson et al. 1967). Elicited aggression is also influenced by its consequences, so that future occurrences of the behavior may not be associated with the noxious antecedent conditions responsible for its acquisition.

Social Learning and Cognitive Factors

A comprehensive review of the social learning view of antisocial behavior has been presented by Bandura (1973). Aggressive behavior may have roots in biological and motivational systems, but antisocial life-styles are learned during human development by processes such as modeling and vicarious reinforcement, a history of reinforcement in the family or subculture for competitive interactions, the use of aversive control by parents or care givers, and material or social gain resulting from such acts.

Patterson and his associates (Patterson 1982; Patterson et al. 1967, 1984) have studied the families of oppositional and conduct disordered children for more than 20 years in the hope of developing a treatment model with the potential to reverse the social learning processes that naturally occur in these troubled families. Their research indicates that patterned irritable social exchanges between the problem child, the child's mother, and siblings provide the training necessary for coercion to emerge as their dominant form of interaction. The research indicates that coercive or negative reinforcement control techniques are mutually acquired by parents and child as a consequence of persistently ineffective parental behavior management strategies. Coercive exchanges gradually escalate into fighting, further disrupting the family and its capacity to serve as a setting for prosocial learning, and eventually influence the manner in which the child interacts with peers and school authorities.

Other researchers have noted the absence of a prosocial behavioral repertoire in children who go on to develop antisocial behavior, psychopathology, and poor school performance (Eron and Huesmann 1984; Huesmann and Eron 1984). Whether displaced by habitual coercive interaction patterns or somehow related to intellectual incompetence, prosocial coping strategies seem to be lacking in individuals with serious conduct disorders. The handicapped child is prone to both influences. Handicapped children are more likely to evoke parental sympathy and to experience less effective corrective discipline than are their nonhandicapped peers. Delayed development results in major limitations on the quality of a child's socialization experience, which is critical to acquiring refined prosocial skills.

The form of antisocial behavior is certainly related to the severity of mental retardation. General disruption and physical aggression are more common forms of antisocial behavior in people with severe and profound mental retardation, whereas more complex antisocial acts require greater overall competence and are more commonly seen in the mild or moderately retarded. Treatment programs for delinquent children and adolescents concentrate a large number of youngsters who function in the mildly mentally retarded range (e.g., Burchard 1967). Obviously, verbal skills and involvement in educational or community settings are required before some kinds of unethical behavior can become a problem (e.g., lying, stealing, cheating, blaming others), and a positive correlation of such behavior with IQ within the population is not surprising (Spivack and Spotts 1965). Additional longitudinal studies are sorely needed to document the range of influence of both social learning and cognitive factors in the development of antisocial behavior among the mentally retarded.

Assessment

Prior to treatment, a thorough assessment must be done. This will involve an examination of problem behavior relative to behavioral antecedents and those consequences that may serve to maintain the behavior. Patient interview, interviews of other family members or close associates, a careful physical examination to rule out relevant biologic factors (including sources of pain and discomfort or sensory deficits that could lead to frustration under some environmental demand conditions), and a careful definition of the problem behavior must be included. The value of electroencephalogram recordings to detect epileptiform discharges, especially in the temporal or frontal lobes, may be controversial, but for selected cases electroencephalography may be crucial to proper diagnosis or treatment. Neurodiagnostic tests (e.g., computed tomography, nuclear magnetic resonance) or neuropsychological testing are important if a structural lesion anywhere in the central nervous system is suspected. Behavioral observation will almost always be required to establish the relationship between behavior and environmental events, and to serve as a baseline against which the effectiveness of treatment can be measured. Cognitive evaluation will help to clarify the relationship between problem behavior and specific cognitive, communication, or social skills deficits.

The classification of antisocial behavior will vary as a function of age. In young children, antisocial behavior is sometimes classified as oppositional disorder and may be diagnosed as early as age three. This category represents an oppositional stance with respect to authority figures, often manifested as disobedience or noncompliance. Conduct disorder can be diagnosed in pre- or postpubertal children on the basis of a persistent pattern of behavior in which others' rights are disregarded and social norms are violated.

If the antisocial behavior persists into adulthood, which is often the case (Patterson 1982), the primary diagnoses are antisocial personality disorder, intermittent explosive disorder, isolated explosive disorder, and adult antisocial behavior. In antisocial personality disorder, a history of chronic norm-violating behavior is required. This pattern of behavior must begin prior to age 15, and in adulthood is associated with poor vocational adjustments, inadequate parenting, unlawful behavior, physical assault, poor financial planning, impulsivity, lying, or recklessness. However, antisocial personality disorder may not be diagnosed in the individual who also meets diagnostic requirements for severe mental retardation.

Intermittent explosive disorder involves several episodes of serious assault to persons or property occurring without clear provocation. Isolated explosive disorder involves physical assault to persons or objects occurring as an isolated incident. To be diagnosed as isolated explosive disorder, the explosive behavior must occur without prior aggressive behavior. Finally, antisocial behavior, as we define it, may be diagnosed as adult antisocial behavior. This is similar to antisocial personality disorder in behavioral criteria but requires adult onset.

The classification process is useful to the extent that it requires the kind of detail that can yield treatment hypotheses. However, the independence of these categories has not been firmly established. The most serious problem for classification may be the tendency for professionals to exhibit classification bias on the basis of the presence of mental retardation (Alford and Locke 1984; Reiss and Szyszko 1983). Another problem is the availability of adequate sources of information. The individual with mental retardation may be a poor source of information and if at all verbal, may respond to language in idiosyncratic ways that are more related to their particular social history than to events under discussion (Sigelman et al. 1982). This is especially a problem in forensic settings, where mental retardation is often unrecognized by examiners (Daniel and Menninger 1983).

Although conduct disorders (broadly defined) can usually be diagnosed in mild or moderately retarded individuals on the basis of existing psychiatric criteria, the classification system is not useful or appropriate for the severe or profoundly retarded. In this group of patients, specific behaviors are better described than defined: for example, physical aggression, destructiveness, noncompliance, irritability, and hyperactivity. For a specific patient, the exact nature of the behavior must be described in an ecobehavioral context.

Treatment

Environmentally based treatment will vary as a function of the age and cognitive ability of the patient, and the setting in which the antisocial behavior occurs. The basic strategy consists of focusing on behavioral excesses (e.g., the specific antisocial acts) and skill deficits (e.g., prosocial acts that could represent appropriate alternative behavior) identified during the initial assessment, and simultaneously restructuring the environment so that the former are either less likely to be elicited or are actively discouraged through negative contingency management, while the latter are taught and subsequently maintained through positive contingency management. This is no mean task, and the managing physician has to work in collaboration with a variety of other professional and nonprofessional care givers. Even the treatment of sources of physical pain and discomfort in mentally retarded patients requires the assistance of care givers in follow-up and assessment of the effects of the medical treatment on antisocial behavior in the natural environment.

Contingency management procedures have been applied successfully to modify a variety of antisocial behavior patterns in people with mental retardation. These behavior modification procedures have been thoroughly reviewed in recent years, and the reader is referred to these sources for more extensive coverage (Mulick and Schroeder 1980; Repp and Brulle 1981). Basic decelerative procedures include time-out from positive reinforcement in which ongoing sources of reinforcement are temporarily interrupted contingent on misbehavior; response cost in which fines or removal of other valued objects are made contingent on misbehavior; overcorrection in which elements of time-out and negative reinforcement for incompatible behavior are combined; and punishment in which noxious stimuli are programmed following the behavior to be decreased. Schedules of positive reinforcement also are used to reinforce either the absence of the target behavior, as in differential reinforcement of other behavior (DRO), or to promote both the absence of the target maladaptive behavior and to maintain the performance of some appropriate or prosocial behavior, as in differential reinforcement of incompatible behavior (DRI). Contingency contracting is a verbal and textual approach to managing agreed on behavioral goals and the positive and negative consequences arranged to produce and maintain them. Contracting is used most effectively with more verbal patients. Direct decelerative procedures produce more rapid and complete suppression of the maladaptive behavior if combined with positive reinforcement procedures and attempts to build and maintain prosocial skills. These procedures are always combined in a comprehensive behavior treatment plan.

Oppositional behavior in younger and more handicapped children will most likely involve parent training and educational programming. Parents and care givers are taught to use appropriate discipline techniques, such as differential attention and planned ignoring (i.e., extinction of negative attention-seeking behavior), and effective decelerative procedures like time-out from positive reinforcement to decrease antisocial acts. Patterson and his colleagues (Patterson 1982; Patterson et al. 1984) have provided convincing evidence that parents of coercive youngsters actually demonstrate a skill deficit in the effective use of punishment, tending to be inconsistent, arbitrary, and poorly controlled in its use. Baker (1983) described a successful comprehensive parent training model for use with parents of handicapped children. In younger patients, the prosocial skills include independent play, positive peer interaction, and assertive verbal communication of desires and intentions.

The same strategy may be effective with some older conduct disordered youngsters who continue to reside at home. The strategy will tend to shift for older patients toward teaching more complex cognitive, social, educational, vocational, and conversational skills, and will involve a larger number of change agents outside of the family. School-based treatment programs necessitate a careful analysis of the instructional approach used because a major source of negative reinforcement for antisocial behavior in school is the avoidance of difficult or inappropriate task demands. Instructional procedures are, in turn, amenable to improvement through the use of better programmed instructional techniques (Weeks and Gaylord-Ross 1981). Techniques to promote the generalization and maintenance of prosocial skills become increasingly important as the older patient at a higher functional level becomes involved in more types of institutional and community settings (Burchard 1967; Huguenin and Mulick 1981; Mulick and Schroeder 1980; Stainback et al. 1983).

Adults with mental retardation and antisocial behavior pose a special problem because of a lack of community acceptance and hence of community-based treatment services. Rarely are community-based mental health services prepared to provide the kind of in vivo training necessary to produce behavior change in the natural environment, although there are examples in the literature suggesting that success for treatment is possible with disorders such as pedophilia (Wong et al. 1982), social aggression in the vocational setting (Gardner et al. 1983), social skill deficits (Brady

1984), and child abuse with associated parenting skill deficits (Goldstein et al. 1985). Imprisonment following serious crimes protects society but does little to produce prosocial skill development, mainly because prison educational and vocational programs are not designed for this population. Reinstitutionalization represents a feasible "treatment" alternative, provided that comprehensive treatment leading to less restrictive placement can be arranged (e.g., Burchard 1967). However, there is presently a substantial shortfall nationwide in the number of openings where effective treatment can be provided.

Commitment to a continuum of treatment services for this population would be a worthy societal goal. The options required include a carefully programmed diagnostic treatment environment with both day and residential placement capacity for the deceleration of dangerous behavior and the development of a long-term plan for prosocial and adaptive skill development. Subsequent follow-up services must include less restrictive but still well-supervised residential options, vocational and recreational options, adult educational services, and flexible staff deployment to provide consultation and actual intervention in a variety of community settings.

Although antisocial behavior and aggression are among the commonest reasons for prescribing psychotropic medications to retarded people, the success of pharmacotherapy is not impressive. Neuroleptics are prescribed most frequently, and may have occasional or temporary utility. Modern psychiatrists tend to prefer lithium or carbamazepine. Stimulants or antidepressants may also be useful, especially in explosive individuals. There is, however, little systematic research on which one can base an informed judgment.

Conclusion

Antisocial behavior in people with mental retardation probably often represents the consequence of inappropriate instrumental social learning. Biologic factors influence the expression of aggression, some of which may be amenable to medical treatment, but medical treatment alone may leave a variety of environmentally maintained behavior patterns unaffected. Treatment strategies include behavior modification, the teaching of prosocial skills to address deficit areas specifically, and preventive efforts directed toward more effective child-rearing approaches in parents of handicapped children. Adult treatment efforts will be more successful with the integration of residential programs and a continuum of community-based therapeutic services.

Chapter 7

Schizophrenia

The relationship between schizophrenia and mental retardation has been described from the very beginning of psychiatry. Indeed, the descriptive clinical picture of Victor, the "Wild Boy of Aveyron," presented by the French psychiatrist Jean-Marc Itard (1801/1962) in the 19th century would today be considered that of an adult psychotic. Despite this clinical picture of both psychosis and severe mental retardation, however, Itard was able to achieve beneficial developmental and behavioral results with the "Wild Boy" and thus initiated decades of hope for the mentally retarded.

In 1896, Dr. Emil Kraeplin, the German descriptive psychiatrist, delineated the relationship between psychosis and mental retardation as one wherein dementia praecox (i.e., schizophrenia) was typically engrafted on previously existing indices of mental retardation. In 1911, the Swiss psychiatrist Dr. Eugene Bleuler proposed the term *propf-schizophrenia* to describe this same relationship. Despite these excellent early descriptions of schizophrenia in the mentally retarded, the condition was not widely discussed in psychiatric literature until the last two decades. The major reason for this period of dormant interest lies in the historical changes that occurred in the field of mental retardation.

Many of the beginnings of modern psychiatry, particularly child psychiatry, were rooted in the asylums for the mentally ill and mentally retarded. Yet by the early 20th century, the mentally ill began to be served in mental hospitals (wherein the focus was placed on active treatment), while the mentally retarded were increasingly placed in custodial institutions (for guardianship of the "helpless and hopeless"). Indeed, by the end of the second decade of this century, three trends had dramatically served to alienate the retarded from the psychiatric profession. First, the wide utilization of the Binet Test for the assessment of general intelligence ushered in exclusive concentration on the IQ score, and the psychiatric case study was viewed as "unnecessary." Second, the popularity of specious case histories of families who were deemed retarded, such as *The Kallikak Family* written by Goddard (1912), underscored the belief that retardation was invariably due to fixed genetic causes (e.g., "some uncle has blighted the family tree"); these individuals were viewed as untreatable, to be permanently sheltered away from the "normal genetic pool." Third, the rapid incorporation of psychoanalysis served to attract American psychiatrists away from the "mundane" needs of the mentally retarded. These three factors, working in concert, produced what has been termed the *tragic interlude* of a field dominated by custodialism. The psychiatrist-superintendent literally became a jailkeeper, and the earlier psychiatric treatment achievements involving Itard (1801/1962) and "The Wild Boy of Aveyron" were forgotten.

An evaluation of the literature covering schizophrenia reveals precious few studies regarding mentally retarded individuals who also display the signs and symptoms of this psychiatric disorder. A major issue, therefore, involves diagnostic clarity. Although Seguin (1846) was the first to describe clearly the association of psychosis with signs and symptoms of mental retardation, diagnostic clarity did not emerge until the last two decades (Beier 1964; Menolascino 1970; Menolascino and McCann 1983). Currently, the relationship is viewed as a literal engrafting of a schizophrenic illness on preexisting indices of mental retardation (i.e., the primary disorder) and is readily classified via the DSM-III-R (American Psychiatric Association 1987) nomenclature system (Eaton and Menolascino 1982). Although schizophrenia is observed at all levels of mental retardation, there has been professional concern expressed as to whether the diagnosis of schizophrenia can be made in a severely retarded individual (Reid 1982). In the experience of some clinicians, however, this concern has not been a major problem. Although the diagnosis may be ambiguous in many cases, there are also many instances of individuals who display both severe mental retardation and symptoms strongly suggestive of schizophrenia. The presence of bizarre behavior, persistent withdrawal, echolalia, and blunted affect in adults who had clearly regressed from a higher level of functioning may be striking. These individuals illustrate the superimposition of schizophrenia (i.e., according to their personal-clinical histories, all had developed schizophrenia between late childhood and early adulthood) on etiologically clear instances of primary mental retardation (e.g., Down's syndrome, fetal rubella, major cranial malformations).

Similarity, it is also within the realm of clinical experience to distinguish the markedly primitive behaviors of severely retarded adults (e.g., severe mental retardation with associated poor language development) from those with schizophrenia superimposed on primary mental retardation. One may note instances of paranoid schizophrenia in nonverbal adult patients who draw their "attackers" on paper, replete with nonverbal gestures. In our experience, one individual tended to label his separate fingers as the "source" of his common delusions, which he portrayed symbolically in crude drawings. Paranoid and catatonic features are the most frequently noted hallmarks of persons with schizophrenia. In individuals who display a dual diagnosis of mental retardation and schizophrenia, the altered affective responses, bizarre rituals, and use of interpersonal distancing devices are suggestive indications of schizophrenic behaviors.

Beyond diagnostic concerns remains the positive challenge of providing modern psychiatry's best treatment intervention approaches to the schizophrenic psychosis that is present. It has been our experience (Menolascino et al. 1985) that retarded citizens with allied schizophrenic psychoses do respond quite rapidly to well-planned treatment approaches, which take into consideration the delayed cognitive and social adaptive dimension of their underlying mental retardation. Within this balanced treatment approach, the judicious and appropriate use of psychoactive agents may produce beneficial results. At all times, the acute aspect of the coexisting schizophrenic psychosis must be aggressively addressed as an entity whose treatment will greatly enhance the retarded citizen's future adaptive potential.

Although the overall prognosis for treatment responses in schizophrenia—in the retarded as well as the nonretarded—is difficult to predict, careful diagnostic understanding and aggressive but balanced treatment intervention will permit a greater likelihood of positive treatment outcome.

Neurobehavioral Syndromes Associated with Mental Retardation

Chapter 8

Introduction

This subsection considers a diverse group of disorders, chosen by virtue of clinical usage, not selected from any single nosologic system. The three eponymic syndromes (Down's, Lesch-Nyhan, and Prader-Willi) are taken from developmental medicine; they are not, as a rule, listed among the psychiatric diagnoses, although the neurobehavioral components of the disorders are of major importance. The other categories are purely behavioral; that is, they represent discrete behavioral problems that frequently require the attention of a neuropsychiatrist, but they are not listed as diagnoses in either the psychiatric-descriptive or etiopathogenic senses of the term.

These neurobehavioral syndromes occur much more frequently in retarded people, especially in the severely retarded. They may also occur in nonretarded individuals: self-injurious behavior, pica, and stereotypy may occur in the chronically mentally ill. Not every patient with Down's syndrome and not every patient with Lesch-Nyhan is mentally retarded; but most are. Although these conditions are not found exclusively in retarded people, they are found most commonly in that population, and they represent some of the most compelling behavioral problems of retarded people. No psychiatric consultant to the retarded can afford to be ignorant of these problems and their proper treatment.

Chapter 9

Down's Syndrome

Down's syndrome (DS) is one of the major known causes of mental retardation in the United States. The incidence is about one per thousand live births, and people with DS comprise 16 percent of the retarded population. [It is possible that the cytogenetic syndrome called "fragile X" may supplant as the major known cause of mental retardation (Fryns et al. 1984).]

A generation ago, people with DS died young, mainly from infectious or cardiac disease, to which they are peculiarly vulnerable. Today, their medical care is much better, and they live longer. Increased longevity, however, has led to the paradoxical discovery of a clear pattern of precocious aging in DS. Somatic and neuropathic changes that characterize the senium may begin in individuals with DS as early as the third decade. The propensity of individuals with DS to the most serious disease of the senium, dementia of the Alzheimer's type (DAT), has been a major area of interest to psychiatrists and other neuroscientists who study dementing diseases, and Alzheimer's disease in particular. The most important advances in our knowledge of DAT will probably come from the careful study of DS. It is ironic that signal advances in the neurobiology of aging may be made by scientists who study a particular class of mentally retarded youths.

Children and adolescents with DS are not often referred to psychiatric consultants because they are not especially prone to serious behavior or emotional problems. (At worst, they are said to be stubborn, but as a group they tend to be happy and well behaved.) But when they begin to develop clinical signs of dementia, in their 30s, 40s, or 50s, they may be well served by neuropsychiatrists or geropsychiatrists who understand how to treat demented patients.

There seems to be little doubt that the ultimate cause of DS is the extra chromosome 21 (hence, Trisomy 21). However, the precise molecular mechanism by which the excess chromosomal material causes an abnormal phenotype is only beginning to be studied (Scott et al. 1983). The neurobiologic basis for mental retardation in DS is probably related to a reduction in dendritic spines, changes in synaptic morphology, and abnormalities in the electric membrane properties of neurons (Scott et al. 1983). The observation of a precocious cessation of growth of dendritic spines during the postnatal period in DS suggests a developmental problem that may be "related to rapid aging," and this idea is reinforced by the clinical observation of dementia and other somatic signs of aging in DS.

The fact that probably all patients with DS develop neuropathic signs of DAT by the age of 40 has led to intense interest in DS as a kind of model for DAT. The fact that abnormalities in the neuronal membrane may be responsible, at least in part, for the intellectual deficits of DS patients has fed speculations about a possible neurochemical treatment for mental retardation.

Although neuropathic findings of a nonspecific nature are not uncommon in the brains of patients with DS, there is no gross or microscopic finding that is specific to or diagnostic of DS. At about age 20, however, the brains of patients with DS begin to show neuropathic changes that are characteristic of DAT: neuronal loss, senile plaques, and neurofibrillary tangles. These lesions are virtually universal in patients with DS who survive to age 40 (Lott 1982).

The clinical manifestations of DAT in individuals with DS may be variable, however. Clinical signs of dementia may develop in patients with DS as young as age 35, although some individuals may have no clinical signs of dementia at age 59 (Thase et al. 1984). Clinical signs of DAT that are noted in older patients with DS include memory loss, aphasia and agnosia syndromes, personality changes, apathy, affective lability, deterioration in personal hygiene, and vocabulary loss. Frontal release signs (facial hyper-reflexia, palmomental reflex, glabellar tap, suck, and snout reflex) occur more frequently in older patients with DS compared to younger patients with DS, and they also show more pathologic reflexes, paroxysmal electroencephalogram abnormalities and developmental regression (Lott 1982). Previously vital, interested, active, music-loving, clean individuals become dull and lose learned tasks. They forget the names of their caretakers and become disoriented, confused, and lethargic. They cannot dress themselves anymore and interest themselves only in eating and drinking (Tolksdorf and Wiedemann 1981).

There are other somatic indices of premature aging in DS: gray hair, baldness, dry skin, fenestration of the cardiac valves, and cataracts (Lott 1982). The mortality curve of individuals with DS from age 40 to 60 resembles to a remarkable degree the mortality curve of the general population from age 60 to 80 (Thase et al. 1984). The characteristic immunologic changes that occur with aging begin about 20 years earlier in individuals with DS than in the general population.

This remarkable association between DS, premature aging, and DAT presents a fertile field for genetic, virologic, immunologic, and neurochemical studies regarding the pathophysiology of DAT (Thase et al. 1984). Reduction in central nervous system levels of serotonin and serotonin metabolites, norepinephrine, and cholinergic activity has been noted both in DAT and in DS (Scott et al. 1983). The loss of cholinergic presynaptic markers in the cortex appears to be the most consistent neurochemical pathology in DAT, and the study of similar changes in DS is an active area of research interest (Price et al. 1982).

There appears to be an excess of DS among relatives of DAT probands (Heston 1982). Individuals with DS are themselves prone to develop certain malignancies, especially leukemias, and there also appears to be an increased incidence of lymphoproliferative disorders among relatives of DS probands (Heston 1982). Heston has speculated that there may be a common genetic matrix to three disorders—DS, DAT, and lymphoproliferative disorders—that may involve a genetically programmed, premature aging process possibly involving a defect in microtubular organization (Scott et al. 1983).

There are also certain immunologic and endocrine abnormalities in DS, which may bear on the physiologic expression of the aging process or the pathophysiology of DAT. Antithyroid antibodies, for example, are commonly elevated in individuals with DS (Walford 1982).

The major psychiatric aspect to DS is DAT, and this association has won far more attention from neurobiologic researchers than from clinical researchers. But if DS is a disease that is typified by an acceleration of the aging process, it is reasonable also to query an association with one other psychiatric concomitant of the senium, major affective disorder. Depression has not been described as a common affliction in the life course of individuals with DS, but whether this represents a lapse in clinical acuity or an actual incompatibility is an open question. It has been suggested that certain forms of affective illness may not occur in patients with DS (Sovner et al. 1985). If this is true, an explanation should be sought. If affective disorders occur in DS with anything approaching normal prevalence rates, clinicians should be making the diagnosis more often and providing appropriate treatment. The fact that major affective disorder, especially depression, occurs with increased frequency in older people suggests that depression might also be frequent in people with DS, and at an earlier age. On the other hand, if depressions do not occur in DS with anything approaching population norms, one would be compelled to look for a reason why. Attempts to explain this counter-intuitive speculation would fuel research on the neurobiology of depression as amply as the DS-DAT association fuels research on the neurobiology of aging.

Chapter 10

Self-Injurious Behavior

Self-injurious behavior (SIB) in mentally retarded persons is usually defined as behavior that potentially or actually causes physical damage to the individual's own body. It consists of idiosyncratic motor acts that repeatedly occur in essentially identical form. The most typical SIB topographies are biting, hitting or banging body parts, pinching, scratching, gouging, hair pulling, and pica. (Pica and a closely related condition, rumination, will be discussed in another chapter.) A number of prevalence studies indicate that SIB is found in 8 to 23 percent of the institutionalized and in 1.5 to 3 percent of the noninstitutionalized retarded population. As a general rule, the relative prevalence and severity of SIB is greater in those persons who also demonstrate aggressive behavior, stereotypies, communication deficits, and specific kinds of neuropathology (Schroeder et al. 1980).

There is an abundance of theories concerning the etiology and maintenance of SIB. No unitary theory, however, describes and embraces such a heterogenous group of conditions. The behaviors are differentially influenced by a variety of organic and psychological factors. It is likely that these factors are accounted for in varying combinations in different individuals and that they partially interact with the individual's developmental level and with the environment.

The self-stimulation or homeostasis-hypothesis suggests that SIB serves to maintain some organismic homeostasis, e.g., to increase central nervous system (CNS) arousal. The need to self-stimulate may be caused by a lack of external stimulation.

Some chromosomal, metabolic, or neurologic disorders, such as the Lesch-Nyhan syndrome and the Cornelia de Lange syndrome, which are associated with the occurrence of SIB are the basis of organic theories. Deficiencies in neurotransmitter systems especially serotonin and dopamine, gross or subtle neuropathologic lesions of the central nervous sytem, or the production of endogenous opiates in response to pain and injury have been related, in theory, to the occurrence of SIB (Cataldo and Harris 1982).

Developmental theories are based on the observation that some types of SIB, for example, head banging, are found in normal infants; it is suggested that some mentally retarded individuals fail to outgrow these behaviors which may be functionally appropriate during certain developmental stages. Head banging is a frequent developmental variant in infants less than two years and even in normal infants it may be self-injurious. The qualitative difference, however, between "developmental" head banging and SIB is dramatic and therefore the developmental hypothesis of pathologic SIB is probably overdrawn.

One organic-developmental hypothesis suggests that some forms of SIB may be caused by the destruction of brain dopaminergic neurons in early development (Breese et al. 1984b). This is discussed in Chapter 11 on Lesch-Nyhan syndrome.

Some psychodynamic and ethologic theories relate SIB to suppressed anger or aggression. It is considered to be displacement behavior resulting from the activation of two "drives" with conflicting goals. It has also been suggested that some SIB may represent a form of affective disorder, a behavioral manifestation of depression.

Operant learning theory has offered some models of SIB maintenance. The discriminative stimulus hypothesis suggests that SIB is maintained by social reinforcement. SIB becomes a discriminative stimulus, or cue, for the attention of the caretaker, who in turn reinforces the SIB by attending to the individual right after or contingent on the occurrence of SIB. Internal positive reinforcement by sensory stimulation is also considered to be a functional variable for some forms of SIB. According to the avoidance hypothesis (or negative reinforcement theory), SIB is maintained by the removal or termination of an aversive stimulus that is contingent on SIB. Demands to engage in a rehabilitative task or transitional periods of the day have been demonstrated to act as aversive stimuli. Individuals manage to avoid these demands by exhibiting SIB, and the behavior is reinforced. The discriminative stimulus and the avoidance hypotheses are well supported by experimental research.

Theories of SIB may be useful for guiding treatment decisions, or for directing treatment research. For example, if some cases of SIB are characterized by an individual's drive for self-stimulation, alternative forms of stimulation may be substituted for acts that are self-injurious. Arousal theories suggest that sedatives or sedating neuroleptics may actually increase levels of self-injury. On the other hand, an individual whose SIB is a form of stereotypy may respond favorably to neuroleptic treatment. If some SIB is a symptom of affective disorder, then antidepressants or lithium treatment may be appropriate. The theory that patients with SIB may be "addicted" to the production of endogenous opiates has led to the development of treatment studies with opiate antagonists (e.g., naltrexone). Theories of SIB based on operant learning theory have been most influential, however, because the only successful treatments of SIB, to date, are behavioral.

For a more thorough discussion of theories of SIB, the reader is referred elsewhere (Baumeister and Rollings 1976; Carr 1977; Singh 1981a).

Treatment

Although there are a number of different treatments for SIB reported in the literature, very few have been demonstrated effective by well-controlled and replicated research.

Behavior Modification

Increased attention to SIB research since the early 1960s can be traced to a few notable studies that demonstrated the control of SIB through the manipulation of external stimuli (e.g., Lovaas et al. 1965a; Tate and Baroff 1966; Wolf et al. 1964). Since that time, behavior modification has become the primary treatment for self-injurious behavior. Behavior modification techniques are usually effective, relatively nonrestrictive, and involve only a low risk factor for the patient.

Behavior modification is based on the tenet that behavior is, at least in part, a function of the presence or absence of specific environmental stimuli. This approach differs considerably from the view reflected in the medical model of aberrant behavior; that is, maladaptive behavior is symptomatic of an underlying, neuropathologic state. It is not impossible, of course, to reconcile these two views, because a preexisting neuropathic disorder may predispose certain individuals to the influence of certain kinds of environmental stimuli. Alternatively, correcting the consequences of a neuropathic state may require an unusual kind of environmental response.

With behavior modification, treatment means changing behavior by manipulating environmental stimuli. The goal of behavior modification is to eliminate a problem behavior or to establish new behaviors that will supplant the problem behavior. In the case of SIB, it is crucial to eliminate the problem behavior due to extraordinary risk to the client's well-being. In addition, the fact that most patients with SIB are retarded and functionally impaired warrants the simultaneous development of adaptive behaviors through behavior-shaping procedures.

An important aspect of behavior modification is its experimental nature in addressing individual clinical problems. The clinical treatment of SIB is actually an experimental approach to operant conditioning in a single case design. The experiment involves careful identification and operational definition of the target behavior(s), continuous behavioral assessment, explicit formulation of treatment goals, and selection of a treatment procedure based primarily on the relationship between the target behaviors and the relevant environmental variables preceding (antecedent) and following (contingent on) the targeted behavior. Treatment effects are then demonstrated through the use of a single subject experimental design.

Operant behavior modification is based on four principles of learning: punishment, reinforcement, extinction, and stimulus control. When a behavior is as seriously maladaptive as self-injury, direct intervention via punishment is frequently sought. Punishment is the presentation (or withdrawal) of a stimulus that results in the suppression of the behavior that precedes its delivery (or withdrawal). *Punishment* is defined in operant terms by its effect on the rate of the target behavior rather than by the intended effect. Several stimuli have been successfully used as punishers in the treatment of SIB (e.g., slaps, water mist, mild electric shock). The application of such interventions, however, is not without its critics, and it may not be permitted in many facilities. Punishment may be an accepted treatment for SIB, considering the severity of the disorder, but a punishment-based program has to be designed by competent professionals, and it has to be carefully monitored.

Although it is generally assumed that the most intense and aversive punishing stimuli produce the most dramatic change in SIB, in fact less aversive but usually more complex punishment procedures have also been demonstrated to be efficacious. Time-out from positive reinforcement involves contingent removal of reinforcement for a specified time. Time-out frequently takes the form of removal from the group or from the desired activity contingent on the occurrence of SIB. Another form of time-out frequently used with self-injurious clients is visual or facial screening. The procedure consists of contingently placing a towel or cover over the client's face (facial screening) or placing one hand over the client's eyes (visual screening). All visual input (reinforcer) is blocked, and the SIB is effectively interrupted.

Positive practice overcorrection is a procedure in which the client is required to practice repeatedly some incompatible or alternative behavior on occurrence of self-injury. Such a procedure for head hitting consists, for example, of repeated, physically prompted, vertical arm movements.

While a behavior that is as potentially dangerous and destructive as SIB frequently warrants intervention focusing directly on behavior reduction, there are some procedures that indirectly reduce undesirable behavior. Indirect reduction of a maladaptive behavior involves the development, increase, and expansion of other desirable behaviors through the differential use of positive reinforcement. Such procedures can be used as an alternative or in addition to the more direct interventions.

The presentation of any stimulus contingent on the occurrence of a particular behavior that results in the increased rate of occurrence of that behavior is positive reinforcement. Thus, analogous to punishment, positive reinforcement is defined by its effect on the future rate of the behavior. Consequences commonly thought of as positive (e.g., hugs, candy, smiles, money, privileges) are positive reinforcers only when a subsequent increase in the preceding behavior occurs.

Differential reinforcement of other behavior (DRO) is the reinforcement of any behavior other than the target behavior given that the target behavior does not occur. Reinforcement is then delivered at a predetermined rate, or schedule. Increasing behaviors directly incompatible with the target behavior is differential reinforcement of incompatible behavior (DRI). One of the first successful attempts to use DRI in the systematic treatment of SIB was reported by Lovaas et al. (1965a). A child who exhibited high rates of multiple self-injurious acts received social reinforcement in the form of smiles and hugs for engaging in hand clapping to music. DRO programs may take advantage of the individual's craving for stimulation by substituting noninjurious forms of stimulation. A brief period of injury-free behavior is rewarded by some form of physical pleasure (e.g., massage, music, a toy). The advantage of such a program over a punishment-based aversive program is obvious.

Extinction refers to the withholding of the stimuli that had previously reinforced a particular response. SIB maintained by sensory reinforcement has been successfully treated through extinction procedures by eliminating the sensory feedback to the client. Ignoring, a commonly used form of extinction, has been used to reduce SIB maintained by social reinforcement. However, extinction by itself may often be inappropriate with SIB because it results in a fairly slow rate of response reduction (depending on the reinforcement prior to treatment). Extinction is frequently paired with reinforcement procedures (DRO, DRI).

Operant behavior modification consists largely of procedures that employ response-contingent stimuli. However, behavior is also influenced by noncontingent or antecedent stimuli, such as the presence of certain persons, the noise level, or the type of environment. This phenomenon is generally known as stimulus control. Ecobehavioral analysis is an approach to identifying relevant antecedents, which can then be systematically altered to decrease SIB (Schroeder et al. 1981). Increased efforts in this area of research will very likely enhance our sophistication with programmed maintenance, generalization, and transfer of treatment gains.

The purpose of behavioral treatment in SIB is to shape the individual's development in directions that are incompatible with self-injury or to allow the individual to learn less destructive ways to attain satisfaction or stimulation. As a form of treatment, behavioral approaches are effective and relatively nonrestrictive and safe; with appropriate aftercare, the results of a successful program may be long lasting. Behavioral treatments are labor intensive, however. A successful program requires a well-trained clinician and a staff of technicians who are committed to making it work. A behavioral program may be sabotaged by cynical or ignorant staff, by medical interventions, or by administrative constraints against some forms of training. The fact that every behavioral program is necessarily experimental means that the directing psychologist has to be a creative and innovative thinker, a confident person who can motivate staff to carry out a program with the necessary energy, consistency, and optimism. The proper kind of behavioral program for a self-injurious person requires highly skilled professional guidance and a well-trained staff. Paper programs concocted for adminstrative purposes serve no useful purpose; they can be demoralizing to care givers and may prejudice staff against the real benefits of effective therapy.

The majority of patients with SIB do not have access to modern behavioral technology, and many of them lead empty lives in woeful circumstances, where the stimulation of self-injury may be the only meaningful stimulation they receive. The most common "treatment" that is given to these unfortunate individuals is restraint. At home, restraint is usually the only treatment; the intense behavioral treatments that are required for SIB are seldom available to retarded patients who live at home, or in small group homes attended by inexperienced staff.

Pharmacotherapy

A review by Radinsky (1984) showed that neuroleptics are frequently administered for control of SIB, but that the reasons for prescribing neuroleptics may vary and may be idiosyncratic or counterproductive. Despite extensive prescription of neuroleptics for the treatment of SIB, there is a paucity of controlled clinical research on their effectiveness. In fact, Campbell et al. (1983) warned that neuroleptics may not specifically reduce SIB in mentally retarded patients but may depress cognitive functions and learning. All the known short- and long-term side effects of neuroleptics, such as drowsiness, motor dysregulation, and tardive dyskinesia, have to be considered. Another psychoactive drug that is used in the treatment of SIB is lithium carbonate. Campbell et al. (1983) cautiously recommended lithium treatment for aggressive behavior and SIB in some mentally retarded people, but only after behavior modification and neuroleptics fail. The administration of naloxone or naltrexone to self-injurious mentally retarded individuals has been reported in just a few case studies. The resulting decrease in pain sensitivity was expected to prevent the clients from engaging in SIB. The data are controversial at best. As of this writing, there is no specific drug treatment known for SIB among mentally retarded persons. The treatment of SIB with dopamine receptor blockade is discussed in another chapter.

Noncontingent Physical Restraint

A traditional form of SIB control has been physical restraint (e.g., camisoles, handcuffs, protective helmets, arm splints). Naturally, these methods are not expected to be therapeutic. They merely prevent injury and should be considered a last resort. Restraints are still widely used, however; in some cases, it is the only treatment available to patients with SIB. Individuals wearing protective helmets, arm splints, or handcuffs are by no means an uncommon sight in many residential facilities for retarded people. Griffin et al. (1984) found in a statewide SIB survey of 13 facilities for the mentally retarded that 27.2 percent of the patients with SIB were in restraints. In addition to their nontherapeutic effect, there are negative side effects associated with restraints. A restrained person may appear to develop a preference to restraints and may resist being released. This resistance may be motivated by protection from self-inflicted injuries as well as increased ability to avoid environmental demands. For the most part, these devices are incompatible with developmental activities and prohibit the acquisition of adaptive behaviors.

The treatment of self-injurious persons usually begins with some kind of restraining, but restraint can only be justified, in medical or in moral terms, if a behavioral program is developed with the likelihood that restraints will be reduced or eliminated. Self-injurious clients can be gradually weaned from restraints. They may prefer to maintain some form of symbolic restraint, like a pair of gloves, but self-injury will not recur as long as positive behavioral programming continues.

Conclusion

Behavior modification offers a highly effective and individually adaptable treatment technology, which makes it the treatment of choice for SIB in mentally retarded persons at the present time (see Favell et al. 1982; Horner and Barton 1980; Singh 1981b). It can be expected, however, that some forms of effective treatment will eventually emerge and particularly on the combination of treatments involving behavior modification techniques and psychopharmacology.

Chapter 11

Lesch-Nyhan Syndrome

The Lesch-Nyhan syndrome (LNS) is an extraordinary disorder characterized by mental retardation, spasticity and choreoathetosis, and a compulsive form of self-mutilation. It is an X-linked recessive disease associated with overproduction of uric acid. The underlying metabolic basis is a congenital deficiency in the enzyme hypoxanthine-guanine phosphoribosyl transferase (HGPRT). The molecular mechanism by which this enzyme deficiency may induce damage in nervous tissue is not known (Lesch and Nyhan 1964; Lloyd et al. 1981). The most striking aspect of the disease is a bizarre pattern of self-mutilation that appears at about two years of age. Finger biting is characteristic; this may cause severe injury, even amputation. Lip biting may also develop, resulting in severe facial deformity and sometimes requiring the extraction of teeth (Anderson et al. 1977).

It is important to emphasize that children with LNS do not appear to be deficient or aberrant in their sensitivity to pain. On the contrary, they are often sorely aggrieved by the consequences of their self-injurious compulsions, and they may be relieved when physical restraints are applied. In addition, they are not as severely impaired cognitively as once was believed; some have normal intelligence and many, if not most, are capable of communicating their grief and distress to other people (Anderson et al. 1977; Sherzer and Ilson 1969).

Although neuropathologic studies of patients with LNS demonstrate no appreciable morphologic abnormalities in any part of the brain, the nature of the associated movement disorders suggests some involvement of structures in the basal ganglia. In fact, discrete biochemical abnormalities have been identified in striatal tissue from afflicted patients, including a general deficit in dopamine-neuron function (Lloyd et al. 1981).

An important animal model of the LNS has been developed in neonatal rats treated with 6-hydroxydopamine, a neurotoxin that selectively disrupts dopaminergic neurons. Severe self-mutilatory behavior may be induced in the rat by an age-dependent reduction in dopamine-containing fibers (Breese et al. 1984a). That, in turn, may lead to a state of dopamine supersensitivity. In support of this contention, it is known that self-mutilatory behavior may be induced by the administration of dopamine agonists (apomorphine, L-dopa) to animals pretreated with neonatal 6-hydroxydopamine (Breese et al. 1984b; Goldstein et al. 1985). Despite dopamine depletion in the brains of patients with LNS, treatment with L-dopa has only a partial or a transient effect on self-mutilatory behavior (Mizuno and Yugari 1974). This behavior is only partially reduced by administration of haloperidol but is completely blocked by cis-flupentixol, a selective D2 dopamine receptor blocking agent. Haloperidol is primarily a D2 blocker. Fluphenazine, a neuroleptic that is commercially available and that does block the D1 receptor, is said to have been clinically effective in at least one patient with LNS (Goldstein et al. 1985). This leap from experimental neuropharmacology to clinical practice may be promising, but it requires careful evaluation.

The neurochemical imbalances found in brains of patients with LNS include disturbances in cholinergic and serotoninergic systems (Lloyd et al. 1981). Since the serotonin precursor, 5-hydroxytryptophan (5-HTP), is known to reduce certain forms of aggressive behavior in rats, it was supposed by Mizuno and Yugari (1974) that 5-HTP treatment might reduce self-mutilatory behavior in patients with LNS. Reductions in spinal fluid 5-hydroxyindoleacetic acid (5-HIAA), a serotonin metabolite, have been noted to occur in patients with LNS (Castells et al. 1979), although increased levels of brain serotonin and 5-HIAA were noted in LNS brains by Lloyd et al. (1981). Mizuno and Yugari (1974) reported three successful treatment cases with 5-HTP. Rapid tachyphylaxis, however, occurred to the therapeutic effects of 5-HTP, and augmentation of drug effects by concomitant administration of carbidopa or imipramine proved to have only a partial, temporary effect (Castells et al. 1979; Nyhan et al. 1980).

The spasticity and dystonia that often afflicts patients with LNS may be treated with drugs like lioresal or benzodiazepines. The systemic effects of hyperuricemia in patients with LNS, the symptoms of gout, respond favorably to treatment with allopurinol, which does nothing, however, to control the neurologic and behavioral symptoms (Dasheiff 1980).

The antenatal diagnosis of LNS may be made from villus biopsy in pregnancies occurring in families afflicted with the disorder (Gibbs et al. 1984).

Physical restraints, to which patients with LNS often respond with profound relief, and behavior modification techniques are virtually the only methods of treatment for the behavioral aspects of the disorder (Anderson et al. 1977, 1978; Dasheiff 1980; Gilbert et al. 1979).

Chapter 12

Fragile X Syndrome

The fragile X syndrome, originally described in 1969, is now recognized as a leading cause of mental retardation. It is second only to Down's syndrome as a cause of mental retardation associated with an identifiable chromosomal abnormality. Although estimates of incidence vary, the fragile X syndrome is believed to affect one in every 1,000 to 1,350 males (Rogers and Simensen 1987). Reports of prevalance among retarded males have ranged from 1.9 to 5.9 percent. Nearly one-third of the female carriers may also be affected. The condition is confirmed cytogenetically by detection of a fragile site at position q27 on the long arm of the X chromosome.

Unlike Down's syndrome, where the phenotype of affected individuals is readily apparent, individuals with the fragile X syndrome show considerable variability in their physical, intellectual, and behavioral characteristics. Still, some common features among fragile X males, as a group, have been described in the literature. These include macro-orchidism (extreme enlargement of the testes in postpubertal males), a prominent jaw, large ears, a broad forehead, and a long, thin face. Other physical characteristics of fragile X males have also been noted, but probably occur less frequently. These include high arched palate, ocular abnormalities (such as strabismus or nystagmus), mitral click, curvature of the spine, hyperextensible joints, and oral-motor incoordination (e.g., difficulty moving the tongue from side to side when it is protruded).

In a report of 67 fragile X positive males, Rogers and Simensen (1987) noted the following physical characteristics in 50 percent or more of their sample: macro-orchidism (100 percent among postpubertal males); prominent jaw (66.2 percent); long, thin faces (63.2 percent); midface hypoplasia (57.3 percent); simple ears (56.9 percent); and a prominent forehead (50 percent). Although other physical measurements (e.g., head circumference and ear length) were greater than two standard deviations above the mean for many subjects, they were comparable to measurements of mentally retarded institutionalized males in general. This suggests that the presence or absence of physical characteristics is of limited value in identifying fragile X positive males.

Likewise, fragile X males display a wide range of cognitive abilities. This is particularly true in affected children, who may function in the average range of intelligence through the severe range of mental retardation. Fragile X adults are generally reported to function in the moderate to severe range of mental retardation (Sutherland and Hecht 1985). There are several reports, however, of normal males with a fragile X trait who show no intellectual impairment (e.g., Rhoads et al. 1982). Attempts to demonstrate a relationship between percentage of fragile X sites (identified through karyotyping) and degree of cognitive impairment have yielded mixed results. Although it is intuitive to suppose that a high percentage of fragile X sites would be associated with a greater degree of congnitive deficit, this hypothesis has not been supported in recent studies (e.g., Rogers and Simensen 1987).

In general, research on the intellectual functioning of fragile X individuals must be interpreted with caution. These reports are likely to include institutionalized males and their family members or those who have sought genetic counseling, thus introducing a bias of ascertainment. There are also wide differences among studies in terms of their assessment of intellectual functioning and classification of subjects.

Several investigators have noted a possible decline in the intellectual functioning of fragile X males with increasing age (Hagerman et al. 1983; Rogers and Simensen 1987). This hypothesis was supported in a retrospective, longitudinal study of 21 noninstitutionalized boys with the fragile X syndrome (Lachiewicz et al. 1987). Thirteen boys in this group showed a significant decline in their level of intellectual functioning from initial to follow-up testing. IQ scores for the group as a whole also dropped significantly. This was the case even though all boys had received some educational intervention and were from middle or upper-middle class families. Larger, prospective studies are needed to provide more conclusive evidence in support of this phenomenon.

A wide variety of behavioral characteristics have also been described in reports of fragile X individuals. These include attentional problems, hyperactivity, impulsivity, hand flapping and other unusual hand movements, poor eye contact, and self-injurious behavior (typically biting hands or arms). In addition, fragile X individuals are often described as shy or timid, prone to temper tantrums, and having difficulty coping with any changes in their routine. Unfortunately, the relevant studies do not employ common diagnostic criteria. As Madison et al. (1986b) pointed out, nearly all investigators have relied on clinical diagnoses, behavioral checklists, or even anecdotal observations as the basis for their reports. Studies of fragile X children and adults employing reliable behavioral observation techniques would be highly desirable. In addition, normative data on the frequency of such aberrant behaviors in mentally retarded persons in general would be vital for purposes of comparison. The use of a control group matched for level of intellectual functioning, but having another specified etiology for their mental handicap (e.g., Down's syndrome), would also be valuable in studies of this kind.

Once again, aberrant behavioral characteristics are not sufficient as sole criteria for detecting the fragile X syndrome. Varying combinations of these behaviors may be observed in any particular individual, as well as a wide range of severity. Manifestation of these behaviors may also vary with age. For example, a fragile X male may exhibit hand flapping at an early age but not during his adolescent or adult years. A detailed history of behavior difficulties is important, as well as reliable behavior observations in a standardized setting.

Investigators have also focused on the speech and language characteristics of fragile X individuals, in addition to their physical, cognitive, and behavioral traits. A number of speech and language dysfunctions have been described in the literature, including articulation errors and errors of omission (Howard-Peebles et al. 1979); repetition of words, phrases, and sentences (perseveration); echolalia; stuttering; and a tendency to speak quickly. More systematic and thorough evaluations of these characteristics are needed in large samples of fragile X individuals. Although speech and language difficulties are not diagnostic in and of themselves, they may be useful in combination with other traits. Once again, the goal is to identify a set of characteristics that may permit early identification of the fragile X syndrome.

Since 1982, when investigators reported on the concurrence of infantile autism and the fragile X syndrome (Brown et al. 1982; Meryash et al. 1982), a growing body of literature has emerged in this area. Reports on the incidence of the fragile X syndrome among autistic males have been variable, with figures ranging from zero (Goldfine et al. 1985) to 5.3 percent (Watson et al. 1984) to 16 percent (Blomquist et al. 1985). More recent studies employing larger samples of autistic males (e.g., Brown et al. 1986) are consistent with the higher incidence rates. Most likely, the variability in these figures is due to the lack of uniform standards for diagnosing autism, the age at which the diagnosis was made, subject selection factors, and the lack of appropriate controls. Although the DSM-III (American Psychiatric Association 1980) criteria for autism were most commonly used, they were not uniformly applied. Still, the available data suggest that the fragile X chromosome abnormality is responsible for an important subgroup of autistic males (Coleman and Gillberg 1985).

Hagerman et al. (1986a) also reported on the incidence of autism among their identified patients with fragile X syndrome. They found that 16 percent of the fragile X males fulfilled all of the DSM-III criteria for infantile autism, while 30 percent of the sample met the criteria for infantile autism, residual state. Some autistic traits were observed in almost all of the 50 fragile X males. These included eye avoidance (90 percent); hand flapping, hand biting, or hand stereotypies (88 percent); and language delays and dysfunctions, such as echolalia (96 percent). Eighteen percent of the males showed a pervasive lack of responsiveness at their present age; 44 percent showed this trait in their early childhood years only. Hagerman et al. (1986a) recommended that chromosome analysis be completed for every child diagnosed as autistic or with autistic traits.

Reiss et al. (1986) reported on a pilot investigation of other psychiatric disabilities that may be associated with the fragile X syndrome. Thirteen relatives representing four generations of a large family with the fragile X chromosome completed a psychiatric evaluation. Three of the four males positive for the fragile X syndrome displayed autistic behavior. The three obligate carrier females all had experienced a major affective or schizoaffective disorder. However, these findings cannot be generalized beyond one particular family because a gentic linkage could exist between the fragile X locus and the locus for the particular psychiatric disabilities.

Investigations of the fragile X syndrome have typically focused on males positive for this chromosomal abnormality. Few studies have examined the characteristics of female carriers. Preliminary work suggests that approximately one-third of heterozygous females may be mildly retarded, or exhibit more serious impairments (Turner et al. 1980). Hagerman (1986) reported as many as 50 percent of heterozygous fragile X females may show some degree of impairment, such as learning disabilities or academic problems with or without retardation.

Fryns' (1986) summary data on 144 obligate female carriers are consistent with these reports. The women in this study were identified following a confirmed diagnosis of the fragile X syndrome in 112 different males. Of these women, 95 were functioning in the average range of intelligence; 46 females were functioning significantly below average. Eleven women were classified as mildly retarded (IQ = 70–55), whereas nine women were believed to be moderately retarded. However, Fryns' criteria for determining level of cognitive functioning were not fully specified. Psychiatric problems were also noted in 10 percent of the females with average intelligence, and 20 percent of the females with some degree of mental retardation. These included psychotic behavior, extreme shyness, problems with social adaptation, and difficulty with child-rearing tasks.

In regard to their physical characteristics, 28 percent of the females examined had facial features similar to those described in fragile X positive males (i.e., long face, prominent forehead, and mandibular prognathism). These facial characteristics were observed more frequently in women with cognitive impairments (55 percent) versus those with averge intelligence (14 percent). Unfortunately, cytogenetic testing of obligate female carriers does not consistently show a fragile X site, making genetic counseling extremely difficult. Previous reports (e.g., Sutherland 1977) indicated that the chromosome abnormality is present in lower proportions in the cells of older women. In Fryns' (1986) sample, all females with at least some characteristic facial features were positive for the fragile X syndrome, regardless of age and level of cognitive functioning. Thus associated physical characteristics may be a more reliable predictor of the condition in females than is true for males.

Another growing area of interest and research has been the effects of folic acid treatment on the aberrant behaviors of fragile X positive males. Anecdotal reports on the treatment's effectiveness in reducing negative behaviors and improving cognitive functioning have prompted more rigorous studies. Hagerman et al. (1986a) reported on a double-blind, crossover study with 25 fragile X positive males ages 1 to 31 years. The patients received 10 mg of folic acid each day during the six-month treatment period, versus a six-month placebo trial. Dependent measures included the males' performance on psychological and language assessments, as well as parent or care taker reports and ratings of their behavior over the 12-month period.

Although the group as a whole did not show changes on these measures, pre-pubertal males on folic acid showed significant improvement in their psychological test scores compared to the placebo controls. Prepubertal males also showed improvement in their behavior over the course of treatment. However, these findings were not supported in a multiple-baseline, placebo-controlled study of three prepubertal boys when the dependent variables were more tightly defined (Madison et al. 1986a). Additional research is clearly needed, with attention to the age, placement (i.e., home vs. institution), and cognitive level of the fragile X males as possible predictors of treatment effectiveness.

The variability in phenotypic expression among fragile X positive individuals, as well as their differing responses to a potential treatment option, has implications for early diagnosis. Affected individuals may exhibit any number of the characteristics described above, or none at all. This makes detection of the syndrome extremely difficult. The cost of cytogenetic studies and the potential for false negatives must also be considered in recommending karyotyping. Still, current investigators in the field suggest that all males with an unknown etiology for mental retardation and/or autism be screened for the fragile X syndrome. This recommendation has been broadened to include females with mental retardation or significant learning disabilities. Turner et al. (1986) recommended a comprehensive program of cytogenetic screening for all currently identified persons with intellectual handicaps, followed by routine screening of children in the school system. Early diagnosis of the fragile X syndrome will facilitate the detection of other family members at risk, such as potential female carriers.

Chapter 13

Rectal Digging, Feces Smearing, and Coprophagy

These are relatively low prevalence chronic behavior problems found mostly among the profoundly retarded living in large public residential facilities (Frieden 1977). There is little literature on this topic, perhaps because of its repugnant nature, and little is known of its etiology and treatment. However, it does have serious consequences (e.g., social ostracism and chronic infestation with intestinal parasites). It often occurs in a chain, starting with either scavenging and pica, then rectal digging, then feces smearing, culminating in coprophagy. However, many variations of this chain have been observed. One cannot assume that coprophagy is always the end point of rectal digging. We have on different occasions found that constipation, hemorrhoids, or masturbation per ano have been the setting factors for rectal digging and feces smearing without coprophagy.

One study (Frieden and Johnson 1979) successfully treated feces smearing and coprophagy in a profoundly retarded boy by removing the positive attention he had been receiving during the showering and clean-up following an incident. Foxx and Martin (1975) successfully used overcorrection, that is, making the client "clean up the mess" as a consequence for the chain of scavenging, pica, rectal digging, and feces smearing. It appears that these behaviors are often jointly under the control of organic and environmental stimuli, and that successful treatment must be based on both rationales. Frieden and Johnson (1979) gave the model for rectal digging, feces smearing, and coprophagy; it seems to be a good one (Table 1).

Table 1. Screening model to determine the motivation and reinforcement for rectal digging, coprophagy, or feces smearing

Part 1
- Screen for physical conditions that could be producing irritations in the anal area.
- Screen for pica problem of ingesting objects that may be irritating the anal area during bowel movements.
- If screening is positive, rectal digging may be maintained by negative reinforcement.
- Feces smearing may be an indirect consequence of rectal digging.

Part 2
- Does the resident attempt to avoid "getting caught" engaging in these types of behavior?
- Are the incidents of feces smearing elaborate?
- Do the types of behavior tend to occur when activities and play materials are unavailable?
- If screening is positive, motivation for all three problems may involve self-stimulation.

(continued)

Table 1.   Screening model to determine the motivation and reinforcement for rectal digging, coprophagy, or feces smearing *(continued)*

Part 3

- Does the problem behavior occur in situations that are known to be aversive to the resident?
- When the behavior occurs, is the resident taken from one place (e.g., program area) to another (e.g., residential area) to be cleaned?
- If screening is positive, feces smearing and coprophagy may be maintained by negative reinforcement.

Part 4

- Does the resident receive little attention for appropriate behavior? Does the resident "present" himself to attending staff after he has smeared feces?
- Does the resident attempt to shower himself or to get into bathtubs by himself at times other than the regular washing time, even if he does not exhibit self-washing skills?
- Even if the resident appears "upset" while he is being washed because of any of the three types of problem behavior, does he appear "cheerful" when the washing and drying are over?
- If screening is positive, feces smearing and coprophagy may be maintained by positive reinforcement.

Chapter 14

Abnormal Stereotyped Behaviors

Stereotyped behaviors (stereotypies) are repetitive, topographically invariant motor behaviors or action sequences in which reinforcement is not specified or is noncontingent, and the performance of which is regarded as pathologic (Schroeder 1970). There are many uses of the term *stereotypy* to describe nonpathologic behaviors in normal individuals and groups (e.g., in ethology, social psychology, and operant conditioning).

Abnormal stereotyped acts, in the clinical sense, refer to deviant behaviors that occur mostly in the mentally retarded, the mentally ill, the autistic, and the blind. They are observed in perhaps two-thirds of these populations (O'Brien 1981). Berkson (1967) offered the following list of stereotypies: 1) whole body movements or postures (body rocking, twirling); 2) other repetitive movements (head rolling, head banging);

3) nonrepetitive movements (limb and body postures, digit sucking, eye poking, gouging); 4) complex hand movements; 5) repetitive manipulation of objects; and 6) repetitious utterance of meaningless sounds. Excluded from the list are dyskinesias due to neuropathology, motor tics, and compulsive behaviors. Different categories of stereotyped behavior are not often clearly delineated in the literature. Stereotypy may be a normal behavior in infancy and in early childhood (Sallustro and Atwell 1978).

We have departed from the usual practice of treating stereotyped behavior as a larger class of which self-injurious behaviors, ruminative vomiting, and self-induced seizures are subsets. Some of these behaviors (e.g., head banging) appear to be topographically related to other stereotyped behavior. However, many retarded self-injurious clients exhibit no stereotyped behaviors at all. In fact, prevalence studies of institutional populations (Maisto et al. 1978; Schroeder et al. 1978) suggest that head banging is accompanied by other stereotypies like rocking, head weaving, and hand waving in only 30 to 40 percent of the subjects. Strategies for managing stereotypies and self-injurious behavior differ considerably (Barron and Sandman 1984, 1985; Frankel and Simmons 1976). The disorders do not covary when one of them is successfully modified, and the severity of their social consequences is of different orders of magnitude. Self-injurious behavior is far more dangerous and disruptive than stereotyped behavior.

Of course, a functional dichotomy does not influence the theoretical speculations as to the origin, development, or adaptive significance of stereotyped behaviors. These have been covered in several excellent reviews (Baumeister 1978; Baumeister and Forehand 1973; Berkson 1967, 1983; Forehand and Baumeister 1976; Lewis and Baumeister, 1982). The two main theoretical positions—the arousal hypothesis and the learning hypothesis—reflect the relative amount of emphasis placed on internal (e.g., neural oscillators) or external (e.g., environmental) influences responsible for development and maintenance of stereotypy. Stereotyped behavior seems to differ from other patterns in that "for the most part, the stimuli which initiate, guide and reward stereotyped behaviors have their origin within the organism performing the act" (Berkson 1983). This feature often makes them highly resistive to intervention because they are only partially responsive to external stimulation. Thus, while conditioned avoidance and attention-getting reinforcement hypotheses have utility with respect to aggression or self-injurious behavior, this is less true for stereotypy.

Most of the intervention research on stereotyped behavior has been on body rocking, head weaving, and hand waving among the institutionalized profoundly retarded or autistic (LaGrow and Repp 1984). There have been a number of interesting correlational studies of incidence and experimental manipulations that have revealed a variety of setting conditions that affect stereotypy in this population; they will be reviewed briefly.

A number of variables have been implicated in the increase of stereotypy. It is negatively related to age and intelligence (Berkson 1964; Berkson and Davenport 1962; Klaber and Butterfield 1968) and positively related to type of physical impairment (Guess and Rutherford 1967; Kaufman and Levitt 1965). In the hearing impaired, head rolling and body rocking are more prevalent; hand waving occurred more frequently in the visually impaired. Responsiveness to the environment (e.g., object manipulation) is negatively related to stereotypy (Berkson and Mason 1964; Guess and Rutherford 1967). Thus complex hand wavers are less affected by competing stimuli such as novel objects than are body rockers, apparently because their hands are occupied.

A number of environmental ecologic conditions tend to increase stereotypy; crib confinement (Warren and Burns 1970); food deprivation (Kaufman and Levitt 1965);

intense ambient noise (Forehand and Baumeister 1970b); emotion-producing restriction of location or movement to novel situations (Berkson and Mason 1964; Berkson et al. 1963); prior movement restraint (Forehand and Baumeister 1970a); reduced sensory stimulation (Higgenbottam and Chow 1975; Tizard 1968); frustration (Baumeister and Forehand 1971); and the presence of certain other patients (Baumeister and Forehand 1970).

Ecologic conditions that provide for enriched visual stimulation, object manipulation, and programmed alternative behaviors tend to decrease stereotypy even if available noncontingently (Berkson and Mason 1964, 1964b; Forehand and Baumeister 1970b, 1971; Warren and Burns 1970).

Contingent punishment has been reported relatively infrequently as a technique to reduce stereotyped behaviors where self-injury or aggression was not involved. Hamilton and Standahl (1969) used contingent direct and remote electrical stimulation to suppress stereotyped growling in a profoundly mentally retarded institutionalized woman. Other vocalizations (mooing and chattering) during treatment were not affected in the treatment. Growling was suppressed over 95 percent during shock but not during shock-free periods. Treatment out-of-doors with the remote device yielded a similar result. Control was then transferred to ward staff, who punished the behavior on an intermittent schedule on a 24-hour basis. Growling declined over three months and remained at a low rate on follow-up one year later.

Baumeister and Forehand (1972) administered contingent electrical stimulation for extremely high-rate rocking in three profoundly mentally retarded institutionalized clients and also achieved dramatic suppression and avoidance but no generalization to other settings on a 10-month follow-up. Suppression in the treatment room was maintained. Risley (1968) reported suppression and avoidance of rocking as a result of a loud "no" and a shake in a severely autistic girl with whom dangerous climbing had been punished previously by electrical stimulation. Symptom substitution was also reported. Another interesting point was that generalized imitative behaviors did not occur in this girl until rocking was inhibited. This was a clear demonstration that stereotyped behaviors sometimes prohibit the development of adaptive behaviors. Differential reinforcement and extinction proved unsuccessful in decelerating her inappropriate behaviors. However, once the stereotyped behavior was inhibited, imitation training proceeded in the laboratory and at home.

Avoidance conditioning was used by Lovaas et al. (1965b) to build prosocial behaviors (approaches, hugs, kisses) and to inhibit a variety of inappropriate behaviors, one of which was rocking, in severely autistic twins. Prosocial contacts increased as rocking and aggression were suppressed. Suppression lasted for more than 10 months but eventually extinguished. Reinstatement of the contingency took only one trial. "No" was acquired as a negative reinforcer. Again little generalization beyond the therapist and the setting was achieved. However, nurses' single-blind ratings indicated an increase in dependency on adults, responsiveness to adults, affection seeking, happiness, and contentment, and a decrease in pathologic behaviors, anxiety, and fear.

Withdrawal of reinforcement for noninjurious stereotyped behaviors has not been used by itself extensively. This is not surprising since environmental impoverishment and reduced sensory stimulation tend to increase stereotypy. Extinction or time-out alone is not likely to be very effective. Extinction plus reinforcement of alternative activities has proven very effective in two experiments (Baumeister and Forehand 1971; Favell 1973). Severely retarded subjects were taken from their wards to an experimental room and reinforced for lever pulling or toy play while stereotypy was ignored. Rocking and head weaving disappeared, but returned when the alternative activity was extinguished or not performed. In the Baumeister and Forehand experiment, a large rebound or "frustration" effect occurred. No generalization or follow-up data were reported.

Time-out from a preferred activity has been effective in a number of experiments. Green et al. (1970) achieved an abrupt 95 percent decrease in rocking in a severely retarded, blind institutionalized subject when distortion of music on her favorite records was made contingent on rocking. Continuous and intermittent schedules were effective, although extensive thinning of the schedule and follow-up were not reported. Laws et al. (1971) found that contingent ignoring of stereotyped head bobbing and hand movements and contingent praise for appropriate eye contact and a handshake gradually decreased these behaviors by 80 percent in two severely autistic children in a language program. Shouting "wrong" for stereotyped movements had no effect. Sachs (1973) timed-out a body twirler, hand waver, and growler who was in a special class. Exclusion time-out decreased the behavior 50 percent, but resulted in screaming and tantrums; withdrawal time-out (turning away) suppressed the behaviors 95 percent. Generalization and follow-up data were not reported. Brawley et al. (1969) achieved a gradual 90 percent reduction of face slapping, hand movements, and garbled talk by contingent withdrawal of attention and by contingently attending to appropriate behaviors in a less structured program for an autistic boy. Anecdotal generalization data suggest that gains were maintained when checked three months later. In a clinic setting, Nordquist and Wahler (1973) trained parents to reinforce appropriate verbalizations and motor imitation in their retarded autistic child while timing him out for stereotypy in his room at home. Gradually, 95 percent suppression occurred at the clinic and at home, especially when television viewing was added to reinforcement during time-in. This result seems similar to that found by Solnick et al. (1977) for time-out of self-injurious behavior under enriched time-in conditions.

The seclusion time-out method was used by Pendergrass (1972) in a thorough study of its effects on stereotyped behaviors of two withdrawn SMR boys. One subject banged toys on the floor or other people and bit himself—an example of self-injurious behavior (SIB). The other twirled strings and emitted a variety of body jerks. The sessions also contained an interesting feature in that one subject could watch the other being secluded. For the first subject, who exhibited mainly SIB, aggression, and destruction, timing-out aggression and destruction abruptly reduced all three misbehaviors and increased his watching of others. For the second subject, who exhibited mainly stereotyped behaviors, time-out of string twirling had a substantial effect but did not generalize to jerking movements or watching others. Aggression increased when the time-out was initiated. The second subject also showed a rebound in punished and unpunished behaviors following the punishment condition. While watching others, appropriate responding, and touching others increased during post-treatment for the first subject, these behaviors decreased for second subject. Pendergrass speculated that the collateral behaviors were more closely chained together for the first subject than for the second. However, the major difference in the two subjects seems more likely to be that the topography of the first subject's behaviors were directed more toward the environment than those of the second subject. This is precisely the distinction between stereotyped behaviors and other maladaptive behaviors to which Berkson (1967) has alluded.

Reinforcement of alternative behaviors has been investigated in a number of laboratory and classroom settings. Mulhern and Baumeister (1971) performed a laboratory experiment with differential reinforcement of incompatible behavior (DRI) on two SMR institutionalized high-rate rockers strapped into a rocking chair. If they sat still for 4 seconds, they received a reinforcement. Subsequently, the differential reinforcement of other behavior (DRO) interval was increased 12 seconds. About a 30 percent reduction in rocking occurred. Apparently, these subjects sometimes assumed a fixed posture to control rocking, only to follow it with a burst of high-rate rocking. This is an example where choosing the apparently perfectly incompatible response (sitting still) did not effect a large decrease in rocking. In a similar laboratory experiment, Lovaas et al. (1971) trained three groups of children (mute autistics, echolalic autistics, and normals) to approach a candy dispenser at the sound of a tone while they were either free of self-stimulating activities or were hand waving, body rocking, finger tapping, fidgeting, or staring at self. All three groups approached the dispenser with the same latency if they had not been self-stimulating, but mute autistic persons took nearly twice as long to approach if they were engaged in self-stimulatory behavior. They also self-stimulated more in a neutral room than in the experimental room and more in the experimental room after satiation with food reinforcement than before it. On the other hand, mute autistic persons did not respond to experimental attempts to satiate self-stimulation. Weisberg et al. (1973) did a well-controlled study on two profoundly retarded, institutionalized men; one was a hand waver and the other stared fixedly at his hand. Food and praise contingent on imitation of specific alternative motor behaviors and the nonimitation of self-stimulatory behaviors effected a gradual 95 percent decrease. Fading, imitative cues, and food reinforcement on an intermittent schedule resulted in a maintained low rate of stereotypy.

DRO was used in a structured classroom setting in two experiments. Repp et al. (1974) reinforced with praise and hugs refraining from lip flapping or rocking in three SMR children. The DRO interval was shaped, beginning with the inverse of the mean rate of stereotypy during baseline and increasing in 10- or 20-second increments contingent on prior performance. More than 90 percent reduction was achieved in all subjects. Barkley and Zuynick (1976) used brief contingent restraint to stop high-rate body contortions in a moderately retarded girl, then progressive DRO intervals for no stereotypy in a structured learning situation. Eventually, two hours of stereotypy-free behavior was maintained, and control was transferred to the teacher.

It should be noted that practically none of the experiments on stereotypy cited thus far except for those using punishment have presented data of generalization, follow-up, or comparisons among different procedures. This is not the case with research on overcorrection.

Foxx and Azrin (1973) have theorized that stereotyped behaviors are dominant "inward-directed" response patterns reinforced mostly by proprioceptive and sensory stimuli incompatible with "outward-directed" social activities. Overcorrection is designed to redirect and reinforce outward activities incompatible with stereotypy. They compared four procedures in suppressing the mouthing behavior of two severely mentally retarded girls in a day-care setting. Order of procedures for one girl was: 1) free reinforcement, 2) reinforcement for nonmouthing, 3) punishment by a slap, 4) free reinforcement, and 5) overcorrection. For the second girl, the order was: 1) free reinforcement, 2) distasteful solution, 3) punishment by a slap, 4) reinforcement for nonmouthing (DRO, 10-sec), and 5) overcorrection. Thus order effects were only partially unconfounded. For the first girl, order of amount of suppression was overcorrection, punishment by slapping, noncontingent reinforcement, and DRO. For the second girl, it was overcorrection, punishment by a distasteful solution, DRO, free reinforcement, and punishment by slapping. A second experiment extended these results to overcorrection for head weaving and hand clapping. In all cases, overcorrection resulted in far more suppression than the other behaviors. Previous results of DRO and physical punishment were not replicated, although the different studies are hardly comparable because of the open day-care setting.

In another study, Azrin et al. (1973) compared the effects of two procedures: reinforcement of alternative outward-directed activities, and reinforcement plus autism reversal overcorrection. Subjects were nine residents in a ward of 32 institutionalized severely and profoundly retarded persons. These residents exhibited body rocking, head weaving, hand waving, pill rolling, string twirling, and staring at fingers. During reinforcement periods, residents were taught how to use toys, and so on. Stereotypy was ignored. During autism reversal, if stereotypy occurred, the resident was reprimanded, removed to another room, and given 20 minutes of gradual guidance in an incompatible behavior. While the reinforcement program alone reduced stereotypy in the ward by 40 percent, reinforcement plus autism reversal almost completely eliminated it in three days. All ward staff were trained in the procedures, but no follow-up is reported. It should be noted that the comparison of the two procedures is confounded with time and exposure to practice. Nevertheless, the results are very impressive.

Other experiments on overcorrection generally confirm these dramatic effects. However, as with overcorrection of self-injurious behavior, poor generalization and substitution frequently occurs (Doke and Epstein 1975; Epstein et al. 1974; Rollings et al. 1977). One particularly well-controlled study (Rollings et al. 1977) achieved dramatic success with a profoundly retarded institutionalized body rocker but not with a head weaver. Strong substitution occurred and new stereotypies emerged once old ones were suppressed. They suggest a much more guarded optimism as to the effectiveness and generality of overcorrection to different behaviors of different subjects and in different settings.

Pharmacotherapy

Stereotyped behavior in laboratory rodents, like gnawing in rats, can be reliably developed by lesions or chemical agents that promote hypersensitivity states in the postsynaptic dopamine receptor (Lewis and Baumeister 1982). These stereotypies can be suppressed by dopamine blockers. In one of the neatest transitions from the laboratory to the clinical setting, the administration of neuroleptic drugs may reliably suppress stereotyped behaviors in retarded, autistic, and schizophrenic patients. In contrast, monoaminergic drugs like stimulants, antidepressants, and the anticonvulsants carbamazepine and valproic acid may increase stereotyped behavior. Low dose neuroleptics may occasionally increase stereotypies by virtue of presynaptic receptor blockade.

The risks of neuroleptic therapy—cognitive blunting, extrapyramidal symptoms, tardive dyskinesia—compromise the utility of pharmacotherapy for stereotypy. Drug treatment is indicated only in severe cases, when stereotypies are severe, disabling, and compromise an individual's adaptation to a habilitative program. The first-line treatment for stereotypy is to change the patient's environment and reduce excessive stimulation, boredom, frustration, sensory deprivation, or other elements that may promote or aggravate the problem. The second step is to initiate a behavioral program. Pharmacotherapy should be limited to severe cases for whom other measures have been ineffective.

Chapter 15

Prader-Willi Syndrome

In 1956, Prader et al. described a syndrome of mental retardation, short stature, obesity, hypogonadism, and muscular hypotonia. More than 200 cases of Prader-Willi syndrome (PWS) have been reported; the estimated incidence is between one in 5,000 and one in 10,000 (Crink et al. 1980). Several specific chromosomal abnormalities have been described in PWS (Goh et al. 1984), although no genetic deficit that is central to the disorder, unique, or pathognomonic of PWS patients has yet been identified. Studies indicate that at least 50 percent of PWS patients have a deletion involving the proximal portion of the long arm of chromosome 15, and some authorities believe that when PWS is diagnosed according to rigid criteria, all patients show the chromosomal abnormality. Etiology and pathophysiology are unknown, although virtually all of the abnormalities observed in PWS point to a disturbance in the development and function of the midline structures of the brain including the thalamus and the hypothalamus.

PWS is another example, like Lesch-Nyhan, of a specific genetic syndrome that is predictably associated with a specific kind of behavioral disturbance. The major behavior problem of PWS patients is hyperphagia, which may be severe, bizarre, and life threatening. Prader-Willi children forage food. They try to consume extraordinary amounts of food with no concern for taste or quality. They may consume garbage, dog food, frozen bread, or other unappetizing things. They are not bulimic; they don't eat on binges, and induced vomiting does not occur in PWS. Their foraging behavior is not pica; they tend to confine their intake to recognized, if unappetizing, foodstuffs. Their behavior around acquiring food may be ingenious and incorrigible. Attempts to control obesity in children with PWS through dietary management have met with limited success (Page et al. 1983). Stealing food may be the modus vivendi of a child with PWS, and parents may have to resort to heroic measures to secure the pantry, cupboards, freezer, and refrigerator. The ingenuity and determination of PWS children in surreptitiously obtaining edibles is almost legendary and belies their cognitive deficits. Serial weighing may be the only way to discover whether such a child is, in fact, stealing food.

Other behavioral manifestations of the disorder include emotional incontinence, dramatic mood swings, temper tantrums, and a tendency to pick, fidget, or scratch at their skin.

Differential diagnosis of PWS is often delayed; the average age of diagnosis in boys is around 10 years and in girls is more than 10 years. Most important to the diagnosis is the fact that PWS obesity is preceded by a phase of apathy, extreme hypotonia, areflexia, and an inability to suck and swallow. These symptoms often necessitate gavage feeding for weeks or even months, and produce a very frustrating period for mothers of PWS infants. Because of the first-phase symptomatology, the second phase of the syndrome, which is characterized by the child's alertness and insatiable appetite, is often welcomed by the mother. She is happy about the changes that have taken place and encourages the newly acquired eating behaviors (Zellweger 1984).

Although the hyperphagia of PWS has been attributed to hypothalamic mechanisms, there is no rational biologic treatment in current use. It is not unreasonable to consider medications that are of occasional use in bulimic patients, such as imipramine or phenelzine. Recently, naloxone was reported useful in the treatment of hyperphagia in obese patients (Wolkowitz et al. 1985). Anabolic steroids have been used to stimulate growth. Anorectic drugs like amphetamine and fenfluramine have only short-term effects on appetite in normal individuals or in obese people, but their effect in PWS is not known.

The only established treatment for hyperphagia in PWS is behavioral. Unfortunately, the effects of even a well-constructed behavioral program may not generalize, and food restriction, in its most draconian form, may be the only solution to a disfiguring and potentially mortal ailment. The behavioral methods described thus far include differential reinforcement of other behavior, contingency contracting, self-monitoring, exercise, contingent social isolation, aversive-shock therapy, and over-correction (Page et al. 1983). Group homes established exclusively for PWS patients have promise, although group homes with both PWS patients and non-PWS patients are not, as a rule, successful.

There is no psychiatric literature to date on the PWS. Since the disorder may not be uncommon, it is not unreasonable to expect at least some psychiatric attention turned to this intriguing problem, perhaps with the development of an effective, rational treatment.

Chapter 16

Pica in the Mentally Retarded

The word *pica* comes from the Latin for magpie, a bird known to pick up and ingest inedible things. The definition of pica refers to eating but sometimes it has also pertained to mouthing or scavenging for inedibles. Such a broad definition is probably responsible for the wide variation of estimates of the prevalence and incidence of pica in retarded and nonretarded populations. Essentially two sets of literature on pica have developed over the years: "developmental" or childhood pica, and pica in the mentally retarded. They overlap considerably, but, until recently, one set of researchers rarely cited the research literature of the other.

Epidemiologic studies of pica (Barltrop 1966; Lourie et al. 1963) suggest that it is quite high (50 percent) in children at one year of age, but decreases rapidly to less than 10 percent by age four. The most frequently ingested items were, in descending order: paper, clothing, dirt, matches, toiletries, plaster, writing materials, tobacco, and other items. Developmental pica is not related to sex, race, family rank, place of birth of parents, nor to the size or social position of the family; it is related to mouthing, bottle feeding, finger sucking, late weaning, bed-wetting, and having siblings who also engaged in pica. These results suggest that home environmental factors affect the occurrence of childhood pica. A similar observation was made by Chisolm and Harrison (1956) that, in many homes, maternal deprivation or disturbed child-parent relationships precipitate the ingestion of nonfood materials. The most serious consequence of childhood pica is the ingestion of lead. Environmental sources of lead include lead-based paint chips and wall dust (Zarkowsky 1976). With respect to the ingestion of lead, the main question is: Does pica cause lead ingestion or vice versa? Both pica and lead intoxication are associated with nutritional deficiencies, especially vitamins C and D, iron, calcium, and phosphorus (Mahaffey et al. 1976; Sorrell et al. 1977). However, there is not good agreement among studies as to the nature of the relationships between pica and nutritional deficiencies (Gutelius et al. 1962; Johnson and Tenuta 1979; Mooty et al. 1975). For instance, Gutelius et al. (1962) found that replenishing an iron-deficient diet with intramuscular injections of iron did not reduce children's pica. Obviously, methodological rigor in this area must cede to ethical considerations, and case-controlled epidemiologic studies in humans will be the only way to address this important question. Animal studies suggest that there could be a nutritional basis for lead-induced pica. Snowdon (1977) showed that rats who had been made deficient in calcium, zinc, and magnesium ingested foods containing more lead, whereas their restoration to a nutritionally adequate diet eliminated lead ingestion. Calcium-deficient rats also failed to form a learned aversion to lead acetate, suggesting that mineral deficiency may be a major factor in producing lead pica. How far such animal models can be generalized to children, for whom pica is also related to early feeding practices and the home environment, needs to be investigated. It is likely that a complex relationship exists between nutritional and sociocultural factors in placing a child at risk for lead pica, and the mental retardation that may develop as a consequence.

The best study of pica in the retarded population was by Danford and Huber (1982), who found that 25.8 percent of a population of 991 institutionalized mentally retarded adults engaged in pica. Pica was negatively correlated with IQ and chronological age, and positively correlated with decreased zinc and iron levels. The primary items ingested (e.g., tobacco, feces, coffee grounds, oak leaves) may be related to dietary insufficiencies, and, in some cases, has been reduced by the appropriate dietary supplements (Danford et al. 1982; Lofts 1986).

There is surprisingly little research on behavioral treatment of pica in the retarded population. However, when one considers the risk involved in any type of experimentation with persons who swallow rocks, razor blades, towels, screws, safety pins, and so on, it is clear why only procedures and settings where risks can be minimized have been investigated. Contingent physical restraint or blindfolding when pica occurs (Singh and Bakker 1984; Singh and Winton 1984) and overcorrection appear to have been successful management procedures with these behaviors (Foxx and Martin 1975; Matson et al. 1978; Mulick et al. 1980a; Rusch et al. 1976). It seems likely that the effectiveness of the overcorrection procedure was related to the fact that the subjects of these experiments were fairly compliant with the oral hygiene positive practice methods used (e.g., brushing the teeth for 15 minutes with mouthwash). It appears that maintenance, but not generalization, is good with overcorrection for pica.

Albin (1977) has criticized the practice of "baiting" the treatment environment to increase an artificial frequency of scavenging and pica, which could then be overcorrected and suppressed. This practice and the consequation of every response during treatment may account for the lack of generalization to the natural setting. Albin raised the speculation that pica is an aberrant generalization of finger feeding beyond which pica patients have not progressed. Thus far this speculation has not been tested experimentally, however.

Chapter 17

Rumination

Ruminative vomiting consists of repeated vomiting, chewing, and reingestion of the vomitus. Ruminative vomiting is not to be confused with other types of vomiting, where vomitus is not reingested. Vomiting is one of the most common symptoms of infancy and early childhood; its occurrence may reflect a variety of maturational problems, illnesses, or family problems (Nelson et al. 1969). It is also an adaptive "reflex" that occurs at all ages as 1) a biologic sentinel of host defense against acute toxicity and infection; 2) a manifestation of altered taste sensitivity related to burns, cancer, renal failure, zinc toxicity, lead toxicity, at least 30 different medications, iron deficiency, vitamin deficiency, diseases of the mouth, hypothalamic malfunctions, and liver disease; and 3) a conditioned emotional response concomitant with depression, anorexia nervosa, or even as the result of a single traumatic incident with a particular food (taste aversion). In such cases, vomiting disappears after the illness is treated or maturation occurs. In contrast, ruminative vomiting seems to have a significant learned component that is maintained by sensory reinforcement. Thus it is a highly complex behavior, chronic and resistant to therapeutic intervention.

Early Childhood Rumination

Early childhood rumination is distinguished from later childhood or adult ruminative vomiting because it may be life threatening, it may or may not be accompanied by mental retardation, and it may simply reflect a disrupted parent-infant relationship around feeding. It rarely occurs beyond the age of two (Richmond and Eddy 1957; Richmond et al. 1958). The prevalence is unknown, although a number of uncontrolled clinical case studies in psychiatric and pediatric settings have been published (reviewed by Kanner 1957). In most cases, the prescribed treatment is hospitalization and copious noncontingent attention to the child by attending staff who attempt to establish a more stable parenting relationship with the infant. Sometimes this tactic is successful (Berlin et al. 1957; Wright and Menolascino 1970); sometimes it is not (Holvoet 1982). It seems that improving the feeding environment with selective approval for eating appropriately may often have a significant effect on ruminative vomiting. However, most of the case reports in the literature lack the experimental rigor to demonstrate a causal link between improved mother-child relationships and decreased ruminative vomiting (Singh 1981b).

Late Childhood and Adult Ruminative Vomiting

Although there are no prevalence studies in the nonretarded population, it is likely that chronic ruminative vomiting is rare. The prevalence studies that have been done (Ross 1972; Singh and Dawson 1980) have been with institutionalized mentally retarded people. It appears to occur in 5 to 10 percent of this population, almost exclusively in the severely and profoundly retarded or in individuals who are autistic. It is often accompanied by sterotyped behaviors, with a duration measured in years. Only rarely is it related to an anatomic or physiologic abnormality. Since the age of onset is usually several years after institutionalization, it does not occur as a continuation of an early infant problem. In older children and adults, it is less likely to be life threatening, although it may be accompanied by severe weight loss, dehydration, respiratory complications, infections, and dental problems (e.g., periodontitis and severe caries). Ruminative vomiting also has an antisocial component; ruminators tend to be socially isolated by virtue of their odor and appearance.

Treatment of Chronic Ruminative Vomiting in Mental Retardation

Since chronic ruminative vomiting in mentally retarded persons involves mainly the severely to profoundly retarded, therapies based on the establishment of a psychotherapeutic relationship have not been very useful. Neither is psychopharmacology, although this question has not been explored very well at all. Programs based on the premise that rumination is maintained by learning principles have been somewhat more successful.

Pavlov (1927) demonstrated that vomiting is a conditional reflex. Rumination can be considered a conditioned reinforced reflex chained to vomiting and therefore can be suppressed by operant procedures.

Several conditioning procedures have been based on the assumption that there are certain stimulus aspects to the consummatory response that can be changed to alter rumination. Procedures based on hypotheses concerning consistency of the food (Rast et al. 1981), proper eating and mastication (Ball et al. 1974), and pacing of the eating by using minimeals (Azrin and Armstrong 1973) seem to show moderately positive results, but often cannot be replicated in different subjects and settings.

The most dramatic effects have been found by the direct application of punishment—for example, bitter substances like lemon juice in the mouth (Sajwaj et al. 1974); electric shock (White and Taylor 1967); overcorrection, such as brushing the teeth with mouthwash (Singh et al. 1982)—contingent on ruminative vomiting. Less dramatic effects have been found with extinction (i.e., ignoring the attention-getting aspects of vomiting) (Wolf et al. 1970) and differential reinforcement of other behaviors (i.e., redirecting or distracting the client when vomiting is about to occur) (Mulick et al. 1980b). All of the above procedures have the limitation of generalizing only with difficulty to other settings. Program follow-up usually has not occurred beyond six months after treatment. We do not really know how long their effects last.

One operant procedure that shows promise is based on the notion put forth by Kanner (1936) that rumination itself is intrinsically reinforcing and can be averted by food satiation. Jackson et al. (1975) applied such a technique to treatment of two severely retarded chronic ruminators. During the treatment condition subjects simply received double portions of their meals, with a large milk shake 90 minutes later. Rumination dropped to 5 percent of baseline in one subject and 50 percent in another. The rationale for this is very simple and perhaps counterintuitive procedure is that vomiting is an initial response in a chain followed by rumination and then by reconsumption of the vomitus. The chain is triggered by a state of deprivation. Satiation, an incompatible state, averts it.

Two experiments (Rast et al. 1981, 1984) carried the satiation rationale even further by allowing their profoundly retarded ruminators to eat large meals until they refused any more food. Rast et al. were able to demonstrate a parametric inverse relationship between amount of rumination and amount eaten. All clients stopped ruminating completely if allowed to eat until satiety. Surprisingly, the amount eaten was three to eight times their single baseline normal adult portions. The portions were in the form of starches, including potatoes, rice, grits, cream of wheat, and bread. Since all of the subjects were underweight, the anticipated weight gain resulting from the satiation procedure was not an issue in the Rast et al. studies. Dietary studies involving biochemical variables concerning the nutritional properties of different foods and their effects on the digestive system are in progress as of this writing, so that this promising procedure can be of more general use in the treatment of chronic rumination.

In summary, it appears that ruminative vomiting is a complex product of organic and learning variables that is difficult to suppress permanently. There may be several factors that maintain it: organic conditions, such as hiatal hernia; social reinforcers, such as attention; consumatory reinforcers, such as mastication; and primary reinforcers, such as satiation related to food deprivation. The relative importance of these factors may be highly individual. Any attempt to suppress it will probably have to take all of these factors into account.

Chapter 18

Rituals, Preoccupation with Sameness, and Tyrannical Behavior

Patients with severe brain disorders like mental retardation, autism, and head injury tend to have little flexibility or adaptability in coping with environmental change. In an extreme form, this may clinically manifest as a preoccupation with sameness, or a preference for rituals, or a tyrannical insistence that circumstances remain exactly as they always have. Autistic children are well known for their rituals and preoccupation with keeping things the same. Moving the furniture in the living room can provoke a catastrophic reaction. Driving to the supermarket or to the sheltered workshop by a different route may provoke an explosive outburst.

Every parent is familiar with ritual behavior in very young children, especially around bedtime. Parents tend to indulge these preferences, which are perfectly normal developmental variants. As the child grows up, the importance of rituals tends to diminish. In retarded people, ritual behavior and preoccupation with sameness may actually increase as the years pass. Repeated patterns of experience and behavior may grow more firmly entrenched, and deviations may be less well tolerated. A recreational drive in the afternoon may turn into a firm expectation and then into an immutable ritual, the occasion for an emotional explosion if it is delayed, altered, or omitted. The same record has to be played at the same time each day. The same food has to be prepared in exactly the same way. A favorite toy or blanket or stuffed animal is expected to last forever; it is precious, indispensable, even after it has grown filthy and decrepit. Bedtime is the occasion of rituals that may be expanded on, extended, and prolonged with each passing year. Nighttime rituals may grow so complex that the hour of sleep is pushed further and further back. By the time the child is in his or her 20s, the clock may have been turned around and sleep may be delayed to the hours of dawn.

Parents who live with such an individual learn that indulging the ritual is the course of least resistance, just as the parents of very young children learn to comply with even the most outlandish rituals. But the retarded person may never outgrow this phase. As the parents grow older and more socially isolated themselves, they are ever less able to contain or control these rituals. They may themselves be forced to participate in endless nighttime rituals. They may go to any heroic lengths to avoid the tantrums that attend interruption or deviation from established routine. As they grow weary from a lifetime of baby-tending, they grow weaker in resisting the accretion of routines, and this simply aggravates the problem.

The preoccupation with sameness of autistic children represents a well-defined symptom that is usually dealt with by energetic young parents and professional counselors. The same problem in retarded or head-injured adults has a more insidious onset and may be less likely to come to professional attention. Retarded adults living with their aged parents may have very little in the way of external activities or professional support. Their families may have grown resigned to living with the problem rather than seeking professional help; they may be too old and weary to fight the system and win new programs for their child. Their weakness, isolation, and despair may simply compound the tyrannical behavior of the child.

The problem is actually rather easy to solve with the proper kind of psychological programming. The major problem is actually obtaining such services for families who need them. Since tyrannical behavior is most likely to develop in individuals whose day is not properly structured and programmed, treatment begins by introducing an appropriate level of programming, especially out of the home, in a sheltered workshop, in social groups, or in recreational activities. This, however, is almost a cynical recommendation. After all, if such services were available to begin with, the condition might never have developed; the fact that they weren't available suggests that attempts at correction will never be made. In practice, this circular arrangement leaves many retarded people to their own ritual devices, and their families are left with little alternative but to oblige and endure. This they do until they are too feeble to carry on or until they die; then their child is remanded, abruptly, to an institution.

Introducing new programs into the life of an older retarded citizen and winning the confidence of the dispirited family requires special tact and a gentle approach. Professionals in the field are more accustomed to families who advocate staunchly for services for their child; they are less accustomed to the business of winning a neglected client and the client's demoralized parents to the world of vocational training, social skills training, and structured recreation. Outreach programs are more familiar with younger children and their families. They are less familiar with dealing with the problems of older retarded people, who may have never had the benefit of a concerted socialization effort.

A profound attachment to environmental sameness, ritual behavior, and tyrannized relationships may sometimes require the administration of a psychotropic medication, and it is not uncommon for physicians to select a sedating neuroleptic. However, this choice should be made only as a temporary measure, to interrupt entrenched patterns of behavior and to allow a new program to gain a foothold. The major treatments over the long-term are behavioral and programmatic.

Chapter 19

Behavior-Related Eating Problems

There are many types and causes of feeding and eating problems and numerous treatment approaches. A variety of bases for classifying these problems and approaches has been proposed.

One factor in classifying feeding problems is the underlying etiology. For example, Springer (1971) reported that feeding problems in mentally retarded children can be due to neurologic impairment, the child's stopping of eating for no known reason, or well-meaning parents keeping the child on the bottle. The first of these implies an organic basis, the latter two a behavioral one. These are important distinctions because different behaviors become manifest, different treatments are implied, and different professional disciplines may be involved in remediation.

Another means of classifying feeding problems is by the component of the feeding process where the problem occurs. Thus there are children who cannot scoop food onto a spoon and bring it to their mouths because of poor neuromuscular coordination, blindness, or profound mental retardation. Others are unable or unwilling to receive solid food into their mouths or have difficulty with chewing or swallowing. Still other children display socially inappropriate or bizarre behaviors in the context of mealtime.

Most available information on eating and drinking abnormalities is from the perspectives of therapy for neuromotor disabilities. Most available information on self-feeding, social skills, and self-injurious eating behaviors is from the perspective of behavioral learning problems. An area of need is a broad information base dealing with drinking and eating problems from a behavioral perspective. This is remarkable because, as will be shown, a significant proportion of retarded students who do not eat normally do not apparently have physical or neuromotor disabilities that would prevent them from doing so.

Causes of Feeding Problems

For a feeding problem taxonomy based on cause to be useful, it is necessary to distinguish clearly among the causes.

Neuromotor Dysfunction

Utley et al. (1977) listed four characteristics, any one of which would indicate that a patient with a feeding problem has a neuromotor dysfunction: 1) spasticity or increased tone, which may result in stiffness of the oral muscles; 2) athetosis or fluctuating tone, which may be evidenced in uncontrolled movement; 3) hypotonia or decreased tone with resulting flaccidity or lack of strength, and 4) the presence of abnormal reflexes, many of which may involve the oral structures. Similarly, Schmidt (1976) considered abnormal tone to be a primary diagnostic indicator of a neurologically based feeding problem. In addition to those on this list, Campbell (1976, 1979) and Morris (1977) mentioned the presence of abnormal movement patterns and oral hypersensitivity or hyposensitivity. If a patient's eating problem is related to substantial neuromotor dysfunction, care givers should seek the assistance of specially trained therapists (Morris 1977).

Ingram (1962) and Ogg (1975) described procedures for evaluating oral functioning in neurologically impaired children. They especially recommended observing the sequence of responses as the children are fed by a care giver. Assessment should include observation of oral-pharyngeal reflexes, oral sensitivity, dental hygiene, and tongue function. Specific therapeutic procedures recommended for children with substantial neuromotor involvement include exercises to normalize "oral-facial imbalance" or hypersensitivity (e.g., "tongue walking" or facial stimulation) and positioning to inhibit abnormal oral reflexes and to facilitate normal oral movements (Campbell 1976, 1979; Morris 1977; Schmidt 1976). A long period of treatment with specialized training may be necessary to implement the therapeutic procedures.

Physical Abnormalities

In addition to distinguishing children with neuromotor impairment, it is necessary to classify feeding problems according to the proposed taxonomy (i.e., whether the problem is physically based). Illingworth and Lister (1964) described several children demonstrating feeding problems caused by obstructions or anatomic abnormalities during the age at which children normally learn to chew. These abnormalities involved deformities of the digestive tract. Campbell (1979) urged the practitioner dealing with feeding problems to be aware of medical reasons that may account for a child's inability to eat normally. She listed anatomic deviations of the oral musculature, congenital internal abnormalities, and multiple food allergies. A. Jones (1978) also gave many examples of physical abnormalities that could result in self-feeding or eating problems. These included cleft lip or palate, muscular dystrophy, and paralysis that interfered with either self-feeding or eating abilities. Ball et al. (1974) and Laidler (1976) discussed how frequent vomiting also could have a physical basis such as an acute infection.

Many physical abnormalities are best diagnosed and treated by a physician. Some eating problems can be ameliorated by surgery or provision of a prosthesis. Otherwise the prognosis for normal eating is very poor. Self-feeding also may be facilitated by prostheses or adaptive equipment such as specially designed utensils (A. Jones 1978; Gertenrich 1970; Hall 1951). Some problems with a physical basis may be successfully treated with behavior modification programs (Ball et al. 1974) or by a change in diet or feeding schedule (Laidler 1976).

Behavior-Related Causes

Where neuromotor dysfunction (as evidenced by clinically abnormal oral reflexes, tone, movement, or sensitivity) and physical abnormalities can be ruled out, feeding and eating problems can be classified as behavioral. A number of such cases have been reported. Remediation is possible with a fairly short-term intervention using behavioral learning principles (Thompson and Palmer 1974).

Behavior-Related Eating Problems

While behavior is often recognized as a factor in problems concerning self-feeding, appropriate social responses, and self-injurious eating behaviors, eating and drinking problems are characterized by some authors as being neuromotor in origin. Although these may be the majority of the cases, there are many isolated examples of children with eating abnormalities for whom oral neuromotor involvement (as well as physical disabilities) can be ruled out.

Extent of the Problem

Although an appreciable incidence of eating problems among severely and profoundly mentally retarded students is generally recognized, there are few reports of prevalence data. McKrensky (1975) noted that a third of the residents in Massachusetts institutions for the mentally retarded exhibited difficulty in swallowing or chewing foods. Of 234 victims of congenital (prenatal) rubella studied at the Rubella Birth Defects Evaluation Project, 53 percent had difficulties in feeding (Chess et al. 1972). In their sample, 59 percent of the children with physical deviations (defined as hearing, vision, cardiac, and/or neurologic defects) demonstrated feeding problems, as did 32 percent of those without such physical deviations. Likewise, 61 percent of those with psychiatric disorders (cerebral dysfunction, mental retardation, reactive behavior disorder, or autism) demonstrated feeding problems, as did 41 percent of those without such disorders. Among referrals to a developmental disabilities center, 35.3 percent had feeding or eating problems (Gouge and Ekvall 1975). Of these, 19.1 percent had difficulties in self-feeding and 47.6 percent had difficulties in eating. In a private hospital for the profoundly retarded in Pennsylvania, 33 percent of the school-age residents were referred by nurses who thought their inability to eat solids was not due to neuromotor or physical abnormalities (T. Jones 1978).

From a broader population, Palmer et al. (1975) reported that 33 percent of the referrals to the nutrition division of a university-affiliated child development center were children who exhibited severe feeding problems. Such problems included "prolonged subsistence on pureed or junior foods . . . bizarre food habits, dislike of many foods, tantrums during meals, or simply refusal to eat" (p. 333). In the sample of 52 children who ate only pureed foods, 78.8 percent of the problems were due to neuromotor dysfunction (including mental retardation), 3.8 percent to mechanical obstruction, and 17.3 percent to behavioral mismanagement. Coffee and Crawford (1971) similarly reported a 13 to 33 percent incidence of feeding problems in their nutrition division population.

Rationale for Treating Eating Problems

Nutrition and Health

From a more practical—and less educational and therapeutic—viewpoint, there is a body of evidence to demonstrate the importance of a solid food diet in enabling optimum nutrition and development. This rationale provides convincing support for emphasizing the intake, chewing, and swallowing of solid food in programming for mentally retarded students. Suggestions for dealing with feeding problems emphasize that not only should a balanced diet be provided but also a variety of textures, including solids to be chewed. To provide a balanced diet, Heffley (1976) recommended using a juicer to liquefy food for deaf-blind children who refuse solids. Nevertheless, there is evidence that liquefied or semiliquid diets at any age do not provide all of the nutrients and other benefits of solid diet.

Gouge and Ekvall (1975) analyzed the nutritional status of 19 handicapped children. Although the nutritional status of the entire sample was generally low, those with mechanical or postnatal (i.e., behavioral) feeding problems had particular nutritional deficiencies. Those with postnatal feeding problems had an abnormally low intake of ascorbic acid, possibly attributable to parents' feeling that food high in ascorbic acid would not be accepted by the child. Children with mechanical feeding problems had an inordinately low iron intake (Gouge and Ekvall 1975).

Burman (1976) found that the weight gain of children on liquid or semiliquid diets was dramatically less than that of children on solid food. Mitchell et al. (1976) noted that it is difficult to keep a reasonable proportion of protein, fat, and carbohydrate in semiliquid diets.

Even if liquid diets provided the necessary range of nutrients, the benefits of food consistency and texture would not be received. It is not possible with human subjects to identify experimentally the effects of diets lacking in texture and consistency, but such studies have been done with animals. For example, Sreebny (1968) found that, in rats, a liquid feeding regimen induced atrophy of the parotid salivary glands. He concluded that mastication stimulates salivation.

Laidler (1976) suggested that diets low in fiber and bulk are one factor in constipation. The foods he recommended included raw fruits and vegetables. One study (T. Jones 1978) involved profoundly retarded residents who learned to eat solids and began having natural and regular bowel movements.

Coffee and Crawford (1971) condemned soft food diets because of their damaging effects on teeth and gums.

The adverse effects of nonsolid diets are even greater when they are prepared by persons who are not fully cognizant of the nutritional needs of children. Parents, nurses, or ward attendants may present food that provides only a few of the necessary nutrients. Compounding the problems, some retarded students may refuse to eat all but a few foods. Bizarre food habits, such as eating butter by the stick or salt by the spoonful, may also upset the balance of a diet (Thompson and Palmer 1974). Stimbert et al. (1977) concluded: "The poor nutritional status of many low functioning children can be directly attributed to their refusal to accept a variety of foods" (p. 528). In such cases, the children involved are deprived of both the nutritional and textural benefits of normal diets.

Normalization

In the literature on feeding problems, the theme consistently recurs that retarded children should function as similarly as possible to their normal nonhandicapped peers. Studies included socially acceptable use of table utensils and the social aspects of the eating process (e.g., messy eating and stealing). In each example, it is not the intrinsic therapeutic benefit to the child as much as the establishment of behaviors to enable the child to conform with societal norms that motivates treatment programs.

It has been noted also that deviation from normal eating patterns puts an extraordinary burden on the retarded child's most important group, the family (Chess et al. 1972; Wing 1966). Parents must spend extra hours preparing special food and feeding and cleaning their handicapped children with feeding problems (Finnie 1974).

Drooling occurs when saliva is not swallowed automatically (Morris 1977). It is a problem that in itself is not detrimental to the child; however, drooling is messy and may inhibit a child's opportunity to interact socially. According to Morris (1977), the drooler's "constant wetness often isolates him from others and reduces the amount of positive social and language stimulation he receives" (p. 1). Both Morris (1977) and Bosley (1966) suggested that learning to handle solid food eliminates the problem of drooling.

Children with feeding problems may significantly deviate from normal in terms of mealtime behaviors, the kinds of food they will eat, the burdens they place on their families, and their appearance. In enabling such children to obtain an existence as close to normal as possible, it is necessary to provide programming to teach the acceptance of socially appropriate solid food diets.

Relationship of Chewing and Speech

In the education of the mentally retarded, chewing and swallowing of solid food are emphasized as part of the curriculum. This emphasis is based on the belief that the oral-facial movements acquired in the development of chewing and swallowing behaviors also facilitate the development of articulation and speech production (Blockley and Miller 1971; Holser-Buehler 1973; Turton 1971).

Chewing exercises are often recommended for improving speech in retarded children who do not necessarily have any feeding problems. This rationale that chewing facilitates speech has been continually reiterated by representatives of a variety of disciplines such as physical and occupational therapists (Finnie 1974).

There is a contrasting viewpoint. Turton (1971) said that there has been virtually no experimental evidence to support the assumption that eating activities facilitate the development of speech. To support his conclusion, Turton cited evidence showing 1) that the major part of articulation learning in normal children continues well past the age when most learn to eat solid food (Crocker 1969); 2) that articulation errors are not always symptomatic of motor deficits (Winitz 1969); 3) that the movements in speech and eating are different (Moll 1965); 4) that the neurologic controls of speech and eating are not the same (Hixon and Hardy 1964); and 5) that awareness of oral structures (as may result from chewing) is not necessary for the improvement of articulation patterns (Shelton et al. 1970).

Despite years of practice to the contrary in several professional disciplines, Turton's (1971) viewpoint may still be valid. This author, personally, has taught several children who had never chewed solid food but who articulated clearly. One was bilingual. Both functions require fine motor movements of the oral structures, however, and improvement of oral motor coordination should benefit both chewing and speech.

Variables in Treatment

Generally effective techniques for treating eating problems related to behavior are difficult to find (Thompson and Palmer 1974). With the exception of therapy approaches for children with oral neuromotor impairments, reports of treatment of eating problems in severely and profoundly mentally retarded children are rare. Some studies describe behaviors characteristic of retarded students, but do not present information about the general intellectual functioning of their subjects. From the studies available on treatment of eating problems, nine related aspects of treatment programs can be identified that might be used with severely and profoundly mentally retarded students. Although several can often be used in combination, each is described separately.

Psychotherapy

Several programs incorporated psychotherapeutic components into their approach to feeding problems. Martin (1973), for example, emphasized that "failure to thrive, rumination, anorexia and strong food dislikes are all symptoms of possible emotional disorders in children in the family function and should alert the clinician to investigate the emotional status of the child and the parent-child interaction" (p. 773).

Bentoviv (1970) used a psychoanalytic approach to feeding disorders. In dealing with the refusal of a 20-pound, three-and-a-half-year-old to eat, Bernal (1972) incorporated socializing activities and psychotherapeutic play (e.g., feeding a doll) into a treatment involving reinforcement and presentation of solid food only. After one month, she was gaining weight and eating strained food; and after one year she was eating a normal diet.

Because of the general lack of applicability of traditional psychotherapeutic approaches to low functioning individuals, and because of the intensive training necessary to implement such approaches, psychotherapy is not a viable approach to treating the eating problems of many severely or profoundly mentally retarded students, especially those in institutional settings.

Hunger

Hunger was a motivating factor in several feeding programs (Clancy et al. 1969; Holser-Buehler 1973; Illingworth and Lister 1964; Spradlin 1964). When only solid food was presented, by the third day the children became hungry enough to begin to eat whatever food they were given. In no case did any physical harm come to the children. This method, in conjunction with a physician's participation, was urged particularly by Holser-Buehler (1973). In other cases, however, the consequences of the children's refusal may be more motivating than the satisfaction from eating (Premack 1959). Refusal to eat may be so concentrated and prolonged that children suffer from dehydration and require hospitalization.

Gradually Increasing Texture

In helping children who refuse solid food, several authors recommended gradually increasing the consistency or texture of food (Hart 1974; Molloy 1961; Wing 1972). This general procedure is recommended by developmental therapists (Campbell 1976; Morris 1977) for children with behavioral eating problems. Morris (1977) and Schmidt (1976) listed a series of stages of increased food textures for children who do not eat solids. Gradually increasing the texture of food is analogous to, but perhaps less systematic than, the principle of successive approximation or shaping utilized by practitioners of behavior modification (Palmer et al. 1975). T. Jones (1978, 1979) used this method with 10 profoundly mentally retarded children and had only a 30 percent success rate after one month.

Blender

Although a blender may be used to increase the texture of a child's diet gradually (Morris 1977), at least one practitioner (Heffley 1976), recommended that a child's meals be liquefied to provide a nutritious diet. In this case, increasing the texture was not suggested. This practice seems questionable on at least two grounds: 1) lack of texture and chewing may be harmful to children and 2) such a procedure assumes that the child's behavior cannot be improved.

Neurodevelopmental Therapy

Much of the literature regarding problems in eating (i.e., actual acceptance, chewing, and swallowing of solids) is from the perspective of physical therapists and other developmental therapists who deal primarily with neurologically damaged, often cerebral palsied, children. Typical recommendations include positioning to facilitate movement, and therapeutic exercises to increase or reduce tone as needed and to normalize oral sensitivity. Holser-Buehler (1973), for example, used therapy to extend the basic sucking reflex into normal eating responses. Such activities require the involvement of trained developmental therapists and are intended to benefit neurologically handicapped children. Several techniques borrowed from developmental therapists are useful in teaching children with behaviorally based feeding problems (Gupta and Wiemann 1977). To teach specific eating and drinking skills, Stainback et al. (1976) used passive therapy techniques such as stroking, brushing, or pressure. Campbell (1976) distinguished between oral hypersensitivity, essentially a neurologic problem, and tactile defensiveness, resulting from misperceiving stimuli. She recommended therapeutic activities to reduce such sensitivity of defensiveness. Holser-Buehler (1973) also recommended specific exercises for dealing with this problem in children who refuse solid food.

A second set of suggestions used by developmental therapists and useful for dealing with behavioral feeding problems are activities that communicate to the child the nature of the normal chewing and swallowing process. Specific suggestions in this area for educators and others have been given by Campbell (1976, 1979), Morris (1977), and Utley et al. (1977), who described jaw control techniques for inhibiting abnormal oral movements and facilitating normal eating behaviors.

Camouflage

A few authors have suggested correcting feeding problems through the use of camouflage, that is, placing the solid food beneath or behind one that is acceptable to the child. Leibowitz and Holcer (1974), for example, reported success with a girl, age 4 years, 11 months, with a Cattell IQ of 41. They hid food under ice cream on the spoon. After 14 hours of training over 15 days, she became an independent eater. Camouflage was also an element in the program described by Clancy et al. (1969). In both cases, this practice was implemented with behavior modification principles. The camouflaging food provided immediate reinforcement for ingestion of the unacceptable food, and the principle of successive approximation was employed. As treatment progressed, the camouflaging food was gradually decreased until it was withdrawn completely. Thompson and Palmer (1974), however, described the results of such procedures as "disappointing."

Behavior Modification

Pervading much of the literature on eating problems are various techniques of behavior modification based on control of the contingencies for desired and undesired behaviors. To be successful, desired behaviors must be elicited from the students by modeling, prompting, physical guidance, or verbal directions. Many developmental therapists recommend reinforcement of desired eating behaviors or ignoring undesirable behavior (Campbell 1976; Morris 1977). In each case, the child's acceptance of a solid food was rewarded with a desired food (e.g., ice cream or juice), a favorite activity (e.g., watching television), or social praise. Refusal of solid food, crying, and other undesirable behaviors were consequated by the instructor's turning his or her back, leaving the room, or otherwise putting such behavior on an extinction schedule. Johnston (1976), for example, used time-out for refusal behaviors, reinforcement of oral ingestion, praise, and recording procedures to establish normal eating behavior in a brain-injured adolescent who had been tube fed. Palmer et al. (1975) used similar procedures successfully with a mildly retarded client. Riordan et al. (1980) used spoonfuls of preferred foods, social praise, and verbal prompts to develop and reinforce selection and consumption of meats, fruits, and vegetables in two clients who had exhibited food refusal and selectivity. The approach of Stimbert et al. (1977) used restitutional overcorrection, positive practice, and fading procedures. Although they were most concerned with teaching self-feeding and correct social behaviors, their program also resulted in dramatic increases in the kinds of foods eaten by children who previously had abnormally limited food preferences.

The basis of the programs of Bernal (1972) and of others was successive approximation or shaping, a behavioral procedure in which behaviors are systematically reinforced as they approach the desired goal. Bernal, for example, identified 10 approximations leading toward the goal of eating a regular family meal. By the 32nd week of treatment her subject, Sandy, a three-and-a-half-year-old weighing 30 pounds, had added 50 new foods to her diet.

A dilemma appears in using reinforcement procedures with some eating problems because implicit in the use of reinforcement concepts to develop eating behavior is the idea that food is a natural reinforcer. Premack (1959), however, showed that eating responses may not change in cases where non-eating responses are conse-quated with events of a higher independent response rate than eating. Similarly, Heffley (1976) pointed out that no procedure will work with some children whose aversion to most food is much stronger than any reinforcer.

Solid Food Only

A few practitioners recommended that the feeding program begin with the pre-sentation of solid food. In these cases, the practice was accompanied by behavior modification procedures, and hunger was probably a motivating factor in the child's beginning to accept solids. In the cases of Holser-Buehler (1973) and T. Jones (1978, 1979), the method was preceded by exercises to reduce oral sensitivity. In the cases of Clancy et al. (1969), camouflaging food was presented. Clancy et al. reported success after three weeks in almost all of 12 cases; Holser-Buehler reported similar success in 20 multihandicapped children with whom the program was attempted.

Presentation of no alternative but acceptance of solid food has come to be known among some practitioners as "forced feeding." In the literature, however, the term is used differently by different writers. Palmer et al. (1975) cited forced feeding as an example of behavioral mismanagement. Bernal (1972) mentioned using hunger to "force" a child to eat solids. Clancy et al. (1969) provided an illustration of a mother force feeding her child. Although no description is given, the picture shows the mother holding the child's head back and pushing food from the front—a pattern not conducive to normal chewing and swallowing patterns. On the other hand, Hart (1972) referred to forced feeding and implied a systematic educational procedure. Used in conjunction with behavior modification procedures, developmental exercises, and facilitative positioning, such a procedure was utilized successfully to teach sal-utary, normal behaviors. In the only study of treatment of eating problems that used an experimental research design, T. Jones (1978) compared a solid food only approach with gradually increasing the food texture. In the solid food only approach, avoidance behaviors were ignored and oral manipulation was used to force normal chewing and swallowing patterns. His subjects were 20 profoundly retarded school-age insti-tution residents. After 15 consecutive meals, eight of the 10 subjects receiving solid food were independently accepting and eating regular table foods, compared to only two of the 10 receiving gradually increasing textures. There was no change in this distribution when the subjects were reevaluated one month later.

Consistency

Related to the use of solid food only is the necessity of a consistent program. Holser-Buehler (1973) suggested that during a program to remediate eating problems, all meals be consistent, that is, that the expectation for the child's responses not vary from meal to meal. T. Jones (1978, 1979) achieved success by using 15 consecutive meals without deviation in texture or consequences to establish normal eating in eight profoundly mentally retarded children. Bernal (1972) trained parents to implement the procedures so training would be consistent across meals. For the same reason, Fingado et al. (1970) used a short-term residential training program.

Conclusion

Mentally retarded individuals present a variety of problems with feeding and eating habits. These problems may involve drinking and eating skills, self-feeding, social behavior during meals, or self-injurious behaviors related to eating. These abnormalities are especially prevalent among the severely and profoundly mentally retarded. Of particular concern to care givers, teachers, and therapists, because of its implications for health and normal functioning, is the refusal or inability of many such children to eat solid food. This problem may have a neuromotor, physical, or behavioral basis. While specific guidelines are available in cases of oral neuromotor or physical disability, information on treatment programs for cases of behavior-related eating problems is scattered. Nine aspects of such programs can be identified. The usefulness of some of them is limited with severely or profoundly mentally retarded people. Four aspects, however, appear to offer viable treatment approaches. They include: 1) oral manipulation techniques borrowed from developmental therapists; 2) behavior modification procedures incorporating successive approximation, reinforcement of desired eating behaviors, and extinction of refusal behaviors; 3) using solid food only rather than attempting to increase the food texture gradually; 4) and following a consistent meal after meal regimen in which expectations do not vary. These four aspects may be combined into an intensive program to establish normal eating behaviors for severely and profoundly mentally retarded children who do not have oral neuromotor or physical impairment. Using such a combination of approaches, T. Jones (1978, 1979) was successful with eight out of 10 profoundly retarded children who received training for 15 consecutive meals.

Because of their social and health implications, the feeding problems of mentally retarded students are serious. A variety of treatment alternatives are available, regardless of whether the students' feeding problems are related to behavioral, neuromotor, or physical disabilities.

Pharmacotherapy

Chapter 20

Introduction

The major thrust in psychopharmacology for retarded people in recent years has been to reduce it. This is largely the consequence of widespread overuse and misuse of neuroleptic drugs, especially in the institutionalized retarded. There has, in fact, been a significant decline in neuroleptic prescription in this population in recent years.

However, the decline in ill-advised pharmacotherapy has not been accompanied by any increase in intelligent, creative drug treatment.

It is likely that the next few years will see a new emphasis on pharmacotherapy for neurobehavioral syndromes in mentally handicapped people. Young psychiatrists are beginning to develop an interest in this clinical frontier. There is a new focus on assessment of psychiatric conditions and neurobehavioral syndromes, on the development of drug-sensitive evaluation instruments, and on the initiation of intelligent clinical trials. There is a new flexibility in prescription, and the dull-witted application of neuroleptics for virtually every behavioral or emotional disturbance is coming to an end. There is a new interest in the behavioral and cognitive effects of anticonvulsant drugs.

Neuropsychiatry is emerging as a creative new discipline for retarded people and other mentally handicapped patients (e.g., severe epileptics, head-injury patients). It incorporates technology from epileptology and behavioral neurology, behavioral psychology, neuropsychology, and, of course, psychopharmacology. The potential benefits of skilled pharmacotherapy ought to be an essential part of the habilitation of retarded individuals with psychiatric disorders or severe neurobehavioral syndromes.

Chapter 21

Monitoring Psychopharmacology in Programs for the Retarded

Neuroleptic drugs are widely used in the mentally retarded, especially adults, in residential centers, community programs, and psychiatric hospitals. The clinical research literature on the subject of neuroleptic treatment has been reviewed by Sprague and Werry (1971) and by Aman (1983). Two summary statements convey the state of the science:

1. Thioridazine appears to improve certain maladaptive behaviors in retarded people and haloperidol appears to be valuable in reducing hyperactivity, aggressive behavior, and stereotyped behavior. The usefulness of chlorpromazine is open to challenge. There is little research to commend the prescription of other neuroleptic drugs (Aman 1983), although the specific efficacy of the D1 blocker fluphenazine for self-injurious behavior is an important new area to explore.
2. The neuroleptic drugs are the most studied psychotropic drugs in retarded people. Despite the volume of research, much of it is uninformative because of poor experimental controls and failure to assess specific functions (Aman 1983; Sprague and Werry 1971).

The fact that neuroleptic drugs are so widely used in retarded individuals may be attributed to the following factors:

1. There is at least some indication of short-term benefit, in some situations, especially with thioridazine and haloperidol (Gualtieri and Keppel 1985).
2. Short-term benefit may become long-term treatment unless careful monitoring programs are in place (Gualtieri and Keppel 1985).
3. No systematic technology for the evaluation of chronic neuroleptic treatment has been translated into actual practice in clinical settings on a national level (Gualtieri and Keppel 1985).

The introduction of a well-designed drug evaluation technology in programs for the retarded is known to reduce neuroleptic prescription, to reduce or eliminate polypharmacy, to lower average doses, and to remove unnecessary medication. For example, Fielding et al. (1980) reported dramatic results from a two-phase drug assessment program at Brainerd State Hospital in Minnesota. Subjects in the study were 192 residents in the hospital's developmental disability unit on one or more psychoactive medications. Eighty-six percent of the patients were severe to profoundly retarded; the mean age was 35 years.

Phase I of Fielding et al.'s (1980) study was a 50-day assessment period, including a 20-day period during which residents received no medication at all. Records of the frequency of maladaptive behaviors were kept throughout. At the end of Phase I, 84 (44 percent) patients showed no increase in maladaptive behaviors and were left medication-free. The remainder of the patients were returned to psychoactive medication, and, after a suitable interval, the Phase I process was repeated. At the end of the second study, 25 (13 percent) additional patients required no further psychoactive medication. Thus, in fewer than four months of actual study time, 109 (57 percent) of the 192 mentally retarded patients had been completely withdrawn from medication and remained medication-free. Two years later, Fielding et al. reported that only 2 of this 109 had to return to psychoactive medication.

Phase II of the study was a minimum effective dose program, which began two to six weeks after the end of Phase I. Ninety-two residents of the same hospital units were observed on medication for 90 days. During this period, the frequency of maladaptive behaviors was monitored. A 30-day dose reduction (by 25-percent decrements) ensued. If maladaptive behaviors did not increase, a second dose reduction occurred.

Sixty-eight of these 92 patients experienced at least one dosage reduction and 46 patients had reduced doses by more than half; 12 patients were taken off medication completely. The average successful dose reduction in Phase II, without a corresponding increase in maladaptive behavior, was 59 percent.

Overall, the assessment program resulted in drug discontinuation for 60 percent of the study participants. This figure coincides neatly with data described in mentally retarded patients by Gualtieri and Keppel (1985), who succeeded in maintaining more than half of subjects drug-free after a prolonged neuroleptic withdrawal trial.

In Fielding et al.'s (1980) study, residents who were taken off medication completely were also felt to improve on measures of adaptive functioning and achievement. This result is supported by research that suggests that neuroleptic drugs impair the acquisition of important self-help skills in mentally retarded people (Gualtieri and Keppel 1985).

The positive results of a psychotropic drug monitoring program can also be seen in the application of monitoring guidelines like those described by James (1983), who studied the systematic application of guidelines derived from the British National Formulary. The program stressed avoidance of polypharmacy, reduction or discontinuance of any drug unless there was clear evidence of its therapeutic value, and reduction of the frequency of administration of drugs with long duration of action.

James (1983) introduced simple, routine assessments to determine drug efficacy. With psychotropic medications, nurses made daily recordings of behavioral difficulties, specified when medication reductions occurred, and rated the severity of the resident's problems on a four-point rating scale. Other routine assessments were made for patients on anticonvulsant and antiparkinsonian medications. In the total population of 270 patients at two mental retardation "hospitals," James reported that 50 percent were receiving drugs affecting the central nervous system. Nine months after implementation of the monitoring system, the number of drug administrations was nearly halved from 2.3 to 1.2 doses per patient per day. There were also reductions in psychotropic drug polypharmacy (5 to 3 percent of the residents) and in the prescription of anticonvulsant drugs (14 to 6 percent).

Similar results were reported three-and-a-half years after the introduction of a drug monitoring program in a Minnesota residential training center for retarded people (LaMendola et al. 1980). The program, which simply consisted of drug evaluations for all residents at the center, resulted in a decrease in the percentage of residents on psychoactive medications from 34 to 21 percent.

Another approach to psychotropic drug monitoring is described by Inoue (1982), who advocated changing the role of the clinical pharmacist on the basis of a study performed at a 400-bed state RRC. Over a five-year period, Inoue reported general dosage reductions (mean 48.6 percent, range 25 to 75 percent) for 91 medication orders and 135 discontinuations of psychotropic medication orders for 121 patients. Of the patients who went through these medication changes, 50 percent were said to have improved in cognitive functioning on the basis of reports by direct care and nursing staff. Only a small fraction of the pharmacist's recommendations resulted in an increase of patient behavior problems.

Ellenor (1977) reported a retrospective analysis of changes in the prescribing habits of physicians at a 475-bed RRC three years after the introduction of a clinical pharmacy program. The total number of patients receiving two or more antipsychotic drugs decreased from 49 to 20, with the mean number of antipsychotics per patient decreasing from 1.31 to 1.12. On an institutional basis, there was a significant decrease (52.3 percent) in antipsychotic polypharmacy.

The use of a consultant pharmacist working in a multidisciplinary patient care team was reported by Berchou (1982), who compared the patient population of an institution prior to and one year after hiring a consultant pharmacist. He found no change in the percentage of patients receiving antipsychotics, but a decrease in polypharmacy from 6.4 to 0.8 percent of the population. There was also a decrease in the use of long-term medications from 76.1 to 56.8 percent.

There has been some very important research in monitoring neuroleptic drug effects in retarded residents, especially for tardive dyskinesia, by John Kalachnick at the Cambridge State Hospital in Cambridge, Minnesota and by Robert L. Sprague at the University of Illinois (Kalachnick et al. 1983a, 1983b; Sprague and Werry 1971). This work has involved the development of a dyskinesia rating system (DIS-CO) with exemplary psychometric properties that can be reliably administered by trained health care technicians. The application of the rating system in a real-life setting has been made in a series of neuroleptic-withdrawal studies involving thousands of ratings on hundreds of retarded patients. Like previous studies done in this vein, the application of systematic monitoring and neuroleptic withdrawal has revealed a high prevalence of tardive dyskinesia among the mentally retarded and a substantial number of patients who do not require the resumption of pharmacotherapy. The pioneering work of Kalachnick and by Sprague has led to a wider availability of their rating system and its adoption by programs for the retarded around the country.

The development of a well-conceived drug evaluation strategy for the mentally retarded will serve to improve medical practice, improve adaptive behaviors, increase the likelihood of successful community placement, and diminish the occurrence of some serious chronic side effects of neuroleptic treatment, especially of tardive dyskinesia. The use of a consulting clinical pharmacist as a team member may be a cost effective way to monitor psychoactive drug practices. The development of a solid monitoring program, however, should rely not only on medical guidelines, but also the proper evaluation of cognitive and adaptive effects of psychoactive drugs. In addition, the neurologic consequences of chronic drug treatment require ongoing monitoring.

Problems with monitoring pharmacology for retarded people are not limited to psychoactive drugs. Proper monitoring procedures would improve anticonvulsant therapy as well. For example, in a survey of 127 residents of an RRC by Kaufman and Kaufman and Katz-Garris (1979), 41 were on anticonvulsants. None had been properly monitored, for example, with anticonvulsant blood levels, folate levels, or complete blood counts. Indeed, there was no documented seizure disorder in no fewer than 24 residents. In a study by Tu (1980) of 26 RRC residents on anticonvulsants and psychoactive drugs for epilepsy with behavior problems, after complete drug withdrawal 35 percent were successfully maintained off anticonvulsants and 65 percent were maintained off psychoactive drugs.

Chapter 22

Neuroleptics

This class of drugs has been the major one used in the treatment of behavioral problems in mentally retarded persons. No doubt part of the initial popularity of this group was based on the apparent similarity of some maladaptive behaviors in mentally retarded people to the symptoms of nonretarded psychotic patients, presumably making these behaviors amenable to antipsychotic drug treatment. An alternative rationale is the short-term tranquilizing effects of neuroleptics, their capacity for reducing negative behaviors by reducing a patient's overall behavioral level, and their acute sedative effects. Three neuroleptics account for the majority of antipsychotic drug usage: chlorpromazine, thioridazine, and haloperidol.

Phenothiazines

Chlorpromazine is one of the oldest and most extensively used psychotropic drugs in mental retardation. Because of its popularity among clinicians, it has served as the comparison drug in numerous studies examining the relative effects of two or more drugs.

Ison (1957) conducted a relatively well-controlled study in which the effects of chlorpromazine and placebo on intelligence were compared. The Wechsler Intelligence Scale for Children (WISC) or the Wechsler Adult Intelligence Scale (WAIS) were used according to the subject's ability. The results of this trial indicated that, of a total of 14 statistical comparisons, only two subtests (comprehension and digit symbol) showed significant drug effects, in both cases in the direction of improvement. This study was unique, not only because it fulfilled appropriate experimental criteria, but because an effort was made to examine the response of diagnostic subgroups. Subjects characterized as brain damaged seemed to show a better response to chlorpromazine than the other groups.

Adamson et al. (1958) compared the effects of chlorpromazine, reserpine, chlor-promazine-plus-reserpine, and placebo. Subjects received each drug for 60 days in a crossover design (i.e., each subject served as his or her own control). The results suggested problem behaviors were reduced most by chlorpromazine, then by reserpine, and least by placebo. Unfortunately, the statistical analysis used was not entirely satisfactory so that these descriptive results could not be confirmed inferentially. It was especially notable that a placebo response was observed in 40 to 70 percent of subjects and lasted up to six weeks. This nonspecific drug response is a phenomenon that all too many researchers choose to ignore, shrugging off the need for untreated controls as unethical or unnecessary.

Wardell et al. (1958) examined the effects of chlorpromazine, reserpine, and placebo in behaviorally disturbed women. Measures of outcome included clinical global impressions plus observations of five behavioral dimensions. The results were essentially nonsignificant, with neither of the drugs producing appreciable benefit. However, the strength of these negative conclusions is mitigated somewhat by low interobserver reliabilities and substantial data loss.

Moore (1960) adopted a novel approach to the assessment of drug effects. The subjects were 90 mentally retarded women who had been chronically treated with chlorpromazine. In half of the subjects, the drug was removed and replaced by placebo; the remainder continued to receive their usual medication. The results indicated that the placebo group made greater gains than the chlorpromazine group on the Stanford achievement tests, although three other categories (Stanford Binet IQ, ratings of behavior, and ratings of academic progress) showed no drug-related differences. This study provides cause for concern in that it suggests that chlorpromazine actually may have been suppressing achievement.

Hollis and St. Omer (1972) conducted a complex study in which four standardized doses of chlorpromazine were compared to a no-drug condition under several types of operant control (discriminative stimulus, fixed ratio schedule, variable interval schedule, and extinction). Unfortunately, the results were reported graphically, selectively, and without inferential statistical analysis. The drug reportedly reduced operant responding, and this effect was directly related to dose. Extinction of a lever response was apparently quickened by chlorpromazine, but so also was extinction of a rocking response, which may be analogous to stereotypic movements. Such measures challenge easy interpretation, but the results can be construed as suggesting both diminished performance under drug (reduction of learned responses) as well as the promotion of improvement (rapid extinction of the rocking).

McConahey (1972) employed a double-blind, crossover design to compare placebo to chlorpromazine. The unique aspect of this study was that the drug was being evaluated against the backdrop of a behavior modification program, which was implemented in the mornings only, with afternoons serving as control periods. The results indicated that chlorpromazine yielded no benefit as compared with placebo. Unfortunately, McConahey failed to report any interaction effects (either enhancement or interference) between drug therapy and behavior modification. This is disappointing because this was one of only two studies that could be located in which drug and behavioral treatments were compared in mentally retarded subjects.

Vaisanen et al. (1974) compared chlorpromazine, sulpiride (another antipsychotic), and placebo in 60 "restless" residents. The design was that of a double-blind, placebo-controlled, crossover trial. Measures of change included ratings of six behavioral categories, two evaluations of sleep, and clinical global impressions. The only variable to show any changes was global impressions, with sulpiride (but not chlorpromazine) significantly better than placebo. There was also a tendency for sulpiride to surpass chlorpromazine, but this was nonsignificant.

Marholin et al. (1979) evaluated the effects of withdrawal of chlorpromazine, using a reversal design procedure, in five chronically treated residents. Objective measures of change were obtained, but the results are difficult to assess because of the small number of subjects and the limited number of crossovers in this study. Response to the drug was highly variable, but in some cases the drug apparently resulted in the worsening of both ward and workshop behaviors.

Sprague and Werry (1971) and Freeman (1970) cited approximately 20 other studies examining chlorpromazine, most of which were poorly controlled or totally uncontrolled. Almost without exception, these studies showed a drug-induced reduction in problem behavior. Such problem behaviors typically included aggressiveness, self-injury, stereotyped movements, and hyperactivity. However, the conclusions of such research must be tempered by the outcome of better controlled studies such as those outlined above.

Despite chlorpromazine's well-entrenched place in the pharmacologic treatment of behavior disorders in mentally retarded people, these earlier, well-controlled studies and other more recent studies challenge its position. Regardless of the already large volume of data, research of high caliber is still required to examine the effects of chlorpromazine on specific cognitive and behavioral functions and also in well-defined subgroups.

Thioridazine (Mellaril) is another drug used extensively in the treatment of behavioral problems. Aman and Singh (1980) comprehensively reviewed 24 studies of this drug in childhood disorders (including mental retardation, hyperactivity, "emotional" disorders, and epilepsy). The studies were evaluated according to six methodological criteria delineated by Sprague and Werry (1971). Only six of these studies fulfilled all the criteria satisfactorily. Furthermore, evaluations tended to be of the clinical global, "better/worse" variety rather than of a standardized form that could reveal meaningful qualitative changes resulting from the drug. Only four of these 24 studies addressed themselves to the cognitive effects of this drug, and two of these suggested that thioridazine tends to impair intellectual performance. Two of the earlier studies and all those appearing since 1970, as of this writing, will be examined here.

Alexandris and Lundell (1968) conducted a double-blind assessment of thioridazine, amphetamine, and placebo in 21 hyperactive residents. The children were rated for drug changes on 14 behavioral dimensions, and their performance was assessed on the WISC, the Visual Motor Gestalt Test, and the Goodenough Draw-A-Person Test. The results indicated that thioridazine caused the greatest social improvement, with 11 of the 14 behavioral categories showing a significant benefit over placebo. Most of these changes were in the area of hyperactivity, attention span, and aggressiveness. Amphetamine produced only two behavioral changes (improved concentration and work interest), but the dose was exceedingly high (mean 52 mg/day) so that this was probably not an appropriate assessment of this drug. None of the psychological tests showed significant changes.

Davis et al. (1969) carried out a double-blind, crossover trial comparing thioridazine, methylphenidate (Ritalin), and placebo. Subjects were nine severely retarded residents selected for high rates of stereotypy. Indices of drug change included amount of stereotypy, nonstereotyped behavior, gross body movement, rocking, and complex hand movements. Thioridazine caused a significant reduction in stereotyped movements, but no changes in other behaviors. Methylphenidate caused no significant changes. This was an exemplary early study that concentrated not only on possible positive changes but also on whether or not reductions occurred in other, adaptive behaviors as well.

In a poorly controlled trial, Le Vann (1970) compared thioridazine, chlorprothixene (Tarasan), and placebo. Both drugs produced a reduction in problem behaviors (hostility, overactivity, sleep problems), with chlorprothixene rendering the greatest improvement.

Davis (1971) carried out a second study examining the effects of thioridazine, methylphenidate, and placebo. Subjects were taught to perform a rocking and a bar-pressing response in the presence of specified discriminative stimuli. The results were essentially nonsignificant, with no drug-related changes. There was, however, some evidence that the drugs caused greater variability in performance.

Heistad and Zimmermann (1979) reported an investigation in which, owing to a court order, all patients had to be taken off medication for a trial period, presumably to determine whether the drug was warranted in individual cases. They exploited the occasion to derive empirical data by substituting placebo when thioridazine was terminated. A double-blind, placebo-controlled, crossover design was used. Measures of drug effect included a nurses' rating scale and an observational, time-sampling technique that rendered 10 categories. Positive changes favoring thioridazine were found on "self-stimulation," a "net adaptive," and two composite categories. The nurses' scale was essentially negative, but there was a significant effect for the combined positive dimensions.

Singh and Aman (1981c) withdrew 19 severely retarded residents from their former thioridazine treatment and stepped them through a trial comparing a low standardized dose of thioridazine (2.5 mg/kg/day), the residents' previous individual doses (mean 5.23 mg/kg/day), and placebo. Measures of outcome included physiologic indices, motor development, instruction following, behavior observations, and behavior ratings. Results showed that few of the measures were actually influenced by the drug conditions. However, where changes did occur, these generally indicated that benefit was derived from the drug (reduced self-stimulation, hyperactivity and bizarre behavior, and increased social behavior). Even more important, however, was the finding that the standardized dose (which was less than half the mean former dose for these residents) was equally beneficial to outcome.

Jakab (1984) compared behavior before and after a mid-morning dose of thioridazine in emotionally disturbed mentally retarded children. Direct observations showed reductions in aggression, stereotypic behavior, self-injury, and emotional lability following medication. Although persuasive of a drug effect, it is also possible that these changes were due in part or whole to temporal effects, which were not controlled.

Schroeder and Gualtieri (1985) phased 23 subjects off their previous medication (mostly thioridazine), using a placebo-controlled, multiple-baseline design. Medication was discontinued either abruptly or over several weeks. Frequency observations, both in the classroom and on the wards, showed no group drug effects. However, behavior ratings did show deterioration, especially in subjects who experienced abrupt withdrawal of medication. Six subjects were withdrawn from the study because of worsened behavior as they came off medication. Behavioral deterioration tended to mirror the appearance of dyskinesia in many of these subjects.

Menolascino et al. (1985) compared thioridazine with thiothixene in retarded and nonretarded schizophrenic patients. "Considerable improvement" was reported in both patient groups, although the study was not controlled. The authors felt that the mentally retarded patients showed a more rapid therapeutic response with thiothixene than with thioridazine. Finally, Aman and White (in press) conducted a dose study of thioridazine and found that the higher of two doses (2.50 versus 1.25 mg/kg/day) was more effective in controlling hyperactivity and self-injury, but at the expense of increased lethargy. They also looked at nondrug levels of stereotypic behavior and found that a higher frequency was associated with a better drug response on average.

In summary, there is some convincing evidence attesting to thioridazine's usefulness in altering certain maladaptive behaviors. However, it is important to note that, even when positive changes have occurred, these were usually outnumbered by the dimensions of social behavior showing no change. Only a few studies have examined the cognitive effects of this drug, but there is evidence that it may depress learning performance. Overall, the evidence with thioridazine appears more positive than that with chlorpromazine, but this may reflect a biased sample of chlorpromazine investigations.

The remaining phenothiazines have been infrequently studied with this clinical population and often with inadequate experimental controls. The reader is referred to the review of Sprague and Werry (1971) and a recent chapter by Schroeder (1988).

Butyrophenones

After chlorpromazine and thioridazine, the other major tranquilizer used extensively in mentally retarded individuals is haloperidol. Research reflects (or perhaps has encouraged) this popularity.

Haloperidol (Haldol, Serenace) was compared to placebo by Burk and Menolascino (1968) in a double-blind study. The results, expressed exclusively in terms of global clinical improvement, suggested that the drug produced significant benefit. Grabowski (1973a), reporting a totally uncontrolled trial, concluded that haloperidol produced a number of therapeutic changes in children and adolescents. In another uncontrolled investigation, Grabowski (1973b) again reported a reduction in hyperactivity, and improvement in social behavior, concentration, and "emotion" because of the drug.

Le Vann (1971) compared the effects of haloperidol to chlorpromazine in children. Haloperidol was significantly superior as assessed by global impressions, and ratings of various behavioral dimensions also suggested superiority of the butyrophenone.

Two other studies (Claghorn 1972; Ucer and Kreger 1975) comparing haloperidol with thioridazine in mentally retarded children showed a general, although often not significant, superiority of the butyrophenone in controlling behavior.

Thus some of the earlier studies suggest that haloperidol may surpass the established phenothiazines in certain respects. However, this is difficult to establish because such differences could be attributable to the particular dosages employed, or may be specific to certain subpopulations. Unfortunately, most of the comparative studies did not incorporate a placebo so that the degree of absolute improvement is impossible to assess. Furthermore, the earliest studies of a drug such as this tend to reflect the enthusiasm of the investigators involved and, as history has shown, subsequent trials are often less optimistic.

Vaisanen et al. (1981) conducted a study of haloperidol and thioridazine in mentally retarded residents. Although placebo phases were included, they were not balanced with active drug conditions, and the study was poorly controlled. Furthermore, the doses used (up to 60 mg/day of haloperidol) were probably much too large for a nonpsychotic sample. A majority of subjects were said to be improved with both haloperidol and thioridazine, with few differences between active treatments. There was no relationship between serum drug concentrations and clinical response.

Finally, Aman et al. (in press) compared low and moderate doses of haloperidol

(0.025 versus 0.05 mg/kg/day) with placebo in residents who had been chronically treated with neuroleptics. It was found that the moderate dose produced improvements in ratings of stereotypy and reduced levels of inactivity as assessed by direct observations. However, most clinical variables were not affected by the drug at either dose. Most importantly, it was noted that nondrug levels of stereotypy were significantly correlated with certain types of clinical response, such that subjects with higher degrees of stereotypy showed a better clinical response on several variables.

Of other butyrophenones, pipamperone (Dipiperon) was assessed in one well-controlled study (Van Hemert 1975) and in another totally uncontrolled trial (Haegeman and Duyck 1978). The former found drug-related improvements in fits of anger, aggressiveness, sleep disorders, and manageability. The latter found improvement in the same categories, as well as in hyperactivity and self-mutilation.

Neuroleptic Drugs and Stereotypic Behavior

Not surprisingly, drug research with mentally retarded individuals has tended to focus on acting-out behavior such as aggression, destructiveness, and self-injury. However, the clinical variable showing the most consistent changes across studies appears to be stereotypic behavior (i.e., the repetitive, voluntary movements with no apparent purpose), so commonly observed in this population. Several studies with mentally retarded individuals have found stereotypic behavior to be the clinical variable most affected by neuroleptic drugs (e.g., Davis et al. 1969; Heistad and Zimmermann 1979; Hollis 1968; Singh and Aman 1981c). This neuroleptic-induced reduction of stereotypy has been a common report in infantile autism as well (Anderson et al. 1984; Campbell et al. 1978). As summarized previously, another pair of studies found that residents having the highest off-medication levels of stereotypic behavior also tended to be among those showing the best clinical response to neuroleptics (Aman et al., in press; Aman & White, in press). This suggests that stereotypic behavior may be a useful variable for predicting clinical response to the neuroleptics, although this idea needs to be replicated and further explored with additional research (see Aman and Singh, 1986). We are not suggesting that the presence of stereotypic behavior should be regarded as a reason for treatment with neuroleptic drugs, but rather, when severe behavioral or psychiatric problems are present, the coexistence of high levels of stereotypy *may* predict a favorable clinical response (Aman and Singh, in press).

Conclusion

The phenothiazine drugs are among the most studied for use in mental retardation. Despite the volume of research, much of it is uninformative because of poor experimental controls and failure to assess specific functions. Nevertheless, thioridazine appears to improve certain maladaptive behaviors, whereas the usefulness of chlorpromazine is open to challenge. Haloperidol, which has been investigated relatively recently, appears to be valuable in reducing hyperactive, aggressive, and stereotyped behavior. There are considerable data from some of the better controlled studies that stereotypic behavior in particular is reduced by neuroleptic drugs, and it is possible that high levels of stereotypy may be predictive of a beneficial response in individuals presenting with severe behavior problems. It is not clear at this time whether the neuroleptics have a somewhat specific effect on certain maladaptive behaviors or whether the clinical changes that do occur are simply part of a more general sedative action.

The quality of the neuroleptic research cited above shows that many essential questions have been left unanswered. There has been a lack of long-term safety and efficacy studies, a dearth of drug/behavioral treatment interaction studies, and a failure of investigators to develop suitable instruments for behavioral and psychological assessment. These shortcomings stand in stark contrast to the frequency with which neuroleptics are prescribed for retarded people, the high doses that are often used, and the long-term nature of neuroleptic maintenance.

These problems have been mitigated at least to a small degree in recent years by the development of new research initiatives in this area, a growing and broadly based awareness of the potential side effects of neuroleptic treatment, and a conservative attitude toward neuroleptics among workers in the field. In fact, the prevalence of neuroleptic treatment in retarded people appears to have declined markedly in recent years. Nevertheless, there will continue to be a small group of retarded people who will require neuroleptic treatment for psychiatric disorders or for severe behavior problems that are refractory to alternative treatments.

Chapter 23

Antidepressant Drugs and Lithium

Although antidepressant drugs—tricyclic antidepressants (TCA), the novel antidepressants, and monoamine oxidase inhibitors (MAOI)—and lithium salts are important chemical agents in adult psychiatry, their use in the developmentally disabled has not been the subject of systematic study. In Lipman's (1970) survey of psychoactive drug use in the institutionalized retarded, fewer than 4 percent of the residents were treated with TCA, and no mention was made of lithium treatment. Cohen and Sprague (1977) reported similar findings in a psychoactive drug survey of two midwestern institutions. In a survey of 184 studies of psychoactive drug treatment of the retarded by Lipman et al. (1978), only 12 (6.5 percent) were concerned with TCA; none with the MAOI or lithium.

It is an open question whether these classes of drugs are underutilized and underresearched, or whether the paucity of available information speaks to their limited utility for the mentally retarded. However, it is our belief that although neuroleptic drugs tend to be overused in the retarded, the antidepressants and lithium may be underprescribed (Sovner and Hurley 1983).

Lithium

Knowledge about the proper use of lithium in retarded people is derived almost entirely from research and clinical experience in nonretarded patients. Lithium is specifically indicated for the treatment of bipolar disorder and for the prophylaxis of recurrent unipolar depression. It may also have a specific indication in the treatment of certain forms of aggression. It may be indicated, in a nonspecific way, to treat any severe behavior problem that does not respond to alternative treatments, just as neuroleptics may be prescribed for nonspecific but severe behavior problems. Unhappily, this latter category (a noncategory, in fact) comprises an enormous number of retarded patients referred for psychiatric consultation.

Hasan and Mooney (1979) reported three case studies of manic-depressive illness in mentally retarded adults. The first patient was a moderately retarded man who had chronic, recurrent bursts of restlessness followed by periods of depression. Following an unsuccessful trial of neuroleptics, lithium was prescribed. After a year on lithium, he was living at home, attending a day program, and no longer a management problem. The second case was a 23-year-old "borderline retarded" woman who was admitted because of "manic" behavior and subsequently diagnosed as "hypomanic." She also responded to lithium, was soon discharged, and continued to function well with only minor relapses. The third case was a mildly retarded 43-year-old woman who had been in a state hospital for 16 years where she had tantrums, was difficult to manage, and attacked the nursing staff. She also had periods of depression. She was placed on fluphenazine and lithium and showed gradual improvement. Six months after discharge, her behavior was under control, and she no longer exhibited mood swings.

Reid and Leonard (1977) reported on the lithium treatment for a 29-year-old mildly retarded woman who suffered recurrent episodes of vomiting, which seemed to occur almost exclusively when she was depressed. She also tended to have brief episodes of talkativeness and excessive friendliness. Data were taken over a two-year span. Comparison was made between the first year, when prochlorperazine and chlorpromazine were prescribed, and the second year, when lithium was added. There was a striking reduction of depression, vomiting, and elation during the second year.

Kelly et al. (1976) described a mildly retarded woman who had displayed a "cyclothymic" behavior pattern since early childhood. She was diagnosed manic-depressive at age 15. Chlorpromazine, haloperidol, and physical restraints were tried unsuccessfully. After chlorpromazine and haloperidol were discontinued and lithium was introduced, her behavior was more controlled, with a gradual "leveling" of her cyclical behavior and an increase in prosocial behavior. After a four-year follow-up, she continued to do well on lithium.

Unfortunately, the bulk of the literature concerned with bipolar disorder and lithium in the mentally retarded is composed of case reports and uncontrolled studies. Naylor et al. (1974), however, conducted a placebo-controlled double-blind study of 14 retarded inpatients, all of whom had a history of cyclical affective or behavioral changes. Each spent a year on lithium and a year on placebo, with order assigned randomly. Based on clinical knowledge and familiarity with the patient, interviewers gave weekly ratings of "normal" or "ill." The number of ill ratings for patients on lithium were significantly fewer than the number of ill ratings during the placebo condition.

The only controlled study of lithium treatment of autistic children provided negative results (Campbell et al. 1972a).

Lithium in the Treatment of Aggression

Lithium has been shown to reduce territorial aggressive behavior in siamese fighting fish, mice, and hamsters (Weischer 1969). In an isolation-induced aggression paradigm, there is less aggressive behavior in lithium-treated rats (Sheard 1970b), and foot-shock-induced aggression decreases in lithium-treated rats (Sheard 1970b). The hyperaggressive and hypersexual behavior of cats and rats treated with p-chlorophenylalanine is inhibited by lithium in doses that do not impair motor activity (Sheard 1970a). Since aggressive behavior is such a common problem in retarded patients, the supposedly specific lithium effect on aggression is of particular interest.

Sheard (1975) conducted a single-blind crossover, placebo-controlled study of lithium in 12 chronically assaultive male prisoners. The subjects had normal IQ scores and showed no overt signs of brain damage or psychosis. In a three-month ABA trial, daily rating scales, clinical interviews, and reports of aggressive behavior were the dependent variables. There was a "significant reduction" in self-rated aggressive affect and in the number of reported aggressive incidents during the lithium treatment period.

Worrall et al. (1975) conducted a double-blind, placebo-controlled study in eight severely retarded women. Nurses rated aggressive behavior during lithium or placebo treatment, alternatively, in four-week blocks over 16 weeks. Two patients had to be withdrawn from the study because of severe toxic effects. Maintenance doses of previously prescribed psychoactive drugs were continued throughout the study. Three patients became less aggressive on lithium, one was more aggressive, and two showed no change.

Dostal and Zvotsky (1970) treated 14 aggressive, hyperactive, phenothiazine-resistant severely retarded adolescents with lithium. Subjects received their usual neuroleptic medication plus lithium at low blood levels (0.3 mEq/L) during the first phase, lithium alone during the second phase (mean 0.6 mEq/L), and, during the third or therapeutic phase, lithium (mean 0.9 mEq/L). There were improvements in affectivity, aggressiveness, psychomotor activity, restlessness, and undisciplined behavior during the latter two phases.

Goetze et al. (1977) reported three case studies of mentally retarded adults treated with lithium for unmanageable, hyperactive, and aggressive behavior. A 20-year-old moderately retarded male was referred to an inpatient psychiatric unit because of aggressive and disruptive behavior that could not be managed in a community-based residential facility. Fluphenazine was tried unsuccessfully and then discontinued. Lithium was prescribed, and a clear behavior change was seen at serum levels around 0.6 to 0.7 mEq/L. He was released to the community-based facility, and after one year maintained his adjustment, even after lithium was discontinued. A 19-year-old moderately retarded woman was admitted to an inpatient unit for uncontrollable, aggressive behavior. Her behavior was characterized by temper outbursts and physical abuse of other patients and nurses. Fluphenazine was tried and discontinued. When lithium serum levels reached 0.8 mEq/L, her behavior was "much improved." She was released, found her own housing, and participated successfully in an outpatient program for two months, when she terminated contact. A 16-year-old "borderline" retarded boy was admitted because of uncontrollable behavior, including fighting with peers and marked agitation. In the hospital, he was agitated and hyperactive and displayed marked pressure of speech and aggressive behavior toward staff and patients. Because neuroleptics had been ineffective during previous hospitalizations, lithium was prescribed. Within two weeks, he was less hyperactive; after a month, however, lithium was discontinued due to side effects (i.e., nausea, vomiting, diarrhea). Within three days, he was again uncooperative, aggressive, and hyperactive. Lithium was reinstated and the negative behavior subsided. He was discharged after two months to a residential treatment center, where the psychiatrist discontinued lithium treatment. Two days later, he was committed to a state mental hospital.

Lion et al. (1975) presented a case report of a 27-year-old moderately retarded male referred because of cyclical temper outbursts that had occurred throughout his life, gradually growing more severe. On admission, he displayed psychomotor restlessness and agitation and made verbal threats. Tranquilizers, sedatives, and stimulants were not helpful. Lithium was chosen because of the cyclical nature of his outbursts. Levels were increased to 1.2 mEq/L and he grew calmer and less active. After discharge, there was a clear reduction in aggressive behavior at home.

Micev and Lynch (1974) reported results of a 12-week, nonblind trial of lithium in 10 severely retarded patients. All displayed aggressive and self-injurious behavior. Rating scales were used. Serum levels were maintained at 0.6 mEq/L. Of nine aggressive patients, five showed "significant" improvement, three improved slightly, and one showed no change. Of the eight patients who engaged in self-injurious behavior, six showed cessation of such behavior, one showed some improvement, and one showed no change. No side effects were noted.

Cooper and Fowlie (1973) report a case study involving self-injurious behavior. A severely retarded girl in her early 20s had been hospitalized for hyperactivity and self-injurious behavior including hand gnawing, head banging, and throwing herself down staircases. Individualized nursing care, tranquilizing drugs, and a restraining jacket all proved ineffective. Lithium was prescribed and within a week the patient "became quiet, docile and cooperative." The self-injurious behavior ceased, and she began to show some interest in other patients. After five years on lithium the patient "continued to be rather negativistic" but showed no self-injurious behavior.

Shader et al. (1974) presented a case study of a 34-year-old nonpsychotic woman of normal intelligence who had been frequently hospitalized for aggressiveness, assaultiveness, and destructiveness. Barbiturates, phenothiazines, benzodiazepines, and TCA were unsuccessful. During her third admission, she exhibited aggression not only against others but against herself (scratching her neck with razor blades, head banging, trying to hang herself). A trial of lithium was initiated, and after one week her mental status and behavior were "markedly improved." She was discharged, and at a two-year follow-up had maintained her improvement.

Lithium may prove to be a useful agent in the management of severely aggressive or self-injurious patients of normal or below normal intelligence who cannot be controlled with less restrictive approaches. However, it is difficult to generalize on the basis of anecdotal reports and poorly controlled studies. For the individual patient, the clinician may do well to consider lithium in circumstances where pharmacologic control is essential and other measures have failed.

Lithium is sometimes used in schizophrenic patients who ordinarily would be treated with neuroleptics but who have developed tardive dyskinesia or transient withdrawal dyskinesias and for whom continued neuroleptic treatment is ill-advised. It may also be a reasonable alternative for retarded patients with tardive dyskinesia.

Lithium: Summary

Lithium is indicated in the treatment of mentally retarded patients with un-equivocal bipolar disorder or in the prophylaxis of recurrent unipolar depressions. It may also be useful in some mentally retarded patients with the following problems: 1) those who have severe, but relatively nonspecific behavior problems, and who also have a family history of manic-depressive illness or of favorable response to lithium; 2) mentally retarded patients whose behavior and emotional disorders occur in clear cycles, with a strong affective component; and 3) mentally retarded patients with explosive, aggressive behavior. Lithium may also be considered in the treatment of schizophrenia, especially for patients who have developed tardive dyskinesia and should no longer take neuroleptic drugs.

The list cited above should, however, be considered "relative indications" for lithium treatment. Considering the potential toxicity of the drug, and the paucity of good research concerning its use in the mentally retarded, it is reasonable practice to confine lithium treatment only to the most severe cases, where behavior management, appropriate programming, and a proper environment are inadequate for control of severe behavior problems. It is likely that lithium will prove to be preferable to the neuroleptic drugs in the treatment of such patients. The fact that neuroleptics are used more frequently than lithium in the retarded speaks more to the prescribing habits of physicians than to any rational guideline.

Tricyclic and Novel Antidepressants

TCA and the novel antidepressants are relatively successful therapeutic agents in the treatment of major depressive disorders in adults, especially depressions characterized by evidence of a genetic predisposition, symptoms of physiologic impairment (psychomotor retardation, sleep disorder, loss of appetite, weight loss, constipation), and recurrent episodes. TCA have also been recommended for the treatment of panic attacks. One TCA, imipramine, is used for the treatment of enuresis nocturna, although the effect of the drug for this disorder is probably related to its effects on autonomic innervation of the bladder, rather than to any psychotropic mechanism. TCA have been used in the treatment of childhood hyperkinesis, school phobia, somnambulism, night terrors, head banging, and encopresis (Gualtieri 1977). Like all psychoactive drugs, TCA have a wide range of biologic activity, but their allegedly successful therapeutic application in such a wide range of disparate disorders warrants a degree of skepticism.

In a review of the literature on depression in the mentally retarded, Gardner (1967) proposed that this condition tends to be underdiagnosed. If such is the case, one would expect that improved diagnostic skills and psychiatric management of mentally retarded patients would ultimately lead to more frequent application of antidepressant drugs. Psychoactive drug treatment in the retarded, however, is more likely to address behaviors that are disturbing or troublesome, rather than those that involve withdrawal, inhibition, psychomotor retardation, or sadness. In our clinical experience, TCA are more commonly prescribed for hyperkinetic and aggressive behaviors. Commonly used doses of TCA can range from 50 to 300 mg/day; doses in the range of 800 to 1,000 mg can be fatal. This extremely low therapeutic-to-lethal dose ratio should clearly limit the use of TCA only to circumstances where the most careful supervision of drug administration is possible.

Although TCA are sometimes used to control behavior disorders in the mentally retarded, empirical data to support their efficacy and safety are sorely lacking. There are conflicting reports on the usefulness of TCA and in the management of enuresis nocturna in the retarded (Fisher et al. 1963; Smith and Gonzalez 1967). There is no a priori reason to suspect that a patient's IQ should influence the efficacy of TCA for enuresis nocturna, but the toxicity of the drugs and the efficacy of alternative behavioral treatments ought to sharply limit their application.

Keegan et al. (1974) described two adults with Down's syndrome who presented with features of psychotic deterioration but who failed to respond to neuroleptic drugs. Both responded favorably to amitriptyline. Kraft et al. (1966) found that amitriptyline was useful in the treatment of four of five mentally retarded boys who had behavior disorders.

Although it was once proposed that imipramine and the MAOI helped withdrawn, autistic children, Campbell et al. (1971) were unable to confirm these findings. Carter (1960) found that nortriptyline was effective as a "standard sedative or tranquilizer in the control of disturbed behavior" in mentally retarded patients 4 to 70 years of age. However, in this study, placebo also exerted a sedative effect.

Pilkington (1962) divided 30 mentally retarded children into two groups: affective (cyclothymic) and nonaffective. In an uncontrolled study, half of the first group improved on imipramine; all of the second group were made worse by the medication.

There are, to the author's knowledge, no controlled studies of novel antidepressants in retarded patients, and no anecdotal reports either. It is not at all clear what impact novel antidepressants like amoxapine, maprotiline, alprazolam, and trazodone will have on the future practice of psychopharmacology because the risk-to-benefit ratio may not be as favorable as originally hoped. Amoxapine is a dopamine blocker that may cause tardive dyskinesia. Maprotiline has a serious proclivity to lower the seizure threshold, a major drawback for retarded patients, many of whom are epileptic. Alprazolam is related to the benzodiazepines and may cause behavioral disinhibition, hyperactivity, and aggression in children and retarded patients. The efficacy profile of trazodone may be somewhat idiosyncratic.

Bupropion is a novel antidepressant that will soon be approved by the Food and Drug Administration. It may prove to be an important drug for hyperactive and conduct-disordered children, in addition to its antidepressant effects. However, bupropion may also lower the seizure threshold, although no more than imipramine does, and probably less than maprotiline.

Nomifensine is the antidepressant that is least likely to alter the seizure threshold, and so may prove to be an important alternative for retarded patients with seizure disorders. But it is not without some serious side effects of its own.

Monoamine Oxidase Inhibitors

Very little has been written concerning MAOI in the treatment of children or the developmentally handicapped. Soblen and Saunders (1961) found that phenelzine was effective in alleviating apathy, withdrawal, low motor activity, and flattened affect in 15 of 20 schizophrenic and behavior-disordered adolescents. Heaton-Ward (1961) found that nialamide had no influence on mental age or behavior in 51 mentally retarded persons. Carter (1960) found that mentally retarded persons treated with isocarboxiazid showed greater alertness, responsiveness, and sociability and increased weight gain. The validity of the findings of these poorly controlled studies is certainly open to question.

Antidepressants: Summary

In cases of major affective disorders, especially when characterized by many of the "biologic" symptoms enumerated above, TCA or nomifensine may clearly be the treatment of choice. Imipramine is effective for enuresis, but is unnecessary in most cases. However, antidepressant drugs have been found to show such variable effects for behavior management in the retarded that it is not now possible to draw any unequivocal conclusions about their efficacy in nonspecific behavior disorders. There are essentially no generalizable research findings, and neither our own clinical experiences nor the experiences of colleagues who work in institutions for the mentally retarded serve to provide any practical guidance in the use of these agents for behavior disorders in the mentally retarded.

Practical Guidelines

Lithium

In mentally retarded persons with an unequivocal diagnosis of bipolar disorder or of recurrent unipolar depression, lithium is the treatment of choice. Lithium may be considered as a treatment measure for patients in the following categories:

1. Mentally retarded patients with nonspecific behavior disorders who have a strong family pedigree of bipolar affective disorder and/or lithium response.
2. Patients with severe behavior disorders that are characterized by cyclicity or a strong "affective flavor."
3. Patients with explosive aggressive behavior.

It is also reasonable to try lithium in cases of the most severe behavior problems simply because all other treatment approaches have failed. In such cases, a combination of lithium and a neuroleptic may also be considered. One cannot be too forceful, however, in maintaining that polypharmacy should be restricted to those extraordinary cases where no other intervention can control an extremely severe behavior problem.

Lithium treatment is usually begun gradually, starting with one tablet (300 mg) and increasing the dose every few days, until therapeutic serum levels are achieved. Lithium is unique among psychoactive drugs in that blood levels have been found to correlate highly with clinical efficacy. After three or four days on a given dose, a blood sample is measured eight to 12 hours after the last dose of lithium. If the blood lithium level is subtherapeutic, the dose can be increased. Therapeutic levels are between 0.7 and 1.5 mEq/L; in adults, an oral dose of 900 to 1,500 mg/day is usually required to achieve these levels. Occasionally, a patient will respond to "subtherapeutic" levels. Levels higher than 2 mEq/L can be dangerous. The early toxic effects of lithium include anorexia, gastric discomfort, diarrhea, vomiting, thirst, polyuria, hyperreflexia, and hand tremor. Toxic effects associated with higher blood levels are more serious and may include muscle fasciculations and twitching, ataxia, somnolence, confusion, disarthyria, and seizures. During the initial treatment with lithium, blood levels must be determined every three to four days; during the maintenance phase, blood levels need be determined only on a monthly basis. Periodic evaluation of the patient's renal, thyroid, and electrolyte status are recommended for patients on chronic lithium treatment because of possible long-term adverse effects; routine assays of weight and urine specific gravity are recommended.

Antidepressants

The only unequivocal indication for the use of antidepressants in the mentally retarded is unipolar depression, characterized by the signs and symptoms listed earlier. Agoraphobia is another reasonable indication for imipramine, but this problem is probably uncommon in the mentally retarded. Imipramine may be effective in the treatment of enuresis. The use of imipramine or other TCA for the routine treatment of hyperactivity and other behavior problems should be discouraged, although there may be exceptional cases where the application of an antidepressant may be warranted. There may also be certain sleep disorders that are appropriately treated with TCA.

Treatment of patients with TCA requires that the physician be aware of the potential cardiotoxicity of these drugs and carefully monitor their use in patients with cardiac disease. While TCA may be safely used in these patients, it is probably best to choose one with a favorable cardiotoxic profile, such as doxepin or desipramine; some of the novel antidepressants may carry even less risk, and would include nomifensine, maprotiline, trazodone, and bupropion.

Treatment of depressed patients with TCA usually begins with low doses, ranging from 25 to 50 mg/day, with gradual upward titration to doses between 150 and 300 mg/day for adults. Plasma level determinations may be obtained and are often helpful when the physician is faced with questions of noncompliance, lack of therapeutic responsiveness, adverse reactions, and high-risk patients. While therapeutic levels have been determined for some TCA (e.g., desipramine, nortriptyline), either linear or curvilinear, for others the relationship between plasma levels and clinical response is much less clear.

Treatment of hyperkinesis, enuresis, and school phobia usually require much lower doses, and correspondingly lower serum levels, than the treatment of depression. The drugs seem to exert an immediate effect in these disorders, whereas their effect on depressive symptoms can be delayed by 2.3 weeks. In light of the cardiotoxicity of TCA, careful monitoring of the patient's cardiac status prior to treatment and during the titration of dose to proper levels is recommended. Blood pressure and pulse should also be measured because hypotension or tachycardia can occur. The drugs can cause a variety of systemic toxic effects such as dry mouth, gastrointestinal symptoms, and weight gain.

In the treatment of a depressive episode, symptoms usually clear within three to six weeks after achieving therapeutic levels. Maintenance antidepressant therapy for depression is usually not necessary, although treatment of agoraphobia with TCA is usually long-term. Tolerance to the therapeutic effects of TCA in the treatment of hyperactivity and enuresis nocturna has been described.

In adults of normal intelligence, lithium and the antidepressants are used primarily in the treatment of affective disorders. In the mentally retarded, they appear to be used more commonly for the treatment of behavior disorders, although their efficacy and safety is less well established. It is sad to reflect that while these drugs provide relief beyond measure to adult patients of normal intelligence who are plagued with affective symptoms, the presence of affective disorders in the mentally retarded is largely ignored, while symptoms that are annoying or irksome to caretakers are the most common indications for psychoactive drugs. It is our belief that sensitive pharmacologic management might increase the number of mentally retarded patients who are treated with lithium and antidepressants for affective disorders, but would probably decrease the number of patients who are treated with these agents for nonspecific behavior problems.

Chapter 24

Antianxiety and Sedative-Hypnotic Agents

In many respects, antianxiety drugs and the sedative-hypnotics are indistinguishable except in terms of the intent of the prescribing clinician. Antianxiety agents are used for the treatment of anxiety and sedative-hypnotic agents are used for the treatment of insomnia, but the actual drug choice may be identical and is most commonly a benzodiazepine. The distinction between the two indications has often been made on the basis of the marketing strategies of pharmaceutical companies and reified by their use in clinical practice. In fact, antianxiety agents are usually sedating and may be used as sedative-hypnotic agents, and sedative-hypnotic agents often have a calming effect and may be used as antianxiety agents.

This situation may change someday with improved understanding of the biology of anxiety and the possibility of more specific and nonsedating antianxiety agents, and with improved understanding of the neurochemistry of sleep, leading to more specific sleep-inducing agents. But that is for the future. For the present, it is appropriate to consider these two classes of psychotropic agents together.

Anxiolytics and sedative-hypnotics are the most widely prescribed medications in the United States, and they are commonly used in mentally retarded people. However, the professional literature concerning their use with the mentally retarded is a virtual desert. The reason for this investigative neglect is not entirely clear, although it may be related to diagnostic difficulties as well as to the fact that neuroleptics have captured the lion's share of what little attention there is in the pharmacotherapy of mental retardation. A reasoned and rational approach to the use of these agents is necessary while further research is encouraged and supported.

Antianxiety Agents (Anxiolytics)

Prevalence of Use

In Lipman's (1970) widely cited survey, he reported that about 8 percent of the institutionalized mentally retarded people in the United States were receiving minor tranquilizers, making this class of agents a distant second to the neuroleptics in terms of psychotropic drug use. Two benzodiazepines, diazepam (Valium) and chlordiazepoxide (Librium), were the most commonly used, and the other agents were meprobamate (Miltown) and hydroxyzine (Vistaril, Atarax).

Subsequent studies have yielded results (e.g., Silva 1979; Tu 1979) placing antianxiety agents second to the much more commonly employed neuroleptics in prevalence of use. For example, in a national survey, Hill et al. (1985) found that 5.4 percent of the institutionalized population and 3.8 percent of the community sample were receiving antianxiety agents. In both populations, benzodiazepines comprised the bulk of these agents. Intagliata and Rinck (1985) reported a prevalence usage rate of minor tranquilizers of 16.9 and 5.5 percent for their institutional and community samples, respectively, again with benzodiazepines comprising the bulk. In the analysis of these findings, they noted that residents of institutions were significantly more likely to be receiving minor tranquilizers, and that the use of these agents was further related to the client's level of medical-physical problems, rebellious behavior, and stereotypic behavior.

Virtually every available study indicates that the antianxiety agents are commonly used in mentally retarded people despite the fact that their proper use in this population is unclear.

Indications and Therapeutic Use

The situation with regard to the clinical use of antianxiety agents in the mentally retarded is peculiar. There are no studies that examine their use for their primary indication of anxiety and very few that examine their use at all, with only one in the past 10 years.

While seldom specifically indicated, it seems clear that these drugs are used primarily for the control of hyperactive, agitated, aggressive, or otherwise disruptive behaviors. This state of affairs appears most unusual; one thing that does emerge from what little research data are available is that anxiolytics have limited usefulness for these types of behaviors. In fact, in the only well-controlled studies, these behaviors do not improve, and often worsen, with the administration of antianxiety agents. For example, Zrull et al. (1963) found no improvement in behavior with the administration of chlordiazepoxide and found similar results with the use of diazepam (1964). Furthermore, LaVeck and Buckley (1961), in their use of chlordiazepoxide, and Walters et al. (1977), in their use of lorazepam, reported that these benzodiazepines actually worsened many of the targeted behaviors and improved none. Therefore, it must be concluded that there is no scientific foundation at this writing to support the use of antianxiety agents for their most commonly employed "indication" in this population. Although success has been reported (Freinha 1985), any use of these agents for the control of hyperactive or aggressive behaviors should be subject to careful scrutiny and cautious interpretation of perceived benefit; it is not unreasonable to recommend placebo-controlled, double-blind conditions even for routine clinical use.

There are no studies available that examine the use of antianxiety agents in the mentally retarded for their primary indication, namely, the short-term treatment of anxiety. This situation is probably attributable to a general underrecognition of anxiety disorders in mentally retarded individuals. There does not appear to be any reason to suspect that these agents would not be effective for this indication, just as they are in the intellectually normal, although in some individuals with obvious or presumed brain damage one may see the well-recognized "paradoxical" effect with their use (see below).

Benzodiazepines

Since their introduction in the 1960s, benzodiazepines have maintained their profile of being extremely safe and effective in the treatment of anxiety disorders, and remain the drugs of choice in this clinical situation. They have essentially replaced the barbiturates and nonbarbiturate, nonbenzodiazepine agents (e.g., propanediols, such as meprobamate) largely because of their superior safety profile and equal or greater therapeutic effectiveness. However, some clinicians, especially in the field of mental retardation, continue to prefer hydroxyzine (Atarax, Vistaril), although problems with this drug include less efficacy than the benzodiazepines and a lowering of the seizure threshold. On the other hand, it does have the advantage of not producing physical dependence.

The benzodiazepines likely exert their therapeutic effects by interacting with an endogenous benzodiazepine receptor that is widespread throughout the brain and that, in turn, interacts with gamma-aminobutyric acid (GABA) receptors as well as with other neuromodulators (Gray 1983; Guidotti 1978; Tallman et al. 1980). The story that is unfolding with respect to these neurochemical events is notably similar to that which occurred with the discovery of the endorphin systems, and we may expect more specific anxiolytic agents to be a product of this work. For the present, however, these drugs are generally quite similar to each other, differing primarily in onset of action and half-life. For example, diazepam (Valium) has a rapid onset of action as well as a long half-life, which may make it preferable in certain situations, whereas oxazepam (Serax), with its slower onset of action and short half-life, may be preferable in others.

The most common untoward effects of the benzodiazepines, including drowsiness and sedation, represent extensions of their pharmacologic actions. In addition, ataxia and psychomotor impairment may appear in some individuals, especially at higher dosages, and would constitute a serious limitation in settings requiring sustained attention and coordination (e.g., vocational workshop).

Increasing concern about the use of benzodiazepines has surfaced over the past several years with the recognition of tolerance and withdrawal reactions to these agents. It is now recognized that such reactions may occur following long-term use of even standard therapeutic dosages as well as following short-term use of high dosages. While the withdrawal phenomena are qualitatively similar to withdrawal from other central nervous system depressants, it remains that these agents are quite safe and that well-monitored use poses little danger to the patient.

Benzodiazepines as Anticonvulsants

Benzodiazepines have an important, but limited, role in the treatment of seizure disorders (Adams and Victor 1985; Schmidt 1983; Trimble 1983). Intravenously administered diazepam continues to play an important part in the emergency treatment of status epilepticus. Furthermore, orally administered clonazepam has a role in the treatment of certain types of epilepsy, particularly generalized absence and myoclonic seizures. It is possible that nitrazepam has a role similar to that of clonazepam, although its use is much less accepted; the drug is not available in the United States. However, beyond these rather specific exceptions, benzodiazepines appear to have little to contribute to the treatment of epilepsy.

Nevertheless, several investigators have noted that the high prevalence of the use of diazepam in the mentally retarded population may be artificially inflated in terms of its role as a psychotropic agent because it is frequently used as an anticonvulsant. If this, in fact, is the case, then it speaks to another problem in the pharmacotherapy of the mentally retarded that has yet to be adequately addressed. In short, because orally administered diazepam has little or no efficacy as a long-term anticonvulsant in the nonmentally retarded population, there appears to be little reason for this to be otherwise in the mentally retarded. The questions that arise include whether epilepsy in the mentally retarded population is significantly different such that diazepam does play an important role as an anticonvulsant, or whether this is yet another instance of inappropriate administration of medication in people with mental retardation.

Other Antianxiety Agents

Diphenhydramine (Benadryl) and hydroxyzine (Atarax, Vistaril) continue to enjoy a certain amount of popularity among clinicians prescribing for mentally retarded individuals. However, despite their relative safety, there is little in the literature to support their efficacy as antianxiety agents in the mentally retarded (Freeman 1970; Rivinus 1980). Therefore, any such use should be carefully monitored and scrutinized.

Two additional agents, imipramine and propranolol, deserve mentioning because of their effects on certain aspects of anxiety. It is now widely accepted that imipramine possesses antipanic activity in a variety of panic-related disorders (Liebowitz 1985). Imipramine is probably the pharmacologic treatment of choice for this panic-related type of anxiety. In addition, other antidepressant drugs appear to possess similar antipanic activity and include other tricyclic agents as well as monoamine oxidase inhibitors (Sheehan 1985). Whether this action is related to their antidepressant activity has yet to be clearly established, although several lines of investigation suggest that the anxiety disorders may be closely related to the affective disorders (depression). Beta-adrenergic blocking drugs, particularly propranolol, appear to be effective in the treatment of the somatic aspects of anxiety (e.g., tachycardia), and may therefore have a special role in those patients in whom such complaints are most prominent (Greenblatt and Shader 1978; Gualtieri et al. 1983; Noyes 1985). However, beta-adrenergic blocking drugs are clearly inferior to the benzodiazepines as general antianxiety agents. In addition, propranolol may have a special role as an "antiaggressive" agent in the treatment of violent outbursts and aggressive behavioral disturbances associated with a variety of brain damage (Gualtieri et al. 1983), including mental retardation (Ratey et al. 1986).

Antianxiety Agents: Summary

Antianxiety agents constitute a commonly employed class of psychotropic agents among the mentally retarded. They are most often used to help control hyperactive and aggressive behaviors, an indication for which their effectiveness has not been demonstrated. In fact, it has usually been shown that they worsen these behaviors. On the other hand, their use in the treatment of anxiety has yet to be examined in the mentally retarded, although it may be expected that these antianxiety psychotropic agents do have a limited role in this situation. Principles of the use of these agents are identical with those in the nonretarded population.

Sedative-Hypnotic Agents

Prevalence of Use

The pattern of use of sedative-hypnotic agents is somewhat more difficult to ascertain from published reports than that of other agents. For example, in Lipman's (1970) survey, he does not mention sedative-hypnotics as a separate category. In addition, the sedative-hypnotics and the anxiolytics often differ only in the intent of the prescribing clinician, and in the reporting of survey data, this intent is not indicated. Therefore, whether a benzodiazepine, a barbiturate, or hydroxyzine is to be viewed as an anxiolytic or as a sedative-hypnotic is often not clear. In addition, one particularly popular medication, phenobarbital, is most often used as an anticonvulsant; often this distinction is not made so that it is even more unclear whether, in specific patients, it is an anxiolytic, a sedative-hypnotic, or an anticonvulsant. For this reason, the data of Silva (1979) and Tu (1979) are uninterpretable because they include phenobarbital with the sedative-hypnotic agents. On the other hand, in the well-reported studies of Hill et al. (1985) and Intagliata and Rinck (1985), prevalence rates for the use of sedative-hypnotic agents are indicated. In their national study of both community and institutional settings, Hill et al. found that 3.9 percent of the community sample and 7.3 percent of the institutional sample were receiving sedative-hypnotic agents. Similarly, Intagliata and Rinck reported that 4.3 percent of the community sample and 9.4 percent of the institutional sample were receiving sedative-hypnotic agents in their survey in Missouri. The two most commonly prescribed agents were chloral hydrate and flurazepam (Dalmane). In the analysis of their findings, Intagliata and Rinck noted that these agents were more likely to be prescribed to individuals with violent or destructive behaviors and to those with lower levels of physical development.

Whether these rates are changing cannot be stated with certainty because the methodological difficulties already mentioned make comparison with earlier studies impossible. Nevertheless, it would appear that sedative-hypnotic agents comprise the third most commonly used class of psychotropic agents among mentally retarded individuals.

Indications and Therapeutic Use

The indication for the use of sedative-hypnotic agents is relatively straightforward, and consists of a desire for short-term sedation, usually in symptomatic treatment of insomnia. In addition, it is a common practice among clinicians who work with mentally retarded individuals to use these agents for short-term sedation during physical examinations and other diagnostic investigations. Beyond these, there appears to be little role for their use.

However, even limiting oneself to these indications, there is essentially no relevant professional literature that speaks to their use in the mentally retarded. Therefore, again, any guidelines must be drawn largely from their use in the general population (Fahs 1985; Gelenberg 1983).

As with the antianxiety agents, benzodiazepines are easily the preferred class of drugs for the pharmacologic treatment of insomnia, as well as for other situations in which short-term sedation is indicated. There are several other possible choices, but probably the only acceptable alternatives would be the chloral derivative (e.g., chloral hydrate) and diphenhydramine (e.g., Benadryl). However, if the patient is already taking one of the traditional antianxiety agents. (e.g., one of the "nonhypnotic" benzodiazepines or hydroxyzine) for the daytime treatment of anxiety, then the dose or scheduling of that agent may be shifted to exploit its sedative effects at bedtime rather than adding another medication.

Since hypnotics play a relatively minor role in the rational treatment of insomnia, management of this symptom should begin with a careful evaluation. When pharmacologic treatment is indicated, it should generally occur within the context of concurrent nonbiologic approaches.

There are currently three benzodiazepines available in the United States that are designated specifically for use as sedative-hypnotic agents: flurazepam (Dalmane), temazepam (Restoril), and triazolam (Halcion). These agents differ primarily in length of half-life, with flurazepam being the longest and triazolam being the shortest. Treatment may be initiated with any of these agents at their lower dosage taken about 30 minutes before retiring. With flurazepam, one may expect greater hypnotic efficacy on the second and subsequent nights of administration as the drug accumulates; with the shorter-acting agents the maximum hypnotic response may be seen on the first night. A transient worsening of sleep may occur following discontinuation of any of the hypnotics, even after short-term administration. Additional difficulties may include daytime sedation, impairment of cognitive and psychomotor function, and the emergence of daytime anxiety. Finally, the cautions with regard to withdrawal and dependence apply to all of the benzodiazepines, and continuous long-term use is to be discouraged. Therefore, these drugs must be prescribed judiciously, for only short periods (usually no more than two weeks), and monitored carefully lest the patient's difficulty be exacerbated.

"Paradoxical" Response to Sedative-Hypnotic Agents

It is well-known that some mentally retarded patients respond to the administration of sedative-hypnotic agents with increased levels of motor activity, restlessness, or other forms of agitated behavior, termed the *paradoxical response*. This response is also observed in elderly patients with dementia, children, and patients with a variety of forms of brain damage. It is this observation that has led many clinicians to caution against the use of these agents in mentally retarded patients. However, the work of Barron and Sandman (Barron and Sandman 1983, 1984, 1985; Sandman et al. 1983) suggests some intriguing possibilities stemming from this observation. They describe a constellation of factors associated with the presence of this paradoxical response in mentally retarded patients, including a history of perinatal trauma, the presence of self-injurious behavior (SIB) and stereotypy, and a beneficial response of their SIB to the administration of the opiate antagonist, naloxone. Although these findings have yet to be replicated and further extended, the implications are clear: there may be a subgroup of mentally retarded individuals whose SIB is etiologically related to an impaired endogenous opiate system and in whom the administration of sedative-hypnotic agents may serve as a pharmacologic marker. Should this prove to be the case, treatment approaches involving manipulation of the opiate system would appear to be quite specific.

Sedative-Hypnotic Agents: Summary

Sedative-hypnotic agents constitute a relatively commonly used class of psychotropic drugs among mentally retarded individuals. The employed indications for use in actual clinical practice cannot be ascertained from the available literature. However, if they are to be viewed as having a primary indication in the short-term treatment of insomnia, then it must be concluded that their use is excessive. Furthermore, because of the possibility of tolerance, dependence, and withdrawal from these agents, long-term use, which is the general practice, should be strongly discouraged. Finally, the presence of a paradoxical response in some individuals may further limit the use of these agents. On the other hand, this paradoxical response may (paradoxically) allow us a window to further understanding of certain behavioral difficulties in mentally retarded patients.

All of these caveats in mind, it is reasonable to assume that sedative-hypnotic drugs, when properly employed, may allow relief in those mentally retarded patients with transient or persistent insomnia, just as they do in the nonretarded population.

Chapter 25

Psychostimulant Drugs

Stimulant drugs are the most commonly prescribed psychoactive drugs for children of normal IQ (Whalen and Henker 1980) and for mentally retarded children who live at home and who attend community schools (Gadow and Kalachnick 1981). On the other hand, they are among the least frequently prescribed psychotropic agents for retarded people who reside in institutions (Aman and Singh 1988; Lipman 1970). The reason for this disparity is not entirely clear, although it suggests that something about the institutionalization decision influences treatment practice. Young mild-to-moderately retarded people without severe behavior problems are more likely to live at home and to be served in community programs. They may also be the most likely group of retarded people to respond well to stimulant treatment. Hyperactivity and inattention are very common problems for retarded people in general. However, the evidence suggests that stimulant treatment seems to work for only a minority of this population.

When given in low to moderate doses, stimulant drugs such as dextroamphetamine and methylphenidate are known to improve performance on some learning measures (Aman 1978, 1980; Douglas 1974; Sprague and Sleator 1977; Sroufe 1975) as well as motor skills (Knights and Hinton 1969) in normal and hyperactive children. They may also enhance memory performance (Rapoport et al. 1978), vigilance performance (Mackworth 1950; Rapoport et al. 1978), and (possibly) physical stamina (Weiss and Laties 1962) in normal adults. This suggests that stimulants have beneficial effects (at least in the short-term) across diagnostic groups and ages and that adverse response or failure to respond is something of an idiosyncrasy.

However, the available evidence indicates that this is not the case. There have been a large number of studies of stimulant medications in retarded persons (Alexandris and Lundell 1968; Anton and Greer 1969; Bell and Zubek 1961; Blacklidge and Ekblad 1971; Christensen 1975; Clausen et al. 1960; Cutler et al. 1940/1941; Davis et al. 1969; Lobb 1968; McConnell et al. 1964; Morris et al. 1955; Spencer 1980; Varley and Trupin 1982). A minority of these investigations (Alexandris and Lundell 1968; Blacklidge and Ekblad 1971; Christensen 1975; Cutler et al. 1940/1941; Varley and Trupin 1982) have shown some improvement. The most typical finding has been a failure of drug effect, at least on a group basis. Some studies (Bell and Zubek 1961; Lobb 1968) have actually documented a net trend in the direction of worsening, especially on learning-related tests. Those few studies to have shown any improvement were usually done in mildly retarded children (Alexandris and Lundell 1968; Blacklidge and Ekblad 1971; Cutler et al. 1940/1941). It is the writer's view that only two of these studies (Blacklidge and Ekblad 1971; Varley and Trupin 1982) reported broadly based improvements of the type observed with hyperactive children of normal IQ. It is interesting to note that the subjects in both of these studies were mildly retarded children living in the community. Most of the stimulant studies listed above have used double-blind, placebo-controlled designs and acceptable statistical analyses. Their results, therefore, have to be taken seriously. The overall impression from these studies is that the probability of detecting a genuinely beneficial clinical response declines as function level declines.

Stimulant drugs have not received extensive evaluation in autistic children. However, it is worth noting in passing that earlier studies that have been done suggest that stimulant medication is contraindicated in this group of children (Campbell 1975; Campbell et al. 1972b, 1976). These studies were conducted with "psychotic" children having "autistic features," who would be diagnosed as having infantile autism using today's nosology. Campbell et al. reported that dextroamphetamine and levoamphetamine caused existing stereotypies to worsen and some stereotypies to appear de novo in these autistic children. In addition, irritability was increased in some children, and there was a general lack of therapeutic effect due to the stimulants. However, two case studies (Geller et al. 1981; Strayhorn et al. 1988) and one uncontrolled group study (Birmaher et al. 1988) reported improvements with methylphenidate on inattention and overactivity, but with some worsening in mood and tantrums in one study (Strayhorn et al. 1988). It is difficult to know how to account for these conflicting outcomes. The following possibilities, however, exist. First, the subjects in the Campbell et al. studies may have been systematically more impaired (and of lower IQ) than in the latter studies. Second, case reports, by their very nature, may tend to recount unusual or idiosyncratic instances of improvement. Third, there may have been marked diagnostic differences across studies. In any case, at this time, the use of stimulants in autism must be regarded as contentious at best. This is obviously an area requiring further empirical group data to determine whether the stimulants have a role to play in this population and, if so, whether clinical response is tied to subject IQ or severity of presenting symptoms.

The data on stimulant drugs and developmental disabilities have been reviewed from a theoretical perspective by Aman (1982). Besides the clinical data summarized above, the following additional facts were noted. First, both mentally retarded and autistic subjects can be characterized as having narrow or "overselective" attention. Second, both clinical populations frequently display stereotypic behavior. Third, it is well established that stimulant drugs can cause stereotypy in laboratory animals as well as in humans, and this action is antagonized by neuroleptic drugs. Furthermore, neuroleptics are often effective in reducing stereotypy in mentally retarded and autistic subjects. Finally, the mechanism whereby stimulants induce stereotypy in animals may be by further constriction or focusing attention. Aman proposed a model that maintains that stimulant drugs cause a constriction of attention regardless of clinical group such that subjects' attentional characteristics are hypothesized to determine the nature of their clinical response to stimulants (Aman 1982). As many mentally retarded and autistic individuals are known to have a narrow (or overselective) focus of attention, and as this presumably becomes more extreme with more severe intellectual impairment, the model suggests that a favorable clinical response becomes less probable with declining IQ.

Gualtieri and Hicks (in press) have made some neuropsychological observations that lead to the same prediction. They argued that stimulant drugs operate therapeutically on frontal lobe structures and, therefore, require an intact frontal system, especially the mesocortical dopamine system. In addition, Chandler et al. (1988) have stated that cortical hypoplasia is the most commonly observed neuropathic finding in severely retarded individuals. Assuming that this mode of therapeutic action is correct and also assuming that frontal system damage is more probable as functional handicap increases, it would be expected, once again, that stimulants are least likely to have a therapeutic effect at very low IQ levels.

Aman et al. (1988) have obtained data that support the idea that there is an interaction between IQ and clinical response. In a group of 30 intellectually subaverage hyperactive children, they found that methylphenidate caused significant improvement in the classroom (as determined by a teacher rating scale) and some gains on performance tests, although parents failed to report therapeutic effects. A series of statistical interactions was found between mental age and drug response, suggesting that children of higher mental age tended to respond better than subjects of low mental age. After breaking the double blind, continued methylphenidate treatment was recommended for several of the children with IQs greater than 48, whereas none of 12 children with IQs below this level appeared to show a positive clinical response. These results support the lines of speculation outlined above, but they also require replication by other investigators.

In summary, on the basis of the published data as well as widespread clinical experience, it is suggested that the stimulants are of limited utility with severely and profoundly retarded people. Both research in this field as well as that with attention deficit hyperactivity disorder (children of normal IQ) would suggest that those mentally retarded people most likely to respond favorably to stimulant drugs may have the following characteristics: 1) being of younger (primary school) age; 2) presenting with mild or moderate retardation; 3) having high levels of inattention, distractibility, impulsivity, and overactivity; and 4) presenting without stereotypies, self-injury, or psychotic symptomatology.

With some justification, Gadow (1985) has criticized previous research with the stimulant drugs for including subjects with a somewhat amorphous collection of symptoms, without focusing on what are now regarded as the core features of hyperactivity. Although the available studies were generally well designed, they were often carried out with samples selected for an ill-defined collection of symptoms. This is obviously an issue that should be addressed in future research. At the same time, the existing data indicate only a limited role for stimulants in mental retardation, and this appears to be mainly among those children and adolescents of higher functional levels.

Chapter 26

Anticonvulsant Drugs

Approximately one-third of institutionalized mentally retarded individuals are on long-term anticonvulsant treatment (Aman 1983), and about 11 percent of noninstitutionalized retardates also receive some form of anticonvulsant therapy (Gadow 1981). Retarded people are prone to seizure disorders, especially the focal epilepsies, which are as a rule much more difficult to treat than generalized epilepsy. By the same token, mental retardation per se is a poor prognostic indicator for epilepsy. Thus many retarded people have to be treated with anticonvulsants for many years, or even an entire lifetime. Since the epilepsies that occur in mentally retarded people tend to be severe, treatment, even with anticonvulsant polypharmacy, is often only partially successful. (The use of more than two anticonvulsants, an example of polypharmacy, is rarely indicated, and in most instances seizures are controlled with one well-chosen drug.)

Anticonvulsants as "Psychotropic" Drugs

Although anticonvulsants are used primarily for the control of epilepsy, there was a period when they were advocated for behavior problems in children and for specific learning problems. This was based on the observation that large proportions of children with behavior disorders seemed to have equivocal or abnormal electroencephalogram (EEG) patterns. The evidence attesting to direct association between brain damage and behavior disorders is somewhat weak, and a direct association with EEG abnormalities has been hotly contested (Gross and Wilson 1964; Lindsley and Henry 1941; Millichap et al. 1969; Walker and Kirkpatrick 1947; Werry 1979). Thus a number of investigators viewed children with behavior problems as having a kind of "epileptic equivalent" as the primary source of their behavioral difficulty. Following this logic, it was argued that since anticonvulsants are effective in suppressing clinical seizures, they may also be effective in cases of subclinical, abnormal discharges. However, the evidence in support of this position is extremely weak.

A number of uncontrolled studies have suggested that antiepileptic drugs, most notably phenytoin, have beneficial behavioral effects in children, especially those described as aggressive and prone to temper outbursts. Selection criteria have frequently included the requirement that subclinical EEG activity be present, but this appears to have made no real difference to outcome. Some of the reports were literally anecdotal accounts, and their conclusions must be treated with caution. Another group of uncontrolled reports have obtained negative results (Cohn and Nardini 1958; Green 1961; Pasamanick 1951).

Only three properly controlled studies of anticonvulsants could be located, all of which looked at the effects of phenytoin. Goldberg and Kurland (1970) compared the drug to placebo in mildly mentally retarded children. The children were observed over an eight-week period. Three measures of learning plus eight factors on a rating scale were measured. The results indicated that one rating scale dimension, distractibility, was improved. Although the authors tried to highlight other positive drug-related changes, it·is worth remarking that this variable alone, out of at least 13 dependent measures, showed significant effects related to the drugs. The two remaining investigations studied delinquent boys (Conners et al. 1971) and children characterized as having periodic temper outbursts (Looker and Conners 1970). A variety of standardized rating scales as well as psychometric tests were used, but no differences could be demonstrated between phenytoin and placebo.

The efficacy of carbamazepine in major affective disorders of the bipolar type is well established in psychiatric patients (see Evans and Gualtieri 1985 for review). Lithium-carbamazepine combination treatment and valproic acid are possible alternatives in refractory patients, although the clinical reports here are anecdotal (Nolen 1983) or based on small clinical studies. There is also a clinical literature on carbamazepine in schizophrenia; aggressive behavior, especially the episodic dyscontrol syndrome; and other behavior problems, including hyperactivity (Evans and Gualtieri 1985). Thus carbamazepine may have some potential as an alternative treatment for patients with severe psychiatric disorders. Its therapeutic potential in retarded patients may also be considerable, but represents a grossly understudied topic.

It is only recently that researchers and clinicians have begun to appreciate the potential deleterious effects of anticonvulsants on cognitive and behavioral function. Unfortunately, the overwhelming majority of this recent research has been done in nonretarded populations. Therefore, making generalizations to the retarded population may be tenuous. Nonetheless, it is important to review these studies because they provide at least some insight about how to monitor the beneficial as well as the harmful consequences of anticonvulsant treatment in the retarded. Presented herein are discussions of: 1) behavioral and cognitive studies of anticonvulsants in normal and clinical populations; 2) suggestions for research on anticonvulsants in the retarded; and 3) clinical considerations for using anticonvulsants in the retarded.

Review of Behavioral and Cognitive Studies

There has been an increased appreciation of the psychological effects of anticonvulsants. Consistent drug-related changes in mental and behavioral performance have been reported in clinical as well as normal populations. Presented in Table 1 are the more frequently cited studies concerning the cognitive and behavioral effects of anticonvulsant treatment.

As indicated in the table, there are few well-controlled studies of differential psychological effects of anticonvulsant treatment in the retarded population. Goldberg and Kurland (1970), in a study with retarded boys, provided initial data to suggest that phenytoin can bring about positive improvements in distractibility without affecting, adversely or favorably, other aspects of cognition.

Phenytoin has recently come under attack for causing possible mental and psychomotor deterioration in patients on long-term treatment. In one study (Smith and Lowery 1972), an increase in IQ due to phenytoin was observed. However, in a number of other studies (Dekaban and Lehman 1975; Dodrill 1975; Idestrom et al. 1972; Matthews and Harley 1975; Stores and Hart 1976; Trimble and Corbett cited in Trimble 1979), deterioration because of the drug was found. Such worsening included decrements on reaction time and vigilance tasks, lowered self-ratings, sedative effects as measured by psychophysiologic measures, reductions in free-recall and memory,

Table 1. Frequently Cited Studies of Anticonvulsant Therapy and Behavioral-Cognitive Response

Authors	Drugs	Subjects	Results
Idestrom et al. 1972	phenytoin	normal adults	decreased reaction time; diminished self-rating
Dodrill 1975	phenytoin	epileptic adults	decreased motor function associated with higher serum level of phenytoin
Trimble 1979	phenytoin and other anticonvulsants	epileptic children	decreased IQ associated with higher serum levels of phenytoin
MacLeod et al. 1978	phenobarbital	epileptic adult males	diminished short-term memory; long-term memory unaffected
Hutt et al. 1968	phenobarbital	normal adults	decreased reaction time, sustained attention, and verbal learning
Schain et al. 1977	carbamazepine	epileptic children	improvement in "cognitive style"
Thompson and Trimble 1982	carbamazepine versus phenytoin	epileptic children	improvement of delayed recall when subjects were switched from phenytoin to carbamazepine
Guey et al. 1967	ethosuximide	epileptic children	initial drop in cognitive functioning, which later stabilized
Butlin et al. 1980	phenytoin versus carbamazepine versus sodium valproate	epileptics	no significant differences among the drugs on memory tests; serum levels of phenytoin noncontributory

depressed reading scores, increased motor tremor, psychiatric illness, and actual intellectual deterioration as measured on IQ tests. However, it is important to note that most of these changes have not been replicated across studies. Further, it is possible that in some instances the deterioration was due to inadequate seizure control or degenerative processes.

It will also be observed that the studies showing the most deterioration were those designated as correlational. These studies employed the strategy of relating performance to the actual level of drug in the bloodstream. The significance of these studies is that deterioration has usually been noted within the range that is generally regarded as therapeutic and nontoxic. This has led to a number of authors (Simmons et al. 1975; Trimble 1979; Trimble and Reynolds 1976) to recommend that it may be better to risk a few seizures than produce oversedation with higher doses.

One study (Wapner et al. 1962) was unable to show any changes due to phenobarbital in epileptic children. However, a group of other investigations (Camfield et al. 1979; Dekaban and Lehman 1975; Hutt et al. 1968; MacLeod et al. 1978; Matthews and Harley 1975; Reynolds and Travers 1974; Trimble and Corbett cited in Trimble 1979) did document adverse effects. Among these were deterioration on tests of attention span, memory, and verbal learning. Intellectual deterioration and psychiatric illness increased with larger serum levels. Again, the warning about risking sedative effects at upper "therapeutic" levels appears appropriate.

Parenthetically it should be mentioned that phenobarbital is reputed to cause hyperactivity in some children (Ounsted 1955; Schain 1979), and an association with aggression and hyperactive behavior has often been noted in the clinical literature. One of the few studies that has examined this issue was unable to document a hyperkinetic reaction due to phenobarbital (Camfield et al. 1979). However, Wolf and Forsythe (1978), who conducted a large-scale investigation, found that 35 percent of children treated with phenobarbital displayed hyperactivity, whereas only 13 percent of a control group showed the behavior pattern. It is important, therefore, that clinicians and others directly involved with such children be aware of the possible association between phenobarbital treatment and behavior disturbance.

Thus far, carbamazepine has not been found to cause decline of cognitive performance at ordinary clinical doses. Although Trimble and Corbett (cited in Trimble 1979) noted adverse effects from the sedative-type anticonvulsants and phenytoin, they could demonstrate no such effects from carbamazepine. Schain and his associates (Schain et al. 1975, 1977) observed actual improvements in cognitive style and IQ when children were switched from their previous medication to carbamazepine. However, this may well reflect a suppression of cognitive function by the previously used sedative drugs rather than a genuine improvement due to carbamazepine.

Carbamazepine treatment is frequently the occasion of behavioral toxicity, and this may be more common in the developmentally handicapped population than in other patients. Behavioral toxicity may include hyperactivity, irritability, combative behavior, insomnia, agitation, or psychosis. Such problems may arise at relatively low doses and do not seem to be related to drug concentration in the blood (Evans et al. 1987). Valproic acid seems to have a pattern of behavioral toxicity similar to that of carbamazepine.

Results with ethosuximide have been mixed. Guey et al. (1967) found that performance on various Wechsler Intelligence Scale for Children subtests, as well as on a test of visual perception, worsened. However, others (Browne et al. 1975; Smith et al. 1968) noted a pattern of no change mixed with improvement. It is very possible that improvements with this drug are due to its effects on seizure activity. Ethosuximide is commonly used in the treatment of absence (or petit mal) seizures, which can substantially interfere with cognitive performance. Hence, improved cognitive function may reflect better seizure control rather than a direct effect on learning-related skills.

Ethosuximide may have behavioral toxicity, including depression.

Research Issues

Research with retarded people in this area is, from a clinical and experimental viewpoint, very difficult. Aman (1983) outlined the major ethical problem of placebo substitution in an epileptic patient as well as some problematic issues in data analysis and interpretation. For example, it is difficult to interpret cognitive-behavioral changes to a direct drug effect and/or to a change in seizure control. These problems do not necessarily militate against employing systematic, placebo-controlled trials but they do highlight the importance of performing responsible, valid assessment of cognitive, behavioral, and even mood effects of anticonvulsants in a population that is especially prone to deficits in these areas.

Anticonvulsant studies, like those reported above, provide a reasonable foundation for research on anticonvulsant effects in the retarded population. Issues that are central to a valid assessment of the psychoactive properties of the anticonvulsants involve:

1. The use of proven drug-sensitive cognitive, behavioral, and mood measures employed within the framework of a controlled (i.e., double-blind, crossover, placebo-controlled) technology.
2. The monitoring of serum levels while on the drug. Research has strongly suggested that dosage and blood level studies do not correlate well with performance levels and that anticonvulsant serum levels are more diagnostic, at least for some anticonvulsants.
3. The continued application of assessment techniques referenced above. It is not uncommon for clinicians and staff treating mentally retarded patients to be misled by the toxic effects of anticonvulsant medications, regarding them rather as a part of the patient's deficit. For example, incoordination, mental confusion, lethargy, and memory impairments can be induced by anticonvulsants; these are symptoms that can easily be misidentified as part of the mental retardation syndrome. Therefore, periodic neurologic and cognitive assessment and serum assays are indicated.

Clinical Issues

Side Effects

The incidence of anticonvulsant side effects are higher and probably occur in greater severity in the retarded population than in the nonimpaired population. Physical effects can include nausea, drowsiness, ataxia, vertigo, blurred vision, and cognitive dysfunction (diminished attention and memory). These effects usually remit if the dosage is decreased. Clinicians who treat retarded people need to be especially conversant with the panoply of specific anticonvulsant drug side effects.

Serum Levels and Dosage Considerations

Because an inverse relationship exists between behavioral-cognitive performance levels and anticonvulsant serum levels, Aman (1983) suggested clinicians should aim for the lowest clinically effective level. Aman also cautioned against using very high doses for seizure management and recommended that clinicians consider changing the medication or consider "chancing a few seizures rather than risk over sedation at higher doses." In any event, periodic serum levels are indicated probably on a six-month basis.

The state of the art in anticonvulsant blood level monitoring is changing, however, with the growing availability of assays of "free" drug (i.e., drug unbound to plasma proteins and therefore therapeutically active).

Drug Substitution and Polypharmacy

A general rule is to avoid anticonvulsant polypharmacy. There is little evidence to suggest that polypharmacy significantly improves seizure control or behavior (although obviously, there are exceptions). The clinician should aim for systematic evaluations of single drugs, at an appropriate dose range, with blood level measurement, prior to considering anticonvulsant polypharmacy. Recent studies have suggested that carbamazepine alone can provide adequate seizure control when phenytoin or phenobarbital have failed. Valproic acid is another second or third alternative in difficult seizure management cases. It should be emphasized that, in general, mental retardation is associated with a poorer prognosis for seizure control. This should not be the occasion for therapeutic nihilism, but rather for careful, systematic efforts to find the right drug or the right combination for each patient.

Chapter 27

Counseling Families of Children with Mental Retardation

According to Henry Leland (Cohen and Leland 1978), services for the mentally retarded can be divided into three categories of treatment approaches: general behavioral counseling services, educational-vocational services, and medical services. The general behavioral counseling services are clinical interventions that are aimed at helping individuals sort out information they already have. These services include therapeutic or rehabilitative interventions. Educational-vocational services are responsible for transmitting new or additional information to create new behavior patterns. The primary educational approaches are behavior modification and special education programs that emphasize training or habilitation. Medical approaches to the treatments of retarded persons generally rely heavily on psychopharmacologic interventions. Since the last approach is described in other chapters, it will not be discussed here.

One of physicians' most important and most difficult roles in providing care to children with mental retardation is communicating with families. Mental retardation is, in most circumstances, a permanent condition. There is nothing that physicians can do to cure the condition. Although therapy is helpful, no medicine or surgery will significantly ameliorate the symptoms. Advances in modern medicine have, however, created a climate where physicians are expected to provide cures or at least dramatic habilitation. Since mental retardation is not a condition where this expectation can be met, both families and physicians can become frustrated. Providing good communication and appropriate counseling are the most important roles for physicians in these circumstances. This chapter will highlight some of the important issues in counseling families of children with mental retardation and provide suggestions for dealing with these issues.

The Initial Interpretive Interview

The physician's first encounter with parents of children with mental retardation is often at the time of diagnosis or not long after that. This is a very important time in the lives of the parents, and can influence the tone of the relationship they develop with their child and their physician. Normal reactions of parents include shock, denial, sadness, anger, adaptation, and reorganization. While parents go through most of these reactions, the intensity and duration of these feelings will vary greatly. For instance, denial may be strong and prolonged in one parent and almost absent in another. The physician should not assume that all parents go through the same reactions in a stereotypic manner. Physicians need to probe and to listen to parents to determine individual reactions.

Most parents also wonder what they did wrong. Feelings of guilt will vary greatly from parent to parent. The role of the physician is to clarify any information that might lead to unrealistic feelings of guilt while assuring the parents that their reaction is understandable. A common mistake made by some physicians is to close the discussion about the parents' guilt feelings by offering information only. Statements like: "You shouldn't feel guilty because . . . " may cause parents to refrain from discussing persistent unrealistic feelings for fear that their physician will think them stupid or incompetent. It is best to clarify the facts, but also to state that the parents may still have persistent feelings of guilt. If so, it is appropriate to discuss those feelings.

The first conference with the parents should focus mainly on the parents' reaction to the diagnosis. Statements such as "I know this must be difficult for you," or "This may be shocking information," will let parents know that their turmoil has been experienced by other parents in the same situation. It is even helpful for physicians to express their own feelings with such statements as: "It is difficult for me to have to tell you." This not only helps to facilitate the discussion, but also conveys the physician's own humanity. There is also a need to help parents identify supportive people to turn to, such as grandparents or clergy. There may be long periods of silence during the initial session. These periods of silence can be uncomfortable for the physician but helpful in allowing the parents to grieve and gather their thoughts. Literally holding a parent's hand, or putting a hand on a parent's shoulder is an extremely effective method for a physician to express empathy quietly.

Content of the Initial Interview

In addition to helping parents deal with their feelings, the initial interview should provide information. Because of the emotional climate, parents will not remember most of what they hear during the first interview. This means information should be limited to essentials. Subsequent interviews will allow time for more in-depth explanations and recommendations. When one parent cannot be present or when information needs to be conveyed quickly, such as when informed consent is required for surgery, using a recorder and providing the audiocassette recordings of the interview to the parents can be helpful. Two studies (Wolraich et al. 1979, 1981) have shown the efficacy of this technique in helping parents learn and retain information. Tape-recording the interview allows the physician to give more detailed information than the parents are likely to remember. The parents can then listen to the tape later when they are more calm. They can also use the tape to explain their child's condition to other close relatives. Sometimes, even though the parents understand their child's problem, it is difficult for them to explain it to others, and they are often asked to do so. Recording the actual session is much more personal and individualized than commercial materials that might be available.

The diagnostic terms used also need to be considered carefully. Terms such as *mental retardation* are likely to cause a strong parental reaction. This does not mean that the terms should be avoided if they are appropriate. It does mean that it is important to determine what the terms mean to the parents. Inaccurate stereotypes or their experience with an atypical case may make them unduly pessimistic. Parents will usually not attempt to clarify the terms themselves unless they are asked, because they are afraid of seeming ignorant.

It is difficult to be the bearer of bad tidings, and most physicians will try to make the situation easier or less traumatic for the parents. Sometimes this can result in misunderstandings. Other terms for mental retardation such as *developmental delay* may not have the same emotional impact, but may not convey the true nature of the disability to the parents. It is best to use the terms the parents are likely to hear in the future and that will most effectively tell them what they are dealing with, while supporting them in their reactions to the term.

Other Support

It is frequently helpful for parents of a newly diagnosed child with mental retardation to speak to other parents of children with mental retardation and to participate in parent groups such as those of the Association of Retarded Citizens. There are aspects of their new experience that can be shared better this way than with professionals. However, parents may not be ready to talk to other parents immediately after finding out about their child's diagnosis. Many times they initially want some privacy and need first to cope with the diagnosis themselves before turning to others. One must also be cautious because mismatches between parents can make for awkward situations. For instance, if the parents that are contacted are extremely enthusiastic and dedicated, it may be difficult for parents who have mixed feelings about their child. Care should be taken in arranging contacts. In arranging the contact, it is also important to have the contact parents call the new parents because the new parents are less likely to make the contact on their own.

Another difficult situation is when parents disagree between themselves. The care and management of children in our society still usually remains the primary responsibility of the mother. This means that she is frequently the person who brings the child in for all the evaluations and treatments. Fathers have less opportunity to learn about their child's condition directly. The mother is then put in the role of not only understanding her child's condition, but also explaining it to her husband. The father may be less able to express his frustrations and emotional distress. It is important for the physician caring for children with mental retardation to encourage the participation of fathers and to meet directly with them.

Counseling Other Family Members

There are other family members the physician needs to consider. Psychiatric difficulties have been found in normal siblings of mentally retarded children (Wasserman 1983). Siblings frequently are misinformed about their sibling's condition and can fear that they are the cause of the handicap or that they may somehow catch the same condition. Siblings can frequently develop anger, resentment, or guilt because the child with mental retardation demands so much of the parents' time and may require additional responsibilities from the brother or sister. Siblings may have no one to talk to about feelings of fear or resentment. They may be hesitant to bother parents, particularly if the parents have difficulty accepting the problem themselves. Parents in such a situation may close off possibilities for communication with their children.

It is particularly difficult for families to cope in situations where mental retardation is felt to be a socially unacceptable condition.

Because the mentally retarded child can have many medical needs, the physician's attention is focused on this family member. However, it is important to identify the emotional conflicts in siblings and to meet with them individually to assess their feelings. Steps can be made to identify counseling needs, and encouragement given to the parents to deal sensitively with siblings. The physician can help parents identify the need for counseling if it is appropriate.

Other Aspects of Counseling

An inordinate emphasis has been placed on making sure that parents accept their child's condition. However, spending a great deal of effort to attain this goal is not always productive. It is not as important to determine how parents describe their child's condition as it is to determine what services they obtain and what demands they place on their child and the professional staff involved in the child's case. It is entirely possible for parents to obtain appropriate services for their child and have realistic short-term goals while refusing to accept the long-term implications of the diagnosis. Time and experience are the keys to parents' acceptance of a child's handicap.

A common complaint voiced by parents is that professionals frequently fail to recognize parents as knowledgeable resources in the decisions that need to be made about the child's care. This is stated eloquently by a group of professionals who are also parents of developmentally disabled children (Turnbull and Turnbull 1978). It is important, where possible, to include the parents in decisions about their child's therapy. It is also important to encourage parents to share any new information they hear about new therapies. This will sometimes help identify new services, but will also help parents avoid spending time and effort on unsubstantiated therapies.

Anticipatory guidance is another important role of the physician. Physicians will follow children and their families from the birth of the child through adulthood. There are certain times that can be anticipated as being stressful in the course of the development of a child with mental retardation. It is helpful to discuss these periods with parents before they occur so that the parents can prepare for them and therefore be better able to cope with the stress that these times create.

In situations where the physicians are caring for children with severe to profound mental retardation, it is also important for the physician to remain as nonjudgmental as possible. Some parents are willing to sacrifice much of their own comforts and way of life while receiving minimal feedback from their severely disabled child. While most individuals may not be willing to make the same sacrifice, it is a mistake to view this automatically as unusual or pathologic behavior. Some families report alienation from physicians who try to convince them that their choice of action is inappropriate. This opinion should only be expressed when other family members, particularly siblings, are being adversely affected by parents who are devoting all their time to the child with mental retardation. By attempting to keep their child at home, the parents are in most cases providing a better and more loving environment than can be provided in any alternative placement and providing it at a lower cost to the state. Helping parents to identify community resources such as day-care and respite care can help the parents to continue to provide care for their child in a way that makes them comfortable.

Children with mental retardation frequently have multiple medical, psychological, language, and educational needs. This requires the families to interact with professionals from a number of disciplines and can be very confusing. The information can be contradictory, or treatment recommendations in one area can impact on other areas. For instance, a change in anticonvulsant medication may change the child's cognitive performance.

To deal with each child as a whole person rather than a collection of separate problems, interdisciplinary communication is essential. This can be difficult, especially when the professionals work for different agencies such as a hospital, a private practice, a school, and a social service department. The importance of developing interdisciplinary services has been the thrust of programs for developmentally disabled children such as the University Affiliated Programs and it has been adopted by the educational system under PL 94-142 (the Education for All Handicapped Children Act). It is important for the physician to see that this approach is utilized with his or her patient. Cooperation with the school system by attending the child's staffing or at least providing a written report can also be helpful. Where no coordinated services are available, the physician may need to take over this responsibility and serve as the professional who pulls the other professionals together to see that coordinated services are provided. Unfortunately, as of this writing, third-party payers have not recognized the importance of this coordination and are not willing to provide the financial support required to compensate adequately for the time it requires. However, the importance of this coordination cannot be stressed too strongly. Care cannot be optimal and can often be an added burden and frustrating to already stressed families if interdisciplinary coordination is not provided.

Chapter 28

General Counseling Services

Robinson and Robinson (1976) reviewed the emotional and behavioral problems most frequently associated with mental retardation. Their review indicated that mild to moderately retarded persons were susceptible to many of the same emotional and personality problems that affect their nonretarded peers. Educable mentally retarded individuals are particularly vulnerable to the emotional and social consequences of educational failure, social rejection, general immaturity, and language retardation. They can have increased anxiety, decreased motivation, lowered frustration tolerance, and low self-esteem. In social situations they can be overly conforming and extremely dependent on external cues. They frequently lack the ability to handle competitive situations.

The behavior problems of individuals who are severely and profoundly retarded are more frequently associated with organic causes. They have a higher incidence of hyperactivity and stereotypic and self-destructive behaviors.

Psychotherapy as a means of addressing these problems has been used primarily with mild to moderately retarded individuals. These interventions have run the gamut from traditional psychotherapy approaches to an emphasis on social skill training from a more behavioral approach in more recent years. Although there is evidence for the need and effectiveness of traditional psychotherapy approaches (Ringelheim and Polotsek 1955; Sternlicht 1966), there has been substantially more evidence for the effectiveness of behavioral treatment approaches in the treatment of mentally retarded individuals (Davis and Rogers 1985). In a direct comparison study, Matson and Senatore (1981) found their behavioral treatment package to be more effective than a traditional psychotherapy group for enhancing the interpersonal functioning of mild to moderately retarded adults.

Regardless of the theoretical orientation of the therapist, the specific individual and group treatment techniques have frequently been altered to meet the unique needs of these clients. In reviewing the psychotherapeutic techniques that have been used with retarded individuals, Nuffield (1983) pointed out several important issues and adaptations. Above all, the therapist must have a positive attitude toward the client and the possibility of improvement through psychotherapy. The approach must be very structured and intervention strategies planned out in advance. Specific goals are necessary, although they can be very modest. The sessions need to be well structured; flexibility in regard to techniques, however, is necessary.

Individual and group therapy approaches have been used to increase socially appropriate behaviors such as greeting others, initiating and maintaining conversations, being assertive, behaving appropriately at mealtime, problem solving, and dating (Bregman 1984; Davis and Rogers 1985; La Greca et al. 1983; Perry and Cerreto 1977; Senatore et al. 1982). Similar approaches have focused on decreasing inappropriate behaviors such as self-injurious behaviors, overactivity, stereotypies, and negative verbal or physical behaviors (Matson and Earnhart 1981; Peterson et al. 1979; Spangler and Marshall 1983).

Individual and group therapy has also been used to help with more traditional areas of stress such as improving self-concept, decreasing anxiety, and providing support during stressful times (e.g., death in family, move to new home).

Successful therapeutic approaches with retarded individuals have several things in common. The strategies involve a great deal of repetition, less reliance on language, and an increased use of visual cues. Direct instruction, modeling, role play, and positive reinforcement for appropriate behaviors are essential. Self-recording has also been used successfully. Senatore et al. (1982) found that active rehearsal further enhanced the effectiveness of the standard social skill program. Therapeutic interventions with mentally retarded individuals are generally more structured and have concrete goals and a limited number of sessions (Nuffield 1983).

Whenever a mentally retarded individual is involved in individual or group therapy, some involvement of the client's parents or other significant adults (teachers or workshop managers) is important (Jakab 1970). These adults often desire help in understanding the retarded person's needs. They also may need support, or specific suggestions on how they can promote the individual's growth at home and in the community. Without family and community support, it is unlikely that the emotional or behavioral skills learned in therapy will generalize from the clinic setting.

Parent Intervention Strategies

Research has shown that some parents of mentally retarded children experience greater stress than parents of developmentally normal children. The stress can be associated with a variety of factors such as the parents' periodic grieving, the strain of the additional caretaking responsibilities, or the financial burden of having a handicapped child. A variety of intervention strategies have been developed to meet the parents' needs for information, support, or technical assistance.

Usually the first level of intervention is one of providing information regarding the child's current level of functioning and information regarding the nature of the disability. Much has been written about the importance of spending time with the parents at the initial diagnostic evaluation to explain the diagnostic techniques and to interpret the results. P. Shew (1984) gave specific suggestions on how to provide support while clearly transmitting to the family members the information they need to understand and assist their child. As the retarded child gets older, new issues arise, and families often find that they need additional information. Life events such as starting school, reaching puberty, or finishing school are often stressful events in the families of normally developing youngsters. Families of developmentally disabled youngsters may find they need additional information to understand and facilitate their child's adaptation to these life events.

The second level of intervention is one of providing support to the families. This support is often provided by professionals in the course of a diagnostic evaluation or during ongoing treatment sessions. In addition, many self-help groups exist where parents of handicapped children get together to share their experiences and to support one another. The formation of the National Association of Retarded Citizens (ARC) during the 1950s has been instrumental in developing support services in local communities for families of retarded individuals.

Some families of disabled children find they need help to develop the skills to teach their children and to manage the behavior problems that may occur. Parent training, whether done individually or in groups, frequently emphasizes teaching parents how to develop appropriate expectations for their child. In addition, parents are taught how to increase positive or appropriate behaviors through the use of verbal praise, concrete reinforcers, or token programs. To decrease negative behaviors such as noncompliance or aggression, the parents are first taught how to reward the youngster for incompatible behaviors (e.g., compliance or playing with another child without hitting). If the negative behaviors persist, the parents are also taught how to use punishment techniques such as time-out in combination with the reward system. In cases of extreme behavior problems, such as self-injurious behavior, a parent may also be taught how to restrain the child physically.

In those cases where a mentally retarded individual is engaged in individual or group therapy, parent sessions are usually done as an adjunct to the child's sessions. During these times, parents are kept informed of the goals and specific techniques being taught to their child so that they can encourage and reinforce the use of these skills outside of the therapy session. As with normally developing youngsters, skills learned in individual therapy sessions often do not generalize to other settings if the adults in these other settings are not informed about the treatment program.

There is a great deal of variability in how families feel about having a handicapped child, and in the coping strategies they employ. Often the information, support, and parent training mentioned previously can meet the needs of these families. However, in some instances, individual, marital, or family therapy may be of help to family members who are having difficulty coping with their feelings related to having a handicapped family member.

Respite care has also been an important resource for families who need some relief from the constant physical and emotional demands of their child. Local ARC groups often coordinate these services.

Community Intervention Strategies

As mentioned previously, to maximize the effects of therapy, all significant adults in the retarded individual's life are included in therapeutic interventions.

For school-age children, their teachers are an invaluable source of data about their social, emotional, and cognitive development. The teacher is best contacted early in the diagnostic process to determine whether there are any specific questions or concerns about the child's behaviors or performance in school. Obtaining any available standardized test data such as the child's scores on national achievement tests or intelligence tests as well as the current school grades will also be helpful. The teacher's general observations about the child's behaviors in the classroom can be supplemented by having the teacher complete a standard behavior questionnaire (Achenbach or the Connors Teacher Questionnaire). Teachers, like parents, often need support and some basic information about the child to maintain appropriate expectations.

A teacher who has participated in the diagnostic evaluation will feel more committed to following up on the treatment recommendations that may result. In addition, if the teacher's input has been used to develop treatment strategies, these strategies are more likely to address the areas seen as concerns. Since the youngster spends about six hours a day in class, the teacher is clearly an essential figure in any intervention program that is designed to change the child's behavior. The teacher can encourage the use of desired behaviors by providing a model of what is expected and by using verbal praise and concrete reinforcers. Behavioral contracts can also be a very effective tool for behavior change in the classroom. The contract clearly states the appropriate behavior the child needs to exhibit as well as the positive consequences of exhibiting that behavior. For example, a mentally retarded boy may be working on increasing his on-task behavior. For every assignment the child completes, he receives a chip; when he has three chips, he earns a short play break. For older youngsters who can work for delayed rewards, the parents can reinforce the child at the end of the day for following through with the contract. Obviously, for this arrangement to work, there needs to be good ongoing communication between the home and the school. Daily or weekly communication between the parents and teacher can be facilitated via a notebook that the child carries to and from school on a regular basis.

Mentally retarded adults who are placed in sheltered workshop settings can also benefit from good communication and consistent programming between their home, the workshop, and the mental health professional. Again, the workshop can provide an important source of data about the mentally retarded individual's behavior. Inappropriate social skills (e.g., constant complaining or poor leisure skills during break times) can interfere with continued employment as much as poor work habits can. To ensure that skills taught in individual or group sessions are generalized, there needs to be good communication between everyone working with the handicapped adult and consistent expectations and behavioral contingencies in all settings.

Chapter 29

Psychotherapy

Pessimism about the usefulness of a psychotherapeutic approach to mentally retarded patients is known to exist among therapists and other mental health professionals. However, psychotherapeutic approaches with the retarded patient are not dissimilar to those used with nonretarded people, although the goals and techniques must be adjusted to the retarded person's developmental level and particular life circumstances.

Individual Psychotherapy

The literature on psychotherapy with the mentally retarded is growing in size and quality. The work of Jakab (1970) and Szymanski (1980) has been important in confronting opposition to psychotherapeutic work with mentally retarded persons. Reviews have been written by Nuffield (1983, 1986) and Stavrakaki and Klein (1986).

Many therapists have contended that individual psychotherapy is not indicated for retarded children and adults (Leland and Smith 1965; Rogers and Dymond 1954). Albini and Demitz (1965) could not demonstrate positive change with a traditional psychotherapeutic approach. However, a growing number of researchers now support innovative psychotherapeutic techniques with mentally retarded people (Burton 1954; Chase 1953; Chess 1962; Denton 1959; Freidman 1965; Hayes 1977; Heiser 1954; Munday 1957; Newcomer and Morrison 1974; Selan 1976; Thorne 1948).

Certainly, there are flaws and shortcomings in the research on psychotherapy effectiveness (Crowley 1965; Matson 1984b). The study of psychotherapy in mentally retarded patients presents many problems in objectively and reliably measuring outcome. Description of the therapeutic process and context is difficult. Matson and Senatore (1981) and others have suggested using multiple assessment instruments to determine psychotherapeutic impact. Matson has urged the use of some means of social validation in gauging the effects of psychotherapy. The "(wo)man on the street" approach and the use of normal peers are two ways to validate change socially (Kazdin and Matson 1981; Matson 1984; Matson et al. 1980).

Mentally retarded patients entering therapy present special issues. Mentally retarded people are often brought to treatment by family or caretakers. The patient may feel little choice about starting treatment. Family members may offer a list of problems they have identified and feel that the patient is persisting in these behaviors out of malice. The identified patient may feel rejected and ridiculed by the people closest to them. Nuffield (1986) listed common problems encountered with the mentally retarded including: 1) a feeling of suspiciousness; 2) low self-esteem; 3) a tendency to avoid responsibility for one's actions; 4) a general clumsiness in interpersonal relationships; and 5) poor impulse control. The patient may deny a handicap but, on the other hand, have difficulty identifying with the therapist due to cognitive deficits.

Understanding individual developmental issues and learning styles is important for well-planned psychotherapy. Some aspects of developmental delay can be conceptualized using mental age. However, the social development of a retarded child is qualitatively different and slower when compared to a child of matched mental age (Capobianco and Cole 1960; Webster 1963, 1970; Weiner and Weiner 1974). Deficits in social action or delayed or strange social behavior is a necessary component of mental retardation (American Psychiatric Association 1980). On the positive side, symbolic play appears to be less impaired in retarded compared to autistic children (matched for chronological and mental age). Mildly retarded children frequently exhibit symbolic play, which is flexible and varied (Riguet et al. 1981).

Mentally retarded people only rarely have special talents. More common is a particular kind of experience that is more organizing and offers more self-esteem. Some patients are more at ease with visual arts or music or stories or kinesthetic experiences such as dance (Sacks 1986).

Realistic goals for psychotherapy include: 1) improvement in grooming and hygiene; 2) improved impulse control; 3) greater ease in interpersonal relationships; 4) improved social skills; and 5) awareness of unconscious wishes and fantasies. The hope is that psychotherapy will increase the patient's wish for independence and improve the patient's self-image. The patient is encouraged and taught to express opinions and feelings appropriately.

While it makes sense to consider specific problems and psychiatric diagnosis in planning a psychotherapeutic approach, there have been no studies of cognitive therapy or particular approaches for phobias or grief in mentally retarded people. However, recent clinical attempts to begin such programs, by groups like Reiss' in Chicago, have reported substantial success.

There are few reports of process material from psychotherapy sessions with mentally retarded patients (Ack 1966; Smith et al. 1976). Schwartz (1979) did present brief case descriptions of analytic work with the mentally retarded.

Most writers agree that therapy should be goal-directed, with the therapist acting as a model for identification, providing limits and sufficient challenge while being flexible, supportive, and empathetic with the retarded person. More emphasis is placed on modeling appropriate behavior, concretely exploring experiences in the present, and building defenses rather than uncovering historically based techniques. Directiveness and therapist activity with clear limit setting is important in relating to retarded people. The therapist may structure several options for play or discussion but must also follow the patient's choices within these limits. Behavior such as person-directed aggression, property destruction, and self-stimulation can be limited in a consistent, concrete, nonjudgmental fashion. Occasional use of simple catharsis has been said to be helpful (Sternlicht 1965; Sternlicht and Wanderer 1963).

Szymanski (1980) recommended verbal approaches, when indicated, to be adapted to the person's level of understanding. The therapy is reality oriented, in the "here and now" with concrete verbal explanations, role-playing, and puppet play to gather information and to help the retarded person learn appropriate ways of experiencing and expressing emotions. Flexibility of technique is required from the therapist. For example, the retarded patient may have difficulty withstanding a full therapeutic hour. In some cases, it is reasonable to use even five-minute contracts while working toward a goal of simply increasing the duration of tolerated interpersonal contact (Stavrakaki and Klein 1986). The mentally retarded person may need to be engaged by action. Trips to practice in various social contexts may be very helpful. Some retarded patients may do best using practice sessions with friends or family under guidance from the therapist, before attempting a particular task in public. Sternlicht

(1965) discussed a variety of useful techniques, including art therapy, music therapy, and dance therapy. A multimedia approach was described by Cantalapiedra et al. (1977).

The therapist must confront the patient's overdependency and self-depreciation, watching for subtle put-downs the patient may place on him- or herself. The therapist cannot become an accomplice in undercutting the patient's potential for progress. Other common themes the retarded person struggles with include being handicapped and being a member of a different, "undesirable" minority group.

Although lack of knowledge is the most common factor in the retarded individual's maladaptive behavior, transference factors and resistance are important, particularly in the treatment of patients referred to psychiatrists after counseling attempts. The primary attachment figure for the retarded patient may have been a depressed, guilt-ridden parent or older sibling. Early relationships may have been characterized by rejection and threats of abandonment. Patient silence may be an effort to prevent discovery of shortcomings or may be the consequence of worries of behaving inappropriately. The patient may expect and fear threats and criticism from the therapist. Of course, an effort is made to understand the particular defense mechanisms or compromise formations. Defenses may be interpreted concretely or demonstrated in play, with respect for the patient's capacities.

Countertransference responses may be induced by the incapacity and dependency of the retarded patient. The therapist must restrain his or her feelings of helplessness and boredom while remaining unconstricted in intellectual and emotional responses. Unconscious fears of being damaged or unconscious guilt may lead to nontherapeutic compromises by the therapist (Schwartz 1979). Omnipotent wishes to cure the retarded patient, overprotectiveness, viewing the patient as too fragile to experience or to talk about emotions, competitiveness and criticism of parents, and unrealistic enthusiasm and setting excessively high goals all may interfere with progress in treatment.

Group Psychotherapy

Observations and therapeutic work with retarded patients in a group setting can provide invaluable information for caretakers and provide direct contact for work with patients on social skills and emotional issues. Early experience with group therapy for retarded people included Cotzin's (1948) sessions with retarded children utilizing Slavson's Activity Interview Therapy. This involved play and open discussion of patients' problems.

The therapist must take care that aggressive members do not overpower more submissive members, who may be less suited for group work (Fisher and Wolfson 1953). As in individual treatment, therapist activity is an important technique. Initiating group activities (e.g., writing, building, drawing) may be helpful. Davis and Shapiro (1979) raised the importance of attending to group process. Adult retarded patients may seek approval from authority figures while avoiding peer relationships. This style must be addressed for group members to develop a sense of coherence and to develop the problem-solving skills of the participants. Mutual acceptance of handicaps and talents is an important group task (Goodman and Rothman 1961). Gradual redirection of patient's attention to other group members and away from reliance on group leaders will help the group and its members become more self-sufficient.

Silence particularly early in treatment may be a difficulty. Silence may not reflect resistance but may more productively be seen as a response to fears of saying something foolish or not knowing what to say. The therapist should not permit long silences to occur and may wish to offer the group suggestions on how to prevent long silences. Szymanski (1980) provided many practical suggestions for leading psychotherapy groups for retarded patients. Issues for discussion in a psychotherapy group include: 1) members' feelings about independence and wishes about their occupation and living situation; 2) members' understanding of their own and others' handicaps; 3) the advantages and disadvantages of disruptive or inappropriate behaviors; 4) sexuality; 5) how to make friends; and 6) recognizing and expressing feelings.

Conclusion

Psychotherapy with mentally retarded patients requires an understanding of the particular developmental and social problems faced by retarded people. Most successful approaches are directive, active, and flexible, with an abiding concern for the functional level of the patient. Successful therapy will, as always, be a function of a creative, empathic therapist; a suitable client; a technique that is individualized; and goals that are realistic.

Chapter 30

Behavior Therapy

Behavior therapy is best defined as a general orientation that uses an empirical problem-solving approach to the areas of skill development and behavior problems. Principles derived from learning theory and psychological experimentation are used to teach new behaviors, to increase appropriate behavior, or to decrease inappropriate behavior. A behavioral approach to treatment involves essentially four steps : 1) definition of desired and undesired behavior in objective, observable terms; 2) assessment of the behaviors in question by observational techniques; 3) the use of intervention methods based primarily on learning principles, and 4) an evaluation of the effectiveness of the treatment program by observational techniques. The old term *behavior modification* refers to the entire process, but it has fallen into disfavor. The more current terms are *behavior analysis*, which refers to steps 1, 2, and 4; and *behavior therapy* or *behavior management*, which refers to step 3.

It is important for clinicians to understand the principles by which behavior is learned and how these principles are used to develop or change behavior. To that end, a behavioral view of human development and of origins of normal and abnormal behavior and a description of different theoretical models of learning will be given.

It is appropriate to emphasize, however, that conceptual bases of behaviorism are, by their very nature, theoretical, and are presented only to illuminate origins and rationale of behavior therapy. Successful application of behavioral treatment in any clinical instance is guided not by theory but by clinical experience and empirical research.

Personality Development from a Behavioral Viewpoint

Behaviorists define personality as the sum total of an individual's behavior and describe it as the likelihood of an individual to behave in similar ways to a variety of situations that comprise day-to-day living (Goldfried and Kent 1972). Focus is on what the person does in various situations. No reference is made to global traits that "make" a person behave a particular way. This is in sharp contrast to most traditional views of personality that assume a person's actions are motivated by certain underlying motives, needs, drives, defenses, or traits. Behaviorists contend that an individual acquires certain behaviors by virtue of interactions with the environment. It is also recognized that an individual inherits certain physical traits and a unique genetic constitution, and these elements may influence the individual's interaction with the environment (Bijou 1970).

Learning

The behavioral point of view holds that most behaviors, with the exception of simple reflexes, are learned. When a functional relationship between a stimulus in the environment and a person's response occurs, learning has taken place. The definition of *learning* is: a relatively permanent change in behavior as a result of practice. Because of the stress on permanence, learning is differentiated from other practice effects like habituation or adaptation and from motivational factors like temperament or incentives. By identifying practice as a key condition for learning, the effects of factors such as heredity and maturation are excluded. The three most basic types of learning are respondent conditioning (sometimes called Pavlovian or classical conditioning), operant conditioning (instrumental conditioning), and observational learning (imitation learning).

Respondent Conditioning

There are several important elements to respondent conditioning. The essentials are: 1) elicitation of a conditioned response by a conditioned stimulus by repeatedly pairing it with the presentation of an unconditioned stimulus that reliably has been eliciting an unconditioned response; and 2) discrimination learning by extinction of the conditioned response to generalized conditioned stimuli. All of these processes have lawful relationships to one another that are relevant to a wide variety of behaviors. There are a variety of types of behavioral treatment today that rely heavily on respondent conditioning—for example, Wolpe's (1969) systematic desensitization, Meichenbaum's (1977) cognitive behavior modification, biofeedback training (Budzynski and Stoyva 1969), and aversion therapies (Rachman and Teasdale 1969). The general term *behavior therapy* is sometimes used to describe treatment based primarily on respondent conditioning.

Operant Conditioning

Among early Pavlovians no distinction was originally made between classical and operant conditioning. The latter term, which was originally known as instrumental conditioning, derived from the work of Thorndike as early as 1898. It was used to emphasize that instrumental conditioning differs form classical Pavlovian procedures in that the subject's behavior is instrumental in producing reward (reinforcement) or avoidance of punishment. But it was Skinner (1938) who made the most forceful case for distinctions between respondent and operant conditioning. First, respondent conditioning occurs basically by association, whereas operant conditioning is under the control of reinforcement. Second, respondent conditioning operates mainly on autonomic responses, whereas operant conditioning works with other responses. Finally, each type of conditioning is subject to a different set of laws. The basic principle of operant conditioning is that behavior is a function of its consequences. Another unique factor of operant conditioning is that its behavioral lawfulness can be examined without reference to other organismic hypotheses such as temperament and that it can be analyzed as single cases in free-responding situations. This approach was unorthodox and it took 25 years to have a strong impact.

A consequence is said to reinforce the connection between the original stimulus and a behavioral response if it increases the probability of its recurrence. If the consequence of the response decreases the probability of its recurrence, then the original stimulus is called a punisher. Note that no inference is made that the punisher is aversive. There is disagreement as to whether it is necessary for punishers to be aversive. The problem seems to be a technical one because some aversive events increase behavior probabilities.

In operant conditioning one can conceive of a discriminative stimulus as being the stimulus that has a higher probability of being followed by the conditioned response when it is present. Likewise, when the discriminative stimulus is absent, the conditioned response is not likely to occur. When this set of relationships prevails, the occurrence of the response is said to be contingent on the presence of the stimulus, and the behavior thus generated is called operant behavior. Operants themselves can be contingent stimuli for other operants so that, with the help of generalization, huge chains of behavior (habits) can be formed. For instance, Skinner (1957) used the notion of chaining as his basic unit of analysis of language.

There are seven basic components of operant conditioning used in behavior therapy. Positive reinforcement is the presentation of a stimulus that increases the probability of a response. Punishment is the presentation of a strong stimulus that decreases the probability of a response. Negative reinforcement or avoidance conditioning increases the probability of a response that removes or avoids an aversive stimulus. Extinction decreases the probability of a response by noncontingent withdrawal of a previously reinforcing stimulus. Time-out involves decreasing the probability of a response by contingent withdrawal of a previously reinforcing stimulus. Differential reinforcement of other behavior (DRO) decreases the probability of a response by reinforcing the omission of it. Satiation decreases the probability of a response by reinforcing it excessively.

There are also many combinations of the above procedures that are sometimes more effective than any one alone. For example, overcorrection has two components: gradual guidance (stopping the undesirable behavior and physically prompting desired behavior) and restitution (repairing the disrupted environment to better than its original condition). These behaviors, however, probably involve punishment, avoidance, time-out, and DRO as well as other components. Thus each of the above actually represents a class of procedures with many variations that can be suited to a particular individual's problem in a particular setting.

Until recently, operant conditioning forms of behavior therapy have focused almost exclusively on managing the consequences of behavior. Currently the influence of ecologic variables, which in operant terminology comprise the area of differential stimulus control, is receiving more attention (Schroeder et al. 1979).

Observational Learning

Observational learning has been treated under a variety of terms, such as modeling, imitation, vicarious learning, identification, copying, social-facilitation, and role-playing. Behavior theorists disagree whether or not it represents a form of learning separate from operant conditioning (Baer and Sherman 1964; Bandura 1969a, 1969b; Miller and Dollard 1941). According to the operant formulation, the necessary conditions for learning through modeling are positive reinforcement for matching the correct responses of a model during a series of initially random, trial-and-error responses. The person is then differentially reinforced for matching the stimulus pattern generated by his or her own responses to the appropriate modeling cues (Baer and Sherman 1964). Divergent cue matching goes unreinforced and, therefore, drops out. Bandura (1969a) rightly pointed out that Baer and Sherman's operant analysis of imitation has difficulty in explaining imitation, when an observer does not overtly perform the model's responses during the acquisition of imitation, when rewards are not administered either to the model or to the observer, and when the first appearance of the newly learned response may be delayed for weeks or months. Bandura's position that observational learning should be distinguished from classical and operant conditioning is the current, prevailing view.

Observational learning plays a key role in socialization. Three main effects of modeling can be distinguished. First, observers can learn new behaviors previously not in their repertoire. Second, the observer's behavior may be inhibited or disinhibited by watching a model. Third, previously learned behaviors can be facilitated by watching a model. Bandura noted (1977) that it is important to make a distinction between learning and performance. An observer may learn the response on one trial without reinforcement of any kind, but may need to be reinforced to perform it.

Some of the factors that Bandura (1977) has shown affect observational learning are: 1) differential reinforcement and punishment of the model; 2) similarity of the observer to the model; 3) status, prestige, power, or expertise of the model; 4) observation of several models versus only one model; and 5) whether the responses to the model are motor, cognitive, attitudinal, or emotional responses. Observational learning can be a very effective therapeutic technique under the appropriate circumstances to desensitize fears, train social skills, and teach new behavior (Kazdin 1974; Meichenbaum 1971; Rachman 1972).

Comparison of Respondent, Operant, and Observational Learning

There really is no fundamental distinction between the three types of conditioning. They are just different forms of the same basic process, but because they respond differently to manipulation by some experimental variables, it is convenient to treat them separately. In fact, it is impossible to perform a purely operant conditioning sequence. When reinforcement occurs, there is always a chance for the responses to reinforcement to become classically conditioned to conditioned stimuli (cues) present at the time. By the same token, it is very difficult to isolate a pure example of classical conditioning because the conditioned response usually has some effect on the probability of recurrence of the unconditioned stimulus. In the complex interactions occurring in the therapy, they may all occur as part of a single therapeutic episode. For instance, a severe reprimand by a mother might simultaneously 1) punish a child's undesirable operant response (e.g., talking-out); 2) elicit a conditioned emotional fear response whenever the mother is subsequently near the offending child; and 3) model for the child a method of dealing with the same behavior of another child that the mother may consider reprehensible in another setting. Behavioral analysis can be a complex and potent method for analyzing learning and performance.

Classification of Psychological Disorders in Behavioral Terms

The intent of a diagnostic label or classification system for psychological disorders is to group together persons who have similar behaviors so that the study and understanding of the etiology, treatment, and prognosis of the behavior can be more effective. In effect, labels help to classify, sort, and put order into the world. For psychological or behavioral disorders, one looks for behaviors that "go together," in other words, are common denominators in describing a group of children's behaviors. To have meaning, one category of behaviors has to be differentiated from another category in terms of what behaviors cluster together (e.g., sex distribution, age of onset, association with other problems, etiology, response to treatment and outcome) (Rutter 1975). For example, the labels hyperactive, autistic, school phobic, and mildly retarded should describe the behavior of a group of children who have similar problems and are distinctly different from other groups of children. Unfortunately, the limited state of knowledge about the significance of particular variables in the development, treatment, and prognosis of most behavior clusters limits the usefulness of any classification system (Quay 1972).

Behaviorists do not have a comprehensive classification system for psychological disorders. The difficulties in developing such a system should be evident given the behavioral focus on an individual's unique interaction with the environment. Any classification system would have to take into account personal and environmental variables without setting critieria for what would be called abnormal behavior. Goldfried and Davison (1976) came close to this in outlining a classification system based on work by Staats and Staats (1963) and Bandura (1968) and Goldfried and Sprafkin (1974). They outlined five general ways in which behaviors could come to be seen as deviant. First, difficulties could result from poor stimulus control of the behavior. Second, the person could have a deficient behavioral repertoire. Third, a person could have a behavioral repertoire that others find aversive. Fourth, there could be difficulties with the incentive systems available to the other person. Fifth, a person could have an aversive self-reinforcing system. A brief examination of each of these categories will help the reader be aware of the importance of a thorough knowledge of the psychological literature on learning in planning a behavioral treatment program.

Difficulties in stimulus control of behavior could result when a person responds inappropriately to social cues or when some environmental stimulus elicits maladaptive emotional responses. For instance, the person may have the appropriate behavioral repertoire but may use it at the wrong time or place.

Deficient behavior repertoires include behavior problems due to a person's lacking the skills needed to deal with situational demands. For example, mentally retarded persons may have never learned to socialize with others or may not know how to organize their time wisely, Goldfried and Davison (1976) pointed out that this skills deficit problem is often complicated by aversive consequences such as ridicule and rejection, which result in the negative subjective attitudes of lack of confidence, anxiety, and so on.

Aversive behavioral repertoires include the person whose behavior is aversive to others. The person with a problem in this category knows what to say or do but is excessive (e.g., talks very loudly), overly aggressive, or does other behavior that is bothersome to others (e.g., stands too close when talking to people).

Difficulties with incentive systems include problem behaviors due to the reinforcing consequences of the behavior. The individual's incentive system may be deficient or inappropriate or the consequences available in the environment may be creating the problem. A deficient incentive system refers to the situation where a person does not respond to the incentives such as approval or disapproval that usually control other people's behavior. On the other hand, the incentive system itself could be maladaptive in that it is harmful or disapproved by society (e.g., drugs or certain sexual practices). The environment can also present conflicting incentive systems whereby a behavior is labeled inappropriate but inadvertently rewarded.

Aversive self-reinforcing systems refer to those problems that result when people do not reinforce their own behavior. Those who view their behavior as continually inadequate or who set excessively high standards for themselves are unlikely to be able to reward themselves regardless of the adequacy of the performance.

Goldfried and Davison's (1976) classification system for categorizing maladaptive behavior within a social learning context provides some guidelines for a behavorial analysis of deviant behavior. A person may have behaviors that fall in several categories or a problem behavior may be complex enough to fall in more than one category. In either case, the system helps pinpoint those personal and environmental variables that should be the focus of treatment.

Some Common Misconceptions

That reinforcement is bribery is a common misperception. Some people see the use of reinforcement to increase a behavior as "buying" the person to perform a behavior. Bribery refers to the illicit use of rewards and gifts to influence someone to do something they should not be doing. The behavioral therapist's use of reinforcement is to reward behavior that is socially desirable. The desired behavior is usually at a low level or nonexistent and the systematic use of reinforcement is intended to strengthen the behavior. The goal should always be to use naturally occurring reinforcers such as more time with other children for improved social skills or more time on the playground for efficient and accurate completion of work. Extrinsic rewards or rewards not usually available in a particular situation (e.g., food, tokens, activities) are often necessary to increase a particular person's behavior but these should always be faded back to the reinforcers that would naturally follow a particular behavior. By now, the reader should understand that people do not do things because they "should"; rather they learn under certain conditions to engage in certain behaviors because of the consequences.

Another concern in this area is that the mentally retarded person will refuse to do anything unless specifically rewarded. Actually this rarely happens. When it does, however, it is usually because the therapist has inadvertently reinforced the manipulative response. For example, if told "If you stop crying, you may have ice cream," a person quickly learns crying will set the stage for getting what he or she wants. Another possible reason for refusing to do things unless rewarded could be that the person is getting only a very low level of reinforcement for other behaviors.

Reinforcing one person might increase the negative behavior of another person to get a reward. This is a concern often voiced by teachers when they have a number of children who are on individual programs or when only one child in a large class is receiving special rewards for increasing desired behavior. O'Leary et al. (1972) reported this happening in a classroom but, in general, there has been little evidence to support this concern. Again, if the reinforcement level is generally high in the classroom, this is less likely to occur. On the other hand, there is evidence for the occurrence of positive side effects of reinforcing one child on the behavior of other children (Bolstad and Johnson 1972; Broden et al. 1970).

Differential Effectiveness of Behavioral Techniques

Which behavioral techniques work best with what kind of problems? How this question is answered depends greatly on how the question is framed. On the one hand, very few treatment failures have been reported in the behavioral literature; on the other hand, there often are successful behavioral techniques reported that are impractical and that exceed the resources of service systems. A second important point is that the behavioral approach does not focus on the form or nature of a disease so much as how a particular behavior problem occurs and what needs to be done to change it directly. It focuses on the symptom rather than the substrate. It holds that the function of a behavior is more important than its form, if one wants to change it. Behavior analysis is mainly a functional analysis. The question usually centers on which procedure works best given the situation; the available resources; and the ecologic, legal, and ethical constraints imposed by society. This view has been established explicitly in several legal precedents from class action right-to-treatment lawsuits and in PL 94-142, all of which hold that all handicapped persons have the right to the most effective treatment in the least restrictive environment. This principle is implemented by behavior modification specialists, but only with the consent of parents, guardians, peers, and internal and/or external review boards who represent outcome values set by the prevailing society in which treatment is conducted.

Restrictive procedures are usually permitted only given the following guidelines: 1) after less restrictive treatments (e.g., positive reinforcement techniques) have been tried and have failed; 2) if a competent professional supervises implementation of the procedure; 3) when the behavior is dangerous to clients or others (as in aggression, self-injurious behavior, destructive outburst); 4) if there is a limit set on the time duration for a trial of the procedure and a frequent external program review; and 5) if restrictive procedures occur only within the context of a positive program to teach acceptable alternative behaviors. Thus it is often the case that an intrusive procedure like severe punishment, although very effective in decelerating a behavior, might not be permitted because it cannot be monitored effectively enough or because it may be considered cruel, given the relative severity of the target behavior, or because free and informed consent cannot be obtained. All of the above factors must be considered when judging effectiveness of a procedure.

Practical Behavior Therapy

Given the above set of guidelines, it is possible to make some general statements about the effectiveness of different behavioral procedures for certain selected behaviors. In general, all other things being equal, for higher functioning clients with appropriate developmental ages, verbal mediation and cognitive behavioral modification techniques—such as rational emotive therapy, social learning, covert sensitization, and relaxation techniques—work no differently than they do for nonhandicapped clients. Since the application of such techniques in borderline or mildly retarded individuals differs little from their application in people of normal intelligence, a detailed explication will not be needed here.

For more severely handicapped clients with communication and sociability problems, the techniques of behavior therapy are quite diferent and do require special attention. In contrast to therapy for high-verbal people, where verbal mediation is paramount, in retarded clients, where nonverbal, directive approaches are necessary, behavioral therapy may be controversial. There is little argument over the common sense basis of the actual practice. This comprises five fundamental principles:

1. The patient is in a stable, humane, and developmentally appropriate environment.
2. There is a consistent approach to training and behavior management, employing standard treatment practices that are individualized to the individual and applied in a creative and enthusiastic manner.
3. There is, in place, a valid and reliable behavior analysis system that permits the periodic evaluation of treatment-induced change and directs the modification of treatment in a lawful manner, around the specific exigencies of individual response.
4. The ecology of the client is well understood prior to and during the application of a behavioral program, and extraneous changes are limited insofar as this is possible.
5. The behavioral program is relevant and generalizable to the client's real world.

The failure of a behavioral program is often attributable to inattention to one or more basic principles: 1) basing treatment strategies on unreliable data; 2) trying to treat individuals whose world is unstable or developmentally out-of-reach; 3) changing medications during a trial of a new behavioral treatment; or 4) applying contingencies in an inconsistent or an unenthusiastic manner. Paper programs that are written only for the sake of external reviewers should not be expected to influence clients' behavior. Perfunctory programs out of textbooks may be inappropriate for an individual client. Behavior therapy, like psychotherapy, requires a creative, individualized approach; it seems to work well only when professionals have faith in its usefulness and are willing to work hard to make it successful.

Unlike most forms of psychotherapy, behavioral treatment is data based and requires some quantitative measure of specific target behaviors. This exercise is usually called behavior analysis. The client's specific problems are defined not in global, diagnostic terms, or in terms descriptive of an individual's personality or temperament. Specific target behaviors are labeled (e.g., self biting, property destruction, aggressive outbursts, hyperactivity) and then defined, operationally (e.g., the client bites his hand) and ecologically (e.g., when required to comply with staff directions). Target behaviors that are relatively infrequent, like explosive episodes, may be counted and graphed as total all-day behavior counts. Frequent behaviors, like head slapping, may be counted only within a specific time period (internal counts). For some behaviors, indirect measures may be appropriate (e.g., time in or out of restraint, number of time-outs, number of tokens earned). Indirect measures, however, are sometimes a more accurate representation of staff behavior than of client behaviors. For target behaviors that are pervasive, like stereotypy or hyperactivity, rating scales may be more appropriate than direct observations. Measures of positive behaviors like social interaction and workshop or classroom performance are also useful for treatment evaluation.

Behavioral data should be summarized and graphed for summary review. Interventions—behavioral, programmatic, pharmacologic—should be coded on the graph. Computerized data systems are used in some clinical settings with considerable success.

Behavioral programs may be written and ignored, or followed only perfunctorily. It is almost trivial to require that the only programs that are written should be those that are likely to be carried out in a consistent manner, but it is also a truism that is honored more in the breach than the keeping. Direct care staff has to be educated in the fine points of behavioral treatment, and their performance has to be monitored closely. Educated, enthusiastic staff are essential. The effective behaviorist has to be a good salesperson, has to win staff to the soundness of the approach, and can design effective programs only if direct care staff finds them sensible, humane, and feasible. Failed programs simply serve to blind staff to the potential utility of an extraordinarily effective treatment approach. The psychiatric consultant is often called on to prescribe medications to a client because "behavioral measures simply haven't worked." Like as not, they were never really given a fair trial.

Behavior therapy is not necessarily a substitute for pharmacotherapy, or vice versa. There is ample evidence, from research literature and from clincial experience, that the two systems are complementary or even synergistic. On the other hand, an irrational, poorly chosen medication may impair a patient's ability to respond to behavior modification.

Although behavior therapy must necessarily be individualized, it is possible to make certain prescriptive statements about the utility of specific techniques for certain classes of behavior problems. An example is self-injurious behavior, which is a severe and sometimes extraordinary disorder that is known to afflict at least 10 percent of all severely retarded people in residential facilities. Self-injurious behavior comprises a heterogeneous group of disorders, in terms of etiology, course, ecology, severity, and response to treatment. Nevertheless, the behavioral approach usually involves certain standard measures. The basic approach is contingent restraint with differential reinforcement of other (DRO) or of incompatible (DRI) behaviors. After positive behaviors are thoroughly shaped through DRO or DRI, restraints may be faded gradually, sometimes persisting only as a token or a symbolic restraining, or even by self-restraint.

For some refractory cases of self-injurious behavior, aversive punishing stimuli may be necessary. These may be mild, like a water mist spray or a very loud "no." In other circumstances, electric shock, slaps, or pinches have been used. Aversive stimuli, however, are always to be considered extraordinary interventions, necessary only for the most severe and refractory cases and requiring close supervision and careful review.

Explosive aggressive behavior or tantrums may respond simply to timeout. Timeout is best introduced as a form of redirection early in the chain of behaviors that lead up to a full-blown outburst. If reliable antecedents cannot be identified, and if the episodes are really unpredictable, the behavior has to be "consequated." An effective consequence may be time-out or a "therapeutic hold." Preventive intervention technique (PIT), the loss of tokens, or the loss of privileges ("response cost") may not be immediate enough to suppress or prevent aggressive outbursts. Aversive punishers may be necessary in severe cases.

Severe stereotyped behavior may be a form of self-stimulation or a tension-discharge phenomenon. In the former instance, the proper approach is to introduce alternative forms of stimulation, preferably in the context of a highly structured activity program.

For pica, overcorrection techniques may be recommended. For chronic rumination vomiting, satiation (multiple small feedings) usually seems to be the most effective formula. An aversive alternative may be a noxious substance (e.g., lemon juice) squirted into the client's mouth.

Hyperactivity is usually so pervasive a problem that consistent, immediate consequences are impossible. The basic approach should be in the direction of attention and compliance training and a highly structured habilitative program. Time-out or response-cost procedures may be linked to severe disruptive behaviors or to episodes of excessive excitement.

Property destruction may be dealt with by PIT, time-out, or overcorrection. For example, a client who engages in excessive clothes tearing may be required to tear rags for five or ten minutes after each infraction.

A form of behavioral intervention that comes close to resembling conventional psychotherapeutic technique is social skills training. This is the specific cultivation of adaptive prosocial behaviors through verbal mediation, role-playing, frequent practice, and generalization from the therapy session to real-world situation. The inculcation of effective interpersonal skills will necessarily diminish the occurrence of peculiar, maladaptive interactions that so often spell rejection and frustration to the retarded person.

It is important to emphasize that aversive treatments are usually unnecessary and should only be developed under the guidance of an experienced, competent behaviorist. Clients who require such extraordinary measures are most often people whose behavior difficulties have become entrenched by virtue of years of neglect and therapeutic inattention.

Comparison of Intervention Procedures

What can be said about the comparative effectiveness of all of these management procedures? With respect to the retarded, the question has been an acute one since clinicians are often charged to use "the most effective treatment in the least restrictive environment." It is apparent that other criteria in addition to scientific research have been used to make such decisions because the technology for deciding the most effective treatment is not agreed on at present by clinical researchers.

Generally, two comparison strategies have been used: enumeration of positive results of different procedures across different experiments and intra-subject comparisons of procedures within the same experiment. There are many problems with both of these strategies. Across-studies comparisons are weak because of the heterogeneity of the subjects and variations in procedures, samples, and parameters of the independent variables. Most intra-subject comparisons across treatments and behaviors fail because multiple baseline and reversal designs tend to confound order of treatment effects related to time and sequence of presentation. In addition, substitution effects and other response generalization effects show that target behaviors and collateral behaviors are clearly not orthogonal. Therefore, only an intra-subject design where time, sequence, and generalization effects can be controlled or at least evaluated by counterbalancing or randomizing the treatment sequences would seem adequate for appropriate comparison of the intervention procedures.

Three criteria that have been applied to judge comparative effectiveness of behavior management procedures are degree and rapidity of suppression, durability of suppression, and covariation (i.e., positive and/or negative side effects). The other criteria that have received attention in recent years are consumer satisfaction, clinical significance, and social validity.

With respect to degree and rapidity of suppression, reviews that have compared results of different procedures across experiments and within the same subjects tend to agree that punishment together with differential reinforcement of alternative positive behaviors produces the most immediate and complete suppression. Other management procedures have not been compared satisfactorily enough to suggest any firm conclusions.

On the question of durability of results, there is too much disagreement to draw a firm conclusion. Bates and Wehman (1977) reported that only 29 percent of the studies reported follow-up results. Contrary to common belief, punishment studies show the least instead of the most permanent suppression, whereas differential reinforcement techniques show the most long-lasting suppression. Investigators have rarely even reported follow-up beyond a year. Thus comparisons between studies should be made with caution when estimates of effectiveness and durability of different interventions are made. Intra-subject comparisons within the same experiment may be more trustworthy.

Other methods for judging comparative effectiveness of an intervention procedure besides statistically significant changes in the dependent variable have been consumer satisfaction and clinical significance. Consumer satisfaction is hardly a cornerstone of scientific inquiry.

Clinical significance or social validity are equally subjective measures used by a number of applied researchers to judge the importance of research. In practice they amount to judging whether intervention produced a substantial change in rate of target behavior. Rate is presumed to reflect response strength (Skinner 1953). However, Herrnstein (1970) and Baum (1977) have argued that choice or time allocation reflect response strength better than rate in terms of their correlation with manipulation of reinforcement contingencies. There are many low-rate behavior problems whose clinical significance cannot be denied (e.g., suicide, murder, some severe self-injurious behavior) that, by their nature, require multidimensional measurement. Finally, the clinical significance criterion does not recognize the heuristic value of research where new domains and procedures are being delineated. Kazdin (1976) has suggested the use of $N=1$ statistics for this purpose. It is not possible at present to evaluate this issue thoroughly. For the time being, measures of social validity may be important and desirable, but they are mostly in the eye of the beholder; reliability of consensus among researchers is low. Therefore, this criterion should be used loosely, taking into account bias and rate of false positives by the raters.

A final consideration is covariation. Initially, this issue arose around the use of intrusive punishment, especially electrical stimulation, as a behavior management procedure and its concomitant, possibly negative physical and conditioned emotional side effects. The latter fears have not been borne out by research. It is clear, however, that "substitution" (Baumeister and Rollings 1976) has been observed recently in a wide variety of settings and with virtually every procedure whose major focus is deceleration of high rate behaviors. Earlier studies did not report such covariation. Most of the research literature on generalization in this area has used the "train-and-hope" procedure and has been biased toward publishing exclusively positive instances of generalization (Stokes and Baer 1977).

Covariation is of two kinds. Transitional changes may occur in the target responses as a function of a change in stimulus conditions or reinforcement contingency (i.e., the contrast effect) (Reynolds 1961). Examples would include rebound effects in follow-up baselines, end-of-session effects, and extinction bursts. Changes in collateral behaviors may occur as a function of changes in the target behaviors and vice versa. As Sajwaj et al. (1972) pointed out, such "side effects" may be of four possible kinds: desirable behaviors may increase or decrease and undesirable behaviors may increase or decrease. The result in any given situation might be a function of: 1) the reinforcing or punishing effects of a particular contingent stimulus used; 2) the membership of a given target behavior in a wider response class; or 3) alterations in setting conditions to the extent that other behaviors are now affected by existing reinforcement contingencies. It is to be hoped that future studies will be designed to take a serious look at the side effects of various intervention strategies, both within treatment settings and at other times.

Research on covariation raises some interesting possibilities. Perhaps an inaccessible target behavior can be indirectly altered by manipulating its covariants. Chained behaviors sometimes can be averted by intervening early in the chain, as was shown with ruminative vomiting (Jackson et al. 1975).

Suppression of inappropriate concurrent behaviors often is negatively related to increases in appropriate behavior. What is the nature of this relationship? For instance, Lovaas et al. (1987) contended that self-stimulatory behavior is so reinforcing for some autistic retarded children that they will endure pain for the opportunity to do it. The inappropriate behavior apparently is so compelling that it reduces the time available for allocation to appropriate behaviors. Does this mean that programming of appropriate behaviors cannot proceed until self-stimulation is inhibited? Probably not if there are enough alternative contingent relationships among covariants specified by the reinforcement schedule (e.g., chained, concurrent, tandem, conjoint, or multiple contingencies). A major implication of this approach is the incorporation of new models that take into account the subject's environment.

Conclusion

A behavioral approach has been defined as a general orientation to clinical and educational work that uses an experimental problem-solving approach to the areas of skills development and behavior problems. Behavior, whether it is labeled normal or abnormal, is seen as learned and maintained by the same principles. The strength of the approach lies in the insistence of defining problems in an objective manner that can be systematically observed and treated (Ross 1980). The principles involved in three types of learning were described and related to intervention strategies in the classroom setting. The specific strategies are less important than the scientific approach that is employed by the behaviorist, which enables new methods to be tested and, consequently, new information to be generated. In essence, a behavior therapist employs an ever-changing and self-correcting approach to the treatment of deviant behavior.

Chapter 31

Special Education

Education for children with mental retardation is not a new idea, but it is an idea that has changed dramatically in recent decades. Interest in the education of all handicapped children is usually traced to a general interest in education during the 18th century and more specifically to the work of Itard whose curriculum for Victor, the "Wild Boy of Aveyron," gave direction and content to these efforts.

Itard's student, Edward Seguin, expanded on this work, calling his technique the "physiological method." Seguin's work in France and his establishment of this country's first residential institution and school in Massachusetts in 1848 had a profound influence on later education. Although this school and the others that soon followed were founded on a sense of optimism and a strategy of short-term residential care, by the early 20th century many state residential institutions were being built for the purpose of lifelong care (Scheerenberger 1983; Wolfensberger 1969). During this period, public school education was seldom available, but day-school programs increased slowly.

By the 1950s, several factors led to a growth in education and other services. One of the primary factors was the formation of the national Association for Retarded Children (now the Association for Retarded Citizens, or ARC) in 1950. ARC developed direct services, such as day-care programs, and mobilized parents into an effective political force. Other factors, such as the presidency of John F. Kennedy, influenced a growth in interest and in services, including education.

Although the number of children with mental retardation who received some form of education grew rapidly during the 1960s and early 1970s, the nature of the services emphasized separate classes (often in separate schools) for those with mild or moderate retardation and exclusion from school programs for the severely or profoundly handicapped. The most dramatic influence on education came in 1975 with the passage of Public Law 94-142, The Education for All Handicapped Children Act, and its 1983 amendments, known as PL 98-199.

The Legal Requirement

PL 94-142 has had profound effects in establishing the legal right to a free appropriate public education. The details of the law have been described by others (e.g., Turnbull and Turnbull 1978), but a summary of the major points is important.

1. Prior to the implementation of PL 94-142, handicapped children could be excluded from school or from other publicly funded education programs. The law now specifies that all children between the ages of three and 21 are entitled to a free, appropriate public education. Although the regulations for this law give some guidance regarding what is "appropriate," some professional judgment is still

required. However, this education must be at public expense and must be available to all children, regardless of handicap.

2. The process of deciding on the appropriate classroom placement must follow certain prescribed procedures. The recommendation of one person, no matter how expert, is not sufficient. A team representing school personnel and parents or parent surrogates makes the decision on educational placement.

3. The classroom placement decision must take into consideration the results of an evaluation conducted by a multidisciplinary team and must not depend solely on one test. The tests or evaluation procedures used must be "nondiscriminatory," must be given "in the child's native language or other mode of communication," and must have been validated for use with mentally retarded children.

4. The goals of each child's education must be specified in the form of an individualized education program (IEP), and these goals must be revised yearly. Short-term objectives, which can be measured, must also be specified. Thus vague goals, such as improving language skills, are not acceptable.

5. Education must take place in the "least restrictive environment." Although this principle is strongly established in law, its implementation requires good judgment and experience with individual cases. Approaches to implementation are addressed later.

6. All of the major elements of PL 94-142 include specific ways in which parents must be involved, and the rights of parents are clearly stated. The 1983 amendments (PL 98-199) provide increased support for parent training and information.

Current Educational Issues

The characteristics and educational needs of students with mental retardation vary widely. Thus a discussion of educational issues should consider the level of severity of mental retardation.

Mild Mental Retardation

Perhaps the most controversy in the education of students with mental retardation has focused on services for the mildly retarded. As school services grew in the 1950s and 1960s, large numbers of children were identified as mildly retarded and placed in special classes with the implicit promise that they would receive a better education than that offered in the regular class. The decision to apply the label of mental retardation is, however, a difficult and controversial one.

Labeling. For many years, children functioning at a mildly retarded level of development have been classified as "educable mentally retarded" in their school programs. A disproportionately large percentage of children so labeled come from ethnic minorities and/or low socioeconomic backgrounds (Mercer 1973). This finding has led to much criticism of the psychological and educational tests used to identify these children. This criticism of cultural bias is further supported by the fact that such children are often situationally retarded. That is, they perform poorly in school but were not labeled before they entered school; they appear to be competent outside of school settings.

Another aspect of this controversy concerns the effects of the label itself on the child. There are indications that the label affects the expectations that teachers and peers hold for the labeled child. Some educators have viewed this effect as positive because it provides an explanation for aberrant behavior and allows children to be more easily accepted. Others view the phenomenon as negative because children are likely to make less progress if expectations for them are low (Ysseldyke and Algozzine 1982).

There is no disagreement that there is social stigma associated with mental retardation in virtually all cultures. However, there is disagreement about whether the school's process of labeling creates stigma and lowers the self-image of students or whether these problems would occur even without a label (Guskin et al. 1975).

Classroom placement. Growth of self-contained classes for the mildly retarded was dramatically interrupted in 1968 when Dunn pointed out controversy associated with labeling and research that failed to show an academic benefit for segregated classes over regular class placement. The following years brought a trend toward mainstreaming, the placement of children with mild learning problems in regular classes with special help for part of the day.

The passage of PL 94-142 gave legal confirmation to the growing trend toward educating handicapped children in the least restrictive environment. Thus a continuum of services should exist from full-time regular class placement to full-time special class placement with in-between steps such as special tutoring and resource rooms. Individual placement decisions must consider the least restrictive placement in which the child can be successful both academically and socially.

Although mainstreaming has been law and educational policy for several years, its effectiveness is still debated. Gottlieb's (1981) review indicated that academic performance is not affected by regular versus special class placement, but social adjustment and peer acceptance may be lower for mainstreamed children. This latter finding may be an indication that just exposing mildly handicapped children to regular classmates will not bring about friendships, peer acceptance, or positive social interaction. More active steps are needed to prepare regular class teachers and students and to train mildly retarded students in the social skills that they need for good social adjustment (Walker 1983; Walker et al. 1983). A combination of such preparation for the handicapped learner, for the regular class teacher, and for the nonhandicapped students is most likely to result in successful mainstreaming.

Curriculum. The content of the education program for mildly retarded students has historically been based very much on that of regular education. Students in mainstreamed settings, of course, follow substantially the same curriculum as their classmates. The extent to which that curriculum can be adapted for the individual is often the key to successful academic mainstreaming. In special classes, the goals for students classified as educable stress independent living and working in nonsheltered adult environments. Traditional academic skills are usually combined with socialization and vocational skills. Abilities among these students vary greatly, and individualization of curriculum is very important.

Teaching methods. Among the many strategies for teaching mildly retarded learners that have been described, the research evidence favors an approach of direct instruction based on learning theory (see reviews by Huguenin et al. 1983; Weisberg et al. 1981). MacMillan (1982) described three components of a behavioral approach to teaching. It must "(1) provide the right situational cues, thereby increasing the likelihood of the desired response, (2) select consequences that are effective for the individual child, and (3) relate the stimuli to the desired response by exerting control over these contingencies" (p. 395). These behavioral principles have been applied successfully to instruction of academic skills—for example, DISTAR approach to teaching reading (Englemann and Bruner 1974)—as well as practical social, self-care, and job skills.

Early intervention.   Mild learning problems are seldom identified until children enter school and are faced with educational demands for the first time. Therefore, early intervention programs for this population are aimed at children at risk for mental retardation. Risk factors include primarily low socioeconomic status and low birth weight.

Early education programs for at risk children are primarily aimed at prevention, rather than treatment (Ramey and Bryant 1983). Research on such programs has been conducted since the early 1960s, and the assumptions about the importance of early experience for later learning on which these programs were based also led to the development of Project Headstart.

Virtually since their beginning, the effectiveness of early intervention efforts has been a subject of controversy. Now that the participants in 12 major studies have been followed into adolescence (Lazar et al. 1982), the long-term effects of early intervention for children at risk for mental retardation can be better understood. Although early intervention is not an inoculation against later problems, the group of children studied by Lazar et al. were more successful than control children in four areas: 1) school competence: they were half as likely to be retained; 2) developed abilities: they had higher IQ scores for up to three or four years after the program and performed better on school-administered achievement tests; 3) children's attitudes and values: they took pride in their achievements; and 4) family outcomes: their mothers were more satisfied with their children's school performance than were mothers of the control children.

These outcomes do not differentiate among approaches to early intervention but do strongly support the value to children and to society of systematic early programs. In 1986 the Education of the Handicapped Act amendments (PL 99-457) provided the legal and funding support to extend early intervention program to all states.

Moderate/Severe Mental Retardation

Children with IQs below 50 with enough basic skills in self-care and communication to function in the usual special classroom setting have been referred to as trainable. The historical expectation for these students has been that education will make them as self-sufficient as possible, but as adults they are likely to require supervision and support in many aspects of living.

Educational placement.   One clearly positive effect of PL 94-142 and its requirement of education in the least restrictive setting has been to challenge the assumption that moderately and severely retarded children have extremely limited potential. Historically such children have been served in settings ranging from special trainable classes in regular schools to special classes in segregated handicapped schools to separate residential programs.

The pressure toward educaton in less restrictive environments has led to more children being served in regular public schools and more integration of severely handicapped learners with their nonhandicapped peers. Although such interactions are not in the context of academic classes, a wide variety of other social, recreational, and nonacademic tasks and roles can be shared in schools (Certo et al. 1984).

Curriculum. Whereas the curriculum for mildly retarded students resembles many aspects of the regular education curriculum, curriculum for severely handicapped students in recent years has focused strongly on practical, applicable, functional skills. Children with severe learning problems are unlikely to generalize an abstract principle and apply it in a practical situation. Thus they must be taught skills in exactly the form that they will use them and have opportunities to learn and practice and apply skills in real-life settings (Horner et al. 1988).

The result of this approach is a dramatic change in what is taught and where teaching takes place. Education for severely handicapped students must stress skills needed in adulthood (Brown et al. 1976). This includes functional communication skills (including nonverbal methods if the student does not speak); basic skills for social interaction; skills needed for work, domestic living, and community functioning; and recreation-leisure skills.

To learn these skills in the settings in which they will be applied, more and more education is taking place outside of schools (Brown et al. 1983). These changes have led to successful acquisition of practical skills and to employment in competitive work settings for people with quite severe handicaps. Many people who only 10 or 15 years earlier would have been candidates for life-long institutional care are now living in their communities with the assistance they need to live productive lives.

Instructional methods. As noted earlier for the mildly retarded, methods of instruction for severely retarded learners rely strongly on behavioral approaches that clearly specify the skills to be taught in small steps, the setting for instruction, and the planned consequences that will effectively reinforce the new skill. Good behavioral teaching methods have become an essential skill for teachers. They complement knowledge of the child's developmental skills, knowledge of functional curriculum, and the ability to involve parents in the education program. A teacher with this broad perspective is able to use behavioral principles systematically but is also able to arrange daily activities that give frequent opportunities to learn in natural settings and to arrange consequences that naturally follow the child's behavior. Teaching in this manner is most likely to foster generalization and spontaneous use of new skills.

Early intervention. Whereas mild learning problems do not become apparent until the child enters school, moderate and severe mental retardation are apparent earlier. Children with Down's syndrome or metabolic disorders are identifiable as newborns. Neurologic disorders such as cerebral palsy are usually recognizable by six months of age and autism can usually be noted within the first 30 months.

Intervention approaches with very young severely handicapped children acknowledge the limitations imposed by biologic or genetic factors but also make environmental interventions available in the belief that they affect development and that programs are more effective if begun earlier. Bricker (1986) noted several goals of such intervention. Early programs can provide the basic skills and experiences on which later learning is based. They can prevent or make less likely problems in later life (e.g., self-stimulation, self-injury, or motor problems), and they can provide support to families during a stressful time when basic information about their children is needed.

It is extremely hard to assess the effectiveness of such programs because they have been in effect for only about 10 years and because ethical concerns make some experimental designs (e.g., control groups) very difficult. Bailey and Bricker's (1984) review highlighted these limitations but also noted that all 13 programs reviewed reported some type of positive outcome. As our society's awareness and concern about severely handicapped infants increase, the need for early intervention will surely increase.

Profound Mental Retardation

School-age children with IQs below approximately 20 who lack basic self-care and communication skills have historically been excluded from public school programs. Accompanying problems (e.g., difficult-to-manage behaviors, seizures, sensory handicaps, severe medical problems) have relegated most such children to state institutions, other residential programs, or special day education settings.

Placement. Public schools and other community-based programs have expanded their services to include lower functioning children than those previously served. At the same time, the deinstitutionalization movement has resulted in a much smaller, much more severely and multiply impaired and somewhat older population remaining in residential care. In most states, children and adults continue to leave institutions each year, and new admissions are approaching zero.

In other words, the option to place children in institutions is seldom available, and the only remaining choice is to develop community-based services. The challenge for the future is to develop the quality and quantity of care that is needed.

Programming. Although great strides have been made in teaching functional skills to children with very low intellectual ability, there remains a population of profoundly retarded, often multiply handicapped, nonambulatory children for whom education in its usual format is not possible. Many such children reside in institutions. Deciding what type of program is appropriate for such children has become very difficult and controversial (e.g., Kauffman 1981).

Children residing in facilities receiving federal funds are required to receive programming regularly. Yet what is a suitable program for children who lack control over their muscles, cannot express preference for or differential response to any potential reinforcer, and whose lives are dominated by medical problems and possibly discomfort and pain? To the extent that consensus exists on this difficult question, educators try to offer opportunities to learn very basic skills, such as expressing a preference by signaling in some way. Successful programs are continued. Unsuccessful programs or those that seem likely only to be annoying the child are changed or discontinued in favor of actions that seem to improve the quality of life. Such actions may be as simple as providing physical comfort and cleanliness, the presence of others (or absence if preferred), physical contact with others, or suitable levels of light and noise.

Because the needs and abilities of children with profound mental retardation are so variable, the educator's credo of individualization is especially important.

Conclusion

Education for children with mental retardation has grown rapidly in the last generation and has dramatically changed its focus since the mid-1970s. PL 94-142 and the commensurate federal role in special education have emphasized every child's right to a free appropriate public education in the least restrictive environment and have given parents substantial steps that they may take to ensure due process in planning their child's education. Accordingly, a wider range of children with learning problems is now receiving an education than ever before.

The combination of behavioral teaching methods, individualized curriculum stressing functional skills and preparation for adult roles, and the active support of parents and community members has led to greater possibilities than ever for children with mental retardation. The most successful schools are achieving the goal that we set for all students: preparation to live the adult years with as much independence and dignity as possible.

Chapter 32

Transition from School to Work

Historically, most of the work with mentally retarded people began with young clients. This was because most professionals in the field had been trained in early childhood development and were more comfortable working with younger children. Moreover, early research on the importance and dramatic benefits of early intervention programs further accelerated this trend.

Now that two decades have passed since John Kennedy's milestone legislation that stimulated so much of the emphasis on services for developmentally handicapped people, many of the children who initially benefited from these new initiatives are becoming adults. As we follow these youngsters, we realize that despite the major advances in the field over the past 20 years, many of them are not as well prepared for adult functioning as we would have liked. Therefore, programs are more seriously reviewing the developmental process from identification through adulthood, trying to develop more coherent and integrated training sequences.

The purpose of this chapter will be to examine each phase of this developmental process, emphasizing those skills that will later be necessary for effective community functioning. Although this will start with the kindergarten years, it in no way minimizes the importance of early identification and intensive infant stimulation programs. In fact, these are essential if a child is to be ready on entering kindergarten to undertake the training sequences that are suggested. However, because this chapter is designed to examine the school-to-work transition, the following periods will be discussed: early school (approximate ages 5 through 10), middle school (approximate ages 11 through 16), and transition to adult programs (approximate ages 17 through 21).

Early School

In general, early school programs are among the strongest for handicapped children so that fewer adjustments in these services are needed. The preacademic and academic focuses of these classrooms are necessary to help these children with disabilities develop their academic capabilities to the furthest extent possible. Those handicapped people who will eventually learn to read, still a most worthwhile goal, will probably receive most of their training during this early school phase. However, some minor adjustments in social, leisure-time, and prevocational training would be quite helpful during this phase.

Social and leisure-time skills are very important for handicapped adults, given the current emphasis on community-based programs. The foundation for these skills should be established early. Social interactive activities with nonhandicapped children should be emphasized and encouraged. However, it is important not just to place handicapped and nonhandicapped children together. There is accumulating evidence that if these activities are to be beneficial, both handicapped and nonhandicapped children need to be adequately prepared, and developmentally appropriate interactive tasks must be carefully selected and prepared.

Leisure-time activities are very important for anyone living in a community, whether handicapped or nonhandicapped. However, these interests and the ability to use one's own leisure-time productively are sometimes problems for handicapped adults. Therefore, it is advisable for classrooms serving younger children to provide opportunities to develop leisure-time interests. These can include field trips to places of interest, hobby times for collecting or examining objects, recreational activities like sports or exercise regimens, or fun times like listening to music or telling jokes. These should not be considered frivolous but rather an important part of every curriculum, with the same emphasis on matching activities to individual strengths and weaknesses as is commonly and effectively done with educational programs.

Preparation for vocational programs would also begin in the early school years. An appropriate and important goal for these children is the development of independent work skills. The process should begin by teaching handicapped children the concept of *finish* and by providing them with opportunities to learn what this means. For example, if a young handicapped child is to be taught to sort red and green chips, a limited number of chips should be placed in front of the child rather than a huge pile. The number selected should be based on the child's capacity with an expectation that the child will be able to finish the task. A place for the child to put completed objects should be provided. This "finish box" should be used for all activities to help children learn this important concept. Under no circumstances should a task involve putting together and taking apart the same objects. For example, a child should not be asked to put erasers on pencils and then be asked to take them off once the first part of the task is completed. Meaningful activities are not disassembled once they are finished.

In addition to learning how to complete tasks, efforts should be made toward independent functioning. This can be facilitated by having materials within children's reach and having them obtain their own work materials. Short work tasks with cues (e.g., picture cards) instructing them on a task's components should replace the teacher-oriented commands that usually predominate in classroom situations. Cues can be used, such as picture cards, so that the child can work independently for longer periods of time. Any tasks that children can do for themselves without explicit teacher instruction represent important steps toward later independent functioning.

Middle School

As handicapped children approach adolescence, they should have a foundation for the further development of social and leisure skills and an ability to work independently. During this next stage, social and leisure activities should continue, and transitional planning must begin in earnest. This will begin a trend of increased time and activities outside of the classroom.

During this period, career alternatives should be explored in earnest. Factors to be considered include the interests and abilities of individual clients, a realistic assessment of local employment prospects, and experiences with other handicapped people. As questions arise about different employment possibilities, answers should be sought through direct observation of students performing those kinds of tasks. Jobs should be considered based on the reported interests of handicapped students, their abilities, and their productivity.

During this phase, it is important for students to have real work experiences outside of the classroom. This can begin in the school on tasks such as working in the library, cleaning or preparing food in the cafeteria, working on general maintenance, cleaning within the school building, outside gardening, or related activities. If opportunities to work in nearby facilities are available, these should be pursued as well. Churches, hospitals, local governmental agencies, and private businesses can provide regular placements for students at these ages.

This is also an important time to begin regular field trips. These can include outings such as swimming or bowling, learning to ride the local transit system, or learning how to purchase groceries or other items in stores. The many skills needed in planning a trip, getting to the appropriate location, and transacting one's business are to be emphasized during these trips. Weekend excursions or even week-long trips are also highly desirable for children of this age, many of whom have very few opportunities to spend a night away from their parents.

Transition to Adult Vocational Programs

By the time adolescents reach this stage, they should have developed some social and leisure skills, participated in a variety of regular community-based activities, and trained in several vocational settings outside the classroom. At this point, they also should each have a very specific career objective with a specific vocation in a specific setting.

The plan for these final years is to implement the transition from school to work. This should occur by having the students spend increasing numbers of hours with supervision in the actual vocational setting where they will be working after school. Increasingly flexible models will be needed to allow teachers to provide the necessary supervision outside the classroom. As an adjunct, further social and leisure training should be pursued so that the skills necessary for adult functioning can be solidified and internalized. Adult living situations should also be located at this point so that the students can move into these settings in ways similar to nonhandicapped students who have completed their formal schooling.

Conclusion

Although great strides have been made in the past few decades in regard to both school and vocational services for handicapped individuals, there remains the problem that many handicapped people are not ready for the adult world on completion of their formal schooling. The problem appears to be that we do not have a coordinated plan for preparing our handicapped students for the realities of the adult world. A developmental model for improving these services has been proposed, including specific suggestions for training goals at each developmental stage.

Chapter 33

Vocational Rehabilitation

Employment is a normal and expected path for persons who are nonhandicapped. Indeed, successful employment experiences are important to both the individual and society. Such employment experiences are no less important to individuals who are mentally handicapped. Unfortunately, achievement of these employment experiences has often been unattainable by these individuals. During the late 1970s and early 1980s, two factors improved the competitive employment prospects of individuals who are mentally handicapped. First, The Education for All Handicapped Children Act (PL 94-142), Section 504 of the Rehabilitation Act, and The Educational Amendments of 1976 (PL 94-482) mandated that functional school programs be offered to handicapped individuals to ensure that they become self-sufficient, productive members of our society. Second, several demonstration projects developed competitive employment models that successfully placed mentally handicapped individuals into community jobs. Today, handicapped individuals who are graduating from schools are now better prepared than previously, and superior training and placement practices are available to them.

Several authors have articulated and implemented competitive employment models (Bates and Pancsofar 1983; Moss et al. 1986; Rusch and Mithaug 1980; Vogelsberg 1984; Wehman 1981). Competitive employment is defined as work that produces valued goods or services at minimum wage or more in a setting that includes nonhandicapped workers and provides opportunities for advancement. Common features of these models include surveying the community for appropriate job openings, training individuals for jobs whose requirements are matched to their skills, placing individuals in these appropriate jobs, and facilitating maintenance of job skills. Certain variations and emphases exist across these five models. Bates and Pancsofar utilized a procedure that rotated students through various jobs to familiarize them with different options and to identify the best match before placement occurred. Vogelsberg focused on the match of job requirements with applicant skills during the placement process. In this model, an agreement is made with the employer that the placement is made on a trial basis and that should the placement be unsuccessful, either party can terminate the agreement. This approach has reduced the stress level on both the employer and the employee and has resulted in successful placement rates. Wehman utilized an approach emphasizing primarily on-the-job training to reduce any mismatch between job requirements and employee's skills.

The five programs cited have had to face similar obstacles to successful employment. Among these obstacles are 1) specific employee skill and behavior deficits, 2) deficient assessment and training procedures, 3) disregard for social validation of work goals and procedures, 4) lack of a systematic approach to service delivery, 5) inadequate training and personnel preparation, and 6) economic and policy considerations deterring efforts to promote competitive employment. The five identified demonstration projects have based their models on several key approaches that have helped to overcome these obstacles. These techniques have included applied behavior analysis (Kazdin 1980), facilitation of maintenance and generalization (Stokes and Baer 1977), parent involvement and awareness (Vogelsberg 1986), social validation of job expectations (Greenspan and Shoultz 1981), and employee-job match (Karan and Schalock 1983). In the course of this chapter, these techniques and others facilitating successful employment of individuals who are mentally handicapped will be explicated.

Vocational Training Model Components

The critical components of the five model programs were described above. Here the components of the competitive employment model are delineated in greater detail.

Assessment

To provide the optimal match between the individual worker and the job into which the worker is placed, assessment of work skills and identification of job requirements are necessary. Assessment of work skills should be based on procedures that most effectively predict progress within the targeted placement setting. These procedures should ideally include 1) collection and interpretation of data within an ecologic framework; 2) identification of specific responses that are required in the projected placement opportunities (especially those most crucial in promoting longevity); 3) selection and training on representative examples of these identified responses; 4) provision of equal emphasis to baseline, formative, and summative phases of assessment; 5) measurements of both quantitative and qualitative varieties; and 6) a deemphasis on developmentally sequenced assessments.

Placement

Within the survey-train-place-maintain (Martin 1986) perspective, the placement component is critical. Martin discussed aspects of the placement process that are keys to its success. First, community placement options must be identified and then surveyed with respect to job availability and requirements. These employment opportunities need to be evaluated; the most favorable opportunities need to constitute the placement pool. Candidates should be matched with the most appropriate job; where necessary, the job can be redesigned. To facilitate placement success, a working relationship with the employer needs to be cultivated; expectations and attitudes need to be considered. Another important contributor to job success is parental support;

thus parents should be included in the placement process. A key step in the placement procedure is the interview process; thus candidates should be prepared specifically so as to enhance the manner in which they present themselves. Finally, consistent feedback in the form of a work performance evaluation form can improve the likelihood of job success by ensuring that employer, worker, and trainer are in agreement with respect to evaluation of job performance.

Skill Training

Within the survey-train-place-maintain model, training has traditionally been the area of greatest research interest. Stainback et al. (1986) underscored the advantages of preparing the individual for placement within community-based training stations, as opposed to programs within sheltered workshops. These advantages include the following:

1. Training of vocational survival skills
2. Opportunities to learn social interaction skills
3. Opportunity for co-workers to serve as role models
4. Development of understanding by co-workers of persons who are handicapped
5. Familiarization with employment consideratons by training personnel
6. Enhancement of generalization
7. More normalized learning experience
8. Positive influence on community members' attitudes toward individuals who are handicapped
9. Enhanced likelihood of successful competitive employment

Social Validation

Recently, certain aspects of the community-based employment model have received increased attention, namely, follow-up issues such as social validation, use of co-workers as change agents, and maintenance and generalization. Social validation provides a measure of the acceptability of work performance as perceived by significant individuals within the workplace (e.g., employers, co-workers). (White and Rusch 1984). Two procedures, social comparison and subjective evaluation, have been used to provide social validation. Social comparison involves comparison of the behavior of the worker who is handicapped with the behavior of nonhandicapped peers within a similar job or situation. Subjective evaluation is the evaluation of a target behavior for its acceptability by experts or significant others who have contact with the target worker. The two methods of social validation can be applied to three components: work goals, work procedures, and work performance. Social validation provides evaluation measures most closely tied to indicators of worker success, that is, worker effectiveness as perceived by supervisors and employers.

Co-workers as Change Agents

In addition to the importance of measuring significant others' perceptions of worker performance, the nature of the interaction of significant others with the worker who is handicapped is often crucial. Specifically, enlisting co-workers as change agents, especially during long-term, follow-up periods, appears to be a promising approach to facilitating enduring placement success (Shafer 1986). Co-workers can be effective in the roles of advocates, observers, and trainers. The importance of co-worker cooperation and involvement is especially great in situations where placement agencies provide little or no sustaining services.

Maintenance and Generalization

Maintenance and generalization of work skills are seen as vocational requirements for which special training strategies must be implemented. Workers must be both autonomous in performing a skill and adaptable to environmental changes in work settings following training (Gifford et al. 1984). Curricula within school settings, as well as on-the-job training, should incorporate strategies that promote autonomy and adaptability. Among the strategies that promote autonomy are self-control procedures, selective withdrawal of cues or reinforcers, use of mediating cues, and traditional behavioral techniques, such as titration of reinforcement schedules (Gifford et al. 1984). General case programming is a technique that presents training examples from across the possible range of skills required in a future job or set of jobs, and thus promotes adaptability to variable work conditions. Curricula within school settings, as well as on-the-job training, should incorporate strategies that promote autonomy and adaptability.

Summary

Topics discussed thus far have primarily involved the individual who is handicapped or those individuals in close contact with the handicapped person. However, other considerations may equally affect employment success. We will now address issues that impinge at diverse system levels on employment of individuals who are mentally handicapped.

Service Delivery Coordination

The service delivery system that is responsible for providing vocational services may not offer appropriate or timely services due to deficiencies in coordination and cooperation. Schalock (1986) identified potential impediments to a coordinated service delivery system:

1. Needed services go beyond the boundaries of traditional generic community services such as health care and education.
2. Continued controversy regarding categorical versus functional definitions.
3. Overlapping legislation and lack of a clear national policy.
4. Multiple funding sources without financial coordination.
5. Multiple planning bodies accompanied by inadequate control and responsibility.
6. Lack of reliable data on program benefits and effectiveness.
7. Lack of adequate resources including facilities, technology, experience, and trained staff.
8. Public attitude that the handicapped person (or the person's family) is responsible for independently obtaining effective services.
9. Competition among service provider for resources.

Despite these potential barriers to service coordination, Schalock (1986) described a technique to improve interagency coordination and intersector (public and private) cooperation. This coordination and cooperation is improved through an Individual Transition Plan (ITP) process, wherein significant others in the handicapped individual's current and future life span share information about environments for which the individual needs to be prepared. The various service delivery systems then plan the means by which the individual will receive these needed services. Over the last few years, Schalock and his associates have used the ITP process to facilitate: 1) students' transition from school to competitive employment, 2) students' transition from school to another service delivery program, and 3) adult developmentally disabled persons' transition from workshop to workplace.

Person-Environment Fit

Karan and Schalock (1983) introduced an ecologic perspective within which to view competitive employment. The individual is considered with respect to the environment; appropriate person-environment match is the goal, achievable by focusing interventions on the person, the environment, or both. Karan and Berger (1986) built on this perspective. They focused on the individual, identifying the characteristics of high risk individuals—for example, social-interpersonal difficulties, excessive influence by external forces, difficulties in emotional expression, negative self-concept (Gardner and Cole 1983), poor social-role development (Martin et al. 1979), and low motivation (Karan and Gardner 1973). The authors identified components of socially accessible environments, which are often essential for successful competitive employment by individuals who are mentally handicapped. Such socially accessible environments include links to key support persons or groups, quality interpersonal transactions, informational feedback focused on satisfying basic psychological and social needs, and reciprocity of need satisfaction. By identifying the characteristics of individuals and environments crucial to successful person-environment fit, the authors made possible the next step: identification of the critical interactions between persons and environment. People influence each other in complex and subtle ways. Karan and Berger emphasized the critical importance of communication in establishing the reciprocal relationships that are the key to developing a support network.

Chadsey-Rusch (1986) proposed an ecobehavioral (Rogers-Warren and Warren 1977; Willems 1977) perspective within which to consider social competence. Social behaviors necessary for successful employment include the ability to communicate at least basic needs, compliance, nondisruption of work setting, and ability to follow directions (Rusch et al. 1982). Social behaviors associated with job loss include character or moral reasons, temperament or affective reasons, and social awareness or not understanding people and work settings (Greenspan and Shoultz 1981).

To unify findings and provide understanding of social competence, Chadsey-Rusch (1986) utilized the conceptual framework of McFall (1982). Within the framework, social competence and social skills are differentiated. Social competency relates to adequacy of performance on a particular social task. Social skills are specific behaviors needed to perform competently on a particular social task. Further, social skills can be divided into three types: social decoding skills, social decision skills, and social performance skills. Social decoding involves understanding the social situation and what the context implies. Social decision involves choosing the appropriate response for the given context. Social performance includes judging whether the response met the demands of the social task. Interventions based on the model depend on identifying social tasks that are critical to the individual in question. Next, the task must be analyzed, which will involve consideration of variables that could potentially influence the task, such as its purpose, task constraints, setting, and performance criteria. Then, assessment of the individual should be conducted on the social tasks identified. The interventions discussed by Chadsey-Rusch are primarily focused on the individual, as opposed to environmental interventions.

Because Chadsey-Rusch's (1986) focus is primarily on the individual and Karan and Berger's (1986) emphasis is on environmental intervention, the two approaches complement each other effectively. Specifically, Chadsey-Rusch's social skill packages, which contain 1) a rationale for why a given social behavior is desirable, 2) an opportunity to observe examples of the behavior, 3) an opportunity to practice the behavior, and 4) feedback regarding performance, complement Karan and Berger's suggested steps to make an environment more socially accessible. These steps include 1) identify key individuals to function as support people, 2) assist in improving successful interactions within the work environment between the high risk individual and the individual's supervisor and co-workers, 3) observe the mentally retarded individual across settings and time to identify both temporally proximate and distant events that may be influencing the individual's inability to function effectively on the job, 4) attempt to ensure that the responsibility for behavioral-change programs is shared by the individual and significant others, and 5) ensure that those providing support to the high risk person have their own sources of support. Combining the two sets of strategies provides a powerful approach toward facilitating person-environment match.

Many of the same issues addressed within areas of support networks and social competence also potentially apply to the topic of parent training and involvement. Again, the ecobehavioral approach allows a systematic analysis of a mentally handicapped person and the person's significant others. In addition to behavioral interventions focusing on the individual and the environment, social validation (White and Rusch 1984) provides a powerful means to enhance person-environment match and development of support networks. Parents constitute one of these key support networks. Schutz (1986) identified inventorying needs of parents, assessing their values and evaluating their level of satisfaction with program delivery as a means to promote the transition process into competitive employment. The parent frequently provides the most important support that a mentally handicapped individual has. Parental support for a child's entrance into competitive employment is critical for success on the job. Utilizing parents to validate socially the employment choices, training means, and placement procedures enhances the likelihood of success on the job.

Policy

Often, successful interventions directed toward mentally handicapped individuals and their environment are thwarted by existing fiscal and administrative policies. Because of various historical, fiscal, and administrative policies, workshop programs for the mentally handicapped have developed into dual-purpose entities: to provide sheltered employment and to move individuals into competitive jobs. These two functions often are combined in one agency within a flow-through model of services. In theory, individuals move through the continuum of services until they become competitively employed. In practice, 75 percent of all consumers placed in competitive employment are transferred during their first three months (Moss 1979). The annual likelihood of placement for individuals who have been in workshop programs longer than two years is 3 percent. The time-limited nature of support for individuals entering competitive employment has reduced the likelihood that more severely handicapped individuals will enter into competitive employment. Bellamy et al. (1986) proposed a two-tiered system: CEP (Competitive Employment Program) and SEP (Supported Employment Program). CEPs are time-limited programs designed to move jobless individuals with disabilities into self-supporting, open employment. SEPs, on the other hand, provide longer-term publicly supported jobs for individuals with handicaps. Through the dual framework, each individual referred to an agency has a chance to obtain work, and the conflicting goals of the agency are reduced considerably. Thus Bellamy et al.'s two-tier system can be considered a refinement of the competitive employment model.

Even if the policy alternative proposed by Bellamy et al. (1986) is successful, an additional policy hurdle is identified by Walls et al. (1986). Movement into competitive employment may be significantly curtailed because of social benefits paid to mentally handicapped individuals. Both a behavioral analysis of disincentives (Rusch and Mithaug 1980) and a microeconomics approach predict decreased job-seeking and work behaviors when guaranteed social benefits are high. When guaranteed social benefit pay is balanced against pay from competitive employment, which has several uncertainties related to it, the social benefit pay is highly attractive. The continued availability of work is uncertain, the ability to be successful on the job is uncertain, and the effects of increased wages on current benefits is particularly uncertain in the eyes of the recipient. Walls et al. suggested that a major overhaul of the social benefit system is needed to produce a consistent system that provides incentives, rather than disincentives. However, the authors indicated the magnitude of such a restructuring in the face of entrenched agencies and political inertia.

Personnel Preparation

Due to the complexity of the task facing practitioners serving the mentally handicapped, personnel preparation will have to provide a more comprehensive and systematic curriculum. Renzaglia (1986) noted that the quality of educational programs for students with handicaps is still poor (Alper and Alper 1980). There is a critical need for the practices developed in model demonstration programs to be incorporated into preservice and inservice preparation programs. The author noted that because of the variety of specialists serving individuals who are mentally handicapped, educators and rehabilitation personnel must become educational team managers (Haring 1982; Mori et al. 1982). In addition, model personnel preparation curriculum should be competency-based, field-based, behaviorally grounded, include community-referenced curriculum development, and provide a focus on transition issues. Further there should be a broadened awareness of medical, legal, and advocacy issues as well as an understanding of service delivery systems that promotes interagency cooperation. Due to the varying types and degrees of handicaps experienced by vocational training program participants, educators must thus have a wider and more sophisticated range of skills.

Quality of Life

Beyond the narrower issue of vocational success, Matson and Rusch (1986) argued for the need to address the issue of quality of life. They identified general descriptors of quality of life, such as self-esteem, self-worth, and independence. These are considered in more operationalized form as the ability to live where one chooses, equal access to services, and opportunity to attend community schools and to engage in other normalized activities. Additionally, the ability to work, experience the feeling of accomplishment, and have the respect of supervisors and co-workers are major steps toward achieving quality of life. Articulating the concept of quality of life is a first step toward its realization. However, policy decisions must come to reflect this concept, community attitudes must be influenced by its message, and its implications must find their way into the day-to-day lives of individuals who are mentally handicapped.

Conclusion

This section introduced several newer and developing approaches to vocational rehabilitation for individuals with mental retardation. Over the past 10 years, significantly different expectations have emerged in regard to employment outcomes of persons with mental retardation. The traditional outcome of sheltered employment has been challenged due to the emergence of an outcome that is more consistent with contemporary professional practice (i.e., competitive employment). These practices have helped to define a new model for program development. The model, sometimes referred to as the survey-train-place-maintain approach, emphasizes the value of the social community and focuses on person-person and person-setting adaptation to facilitate fuller participation in society by individuals who are mentally retarded.

Chapter 34

Normalization and Deinstitutionalization: Philosophy, Public Policy, and Personal Decision

Since the mid-1950s, a controversy has been waged over whether mentally retarded individuals are appropriately and humanely served in large institutions. This controversy has been accompanied by claims of abusive treatment and neglect in the institution, related class-action lawsuits, the movement of large numbers of people out of institutions, and the concomitant development of "normalized" community-based systems of care. In this chapter, the concepts of normalization and deinstitutionalization will be reviewed and critiqued from three perspectives: as philosophy, as public policy, and as a personal dilemma for families with retarded members. The purpose of the discussion is to de-simplify the arguments for and against institutionalization and, secondly, to suggest that the highly vocal proponents of normalization and deinstitutionalization may unintentionally impede the adjustment of the family coping with mental retardation.

Definition of Terms

Although there is wide agreement about the meaning of normalization and deinstitutionalization, it is worthwhile to clarify the way in which these and some other terms will be used in this discussion.

Institution.   Institution refers to large (e.g., 100 to 200 beds) government-operated residential facilities providing continuous 24-hour residential care for the retarded. Client services rendered in these facilities typically include medical, nursing, occupational therapy, physical therapy, education, psychology, recreation, psychosocial, and case management services, which are provided by facility staff primarily on the institution's grounds. Although these institutions have different names in different locations, they are usually designated as state hospitals, state schools, or developmental centers.

Normalization. Normalization is a philosophy that essentially holds that humane and ethical treatment of retarded people demands that they will live in ordinary homes in community neighborhoods with the same degree of social integration and basically the same style of life as the general population. The philosophy also incorporates such values as respect for individual rights, freedom from stigma, and personalization of the environment. It is important to recognize that normalization philosophy grew out of extreme dissatisfaction with care in physical institutions (i.e., specific settings where care was delivered). As a result, normalization has become, for all practical purposes, synonymous with the alternative physical arrangement of community-based domiciles.

Even a brief definition of the philosophy of normalization is incomplete without some comment on whether or not there is an opposing or comparative philosophy. There is indeed a field of driving and restraining forces relative to the normalization philosophy, especially insofar as that philosophy is anti-institutional. On the one hand, normalization proponents are vocal, active, and organized. They are influential in the political arena, have been key actors in the development of their preferred community-based system of care, and have developed much of the program evaluation and training methodology in the field of mental retardation. On the other hand, although there is not a highly organized group that opposes normalization, there is a somewhat passive but powerful set of factors that keep institutional placement viable.

First, there is a sizable group of moderate thinkers who take the position that the preferred placement depends on a number of individual client, service system, and environmental variables. Proponents of this moderate position constitute a loosely coupled group whose ideas have not crystallized to the extent that they have been given a philosophical label; nevertheless, their influence at the level of client care is formidable. This relatively silent group includes a large number of practicing clinicians and families of the retarded, many of whom have very limited interest in political activism. A second reason for the continued viability of the institution is that reforms of considerable magnitude have taken place within them, so that many provide state-of-the-art care. Finally, the institution remains viable because of deficiencies in the community system, both in terms of the quality of care provided in that setting and the absence of placements for specific types of retarded people.

Deinstitutionalization. Deinstitutionalization refers to the policy decisions of government that lead to the movement of retarded people out of large hospitals and residential schools into community-based placements. It involves a vast restructuring of the public service delivery system, including (at the minimum) the development of community-based systems of care, new policy and legislation, and new mechanisms for financing services.

Deinstitutionalization can be seen as the administrative counterpart of the normalization movement. But the motives and forces behind deinstitutionalization are only partly philosophical. One of the primary political motives for deinstitutionalization policy is anticipated savings. It is widely held that care in the community is cheaper than care in the institution, although there is little evidence to support this idea. The reasons for the tenacity of the cost-effectiveness belief will be discussed later.

Despite the connection between normalization and deinstitutionalization, the methods through which deinstitutionalization is accomplished are often at direct odds with concepts of normalization. This occurs when, for example, groups of retarded people who have spent years of their lives in the institution are moved out en masse with little participation in decision making and little preparation for the new environment. That this sort of practice is contrary to any humane policy is evidenced by the deaths that have been reported from such uprootings (Marlowe 1976).

Institutionalization.   Institutionalization refers here to the decision to deliver the care of a mentally retarded family member over to an institution. This is often a personal family decision. The decision has two parts: the election of out-of-home care and a choice from among placement alternatives.

Retarded people.   Here we are talking about a population with an extremely broad range of severely handicapping conditions in addition to subnormal intelligence. The onset of their disabilities occurs prior to adulthood and often is evident from birth. At one end of the continuum, we are talking about ambulatory, semi-independent children and adults. At the other end, we are talking about nonambulatory or bedridden adults and children who are entirely dependent on other human beings for the sustenance of life from minute to minute.

Deinstitutionalization and Normalization as Philosophy

It is difficult to criticize a philosophy of normalization, the cornerstone of which is equal rights for retarded people. Nevertheless, some aspects of the philosophy need to be called into question. Among other things, this involves an assessment of how the philosophy has played out in the real world of community living.

The first point to be made is that normalization should refer to a set of environmental conditions, not to a physical location. It follows that institutionalization is not the opposite of normalization, nor is community placement synonymous with normalization. At the present time, there are normalizing factors in the institutional environment that are difficult or impossible to replicate in community environments. These include: 1) easily accessible, proximal, social activities among a community of people that resembles any other community with its young and old and its various races, nationalities, and creeds; 2) a large pool of peers to whom the retarded person can relate, can compete with at the same level, can be accepted by, and can make friends with; 3) the availability of volunteer, foster grandparent, student, and other hands to enrich personal contacts and to increase opportunities for the retarded person; 4) freedom from stigma; 5) the availability of state-of-the-art adaptive equipment and adaptive recreational, social, and educational experiences because of the special emphasis on innovation within the institution; and 6) increased freedom of movement because of special safeguards in the environment.

It is time for a new evaluation of institutions. They have changed since the days when Rene Spitz identified anaclitic depression and when people with dangerous behaviors were kept for long hours in physical restraints. Most no longer deserve the criticisms that have been leveled against them in the past. If normalization philosophy is to survive to benefit the retarded citizen, it must detach itself from physical locations and must abandon its traditional vendetta with the institution.

The second point to be made is in regard to the psychology of normalization. Perhaps these comments are best introduced by what is quite simply a folk adage, that is, what is normal for one person, may not be for another. The possibility that normalization, as currently defined, is a burden to retarded people cannot be overlooked. The expectations underlying normalization, established by intellectually and physically "normal" people, may constitute for the retarded person who stretches to meet them a pathologic denial of differentness. Wright (1960) wrote eloquently about the psychodevelopmental tasks of the handicapped individual evolving a positive self-concept. This task involves full recognition and acceptance of differentness, limitations, and special needs in place of denial and "splitting off" of the handicap from the worthy self, resulting in the renunciation of special helps. We must take care in promoting normalization philosophy that we are not promoting devaluation and denial of "differentness" by insisting that the retarded person strive to replicate our own image and value system. Then, from the prespective of social and political psychology, we should recall that normalization grew out of an era broadly concerned with the protection of human civil rights. That movement has led us to question the value of "melting pot" concepts and to recognize the personal, social, and political power connected with cultural pluralism and the maintenance of a distinct group identity.

Deinstitutionalization as Public Policy

It is widely assumed that care in the community and in the home is less costly than care in institutions. Most people think the high cost of institutional care is attributable to the necessity of maintaining complex, sometimes century-old, institutional infrastructures. Cost effectiveness, then, is an acceptable rationale for deinstitutionalization and a politically attractive position because no one is interested in wasting money. To ensure that the rights of the retarded are not sacrificed in the interests of government savings, federal standards prohibit their movement except when the move is to an "equal or better" treatment milieu. With these safeguards in place, it is tacitly assumed that deinstitutionalization results in retarded people living in environments more favorable than the institution and living at a lower cost. There is little evidence that either of these assumptions is correct.

The assumption that community facilities are equal to or better than the institution has simply not been tested. In the great majority of states, there is no regular monitoring of the quality of care in community facilities, many of which are operated on a proprietary basis. In addition, there is generally no attempt to assess the quality of the environment into which a retarded person is to be moved before the move occurs. Equal or better is rhetoric only, and no attempt has been made to operationalize the standard. This is not to say that concerned professionals do not "eyeball" a potential community living arrangement before a retarded person is moved to it, but there is no standard quality assurance system that guarantees this. There are plenty of reasons to believe that the equal-or-better standard is not being met. The most obvious reasons are reported in newspaper articles that tell of scandals in unmonitored homes. Then there is mounting evidence that psychotropic drug use is unnecessarily high in community facilities and not well monitored. The reasons for this are complex (Mouchka 1985) and probably include the fact that the use of drugs as a means of controlling behavior is less labor intensive, thus less costly, than other means. There is also reason to believe that services are not delivered with the same frequency and intensity in the community as in institutional settings (Mouchka 1985). The organizational

structure of institutions and the continued surveillance of their compliance with established standards of care create a system of services delivered by trained professionals and characterized by availability, accessibility, and coordination.

The second assumption, that community is less costly than institution, is as
untested as the equal-or-better hypothesis. This is not to say that cost studies have
not been done (e.g., Bruininks et al. 1980; Mayeda and Wai 1975; Mouchka 1985;
Rotegard et al. 1984). At first glance, all of these studies confirm the cost effectiveness
of community placement. But these and other similar studies have two major weaknesses. First, they have not been able to capture all community costs because of the
multitude of administrative entities and funding sources involved in the provision of
services, the differences in the systems of accounting used by these entities, and the
various levels of government (federal, state, county) involved. Second, there has been
no satisfactory way of determining whether comparable clients in varied placements
are receiving comparable-appropriate levels of service. One study involved an exhaustive attempt to collect all costs incurred by comparable clients in three settings
(hospital, home, community) over a one-year period (Mouchka 1985). In this study,
the total costs for care delivered, for any and all client types, was greater in the
institution than in the community. What was not assessed was the extent to which
the clients' actual service needs were being met in the varied placement settings.
Neither was the quality of the respective environments assessed, nor the coordination
and accessibility of the services. All of these are client benefits purchasable with the
available dollar. These measures were considered beyond the scope of the study,
even though they are an essential part of the cost-effectiveness equation. The great
majority of cost studies involve the simple totaling of dollars spent, with little or no
attention to the quality or adequacy of the program the dollar has purchased in the
varied systems of care.

One of the most interesting findings in studies of institutional costs is that the
maintenance of institutional infrastructures and support services accounts for only a
tiny percentage of the institutional cost differential. In states that elect to qualify their
institutions for federal reimbursement, a large proportion of the difference in cost
between institution and community is attributable to the maintenance of quality standards of care on which federal reimbursements are contingent. These standards of
quality care are far too extensive to enumerate here, but one of the most costly of
them is the maintenance of staffing standards. These standards dictate the number,
training, and qualifications of staff for each institutional unit. Except in the unusual
case, the community has no such staffing standards at this time. It is not unusual for
a retarded person in the community to receive care from someone who has had no
education, training, or experience in the field of mental retardation; who is paid a
minimum wage by the proprietary provider; and who may be gone as soon as a more
agreeable minimum wage job turns up. At the highest end of the pay continuum,
physicians who provide community care also have little or no training in the field.
This obviously has an impact of the greatest magnitude on the quality of care.

Assuming for a moment that the inclusion of benefit measures would show
community care to be more cost effective, there is still the question of whether government would act responsibly to use savings from hospital closures to actually create
an equal or better community system. If deinstitutionalization of the mentally ill is
any indicator, once savings are realized there is no guarantee that they will be turned
back into expenditures that enhance the quality of alternative care.

A number of factors that keep the institution viable have been mentioned earlier.
At least three other factors have prevented wholesale deinstitutionalization in the
interest of cost cutting, none of them involving interests in normalization or in equal

or better care. First, the institutions are often a major source of economic stability for the surrounding community. As a result, there are powerful political pressures to maintain these facilities. Second, systems for the finance of care, including public and private reimbursement programs, often embody incentives for institutional care. Finally, the states have failed to innovate adequate programs of care in community settings for specific types of clients. This is evident from the types of clients who remain in the institution for lack of community option. For example, institutions have a much higher percentage of residents with severe maladaptive behaviors, profound mental retardation, minimal self-help skills, and severe physical disability than does the community system.

Institutionalization as Personal Decision

The great majority of retarded people and their families are not concerned with philosophers and public policymakers, to whom the words deinstitutionalization and normalization belong. They are dealing with individual concerns, problems, stressors, opportunities, and values within a unique family system. Under the best of circumstances, the individual family will engage in a healthy problem-solving process that involves constructing an optimal solution for itself as a system, with all members sharing in the personal compromises and adjustments that are inevitable when the special challenges of retardation in the family must be met. In the normal course of things, the family decision-making process is at high risk of pathology. The essence of the pathology is the repression of certain adaptive options for the family (i.e., the failure to consider certain options) because they carry with them the threat of criticism, shame, and guilt. Anti-institutional rhetoric and normalization banner waving, while acting as potent sources of social reform in the field of retardation, have exacerbated this problem for the family. In addition, they have obscured the need for a realistic evaluation of whether the aims of normalization have been met in existing community systems of care.

Certainly the option to place the retarded family member outside the home and the choice of a placement are two of the most emotionally complex options that the family will consider. These are also the most critical decisions because they will affect the entire social, psychological, and economic life of the family.

Let us consider some dynamics of the family coping with retardation and some of the reasons why constructive consideration of placement options is so difficult.

The guilt that families feel around the possibility of placing the retarded family member outside the home can be of such intensity that the issue can barely be discussed. The failure to do so may commit family members to a lifetime of diminished self-actualization and may even attenuate the development of the retarded member. This sense of guilt has both intrapsychic and social origins; it is not limited to parents but applies equally to siblings of the retarded.

Society, and this includes the extended family, may see the decision to place out-of-home as a failure of caring, as either rejection of the retarded member or as abdication of responsibility. Then, too, acknowledging that someone else is needed to care for the retarded member may carry with it a sense of personal failure. This complex of guilt and shame is greatly complicated by the inevitable, but strictly repressed, ambivalence of the family toward the retarded member. The unacceptability of their own ambivalence makes the societal charge "you don't care" all the more searing.

The point is that the family suffering from these sequelae must be freed up from them to make a good decision about placement and to achieve optimal long-lasting family adjustment. The concern here is not only that the family will reject adaptive consideration of out-of-home placement or of respite. There is equal concern that, if a decision to place is made before it is found to be a fully acceptable option, it will result in alienation. The family will reject further contact with the retarded member because such contact renews the unresolved shame and guilt over the decision. These problems are exacerbated by anti-institutional diatribes, when the institution is the only available placement or when it is the placement of choice in terms of quality care.

For what reasons should families be encouraged or want to consider the institution a viable option? A number of reasons are obvious from the previous discussion. To these should be added several others.

First, the institution has a history of stability. Families want to know that their dependent loved one will not be removed from his or her home and shuffled about when a care provider goes out of business. They want to know that when they are gone some reliable authority will take their place in monitoring the quality of life of their son, daughter, brother, or sister. They feel even more secure if there are standards of care set forth that they can review and with which they agree. They want also to be assured that their relative will not live in a community where he or she is subjected to ridicule and exclusion. They would also like their relative to be cared for and become attached to people who will not leave tomorrow and who have chosen to be educated and trained in the special skills necessary to meet the necessary needs. They hope that their relative will be in an environment where some freedom of movement can be experienced without excessive risk despite the dangers the person may at times pose to him- or herself.

Conclusion

The decision whether institutional or community placement is the better choice for an individual is a decision that should be made in terms of the wishes of the individual and the family. It must also be based on a realistic appraisal of the quality of the environments, the availability of appropriate services, the amount of programming, and the stability of the facility. It is not "normalization" to consign a retarded person to a nursing home or to home care if the necessary services will not be there. And it is not "institutionalization" to retain, at least for the present, residential facilities of substantial size, that can provide specialized services for retarded people who are medically unstable, or multiply handicapped, or behaviorally disturbed. An ideological preference for one type of service, opposed to another, should play only a small role in the destiny of the individual.

Community placement is not necessarily high-quality placement. We must be as critical of deficiencies in community placement as we have been of deficiencies in institutions. We must develop the same safeguards for community care as we have tried to do for institutional care. Ideology should not blind our critical judgment.

But it is not ideology that guides our belief that the weakness of the community movement, in some areas, and the continued need for institutions, in some places, is only an unfortunate deflection of the central thrust. The future will only bring a firmer resolve to advance community programs for handicapped people. As the strength of community placement grows around the country, large institutions will continue to shrink, and then they will disappear. It is our resolve to speed that process. But that resolve should be made of equal parts: to be alive to the deficiencies of institutional care, so to dismantle the institutions; and to be alive to the weaknesses of community programs, so to make them better.

Chapter 35

The Association for Retarded Citizens

In the fall of 1950, a group of 11 parents who had one feature in common—a retarded son or daughter—met to share their frustrations and hopes. Their frustrations revolved around persistent professional and societal disinterest in the educational, medical, and developmental needs of their children. Their hopes stemmed from the developmental attainments that were readily observable in their children. Their own personal investment had directly produced these attainments, which were viewed as impossible by the professional community in the early 1950s in America. This group of parents founded the national Association for Retarded Children (ARC). Within five years, the organization had spread into half of the states; state chapters organized into local chapters and, building on the grassroots support, became a major voice of help and hope for retarded citizens everywhere.

Achievements were made toward the original organizational goal of prevention and amelioration of mental retardation. The group commissioned a benchmark study of all known research findings concerning mental retardation and published its results in the book *Mental Subnormality* by Masland et al. (1958). This book outlined what was known in world literature regarding research dimensions of mental retardation. Following its wide national distribution, *Mental Subnormality* became the template for the founding of the series of Mental Retardation Research Centers by President John Kennedy in 1960. The issue of hope had been recast into a national research commitment aimed at understanding the preventive aspects of mental retardation.

The allied goal of "amelioration" was initiated in a series of opportunity centers (i.e., parent-operated developmental centers), which were the forerunners of the "schools for the trainable" of the early 1960s. These opportunity centers became living laboratories that clearly showed that young retarded children did grow, albeit slowly and at a developmental pace different from the norm.

These national activities gained enormous strength in the national ARC movement in the early 1960s. By the end of that decade, there was an association in every state, and its local units numbered more than 1,000. Recruitment of members became easier as public education and research grew and, most importantly, as parents of the retarded witnessed concrete examples of a program that actually helped their sons and daughters. This era of the ARC movement has been termed the "provide" phase of the national organization. The association reached out to provide services for the mentally retarded amid a national professional landscape of disinterested service providers. While diffident professionals could no longer argue against the significant and demonstrable indices of developmental advancement seen in the retarded citizens who participated in ARC programs, the ARC realized that unless their organizations obtained some significant local, state, and national legislative changes, their opportunity centers could end up as isolated islands of developmental excellence for mentally retarded people.

This shift in ideology prompted major reinvestments by the ARC, both in parental power and financial contributions. They established governmental affairs offices throughout the country. They decided that, if need be, the rights of their children would be aggressively reaffirmed in the courts and codified into federal and state laws so that a "local privilege" (i.e., to attend school, if one is available) would become a right (i.e., to enter into school like their nonretarded peers).

The "obtain" phase of the ARC movement in our country is a remarkable example of the awesome power of citizens who band together to "change the system" via proven pathways of public education, individualized and group lobbying efforts, and remarkable persistence. This phase brought the enlightened right to education for all retarded citizens (i.e., PL 94-142), the Social Security amendments to help provide retarded citizens with the financial wherewithal for their basic human needs, and the major push for the right to a community-based, rather than institutional-based, system of services, which includes residential settings of a normalized size.

In the mid-1970s, the association changed its name to the Association for Retarded Citizens of the United States—a change that directly reflected the parents' awareness that the children of the 1950s were now adults and needed further attention within autonomous settings away from the primary family. This was a courageous step, beyond the mere changing of a title, for it directly attacked the societal prejudice of viewing adult retarded persons as incompetent or nonproductive. Providing the key personal and social ingredients for the adult retarded citizen (i.e., opportunities for work and autonomous living management) became the main thrust of the ARC movement of the 1970s (Menolascino 1977).

The 1980s continue to witness a very strong ARC presence in our nation's ongoing commitment to provide modern services for all of its retarded citizens. Increasingly, the obtain phase of the ARC national movement is being replaced by a strong focus on monitoring. There is a push to provide active monitoring of the quality of care provided in institutional- or community-based programs. Behavioral treatments are monitored to eliminate aversive techniques, and educational programs are monitored so as to ensure that they are of high quality and as generically integrated as possible. The goal that permeates the current agenda of national activity of the ARC has provided the vital difference in the progression of community-based, human-scale living and working opportunities for the retarded. It has been the key to avoiding the nontreatment posture that continues to plague the care of the chronically mentally ill in our country, and it has clearly shown that the presence of strong advocacy constitutes an important difference in national perceptions and commitments to the care of its chronically handicapped citizens.

References

Section 1
Mental Retardation

Ack M: Julie: The treatment of a case of developmental retardation. Psychoanal Stud Child 21:127–141, 1966

Adams RD, Victor M: Epilepsy and other seizure disorders, in Principles of Neurology (3rd ed). New York, McGraw-Hill, 1985

Adamson WC, Nellis BP, Runge G, et al: Use of tranquilizers with mentally deficient patients. Am J Dis Child 96:159–164, 1958

Albin J: The treatment of pica (scavenging) behavior in the retarded: a critical analysis and implications for research. Ment Retard 15:14–18, 1977

Albin JL, Demitz S: Psychotherapy with disturbed and defective children: an evaluation of changes in behavior and attitudes. Am J Ment Defic 69:560–567, 1965

Alexandris A, Lundell FW: Effect of thioridazine, amphetamine, and placebo on the hyperkinetic syndrome and cognitive area in mentally deficient children. Can Med Assoc J 98:92–96, 1968

Albini J, Dinitz S: Psychotherapy with disturbed and defective children: an evaluation of changes in behavior and attitudes. Am J Ment Def 69:560–567, 1965

Alford JD, Locke BJ: Clinical responses to psychopathology of mentally retarded persons. Am J Ment Defic 89:195–197, 1984

Alper S, Alper J: Issues in community-based vocational programming: institutionalization of staff, in Expanding Opportunities: Vocational Education for the Handicapped. Edited by Hansen C. Seattle, Wash, University of Washington, PDAS, 1980, pp 121–143

Aman MG: Drugs, learning and the psychotherapies, in Pediatric Psychopharmacology: The Use of Behavior Modifying Drugs in Children. Edited by Werry JS. New York, Brunner/Mazel, 1978

Aman MG: Psychotropic drugs and learning problems: a selective review. Journal of Learning Disabilities 13:87–96, 1980

Aman MG: Stimulant drug effects in developmental disorders and hyperactivity: toward a resolution of disparate findings. J Autism Dev Disord 12:385–398, 1982

Aman MG: Psychoactive drugs in mental retardation, in Treatment Issues and Innovations in Mental Retardation. Edited by New York, Plenum Press, 1983, pp 455–513

Aman MG, Singh NN: The usefulness of thioridazine for treating childhood disorders: fact or folklore? Am J Ment Defic 84:331–338, 1980

Aman MG, Singh NN: Aberrant Behavior Checklist. Canterbury, New Zealand, University of Canterbury, 1985

Aman MG, Singh NN: A critical appraisal of recent drug research in mental retardation: the Goldwater studies. J Ment Defic Res 30:203–216, 1986

Aman MG, Singh NN: Patterns of drug use, methodological considerations, measurement techniques, and future trends, in Psychopharmacology of the Developmental Disabilities. Edited by Aman MG, Singh NN. New York, Springer-Verlag, 1988

Aman MG, Singh NN: Pharmacological intervention: an update, in Handbook of Mental Retardation (2nd ed). Edited by Matson JL, Mulick JA. New York, Pergamon Press, in press

Aman MG, White AJ: Thioridazine dose effects with reference to stereotypic behavior in mentally retarded residents. J Autism Dev Disord, in press

Aman MG, Marks R, Turbott SH, et al: The clinical effects of methylphenidate and thioridazine in intellectually subaverage children with behavior disorders. Manuscript in preparation. Columbus, Ohio State University, 1988

Aman MG, Teehan CJ, White AJ, et al: Haloperidol treatment with chronically medicated residents: dose effects on clinical behavior and reinforcement contingencies. Am J Ment Retard, in press

American Psychiatric Association: Diagnostic and Statistical Manual of Mental Disorders, 1st ed (DSM-I). Washington, DC, American Psychiatric Association, 1952

American Psychiatric Association: Diagnostic and Statistical Manual of Mental Disorders, 2nd ed (DSM-II). Washington, DC, American Psychiatric Association, 1968

American Psychiatric Association: Diagnostic and Statistical Manual of Mental Disorders, 3rd ed (DSM-III). Washington, DC, American Psychiatric Association, 1980

American Psychiatric Association: Diagnostic and Statistical Manual of Mental Disorders, 3rd ed, revised (DSM-III-R). Washington, DC, American Psychiatric Association, 1987

Anderson LT, Dancis J, Alpert M, et al. Punishment learning and self-mutilation in Lesch-Nyhan disease. Nature 265:461–463, 1977

Anderson LT, Dancis J, Alpert M: Behavioral contingencies and self-mutilation in Lesch-Nyhan disease. J Consult Clin Psychol 46:529–536, 1978

Anderson LT, Campbell M, Grega DM, et al. Haloperidol in the treatment of infantile autism: effects on learning and behavioral symptoms. Am J Psychiatry 141:1195–1201, 1984

Anton AH, Greer M: Dextroamphetamine, catecholamines and behavior. Arch Neurol 21:248–252, 1969

Azrin NH, Armstrong PM: The "mini-meal"—a method for teaching eating skills to the profoundly retarded. Ment Retard 11:9–13, 1973

Azrin NH, Kaplan SJ, Foxx RM: Autism reversal: eliminating stereotyped self-stimulation of retarded individuals. Am J Ment Defic 78:241–248, 1973

Baer DM, Sherman JA: Reinforcement control of generalized imitation in young children. J Exp Child Psychol 1:37–49, 1964

Bailey EJ, Bricker D: The efficacy of early intervention for severely handicapped infants and young children. Topics in Early Childhood Special Education 4:30–51, 1984

Baker BL: Parents as teachers: issues in training, in Parent-Professional Partnerships in Developmental Disability Services. Edited by Mulick JA, Pueschel SH. Cambridge, Mass, Academic Guild Publishers, 1983

Ball TS, Hendrickson H, Clayton J: A special feeding technique for chronic regurgitation. Am J Ment Defic 78:486–493, 1974

Bandura A: A social learning interpretation of psychological dysfunctions, in Foundations of Abnormal Behavior. Edited by London P, Rosehan D. New York, Holt, Rinehart & Winston, 1968

Bandura A: Principles of Behavior Modification. New York, Holt, Rinehart & Winston, 1969a

Bandura A: Social Learning Theory. Englewood Cliffs, NJ, Holt, Rinehart & Winston, 1969b

Bandura A: Aggression: A Social Learning Analysis. Englewood Cliffs, NJ, Prentice-Hall, 1973

Bandura A: Self-efficacy: toward a unifying theory of behavior change. Psychol Rev 191–215, 1977

Barkley RA, Zuynick S: Reduction of stereotypic body contortions using physical restraint and DRO. J Behav Ther Exp Psychiatry 7:167–170, 1976

Barltrop D: The prevalence of pica. Am J Dis Child 112:116–123, 1966

Barron J, Sandman CA: Relationship of sedative/hypnotic response to self-injurious behavior and stereotypy by mentally retarded clients. Am J Ment Defic 88:177–186, 1983

Barron J, Sandman CA: Self-injurious behavior and stereotypy in an institutionalized mentally retarded population. Appl Res Ment Retard 5:499–511, 1984

Barron J, Sandman CA: Paradoxical excitement to sedative/hypnotics in mentally retarded clients. Am J Ment Defic 90:124–129, 1985

Bates P, Pancsofar E: Project EARN. British Journal of Mental Subnormality XXIX, 29 (Part 2):97–103, 1983

Bates P, Wehman P: Behavior management with the mentally retarded: an empirical analysis of the research. Ment Retard 15:9–12, 1977

Baum WM: The correlation-based law of effect. J Exp Anal Behav 10:137–153, 1977

Baumeister AA: Origins and control of stereotyped movements, in Quality of Life in Severely and Profoundly Retarded People: Research Foundations for Improvement (Monograph No 3). Edited by Meyers LE. The American Association on Mental Deficiency, 1978

Baumeister AA, Forehand R: Social facilitation of body rocking in severely retarded patients. J Clin Psychol 26:303–305, 1970

Baumeister AA, Forehand R: Effects of extinction of an instrumental response on stereotyped body rocking in severe retardates. The Psychological Record 21:235–240, 1971

Baumeister AA, Forehand R: Effects of contingent shock and verbal command on body rocking of retardates. J Clin Psychol 28:586–590, 1972

Baumeister AA, Forehand R: Stereotyped acts, in International Review of Research in Mental Retardation, Vol 6. Edited by Ellis NR. New York, Academic Press, 1973, pp 55–96

Baumeister AA, Rollings P: Self-injurious behavior, in International Review of Research in Mental Retardation, Vol 9. Edited by Ellis NR. New York, Academic Press, 1976

Beier DC: Behavioral disturbances in the mentally retarded, in Mental Retardation: A Review of Research. Edited by Stevens HÁ, Heber R. Chicago, University of Chicago Press, 1964

Bell A, Zubek JP: Effects of deanol on the intellectual performance of mental defectives. Can J Psychol 15:172–175, 1961

Bellamy GT, Inman DP, Yeates J: Workshop supervision: evaluation of a procedure for production management with the severely retarded. Ment Retard 16:317–319, 1979

Bellamy GT, Rhodes LE, Bourbeau PE, et al: Mental retardation services in sheltered workshops and day activity programs: consumer benefits and policy alternatives, in Competitive Employment: Issues and Strategies. Edited by Rusch FR. Baltimore, Paul H. Brookes Publishers, 1986, pp 257–271

Bentoviv A: The clinical approach to feeding disorders of childhood. J Psychosom Res 14:267–276, 1970

Berchou RC: Effect of a consultant pharmacist on medication use in an institution for the mentally retarded. Am J Hosp Pharm 39:1671–1674, 1982

Berkson G: Stereotyped movements of mental defectives, V: ward behavior and its relation to an experimental task. Am J Ment Defic 69:253–264, 1964

Berkson G: Abnormal stereotyped motor acts, in Comparative Psychopathology. Edited by Zubin J, Hunt HF. New York, Grune & Stratton, 1967, pp 76–9

Berkson G: Repetitive stereotyped behaviors. Am J Ment Defic 88:239–246, 1983

Berkson G, Davenport RK, Jr: Stereotyped movements of mental defectives, I: initial study. Am J Ment Defic 66:849–852, 1962

Berkson G, Mason WA: Stereotyped movements of mental defectives, IV: the effects of toys and the character of the acts. Am J Ment Defic 68:511–524, 1964

Berkson G, Mason WA, Saxon SV: Situation and stimulus effects on stereotyped behaviors of chimpanzees. J Comp Physiol Psychol 56:786–792, 1963

Berlin I, McCullough G, Lisha E, et al: Intractable episodic vomiting in a three-year-old child. Psychiatr Q 31:228–249, 1957

Bernal ME: Behavioral treatment of a child's eating problem. J Behav Ther Exp Psychiatry 3:43–50, 1972

Bialer I: Psychotherapy and other adjustment techniques with the mentally retarded, in Mental Retardation, Appraisal, Education and Rehabilitation. Edited by Baumeister AA. Chicago, Aldine, 1967

Bijou S: What psychology has to offer education—now. J Appl Behav Anal 3:63–71, 1970

Birmaher B, Quintana H, Greenhill LL: Methylphenidate treatment of hyperactive autistic children. J Am Acad Child Adolesc Psychiatry 27:248–251, 1988

Blacklidge VY, Ekblad RL: The effectiveness of methylphenidate hydrochloride (Ritalin) on learning and behavior in public school educable mentally retarded children. Pediatrics 47:923–926, 1971

Blockley J, Miller G: Feeding techniques with cerebral palsied children. Physiotherapy 57:300–308, 1971

Blomquist HK, Bohman M, Edvinsson SO, et al: Frequency of the fragile X syndrome in infantile autism. Clin Genet 27:113–117, 1985

Boe RB: Economical procedures for the reduction of aggression in a residential setting. Ment Retard 15:25–28, 1972

Bolstad OD, Johnson SM: Self-regulation in the modification of disruptive behavior. J Appl Behav Anal 5:443–454, 1972

Bosley E. Teaching the cerebral palsied to chew. Cerebral Palsy Journal 25:9–10, 1966

Brady, JP: Social skills training for psychiatric patients, II: clinical outcome studies. Am J Psychiatry 141:491–498, 1984

Brawley E, Harris F, Allen K, et al: Behavior and modification of an autistic child. Behavior Sci 4:87–97, 1969

Breese GR, Baumeister A, McCown TJ, et al: Behavioral differences between neonatal and adult 6-hydroxydopamine-treated rats to dopamine agonists: relevance to neurological symptoms in clinical syndromes with reduced brain dopamine. J Pharmacol Exp Ther 231:343–353, 1984a

Breese GR, Baumeister A, McCown TJ, et al: Neonatal-6-hydroxydopamine treatment: model of susceptibility for self-mutilation in the Lesch-Nyhan syndrome. Pharmacol Biochem Behav 21:459–461, 1984b

Bregman S: Assertiveness training for mentally retarded adults. Ment Retard 22:12–16, 1984

Bricker DD: An analysis of early intervention programs: attendant issues and future directions, in Special Education: Research and Trends. Edited by Morris R, Biatt B. New York, Pergamon Press, 1986

Broden M, Bruce C, Mitchell MA: Effects of teacher attention of attending behavior of two boys at adjacent desks. J Appl Behav Anal 3:199–203, 1970

Brown L, Nietupski J, Hamre-Nietupski S: The criterion of ultimate functioning and public school services for the severely handicapped student, in Hey, Don't Forget About Me: Education's Investment in the Severely, Profoundly and Multiply

Handicapped. Edited by Thomas MA. Reston, Virg, Council for Exceptional Children, 1976, pp 2–15

Brown L, Nisbet J, Ford A, et al: The critical need for nonschool instruction in educational programs for severely handicapped students. Journal of the Association for the Severely Handicapped 8:71–77, 1983

Brown WT, Jenkins EC, Friedman E, et al: Autism is associated with the fragile X syndrome. Autism Dev Disord 12:303–308, 1982

Brown WT, Jenkins EC, Cohen IL, et al: Fragile X and autism: a multicenter survey. Am J Med Genet 23:341–352, 1986

Browne TR, Dreifuss FE, Dyken PR, et al: Ethosuximide in the treatment of absence (petit mal) seizure. Neurology 25:515–524, 1975

Bruininks RH, Hauber FA, Kudls MJ: National survey of community residential facilities: a profile of facilities and residents in 1977. Am J Ment Defic 4:470–478, 1980

Budzynski TH, Stoyva JM: An instrument for producing deep muscle relaxation by means of analog information feedback. J Appl Behav Anal 2:231–238, 1969

Burchard JD: Systematic socialization: a programmed environment for the habilitation of antisocial retardates. The Psychological Record 17:461–476, 1967

Burchard J, Tyler V: The modification of delinquent behavior through operant conditioning. Behav Res Ther 2:245–250, 1965

Burk HW, Menolascino FJ: Haloperidol in emotionally disturbed mentally retarded individuals. Am J Psychiatry 124:1589–1591, 1968

Burman D: Nutrition in early childhood, in Textbook of Pediatric Nutrition. Edited by McLaren DS, Burman D. New York, Churchill Livingston, 1976

Burton A: Psychotherapy with the mentally retarded. Am J Ment Defic 58:486–489, 1954

Butlin AT, Wolfendale L, Danta G: The effects of anticonvulsants on memory function in epileptic patients: preliminary findings. Clin Exp Neurol 17:79–84, 1980

Camfield CS, Chaplin S, Doyle A, et al: Side effects of phenobarbital in toddlers: behavioral and cognitive aspects. J Pediatr 95:361–365, 1979

Campbell M: Pharmacotherapy in early infantile autism. Biol Psychiatry 10:399–423, 1975

Campbell M, Fish B, Shapiro T, et al: Imipramine in pre-school autistic and schizophrenic children. Journal of Autism and Childhood Schizophrenia 1:267–282, 1971

Campbell M, Fish B, Korein J, et al: Lithium and chlorpromazine: a controlled crossover study of hyperactive severely disturbed young children. Journal of Autism and Childhood Schizophrenia 2:234–263, 1972a

Campbell M, Fish B, David R, et al: Response to tri-iodothyronine and dextroamphetamine: a study of preschool schizophrenic children. Journal of Autism and Childhood Schizophrenia 2:343–358, 1972b

Campbell M, Small AM, Collins, PJ, et al: Levodopa and levoamphetamine: a crossover study in young schizophrenic children. Current Therapeutic Research 19:70–86. 1976

Campbell M, Anderson LT, Meier M, et al: A comparison of haloperidol and behavior therapy and their interaction in autistic children. J Am Acad Child Psychiatry 17:640–655, 1978

Campbell M, Anderson LT, Green WH: Behavior-disordered and aggressive children: new advances in pharmacotherapy. Developmental and Behavioral Pediatrics 4:265–271, 1983

Campbell PH: Problem-Oriented Approaches to Feeding the Handicapped Child. Akron, Ohio, The Children's Hospital of Akron, 1976

Campbell PH: Assessing oral-motor skills in severely handicapped persons: an analysis of normal and abnormal patterns of movement, in Teaching the Severely Handicapped, Vol 4. Edited by York RL, Edgar E. Seattle, American Association for the Severely and Profoundly Handicapped, 1979

Cantalapiedra MA, DeWeerdt C, Frederick F: Le role psychotherapique de l'educateur dans un externat pour jeunes enfants. Revue de Neuropsychiatrie Infantile 25:787–811, 1977

Capobianco RJ, Cole DA: Social behavior of mentally retarded children. Am J Ment Defic 64:638–651, 1960

Carr EG: The motivation of self-injurious behavior. Psychol Bull 84:800–816, 1977

Carter C: Nortriptyline HCL as a tranquilizer for disturbed mentally retarded patients: a controlled study. Am J Med Sci 251:465–467, 1960

Castells S, Chakrabarti C, Winsberg BG, et al: Effects of L.5-hydroxytryptophan on monoamine and amino acids turnover in the Lesch-Nyhan syndrome. J Autism Dev Disord 9:95, 1979

Cataldo MG, Harris J: The biological basis for self-injury in the mentally retarded. Analysis and Intervention in Developmental Disabilities 2:21–39, 1982

Certo N, Haring N, York R: Public School Integration of Severely Handicapped Students. Baltimore, Paul H. Brookes, 1984

Chadsey-Rusch J: Identifying and teaching valued social behaviors, in Competitive Employment Issues and Strategies. Edited by Rusch FR. Baltimore, Paul H. Brookes Publishers, 1986

Chandler M, Gualtieri CT, Fahs JJ: Other psychotropic drugs: stimulants, antidepressants, the anxiolytics, and lithium, in Psychopharmacology of the Developmental Disabilities. Edited by Aman MG, Singh NN. New York, Springer-Verlag, 1988

Chase MD: The practical application of psychotherapy in an institution for the mentally deficient. Am J Ment Defic 58:337–341, 1953

Chess, RS: Psychiatric treatment of the mentally retarded child with behavior problems. Am J Orthopsychiatry 32:863–869, 1962

Chess S, Korn SJ, Fernandez PB: Psychiatric Disorders of Children with Congenital Rubella. New York, Brunner/Mazel, 1972

Chisolm JJ, Harrison HE: The exposure of children to lead. Pediatrics 18:943–957, 1956

Christensen DE: Effects of combining methylphenidate and classroom token system in modifying hyperactive behavior. Am J Ment Defic 80:266–276, 1975

Claghorn JL: A double-blind comparison of haloperidol (Haldol) and thioridazine (Mellaril) in outpatient children. Current Therapeutic Research 14:785–789, 1972

Clancy H, Entsch M, Rendle-Short J: Infantile autism: the correction of feeding abnormalities. Dev Med Child Neurol 11:569–578, 1969

Clausen J, Fineman M, Henry CE, et al: The effect of Deaner (2-dimethyl-aminoethanol) on mentally retarded subjects. Training School Bulletin 57:3–12, 1960

Cleland CC, McGavern ML, Case JC: Daybook analysis of disruptive behaviors of the profoundly retarded. Ment Retard 14:33–35, 1976

Coffee K, Crawford J: Nutritional problems commonly encountered in the developmentally handicapped, in Feeding the Handicapped Child. Edited by Smith MA. Memphis, University of Tennessee Child Development Center, 1971

Cohen HG, Leland H: The workshop group: a case history of group processes among institutionalized mentally retarded men. Ment Retard 15:45–46, 1978

Cohen MN, Sprague RL: Survey of Drug Usage in Two Midwestern Institutions for the Retarded. Presented at the Gatlinburg Conference on Research in Mental Retardation. Gatlinburg, Tenn, 1977

Cohn R, Nardini JE: The correlation of bilateral occipital slow activity in the human EEG with certain disorders of behavior. Am J Psychiatry 115:44–48, 1958

Coleman M, Gillberg C: The Biology of the Autistic Syndromes. New York, Praeger, 1985

Conners CK, Kramer R, Rothschild GH, et al: Treatment of young delinquent boys with diphenylhydantoin sodium and methylphenidate. Arch Gen Psychiatry 24:156–160, 1971

Conroy JW: Trends in deinstitutionalization of the mentally retarded. Ment Retard 15:44–46, 1977

Cooper AF, Fowlie HC: Control of gross self-mutilation with lithium carbonate. Br J Psychiatry 122:370–371, 1973

Corbett JA: Psychiatric morbidity and mental retardation, in Psychiatric Illness and Mental Handicap. Edited by James FE, Smith RP. London, Gaskell Press, 1979

Cotzin M: Group therapy with mentally defective problem boys. Am J Ment Defic 53:268–283, 1948

Craft M: Mental disorder in the defective: a psychiatric survey among in-patients. Amer J Ment Def 63:829–834, 1959

Crink KA, Sulzbacher S, Snow J: Preventing mental retardation associated with gross obesity in the Prader-Willi syndrome. Pediatrics 66:787–798, 1980

Crocker J: A phonological model of children's articulation competence. J Speech Hear Disord 34:203–213, 1969

Crowley FJ: Psychotherapy for the mentally retarded: a survey and projective consideration. Training School Bulletin (Vineland) 62:5–11, 1965

Cutler M, Little JW, Strauss AA: The effect of Benzedrine on mentally deficient children. Am J Ment Defic 45:59–65, 1940/1941

Danford DE, Huber AM: Pica among mentally retarded adults. Am J Ment Defic 87:141–146, 1982

Danford DE, Smith JC, Huber AM: Pica and mineral status in the mentally retarded. Am J Clin Nutr 35:958–967, 1982

Daniel AE, Menninger K: Mentally retarded defendants: competency and criminal responsibility. The American Journal of Forensic Psychiatry 4:145–156, 1983

Dasheiff RM: Benzodiazepine treatment for Lesch-Nyhan syndrome? Dev Med Child Neurol 22:101, 1980

Davis KR, Shapiro LJ: Exploring group process as a means of reaching the mentally retarded. Social Casework 60:330–337, 1979

Davis KV: The effect of drugs on stereotyped and nonstereotyped operant behaviors in retardates. Psychopharmacology (Berlin) 22:195–213, 1971

Davis KV, Sprague RL, Werry JS: Stereotyped behavior and activity level in severe retardates: the effect of drugs. Am J Ment Defic 73:721–727, 1969

Davis RR, Rogers ES: Social skills training with persons who are mentally retarded. Ment Retard 23:186–196, 1985

Dekaban AS, Lehman EJB: Effects of different dosages of anticonvulsant drugs on mental performance in patients with chronic epilepsy. Acta Neurol Scand 52:319–330, 1975

Denton LR: Psychotherapy with mentally retarded children. Bulletin of the Maritime Psychological Association 8:20–27, 1959

Dodrill C: Diphenylhydantoin serum levels, toxicity and neuropsychological performance in patients with epilepsy. Epilepsia 16:593–600, 1975

Doke LA, Epstein LH: Oral overcorrection: side effects and extended applications. J Exp Child Psychol 20:496–511, 1975

Dostal T, Zvotsky P: Antiaggressive effect of lithium salts in severe mentally retarded adolescents. International Psychopsychiatry 5:302–307, 1970

Douglas VI: Differences between normal and hyperkinetic children, in Clinical Use of Stimulant Drugs in Children. Edited by Conners C. Amsterdam, American Elsevier, 1974

Dunn, LM: Special education for the mildly retarded: is much of it justifiable? Except Child 35:5–22, 1968

Eaton LF, Menolascino FJ: Psychiatric disorders in the mentally retarded: types, problems and challenges. Am J Psychiatry 139:1297–1303, 1982

Eleftheriou BE, Scott JP: The physiology of aggression and defeat. New York, Plenum Press, 1971

Ellenor GL: Reducing irrational antipsychotic polypharmacy prescribing. Hospital Pharmacy 12:369–376, 1977

Englemann S, Bruner E: DISTAR Reading Level 1. Chicago, Science Research Associates, 1974

Epstein H, Doke L, Sajwaji T, et al: Generality and side effects of overcorrection. J Appl Behav Anal 7:385–390, 1974

Eron LD, Huesmann LR: The relation of prosocial behavior to the development of aggression and psychopathology. Aggressive Behavior 10:201–211, 1984

Evans RW, Gualtieri CT: Carbamazepine: a neuropsychological and psychiatric profile. Clin Neuropharmacol 8:221–241, 1985

Evans RW, Clay T, Gualtieri CT: Carbamazepine in pediatric psychiatry. J Am Acad Child Psychiatry 2:2–8, 1987

Fahs JJ: Insomnia, in Manual of Clinical Problems in Adult Ambulatory Care. Edited by Dornbrand L, Hoole AJ, Fletcher RH, et al. Boston, Little, Brown & Co, 1985

Favell J: Reduction of stereotypies by reinforcement of toy play. Ment Retard 11:21–23, 1973

Favell JE, Azrin NH, Baumeister AA, et al: The treatment of self-injurious behavior. Behavior Therapy 13:529–554, 1982

Fielding LT, Murphy RJ, Reagan MW, et al: An assessment program to reduce drug use with the mentally retarded. Hosp Community Psychiatry 31:771–773, 1980

Fingado ML, Marta L, Kini JF, et al: A thirty-day residential training program for retarded children. Mental Retardation 8:42–45, 1970

Finnie NR: Handling the Young Cerebral Palsied Child at Home (2nd ed). New York, EP Dutton & Co, 1974

Fisher L, Wolfson I: Group therapy of mental defectives. Am J Ment Defic 57:463–476, 1953

Fisher GW, Murray F, Walley MR, et al: A controlled trial of imipramine in the treatment of nocturnal enuresis in mentally subnormal patients. Am J Ment Defic 67:536–538, 1963

Forehand R, Baumeister AA: Body rocking and activity level as a function of prior motion restraint. Am J Ment Defic 74:608–610, 1970a

Forehand R, Baumeister AA: Effect of frustration on stereotyped body rocking: follow-up. Percept Mot Skills 31:894, 1970b

Forehand R, Baumeister AA: Stereotyped body rocking as a function of situation, IQ and time. J Clin Psychol 27:324–326, 1971

Forehand R, Baumeister AA: Deceleration of aberrant behavior among retarded individuals, in Progress in Behavior Modification, Vol 2. Edited by Hersen M, Eisler RM, Miller PM. New York, Academic Press, 1976, pp 223–278

Foster WS: Adjunctive behavior: an under-reported phenomenon in applied behavior analysis. J Appl Behav Anal 11:545–546, 1978

Foxx RM, Azrin NH: The elimination of autistic self stimulatory behavior by overcorrection. J Appl Behav Anal 6:1–14, 1973

Foxx RM, Martin ED: Treatment of scavenging behavior (coprophagy and pica) by overcorrection. Behav Res Ther 13:153–162, 1975

Frankel F, Simmons JQ: Self-injurious behavior in schizophrenic and retarded children. Am J Ment Defic 80:512–522, 1976

Frederiksen LW, Peterson GL: Schedule-induced aggression in humans and animals: a comparative parametric review. Aggressive Behavior 3:57–75, 1977

Freeman RD: Psychopharmacology and the retarded child, in Psychiatric Approaches to Mental Retardation. Edited by Menolascino FJ. New York, Basic Books, 1970

Freidman E: Individual therapy with defective delinquents. Am J Psychiatry 121:1014–1020, 1965

Freinhar JP: Clonazepam treatment of a mentally retarded woman. Am J Psychiatry 142:1513, 1985

Frieden BD: Clinical issues on the physical restraint experience with self-injurious children. Research and the Retarded 4:1–6, 1977

Frieden BD, Johnson HK: Treatment of a retarded child's feces smearing and coprophagic behavior. J Ment Defic Res 23:55–61, 1979

Fryns J: The female and the fragile X. Am J Med Genet 23:157–169, 1986

Fryns JP, Kleczkowska A, Kubien E, et al: Cytogenetic findings in moderate and severe mental retardation. Acta Paediatrica Scandinavica Supplement 313:3–23, 1984

Gadow KD: Prevalence of drug treatment for hyperactivity and other childhood behavior disorders, in Psychosocial Aspects of Drug Treatment for Hyperactivity. Edited by Gadow KD, Loney J. Boulder, Colo, Westview Press, 1981

Gadow KD: Prevalence and efficacy of stimulant drug use with mentally retarded children and youth. Psychopharmacol Bull 21:291–303, 1985

Gadow KD, Kalachnik J: Prevalence and pattern of drug treatment for behavior and seizure disorders of TMR students. Am J Ment Defic 85:588–595, 1981

Gandelman R: Relative contributions of aggression and reproduction to behavioral endocrinology. Aggressive Behavior 10:123–133, 1984

Gardner WI: Occurrence of severe depressive reactions in the mentally retarded. Am J Psychiatry 124:386–388, 1967

Gardner WI, Cole CL: A structured learning habilitation approach: use with the mentally retarded presenting emotional and behavioral disorders, in Habilitation Practices with the Developmentally Disabled Who Present Behavioral and Emotional Disorders. Edited by Karan OC, Gardner WI. Madison, Wis, Rehabilitation Research and Training Center in Mental Retardation, 1983, pp 39–60

Gardner WI, Cole CL, Berry DL, et al: Reduction of disruptive behaviors in mentally retarded adults. Ment Retard 7:76–96, 1983

Gelenberg AJ: Anxiety, in The Practitioner's Guide to Psychoactive Drugs (2nd ed). Edited by Bassuk EL, Schoonover SC, Gelenberg AJ. New York, Plenum Press, 1983

Geller B, Guttmacher LB, Bleeg M: Coexistence of childhood onset pervasive developmental disorder and attention deficit disorder with hyperactivity. Am J Psychiatry 138:388–389, 1981

Gertenrich RL: A simple, adaptable drinking device for mental retardates lacking arm/hand control. Ment Retard 8:51, 1970

Gibbs DA, McFadyen IR, Crawford MD, et al. First-trimester diagnosis of Lesch-Nyhan syndrome. Lancet 1180–1183, 1984

Gifford JL, Rusch FR, Martin JE, et al: Autonomy and adaptability in work behavior of retarded clients, in International Review of Research on Mental Retardation, Vol 12. Edited by Ellis N, Bray N. New York, Academic Press, 1984, pp 285–318

Gilbert S, Spellacy E, Watts RWE: Problems in the behavioral treatment of self-injury in the Lesch-Nyhan syndrome. Dev Med Child Neurol 21:795–800, 1979

Goddard H: The Kallikak Family. New York, MacMillan, 1912

Goetze U, Grunberg F, Berkowitz B: Lithium carbonate in the management of hyperactive aggressive behavior of the mentally retarded. Compr Psychiatry 18:599–606, 1977

Goh K, Herrmann MA, Campbell RG, et al: Abnormal chromosome in Prader-Willi syndrome. Clin Gen, 26:597–601, 1984

Goldberg JB, Kurland AA: Dilantin treatment of hospitalized cultural-familial retardation. J Nerv Ment Dis 150:133–137, 1970

Goldfine PE, McPherson PM, Heath A, et al: Association of fragile X syndrome with autism. Am J Psychiatry 142:108–110, 1985

Goldfried MR, Davison GC: Clinical behavior therapy. New York, Holt Rinehart & Winston, 1976

Goldfried MR, Kent RN: Traditional versus behavioral personality assessment: a comparison of methodological and theoretical assumptions. Psychol Bull 77:490, 1972

Goldfried MR, Sprafkin JN: Behavioral Personality Assessment. Morristown, NJ, General Learning Press, 1974

Goldstein AP, Keller HR, Erne D: Changing the Abusive Parent. Champaign, Ill, Research Press, 1985

Goldstein M, Anderson LT, Reuben R, et al. Self-mutilation in Lesch-Nyhan disease is caused by dopaminergic denervation. Lancet 338–339, 1985

Goodman L, Rothman R: The development of a group counseling program in a clinic for retarded children. Am J Ment Defic 65:789, 1961

Gostason R: Psychiatric illness among the mentally retarded: a Swedish population study. Acta Psychiatr Scand 71(Suppl 318):1–117, 1985

Gottlieb J: Mainstreaming: fulfilling the promise? Am J Ment Defic 86:115–126, 1981

Gouge AL, Ekvall SW: Diets of handicapped children: physical, psychological and socioeconomic correlations. Am J Ment Defic 80:149–157, 1975

Grabowski SW: Haloperidol for control of severe emotional reaction in mentally retarded patients. Diseases of the Nervous System 34:315–317, 1973a

Grabowski SW: Safety and effectiveness of haloperidol for mentally retarded behaviorally disordered and hyperkinetic patients. Current Therapeutic Research 15:856–861, 1973b

Gray JA: Gamma-aminobutyrate, the benzodiazepines and the septohippocampal system, in Benzodiazepines Divided: A Multidisciplinary Review. Edited by Trimble MR. New York, John Wiley & Sons, 1983

Green JB: Association of behavior disorder with an electroencephalographic focus in children without seizures. Neurology 11:337–344, 1961

Green RJ, Hoats DL, Hornick AJ: Music distortion: a new technique for behavior modification. The Psychological Record 20:107–109, 1970

Greenblatt DJ, Shader RI: Pharmacotherapy of anxiety with benzodiazepines and beta-adrenergic blockers, in Psychopharmacology: A Generation of Progress. Edited by Lipton MA, DiMascio A, Killam KF. New York, Raven Press, 1978

Greenspan S, Shoultz B: Why mentally retarded adults lose their jobs: social incompetence as a factor in work adjustment. Appl Res Ment Retard 2:23–38, 1981

Griffin JC, Williams DE, Stark MT, et al: Self-injurious behavior: a statewide prevalence survey, assessment of severe cases and follow-up of aversive programs, in Advances in the Treatment of Self-Injurious Behavior. Edited by Griffin JC, Stark MT, Williams DE, et al. Austin, Tex, Department of Health and Human Services, Texas Planning Council for Developmental Disabilities, 1984

Gross MD, Wilson WC: Behavior disorders of children with cerebral dysrhythmias. Arch Gen Psychiatry 11:610–619, 1964

Gualtieri CT: Imipramine and children: a review and some speculations about the mechanism of drug action. Diseases of the Nervous System 38:368–375, 1977

Gualtieri CT, Hicks RE: The neuropsychology of stimulant effects in attention deficit disorder, in Attention Deficit Disorder, Vol 3. Edited by Bloomingdale L. New York, Spectrum Publications, in press

Gualtieri CT, Keppel JM: Psychopharmacology in the mentally retarded and a few related issues. Pscyhopharmacol Bull 21:304–309, 1985

Gualtieri CT, Golden RN, Fahs JJ: New developments in pediatric psychopharmacology. Developmental and Behavioral Pediatrics 4:202–209, 1983

Guess D, Rutherford G: Experimental attempts to reduce stereotyping among blind retardates. Am J Ment Defic 71:984–986, 1967

Guey J, Charles C, Coquery C, et al: Study of psychological effects of ethosuximide (Zarontin) on 25 children suffering from petit mal epilepsy. Epilepsia 8:129–141, 1967

Guidotti A: Synaptic mechanisms in the action of benzodiazepines, in Psychopharmacology: A Generation of Progress. Edited by Lipton MA, DiMascio A, Killam KF. New York, Raven Press, 1978

Gupta C, Wiemann G: A Model for Incorporating Therapeutic Feeding Techniques into the Skill Repertoire of Teachers and Aides in a Residential School Setting for the Severely Multihandicapped. Cambridge, Minn, CADRE Center, 1977

Guskin SL, Bartel NR, MacMillan DL: Perspective of the labeled child, in Issues in the Classification of Children, Vol 2. Edited by Hobbs N. San Francisco, Jossey-Bass, 1975, pp 189–212

Gutelius MF, Millican FK, Layman EM, et al: Nutritional studies of children with pica. Pediatrics 29:1012–1023, 1962

Hagerman RJ, Duyck F: A retrospective evaluation of pipamperone (Dipiperon) in the treatment of behavioral deviations in severely mentally handicapped. Acta Psychiatr Belg 78:392–398, 1978

Hagerman RJ: Misconceptions concerning the fragile X syndrome, in The Fragile X Foundation Newsletter Winter 1986 (Available from The Fragile X Foundation, PO Box 300233, Denver, CO 80203)

Hagerman RJ, Smith AC, Mariner R: Clinical features of the fragile X syndrome, in the Fragile X Syndrome: Diagnosis, Biochemistry and Intervention. Edited by Hagerman RJ, McBogg PM. Dillon, Colo, Spectra Publishing Co, 1983

Hagerman RJ, Jackson AW, Levitas A, et al: The analysis of autism in fifty males with The fragile X syndrome. Am J Med Genet 23:359–374, 1986a

Hagerman RJ, Jackson AW, Levitas A, et al: Oral folic acid versus placebo in the treatment of males with the fragile X syndrome. Am J Med Genet 23:241–262, 1986b

Hall ME: Two feeding appliances. Am J Occup Ther 5:52, 1951

Hamilton J, Standahl J: Suppression of stereotyped screaming behavior in a profoundly retarded institutionalized female. J Exp Child Psychol 7:114–121, 1969

Haring N: Review and analysis of professional preparation for the severely handicapped, in Quality Education for the Severely Handicapped. Edited by Wilcox B, York R. Falls Church, Va, Counterpoint Handcrafted Books, 1982

Hart V: A Team Teaching Practicum for Multiple Handicaps: A Final Report. Nashville, Peabody College, 1972

Hart V: Beginning with the Handicapped. Springfield, Ill, Charles C Thomas, 1974

Hasan MK, Mooney RP: Three cases of manic-depressive illness in mentally retarded adults. Am J Psychiatry 136:1069–1071, 1979

Hayes M: The responsiveness of mentally retarded children to psychotherapy. Smith College Studies in Social Work 47:112–153, 1977

Heaton-Ward WA: Inference and suggestion in a clinical trial (Niamid in mongolism). J Ment Sci 107:115–118, 1961

Heaton-Ward WA: Psychosis in Mental Handicap. The tenth Blake Marsh lecture delivered before the Royal College of Psychiatrists, February 2, 1976. Br J Psychiatry 130:525–533, 1977

Heffley J: Improving nutrient supply for deaf-blind children, in Proceedings: The

Deaf-Blind Child and the Nutritionist, the Social Worker and the Public Health Nurse. Edited by Bomin C. Sacramento, Calif, Southwestern Regional Deaf-Blind Center, 1976

Heiser KF: Psychotherapy in a residential school for mentally retarded children. Training School Bulletin 50:211–218, 1954

Heistad GT, Zimmermann RL: Double-blind assessment of Mellaril in a mentally retarded population using detailed evaluations. Psychopharmacol Bull 15:86–88, 1979

Herrnstein RJ: On the law of effect. J Exp Anal Behav 13:243–266, 1970

Heston LL: Alzheimer's dementia and Down's syndrome: genetic evidence suggesting an association. Ann NY Acad Sci 396:29–37, 1982

Higgenbottam JA, Chow B: Sound-induced drive, prior motion restraint and reduced sensory stimulation effects on rocking behavior in retarded persons. Am J Ment Defic 80:231–233, 1975

Hill BK, Bruininks RH: Maladaptive behavior of mentally retarded individuals in residential facilities. Am J Ment Defic 88:380–387, 1984

Hill BK, Balow EA, Bruininks RH: A national study of prescribed drugs in institutions and community residential facilities for mentally retarded people. Psychopharmacol Bull 21:179–284, 1985

Hixon TJ, Hardy JC: Restricted mobility of the speech articulators in cerebral palsy. J Speech Hear Disord 29:243–306, 1964

Hollis JH: Chlorpromazine: direct measurement of differential behavioral effect. Science 159:1487–1489, 1968

Hollis JH, St. Omer VV: Direct measurement of psychopharmacologic response: effects of chlorpromazine on motor behavior of retarded children. Am J Ment Defic 76:397–407, 1972

Holser-Buehler P: Correction of infantile feeding problems. Am J Occup Ther 24:331–335, 1973

Holvoet JF: The etiology and management of rumination and psycho-genic vomiting: a review, in Life-Threatening Behavior (Monograph No 5, AAMD Monograph Series 29–77). Edited by Hollis J, Meyers CE. Washington, DC, AAMD 1982

Horner RD, Barton ES: Operant techniques in the analysis and modification of self-injurious behavior: a review. Behavior Research of Severe Developmental Disabilities 1:61–91, 1980

Horner RH, Dunlap G, Koegel RL: Generalization and maintenance: life-style changes in applied settings. Baltimore, Paul H. Brookes, 1988

Howard-Peebles PN, Stoddard GR, Mims MG: Familial X-linked mental retardation, verbal disability, and marker X chromosomes. Am J Hum Genet 31:214–222, 1979

Huesmann LR, Eron LD: Cognitive processes and the persistence of aggressive behavior. Aggressive Behavior 10:243–251, 1984

Huguenin NH, Mulick JA: Nonexclusionary timeout: maintenance of appropriate behavior across settings. Appl Res Ment Retard 2:55–67, 1981

Huguenin NH, Weidenmann LE, Mulick JA: Programmed instruction, in Handbook of Mental Retardation. Edited by Matson JL, Mulick JA. New York, Pergamon Press, 1983, pp 443–453

Hurley AD, Sovner R: Diagnosis and treatment of compulsive behaviors in mentally retarded persons. Psychiatric Aspects of Mental Retardation Reviews 3:37–40, 1984

Hutchinson RR: The environmental causes of aggression, in Nebraska Symposium on Motivation: 1972. Edited by Cole JK, Jensen DO. Lincoln, Nebr, University of Nebraska Press, 1973

Hutt SJ, Jackson PM, Belsham A, et al: Perpetual-motor behavior in relation to blood phenobarbitone level: a preliminary report. Dev Med Child Neurol 10:626–632, 1968

Idestrom CM, Schalling D, Carlquist U, et al: Acute effects of diphenylhydantoin in relation to plasma levels. Psychol Med 2:111–120, 1972

Illingworth R, Lister J: The critical or sensitive period with reference to certain feeding problems in infants and children. J Pediatr 65:839–848, 1964

Ingram TTS: Clinical significance of the infantile feeding reflexes. Dev Med Child Neurol 4:159–169, 1962

Inoue F: A clinical pharmacy service to reduce psychotropic medication use in an institution for mentally handicapped persons. Ment Retard 20:70–74, 1982

Intagliata J, Rinck C: Psychoactive drug use in public and community residential facilities for mentally retarded persons. Psychopharmacol Bull 21:268–278, 1985

Ison MG: The effect of 'Thorazine' on Wechsler scores. Am J Ment Defic 62:543–547, 1957

Itard J: The Wild Boy of Aveyron (1801). Translated by Humphrey G, Humphrey M. New York, Appleton-Century-Crofts, 1962

Jackson GM, Johnson CR, Ackron GS, et al: Food satiation as a procedure to decelerate vomiting. Am J Ment Defic 80:223–227, 1975

Jacobs PA, Brunton M, Melville MM, et al: Aggressive behavior, mental subnormality and the XYY male. Nature 208:1351, 1965

Jacobson JW: Problem behavior and psychiatric impairment within a developmentally disabled population, I: behavior frequency. Appl Res Ment Retard 3:121–139, 1982

Jakab I: Psychotherapy of the mentally retarded child, in Diminished People. Edited by Bernstein NR. Boston, Little, Brown & Co, 1970, pp 223–261

Jakab I: Short-term effect of thioridazine tablets versus suspension on emotionally disturbed/retarded children. J Clin Psychopharmacol 4:210–215, 1984

James DH: Monitoring drugs in hospitals for the mentally handicapped. Br J Psychiatry 142:163–165, 1983

Johnson NE, Tenuta K: Diets and lead blood levels of children who practice pica. Environmental Health Research 369–376, 1979

Johnson RN: Aggression in man and animals. Philadelphia, WB Saunders Co, 1972

Johnston M: Behavioral treatment of an eating problem. Nursing Times 72:1098–1099, 1976

Jones AM: Overcoming the feeding problems of the mentally and physically handicapped. Journal of Human Nutrition 32:359–367, 1978

Jones TW: An Experimental Comparison of Two Methods for Remediating Behavioral Eating Problems of Handicapped Children. Doctoral dissertation. Pittsburgh, University of Pittsburgh, 1978 (Dissertation Abstracts International 39, 1978; University Microfilms No 7902707)

Jones TW: An experimental comparison of two methods for remediating behavioral eating problems, in The Profoundly Mentally Retarded: Fifth Annual Conference Proceedings. Edited by Duckett J, Cleland CC, Zucker SH. 1979

Kalachnick JE, Miller RF, Jamison AG, et al: Results of a system to monitor effects of psychotropic medication in an applied setting. Psychopharmacol Bull 19:12–15, 1983a

Kalachnick JE, Larum JG, Swanson A: A tardive dyskinesia monitoring policy for applied facilities. Psychopharmacol Bull 19:277–282, 1983b

Kanner L: Historical notes on rumination in man. Medical Life 43:27–60, 1936

Kanner L: Child Psychiatry. Springfield, Ill, Charles C Thomas, 1957

Karan OC, Berger C: Developing support networks for individuals who fail to achieve competitive employment, in Competitive Employment Issues and Strategies. Edited by Rusch FR. Baltimore, Paul H Brookes Publishers, 1986, pp 241–255

Karan OC, Gardner WI: Vocational rehabilitation practices: a behavioral approach. Rehabil Lit 34:290–298, 1973

Karan OC, Schalock RL: An ecological approach to assessing vocational and community living skills, in Habilitation Practices with the Developmentally Disabled Who Present Behavioral and Emotional Disorders. Edited by Karan OC, Gardner WI. Madison, Wis, Rehabilitation Research and Training Center in Mental Retardation, 1983, pp 121–173

Kauffman JM: Are all children educable? (Special Issue). Analysis and Intervention in Developmental Disabilities 1(1), 1981

Kaufman KR, Katz-Garris L: Epilepsy, mental retardation and anticonvulsant therapy. Am J Ment Defic 84:256–259, 1979

Kaufman ME, Levitt H: A study of three stereotyped behaviors in institutionalized mental defective. Am J Ment Defic 69:467–473, 1965

Kazdin AE: Covert modeling, model similarity, and reduction of avoidance behavior. Behav Ther 5:325–340, 1974

Kazdin AE: Statistical analysis for single-case experimental designs, in Single Case Experimental Designs. Edited by Hersen H, Barlow D. New York, Pergamon Press, 1976

Kazdin AE: Behavior Modification in Applied Settings (rev). Homewood, Ill, Dorsey Press, 1980

Kazdin AE, Matson JL: Social validation in mental retardation. Appl Res Ment Retard 2:39–53, 1981

Kazdin AE, Matson JL, Senatore V: Assessment of depression in the mentally retarded. Am J Psychiatry 140:1040–1043, 1983

Keegan DL, Pettigrew A, Parker Z: psychosis in Down's syndrome treated with amitriptyline. Can Med Assoc J 110:1128–1129, 1974

Kelly JT, Koch M, Buegel D: Lithium carbonate in juvenile manic-depressive illness. Diseases of the Nervous System 37:90–92, 1976

Klaber MM, Butterfield EC: Stereotyped rocking: a measure of institution and ward effectiveness. Am J Ment Defic 73:13–20, 1968

Knights RM, Hinton GG: The effects of methylphenidate (ritalin) on the motor skills and behavior of children with learning problems. J Nerv Ment Dis 148:643–653, 1969

Koller H, Richardson SA, Katz M: Behavior disturbance since childhood among a 5-year birth cohort of all mentally retarded young adults in a city. Am J Ment Defic 87:386–395, 1983

Kraft IA, Ardali C, Duffy J, et al: Use of amitryptiline in childhood behavior disturbances. International Journal of Neuropsychiatry 2:611–614, 1966

Lachiewicz AM, Gullion CM, Spiridigliozzi GA, et al: Declining IQs of young males with the fragile X syndrome. Am J Ment Retard 92:272–278, 1987

La Greca A, Stone W, Bell C: Facilitating the vocational-interpersonal skills of mentally retarded adults. Am J Ment Defic 88:270–278, 1983

LaGrow SJ, Repp AC: Stereotypic responding: a review of intervention research. Am J Ment Defic 88:595–609, 1984

Laidler J: Nutritional assessment of common problems found among the developmentally disabled. Ment Retard 14:24–28, 1976

LaMendola W, Zaharia ES, Carver M: Reducing psychotropic drug use in an institution for the retarded. Hosp Community Psychiatry 31:271–272, 1980

LaVeck GD, Buckley P: The use of psychopharmacologic agents in retarded children with behavior disorders. J Chronic Dis 13:174–183, 1961

Laws DR, Brown RA, Epstein J, et al: Reduction of inappropriate social behavior in disturbed children by an untrained paraprofessional therapist. Behavior Therapist 2:519–533, 1971

Lazar I, Darlington R, Murray H, et al: Lasting effects of early education: a report from the consortium for longitudinal studies. Monogr Soc Res Child Dev 47(2–3, serial no 195), 1982

Leibowitz JM, Holcer P: Building and maintaining self feeding skills in a retarded child. Am J Occup Ther 28:545–548, 1974

Leland H, Smith DE: Play Therapy with Mentally Subnormal Children. New York, Grune & Stratton, 1965

Lesch M, Nyhan WL: A familial disorder of uric acid metabolism and central nervous function. Am J Med 36:561–570, 1964

Le Vann LJ: Clinical experience with Tarasan and thioridazine in mentally retarded children. Applied Therapeutics 12:30–33, 1970

Le Vann LJ: Clinical comparison of haloperidol with chlorpromazine in mentally retarded children. Am J Ment Defic 75:719–723, 1971

Levine HG: Situational anxiety and everyday life experiences of mildly mentally retarded adults. Am J Ment Defic 90:27–33, 1985

Levine HG, Langness LL: Context, ability and performance: comparison of competitive athletics among mildly mentally retarded and nonretarded adults. Am J Ment Defic 87:528–538, 1983

Lewis MH, Baumeister AA: Stereotyped mannerisms in mentally retarded persons: animal models and theoretical analyses, in International Review of Research on Mental Retardation, Vol 2. Edited by Ellis NR. New York, Academic Press, 1982

Liebowitz MR: Imipramine in the treatment of panic disorder and its complications. Psychiatr Clin North Am 8:37–47, 1985

Lindsley DB, Henry CE: The effect of drugs on behavior and the electroencephalograms of children with behavior disorders. Psychosom Med 4:140–149, 1941

Lion JR, Hill J, Madden DJ: Lithium carbonate and aggression: a preliminary report. Diseases of the Nervous System 36:97–98, 1975

Lipman RS: The use of psychopharmacological agents in residential facilities for the retarded, in Psychiatric Approaches to Mental Retardation. Edited by Menolascino FJ. New York, Basic Books, 1970

Lipman RS, Dimascio A, Reatig N, et al: Psychotropic drugs and mentally retarded children, in Psychopharmacology: A Generation of Progress. Edited by Lipton MA, Dimascio A, Killman KF. New York, Raven Press, 1978

Lloyd KG, Hornykiewicz O, Davidson L, et al: Biochemical evidence of dysfunction of brain neurotransmitters in the Lesch-Nyhan syndrome. N Engl J Med 305:1106–1111, 1981

Lobb H: Trace GSR conditioning with benzedrine in mentally defective and normal adults. Am J Ment Defic 73:239–246, 1968

Lofts R: Effect of zinc on pica in a mentally retarded female. Presented at the Annual Gatlinburg Conference on Mental Retardation and Developmental Disabilities. Gatlinburg, Tenn, March 1986

Looker A, Conners CK: Diphenylhydantoin in children with severe temper tantrums. Arch Gen Psychiatry 23:80–89, 1970

Lott IT: Down's syndrome, aging, and Alzheimer's disease: a clinical review. Ann NY Acad Sci 396:15–27, 1982

Lourie RS, Layman EM, Millican FK: Why children eat things that are not food. Children 10:143–146, 1963

Lovaas OI, Freitag G, Gold VJ, et al: Experimental studies in childhood schizophrenia: analysis of self-destructive behavior. J Exp Child Psychol 2:67–84, 1965a

Lovaas OI, Schaeffer R, Simmons JQ: Experimental studies in childhood schizophrenia: building social behavior in autistic children by the use of electric shock. Journal of Experimental Research in Personality 1:99–109, 1965b

Lovaas OI, Litrownik A, Mann R: Response latencies to auditory stimuli in autistic children engaged in self stimulatory behavior. Behav Res Ther 9:39–49, 1971

Lovaas OI, Newsom C, Hickman C: Self-stimulatory behavior and perceptual development. J Appl Behav Anal 20:45–68, 1981

Lyon R, Bland W: The transfer of adult mental retardates from a state hospital to nursing homes. Ment Retard 7:31–36, 1969

Mackworth NH: Researches on the measurement of human performance. London, His Majesty's Stationery Office, 1950

MacLeod CM, Dekaban AS, Hunt E: Memory impairment in epileptic patients: selective effects of phenobarbital concentration. Science 202:1102–1104, 1978

MacMillan DL: Mental retardation in school and society (2nd ed). Boston, Little, Brown, 1982

Madison LS, Wells TE, Fristo TE, et al: A controlled study of folic acid treatment in three fragile X syndrome males. Developmental and Behavioral Pediatrics 7:253–256, 1986a

Madison LS, Mosher GA, George CH: Fragile X syndrome: diagnosis and research. J Pediatr Psychol 11:91–102, 1986b

Mahaffey KR, Treloar S, Banis TA, et al: Differences in dietary intake of calcium and phosphorus in children having normal and elevated blood lead concentrations. J Nutr 106:107, 1976

Maisto CR, Baumeister AA, Maisto AA: An analysis of variables related to self-injurious behavior among institutionalized retarded persons. J Ment Defic Res 22:27–36, 1978

Marholin D, Touchette PE, Stewart RM: Withdrawal of chronic chlorpromazine medication: an experimental analysis. J Appl Behav Anal 12:159–171, 1979

Mark VH, Ervin FR: Violence and the Brain. New York, Harper and Row, 1970

Marlowe RA: When they closed the doors at Modesto, in State Mental Hospitals: What Happens When They Close. Edited by Ahmed P, Plog S. New York, Plenum Press, 1976

Martin A, Flexer R, Newberry J: The development of a work ethic in the severely retarded, in Vocational Rehabilitation of Severely Handicapped Persons: Contemporary Service Strategies. Edited by Bellamy T, O'Conner G, Karan O. Baltimore, Md, University Park Press, 1979, pp 136–159

Martin HP: Nutrition: its relation to children's physical, mental and emotional development. Am J Clin Nutr 26:766–775, 1973

Martin JE: Identifying potential jobs, in Competitive Employment: Supported Work Models, Methods and Issues. Edited by Rusch FR. Baltimore, Md, Paul H. Brookes Publishers, 1986

Martin PL, Foxx RM: Victim control of the aggression of an institutionalized retardate. J Behav Ther Exp Psychiatry 4:161–165, 1973

Masland RL, Sarason SB, Gladwin T: Mental Subnormality. New York, Basic Books, 1958

Matson JL: The treatment of behavioral characteristics of depression in the mentally retarded. Behavior Therapy 13:209–218, 1982

Matson JL: Depression in the mentally retarded: research findings and future directions. Prog Behav Modif 15:57–79, 1983

Matson JL: Exploration of phobic behavior in a small child. J Behav Ther Exp Psychiatry 19:185–190, 1983b

Matson JL: The behavioral treatment of psychosomatic complaints in the mentally retarded. Am J Ment Defic 88:639–646, 1984a

Matson JL: Psychotherapy with persons who are mentally retarded. Ment Retard 22:170–175, 1984b

Matson JL, Barret RP: Psychopathology in the Mentally Retarded. New York, Grune & Stratton, 1982

Matson JL, Earnhart T: Programming treatment effects to the natural environment. Behav Modif 5:27–37, 1981

Matson JL, Rusch FR: Quality of life: does competitive employment make a difference? in Competitive Employment Issues and Strategies. Edited by Rusch FR. Baltimore, Md, Paul H. Brookes Publishers, 1986, pp 331–337

Matson JL, Senatore V: A comparison of traditional psychotherapy and social skills training for improving interpersonal functioning of mentally retarded adults. Behavior Therapy 12:369–382, 1981

Matson JL, Stephens RL, Smith C: Treatment of self-injurious behavior with overcorrection. J Ment Defic Res 22:175–178, 1978

Matson JL, Kazdin AE, Esveldt-Dawson K: Training interpersonal skills among mentally retarded and socially dysfunctional children. Behav Res Ther 18:419–427, 1980

Matthews CG, Harley JP: Cognitive and motor-sensory performances in toxic and nontoxic epileptic subjects. Neurology 25:184–188, 1975

Mayeda T, Wai F: The Cost of Long-Term Developmental Disabilities Care. (Report prepared for the Office of the Assistant Secretary for Planning and Evaluation, US Department of Health, Education and Welfare.) Pomona, Calif, University of California at Los Angeles Research Group at Pacific State Hospital, 1975

McConahey OL: A token system for retarded women: behavior modification, drug therapy and their combination, in Behavior Modification of the Mentally Retarded. Edited by Thompson T, Grabowski J. New York, Oxford University Press, 1972

McConnell TR, Cromwell RL, Bialer I, et al: Studies in activity level, VII: effects of amphetamine drug administration on the activity level of retarded children. Am J Ment Defic 68:647–651, 1964

McFall RM: A review and reformulation of the concept of social skills. Behavioral Assessment 4:1–33, 1982

McKrensky M: After nutrition legislation and guidelines, what? Presented at the 57th Annual American Dietetic Association Meeting. Philadelphia, 1974. Cited in Palmer S, Thompson RJ, Jr, Linschied TR: Applied behavior analysis in the treatment of childhood feeding problems. Dev Med Child Neurol 17:333–339, 1975

Meichenbaum DH: Examination of model characteristics in reducing avoidance behavior. J Pers Soc Psychol 17:298–307, 1971

Meichenbaum DH: Cognitive-behavior modification: an integrative approach. New York, Plenum Press, 1977

Menolascino FJ: The research challenge of delineating psychiatric syndromes in mental retardation, in Psychiatric Approaches to Mental Retardation. Edited by Menolascino FJ. New York, Basic Books, 1970

Menolascino FJ: Challenges in Mental Retardation. New York, Human Sciences Press, 1977

Menolascino FJ: Schizophrenia in the Mentally Retarded. New York, Pfizer, 1983a

Menolascino FJ: Overview: bridging the gap between mental retardation and mental illness, in Mental Health and Mental Retardation: Bridging the Gap. Edited by Menolascino FJ, McCann BM. Baltimore, University Park Press, 1983b

Menolascino FJ: Mental illness in the mentally retarded: diagnostic and treatment issues, in Mental Retardation and Mental Health: Classification, Diagnosis, Treatment, Services. Edited by Stark JA, Menolascino FJ, Albarell MH, et al. New York, Springer-Verlag, 1988

Menolascino FJ, McCann BM: Mental Health and Mental Retardation: Bridging the Gap. Baltimore, University Park Press, 1983

Menolascino FJ, Ruedrich S, Golden C, et al: Schizophrenia in the mentally retarded. Psychiatric Hospital 12:16, 21–25, 1985

Mercer JR: Labeling the mentally retarded. Berkeley, University of California Press, 1973

Meryash DL, Szymanski LS, Gerald PS: Infantile autism associated with the fragile X syndrome. J Autism Dev Disord 12:295–301, 1982

Meyer-Bahlburg HFL, Ehrhardt AA: Prenatal sex hormones and human aggression: a review and new data on progestogen effects. Aggressive Behavior 8:39–62, 1982

Micev V, Lynch DM: Effect of lithium on disturbed severely mentally retarded patients. Br J Psychiatry 125:110, 1974

Miller NE, Dollard J: Social Learning and Imitation. New Haven, Yale University Press, 1941

Millichap JG, Egan RW, Hart ZH, et al: Auditory perceptual deficit correlated with EEG dysrhythmias: response to diphenylhydantoin sodium. Neurology 19:870–872, 1969

Mitchell HS, Rynberger HJ, Anderson L, et al: Nutrition in Health and Disease. Philadelphia, JB Lippincott Co, 1976

Mizuno T, Yugari Y: Self-mutilation in Lesch-Nyhan syndrome. Lancet 761, 1974

Molloy JS: Teaching the Retarded Child to Talk. New York, John Day, 1961

Moore JW: The effects of a tranquilizer (Thoraxine) on the intelligence and achievement of educable mentally retarded women. Dissertation Abstracts 20:3200, 1960

Mooty J, Ferrand CF, Harris P: Relationship of diet to lead poisoning in children. Pediatrics 55:636–639, 1975

Mori A, Rusch F, Fair G: Vocational Education for the Handicapped: Perspectives on Special Populations/Severely and Moderately Handicapped. (Personnel Development Series: Document 1) Champaign, Ill, Office of Career Development for Special Populations, University of Illinois, 1982

Morris JV, MacGillivray RC, Mathieson CM: The results of the experimental administration of amphetamine sulfate in oligophrenia. Psychiatry 101:131–140, 1955

Morris S: Program Guidelines for Children with Feeding Problems. Edison, NJ, Childcraft, 1977

Moss JW: Post Secondary Vocational Education for Mentally Retarded Adults. Final Report to the Division of Developmental Disabilities, Rehabilitation Services Administration, Department of Health, Education and Welfare, Grant No. 50281/0, 1979

Moss JW, Dineen JP, Ford LH: University of Washington employment training program, in Competitive Employment Issues and Strategies. Edited by Rusch FR. Baltimore, Paul H. Brookes Publishers, 1986, pp 77–85

Moyer KE: Physiology of Aggression and Implications for Control. New York, Raven Press, 1976

Mouchka S: Analysis of the costs of hospital and community programs for comparable developmentally disabled persons. Office of Planning and Policy Development, California State Department of Developmental Services, 1985

Mulhern T, Baumeister AA: Effects of stimulus-response compatibility and complexity upon reaction times of normals and retardates. Journal of Comparative and Physiological Psychology 75:459–463, 1971

Mulick JA, Schroeder SR: Research relating to management of antisocial behavior in mentally retarded persons. The Psychological Record 30:3997–4417, 1980

Mulick JA, Barbour R, Schroeder SR, et al: Overcorrection of pica in two profoundly retarded adults: analysis of setting effects, stimulus and response generalization. Appl Res Ment Retard 1:241–252, 1980a

Mulick JA, Schroeder SR, Rojahn J: Chronic ruminative vomiting: a comparison of four treatment procedures. J Autism Dev Disord 10:203–213, 1980b

Munday L: Therapy with physically and mentally handicapped children in a mental deficiency hospital. J Clin Psychol 13:3–9, 1957

Narabayashi K, Nagao T, Saito Y, et al: Stereotaxic amygdalotomy for behavior disorders. Arch Neurol 9:1–16, 1963

Naylor GJ, Donald JM, LePoidevin D, et al: A double blind trial of long-term lithium therapy in mental defectives. Br J Psychiatry 124:52–57, 1974

Nelson WE, Vaughan VC, McKay RJ: Textbook of Pediatrics. Philadelphia, WB Saunders Co, 1969

Newcomer RB, Morrison TL: Play therapy with institutionalized mentally retarded children. Am J Ment Defic 76:727–733, 1974

Nolen WA: Carbamazepine: a possible adjunct or alternative to lithium in bipolar disorder. Acta Psychiatr Scand 67:218–225, 1983

Nordquist VM, Wahler RG: Naturalistic treatment of an autistic child. J Appl Behav Anal 6:79–87, 1973

Noyes R: Beta-adrenergic blocking drugs in anxiety and stress. Psychiatr Clin North Am 8:119–132, 1985

Nuffield EJ: Psychotherapy for the retarded, in Handbook of Mental Retardation. Edited by Matson JL, Mulick JA. New York, Pergamon Press, 1983, pp 351–368

Nuffield EJ: Counseling and psychotherapy in severe behavior disorders in the mentally retarded, in Non-drug Approaches to Treatment. Edited by Barret RP. New York, Plenum Press, 1986, pp 207–234

Nyhan WL, Johnson HG, Kaufman IA, et al: Serotonergic approaches to the modification of behavior in the Lesch-Nyhan syndrome. Appl Res Ment Retard 1:25–40, 1980

O'Brien F: Treating self-stimulation behavior, in Handbook of Behavior Modification with the Mentally Retarded. Edited by Matson JL, McCartney JR. New York, Plenum Press, 1981

Ogg HL: Oral-pharyngeal development and evaluation. Phys Ther 55:235–241, 1975

O'Leary KD, Paulos RW, Devine OT: Tangible reinforcers: bonus or bribes? J Consult Clin Psychol 38:1–8, 1972

Ollendick TH, Ollendick DG: Anxiety disorders, in Psychopathology in the Mentally Retarded. Edited by Matson JL, Barrett RP. New York, Grune & Stratton, 1982

Ounsted C: The hyperkinetic syndrome in epileptic children. Lancet 2:303–311, 1955

Page TJ, Finney JW, Parrish JM, et al: Assessment and reduction of food stealing in Prader-Willi children. Appl Res Ment Retard 4:219–228, 1983

Pagel S, Whitling C: Readmissions to a state hospital for mentally retarded persons: reasons for community placement failure. Ment Retard 16:164–166, 1978

Palmer S, Thompson RJ, Jr, Linschied TR: Applied behavior analysis in the treatment of childhood feeding problems. Dev Med Child Neurol 17:333–339, 1975

Paluck RJ, Esser AH: Controlled experimental modification of aggressive behavior in territories of severely retarded boys. Am J Ment Defic 76:284–290, 1971

Pasamanick B: Anticonvulsant drug therapy of behavior problem children with abnormal electroencephalograms. Arch Gen Psychiatry 65:752–766, 1951

Patterson GR: Coercive Family Process. Eugene, Oreg, Castalia, 1982

Patterson GR, Littman RA, Bricker W: Assertive behavior in children: a step toward a theory of aggression. Monogr Soc Res Child Dev 32(5, Serial No 113), 1967

Patterson GR, Kishion TJ, Bank L: Family interaction: a process model of deviancy training. Aggressive Behavior 10:253–267, 1984

Pavlov EP: Conditioned Reflexes: An Investigation of the Physiological Activity of the Cerebral Cortex: Lecture 3. Oxford, Oxford University Press, 1927

Pendergrass VE: Time-out from positive reinforcement following persistent, high-rate behavior in retardates. J Appl Behav Anal 5:85–91, 1972

Perry MA, Cerreto MC: Structured learning training of social skills for the retarded. Ment Retard 15:31–34, 1977

Peterson GA, Austin GJ, Lang RP: Use of teacher prompts to increase social behavior: generalization effects with severely and profoundly retarded adolescents. Am J Ment Defic 84:82–86, 1979

Philips I, Williams N: Psychopathology and mental retardation: a study of 100 mentally retarded children, I: psychopathology. Am J Psychiatry 132:1265–1271, 1975

Philips I, Williams N: Psychopathology and mental retardation: statistical study of 100 mentally retarded children treated at a psychiatric clinic, II: hyperactivity. Am J Psychiatry 134:418–419, 1977

Pilkington TL: A report on "Tofranil" in mental deficiency. Am J Ment Defic 66:729–732, 1962

Potter HW: The needs of mentally retarded children for child psychiatry services. J Am Acad Child Psychiatry 3:352–374, 1964

Potter HW: Mental retardation: the Cinderella of psychiatry. Psychiatr Q 39:537–549, 1965

Prader A, Labhart A, Willi H: Ein syndrom von adipositas, kleinwuchs, kryptorchismus und oligophrenie nach myatoneartigem zustand im neugeborenenaltr. Schweiz Med Wochenschr 86:1260, 1956

Premack D: Toward empirical laws of behavior, I: positive reinforcement. Psychol Rev 66:219–233, 1959

Price DL, Whitehouse PJ, Struble RG, et al: Alzheimer's disease and Down's syndrome. Ann NY Acad Sci 396:145–164, 1982

Quay HC: Patterns of aggression, withdrawal and immaturity, in Psychopathological Disorders of Childhood. Edited by Quay H, Werry JW. New York, Wiley Press, 1972

Rachman S: Clinical applications of observational learning, limitation and modeling. Behavior Therapy 3:379–397, 1972

Rachman S, Teasdale J: Aversion therapy and behavior disorders. Coral Gables, Fla, University of Miami Press, 1969

Radinsky AM: A Descriptive Study of Psychotropic and Antiepileptic Medication Use with Mentally Retarded Persons in Three Residential Environments. Doctoral dissertation, Pittsburgh, University of Pittsburgh, 1984

Ramey CT, Bryant DM: Early intervention, in Handbook of Mental Retardation. Edited by Matson JL, Mulick JA. New York, Pergamon Press, 1983, pp 467–478

Rapoport JL, Buchsbaum MS, Zahn TP, et al: Dextroamphetamine: cognitive and behavioral effects in normal prepubertal boys. Science 199:560–563, 1978

Rast J, Johnston JM, Drum C: The relation of food quantity to rumination behavior. J Appl Behav Anal 14:121–130, 1981

Rast J, Johnston JM, Drum C: A parametric analysis of the relationship between food quantity and rumination. J Exp Anal Behav 41:125–134, 1984

Ratey JJ, Mikkelsen EJ, Smith GB, et al: Beta-blockers in the severely and profoundly mentally retarded. J Clin Psychopharmacol 6:103–107, 1986

Reid AH: Diagnosis of psychiatric disorder in the severely and profoundly retarded patient. Journal of Royal Society of Medicine 73:607–609, 1980a

Reid AH: Psychiatric disorders in mentally handicapped children: a clinical and follow-up study. J Ment Defic Res 24:287–298, 1980b

Reid AH: The Psychiatry of Mental Handicap. Oxford, Blackwell Scientific Publications, 1982

Reid AH: Prevalence of mental illness among mentally handicapped people (letter to the editor). Journal of the Royal Society of Medicine 77:894–895, 1984

Reid AH, Leonard A: Lithium treatment of cyclical vomiting in a mentally defective patient. Br J Psychiatry 130:316, 1977

Reiss AL, Feinstein KE, Goldsmith TB, et al: Psychiatric disability associated with the fragile X chromosome. Am J Med Genet 23:393–401, 1986

Reiss S: Psychopathology and mental retardation: survey of a developmental disabilities mental health program. Ment Retard 20:128–132, 1982

Reiss S, Szyszko J: Diagnostic overshadowing and professional experience with mentally retarded persons. Am J Ment Defic 87:396–402, 1983

Reiss S, Levitan GW, Szyszko J: Emotional disturbance and mental retardation: diagnostic overshadowing. Am J Ment Defic 86:567–574, 1982

Renzaglia A: Preparing personnel to support and guide emerging contemporary service alternatives, in Competitive Employment Issues and Strategies. Edited by Rusch FR. Baltimore, Paul H. Brookes Publishers, 1986, p 303

Repp AC, Brulle AR: Reducing aggressive behavior of mentally retarded persons, in Handbook of Behavior Modification with the Mentally Retarded. Edited by Matson JL, McCartney JR. New York, Plenum Press, 1981

Repp AC, Deitz SM, Speir NC: Reducing stereotypic responding of retarded persons by the differential reinforcement of other behavior. Am J Ment Defic 79:279–284, 1974

Reynolds EH, Travers RD: Serum anticonvulsant concentrations in epileptic patients with mental symptoms. Br J Psychiatry 124:440–445, 1974

Reynolds GS: Behavioral contrast. J Exp Anal Behav 4:57–71, 1961

Rhoads FA, Oglesby AC, Mayer M, et al: Marker X syndrome in an Oriental family with probable transmission by a normal male. Am J Med Genet 12:205–217, 1982

Richardson SA, Katz M, Koller H, et al: Some characteristics of a population of mentally retarded young adults in a British city: a basis for estimating some service needs. J Ment Defic Res 23:275–283, 1979

Richmond J, Eddy E: Rumination: a psychosomatic syndrome. Psychiatric Research Reports 8:1–11, 1957

Richmond J, Eddy E, Green M: Rumination: a psychosomatic syndrome in infancy. Pediatrics 22:49–55, 1958

Riguet CB, Taylor ND, Benaroya S, et al: Symbolic play in autistic, Down's and normal children of equivalent mental age. J Autism Dev Disord 11:439–448, 1981

Ringelheim D, Polotsek I: Group therapy with a male defective group. Am J Ment Defic 60:157–162, 1955

Riordan MM, Iwata BA, Wohl MK, et al: Behavioral treatment and food refusal and selectivity in developmentally disabled children. Appl Res Ment Retard 1:95–112, 1980

Risley TR: The effects and side effects of punishing the autistic behaviors of a deviant child. J Appl Behav Anal 1:21–34, 1968

Rivinus TM: Psychopharmacology and the mentally retarded patient, in Emotional Disorders of Mentally Retarded Persons. Edited by Szymanski LS, Tanguay PE. Baltimore, University Park Press, 1980

Robinson N, Robinson H: The Mentally Retarded Child (2nd ed). New York, McGraw-Hill, 1976

Rogers CR, Dymond RF: Psychotherapy and Personality Change. Chicago, University of Chicago Press, 1954

Rogers RC, Simensen RJ: Fragile X syndrome: a common etiology of mental retardation. Am J Ment Defic 91:445–449, 1987

Rogers-Warren A, Warren SF: The developing ecobehavioral psychology, in Ecological Perspectives in Behavior Analysis. Edited by Rogers-Warren A, Warren SF. Baltimore, University Park Press, 1977, pp 3–8

Rollings JP, Baumeister AA, Baumeister AA: The use of overcorrection procedures to eliminate the stereotyped behaviors of retarded individuals: an analysis of collateral behaviors and generalization of suppressive effects. Behav Modif 1:29–46, 1977

Ross AO: Psychological Disorders of Children. New York, McGraw, 1980

Ross RT: Behavioral correlates of levels of intelligence. Am J Ment Defic 76:545–549, 1972

Rotegard LL, Bruininks RH, Krantz GC: State operated residential facilities for people with mental retardation: July 1, 1978–June 30, 1982. Ment Retard 22:69–74, 1984

Rusch FR, Mithaug DE: Vocational Training for Mentally Retarded Adults: A Behavior-Analytic Approach. Champaign, Ill, Research Press, 1980

Rusch FR, Close D, Hops H, et al: Overcorrection: generalization and maintenance. J Appl Behav Anal 9:498, 1976

Rusch FR, Schutz RP, Agran M: Validating entry-level survival skills for service occupations: implications for curriculum development. The Journal of the Association for the Severely Handicapped 1:32–41, 1982

Russell AT, Forness SR: Behavioral disturbance in mentally retarded children in TMR and EMR classrooms. Am J Ment Defic 89:338–344, 1985

Rutter M: Helping Troubled Children. New York, Plenum Press, 1975

Rutter M, Tizard J, Yule W, et al: Isle of Wight studies, 1964–1974. Psychol Med 6:313–332, 1976

Sachs DA: The efficacy of time-out procedures in a variety of behavior problems. J Behav Ther Exp Psychiatry 4:237–242, 1973

Sacks O: The Man Who Mistook His Wife for a Hat. New York, Summit Books, 1986

Sajwaj T, Twardosz S, Burke M: Side effects of extinction procedures in a remedial school. J Appl Behav Anal 5:163–175, 1972

Sajwaj T, Libet J, Agras S: Lemon juice therapy: the control of life-threatening rumination in a six-month-old infant. J Appl Behav Anal 7:557–563, 1974

Sallustro F, Atwell C: Body rocking, head banging and head rolling in normal children. J Pediatr 93:704–708, 1978

Sandman CA, Datta P, Barron J, et al: Naloxone attenuates self-abusive behavior in developmentally disabled clients. Appl Res Ment Retard 3:5–11, 1983

Schain RJ: Problems with the use of conventional anticonvulsant drugs in mentally retarded individuals. Brain Dev 1:77–82, 1979

Schain RJ, Riehl JP, Ward J: Analysis of cognitive effects of withdrawal of sedative anticonvulsants in epileptic children. Pediatr Res 9:384, 1975

Schain RJ, Ward JW, Guthrie D: Carbamazepine as an anticonvulsant in children. Neurology 27:476–480, 1977

Schalock RL: Comprehensive community services: a plea for interagency collaboration, in Living and Learning in the Least Restrictive Environment. Edited by Bruininks R. Baltimore, Md, Paul H. Brookes Publishers, 1986

Scheerenberger RC: A history of mental retardation. Baltimore, Paul H. Brookes, 1983

Schiavi RC, Theilgard A, Owen DR, et al: Sex chromosome anomalies, hormones and aggressivity. Arch Gen Psychiatry 41:93–99, 1984

Schmidt D: How to use benzodiazepines, in Antiepileptic Drug Therapy in Pediatrics. Edited by Morselli PL, Pippinger CE, Penry JK. New York, Raven Press, 1983

Schmidt P: Feeding assessment and therapy for the neurologically impaired. AAESPH Review 1:19–27, 1976

Schroeder SR: Usage of stereotypy as a descriptive term. The Psychological Record 20:4457–4464, 1970

Schroeder SR: Neuroleptic medications for persons with developmental disabilities, in Psychopharmacology of the Developmental Disabilities. Edited by Aman MG, Singh NN. New York, Springer-Verlag, 1988, pp 82–100

Schroeder SR, Gualtieri CT: Behavioral interactions induced by chronic neuroleptic therapy in persons with mental retardation. Psychopharmacol Bull 21:310–315, 1985

Schroeder SR, Mulick JA, Schroeder CS: Management of severe behavior problems of the retarded, in Handbook of Mental Deficiency (2nd ed). Edited by Ellis NR. New York, Lawrence Erlbaum Associates, 1979

Schroeder SR, Mulick JA, Rojahn J: The definition, taxonomy, epidemiology and ecology of self-injurious behavior. J Autism Dev Disord 10:417–432, 1980

Schroeder SR, Schroeder CS, Smith B, Dalldorf J: Prevalence of self-injurious behaviors in a large state facility for the retarded: a three-year follow-up study. J Autism Child Schizophr 8:261–269, 1978

Schroeder SR, Schroeder CS, Rojahn J, et al: Self-injurious behavior: an analysis of behavior management techniques, in Handbook of Behavior Modification with the Mentally Retarded. Edited by Matson JL, McCartney JR. New York, Plenum Press, 1981, pp 61–115

Schutz RP: Establishing a parent-professional partnership to facilitate competitive employment, in Competitive Employment Issues and Strategies. Edited by Rusch FR. Baltimore, Md, Paul H. Brookes Publishers, 1986, pp 289–302

Schwartz C: The application of psychoanalytic theory to the treatment of the mentally retarded child. Psychoanal Rev 66:133–141, 1979

Scott BS, Becker LE, Petit TL: Neurobiology of Down's syndrome. Prog Neurobiol 21:199–237, 1983

Selan BH: Psychotherapy with the developmentally disabled. Health Soc Work, 1:74–84, 1976

Senatore V, Matson JL, Kazdin AE: A comparison of behavioral methods to train social skills to retarded adults. Behavior Therapy 13:313–324, 1982

Sequin E: The Moral Treatment, Hygiene and Education of Idiots and Other Backward Children. New York, Columbia University Press, 1846

Shader RI, Jackson AH, Dodes LM: The antiaggressive effects of lithium in man. Psychopharmacologia 40:17–24, 1974

Shafer MS: Utilizing co-workers as change agents, in Competitive Employment Issues and Strategies. Edited by Rusch FR. Baltimore, Md, Paul H. Brookes Publishers, 1986, pp 215–224

Sheard MH: Behavioral effects of p-chlorophenylalanine: inhibition by lithium. Behavioral Biology 5:71–73, 1970a

Sheard MH: Effect of lithium on footshock aggression in rats. Nature 228:284–285, 1970b

Sheard MH: Effect in the treatment of aggression. J Nerv Ment Dis 160:108–118, 1975

Sheehan DV: Monoamine oxidase inhibitors and alprazolam in the treatment of panic disorder and agoraphobia. Psychiatr Clin North Am 8:49–62, 1985

Shelton RL, Knox AW, Elvert M, et al: Palate awareness and non-speech voluntary palate movement, in Second Symposium of Oral Sensation and Perception. Edited by Bosma J. Springfield, Ill, Charles C Thomas, 1970

Sherzer AL, Ilson JM: Normal intelligence in the Lesch-Nyhan syndrome. Pediatrics 44:116–120, 1969

Shew P: Explaining mental retardation and autism to parents, in The Effects of Autism on the Family. Edited by Schopler E, Mesibov GB. New York, Plenum Press, 1984

Sigelman CK, Budd EC, Winer JL, et al: Evaluating alternative techniques of questioning mentally retarded persons. Am J Ment Defic 86:511–518, 1982

Silva DA: The use of medication in a residential institution for mentally retarded persons. Ment Retard 17:285–288, 1979

Simmons JQ, Tymchuk AJ, Valente M: Treatment considerations in mental retardation. Curr Psychiatr Ther 15:15–24, 1975

Singh NN: Current trends in the treatment of self-injurious behavior, in Advances in Pediatrics, Vol 28. Edited by Barnes CA. Chicago, Year Book Medical Publications, 1981a

Singh NN: Rumination, in International Review of Research in Mental Retardation, Vol 10. Edited by Ellis NR. New York, Academic Press, 1981b

Singh NN, Aman MG: Effects of thioridazine dosage on the behavior of severely mentally retarded persons. Am J Ment Defic 85:580–587, 1981c

Singh NN, Bakker LW: Suppression of pica by overcorrection and physical restraint: a comparative analysis. J Autism Dev Disord 14:331–341, 1984

Singh NN, Dawson MJ: The prevalence of rumination in institutionalized mentally retarded children. Unpublished manuscript. Auckland, NZ, Mangere Training School, 1980

Singh NN, Winton AS: Effects of a screening procedure on pica and collateral behaviors. J Behav Ther Exp Psychiatry 15:59–65, 1984

Singh NN, Manning DJ, Angell MJ: Effects of an oral hygiene punishment procedure on chronic rumination and collateral behaviors in monozygous twins. J Appl Behav Anal 15:309–314, 1982

Skinner BF: The Behavior of Organisms. New York, Appleton-Century-Crofts, 1938

Skinner BF: Science and Human Behavior. New York, Macmillan, 1953

Skinner BF: Verbal Behavior. New York, Appleton Century Crofts, 1957

Smith EH, Gonzalez R: Nortriptyline hydrochloride in the treatment of enuresis in mentally retarded boys. Am J Ment Defic 71:825–827, 1967

Smith EH, McKinnon R, Kessler JW: Psychotherapy with mentally retarded children. Psychoanal Stud Child 31:493–514, 1976

Smith WL, Lowery JB: The effects of diphenylhydantoin on cognitive functions in man, in Drugs, Development and Cerebral Function. Edited by Smith WL. Springfield, Ill, Charles C Thomas, 1972

Smith WL, Philippus MJ, Guard HL: Psychometric study of children with learning problems and 14–6 positive spike EEG patterns, treated with ethosuxmide (zarontin) and placebo. Arch Dis Child 43:616–619, 1968

Snowdon CF: A nutritional basis for lead pica. Physiol Behav 18:885–893, 1977

Soblen RA, Saunders JC: Monoamine oxidase inhibitor therapy in adolescent psychiatry. Diseases of the Nervous System 22:96–100, 1961

Solnick JV, Rincover A, Peterson CR: Some determinants of the reinforcing and punishing effects of time out. J Appl Behav Anal 10:415–424, 1977

Sorrell M, Rosen JF, Roginsky MR: Interactions of lead, calcium, vitamin D and nutrition in lead-burdened children. Arch Environ Health 32:160–164, 1977

Sovner R, Hurley AD: Do the mentally retarded suffer from affective illness? Arch Gen Psychiatry 40:61–67, 1983

Sovner R, Hurley AD, Labrie R: Is mania incompatible with Down's syndrome? Br J Psychiatry 146:319–320, 1985

Spangler P, Marshall A: The unit play manager as facilitator of purposeful activities among institutionalized profoundly and severely retarded boys. J Appl Behav Anal 16:345–349, 1983

Spencer DA: Ronyl (pemoline) in overactive mentally subnormal children. Br J Psychol 8:491–500, 1980

Spivack G, Spotts J: The Devereux Child Behavior Scale: symptom behaviors in latency age children. Am J Ment Defic 69:839–853, 1965

Spradlin JE: The Premack hypothesis and self-feeding by profoundly retarded children: a case report (working paper 79). Parsons, Kans, Parsons Research Center, 1964

Sprague RL, Sleator EK: Methylphenidate in hyperkinetic children: differences in dose effects on learning and social behavior. Science 198:1274–1276, 1977

Sprague RL, Werry JS: Methodology of psychopharmacological studies with the retarded, in International Review of Research in Mental Retardation, Vol 5. Edited by Ellis NR. New York, Academic Press, 1971, pp 148–219

Springer NS: Proceedings of a Conference on Nutrition and Mental Retardation. Ann Arbor, Mich, University of Michigan, 1971

Sreebny LM: Effect of food consistency and decreased food intake on rat parotid and pancreas. Am J Physiol 215:455–460, 1968

Sroufe L: Drug treatment of children with behavior problems, in Review of Child Development Research, Vol 4. Edited by Horowitz F. Chicago, University of Chicago Press, 1975

Staats AW, Staats CK: Complex Human Behaviors: A Systematic Extension of Learning Principles. New York, Holt, Rinehart & Winston, 1963

Stainback S, Healy H, Stainback W, et al: Teaching basic eating skills. AAESPH Review 1:26–35, 1976

Stainback W, Stainback S, Strathe M: Generalization of positive social behavior by severely handicapped students: a review and analysis of research. Education and Training of the Mentally Retarded 18:293–299, 1983

Stainback W, Stainback S, Nietupski J, et al: Establishing effective community-based training stations, in Competitive Employment Issues and Strategies. Edited by Rusch FR. Baltimore, Md, Paul H. Brookes Publishers, 1986, pp 103–113

Stavrakaki C, Klein J: Psychotherapies with the mentally retarded. Psychiatr Clin North Am 9:733–743, 1986

Sternlicht M: Psychotherapy techniques useful with mentally retarded: a review and critique. Psychiatry Q 39:84–90, 1965

Sternlicht M: Psychotherapeutic procedures with the retarded, in International Review of Research in Mental Retardation, Vol 2. Edited by Ellis NR. New York, Academic Press, 1966

Sternlicht M, Wanderer ZW: Group Psychotherapy with Mental Defectives. Presented at Annual Conference of the American Group Psychotherapy Association, Washington DC, January, 1963

Stimbert VE, Minor JW, McCoy JF: Intensive feeding training with retarded children. Behav Modif 1:517–530, 1977

Stokes TF, Baer DM: An implicit technology of generalization. J Appl Behav Anal 10:349–367, 1977

Stores G, Hart J: Reading skills of children with generalized or focal epilepsy attending ordinary school. Dev Med Child Neurol 18:705–716, 1976

Strayhorn JM, Rapp N, Donina W, et al: Randomized trial of methylphenidate for an autistic child. Am Acad Child Adolesc Psychiatry 27:244–247, 1988

Sutherland GR: Marker X chromosomes and mental retardation. N Engl J Med 296:1415, 1977

Sutherland GR, Hecht F: Fragile Sites on Human Chromosomes. New York, Oxford University Press, 1985

Sutter P, Mayeda T, Call T, et al: Comparison of successful and unsuccessful community-placed mentally retarded persons. Am J Ment Defic 85:262–267, 1980

Szymanski LS: Individual psychotherapy with retarded persons, in Emotional Disorders of Mentally Retarded Persons. Edited by Szymanski LS, Tanguay PE. Baltimore, University Park Press, 1980, pp 131–147

Talkington LW, Riley J: Reduction diets and aggression in institutionalized mentally retarded. Am J Ment Defic 76:370–372, 1971

Tallman JF, Paul SM, Skolnick P, et al: Receptors for the age of anxiety: pharmacology of the benzodiazepines. Science 207:274–281, 1980

Tate BG, Baroff GS: Aversive control of self-injurious behavior in a psychotic boy. Behav Res Ther 4:281–287, 1966

Thase ME, Tigner R, Smeltzer DJ, et al: Age-related neuropsychological deficits in Down's syndrome. Biol Psychiatry 19:571–585, 1984

Thompson RJ, Palmer S: Treatment of feeding problems: a behavioral approach. Journal of Nutrition Education 6:63–66, 1974

Thompson RJ, Trimble MR: Anticonvulsant drugs and cognitive functions. Epilepsia 23:531–544, 1982

Thorne FC: Counseling and psychotherapy with mental defectives. Am J Ment Defic 52:263–271, 1948

Thurston JH, Thurston DL, Hixon BB, et al: Prognosis in childhood epilepsy. N Engl J Med 306:831–836, 1982

Tizard B: Observations of overactive imbecile children in controlled and uncontrolled environments, II: experimental studies. Am J Ment Defic 72:548–553, 1968

Tolksdorf M, Wiedemann H: Clinical aspects of Down's syndrome from infancy to adult life. Hum Genet [Suppl] 2:3–81, 1981

Trimble MR: The effect of anti-convulsant drugs on cognitive abilities. Pharmacol Ther 4:677–685, 1979

Trimble MR: Benzodiazepines in epilepsy, in Benzodiazepines Divided: A Multidisciplinary Review. Edited by Trimble MR. New York, John Wiley & Sons, 1983

Trimble MR, Reynolds EH: Anticonvulsant drugs and mental symptoms. Psychol Med 6:16, 1976

Tu JB: A survey of psychotropic medication in mental retardation facilities. J Clin Psychiatry 40:125–128, 1979

Tu JB: Drug holiday for the disturbed-retarded epileptics. J Clin Psychiatry 41:324, 1980

Turnbull AP, Turnbull HR: Parents Speak Out—Views from the Other Side of the Two-Way Mirror. Columbus, Ohio, Charles E. Merrill Publishing Co, 1978

Turnbull HR, Turnbull AP: Free Appropriate Public Education: Law and Implementation. Denver, Love, 1978

Turner G, Brookwell R, Daniel A, et al: Heterozygous expression of X-linked mental retardation and the X-chromosome marker fra(X)(q27). N Engl J Med 303:662–664, 1980

Turner G, Robinson H, Laing S, et al: Preventive screening for the fragile X syndrome. N Engl J Med 315:607–609, 1986

Turton LJ: Interdisciplinary panel presentation solving feeding problems of mentally retarded children, in Proceedings of a Conference on Nutrition and Mental Retardation. Edited by Springer NS. Ann Arbor, Mich, University of Michigan, 1971

Ucer E, Kreger C: A double-blind study comparing haloperidol with thioridazine in emotionally disturbed retarded children. Current Therapeutic Research 17:202–205, 1975

Utley BL, Holvoet JF, Barnes J: Handling, positioning and feeding the physically handicapped, in Educational Programming for the Severely and Profoundly Handicapped. Edited by Sontag E. Reston, Va, Division on Mental Retardation Council for Exceptional Children, 1977

Vaisanen K, Kainulainen P, Paavilainen MT, et al: Sulpiride versus chlorpromazine and placebo in the treatment of restless mentally subnormal patients: a double-blind crossover study. Current Therapeutic Research 78:640–648, 1974

Vaisanen K, Viukari M, Rimon R, et al: Haloperidol, thioridazine and placebo in mentally subnormal patients: serum levels and clinical effects. Acta Psychiatr Scand 63:262–271, 1981

Van Hemert JC: Pipamperone (Dipiperon, R3345) in troublesome mental retardates: a double-blind placebo controlled crossover study with long-term follow-up. Acta Psychiatr Scand 52:237–245, 1975

Varley CK: Schizophreniform psychoses in mentally retarded adolescent girls following sexual assault. Am J Psychiatry 141:593–595, 1984

Varley CK, Trupin EW: Double-blind administration of methylphenidate to mentally retarded children with attention deficit disorder: a preliminary study. Am J Ment Defic 86:560–566, 1982

Vogelsberg RT: Competitive employment programs for individuals with mental retardation in rural areas, in Proceedings from the National Symposium on Employment of Citizens with Mental Retardation. Edited by Wehman P. Richmond, Va, Virginia Commonwealth University, 1984

Vogelsberg RT: Competitive employment programs in Vermont, in Competitive Employment Issues and Strategies. Edited by Rusch FR. Baltimore, Md, Paul H Brookes Publishers, 1986, pp 35–50

Walford RL: Immunological studies of Down's syndrome and Alzheimer's disease. Ann NY Acad Sci 396:95–106, 1982

Walker CF, Kirkpatrick: Dilantin treatment for behavior problem children with abnormal encephalograms. Am J Psychiatry 103:484–492, 1947

Walker HM: The social behavior survival program: a systematic approach to the integration of handicapped children into less restrictive settings. Education and Treatment of Children 6:421–441, 1983

Walker HM, McConnell S, Holmes D, et al: The Walker social skills curriculum: the ACCEPTS program. Austin, Tex, Pro-Ed, 1983

Walls RT, Zawlocki RJ, Dowler DL: Economic benefits as disincentives to competitive employment, in Competitive Employment Issues and Strategies. Edited by Rusch FR. Baltimore, Md, Paul H. Brookes Publishers, 1986, pp 317–329

Walters A, Singh N, Beale IL: Effects of lorazepam on hyperactivity in retarded children. 86:473–475, 1977

Wapner I, Thurston DI, Holowach J: Phenobarbital: its effect on learning in epileptic children. JAMA 182:937, 1962

Wardell DW, Rubin JK, Ross RT: The use of reserpine and chlorpromazine in disturbed mentally deficient patients. Am J Ment Defic 63:330–344, 1958

Warren SA, Burns NR: Crib confinement as a factor in repetitive and stereotyped behavior in retardates. Ment Retard 8:25–28, 1970

Wasserman R: Identifying the counseling needs of the siblings of mentally retarded children. Personnel and Guidance Journal 61:622–627, 1983

Watson MS, Leckman JF, Annex B, et al: Fragile X in a survey of 75 autistic males (letter to the editor). N Engl J Med 310:1462, 1984

Webster TG: Problems of emotional development in young retarded children. Am J Psychiatry 120:37–43, 1963

Webster TG: Unique aspects of emotional development in mentally retarded children, in Psychiatric Approaches to Mental Retardation. Edited by Menolascino FJ. New York, Basic Books, 1970

Weeks M, Gaylord-Ross R: Task difficulty and aberrant behavior in severely handicapped students. J Appl Behav Anal 14:449–463, 1981

Wehman P: Competitive Employment: New Horizons for Severely Disabled Individuals. Baltimore, Md, Paul H. Brookes Publishing, 1981

Weiner EA, Weiner BJ: Differentiation of retarded and normal children through toy-play analysis. Multivariate Behavioral Research 9:245–252, 1974

Weisberg P, Passman RH, Russell JE: Development of verbal control over bizarre gestures of retardates through imitative and nonimitative reinforcement procedures. J Appl Behav Anal 6:487–495, 1973

Weisberg P, Packer RA, Weisberg RA: Academic training, in Handbook of Behavior Modification with the Mentally Retarded. Edited by Matson JL, McCartney JR. New York, Plenum Press, 1981, pp 331–411

Weischer ML: Uber die antigressive wirkung von Lithium. Psychopharmacologia 15:245–254, 1969

Weiss B, Laties VG: Enhancement of human performance by caffeine and the amphetamines. Psychol Rev 14:1–36, 1962

Werry JS: Organic factors, In Psychopathological Disorders of Childhood (2nd ed). Edited by Quay HC, Werry JS. New York, John Wiley & Sons, 1979

Whalen CK, Henker B: Hyperactive Children: the Social Ecology of Identification and Treatment. New York, Academic Press, 1980

White DM, Rusch FR: Social validation in competitive employment: evaluating work performance. Appl Res Ment Retard 4:343–354, 1984

White JC, Taylor DJ: Noxious conditioning as a treatment for rumination. Ment Retard 5:30–33, 1967

Willems EP: Steps toward an ecobehavioral technology, in Ecological Perspectives in Behavior Analysis. Edited by Rogers-Warren A, Warren SR. Baltimore, Md, University Park Press, 1977, pp 39–61

Wing, JK: Early Childhood Autism: Clinical, Educational and Social Aspects. New York, Pergamon Press, 1966

Wing L: Autistic Children: A Guide for Parents. New York, Brunner/Mazel, 1972

Winitz H: Articulatory Acquisition and Behavior. New York, Appleton-Century-Croft, 1969

Witkin HA, Mednick SA, Schulsinger R, et al: Criminality in XYY and XXY men. Science 193:547–555, 1976

Wolf M, Risley T, Mees P: Application of operant conditioning procedures to the behavior problems of an autistic child. Behav Res Ther 1:305–312, 1964

Wolf M, Birnbauer JF, Lawler J, et al: The operant extinction, reinstatement and re-extinction of vomiting behavior in a retarded child, in Control of Human Behavior: From Cure to Prevention, Vol. 2. Edited by Ulrich R, Staknik T, Mabry J. Glenview, Ill, Scott, Foresman and Co, 1970

Wolf SM, Forsythe A: Behavior disturbance, phenobarbital and febrile seizures. Pediatrics 61:728–731, 1978

Wolfensberger W: The origin and nature of our institutional models, in Changing Patterns in Residential Services for the Mentally Retarded. Edited by Kugel RB, Wolfensberger W. Washington, DC, President's Committee on Mental Retardation, 1969

Wolkowitz OM, Doran AR, Cohen MR, et al: Effect of naloxone on food consumption in obesity (letter). N Engl J Med 313:327, 1985

Wolpe J: The Practice of Behavior Therapy. New York, Pergamon Press, 1969

Wolraich M, Healy A, Henderson M: Audiocassette recordings: an aid to parent counseling. Spina Bifida Therapy 1:96–99, 1979

Wolraich M, Lively S, Schultz, F, et al: Effects of intensive initial counseling on the retention of information by parents of children with meningomyelocele. Journal of Developmental and Behavioral Pediatrics 2:163–165, 1981

Wong SE, Gaydon GR, Fuqua RW: Operant control of pedophilia. Behav Modif 6:73–84, 1982

Worrall EP, Moody JP, Naylor GJ: Lithium in nonmanic depressives: antiaggressive effect and red blood cell lithium values. Br J Psychiatry 126:464–468, 1975

Wright B: Physical Disability: A Psychological Approach. New York, Harper & Row, 1960

Wright MW, Menolascino FJ: Rumination, mental retardation and interventive therapeutic nursing, in Psychiatric Approaches to Mental Retardation. Edited by Menolascino FJ. New York, Basic Books, 1970, pp 205–223

Ysseldyke JE, Algozzine B: Critical Issues in Special and Remedial Education. Boston, Houghton Mifflin, 1982

Zarkowsky H: The lead problem in children: dictum and polemic. Curr Probl Pediatr 6:1–47, 1976

Zellweger H: The Prader Willi syndrome (letter). JAMA 251:1835, 1984

Zrull JP, Westman JC, Arthur B, et al: A comparison of chlordiazepoxide, d-amphetamine and placebo in the treatment of hyperkinetic syndrome in children. Am J Psychiatry 120:590–591, 1963

Zrull JP, Westman JC, Arthur B, et al: A comparison of diazepam, d-amphetamine and placebo in the treatment of hyperkinetic syndrome in children. Am J Psychiatry 121:388–389, 1964

SECTION 2

Pervasive Developmental Disorders

Chapter 36

Introduction

The contributors to this section offer a comprehensive presentation of the state of the art of psychosocial and pharmacologic therapeutic interventions in pervasive developmental disorders. From a theoretical perspective, the section reflects an important shift from the psychodynamic concepts based on psychoanalytic theories, dominant during the post-World War II period. These have been replaced by an increased emphasis on empirical research based on cognitive and behavior theory, discussed in lucid, historical perspective by Gardner (1985). The resulting increase in knowledge about this disorder is reflected in its reformulation as a pervasive developmental disorder in the DSM-III (American Psychiatric Association 1980) and the DSM-III-R (American Psychiatric Association 1987), where it encompasses autistic disorder and pervasive developmental disorder not otherwise specified. Little is known about the validity of the latter diagnosis: the literature and experience are based on work and research conducted in patients diagnosed as autistic disorder or autism. However, some of the earlier literature reviewed here refers to autistic children as schizophrenic, or schizophrenic with autistic features, since DSM-II (American Psychiatric Association 1968) did not contain the diagnosis of autistic disorder: it had only schizophrenia, childhood type.

Since Kanner's (1943) historical article on the syndrome of early infantile autism, considerable progress has been made:

1. autistic disorder is now in DSM-III-R with both inclusion and exclusion criteria;
2. various research is directed to detect the biologic abnormalities underlying the behavioral and cognitive problems;
3. various therapeutic interventions directed toward both behavioral and cognitive abnormalities were developed and research strategies devised;
4. attempts are being made to assess more critically the efficacy of various treatment modalities;
5. classrooms and programs were developed and tailored for the needs of autistic individuals, who are both behaviorally and cognitively heterogeneous.

Chapter 37

Diagnosis and Evaluation for Treatment Planning

As noted in Chapter 36, the category of pervasive developmental disorders (PDD) was first introduced in DSM-III (American Psychiatric Association 1980) and it remains in DSM-III-R (American Psychiatric Association 1987). (The following diagnostic entities from DSM-III were included under PDD: infantile autism, full syndrome present; infantile autism, residual state; childhood onset PDD, full syndrome present; and atypical PDD.) These disorders are characterized by severe abnormalities and/or delays and unevenness in the development of all behaviors, particularly social, language, and cognitive areas, with onset of symptoms in infancy or before puberty. For details on the history; diagnostic criteria and symptoms; genetic, biologic, and environmental contributory factors; theories; and differential diagnosis, the reader is referred to reviews elsewhere (Campbell and Green 1985; DeMyer et al. 1981; Rutter 1985).

In DSM-III-R, the symptoms of these conditions are well defined and clearly described. With the help of a detailed developmental history, an accurate diagnosis is possible in most cases. The *DSM-III Training Guide for Diagnosis of Childhood Disorders* (Rapoport and Ismond 1984) was helpful for the use of DSM-III with children. However, a revision of DSM-IV is underway, although as of this writing it is not yet decided what will be the changes or additional criteria for autistic disorder.

As we are approaching DSM-IV, there is a great deal of work, discussion, and controversy concerning the group of PDDs (Cohen et al. 1986a, 1986b; Dahl et al. 1986; Denckla 1986; Volkmar et al. 1986; Rutter and Schopler 1988), without reference to discrete treatment approaches. Infantile autism is the only diagnostic entity we found in the literature, in regard to treatment, from this group of disorders. The validity of childhood onset PDD (DSM-III) has not yet been demonstrated. There is an increasing interest in Asperger's syndrome (Asperger 1944), also called autistic psychopathy, a severe personality disorder similar to autism but without a psychosis. Wing (1981, 1982), Burgoine and Wing (1983), and others feel that there is considerable overlap between Asperger's syndrome and infantile autism, or autistic disorder, whereas Cohen et al. (1986a) believe that some patients with Asperger's syndrome could be included in the category of autism.

At the time when this chapter was written, there was not one single report in the literature on autistic patients who were diagnosed by DSM-III-R criteria. Therefore, all discussions in this chapter will refer to infantile autism; its diagnostic criteria are listed in Table 1. It also should be noted that in some of the earlier literature, particularly on studies involving psychoactive drugs, infantile autism was referred to as schizophrenia, childhood type, using DSM-II (American Psychiatric Association 1968) criteria, usually with the qualification that patients, or the sample, had autistic features. However, those children met Kanner's (1943) and Rutter's (1972, 1978) criteria and the criteria of DSM-III for (early) infantile autism. Schizophrenia, with onset

Table 1. DSM-III-R Diagnostic Criteria for Pervasive Developmental Disorders

Autistic Disorder

At least eight of the following sixteen items are present, these to include at least two items from A, one from B, and one from C.

Note: Consider a criterion to be met *only* if the behavior is abnormal for the person's developmental level.

A. Qualitative impairment in reciprocal social interaction as manifested by the following:

(The examples within parentheses are arranged so that those first mentioned are more likely to apply to younger or more handicapped, and the later ones, to older or less handicapped, persons with this disorder.)

   (1) marked lack of awareness of the existence or feelings of others (e.g., treats a person as if he or she were a piece of furniture; does not notice another person's distress; apparently has no concept of the need of others for privacy)

   (2) no or abnormal seeking of comfort at times of distress (e.g., does not come for comfort even when ill, hurt, or tired; seeks comfort in a stereotyped way, e.g., says "cheese, cheese, cheese" whenever hurt)

   (3) no or impaired imitation (e.g., does not wave bye-bye; does not copy mother's domestic activities; mechanical imitation of other's actions out of context)

   (4) no or abnormal social play (e.g., does not actively participate in simple games; prefers solitary play activities; involves other children in play only as "mechanical aids")

   (5) gross impairment in ability to make peer friendships (e.g., no interest in making peer friendships; despite interest in making friends, demonstrates lack of understanding of conventions of social interaction, for example, reads phone book to uninterested peer)

B. Qualitative impairment in verbal and nonverbal communication, and in imaginative activity, as manifested by the following:

(The numbered items are arranged so that those first listed are more likely to apply to younger or more handicapped, and the later ones, to older or less handicapped, persons with this disorder.)

   (1) no mode of communication, such as communicative babbling, facial expression, gesture, mime, or spoken language

   (2) markedly abnormal nonverbal communication, as in the use of eye-to-eye gaze, facial expression, body posture, or gestures to initiate or modulate social interaction (e.g., does not anticipate being held, stiffens when held, does not look at the person or smile when making a social approach, does not greet parents or visitors, has a fixed stare in social situations)

   (3) absence of imaginative activity, such as playacting of adult roles, fantasy characters, or animals; lack of interest in stories about imaginary events

   (4) marked abnormalities in the production of speech, including volume, pitch, stress, rate, rhythm, and intonation (e.g., monotonous tone, questionlike melody, or high pitch)

   (5) marked abnormalities in the form of content of speech, including stereotyped and repetitive use of speech (e.g., immediate echolalia or mechanical repetition of television commercial); use of "you" when "I" is meant (e.g., using "You want cookie?" to mean "I want a cookie"); idiosyncratic use of words or phrases (e.g., "Go on green riding" to mean "I want to go on the swing"); or frequent irrelevant remarks (e.g., starts talking about train schedules during a conversation about sports)

   (6) marked impairment in the ability to initiate or sustain a conversation with others, despite adequate speech (e.g., indulging in lengthy monologues on one subject regardless of interjections from others) *(continued)*

Table 1.   DSM-III-R Diagnostic Criteria for Pervasive Developmental Disorders (continued)

C. Markedly restricted repertoire of activities and interests, as manifested by the following:

  (1) stereotyped body movements, e.g., hand-flicking or -twisting, spinning, head-banging, complex whole-body movements

  (2) persistent preoccupation with parts of objects (e.g., sniffing or smelling objects, repetitive feeling of texture of materials, spinning wheels of toy cars) or attachment to unusual objects (e.g., insists on carrying around a piece of string)

  (3) marked distress over changes in trivial aspects of environment, e.g., when a vase is moved from usual position

  (4) unreasonable insistence on following routines in precise detail, e.g., insisting that exactly the same route always be followed when shopping

  (5) markedly restricted range of interests and a preoccupation with one narrow interest, e.g., interested only in lining up objects, in amassing facts about meteorology, or in pretending to be a fantasy character

D. Onset during infancy or childhood.

Specify if childhood onset (after 36 months of age).
Specify: 299.00   infantile onset (before 36 months of age)
         299.90*   childhood onset (after 36 months of age)
         299.90*   age at onset unknown or NOS
         299.80   pervasive developmental disorder NOS

Note. From American Psychiatric Association (1987).

---

before puberty, seems to be a discrete clinical entity (Green et al. 1984; Kolvin 1971; Rutter 1985).

Purposes of Evaluation

Establishment of Diagnosis

A thorough evaluation and workup is required to establish a correct diagnosis to identify possible known or contributory factors to autism or coexisting conditions (e.g., partial deafness, seizure disorder), and to plan appropriate and effective treatment. The reasons for this are as follows: there is increasing evidence that the disorders under discussion, and specifically infantile autism, are behavioral syndromes that are etiologically heterogeneous. Furthermore, children who have conditions with detectable (or identifiable) etiology and require additional or other types of treatments may also display autistic-like symptoms. Pediatric and neurologic workup, biochemical studies, tests for inborn errors of metabolism, and chromosome studies including for fragile X are discussed elsewhere (Coleman and Gillberg 1985).

Evaluation includes the following:

- Developmental, prenatal and perinatal, medical, and other past history; family history; birth records and medical records (Campbell and Palij 1985b)
- History of prior medication, including psychoactive drugs (Campbell and Palij 1985c)
- Pediatric examination
- Pediatric neurologic evaluation

- Hearing and speech evaluation
- Psychiatric observation and evaluation
- Psychological testing
- Laboratory studies (Evaluation for inborn errors of metabolism and baseline electroencephalogram should be obtained in each case. Chromosome studies and brain scans are indicated for selected cases with atypical presentations.)
- Examination for abnormal movements (stereotypies, tics, chorea, Tourette's disorder, and tardive or withdrawal dyskinesias)

Developmental and Cognitive Functioning

Determining patterns of strengths and weaknesses (i.e., a profile) is only the initial step in conceptualizing an intervention program. More important is the individualization of the developmental profile, the unique pattern of strengths and weaknesses. What characterizes PDD is the heterogeneity in developmental functioning despite certain commonalities in abnormalities and symptoms. For example, although communication disturbances are present in all PDD cases, the range and variety of language problems and skills cover a wide spectrum from muteness and virtually no abstract concepts to elaborate conversational speech but with rigid content and perseveration. Similarly, many individuals may have fairly intact motor skills while others are awkward in movement or have motor planning difficulties. Thus each area of development needs assessment and comparison with each other and with normative standards for that chronological age. By delineation of how the individual lags behind or approximates the norm on the one hand, and is variable across his or her own profile on the other, the clinician can begin to individualize a treatment plan.

Family Needs and Priorities

An essential component of a comprehensive evaluation is the assessment of the concerns of the family of an individual with PDD. As noted above, families represent a critical support system. The role of the helping clinician involves strengthening that system and enhancing its coping abilities. Individuals with PDD typically have difficulty generalizing learning from one setting to another; the parental role is crucial in facilitating such a process. The initial phase in this process involves identifying the needs and priorities of the family. Also required is an evaluation of the resources available to the family, including its own capabilities to carry out necessary tasks (e.g., advocacy, home teaching and behavior management, mutual emotional support). This aspect of evaluation requires understanding the family in relation to the handicapped individual, that is, both recognizing how the handicapped child has affected the family and assessing the family's adaptive mechanisms and strategies of coping (Schopler and Mesibov 1984).

Community Resources

In addition to the family, the broader community context in which the PDD individual functions must be understood. This context includes school and day-care programs, various helping agencies such as social services and health care programs, recreational programs, after school programs, and summer programs. For the older individual, community resources needed to be evaluated include residential and vocational services. The rationale for incorporating the community into an evaluation lies in the pervasiveness of the disorder, its presence across all settings, and the necessity of providing consistent intervention in each setting. The assessment of community context should also have a longitudinal perspective to take into account the chronicity of the disorder. For example, if the evaluation of a young child indicates severe impairments, then specialized schooling will be needed for an extended period, and an exploration of the availability of continuity of such services should be made. Another aspect to the longitudinal perspective is the awareness that over time there will be a shift of responsibility from the family to the community for provision of care and decision making.

Clarification of Prognosis

As is evident from this discussion, there is an interaction among the goals of evaluation. An assumption that can be made is that consideration of the relevant data will lead to a reasonable prediction regarding future outcome of the individual. The literature has clarified what makes for relatively good or poor outcomes, and those indices (e.g., IQ, severity of impairment, family organization, availability of community resources) can be assessed as earlier described (Rutter 1977). Although it is neither necessary nor clinically wise to draw and assert definitive conclusions regarding prognosis for the young PDD child and the child's family, preliminary evidence can be ascertained and the groundwork laid for later discussion. Parents often raise this issue; honest, if tentative, opinions should be shared. Over time, particularly if data have been candidly presented all along, parents will become increasingly aware of the chronicity of their child's disorder, and the question of prognosis will focus on concrete plans.

Clinical experience and a review of the literature indicate that the majority of autistic children remain severely handicapped adults and may have to be institutionalized (Campbell and Green 1985; Campbell et al. 1978d; DeMyer et al. 1973; Eisenberg, 1956; Lockyer and Rutter 1969; Rutter and Lockyer 1967; Rutter et al. 1967). Acquisition of communicative language and good IQ remain the best predictors for outcome. There is no systematic research to assess critically what effect treatment(s) may have on the long-term outcome, or what is the best single treatment or combination of treatments in this condition. Most subjects who participated in long-term follow-up studies received a variety of treatments, and there were no controls. Preliminary results of a prospective longitudinal study of haloperidol in young autistic children suggest that when this drug is administered judiciously, it does not affect adversely IQ, and that some children have shown marked increases in IQ over time (Die Trill et al. 1984).

Strategies of Evaluation

In attempting to implement the goals of evaluation, there are essentially three basic sources of information: direct observation, verbal reports, and direct assessment. Observations can be made in a natural context, such as the school or home, or under more controlled circumstances in these settings by having a predetermined task set up or having the observer intervene. Although it is often quite useful to observe the individual in a natural setting, it is not always essential nor practical; comparable information can be obtained by written report or interviews with reliable informants. Discussed below are basic strategies for generating the data useful for treatment planning.

Behavioral Scales

A variety of objective and clinical scales have been developed in recent years to help in arriving at a behavioral profile or a diagnostic decision. Table 2 summarizes the main features of these instruments; more detailed review and evaluation can be found elsewhere (Campbell and Palij 1985b; Parks 1983). As can be noted from the table, each scale has evolved from a different perspective and orientation and intended for somewhat different purposes. For example, the E-2 (Rimland 1971) gathers its information from parent report and is intended to identify Kanner's syndrome or "classic" autistic children.

The Childhood Autism Rating Scale (CARS) (Schopler et al. 1980b, 1985) was developed in the context of direct observation in a clinical setting and serves the purpose of objectifying clinical observations of behaviors associated with autism and PDD. The 15 CARS items incorporate 1) Kanner's (1943) primary autism features; 2) other characteristics noted by Creak (1964), which are found in many but not all children who may be considered autistic; and 3) additional scales useful in tapping the symptoms characteristic of the younger child. The scale can be used in different settings (e.g., clinic assessment, classroom, report, observation in the home), and the results provide the most effective diagnostic screening in terms of presence or absence of autism. If autism is diagnosed, the degree of severity is classified as mild-moderate or moderate-severe. The CARS is not intended to be the sole source of determination of diagnosis, but has been shown to be a useful measure in conjunction with other relevant information.

Developmental and Educational Assessment

Because the essential problems in PDD are developmental, the most useful methods to pinpoint those dysfunctions should focus on developmental areas as well as examine deviations from normal patterns. Historically, evaluations of children with PDD or autism have utilized informal play techniques or traditional psychological tests with heavy emphasis on language. Neither has proved satisfactory. Nondirective play observations fail to provide the structure required to assess the child's abilities or disabilities objectively. This approach can typically lead to false conclusions, including an overestimate of intellectual potential. Traditional psychological tests require an understanding and expressive use of language that is often the major handicap for individuals with PDD. A session based on such tests typically yields little useful information and, worse, the mistaken notion that the child is "untestable" (Alpern 1967; Marcus and Baker 1986).

One instrument that has been designed to avoid these problems and to obtain information about developmental functioning and deviations is the Psychoeducational Profile (PEP) (Schopler and Reichler 1979; Mesibov et al. 1988). In contrast to traditional standardized tests, the PEP has a flexible administration and scoring system that permits the clinician to explore the unique and idiosyncratic learning patterns so characteristic of PDD individuals. In contrast to informal play techniques, the PEP provides a structured set of tasks to measure basic developmental skills such as imitation, eye-hand integration, and verbal and nonverbal cognition. In addition, there are many items keyed to the behavioral abnormalities of autism and PDD to allow for diagnostic inferences. Finally, interpretation of the findings leads to the development of an individualized treatment program (Schopler et al. 1980a).

There are several developmental screening instruments that are not specific to autistic or PDD individuals, but can provide useful information on developmental

Table 2. Characteristics of Diagnostic and Behavior Rating Scales for Autistic Children

Scale	Domains	Age range	Mode of administration	Scoring
Autism Screening Instrument for Educational Planning (Krug et al. 1979)	Sensory, relating, body, and object use language; social and self-help	18 months	Checklist	57 items sums of weighted items
Behavior Observation Scale (Freeman et al. 1978)	General language; language; response to stimuli; attending response; response to being helped; response to ball play; inappropriate response to pain; motility disturbances to stimuli	30–60 months	Observation in 9 3-minute intervals; combination of structured and unstructured; checklist	67 items frequency count
Behavior Rating Instrument for Autistic and Atypical Children (Ruttenberg et al. 1977)	Relationship to adult; communication; drive for mastery; vocalization and expressive speech; sound and speech reception; social responsiveness; body movement; psychobiologic development	Up to 54 months	Descriptive ratings based on observations	10 scale score from severe autism to normal; 3½ to 4 year level: cumulative score and profile
Childhood Autism Rating Scale (Schopler et al. 1980)	Relationship with people; imitation; affect; body awareness; relation to nonhuman objects; adaptation to environmental change; visual responsiveness; near receptor responsiveness; anxiety reaction; verbal communication; nonverbal communication; activity level; intellectual functioning; general impressions	All ages; has been used mostly with preadolescents	7-point rating scale based on observation of testing	a. scale scores (1–7) b. total score (15–60) c. 3 categories: no autism; mild to moderate autism; severe autism
E-2 Checklist (Rimland 1971)	Social interaction and affect; speech motor manipulative ability; intelligence and reaction to sensory stimuli; family characteristics; illness development; physiological and biologic data	Up to 7 years	Checklist based on parental report, including retrospective recall	Multiple choice; items scored + or –; autism score the difference between pluses and minuses; + 20 considered cutoff for Kanner's syndrome

functioning. These scales also include sections on self-help and adaptive skills. Among the better instruments available are the Vulpe Assessment (Vulpe 1977), particularly useful with younger or lower-level children; the Learning Accomplishment Profile (Sanford 1984), easy to administer for teachers and others in classroom or day-care settings; and the Brigance Diagnostic Inventory of Early Development (Brigance 1978), useful for its sequential arrangement of functional levels of a variety of skills. The main limitation of these tests is the inapplicability of certain items or scoring criteria to autistic children.

Psychological and Other Assessment Scales

Although traditional psychological tests such as the Wechsler (1974a, 1974b) intelligence scales may be appropriate for only approximately 10 to 15 percent of individuals with PDD because of their level of functioning and limited language skills, there are several standardized IQ measures that can be used effectively. Table 3 summarizes characteristics of the more popular psychological tests and their advantages and disadvantages with autistic and PDD individuals. These instruments can be used to supplement the developmental and clinical information reported above. In addition, they can provide IQ measures that, as has been reported in the literature, can aid in estimating future functioning and outcome. Since standardized IQ tests are also predictive of successful school achievement, their use with PDD cases can help identify those individuals whose chances for mainstreaming are more likely. Periodic retesting can establish the stability of cognitive growth or document spurts that may require a shift in educational planning.

Language assessment (see Chapter 39) can facilitate clarification of specific language and speech problems not completely delineated by the developmental or psychological tests. For children whose language falls below four years, the Sequenced Inventory for Communication Development (Hedrick et al. 1975) has been found useful. Assessing communication in natural settings is becoming recognized as having central importance (Watson and Lord 1982; Watson et al. 1989).

Measures of adaptive functioning are essential adjuncts because they can objectify home-living, personal self-care, and independent functioning abilities. The Vineland Social Maturity Scale (Doll 1965) and its revision, the Vineland Adaptive Behavior Scales (Sparrow et al. 1984), are excellent inventories for covering these important areas at home or school.

Family Interview

Of equal importance to assessing the individual with PDD is the assessment of the concerns, priorities, and resources of the family. The clinician should not only gather information about the child's functioning at home to round out the diagnostic picture, but also establish a working partnership with the parents based on a sensitivity to their needs and role as primary support system. The parent interview should cover at least three areas: early history, focusing on developmental and medical factors; major parental concerns and problems about the child; and current home functioning of the child, including adaptive skills, communication, socialization, and play skills. Traditionally, in an effort to identify the psychogenic origins in the family system, clinicians would focus on history factors such as parental feelings, infantile sexual experiences, and toilet training, issues now recognized as usually unrelated to the development of autism. Such a focus not only failed to clarify the child's problems, but usually increased the parents' sense of guilt and helplessness. This

Table 3. Summary of General Intelligence Tests

Test	Age range	Description	Autistic children for whom test is best suited	Advantages	Disadvantages
Bayley Mental Scale of Infant Development (Bayley 1969)	2 to 30 months	Motor, language, and social skills assessed in tasks designed to measure small increments of ability.	Young or severely delayed children, particularly if attentional and behavior skills are poor.	Breaks down social and language skills into small components. Tasks require only brief attention.	For children with poor language and social skills but good visual-motor skills, range of visual-motor tasks may be too low.
Merrill-Palmer Test of Mental Abilities (Stutsman 1948)	18 months to 6 years	Wide range of visual-motor tasks, smaller number of language items.	Children whose conceptual and language deficits make higher tests inappropriate, but who have relatively good visual-motor skills.	Attractive materials. Language and nonlanguage items fairly well separated.	Language skills not comprehensively assessed. Autistic children with good visual-motor skills may score misleadingly high. No derived IQ.
Leiter International Performance Scale (Leiter 1969)	3 to 18 years	Nonlanguage test used with deaf children. Child demonstrates understanding of concepts by matching blocks to a pictorial key.	Children whose conceptual abilities greatly exceed their language or who have difficulty with tasks requiring social interaction.	Little interaction with examiner required. Repetitive routine of administration minimizes stress for many autistic children.	No language assessment. Very little assessment of interpersonal skills, so score may not be accurate reflection of ability in "real life" situations.
Hiskey-Nebraska Test of Learning Aptitude (Hiskey 1966)	3 to 16 years	Nonlanguage test used with deaf children. Various subtests involve imitation and memory as well as matching.	Children whose conceptual abilities greatly exceed their language, and who can sustain attention to and interaction with examiner.	Tests wide range of concepts and interpersonal skills with no language demands. Can be given with or without verbal instructions.	No language assessment. Longer and more demanding than Leiter scale. No derived IQ.

Test	Age range	Description	Population	Advantages	Disadvantages
McCarthy Scales of Children's Abilities (McCarthy 1972)	2½ to 8½ years	Five subscales, partially overlapping, measure verbal, perceptual-performance, quantitative, motor, and memory skills.	Children whose language skills are not severely delayed and who have relatively good attentional and behavioral skills.	2½ to 8½ year range better suited to many children than Wechsler tests. Fewer tasks dependent on language. Attractive materials. Administration allows for repeated demonstration and encouragement.	Language and conceptual demands too difficult for many autistic children. Comparison of subtest scores difficult.
Wechsler Preschool and Primary Scale of Intelligence (WPPSI) (Wechsler 1974a)	4 to 6½ years	Verbal and performance subscales. Emphasis on language skills. Several subtests assess formally acquired knowledge (e.g., arithmetic, information).	Higher-level autistic children, whose language skills are only mildly delayed, and who have good attentional and behavioral skills.	Well designed and well standardized. Several subtests assess skills emphasized in school. Alternation of verbal and performance subtests helps reduce language demands.	Language and conceptual demands too difficult for most autistic children. Receptive language important even on performance subtest. Administration guidelines fairly rigid.
Wechsler Intelligence Scale for Children—Revised (WISC-R) (Wechsler 1974b)	6 to 17 years				
Kaufman Assessment Battery for Children (K-ABC) (Kaufman and Kaufman 1983)	2½ to 12 years	Separates abilities from acquired knowledge; format requires simple motor responses or short verbal answers; measures variety of cognitive and achievement skills.	Similar to Wechsler group—need for further study as test becomes more widely used.	Well designed and standardized; age range wider than Wechsler or McCarthy scales; teaching items for each subtest allows for flexibility of administration; expressive language demands minimal; visually oriented format; easy to administer.	Does not allow for assessment of language peculiarities and problems picked up by Wechsler scales; neuropsychology model (sequential-simultaneous dichotomy) of questionable value for autistic group; lack of research and clinic use with this population warrants cautious approach to interpretations.

Note. Adapted from Baker (1983).

type of destructive approach should be replaced with the attitude that parents are the victims of the child's handicap in many respects and require support and guidance from the clinician. This attitude can be conveyed in an initial interview, which should be problem-focused, cover development and skills, and allow for full expression of the parental feelings about their situation. As mentioned earlier, an objective adaptive measurement instrument can be used in the interview integrated with the clinical assessment.

Assessing Community Contexts

The final source of information comes from the community. If a child is not yet in any program, then the focus becomes the identification of possible programs or individual therapists in the community. If a school is involved, it helps to evaluate the structure of the classroom—that is, its behavioral and instructional methods, including the emphasis on communication and social-skills training, central issues to PDD. If the individual has been served in a program, it becomes crucial to involve a knowledgeable representative from that program in the assessment. Comparable to the parent interview, emphasis is on identifying problems and concerns of the program and how the individual functions in this setting in terms of behavior, communication, and socialization. This information can be gathered through verbal report, written records, or direct observation of the program. If the clinician visits the program, effort should be made to observe several parts of the schedule, such as individual sessions, formal group work, and informal play or recreation periods. Another feature of this assessment component is the evaluation of the relationship between home and the community program. It is common for tension to develop between these settings based on misunderstandings of the different priorities and requirements as well as the strong emotional involvement and commitment of each. The clinician will find maintenance of clear communication among all parties a necessary function for successful treatment of the child. An effective treatment plan has to be concerned with both home and school or other community program. Consistent viewpoints, if not actual intervention strategies, have to be established.

Objective assessment techniques include comparable adaptive scales discussed above, behavioral observation methods used in research studies (Powers and Handlemann 1984), and ecologic inventories that evaluate natural environments in terms of what skills may be required of the PDD individual (Brown et al. 1979).

Implementing a Treatment Plan

Once the diagnosis is established and a profile of the individual is determined, with its deficits and assets (if any), a detailed treatment plan for the patient and for involvement of the family or of the school, if applicable to appropriate, is to be developed. Goals are set for both the child and for the parents, or for the entire family. Both immediate and long-term goals should be established.

While diagnostic clarification and individualized assessment yield useful information, evaluation should lead logically to a meaningful treatment plan. Consideration of the strategies described above can provide the basis for treatment decisions.

With the PDD population, treatment is defined in terms of structured intervention, with an emphasis on education and consultation. Elsewhere in this volume treatment strategies are discussed more fully. They are based on a sound understanding of the fundamental problems of autism and PDD. These include its chronic and pervasive nature, deficits in communicative and social functioning, accompanying behavioral difficulties, and associated learning weaknesses.

Interpreting Results

Prior to the implementation of such a plan, a thorough and open discussion of the individual's problem and condition needs to be held with the family. Because parents have to be in collaboration with professionals in the treatment of their handicapped child, complete disclosure under most circumstances is required. Candid sharing of findings helps build trust and a sense of confidence in the professional and can facilitate implementation of intervention strategies. Thus the actual first step in the treatment process is the diagnostic interpretative conference. This process is discussed in detail elsewhere (Morgan 1984; Shea 1984).

Establishing Goals

Treatment goals should be discussed as part of the interpretative conference. These goals should include the priorities and needs of the family, the needs of the school or related community setting, and the diagnostic and assessment profile of the child. Goals may vary from setting to setting. For example, the family may have as its highest priority self-help skills or improving sleep habits, whereas the school might emphasize task performance. Goals may even appear to be in conflict. For example, a teacher or speech therapist may feel that sign language may be more useful than speech, whereas the parents may wish to emphasize speech training. At times the clinician may have goals that cannot realistically be achieved in either the home or school because of limited resources. Thus goals may need to be altered or reduced in scope to accommodate environmental circumstances.

Goals should have both short- and long-term components. The short-term goals are derived from the current assessment data, such as deficits and strengths in communicative functioning, social skills, and behavior problems. They may emphasize the improvement in these skill areas (e.g., ability to focus on a task, vocabulary, self-feeding, using utensils, sitting at the table during meals) or reduction of maladaptive behaviors (e.g., aggressiveness, self-mutilation, hyperactivity, stereotypies, insomnia). Specific intervention strategies can be geared to the home or school setting.

Depending on the individual's chronological and maturational age and intellectual functioning, long-term goals may include developing self-care; social, adaptive, and language skills; and academic or other skills. They are based on an understanding of the future implications of the severity of the disorder. If it appears quite likely that the affected individual will require specialized education, sheltered work, and eventual alternative residential placement, then long-range planning should be directed toward effective and timely development of these services.

The child's, adolescent's, or even adult's needs may change with time: at some point special education or pharmacotherapy will have to be replaced by vocational training or individual psychotherapy, geared to the individual's cognitive and verbal skill level.

Evaluating Treatment Effectiveness

The final step in treatment planning is the ongoing assessment of treatment effectiveness. Measurement can focus on short-term objectives, such as the successful mastery of a communication skill or self-help activity, or on larger goals, such as integration into a mainstream school setting or living at home without requiring institutional care. The key to a fair evaluation of treatment effectiveness is the recognition that PDD and autism are chronic, developmental disorders for which the likelihood of completely normal adjustment is extremely small. Outcome success should be based on a realistic appraisal of each individual's potential and factors such as the ability of the child to cope and survive at home and in the community. The heterogeneity of this population and the unpredictability of development patterns for many of them require an ongoing evaluation process that is highly individualized.

Chapter 38

Education for Children with Autism

The education of children and youth with autism and related pervasive development disorders has progressed from a few isolated private programs just 20 years ago to a legal requirement for a free appropriate public education. Education is now the most prevalent form of treatment and the one that has shown the most consistent long-term effectiveness (Wilcox and Thompson 1980). Early research (e.g., Brown 1960) showed psychotherapy for autistic children to be ineffective. These changes are the results of research, demonstration programs, and parent and professional advocacy.

This chapter reviews the role that education plays in the treatment plan for children with autism. Unlike some other treatment approaches, many aspects of education for handicapped children are determined by a combination of federal, state, and local laws and regulations. These rulings in combination with professional judgment and the wishes of parents determine the nature of each child's education.

In addition to knowledge of legal prescriptions, those providing education and related services to children must be familiar with other key issues noted in this chapter. Education must be based on a thorough assessment of the child's strengths, weaknesses, and interests. Many instructional methods have been promoted for this population. The most effective methods are reviewed. The curriculum or the content of the educational program is of great importance in preparing students for life outside the classroom. Closely related to curricular issues are concerns related to the setting in which education takes place. This chapter provides a discussion of the "least restrictive environment" and approaches to applying this principle to children with autism. The chapter concludes with a review of the roles that parents may play in the education of their autistic child and some observations on the physician's role in education programs.

Goals of Education

In many respects the goals of education for children with autism are similar to those for all children. Education is intended to prepare students to function as independently, as productively, and with as much dignity as possible in adulthood. Because children with autism learn slowly and are likely to require supervision throughout their lives, education must focus on essential skills. It is indefensible to spend many hours teaching a skill for which the student will never have a use.

Not long ago the success of school programs was often judged by the number of skills taught, or the rate of acquisition of new skills, or the decrease in "odd" behaviors, or the purported happiness of the children, or the extent to which they were compliant or did not bother others. These are not the central goals of education. Today education is judged successful if students can function well outside of school and throughout their lives.

Elements of Education Services Determined by Law

Today many elements of appropriate education are specified by The Education for All Handicapped Children Act of 1975 (PL 94-142) and by state and local laws and regulations. The effective professional must be aware of which elements are legally required and which elements depend on judgment of best current educational practice. Those elements of a quality education that are determined by federal law are as follows.

1. Whereas prior to the implementation of PL 94-142, children with autism or other handicaps could be excluded from school, the law now requires that *all* children between the ages of three and 21 be given a free, appropriate public education. Professional judgment is still required to determine what is "appropriate," but education must be at public expense and available to all children, regardless of handicap.
2. The process of deciding on the appropriate classroom placement must follow certain prescribed procedures. The recommendation of one person, no matter how expert, is not sufficient. A team representing school personnel and parents or parent surrogates makes the decision on educational placement.
3. The classroom placement decision must take into consideration the results of an evaluation conducted by a multidisciplinary team and must not depend solely on one test. The tests or evaluation procedures used must be "nondiscriminatory," must be given "in the child's native language or other mode of communication," and must have been validated for use with autistic children. Thus a test such as the third edition of the Stanford-Binet Intelligence Scale (Terman and Merrill 1973), which is highly weighted toward verbal skills and has not been validated for use with autistic students would be inappropriate under the law for evaluation of most children with autism. A test such as the Psychoeducational Profile (Schopler and Reichler 1979), which allows for the individual's preferred mode of communication and has been validated for use with autistic children, would meet the requirements of the law when evaluating for classroom placement.

4. The goals of each child's education must be specified in the form of an individualized education program (IEP), and these goals must be revised yearly. Short-term objectives that can be measured must also be specified. Thus vague goals, such as improving language skills, are not acceptable.

5. Education must take place in the "least restrictive environment." Although this principle is strongly established in law, its implementation requires good judgment and experience with individual cases. Approaches to implementation are addressed in a later section.

6. All of the major elements of PL 94-142 include specific ways in which parents must be involved. The law and its regulations also make clear the due process rights of parents. This emphasis is a major change from the years when parents' behavior was believed to cause autism.

The Effectiveness of Education

Studies by Halpern (1970) and Rutter and Bartak (1973) reported several approaches to education, all of which resulted in some progress for autistic children. Such findings require refinement, however. What are the elements that make some classroom approaches more effective than others?

In 1971, Schopler et al. took a substantial step toward clarifying this issue in a study that demonstrated clearly that autistic children's behavior is more appropriate and organized in a structured rather than an unstructured treatment approach. Rutter and Bartak (1973) confirmed and extended these findings to a classroom setting. Their study compared the progress of children in three programs using different educational approaches over a three-and-a-half to four-year period. The program that used a structured approach to teach specific skills led to superior academic progress compared to two unstructured programs stressing interpersonal relationships.

Rutter and Bartak's (1973) extensive comparisons of these three groups highlighted some important issues that have been studied further in recent years. Many of these early findings and clinical suggestions have been confirmed by later research. For instance, although Rutter and Bartak found that a structured approach to direct instruction led to good academic progress, measures of social responsiveness and deviant behavior outside of the classroom were not affected. Even academic skills had limited generalization beyond the classroom.

These findings led Rutter (1970) and Rutter and Bartak (1973) to several recommendations that have stood the test of later research. They suggested a practical, life skills approach emphasizing communication, social skills, and basic skills needed to hold a job. They noted that education should start early (before age four or five), continue through adolescence, involve social contacts with children who are not autistic, and actively involve parents.

Instructional Methods

Behavioral Approach

Specific methods to structure teaching activities and to reduce problem behaviors were defined in a variety of settings (Rutter 1970; Schopler et al. 1971). One school of thought (e.g., Lovaas 1977, 1981) advocated the elimination of virtually all odd or self-stimulating behavior and the teaching of eye contact and compliance to teacher instructions as prerequisites for teaching other skills to autistic children. This approach has also emphasized a rigid format of instruction in which the child must achieve a predetermined level of mastery on each skill before moving to the next step.

Although all teaching approaches apply behavioral principles of learning (whether or not they do it purposely or systematically), this approach to behavioral instruction achieves precision by following exact lesson plans that specify both the teacher's and the student's correct behaviors. The activity, its objectives, and the motivational system (often a tangible reinforcer) are determined by the adult. The skills taught are seldom chosen with a strong concern for their functional application.

This approach has succeeded in demonstrating the teaching of a variety of discrete skills (see review by Egel et al. 1980), but as in Rutter and Bartak's (1973) earlier research, these skills have generalized beyond the classroom in only a limited way (Carr 1980). In addition, this strategy has shown little success in teaching initiation or spontaneity of behavior. Problems in these areas are common for autistic students and limit the practical application of school skills in home, work, recreation, or other community settings.

Incidental Teaching

To avoid these limitations, recent studies have retained the precision and objectivity of behavioral methods while making the teaching sequence less rigid. For instance, it is possible for the teacher to specify the goals and objectives and also capitalize on naturally occurring learning opportunities. This strategy still requires considerable planning, but instead of requiring a fixed set of behaviors, the teacher plans a learning environment that takes advantage of student interests, abilities, and estabished routines as well as the natural consequences of behavior. This approach improves learning, reduces behavior problems, and produces more spontaneous, generalizable skills.

For instance, one child's favorite activity during a free-choice period in school was needlepoint. The teacher's goal was for the student to ask for help when he needed it. To achieve this the teacher would occasionally misplace the needle or another piece of essential material, thus giving the student a natural occasion to ask "Where is the needle?" This plan took advantage of the student's interest and involved a familiar task. Asking for help led to a natural consequence; the child received an answer and was able to complete an enjoyable activity.

Many variations on this theme exist. Students are required to ask for help, get needed materials, involve another student, clean up and put away, use basic math skills, follow a schedule, and so on as part of practical, useful, and interesting activities. Children are asked systematically to learn one new skill in order to combine it with several old, familiar skills to complete a practical task.

These problems have been addressed in recent research by considering several aspects of the setting and methods of teaching. For instance, generalization has been shown to improve when the skill is taught in several real settings in which it will actually be used, rather than doing all teaching at a table in the classroom (Carr 1980; Handleman and Harris 1983). Studies of "incidental teaching" of communication skills (Carr and Kologinsky 1983; McGee at al. 1983, 1985) have shown greater generalization and spontaneity when the teaching takes place in natural communication settings, when it involves material of interest to the child and selected by the child, and when the activity leads to a meaningful consequence. Peck (1985) used a similar approach to increase spontaneous social language production and to improve the perceived social climate of two classrooms. When students with autism were offered more choices and more communicative opportunities and when teachers responded more often to student initiatives during instruction, the students' social communication increased.

Incidental teaching is one term for this approach, usually applied to teaching language. It is an example of a strategy that considers the unique learning, behavior, motivation, social, and communication problems of autism and designs a learning experience with these difficulties in mind.

Planned Learning Environments

An understanding of the central problems or deficits in autism and their implications for teaching helps the teacher to plan a total learning environment in which the demands of the task are clearer and in which the child can be successful. This approach involves careful planning of each activity and the whole learning environment as well as planning appropriate consequences for learning. A well-planned lesson is one that clearly communicates the nature of the task to the child, has a clear beginning and end, is interesting for the child and the child's peers, is appropriate for the child's developmental level, and has a clear use or application in the child's life.

Planning the learning environment may involve the choice of materials, arrangement of space, limiting distractions, scheduling the length and sequence of activities, and providing some predictability or routine. The appropriate environment for learning some skills may be a table in the classroom; for others it may be the cafeteria, or the hallway, or the playground. Some skills (e.g., restaurant skills, job skills) are best taught in nonschool settings. An effective teacher plans the task and the setting to ensure success, interest, opportunity to apply the skills, and generalization to other practical settings. An awareness of the special problems of autism is important in this planning because it can facilitate pleasant, productive, and practical learning without the need to punish or suppress every odd behavior.

Reduction of Behavior Problems

This broader issue has been addressed by Schopler and Bristol (1980), who described many common problems associated with autism. Their observations are especially valuable when considering the need to reduce difficult behaviors. For instance, autistic students may engage in temper tantrums, hitting others, or throwing materials. Instead of immediately punishing these behaviors, it is important to see them as manifestations of the central problems of autism. Children with no effective means of communication may engage in tantrums or aggression because they have no other ways to express their wishes or their frustrations. Such behavior may also be related to deficits in social skills or sensory perceptions. Refusal to eat certain foods may be related to resistance to change or to impaired sensory perceptions. Inability to play with others or use toys appropriately may be manifestations of the autistic child's difficulties in relating to others or to materials or may be a reflection of cognitive limitations.

There are, of course, times when self-stimulation or other behavior problems are so severe that they interfere with the child's learning or the broader classroom program. The question of whether to target a certain behavior for reduction is a complex but important one. Schopler (1976; Schopler et al. 1980) and Evans and Meyer (1985) urged teachers to consider such issues as whether the behavior in question is dangerous, whether it truly interferes with learning, whether it increases the child's risk of institutionalization, and whether it makes other people avoid social contact with the child. Only when these and other issues have been thoroughly considered can the teachers and parents decide whether the use of behavior reduction procedures, particularly punishment, is justified.

The occurrence of problem behavior in students with autism has led to many research studies using punishment to reduce such behavior. Studies of aversive procedures ranging from mild reprimands to electric shock have been reported and have led to serious concerns about the ethical and legal use of these procedures. Teachers should be aware of state laws and local school system policies regarding punishment. Those who train and advise teachers should also be familiar with the extensive literature on the pros and cons of punishment (Matson and DiLorenzo 1984). As a rule of thumb, parent permission must be obtained, and punishment should not be tried until it has been convincingly demonstrated that positive approaches, such as teaching alternative behaviors, are unsuccessful.

Linking Assessment to Teaching

Although a thorough understanding and mastery of teaching methods is essential, these methods cannot be applied effectively without information about individual students. All teaching methods must be individualized. This information may come from a formal test designed for autistic children (e.g., Schopler and Reichler 1979), or from a behavioral assessment (Powers and Handleman 1984), or some combination. The teacher's task is then to use this information to structure teaching activities at a developmental level that is appropriate for the child and to accommodate for the unique problems of autism to ensure the child's success.

An appropriate assessment of the child is one that provides the teacher with the information needed to individualize instruction. Schopler et al. (1980) described in detail this process of applying assessment information to school and home programs.

Curriculum

Although the topics of teaching methods and child assessment in autism have been addressed for several years, the content of school programs has received attention only recently. Until the last few years, nearly all school programs for autistic students had been for young children and had borrowed their curricula from early education for nonhandicapped students. As these children have grown older and it has become clear that few autistic students have benefited from an academically oriented curriculum, the emphasis has changed. Classes for adolescent students have increased, and the emphasis has shifted toward the teaching of practical life skills, as Rutter (1970) suggested earlier. Such skills should have immediate application outside of school and in the adult years and should prepare students for employment. Examples of this change can be seen in the increased efforts to teach communication and social skills.

Communication

Although difficulties in language and virtually all forms of communication are recognized to be central to autism, educational approaches to language have been limited until recently. Fay and Schuler (1980) recognized the failure of traditional speech therapy methods and other approaches to improve the form of speech in autistic children. They emphasized instead a pragmatic approach designed to give students some effective means of communication, even if it is not standard speech.

This change in emphasis has led to a growth in alternative communication systems, such as signing, use of informal gestures, pictures, written words, and other individualized strategies. For autistic students who do speak, the emphasis is on spontaneous use of simple appropriate messages rather than perfect articulation. These approaches have been combined with the advantages of incidental teaching to provide a practical curriculum in communication skills (Watson 1985; Watson et al. 1989).

Social Skills

Even high functioning autistic students who have mastered difficult academic skills and who have good speech face serious adjustment problems in adulthood. Autistic adults almost always continue to have difficulties in the communication patterns and social interactions. Recognizing this problem, many school programs have begun to teach social skills as early as possible. These efforts involve both specific teaching activities stressing the social behavior expected in our culture and exposure to broader social experiences that allow students to practice and generalize these skills.

Olley (1986) described a curriculum for social skills training in the classroom that takes into account the individual autistic child's social difficulties as well as the various settings in which social skills must be used. The move toward education in the least restrictive environment has provided many children with increased social opportunities. For instance, McHale (1983) described the social changes in young autistic students who participated in daily play groups with nonhandicapped children in their school. Strain (1983) documented benefits in social skills and generalization associated with interaction with nonhandicapped peers.

As school services grow and change and special education curriculums become more sophisticated, Rutter's (1970) suggestion that communication and social skills form a core of education in practical life skills for autistic students is coming close to reality.

Early Education

Despite the fact that autism is usually identifiable in the first 30 months of life, and Rutter (1970) pointed out the need for early education, surprisingly little research exists on the effectiveness of early versus later treatment. In a review of this literature, Simeonsson et al. (1987) concluded that although many individual studies of young children with autism exist, few studies have examined comprehensive early education efforts.

These few strong studies involved relatively small numbers of children and will require replication and follow-up. On the basis of current research, however, Simeonsson et al. (1987) concluded that early education can be effective if it 1) uses a structured, behavioral approach; 2) involves parents; 3) is intensive and available virtually every day; and 4) emphasizes generalization of skills to practical settings. This area is one in which we may expect to see a great deal of future research.

Education in the Least Restrictive Environment

Although education in the least restrictive environment is required by law and well agreed on in principle, its implementation is subject to much debate. It is an area requiring substantial professional judgment.

The law requires that, to the maximum extent possible, handicapped children be educated in the same settings as their nonhandicapped age-mates. Although a continuum of services from more restrictive or separate services to minimally restrictive classroom placements should be available, placement in a more restrictive setting may take place only if it has been shown that the child cannot progress satisfactorily in a less restrictive setting.

This provision of the law has led to an increase in services for autistic students in regular public schools and increased contacts between autistic and nonhandicapped students. Although autistic students are seldom able to profit academically from mainstreaming into regular classes, other carefully planned contacts such as interaction on the playground, in physical education, in the cafeteria, or in peer tutoring sessions are becoming commonplace in many schools (Arick et al. 1983; Gaylord-Ross et al. 1984; McHale 1983; McHale at al. 1981).

Developing Classroom Programs

The great heterogeneity of characteristics in autism and the low prevalence of the disorder make educational planning in the least restrictive environment very difficult for most school systems. In very rural areas, children with autism must, by necessity, be educated with other students whose learning characteristics are quite different. Teachers in such settings may find it very valuable to receive classroom consultation from someone experienced in individualizing instruction for this population. Such consultation is also valuable in reducing the frustration and sense of isolation faced by teachers in rural areas. In urban school districts, more flexibility in planning and grouping students is possible.

In North Carolina more than 65 public school classrooms are affiliated with Division TEACCH at the University of North Carolina at Chapel Hill and compose the largest statewide system of classes for children with autism and related disorders. The classes provide the specialized educational approaches needed to compensate for the learning and communication problems of autism. By being located in public schools, they also allow opportunities for less restrictive experiences, and such activities can be planned according to children's individual needs and abilities. Even for children whose education programs take place entirely in the self-contained class, their experiences are broadened by the normal school experiences and incidental contacts with nonhandicapped children. In addition, this format allows children in regular classes to gain a better understanding of autism (McHale and Simeonsson 1980). Thus the North Carolina approach individualizes the concept of least restrictive environment for children at all levels of ability.

Planning an Individualized Program

The process of planning an individualized program of instruction has been described in detail by Schopler and Bristol (1980). This strategy begins with an assessment of each child's abilities and interests and involves the parents in all stages. The information gained in the assessment contributes to the development of initial individualized teaching objectives that can be included in the IEP. Ongoing measurement of classroom progress provides data for revising the instructional curriculum and methods.

To accomplish these individualized activities in a classroom containing perhaps six students and only one teacher and one aide, the class must be very well organized and structured. An emphasis from an early age on a predictable schedule and routine for the day combined with very clear instructions, consequences, and physical structure can make the demands of the class more readily understood for students with autism. Within this structured approach, teachers emphasize independent work for all students, beginning as young as possible. The result is that a teacher and aide can plan instruction to accomplish individualized objectives. A balance of one-to-one instruction for teaching new skills; instruction for practicing old skills in independent work or group settings; instruction in engaging in leisure or activities earned as reinforcers, activities in other classes, physical education, music, and art; and instruction in functional skills outside the classroom or school are used to achieve both individual and group goals.

Most of the research literature on behavioral instruction has involved one-to-one teaching. Lovaas (1981) and others have described careful plans that begin with intensive one-to-one instruction and systematically prepare students to work independently and in groups. However, the reality for most teachers is that students are placed in classes without this preparation, and the teachers must manage the activities of the whole class with little time available for one-to-one teaching.

Reid and Favell (1984) reviewed the literature on group instruction and concluded that it is a practical and useful approach for many students. However, the research does not allow teachers to match individual students to the best method of instruction. In general, group instruction is more likely to be effective for mild or moderately handicapped students than for the severely impaired.

Parent Involvement

The active and meaningful involvement of parents in school programs is required by PL 94-142 and is widely supported. The 1983 amendments (PL 98-199) provide further support for parent training and information. Parents have played many roles and had services provided for them in many ways. They have been trained in behavior modification, in speech instruction, and in teaching a wide variety of skills at home. They have been the primary teachers for their children, and they have assisted classroom teachers. They have provided key information and assistance in their children's evaluations. They have gone to clinics and allowed professionals to visit their homes. They have assisted each other, helped to train professionals, and formed organizations that have advocated effectively for their children.

In general, the role of parents has shifted in recent years from one of receiving training or counseling from professionals to a diversity of roles representing true collaboration with professionals.

The Psychiatrist's Role in the Classroom

Although the stereotype of the autistic child is that of an attractive and apparently physically healthy youngster, in fact many children and youth with autism have medical concerns that affect their school programs. Autism that coexists with mental retardation syndromes, seizures, odd sleep patterns, and many other difficulties makes the psychiatrist's close work with parents and teachers essential.

At the time that parents learn of their child's disorder, they will likely seek the advice of their pediatrician or family physician regarding both medical concerns and other problems in planning for the child's future. Although many physicians will refer the family to others who specialize in pervasive developmental disorders, the initial information given, the support for the family, and the attitude toward the future that the physician conveys may have lasting impact. The family physician may continue to provide support for many years, even if specialized medical care is given elsewhere.

When considering classroom placement, in many states a physical examination and perhaps a screening for neurologic problems are required. The psychiatrist may participate in the school-based committee that makes a formal recommendation for classroom placement. Recommendations and information are generally welcomed, particularly with regard to seizures and the goals and effects of particular drugs. A knowledge of the effects and side effects of a student's medication can help both parents and teachers understand the child's behavior and teach more effectively.

At an earlier time, the psychiatrist's role in the classroom was seen as an extension of psychotherapy provided for the child and/or the parents. As the primary treatment has shifted from psychotherapy to education, physicians have assumed a different, if no less important, role in interdisciplinary school services. Supportive counseling or psychotherapy may still be appropriate for some families to help them to cope with the difficulties of a severely handicapped child (or other unrelated difficulties).

The psychiatrist's current contributions in monitoring and treating medical problems and informing and supporting both parents and teachers are important complements to the school program.

Chapter 39

Language and Communication Therapy

Goals of Therapy

Language Therapy Versus Communication Therapy

There has been a major shift over the past 10 years in the focus of therapy for language problems in children with autism and related disorders. The shift has come about in part because autism is now viewed as a developmental disorder. In the treatment of language problems in autism as well as in other developmental disorders affecting language (e.g., mental retardation, developmental language delay), therapists have increasingly relied on concepts derived from the study of normal language acquisition (e.g., Bloom and Lahey 1978; MacDonald 1978; McLean and Snyder-McLean 1978). Further, problems of language development in autism and related disorders have been increasingly viewed from the broader perspective of the communication and social interaction deficits characteristic of these disorders. Thus, in treating this population, goals of language therapy are now subsumed under goals of communication therapy.

Maximizing Communication Skills at the Child's Current Developmental Level

The first broad goal of such therapy is to maximize communication skills at the child's current developmental level. By communication skills, we refer here to a person's ability to send messages that others can interpret and to interpret messages that other people send. Messages are often communicated, either in whole or in part, by means of a formal language (e.g., English, Chinese, American Sign Language), but communication can also be nonverbal, achieved through gestures, facial expression, gaze, pictures, or other nonlanguage means.

At the most basic level, autistic children seem to be less aware of the potential power of communication than are normal children and children with other handicapping conditions. Thus a major task in communication therapy is to help autistic children understand that by communicating they can get other people to act and react in ways the children find desirable.

To maximize communication skills, the therapist must begin by identifying the means or form(s) of communication that are easiest for the child to use. The therapist must also identify what the child is most likely to be interested in communicating about (i.e., what does the child like or need?), help the child to communicate those messages appropriately, and then ensure that the messages achieve the desired response from people in the child's environment.

This approach contrasts with earlier efforts to have a direct therapeutic impact on the language skills of autistic children. In early behavior modification programs, teaching speech was an end goal in itself, abstracted from its potential role as a means to communicate (e.g., Hewitt 1965; Lovaas et al. 1966; Risley and Wolf 1967; Wolf et al. 1964). Thus the child was typically taught to imitate sounds and words, and to pair words discriminatively with the appropriate referent. Food rewards, tokens, and praise were given to reinforce "correct" responses. There was no inherent relation between the speech and the consequence (reinforcer), as would be the case in natural communicative exchanges.

One advantage of the current approach, which permits any (socially acceptable) form as a means to the end of communicating successfully, is that the list of prerequisite skills can be greatly reduced. To participate in a structured stimulus-response reinforcement program to acquire speech skills, the child was generally required to demonstrate first a range of "prerequisite" skills such as sitting in a chair for a specified length of time, giving eye contact on command, imitating a variety of nonspeech behaviors, and refraining from self-stimulatory or other "bizarre" behaviors. All of the above may be desirable goals in intervention with autistic children, but none are prerequisites for learning to communicate. Furthermore, it is now believed that learning to communicate will generally have favorable effects in these other areas (e.g., Casey 1978).

Establish Flexibility of Communication Across Everyday Contexts

Once the therapist has identified the easiest socially acceptable means of communication for a child and the child has learned to use those means to communicate some wants and needs to others, therapy goals should expand to include a concern with the flexibility or generalization of communication skills. The child needs to learn to use communication skills in as many contexts encountered during everyday life as are appropriate for communicating a given message.

The problem that autistic children have in generalizing skills to new situations is well recognized (Fay and Schuler 1980). While there is much documentation showing that specific language training programs have improved specific skills of autistic children in specific contexts (Churchill 1978; Lovaas 1977), there is little evidence that these skills lead to self-initiated communicative efforts in other contexts (Bartak and Rutter 1973; Lovaas 1977; Lovaas et al. 1973).

Shane (1979) conceptualized communication therapy as entailing two broad aspects. Vertical programming is concerned with increasing the child's knowledge of the symbolic systems of communication. Horizontal programming is concerned with increasing the range of situations in which the child's communicative attempts are relevant and effective. Because of the social deficit associated with autism, understanding how communication is used is at least as difficult as the acquisition of knowledge of symbolic systems. Therefore, it is imperative that communication therapy for these children incorporate horizontal programming as well as vertical programming on a continuous basis. Historically, this need was largely ignored in language training programs for autistic and other developmentally handicapped children, leading Guess et al. (1977) to conclude that "the issue of generalization is certainly the most current and pressing problem re: language training" (p. 363). It is encouraging to note that this situation has improved. In reviewing 24 programs designed for children with severe communication handicaps, Musselwhite and St. Louis (1982) found that about half of the programs included generalization as an explicit goal of therapy.

Moving Toward Independence in Communication

A third major goal of communication therapy is to help the child become as independent in communicative functioning as possible. There is a great deal of overlap between the issues pertaining to the goals of independence and issues raised earlier. First of all, to function independently of the communication therapist, the child must have a means of communication that is comprehensible to the people the child encounters in everyday life. The process of selecting a system of communication must involve those people who are with the child and responsible for the child on a daily basis (e.g., parents, teachers, group home staff). If the system of communication being considered is not one that parents, teachers, and others can interpret and use without training, then the therapist needs to determine whether these important people in the child's everyday life are willing to learn to interpret and use a new means of communication themselves. In general, parents and most special education teachers are willing to do so if they are convinced it will help the child learn to communicate.

As the child becomes capable of increasing independence in noncommunicative areas of development, however, there is an increasing need to consider whether the child's communication will be successful with people who have little or no knowledge of the child and little or no commitment to accommodating themselves to the needs of the child. At this point, problems may arise with communication systems that were quite adequate in the more supportive settings of clinic, home, or classroom. For instance, a child with poorly articulated speech may be understood by his parents and teacher, but incomprehensible to a cafeteria worker or school secretary. An adolescent who has learned to communicate with her therapist and parents using sign language may be a candidate for employment in a setting where supervisors and staff are unlikely to know sign language or unlikely to desire to learn it. Thus, in addition to the goal of generalizing communication skills to different settings, therapy must be concerned with ensuring that the child has the means to communicate effectively in the various settings he or she is likely to be in (Watson et al. 1989).

Another facet of independence is the ability to initiate communication as well as to respond to the communication of others (Prizant 1982). Cue dependency is an oft-cited problem in therapy with autistic children. When the therapist holds up a cup and asks, "What do you want?" an autistic child might reliably respond, "juice," yet fail to request juice from his mother when he sees the pitcher on the kitchen counter. If skills can be used only when someone else has decided what the child wants to or should say, then they are of limited value to the child. The goal of teaching the child to initiate communication is another facet of skill generalization. That is, the child needs to learn not only to use communication skills in different places with different people, but also in response to a variety of cues including internal cues (feeling thirsty) and natural external cues (seeing the juice pitcher on the counter).

Facilitate Appropriate Modification of Communicative Input by Persons in the Child's Everyday Environments

The goal of maximal independence is clearly an important one. At the same time, it is important to recognize that children with autism or other pervasive developmental disorders suffer from severe lifelong communication handicaps. Thus a final goal of therapy is to assist those persons who are major figures in the child's life in understanding the nature of the child's problem and in discovering what adaptations they can make to alleviate the child's handicaps. In communication therapy, adaptations might include learning to use and understand an alternative communication system; learning to utilize gestures or other visual cues (e.g., physical arrangement of the environment, objects in the environment) to aid the child in understanding communicative messages; and learning to adjust the complexity of communicative messages to a level more compatible with the child's ability to understand. It is also highly desirable for parents to assume the role of cotherapists in the child's communication therapy as in other aspects of therapy, and in this role to learn and develop effective teaching strategies for their child.

Assessment as the Starting Point for Therapy

Production of Messages

For the purposes of planning communication therapy, the core assessment information should be drawn from observing the child's communication skills in natural and naturalistic settings (Bloom and Lahey 1978; Crystal et al. 1976; Lee and Canter 1971; Watson 1985; Watson and Lord 1982). In this way, assessment is linked most directly to the goals of therapy: that is, to improve the child's everyday communication skills.

These observations can be analyzed according to the various dimensions of communication (to be discussed below), but also provide the therapist with a wholistic and socially valid picture of the child's communication skills. Observing and analyzing the child's everyday communication will likely leave the therapist with some unanswered questions, but such observations provide direction for asking further questions and selectively using more structured procedures for obtaining answers to specific questions.

A detailed discussion of procedures for analyzing language and communication is beyond the scope of this chapter. The overview presented here will be based largely on assessment and programming procedures developed at Division TEACCH to meet the needs of lower functioning autistic children and adolescents (Watson et al. 1989; Watson and Lord 1982). There are two other resources for analyzing language produced in naturalistic settings (Bloom and Lahey 1978; Miller 1981). Both of these focus on children who are using spoken language, beginning at the one-word level and continuing through the expression of complex concepts in complex sentence forms.

In assessing the communication of children with pervasive developmental disorders, there are (at least) four general questions to be addressed:

1. How does the child communicate?
2. What does the child communicate?
3. Why does the child communicate?
4. Where, when, to whom, and under what conditions does the child communicate?

These questions reflect the various dimensions of skills that comprise one's communicative competence. All these dimensions are at risk for moderate to severe impairment in autistic children. We elaborate on each dimension below.

How does the child communicate?   What form or forms of communication are used by the child? There are two somewhat different aspects of this question. First, form refers to the mode(s) or system(s) of communication used by the child. Examples of modes are motoric acts (e.g., pulling a person to a location), gestures (e.g., pointing, nodding, pantomiming), picture communication systems, sign language, and spoken language. A child may use only one mode of communication or may use several modes.

A second aspect of the form of communication is the complexity of the communication in any given mode. For example, a child who uses motoric acts to communicate might simply hand a peanut butter jar to his mother, or he might give his mother the jar and place her hand on the lid that he would like to have removed. A child using spoken language might communicate in the same situation with a one-word utterance such as "open" or might use a more complex utterance such as "open jar" or even "Could you open the peanut butter for me please?"

What does the child communicate?   What is the meaning or semantic content of the child's communication? Again the question is divided into its subcomponents. The first deals with the child's vocabulary: what words or word-equivalents does the child use in communicating? The second has to do with the categories of meaning or semantic categories the child expresses. A set of semantic categories commonly reported for normal children in the early stages of language development is given in Table 1. These categories have been found adequate for most of the communication observed in autistic children and adolescents whose language is at the level of simple sentences or below (Watson et al. 1989; Watson and Lord 1982).

Table 1.   Semantic Categories

Object that is wanted, is being acted on, or is being described
Action of a person or an object
Actor or the person doing something
Location of a person or a thing
Attribute of a person or a thing
State or experience of a person or thing
Social words used in routine greetings, farewells, apologies, etc.
Experiencer or the person feeling something
Possessor or the person having or owning something
Recipient or the person being given something
Person called or addressed
Recurrence of an object or event
Negatives used to refuse, reject, deny, or talk about disappearance or nonexistence
Agreement words used to agree with another person or to affirm something
Time or duration of an event
Manner in which an action is carried out

Table 2.   Communicative Functions

Requesting
  • an object
  • an action
  • attention
  • permission
Refusing or Rejecting
Commenting
  • on objects
  • on self
  • on others
Giving Information
Seeking Information
Expressing Feelings
Engaging in a Social Routine

Why does the child communicate?   This question examines the purposes for the child's communication. Here the therapist must make inferences about the communicative intent of the child. At the first level of inference, the therapist must decide whether there was any communicative intent associated with each act or utterance observed. Then, having decided that the child did intend to communicate something, the therapist must make a judgment about the specific purpose the child had in mind. Table 2 lists communicative functions that have been observed in the behavior of young normal children and moderately to severely impaired autistic children.

Where, when, to whom, and under what conditions does the child communicate?   The child may be observed to communicate during mealtime and snack time, but rarely on other occasions. The child's communication may be directed almost exclusively toward parents and teachers, and rarely toward siblings or peers. The child may communicate fairly consistently when someone else initiates communication, but rarely initiate it. Or the child may initiate communication if someone looks at him or her, but rarely approach someone or "call" for attention in any way. These questions are the most open-ended of the assessment questions we have posed, but the lack of finiteness should not discourage the therapist from addressing the questions and generating hypotheses about the answers, based on observation of the child and discussions with the parents, teachers, and significant others in the child's life.

After conducting an observation of the child during everyday activities, the therapist may wish to supplement the observation with some further, more structured interaction or testing (Bloom and Lahey 1978; Fay and Schuler 1980; Wetherby and Prutting 1984). The biggest "error" inherent in this observational approach appears to be the possibility of missing communication skills that the child has, but does not exhibit during the period of observation. In terms of planning therapy, the consequences of this are not disastrous. If the therapist generates an objective that is redundant with skills the child already has, then the child will simply attain the objective rapidly, and the therapist can move on to the next objective.

Comprehension of Messages

As with production, the assessment of communicative comprehension includes more than the assessment of linguistic skills. The naturalistic observation recommended for assessing an autistic child's production of messages will also give the therapist some hypotheses about what the child understands and doesn't understand in everyday communication. Additional systematic testing will probably be necessary, however, to test out these hypotheses and to provide the therapist with a clear picture of what limits and what facilitates a particular child's communicative comprehension.

Again, assessment should consider factors in the various dimensions of communication that we listed above—that is, how is the child's comprehension of messages affected by variations in the form, content, purpose, and context of communication? A more complete discussion of comprehension and its assessment and remediation in autism appears elsewhere (Lord 1985). The fact that a child (autistic or normal) responds appropriately to a message during everyday interaction does not mean that all dimensions of the message are fully understood. For example, a toddler's father may say to her "Throw the ball to Daddy," and glance toward the ball that he has just rolled to her. The child throws the ball to her father, completing a communicative interaction that is fully successful from the point of view of the participants. We cannot be at all sure, however, what to infer about the child's comprehension. Does she understand five-word imperative verbal utterances? Does she understand *each* of the words? Does she understand generally the concepts of actions on objects, and recipients of objects? Does she understand that one purpose of communicating is to get people to carry out actions? The answer to all of these questions is "not necessarily." The child may have responded to the message appropriately by using some of the very earliest comprehension strategies: to look where the other person is looking and to do what the other person has done (Chapman 1978). Unfortunately, the impairments of autistic children include difficulties with both following the gaze of others and with imitation, so that even these very "simple" means of responding to messages may not be available to the child with autism (Lord 1985). Suggestions for exploring the various dimensions of message comprehension in autistic children follow.

How is the child's comprehension affected by the form of the message? The therapist ideally would like to know what mode(s) of communication the child is best able to understand, and what level of complexity is best matched to the child's abilities. If the child is verbal and has been tested on some of a variety of tests of mental and language development, the therapist may be able to address this first question by regrouping test information and information from the naturalistic observation. For example, a number of standardized tests include some receptive vocabulary items. If the child clearly "knew" at least some of these items, then there is evidence that the child can respond to messages in a verbal mode at a single word level of complexity in situations where the correct response presumably cannot be made based purely on contextual information. Several tests that were developed primarily for assessing children's comprehension of increasingly complex verbal utterances are available: Test for Auditory Comprehension of Language (Carrow 1973), Northwest Syntax Screening Test (Lee 1971), Test of Language Development (Newcomer and Hammill 1977), Preschool Language Scale (Zimmerman et al. 1969), and Assessment of Children's Language Comprehension (Foster et al. 1972).

For the majority of autistic children, the comprehension of speech will be significantly limited, and the therapist will want information on how other modes of communication are comprehended, either in conjunction with speech or alone. The Sequenced Inventory of Communication Development (Hedrick et al. 1975) is a standardized test that includes some items assessing understanding of speech combined with gesture.

One concern regarding the use of standardized tests to assess how well autistic children understand language is that the objects, people, and activities focused on in these tests may not be meaningful for individual autistic children. Another concern is that no standardized tests are currently available that systematically explore comprehension of alternative modes of communication, which is a crucial area in providing therapy to many autistic children. Thus the therapist may wish to custom-design a comprehension assessment for the child that can supplement or possibly substitute for standardized testing. In developing such an assessment, the therapist would choose objects, activities, and people from the child's everyday experiences. To assess the impact of message form on comprehension, the therapist would develop messages about individually selected people, objects, and activities that vary in mode and complexity, and ask the child to respond to the messages in situations where the messages could not be understood from contextual cues alone. The messages might vary in the following ways:

1. Verbal mode only
   - single word level
   - two and three word combinations
   - simple sentences, using different sentence types: declarative, imperative, interrogative
   - complex sentences
2. Verbal mode plus alternative mode
   - using gestures to accompany speech
   - using pictures to accompany speech
   - using signs, visual symbols, or written words to accompany speech, if the child has prior exposure to these alternative modes of communication
3. Alternative mode only
4. Verbal mode with varied intonation—for example, does child respond to neutral tone? Does child respond better to question (rising) intonation than statement (falling) intonation or better to loud voice than whisper?

How is the child's comprehension affected by the content (meaning, concepts) of the message?   Normal children who are just beginning to acquire language rely heavily on what they know about the world at a nonverbal level to interpret language messages (Chapman 1978; Clark and Clark 1977; MacNamara 1972). From the deficiencies and oddities that characterize the interaction of autistic children with both people and objects, we can infer that autistic children generally understand the world less well or in a different way from normal children. Thus, when an autistic child is having difficulty understanding communicative messages, one aspect of assessment involves determining whether the child understands the nonverbal world in a conventional way. For example, if an autistic child fails to respond to a message such as "Give the baby a ride" when a doll and doll carriage are available, then one should consider the child's knowledge of the doll and doll carriage as indicated by his interaction with these objects. They may not be objects that the child plays with at all, or if the child does play with the objects, it may be in quite unconventional ways. For instance, the child might be fascinated with opening and closing the doll's eyes, and do this repeatedly. Or he may spin the wheels on the carriage, or flip the bonnet from side to side. In such a case, it is unlikely that the child has the nonverbal basis for understanding the message "Give the baby a ride."

A second area of assessment pertaining to the child's understanding of message content is the determination of the child's receptive vocabulary skills—that is, to what extent can the child pair words (or other symbols) with the objects, activities, and relations they represent. Again, there are standardized tests, such as the Peabody Picture Vocabulary Test—Revised (Dunn and Dunn 1981), that are designed to test how a child's vocabulary comprehension compares to that of normal children. If an autistic child's vocabulary comprehension is near normal, then it is unlikely to be the factor most responsible for difficulty in understanding communicative messages. Usually, however, vocabulary knowledge is severely deficient in autistic children. Thus it may be more therapeutically relevant to test the child's understanding of vocabulary contained in messages addressed to the child in the course of everyday life, rather than try to determine how the child's skills compare to those of normal children. In assessing the understanding of vocabulary items, the therapist should be sensitive to the type of concept represented by various words. Generally, children will understand words referring to specific people (e.g., Mommy, Daddy) and concrete objects best, and have more difficulty with words referring to actions (e.g., run, give), spatial relations between objects (e.g., in, on, under), and other relational concepts. There is some evidence suggesting that autistic children have a disproportionate amount of difficulty acquiring relational concepts, compared to their comprehension of concrete concepts (Menyuk and Quill 1985).

How well is the child able to understand the varying purposes of communicative messages? To date, no systematic procedures have been developed to assess the comprehension of message purpose. Thus the suggestions for assessment in this area are tentative and incomplete. In observing the child, the therapist should consider the following questions:

1. To what extent does the child give evidence of an awareness of other people's efforts to communicate (e.g., momentarily ceases ongoing activity, looks toward speaker, echoes messages addressed to him or her but not other speech)?
2. Does the child show an understanding of the basic purposes of various messages? For instance, if a child is asked to do carry out some action, does the child try to do something (even if it is not the totally correct action) or does the child respond only verbally, without giving evidence of understanding the speaker's intention? For example, Mother says, "Danny, time to go home." Danny glances at her; says, "go home," and wanders over to the record player. If someone asks for information, does the child interpret the speaker's intention as a request

or invitation to carry out an action? For example, Examiner: "What makes a train go?" Child: "Yes, thanks, I'll make it go."
3. Does the child show a marked pattern of recognizing some types of communicative intentions and not recognizing others (e.g., often makes an effort to carry out actions when asked, but frequently misinterprets or fails to respond to requests for information)?

How is the child's understanding affected by the context of communication? Often autistic children respond to communicative messages that occur as predictable parts of familiar routines, but have difficulty responding to the same messages in a different context. Related to this, an autistic child may respond to certain messages if communicated by a familiar person, but not to the same messages communicated by an unfamiliar person.

Given the severe difficulties that autistic persons have in language acquisition and comprehension, developing the ability to use contextual cues to decipher message meaning is an important skill. As noted earlier, the ability to interpret the physical context and the behavior of other persons in terms of their social and communicative relevance is not an area of strength in autistic persons; however, progress in this area should be expected to precede developmentally any significant progress in understanding language in the absence of contextual cues.

Again, no formal procedures have been developed to assess the role of context in children's comprehension. Some suggestions for organizing and expanding on observations made of the child's behavior during everyday events are given below.

1. What messages communicated by others did the child seem to understand? What sorts of contextual cues accompanied those messages? For example, was someone else doing the activity being communicated about? Were objects being communicated about visible in the environment? Was the communication related to an activity or to a routine which the child was familiar?
2. What happens when the contextual cues accompanying the "understood" message above are changed (e.g., a different person delivers the message; objects are not visible; message is communicated at an unexpected time or in connection with a different activity)?
3. What were some messages that occurred during everyday events that the child did not appear to understand?
4. If the "not-understood" messages are delivered with more or different contextual cues, is the child able to interpret them correctly? For example, during the observation, a mother said to her autistic daughter, "Ann, get your coat. It's time to go." The mother pointed to Ann's coat as she spoke. Ann did not respond. In structuring a follow-up observation, the therapist asked Ann's mother to deliver the same message as the mother put on her coat. Ann looked at her mother's action, then put on her coat. From this and similar episodes, the therapist concluded that Ann was able to attend to nonverbal cues in the environment, although she seemed to have little understanding of language.

Treatment Methods

Determination of Objectives

Objectives should be developed for the child that are consistent with the child's current developmental level and consistent with priorities for improving the child's ability to function communicatively in everyday life. Knowledge of the patterns and processes involved in normal development of communication skills can provide the therapist with general guidelines for establishing developmentally appropriate objectives (Bloom and Lahey 1978). The information from the assessment can be used to determine the autistic child's general developmental level and, in addition, will provide information about the child's individual developmental patterns that will aid the therapist in fine-tuning objectives so that the chances of the child attaining therapeutic objectives are increased. The principle to be followed here is to utilize the child's existing skills as much as possible in teaching new skills. The analysis of a communication sample, as described above, will indicate the relative strengths and weaknesses of the individual child across the various dimensions of communicative ability. In therapy, an objective should focus on only one weak area, and incorporate the strengths the child shows across other dimensions of communication. For instance, the therapist may observe that the content of the child's communicative production is limited mainly to words for concrete objects. The therapist chooses the acquisition of action concepts as an objective. Looking at the other dimensions of the child's spontaneous communication, the therapist observes that 1) the *form* of the child's communication is predominantly single signs, 2) the *purpose* of the child's communication is usually to make requests, and 3) a predominant *contextual* feature is that the child communicates when a wanted object is visible.

One typical approach to teaching new action concepts would be to choose a set of pictures showing the chosen actions and teach the child to label the pictures. This is unlikely to be the most successful approach for the child described above, however. It would ask the child to communicate for a purpose (labeling) and in a context (pictured stimuli) that are not strengths. To fine-tune the objective to the child, the therapist could identify some actions the child cannot carry out but seems to enjoy (e.g., blowing bubbles, being tickled, swinging). The therapeutic treatment would be structured so that the child would first be made aware that the action was "available" (e.g., the therapist would blow bubbles, or tickle or swing the child). Then the child would be put under some pressure to communicate to have the action repeated (e.g., by pausing). Then initially, the therapist would physically prompt the child to produce the sign for the desired action. Structured in this way, the therapeutic objective would be for the child to learn a new concept, expressed for an "old" purpose (requesting), in an "old" form (single word signs) when visible contextual cues are available.

To determine priorities for improving the child's communication skills, the therapist should consider both the child's point of view and the point of view of parents, teachers, and others who are in an ongoing relation with the child. From the child's point of view, this means the therapist must infer what the child would most likely want to communicate about (i.e., the child's own interests, wants, and needs). Parents are usually also concerned that the child learn to communicate about these things and can provide much insight into what the child's interests, wants, and needs are. Parents may have additional priorities that relate to their own needs in parenting the child (e.g., need for the child to respond to them calling when the child is out of sight and they want to check on the child's whereabouts).

Therapeutic Settings and Agents

Because of the difficulty autistic children have in generalizing language and communicative skills from person to person and from setting to setting, it is essential that communication therapy take place in a variety of settings that the children encounter in their home, school, and community, and that the children's parents and teachers, as well as perhaps siblings, peers, and others, act as therapeutic agents. Thus a communication specialist may assume primary responsibility for assessing the child and planning objectives and strategies, but successful implementation of the therapy requires a specialist with skills in providing consultation and coordination to the client's family and school.

Content of Communication Therapy

The content of therapy must be individualized to meet the specific objectives that are developed for a given child following the assessment process. As noted earlier, most autistic children show difficulties in all dimensions of communication, although the patterns of relative strengths and weaknesses vary greatly from one child to the next. We will now discuss approaches to facilitating development in the different communicative dimensions described above.

Treatment of how the child communicates. One of the most exciting developments in the treatment of the language and communication handicaps of autistic children over the past decade has been the increased use of alternative systems of communication. Most research and clinical reports have been concerned with teaching autistic children to use manual signs (Barrera et al. 1980; Benaroya et al. 1977; Bonvillian and Nelson 1976; Carr and Dores 1981; Carr et al. 1978; Casey 1978; Creedon 1982; Fulwiler and Fouts 1976; Konstantareas et al. 1977; Layton and Helmer 1981; Watters et al. 1981; Webster et al. 1973). Undoubtedly these treatment approaches have resulted in some autistic children acquiring language skills that would not have been learned in a strictly oral approach to language treatment. In a recent review, Layton (1987) identified some variables that appear to be predictive of how well autistic children will do in manual or "simultaneous communication" (speech plus manual sign language) programs versus speech-only programs. Children who have nonverbal IQs above 55 and who are echolalic or have verbal imitation skills are most likely to acquire speech. These children also do relatively well in simultaneous communication programs in acquiring signs as well as speech. Thus far there is no evidence that the acquisition of a manual system of communication impedes in any way the acquisition of speech skills, an issue that is of great clinical concern to parents and therapists alike. While autistic children with lower IQs are less likely to acquire speech, children with nonverbal IQs as low as 20 have been reported to have learned some signs (Creedon 1982; Layton and Helmer 1981; Watters et al. 1981). In some cases, previously nonverbal children who had a history of failure in verbal imitation treatment programs were reported to develop some oral language following the acquisition of signs (Carr and Dores 1981; Creedon 1982; Layton and Baker 1981).

Thus teaching autistic children to use manual signs has been documented as an effective treatment approach for large numbers of autistic children. One caution is that this therapy is focused on finding a system of communication that is easier for nonverbal and low-verbal autistic children to learn than is speech. However, in teaching signs to autistic children, the therapist must remain sensitive to the other dimensions of communication as well. Similar to reports of speech training with autistic children, the major weaknesses of the literature on sign training lie in failures to examine whether the signing skills generalized to a variety of settings, and to what extent signs were used by the children in their spontaneous, everyday communication.

Other alternative systems of communication have been used with autistic children as well, although there is less documentation of these approaches than is available for signed communication. For instance, autistic children have been taught to communicate using objects, pictures (Lancioni 1983; Murphy et al. 1977), representational symbols or pictographs (e.g., Rebus, Blissymbolics), abstract symbols (Carrier 1976; DeVilliers and Naughton 1974; Kiernan and Jones 1985; McLean and McLean 1974; Premack and Premack 1974) and written words (LaVigna 1977; Ratusnik and Ratusnik 1974). In addition, Colby (1973) reported positive effects of a computer-interaction language program for 13 of 17 nonverbal children.

A major issue with autistic children is how to decide what system of communication is best suited to the individual child. As mentioned earlier, children with higher nonverbal IQs who are echolalic or have good verbal imitation skills are likely to progress as well with the acquisition of speech as with an alternative system of communication. Because speech is the predominant means of social communication in our society, the selection of speech training for these children is indicated. For mute or nonimitative children and children with lower IQs, however, clinicians are in need of some basis for decision making. Most of the available discussions emphasize fitting a handicapped individual with an alternative means of communication that is adapted to the person's physical or sensory handicaps. For some autistic children, these issues will also need to be considered, but in most cases the system best suited to the autistic child will depend on the child's general cognitive level and specific perceptual and cognitive characteristics (Alpert 1980). The naturalistic observation of a child's communication can be used to address certain questions; for instance, what is (are) the child's current system(s) of communication? How frequently does the child communicate with each system? If the child has a history of training utilizing a specific system of communication (e.g., speech, sign, pictures), does the child utilize this form in spontaneous communication?

Other questions cannot be addressed through naturalistic observation. In particular, it is not possible to predict from this how readily a child will learn an alternative system of communication to which he or she has never been exposed.

If the child has one or more functional systems of spontaneous communication, the clinician's first concern should be with how to expand the use of these systems (through teaching the child to express new meanings, to communicate for different purposes, and to communicate in a variety of natural situations). A typical observation of a low-functioning child might reveal, for instance, that the child occasionally communicates by giving another person an object or placing another person's hand on an object. There are generally a good many possibilities for teaching such children to communicate more using a wider variety of objects with more people in more different settings.

In some cases, the child will exhibit no functional system of communication. In other cases, the child communicates functionally in some way, but the therapist feels that the child would be capable of communicating more complex ideas, or could communicate more clearly in a greater variety of settings with a different system of communication. In these cases, the therapist can collect other sorts of information to help narrow down the possibilities for an alternative system. For instance, can the child scan a visual array of objects or pictures? Can the child match objects to objects, pictures to objects, or pictures to pictures? Can the child categorize based on perceptual characteristics or functional characteristics? Does the child seem to have a fascination with pictures? Does the child have peak drawing skills? Does the child have signs of hyperlexia (reading skills beyond what would be predicted based on general cognitive level)? Can the child imitate motor movements? Does the child withdraw or become distressed when physically prompted?

Once the therapist has decided on one or two alternative systems as the most likely possibilities for a child, then a trial therapy period is recommended, during which the child's ability to acquire the new system(s) of communication is carefully evaluated before a long-term commitment is made to teaching the child using a particular alternative communication system.

The other aspect of treatment of how a child communicates is concerned with teaching the child to communicate in a structurally more complex way within a given system. For instance, the therapist might wish to teach a child who is using single signs to combine two or more signs; or to teach a child who is using simple sentences (e.g., I want a cracker) to use coordinated sentence structures (e.g., I want a cracker and some juice). The danger here is in moving to more complex structures without the child fully understanding them. With autistic children it is often possible to teach the use of rote sentence patterns that sound more mature than single words or telegraphic word combinations, but that are not analyzed by the child. These patterns represent isolated behaviors the child has learned, not language knowledge that can be built on to express own ideas in increasingly more flexible and more complex ways. Again, the general order of priorities is to expand the child's communication abilities in the other dimensions prior to moving the child to more complex forms of communication.

Treatment of what the child communicates.　Particularly with children at lower levels of language abilities, therapy has traditionally been concerned with expanding vocabulary. Intuitively this is a legitimate practice because a child's ability to communicate will obviously be limited by the different word-type units (e.g., words, signs, pictures) that are known. But it is probably in this aspect of therapy more than in any other that vast discrepancies have been noted between what the child appears to know in a structured therapeutic setting and what the child uses when communicating during everyday activities. There are several possible explanations for these discrepancies. First, in some cases vocabulary is taught in structured settings with little attention to what the child may need or want to communicate about in everyday life. For example, a young urban child is not likely to have many real life encounters with cows, pigs, or chickens. As another example, some autistic children may have an interest in colors, but most appear to have little internal motivation to describe an object's color, and few naturally occurring events impose an external need to specify color. Yet vocabulary for animals and colors have frequently been included in initial language programs.

A second explanation for discrepancies between vocabulary skills exhibited in therapy versus everyday settings may be that some vocabulary items taught in therapy represent concepts that the child does not understand, at least not in a conventional way. The child learns, for instance, to identify correctly pictures exemplifying the locational terms *in*, *on*, and *under* by attending to specific features of the pictures and learning to associate the correct response with each picture. But the child has failed to derive the essential locational concepts of these terms from the experiences in therapy, and, because the child never encounters the therapy pictures in everyday life, there is never any occasion to use the three terms outside of the therapy setting. In some such cases, the conventional concepts expressed by certain vocabulary may be beyond the child's current cognitive abilities. In other cases, the failure is simply due to an incompleteness of the therapeutic strategy in teaching the child that the same word applies to a variety of stimuli and can be used to communicate with different people, for different purposes, and so forth. For instance, often in therapy the child is taught new words by learning labeling responses (e.g., to respond to "What is that?" "What is he doing?"). In natural spontaneous communication, however, the child may be observed never to label objects or actions, but frequently to request them. If this is the case, then the therapist needs either to teach new vocabulary originally in situations where the child is making requests or else to follow training in labeling with training in using the new vocabulary for requesting.

In addition to expanding the number of words a child understands and uses, therapy should be planned to expand the variety of semantic categories that the child expresses in communicative messages (Table 1), and the different ways these categories are combined in messages. For example, a child may be able to use words in labeling objects ("That is a truck," "That is a block"), people ("Mommy," "That is a man"), and actions ("Push," "Ride"). Therapy objectives include teaching the child to use these words to express a variety of semantic concepts, such as action + object ("push truck"); person + location ("man in truck"); object + location ("block in truck"); person possessing + object ("man's truck"); and so forth. This approach to treatment is described by MacDonald (1978) and MacDonald and Blott (1974).

Treatment of why the child communicates.   The need to expand the functions of communication for the autistic child has been addressed by numerous authors (Beisler and Tsai 1983; Fay and Schuler 1980; O'Neill and Lord 1982; Prizant 1982; Seibert and Oller 1981; Watson and Lord 1982). Some evidence that intervention can facilitate the use of communication for a broader range of purposes is provided by O'Neill and Lord (1982) and Schopler (1984). Interestingly, in a study of a home-based language intervention study with autistic children, Howlin (1981) found that children in the treatment group significantly increased their use of functional, communicative speech compared to children in the control group, but did not develop significantly more complex forms of language than did the control group. Thus treatment aimed at increasing the general communicativeness of autistic children and their range of purposes for communication, which is critical to ameliorating the social disabilities associated with autism, can be implemented with reasonable expectation of a beneficial outcome for the child.

Treatment of the contexts of the child's communication.   As discussed previously, it is becoming increasing clear that communication therapy with autistic children should involve training with multiple exemplars, with multiple therapists, and in multiple settings. These strategies have been implemented in several programs involving autistic children (Barrera et al. 1980; Carr et al. 1978; Fulwiler and Fouts 1976; Handleman 1979; Handleman and Harris 1980; Helmer and Layton 1980). Beyond this necessity to facilitate generalization by training in a variety of contexts, however, there is a need to provide therapy to expand autistic children's communication to new contexts. For instance, if a child is observed to communicate rarely or never with peers or with unfamiliar adults even though there are frequent opportunities to do so, then expanding the child's communication skills to these contexts is an important therapeutic goal. One program (Watson 1985; Watson and Lord 1982) explicitly includes this dimension in its treatment approach, but no systematic evaluation has been carried out on the effectiveness of this aspect of treatment.

Therapeutic Strategies

Structure.   The importance of structured situations in decreasing children's autistic behaviors and increasing the acquisition of new skills has been demonstrated (Bartak 1978; Clark and Rutter 1981; Ney et al. 1971). By making cues consistent, explicitly modeling and shaping the desired behavior, and responding to the child's behavior in a predictable fashion, the therapist greatly reduces the potential for confusion and frustration on the part of the child. The work of Schopler et al. (1971) suggested that structure is especially beneficial for lower-functioning autistic children.

For some purposes (e.g., certain problems of behavior management), an ongoing reliance on structure may be a practical means of accomplishing therapeutic goals. In communication therapy, however, the child must be weaned from reliance on artificially imposed structure and come to rely on natural cues available in the everyday environment. Thus, in addition to understanding how to use structure, the communication therapist must understand how to modify and reduce structure so that the autistic child adapts to the more unpredictable features of the natural environment and becomes flexible enough to communicate in these less structured situations. Because the ultimate goal of therapy is improving communication in everyday life, the transition is easiest when the therapist incorporates the objects and activities encountered in the everyday world into the structured therapy sessions insofar as is possible.

Motivation.   The emphasis on motivation in language and communication therapy with autistic children has undergone a shift from the use of artificial, extrinsic reinforcers to the use of natural consequences (Beisler and Tsai 1983; Carr 1982; Goetz et al. 1979; Helmer and Layton 1980; Prizant 1982; Watson 1985). In the past, the child may have been asked, for example, "What is this?" and shown an object. If the child labelled the object appropriately, then the child would be praised and perhaps given a token or an edible as a positive consequence for correct responding. Then the therapist would move on to the next trial, presenting a different stimulus to the child. Although procedures such as these have been effective in teaching autistic children to give consistent, correct answers in structured therapy sessions, it makes no sense communicatively for a child to label a ball and then get a piece of candy. The therapist needs to structure communication therapy for the autistic child so that the natural consequences of the communicative behavior will be motivating. For instance, if the child has an interest in balls, then the child can learn to ask for "ball" to have a few moments to play with it. If the therapist wants to teach a child to ask questions, such as "What is this?' then an activity must be designed in which the child is given a reason to seek such information. For instance, one teacher gave an autistic student the writing assignment of making labels for a series of pictures. The series included a number of pictures that the teacher was sure the student would not recognize. Thus the student needed to ask for information on the identity of the pictures to finish the assignment. In this case, the desire to finish the work was sufficiently motivating that the student learned to ask the teacher for information when it was needed. The point of this example is that motivating consequences for autistic children are not limited to food, tickles, and so on, although these may be powerful motivators. There is also motivation inherent in the drive to complete an activity, to carry out a routine, to get an unpleasant stimulus removed, or (for some children) to continue a pleasant social interaction. Beisler and Tsai (1983) presented a detailed description of a program using natural communicative consequences that was carried out with autistic children.

Moving toward independence.   Providing physical prompts, modeling the desired communicative behavior, using verbal cues, and so forth are all important strategies in shaping the communicative responses of autistic children. As noted earlier, if the therapist is to avoid confusing and frustrating the child, then it is important to make it very clear to the child what is expected when a given situation is encountered. On the other hand, autistic children readily become cue-dependent, and frequently the cues depended on are not the ones most readily available under ordinary circumstances. Thus the autistic child may sit at snack time and wait for the familiar "What do you want?" before saying "I want some juice." To move the child toward greater independence and self-initiated spontaneous communication, the therapist must back off further from cuing the child. For instance, the therapist might use a less direct verbal cue, such as "Time for snack" or (serving and talking about another child) "Brenda wants some juice." A further step away from artificial cues would be to serve the other children and stare at the target child expectantly. In these steps, as in all efforts to shape behavior, the therapist must be sensitive to the need to drop back down to more explicit cues at times. But the eventual goal should be to have children who communicate under the most ordinary of conditions, and who are capable of initiating communication when they want to, as well as responding to the communication that others direct toward them.

Chapter 40

Behavior Modification

Autistic children were among the first patients to benefit from applied behavior therapy (Ferster and DeMyer 1961). During the last two decades more than 300 articles have appeared exploring the behavioral approach to the problems associated with this syndrome. There is little question that behavior therapies are a very significant development in the psychosocial treatment of infantile autism (DeMeyer et al. 1981).

It must be stressed that by no means is behavior modification a cure for infantile autism. Progress, even under the best of conditions, is often slow and disappointing. There is also no question that by the use of a systematic and highly directive approach that there can be significant expansion of the behavioral repertoires of these children.

Treatment Strategy

In designing a program, the therapist's attention should not be focused on techniques of therapy but rather on the techniques of a proper functional analysis. Observation and hypothesis formation is the starting point for any decisions about intervention. Clues to the most effective environmental manipulation are most efficiently gathered by simple observation. The therapist attempts to discover the functional relationship between the environment and the child's actions during observation sessions. As the literature on overselective responding attests (Koegel and Schreibman 1977), each child tends to respond in a highly idiosyncratic way to the environment. The normal course of daily events should provoke hypotheses as to the nature of the child's selective responding and the ability to be controlled by various situational factors. For example, does the child engage in stereotypies when alone, or when pressured to behave? Do maladaptive behaviors occur more frequently during tasks that are cognitive and language-oriented, or when the task is motoric in nature (e.g., block building)? Do tantrums or self-injury occur in the presence of certain individuals or at certain times of the day? Is the child's behavior different at mealtimes? What situations are associated with increases in behavior and which are associated with decreases? The child's behavior is observed during solitary play, interaction with other children, interaction with adults, different times of the day, home and school, structured versus nonstructured situations, and so on. Finally, can reinforcers be identified that are durable and practical for use during therapy? Does the child respond to social stimulation or must one rely on more basic reinforcing events such as food or sensory stimulation?

Once hypotheses are formed, they are tested by manipulation of the learning situation. For example, parents and teachers can be asked to alter their usual response to misbehavior to observe the corresponding effect, if any, on the frequency and intensity of the behavior in question. Hypotheses about the failure to generalize can be tested by selectively manipulating limited portions of those environmental events to which the child responds. The answers to these questions in combination with a decision about which behaviors seem most consistent with the abilities of each child are the starting point in developing a behavioral program.

Following the completion of the functional analysis, a strategic decision is made that conceptualizes treatment as either a strengthening of positive behaviors or as an elimination of negative behaviors. Both have their advantages. For example, Wolf et al. (1964) demonstrated that the elimination of maladaptive behaviors automatically permitted more normal behaviors to appear. Also, once maladaptive behaviors are at a low ebb, positive behaviors can more easily be approached. Frankel and Simmons (1976) demonstrated that the establishment of simple and basic communication skills substantially reduces the tendency to self-injure and to engage in stereotypies. Similarly, Butcher and Lovaas (1968) demonstrated a positive "side effect" of a punishment procedure for the elimination of severe self-injury. Once the self-injury was controlled, the child became more manageable and was more accessible to the establishment of positive behaviors.

If the child displays very severe self-injury or engages in constant stereotypies, the initial approach will be to reduce the frequency and intensity of the problem behavior. Alternatively, if the child is functioning on a higher level, the initial choice will be to conceptualize the treatment as consisting of establishing prosocial behavior. Practically speaking the therapist will probably choose a midway point between these two alternatives. The objectives of therapy must be clearly stated by identifying the behaviors to be created, those to be eliminated, and the sequence in which they will be approached (Frankel and Graham 1976).

Behavior Modification Procedures

Rewards

In behavior therapy, rewards are given to the child in such a way as to increase the likelihood of a specified behavior. The simplicity of the reinforcement concept is illusive, and close supervision and extensive experience is necessary to maintain a reinforcement program properly. The following discussion focuses on some of the common mistakes and misuses of rewards.

Discovering a reinforcer. A reinforcer may not necessarily be that which children typically like. A common mistake of therapists is to assume that an event such as touching and holding the child is reinforcing to that child. For many children it is, but for some it may have the opposite effect. For some autistic children, social attention contingent on a desired behavior can make that behavior less likely to occur, whereas being left alone is actually a more effective reinforcing event.

The technique developed by Premack (1965) can be helpful in identifying reinforcers in autistic children. The Premack principle states that contingent access to any high probability behavior can serve as a reinforcer. Because it is sometimes difficult to discover a "traditional" reinforcer that is effective for a socially unrelated child, and because these children often engage in some frequent behavior such as self-stimulation, the Premack technique can be effective. For example, a child may be allowed to self-stimulate as a reinforcer for language acquisition (Hung 1978).

As a general rule, it is advisable to select a reinforcer that is as developmentally advanced as possible. If a child has some ability to relate to adults, the therapist would want to utilize this skill and attempt to rely on social events as reinforcers for adaptive behaviors. Social events are highly desirable for practical as well as therapeutic reasons. Practically, it is easier to present a reinforcer exactly timed to have maximum effect if it is a response such as "good boy," a tickle, or a hug. Social reinforcers are durable and have the effect of making social events more salient to the child. Not only does the social interaction serve to strengthen behavior but it also serves to focus the child's attention on the social aspects of the therapist.

Food can almost always be used as a reinforcer, and is thus an effective tool to be used when social events are not effective. On the negative side, food tends to distract the child from the social nature of the therapy, tends to build an overreliance on tangible rewards, and quickly satiates.

The particular type of food that each child prefers must first be established and care taken to ensure that satiation to that food item does not occur. A cafeteria-style selection can be used. The therapist has available several items the child enjoys and the child is allowed to select the particular item preferred at the moment of reinforcement. Some therapists will prefer to work at mealtimes, essentially feeding lunch to the child contingent on behavioral progress. Preferably, the food item should be small and quickly consumable. Alternatively, it is possible to place the food item in a container that the child can take at the end of the session for consumption later. The food container should be clearly visible, and the therapist should comment on the reward as it is given. If the dish becomes a distraction, briefly removing the food container from the child's vision might be an effective method to control the problem.

Moving the child along the path toward more mature reinforcers and breaking the habit of food reinforcers can best be accomplished by close attention to the details of the therapist-child interaction. It has been found (Rincover et al. 1977) that pairing of a food reward with a social interaction establishes the social event as an effective reinforcer. Initially, the therapist rewards each positive behavior with food while concomitantly making some social comment. For example, as the food item is given, the therapist touches and speaks to the child. Once the child is working well, the therapist begins to eliminate the food reward systematically while continuing with the social reward. This must be accomplished by using schedules of reinforcement that maximize retention of behavior.

Because some autistic children are refractory to social interaction and even seem to find it aversive, the use of sensory rewards has been studied. The nature of sensory rewards are limited only by the creativity of the therapist. Flashing lights, tape-recorded music, clicking sounds, and skin vibration are examples. Multimedia events in the form of light and sound bursts have proved effective in our facility. Besides the practical effect of achieving a reinforcing effect, sensory rewards have some additional advantages. They can be easily timed to correspond to the child's response, the duration of the reward can be specified, and the reward can be automated for use with a computer. An additional advantage is that relatively small changes in the sensory input can alter the satiating effects of one particular sensory experience, thus rendering the child more capable of sustaining longer therapy sessions (Rincover et al. 1977). Despite their efficacy, sensory stimulation and the Premack technique are not treatments of choice because they tend to strengthen the very characteristics (e.g., stereotypies, lack of social relatedness) that the therapist is attempting to change.

Timing of the reward. A reward will strengthen the behavior that it follows. This rule is often misapplied by beginning behavior therapists and almost always broken by parents. In doing behavior therapy, the therapist must always wait for the response to occur before delivering the reinforcer. It is a mistake to use the reward as a "bribe" in an attempt to coax the child into performing the response. For example, if the child is engaged in some isolated activity and the therapist wishes to draw the child into a group activity, tying delivery of the reward to the child's performance is critical. The temptation is to call to the child, go to the child, and direct his or her attention to the group, saying something like "wouldn't you like to join the rest of the children, why don't you come and play." If the teacher's words are a reinforcer, the timing of this interaction will serve the opposite intention of the therapy, actually making it more likely that the child will remain in isolated play. The correct timing of the teacher's social interaction requires that the child first make some minimal movement away from isolation and toward the group before the child is spoken to. If the child immediately retreats into isolation, the teacher's words are broken off immediately and resumed only when the child once again makes some minimal approach toward the group activity. Another example of this error often is seen in a parent's attempt to stop an unwanted behavior. Whenever there is a high rate of some unwanted behavior, the parents' attempt to make the child stop is probably serving to keep it going. Coaxing a child to eat will result in the child not eating; holding a child each time stereotypies are engaged in will only result in more stereotypies. The parent must wait for the child to take a bite of food and then speak; the therapist must wait for the child to stop the unwanted mannerism and then touch and cuddle.

If the child does not engage in the behavior that the teacher wishes to strengthen, a shaping procedure or a prompt and fading procedure is the next alternative to be used. A prompt can, however, easily become a part of the problem unless used carefully. The act of prompting can accidentally reward the absence of the behavior.

Duration of reward. Not only should the reward be closely timed to immediately follow the behavior, it should also be short and discrete. "Good boy," a small bite of food, or a one- or two-second burst of sensory stimulation are most common. Short rewards make the nature of the timing of the delivery all the more salient. All types of rewards tend to become satiated, and keeping the reward short helps to maintain the durability of the reward.

Reward frequency. A characteristic of autistic children is that it is very difficult to move them from a dense schedule of reinforcement toward the rate of reinforcement necessary to maintain responding in the real world. The failure to maintain responding across short periods of nonreward, the failure to generalize and maintain a response, and the tendency to "overselect" while forming discriminations may all be related.

The consistency with which the reward follows the behavior is known as the schedule of reinforcement. Depending on the goals of a particular therapeutic exercise, the therapist can choose to deliver a reward contingent on each correct response, every other correct response, or only very occasionally on a correct response. Because the world is not consistent in delivery of reinforcement and because normal children and adults do not require constant rewards to maintain behavior, it is the goal of the therapist to reduce the flow of reinforcers to a minimum while still maintaining the behavior of the autistic child. The density of reinforcement must be maintained at a one-to-one ratio during the early stages of training: each correct response should produce a reinforcement. As the behavior becomes firmly established, the ratio of correct response to the number of reinforcers increases in gradual steps. It is possible, although difficult, to reach a point where correct responding is in itself a reward (Koegel and Egel 1979).

In the first stages of therapy, the therapist should attempt to reinforce each correct response. A nonrewarded response is an extinction trial, and this affects an autistic child much more profoundly than a normal child. If a correct response is not made, the criterion must be lowered and the child gradually shaped back toward the desired behavior. The learning situation should always produce rewards for some level of correct responding. If the child is not receptive, the session should be ended. This effect is particularly important in language training. Lovaas (1977) reported a demonstration using two children who were consistently producing correct verbal responses when reinforcement was consistent and immediate. When the relationship between the reward and the response was broken and thus made noncontingent, the children's use of language sharply declined.

Extinction

The term *extinction* refers both to a procedure and to an effect. Directing a parent to ignore temper tantrums would constitute an extinction procedure. If the child has fewer temper tantrums, the behavior would have undergone extinction. Identifying and implementing extinction procedures constitutes a main occupation of behavior therapists. Once a pattern of reinforcement has been identified as being responsible for some unwanted behavior, the job of the therapist very often becomes one of educating those responsible for the effect. Parents and teachers easily fall into the trap of giving attention to the child contingent on misbehavior. This can be a result of the physical touching used to get the child to stop or the words spoken in the process of "correcting the child." An example would be an interaction with a child engaged in self-injury. The temptation is to hold the child while talking about the problem or to distract the child with a toy or activity. The timing of physically touching or talking in an attempt to stop a behavior is perhaps the most common of all interaction errors.

The therapist tests the hypothesis that the adult's intervention is actually serving to maintain the behavior by convincing the parent or staff member to ignore the problem and noting the effect on the rate of the behavior. If the problem behavior is not severely disruptive or dangerous, it is possible to ignore the behavior and wait for the child to stop before resuming a reinforcing activity. Extinction is usually accompanied by an increase in the intensity of behavior. Thus if the behavior is such that it cannot be ignored, alternative methods of intervention must be utilized.

It is frequently the case that the removal of the event that is hypothesized to be a reinforcer has little or no effect on the autistic child's behavior. A therapist may design an extinction intervention based on the fact that self-injury or a stereotypy is displayed in association with some social interaction. Believing that the social interaction is responsible for the behavior, the social event is removed and the child is allowed to continue while being ignored. The therapist soon discovers that the manipulation has had little or no effect on the rate of the behavior problem. In these cases, it has been hypothesized (Carr 1977) that the reinforcer that is actually maintaining the behavior is an "internal" reinforcer, perhaps resulting from the pleasure of self-stimulation. Self-stimulation or self-injury that results from an internal reward is particularly difficult to eliminate.

One possible intervention is to establish some new event as a reward and then remove that reward contingent on the unwanted behavior. If the new artificial reinforcer is more potent than the act of self-stimulation, then the behavior could be controlled. We have successfully used a skin vibrator as a reward that could be switched off whenever the child attempted to self-stimulate. Another technique we have used with success has been to engage the child in some play activity such as swinging and then immediately to stop the swing whenever self-stimulation occurs. In another intervention, Rincover (1978) demonstrated the ability to control self-stimulatory behavior through removing auditory feedback by installing carpeting on the table where the child would normally spin and bang plates. The above examples demonstrate the utility of the approach. Each therapist must understand the general principle that is being demonstrated and be able to create their own specific manipulation that best meets situational realities and the idiosyncratic needs of the individual child.

Time-Out

Time-out is one of the most common procedures used for all types of children. It refers to the momentary loss of reinforcement and is intended to reduce the likelihood of an unwanted behavior. To apply time-out, the therapist most typically would simply stop talking and looking at the child for a brief period of time. This momentary loss of social interaction is preferable to the use of a "quiet room" because the act of removing the child to a special location can inadvertently reinforce the unwanted behavior. Although frequently used with autistic children, its effect is often less satisfactory than with normal or retarded children. For some autistic children, time-out, perhaps because it reduces the stress of interaction and removes the child from a demanding therapy session, can serve as a negative reinforcer and actually strengthen behavior. Another explanation is that time-out may be a positive reinforcer because of the self-stimulation that autistic children easily fall into when placed in isolation. The procedure becomes more effective if behavior such as self-stimulation is prevented while in time-out (Solnick et al. 1977). Numerous studies have questioned the use of time-out with autistic children by demonstrating its limited value with this population (Husted et al. 1971; Martin 1975; Plummer et al. 1977). If it is to be used at all, time-out should be used with caution while carefully monitoring its effects on the behavior in question.

Shaping

In operant conditioning, the response to be strengthened must occur before the reinforcer is presented. If the response does not occur spontaneously, it must be shaped. In shaping, the therapist divides the terminal behavior into smaller units that are more likely to be spontaneously emitted by the child. The creation of prosocial behavior, for example, must be shaped in autistic children. When attempting to establish language or interaction skills, the therapist must often start with existing behaviors that are very limited or altogether absent. If social and communication skills are to be shaped, the process may begin by shaping the child to attend to the therapist or to enter the therapy room. The act of sitting in a chair while looking at the therapist may be the first shaping step along the path to language acquisition. Before teaching the child to say a particular word, it might first be necessary to teach the child to open his or her mouth and then to utter any sound. Then the sound in turn must be gradually altered to produce a word.

For each child and for each behavior, the process of training must be broken down into as many component units as is necessary for the child to begin to display some movement toward the ultimate goal. The therapist can recognize the appropriate size of each individual shaping step by noting if the behavior being taught is actually being learned. When moving from one step to the next, the behavior may be suddenly lost. If the child is not learning, stop trying. Each nonresponse is an extinction trial in following commands, thus making it more difficult for the therapist to regain the child's attention. When this happens, the therapist must quickly move back along the line of shaping until a level is reached that allows the child to respond again correctly. If the child still fails to respond correctly, the session should be ended.

The Use of Prompts

Because the shaping process can be so laborious, an alternative method known as prompting and fading has been explored (Lovaas 1977). A prompt is a stimulus that cues the desired response prior to training. The prompt is intended to ensure that the correct response is made during the training sequence. Prompting can be done in several ways: the therapist may model the correct response, the therapist may physically guide the behavior, or the therapist can tell the child the correct response. Before starting a prompting procedure, the therapist must have decided in advance how the prompt is to be gradually faded so the child does not come to rely on the prompt. After the prompt has been used for several trials and the child is responding correctly, the prompt is gradually faded so that only the training stimulus remains. Prompting must be carefully used because the danger exists that the physical act of touching or speaking to the child may accidentally result in a reinforcement of nonresponding.

Generalization and Maintenance

Perhaps the most important and also most difficult aspect of teaching autistic children is the problem of generalizing and maintaining the learned response outside the therapy situation. If a desired behavior occurs only in the therapy situation and does not generalize to the extra therapeutic setting, the effort is of limited or no value. The autistic child's problem of overselective responding or the inability to respond to multiple cues is related to the failure to generalize a learned response (Koegel and Schreibman 1977). Autistic children have a strong tendency to focus attention on some limited and often irrelevant aspect of the training situation. Because behavior is elicited by the stimuli that have been associated with reinforcement, a major problem arises when the child has attended to only one very narrow aspect of the reinforcement setting. The color of the room in which the training occurs, for example, may be the only stimuli in the therapy setting that the child has noted. When the child is moved to another room, the response that was readily emitted in the first setting will not occur in the second. This tendency can hide the fact that the child has not learned correct response; for example, the child may respond "ball" each time the ball is held up, but the child also says "ball" when the therapist holds up an empty hand.

There are several ways to overcome this problem. First, the functional aspects of the training environment need to be identified and the child selectively forced to attend to a broader array of stimulus events. Second, by identifying the functional stimuli in the training setting, these stimuli can then be moved into the new setting (Koegel and Rincover 1977; Rincover and Koegel 1975). Third, the new stimuli can be moved into the training situation. If, for example, a child will talk only while in the presence of a parent or a particular therapist, generalization can be created by gradually fading in other persons while the child is talking. A cue for talking in the presence of other people can then be created.

Even when generalization of the response is achieved, the behavior may quickly extinguish, and a failure of maintenance will occur. Autistic children require a dense schedule of reinforcement to maintain responding. In the extra therapy setting, it is not likely that the necessary ratio of reinforcement to correct responding will automatically occur. Maintenance can best be achieved if, during the therapy session, time is taken to move the child from a continuous reinforcement schedule to a much less dense schedule before attempting generalization and maintenance. It has also been demonstrated that noncontingent reinforcers in the extra-therapy environment can increase generalization (Koegel and Rincover 1977).

Punishment

Technically, a punisher is any stimulus that, when presented contingent on a behavior, reduces the probability of that behavior. Using this definition, the two procedures used with autistic children that are punishment techniques would be overcorrection (Foxx and Azrin 1973) and some form of aversive stimulation such as electric skin shock (Butcher and Lovaas 1968; Lovaas et al. 1974).

Overcorrection.　Overcorrection is most commonly used to reduce maladaptive self-stimulation that is clearly interfering with the acquisition of more adaptive skills. The procedure involves forcing the child to engage for several minutes in unpleasant physical "exercise" each time the unwanted behavior occurs. Azrin and Nunn (1973) recommended that the exercise be in the same topography as the unwanted behavior. For example, if hand flapping is to be targeted, each time it occurs, the child is required to hold the hand over the head or out to the sides. When applied consistently, overcorrection is quite effective in reducing a wide variety of unwanted motor mannerisms. The difficulty with the technique is that it is sometimes hard to obtain the necessary staff compliance to engage the child in the physical activity. If done in an incomplete way the interaction could serve to facilitate the unwanted behavior.

Skin shock.　Electric skin shock should not be considered for any behavior other than severe self-injury. The development of self-injury stems from the tendency to self-stimulate and from the operant effects created by attempts to make the child stop

(Carr and McDowell 1980). The control of self-injury tends to be a greater problem in autism than in the retarded. In the retarded, self-injury is often clearly related to its reinforcing effects. During periods of staff inattention or because of desperate attempts on their part to help, the child's limited communication skills result in self-injury becoming a form of interaction with caretakers. It is much like the traditional temper tantrum that is exaggerated into self-injury. For example, if being held is a reinforcer, the retarded child will learn to self-injure when an adult holds the child to stop the behavior; if going outside is reinforcing, caretakers might report that they get the child to cease the self-injury by taking the child for a walk. This effect is clearly a factor in the self-injury of autistic children (Lovaas et al. 1974). In addition, however, self-injury may be intrinsically rewarding for autistic children (Carr 1977). In the retarded, self-injury is usually easily correlated with situational events. In the autistic, self-injury may appear to occur at random times, appearing to be detached from any external event. We have observed self-injurious behavior in autistic children to be decreased by changing the adult interaction associated with the self-injury, only to have self-injury drift back to beginning rates in subsequent days despite the maintenance of the new adult interaction pattern.

From a totally pragmatic position, electric skin shock is a reliable and rapidly effective means of eliminating self-injury. In a review of the skin shock literature, the only instance of its failure was in Lesch-Nyhan disease (Anderson et al. 1977). Skin shock procedure may often fail to generalize, and maintenance of the effect may be limited, but it does stop a serious self-injury problem quickly.

Physical punishment has unquestionably been used inappropriately and in highly unethical ways. It is proper that community groups monitor such programs to ensure professional integrity. The use of punishment is almost certain to create controversy, and the director of the treatment facility must be familiar with the debate. It should be noted that some states (e.g., New York) have made the use of electric skin shock illegal under any conditions. Thus the therapist must be aware of institutional, local, and state regulations regarding its use.

Before discussing punishment procedures, it must be made clear that if the intensity and frequency of self-injury is not severe, a program that eliminates the inadvertent reinforcement of self-injury while creating adaptive and appropriate behaviors is the therapy of choice (Frankel and Simmons 1976). If, however, self-injury is quite serious, a punishment procedure delivered by a therapist well trained in its use should be considered. If the self-injury is on the verge of becoming a serious problem, a punishment procedure may also need to be considered because of the typical extinction effect that follows removal of reinforcement. If the self-injury has a component that is maintained by its functional relationship to a reinforcer, the removal of the reinforcer is almost always accompanied by an increase in the intensity and frequency of the behavior. If the topography and intensity of the self-injury is at all problematic, an extinction procedure should be used with the utmost of caution.

Lovaas et al. (1974) were the first to use a punishment procedure to suppress serious self-injury. They felt that the use of such a drastic measure was justified when the alternative was continued severe, frequently life-threatening, self-abuse. The technique is to touch the child's skin with a shock source immediately on the act of self-injury. A serious and long-standing problem can be suppressed in a few applications of shock. The child should react with an intense startle response after the initial shock. After the second or third shock, there should be a substantial lowering of the rate of self-injury. There should be a complete elimination of the response by perhaps the tenth shock. The process should be stopped if this general pattern is not shown by the child.

Like any therapy that does not correct the basic mechanism that maintains the unwanted behavior, this procedure should not be considered a cure. While the literature on skin shock is unanimous in reporting an initial elimination of the self-injury, the process often fails to generalize to the extra-therapy setting. Even maintenance within the therapy session itself is often difficult. Electric skin shock must be viewed as a temporary measure that allows the therapist to proceed with the creation of more adaptive responses and to eliminate the social interaction that helped maintain self-injury.

Drug and Behavior Therapy Interactions

Unlike the retarded, where the use of medication may result in a deterioration of performance (Werry and Aman 1975), the use of haloperidol has proved helpful even in the lowest functioning autistic children (Anderson et al. 1984). Haloperidol in combination with behavior therapy has been shown to facilitate language acquisition beyond that expected from behavior therapy alone (Campbell et al. 1978a). These issues are discussed and the data presented in the following chapter on pharmacotherapy.

Chapter 41

Pharmacotherapy

Goals of Pharmacotherapy: General Principles

The two pervasive developmental disorders—autistic disorder and pervasive developmental disorder not otherwise specified—are characterized by behavioral symptoms and cognitive deviations, usually delays. According to DSM-III-R (American Psychiatric Association 1987), essential features are qualitative impairment in reciprocal social interactions, in communication (both verbal and nonverbal), and in imaginative activity, as well as a severely restricted repertoire of activities and interests. In addition, stereotypies, hyperactivity, hypoactivity, and aggressiveness may be displayed. The goal of treatment is to decrease the behavioral symptoms and to promote cognitive development.

In severe psychiatric disorders that become manifest in adults, the purpose of treatment, particularly of pharmacotherapy, is to decrease or to control symptoms and to enable patients to return to their previous level of functioning. However, children and adolescents affected with pervasive developmental disorders 1) have never or only rarely functioned in a normal, age-expected manner, and a regression from some previously achieved level is infrequent, and 2) are still developing and maturing organisms who have not achieved the adult level maturational organization. For them, treatment is expected not only to decrease behavioral symptoms, but also to promote development. Ideally, this is the goal of pharmacotherapy. Because there is some supportive evidence that certain drugs at certain doses may interfere with or cause deterioration in cognitive functioning, in the past few years the following have been the goals in research: 1) to assess critically the behavioral efficacy of certain psychoactive drugs, 2) to assess their effect on learning, and 3) to determine their safety.

Indications

Pharmacotherapy is viewed as one of the treatment modalities in the comprehensive treatment program tailored for the needs of the individual child. Hyperactivity, stereotypies, withdrawal, aggressiveness directed against others or self-mutilation, irritability, and temper tantrums are among the target symptoms that often, but not always, respond to drug therapy. When effective in decreasing such target symptoms and when safe, a drug can quickly render the autistic child more amenable to psychosocial treatments and to special education.

Drug therapy should be prescribed only when all other treatments failed. It should be considered if the child displays certain target symptoms (such as those listed above), and it should be included, along with other therapeutic interventions, after the initial careful and exhaustive evaluation of the child.

A two-week period is usually required to establish a stable baseline (variation and range of behavioral symptoms, eating and sleeping pattern, and in some cases blood pressure and pulse rate) prior to commencing drug administration.

Contraindications

As a rule, a child with mild symptoms should be prescribed medication under careful observation by someone with considerable experience in these cases who can weigh the benefits against the risks. Furthermore, known allergy or sensitivity to a particular drug is a contraindication. An exclusively hypoactive child usually does not respond well to a neuroleptic. If the child has an associated seizure disorder, chlorpromazine administration is contraindicated because it is known to increase the frequency to seizures and to decrease seizure threshold in seizure-prone individuals (Tarjan et al. 1957). As a rule, the parents must be responsible and cooperative.

Goals

As in all treatments of chronic conditions, for pharmacotherapy too, both immediate and long-term goals should be established. For example, a short-term goal can be the decrease of such maladaptive behaviors as aggressiveness, self-mutilation, hyperactivity, stereotypies, and insomnia, and the increase in the ability to focus on a task. It is in achieving this type of goal that an effective drug can be very helpful, in conjunction with milieu, behavior, and other psychosocial treatments in a highly structured environment. Some autistic children may require long-term drug maintenance to remain with their families or in a good educational program or class. For example, if the addition of an effective drug to special education can clinically significantly reduce hyperactivity, aggressiveness, or other symptoms that interfere with a child's functioning and learning and can prevent (or control) disruptiveness in the classroom, then it is justified and judicious to maintain the child on pharmacotherapy, provided it is discontinued and reevaluated at certain regular intervals (e.g., every six months). This is necessary to determine whether further continuous pharmacotherapy is warranted and whether certain withdrawal phenomena may develop. The only alternative to pharmacotherapy may be to place the child in a residential treatment center, an alternative that some parents may not wish to choose.

Certainly in no case should pharmacotherapy be thought of as a permanent treatment. Experience has shown that many children with the most severe and disruptive symptoms may cease to display maladaptive behaviors as they mature or as psychosocial treatments take effect, and further drug administration becomes unnecessary. However, it is important to monitor and evaluate at regular intervals not only the efficacy (and safety) of pharmacotherapy but also that of other treatments. The child's, adolescent's, or even adult's needs may change with time; at some point, special education or pharmacotherapy will have to be replaced by vocational training or individual psychotherapy.

Pharmacotherapy has a role in the treatment of the individual patient only if it makes sufficient impact on the maladaptive behavior to outweigh the possible short-term, and particularly the long-term, side effects, and if the outcome compares favorably to what would have been possible without employing this particular treatment modality.

Assessment of the Efficacy and Safety of Pharmacotherapy

No matter what type of assessment or documentation of changes associated with pharmacotherapy is employed, a brief but careful and accurate written documentation and stable baseline is essential prior to commencing drug administration. This involves behavioral, cognitive, physical, and laboratory evaluation of the patient (Campbell et al. 1985). In the absence of these measures, it is impossible to evaluate meaningfully the (possible) therapeutic effects and side effects of drug intervention. Particularly in inpatients, every attempt is made to conduct assessments (including blood pressure, pulse rate, weight) at fixed times of the day and to carry out formal assessments (behavioral and cognitive ratings and videotaping of the patient) at fixed times in relationship to drug administration (ingestion).

These issues will be only briefly discussed here. Elsewhere there are extensive reviews on assessment of demographic data, and side effects in children and measures used (Campbell and Palij 1985a, 1985c; Campbell et al. 1985), as well as behavioral and cognitive measures used in psychopharmacologic studies of autistic children (Campbell and Palij 1985b; Campbell et al. 1985).

Clinical Methods

1. *Documentation by reports.* In daily practice, both the positive and untoward effects of drug intervention are usually evaluated by reports from parents, teachers, and/ or hospital and residential treatment facility staff, or by other caretakers of the patient.
2. *Observation of patient.* Patient observations can be kept in the form of written notes by the parents or other adults involved in the patient's care or therapy (e.g., Ritvo et al. 1983).

3. *Interview of patient.* Depending on the patient's maturational or chronological age, unstructured and various semistructured interview methods were conducted in research (Campbell et al. 1978a, 1978b).
4. *Examination of patient.* This method is usually employed for the assessment of certain side effects, including for parkinsonian side effects and for tardive dyskinesia.

Rating Scales

The above methods of assessment can be supplemented by the use of various rating scales, or the findings can be transferred on certain scales (e.g., tardive dyskinesia can be documented on one of the scales developed for the ratings of abnormal involuntary movements). In research, invariably, rating scales and multiple raters are employed. They include:

Behavioral and Cognitive Measures (for a review, see Campbell and Palij 1985b)
- Behavioral Rating Scales (subjective and objective, used in psychopharmacologic studies involving autistic subjects)
  - The Children's Psychiatric Rating Scale (CPRS)
  - Clinical Global Impressions Scale (CGI)
  - The Nurse's Global Impressions Scale (NGI)
  - The Conners' Parent-Teacher Questionnaire (PTQ)
  - The Ritvo-Freeman Real Life Rating Scale for Autism (Freeman et al. 1986)
  - The Childhood Autism Scale (CARS) (Schopler et al. 1985)
  - The Timed Stereotypies Rating Scale (Campbell 1985a)
- Electronic Devices
  - Measurement of Stereotypies and Their Duration
  - Measurement of Motor Activity
- Videotaping and Ratings of Videotapes
- Cognitive Measures (used in psychopharmacologic studies involving autistic subjects, as shown in Table 1)
  - Learning and Performance Tasks (for short-term studies)
  - Intelligence Tests (age appropriate, for long-term studies)

Measures for Untoward Effects of Drugs (for a review, see Campbell and Palij 1985c; Campbell et al. 1985)
- Measures for Behavioral Toxicity (psychomotor, cognitive, gross behavior, and mood)
- Measures of Behavioral and Other Effects of Drug Withdrawal
- Measures of Central Nervous System Untoward Effects (including those of tardive dyskinesia)
- Measures for Autonomic Nervous System Untoward Effects
- Laboratory Studies
- IQ Tests
- Growth Charts (for linear growth and weight)

Experimental Study Design and Methodology

The experimental design, methodology, and assessment in general have to be at least as rigorous and critical in studies of infantile autism as in those of other psychopath-

Table 1. Cognitive and Learning Measures in Clinical Drug Trials Involving Autistic Children

| Measure | Duration of study | Subjects | | Reference |
		Ages (years)	Sample size	
Cognitive Battery (based on items from Gesell, Developmental Schedules, WPPSI, and Stanford-Binet)	(1) 12 weeks	2.6–7.2	40	Campbell et al. (1978a)
	(2) 14-21 weeks	2.3–7.2	30	Campbell et al. (1978b)
Language acquisition	12 weeks	2.6–7.2	40	Campbell et al. (1978a)
Discrimination Learning (Auditory and Visual Stimuli)	(1) 14 weeks	2.33–6.92	40	Anderson et al. (1984)
	(2) 14 weeks	3.2–7.6	42	Anderson et al. (1979)
Serial IQ Testing (Merrill-Palmer Preschool Performance, Cattell or Stanford-Binet Scales, age-appropriate Wechsler scale)	(1) 7.5 months (Note: IQ measured once every month)	3–18	14	Ritvo et al. (1983)
	(2) Same as 1 above	5–13	9	August et al. (1985)
	(3) Same as 1 above	3–12	16	Leventhal (1985)
IQ and/or DQ Testing (Gesell Developmental Schedules, age-appropriate Wechsler scale, Stanford-Binet)	9 months to 3.8 years (mean 3.0 years) (Note: IQ measured twice: on baseline and after 9 months to 3.8 years)	3.3–8.11	15	Die Trill et al. (1984)

Note. Reproduced with permission from Campbell (1987).

ologies in children. Whereas, for example, in attention deficit disorder with hyperactivity, many such psychopharmacologic studies exist, rigorous and systematic research in autistic children began only about 10 to 15 years ago (for a review, see Campbell et al. 1984b). The exception is a carefully designed study involving trifluoperazine (Fish et al. 1966). Therefore the methodology or the use of behavioral rating scales may not be as well researched in psychopharmacology involving autistic children, leaving certain unresolved methodological problems. The choice of experimental design is one such issue. Because autism is a rare condition and because autistic children may be heterogeneous concerning etiology, severity or types of symptoms, intellectual functioning, and status at the time of the study (full syndrome present versus residual state [American Psychiatric Association 1980]), it was thought that a combination of single-subject design with intensive study of each subject (Chassan 1960) and an extensive evaluation across all subjects in the sample (Turner et al. 1974) would be desirable, and preferable over a lengthy crossover design, where time itself may be a decisive factor in influencing outcome (Campbell et al. 1978b). This choice has been shown to be a good one in more than one study (Anderson et al. 1984; Campbell et al. 1982a; Cohen et al. 1980a). However, because of such issues as carryover (Cochran and Cox 1957; Laska et al. 1983), perhaps parallel design is the design of choice for carefully diagnosed children, who are relatively homogeneous in terms of chronological age, who are properly monitored, and who are randomly assigned to treatment conditions to reduce bias (Campbell et al. 1978a, 1987a). Certainly randomization is much preferred to matching of subjects (Campbell et al. 1972b, 1976) when we do not know with certainty on what variables these children should be matched (Fish 1968).

Since Fish's (1968) historic article on methodology, with particular emphasis on autistic children, the following progress has been made in methodology relating to psychopharmacologic studies of autistic children:

- Adequate sample sizes;
- Patients diagnosed by specific DSM-III (American Psychiatric Association 1980) criteria;
- Enrollment of patients who are relatively homogeneous in terms of chronological age;
- Employment of appropriate (for the population) and drug sensitive behavioral rating scales;
- Use of multiple trained raters;
- Videotaping of patients' ratings and rating of videotapes;
- Assessment of drug effects both on behavioral symptoms and on cognition and/or learning;
- Employment of appropriate experimental designs with placebo control;
- Attention to ecologic variables;
- Provision of good and detailed documentation of safety (both short-term and long-term side effects);
- Use of various rating scales for (quantification of) side effects;
- Exploration of relationship between change in behavioral symptoms and drug levels in plasma;
- Assessment of both short- and long-term therapeutic efficacy of drug;
- Comparison of drug-to-psychosocial (behavior modification) treatment.

Rating Conditions

Rating conditions may, and in most cases will, influence the outcome of pharmacotherapy. This is certainly true for many psychiatric conditions in children, but particularly for infantile autism. The younger the child, the more variable is the child's behavior from minute to minute or from one place to another. The same is true for those who are functioning on a retarded level. Furthermore, autistic children are known to have unpredictable maladaptive behaviors. Thus, when assessing (or determining) the efficacy of a psychoactive agent, certain variables or conditions have to be made as constant as possible to reduce variability or the role of chance. The same is true for the assessment of certain side effects, particularly of drug-related tardive or withdrawal dyskinesias. Therefore, evaluations, particularly when rating scales and videotaping are employed, should be made at certain fixed times after drug ingestion, and the ratings should be conducted at the same sites (e.g., classroom, playroom, other familiar environment) and after meals. Young children may be particularly upset when taken to a strange, unfamiliar environment. A child should not be removed from group play or any enjoyable activity (e.g., play with sand or water, gross motor activity) to be formally assessed. Physical examination, venipuncture, finger prick, or any other potentially painful or frightening procedures should not be scheduled immediately prior to such formal assessments. The ideal time for formal ratings is the morning hours. However, as noted above, there can be no valid assessment of treatment efficacy without a stable baseline assessment: this should be done under the same conditions as post-drug evaluations.

Special Issues with Children

Prior to prescribing a psychoactive drug for a child, the possible benefits and untoward effects should be discussed with parents and, if appropriate, with the child's teachers. Noncompliance or improper administration are relatively frequent reasons for failure to respond to a drug; this issue should be explained to the parents.

It has not been demonstrated that the combination of two drugs is more effective than one single drug. Furthermore, combining two or more drugs can escalate untoward effects. Therefore, polypharmacy is considered to be poor medical practice.

The initial starting dose should be small, and it is usually ineffective. Increments should be gradual, and dose should be increased and titrated until positive or side effects occur, and then the optimal dose established. However, the maximum dose should not exceed the one recommended by the *Physician's Desk Reference* (PDR). Unlike in hyperactive children, where usually a fixed dosage of stimulant (mg/kg) is being used, dosage titration is recommended in autistic children. Both research and clinical experience have shown that in these children, of the drugs currently in use, the optimal doses show a wide range and are not necessarily related to chronological age, weight, or severity of symptoms. The exception may be fenfluramine, which was administered in a fixed daily dose (1.5 mg/kg) to a large number of autistic children in multicenter study (Ritvo et al. 1986). However, its use in infantile autism is recent, and the findings have to be replicated.

Behavioral toxicity (i.e., worsening of preexisting symptoms or the development of new symptoms) is frequently the first sign of excess dose in children. It should be looked for and recognized as such to eliminate unnecessary dose escalation and further increase of behavioral toxicity. At first dividing the dosage into two or three parts—given morning, noon, and afternoon—can increase the effectiveness of a drug and help to eliminate untoward effects. Frequently the drug can later be given in a single dose, in the morning. In general, drug administration in the evening prior to sleep is not recommended because the purpose of pharmacotherapy is usually to decrease disruptive and other behavioral symptoms usually manifested at daytime.

Duration of Drug Treatment

Usually a trial of one month is required to evaluate whether a drug is effective. Minimal improvement, or improvement only in sleep pattern, does not justify administration of a psychoactive drug, particularly if there is a risk for the development of long-term side effects (e.g., as in the case of a neuroleptic). In some cases, a period of three months will be sufficient to administer a drug. During this time, with the aid of the drug, some children may acquire adaptive skills and be able to function further without drug treatment. If longer drug administration is required, the drug should be discontinued every six months to determine whether further drug treatment is necessary, as well as to establish the presence of tardive or withdrawal dyskinesias.

Pharmacotherapy and Psychosocial Treatments

Certainly experience strongly supports the view that pharmacotherapy can be a very useful treatment modality in a comprehensive treatment program tailored for the individual needs of the autistic child, and that includes behavior modification and special education in a highly structured environment. It is believed that the only lasting side effect of a drug is indirect, and it is a result of the modified interaction of the patient with the environment due to concurrent psychosocial interventions (Irwin 1968). In one study, a combination of haloperidol and behavior modification focusing on language acquisition was significantly superior to either treatment administered alone (Campbell et al. 1978a). These treatments were given over 12 weeks; the study was double-blind and placebo controlled, and involved 40 autistic children 2.6 to 7.2 years of age, all of whom were inpatients placed in a therapeutic nursery program. Behavior therapy in this study was conducted daily by professional and highly trained therapists on a one-to-one basis. However, behavior modification is an expensive procedure and requires highly trained staff or parents (Schopler and Reichler 1971a). As in the above study (Campbell et al. 1978a), most research and many clinical intervention programs are based on one-to-one therapist-child ratios (Lovaas et al. 1976) and are therefore, for the most part, prohibitive for many hospitals, school programs, and institutions. Combining behavior modification with drug therapy was thought to be more effective than either treatment alone in other populations as well (Sprague 1972; Sprague and Werry 1971).

Ideally, symptoms should be decreased by drug therapy, whereas development is hoped to be promoted with the aid of concurrent psychosocial treatments. Development is a dynamic interaction between the maturing central nervous system (CNS) and the psychosocial environment. Thus the psychoactive drug acts on the CNS, decreases symptoms, and promotes development in interaction with psychosocial treatment.

Current Status of Pharmacotherapy in Infantile Autism

Pharmacotherapy is not viewed as a popular, or even a desirable, method of treatment for autistic children by many professionals. Often it is sought when other methods have failed or when the child's behavior is so disruptive or intolerable that the child cannot be maintained with parents, in a classroom, or even in a residential treatment center. This is so despite the fact that it has been repeatedly demonstrated that certain drugs (e.g., haloperidol) are both clinically and statistically superior to placebo effect in decreasing behavioral symptoms when dosage is individually regulated and when given on a short-term basis over a period of one and up to three months (Anderson et al. 1984; Campbell et al. 1978a, 1982a, Cohen et al. 1980), and on a long-term basis when administered over a period of up to 42½ months (Campbell et al. 1982b, 1983a; Perry et al. 1989). Haloperidol is also a safe drug at doses at which maladaptive behaviors decrease; side effects, when given over a period of up to 56 days occur only above therapeutic doses.

Perhaps the following are the reasons for this reluctance to use pharmacotherapy, or at times even hostility toward drug treatment. First, there is a greater concern about the safety of treatments, particularly drugs, when the patient is a child. Because infantile autism is a developmental disorder and, according to DSM-III (American Psychiatric Association 1980), its symptoms are displayed before the age of 30 months, these children are diagnosed at an earlier age (e.g., three to five years) than youngsters with other diagnoses who may be considered for psychopharmacologic intervention (e.g., attention deficit disorder with hyperactivity, schizophrenic disorder). Infantile autism is a disorder with a chronic course, and safety is a serious concern when considering long-term drug administration (e.g., the possibility of tardive or withdrawal dyskinesias, adverse effect on height and weight). Second, because drugs are thought to be dangerous (or less safe) when given to children, it is believed that, to prescribe them, their therapeutic efficacy has to be greater than the efficacy of psychosocial treatments (e.g., behavior modification) because these later treatments are considered harmless (or free of side effects).

There are those who state that positive response to neuroleptics characterizes children diagnosed as schizophrenic and can be used to differentiate them from those with infantile autism, who typically fail to respond to such drug treatment (Hanson and Gottesman 1976). This statement has not been supported by research evidence, and even clinical experience has not confirmed this belief. A review of the literature suggested that perhaps no more than five reports exist on the effect of neuroleptics on schizophrenic children and adolescents five to 22 years of age (Campbell 1985). Only in two of the five studies were the samples diagnostically homogeneous, and only one of the five was double-blind and placebo controlled, involving a large sample size (75 acute schizophrenics or chronic schizophrenics with acute exacerbation) (Pool et al. 1976). It is of interest that the study, which involved 21 chronic schizophrenic adolescents, indicated that this population showed fairly poor response to thiothixene, and even worse to thioridazine (Realmuto et al. 1984). Furthermore, side effects appeared even at "therapeutic" doses, as was the case with the neuroleptic haloperidol in children with conduct disorder, aggressive type (Campbell et al. 1984a), whereas in autistic children two to seven years of age, with careful clinical monitoring, haloperidol yielded no untoward effects at daily therapeutic doses (0.5 to 4.0 mg) when given over one to two months (Anderson et al. 1984, 1989; Campbell et al. 1978a, 1982a) and up to 56 days (Campbell et al. 1982b, 1983a, 1983b; Perry et al. 1985). The concern with haloperidol is its long-term safety; its administration in a prospective study (for three-and-a-half months or longer) is associated with the development of tardive or withdrawal dyskinesias, so far reversible (Campbell et al. 1982b, 1983a, 1983b, 1988a; Meiselas et al. 1989; Perry et al. 1985).

Review of the Literature

This is not intended to be an exhaustive review but rather a summary of what is known to be the (short-term or, if data are available, long-term) therapeutic efficacy and safety of drugs in this population. An attempt will be made to state what is based on hard data and what is based on open, pilot studies or methodologically weak research. It is now firmly believed that infantile autism is etiologically heterogeneous (for a review, see Panksepp and Sahley 1987; Young et al. 1982). Whenever feasible, a rationale for the exploration or for the use of a drug or class of drugs will be given, as well as some speculation as to how the biochemical action of a drug may relate to (affect) the possible (putative) biochemical abnormalities underlying the behavioral and cognitive abnormalities found in (subgroups) autistic children (Table 2). The classification of the drugs will be somewhat arbitrary, and they will not necessarily be grouped on the basis of their mode of action. Daily dosages of the most frequently used drugs are listed in Table 3.

As emphasized above, systematic research in this area has begun only in the past decade or so (for a review, see DeMyer et al. 1981), and many of the published studies require replication or future research employing more rigorous and sophisticated methodology.

Hallucinogens

In the early 1960s, psychotomimetics were explored in the treatment of infantile autism in attempts to stimulate the apathetic, anergic child who functions on a retarded level, and to promote the development of rudimentary or nonexistent language or other skills. At that time, other available drugs were mainly the standard phenothiazines and the amphetamines. Methysergide, an antiserotonergic agent and a methylated derivative of 1-methyl-D-lysergic acid butanolamide bimaleate (LSD) was reported to have both stimulating and tranquilizing effects, as well as psychotomimetic properties in adults.

In autistic and schizophrenic children six to 12 years of age, Bender and associates reported positive effects associated with open administration of either LSD or methysergide. Stimulation of affect, motor behavior, and communicative speech, as well as increase of alertness and decrease of stereotypies, were reported (Bender et al. 1962, 1963, 1966). Subsequently, in an acute dose range study of methysergide, positive changes were noted, as in Bender's trial; however, these therapeutic effects were accompanied by toxic behavioral changes, which included excessive sedation; increases in hyperactivity, irritability, psychotic language, and disorganized behavior; and deterioration in performance tasks in addition to autonomic side effects (Fish et al. 1969b). When these 11 children, whose ages were under five years, were placed on maintenance doses of methysergide for a mean number of 42 days in an open trial, ratings showed initial improvement followed by significant worsening at termination; side effects were similar to those during the acute dose range trial. In general, the positive changes observed in the maintenance study seemed to be of a lesser degree than in the acute trial, whereas tolerance to the drug and worsening of psychosis were marked (Fish et al. 1969b). In a sample of 17 children, Simmons et al. (1972) found positive changes (e.g., smiling, euphoria, and prolonged physical contact with adults) associated with administration of LSD-25. Negative effects were strong and included fear and panic responses.

Thus antiserotonergic property of a drug is not necessarily associated with therapeutic effects in infantile autism, even though perhaps one-third of these children show evidence of hyperserotonemia (Campbell et al. 1975; Ritvo et al. 1970).

Antidepressants

Drugs of this class were explored because they possess both tranquilizing and stimulating properties, which seem to be desirable features, particularly for very withdrawn, anergic, and hypoactive autistic children who function on a retarded level, who have little motor initiation, and who have little or no language or other adaptive skills.

Table 2. Clinical Response to Psychoactive Agents and Its Relationship to Relevant Biochemical Findings in Subgroups of Autistic Children

Relevant biochemical findings	Psychoactive drugs	Clinical response	Main side effects	Representative references
Elevated serotonin levels (Campbell et al. 1975; Ritvo et al. 1970; for a review, see Young et al. 1982)	**Serotonin antagonists**			
	Methysergide	In general poor; mixture of stimulating, disorganizing, and sedative effects; tolerance developing; improvement in 2 of 9 patients	Excessive sedation, vomiting, insomnia, increased irritability	Fish et al. (1969b)
	L-dopa	In general some positive response: mainly stimulating effects; improvement in 5 of 12 patients	Vomiting, decreased appetite, increased irritability, motor retardation, increase of stereotypies and stereotypies de novo	Campbell et al. (1976)
	Fenfluramine	Conflicting reports	Excessive sedation, transient loss of weight, and irritability	August et al. (1985); Campbell et al. (1986a; 1988c); Geller et al. (1982); Leventhal (1985); Ritvo et al. (1983; 1986)
	Serotonin agonists Imipramine (?)	Poor: mixture of stimulating, tranquilizing, and disorganizing effects; 2 of 10 children improved	Worsening of psychotic symptoms, excessive sedation, irritability, insomnia, catatonic-like state, lowering of seizure threshold, transient increase of SGOT and SGPT	Campbell et al. (1971b)
	Lithium (?)	Minimal effect on symptoms except on aggressiveness and explosiveness	Motor retardation, motor excitation, vomiting, polydipsia, polyuria, leukocytopenia, decrease of T_4 and electrocardiogram changes	Campbell et al. (1972b)

Dopaminergic abnormalities *Elevated dopamine levels* (Cohen et al. 1974, 1977; for review, see Young et al. 1982); alteration of hypothalamic dopamine receptor sensitivity (Deutsch et al. 1985, 1986)			
Dopamine antagonists Sedative type of neuroleptics: chlorpromazine	In general poor: some decrease of symptoms accompanied by excessive sedation; narrow therapeutic margin	Excessive sedation, motor retardation, irritability, and catatonic-like state	Campbell et al. (1972b)
High potency neuroleptics: thiothixene, molindone, fluphenazine, trifluoperazine, and haloperidol	In general good: marked decrease of symptoms, wide therapeutic margin; with haloperidol, marked decrease of symptoms, enhancement of learning without untoward effects (when administered over a period of 3½ months cumulatively)	Excessive sedation, acute dystonic reaction, parkinsonian side effects, excessive weight gain and tardive and withdrawal dyskinesias	Anderson et al. (1984; 1989); Campbell et al. (1970, 1971a, 1978a, 1982a, 1982b, 1983a, 1983b); Engelhardt et al. (1973); Faretra et al. (1970); Fish et al. (1966); Perry et al. (1985)
Dopamine agonists D-amphetamine	In general, only slight decrease of hyperactivity and increases of attention span and verbal production accompanied by side effects	Irritability, motor excitability, worsening of stereotypies and stereotypies de novo, loss of appetite, excessive sedation	Campbell et al. (1972a, 1972c)
L-amphetamine	Poor: only decrease in hyperactivity, in 5 of 11 patients	Increase of preexisting stereotypies and stereotypies de novo, decrease of appetite, loss of weight, excessive sedation and worsening of preexisting symptoms	Campbell et al. (1976)
L-dopa	[see above]	[see above]	[see above]

Table 2. Clinical Response to Psychoactive Agents and Its Relationship to Relevant Biochemical Findings in Subgroups of Autistic Children (continued)

Relevant biochemical findings	Psychoactive drugs	Clinical response	Main side effects	Representative references
Hypothalamic dysregulation abnormal response to TRH (Campbell et al. 1978b); elevated triiodothyronine levels (Campbell et al. 1980, 1982c; Deutsch et al. 1985, 1986)	Triiodothyronine (T$_3$)	Decrease of stereotypies and overall improvement at home	Fluctuating blood pressure, tachycardia, and irritability	Campbell et al. (1978c)
Abnormalities of endogenous opiate system[a] Reduction of urinary free catecholamines and MHPG (Young et al. 1978, 1979) Reduction of H-endorphin in plasma (Weizman et al. 1984); elevated endorphin fraction II levels in cerebrospinal fluid (Gillberg et al. 1985)	*Opiate antagonists:* Naloxone[b] Naltrexone[b]	Tranquilizing and stimulating effects: decreases in hyperactivity, impulsivity, stereotypies, and aggressiveness; increases in language production and social behavior	Hypoactivity and "as if dazed"	Campbell (1985)
Correlation between high endorphin fraction II levels, self-destructiveness, and decreased pain sensibility (Gillberg et al. 1985)				

Note. Reproduced with permission of Plenum Publishing Corp; from Campbell et al. (1987). SGOT = serum glutamic-oxaloacetic transaminase; SGPT = serum glutamic-pyruvic transaminase; TRH = thyrotopin-releasing hormone; MHPG = 3-methoxy-4-hydroxyphenylglycol.
[a]See Kalat (1978) and Panksepp (1979).
[b]For a review of literature in normal adults and psychiatric patients, see Verebey et al. (1978). For effects on self-injurious behavior, see Bernstein et al. (1984), Davidson et al. (1983), and Sandman et al. (1983).

Table 3. Dosages[a] of Psychoactive Drugs

Drug	Therapeutic daily dose range	
	mg	mg/kg
Chlorpromazine	10–200	0.441–2.0
Trifluoperazine	2–20	0.11–0.69
Fluphenazine	2–16	
Haloperidol	0.5–16	0.019–0.217
Thiothixene	1–30	
Molindone	1–40	
Fenfluramine[b]	15–40	1.093–1.787

Note. Adapted with permission from Campbell et al. (1987).
[a]For children under 12 years of age.
[b]Given twice a day, at 8 A.M. and 12 noon (or 4 P.M.).

Nortriptyline was administered to 16 children, four to 15 years of age, who failed to respond in the past to other drugs (Kurtis 1966). Aggressiveness, hyperactivity, and destructive behavior were reported to have decreased.

Imipramine was administered to 10 children, two to six years of age, most of whom functioned on a retarded level (Campbell et al. 1971a). In general, the response was poor: according to psychiatrist's blind global ratings, only two children improved markedly, and the remaining eight were rated as unchanged or worse. The total mean syndrome severity score was 59.9 on baseline and decreased to 50.5 at the end of treatment with imipramine; this was not statistically significant. As in children diagnosed as having attention deficit disorder with hyperactivity according to DSM-III criteria (American Psychiatric Association 1980), in these patients hyperactivity decreased, but it did not reach statistical significance. In general, initial improvements in six patients were only transient. The clinical effects observed were a mixture of stimulation, tranquilization, and disorganization. One of the good responders was a very explosive, assaultive girl with noncommunicative speech whose intellectual functioning was low average. However, the beneficial effects were outweighed in most cases by toxic effects, which included epileptogenic effects (Petti and Campbell 1975). It should be emphasized that neither of the studies was controlled or double-blind. Imipramine potentiates the effects of serotonin and increases serotonin levels in the brain (Costa 1960): one may speculate that this is an undesirable effect in infantile autism, where about 30 percent of children have increased serotonin levels in blood. Because hyperserotonemia is thought to be related to some of the clinical manifestations of the syndrome (Campbell et al. 1975; Young et al. 1982), worsening of preexisting symptoms in general and a significant increase of blunted affect at termination ($t - 2.715$, 9 df, $p < .50 - > .02$) could be related to the effect of imipramine on serotonin.

Lithium

Since the effects of lithium in counteracting aggressiveness and hyperexcitability were established in animals, human adults, and psychiatric patients (for a review, see Campbell et al. 1984c), it was thought that this action should be explored in hyperactive autistic children and compared to the effects of chlorpromazine (Campbell et al. 1972b). There were no significant differences between the two drugs and improvements were only slight with both. However, more individual symptoms decreased with chlorpromazine than with lithium. It is of interest that while there was no significant change in hyperactivity or in any of the symptoms characteristic of autism, explosiveness and self-mutilation ceased in one child receiving lithium (600 mg/day, blood level 0.593 to 0.760 mEq/l). This six-year-old boy previously had failed to respond to a variety of psychoactive drugs. Lithium merits further studies in autistic children in whom excitability, explosiveness, and aggressiveness directed against self or others is a prominent symptom.

Thyroid Hormone

In adult psychiatric patients, the interrelations of hormones and psychoneuroendocrine systems, their abnormalities, and psychiatric disorders have been studied for several decades (Gjessing 1938; Hoskins 1946; Prange 1974; Prange and Lipton 1972; Sachar 1975, 1976). It was suggested that simultaneous treatment of both hormonal and related psychiatric disorders will result in clinical improvement of patients (Reiss 1958); therefore hormones were administered as psychoactive drugs. In child psychiatry, neuroendocrine investigations are few and recent, having begun only in the past 15 years or so. However, thyroid hormone has a particularly significant role in the maturation and development of the CNS in both animals and humans (Eayrs 1968; Schapiro 1971; Sokoloff and Roberts 1971).

Studies of triiodothyronine (T_3) in autistic children were prompted by a brief report of Sherwin et al. (1958) on the encouraging behavioral results of T_3 in two clinically euthyroid, autistic children. The positive effects of this hormone included improvement in affective contact and speech. Studies of T_3 were begun since Fish (1970), in her psychopharmacologic studies of autistic children, was searching for drugs with stimulating effects. The first study involving 16 clinically euthyroid children showed a statistically significant decrease in overall symptoms while on T_3 ($p \le .01$). The decrease of individual symptoms (withdrawal, decreased attention span, negativism, verbal production, psychotic speech, flat affect, explosiveness, motor retardation), however, did not reach statistical significance (Campbell et al. 1972c, 1973). In general, the effects of T_3 appeared to be both stimulating and antipsychotic. This clinical trial had methodological weaknesses, and therefore a new, more rigorous study was designed with a larger and diagnostically homogeneous patient sample, employing new rating scales, developed by the Psychopharmacology Research Branch of the National Institute of Mental Health (NIMH) (Psychopharmacology Bulletin, 1973). Unlike the previous study, this trial of T_3 was placebo controlled and double blind. It consisted of 30 children and involved five raters and six behavioral rating scales. In this crossover design, T_3 did not differ from placebo except for a few symptoms using the two child psychiatrists' ratings. On the CGI, the more retarded children responded better than the higher functioning patients. There was a significant ($p < .05$) decrease of the total score of the PTQ, as rated by the parents (Campbell et al. 1978b) When the weekly ratings of the CPRS were analyzed for all 30 subjects, only four showed clear-cut evidence of improvement on T_3, although no child became worse on this drug. Thus, when T_3 was critically assessed, its earlier strong effects could not be replicated.

What we learned from both studies is that a subgroup of clinically euthyroid autistic children have elevation of thyroxine (T_4) and/or T_3 on baseline (Campbell et al. 1972c, 1973, 1982c). Furthermore, the results of administration of synthetic thyrotropin-releasing hormone (TRH) to 10 children suggested that a hypothalamic dysfunction may exist in these children (Campbell et al. 1978c). Others did not confirm these findings (Abassi et al. 1978; Cohen et al. 1980); the reason for this might be in certain demographic differences.

Megavitamins

The use of large, "mega" doses of vitamins as a treatment modality in this population is based on the concept that deficiencies of certain substances vital for the functioning of the organism, particularly of the brain, may lead to mental illness. It was Linus Pauling (1968) who introduced the concept called orthomolecular treatment into psychiatry (Hawkins and Pauling 1973). Roukema and Emery (1970) and Rimland (1973) reported encouraging results in autistic children. Rimland's open study involved 190 outpatients who received megadoses of ascorbic acid, niacinamide, pyridoxine, pantothenic acid, and multiple vitamin B tablets over a two-year period followed by a one-month drug-free period. Improvements were rated by parents and physicians and consisted mainly of increased alertness and socialization; with vitamin B6 there were particular gains in language. Definite improvements were reported in 45.3 percent of the children. However, it is not clear how many subjects were receiving psychoactive drugs simultaneously; for example, among the best responders were six children receiving phenytoin (Dilantin).

Greenbaum (1970) did not confirm the above finding in a double-blind study that involved random assignment of 17 children to niacinamide, 24 to placebo, and 16 to niacinamide and a tranquilizer. The children were four to 12 years of age and were receiving treatment over six months. Subsequently, Rimland et al. (1978) conducted a placebo-controlled study of vitamin B6 in subjects four to 19 years of age; 15 completed this double-blind trial. The children were rated to have significant worsening of symptoms by parents and teachers when B6 was withdrawn. However, these results are inconclusive because of methodological problems: choice of patients, concurrent medications (other vitamins and psychoactive drugs), varied length of treatment, design, lack of randomization, manner of ratings, and ecologic factors.

A task force of the American Psychiatric Association (Lipton et al. 1973) and of the American Academy of Pediatrics (Barness 1976) came to the conclusion that megavitamins have no role in the treatment of adult psychiatric patients and children with behavioral disorders. Furthermore, certain vitamins may have untoward effects (Rimland 1973; Rimland et al. 1978) or even toxic effects (Schaumburg et al. 1983).

Stimulants

This class of drugs has been shown repeatedly, in well-designed and carefully controlled studies, to decrease hyperactivity and impulsivity, to increase attention span, and, in the laboratory, to improve performance on a variety of tasks in children diagnosed as having attention deficit disorder with hyperactivity. Levoamphetamine was said to have a differential effect on aggressiveness in children with such symptoms (Arnold et al. 1972, 1973). This was the rationale for exploring dextroamphetamine and levoamphetamine in infantile autism. With both drugs, and particularly with levoamphetamine, the few positive effects observed in autistic children were usually outweighed by side effects (Campbell et al. 1972a, 1972c, 1976). In 11 children treated with levoamphetamine, only hyperactivity decreased; on the CGI seven of the children showed worsening (Campbell et al. 1976). Untoward effects were many and were observed in all children; they included loss of weight, worsening of aggressiveness directed against self or others, excessive sedation, and, above all, worsening of preexisting stereotypies and stereotypies de novo. With dextroamphetamine, there were slightly more positive changes but the untoward effects were of the same type and were frequent (Campbell et al. 1972a, 1972c). The rare reports on the usefulness of stimulants in autistic children are based on single cases or on only a few patients (Geller et al. 1981).

The adverse effects of this class of drugs can be interpreted on the basis of their action: they are dopamine agonists. There is a suggestion that excess dopaminergic activity exists in infantile autism (Cohen et al. 1977; for a review, see Young et al. 1982).

Neuroleptics

If further systematic studies confirm that there is excess dopaminergic activity in at least a subgroup of autistic children, as evidenced by biochemical findings accompanied by certain behavioral symptoms and cognitive abnormalities (e.g., stereotypies, hyperactivity, attentional difficulties), then the use of neuroleptics or antipsychotic drugs represents a rational therapeutic approach in this population. Fish (1970) first made the observation that the sedative type neuroleptic, such as chlorpromazine, has little therapeutic value, particularly in the retarded, anergic, and apathetic autistic child, and that this drug even at low doses yields excessive sedation and therefore may impair functioning and learning. Subsequent studies have confirmed this (Campbell et al. 1969a, 1972a, 1972b). Furthermore, Fish demonstrated that the less sedative type of neuroleptics, with high potency and low dose such as trifluoperazine (Fish et al. 1966) and trifluperidol (Fish et al. 1969a) are capable of decreasing behavioral symptoms and have a wide therapeutic margin. The controlled study of trifluoperazine was followed by pilot, or single-blind studies of several high potency, low dose neuroleptics, each involving small samples of children, confirming the above positive findings. These were trials of thiothixene (Campbell et al. 1970; Simeon et al. 1973; Waizer et al. 1972), fluphenazine and haloperidol (Engelhardt et al. 1973; Faretra et al. 1970), and of molindone (Campbell et al. 1971b). Pimozide was found therapeutically effective in a double-blind, placebo-controlled study, with random assignment to treatment conditions: 34 of the 87 children were autistic (Naruse et al. 1982). While in older autistic children these drugs sometimes produced parkinsonian extrapyramidal side effects at therapeutic doses, this was rarely the case in the preschool-age child. The only exception was trifluperidol, an experimental drug that had a very high incidence of extrapyramidal effects not only in adult patients but even in this young age group (Fish et al. 1969a) and was subsequently withdrawn from experimental use in this country.

Of all these psychoactive agents, trifluperidol, a butyrophenone, seemed to yield the most marked therapeutic changes. However, because of its toxicity and withdrawal from research, another butyrophenone, haloperidol, was systematically studied subsequently. The early studies of haloperidol by Faretra et al. (1970) and Engelhardt et al. (1973) involved large samples of carefully diagnosed patients, but both had some methodological weaknesses and showed disagreements concerning therapeutic dosage. While Faretra et al. achieved marked improvement in inpatients at conservative daily doses of haloperidol (0.75 to 3.75 mg), Engelhardt et al. administered much higher daily doses to outpatients (mean 11.9 mg, highest dose 16 mg). The following therapeutic changes were obtained. Faretra et al. found decreases in autism, assaultiveness, provocativeness, and anxiety by four weeks of treatment. Reduction in hyperactivity and stereotypies and improvements of attention span, adaptive skills, and self-care skills were among the significant gains in the clinical trial of Engelhardt et al. Subsequent carefully designed, double-blind, and placebo-controlled studies involving preschool-age inpatients confirmed the short-term beneficial effects of haloperidol. One of these studies involved 10 children (Cohen et al. 1980a), and other studies consisted of 40 children each (Anderson et al. 1984; Campbell et al. 1978a) or 45 children (Anderson et al. 1989). In addition to decreases of behavioral symptoms, which included withdrawal, hyperactivity, stereotypies, and abnormal object relations, there was a facilitation of learning in the laboratory at daily doses of 0.5 to 4.0 mg (mean 1.11 to 1.65 mg) or 0.019 to 0.217 mg/kg when dosage was individually regulated. At the doses on which these positive effects were obtained, no untoward effects were observed when the drug was administered over one month and up to 56 days. In only above therapeutic doses was excessive sedation noted with other behavioral toxicity; parkinsonian side effects were practically absent. Acute dystonic reaction was seen during dose regulation; its incidence could have been reduced using a lower starting dose and employing more gradual and slower dose increments (e.g., starting with 0.25 mg/day, and small increments twice weekly only: 0.5 mg/day, 0.5 mg bid, and so on).

It has been reported that today haloperidol is relatively commonly used in the treatment of autistic children and that parents view it as being most therapeutic (Rimland 1980, cited by DeMyer et al. 1981).

The concern with haloperidol, as with other neuroleptics, is its long-term safety, specifically the development of tardive and withdrawal dyskinesias (for a review, see American Psychiatric Association Task Force on Tardive Dyskinesia 1985; Campbell et al. 1983b; Gualtieri et al. 1980). In adults, there is a wide disagreement as to the incidence of tardive dyskinesia: a review of the literature gives a range of 0.5 to 67.6 percent (Gardos and Cole 1980a, 1980b; Gardos et al. 1977; Kane and Smith 1982). In children, the reported risk ranges from 8 to 51 percent (for a review, see Campbell et al. 1983b, 1985). This great discrepancy is thought to be due to a variety of methodological problems and is discussed elsewhere (Campbell et al. 1983b; Gardos and Cole 1980a; Gardos et al. 1977). In a carefully designed prospective study of autistic children receiving haloperidol, about 29 percent developed reversible tardive or withdrawal dyskinesias (Campbell et al., 1988a). This is in agreement with carefully conducted studies of adult patients (Kane and Smith 1982). The majority of autistic children, particularly those who function on a retarded level (Bartak and Rutter 1976; Campbell et al. 1975; Freeman et al. 1981), have abnormal movements (i.e., stereotypies, grimacing, posturings) as part of their behavioral syndrome. It is crucial to differentiate these abnormal movements present at baseline from abnormal involuntary movements associated with neuroleptic administration. It has been demonstrated repeatedly under double-blind conditions that haloperidol can reduce or control stereotypies, and these will reemerge or return when the child is placed on placebo (Anderson et al. 1984; Campbell et al. 1978a, 1983a; Cohen et al. 1980a). In our studies, more autistic children developed withdrawal dyskinesias than dyskinesias during neuroleptic treatment (Campbell et al., 1988a). The same was true for other studies involving autistic children (Engelhardt and Polizos 1978; Polizos and Engelhardt 1980; Polizos et al. 1973).

Most studies agree that the topography of drug-related abnormal involuntary movements is the same in children as in adults; most frequently it involves the muscles of mouth, jaw, and tongue (Campbell et al. 1982b, 1983a, 1983b, 1988a; Gualtieri et al. 1980, 1984), although not all concur (Polizos et al. 1973). Many autistic children have on baseline a high rate of stereotypies involving the same areas (Meiselas et al. 1989, in press). Furthermore, it was demonstrated that normal controls, matched for age, sex, socioeconomic status, and race, also have abnormal movements in the same areas, although significantly less than autistic children when rated on objective rating scales (Campbell et al. 1983b; Cohen et al. 1980b). This is in agreement with another comparison of autistic (high and low IQ) and normal control children (Freeman et al. 1981). Furthermore, retarded subjects, another population in which tardive and withdrawal dyskinesias were studied, also may have a high rate of stereotypies on baseline (Bicknell and Blowers 1980; Freeman et al. 1981). It is for these reasons that each autistic child should be rated prior to neuroleptic or even other psychoactive drug administration on one or both of the following scales: the Abnormal Involuntary Movements Scale (AIMS), developed by the Psychopharmacology Research Branch of the NIMH (Psychopharmacology Bulletin, 1985), or the abridged Simpson Scale (Simpson et al. 1979). Since methodological variables will significantly influence the rate of abnormal involuntary movements associated with pharmacotherapy, procedures for examination and ratings are described elsewhere (Campbell and Palij 1985c). For this population of autistic children, we found the AIMS to be more useful than the abridged Simpson Scale (Perry et al. 1985).

At our present state of knowledge, the following statements can be made concerning tardive and withdrawal dyskinesias in children:

1. The topography is the same as in adults: the abnormal involuntary movements involve most frequently the muscles of the mouth, jaw, and tongue, although any part of the body can be affected, including the muscles of the diaphragm and larynx (Campbell et al. 1982b, 1983a, 1983b, 1988a; Perry et al. 1985). However, in one study, mainly the lower extremities were involved and a high rate of choreoathetotic movements were reported (Engelhardt and Polizos 1978; Polizos and Engelhardt 1980; Polizos et al. 1973).

2. In most cases the movements are reversible; however, irreversible movements were also reported (Paulson et al. 1975).

3. Both administration of conservative daily doses (haloperidol, 0.5 to 3.0 mg) (Campbell et al. 1982b, 1983a, 1983b, 1988a; Perry et al. 1985) and relatively high daily doses (Engelhardt and Polizos 1978; Polizos and Engelhardt 1980; Polizos et al. 1973) are associated with development of these abnormal movements. Two studies suggest that higher doses are more likely to be associated with abnormal movements (Gualtieri et al. 1984; McAndrew et al. 1972).

4. It is not clear whether length of neuroleptic treatment is a contributing factor to the development of movements; however, as early as after 56 days of cumulative neuroleptic administration, withdrawal dyskinesias were rated (Campbell et al. 1988a).

5. Abrupt or gradual drug withdrawal does not seem to influence the outcome (Gualtieri et al. 1984; Polizos et al. 1973).

6. Continuous or discontinuous neuroleptic administration (haloperidol for seven days a week versus five days a week of haloperidol and two days a week of placebo in a double-blind prospective study with random assignment to treatment) did not influence the outcome (Campbell et al. 1983a, 1983b; Perry et al. 1985; 1989).

7. There is no significant difference between males and females, although females were overrepresented (Campbell et al. 1983a, 1983b, 1988a; Perry et al. 1985). In a sample of 82 autistic children, there was only a trend toward increased risk in females (Campbell et al., 1988a). The results of one study suggest that females receiving higher doses tended to develop drug-related movements (Gualtieri et al. 1984). It should be noted that in these studies the sample sizes are modest, and that in these samples there are fewer females than males.

8. Both tardive and withdrawal dyskinesias are seen in children.

In addition to abnormal movements, behavioral and other withdrawal phenomena were also reported (Campbell et al. 1983a; Gualtieri et al. 1984). One autistic girl developed supersensitivity psychosis (Campbell et al. 1983a).

In a prospective but uncontrolled study, IQ did not seem to be adversely affected; actually some children showed an intellectual spurt during long-term administration of haloperidol when given in daily doses of 0.5 to 3.0 mg (mean 1.313 mg) (Die Trill et al. 1984).

Height and weight were also studied in a prospective fashion during long-term administration of haloperidol in preschool-age autistic children. There was a significant increase in weight after six months of maintenance ($p < .05$). Height decreased by 4.7 points on the growth charts of the National Center of Health Statistics (Hamill et al. 1976), although this was not significant (Campbell et al. unpublished data).

Clearly haloperidol, and perhaps some other high potency neuroleptics, can be an important part of a comparative treatment program for hyperactive and normoactive autistic children (or for those in whom hyperactivity alternates with hypoactivity) when prescribed judiciously, monitored carefully, and given up to two months, cumulatively. Some of these children may acquire some adaptive skills during this period with the aid of the drug, and may not need further drug therapy. Certainly, it was demonstrated that haloperidol facilitates learning in the laboratory. However, there are those children whose chronic disruptive behavior will require prolonged drug maintenance. These children should be carefully monitored; the lowest effective dose should be prescribed, and the drug should be discontinued every six months for a minimum of four weeks. Discontinuation of drug therapy is required to determine whether further drug administration is warranted and to assess possible withdrawal phenomena. In general, it is not recommended to prescribe a neuroleptic to a child who developed tardive and withdrawal dyskinesias.

Antiserotonic Agents

Only L-dopa and fenfluramine will be discussed here, although there are other drugs that have antiserotonergic properties, some of which were mentioned above. The reason for this is that these two drugs were explored first by Ritvo and his associates in autistic children only for one reason: because of their antiserotonergic properties. The serotonergic system, as measured in blood, was systematically studied in infantile autism: actually, serotonin is the most extensively studied neurotransmitter in this condition. The majority of studies indicate that about one-third of autistic children have high levels of serotonin in blood as compared to controls (Campbell et al. 1975; Ritvo et al. 1970; for a review, see Coleman and Gillberg 1985). Serotonin has been implicated in a variety of functions, which include certain normal and abnormal behaviors and cognition. There is suggestive evidence that hyperserotonemia is associated with lower IQs, stereotypies, and, in general, more florid psychoses (Campbell et al. 1975), and that autistic children with higher IQs have low serotonin levels in peripheral blood (Ritvo et al. 1984, 1986).

It should be noted, however, that autistic children are heterogeneous concerning serotonin levels in blood; the variability of serotonin levels is greater in autistic children than in controls (Campbell et al. 1975; Goldstein et al. 1976; for a review, see Coleman and Gillberg 1985).

There is also considerable disagreement as to the platelet uptake of serotonin and efflux of serotonin from the platelets (for a review, see Coleman and Gillberg 1985). Furthermore, the levels of 5-hydroxyindoleacetic acid (5-HIAA) in cerebrospinal fluid of autistic children may not be related to serotonin levels in blood (Cohen et al.

1977; for a review, see Coleman and Gillberg 1985). Serotonin in blood may not reflect serotonin in the brain and certainly does not reflect dynamic events in the brain. Furthermore, hyperserotonemia was also found in a large number of mentally retarded individuals (Partington et al. 1973). It should also be noted that there are unresolved methodological problems in measuring serotonin in autistic children and in interpreting the findings.

It is against this background that Ritvo's attempt to develop a more rational pharmacotherapy for autistic children should be viewed. Ritvo has suggested that if hyperserotonemia represents the biochemical correlate of some symptoms in austistic children, then a potent serotonin antagonist, for example, L-dopa (Ritvo et al. 1971) or fenfluramine (Geller et al. 1982), should simultaneously yield decreases of serotonin and of behavioral abnormalities in these patients.

L-Dopa

Significant lowering of serotonin levels by L-dopa was not associated with behavioral changes when it was given to four children over six months (Ritvo et al. 1971). L-dopa's biochemical actions include elevation of dopamine; this may be related to its clinical effects observed in patients with Parkinson's disease, which include awakening-alerting effects, psychomotor activation, and improvement in cognitive functions (for a review, see Campbell 1973). These encouraging findings in Parkinson's disease led to administration of L-dopa to 12 young children in a crossover comparison with L-amphetamine (Campbell et al. 1976). Although improvements with L-dopa did not reach statistical significance, nonblind ratings suggested that good clinical response included stimulation of motor activity, energy, and play in hypoactive children and increases in verbal production, vocabulary, and affective responsiveness. These effects are particularly desirable in preschool-age, apathetic and hypoactive autistic children, who show delays in all areas of development. However, above optimal daily doses (range 900 to 2,250 mg) and even at therapeutic doses numerous untoward effects were observed: these included vomiting, decrease of appetite, worsening of irritability, and worsening of preexisting stereotypies and stereotypies de novo (Campbell et al. 1976). Both studies had methodological flaws: clearly, well-designed studies with larger patient samples are needed to assess critically the therapeutic role of L-dopa in autism.

Fenfluramine

Fenfluramine is a drug with amphetamine-like properties; it is a potent antiserotonergic and a mild antidopaminergic agent—hence its tranquilizing effects. After impressive therapeutic effects and an increase in IQs in three autistic children (Geller et al. 1982), a multicenter study of fenfluramine has begun under the leadership of Ritvo. Two reports indicated that fenfluramine is superior to placebo in children with higher IQs and that behavioral improvements are associated with a rise in verbal and cognitive skills (Ritvo et al. 1983, 1984). The sample consisted of 14 children three to 18 years of age. As a group, the responders had lower serotonin levels than the nonresponders, though there was significant decrease of serotonin associated with administration of fenfluramine in all subjects. Ritvo et al. (1986) reported that of the 81 subjects in a multicenter study, about 33 percent improved unquestionably: they showed decreases in hyperactivity, stereotypies, and withdrawal and increases in eye contact and social relatedness. Untoward effects were minor and included transient irritability, anorexia, and weight loss. However, August et al. (1985) reported only behavioral improvement without changes in cognition in nine children five to 13 years of age. Furthermore, Leventhal (1985) found no clinical response to fenfluramine in 16 children three to 12 years of age; the only change rated was significant decrease of serotonin levels in blood. All 81 children reported on participated in the multicenter study and were outpatients; they were receiving a fixed daily dose of 1.5 mg/kg of fenfluramine. The design of the study had some methodological weaknesses; therefore replication of these findings is required.

In an open pilot study involving inpatients three to five-and three-quarter years of age, fenfluramine had both stimulating and tranquilizing effects at therapeutic daily doses, which ranged from 1.093 to 1.787 mg/kg (mean 1.413 mg) (Campbell et al. 1986a). The highest daily dose explored was 3.625 mg/kg. On the CPRS there was a significant decrease of symptom scores; on the CGI there was a significant decrease of severity of illness. Clinically, the most marked effects were increases in relatedness and animated facial expression, decreases in temper tantrums, aggressiveness directed against self or others, irritability, hyperactivity, and improved sleep pattern. Four of the 10 children improved markedly; they were of low IQs. Untoward effects were rated above optimal doses: drowsiness, lethargy, and uncontrollable irritability were most frequent. There was a transient weight loss at the end of the first month of fenfluramine administration, which was followed by weight gain at the end of the second month. However, the behavioral improvements were only transient in some children. Laboratory studies remained within normal limits, and there were no electrocardiogram changes under careful clinical monitoring.

Because of the controversy over the therapeutic usefulness of fenfluramine, a carefully designed (parallel groups design with randomization) and placebo-controlled study was commenced to assess critically the effects of this drug on maladaptive behaviors, on discrimination learning in an automated laboratory, and its safety. In 28 children, ages 2.56 to 6.66 years, fenfluramine was not superior to placebo in reducing behavioral symptoms (Campbell et al., 1988c). When compared to placebo, fenfluramine had a retarding effect on discrimination learning in the laboratory.

Naltrexone

The search for biologic markers or biochemical abnormalities underlying (or contributing) to the developmental, behavioral, and cognitive deviances in infantile autism and for developing more rational, more effective, and safer psychopharmacologic interventions at a young age continues. Efficacy is not necessarily associated with safety; safety may be lacking in a drug that has been shown to be statistically and clinically effective. This is the case with neuroleptic long-term maintenance. Although educational and psychosocial interventions are a must in autistic children, many require and would benefit from a therapeutically effective and safe psychoactive agent.

In the past few years, following the discovery of endogenous opiates and their influential regulatory roles in animals and in human adults, research has also begun in autistic children. There are only a few published studies: the data are exciting and warrant further research to replicate the findings in larger sample sizes of patients and under more rigorous controls.

Abnormal levels or activity of the endogenous opioids in the brain (opiate excess or hypofunction) is implicated in the pathogenesis of schizophrenic and of major affective disorders (Berger et al. 1980; Brambilla et al. 1984; for a review, see Verebey et al. 1978). In 10 autistic patients seven to 17 years of age and in 12 schizophrenics, humoral (H)-endorphin levels in blood were lower than in 11 healthy controls (Weizman et al. 1984). The three groups were matched for age and sex. While in the autistics the levels were significantly reduced as compared to normals, the difference between schizophrenics and normals did not reach statistical significance. Endorphin fractions I and II in cerebrospinal fluids were also investigated in 20 autistics, four children with "other" psychoses, and eight normals (Gillberg et al. 1985). The subjects, both males and females, ranged in age from six months to 13 years. Both patient groups had signficantly higher fraction II levels than the controls; however, the differences between the two patient groups did not reach statistical significance, and the scatter was great. In the combined patient groups, those children with the symptom of self-destructiveness had significantly higher levels of endorphin fraction II ($p < .05$); a positive correlation was found between fraction II levels and decreased sensitivity to pain ($p < .05$). No definitive statements can be made on the basis of these two studies, taking into account that the autistic samples studied may not have been representative, that infantile autism is an etiologically heterogeneous syndrome, that the endogenous opioid system is heterogenous too, and that the blood or cerebrospinal fluid levels of opioids may not reflect the events in the brain. However, the hypotheses of Kalat (1978) and of Panksepp (1979) are interesting. They suggest that abnormal brain opioid activity is the neurochemical basis of infantile autism and that various behavioral symptoms and other abnormalities in autistic children show analogies with opiate addiction; therefore, an opiate antagonist should simultaneously decrease endogenous opiates and their behavioral and other correlates. It was suggested (Panksepp 1979; Panksepp and Sahley 1987) that naltrexone should be explored in these children. Naltrexone is a potent, long-acting oral opiate antagonist; data suggest that it is relatively safe in adults (Willette and Barnett 1981). Furthermore, naloxone, the intravenous opiate antagonist, was reported to be effective in decreasing self-injurious behavior in a few retarded individuals (Bernstein et al. 1984, 1985; Davidson et al. 1983; Richardson and Zaleski 1983; Sandman et al. 1983). Finally, a synergism was reported between naloxone and neuroleptics in adult patients (Pickar et al. 1982). As noted above, haloperidol was found to be a potent therapeutic agent in autistic children (Anderson et al. 1984; Campbell et al. 1978a; Cohen et al. 1980a; Faretra et al. 1970; Engelhardt et al. 1973).

The hypotheses of Kalat and of Panksepp and supportive data provided a rationale for exploring naltrexone in autistic children, employing an acute dose range tolerance study design. A single morning dose of naltrexone HCl syrup was given, only once a week, in increasing daily doses (0.5, 1.0, and 2.0 mg/kg); a variety of rating scales were used by multiple raters under different conditions, and careful laboratory and behavioral monitoring were conducted by two groups of investigators (Campbell et al. 1988b; Herman et al. 1986). Decreases of stereotypies and increases of positive social behaviors were rated (Herman et al. 1986), as well as increases of verbal production (Campbell et al. 1988b). In general, therapeutic effects were both tranquilizing and stimulating; mild sedation was the only untoward effect (Campbell et al. 1986a, 1988b). These results warrant further studies of naltrexone, and it is hoped that its efficacy and safety will be assessed under rigorous conditions.

Chapter 42

The Family in the Treatment of Autism

Change in the Role of the Family

The role of the family in treatment programs for autistic children and adults is shaped by professional perceptions of the nature of autism. With increasing recognition of a biologic basis for autism and the failure of empirical research to support early psychogenic theories regarding autism, there has been a dramatic shift in treatment programs for family members.

Theories of parental causation based mainly on case studies or clinical anecdotes have not been supported by susequent empirical research. The early trauma hypothesis was not substantiated when histories of autistic children were studied. Parents of autistic children did not report more maternal depression during the child's first two years, and parental deaths, divorces, separations from the child, or financial, health, or housing stresses were not more common for parents of autistic children than for a comparison group of parents of dysphasic children (Cox et al. 1975). DeMyer and Goldberg (1983) noted a lower than average rate of divorce among a sample of families of autistic adolescents and adults. Similarly, in studies of consecutive admissions to a free, statewide program for autistic children (Bristol 1987a; Bristol et al. 1988), the parents of autistic children did not differ from parents of communication-impaired children in maternal depression, or marital satisfaction.

Alternatively, follow-up of children known to have experienced severe early deprivation revealed substantial increases in other psychiatric disorders, but cases of autism in this population were virtually nonexistent (Rutter 1968).

Perhaps the most persuasive data challenging the early trauma hypothesis were found by Folstein and Rutter (1978). They studied sets of twins in which one twin was autistic and the other was normal. No differences were found in psychosocial factors for autistic or nonautistic twins, but autistic twins were significantly more likely to have suffered biologic complications at birth.

The majority of well-designed studies have also failed to support hypotheses regarding the etiologic significance of parental attitudes (DeMyer et al. 1972), incidence of parental schizophrenia (Kolvin et al. 1971); Lotter 1967; McAdoo and DeMyer 1977), personality deviance (Block 1969; Cantwell et al. 1978), or deviant parent-child language (Cantwell et al. 1977).

Similarly, when appropriate comparison groups have been used, empirical support has not been found for deviant interpersonal relationships in these families either when paper and pencil assessment measures (Koegel et al. 1983) or more direct observational measures were used (Bristol 1987b). In research with mothers of autistic children ranging from two to nine years of age, family ratings (completed after a two-to-three-hour in-home visit) demonstrated that families of autistic children did not differ in degree of acceptance of the child and quality of parenting from families of communication-impaired children (Bristol 1987b; Bristol et al. 1988). Furthermore, persistent assumptions that parents of autistic children come from the higher social classes have not been substantiated by research with large samples once selective referral factors have been controlled (Schopler et al. 1979). Ritvo and Freeman (1984) stated that "autism occurs with the same incidence throughout the world, in all social classes, in all types of families and in remarkably similar clinical form" (p. 298).

In a review of more than 150 studies since 1960, Cantwell and Baker (1984) concluded that, if an appropriate diagnosis of autism is used and comparison groups of parents of children with other handicaps are included to control for the increased stress due to the child's developmental problems, there is no basis for concluding that parents caused autism in an otherwise normal infant.

Parents as Cotherapists

Although there is no evidence at this time that parents could have caused their child's disorder through psychosocial or environmental means, there is accumulating evidence that parents, when accepted as partners in treatment, can positively affect the course of the child's disorder.

Goals of Training Parents as Cotherapists

The purpose or goals of training parents as cotherapists in the treatment of their autistic children are:

1. To capitalize on the parent's knowledge of this particular child's characteristics, motivators, and home environment;
2. To equip the parent with the knowledge and skills necessary to understand the child's disorder and to communicate and interact effectively with the child;
3. To increase the child's responsiveness to the parent and other family members;
4. To increase the child's appropriate behavior and decrease the child's inappropriate behavior in settings outside the clinic or school; and
5. To build a parent-professional partnership that will be effective in mobilizing community resources on behalf of the autistic child.

With accumulating evidence of a biologic basis for autism and the failure of empirical studies to support psychogenic theories of autism, the definition of the parent as the cause of autism is no longer tenable. Instead, if autism is assumed to have a biologic basis, the parent is defined, not as the patient, but as a cotherapist or partner in intervention with the focus on the primary client, the autistic child. Diagnosis, assessment, and behavioral and educational interventions for autistic children are described in previous chapters. This chapter will summarize the parent's role as cotherapist in those processes as it affects the child's adaptation to the home, school, and community. Although parent counseling is often an integral part of training programs for parents, counseling is discussed separately below with a focus on family adaptation to the child as distinct from this section's focus on child change.

The Parent as Trainee

For parents to function effectively as cotherapists, they must begin by learning the special educational and behavioral interventions described above. In this case, the professionals function as trainers and the parents as trainees. Professionals draw on their knowledge of the field, the literature, and their experience with a wide range of children. Parents learn to carry out and evaluate both special education procedures and behavior modification techniques at home. A detailed description of the process can be found elsewhere (Schopler and Reichler 1971b; Schopler et al. 1984). In most intervention programs, this is done through individual educational sessions, which include one-to-one modeling, reinforcement, and guided feedback for the parent. Interventions with the child are first modeled by the therapist with the parent observing, usually through a one-way mirror. The parent then demonstrates the techniques with the therapist observing and coaching, and then practices the techniques at home for a period of time before returning to demonstrate proficiency to the therapist. The professional's role is gradually faded as the parent gains both skills and confidence in applying the techniques to both practiced and novel situations in the clinic and home setting. In some programs, experienced parents then become trainers for other parents. In others, this type of parent-professional collaborative training and intervention is also extended to the child's classroom. Here parental collaboration with teachers is carried out at different levels, depending on family and school circumstances. At the most intense level, the parent may function as an assistant teacher on a part-time but regular basis. Alternately the parent may assist in the classroom periodically or on special occasions. Parents also collaborate with teachers in specific teaching programs, teaching and reinforcing at-home interventions that are similar to or coordinated with those in the classroom. This parent-teacher collaboration plays an important role in generalizing the autistic child's learning from one setting to another. At a minimum, parents and teachers need to meet on a regular or periodic basis to establish priorities and to coordinate home and school learning experiences (Bristol and Wiegerink 1979). Such home-school cooperation is often facilitated by a professional who encourages this type of collaboration and provides ongoing consultation to both the parent and the teacher.

Discussion thus far has focused on the role of parent as trainee. An equally important role for the parent who is a cotherapist is that of trainer.

The Parent as Trainer

If parents are cotherapists, it is assumed that they, too, bring expertise to the collaboration. In this aspect of the parent-professional relationship, the parents are the trainers and the professionals the trainees. This assumes that parents are the foremost experts on their own child. They have spent more time with the child than anyone else, and they usually are highly motivated for the child to succeed at skills that are valued by the family. In this role, parents provide valuable input into diagnosis, assessment, and program planning.

Diagnosis and assessment. In addition to providing a detailed history of the child's disorder, parents can also comment on whether the child's behavior in the unfamiliar clinic testing situation is typical. They may also identify motivators (e.g., music, favorite snacks, activities) that will enable the professional to coax optimal performance from the child during assessment to distinguish deficits in competence from deficits in performance. Directly observing the child interacting with the parent during the diagnostic and assessment process also yields valuable information regarding the child's performance with a familiar adult. For children who resist change and often react badly to novel situations, this opportunity may be particularly valuable. Certainly enlisting parents in these early asssessment processes communicates to the parents that the professional respects them and is genuinely offering an opportunity for collaboration.

Priorities for program planning. If parents are expected to be cotherapists in carrying out intervention programs, their expertise and advice regarding priorities for intervention must be respected. Parents of a child who sets fires in the night can hardly be faulted for balking at spending time working on a shape discrimination task with the youngster. Parental input in establishing a hierarchy of problems for intervention is essential both because the parents are usually well aware of the major risks the child is facing daily and because there is apt to be little parental compliance or follow-through unless the problems to be addressed or skills to be learned are ones that the parents value. Parents and professionals can usually agree on the following hierarchy of risks:

1. Risks to the child's life,
2. Risks to the child's survival within the family,
3. Risks to inclusion in (or expulsion from) the best available educational program, and
4. Risks to community acceptance.

Risks to the child's life. Given first priority in targeting intervention are problems that risk the child's life. These include eating poisonous or dangerous substances, running into busy streets, playing with fire, or self-destructive behavior. Parents and professionals can work out a program to change the child's behavior, can change the conditions that create the risk, or can develop a combination of both approaches. For example, if the risk occurs because of a child's inability to cope with traffic hazards, the risk may be reduced by teaching traffic signals, keeping the child in the house when unattended, or fencing in the outside play area. Teaching the child spoken, written, and visual signals for traffic danger is simpler and cheaper than building fences. On the other hand, in certain circumstances, building a fence will be more appropriate than keeping the child indoors or under constant adult supervision outdoors. In any case, solving the problem usually requires first recognizing the problem, making that problem a priority, and then mutually agreeing on both immediate and long-term solutions.

Risks to the child's survival within the family. Direct threat to the child's life is less common than threat to the child's survival in the family. Only the life-style the family is committed to can define these survival problems. Common among them are temper tantrums, persistent sleep difficulties, strange food preferences, poor toileting habits, strange repetitive sounds, and interference with or aggression against siblings. Only parents or other family members can help in identifying these priorities.

Risks to inclusion in (or expulsion from) the best available educational programs. Certain behaviors are considered prerequisites for success in the least restrictive educational programs available for the child. Particularly for the higher functioning autistic child, inclusion in higher level classes may be jeopardized by an inability to wait in line, use the toilet, show responsiveness to the teacher, or eat appropriately in the cafeteria. Parents and professionals often focus on academic prerequisites and neglect these survival skills, which may spell the difference between acceptance and rejection in a classrooms or vocational placement. Working together, parents and professionals can both recognize and reduce these risks to survival.

Risks to community acceptance. Parents can readily identify situations in which people stared at their child or excluded the child from church, recreation programs, other community services, or neighborhood play groups, or when the parent was unable to obtain appropriate medical or dental care for the child because of the child's behavior. In addition to being able to describe negative behaviors that interfere with community participation, parents can also identify strengths or interests their child has (e.g., music, artistic ability, interest in maps) that could be developed to facilitate the child's integration in the community.

In accepting the role of trainee in establishing these priorities, professionals allow themselves to learn about the context of the child's life and the behaviors that are likely to be reinforced in the child's real world.

Efficacy Data

Research has demonstrated that parents are, in fact, good judges of the current developmental status of their autistic children (Schopler and Reichler 1972). It has also been shown that training mothers as cotherapists or teachers of their own children is superior to direct instruction of the child (Koegel et al. 1981). Such training increases parent teaching skills and appropriate child behaviors and decreases inappropriate child behaviors (Marcus et al. 1978). Training parents as therapists has also been shown to result in improvements in autistic children's cooperation and socialization (Hemsley et al. 1978; Kozloff 1976), speech (Harris et al. 1981), and language and self-help skills (Kane et al. 1976). Parent training also results in the generalization of treatment gains from clinic to home (Short 1984) and in maintenance of gain over time (Koegel et al. 1981; Lovaas et al. 1973) and is related to reduced family stress (Bristol 1985).

With a few notable exceptions (e.g., Hemsley et al. 1978; Schopler et al. 1982), most of these studies involve single subject designs with a small number of subjects. Thus they demonstrate the efficacy of particular procedures—some over time intervals from two months (Marcus et al. 1978) to four years (Lovaas et al. 1973)—but do not, in general, demonstrate generalizability to larger populations of subjects. In most of these studies, subjects act as their own controls.

However, the British studies (Hemsley et al. 1978; Howlin 1981; Rutter 1980) demonstrated the efficacy of training parents to improve language and social behavior for large groups of children using a research methodology that includes matched untreated and clinic-treated control groups of autistic children. Long-term as well as immediate efficacy of treatment has been demonstrated for children in this program.

In another large-scale study, Schopler et al. (1982) followed up 348 families served through the TEACCH program and found a high degree of parental satisfaction with the program and evidence of a rate of out-of-home placement of only 8 percent compared to commonly reported rates of 39 to 74 percent (Lotter 1978). The TEACCH program is a comprehensive, statewide service program involving parent training, direct classroom instruction of the child, parent counseling, support and advocacy groups, and a variety of other features such as open-ended parent telephone consultation, teacher training, and ongoing school consultation. It is not clear at this time which specific component or combination of components other than direct parent training is critical for successful child and family outcomes.

Conclusions

There is little evidence of either transfer of skills from clinic to home or of long-term maintenance of gain for autistic children without ensuring that parents or parent surrogates have the specific skills necessary to help their children overcome their very real cognitive and social disabilities. Such parental training is necessary, not because these parents are poor parents but because autistic children do not spontaneously respond to parental techniques such as modeling, social reinforcement, and incidental learning that are effective with most normal children. This approach to treatment not only provides parents with opportunities for training in special education and behavior modification, but also emphasizes the importance of parental input in the assessment of the child's current status and the selection of target behaviors for intervention (Schopler and Reichler 1971a). Additional research is needed to determine the optimal type, duration, or amount of parent or parent surrogate involvement needed and to determine the extent to which ancillary services such as counseling or support groups make a difference in long-term outcome.

Parent Counseling

Although parents of autistic children have been found to have a normal range of personalities, they may seek counseling for themselves or other family members because of the severe chronic stress engendered by the child's autism.

Counseling Versus Psychotherapy

Although both counseling and psychotherapy are similar, they differ in many important ways. George and Christiani (1981) stated that the purpose of psychotherapy is "more likely to involve a quite complete change of basic character structure; the goals of counseling are apt to be limited, . . . more aimed at helping the individual function adequately in appropriate roles" (p. 8). Pietrotesa et al. (1984) concluded that counseling, as opposed to psychotherapy, does not deal with the more serious problems of the mentally ill; emphasizes the present rather than the past; emphasizes change rather than insight; encourages therapists to reveal rather than conceal personal values and feelings; and expects the therapist to act as a sharing partner with the client rather than the expert.

As Powell and Ogle (1985) indicated for siblings, most parents will not require intensive psychotherapy to deal with their feelings or concerns or to learn new ways to solve their problems.

Goals of Parent Counseling

The purpose or goals of parent counseling are:

1. To assist parents or other family members in achieving a clearer understanding of the nature and etiology of the autistic child's disorder;

2. To assist parents or other family members in the process of accepting the autistic child's disability; and
3. To facilitate parental coping with the chronic stress of having a developmentally disabled child.

Counseling, whether individual or group, for families of autistic children requires all of the structural, procedural, and process elements specified for good counseling. In addition, counseling for these families should address a number of issues that are unique to or especially salient for this population.

Counseling as an Option

Research cited above indicates that parents of autistic children do not differ significantly from other parents. Therefore, assumptions that counseling is necessarily either wanted or warranted are not valid. Parents may seek counseling, however, to get a clearer understanding of autism, to assist them in accepting the child's disability, or to obtain help in coping with the stress of having a difficult, developmentally disabled child. Special issues to be dealt with in counseling parents of autistic children are similar in most respects to those addressed in counseling for parents of mentally retarded children.

Clarification of Information

Until parents have a clear understanding of the nature of the child's disorder and reassurance that their child is receiving appropriate services, efforts at reducing stress will be futile. In the past, parents came seeking services for their children and instead were treated as patients themselves. Parental requests for candid, but sensitive explanations of their child's condition, for information regarding services available for their child, and for concrete suggestions for dealing with their child's specific problems must be honored if more general counseling is to succeed. A number of publications written expressly for lay audiences may be helpful in this regard (Paluzny 1979; Schopler and Bristol 1980; Wing 1975). It is particularly important that parents understand that there is a biologic basis for autism so that they are relieved of unwarranted self-blame.

Individual Versus Group Counseling

Since counseling has a future orientation and focuses on problem solving, individual or family counseling may be optimum for dealing with problems specific to one individual or one family. Where it is appropriate, however, group counseling may be both more efficient and more effective. Powell and Ogle (1985) summarized the advantages and limitations of group versus individual counseling (Table 1, adapted for parental counseling). The choice of group versus individual counseling depends on the needs of the particular parents (or other members of the extended family or significant friends), the goals of the counseling, and the training and skills of the counselor.

Table 1. Advantages and Disadvantages of Group Counseling

Advantages

- Efficiency
- Parent-to-parent support provided
- Provides interpersonal setting to experiment with new behaviors
- Parental acceptance from peers, not just counselors
- Parents learn interpersonal skills beyond those possible in a one-to-one relationship
- Parents discover both how similar and unique their own problems are
- Parents may be more receptive to suggestions from other parents who have a unique credibility for them
- Parents can provide as well as receive help

Disadvantages

- Particular personality types (shy or manipulative) may either get "lost in the crowd" or dominate the group
- Some parents have problems that require in-depth attention
- The mechanics of the group process may detract from individual concerns
- Cliques may develop and individual members may feel excluded
- Some parents may find it difficult to express feelings, thoughts, and concerns in a group
- Effective group counseling may require more advanced professional skill

Note. Adapted with permission from Powell and Ogle (1985).

Genetic Counseling

One issue that may arise is genetic counseling, that is, questions regarding the heritability of autism and the likelihood that either current or potential siblings of the autistic child will be autistic. The DSM-III (American Psychiatric Association 1980) stated that "the prevalence of Infantile Autism is 50 times as great in siblings of children with the disorder than in the general population" (p. 89). However, this prevalence meant that only 2 percent of siblings of autistic children have autism (Folstein and Rutter 1978). The DSM-III-R (American Psychiatric Association 1987) simply stated that "Autistic Disorder is apparently more common in the siblings of children with the disorder than in the general population" (p. 37).

From limited studies of multiple-incidence families, it can be concluded that siblings may be at higher-than-normal risk for autism (Folstein and Rutter 1978; Ritvo et al. 1985a). They are even more likely to be at greater risk for a broad spectrum of cognitive disabilities, including disturbances in language, learning disabilities, or mental retardation (August et al. 1981; Folstein and Rutter 1978). More definitive information will be available at the conclusion of a national study of multiple-incidence families by Ritvo et al. (1982) at the UCLA Neuropsychiatric Institute. They are studying a national sample of families of autistic children in which there is any relative with a mental, neurologic, developmental, or serious medical condition. Studies such as this suffer from the problem of selective referral, that is, only those families with multiple incidence are referred, limiting predictions of prevalence of the problem in the more general autistic population. However, preliminary data from the UCLA Registry project (Ritvo et al. 1985b) indicate that there is a subgroup of autistic families in which genetic transmission of autism is likely, and/or a subgroup of families in which defective immunogenetic defense systems render children more vulnerable to central nervous system damage. Reviews of empirical studies by Hanson and Gottesman (1976) and by Cantwell and Baker (1984) concluded that findings to date are too limited to have practical significance for genetic counseling. Until more evidence is in, it seems prudent to acknowledge some increased risk of disability in siblings of autistic children, but to admit frankly the limited basis for such speculations. There is presently not enough information even to speculate about whether the offspring of nonautistic siblings are more likley to have autistic or disabled children themselves (Folstein and Rutter 1978, 1988).

Acceptance of the Child's Disability

Some professionals speak easily of acceptance of the child's disability and often suggest that such acceptance is the desired outcome of the initial interpretive conference in which the diagnosis is explained to the parents. Parents and more experienced professionals know that acceptance is a lifelong process that must be renegotiated as the reality of the child's disability and the level of community acceptance changes with the child's changing developmental status.

Professionals facilitate this process of parental acceptance initially in the diagnostic interpretive or informing conference by being as responsive to parental feelings as to the technical information conveyed. A thoughtful and explicit discussion of the structure, content, and process of the interpretive conference for parents of autistic children is available elsewhere (Shea 1984).

Stress Management

A number of excellent texts deal with therapeutic procedures for managing stress in general. In the context of these more general procedures, a number of issues are particularly appropriate for counseling parents of autistic children (Bristol 1987a).

"Normal" family stress. It is not surprising that parents of autistic children should experience stress, but it is important to acknowledge to the family that such stress is a normal response to parenting a difficult child such as theirs. The challenge in interpreting this stress is to see it, and help parents see it, in the context of a normal family response to stress. A healthy normal response to stress also allows for a temporary period of family disequilibrium followed by a period of reorganization and eventual recovery. For parents of autistic and other developmentally disabled children, this reorganization is a cyclical pattern that may occur at the time of initial diagnosis and reoccur at the child's transitions to school age, adolescence, and so on. At each stage, readjustment to the child's and family's changed needs, as well as to differences in community acceptance of their child, will take some time (Bristol and Schopler 1984). Families should be allowed to go through this normal readjustment without being labeled pathologic.

Factors affecting stress and adaptation. Some aspects of particular child and family resources and beliefs appear to affect the level of family stress and the likelihood of successful adaptation to the child (Table 2). Particular child characteristics that have been found to be related to family stress include child's age, gender, difficult individual child characteristics, social obtrusiveness, and lack of activities and prospects for independent living (Bristol and Schopler 1984).

Older autistic children are more stressful when compared with matched younger autistic children (Bristol and Schopler 1983) or when contrasted with same-age retarded or normal children (Donovan 1985). The reality of the permanence and severity of the child's handicap, the decrease in community tolerance of bizarre behavior in

Table 2.   Factors Predicting Better Adaptation in Families of Autistic Children

- Age of the child (younger child)
- Female child
- Less difficult child
- Less socially obtrusive child
- More activities
- Better prospects for independent living
- Clarity of the child's handicap
- Lack of unwarranted self-blame for the autistic child's condition
- Absence of other family stresses
- Perceived adequacy of social support from immediate and extended family, especially from the child's father
- Active coping strategies, including:
  - maintaining family integration and an optimistic definition of the situation
  - maintaining self-esteem and soliciting social support
  - active contact with other parents and professionals in seeking information and services for the child

an adult-sized person, problems associated with the child's physical size and emerging sexuality, and, often, the dearth of adequate services, especially community residential services for autistic adolescents and adults, all contribute to greater family stress as both the child and parent age.

As Farber (1959) noted for families of retarded children, parents of autistic sons express greater distress than parents of autistic daughters (Bristol 1987a). It is not clear whether this is related to the greater physical size and difficulty of boys, or as Farber suggested, to greater disappointment that sons will not achieve the vocational aspirations the family anticipated for them.

Difficult individual child characteristics such as noncompliant behavior and inability to communicate are particularly stressful for parents. Such difficult child characteristics, together with the child's social obtrusiveness (e.g., hand flapping, twirling, strange noises in public), a lack of activities for the child, and poor prospects for independent vocational and living skills, predicted three-quarters of the variance in maternal reports of stress (Bristol and Schopler 1984). These findings suggest the importance to reduced stress of directing efforts at specific behaviors or specific skill or service needs of the child, especially those identified as stressful by the child's family. Recognition of the stress potential of other child characteristics not amenable to intervention (e.g., age, gender) should help clinicians to deal with the ramifications of these issues in counseling.

The pileup of other stresses unrelated to the child has also been shown to be a significant predictor of family stress and adaptation to the child (Bristol 1987a). Counseling parents may involve helping them solve financial, housing, vocational, or other family problems that may exacerbate the stress of having an autistic child.

Effective counseling of parents will also include helping family members identify and access ongoing sources of social support in their immediate or extended families, their neighborhoods, or from other families with similar children. The perceived adequacy of such social support, especially support from the child's father, distinguished otherwise comparable high stress and low stress mothers of autistic children (Bristol 1984). Such support also predicted quality of parenting in the home more strongly than did the severity of the child's handicap (Bristol 1987b; Bristol et al. 1988). Such support can be facilitated formally through family and group counseling and informally through encouragement of parents' participation in parent organizations such as the National Society for Autistic Children and Adults or more simply through parent-to-parent contact in shared activities.

Counseling can also be directed toward facilitating active coping rather than passive acceptance of the stress of the autistic child. Active coping strategies, which involved maintaining an optimistic attitude, remaining involved in family activities other than just the child's care, and actively seeking emotional support, information, and advice from other parents and professionals, significantly predicted successful family adaptation to autistic children (Bristol 1987a).

Anticipatory coping: a developmental progression of stresses.　As in coping with many types of chronic stress, it is helpful for parents to be able to anticipate problems and to discuss and even role play solutions to such problems before they occur. Parents of autistic children have identified a series of stresses across their child's development (Bristol and Schopler 1984; Dewey 1983; Marcus 1977) (Table 3). Some of these stresses, such as parental fatigue and the need for appropriate educational services, are common across all developmental stages. Some, such as the need for a clear diagnosis, may be resolved in the preschool stage. Others, such as embarrassment in public, may first emerge during the child's preschool years, diminish somewhat during the elementary school years, and then resurface during adolescence when the growing child's deviant behavior may be both more conspicuous and less accepted in public.

In a retrospective study of service needs of families of autistic children, DeMyer and Goldberg (1983) found a corresponding developmental pattern of intervention needs. Table 4 summarizes the five most frequently cited service needs for each developmental period. One important function of counseling is to provide information and referral to appropriate services to meet these needs.

Advocacy as a form of coping.　In studies of families coping with the stress of having husbands or fathers who were prisoners of war or missing in action, McCubbin (1979) demonstrated the importance of advocacy as a form of coping. Families who did more than endure, who used collective action to change resources available to them (e.g., college tuition for their children, obtaining access to government information) were more able to cope with their spouse- or father-missing situation. Similar collective action for parents of autistic children effectively increases resources for families (e.g., additional school services, summer camp) and gives parents a sense of potency. Such collective action also provides parents with a valuable norm reference group on whom they can depend for emotional support, advice, and affirmation of their efforts on behalf of their autistic child. Professionals can be effective in facilitating the efforts of both individuals and organizations in such advocacy efforts.

Other stress management techniques.　A variety of other techniques can be used to assist parents in coping with the stress of having an autistic child, including those involving changes in cognitive appraisal or attitude toward the situation (Lazarus and Delongis 1983); time management techniques to assist parents in meeting the many demands of the child for assistance, professional services, and advocacy (Turnbull et al. 1985); and, where appropriate, specific stress reduction techniques such as biofeedback, exercise programs, or developing hobbies or other outside interests to promote relaxation. Involvement of parents in recreational activities that do not involve the autistic child has been shown to be related to better marital adjustment in these families and to better in-home ratings of quality of parenting (Bristol 1984).

Table 3.   Major Family Stresses Identified During Specific Developmental Periods

Developmental period	Family stress
Preschool Years	• Ambiguity of child's handicap • Lack of consistent diagnoses • Chronic parental fatigue caused by child's irregular sleep patterns and high activity level • Child's lack of effective communication system to express needs • Child's behavior management problems • Child's lack of fear • Child's peculiar food habits • Child's lack of response to family members • Embarrassment in public • Lack of adequate babysitters or respite care
School Years	• Lack of appropriate services • Increasing parental recognition of severity of child's handicap • Lack of acceptance of child by peers, general public • Continued difficulty with toileting, eating routines • Child's hyperactive, destructive behavior • Draining of family financial and emotional sources to cope with child • Interference with family goals such as maternal employment, father's job relocation to area, where services for child not available • Concerns about impact of time demands on siblings, marital relationship • Lack of adequate babysitters or respite care
Adolescence and Adulthood	• Child's sexuality • Embarrassment in public • Child's lack of vocational skills • Concern about living arrangements, guardianship for child after parents unable to care for child • Onset of seizures in child • Lack of appropriate community services

Note. Reproduced with permission from Bristol and Schopler (1984).

Other coping strategies that parents have reported as helping them cope with the stress of their autistic children include (Bristol 1984) personal belief in God (but much dissatisfaction with the lack of response of organized religion to their child's needs) and confidence that their child will improve. Despite having a child with a handicap, successful parents indicate that they have many things for which to be thankful. Counseling can help parents identify both resources and cognitions that will enable them to cope with the stress of having a difficult, disabled child.

"Invulnerable" parents.   Clearly some parents or families may be more resilient to stress than others. Paraphrasing Anthony's (1974) description of the "invulnerable" child, Akerly (1975) described "invulnerable" parents of autistic children who are healthy, competent, resilient persons despite an environment that is stressful in the extreme. She described these parents as having a "stubborn resistance to the process of being engulfed by the illness; a curiosity in studying the etiology, diagnosis, symptoms, and treatment of the illness" (p. 275), often reaching a level of knowledge that

Table 4. The Five Most Frequently Reported Family Service Needs for Each Developmental
Period in the DeMyer and Goldberg (1983) Study

Age group (years)	N	Service needs
1–5	23	Early and consistent diagnosis Respite services Parent or sibling counseling Good day- and year-long educational program Babysitting[a] Financial assistance[a]
6–12	23	Curriculum additions to educational programs Respite services Good day- and year-long educational program Financial assistance Better teacher and staff attitudes
13–17	11	Good residential treatment Sex management and training Financial assistance Respite services Good day- and year-long educational program[b] Community acceptance[b]
Adult (18+)	18	Good residential treatment Financial assistance Sex management and training[c] Knowledgeable and concerned professionals[c] Contact with other parents[c] Community acceptance[d] Good day- or year-long education program[d] Curriculum additions to educational program[d]

[a]Tied for fifth rank, 1–5 year age period.
[b]Tied for fifth rank, 13–17 year age period.
[c]Tied for third rank, adult period.
[d]Tied for fifth rank, adult period.

is equal to that of many professionals. She noted that invulnerable parents are able
to develop an objective, realistic, and yet distinctly compassionate approach to the
child's handicap. They typically have a history of successfully dealing with other
stresses. Akerly noted the special encouragement and support these parents draw
from their successful parenting experiences with their other normal children and their
ability to understand the child's handicap as both a personal experience invading
their lives and a phenomenon to be investigated and treated. Counseling can increase
the number of such invulnerable parents by assisting them in obtaining needed information, coping with the strong emotions having a disabled child engenders, identifying family strengths, and increasing their confidence in dealing with their child.

Burnout.   The vast majority of parents of autistic children cope adequately with
the continuing stress. Some, however, particularly those for whom child services are
unavailable or inadequate, experience emotional overload or burnout. This response,
to be distinguished from expected periods of sadness or discouragement because of

the child's limitations, impairs the parents' ability to carry out their necessary functions of everyday life. An extensive discussion of burnout in parents of autistic children can be found elsewhere (Marcus 1984). If this condition persists after meeting the child's needs for services and the parents' needs for information and minimal support, more focused intervention may be necessary. A brief period of respite care for the child or, in some cases, longer-term alternative living arrangements for the child (especially older adolescents and adults) may be called for. If the parent does not improve significantly after this lifting of some or most of the burden of the child's care, referral for more in-depth counseling or psychotherapy to deal with problems such as persistent depression may be warranted. Treatment would be similar to that recommended for adjustment reactions, but services should be provided by a professional who is cognizant of and sensitive to the very real physical and emotional demands that may have precipitated the crisis.

Efficacy Data

Although there are numerous clinical accounts from both parents and professionals regarding the efficacy of parent counseling, there are few empirical data that unequivocally demonstrate its efficacy. In some cases of anecdotal success, systematic studies of efficacy have not been done. In other cases (e.g., Schopler et al. 1982), data are presented indicating that a program of which counseling is an integral part appears to be effective in maintaining autistic children in their homes and communities. On the basis of data presented as of this writing, however, it is not possible to specify the extent to which counseling per se contributed to the successful outcome in this program that included a variety of other child and parent services.

Sibling Services

Services for siblings of autistic children will now be discussed. For reasons of clarity, the term *sibling* will be used here to refer only to the brothers and sisters of the autistic child and not to the autistic child.

Importance of Sibling Relationship

For most children, and especially for disabled children who often have limited contact with nonhandicapped peers, siblings may be the most important socialization agents outside of parents. This permanent relationship between brothers and sisters is becoming even more important as social changes increase sibling contact and interdependence. Bank and Kahn (1982) attributed this greater importance of the closeness and continuity of sibling relationships to decreasing family size, greater longevity with siblings providing support especially in later years, mobile families that force siblings to rely more on each other, divorce and remarriage, and maternal employment with siblings often alone together without adult supervision. Professionals can facilitate this relationship between siblings and their autistic brothers and sisters.

Goals of Sibling Services

The purpose or goals of providing counseling and training for siblings are:

1. To assist the sibling in achieving a clearer understanding of the nature and heritability of autism;

2. To assist the sibling in clarifying and coping with both positive and negative emotional reactions to having an autistic brother or sister;
3. To teach the sibling skills in dealing with the specific behaviors of his or her autistic brother or sister; and
4. To assist the sibling in receiving an equitable share of family resources and responsibilities.

Some of the issues involved in providing services for siblings are similar to those discussed above under parents. These include 1) recognition that services for siblings are not universally either wanted or warranted; 2) a shared parental and sibling concern for heritability of autism, 3) need for information and skills in dealing with specific behaviors of the autistic child, and 4) concern about the long-term care of the autistic person after the parent is no longer able to care for the child.

Sibling Services as an Option

As noted above, families of autistic children do not differ significantly from families with other types of developmentally disabled children. Despite causing reduced maternal time for siblings (McHale et al. 1984), autistic children do not necessarily have a negative overall effect on their siblings. Three studies assessing impact on siblings found positive results of having an autistic brother or sister. Siblings of autistic children were rated by mothers as more supportive, less hostile, and more accepting of their brother or sister than normal siblings (McHale et al. 1984). Siblings of autistic children also had self-esteem, and home and school adjustment and achievement scores similar to the norms for the instruments used (Mates 1982).

DeMyer (1979) found that 54 percent of the parents of autistic children in her study thought that siblings were positively affected by the presence of the autistic child, 30 percent negatively affected, and the remainder somewhere in between. Although average scores for matched groups of siblings of both autistic and retarded children were comparable to averages for siblings of nonhandicapped children, McHale et al. (1984) noted that, unlike the siblings of normal children, about half of the siblings in each of the handicapped groups gave very positive and half very negative views about their relationship to the handicapped child. In some cases, then, there is no basis for assuming a need for special services for siblings. In others it appears that sibling counseling or training should be an optional part of a comprehensive program for autistic children. At the very least, professionals should be able to recommend books about siblings of autistic children. Both fiction (Gold 1975; Parker 1974; Spence 1977) and nonfiction (Bodenheimer 1979) books are available.

Sibling Counseling

Powell and Ogle (1985) identified six areas of concern to siblings of disabled children regardless of the type of the child's handicap. These concerns relate to the disabled child, their parents, siblings themselves, their friends, the community, and adulthood. Dealing with these concerns can serve as the focus for sibling counseling.

The major concerns of siblings regarding the disabled child identified by Powell and Ogle include:

1. Cause of and blame for child's handicap,
2. Curiosity about the disabled child's unspoken feelings and thoughts,
3. The child's prognosis,
4. Services needed,

5. How the sibling can help,
6. Pros and cons of the child's living at home or away,
7. The disabled child's future.

Concerns regarding parents (Powell and Ogle 1985) include:

1. Parental expectations for the normal sibling,
2. Discussing the disabled child with parents,
3. Parents' feelings regarding both the disabled child and sibling,
4. Shortage of parental time for sibling,
5. Helping parents in general,
6. The sibling's role in child rearing.

Concerns regarding siblings themselves (Powell and Ogle 1985) include:

1. The sibling's mixed feelings toward the disabled child,
2. Health of sibling, "contagion" of handicap,
3. Getting along with their disabled brother or sister.

Concerns involving friends (Powell and Ogle 1985) include:

1. Telling their friends about the disabled child,
2. Teasing by friends and acquaintances,
3. Their friends' acceptance of the disabled child and family,
4. Dating and having a disabled brother or sister.

Community concerns (Powell and Ogle 1985) include:

1. School—special education and the sibling's school,
2. Community acceptance of the disabled child,
3. Community living opportunities for the disabled child.

Concerns related to adulthood (Powell and Ogle 1985) include:

1. Guardianship—legal and financial responsibility for the disabled person,
2. The sibling's own spouse and family and the disabled person,
3. Continuing involvement, if any, with the disabled person.

Siblings need honest and understandable information regarding these issues and, at the same time, respect for and acknowledgment of the normalcy of varied emotions evoked by the disabled child and by these concerns. Approaches to two such emotionally charged issues, the heritability of autism and providing for the autistic person's future, are given below as examples.

1. Heritability of autism. Concern regarding family transmission of autism is of particular importance to both parents and siblings. Younger children may need to be reassured that they will not "catch" autism or that, despite the fact that they resemble their autistic brother or sister in many ways, they will not become autistic as they grow older. Older siblings are concerned about the prospects of having autistic offspring themselves. In a manner appropriate to their level of maturity, information on genetic counseling covered above should be shared with adolescent and adult siblings.

2. Providing for the autistic person's future.   Particularly as the autistic person and the parents age, both parents and siblings are concerned about who will bear responsibility for the autistic person once the parents are no longer available to do so. There is often an unspoken assumption that the sibling, especially if the sibling is a daughter, will become the guardian and care for the autistic person for the rest of his or her life. Such an arrangement may be mutually agreeable and the best arrangement for the continued care of the autistic person. In other cases, however, a different sibling, a friend, or an agency or organization may better suit the guardianship needs of the autistic person and the familes involved. Since guardianship involves such things as giving or withholding consent for treatment and program admission and seeking, advocating for, monitoring, and paying for services from funds for the autistic person, the guardian chosen must be a person or agency willing to serve in this capacity, accessible to the autistic person, and free from any conflict of interest, particularly in the dispersement of funds from the autistic person's estate. In some cases, someone other than a sibling may be a more appropriate guardian, with the sibling serving as a conservator who manages the financial affairs. Professionals can help parents in developing a plan for the autistic person's long-term care, encourage them to obtain the consent of the persons involved, and assist them in finding an attorney who is experienced in guardianship and estate planning for disabled persons. Whether the sibling is the guardian or conservator should be a carefully planned matter and not merely an assumption or a task that falls to a sibling by virtue of birth order or gender. A detailed discussion of issues of guardianship and estate planning for disabled persons can be found elsewhere (Russell 1983).

Individual Versus Group Counseling

Whether it is most appropriate and most effective to counsel siblings individually, in family units, or in peer groups depends on the particular sibling and family, the specific counseling or training needs being addressed, the other siblings or families available and needing services, and the training and skill of the counselor. (See Table 1 for advantages and disadvantages of group counseling.)

3. Sibling training.   Because the autistic child's behavior impacts on all aspects of family life, it is important that the family be able to help the child communicate, take care of self-care needs as much as possible, and behave appropriately in social situations at home and in public. Although parents and teachers carry the heaviest burden of responsibility for this training, siblings may also play an important role. Whether as a substitute for or supplement to parental training, siblings have unique opportunities to influence their autistic brother's or sister's behavior, especially social behavior. In doing so, they can make life at home and in the community easier for the siblings and the family.

Usually training of siblings is done informally by parents who have learned through training and experience how best to work with their child. More formal training may be warranted if the sibling already bears a large part of the child-care responsibility for an autistic brother or sister and needs to make that time more manageable (e.g., after-school child care), if lack of such skills leads to repeated clashes between the sibling and the autistic child, or if the sibling appears to have a special relationship with the autistic child and is able to motivate the child to learn things parents or others cannot. Sibling training may be contraindicated if the sibling is unwilling or if it appears that such training will encourage parents to shift excessive child-care demands to siblings already overburdened for their age. For some siblings, it will be necessary to deal with their strong emotional reactions to the autistic child before they are encouraged to share responsibility for changing the child's behavior. Training procedures and issues identified above for parents are appropriate for siblings if the instructions and expectations are geared to the sibling's developmental level and willingness to participate.

Efficacy Data

Although anecdotal accounts from parents and clinicians attest to the efficacy of information sharing and counseling in facilitating sibling acceptance and reducing sibling stress regarding the autistic child, systematic data regarding efficacy are lacking.

There are data, however, that demonstrate the efficacy of sibling training in making positive changes in the autistic child's behavior (Colletti and Harris 1977; Schreibman et al. 1983). The Schreibman et al. study also found that the efficacy of siblings in changing their autistic brother's or sister's behavior led to sibling expressions of positive sentiment about themselves. Siblings not only helped their autistic brother or sister learn new behaviors, they felt better themselves for having been able to do it.

Chapter 43

Other Treatment Modalities

Individual Therapy

Early views of autism as an emotional disorder caused by cold and rejecting parents resulted in open-ended play therapy as the treatment of choice. The ineffectiveness of this approach and the accumulation of overwhelming evidence that autism is in reality a developmental disability has virtually eliminated open-ended play therapy as a viable option for autistic people. Psychoanalytically based, insight-oriented approaches to the treatment of autistic adolescents and adults are also rarely reported because of these clients' difficulties with language and conceptualization. The most common approaches today are structured counseling and social skills training. The social skills training component is more effectively carried out in the context of a larger group so that skills learned can be practiced immediately. The purpose of individual therapy and social skills training is to increase the ability of autistic adolescents and adults to cope with normal life stresses and to increase their enjoyment of other people in community-based settings.

Individual counseling is generally only possible with more verbally oriented autistic adolescents and adults. For those without the skills to participate in a counseling relationship, a combination of behavior management and special education interventions has been most effective.

Although insight-oriented psychotherapy is not a treatment of choice for autistic individuals, counseling can be a very helpful adjunct to a treatment regimen. However, rather than focusing on psychodynamics, a counseling approach must emphasize the understanding of real-life problems and situations as well as the development of effective coping strategies.

One of the major difficulties facing autistic people is their inability to understand their environment in the same way that nonhandicapped people do. This leads to considerable anxiety and frustration, which are generally maladaptive and can serve to exacerbate an autistic person's difficulties. A counseling relationship can be most helpful in clarifying subtleties of interpersonal relationships and life situations and providing a forum for understanding and reconciling incompatible ideas.

For example, many autistic people are confused about the nature of their disability. Higher functioning adolescents and adults realize that they differ from nonhandicapped students in the school courses they take and the special assistance they receive. Frequently they are educated with mildly retarded or orthopedically handicapped youngsters in public school settings. The autistic students often realize that they do not have the same problems as mentally retarded or orthopedically handicapped youngsters in these programs.

For autistic people who have questions and concerns about these situations, a counseling relationship can help them to understand their disability. This is often helpful in providing opportunities to maximize their potential. Autistic individuals who do not understand their handicap will sometimes reject special assistance because they associate this with being mentally retarded. An understanding of their situation and the reason they need assistance is often helpful in having them accept the extra help that they need.

The understanding of emotions is also problematic for autistic adolescents and adults. Feelings of confusion, frustration, and anxiety are often present, but very abstract and difficult to comprehend. Although autistic people frequently exhibit these emotions, their inability to identify them in themselves and others is a constant source of frustration and difficulty. A counseling relationship can be very helpful for clarifying these emotional labels and feelings as well.

Autistic people are generally very good candidates for a counseling relationship. The regularity and familiarity of weekly sessions is something they can depend on and enjoy. Moreover, higher functioning autistic people generally enjoy talking and questioning, but are frequently cut off by others who have neither the patience nor understanding to deal with their incessant questioning. A counselor with experience in autism can be instrumental in assisting them to work through some of these concerns.

It has been established recently that autistic people develop social interests and involvement as they get older. Therefore, attachments that generally form to counselors facilitate communication and can also be helpful in managing some difficult situations. Autistic people can be very stubborn and difficult to work with when they establish certain patterns in community-based living situations. A positive relationship with a counselor can provide a means of intervening in these situations and can often get the autistic person to change maladaptive behaviors in ways that would not otherwise be possible.

Social Skills Training

A recent successful therapeutic intervention approach with autistic adolescents and adults has been social skills training. This is important because social and interpersonal deficits are the most obvious and characteristic of the autism syndrome, and the growing literature suggests that they improve significantly as autistic children get older (Mesibov 1983; Rutter 1970; Schopler and Mesibov 1983). In developing a social skills program, the main issues involve what to teach and how to teach it.

Working with low functioning and younger autistic children, Lord (1984) emphasized several basic skills. In general, she teaches younger autistic children how to play in the presence of others and be more aware of them. Her expectation is that positive social experiences in the presence of others will stimulate social interests more quickly and facilitate the later acquisition of social skills.

Working with older and more verbal autistic adolescents, McGee et al. (1984) emphasized positive and negative assertions. They argued that these skills will improve the conversational abilities of autistic youngsters. Mesibov (1986) also targeted conversational skills in his program in addition to attentional skills and the ability to interact in games and eating situations. Social interactions are also stressed by the San Diego program developed by Kilman (1981).

To achieve the above-mentioned goals, several intervention techniques have been used. Behavioral rehearsal with feedback are crucial elements in several of the programs (McGee et al. 1984; Mesibov 1984). Highlighting specific objectives and allowing autistic people to practice them in carefully controlled situations optimize the structured teaching approach that is generally so effective with autistic youngsters. Another important aspect of several social skills programs is the positive nature of the environment that is created. Lord (1984) convincingly argued that a major difficulty confronting autistic people is the negative feedback they have received in social situations. Therefore, her program emphasizes making these activities as positive as possible. This has also been followed by Kilman (1981), who stressed social outings, and Mesibov (1984), who used social outings and humor. One implication of these approaches is that inappropriate interpersonal behaviors are not targeted directly so as to maintain the positive nature of the groups.

Although a relatively new model, social skills training with autistic people promises to receive increasing attention in the years ahead. Although many have acknowledged the salience of this difficulty and the problems that it presents, until recently social behaviors have received less attention than any other aspect of the disorder. The recent development of social skills programs should be only the start of an increasing trend in this direction.

Residential Options

Approximately 10 years ago, the only residential options for autistic people were to live in their homes or large, depersonalized institutions. However, there has been a dramatic increase in residential programs, and there are now several options on a continuum from home to institutional care. Although these options are not yet available to many of the autistic people and their families in dire need, the development of these programs is an encouraging symbol of hope for the future. The purpose of these residential options is to allow autistic adolescents and adults to live as independently as their skills allow in community-based settings.

An initial residential program along this continuum is called respite care. Although not a separate residential program, respite care has enabled many families to keep their autistic children in their homes for longer periods of time. The goal of respite care programs is to provide relief for families so that they may return to the duties of managing an autistic youngster with renewed rest and energy. This relief can range anywhere from two hours for an evening on the town to 30 days for an extended vacation.

There are two basic respite care models: center-based and home-based. The center-based model is similar to a group home where families can bring their autistic youngsters for periods of a few hours to a month. These centers operate like group homes except for the fact that no one is a permanent resident. There is usually a maximum number of days each year that a family is able to use these services.

Although center-based programs are very popular in the comprehensive services they can provide, they are considered by some to represent an expensive and inefficient service delivery model. The problem is that these homes are not always fully used because there are periods when no families are using this service. The cost of the home remains constant, however, irrespective of whether it is being fully used. The alternative to this center-based model is a home-based model. This involves fully trained respite workers who offer to go into the homes of the needy families. Although less expensive than the respite care models, the problem with these programs is that the family must leave home to avail themselves of respite care. This can impose an accumulating financial burden on these families over time. Some home-based programs have care providers who will take autistic people into their homes for periods of time. This model combines the advantages of home- and center-based programs.

Following respite care along the continuum from family to institutional services, there are several programs around the country that are developing community-based group homes for autistic youngsters. These consist of either individual homes or apartments where groups of four to eight autistic people live under the supervision of a 24-hour-a-day staff. These programs are located directly in the community and most residents use community-based programs during the day. The oldest and best known of the group home programs are Division TEACCH in North Carolina, the Jay Nolan Center in California, and Community Services for Autistic Citizens (CSAC) in Maryland.

Beginning as a research project funded by the National Institute of Mental Health and the US Office of Education in the mid 1960s, Division TEACCH became the first legally mandated statewide program for autistic children in 1972 and now includes a network of five regional centers, 55 public school classrooms, and eight group homes exclusively for autistic individuals located throughout the state of North Carolina.

The TEACCH group home system represents a continuum of services, based on client needs. The most severely retarded and autistic clients, requiring the most intensive programing and staffing efforts, live in Intermediate Care Facility-Mentally Retarded (ICF-MR) group homes. These are the most heavily financed and intensively staffed of the programs, serving approximately 15 clients in three programs around the state.

Another intensely staffed group home model within the TEACCH Program, although the clients in these homes are not as severely handicapped as those in the

ICF-MR programs, are state-funded group homes for autistic people. There are three of these programs in North Carolina serving a total of 15 autistic youngsters. These programs also have intensive individualized programing capabilities, although they are not quite as intensive as the ICF-MR programs.

Group homes for mildly to moderately retarded adults are often appropriate for higher functioning autistic clients as well, and in fact there are more autistic people in North Carolina residing in these programs than any other kind. Approximately 26 autistic people live in these kinds of homes around the state. Although these homes are not always willing to accept autistic people, those that do generally find them to be acceptable clients if appropriate consultation and training are available. Generally one autistic client will reside in a home with four or five mild to moderately retarded individuals. These homes tend to be concentrated in the counties around the state that are more receptive to this model.

A final residential model was recently funded by the North Carolina State Legislature. This program is for higher functioning autistic people with the potential for competitive employment. Clients able to benefit from intensive training and capable of competitive employment are considered suitable for this model. There is at this writing one program of this kind serving six autistic adolescents and adults.

Another community-based program is the Jay Nolan Center in southern California (LaVigna 1983). The Jay Nolan Center is a private program for autistic adolescents and adults whose goal is the development of a continuum of residential, vocational, recreational, and educational services. The center is a collaborative effort between a private board and the Los Angeles Chapter of the National Society for Autistic Citizens. The residential programs run by this center include small group homes and apartment living alternatives.

The normalization principle (Wolfensberger 1972) guides the Jay Nolan Center's apartment and group home programs. Following this principle, activities pursued are community-based, involving nonhandicapped peers and located in age-appropriate settings to the extent possible. For this reason, the group homes never have more than six clients and no two homes are closer than one mile from each other. The homes themselves have no outward signs that they are different from any other homes (e.g., no signs), and care is taken to ensure that the clients are dressed in a similar fashion to other people of their age. In addition, school-aged children attend public school, and adults attend vocational training programs located in an industrial park.

Community Services for Autistic Citizens (CSAC) is located in Rockville, Maryland. The main goal of this program is to provide community-based services for autistic people who would otherwise have to reside in residential institutions. The residential component of this program consists primarily of apartment living situations in which autistic adults live under the close supervision of residential counselors. A group of autistic people will live in an apartment complex along with these residential counselors. The combination of an apartment living situation and vocational programs with adequate supervision and support have demonstrated that previously institutionalized autistic adults are able to function appropriately in community-based programs.

In addition to the community-based models already described, two alternative residential programs have evolved. Although these use many principles similar to those in the TEACCH, Jay Nolan Center, and CSAC programs, the primary difference is their greater isolation from the surrounding communities. Although both programs emphasize interaction with community members, their residential programs are primarily self-contained.

Benhaven is both a day and a residential school community in New Haven,

Connecticut (Lettick 1983). Founded in 1967, it was designed to avoid institutionalization in large state facilities by maximizing independence and competence in vocational, residential, and recreational skills. Benhaven is primarily an educational and behavioral program, focusing on individualized instruction with continual measurement and adjustment.

The residential programs at Benhaven are similar to the group homes already described under the community-based programs. However, the major difference is that these homes are not in communities, but rather in the self-contained residential environment that includes the vocational, recreational, and other programs involving these autistic people. The Benhaven program is one of the oldest and most successful in serving autistic adults in the United States.

Another self-contained alternative is called Bittersweet Farms in Toledo, Ohio. Established by a group of concerned parents and professionals who formed a nonprofit corporation in 1975, this program has already established itself as a potential new model for providing a comprehensive and wholistic living environment for autistic adolescents and adults.

Bittersweet Farms is modeled after Sybil Elgar's (1975) program in England, emphasizing a cooperative relationship between staff and clients, which facilitates ongoing training and supervision. The model is a farm community where residents and staff contribute to all aspects such as self-care, leisure, housekeeping, building and grounds maintenance, gardening and keeping of small animals, as well as special tasks such as weaving and printing. In addition, residents produce and prepare their own food and hope one day to operate shops to sell their surplus.

There are several aspects of the Bittersweet Farms program that are especially appealing. First, it creates an environment where autistic people can live meaningfully and productively without major stress. This is a difficult combination to achieve with a group of youngsters who are so easily disoriented and upset. Second, Bittersweet Farms represents an excellent learning environment because all aspects of the community are related to one another (e.g., the residents actually eat what they grow). For this reason the meaning of specific activities in a larger scheme is more easily understood. Finally, the activities of this farm community emphasize the visual, fine motor, and gross motor skills that are usually the strongest that autistic adolescents and adults possess. Although some might criticize this model because it is separated from the mainstream, a farm environment does not preclude extensive contact with the local community.

Early reports suggest that Bittersweet Farms represents a humane and cost-effective alternative to current services for handicapped people. It is likely that many programs in this country will be observing their progress and new models based on their initiatives are quite likely to appear.

The group home programs described in this section do not represent an exhaustive list of the programs around the country. Many other states are developing residential alternatives to large state institutions, and this encouraging trend seems to be accelerating of late. However, the programs described in this section are representative of those being developed around the country and represent the oldest and most established.

Vocational Issues

With the enactment of the 1973 amendment to the Rehabilitations Act, there has been increasing interest in providing vocational rehabilitation and counseling services to severely handicapped clients. These efforts have been further encouraged by recent demonstrations of the capabilities of severely handicapped individuals to learn and complete complex vocational tasks (Bellamy et al. 1980; Gold 1976; Wehman and Hill 1981). Techniques such as task analysis, systematic training, and behavior modification have shown considerable potential for breaking down complex tasks so that severely handicapped individuals can learn and perform them. The purpose of these vocational training efforts is to provide autistic adolescents and adults with the skills they will need to function as independently as possible in community-based settings.

Unfortunately, the implementation of ongoing vocational programs for severely handicapped clients has not kept pace with this interest and demonstrations of their capabilities. Rather than using the potential that these recent developments have revealed, most states serve severely handicapped people in day programs with a minimal work component if any. The average annual wage for a severely handicapped client in one of these programs is less than $200. The problem is especially pronounced for individuals with autism whose behavior, social, and communication problems make employment outside of these workshop settings an unlikely possibility. However, recent studies suggest that autistic individuals might indeed be capable of effective functioning in more vocationally oriented programs such as sheltered workshops, supported employment situations, or even competitive employment.

The sheltered workshop programs in this country are generally of two types: work activity centers and sheltered employment situations. Work activity programs are primarily designed to meet the needs of lower functioning clients. These programs provide basic prevocational, self-help, and socialization training in addition to recreational opportunities. Clients in these programs generally are capable of producing only about a quarter of what a normal, nonhandicapped worker can produce. These programs sometimes have a legitimate work component, but more often emphasize activities such as making crafts (not for sale), playing games, watching television, and taking field trips.

Sheltered workshops are nonprofit rehabilitation facilities providing a controlled work environment for handicapped people to achieve their maximum potential. These are conceptualized as transitional programs that should provide training for handicapped employees to function in less restrictive settings. Sheltered workshops have been criticized on several counts. They are not viewed as good work environments because tasks performed are overly simplified and repetitive. An interesting and productive work environment should have a wider variety of tasks corresponding to different levels of skills. These programs have also been criticized for their lack of a production orientation. Those criticizing this aspect argue that successful work environments emphasize production and handicapped people suffer when this orientation is missing from their programs. Finally and most importantly, the major problem with these programs is that they are not actually transitional for many clients. Rather, there is a tendency to hold on to the higher functioning handicapped clients so that the workshop will be better able to meet its contractual obligations. Those clients most capable of employment outside these workshops are the same ones these programs try hardest to retain. It seems that sheltered workshops frequently interfere with the transition to nonsheltered employment because of their own production needs.

For those handicapped people able to function outside of work activity centers and sheltered workshops but still in need of some assistance, the agency for providing this support is the US Government's Department of Health and Human Service's Vocational Rehabilitation Division. The problem with this agency, from the perspective of autistic citizens, is that it is designed for people needing only short-term help to become fully employed. Therefore, vocational rehabilitation emphasizes short-term training programs and is not able to provide the longer-term, less intensive assistance that some autistic people need to obtain better employment prospects.

For example, if a handicapped person were capable of learning carpentry, vocational rehabilitation could potentially sponsor this person in a very intensive carpentry training program. Once this skill was learned, the same person would probably be capable of functioning as a carpenter. The problem with autistic adults is that the extensive training probably would not be enough. In addition, they would need some long-term assistance in applying these carpentry skills to a variety of settings. This assistance might not have to be full-time, but it would need to be available for problems that would likely occur intermittently.

Supported employment is a new concept being developed by the Office of Special Education and Rehabilitative Services to fill this void. Supported employment would allow day services for people who are not viewed as eligible for competitive employment under the traditional vocational rehabilitation model. Supported employment is designed to provide continual training and supervision for severely handicapped clients in employment settings. This concept could prove quite beneficial for autistic clients because it could provide the less intensive yet longer-term support that they need to be maximally productive. Final approval and funding for this concept is still pending.

The Bittersweet Farms and Somerset Court models described under residential programs provide another vocational option for autistic individuals. In these programs, the ongoing requirements of the community provide the daily vocational activities. Therefore, the planting, growing, and preparation of food in addition to animal care, facility maintenance and development, and related activities comprise most of the clients' daily routines. An advantage of this model is its simplicity and clarity for these autistic clients who have so much difficulty with understanding their environment. These clients actually plant the seeds, then cultivate the gardens, then pick the crops that they finally eat. Compared to another client who might live in a group home and travel to a workshop to assemble parts to a machine never seen nor understood, this situation is much clearer and more easily comprehensible.

A final vocational option for autistic individuals is competitive employment. Although some of the problems these clients have in sheltered work settings might suggest that competitive employment is an unrealistic goal, evidence is accumulating to suggest this might not be true. Even though sheltered workshop settings are specifically designed for handicapped people, the large numbers of workers, general noise level, and poor staff-to-client ratios have made these programs difficult for many autistic people. Moreover, many staff of these programs are trained to work with physically handicapped or mentally retarded adults without autism and are not sensitive to the unique skills and needs of autistic clients.

Competitive employment situations provide an opportunity to individualize tasks and situations to meet the needs of autistic adults and employers. Margaret Dewey (1983) and Clara Park (1983) have written about the employment successes of their children: Jack Dewey and Jessie Park. These two children are similar in that they are working at tasks that maximize their skills, allow for individualized training, and are performed in relatively nondistracting, structured environments. Jack's success as a piano tuner and Jessie's successful functioning in a university mailroom suggest that employment options for many autistic people might be more varied than originally had been thought.

Other programs are using similar approaches and training strategies. Division TEACCH is employing a trainer-advocate approach to placing autistic people into competitive employment situations. Adapted from the work of Bellamy et al. (1980)

and Wehman and Hill (1981) with severely mentally handicapped clients (Levy 1983; Mesibov et al. 1983), the trainer-advocate is a person who first learns a job and then teaches it to an autistic client until the client has learned the job and is able to perform successfully without supervision. Jobs generally begin on a volunteer or part-time basis and then gradually expand as the skills of the clients allow. A similar model is being employed by the CSAC program in Maryland. This model has allowed TEACCH and CSAC to place autistic clients in printing offices, libraries, food services, and industrial settings.

Although none of the vocational models is perfect for all autistic adults, each one has demonstrated that it can appropriately serve some of these clients. Future success will depend on using this continuum effectively in developing a comprehensive service system and expanding it to include models not yet developed.

References

Section 2
Pervasive Developmental Disorders

Abbassi V, Linscheid T, Coleman M: Triiodothyronine (T_3) concentration and therapy in autistic children. Journal of Autism and Childhood Schizophrenia 8:383–387, 1978

Akerley M: The invulnerable parent. Journal of Autism and Childhood Schizophrenia 5:275–281, 1975

Alpern GD: Measurement of "untestable" autistic children. J Abnorm Psychol 72:478–486, 1967

Alpert C: Procedures for determining the optional nonspeech mode with the autistic child, in Nonspeech Language and Communication. Edited by Schiefelbusch RL. Baltimore, University Park Press, 1980, pp 389–420

American Psychiatric Association: Diagnostic and Statistical Manual of Mental Disorders, 2nd ed (DSM-II). Washington, DC, American Psychiatric Association, 1968

American Psychiatric Association: Diagnostic and Statistical Manual of Mental Disorders, 3rd ed (DSM-III). Washington, DC, American Psychiatric Association, 1980

American Psychiatric Association: Diagnostic and Statistical Manual of Mental Disorders, 3rd ed, revised (DSM-III-R). Washington, DC, American Psychiatric Association, 1987

American Psychiatric Association Task Force For Tardive Dyskinesia (letter). 1985

Anderson LT, Dancis J, Alpert M: Punishment learning and self-mutilation in Lesch-Nyhan disease. Nature 265:461, 1977

Anderson LT, Campbell M, Grega DM, et al: Haloperidol in the treatment of infantile autism: effects on learning and behavioral symptoms. Am J Psychiatry 141:10, 1195–1202, 1984

Anderson LT, Campbell M, Adams P, et al: The effects of haloperidol on discrimination learning and behavioral symptoms in autistic children. J Autism Dev Disord (1989, in press)

Anthony EJ: The syndrome of the psychologically vulnerable child, in The Child in His Family, Vol 3: Children at Psychiatric Risk. Edited by Anthony EJ, Koupernik C. New York, John Wiley & Sons, 1974

Arick JR, Almond PJ, Young C, et al: Effective Mainstreaming in the Schools. Portland, Oreg, ASIEP Education, 1983

Arnold LE, Wender PH, McCloskey K, et al: Levoamphetamine and dextroamphetamine: comparative efficacy in the hyperkinetic syndrome. Arch Gen Psychiatry 27:816–822, 1972

Arnold LE, Kirilcuk V, Corson SA, et al: Levoamphetamine and dextroamphetamine: differential effect on aggression and hyperkinesis in children and dogs. Am J Psychiatry 130:165–170, 1973

Asperger H: Die "Autistischen Psychopathen" Kinderalter. Archiv for Psychiatrie Nervenkrankheiten 117:76–136, 1944

August GJ, Stewart MA, Tsai L: The incidence of cognitive disabilities in the siblings of autistic children. Br J Psychiatry 138:416–422, 1981

August GJ, Raz N, Baird TD: Brief report: effects of fenfluramine on behavioral, cognitive, and affective disturbances in autistic children. J Autism Dev Disord 15:97–107, 1985

Azrin NH, Nunn RG: Habit reversal: a method of eliminating nervous habits and tics. Behav Res Ther 11:619–628, 1973

Baker A: Psychological assessment of autistic children. Clinical Psychology Review 3:41–59, 1983

Bank S, Kahn MD: The Sibling Bond. New York, Basic Books, 1982

Barness LA: Megavitamin therapy for childhood psychoses and learning disabilities. Pediatrics 58:910–911, 1976

Barrera RD, Lobato-Barrera D, Sulzer-Azaroff B: A simultaneous treatment comparison of three expressive language training programs with a mute autistic child. J Autism Dev Disord 10:21–37, 1980

Bartak L: Educational approaches, in Autism: A Reappraisal of Concept and Treatment. Edited Rutter M, Schopler E. New York, Plenum, 1978, pp 423–438

Bartak L, Rutter M: Special educational treatment of autistic children: a comparative study, I: design of study and characteristics of units. J Child Psychol Psychiatry 14:161–179, 1973

Bartak L, Rutter M: Differences between mentally retarded and normally intelligent autistic children. Journal of Autism and Childhood Schizophrenia 6:109–120, 1976

Bayley N: Bayley Scales of Infant Development. New York, Psychological Corporation, 1969

Beisler JM, Tsai LY: A pragmatic approach to increase expressive language skills in young children. Journal of Autism and Development Disabilities 13:287–303, 1983

Bellamy T, Sheehan M, Horner R, et al: Community programs for severely handicapped adults: an analysis. Journal of the Association for the Severely Handicapped 5:307–324, 1980

Benaroya S, Wesley S, Ogilvie H, et al: Sign language and multisensory input training of children with communication and related developmental disorders. Journal of Autism and Childhood Schizophrenia 7:23–31, 1977

Bender L, Goldschmidt L, Sankar DVS: Treatment of autistic schizophrenic children with LSD-25 and UML-491, in Recent Advances in Biological Psychiatry, Vol 4. Edited by Wortis J. New York, Plenum, 170–177, 1962

Bender L, Faretra G, Cobrinik L: LSD and UML treatment of hospitalized disturbed children, in Recent Advances in Biological Psychiatry, Vol 5. Edited by Wortis J. New York, Plenum, 84–92, 1963

Bender L, Cobrinik L, Faretra G, et al: The treatment of childhood schizophrenia with LSD and UML, in Biological Treatment of Mental Illness. Edited by Rinkel M. New York, LC Page & Co., 1966, pp 463–491

Berger PA, Watson SJ, Akil H, et al: β-endorphin and schizophrenia. Arch Gen Psychiatry 37:635–640, 1980

Bernstein GA, Hughes JR, Thompson T: Naloxone Reduces the Self-Injurious Behavior of a Mentally Retarded Adolescent. Presented at the Annual Meeting of the American Academy of Child Psychiatry. Toronto, Canada, October 10–14, 1984

Bernstein GA, Hughes JR, Mitchell JE, et al: Effects of Naltrexone on Self-Injurious Behavior: A Case Study. Proceedings for Papers and New Research Posters, American Academy of Child Psychiatry, 32nd Annual Meeting. San Antonio, Texas, October 23–27, 1985, p 33

Bicknell DJ, Blowers AJ: Tardive dyskinesia and the mentally handicapped. Br J Psychiatry 136:315–316, 1980

Block J: Parents of schizophrenic, neurotic, asthmatic, and congenitally ill children: a comparative study. Arch Gen Psychiatry 20:659–674, 1969

Bloom L, Lahey M: Language Development and Language Disorders. New York, John Wiley & Sons, 1978

Bodenheimer C: Everybody Is a Person: A Book for Brothers and Sisters of Autistic Kids. Syracuse, NY, Jowonio: The Learning Place, 1979

Bonvillian J, Nelson K: Sign language acquisition in a mute autistic boy. J Speech Hear Res 41:339–347, 1976

Brambilla F, Facchinetti F, Petraglia F, et al: Secretion patterns of endogenous opioids in chronic schizophrenia. Am J Psychiatry 141:1183–1189, 1984

Brigance AH: Brigance Diagnostic Inventory of Early Development. Woburn, Mass, Curriculum Associates, 1978

Bristol MM: Family resources and successful adaptation to autistic children, in The Effects of Autism on the Family. Edited by Schopler E, Mesibov G. New York, Plenum, 1984, pp 289–309

Bristol MM: Designing programs for young developmentally disabled children: a family systems approach to autism. Remedial and Special Education 4:46–53, 1985

Bristol MM: The home care of children with developmental disabilities: empirical support for a model of successful family coping with stress, in Living Environments and Mental Retardation. Edited by Vietz P, Landesman S. Washington, DC, American Association on Mental Retardation, 1987a, pp 401–422

Bristol MM: Mothers of children with autism or communication disorders: successful adaptation and the double ABCX model. J Autism Dev Disord 17:469–486, 1987b

Bristol MM, Schopler E: Coping and stress in families of autistic adolescents, in Autism in Adolescents and Adults. Edited by Schopler E, Mesibov G. New York, Plenum, 1983, pp 251–279

Bristol MM, Schopler E: Developmental perspective on stress and coping in families of autistic children, in Families of Severely Handicapped Children: Review of Research. Edited by Blacher J. New York, Academic Press, 1984, pp 91–134

Bristol MM, Wiegerink R: Parent involvement, in Autism: A Practical Guide for Parents and Professionals. Edited by Paluzny MJ. Syracuse, Syracuse University Press, 1979

Bristol MM, Gallagher JJ, Schopler E: Mothers and fathers of young developmentally disabled and nondisabled boys: adaptation and spousal support. Dev Psychol 24:240–247, 1988

Brown JL: Prognosis from presenting symptoms of pre-school children with atypical development. Am J Orthopsychiatry 30:383–390, 1960

Brown L, Branston M, Hamre-Nietupski S, et al: A strategy for developing chronological age appropriate, functional curriculum for severely handicapped adolescents and adults. Journal of Special Education 13:81–90, 1979

Burgoine E, Wing L: Identical triplets with Asperger's syndrome. Br J Psychiatry 143:261–265, 1983

Butcher B, Lovaas IO: Use of aversive stimulation in behavior modification, in Miami Symposium on The Prediction of Behavior 1967: Aversive Stimulation. Edited by Jones MR. Coral Gables, Fla, University of Miami Press, 1968

Campbell M: Biological interventions in psychoses of childhood. Journal of Autism and Childhood Schizophrenia 3:347–373, 1973

Campbell M: Timed Stereotypies Rating Scale. Psychopharm Bull 21:1082, 1985a

Campbell M: Pervasive developmental disorders: autistic and schizophrenic disorders, in Diagnosis and Psychopharmacology of Childhood and Adolescence. Edited by Wiener JM. New York, John Wiley & Sons, 1985b, pp 113–150

Campbell M: Drug treatment of infantile autism: the past decade, in Psychopharmacology: The Third Generation of Progress. Edited by Meltzer HY. New York, Raven Press, 1987, pp 1225–1231

Campbell M: Fenfluramine treatment of autism: annotation. J Child Psychol Psychiatry 29:1–10, 1988

Campbell M, Green WH: Pervasive developmental disorders of childhood, in Comprehensive Textbook of Psychiatry, Vol 2 (4th ed). Edited by Kaplan HI, Sadock BJ. Baltimore, Williams & Wilkins Co, 1985, pp 1672–1683

Campbell M, Palij M: Documentation of demographic data and family history of psychiatric illness. Psychopharmacol Bull 21:719–733, 1985a

Campbell M, Palij M: Behavioral and cognitive measures used in psychopharmacological studies of infantile autism. Psychopharmacol Bull 21:1047–1053, 1985b

Campbell M, Palij M: Measurement of untoward effects including tardive dyskinesia. Psychopharmacol Bull 21:1063–1082, 1985c

Campbell M, Fish B, Shapiro T, et al: Thiothixene in young disturbed children: a pilot study. Arch Gen Psychiatry 23:70–72, 1970

Campbell M, Fish B, Shapiro T, et al: Imipramine in preschool autistic and schizophrenic children. Journal of Autism and Childhood Schizophrenia 1:267–282, 1971a

Campbell M, Fish B, Shapiro T, et al: Study of molindone in disturbed preschool children. Current Therapeutic Research 13:28–33, 1971b

Campbell M, Fish B, Shapiro T, et al: Acute responses of schizophrenic children to a sedative and a "stimulating" neuroleptic: a pharmacologic yardstick. Current Therapeutic Research 14:759–766, 1972a

Campbell M, Fish B, Korein J, et al: Lithium and chlorpromazine: a controlled crossover study of hyperactive severely disturbed young children. Journal of Autism and Childhood Schizophrenia 2:234–263, 1972b

Campbell M, Fish B, David R, et al: Response to triiodothyronine and dextroamphetamine: a study of preschool schizophrenic children. Journal of Autism and Childhood Schizophrenia 2:343–358, 1972c

Campbell M, Fish B, David R, et al: Liothyronine treatment in psychotic and nonpsychotic children under 6 years. Arch Gen Psychiatry 29:602–609, 1973

Campbell M, Friedman E, Green WH, et al: Blood serotonin in schizophrenic children: a preliminary study. Int Pharmacopsychiatry 10:213–221, 1975

Campbell M, Small AM, Collins PJ, et al: Levodopa and levoamphetamine: a crossover study in young schizophrenic children. Current Therapeutic Research 19:70–86, 1976

Campbell M, Anderson LT, Meier M, et al: A comparison of haloperidol, behavior therapy and their interaction in autistic children. J Am Acad Child Psychiatry 17:640–655, 1978a

Campbell M, Small AM, Hollander CS, et al: A controlled crossover study of triiodothyronine in autistic children. Journal of Autism and Childhood Schizophrenia 8:371–381, 1978b

Campbell M, Hollander CS, Ferris S, et al: Response to thyrotropin releasing hormone stimulation in young psychotic children: a pilot study. Psychoneuroendocrinology 3:195–201, 1978c

Campbell M, Hardesty AS, Breuer H, et al: Childhood psychosis in perspective: a follow-up of 10 children. J Am Acad Child Psychiatry 17:14–28, 1978d

Campbell M, Petti TA, Green WH, et al: Some physical parameters of young autistic children. J Am Acad Child Psychiatry 19:193–212, 1980

Campbell M, Anderson LT, Small AM, et al: The effects of haloperidol on learning and behavior in autistic children. J Autism Dev Disord 12:167–175, 1982a

Campbell M, Anderson LT, Cohen IL, et al: Haloperidol in autistic children: effects on learning, behavior, and abnormal involuntary movements. Psychopharmacol Bull 18:110–112, 1982b

Campbell M, Green W, Caplan R, et al: Psychiatry and endocrinology in children: early infantile autism and psychosocial dwarfism, in Handbook of Psychiatry and Endocrinology. Edited by Beaumont PJV, Burrows GD. Amsterdam, Elsevier Biomedical Press, 1982c, pp 15–62

Campbell M, Perry R, Bennett WG, et al: Long-term therapeutic efficacy and drug-related abnormal movements: a prospective study of haloperidol in autistic children. Psychopharmacol Bull 19:80–83, 1983a

Campbell M, Grega DM, Green WH, et al: Neuroleptic-induced dyskinesias in children. Clin Neuropharmacol 6:207–222, 1983b

Campbell M, Small AM, Green WH, et al: Behavioral efficacy of haloperidol and lithium carbonate: a comparison in hospitalized aggressive children with conduct disorder. Arch Gen Psychiatry 41:650–656, 1984a

Campbell M, Anderson LT, Deutsch SI, et al: Psychopharmacological treatment of children with the syndrome of autism. Pediatr Ann 13:309–316, 1984b

Campbell M, Perry R, Green WH: The use of lithium in children and adolescents. Psychosomatics 25:95–106, 1984c

Campbell M, Green WH, Deutsch SI: Childhood and Adolescent Psychopharmacology. Beverly Hills, Calif, Sage Publications 1985

Campbell M, Small AM, Perry R, et al: Pharmacotherapy in infantile autism: efficacy and safety, in Biological Psychiatry, 1985: IV World Congress of Biological Psychiatry. Edited by Shagass C, Josiassen RC, Bridger WH, et al. New York, Elsevier, 1986a, pp 1489–1491

Campbell M, Deutsch SI, Perry R, et al: Short-term efficacy and safety of fenfluramine in hospitalized preschool-age autistic children: an open study. Psychopharmacol Bull 22:141–147, 1986b

Campbell M, Perry R, Small AM, et al: Overview of drug treatment in autism, in Neurobiological Issues in Autism. Edited by Schopler E, Mesibov GB. New York, Plenum, 1987, pp 341–356

Campbell M, Adams P, Perry R, et al: Tardive and withdrawal dyskinesia in autistic children: a prospective study. Psychopharmacology Bull 24(2), 1988a

Campbell M, Adams P, Small AM, et al: Naltrexone in infantile autism. Psychopharmacol Bull, 24:135–139, 1988b

Campbell M, Adams P, Small AM, et al: Efficacy and safety of fenfluramine in autistic children. Journal of the American Academy of Child and Adolescent Psychiatry 27(4):434–439, 1988c

Cantwell DP, Baker L: Research concerning families of children with autism, in The Effects of Autism on the Family. Edited by Schopler E, Mesibov G. New York, Plenum Press, 1984, pp 41–63

Cantwell DP, Baker L, Rutter M: Families of autistic and dysphasic children, II: mothers' speech to the children. Journal of Autism and Childhood Schizophrenia 7:313–327, 1977

Cantwell DP, Baker L, Rutter M: Family factors in the syndrome of infantile autism, in Autism: a Reappraisal of Concepts and Treatments. Edited by Rutter M, Schopler E. New York, Plenum, 1978

Carr EG: The motivation of self-injurious behavior: a review of some hypotheses. Psychol Bull 84:800–816, 1977

Carr EG: Generalization of treatment effects following educational intervention with autistic children and youth, in Critical Issues in Educating Autistic Children and Youth. Edited by Wilcox B, Thompson A. Washington, DC, US Department of Education, Office of Special Education, 1980, pp 118–134

Carr EG: How to Teach Sign Language to Developmentally Disabled Children. Lawrence, Kans, H & H Enterprises, 1982

Carr EG, Dores PC: Patterns of language acquisition following simultaneous communication with autistic children. Analysis and Intervention in Developmental Disabilities 1:347–361, 1981

Carr EG, Kologinsky E: Acquisition of sign language by autistic children, II: spontaneity and generalization effects. J Appl Behav Anal 16:297–314, 1983

Carr EG, McDowell JJ: Social control of self-injurious behavior of organic etiology. Behav Ther 11:402–409, 1980

Carr EG, Binkoff JA, Kologinsky E, et al: Acquisition of sign language by autistic children: expressive labeling. J Appl Behav Anal 11:489–501, 1978

Carrier JK Jr: Application of a nonspeech language system with the severely handicapped, in Communication Assessment and Intervention Strategies. Edited by Lloyd LL. Baltimore, University Park Press, 1976, pp 523–547

Carrow E: Test for Auditory Comprehension of Language (TACL) (5th ed). Hingham, Mass, Teaching Resources Corporation, 1973

Casey L: Development of communicative behavior in autistic children: a parent program using manual signs. Journal of Autism and Childhood Schizophrenia 8:45–59, 1978

Chapman RS: Comprehension strategies in children, in Speech and Language in the Laboratory, School, and Clinic. Edited by Kavanagh JF, Strange W. Cambridge, Mass, MIT Press, 1978

Chassan JB: Statistical inference and the single case in clinical design. Psychiatry 23:173–184, 1960

Churchill D: Language: the problem beyond conditioning, in Autism: A Reappraisal of Concepts and Treatment. Edited by Rutter M, Schopler E. New York, Plenum, 1978, pp 71–84

Clark HH, Clark EV: Psychology and Language. New York, Harcourt Brace Jovanovich, 1977

Clark P, Rutter M: Autistic children's responses to structure and to interpersonal demands. J Autism Dev Disord 11:201–217, 1981

Cochran WG, Cox GM: Experimental Designs (2nd ed). New York, John Wiley & Sons, 1957

Cohen DJ, Shaywitz BA, Johnson WT, et al: Biogenic amines in autistic and atypical children. Arch Gen Psychiatry 31:845–853, 1974

Cohen DJ, Caparulo BK, Shaywitz BA, et al: Dopamine and serotonin metabolism in neuropsychiatrically disturbed children. Arch Gen Psychiatry 34:545–550, 1977

Cohen DJ, Young JG, Lowe TL, et al: Thyroid hormone in autistic children. J Autism Dev Disord 10:445–450, 1980

Cohen DJ, Volkmar FR, Paul R: Introduction: issues in the classification of pervasive and other developmental disorders: history and current status of nosology. J Am Acad Child Psychiatry 25:158–161, 1986a

Cohen DJ, Paul R, Volkmar FR: Issues in the classification of pervasive and other developmental disorders: toward DSM IV: J Am Acad Child Psychiatry 25:213–220, 1986b

Cohen IL, Campbell M, Posner D, et al: Behavioral effects of haloperidol in young autistic children: an objective analysis using a within-subjects reversal design. J Am Acad Child Psychiatry 19:665–677, 1980a

Cohen IL, Campbell M, McCandless W, et al: A Timed Objective Rating Scale for Autistic Children: Comparison of Preschool-Age Patients and Normal Controls. Presented at the Annual Meeting, American Academy of Child Psychiatry. Chicago, Illinois, October, 1980b

Colby KM: The rationale for computer-based treatment of language difficulties in nonspeaking autistic children. Journal of Autism and Childhood Schizophrenia 3:254–260, 1973

Coleman M, Gillberg C: The Biology of the Autistic Syndromes. New York, Praeger, 1985

Colletti G, Harris SL: Behavior modification in the home: siblings as behavior modifiers, parents as observers. J Abnorm Child Psychol 5:21–30, 1977

Costa E: The role of serotonin in neurobiology. Int Rev Neurobiol 2:175–227, 1960

Cox A, Rutter M, Newman S, et al: A comparative study of infantile autism and specific developmental receptive language disorder: parental characteristics. Br J Psychiatry 126:146–159, 1975

Creak M: Schizophrenic syndrome in childhood: further progress report of a working party. Dev Med Child Neurol 6:530–535, 1964

Creedon M: Program Follow-Up Report: Using Simultaneous Communication Model. Presented at the Sixth International Meeting of the Association for the Scientific Study of Mental Deficiency. Toronto, Canada, 1982

Crystal D, Fletcher P, Garman M: The Grammatical Analysis of Language Disability. London, Edward Arnold, 1976

Dahl EK, Cohen DJ, Provence S: Clinical and multivariate approaches to the nosology of pervasive developmental disorders. J Am Acad Child Psychiatry 25:162–169, 1986

Davidson PW, Kleene BM, Carroll M, et al: Effects of naloxone on self-injurious behavior: a case study. Appl Res Ment Retard 4:1–4, 1983

DeMyer M: Parents and Children in Autism. Washington, DC, VH Winston & Sons, 1979

DeMyer M, Goldberg P: Family needs of the autistic adolescent, in Autism in Adolescents and Adults. Edited by Schopler E, Mesibov GB. New York, Plenum, 1983, pp 225–250

DeMyer M, Pontius W, Norton J, et al: Parental practices and innate activity in autistic and brain-damaged infants. Journal of Autism and Childhood Schizophrenia 2:49–66, 1972

DeMyer MK, Barton S, DeMyer WE, et al: Prognosis in autism. Journal of Autism and Childhood Schizophrenia 3:199–246, 1973

DeMyer MK, Hintgen JN, Jackson RK: Infantile autism reviewed: a decade of research. Schizophr Bull 7:388–451, 1981

Denckla MB: New diagnostic criteria for autism and related behavioral disorders: guidelines for research protocols: editorial J Am Acad Child Psychiatry 25:221–224, 1986

Deutsch SI, Campbell M, Sachar EJ, et al: Plasma growth hormone response to oral L-dopa in infantile autism. J Autism Dev Disord 15:205–212, 1985

Deutsch SI, Campbell M, Perry R, et al: Plasma growth hormone response to insulin-induced hypoglycemia in infantile autism: a pilot study. J Autism Dev Disord 16:59–68, 1986

DeVilliers JG, Naughton JM: Teaching a symbol language to autistic children. J Consult Clin Psychol 42:111–117, 1974

Dewey MA: Parental perspective of needs, in Autism in Adolescents and Adults. Edited by Schopler E, Mesibov GB. New York, Plenum, 1983

Die Trill ML, Wolsky BB, Shell J, et al: Effects of Long-Term Haloperidol Treatment on Intellectual Functioning in Autistic Children: A Pilot Study. Presented at the 31st Annual Meeting of the American Academy of Child Psychiatry. Toronto, Canada, October 10–14, 1984

Doll E: Vineland Social Maturity Scale. Circle Pines, Minn, American Guidance Service, 1965

Donovan A: A Comparative Study of Stress and Coping in Families of Autistic,

Retarded, and Normal Adolescents. Doctoral Dissertation. Chapel Hill, NC, University of North Carolina at Chapel Hill, 1985

Dunn LM, Dunn LM: Peabody Picture Vocabulary Test—Revised. Circle Pines, Minn, American Guidance Service, 1981

Eayrs JT: Developmental relationships between brain and thyroid, in Endocrinology and Human Behavior. Edited by Michael RP. London, Oxford University Press, 1968, pp 239–255

Egel AL, Koegel RL, Schreibman L: A review of educational treatment approaches for autistic children, in Fourth Review of Special Education. Edited by Mann L, Sabatino DA. New York, Grune & Stratton, 1980. pp 109–149

Eisenberg L: (1956). The autistic child in adolescence. Am J Psychiatry 112:607–612, 1956

Engelhardt DM, Polizos P: Adverse effects of pharmacotherapy in childhood psychosis, in Psychopharmacology: A Generation of Progress. Edited by Lipton, MA, DiMascio A, Killam KF. New York, Raven Press, 1978

Engelhardt DM, Polizos P, Waizer J, et al: A double-blind comparison of fluphenazine and haloperidol. Journal of Autism Childhood Schizophrenia 3:128–137, 1973

Evans IM, Meyer LH: An Educative Approach to Behavior Problems: A Practical Decision Model for Interventions with Severely Handicapped Learners. Baltimore, Brookes, 1985

Farber B: Effects of a severely mentally retarded child on family integration. Monogr Soc Res Child Dev 24:(2, Serial No 71), 1959

Faretra G, Dooher L, Dowling J: Comparison of haloperidol and fluphenazine in disturbed children. Am J Psychiatry 126:1670–1673, 1970

Fay WH, Schuler AL: Emerging Language in Autistic Children. Baltimore, University Park Press, 1980

Ferster CB, DeMyer MK: The development of performance in autistic children in an automatically controlled environment. J Chronic Dis 13:312–345, 1961

Fish B: Methodology in child psychopharmacology, in Psychopharmacology: A Review of Progress 1957–1967. Edited by Efron DH, Cole JO, Levine J, et al. (Public Health Service Publication No. 1836) Washington, DC, US Government Printing Office, 1968, pp 989–1001

Fish B: Psychopharmacologic response of chronic schizophrenic adults as predictors of responses in young schizophrenic children. Psychopharmacol Bull 6:12–15, 1970

Fish B, Shapiro T, Campbell M: Long-term prognosis and the response of schizophrenic children to drug therapy: a controlled study of trifluoperazine. Am J Psychiatry 123:32–39, 1966

Fish B, Campbell M, Shapiro T, et al: Comparison of trifluperidol, trifluoperazine, and chlorpromazine in preschool schizophrenic children: the value of less sedative antipsychotic agents. Current Therapeutic Research 11:589–595, 1969a

Fish B, Campbell M, Shapiro T, et al: Schizophrenic children treated with methysergide (Sansert). Diseases of the Nervous System 30:534–540, 1969b

Folstein SE, Rutter ML: Autism: Familial aggregation and genetic implication. J of Autism Dev Disord 18:3–30, 1988

Folstein SE, Rutter ML: A twin study of individuals with infantile autism, in Autism: a Reappraisal of Concepts and Treatment. Edited by Rutter M, Schopler E. New York, Plenum, 1978, pp 219–243

Foster R, Giddan JJ, Stark J: Assessment of Children's Language Comprehension. Monterey, Calif, Publishers Test Service, 1972

Foxx RM, Azrin NH: The elimination of autistic self-stimulatory behavior by overcorrection. J Appl Behav Anal 6:1–14, 1973

Frankel F, Graham V: Systematic observation of classroom behavior of retarded and autistic preschool children. Am J Ment Defic 81:73–84, 1976

Frankel F, Simmons JQ: Self-injurious behavior in schizophrenics and retarded children. Am J Ment Defic 80:512–522, 1976

Freeman BJ, Ritvo ER, Guthrie D, et al: The Behavior Observation Scale for Autism: initial methodology, data analysis, and preliminary findings on 89 children. J Am Acad Child Psychiatry 17:576–588, 1978

Freeman BJ, Ritvo ER, Schroth PC, et al: Behavioral characteristics of high- and low-IQ autistic children. Am J Psychiatry 138:25–29, 1981

Freeman BJ, Ritvo ER, Yokota A, et al: A scale for rating symptoms of patients with the syndrome of autism in real life settings. J Am Acad Child Psychiatry 25:130–136, 1986

Fulwiler R, Fouts R: Acquisition of American Sign Language by a noncommunicating autistic child. Journal of Autism and Childhood Schizophrenia 6:43–51, 1976

Gardner H: The Mind's New Science. Basic Books, New York, 1985

Gardos G, Cole JO: Problems in assessment of tardive dyskinesia, in Tardive Dyskinesia Research and Treatment. Edited by Fann WE, Smith RC, Davis JM, et al. New York, SP Medical & Scientific Books, 1980a, pp 201–214

Gardos G, Cole JO: Overview: public health issues in tardive dyskinesia. Am J Psychiatry 137:776–781, 1980b

Gardos G, Cole JO, La Brie R: The assessment of tardive dyskinesia. Arch Gen Psychiatry 34:1206–1212, 1977

Gaylord-Ross RJ, Haring TG, Breen C, et al: The training and generalization of social interaction skills with autistic youth. J Appl Behav Anal 17:229–247, 1984

Geller B, Guttmacher LB, Bleeg M: Coexistence of childhood onset pervasive developmental disorder and attention deficit disorder with hyperactivity. Am J Psychiatry 138:388–389, 1981

Geller E, Ritvo ER, Freeman BJ, et al: Preliminary observations on the effect of fenfluramine on blood serotonin and symptoms in three autistic boys. N Engl J Med 307:165–169, 1982

George RL, Christiani TS: Theory, Methods and Processes of Counseling and Psychotherapy. Englewood Cliffs, NJ, Prentice-Hall, 1981

Gillberg C, Terenius L, Lönnerholm G: Endorphin activity in childhood psychosis: spinal fluid levels in 24 cases. Arch Gen Psychiatry 42:780–783, 1985

Gjessing R: Disturbances of somatic functions in catatonia with a periodic course, and their compensation. J Ment Sci 84:608–621, 1938

Goetz L, Schuler A, Sailor W: Teaching functional speech to the severely handicapped: current issues. J Autism Dev Disord 9:325–343, 1979

Gold M: Task analysis of a complex assembly task by the retarded blind. Except Child 43:78–87, 1976

Gold P: Please Don't Say Hello. New York, Human Services, 1975

Goldstein M, Mahanand D, Lee J, et al: Dopamine-beta-hydroxylase and endogenous total 5-hydroxyindole levels in autistic patients and controls, in The Autistic Syndromes. Edited by Coleman M. Amsterdam, North-Holland, 1976, pp 57–63

Green WH, Campbell M, Hardesty AS, et al: A comparison of schizophrenic and autistic children. J Am Acad Child Psychiatry 23:399–409, 1984

Greenbaum GH: An evaluation of niacinamide in the treatment of childhood schizophrenia. Am J Psychiatry 127:129–132, 1970

Gualtieri CT, Barnhill J, McGimsey J, et al: Tardive dyskinesia and other movement disorders in children treated with psychotropic drugs. J Am Acad Child Psychiatry 19:491–510, 1980

Gualtieri CT, Quade D, Hicks RE, et al: Tardive dyskinesia and other clinical consequences of neuroleptic treatment in children and adolescents. Am J Psychiatry 141:20–23, 1984

Guess D, Sailor W, Baer D: A behavioral-remedial approach to language training for the severely handicapped, in Educational Programming for the Severely and Profoundly Handicapped. Edited by Sontag E. Reston, Va, Division on Mental Retardation, Council for Exceptional Children, 1977, pp 360–377

Halpern WI: The schooling of autistic children: preliminary findings. Am J Orthopsychiatry 40:665–671, 1970

Hamill PVV, Drizd TA, Johnson CL, et al: N.C.H.S. Growth Charts, 1976. Monthly Vital Statistics Report, Health Examination Survey Data, National Center for Health Statistics Publication (HRA) 25:76–1120, (suppl 3, 1–22) 1976

Handleman JS: Generalization by autistic-type children of verbal responses across settings. J Appl Behav Anal 12:273–282, 1979

Handleman JS, Harris SL: Generalization from school to home with autistic children. J Autism Dev Disord 10:323–333, 1980

Handleman JS, Harris SL: Generalization across instructional settings by autistic children. Child and Family Behavior Therapy 5:73–83, 1983

Hanson DR, Gottesman II: The genetics, if any, of infantile autism and childhood schizophrenia. Journal of Autism and Childhood Schizophrenia 6:209–234, 1976

Harris SL, Wolchik SA, Weitz S: The acquisition of language skills by autistic children: can parents do the job? Journal of Autism and Childhood Schizophrenia 6:209–234, 1981

Hawkins D, Pauling L (eds): Orthomolecular Psychiatry. San Francisco, WH Freeman & Co, 1973

Hedrick DL, Prather EM, Tobin AR: Sequenced Inventory of Communication Development. Seattle, University of Washington Press, 1975

Helmer SH, Layton T: Language Program for Autistic Children: Experimental Edition. Research supported by grant No. 1-NS-9-2305, National Institute of Neurological and Communicative Disorders and Stroke, University of North Carolina at Chapel Hill, 1980

Hemsley R, Howlin P, Berger M, et al: Treating autistic children in a family context, in Autism: A Reappraisal of Concepts and Treatment. Edited by Rutter M, Schopler E. New York, Plenum, 1978

Herman BH, Hammock MK, Arthur-Smith A, et al: Effects of Naltrexone in autism: correlation with plasma opioid concentrations, in Scientific Proceedings for the Annual Meeting of the American Academy of Child and Adolescent Psychiatry. Los Angeles, CA, volume II, 1986, pp 11–12

Hewitt PM: Teaching speech to an autistic child through operant conditioning. Am J Orthopsychiatry 35:927–936, 1965

Hiskey M: Hiskey-Nebraska Test of Learning Aptitude. Lincoln, Nebr, Union College Press, 1966

Hoskins RG: The Biology of Schizophrenia. New York, WW Norton and Co, 1946

Howlin P: The effectiveness of operant language training with autistic children. Journal of Autism and Developmental Disabilities 11:89–105, 1981

Hung DW: Using self-stimulation as reinforcement for autistic children. Journal of Autism and Childhood Schizophrenia 8:355–366, 1978

Husted JR, Hall P, Agin B: The effectiveness of time-out in reducing maladaptive behavior of autistic and retarded children. J Psychol 79:189–196, 1971

Irwin S: A rational framework for the development, evaluation and use of psychoactive drugs. Am J Psychiatry (Suppl) 124:1–19, 1968

Kalat JW: Letter to the editor: speculations on similarities between autism and opiate addiction. Journal of Autism and Childhood Schizophrenia 8:477–479, 1978

Kane G, Kane JF, Amorosa H, et al: Parents as participants in the behavior therapy of their mentally retarded children. Perspectives Psychiatriques 58:293–303, 1976

Kane JJ, Smith JM: Tardive dyskinesia: prevalence and risk factors, 1959 to 1979. Arch Gen Psychiatry 39:473–481, 1982

Kanner L: Autistic disturbances of affective contact. Nervous Child 2:217–250, 1943

Kaufman AS, Kaufman NL: K-ABC Kaufman Assessment Battery for Children: Interpretive Manual. Circle Pines, Minn, American Guidance Service, 1983

Kiernan CC, Jones MS: The Heuristic Programme: a combined use of signs and symbols with severely mentally retarded autistic children. Australian Journal of Human Communication Disorders 13:153–168, 1985

Kilman BA: Developing social skills, in Proceedings of the 1981 International Conference on Autism. Edited by Park D. Washington, DC, National Society for Autistic Children, 1981, pp 318–327

Koegel RL, Egel AL: Motivating autistic children. J Abnorm Psychol 88:418–426, 1979

Koegel RL, Rincover A: Research on the difference between generalization and maintenance in extra-therapy responding. J Appl Behav Anal 10:1–12, 1977

Koegel RL, Schreibman L: Teaching autistic children to respond to simultaneous multiple cues. J Exp Child Psychol 24:299–311, 1977

Koegel RL, Schreibman L, Britten KR, et al: A comparison of parent training to direct child treatment, in Educating and Understanding Autistic Children. Edited by Koegel RL, Rincover A, Egel AL. San Diego, College-Hill 1981, pp 260–279

Koegel RL, Schreibman L, O'Neill RE, et al: The personality and family-interaction characteristics of parents of autistic children. J Consult Clin Psychol 51:683–692, 1983

Kolvin I: Psychoses in Childhood: A Comparative Study, in Infantile Autism: Concepts, Characteristics, and Treatment. Edited by Rutter M. Edinburgh, Churchill Livingstone, 1971, pp 7–26

Kolvin I, Ounsted C, Richardson L, et al: Studies in childhood psychosis, III: the family and social background in child psychoses. Br J Psychiatry 118:396–402, 1971

Konstantareas M, Oxman J, Webster C: Simultaneous communication with autistic and other severely dysfunctional nonverbal children. J Commun Disord 10:267–282, 1977

Kozloff MA: Systems of structured exchange: changing families of severely deviant children. Sociological Practice 1:86–104, 1976

Krug DA, Arick JR, Almond PJ: Autism Screening Instrument for Educational Planning: background and development, in Autism: Diagnosis, Instruction, Management, and Research. Edited by Gilliam J. Austin, University of Texas at Austin Press, 1979

Kurtis LB: Clinical study of the response to nortriptyline on autistic children. International Journal of Neuropsychiatry 2:298–301, 1966

Lancioni GE: Using pictorial representations as communication means with low-functioning autistic children. J Autism Dev Disord 13:87–105, 1983

Laska E, Meisner M, Kushner HB: Optimal crossover designs in the presence of carryover effects. Biometrics 39:1087–1091, 1983

La Vigna GW: Communication training in mute, autistic adolescents using the written word. Journal of Autism and Childhood Schizophrenia 7:135–149, 1977

La Vigna GW: The Jay Nolan Center: a community-based program, in Autism in Adolescents and Adults. Edited by Schopler E, Mesibov GB. New York, Plenum, 1983, pp 381–410

Layton TL: Manual communication, in Language and Treatment of Autistic and Developmentally Disordered Children. Edited by Layton TL. Springfield, Ill, Charles C Thomas, 1987, pp189–213

Layton TL, Baker PS: Description of semantic-syntactic relations in an autistic child. J Autism Dev Disord 11:385–399, 1981

Layton TL, Helmer S: The Use of Manual Signs in a Communication Training Program with Autistic Children. Presented at the American Association on Mental Deficiency. Detroit, Mich, 1981

Lazarus RS, Delongis A: Psychological stress and coping in aging. Am Psychol 38:245–254, 1983

Lee L: Northwestern Syntax Screening Test. Evanston, Ill, Northwestern University Press, 1971

Lee L, Canter SM: Developmental sentence scoring: a clinical procedure for estimating syntactic development in children's spontaneous speech. J Speech Hear Disord 36:315–340, 1971

Leiter RG: Leiter International Performance Scale. Los Angeles, Western Psychological Services, 1969

Lettick AL: Benhaven, in Autism in Adolescents and Adults. Edited by Schopler E, Mesibov GB. New York, Plenum, 1983, pp 355–380

Leventhal BL: Fenfluramine Administration to Autistic Children: Effects on Behavior and Biogenic Amines. Presented at the 25th NCDEU Annual (Anniversary) Meeting. Key Biscayne, Florida, May 1–4, 1985

Levy SM: School doesn't last forever: then what? Some vocational alternatives, in Autism in Adolescents and Adults. Edited by Schopler E, Mesibov GB. New York, Plenum, 1983, pp 133–148

Lipton MA, Ban TA, Kane FJ, et al: Megavitamin and Orthomolecular Therapy in Psychiatry. Washington, DC, American Psychiatric Association, 1973

Lockyer L, Rutter M: A five to fifteen-year follow-up study of infantile psychosis. Br J Psychiatry 115:865–882, 1969

Lord C: A Developmental Approach to Social Training for Autistic People. Presented at the annual meeting of the National Society for Children and Adults with Autism. San Antonio, Tex, July 1984

Lord C: The comprehension of language and autism, in Communication Problems in Autism. Edited by Schopler E, Mesibov GB. New York, Plenum, 1985, pp 257–281

Lotter V: Epidemiology of autistic conditions in young children. Some characteristics of the parents and children. Soc Psychiatry 1:163–163, 1967

Lotter V: Follow-up studies, in Autism: A Reappraisal of Concepts and Treatment. Edited by Rutter M, Schopler E. New York, Plenum, 1978

Lovaas OI: The Autistic Child: Language Development Through Behavior Modification. New York, Irvington, 1977

Lovaas OI: Teaching Developmentally Disabled Children: The ME Book. Baltimore, University Park Press, 1981

Lovaas OI, Berberich JB, Perloff BF, et al: Acquisition of imitative speech by autistic children. Science 151:705–707, 1966

Lovaas OI, Koegel R, Simmons JL, et al: Some generalizations and followup measures on autistic children in behavior therapy. J Appl Behav Anal 6:131–165, 1973

Lovaas OI, Schreibman L, Koegel RI: A behavior modification approach to the treatment of autistic children. Journal of Autism and Childhood Schizophrenia 4:111–129, 1974

Lovaas OI, Schreibman L, Koegel RL: A behavior modification approach to the treatment of autistic children, in Psychopathology and Child Development: Research and Treatment. Edited by Schopler E, Reichler RJ. New York, Plenum, 1976

MacDonald JD: Environmental Language Inventory: A Semantic-Based Assessment and Treatment Model for Generalized Communication. Columbus, Ohio, Charles E. Merrill, 1978

MacDonald JD, Blott JP: Environmental language intervention: the rationale for a diagnostic and training strategy through rules, context, and generalization. J Speech Hear Disord 39:244–256, 1974

MacNamara J: Cognitive basis of language learning in infants. Psychol Rev 79:1–13, 1972

Marcus LM: Patterns of coping in families of psychotic children. Am J Orthopsychiatry 47:388–399, 1977

Marcus LM: Coping with burnout, in The Effects of Autism on the Family. Edited by Schopler E, Mesibov G. New York, Plenum, 1984, pp 311–326

Marcus LM, Baker AF: Assessment of autistic children, in Psychological Assessment of Special Children. Edited by Simeonsson RJ. 1986

Marcus LM, Lansing M, Andrews C, et al: Improvement of teaching effectiveness in parents of autistic children. J Am Acad Child Psychiatry 17:625–639, 1978

Martin G: Brief time-outs as consequences for errors during training programs with autistic and retarded children: a questionable procedure. The Psychological Record 25:71–89, 1975

Mates TE: Siblings of Autistic Children: Their Adjustment and Performance at Home and School as a Function of Their Sex and Family Size. Doctoral dissertation. Chapel Hill, NC, University of North Carolina at Chapel Hill, 1982

Matson JL, DiLorenzo TM: Punishment and Its Alternatives: A New Perspective for Behavior Modification. New York, Springer, 1984

McAdoo WG, DeMyer MK: Research related to family factors in autism. J Pediatr Psychol 2:162–166, 1977

McAndrew JB, Case Q, Treffert DA: Effects of prolonged phenothiazine intake on psychotic and other hospitalized children. Journal of Autism and Childhood Schizophrenia 2:75–91, 1972

McCarthy D: McCarthy Scale of Children's Abilities. New York, Psychological Corporation, 1972

McCubbin H: Integrating coping behavior in family stress theory. Journal of Marriage and the Family 42:237–244, 1979

McGee GG, Krantz PJ, Mason D, et al: A modified incidental-teaching procedure for autistic youth: acquisition and generalization of receptive object labels. J Appl Behav Anal 16:329–338, 1983

McGee GG, Krantz PJ, McClannahan LE: Conversational skills for autistic adolescents: teaching assertiveness in naturalistic game settings. J Autism Dev Dis 14:319–330, 1984

McGee GG, Krantz PJ, McClannahan LE: The facilitative effects of incidental teaching on preposition use by autistic children. J Appl Behav Anal 18:17–31, 1985

McHale SM: Social interactions of autistic and nonhandicapped children during free play. Am J Orthopsychiatry 53:81–91, 1983

McHale SM, Simeonsson RJ: Effects of interaction on nonhandicapped children's attitudes toward autistic children. Am J Ment Defic 85:18–24, 1980

McHale SM, Olley JG, Marcus LM, et al: Nonhandicapped peers as tutors for autistic children. Except Child 48:263–265, 1981

McHale SM, Simeonsson RJ, Sloan JL: Children with handicapped brothers and sisters, in The Effects of Autism on the Family. Edited by Schopler E, Mesibov GB. New York, Plenum, 1984, pp 327–342

McLean JE, Snyder-McLean LK: A Transactional Approach to Early Language Training. Columbus, Ohio, Charles E. Merrill, 1978

McLean LP, McLean JM: A language training program for nonverbal autistic children. J Speech Hear Disord 39:193–196, 1974

Meiselas KD, Spencer EK, Oberfield R, et al: Differentiation of stereotypies from neuroleptic-related dyskinesias in autistic children. J Clin Psychopharmaco, 1989, in press

Menyuk P, Quill K: Semantic problems in autistic children, in Communication Problems in Autism. Edited by Schopler E, Mesibov G. New York, Plenum, 1985, pp 127–145

Mesibov GB: Current perspectives and issues in autism and adolescence, in Autism in Adolescents and Adults. Edited by Schopler E, Mesibov GB. New York, Plenum, 1983, pp 37–53

Mesibov GB: Social skills training with verbal autistic adolescents and adults: a program model. J Autism Dev Disord 14:395–404, 1984

Mesibov GB: A cognitive program for teaching social behaviors to verbal autistic adolescents and adults, in Social Behavior in Autism. Edited by Schopler E, Mesibov GB. New York, Plenum, 1986, pp 265–283

Mesibov GB, Schopler E, Sloan JL: Service development for adolescents and adults in North Carolina's TEACCH program, in Autism in Adolescents and Adults. Edited by Schopler E, Mesibov GB. New York, Plenum, 1983, pp 411–432

Mesibov GB, Schopler E, Schaffer B, et al: Adolescent Adult Psychoeducational Profile. Austin, Texas, Proed, 1988

Miller JF: Assessing Language Production in Children: Experimental Procedures. Baltimore, University Park Press, 1981

Morgan SB: Helping parents understand the diagnosis of autism. Developmental and Behavioral Pediatrics 5:78–85, 1984

Murphy GH, Steele K, Gilligan T, et al: Teaching a picture language to a non-speaking retarded boy. Behav Res Ther 15:198–201, 1977

Musselwhite CR, St. Louis KW: Communication Programming for the Severely Handicapped: Vocal and Non-Vocal Strategies. San Diego, Calif College Hill, 1982

Naruse H, Nagahata M, Nakane Y, et al: A multicenter double-blind trial of pimozide (Orap), haloperidol and placebo in children with behavioral disorders, using crossover design. Acta Paedopsychiatr (Basel) 48:173–184, 1982

Newcomer PL, Hammill DD: Test of Language Development—Primary (TOLD-P). Allen, Tex, DLM Teaching Resources, 1977

Ney PG, Palvesky A, Markley J: Relative effectiveness of operant conditioning and play therapy in childhood schizophrenia. Journal of Autism and Childhood Schizophrenia 1:337–343, 1971

Olley JG: The TEACCH curriculum for teaching social behavior to children with autism, in Social Behavior and Autism. Edited by Schopler E, Mesibov GB. New York, Plenum, 1986, pp 351–373

O'Neill PJ, Lord C: A Functional and Semantic Approach to Language Intervention for Autistic Children and Adolescents. Presented at the Symposium on Research in Child Language Disorders. Madison, Wisc, 1982

Paluzny M: Autism: A Practical Guide for Parents and Professionals. Syracuse, NY, Syracuse University Press, 1979

Panksepp J: A neurochemical theory of autism. Trends in Neuroscience 2:174–177, 1979

Panksepp J, Sahley TL: Possible brain opioid involvement in disrupted social intent and language development in autism, in Neurobiological Issues in Autism. Edited by Schopler E, Mesibov GB. New York, Plenum Press, 1987, pp. 357–372

Park CC: Growing out of autism, in Autism In Adolescents and Adults. Edited by Schopler E, Mesibov GB. New York, Plenum, 1983, pp 279–295

Parker R: He Is Your Brother. Nashville, Tenn, Thomas Nelson, 1974

Parks SL: The assessment of autistic children: a selective review of available instruments. J Autism Dev Disord 13:255–267, 1983

Partington MW, Tu JB, Wong CY: Blood serotonin levels in severe mental retardation. Dev Med Child Neurol 15:616–627, 1973

Pauling L: Orthomolecular psychiatry. Science 160:265–271, 1968

Paulson GW, Rizvi CA, Crane GE: Tardive dyskinesia as a possible sequel of long-term therapy with phenothiazines. Clin Pediatr (Phila) 14:953–955, 1975

Peck CA: Increasing opportunities for social control by children with autism and severe handicaps: effects of student behavior and perceived classroom climate. Journal of the Association for Persons with Severe Handicaps 10:183–193, 1985

Perry R, Campbell M, Green WH, et al: Neuroleptic-related dyskinesias in autistic children: a prospective study. Psychopharmacol Bull 21:140–143, 1985

Petti TA, Campbell M: Imipramine and seizures. Am J Psychiatry 132:538–540, 1975

Physicians' Desk Reference (PDR). Oradell, NJ, Medical Economics Co, 1988

Pickar D, Vartanian F, Bunney WE Jr, et al: Short-term naloxone administration in schizophrenic and manic patients: a World Health Organization collaborative study. Arch Gen Psychiatry 39:313–319, 1982

Pietrofesa JJ, Hoffman A, Splete HH: Counseling: An Introduction. Boston, Houghton Mifflin, 1984

Plummer S, Baer DM, LeBlanc JM: Functional considerations in the use of procedural timeout and an effective alternative. J Appl Behav Anal 10:689–705, 1977

Polizos P, Engelhardt DM: Dyskinetic and neurological complications in children treated with psychotropic medication, in Tardive Dyskinesia: Research and Treatment. Edited by Fann WE, Smith RC, Davis JM, et al. Jamaica, NY, Spectrum Publications, 1980, pp 193–199

Polizos P, Engelhardt DM, Hoffman SP, et al: Neurological consequences of psychotropic drug withdrawal in schizophrenic children. Journal of Autism and Childhood Schizophrenia 3:247–253, 1973

Pool D, Bloom W, Mielke DH, et al: A controlled evaluation of loxitane in seventy-five adolescent schizophrenic patients. Current Therapeutic Research 19:99–104, 1976

Powell TH, Ogle PA: Brothers and Sisters—A Special Part of Exceptional Families. Baltimore, Md, Brookes Publishing Co, 1985

Powers MD, Handlemann JS: Behavioral Assessment of Severe Developmental Disabilities. Rockville, Md, Aspen Systems Corp, 1984

Prange AJ Jr: The Thyroid Axis, Drugs, and Behavior. New York, Raven Press, 1974

Prange AJ Jr, Lipton MA: Hormones and behavior: some principles and findings, in Psychiatric Complications of Medical Drugs. Edited by Shader RI. New York, Raven Press, 1972

Premack D: Reinforcement Theory, in Nebraska Symposium On Motivation. Edited by Levine D. Lincoln, University of Nebraska Press, 1965

Premack D, Premack AJ: Teaching visual language to apes and language-deficient persons, in Language Perspectives—Acquisition, Retardation, and Intervention. Edited by Schiefelbusch RL, Lloyd LL, Baltimore, University Park Press, 1974, pp 347–376

Prizant B: Speech-language pathologists and autistic children: what is our role? part II. ASHA 24:531–537, 1982

Psychopharmacol Bull, Special Issue: Pharmacotherapy of Children, 1973

Psychopharmacol Bull, Special Feature: Rating scales and assessment instruments for use in pediatric psychopharmacology research. 21:4, 1985

Rapoport JL, Ismond DR: DSM-III Training Guide for Diagnosis of Childhood Disorders. New York, Brunner/Mazel, 1984

Ratusnik CM, Ratusnik DL: A comprehensive communication approach for a ten year old nonverbal child. Am J Orthopsychiatry 44:396–403, 1974

Realmuto GM, Erickson WD, Yellin AM, et al: Clinical comparison of thiothixene and thioridazine in schizophrenic adolescents. Am J Psychiatry 141:440–442, 1984

Reid DH, Favell JE: Group instruction with persons who have severe disabilities: a critical review. Journal of the Association for Persons with Severe Handicaps 9:167–177, 1984

Reiss M: Psychoendocrinology. New York, Grune & Stratton, 1958

Richardson JS, Zaleski WA: Naloxone and self-mutilation. Biol Psychiatry 18:99–101, 1983

Rimland B: The differentiation of childhood psychoses: an analysis of checklists for 2,218 psychotic children. Journal of Autism and Childhood Schizophrenia 1:161–174, 1971

Rimland B: High-dosage levels of certain vitamins in the treatment of children with severe mental disorders, in Orthomolecular Psychiatry. Edited by Hawkins D, Pauling L. San Francisco, WH Freeman & Co, 1973, pp 513–539

Rimland B, Callaway E, Dreyfus P: The effect of high doses of vitamin B6 on autistic children: a double blind crossover study. Am J Psychiatry 135:472–475, 1978

Rincover A: Sensory extinction: a procedure for eliminating self-stimulatory behavior in developmentally disabled children. J Abnorm Child Psychol 6:299–310, 1978

Rincover A, Koegel RL: Setting generality and stimulus control in autistic children. J Appl Behav Anal 8:235–246, 1975

Rincover A, Newsom CD, Lovaas OI, et al: Some motivational properties of sensory stimulation in psychotic children. J Exp Child Psychol 24:312–323, 1977

Risley JR, Wolf MM: Establishing functional speech in echolalic children. Behav Res Ther 5:73–88, 1967

Ritvo ER, Freeman BJ: A medical model of autism: etiology, pathology, and treatment. Pediatr Ann 13:298–305, 1984

Ritvo ER, Yuwiler A, Geller E, et al: Increased blood serotonin and platelets in early infantile autism. Arch Gen Psychiatry 23:566–572, 1970

Ritvo ER, Yuwiler A, Geller E, et al: Effects of L-dopa in autism. Journal of Autism and Childhood Schizophrenia 1:190–205, 1971

Ritvo ER, Ritvo EC, Mason-Brothers AM: Genetic and immunohematologic factors in autism. J Autism Dev Disord 12:109–114, 1982

Ritvo ER, Freeman BJ, Geller E, et al: Effects of fenfluramine on 14 outpatients with the syndrome of autism. J Am Acad Child Psychiatry 22:549–558, 1983

Ritvo ER, Freeman BJ, Yuwiler A, et al: Study of fenfluramine in outpatients with the syndrome of autism. J Pediatr 105:823–828, 1984

Ritvo ER, Freeman BJ, Mason-Brothers A, et al: Concordance of the syndrome of autism in 40 pairs of afflicted twins. Am J Psychiatry 142:74–77, 1985a

Ritvo ER, Spence A, Freeman BJ, et al: Evidence for autosomal recessive inheritance in 46 families with multiple incidences of autism. Am J Psychiatry 142:187–192, 1985b

Ritvo ER, Freeman BJ, Yuwiler A, et al: Fenfluramine treatment of autism: UCLA collaborative study of 81 patients at nine medical centers. Psychopharmacol Bull 22:133–140, 1986

Roukema RW, Emery L: Megavitamin therapy with severely disturbed children. Am J Psychiatry 127:249, 1970

Russell LM: Alternatives: A Family Guide to Legal and Financial Planning for the Disabled. Evanston, Ill, First Publications, 1983

Ruttenberg BA, Kalish BI, Wenar C, et al: Behavior Rating Instrument for Autistic and Other Atypical Children, revised. Philadelphia, Developmental Center for Autistic Children, 1977

Rutter M: Concepts of autism: a review of research. J Child Psychol Psychiatry 9:1–25, 1968

Rutter M: Autism: educational issues. Special Education 59:6–10, 1970

Rutter M: Autistic children: infancy to adulthood. Seminars in Psychiatry 2:435–450, 1970

Rutter M: Childhood schizophrenia reconsidered. Journal of Autism and Childhood Schizophrenia 2:315–337, 1972

Rutter M: Infantile autism and other child psychoses, in Child Psychiatry Modern Approaches. Edited by Rutter M, Hersov L. London, Blackwell Scientific Publications, 1977

Rutter M: Diagnosis and definition, in Autism: A Reappraisal of Concepts and Treatment. Edited by Rutter M, Schopler E. New York, Plenum Press, 1978, pp 1–25

Rutter M: Language training with autistic children: how does it work and what does it achieve? in Language and Language Disorders in Childhood. Edited by Hersov L, Berger M, Nicol AR. New York, Pergamon Press, 1980

Rutter M: Infantile autism and other pervasive developmental disorders, in Child and Adolescent Psychiatry (2nd ed). Edited by Rutter M, Hersov L. Oxford, Blackwell Scientific Publications, 1985, pp 545–566

Rutter M, Bartak L: Special educational treatment of autistic children: a comparative study, II: follow-up findings and implications for services. J Child Psychol Psychiatry 14:241–270, 1973

Rutter M, Lockyer L: Five to fifteen-year follow-up study of infantile psychosis: I. Br J Psychiatry 113:1169–1182, 1967

Rutter M, Schopler E: Autism and pervasive developmental disorders: concepts and diagnostic issues, in Diagnosis and Assessment in Autism. Edited by Schopler E, Mesibov GB. New York, Plenum Press, 1988, pp 15–30

Rutter M, Greenfield D, Lockyer L: A five to fifteen-year follow-up study of infantile psychosis: II. Br J Psychiatry 113:1183–1199, 1967

Sachar EJ: Neuroendocrine abnormalities in depressive illness, in Topics in Psychoendocrinology. Edited by Sachar EJ. New York, Grune and Stratton, 1975

Sachar EJ (ed): Hormones, behavior and psychopathology. New York, Raven Press, 1976

Sandman CA, Datta PC, Barron J, et al. Naloxone attenuates self-abusive behavior in developmentally disabled clients. Appl Res Ment Retard 4:5–11, 1983

Sanford AR: Learning Accomplishment Profile. Winston-Salem, NC, Kaplan Press, 1984

Schapiro S: Influence of hormones and environmental stimulation on brain development, in Influence of Hormones on the Nervous System. Edited by Ford DH. Basel, S Karger, 1971, pp 63–73

Schaumburg H, Kaplan J, Windebank A, et al: Sensory neuropathy from pyridoxine abuse: a new megavitamin syndrome. N Engl J Med 309:445–490, 1983

Schopler E: Towards reducing behavior problems in autistic children, in Early Childhood Autism (2nd ed). Edited by Wing L. New York, Pergamon, 1976, pp 221–245

Schopler E: Model Educational Programs for Autistic Children and Youth: Final Report. Contract Number 300-80-0841, Special Education Programs, US Department of Education, Division TEACCH, University of North Carolina at Chapel Hill, 1984

Schopler E, Bristol M: Autistic Children in Public School: Exceptional Child Education Report. Reston, Va, Council for Exceptional Children, 1980

Schopler E, Mesibov GB: Autism in Adolescents and Adults. New York, Plenum, 1983

Schopler E, Mesibov GB: The Effects of Autism on the Family. New York, Plenum, 1984

Schopler E, Reichler RJ: Parents as cotherapists in the treatment of psychotic children. Journal of Autism and Childhood Schizophrenia 1:87–102, 1971a

Schopler E, Reichler RJ: Developmental therapy by parents with their own autistic child, in Infantile Autism: Concepts, Characteristics, and Treatment. Edited by Rutter M. London, Churchill Livingstone, 1971b, pp 206–227

Schopler E, Reichler RJ: How well do parents understand their own psychotic child? Journal of Autism and Childhood Schizophrenia 2:387–400, 1972

Schopler E, Reichler RJ: Individualized Assessment and Treatment for Autistic and Developmentally Disabled Children, vol 1, Psychoeducational Profile. Austin, Tex, Pro-Ed, 1979

Schopler E, Brehm SS, Kinsbourne M, et al: Effect of treatment structure on development in autistic children. Arch Gen Psychiatry 24:415–421, 1971

Schopler E, Andrews CE, Strupp K: Do autistic children come from upper-middle-class parents? J Autism Dev Disord 9:139–152, 1979

Schopler E, Reichler RJ, Lansing MD: Individualized Assessment and Treatment for Autistic and Developmentally Disabled Children, vol 2: Teaching Strategies for Parents and Professionals. Austin, Tex, Pro-Ed, 1980a

Schopler E, Reichler RJ, DeVellis RF, et al: Toward objective classification of childhood autism: Childhood Autism Rating Scale (CARS). J Autism Dev Disord 10:91–103, 1980b

Schopler E, Mesibov G, Baker A: Evaluation of treatment for autistic children and their parents. J Am Acad Child Psychiatry 21:262–267, 1982

Schopler E, Mesibov GB, Shigley RH, et al: Helping autistic children through their parents: the TEACCH model, in The Effects of Autism on the Family. Edited by Schopler E, Mesibov GB. New York, Plenum, 1984, pp 65–81

Schopler E, Reichler RJ, Renner BR: The Childhood Autism Rating Scale (CARS). New York, Irvington, 1985

Schreibman L, O'Neill RE, Koegel RL: Behavioral training for siblings of autistic children. J Appl Behav Anal 16:129–138, 1983

Seibert JM, Oller DK: Linguistic pragmatics and language intervention strategies. Journal of Autism and Developmental Disabilities 11:75–88, 1981

Shane H: Approaches to communication training with the severely handicapped, in Teaching the Severely Handicapped. Edited by York R, Edgar E. Columbus, Ohio, Special Press, 1979

Shea V: Explaining mental retardation and autism to parents, in The Effects of Autism on the Family. Edited by Schopler E, Mesibov GB. New York, Plenum, 1984

Sherwin AC, Flach FF, Strokes PE: Treatment of psychoses in early childhood with triiodothyronine. Am J Psychiatry 115:116–167, 1958

Short AB: Short-term treatment outcome using parents as cotherapists for their own autistic children. J Child Psychol Psychiatry 25:443–458, 1984

Simeon J, Saletu B, Saletu M, et al: Thiothixene in Childhood Psychoses. Presented at the Third International Symposium on Phenothiazines. Rockville, Maryland, 1973

Simeonsson RJ, Olley JG, Rosenthal SL: Early intervention for children with autism, in The Effectiveness of Early Intervention for At-Risk and Handicapped Children. Edited by Guralnick MJ, Bennett FC. New York, Academic Press, 1987, pp 275–296

Simmons JQ, Benor D, Daniel D: The variable effects of LSD-25 on the behavior of a heterogeneous group of childhood schizophrenics. Behav Neuropsychiatry 4:10–16, 1972

Simpson GM, Lee JH, Zoubok B, et al: A rating scale for tardive dyskinesia. Psychopharmacology 64:171–179, 1979

Sokoloff L, Roberts P: Biochemical mechanism of the action of thyroid hormones in nervous and other tissues, in Influence of Hormones on the Nervous System. Edited by Ford DH. Basel, S Karger, 1971

Solnick JV, Rincover A, Peterson CR: Some determinants of the reinforcing and punishing effects of timeout. J Appl Behav Anal 10:415–424, 1977

Sparrow S, Balla DA, Cicchetti DV: The Vineland Adaptive Behavior Scales. Circle Pines, Minn, American Guidance Service, 1984

Spence E: The Devil Hole. New York, Lothrop, Lee & Shepard Books, 1977

Sprague RL: Psychopharmacology and learning disabilities. Journal of Operational Psychiatry 3:56–67, 1972

Sprague RL, Werry JS: Methodology of psychopharmacological studies with the retarded, in International Review of Research in Mental Retardation, vol 1. Edited by Ellis NR. New York, Academic Press, 1971, pp 147–219

Strain PS: Generalization of autistic children's social behavior change: effects of developmentally integrated and segregated settings. Analysis and Intervention in Developmental Disabilities 3:23–34, 1983

Stutsman R: Merrill-Palmer Scale of Mental Tests. Los Angeles, Western Psychological Services, 1948

Tarjan C, Lowery VE, Wright SE: Use of chlorpromazine in two hundred seventy-eight mentally deficient patients. AMA Journal of Disturbed Children 94:294–300, 1957

Terman LM, Merrill MA: Stanford-Binet Intelligence Scale: Manual for the Third Revision—Form L-M. Boston, Houghton Mifflin, 1973

Turnbull AP, Brotherson MJ Summers JA: The impact of deinstitutionalization on families: a family system approach, in Living and Learning in the Least Restrictive Environment. Edited by Bruininks RH. New York, Brookes Publishing Co, 1985

Turner DA, Purchatzke G, Gift T, et al: Intensive design in evaluating anxiolytic agents, in Principles and Techniques of Human Research and Therapeutics, vol 8: Psychopharmacological Agents. Edited by Levine J, Schiele BC, Taylor WJR. Mt. Kisco, NY, Futura Publishing Co, 1974, pp 105–118

Verebey K, Volavka J, Clouet D: Endorphins in psychiatry. Arch Gen Psychiatry 35:877–888, 1978

Volkmar FR, Cohen DJ, Paul R: An evaluation of DSM-III criteria for infantile autism. J Am Acad Child Psychiatry 25:190–197, 1986

Vulpe SG: Vulpe Assessment Battery. Toronto, National Institute on Mental Retardation, 1977

Waizer J, Polizos P, Hoffman SP, et al: A single-blind evaluation of thiothixene with outpatient schizophrenic children. Journal of Autism and Childhood Schizophrenia 2:378–386, 1972

Watson LR: The TEACCH communication curriculum, in Communication Problems in Autism. Edited by Schopler E, Mesibov GB. New York, Plenum, 1985, pp 187–206

Watson LR, Lord C: Developing a social communication curriculum for autistic students. Topics in Language Disorders 3:1–9, 1982

Watson LR, Lord C, Schaffer B, et al: Teaching Spontaneous Communication to Autistic and Developmentally Handicapped Children. New York, Irvington Press, 1989

Watters RG, Wheeler LJ, Watters WE: The relative efficiency of two orders for training autistic children in the expressive and receptive use of manual signs. J Commun Disord 14:273–285, 1981

Webster C, McPherson H, Sloman L, et al: Communicating with an autistic boy by gestures. Journal of Autism and Childhood Schizophrenia 3:337–346, 1973

Wechsler D: Wechsler Intelligence Scale for Children, revised. New York, Psychological Corporation, 1974a

Wechsler D: Wechsler Preschool and Primary Scale of Intelligence. New York, Psychological Corporation, 1974b

Wehman P, Hill JW: Competitive employment for moderated and severely handicapped individuals. Except Child 47:338–345, 1981

Weizman R, Weizman A, Tyano S, et al: Humoral-endorphin blood levels in autistic, schizophrenic and healthy subjects. Psychopharmacology 82:368–370, 1984

Werry JS, Aman MG: Methylphenidate and haloperidol in children: effects on attention, memory and activity. Arch Gen Psychiatry 32:790–795, 1975

Wetherby AM, Prutting CA: Profiles of communicative and cognitive-social abilities in autistic children. J Speech Hear Res 27:364–377, 1984

Wilcox B, Thompson A: Critical Issues in Educating Autistic Children and Youth. Washington, DC, US Department of Education, Office of Special Education, 1980

Willette RE, Barnett G (eds): Narcotic antagonists: naltrexone pharmacochemistry and sustained release preparations. NIDA Research Monograph 28, 1981

Wing L: Autistic Children: A Guide for Parents (rev ed). London, Constable, 1975

Wing L: Asperger's syndrome: a clinical account. Psychol Med 11:115–130, 1981

Wing L: Development of concepts, classification, and relationship to mental retardation, in Handbook of Psychiatry, vol 3, Psychoses of Uncertain Aetiology. Edited by Wing JK, Wing L. Cambridge, Cambridge University Press, 1982, pp 185–190

Wolf MM, Risley JR, Mees HL: Application of operant conditioning procedures to the behavior problems of an autistic child. Behav Res Ther 1:305–312, 1964

Wolfensberger W: The Principle of Normalization in Human Services. Toronto, National Institute on Mental Retardation, 1972

Young JG, Cohen DJ, Brown S-L, et al: Decreased urinary free catecholamines in childhood autism. J Am Acad Child Psychiatry 17:671–678, 1978

Young JG, Cohen DJ, Caparulo BK, et al: Decreased 24-hour urinary MHPG in childhood autism. Am J Psychiatry 136:1055–1057, 1979

Young JG, Kavanagh ME, Anderson GM, et al: Clinical neurochemistry of autism and associated disorders. J Autism Dev Disord 12:147–165, 1982

Zimmerman IL, Steiner VG, Pond RE: Preschool Language Scale. Columbus, Ohio, Charles E. Merrill, 1969

SECTION 3

Specific Developmental Disorders

Chapter 44

Overview of the Specific Developmental Disorders

Prior to the late 1950s, many pediatricians and child psychiatrists were fairly confident that most children of average IQ could learn if they wanted to and if they were exposed to an appropriate curriculum.

Thus anyone of normal intelligence presenting with learning problems was easily placed into a category of emotional difficulty with secondary problems in learning. Early psychiatric literature on learning difficulties therefore focused on the encroachment of conflict on the learning situation. The adaptive significance of the learning difficulty frequently was seen as a way of working out hostilities toward parents and adults. Additional formulations included defenses against the danger of competition with peers and siblings and the child's symbolic view of the teacher as a parent substitute with whom there was an intolerable or difficult relationship. In addition to these factors, exhibitionistic and performance anxiety were cited as determinants (Blanchard 1946).

While these trends were predominant, Orton (1937) invoked developmental reasons for learning problems, thereby introducing a new concept within psychiatry that did not take hold until later. They viewed children with learning problems as having specific learning difficulties. Labels such as strephosymbolia and dyslexia began to appear in the psychiatric and educational literature. These learning difficulties were seen as neurodevelopmental problems, maturational lags, or incapacities that were familial. Perinatal factors were also explored, and the relationship to conduct disorders and behavioral problems of all sorts was studied. More global concepts such as minimal brain dysfunction spanned not only what we now call attention-deficit hyperactivity disorder, but also included other varieties of behavioral and learning problems viewed as secondary to insult around the birth process. The continuum of reproductive casualty (Lilienfeld et al. 1955) became child psychiatry's most frequent etiologic inference. In addition to these "toxic" elements in the history, other environmental factors (e.g., lead, sugar, red dye) were invoked as causative. While the struggle to determine etiology still rages, there are firm grounds to indicate that most learning disabilities and language and speech problems can well be assigned to a category currently described as developmental disability.

As early as 1974, Rutter wrote that emotional disturbances may lead to under-achievement, but that the studies are not conclusive. However, more extensive studies of reading retardation showed emotional disorder does not play an important role etiologically. At the same time, motivational factors may be influential in the contin-uation of difficulties as children age. He then cited the earlier epidemiologic study of the Isle of Wight (Rutter et al. 1970), which showed that one-third of the subjects with specific reading disorders also had conduct disorders, and one-third of the subjects with conduct disorders had reading disorders. At about the same time in the United States, Chess and Rosenberg (1974) reported on the frequent occurrence of speech and language complaints at intake in a private practice sample of middle-class children seeking psychiatric consultation. The records revealed that during a three-year period, 24 percent of 563 children examined had some kind of language difficulty, with boys showing a 3:1 predominance over girls as compared to a 2:1 boy:girl ratio of the entire sample. Clinicians have since repeatedly attested to these early findings. When Silver (1981) examined three populations—a learning disabled school population, a pediatric group of hyperactive children, and a mental health population of emotionally disturbed youngsters—he found significant overlap of symptoms between hyperkinetic children and the learning-disabled school popula-tion. However, the emotionally disordered children from the psychiatric clinic showed little overlap in symptom pictures with the other two. This represents a radical turn-about from the earliest views of psychiatrists.

These background discoveries have laid the groundwork for recent work in which a variety of professionals have taken important roles in the study and care of devel-opmentally disabled children. Although in many communities there is a paucity of services for children, in other communities in the United States children are potentially beset by more professionals than any other population. It is nowhere more vital than in the area of developmental disabilities that all professionals interact cooperatively and share information and skill for the good of the children.

The DSM-III (American Psychiatric Association 1980) has designated Axis II as the area where child psychiatrists can categorize one of our largest groups of disability and disorder. Child psychiatrists confronted with this array have to achieve knowl-edge often not included within their training. For example, language and speech disorders include varieties of articulation problems and dysfluencies as well as lan-guage problems (articulation disorder, stuttering, cluttering, receptive language dis-order, and selective mutism). Academic skill disorders are also listed in reading, writing, and arithmetic, as well as coordination disorders. While child psychiatrists may be expected to recognize such disorders clinically, they receive much comple-mentary aid, historical input, and therapeutic assistance from regular and special educators, speech and hearing specialists, psychologists, educational psychologists, speech pathologists, and parents. Each of these disciplines has a role in diagnosis, care, and treatment.

The Axis I of DSM-III also included a number of developmental diagnoses (e.g., the pervasive developmental disorders, autism, and mental retardation), and the "other" developmental disabilities were listed in Axis II of the World Health Orga-nization (WHO) scheme prior to DSM-III. Whatever the wisdom of the initial decision, we may remember that the immediate progenitor to the DSM-III multiaxial system was a triaxial system first recommended by a WHO study group of child psychiatrists (Rutter et al. 1969). They suggested that psychiatric diagnosis, developmental level (i.e., IQ), and organic substrate disease were needed to provide a complete picture of the child clinically. Axis II was designated as the axis in which diagnosis of de-velopmental problems as reflected in IQ was to be recorded. It is interesting that

DSM-III initially retained Axis II as a developmental sector, but halfheartedly. Subsequently, recommendations were made for a separate developmental axis to be included as an axis for children substituting for Axis V or adding an optional Axis VI. DSM-III-R (American Psychiatric Association 1987) now provides some variant of these considerations prior to the later DSM-IV or ICD-10. At the 1985 DSM-III-R hearings on multiaxial system, the revisions recommended were adopted so that pervasive developmental disorders and mental retardation are now listed in Axis II along with the specific developmental disorders, which is consonant with the initial intentions of the WHO group.

Because children are in a developmental flux, true disorders of development must be distinguished from simple lags in development or those disorders of development that seem to be secondary to Axis I diagnoses. For example, it might be important to know whether the conduct disorder on Axis I is secondary to a learning disability in Axis II or whether the learning disability on Axis II is further impaired by an attentional-deficit hyperactivity disorder, which does not permit the child to attend in school. It is also clear that in Axis IV, social and familial problems might influence capacity or temporarily impair the child's learning. Biologic factors also operate at varying stages of development, impeding the pace of learning. In fact, Cantwell and Baker (1987) argued that when effects of marital discord and IQ are controlled, social class variables diminish in importance. Anyone using a nomenclature of this sort for treatment planning should take heed of Piaget's warning about the American tendency to pack more in than is cognitively indicated by the normal sequence and progression of cognitive maturation. David Elkind's (1984) concept of the hurried child is a relevant indictment of thoughtless pacing of early education. This warning notwithstanding, Rutter et al.'s (1979) study of secondary schools emphasized the importance of academic variables and incentives to learning in the school-aged child, suggesting that warmth is not enough. These factors lead the practitioner to a view of diagnostics that includes not only the index patient but the relevant surroundings of teachers, parents, and peers as well as the developmental stage.

In this section on treatments we will illustrate the uniqueness of the vantage of each discipline and the mutual respect and common vocabulary that will have to develop among professionals so that communication is increased and competition decreased. While the "whole child" cliché may be overused, it is important that a coordinated treatment plan among professionals be secured and time made available for the development of such treatment plans with an appropriate division of labor if adequate care is to be delivered.

If we view the child's developmental course from early infancy on, it is easy to determine that early contact between parent and child focuses on bodily care and feeding. These interactions with parent or caretaker also include affection, socialization, and the development of social routines (Stern 1977). Ninio and Bruner (1978) used book reading as a central model of the setting in which language is learned. They suggested that rules of pragmatic interaction and the structure of such exchanges may be projected from the initial context to all future learning. Verbal and pointing interactions in such sequences of mutual regard between parent and child become a model for school learning as well (Bruner 1984). Thus it seems that competent language use is vital to socialization. This developmental fact is complemented by large-scale epidemiologic studies in Britain (Stevenson et al. 1985). While polysymptomatic disorders among three-year-olds have a prevalence rate of about 7 percent, if early language disability is present it increases the likelihood of a child having a disorder (i.e., there is a strong association between language delay and behavior problems). Of 22 children with such delays, 59 percent had symptomatic states as compared with

7 to 15 percent of the larger sample. These disruptive behaviors also persist later into childhood.

Cantwell and Baker (1977; 1987) approached the problem from another angle. They showed that 53 percent of children seen initially in a speech and hearing clinic had a psychiatric diagnoses. Of these, 19 percent were attention-deficit hyperactivity disorders. Follow-up studies four years later also showed persistence of disorder with the further suggestion that no social correlate was stronger than having a language problem. Of this population, 16 percent was diagnosed as attention-deficit hyperactivity disorder with a variety of conduct and oppositional disorders, following with only 2 percent categorized in the emotional disorder category.

A school-age normal population has also been studied in Ottowa-Carleton, Canada by Beitchman et al. (1986a, 1986b). A one-in-three population study of 1,655 five-year-olds revealed a prevalence rate of 142 (8.6 percent) children with language and learning problems who reached the third stage of the study, which included direct testing and interviews. Of these, 22 to 48 percent had psychiatric disorders. The initial figure is by parent report, the latter by direct psychiatric evaluations. Of this group, 30 percent were attention-deficient hyperactivity disorder. These studies give some greater statistical force to the proposition that developmental disorders are widespread in our community and need the attention of professionals.

The school may be the first to notice and isolate the disordered child. Moreover, the law governing the Education for All Handicapped Children (PL 94-142) determines where the psychiatrist and the special educator enter into the investigation and treatment. Families may not naturally consult psychiatrists, but schools may require them to do so once the child is noticed in the school system. More significantly, anyone working in a child psychiatric clinic has come to understand that what Chess and Rosenberg (1974) found earlier is indeed true. School difficulties and failure are among the most frequent complaints.

But school failure alone or difficulties in learning alone do not automatically point to the appropriate intervention. As will be shown throughout this text, there is a necessary overlap in the process of learning with the difficulties children have in their sense of achievement, their self-esteem, peer interaction, and so on. Moreover, busy educators have found that whatever the perceptual difficulties are that contribute to learning problems, there are secondary concomitants to all developmental disabilities. High or low IQ or socioeconomic status may provide mitigating effects, but each professional must be cognizant of the possibility that a more holistic approach to treatment has to be considered. Although special placement in a special classroom or tutoring is appropriate, and sufficient sometimes, at other times or at later ages other methods may become more appropriate.

A recent review of remedial approaches shows the greater likelihood of effect of such intervention early on, with more difficulties in gaining effect later (Watson et al. 1982). Identification of subtypes and etiology is still in its infancy (Cantwell and Forness 1982). Such findings suggest that tutors may have to modify their favored approaches if emotional disorder is also present. The psychiatrist's role in the team frequently is greater than that provided by PL 94-142 (i.e., diagnosis alone). In that sense, the student or client may sometimes become a patient, and the social system that pays for the client's studentship and patientship must take cognizance of other multiple needs for aid. On the other hand, a psychiatrist invited to take a role in the mélange of professionals need not be overly zealous in the direction of medical treatment. Thus just because a good percentage of children with attention-deficit hyperactivity disorder respond to methylphenidate and amphetamine does not mean that children who have learning disabilities and reading problems necessarily will respond similarly. Gittleman and Feingold (1983a, 1983b) have shown that tutoring alone is superior to tutoring plus medication for straightforward uncomplicated learning disabilities. It is also true, however, that when learning disabilities are a concomitant of attention-deficit hyperactivity disorder, then medication is indicated. Moreover, these models show that medical and psychiatric approaches can gain in their impact if the information available from other disciplines is used to complement the usual information sources. Future research not only in treatment but in the mechanism of disability will require more careful complementary rather than focused intervention without consultation.

Chapter 45

Early Developmental Environment of the Child with Specific Developmental Disorder

The literature on normal infant development is extensive, spanning several decades of research and clinical observation. In particular, study of the attention, visual perceptual, language, and social skills of infants up to three months of age has demonstrated the remarkable progression in skills characteristic of these early years. Children in the three-to-six-year age range have been the subject of considerable child development research for a half century. They are conveniently accessible to researchers and have had group experiences that make standardized procedures more easily accomplished and reliable.

Recently there has been increased interest in the effects, on development, of neurologic deficits and/or sensory or motor impairments. The assumption that the learning process is disrupted or distorted has, in fact, been supported by a number of studies.

Fraiberg (1975), for example, investigated the unfolding of various developmental skills in congenitally blind infants, who were otherwise intact. Early in her project, Fraiberg became alarmed at the large number of blind children who exhibited abnormal ego development, autistic behaviors, and failure to use their hands effectively for exploration. She found that when researchers facilitated parent-infant dialogue, with vocal and tactile interchanges, relationship skills developed normally. Strategies were also devised to encourage bringing the hands to midline, reaching, grasping, and exploring. Fraiberg demonstrated that motor, communication, and tactile perceptual skills could also be facilitated.

Mindel and Vernon (1971) reported that in deaf infants the absence of full communication with the mothers led to early alterations in personality development, often including a limited capacity to relate closely to others. The tendency of older deaf infants to be temperamentally difficult, expressing their frustration physically, is well known; as with young blind children, there is serious risk that the child will be withdrawn from the caretakers, who are, of course, the child's first teachers.

Interaction of Specific Developmental Disorder and Development

There is a circular, transactional relationship between specific developmental disorder and development in which the direct effects of the disability (e.g., not mastering a concrete skill) affect the child's experience and interactions (e.g., social). These modify the attitudes of others toward the child, influencing in turn the child's motivation and self-esteem, which leads to compensatory defenses and will ultimately affect adversely the learning process. Thus the emotional behavioral patterns of these children are not fixed, but undergo a continuous, dynamic change. Children with specific developmental disorder will suffer from 1) primary deficiencies: the specific developmental disability itself (e.g., inefficient verbal communication); 2) secondary deficiencies: lack of skill acquisition due to interference from the primary deficiency (e.g., academic backwardness in a child with dyslexia); and 3) tertiary ones: complications in another area (e.g., a behavioral disorder).

Language and speech disorders are probably most important among these disabilities. Verbal language is what permits the child to communicate with others as well as serves as the chief avenue for acquiring new knowledge. Thus interaction with others as well as academic learning will be affected. A disability in the motor area will adversely affect a child's learning self-care (e.g., dressing) and play skills.

Effects of these deficiencies on a child's social development and interaction are important and handicapping. A child who had language and speech problems will have difficulties in communicating with playmates and in understanding the rules of the game. Associated motor deficits, poor motor coordination, and clumsiness will interfere with the child's integration in sports-oriented games. These children may also have problems with symbolic, imaginative play, which is so important for growth and the learning of social skills (Millar 1968). Closer to school age, failure to acquire academic skills (e.g., early reading and counting) further differentiates them from other children. In peer groups these children stand out and are often considered different or slow. The secondary behavioral problems further reinforce these impressions.

Since these children have no visible "deficits," appear normal, and are not "sick," the parents are usually confused and puzzled. The child may be seen as lazy. Lack of compliance with limits due to receptive language problems may be labeled as disobedience. The parents may exert increasing pressure on the child to learn to speak properly, to master letters and counting, and to practice sports. This drilling in skills may eventually dominate parent-child interaction, leaving little room for mutually gratifying activities. The parents may become increasingly frustrated and angry. Guilt for "causing" the problems may be present, especially since parents of these children often have a history of a learning disability themselves. They may tend to overprotect, for example, may guess the needs of the child with a language disability before these needs are verbalized (Beckey 1942). At the same time, a sort of double message may be given through insistence that the child can do well if he or she only tries hard enough. The child's preschool teacher may feel similarly confused, puzzled by an apparently normal child who doesn't learn and who threatens the self-image of a competent educator. There are several mechanisms through which the behavioral and emotional development of children with specific developmental disorder may be affected. Attitudes of those in their environment are important. These children can well perceive the dissatisfaction of their parents and teachers as well as the rejection and ridicule of their peers. They are also aware of their own deficiencies. Various compensatory and defense mechanisms may be employed, and behavior problems may be frequent. This has been particularly well documented in children with speech and language disorders (Cantwell et al. 1979).

The behavioral disorders in these children might also be linked to the mechanism associated with the specific developmental disorder (Cantwell and Baker 1987). A child with a language disability and attention-deficit hyperactivity disorder may serve as an example.

The early manifestations will depend on the nature of the specific developmental disorder and of the associated conditions that are frequently present. In a child with specific disturbance in motor development, poor sucking and feeding may be first noticed, followed by delayed developmental motor milestones. These will obviously alarm the parents inasmuch as interaction around feeding is one of the cornerstones of parent-child bonding at this stage, and motor milestones are usually anticipated as an early proof of a child's normalcy. A child with an associated attention-deficit hyperactivity disorder may present early as a restless and overactive infant. The parents' reaction in these cases will be different than it would be if the child had a visible, obvious, and serious developmental disability, such as Down's syndrome or blindness. These parents are often confused, puzzled, dismayed, and anxious. Unfortunately, since an accurate diagnosis is usually not made as yet at this stage, their concerns are dismissed and they are labeled neurotic and expecting too much of the child.

Abnormalities in play patterns may be noticed early. The play may be unimaginative, concrete, and different from age peers.

An early warning sign in the child with developmental language disability is poor response to limit setting. When the child's ability to understand verbal commands and constraints is limited, physical punishment is sometimes used, even in families where this is not the pattern for other children. The child's activity level and ability to wreak havoc on the home, when not supervised, may prompt the parents to such measures as special locks, bars on windows, and fenced-in areas. At the very least, they may alter their patterns of daily living, making fewer social calls, leaving the child with a friend while the mother shops, and so on.

Parent Variables in Early Identification

The fit between an infant's temperament and parental expectations of how he or she should behave is a critical factor in early referral for evaluation of mild learning disabilities. When the parental expectation for a male infant is that he will be active, strong willed, noisy, and perhaps aggressive, the presence of these characteristics is not viewed as alarming. In such families boys are not socialized to be docile or quiet, and the parents may be quite surprised when the child at age five is considered a problem at school. Obviously, teachers' expectations of what is normal are also highly pertinent.

Parents whose expectations for infant and young child behavior include steadily increasing attention to pictures and books, adaptability to situations that demand relative inactivity, and self-modulation of behavior may seek professional opinion quite early with concerns that their child is hyperactive or difficult to manage. Such parents may also be alert to delays in auditory attention and expressive language skills. The availability of hearing screening for young children may reassure them that the child hears, and skill development in other areas may also negate mental retardation. But if, by age three, the child does not express himself or herself appropriately, or, worse still, does not appear to process others' directions or comments, these parents will refer the child to a clinic or to the school evaluation team.

Special education laws, in particular PL 94-142, prescribe interdisciplinary evaluation of children who exhibit developmental problems. This type of review is particularly appropriate because it 1) provides for the gathering of multiple professional opinions and 2) assumes responsibility for providing a program or therapeutic services (e.g., speech therapy, occupational therapy) (see Chapter 52).

Educational Planning and Programs

The recognition of specific developmental disorders as a separate entity from other developmental disabilities is quite recent. Programs for these children at the elementary school level were uncommon until the 1960s. In the early special programs, pupils received training in visual-motor-perceptual tasks and individualized instruction in reading and mathematics. But few of the teachers had any understanding of language disorders (nor did speech therapists at that time).

Since there were no public school programs for three- and four-year-old children, the available choices were Head Start Programs (for disadvantaged children), therapeutic programs operated by clinics or universities; and the private nursery programs, which ranged from play schools run by the parents to academically challenging preschools that served upper middle-class children. There were, of course, clinical nurseries for various populations of handicapped children, but these were not usually open to, or appropriate for, children with specific developmental disorder. As public school preschool programs began to proliferate, this situation improved; however, the adequacy of educational resources still varies widely from one locale to another.

The majority of children with learning disabilities will be served in preschool programs for normal children. A review of child development textbooks suggests that knowledge of what is normal for a particular age is still considered enough for most teachers to know. The experience of clinics that see preschool children is that many teachers use referrals as a way to answer questions about relatively minor deviations from normal development, exaggerating the significance of such delays and frightening the parents. Clinical professionals may exacerbate the problem by using terminology that suggests a serious handicapping condition.

Contrary to this latter trend, most parents and professionals agree that labeling a child as handicapped should be avoided if possible. Formal testing revealing delays at age three sometimes are inconspicuous by age five. However, if a child appears to need early education services offered by the school district, a formal diagnostic label is sometimes required for eligibility. The preschool child is now said to be "at risk" and the degree of risk is dependent on subsequent maturation, the nature of the disability, and the appropriateness of service at the primary school level. With relatively little supporting data, educators hope that the majority of children identified early and given services will become normal learners by school age.

Parents, teachers, and indeed psychotherapists may each have a different view of the troubled preschool child; each may also have a different agenda for what early education should accomplish. The parents may hope that their child will "catch up" and become more manageable and able to interact with other children. The teacher may seek to advance preacademic skills. The therapist may be looking for healthy personality development in the face of learning difficulties that threaten self-esteem, or may even hope that the child is only "pseudo-handicapped" and may be "cured" by psychotherapy. Obviously, these goals are not mutually exclusive, but it is important that the differing expectations be recognized and discussed. Otherwise, the school experience may be viewed positively by one party and negatively by another.

Parent, Pupil, Teacher, School

Nowhere is the fit between pupil and teacher more critical than with the learning-disabled child. The teacher's pedagogic style, personality characteristics, energy level, and even voice and appearance affect these children disproportionately. In addition, the learning environment, as it is structured by the teacher, can facilitate or hinder the child's ability to attend and learn. Obviously, physical factors in the classroom, the number and types of children, and the general philosophy and policies of the school are also relevant.

Parents may express the desire that the child be educated with peers who present the same difficulties; on the other hand, they hope that their child will have normal peer models. There is often a hope that their child will be placed with children who are more advanced developmentally. With the emphasis on mainstreaming, they often hope that the school will provide opportunities for their child to observe and be with normal age peers.

There are undeniable advantages to both homogenous and heterogenous groupings. In a class where all children present with serious language disorders, the focus of instruction will be the development of more adequate communication skills. Sometimes the teacher will be a certified speech pathologist, or a speech therapist may provide individual and group therapy as well as consultation to other members of the educational team. However, the children will not experience the stimulation and challenge of interacting with normally verbal peers. The advantage of highly specific, appropriate educational treatment and the reduced frustration of a communication-facilitating environment must be balanced, at least temporarily, against the advantage of integration.

Increasing numbers of children from all social classes attend center-based or family day-care where structured learning experiences are provided for a portion of the day. Like public schools of an earlier era, day-care programs have a homogenizing effect on children, familiarizing them with experiences and materials that some might not otherwise have. Young children with specific learning disabilities may become visible at an earlier age and be referred for evaluation and special services.

Home-based programs for developmentally disabled or at risk infants and toddlers have much to recommend them. They involve both parent and child at a time when it is most appropriate for the mother to be the "chief programmer." The child is more comfortable and responsive in familiar surroundings and the mother can relate her concerns in privacy. The drawbacks of home-based programs are that a relatively isolated or depressed mother will not receive the support of other mothers. Also, the home programmer must often assume the roles of several professionals; he or she must be a generalist.

Approaches to teaching the young child with emotional and learning disabilities reflect several theoretical and philosophical positions. A program attached to or closely affiliated with a psychiatric clinic or institute will serve the population referred to those professionals; parent and child therapeutic services, as well as educational services, will have a unity that can scarcely be duplicated by public school programs. The clientele of the therapeutic school will tend to remain similar from year to year because of the selection factors operating; in contrast, public schools are obligated under PL 94-142 to serve all children with special needs.

Over the last decade the best teacher training programs have begun, including course work on the origins and nature of handicapping conditions as well as on the educational management of children's disabilities. The choice of materials, the structuring of the learning environment, the pupil-teacher ratio, and behavioral management techniques all assume a sophistication on the part of the educator. This sophistication has been conspicuously lacking among more traditionally trained preschool teachers, except in therapeutic or university-affiliated preschools.

It is especially helpful when the pediatrician, psychiatrist, or other involved professional can visit the school and have a continuing dialogue with the staff. Communication that involves only the transmittal of written information and recommendations to the teacher is less helpful because there is no opportunity for mutual questioning. The therapist or other professional is likewise unable to judge the competence, sensitivity, and teacher-pupil compatibility of a client's teacher. On the other hand, the teacher may be worried that the child's therapist will not recognize the child's problems and may be uncomfortable being observed by a visiting therapist, particularly when there is already a question of whether the placement is appropriate for the child.

Ideally, the teacher can play an important role in helping the young child with emotional difficulties. In contrast to a therapist, the teacher has contact several times a week. If the therapist suggests collaborative efforts, it is critical that there be follow-through. The teacher will be discouraged if the therapist is vague or unresponsive when telephoned with a problem.

Joint conferences of educators, parents, and clinicians at which the child's needs and progress are discussed enhance consistency and ensure appropriate expectations of what can be accomplished. The parent can be reassured that the child is responding and making gains, if that is the case; new strategies can be planned if the child is not progressing as expected. Some parents seem particularly sensitive to the type of program best suited to their child's need; others have preconceived notions about what is best of all children and seem unaware of their own child's particular needs.

Optimally the psychiatrist should be involved early, for instance as a member of an interdisciplinary developmental disabilities team. This would allow early assessment of risk factors for emergency of behavioral and emotional problems and recommendations for anticipatory parental guidance and other preventive measures. Typically, however, psychiatric referral is made only after behavioral problems develop, and managing the child is difficult. Often the referral question is a differential diagnosis between, for example, a language disorder and infantile autism or schizophrenia. Language and speech disorders, as well as other developmental abnormalities, are an integral part of the clinical presentation of many Axis I diagnoses (Cantor 1982; Cantwell et al. 1979; Shapiro and Fish 1969). The referral to the psychiatrist is often linked to two agendas: the manifest and the hidden (Szymanski 1977, 1980). An example of the latter would be a teacher hoping that the "difficult to teach" child with specific developmental disorder will be labeled mentally ill and removed to another class.

An accurate psychiatric diagnostic assessment is necessary, along the lines delineated for mentally retarded children (Szymanski 1980). The psychiatrist should avoid the common mistake of becoming preoccupied with the diagnosis of specific developmental disorder and should focus instead on the assessment of the emotional and behavioral symptoms and their relationship with the disorder. These symptoms may warrant referral for psychotherapy. The indications for pharmacologic treatment of attention deficit, if present, should be carefully assessed.

As is the case with children with a global developmental disability mental retardation, the psychiatric treatment has to be a part of a comprehensive program, uniting behavioral, educational, family, and other interventions (Szymanski 1980). Most importantly, to be effective, the therapist should be a part of an interdisciplinary team comprising educators, parents, and other involved persons.

Clinical Description

Chapter 46

Learning Problems

Learning disabilities is a generic term that refers to a heterogeneous group of disorders manifested by significant difficulties in acquisition and use of listening, speaking, reading, writing, reasoning, or mathematical abilities. These disorders are intrinsic to the individual and presumed to be due to central nervous system dysfunction. Even though a learning disability may occur concomitantly with other handicapped conditions (e.g., sensory impairment, mental retardation, social and emotional disturbances) or environmental influences (e.g., cultural differences, insufficient or inappropriate instructions, psychogenic factors), it is not the direct result of those conditions or influences.

Professionals in special education classify the disabilities either in general, descriptive terms or by identifying the specific learning disabilities. Generalists would label a difficulty with reading as dyslexia, with writing as dysgraphia, and with arithmetic as dyscalculia. On the other hand, a classification of specific learning disabilities would include categories like perceptual, central processing, memory, motor, or language dysfunctions.

The DSM-III (American Psychiatric Association 1980) did not use the educational terminology, but referred to these disabilities as specific developmental disorders. They are subgrouped as developmental reading disorders, developmental arithmetic disorders, developmental language disorders, developmental articulation disorders, or as mixed specific developmental disorders.

DSM-III-R (American Psychiatric Association 1987) maintains the focus on specific developmental disorders and on general areas of difficulty. However, the subgroupings are different than in DSM-III, as shown below.

Academic skills disorders
- Developmental arithmetic disorder
- Developmental expressive writing disorder
- Developmental reading disorder

Language and speech disorders
- Developmental articulation disorder
- Developmental expressive language disorder
- Developmental receptive language disorder

Motor skills disorder
- Developmental coordination disorder

DSM-III-R differs significantly from federal and state classification systems for children and adolescents with learning disabilities. The latter systems state in their definition that such individuals are of at least average intelligence. In DSM-III-R a child who is performing academic skills below his or her intellectual potential is diagnosed as having an academic skills disorder even if the child is mentally retarded.

There are related clinical difficulties that individuals with a specific developmental disorder might have. Some will be hyperactive and/or distractible (attention-deficit hyperactivity disorder). Many show evidence of emotional, social, and family difficulties. The emotional problems may be independent of the academic difficulties, may be a reflection of the frustrations and failures experienced because of the academic difficulties, or may be another reflection of a dysfunctional central nervous system. Concerning this latter group, difficulty with impulsivity and impulse control along with the cognitive difficulties might contribute to the formation of a conduct disorder or a borderline personality disorder.

Thus it is critical to assess the total child or adolescent in his or her total environment before designing a treatment plan. This chapter will focus only on the specific developmental disorders; however, the clinician must be aware of any other related disorders that must also be treated. If the learning problem is secondary, treatment of the primary disorder will have a positive effect on the school-related problem.

As noted above, the primary disorder is the specific learning disability. However, some children or adolescents will be hyperactive and/or distractible. Others will show emotional, social, and family problems.

Specific Learning Disabilities

Learning is a complex function that can be described in terms of input, central integration, storage, and output or expression. A child or adolescent might have difficulty with input (i.e., receiving information into the brain). These difficulties comprise the group of perceptual problems and might involve any of the five senses. Visual and auditory perceptual disabilities are the two most commonly found. A child with a visual-perceptual disability may have difficulty organizing a percept in space; faced with a symbol, the child may reverse it or transpose it. Or the child may have difficulty with spatial relationships, confusing left and right or position in space. Another variety of problems relates to difficulty in distinguishing the significant elements of a scene from the background, referred to as a figure-ground problem. Depth perception may also be affected by visual-perceptual problems.

A child with auditory-perceptual problems may have difficulty distinguishing subtle differences in sounds and may misunderstand what is being said and perhaps respond incorrectly. The child may have difficulty with sound figure-ground or sound depth perception. Some children have difficulty processing sound as quickly as ordinary speech requires; this auditory lag causes them to miss part of what they hear.

In addition to input difficulties, the child may have problems relating to the central integration of information after it has been processed by the brain. The child may assign incorrect sequence to the symbols or have difficulty inferring abstract meaning from the literal percepts. These sequencing and abstraction problems may relate to visual or auditory inputs, or both. Another integrative task is the ability to organize the information being processed. Some may have difficulty organizing parts of information into whole concepts.

Once perceived and integrated, information must be stored, later to be retrieved. Some children have difficulty with memory. In learning disabilities, the storage problem involves only short-term memory (i.e., memory that is retained only as long as one attends to the information). Again, these disabilities can relate to visual, auditory, or both forms of input.

A final area of possible disability involves the process of getting information out of the brain. This output disability may include difficulty in expressing oneself by words, a language disability, or in expressing oneself through muscle activity, a motor disability. Language disabilities usually involve difficulty with demand language. The child may have no difficulty initiating a conversation, but finds it hard to organize thoughts or to find the correct words when language is demanded (e.g., when asked a question).

A child with a motor output disability may have difficulty with gross or fine motor performance. Gross motor problems may cause the child to be clumsy or to have difficulty riding a bike. The child or adolescent with fine motor disabilities will have trouble organizing combinations of muscles to work together. In school, the most commonly noted fine motor disability is in the area of written language. In the same category of disability, the child may have a problem coordinating the many muscles involved in speech production, referred to as dysarthria.

Hyperactivity and/or Distractibility

Of children with specific developmental disabilities, 20 to 40 percent will be hyperactive and/or distractible (Silver 1981). Those who are distractible will consequently have a short attention span. It is significant to note that most children with specific developmental disorder will demonstrate the specific characteristics of learning disabilities but will not be hyperactive and/or distractible.

Hyperactivity.   These children's increased motor activity is physiologically based; it is not an anxiety-based motor response. This is a differentiation of very considerable significance. With the child who utilizes an increase in motor activity as a means of coping with anxiety, the behavior usually relates to a specific life-space experience. The history will suggest that hyperactivity began during the first grade or that it happens only in school but not at home. With physiologically based hyperactivity, there is a chronic and pervasive history of such activity. In some cases, the parent might report that the child kicked more than usual in utero. The child squirmed in his or her mother's arms, rolled in the crib, ran before walking and has been in almost constant motion since birth. This motor hyperactivity does not relate to any specific events. It certainly is not limited to school hours; it occurs all the time and any place.

Distractibility.   Some children with this disorder have difficulty filtering sensory inputs; thus most or all inputs reach the cortex and compete for full attention. The distractibility may relate more to visual inputs, to auditory inputs, or to both. The child with this disability might try to attend and work, but other visual and/or auditory inputs continue to distract. With each distraction, there is the need to reattend. Thus they have a short attention span.

The distractibility caused by external stimuli is clinically different from internal distractibility. This might be daydreaming or cognitive dysinhibition. The latter, seen in pervasive developmental disorder, is characterized by difficulty inhibiting internal thoughts from intruding on external thoughts and behavior. It is helpful to distinguish between distractibility and dysinhibition as a cause for the clinical behavior. The former, as will be discussed later, often improves with the use of psychostimulants; the latter will not.

Social, Emotional, and Family Problems

Because of the specific learning disabilities as well as, with some, the hyperactivity and/or distractibility, these children become frustrated, experience many failures, and have difficulty coping in a number of situations. Thus they often develop social and emotional problems. This child's behavior may lead to stress within the family. All too often, the learning disabilities are not recognized or treated, and the child continues to experience repeated frustrations and failures. Finally, the child develops conspicuous emotional problems and is referred for an evaluation. To view such a child as having a primary emotional difficulty rather than an emotional problem secondary to the unrecognized learning disabilities is to miss a significant etiologic factor and to plan an incomplete treatment program. It is critical to differentiate between a child whose emotional problems are causing the academic difficulty and a child whose emotional problems are a consequence of the academic difficulties.

These children have difficulty with all stages of psychosocial development (Gardner 1969; Silver 1974a; Silver and Brunstetter; 1987). The learning disabilities, hyperactivity, or distractibility may interfere with mastery of many different developmental tasks. The child's difficulties, in turn, weigh heavily on the parents, who may become frustrated, helpless, and dysfunctional (Gardner 1969; Poznanski 1969; Silver 1974b; Silver and Brunstetter 1987).

It is beyond the scope of this chapter to describe the multiple types of social, emotional, and family difficulties. These difficulties have been described elsewhere (Silver 1979; see also Chapter 45).

Briefly, the frustrations and failures can lead to any form of expression. The child might externalize these feelings (causing behavioral problems), might internalize these feelings (causing depression or physiologic symptoms), or might try to manipulate the environment to avoid these feelings (e.g., becoming the person in the class who disrupts lesson plans or who gets removed from class). The social problems can relate to difficulty picking up social cues, resulting in inappropriate behavior and poor peer relationships, or to difficulty doing the activities of their peer group, resulting in a preference for playing with younger children. The stress on the family can result in difficulty with either or both parents or with the siblings. Parents and siblings struggle with their anger, guilt, and sadness.

It is important to be aware of parents' reactions to finding out that their child has a disability (Silver 1974b, 1979; Silver and Brunstetter 1987; Solnit and Stark 1961). Briefly, the parents of these children may go through a normal grief reaction similar, albeit of lesser intensity, to that experienced with a loss by death. They must give up an image of their child; an ambition that may now never be fulfilled. They may indeed react in a manner that tends to alienate their physician. In particular, they may seek a quick cure or magic pill.

As with other grief reactions, denial is often the initial phase of this response. They insist it cannot be true. It must be a mistake. "I don't believe it!" A parent may doubt the professional's competence or castigate him or her. Frequently, another opinion is sought. Unfortunately, while consultation is often useful, doctor shopping for someone who will tell the parents what they want to hear is not. Another form of denial may be the cover-up reaction. One parent, usually the mother, will want to protect the other parent by concealing the results of the studies or by minimizing the problems. Some parents successfully cover up special school problems for years. Sadly, the unknowing parent builds up unrealistic expectations or makes demands that the child cannot fulfill. Children often see through this cover-up and perceive the true reason, that their parents cannot accept them and have to deny them as they are and pretend they are different. The child may react with anger or sadness. To the extent that they feel the parents do not accept them, they will surely have difficulty accepting themselves.

The parental denial stage may be followed by a period of anger. This angry reaction is not uncommon. It may be directed inward or projected outward. On learning of a child's disability, it is normal for parents to feel anger and to express (or think) such sentiments as, "Why me?" or "How could God do this to me?" This initial reaction often reflects feelings of helplessness and frustration.

The initial anger may turn inward; the attack is against the self, resulting in a feeling of depression. Along with this reaction, there is often a feeling of guilt and a belief that it is all "my own fault." A parent may berate oneself, saying "God is punishing me because I didn't follow my doctor's advice," or "I've been given this extra burden to prove my worthiness."

If the depression is allowed to continue, the parent might withdraw from the child or from the other parent just at the time that he or she is most needed. For some parents, the guilt feeling might be an attempt to establish control over a situation that is experienced as hopeless. By attributing the cause to themselves, the parents put into their own hands the power to understand the situation and to control it. The rationale is that if they are not again guilty of transgression, the situation will not happen again.

If, on the other hand, the initial anger is displaced outward, the parent enters into a pattern of blaming or attributing the fault to someone else. Like the guilt reaction, it places responsibility in the hands of humanity and protects one against feelings of helplessness. The parent might blame the obstetrician because he or she did not get to the hospital fast enough or might recall that on one occasion the pediatrician did not see the child when he or she had a high fever and instead prescribed over the phone. This reaction might be generalized to all professionals, who are then considered bunglers, incompetents, and charlatans. The professional may never hear the parent's complaints, but the child may never be allowed to forget them. Such reactions may undermine the child's faith in or respect for the very people the child must turn to for help and for hope.

Some parents may attempt to suppress their feelings of guilt by overprotecting the child. The natural thing to do when a child is hurt is to reach out and protect. This is necessary and helpful. But the goal is to protect the child where the child needs the protecting. Too wide a blanket of protection may cushion the weaknesses, but it also blunts the strengths. Not only does this behavior keep the child immature or delay areas of growth, it also makes the child feel inadequate. The child knows what is happening. When everyone else has a chore to do and he or she does not, when everyone takes turns clearing the table but he or she never has to, the child might conclude that the parents regard the child as inadequate.

Most parents of such handicapped children go through this sequence of denial, anger, and guilt. Parents may need to review the clinical findings again or they may ask repeated questions about their child, as if they have to overinvest in the symptoms and treatment programs before they can accept them. Some parents express relief that they are not directly responsible and that the disorder as described seems reasonable and subject to intervention.

Chapter 47

Developmental Language, Phonologic, and Fluency Problems

Developmental Language Problems

In 1979 the National Institute of Neurological and Communicative Disorders and Stroke estimated that 31 per 1,000 three-year-old children "have some form of language disorder" and 23 per 1,000 "are severely impaired in their language expression [with] their language age less than two thirds of their chronological" and mental ages. The prognosis for many of these children with respect to academic and social functioning is not good (Aram and Nation 1980). By age nine, of 50 children who were language disordered prior to their fifth years, one-half to three-quarters displayed significant reading and expressive language difficulties (Strominger and Bashir 1977). More often than not, some sort of speech production problem accompanies expressive and receptive language disorders. Articulation deficits continue to remain the most prevalent handicapping condition throughout the primary school years (Schwartz 1983). Many children who present with developmental speech or language deficits in the preschool years become the learning-disordered and emotionally disordered youngsters that special educators, psychologists, and speech and language pathologists encounter during the elementary and secondary school years (Aram et al. 1984; Wallach and Liebergott 1984). The emotional problems displayed by this population are generally secondary to language-learning problems. They often surface as a result of frustrations and anxieties that arise in response to the taxing demands of and failures in the academic world. Estimates of the number of identified language and learning-disordered children in the United States have ranged as high as 14 percent for school-aged children. Only 1.4 to 2.6 percent of those are in special classes receiving the help they need (Gaddes 1976). These numbers do not reflect those children who receive help privately, nor those who have not been classified or who have been mainstreamed.

Definition

To be able to recognize the presence of a speech and/or language disorder, a definition of what language is will be helpful. The definition below has been adopted by the American Speech-Language and Hearing Association (1983).

Language is a complex and dynamic system of conventional symbols that is used in various modes for thought and communication. Contemporary views of human language hold that:

- language evolves within specific historical, social, and cultural contexts;
- language, as rule governed behavior, is described by at least five parameters—phonologic, morphologic, syntactic, semantic, and pragmatic;
- language learning and use are determined by the interaction of biological, cognitive, psychosocial, and environmental factors;
- effective use of language of communication requires a broad understanding of human interaction including such associated factors as non-verbal cues, motivation, and sociocultural roles. (p. 44)

Several implications follow from the above definition. First, although language is generally thought of as occurring through an oral mode, this description does not preclude gestural systems.

Language variation resulting from social, cultural, and geographic differences is acknowledged. Thus differences in learners and human behavior is rule governed. It is deviation from expected and acceptable patterns of communicative behavior that signals the presence of a disorder. Deviations in sound production (phonology) in the form of utterances (syntax), in the meaning system of lexical items and connected speech (semantics), and in the use of language in social situations (pragmatics) signal the presence of a speech or language disorder. Any one or combination of the components of the language system can be affected.

Articulation disorders, while frequently viewed as a separate category of communicative problem, often occur in conjunction with a language disorder. Most school-aged children who present with speech sound production problems reveal no clear-cut etiology of physical problems. In recent years they have been described as displaying a disorder of the phonologic component of the language system.

Developmental Phonologic Disorders

Developmental phonologic disorders comprise the majority of communication problems in children. They can arise from obvious organic factors (e.g., cleft palate and other orofacial anomalies), neurologic deficits (e.g., cerebral palsy, dysarthria, apraxia), or sensory deficits (e.g., deafness, hearing impairment). A large percentage of speech sound production disorders, however, have no clear-cut etiology, and it is that category of developmental articulation disorder that will be discussed here.

A speech sound production disorder frequently accompanies a developmental language disorder. Conversely, subtle language or learning problems often accompany developmental phonologic disorders. Indeed, it is typically the case that a child's speech unintelligibility rather than a language deficit is of primary concern to parents. It is not unusual to find that language deficits become apparent as a speech sound production disorder is remediated and a child's speech becomes more intelligible.

The philosophy of assessment and intervention for developmental phonologic disorders has shifted in recent years from a phoneme-by-phoneme error analysis model to a developmental process model. The transition in approaches has evolved from the plethora of research in normal and disordered child language and from the recognition that articulatory production, like other aspects of complex human behavior, is rule governed and patterned. Adherence to the philosophy of one or the other of these models has significantly different implications for assessment and intervention of articulation disorders.

A clinical rule of thumb for judging the adequacy of a child's articulatory system is that by age three the child should be intelligible to persons other than just members of the immediate family. Typical complaints of parents of speech-disordered children between the ages of two-and-one-half to four are "she speaks like a foreigner." "No one but me can understand him." "All the other children speak so clearly and we hardly understand her." If there is parental concern about a child's speech intelligibility, that child should be assessed by a speech and language pathologist. The parents should not be told to wait, that their child will grow out of it. It is more often than not the case that children with developmental articulation problems do not grow out of their speech difficulties. Typically these children present with a history of delayed onset of speech and language but little else that will shed light on etiology. Their speech production may be perceived as too rapid. Often production of single words is more intelligible than connected speech. Parents feel that their speech-disordered child understands everything and only presents difficulty with sound production. The frequency with which young severely speech-impaired children display language disorders, when components of language other than phonology can be measured, is in sharp contrast to initial impressions of the presence of just an articulation disorder (Aram and Nation 1975; Aram et al. 1984; Denkla 1979; McReynolds and Elbert 1982).

Disorders of Fluency

Stuttering is a disorder that has its onset between the ages of two and six years. Many normally developing children experience a period of disfluency during the early language development years. Thus it is important to be able to discriminate stuttering behavior from normal disfluencies and to be able to recognize the warning signs that characterize childhood stuttering.

A recent publication of the Speech Foundation of America (1981, pp. 3–5) lists eight "warning signs" that are characteristic of the development of stuttering. They are listed below.

1. "Multiple repetitions" of words, fillers ("uh, um"), and the first syllables of words.
2. Insertion of the "shwa vowel ("guh, guh, goat" or "uh, uh, over" rather than go, go, goat or oh, oh, over).
3. Prolongations of sounds at the beginning of words.
4. Tremors around the mouth and jaw.
5. Increase in pitch and loudness of voice as sounds are prolonged.
6. Signs of struggle or tension as a child begins to speak.
7. Signs of fear in the child's face in anticipation of difficulty producing a word.
8. Avoidance of particular words and an increase in the number of pauses during speaking.

Any combination of these warning signs indicate the possibility of a real stuttering problem and the need for clinical evaluation.

All speakers are disfluent from time to time, but not all disfluent speakers are stutterers. Clinicians and researchers agree that it is the "broken word" not the "broken or repeated phrases or sentences" that are characteristic of stuttering behavior (Freeman 1983; Van Riper 1982). Van Riper proposed the following definition of stuttering behavior: "Stuttering occurs when the forward flow of speech is interrupted by a motorically disrupted sound, syllable, or word or by the speaker's reaction thereto" (p. 15). Thus it is not just the speech of a stutterer, but also the concomitant motor behaviors and facial expressions in response to listener reactions, and the stutterer's reaction to his or her own speech, that constitute stuttering behaviors. These motor behaviors and facial expressions tend to occur in older (school-age and above) individuals.

Stuttering, or disfluent speech, may accompany a language or speech disorder. Similarly, a stutterer may have mild articulation problems as well as a subtle language disorder. For this reason, it is essential that a child who is referred for a disfluency problem be given a comprehensive speech and language evaluation.

Assessment Issues and Principles

The etiology of stuttering is unclear, but the disorder is considered to arise from a combination of biologic, neurologic, and social variables. Current views hold that the cause of stuttering may be attributed to organic factors such as a hereditary predisposition (Andrews and Harris 1964; Kidd 1977; Kidd and Records 1979), or possibly a lack of strong cerebral dominance for speech (Brady and Berson 1975; Curry and Gregory 1967; Sommers et al. 1975). There is recent evidence that stutterers have a deficit in the coordination of timing and intensity of the musculature used for phonation and articulation (Conture et al. 1977; Freeman 1979; Hillman and Gilbert 1977; Zimmerman 1980). Stuttering has also been viewed as learned behavior that develops as a function of a complex system of reinforcement of normal disfluencies. Combinations of classical and operant conditioning (Brutten and Shoemaker 1967) and reduction of anxiety in conflict situations (Sheehan 1958; Wishner 1950, 1952) are posited as causal and maintaining factors in the development of disfluent speech. Finally, stuttering behavior is influenced by situational variables (e.g., environmental stress), communicative responsibility, and linguistic factors (e.g., particular words or sounds). Given the variety of factors that may be related to any individual's stuttering problem, Freeman (1983) proposed investigating four different levels of cause as part of the assessment and intervention process:

1. The underlying cause(s)—the genetic, neurological, physiological, and psychological factors that may predispose a child to fluency disruption problem (Conture 1982).
2. The environmental cause(s)—the . . . factors associated with the onset and development of stuttering symptoms.
3. The precipitating cause(s)—when, where, and under what conditions moments of stuttering are likely to occur.
4. The vocal tract cause(s)—the vocal tract events that generate the disrupted speech patterns. (p. 678)

As with assessment of any communicative behavior, part of the intake process will be comprised of obtaining complete historical and developmental information. In addition, because of the role of environmental influences and the fluctuating nature of this disorder, it is essential to learn about parental perceptions of the disorder, to learn about the course of the disorder, and to obtain a clear picture of the family dynamics and family communication patterns. Collection and analysis of a language sample will yield information not only about the overall state of a child's speech and language skills, but also about the location, type, and consistency of stuttering events in the speech signal. A variety of situations for communicating should be constructed. This affords a clinician opportunities to observe variations in fluency as a function of differing contexts. Communicative situations should vary along a continuum of least stressful (i.e., little speaker responsibility) to more stressful (i.e., increased speaker responsibility). The Stocker (1976) probe technique is an assessment tool that has just such a pragmatic variable built into it. Careful analysis and a tally of the number of within-word disfluencies across a variety of situations is a telling figure. Three or more within-word disfluencies per 100 is suggestive of a stuttering problem (Conture 1982).

Chapter 48

Specific Mathematics Disorder

Primary mathematical disorders (dyscalculia), estimated to occur in 6 percent of the population with normal intelligence, are due to reading-language, perceptual, memory deficits, and/or disorders in quantitative thinking. Language ability is seen as a strong correlate of mathematical understanding, or, as Cohn (1971) suggested, mathematical skills are a subset of language functioning. Johnson and Mykelbust (1967) stated that

> There are inner, receptive and expressive aspects of math language as with other forms of symbolic behavior, a child first assimilates and integrates non verbal experiences, then learns to associate numerical symbols with the experience and finally expresses ideas of quantity, space and order by using the language of math. (p. 245)

More than in the case of reading, mathematical problems are often related to inadequate instruction, in which case there is a poor match between the learner, the method of teaching, and the ecology of mathematics learning (Wiederholt et al. 1978). Prerequisite skills are not mastered adequately to provide a base for more advanced learning. Affective factors (e.g., anxiety, self-confidence, motivation) also play a role. While these instructional and emotional issues are important variables, a primary math disability is, in most cases, intrinsic to the child.

Difficulties with language or symbolic thought interfere directly with comprehension and use of abstract mathematical concepts. The need to generate formal hierarchies and principles and relate concepts to their representation in the number system (e.g., 1-1 correspondence, seriation, flexibility, reversibility, conservation) is central.

Language problems typically increase with grade level as vocabulary, syntactic complexity, and the length and structure of mathematical problems change. Additionally, mathematical terms have limited redundancy; complex concepts are contained in few words so that semantic understanding depends on specific and technical knowledge. There is little opportunity to utilize context, so helpful in reading of content-related material. Typical syntactic difficulties relate to changes in active-passive voice. For example, at the elementary level, difficulty with division is seen to be related to the fact that mathematical expressions are stated in the passive voice (Sharma 1981).

Cognitive-perceptual delays (e.g., auditory processing and memory problems) interfere with mental computation and maintenance of counting and temporal order. Speed and accuracy of processing as well as retention in short-term memory is critical for problem solving (e.g., retaining numerical information while focusing on specific operations). Visual-perceptual problems take the form of reversals, rotations that interfere with written work, and with perception of nonverbal information related to shape, size, length, temporal (first, last), spatial (under, between) order, and directionality.

As in all other areas of learning, interference with concentration, retention, and carefulness will also affect mathematics performance. Thus clinically significant depression, anxiety, and attention-deficit hyperactivity disorder might show secondary effects on mathematics test results and competence.

Chapter 49

Evaluation and Treatment: A Psychiatric Perspective

During the evaluation, the data from the history obtained from the parents may begin to suggest a disorder of development. Descriptions of behavior or inconsistencies in the child's performance or delays in motor or language development should alert the clinician to the possibility of specific learning disabilities. Continuous increased motor activity might reflect hyperactivity. A short attention span might be caused by distractibility. Behavioral problems beginning with the first year of school associated with poor academic performance should suggest the possibility that the emotional difficulties might be related to a learning disability.

When the clinician meets the child at an evaluation, the child's behavior in the waiting room may give the first clinical clue to hyperactivity or distractibility. As one walks to the room, it is sometimes possible to note gross motor difficulties, an awkward gait, or some difficulty walking up or down stairs. Observations during the session also might suggest a learning disability (Silver 1974a). The following represent some clues to categorizing the problem for clinical use.

Input Disabilities

If a child appears to be using any one sensory modality beyond what might be age appropriate, one needs to ask why. Possibly the child who uses vision predominantly has auditory deficits, or the child who uses mainly auditory inputs to attend and relate has visual deficits. If a child prefers tactile or taste or smell, the clinician must consider that one possibility might be visual and/or auditory deficits.

A child with visual-perceptual disabilities might have difficulty organizing activities in the diagnostic session. The child might bump into things or knock them over. If one asks the child to do one of the games requiring placing geometric figures into spaces or concentric cups into one another, these difficulties might become more apparent. If one wishes, the child could be asked to copy a circle, square, rectangle, and diamond, or given the Bender-Gestalt Test. Some children with visual-perceptual problems walk about the room apparently talking to themselves. They seem to subvocalize, naming objects or saying what they are doing as a means of getting the thoughts in through the ears to compensate for uncertain visual inputs.

Auditory perception problems might be discerned if the child misunderstands comments or questions and seems to be confused by what is being said. Thus the child might ignore the question or comment or might answer a question slightly incorrectly. This behavior might be seen as resistance or avoidance; it should also be viewed as a possible clinical clue of a learning disability.

Integrative Disabilities

The child might have difficulty organizing activities or using play objects. The child might tell you something that appears confusing because the sequencing of the events is wrong. Games that require moving objects along a specific sequence (e.g., Candyland, Chutes and Ladders) might be difficult. The child might have difficulty abstracting concepts or learning new games or activities. Such behavior might be misunderstood as evidence of a thinking disorder.

Memory Disabilities

This type of disability is more difficult to observe. The child might have difficulty remembering how to do an activity or game. If the history and clinical observations suggest such disabilities, one can set up various games or activities requiring short-term memory (e.g., showing several objects, then covering them and asking the child to recall them, or saying several words or numbers and asking the child to repeat them).

Output Disabilities

Some children with expressive language difficulties flood the room with conversation. It is as though they talk continuously to prevent the other person from asking or saying something. If one tries to ask a question, the child might not answer or will answer in a few hesitant words. Children might ask to have the questions repeated or might repeat statements to themselves to organize their thoughts prior to responding. Such behavior might be incorrectly seen as echolalia, or might be misinterpreted as autistic-like behavior. Older children or adolescents might begin to talk about something, then, in midparagraph, stop and say, "Oh, forget it." On detailed questioning, these children might admit that they forgot what they were trying to say. Too embarrassed to admit this, they simply say, "Oh, forget it."

Differential Diagnosis

A careful, detailed developmental history is most important to rule out a primary psychiatric disorder with the effect on learning. If the history plus clinical assessment suggests a specific developmental disorder, it is important to differentiate it from other clinical conditions. The presenting academic difficulties might initially be attributed to mental retardation. Children with maturation lags in motor or language development usually present with the same academic problems plus, possibly, hyperactivity and distractibility. The perceptual distortions and thinking disorders that occur in pervasive developmental disorder might appear initially to be clinical evidence of a specific learning disability. It may not be until the full clinical picture develops that the correct diagnosis becomes apparent. Some children with these disorders, when evaluated at ages one to three, resemble an autistic child. The underlying learning and language disabilities interfere with normal psychosocial development. Especially when under stress, these children appear to function as though they were in the early stages of establishing object constancy. By age three they usually achieve object constancy, but they remain psychosocially immature. With children who have a degenerative disease of the central nervous system (e.g., Schilder's disease), the earliest clinical findings are often a loss of memory and cognitive skills. These clinical findings start in early latency. The associated academic problems may initially be diagnosed as a specific developmental disorder, the fuller picture of degeneration of the central nervous system only becoming apparent with time.

Once these disorders are suspected, specific studies will confirm their presence and clarify treatment needs. The primary clinician needs to make the necessary referrals and coordinate the integration of the findings into a final diagnosis and treatment plan.

Psychological Testing

An intellectual assessment can rule out mental retardation. The child with specific learning disabilities will do well on subtests that utilize the areas of learning strengths, but will do poorly on subtests requiring the use of areas of learning weakness. Thus a subtest scatter might suggest this disorder. For example, a child with visual-perceptual, visual-integrative, and visual-motor disabilities might score below average on subtests requiring such skills (e.g., Wechsler Intelligence Scale for Children [WISC-R] performance scores), but might score well above average on subtests not requiring such skills (e.g., WISC-R verbal scores).

Specific visual-motor tests can be given. Projective tests might help to rule out a thinking disorder. Neuropsychological tests might also clarify the areas of disability.

Educational Evaluation

If one suspects a learning disability, an educational diagnostician can do a learning disability evaluation to clarify if such exists and, if so, which ones. These data, along with the psychological evaluation, can be invaluable in understanding the observations made in the clinical evaluation session and in finalizing the clinical diagnosis.

Neurologic Evaluation

Clinical neurologic evaluations are frequently useful in diagnosis. However, it should be kept in mind that many of these children have no evidence of neurologic deficits other than soft signs; that is, there are no clear clinical findings (hard signs). However, information from the educational and psychological test materials plus specific clinical neurologic findings suggest that the brain is not functioning normally. There is no specific electroencephalogram (EEG) pattern that would establish the diagnosis.

TREATMENT

The term *specific development disability* may suggest that there are only school-related problems. However, the pathologic processes underlying specific learning disabilities often interfere with all aspects of psychosocial development as well as with functioning in the family and with peer interactions and activities. It is critical to address all aspects of the child's or adolescent's life when designing a treatment plan. The clinician will have to work with the school professionals to develop the necessary educational programs and interventions. Family education and counseling are essential. Individual-dynamic, behavioral, group, or family therapy may be needed if emotional, social, or family problems exist.

The School Environment

If the school concurs that the disabilities are of such nature and severity that the child cannot, in his or her best interests, be maintained in a regular school program without special help, the child will be classified as learning disabled (under PL 94-142, Education for All Handicapped Children Act).

Several kinds of programs are available. Which one is selected will depend on the degree of the child's disability and level of current academic performance and the availability of programs.

The best program offers what the child needs academically and behaviorally in the least restrictive environment possible. The least restrictive environment is not necessarily the program closest to a regular program. For some children and adolescents, the least restrictive environment that will do the job might be the most restrictive environment available. For example, a child with multiple learning disabilities who is several years behind in basic skills might feel most relaxed and safe in a small, self-contained, special education classroom.

There are several levels of placement. Briefly, the child or adolescent can be in a regular classroom program with a daily half-hour or hour of supplemental special education help. The program at the second level of intensity is often called mainstreaming. The child or adolescent is assigned basically to a resource room staffed with a special educator, then mainstreamed into regular classroom programs for as much of the day as the child can handle. If a yet more intensive, third-level program is needed, the child might be assigned full-time to a self-contained classroom.

Work with the Family

The primary clinician or another member of the treatment team must educate the family. Parents need to understand their child's learning disabilities as well as their learning abilities. They must know how to build on strengths rather than magnify weaknesses. Such knowledge helps them plan home activities, chores, outside activities, sports, and camps in a way that is most likely to be successful and to lead to positive psychological and social growth.

Educational family counseling.   The full evaluation should be reviewed in detail with the parents. They need to know their child's intellecutal potential, level of academic performance, and why the child is underachieving. Any existing emotional, social, or family problems must be clarified. A treatment plan should be presented, clarifying what the parents must do. Next, the full evaluation should be shared with the child. Children must understand their academic difficulties. They are confused about their lack of success and might fear that they are bad or dumb. They must also understand the treatment plan.

Parents have a critical role to play in helping their child or adolescent (Silver 1984). The specific learning disabilities will be apparent at home. Parents need to tell their child that they understand. They should reassure their daughter or son that they are glad that she or he is getting help. They should ask for their child's own advice on how they can help best. With knowledge, parents can best avoid problems and assist their child. For example, in talking to a child with an auditory figure-ground problem (i.e., difficulty selecting what sounds to focus on), they may need to establish eye contact before speaking. They will have to go into the room where the child is and call out the child's name, speaking to the child only after she or he has looked up. If the child has difficulty with sequencing (i.e., getting the steps of a task in the right order), they might need to help their child get started. They do not do the job for the child, but help the child get organized. If they want the table set, for example, they might put a sample setting down (plate here; fork, knife, and spoon there; glass here). If their child has trouble dressing in the morning because it is hard to figure out what goes first, a parent can place the clothes out on the bed in sequence. If the child has fine motor problems and difficulty with buttons or shoelaces or slipover tops, Velcro fasteners or loafers might be tried. Such behaviors communicate acceptance and encourage independence and growth.

Parents might make a list of the areas in which their child is strong and weak. Next to each strength, they can write out all of the things the child is capable of doing. Next to the weaknesses, they can write out all of the things that they notice that a disability interferes with. Then, by thinking creatively, they can build on the child's strengths while helping to compensate for weaknesses. For example, what household chores can the child do? If motor problems result in frequent accidents when the child takes out the trash, can some other task be assigned? The special educator might help by offering suggestions. The goal is to find chores rather than to excuse the child from family participation.

If the parents want to take a more active part in helping their child work on the areas of disability, they should consider using normal household activities to reinforce learning. The clinician cannot write out a recipe for helping each child or adolescent, but can suggest a way of thinking. Many kitchen activities, for example, require reading, measuring, counting, and following directions. These provide good practice in sequencing. Chopping and stirring make good gross motor exercises. Auditory memory can be worked on when a parent takes the child shopping. At first, while near the correct shelf, the parent can ask the child to pick up one item (e.g., a can of peas). Later, the parent can make it two or three items. Still later, the parent can make it an item an aisle over, then two aisles. Parents can think of many other situations that come up in their daily life where the child can practice the skills that the child lacks.

The same technique can be applied outside the home in sports, at clubs, and in other activities. Each sport requires different strengths. If the child has sequencing, fine motor, and visual-motor disabilities, games with elaborate rules or those that require eye-hand coordination skills (e.g., baseball and basketball) will be difficult. The child's poor performance also adds to the social and peer problems. But let us say that the child has good gross motor strengths. Swimming, diving, soccer, horseback riding, skiing, bowling, or certain field and track events, all of which rely on gross motor abilities, may be successes. The same 10-year-old who stopped playing baseball because he could not catch, throw, or hit well, and who did no better at basketball, might do very well in soccer or might become an excellent swimmer. The child may find success and peer acceptance with these sports.

Some children find all sports difficult. But it might be possible to improve some of the required skills through practice. Most of the child's age peers won't take the time or have the patience to help. But a parent or an older sibling can go into the yard, or any place else where the other kids won't see, and practice catching, throwing, or hitting.

Because of difficulty following directions or because they simply play so badly, some children never learn the basic rules of a game. Once again, someone in the family may need to sit down and teach the child how to play baseball or hopscotch from the ground up, going back over the rules until the child catches on.

This approach can be used with all of the child's outside activities. The goal for parents is to build on strengths rather than to magnify weaknesses. Picture a 10-year-old with fine motor, sequencing, and visual-motor disabilities at a Cub Scout or an Indian Princess meeting. Everyone is cutting out a pumpkin or a turkey, and this child's is not good. Everybody laughs at the cutouts. With another failure, the child doesn't want to go to any more meetings. But if the activity leaders had known what the child could do, they could have tapped the gross motor abilities the child does have. The child could hand out the paper, squirt the glue, or smear the paste. Failure could be turned into success. Similarly, on parent night, this child shouldn't have to demonstrate knot tying; the child could march, carrying the flag.

When such children go to the local youth center, they should not wander around and select what they want to do at random. Whether they should be in arts and crafts or photography depends on what they are able to do reasonably well. Many crafts require good visual perception and eye-hand coordination, whereas many aspects of photography involve gross motor skills. Parents must plan ahead for those occasions.

The club, group, or activity leaders can be helpful if informed. Such people should understand that this child does not always hear every instruction given; they must know in advance to check with the child and repeat things if necessary. The child may appear quiet or indifferent because language does not come easily. The leaders need to understand that the child is not mentally retarded or lazy. The disability is simply invisible. The same advice holds for Sunday school and religious education programs. The staff must know all about the child so that they can design appropriate classroom and activity programs.

Choosing a camp, whether day or sleep-away, requires the same attention. Parents may need to consider a camp designed for children with special needs, or they might be able to use a carefully selected regular camp. They need to think about whether this child can handle a large or small camp. What strengths and abilities does the child have, and how do they match with the offerings of a camp? Some camps focus on drama or arts and crafts. Are these activities that will build on strengths or is the child likely to fail? Some camps are sports-oriented and competitive. Woe to the child who drops a ball and causes his or her cabin to lose the game! But there are camps that do focus on noncompetitive activities or on gross motor sports. A clumsy, nonathletic son or daughter might do very well at a camp that focuses on horseback riding or on waterfront activities. Swimming, rowing, and sailing are gross motor activities that require minimal eye-hand coordination.

Before selecting a camp, parents need to talk with the director at length. Is that person flexible? Can the director describe programs that might work for their particular child? They should not hesitate to educate the counselors, either. The counselors will appreciate the information, and the child will benefit from the understanding of such important people.

The above examples are meant to illustrate a style of thinking and problem solving that can be helpful to families. The primary clinician must be sure that the parents know their child's areas of learning disabilities and learning abilities so that they can use these strategies to build on these strengths to maximize psychosocial growth and peer successes.

Psychological Interventions

Types of intervention. It is critical to differentiate any emotional, social, or family problems as primary or secondary. Are they causing the academic difficulties or are they a consequence of the academic difficulties and the resulting frustrations and failures. If they are secondary, the initial phase of treatment should focus on the cause (i.e., establishing the necessary educational programs and educating the individual and family). If the secondary psychological problems have become so established that they now have a life of their own, they must also be handled.

If intrapsychic difficulties exist, psychoanalytically oriented psychotherapy may be necessary. If the patterns of learned or reinforced behaviors are dysfunctional or if performance anxiety is high, a behavioral mangaement plan or cognitive or behavioral therapy approach may be needed. If interpersonal skills are poor, group therapy or a social learning skills group might be useful. If a parent has developed dysfunctional patterns for handling the child, parent counseling may be helpful. If there is family dysfunction, family therapy might be indicated. Often a multimodal approach is used. Whichever interventions are needed, the primary clinician must coordinate the efforts with the school and provide initial educational family counseling.

If the child has emotional problems that are secondary to the frustrations and failures experienced due to the specific developmental disorder, psychotherapy alone may not succeed. One or two hours a week of therapy cannot undo 20 or more hours a week of school experiences that reinforce the poor self-image or cause anxiety or depression. The educational needs must be addressed. Even if psychotherapy is needed, it might be better to delay starting until all negotiations with the school are complete. To start before this is done might give the school personnel grounds for saying that the academic problems are emotionally based and thus not the school's responsibility.

The therapeutic process. If any therapy is initiated—individual, cognitive, behavior, group, family—the clinician must understand the learning disabilities and how they might interfere with the therapeutic process. This concern is especially true if the disabilities are in the auditory and language areas, and the therapeutic interaction primarily requires listening and talking. A child who also is distractible will have further problems attending.

If the child appears to misunderstand the clinician's comments or questions or has difficulty with word finding or organizing thoughts, the clinician should explain that he or she understands the disabilities. Then a therapeutic alliance can be established by asking the child how the clinician can help by modifying the style of interaction. One might need to talk slower, to make shorter or more simple comments, or to use paper and pencil to draw illustrations.

Other children might have difficulty when play is used as a vehicle for therapy. Reading cards or instructions, following sequences, or doing motor tasks (e.g., building blocks) might be difficult.

Before the therapist doing dynamic therapy concludes that the child is blocking or resisting, or the behavioral therapist decides that the child is not responding to a reinforcement system, the possible interference of the learning disabilities should be considered and can suggest models for interacting or doing tasks.

Pharmacotherapy. If the child with a specific development disorder is also hyperactive or distractible, stimulant medication will be of help. Such medication will make the child more available for attending and learning and may improve some forms of fine motor difficulties; however, it does not treat the underlying learning disabilities (Gadow 1983). Educational therapy is still essential.

Piracetam has been suggested as having a specific ability to improve cognitive and memory functioning (Rudel and Helfgott 1984; Simeon et al. 1980; Wilsher et al. 1979). As of the time of preparing this chapter, the data remain unclear.

Controversial Therapies

There are several to be considered.

Patterning. This is a neurophysiologic approach to stimulating and retraining the central nervous system developed by Doman and Delacato (1968). It has not been found to improve the basic learning disabilities (American Academy of Pediatrics 1982; Silver 1987).

Ophthalmology versus optometry. The clinican and families may be confused by the different views on treating learning disabilities held by ophthalmologists and by optometrists. Ophthalmologists and optometrists believe that when a child or adolescent with learning disabilities is referred to them they should check for problems with vision (e.g., nearsightedness, farsightedness, astigmatism), for eye-muscle imbalance, and for any ocular disease. If they find any of these problems, they treat it. The ophthalmologists believe that the child should be referred to a special educator or some other appropriate specialist for treatment of his or her learning disabilities. The optometrists believe they can treat the learning disability.

Optometrists evaluate the child's visual abilities and may prescribe glasses or the use of visual-training or eye-muscle training techniques. They may also use a developmental vision approach for treating the learning problems (Carlson and Greenspoon 1968). They feel that learning in general and reading in particular require high levels of visual perception. They point out that visual-perceptual processes are also related to the child's sensory-motor coordination. To correct visual-perceptual problems, they employ a wide variety of educational and sensory-motor perceptual training techniques in an attempt to correct educational problems in children. Several reviews question the effectiveness of these approaches (e.g., Metzger and Werner 1984).

The American Academy of Pediatrics, the American Academy of Ophthalmology and Otolaryngology, and the American Association of Ophthalmology issued a joint statement that criticized this approach (American Academy of Pediatrics 1972). This statement emphasized the need for a multidisciplinary approach to learning disabilities. No one professional can evaluate and treat the whole child. The statement further cautioned that there are no peripheral eye defects that can produce dyslexia and associated learning disabilities. This position statement was futher supported by the American Academy for Pediatric Ophthalmology and Strabismus (American Academy of Ophthalmology 1984).

Cerebellar-vestibular therapy. Dr. Harold Levinson published several books in which he suggested that some forms of dyslexia are caused by cerebellar-vestibular dysfunction (Levinson 1981, 1984). He proposed that this disability can be corrected by using medication such as those used for motion sickness. He reported that the dyslexia improves or disappears in patients on this medication. His theory and methodology are in question (Silver 1987). Polatajko (1985) failed to find a relationship between vestibular function and learning disabilities.

Applied kinesiology. Dr. Carl A. Ferreri, a chiropractor, stated that learning disabilities are due to the shift in position of two cranial bones, the sphenoid and the temporal, resulting in an ocular muscle imbalance called an "ocular lock" and other nervous system dysfunctions (Ferreri and Wainwright 1984). They propose treatments focused on correcting these shifts in anatomic position. This approach is new and not yet fully researched. There is no research basis for the theory or claims. Many of the anatomical concepts stated in the book are not held by information in anatomical texts.

Megavitamins. The use of massive doses of vitamins to treat emotional and thinking disorders began with the treatment of schizophrenia. Two researchers, Osmond and Smythies, suggested that schizophrenia was caused by an improper breakdown of certain chemicals normally found in the brain (Hoffer and Osmond 1960; Hoffer et al. 1954). Hoffer and Osmond proposed that administration of large quantities of certain B vitamins could stop this faulty breakdown. To date, no documented biochemical studies on schizophrenic patients have confirmed this theory. After reviewing the history and literature relating to this subject, the members of an American Psychiatric Association (1973) task force concluded that there is no valid basis for the use of megavitamins in the treatment of mental disorders. The American Academy of Pediatrics (1976) has also reported no validity to this concept.

Cott (1971, 1985) suggested megavitamin treatment for children with learning disabilities. His conclusion that megavitamins can help these children has not been confirmed by other researchers. Despite these negative results, the approach remains popular.

Trace elements. Certain trace elements (e.g., copper, zinc, manganese, magnesium, chromium), along with more common elements (e.g., calcium, potassium, sodium, and iron), are necessary nutrients—that is, their presence is essential for maintenance of normal physiologic function. Deficiency in specific trace elements has been proposed as a cause of learning disabilities (Cott 1971). In many parts of the United States, children are treated with trace-element replacement therapy. To date, no research has shown that such treatment can correct learning disabilities.

Hypoglycemia. It has been proposed that learning disabilities may be secondary to hypoglycemia (Cott 1971). The proposed treatment is to place the child on a hypoglycemic diet. There are no research findings that establish hypoglycemia as a cause of learning disabilities.

Allergic reactions. Several researchers have suggested that some types of learning disabilities may result from an allergic sensitivity of the central nervous system to specific foods. They discuss specific test procedures for establishing this as a possible factor. The relationship between food allergies and learning disabilities is still under investigation. No consistent findings have been established, nor are there consistent findings that reliably connect a variety of yeasts such as *Candida* to learning problems.

Chapter 50

Evaluation and Treatment of Reading, Learning, and Mathematics Disabilities: A Special Education Perspective

Although diagnosis traditionally refers to the process of observing symptoms and symptom clusters to classify a dysfunction, within the field of special education diagnosis is used to describe a broader process and serves as a generic referent for identification, evaluation, and placement (Kauffman and Hallahan 1974).

The purpose of an educational evaluation is to provide data on cognitive and academic functioning to confirm the existence of a problem and to understand the nature, extent, and specificity of the difficulties. Attention is given to interpretation of characteristics, level of performance, learning style, and patterns evident within the framework of the child's "current ecology" (Salvia and Ysseldyke 1981). In addition, developmental and psychosocial data are considered.

Such evaluative information provides the basis for decision making regarding school, classroom placement, and instructional and therapeutic needs. The special educator compiles and interprets test findings, which include both normative and qualitative data, and writes a prescription or set of guidelines. These data are utilized by classroom and remedial teachers for "diagnostic-prescriptive teaching," a model in which instructional techniques and materials are matched to the academic skill profile of the child so that instruction is appropriate to the child's needs.

Classroom teachers and school psychologists are the primary sources of referral for testing because they are in the best position to detect behavioral problems or difficulties related to school learning. Referrals for the preschool child are more likely to come from other professionals, such as speech and language pathologists and physicians, or from parents because speech and language delays are the first warning signs of problems in this age group.

Diagnostic information should be shared with parents so that the recommendations and goals can be established and operationalized. Adequate conference time and follow-up is critical and must be geared to meeting the child's and family's needs. Team conferences involving those professionals who participate in or are part of the diagnostic process are most effective.

The special educator is someone with a master's degree or higher, with specific training in reading and learning disabilities. This training allows one to work as a classroom teacher, resource room specialist, or remedial teacher, or as part of the evaluative team. As such, the special educator is in an excellent position to coordinate services and to provide ongoing monitoring of a child's progress and placement in school. In fact, the special educator is often the one to provide the primary treatment, and only when learning problems become more complex are other professionals involved.

While children with reading and learning problems are evaluated with a broad array of test measures, the approach to test use and interpretation reflects to some degree the varying theoretical positions in use. For example, testing "processes" or "abilities" (e.g., linguistic, perceptual, memory) that are said to interfere with or underlie academic difficulties is one approach. Other approaches focus on testing achievement of specific skills within the content areas. This ties in more closely to the development of instructional guidelines within the skill areas. While there remains a lack of research to support the efficacy of developing instruction to parallel diagnostic findings specifically within the process areas, there is evidence that these processes are involved in the acquisition of reading and mathematics skills. Therefore, if used cautiously within an academic context, this information can guide instruction.

Relying solely on either approach tends to provide a fractional view of the child's performance and behavior. It would follow then that a psychoeducational evaluation should utilize a model that addresses both sets of data (i.e., looks at the child's performance on a range of test types and formats). Along with qualitative information, a more comprehensive view of the child surfaces. Instructional plans are then developed based on this diagnostic information and serve as an initial guide for intervention. Plans need ongoing modification within two- to three-month periods as teaching and maturation takes place.

Test Measures

Cognitive, language, and academic tests are standardized approaches to the measurement of skills and abilities. Most of these tests have been developed for normal populations so that modifications are often needed when working with children with reading and learning problems. Such changes include adapting time constraints, directions, and demonstration items appropriately. Since test norms are not applicable under such conditions, it becomes especially important to compile sufficient qualitative and comparative data on this population.

The following provides a brief guide to some of the more frequently used assessment instruments. It will be apparent that the special educator shares some of these instruments with other professionals. However, many tests have been developed specifically to address academic and skill development, which is the special province of the special educator.

Standardized Tests

Standardized tests provide normative data (i.e., individual scores are compared to a normative sample) by translating standardized scores into grade, age scores, percentiles, and stanines. Thus the standing of an individual is provided relative to his or her peers. Cognitive, language, perceptual, and achievement tests are reported in this form.

Cognitive and Language Tests

The Wechsler Intelligence Scale for Children-Revised (WISC-R) (Wechsler 1974) is the most widely used instrument for cognitive testing. Individually administered, the test measures ability on verbal (auditory-verbal, auditory-memory) and performance or perceptual (visual, visual-motor) tasks. The 10 or 11 subtests (one is optionally given) are viewed individually as well as in terms of a composite IQ score. Response patterns and inter- and intratest data can then be compared and correlated to other instruments. The oldest measure of IQ, the Stanford–Binet Intelligence Scale (Terman and Merrill 1973), is also in use but does not provide as broad a sampling of behavior and as such is not as useful for learning-disabled populations. State guidelines mandate the use of individually administered intellectual tests for decision making within special education.

While special educators refer to speech and language pathologists for in-depth testing when significant language problems are noted, a number of language measures are included in an educational battery. Language functioning is assessed on both receptive and expressive levels through tests of vocabulary knowledge and grammatic understanding and use. The Peabody Picture Vocabulary Test Revised (PPVTR) (Dunn and Dunn 1981) measures receptive vocabulary. The Illinois Test of Psycholinguistic Abilities (Kirk et al. 1968), the Test of Language Development (TOLD) (Newcomer and Hammill 1977), the Clinical Evaluation of Language Functions-Revised (CELF-R) (Semel and Wiig 1980), and the Essentials of English tests (Smith and McCullough 1961) measure vocabulary, recall, and grammatic ability through auditory and visual tasks.

Perceptual (discrimination, blending, sequencing, memory) and perceptual-motor tests measure auditory-motor and visual-motor functioning. The Bender (1938) Visual Motor Gestalt Test and the Developmental Test of Visual-Motor Integration (Beery and Buktenica 1967) are widely used. The Bender is often used more broadly by some to estimate IQ and personality variables. Since these tests provide a limited sampling of behavior, caution must be exercised in extending the applicability of this information, especially for use with reading and learning-disabled children, regarding placement decisions.

Achievement and Diagnostic Tests

Achievement and diagnostic tests measure skill development in the content areas and subsequently the student's ability to profit from instruction. Individually or group-administered achievement tests tap a range of academic skills; diagnostic tests focus on single content areas (e.g., reading). Both are useful for initial planning information and for monitoring progress within the instructional area. These results are reported in terms of grade or age scores.

Reading Tests

Reading tests sample behavior across beginning and later reading tasks. Widely used measures, such as the Gates-McKillop-Horowitz Reading Diagnostic Tests (Gates et al. 1981) and the Gray Oral Reading Test (Gray and Robinson 1981), tap decoding and word attack skills through tests of oral reading, letter and sound recognition, sight recognition, and other subtests. The Gates-MacGinitie Reading Tests (MacGinitie 1978) and the Stanford Achievement Test (Madden et al. 1973), for example, measure silent reading comprehension and vocabulary knowledge through varying formats (e.g., multiple choice and cloze questions). Specific questions tap the ability to extract literal, critical, or inferential information.

A careful assessment of reading should consider the range of skills involved in the reading process, from beginning levels of decoding to more advanced stages of comprehension. Relying on composite scores or subtest scores in isolation leads to erroneous or incomplete judgments concerning the child's reading skills and/or the child's ability to transfer these to the classroom setting.

Mathematics Tests

Tests within the area of mathematics measure comprehension of computational processes, verbal problems, and ability to apply this knowledge through computation. Commonly used instruments include the Key Math Diagnostic Arithmetic Test Revised (Connolly et al. 1988), the Stanford Diagnostic Arithmetic Test (Beatty et al. 1966), and the Wide Range Achievement Test (Jastak and Jastak 1978). Test formats include visual and auditory questions as well as pencil-and-paper tasks. Again, a careful assessment requires attention to the range of skills involved in mathematical learning.

Spelling Tests

Spelling tests measure the ability to record words from dictation or to correct errors in written format. Both types of tasks involve knowledge of vowel and consonant patterns, sight words, and spelling rules. Spelling subtests of the Wide Range Achievement Test (Jastak and Jastak 1978) and the Test of Written Spelling (Larsen and Hammill 1976) are some examples of tests used in this area.

Criterion-Referenced Tests

Criterion-referenced measures are either selected from published systems or are teacher constructed. Criterion-referenced tests measure the level and mastery of specific skills within the academic areas and against specific curriculum goals. These tests do not provide normative information but do have high levels of content validity because they are developed in line with course content, developmental levels, and instructional planning. For example, to measure the acquisition of simple addition, a test might include 10 one-digit × one-digit (e.g., 9 + 3 =) problems; criterion or mastery would be assumed if nine out of 10 problems were answered correctly.

Nonstandardized and Informal Measures

Informal measures are used to supplement information from both standardized and criterion-referenced tests. They provide the opportunity to engage in trial teaching using varying techniques and to use tasks outside of standardized formats and time constraints. Observation or demonstrations of strategy use can be included.

Recent developments have directed researchers to an inquiry of how children arrive at answers and what strategies they employ in doing so. This area is referred to as metamemory and includes the child's repertoire of strategies and techniques for learning and remembering as well as the child's self-knowledge as a learner and rememberer. This rich area of inquiry within education provides us with a new approach to testing and teaching. There are, however, no standardized tests yet available, but examiners can begin to utilize preliminary descriptions in the literature (Baker and Brown 1983; Shapiro 1982).

Thus, in summary, a psychoeducational evaluation provides a complete profile of a child's performance on both formal and informal measures. This information allows one to consider cognitive functioning, estimates of potential, and academic ability. There is no doubt that we must work toward the continued application of research findings to test development and use and study of the relationship between postulated underlying abilities and observable skills. Nonetheless, diagnostic tools now available provide us with the opportunity to view a child's learning from varying perspectives. Knowledgeable use of a wide range of tests is central to our understanding of a child's problems and for appropriate educational programming and treatment.

Remediation and Educational Treatment

The child with reading and learning disabilities should be treated with a broad-based approach that includes diagnostic information, educational planning, remedial intervention, and family involvement. School and classroom placement are judged in accord with the nature and degree of the problem and the age and developmental level of the child. While the goal of special education is to provide least-restrictive or mainstreamed settings, more intensive help is often indicated and takes the form of special school, classroom, or resource room placement in which small group or individual instruction is available. In many cases, tutoring on an individual basis is needed to supplement classroom instruction regardless of placement.

Remedial instruction is reserved for children who are performing substantially below their capacity level and who require intensive help beyond that provided within a developmental setting in the schools. Remedial instruction is geared to the development of skills and compensatory strategies that will allow the child to function as effectively and independently as possible. Rate of learning, sequencing of skills, level of material, mode of presentation, and type and degree of reinforcement are developed in line with diagnostic information and according to individual needs. Remediation must parallel and be in phase with developmental instruction so that the child can participate in programs to the fullest extent and be mainstreamed for instruction, when possible.

Because of the heterogeneous nature of the reading and learning-disabled population, a unitary approach is not used for remediation (Johnson and Mykelbust 1967). Moreover, there are a wide range of materials and approaches in use so that remediation is based, for the most part, on an eclectic model that includes varying combinations of both formal and informal programming. However, over the past 20 to 30 years, several theoretical models have become popular, leading to the specialized testing mentioned and specific instructional programs.

One mode, ability or process training, invokes a causal relationship between psychological processes (e.g., perception, memory, and linguistic skills) and the acquisition of more advanced learning within the academic areas. Therefore, perceptual and linguistic development is approached through specific testing and stage-related training as a prerequisite to achievement at higher levels, especially with tasks such as reading. Process training has been used widely within the field of special education, although over the last 10 to 15 years research findings have consistently shown that 1) the underlying abilities presumed important for school learning are remarkably resistant to improvement through training (Arter and Jenkins 1979); 2) there appears to be no empirical support that basic process training (e.g., perception) is a prerequisite to the acquisition of academic skills (Salvia and Ysseldyke 1981); and 3) there is no evidence of transfer of such training to academic skills per se (Hammill and Larsen 1974; Hammill et al. 1974). While perceptual and linguistic programs continue to be included in instruction, gains are evident if process training is specifically incorporated into subject areas, such as reading or mathematics. For example, in the areas of reading, training discrimination of letters is emphasized rather that nonsymbolic geometric forms.

Academic skill training, another model, approaches instruction through the analysis of task components and goals and the development of a hierarchy of skills. Mastery of beginning level tasks are assumed to underlie more complex learning. Instruction moves through a specific sequence. For example, in mathematics, concepts and computational skills for addition would have to be mastered before multiplication is taught. Similarly, mastery of basic phonetic rules would underlie oral reading. Because of the variability and scatter so evident in the skill development and profile of reading and learning-disabled children, this approach is central within special education. Such attention to discrete steps may obscure more overriding factors in learning such as application of strategies, bringing into question whether this approach alone is sufficient to remediate academic difficulties.

Modality matching (Johnson and Myklebust 1967; Lerner 1971), or matching instruction and techniques to the child's area of strength (e.g., visual, auditory, tactile-kinesthetic), has also been widely used, especially for reading instruction. For example, a phonic approach emphasizing the sound system would be utilized with a child with strong auditory perceptual skills, whereas a sight approach would be matched to strengths in the visual modality. In a review of research studies utilizing modality-specific approaches, Arter and Jenkins (1979) reported limited gains in overall reading skills. While there are advantages to these approaches, these findings underscore the fact that reading is a complex skill that is highly dependent on cross-modal integration and linguistic understanding. Some children do learn best through modality-specific techniques, but the need for generalizable skills is overriding.

Most recently, information theory and development of cognitive models outlining schematic organization and strategic control over learning has had a major impact on research and more gradually on instruction as well. It is hypothesized that the development of a schematic framework is essential for comprehension, storage, and retrieval. This is operationalized by an executive that takes control over learning in the form of metacomprehension and strategy use. A strategy is a set of processes or steps that facilitate acquisition, storage, and retrieval (e.g., rehearsal, self-monitoring, or association). Thus metaknowledge, rather than process factors, are seen as central to academic performance. Since reading and learning-disabled children have consistently been shown to be passive learners whose performance suggests immature rather than deviant metaknowledge and strategy use, this approach to instruction holds great promise. In fact, Brown et al. (1974), Torgesen and Goldman (1977), Wong et al. (1977), and the Institute for the Study of Learning Disabilities (1983), working with retarded and reading-disabled groups, have demonstrated that strategic instruction has had a dramatic and positive effect on performance variables. Torgesen and Goldman further suggested that strategy deficits rather than reading problems per se may be at issue.

Remediation of Reading Disorders

Reading is a complex skill that is dependent on adequate development in perception, language, memory, and strategic functioning. Different levels of processing and clusters of skills are needed at each stage. While the beginning stage of reading emphasizes perceptual learning, more mature reading is highly dependent on linguistic understanding and strategic monitoring.

Reading is considered to be a second language skill that builds on basic linguistic competence acquired over the first six years of life. At this time, vocabulary and basic syntactic structures are internalized and used competently on both a receptive and an expressive level. While the initial language is learned gradually through the aural-verbal mode, reading requires comprehension of a visual symbol system acquired through direct instruction.

Specifically, initial or beginning reading (approximately first to third grade) requires perceptual attention (visual and auditory) to letter names, sounds, and words. Words are formed by integrating sounds and symbols, which are then attached to semantic labels and meaning. Once this stage becomes automatic, the vocabulary store builds from words learned through sound analysis or memory and provides a base for comprehension of meaning. This early stage requires attention to surface analysis or decoding (i.e., translation of written language into meaning).

However, as written language structures become more complex and as vocabulary and meaning become more abstract, the reader needs strong language skills essential to meet this shift in instruction and content. From approximately third grade on, reading requires processing of more complex auditory and visual symbolic material along with parallel processing of semantic syntactic structures and content-related information. Thus the use of linguistic and contextual cues underlies more efficient reading.

Historically, reading comprehension was considered to be a passive process. Recently, however, information theory has directed our attention to the active role of the reader and the reader's ability to utilize language and contextual cues. Interaction between the reader and text involves continued alterations of meaning as new representations are formed. This change in theory places more responsibility on the strategic role of the reader within the reading and learning process.

Beginning Reading (Decoding)

Most reading methods are intended for use in regular classrooms and with elementary-age children and fall roughly into either "meaning-emphasis" or "code-emphasis" approaches (Chall 1967). However, they have been and are adapted for use with children with reading and learning problems.

A meaning-emphasis approach views early comprehension as critical. As such, focus is placed on the acquisition of a controlled vocabulary, which is then integrated into story material for reading exercises. Vocabulary is learned as whole words through sight recognition. Instruction in decoding is provided through either a phonic (e.g., b-a-t) or linguistic (e.g., b-at) method. Basal programs and language experience approaches utilize this early emphasis on language and content. From a modality point of view, this approach appears to be suited to children with strengths in the visual modality (especially visual memory). Readers and workbooks are used selectively, either as basic reading material or as supplements to other approaches.

A code-emphasis approach focuses initially on instruction in sound-symbol correspondence, thereby attending less to meaning. Letter names and sounds are taught either phonically, with each letter in isolation (e.g., b-a-t) or through linguistic patterns. In either case, letters then must be blended into whole words. Vocabulary learning of phonetically irregular words must be approached through sight recognition. A word bank is developed to build a sufficient language vocabulary base with which to construct sentences and reading material. Since code approaches are more demanding of the auditory modality, they have been used more extensively with children with strengths in this area. Phonic and lingusitic programs fall under this category. Of the two, the linguistic method is more rule governed than the phonic method and therefore less dependent on rote memory skills. However, after extensive review of beginning reading methods, Chall (1967) reported that code emphasis approaches produce significantly greater gains, at least up to the third grade, when research evidence is available.

Programs developed specifically for children with reading problems include the Gillingham and Stillman (1965) method, geared to subgroups of visual dyslexics. As such, phonic and alphabetic instruction utilizes multisensory stimulation as a means for learning letters, sounds, and words. Research (Childs 1964; Kline and Kline 1975; Rawson 1968) suggests positive gains, although critics point to the overemphasis on auditory skills (Wepman 1960). The Fernald (1943) approach also uses multisensory stimulation. Words, chosen by the child, are taught through tracing and saying each part aloud until the word can be traced strictly from memory. Phonic principles taught secondarily are acquired from reading material. Myers and Hammill (1968) indicated that the success of the approach depends on stimulation of auditory and visual pathways and Harris (1970) underscored the careful and systematic study of words. Structural reading (Stern 1963) emphasizes phonic elements within the context of spoken vocabulary that provides a sound basis for the reading of words and sentences.

Color coding has been utilized as a means of helping children learn to read both through formal programs (Bannatyne 1966; Frostig 1965; Gattegno 1962) and through informal techniques. Modified alphabets (Pitman 1963; Woodcock 1967) have been used with reading and learning-disabled children as well as Distar (Englemann and Bruner 1969) and programmed readers; the latter are two variants in programming.

Most of the support for the efficacy or failure of the varying reading programs comes from clinical data. At present there is a lack of controlled empirical research across programs so that the effects of method, maturation, and instruction have not been factored out for study and therefore cannot be used to explain improvement or gains in reading performance.

The sequence of sounds and sight words taught varies only minimally regardless of what reading program is used. Each program proceeds from the presentation of consonants, short and long vowels, and consonant and vowel clusters to multisyllable words. Oral reading is used initially to help integrate sounds and symbols at both a letter and word level and within a contextual framework. Early attention to syntactic structure and phrasing rather than word calling (word-by-word reading) is an important precursor to comprehension. Knowledge of sound-symbol correspondence is reinforced through exercises that train visual-motor (words copied from models) and auditory-motor learning (spelling from dictation). Early reading problems typically involve difficulty learning and retrieving sounds or symbols, such as vowels.

Perceptual errors, reversals, rotations (e.g., b/d, on/no), poor discrimination of distinctive features, confusion of words of similar configuration (e.g., then, there), and sequencing errors are treated with color-coding techniques (coding errors or patterns), deletion exercises (e.g., the-e, t--re, th---, there), verbal mediation, and cross-modal stimulation (e.g., tracing, use of textured letters, oral spelling). If strategies can be incorporated at the initial learning stage, problems are often circumvented (e.g., teaching the child different writing approaches to form b/d to help avoid reversals).

Decoding places heavy demands on integrative learning. Instruction must provide the child with the skills to integrate sounds and symbols within a meaningful context. This is especially important with the reading-delayed child whose information store tends to be fragmented and context-bound and who does not spontaneously transfer or conceptualize tasks within a larger framework. Ideally, knowledge of sounds, letters, and words should be automatic across all modes so that later reading stages can be acquired competently and accurately. Regardless of approach or special method used, the communicative nature of reading and the relevance of linguistic content should be addressed so that the child is prepared to continue to more advanced levels.

Reading comprehension (associated with silent reading) requires the use of sound and symbol information to extract semantic, syntactic, and conceptual information. Because written language requires processing of more abstract forms and ideas, a strong vocabulary and language base is needed to make the shift from the oral reading stage.

Information processing and theories related to cognitive organization have been translated into instructional techniques and materials, making a significant impact on approaches to reading comprehension.

Later Reading (Comprehension)

Comprehension is described as an interactive, bidirectional process (Rumelhart and Ortony 1977) operating through top-down (conceptually driven) and bottom-up (text-driven) processing. While reading requires ongoing interaction, the more proficient reader is able to utilize schematic organization and contextual cues to advantage. This is achieved through the development of anticipatory schemas and hypotheses that allow for ongoing questioning, matching, and storage. The skilled reader draws simultaneously from different sources of knowledge so that meaning is constructed through an analysis of author's intent, context, and knowledge base. All levels of analysis are needed.

The child with limited language or beginning reading skills often remains fixed at the decoding and bottom-up processing level and is less able to extract meaning or comprehend conceptual information. Given the high level of activity that is postulated to accompany reading comprehension, we can see that motivation, attention, independent work habits, and strategic monitoring are also central to efficient performance. If impaired concentration secondary to psychiatric disorder is found, treatment directed toward the primary disorder is indicated.

Traditionally, teaching comprehension has a briefer history than teaching of other reading skills. This has been partly due to the fact that conceptually there has been less certainty about the nature of comprehension, how it is acquired, and subsequently the means to teach it. While vocabulary and content-related information have always been included in instruction, comprehension in both classroom and remedial settings has been measured through questions geared to different types of information (e.g., vocabulary, main ideas, inference), thus tapping, for the most part, effective memory skills. Comprehension was not defined as a skill to be taught.

However, instructional approaches have been directed toward the development of the student's knowledge base and strategic repertoire. Instruction ranges from facilitating comprehension of specific content to teaching metacognitive skills that are generalizeable and provide control over comprehension tasks. While comprehension depends on stored meaning, integration and elaboration are critical. As such, variables such as text structure, instructor's role, and strategic control by the reader are central. Brown (1975) suggested that children are "universal novices," needing self-generating strategies as well as insight as to when external mediators are appropriate. This development is now thought to be even more critical with reading and learning-disabled children and has enabled educators to approach instruction with a firmer theoretical base.

Research has shown that text characteristics such as coherence and style affect comprehension. Mandler and Johnson (1977) reported that memory for stories is superior when content is organized according to story grammar. Meyer's (1979) research also points out that learning is affected by clarity of text structure (e.g., introductory statements, cue words). Structure that includes explicit rather than inferred connectives is also easier to comprehend. While this research has been primarily based on normal populations, these findings are especially relevant to reading-disabled groups.

Studies from the Institute for the Study of Learning Disabilities (1983) indicate that although learning-disabled children were found to be competent in their ability to comprehend and use main idea and text macrostructure, they had difficulty when presented with contrast structures (adversatives) or were found to use inappropriate processing strategies. Thus they relied on fixed hypotheses or on prior information without adapting strategies to understand more complex information better. Remedial strategies have been developed by this institute as well as others, and specifically include exercises to modify these problems.

Strategic instruction has also focused on the use of elaboration (forming representations of ideas) (Reder 1980) and comprehension monitoring through self-questioning and self-reflective strategies, with positive gains reported (Brown 1978; Meichenbaum and Asarnow 1979; Wong and Jones 1982). Brown and Day (1980) approached comprehension through the use of written summaries that demand active, explicit reformulation of information, and have shown its effect on learning.

Vocabulary development, an essential part of comprehension, is encouraged through activities that utilize multiple definitions, integration, and transfer of vocabulary knowledge to reading and writing tasks. Cloze techniques (supplying missing words), multiple choice, and written exercises are some of the tasks used to strengthen these skills.

In general, there has been less attention given to instruction in word attack or language skills in the middle and upper grades within the normal classroom setting. The adolescent with problems has particular difficulty, then, maintaining and acquiring the skills needed to make the transition to content area reading. For this age group, instruction in basic skills and strategy use must be included in curricular goals. Of importance as well is the choice of materials that are compatible with reading level, while providing the information needed across subject areas.

Regardless of age, remediation must provide needed support in the area of reading and language so that content-related information and academic subjects can be acquired effectively. The overall goal is to build skills and a knowledge base to maximize transfer of remedial work to classroom learning. Through evidence of skill development and academic success, interest and motivation in learning can be mobilized.

Remediation of Specific Mathematics Disorders

Specialized instruction in mathematics generally involves a dual approach that focuses 1) on the development of metacomprehension skills and problem-solving strategies that underlie executive control and 2) on the development of skills through direct instruction or task analyses. Learning-disabled students are consistently reported to be passive learners who lack the varied repertoire of strategies seen in the nonlearning-disabled population. Thus, while they do not use idiosyncratic approaches to problem solving, they do employ more primitive methods that are not appropriate to task demands (Institute for the Study of Learning Disabilities 1983). The institute has also been involved in research studying the effects of direct instruction. Concepts and facts are presented according to a developmental or hierarchical scale. Basic skills are reinforced and assumed to be secure before more advanced levels can be achieved. Such instruction in basic facts (e.g., with computational skills) has resulted in positive gains.

Patterson (1974) noted that instruction should involve the analysis of language and reading elements in mathematical problems. For example, vocabulary should be highlighted to effect greater understanding. Vocabulary terms (e.g., cue words, symbols, number concepts) should be taught both in isolation and in the context of word problems. Dahmus (1970) and Aiken (1972) have suggested that verbal problems be translated into equivalent mathematical statements, with a gradual move from concrete to abstract levels. Problems that use alternate forms to express the same process are suggested to help the student detect and utilize the overriding principles, encouraging the transfer of a verbal problem such as "Mary had eight apples, gave three away, how many are left?" into a number sentence "$8 - 3 =$." Ashlock (1972) recommended encouraging students to verbalize their procedure and set of rules because defective algorithms are seen as one of the major causes of computational inaccuracy.

Two- to- three-dimensional objects and concrete manipulative materials (e.g., Cuisenaire rods, coins) are utilized to highlight and help the student detect the relationship between concrete and abstract problems. In addition, these nonverbal materials encourage active problem solving and provide the poor reader with alternative means of conceptualization. Precise and carefully sequenced instructions should positively affect comprehension of verbal problems.

Other activities involve attention to the order of numbers in a series or in sets, work with spatial concepts (e.g., sets and fractions), and work with arithmetic processes (e.g., addition, subtraction, multiplication, and division). Classification activities utilize varying criteria (e.g., color, shape, size). Principles of conservation are reinforced through activities that demonstrate that basic number units remain the same in a set regardless of physical arrangement.

The following are a series of structured approaches that are used widely. The structural arithmetic program (Stern 1965), used within normal settings and for special populations, stresses a problem-solving approach. A sequence of concrete materials and workbook illustrations provide an initial base for the construction of facts and principles before verbal problems are presented. The Nuffield math project (Reid and Hresko 1981) details a child-centered, discovery approach to learning. The Cuisenaire rods (Davidson 1969) were similarly designed to teach problem-solving and conceptual skills rather than rote memorization.

At the high school level, Cawley's (1978) guidelines include diagnostically based instruction and task-specific remedial modules. Similarly, the Distar instructional system (Englemann et al. 1976) and the diagnostic-prescriptive teaching model (Glennon and Wilson 1972) stress direct instruction, ongoing evaluation, and careful monitoring of progress.

Thus instruction in mathematics for young children as well as adolescents centers on executive control, strategic use, and skill development. Systematic instruction geared to a cumulative store of knowledge and skills remains the goal, regardless of program model and use.

Conclusion

Remedial instruction across the skill areas is geared to individual learning needs and performance levels. The goal is to help the student meet academic demands and function as effectively as possible within the school setting. Research continues to be needed regarding the relationship between cognitive modes, test construction, and instructional programming. A more consistent research methodology must be developed to factor out variables such as age, disability, length, and type of remedial treatment for study. Data concerning prognosis for children with learning problems strongly suggest that early identification and remediation is critical. While classroom options and instructional planning have centered around the preschool- and elementary-age child, only recently has attention been directed toward problems more specific to the adolescent. Certainly more consistent and appropriate help across ages is needed for initial and long-range planning for children with reading and learning problems.

Chapter 51

Evaluation and Treatment of Language, Articulation, and Fluency Problems: A Speech Pathology Perspective

Assessment

The first step in the assessment process, the face-to-face parent interview, affords the clinician the opportunity to observe parent-child interaction, to investigate parental attitudes and perceptions of "the problem," and to gather information about medical, familial, developmental, social, and educational history and its impact on the child's speech and language skills. Information obtained during the interview establishes initial hypotheses about the patient that will need to be confirmed or disconfirmed during the course of the evaluation session. Typically, evaluation and reevaluation continues beyond this initial session and throughout the intervention process.

Parents' descriptions of the problem are generally accompanied by the qualifying statement that the child understands everything that is said, knows what is expected, but is stubborn and intentionally does not listen. These are classic indications of developmental language (and many language learning) disorders.

For those children referred by psychologists and psychiatrists, it is not unusual to find that their formal tests reveal verbal scores that reflect adequate performance. This finding often occurs in the face of clinical observations that negate an intact language system. Children with learning and language problems typically fall into this category. Their language problems are subtle and require the expertise of a speech and language diagnostician who has had extensive experience with normal language development and child language disorders.

Formal Versus Informal Evaluation Procedures

Several trends have evolved in the field of speech and language pathology in recent years that have had a significant impact on the ways in which diagnosis gets done. The influence of speech act theory and the pragmatics of language has had a major impact on shifting attention from syntactic structures to the use of language in a situational context (Dore 1985; Duchan 1985; Gallagher and Prutting 1983). Behaviorism was replaced by cognitive psychology and information processing, transforming the evaluation session from one of a stimulus-response paradigm to a dynamic, naturalistic, problem-solving series of situations (Muma 1973). Attention is now paid to parent-infant interaction and the effects of socialization on linguistic behaviors (Bates 1979; Brazelton and Tronick 1980; Brazelton et al. 1974; Bruner 1977; Ochs and Schieffelin 1979; Stern 1977). The impact of this work has been powerful.

Although the comprehensive evaluation still often includes the use of standardized testing instruments, more opportunities for interaction via dialogue, story telling, narrative, game playing, and verbal and nonverbal problem solving have been built into the process. Language sampling that includes child and adult utterances along with contextual description is the method of choice for analyzing the structures and functions of child language. Reproduction of naturalistic settings has become commonplace in the clinic (as opposed to the structured unnaturalness of the formalized testing context). The naturalistic setting affords opportunities for a wide range of language structures and functions to surface. Contextual situations are varied to include activities such as symbolic play, story telling, narration, descriptions of events, and organizational activities, each of which allows a range of psychological processes and strategies to be examined. In addition to speech and language data collection, the more informal setting gives information about the child's attentional skills, concentration, organization skills, cognitive style, interests, willingness to take risks, and interpersonal style in a more real-world-type setting.

Standardized tests that are used to assess a child's language and cognitive skills offer little to no opportunity for investigation of strategies or reasoning that motivates a child's responses. Piaget's (1972a, 1972b) clinical method and Vygotsky's (1962, 1978) "zone of proximal development" do. Although both are rarely used by speech and language pathologists, both should be. The clinical method allows for a good deal of conversational interaction and reveals information about a child's logical mental structures. The perspective of the zone of proximal development gives rich information about techniques for facilitating performance and potential for learning. Information from both sources readily becomes the basis for intervention.

Approaches to Language Intervention

Three general categories of philosophies of intervention will be discussed below. Each in turn reflects changes in our ideas about language, its development, its function, and its relation to the functioning of the whole child. Whether an intervention approach is behavioral, cognitive-linguistic, or holistic, it is not viewed as useful only for a specific disorder. These intervention approaches cut across diagnostic categories. Combinations of each are often used simultaneously.

Behavioral Approach

The assumption of behaviorism is that teaching the forms of language will ultimately lead to internalization of rules of grammar. Communicative behavior including eye gaze, motor imitation, and speech and language comprehension and production are analyzed into behavioral units and subsequently taught by using reinforcement principles. Children "learn" to respond to specific gestures and verbalizations in clearly specified contexts. Production of desired communicative behavior is rewarded on various frequency schedules. Rewards are initially tangible and gradually grow into secondary reinforcers. The goal of an operant conditioning paradigm is to have language accomplish some end. Hence language becomes its own socially rewarding behavior.

Cognitive-Linguistic Approach

In contrast to the behavioral approach, the cognitive-linguistic model posits that particular cognitive structures are necessary prerequisites to the formulation of a language symbol system (Bates 1979; Moorhead and Moorhead 1974; Piaget 1963). Clinicians adhering to this model expose an infant or young child to experiences that foster, for example, cognitions such as object permanence, tool use, classification, and identity, before attempting to teach the child the linguistic symbols that code conceptual events. As language develops, these nonlinguistic conceptual structures become the semantic content of the symbol system. Thus early linguistic and semantic forms that are taught to a language-disordered child will code the nonlinguistic concepts the child has already constructed or is in the process of constructing about the world. Labels for readily manipulable objects, words that code social events (e.g., hi, bye-bye), and semantic relations such as recurrence (more), non-existence (no), and disappearance (all gone) are some of the functional symbols that are taught to the developmentally (language) disordered toddler. The older language-disordered child needs language that codes, for example, concepts such as space, time, quantity, and sequence. The child also requires the linguistic means to communicate sophisticated ideas. Language is needed for learning, for constructing narratives, and for academic problem solving. Language is needed for functioning as an appropriate social being. In this model, children's experiences of living in the world and interacting with and on persons and objects are coupled with talk that refers to meaningful and functional events. Language also serves to engage a child's attention and to focus and reorganize perceptions. Language intervention is planned based on a combination of what we know about normal developmental progress and the language needs relevant to each disordered child's world (Bloom and Lahey 1978; Cole 1982).

As cognitive structures develop, new language forms are required. As understanding and use of new language and meaning forms increases, cognitions are reorganized and enriched. This reciprocity between language and cognition occurs in a setting where interaction between clinician and child becomes an educational and social model for learning the rules and forms for communicating. The goal of the cognitive-linguistic approach as an intervention strategy is to increase the child's understanding and production of language form (i.e, phonology, morphology, and syntax), content (i.e., semantics), and use (i.e., appropriate integration of form and meaning in a variety of situational contexts) (Bloom and Lahey 1978). The primary focus throughout intervention is on the acquisition of language forms and the uses to which language can be put.

Holistic Approach

Development of communicative competence is dependent on more than just knowledge of linguistic form. For language to develop it is necessary to have intact biologic, neurologic, cognitive, auditory, and visual systems. Healthy interpersonal dynamics provide the social environment from which language data and discourse rules are abstracted. A dysfunction or disruption in any one of these systems can have negative effects on the functioning of the linguistic system. A dysfunction in one's linguistic system can, in turn, have negative impact on social, cognitive, emotional, and academic functioning. A holistic or "ecologic perspective" (Waryas and Crowe 1982; Woolfolk et al. 1982) with respect to language intervention attends to the variety of functional systems that contribute to maintaining a language disorder. Thus, if socialization deficits are paramount, pragmatics (ideally in individual and group situations) will receive intensive training. If cognitive deficits are the primary problem, then a program that focuses on logical problem solving will be constructed. The notion of making use of one's functional system to help compensate for deficit skills in related systems is the basis of Luria's (1963, 1968, 1980) work with brain-injured adults. The goal of intervention is not to "cure" the system or systems that are dysfunctional. Rather it is to teach compensatory strategies that will enable a child to function to the fullest potential. The processes may consist of initially teaching the use of different concrete external means for facilitating memory, organization of thought and language, categorization, motor performance, or other dysfunctional skills. Ultimately social, cognitive, linguistic, and academic behaviors are reorganized internally and can be handled by the child's strengths and developmental readiness. Ideally the end result of this sort of intervention is the reorganization of interrelated systems— general cognitive, linguistic, and social. Changes in cognitive strategies effect changes in cognitive structures. Changes in cognitive structures influence vocabulary, semantics, syntax, and pragmatics. Social interaction has input on and increases the production of various forms and uses of language (Duchan 1985; Lund and Duchan 1988). Language, the educational and social tool used across all knowledge domains, influences social skills and knowledge structures. Experiences of success in one or more developmental domains, as various skills and performances are facilitated and increased, can lead to feelings of confidence and competence. The whole child is being treated because a variety of aspects of the worlds in which the child functions are being addressed simultaneously. Language is the tool or medium used to accomplish reorganization of functional systems. Particular forms of language may not be focused on during initial training.

> If the child lacks the rudimentary social skills of influencing and controlling others through some form of communication, then primary emphasis should be placed on teaching him/her the basic principle that "language works" to get things done by influencing the behavior of others. (Waryas and Crowe 1982, p. 776)

Developmental Articulation Disorders

Developmental articulation disorders comprise the majority of communication problems in children. They can arise from obvious organic factors (e.g., cleft palate, other orofacial anomalies), neurologic deficits (e.g., cerebral palsy, dysarthria, aproaxia), or sensory deficits (e.g., deafness, hearing impairment). A large percentage of speech sound production disorders, however, have no clear-cut etiology, and it is that category of developmental articulation disorder that will be discussed here.

The goals of any speech sound production evaluation are to determine whether there is a problem, to ascertain the nature of the problem, and to initiate a program of effective intervention. It is the last two of these issues that is most affected by clinicians' theoretical perspectives. The description that an articulation disorder is developmental in nature tells us only that a child's speech production repertoire is not adequate compared to that of the child's peers. This sort of diagnostic information is easily obtained even without formal testing during the first few minutes of an evaluation session in conversation with the patient. In fact, most articulation tests available today are based on developmental acquisition norms and offer little information beyond age-appropriate speech production tables. Current approaches to assessment have moved away from error sound identification to identification of the organization of the sound system and of production processes that reflect normal developmental progress. Two approaches that are widely used today are distinctive features analysis and phonologic process analysis. Both of these approaches differ from the traditional sound-by-sound assessment and intervention procedures employed before the early to mid-1970s.

Distinctive Features: Assessment and Intervention

An analysis of a child's phonologic system that relies on discovering and describing the acoustic or articulatory features bundles that are common to groups of phonemes is the distinctive features approach to articulatory assessment. Vocalic, for example, is a distinctive feature that is characteristic of a group of sounds produced orally and have as their primary sound source the glottis (Jakobson et al., 1952). The sounds *o, a, e, u, l*, and *r* fall into this category. Tense is a feature described as "more sharply defined resonance regions in the spectrum . . . and greater deformation of the vocal tract away from its rest position" (Winitz 1969, p. 83). Examples of tense sounds are *sh, ch, f*, and *p*. Theoretically one ought to be able to identify a feature or features that are used erroneously or are omitted from a child's repertoire. That is the goal of assessment. Following this, the elusive feature(s) would be taught. Gradually, other phonemes containing the target feature will evolve as a function of the child's having "learned" a feature common to several phonemes. This is a far more economical method than teaching one sound at a time to a child who displays multiple articulation problems.

Walsh (1974) criticized the usefulness of the abstract feature system for clinicians. He presented an argument for describing articulatory rather than acoustic features for clinical use. Identification of acoustic features such as stridency, coronal, diffuse, grave, and tense (Jakobson et al. 1952) are difficult for clinicians to make. In contrast, it is simpler and clinically more useful for the speech and language pathologist to observe and describe the articulatory postures a child uses during production of speech. Articulatory postures such as an open versus constricted vocal tract, tongue position in relation to lips and teeth and palate, and lip rounding and voicing are described in relation to production of groups of phonemes. Therapy is targeted at modifying erroneous articulatory postures that reflect abstract distinctive features. Here, too, the assumption is that particular articulatory postures are common to several phonemes. Thus learning new, more appropriate postures should generalize to several phonemes, some of which have not been specifically taught.

The Fisher-Logeman Test of Articulation Competence (Fisher and Logeman 1971) is the only formal instrument on the market at this writing whose theoretical construct is based on distinctive feature theory. Error analysis is accomplished by identification of articulatory distinctive features. This quite naturally provides a structure for planning an intervention program (Meecham 1979).

Phonologic Process Approach: Assessment and Intervention

As children go about the business of developing a phonologic system, they display the use of simplification processes of the adult speech sound system. Ingram (1976) and Hodson and Paden (1983) described a variety of these simplification processes. Both provide data and case studies that support the notion that articulation disorders result from the systematic prolonged use of phonologic simplification processes. Simplification processes such as consonant cluster reduction, final consonant deletion, weak syllable deletion in multisyllabic words, stopping, and fronting result in predictable patterns of errors within a child's phonologic system. Identification of processes that occur on sounds in single words and/or running speech is the goal of assessment. Intervention would consist of the modification of phonologic processes. The focus then is on the child's whole phonologic system rather than on the child's correct sound-by-sound phonetic production. In fact, with Hodson and Paden's intervention program, clinicians are advised initially not to be concerned about on-target production of particular sounds. Instead, the goal is to have the child become aware of a new process. Acquisition of a process should generate more appropriate rules for the combination of sounds to form adult-like speech. For example, a child who deletes final consonants from all words will be taught that it is necessary to produce a consonant, any consonant, at the end of a single-syllable word. Once that particular process is established across several words, the next process in the cycle of remediation is initiated. Hodson and Paden have found that, in the course of bombarding their patients with listening and practicing new phonologic processes, other processes begin to evolve spontaneously.

Identification of simplification processes can be accomplished by using available articulation tests such as the Goldman-Fristoe Test of Articulation (Goldman and Fristoe 1972). Although this instrument was not constructed based on phonologic theory and looks at motor production of individual sounds, a creative clinician can use the stimulus items to do a phonologic process analysis. An advantage of the Goldman-Fristoe test is that preschool children enjoy the colorful, large pictures, which often evoke additional chatter that provides more data for linguistic analysis.

The Mildly Impaired Child

Neither the distinctive features approach nor the phonologic process approach is necessary, or suggested, for mildly articulatory disordered children. Both approaches are time consuming initially, but the economy of these approaches for intervention with the unintelligible child ends up being cost effective in terms of time, success, and money. For the mildly speech disordered child, a spontaneous speech sample is generally sufficient for identification of phonetic errors. Phonetic errors, in contrast to phonologic errors, are defined as off-target motor productions of certain speech sounds. The child who displays an interdental lisp, a *w* for *r* substitution, manifests a phonetic disorder. This child is still best helped by traditional articulation therapy, such at that described by Van Riper and Irwin (1958). With this approach, the child progresses from isolated sound production to sound in syllable production, to sound in word production, to sound in sentence production.

Treatment of Stuttering

Many children who display symptoms of stuttering do spontaneously recover from the disorder. The percentage of spontaneous recoveries can occur at a rate as high as 79 percent (Andrews and Harris 1964; Cooper 1972; Wingate 1964). Just as the onset of the disorder is gradual, so is the transition to fluency and normal speech. Most spontaneous recovery occurs during the preschool or elementary school years (Van Riper 1982). The second major spontaneous recovery period is during the teen years (Martyn and Sheehan 1968). Given this knowledge—that a child may or may not gradually recover from the disorder—the clinician is faced with decisions, such as 1) whether to intervene or to observe the course of the suspected disorder for a time, and 2) how to intervene (e.g., direct or indirect therapy).

These decisions will ultimately be based on a combination of factors: the clinician's theoretical orientation, perceived parental concern and coping behaviors, and the child's speech behaviors along with motivation for intervention. If, for example, a child is resistant to therapy or if the problem is more one of distorted parental perceptions than it is child behavior, a holding pattern may be chosen. An indirect treatment plan consisting of contact with and counseling of the parents can be initiated. The child's speech behavior at home and in a variety of communication situations will be observed and monitored. During this time, parents are counseled to notice their child's fluent speech, to modify their expectations for the child's speech and language development, and to help reduce environmental stresses that may be contributing to disfluent speech. Suggestions for carrying out this indirect form of intervention are contained in The Speech Foundation of America (1981) pamphlet and in Van Riper's (1973) text. Oftentimes counseling with respect to modification of family communicative interaction patterns is sufficient to mitigate childhood disfluency in a short period of time.

In those cases where a direct approach is taken, the child is worked with and the parents are also involved in the intervention program. A direct intervention approach with preschool children may employ the philosophical construct behind Stocker's (1976) communicative responsibility probe. Puppets, toys, and parallel play settings in which the child's talk is indirectly focused on may be used. The level of communicative responsibility given to the child can be systematically varied by the clinician to maintain a high level of fluency. Parents may observe these sessions and can be taught how to frame their talk so as to lessen elicitation of disfluent speech from their child.

Whether an indirect or a direct approach to stuttering intervention is initiated, the difficulty a child is experiencing talking should be gently but honestly acknowledged. All speakers are disfluent from time to time. All speakers' mouths get "stuck" at times. Children should not be made to feel that their speech is something to be hidden or about which they should be embarrassed.

As mentioned above, in addition to a stuttering problem, some children may also present with a speech sound production or language disorder. In cases where this occurs, intervention with the language disorder should take priority over the disfluency problem.

An older child who stutters presents some different issues from those of a younger child. Factors such as motivation to change and peer pressures need to be considered. Stuttering resulting from tensions that arise in response to specific situations can be more easily identified by the older child. Such tensions can be lessened by systematic desensitization procedures (Brutten and Shoemaker 1967; Van Riper 1973). Direct modification of within-word disfluencies and sound prolongations may be accomplished through relaxation techniques and biofeedback (Guitar et al. 1979). Techniques such as Van Riper's (1973) cancellation and pull-out or the process of precision fluency shaping (Webster 1979) may be used for direct modification of stuttering behaviors.

Working with stutterers and their families requires a special expertise. There are speech and language clinicians who either do not have wide experience with this population or who feel uncomfortable working with stutterers. Thus the clinician who will be working with the stutterer—preschool or school-age—should be chosen with care.

Conclusion

Behavioral techniques are perfectly acceptable to use with any articulation or fluency training approach as well as with cognitive and holistic language intervention approaches. Can one deny the benefits of data collection to assess progress, or the social advantages of interpersonal rewards for successful communication and problem solving? The rigidity and formal structure that characterized behavioral language intervention in the past have been replaced today by naturalistic settings that emulate spontaneous, functional, real-world situations. A wide variety of communicative functions (e.g., attentional devices, commands, requests, negation, informing, pretending) get expressed in those settings. The fact that language is used in a functional way to manipulate the world is not just reinforcing; it also enhances a child's cognitive and social awareness of the ways and means of human learning and interaction.

Regardless of whether disfluent, dysphasic, language delayed, autistic, retarded, learning disabled, or phonologically impaired, the child needs to be educated about how to express and understand the meaning underlying any communicative act. For the developmentally speech and language-disordered child, intervention strategies based on normal developmental progress and processes are typical. The child's quality and level of performance within and across skill areas will help to determine where and how intervention is to get done. The child's skill repertoire will dictate how and which functional systems need to be reorganized.

Early intervention for communicatively handicapped children is standard practice today. Infant programs where parents, siblings, language pathologists, physical therapists, psychiatrists, social workers, and psychologists work together as a team are common. Early identification and intervention of language-based learning disorders may reduce, or at the very least provide coping strategies for, many of the social and academic problems that can arise from speech- and language-based learning disorders. Integrated, holistic intervention programs that treat the communicative skills of these children along with their familial, social, cognitive, and educational needs give them their best chance to be integrated, dynamic, functional individuals.

Chapter 52

Treatment and Education: Effect of Public Law 94-142

Some schools may potentiate disturbed behavior, whereas others may protect against disturbed behavior and foster academic and psychosocial success (Rutter 1980). The importance of schools as facilities that may provide psychoeducational programming and offer a protective environment has been highlighted by the Education of All Handicapped Children Act of 1975 (Public Law [PL] 94-142). It represents the culmination of legal attempts to grant educational opportunities and rights to handicapped children and is similar in intent to major civil rights legislation passed during the past three decades.

Handicapping conditions that have been identified by the law include 1) serious emotional disturbance, 2) mental retardation, 3) specific learning disabilities, 4) speech impairments, 5) hearing and visual handicaps, 6) orthopedic handicaps, and 7) "other health impaired."

The first category is an Axis I diagnosis in DSM-III-R (American Psychiatric Association 1987) and the next three are Axis II categories. The other categories are frequently associated with psychiatric disorders.

Medical and counseling services are recommended by law as related services. However, it is specifically stated that "such medical services shall be for diagnostic and evaluation purposes only" as required to assist a handicapped child to benefit from special education. The provision of ongoing treatment for children identified through the evaluation process is not addressed in the public law. However, increased responsibility and "ownership" of the problems of exceptional children leads naturally to treatment. Children referred to learning disability programs have a similar behavioral profile to those in a special school for the emotionally disturbed, although their problems are less severe (Harris et al. 1984). Schools have traditionally focused on school conduct and peer relations but not on psychoeducational programs that address the academic progress of severely disordered children. Nor have specific parent-child problems, although having impact on academic performance, been systematically addressed. The issue of psychiatric diagnosis as a factor in the makeup of classroom composition also is not ordinarily considered. So as diagnostic and evaluation services identify diagnostic categories, recognize parent-child problems, and clarify the child's affective interactions within the school, then issues in treatment will be further highlighted. Psychiatric participation in team meetings is essential to specify treatment approaches.

In this chapter, I will 1) emphasize the impact of PL 94-142 on psychiatry and education, 2) review the relationship of DSM-III-R to special education categories, and 3) discuss the development of special schools that provide comprehensive psychoeducational programs for designated handicaps.

PL 94-142: An Overview

This law mandates that every educationally handicapped child must have the opportunity for free and appropriate educational services. Extensive evaluation studies are lacking but the more impressionistic reports (Ballard and Zettel 1977; Harvey and Siantz 1979; Henderson and Hage 1979; Kaplan 1978; Kaye and Aserlind 1979) suggest positive effects. Much of the psychiatric, pediatric, and psychological literature is descriptive and focuses on how practitioners might relate to the law (McCoy and Glazzard 1975; Palfrey et al. 1978; Safford 1978; Silverman 1979).

Keith and Epanchin (1983), a child psychiatrist and a county school psychologist, reviewed their four years of experience with PL 94-142 in their local school system. They commented on the development of screening teams whose task it is to draw up the individualized education program (IEP) for a particular child. These teams have streamlined the planning process, and the number of child psychiatric referrals for evaluation has increased. The psychiatrist and psychologists from the local mental health center are integrally involved in the screening team process, and these teams have allowed them to have an impact at one interface with the public school system. They reported the following:

1. There was an increased "ownership" by the school system of several groups of exceptional children. For example, a sincere effort has been made to plan for regular classroom programs for the children coming out of the state children's psychiatric units, for community and private programs for the deaf, and for the mentally retarded who have been "taken back" into the school system. Special classes and resource rooms for the emotionally disturbed, including autistic children, increased from none to seven over a three-year period.
2. The number of "officially designated" exceptional and handicapped children increased by 38 percent (from 1,400 to 1,800) between 1974 and 1979 while the school population increased less than 5 percent. The increase was primarily in the learning disability category.

The stress on least-restrictive environment, provision of regular IEP reviews, and the due process provisions in the law mitigate the effects of early labeling and its presumed prejudicial effect. This focus may lead to the ecologic approach to classification that Hobbs (1975) recommended, where the child's particular problem is specified and procedures are outlined for its remediation. This approach is similar to the development of a treatment plan (Group for the Advancement of Psychiatry 1973; Looney 1984) in child psychiatric practice. Concerns about labeling, confidentiality, and inadequate remedial programming existed before the law was passed and, with its passage, now must be directly approached in individual cases.

Since the inception of the law, there have been concerns that excessive service demands may drain the resources of school systems. However, the screening system ordinarily attempts to deal with fair and realistic solutions given that the "ideal" program may not be available. Reasonable services based on community standards are the general intent of the legislation. The civil rights focus of the legislation leads to reevaluation of resources and priorities for service for handicapped children.

DSM-III and DSM-III-R and Special Education

The school and mental health programs are separate but need a common language to define emotional and behavioral problems. Both groups use behavior as a means of categorization. DSM-III (American Psychiatric Association 1980) has led to the introduction of a diagnostic system into the school-hearing procedure that decides special school placement. DSM-III's strengths and limitations for schools have been widely argued, and DSM-III-R has, in part, been responsive to child psychiatrists' involvement with the schools.

The usual behavioral focus in schools has been on classroom deportment and on peer relations rather than on the academic progress of disturbed students or in viewing school programs as preventive interventions with disturbed and behaviorally disordered students. Although behavior at school in first grade has been suggested by Kellam et al. (1975) to predict antisocial behavior and substance abuse in adolescent boys, schools traditionally have not seen their programs as having a mental health focus or impact. This may be changing now that "affective education" and "social cognition" programs are entering the curriculum and PL 94-142 is leading to more interaction with mental health professionals. The need to establish specific treatment goals for learning-disabled and emotionally disturbed children leads to a closer look at how both schools and mental health professionals define disturbed behavior. It places a renewed focus on how the educational process may influence behaviorally and emotionally disturbed children.

Although special educational categories vary among the different states, such categories as learning disabled and educationally handicapped, behavioral disordered and emotionally handicapped, severely emotionally disturbed, educable mental retardation, trainable mental retardation, severe or profound mental retardation, developmentally handicapped, speech and hearing handicapped, other health impairment, and ineligible for special education services are commonly used. Educators may classify autistic children alone as a unique category, under one of the behavioral or developmental categories, or in the other health related category. There also may be special categories for aphasia and orthopedic handicaps. These designations are used by schools to determine the level of educational services needed (e.g., class size and teacher-to-pupil ratio).

The severity of the problem is frequently the major consideration for the school in making these determinations. This was demonstrated by Harris et al. (1984) when teachers were asked to complete behavioral questionnaires in two special educational settings, one for learning disabled and one for severely emotionally disturbed. The populations of students had similar behavioral profiles, but those students referred to the severely emotionally disturbed program had more frequent and severe emotional and behavioral disturbances. The school referral process based on severity rather than diagnostic considerations results in mixing severely conduct-disordered children with children who have major psychiatric diagnoses (e.g., affective disorder or schizophrenia). This often complicates programming.

To review, in contrast to general descriptions, the psychiatric diagnostic system uses specific definitions designating essential features for each diagnosis, often with criteria for duration of symptoms. Associated features (e.g., age of onset, course, outcome, prevalence, sex ratio, family pattern) are specified, and differential diagnostic considerations are listed. To be included as an Axis I diagnosis, there must be evidence of a disorder as indicated by distress or disability. Because of associated problems with adaptive function, mental retardation was included on Axis I in DSM-III. DSM-III-R has created a developmental axis and places mental retardation on Axis II.

The more severe developmental disorders (e.g., autism) are designated in the category pervasive developmental disorders and are now coded on Axis II. There is also a provision in the classification for interactional problems between persons that may require therapeutic intervention, although neither the child nor adult meets criteria for a specific diagnosis. These difficulties may be classified using categories such as parent-child problem in a clinic but may not be recognized in the school setting, although they are categorized in DSM-III-R. Axis II diagnoses may be designated as the primary diagnosis. Although not required by DSM-III-R for general use, Axis IV (severity of psychosocial stressors) and Axis V (global assessment of functioning scale) may be included in the diagnostic profile. This information may be helpful in considering the prognosis of the child's condition and facilitate appropriate school placement.

Clinicians are in better agreement about the more general categories, such as conduct or emotional disorders. However, specific subcategorizing meets with less agreement. For example, a child who does not meet all the essential features for a disorder may be placed in a residual category, but for the school the general category may be adequate for placement. The classification itself is in the process of continual review. The dimensions provided by the multiaxial system are of importance in treatment planning and more extensive than those used by the school. Individual interviews with the child and parent also provide data not available to the school that may be of importance in treatment planning.

A psychiatric diagnosis alone is not enough to guarantee special educational programming. Forness et al. (1982) found that children with the same psychiatric diagnosis might be categorized differently by the school program. For example, three children with attention-deficit hyperactivity disorder were each categorized differently; one was placed in the learning-disabled class, another in the severely emotionally disturbed class, and a third was ineligible for special education. The severity of classroom management problems and the results of the school's educational assessment are more critical features for the school in determining classroom placement.

Communication with schools must include assessment information gathered from the multiaxial diagnostic system and the case formulation. A meaningful report that clarifies the child's needs in the language required by 94-142 and advocates a program tailored to the child's multiple needs should be sent to the school. In some instances, a child may fit into more than one educational category. For example, a child with a diagnosis of conduct disorder, attention-deficit hyperactivity disorder, and learning disability may require programming that takes into account both behavioral and learning difficulty. The study by Harris et al. (1984) found that children placed in special programs for severe emotional disturbance also had educational needs that required special programming and that children in a learning-disabled school program needed additional services for their behavior disorders. They also noted that teachers tended to bring children with externalizing symptoms to attention and be less concerned about the more withdrawn child who might be depressed. The teacher questionnaire, Child Behavior Checklist (CBCL) teacher report, does not include a grouping for depression as rated by teachers, thereby permitting this important diagnostic entity to receive less emphasis.

The DSM-III-R categories and the use of multiaxial classification provide more precision and lend more complexity to the development of IEPs. However, more careful consideration of the psychoeducational needs of children in schools based on psychiatric diagnostic considerations may lead to better understanding by teachers of the child's needs and provide the clinician with a new perspective on how the school may participate in treatment planning.

Special Classes and Special Schools

The earliest model for child psychiatric consultation to schools was the Wellesley model, which was based on the work preventive model of Gerald Caplan. The main focus is on consultation with the teachers in the school, who are helped to clarify the child's problem and develop strategies for dealing with the child in the classroom. With PL 94-142, schools are also asking for additional individual psychiatric assessments of children at school since the child is already identified as having a disturbance. School systems are under pressure to provide services locally. This has led to the development of special classes in the school where the child may remain all day or may spend part of each day in other classes with other students in a regular classroom setting (i.e., mainstreaming). Alternatively, the student may be referred to a special school program in his or her home state or out of state. These programs are ordinarily administered by the school; however, there may be special arrangements, such as a program in San Antonio, Texas, where the school has contracted with the child psychiatrists to provide day hospital services for emotionally disturbed and behaviorally disordered children (Serrano 1984).

Children with learning disabilities make up the largest segment of the population requiring special schooling. If their needs cannot be met in regular classrooms or in special classes in regular schools, they may be referred to special school programs. A special school program might lead to improvement in both behavior and learning and prevent further progression of conduct difficulties. Some of the complexities in defining services in special schools were demonstrated by Harris et al. (1984). Achenbach (Achenbach and Edelbrock 1981) behavior profiles filled out by teachers showed similar patterns but were different for the two groups in that the students in the emotionally handicapped school had statistically higher total scores, higher externalizing and internalizing scores, and higher scores on the social withdrawal, self-destructive, inattentive, and nervous-overanxious subscales. They were 2.6 years behind in reading compared to 3.3 years behind for the learning-disabled group. Despite their differences, the learning-disabled group were a relatively disturbed population, scoring at the 85th percentile on the CBCL. It was concluded that the emotionally handicapped group required additional instruction for their learning difficulties and the learning-disabled group required additional services for behavioral disorders. Both school programs provided settings where preventive interventions could be carried out, with the eventual goal of mainstreaming back into regular school programs.

Special school programs allow the development of comprehensive models of care. Preadmission evaluations including both child and parent provide diagnostic information important for treatment planning. Decisions can then be made regarding individual and group psychotherapy with children during the school day; strategies for working with families during the school year can be developed. A special school setting provides an opportunity for students to participate in the student council or in the school paper and to be involved in peer tutoring—socializing experiences ordinarily not available to them in regular school programs. Periodic reevaluation of each student is ongoing, with teachers involved in both group and individual discussion regarding students in their classes.

References

Section 3
Specific Developmental Disorders

Achenbach TM, Edelbrock SC: Behavioral problems and competencies reported by parents of normal and disturbed children aged four through sixteen, (Serial no 188). Monogr Soc Res Child Dev 46:1–81, 1981

Aiken LR Jr: Language factors in learning mathematics. Review of Educational Research 42:359–385, 1972

American Academy of Ophthalmology: Policy Statement: Learning Disabilities, Dyslexia and Vision. San Francisco, American Academy of Ophthalmology, 1984

American Academy of Pediatrics: Joint organizational statement: the eye and learning disabilities. Pediatrics 49:454–455, 1972

American Academy of Pediatrics: Committee on Nutrition: megavitamin therapy for childhood psychoses and learning disabilities. Pediatrics 58:910–911, 1976

American Academy of Pediatrics: The Doman-Delacato treatment of neurologically handicapped children: a policy statement by the American Academy of Pediatrics. Pediatrics 70:810–812, 1982

American Psychiatric Association: Task Force on Vitamin Therapy in Psychiatry: Megavitamin and Orthomolecular Therapy in Psychiatry. Washington, DC, American Psychiatric Association, 1973

American Psychiatric Association: Diagnostic and Statistical Manual of Mental Disorders, 3rd ed. Washington, DC, American Psychiatric Association, 1980

American Psychiatric Association: Diagnostic and Statistical Manual of Mental Disorders, 3rd ed, revised. Washington, DC, American Psychiatric Association, 1987

American Speech-Language and Hearing Association Journal 25:43 June 1983

Andrews G, Harris M: The Syndrome of Stuttering. London, William Heinemann Medical Books, 1964

Aram DM, Nation JE: Patterns of language behavior in children with developmental language disorders. J Speech Hear Res 18:229–241, 1975

Aram DM, Nation JE: Preschool language disorders and subsequent language and academic difficulties. J Commun Dis 13:159–270, 1980

Aram DM, Eckelman B, Nation JE: Preschoolers with language disorders 10 years later. J Speech Hear Res 27:232–244, 1984

Arter JA, Jenkins JR: Differential diagnosis: prescriptive teaching: a critical appraisal. Review of Educational Research 49:517–555, 1979

Ashlock RB: Error Patterns in Computations: A Semi-Programmed Approach. Columbus, Ohio, Charles E. Merrill, 1972

Baker L, Brown AS: Cognitive monitoring in reading and studying, in Understanding Reading Comprehension. Edited by Flood J. Newark, Del, International Reading Association, 1983

Ballard J, Zettel JJ: Public law 94-142 and section 504: What they say about rights and protection. Except Child 44:177–184, 1977

Bannatyne A: The color phonics system, in The Disabled Reader. Edited by Money J, Schiffman G. Baltimore, Johns Hopkins University Press, 1966

Bates E: The Emergence of Symbols. New York, Academic Press, 1979

Beatty LD, Madden R, Gardner EF: Stanford Diagnostic Arithmetic Test (Level I and Level II). New York, Harcourt Brace Jovanovich, 1966

Beckey RE: A study of certain factors related to retardation of speech. Journal of Speech Disorders 7:223–249, 1942

Beery ED, Buktenica N: Developmental Test of Visual-Motor Integration. Chicago, Follett Publishing Co, 1967

Beitchman JH, Nair R, Clegg M, et al: Prevalence of psychiatric disorders in children with speech and language disorders. J Am Acad Child Psychiatry 25:528–535, 1986a

Beitchman JH, Nair R, Clegg M, et al: The prevalence of speech and language disorders in 5-year-old kindergarten children. J Speech Hear Res 51:98–110, 1986b

Bender LA: Visual Motor Gestalt Test and Its Clinical Use. New York, American Orthopsychiatric Association, 1938

Blanchard P: Psychoanalytic contributions to the problems of reading disabilities. Psychoanal Study Child 2:163–187, 1946

Bloom L, Lahey M: Language Development and Language Disorders. New York, John Wiley & Sons, 1978

Brady JP, Berson J: Stuttering, dichotic listening, and cerebral dominance. Archives of General Psychiatry 32:1449–1452, 1975

Brazelton TB, Tronick E: Preverbal communication between mothers and infants, in The Social Foundations of Language and Thought. Edited by Olson D. New York, WW Norton & Co, 1980

Brazelton TB, Koslawski B, Main M: The origins of reciprocity: the early mother-infant interaction, in The Effect of the Infant on Its Caregiver. Edited by Lewis M, Rosenblum LA. New York, John Wiley & Sons, 1974

Brown AL: The development of memory: knowing, knowing about knowing and knowing how to know, in Advances in Child Development and Behavior. Edited by Reese H. New York, Academic Press, 1975

Brown AL: Knowing when, where and how to remember: a problem of meta-cognition, in Advances in Instructional Psychology. Edited by Glaser R. Hillsdale, NJ, Lawrence Erlbaum Associates, 1978

Brown AL, Day JD: Strategies and knowledge for summarizing texts: the development of expertise. Unpublished manuscript. Chicago, University of Illinois, 1980

Brown AL, Campione JC, Murphy MD: Keeping track of changing variables: long-term retention of a trained rehearsal strategy by retarded adolescents. J Ment Defic Res 78:446–453, 1974

Bruner J. Interaction, communiction, and self. J Am Acad Child Psychiatry 23:1–7, 1984

Bruner J: The ontogenesis of speech acts, in Social Rules and Social Behavior. Edited by Collet P. Oxford, Basil Blackwell, 1977

Brutten E, Shoemaker D: The Modification of Stuttering. Englewood Cliffs, NJ, Prentice-Hall, 1967

Cantor S: The Schizophrenic Child. Montreal, Eden Press, 1982

Cantwell DP, Baker L: Psychiatric disorder in children with speech and language retardation. Arch Gen Psychiatry 34:583–591, 1977

Cantwell DP, Baker L: Developmental Speech and Language Disorders. New York, Guilford Press, 1987

Cantwell DP, Forness SR: Learning disorders. J Am Acad Child Psychiatry 21:417–419, 1982

Cantwell DP, Baker L, Mattison RE: The prevalence of psychiatric disorder in children with speech and language disorders: an epidemiological study. J Am Acad Child Psychiatry 18:450–451, 1979

Carlson PV, Greenspoon NK: The uses and abuses of visual training for children with perceptual-motor learning problems. American Journal of Optometry 45:161–169, 1968

Cawley JF: An instructional design in secondry school mathematics for learning-disabled students, in Learning Disabilities in the Secondary School. Edited by Mann L, Goodman L, Wiederholt JL. Boston, Houghton Mifflin, 1978

Chall J: Learning to Read: The Great Debate. New York, McGraw-Hill, 1967

Chess S, Rosenberg M: Clinical differentiation among children and initial language complaints. Journal of Autism and Childhood Schizophrenia 4:99–110, 1974

Childs S: Teaching the Dyslexic Child: Dyslexia in Special Education. Pomfret, Conn, The Orton Society, 1964

Cohn R: Arithmetic and learning disabilities, in Progress in Learning Disabilities. Edited by Mykelbust H. New York, Grune & Stratton, 1971

Cole P: Language Disorders in Preschool Children. Englewood Cliffs, NJ, Prentice-Hall, 1982

Connolly AJ, Nachtman W, Pritchett EM: Key Math Diagnostic Arithmetic Test. Circle Pines, Minn, American Guidance Service, 1988

Conture E: Stuttering. Englewood Cliffs, NJ, Prentice-Hall, 1982

Conture E, Brewer D, McCall G: Laryngeal behavior during stuttering. Journal of Fluency Disorders 4:79–89, 1977

Cooper EB: Recovery from stuttering in a junior and senior high school population. J Speech Hear Disord 15:632–638, 1972

Cott A: Orthomolecular approach to the treatment of learning disabilites. Schizophrenia 3:95–107, 1971

Cott A: Help for Your Learning Disabled Child: The Orthomolecular Treatment. New York, Times Books, 1985

Curry FK, Gregory HH: A comparison of stutterers and nonstutterers on three dichotic listening tasks. Convention Address, American Speech-Language Hearing Association, 1967

Dahmus NE: How to teach verbal problems. School, Science and Mathematics 70:121–138, 1970

Davidson J: Using the Cuisenaire Rods. New Rochelle, NY, Cuisenaire, 1969

Denkla M: Childhood learning disorders, in Clinical Neuropsychology. Edited by Heilman KM, Valenstein E. New York, Oxford University Press, 1979

Doman G, Delacato C: Doman-Delacato philosophy. Human Potential 1:113–116, 1968

Dore J: The development of communicative competence, in Language Competence: Assessment and Intervention. Edited by Schiefelbusch R. San Diego, College Hill Press, 1985

Duchan J: Language intervention through sensemaking and fine tuning, in Language Competence: Assessment and Intervention. Edited by Schiefelbusch R. San Diego, College Hill Press, 1985

Dunn L, Dunn L: Peabody Picture Vocabulary Test. Circle Pines, Minn, American Guidance Service, 1981

Elkind D: The Hurried Child: Growing Up Too Fast, Too Soon. Reading, Mass, Addison-Wesley, 1984

Englemann S, Bruner EC: Distar Reading: An Instructional System. Chicago, Science Research Associates, 1969

Englemann S, Carnine D: Distar: An Instructional System: Arithmetic I, II, and III. Chicago, Science Research Associates, 1976

Fernald G: Remedial Techniques in Basic School Subjects. New York, McGraw-Hill, 1943

Ferreri CA, Wainwright RB: Breakthrough for Dyslexia and Learning Disabilities. Pompano Beach, Fla, Exposition Press of Florida, 1984

Fisher HA, Logeman JA: The Fisher-Logeman Test of Articulation Competence. New York, Houghton-Mifflin Co, 1971

Forness SR, Cantwell DT: DSM-III Psychiatric Diagnosis and Special Education Categories. Journal of Special Education 16:49–63, 1982

Fraiberg S: Intervention in infancy: a program for blind infants, in Exceptional Infant, vol 3. Edited by Freidland B, Sterrit G, Kirk G. New York, Brunner/Mazel, 1975

Freeman F: Phonation in stuttering: a review of current research. Journal of Fluency Disorders 4:79–89, 1979

Freeman F: Stuttering, in Speech, Language and Hearing, vol 2. Edited by Lass N, McReynolds LV, Northern JL, et al. Philadelphia, WB Saunders Co, 1983

Frostig M: Corrective reading in the classroom. The Reading Teacher 18:573–580, 1965

Gaddes W: Prevalence estimates and the need for definition of learning disabilities, in Neuropsychology of Learning Disorders. Edited by Knights RM, Bakker DJ. Baltimore, University Park Press, 1976

Gadow KD: Pharmacotherapy for learning disabilities. Learning Disabilities 2:127–140, 1983

Gallagher T, Prutting C (eds): Pragmatic Assessment and Intervention Issues in Language. San Diego, College Hill Press, 1983

Gardner TA: The guilt reaction of parents of a child with severe physical disease. Am J Psychiatry 126:636–644, 1969

Gates IA, McKillop AS, Horowitz EC: Gates-McKillop-Horowitz Reading Diagnostic Tests. New York, Teachers College, 1981

Gattegno C: Words in Color. Chicago, Learning Materials, 1962

Gillingham A, Stillman B: Remedial Work for Reading, Spelling and Penmanship, 7th ed. Cambridge, Mass, Educators Publishing Service, 1965

Gittelman R, Feingold I: Children with reading disorders, I: efficacy of reading remediation. J Child Psychol Psychiatry 24:167–191, 1983a

Gittelman R, Feingold I: Children with reading disorders, II: effects of methylphenidate in combination with reading remediation. J Child Psychol Psychiatry 24:193–212, 1983b

Glennon VJ, Wilson JW: Diagnostic-prescriptive teaching, in The Slow Learner in Mathematics: Thirty-Fifth Yearbook of the National Council of Teachers of Mathematics. Edited by Lowrey WC. Washington, DC, National Council of Teachers of Mathematics, 1972

Goldman R, Fristoe M: Goldman-Fristoe Test of Articulation. Circle Pines, Minn, American Guidance Service, 1972

Gray WS, Robinson HM: Gray Oral Reading Test. Indianapolis: Bobbs-Merrill, 1981

Group for the Advancement of Psychiatry: From Diagnosis to Treatment: An Approach to Treatment Planning for the Emotionally Disturbed Child. Monograph no. 87, 1973

Guitar B, Adams M, Conture E: Clinical feedback. Journal of Childhood Communication Disorders 3:3–12, 1979

Hammill DD, Larsen SL: The relationship of selected auditory perceptual skills and reading ability. Journal of Learning Disabilities 7:429–435, 1974

Hammill DD, Goodman L, Wiederhold JL: Visual-motor processes: can we train them? The Reading Teacher 27:469–478, 1974

Harris A: How to Increase Reading Ability, 5th ed. New York, David McKay, 1970

Harris J, King S, Reifler J, et al: Emotional and learning problems in 6–12 year old boys attending special schools. J Am Acad Child Psychiatry 23:431–436, 1984

Harvey J, Siantz J: Public education and the handicapped. Journal of Research and Development in Education 12:1–9, 1979

Henderson R, Hage R: Economic implications of public education of the handicapped. Journal of Research and Development in Education 12:71–79, 1979

Hillman RE, Gilbert HH: Voice onset time for voiceless stop consonants in the fluent reading of stutterers and non-stutterers. J Acoust Soc Am 61:610–611, 1977

Hobbs N (ed): Issues in the Classification of Children, vols 1 & 2. San Francisco, Jossey-Bass, 1975

Hodson BW, Paden EP: Targeting Intelligible Speech. San Diego, College Hill Press, 1983

Hoffer A, Osmond H: The Clinical Basis of Clinical Psychiatry. Springfield Ill, Charles C Thomas, 1960

Hoffer A, Osmond H, Smythies J: Schizophrenia: a new approach, II: results of a year's research. Journal of Mental Science 100:29–54, 1954

Ingram D: Phonologic Disability in Children. New York, Elsevier, 1976

Institute for the Study of Learning Disabilities: Final Report. New York, Teachers College, Columbia University, 1983

Jakobson R, Fant GM, Halle M: Preliminaries to Speech Analysis. Technical report 13. Acoustics Laboratory, Boston, Massachusetts Institute of Technology, 1952

Jastak JE, Jastak SR: The Wide Range Achievement Test. Wilmington, Del, Jastak Associates, 1978

Johnson DG, Mykelbust HR: Learning Disabilities: Educational Principles and Practices. New York, Grune & Stratton, 1967

Kaplan L: Special education Public Law 94-142: what's happening? Journal of Special Education 29:74–75, 1978

Kauffman JM, Hallahan DP: The medical model and the science of special education. Exceptional Children 41:97–102, 1974

Kaye N, Aserlind R: The IEP, the ultimate process. Journal of Special Education 13:137–143, 1979

Keith C, Epanchin A: Child Psychiatric Perspectives on Public Law 94-142: Four Years of Experience in an Average School System. Presented at the Annual Meeting of the American Academy of Child Psychiatry. 1983

Kellam SG, Branch JD, Agrawal KC, et al: Mental Health and Going to School: The Woodlawn Program of Assessment, Early Intervention, and Evaluation. Chicago, University of Chicago Press, 1975

Kidd KK: A genetic perspective on stuttering. Journal of Fluency Disorder 2:259–269, 1977

Kidd KK, Records MA: Genetic methodologies for the study of speech, in neurogenics: Genetic Approaches to the Nervous System. Edited by Breakfield N. New York, Elsevier, 1979

Kirk S, McCarthy J, Kirk W: Illinois Test of Psycholinguistic Abilities. Urbana, University of Illinois Press, 1968

Kline C, Kline C: Follow-up study of 216 dyslexic children. Bulletin of the Orton Society 25:127–144, 1975

Larsen S, Hammill D: Test of Written Spelling. Austin, Tex, Pro-Ed, 1976

Lerner J: Children with Learning Disabilities. New York, Houghton Mifflin Co, 1971

Levinson HN: A Solution to the Riddle Dyslexia. New York, Springer-Verlag, 1981

Levinson HN: Smart but Feeling Dumb. New York, Warner Books, 1984

Lilienfeld AM, Pasamanick B, Rogers M: Relationships between pregnancy experience and the development of certain neuropsychiatric disorders in childhood. Am J Public Health 45:637–643, 1955

Looney JL: Treatment planning in child psychiatry. J Am Acad Child Psychiatry 23:529–536, 1984

Lund N, Duchan J: Assessing Children's Language in Naturalistic Contexts. Englewood Cliffs, NJ, Prentice-Hall, 1988

Luria A: Restoration of Function After Brain Injury. New York, Macmillan, 1963

Luria A: The Working Brain. New York, Basic Books, 1968

Luria A: Higher Cortical Functions in Man. New York, Basic Books, 1980

MacGinitie W: Gates-MacGinitie Reading Tests. Boston, Houghton Mifflin Co, 1978

Madden R, Gardner ER, Rudman HC, et al: Stanford Achievement Test. New York, Harcourt Brace Jovanovich, 1973

Mandler JM, Johnson NS: Remembrance of things parsed: story structure and recall. Cognitive Psychology 9:111–151, 1977

Martyn MM, Sheehan J: Onset of stuttering and recovery. Behav Res Ther 6:295–307, 1968

McCoy S, Glazzard P: Winning the case but losing the child: interdisciplinary experiences with P.L. 94-142. Journal of Clinical Child Psychology 7:205–208, 1975

McReynolds LV, Elbert MF: Articulation disorders of unknown etiology and their remediation, in Speech, Language and Hearing, vol. 2. Edited by Lass N, McReynolds LV, Northern JL, et al. Philadelphia, WB Saunders Co, 1982

Meecham MM: Evaluating of Appraisal Techniques in Speech Language Pathology. Edited by Darley F. Reading, Mass, Addison-Wesley, 1979

Meichenbaum N, Asarnow J: Cognitive-behavioral modification and metacognitive development: implications for the classroom, in Cognitive-Behavioral Intervention: Theory, Research and Procedures. Edited by Kendall PC, Hollson SD. New York, Academic Press, 1979

Metzger RL, Werner DB: Use of visual training for reading disabilities: a review. Pediatrics 73:824–829, 1984

Meyer BJ: Organizational patterns in prose and their use in reading, in Reading Research: Studies and Applications: Twenty-Eighth Yearbook of the National Reading Conference. Edited by Kamil ML, Moe AJ. 1979, pp 109–117

Meyers PI, Hammill DD: Methods for Learning Disorders. New York, John Wiley & Sons, 1976

Millar S: The Psychology of Play. London, Penguin Books, 1968

Moorhead D, Moorhead A: From signal to sign: a Piagetian view of thought and language during the first two years, in Language Perspectives: Acquisition, Retardation, Intervention. Edited by Schiefelbusch RL, Loyd LL. Baltimore, University Park Press, 1974

Muma J: Language Handbook: Concepts, Assessment and Intervention. Englewood Cliffs, NJ, Prentice-Hall, 1973

Newcomer PL, Hammill DD: The Test of Language Development. Austin, Tex, Empiric Press, 1977

Ninio A, Bruner J: The achievement and antecedents of labelling. Journal of Child Language 5:1–16, 1978

Ochs E, Schieffelin B: Developmental Pragmatics. New York, Academic Press, 1979

Orton S: Reading, Writing, and Speech Problems in children. New York, WW Norton & Co, 1937

Palfrey JS, Mervis RC, Butler JA: New directions in the evaluation and education of handicapped children. N Engl J Med 298:819–824, 1978

Patterson JH: Technique for improving comprehension in mathematics, in Reading in the Middle School. Newark, Del, International Reading Association, 1974

Piaget J: The Origins of Intelligence in Children. New York, WW Norton & Co, 1963

Piaget J: The Child's Conception of the World. Totowa, NJ, Littlefield, Adams & Co, 1972a

Piaget J: Judgment and Reasoning in the Child. Totowa, NJ, Littlefield, Adams & Co, 1972b

Pitman J: Initial Teaching Alphabet. London, 1963

Polatajko HJ: A critical look at vestibular dysfunction in learning-disabled children. Dev Med Child Neurol 27:283–292, 1985

Poznanski E: Psychiatric difficulties in siblings of handicapped children. Clin Pediatr (Phila) 8:232–234, 1969

Rawson M: Developmental Language Disability: Adult Accomplishments of Dyslexic Boys. Baltimore, Johns Hopkins Press, 1968

Reder LM: The role of elaboration in the comprehension and retention of prose. A Critical Review of Educational Research 50:5–53, 1980

Reid DK, Hresko WP: A cognitive approach to learning disabilities. New York, McGraw-Hill, 1981

Rudel RG, Helfgott E: Effect of piracetam on verbal memory of dyslexic boys. J Am Acad Child Psychiatry 23:695–699, 1984

Rumelhart DE, Ortony A: The representation of knowledge in memory, in Schooling and the Acquisition of Knowledge. Edited by Anderson RC, Spiro RJ, Montague WE. Hillsdale, NJ, Lawrence Erlbaum Associates, 1977

Rutter M: Emotional disorder and educational underachievement. Arch Dis Child 49:249–266, 1974

Rutter M: School influences on children's behavior and development. Pediatrics 65:208–220, 1980

Rutter M, Lebovki S, Eisenberg L: A triaxial classification of mental disorders in childhood. J Child Psychol Psychiatry 10:41–61, 1969

Rutter M, Tizard J, Whitemore K: Education, Health and Behavior. London, Longmans, 1970

Rutter M, Maughan B, Mortinore P, et al: Fifteen thousand hours. London, Open Books, 1979

Safford P: Mental health counseling dimensions of special education programs. J Sch Health 48:541–547, 1978

Salvia J, Ysseldyke E: Assessment in Special and Remedial Education, 2nd ed. Boston, Houghton Mifflin Co, 1981

Schwartz RG: Diagnosis of speech sound disorders in children, in Diagnosis in Speech-Language Pathology. Edited by Meitus IJ, Weinberg B. Baltimore, University Park Press, 1983

Semel EM, Wiig EH: Clinical Evaluation of Language Functions. New York, Bell & Howell, 1980

Serrano A: Symposium on School Consultation. American Academy of Child Psychiatry, Toronto, 1984

Shapiro J: Metamemory and the Metamemory-Memory Relationship in Learning Disabled and Nonlearning Disabled Children. Doctoral dissertation. New York, Teachers College, Columbia University, 1982

Shapiro T, Fish B: A method to study language deviation as an aspect of ego organization in young schizophrenic children. J Am Acad Child Psychiatry 8:36–56, 1969

Sharma M: Using word problems to aid language and reading comprehension. Topics in Learning Disabilities 1:61–77, 1981

Sheehan J: Conflict theory of stuttering, in Stuttering: A Symposium. Edited by Eisenson J. New York, Harper & Row, 1958

Silver LB: Emotional and social problems of children with developmental disabilities, in Handbook of Learning Disabilities. Edited by Weber RE. Englewood Cliffs, NJ, Prentice-Hall, 1974a, pp 97–120

Silver LB: Emotional and social problems of the family with a child who has developmental disabilities, in Handbook of Learning Disabilities. Edited by Weber RE. Englewood Cliffs, NJ, Prentice-Hall, 1974b, pp 121–130

Silver LB: Minimal brain dysfunction, in Basic Handbook of Child Psychiatry, vol. 2. Edited by Noshpitz J. New York, Basic Books, 1979, pp 416–439

Silver LB: The relationship between learning disabilities, hyperactivity, distractibility, and behavioral problems. J Am Acad Child Psychiatry 20:385–397, 1981

Silver LB: The Misunderstood Child: A Guide for Parents of Learning Disabled Children. New York, McGraw-Hill, 1984

Silver LB: "The magic cure": a review of the current controversial approaches for treating learning disabilities. Journal of Learning Disabilities 20:498–512, 1987

Silver LB, Brunstetter RW: Learning disabilities: current therapeutic methods, in Basic Handbook of Child Psychiatry, vol 5. Edited by Noshpitz J. New York, Basic Books, 1987, pp 494–502

Silverman M: Beyond the mainstream: the special needs of the chronic child patient. Am J Orthopsychiatry 49:62–68, 1979

Simeon J, Waters B, Resnick M: Effects of piracetam in children with learning disorders. Psychopharmacol Bull, 16:65–66, 1980

Smith DV, McCullough CM: Essentials of English Tests. Circle Pines, Minn, American Guidance Service, 1961

Solnit AJ, Stark MH: Mourning and the birth of a defective child. Psychoanal Study Child 16:523–537, 1961

Sommers RK, Briady WA, Moore WR: Dichotic ear preference of stuttering children and adults. Percept Mot Skills 41:931–938, 1975

The Speech Foundation of America: If your child stutters: A guide for parents: November 11. Memphis, Tenn, 1981

Stern C: The Structural Reading Series. Syracuse, NY, Singer, 1963

Stern C: Structural Arithmetic. Boston, Houghton Mifflin Co, 1965

Stern D: The First Relationship: Infant and Mother. Cambridge, Harvard University Press, 1977

Stevenson J, Richman N, Graham P: Behavior problems and language abilities at three years and behavioral deviance at eight years. J Child Psychol Psychiatry 26:215–230, 1985

Stocker B: Stocker Probe Technique for Diagnosis and Treatment of Stuttering in Young Children. Tulsa, Okla, Modern Education Corporation, 1976

Strominger AZ, Bashir AS: A nine year follow-up of 50 language delayed children. Presented at the Annual Meeting of the American Speech and Hearing Association. Chicago, November 1977

Szymanski LS: Psychiatric diagnostic evaluation of mentally retarded individuals. J Am Acad Child Psychiatry 16:67–87, 1977

Szymanski LS: Psychiatric diagnosis of retarded persons, in Emotional Disorders of Mentally Retarded Persons. Edited by Szymanski LS, Tanguay PE. Baltimore, University Park Press, 1980

Terman LM, Merrill MA: Stanford-Binet Intelligence Scales, 3rd revision. Boston, Houghton Mifflin Co, 1973

Torgesen JK, Goldman T: Rehearsal and short-term memory in reading disabled children. Child Dev 48:56–60, 1977

Tower DB: Foreword, Natl. Inst. Neurol. and Commun. Dis. and Stroke. Monograph no. 22. U.S. Dept. Health Human Services, Bethesda, 1979

Van Riper C: The Treatment of Stuttering. Englewood Cliffs, NJ, Prentice-Hall, 1973

Van Riper C: The Nature of Stuttering. Englewood Cliffs, NJ, Prentice-Hall, 1982

Van Riper C, Irwin J: Voice and Articulation. Englewood Cliffs, NJ, Prentice-Hall, 1958

Vygotsky L: Thought and Language. Cambridge, Mass, MIT Press, 1962

Vygotsky L: Mind, in Society. Edited by Cole M, John-Steiner F, Scribner E, et al. Cambridge, Mass, Harvard University Press, 1978

Wallach GP, Liebergott JW: Who shall be called "learning disabled": some new directions, in Language and Learning Disabilities in School-Age Children. Edited by Wallach GP, Butler KG. Baltimore, John Wiley & Sons, 1984

Walsh H: On certain practical inadequacies of distinctive feature systems. J Speech Hear Disord 39:32–43, 1974

Waryas CL, Crowe TA: Language delay, in Speech, Language and Hearing, vol 2. Edited by Lass N, McReynolds LV, Northern JL, et al. Philadelphia, WB Saunders Co, 1982

Watson BU, Watson CS, Fredd R: Followup studies of specific reading disability. J Am Acad Child Psychiatry 21:376–382, 1982

Webster RL: Empirical considerations regarding stuttering therapy, in Controversies About Stuttering Therapy. Edited by Gregory H. Baltimore, University Park Press, 1979

Wechsler D: Wechsler Intelligence Scale for Children–Revised. New York, The Psychological Corporation, 1974

Weiderholt JL, Hammill DD, Brown U: The Resource Teacher. Guide to Effective Practices. Boston, Allyn and Bacon, 1978

Wepman JM: Auditory discrimination, speech and reading. The Elementary School Journal 9:325–333, 1960

Wilsher CR, Atkins G, Manfield P: Piracetam as an aid to learning in dyslexia: preliminary report. Psychopharmacologia 65:107–109, 1979

Wingate ME: Recovery from stuttering. J Speech Hear Disord 29:312–321, 1964

Winitz H: Articulatory Acquisition and Behavior. New York, Appleton-Century-Crofts, 1969

Wishner GJ: Stuttering behavior and learning. J Speech Hear Disord 15:324–325, 1950

Wishner GJ: Experimental approach to expectancy and anxiety in stuttering behavior. J Speech Hear Disord 17:139–154, 1952

Wong BY, Jones W: Increasing metacomprehension in learning disabled and normally-achieving students through self-questioning training. Unpublished manuscript. Simon Fraser University, 1982

Wong B, Wong W, Foth D: Recall and clustering of verbal materials among normal and poor readers. Bulletin of the Psychonomic Society 10:375–378, 1977

Woodcock RW: Peabody Rebus Reading Program. Circle Pines, Minn, American Guidance Service, 1967

Woolfolk E, Carrew X, Lynch J: An Integrative Approach to Language Disorders in Children. New York, Grune & Stratton, 1982

Zimmerman GN: Articulatory dynamics of fluent utterances of stutterers and non-stutterers. J Speech Hear Res 23:95–107, 1980

SECTION 4

Attention-Deficit Hyperactivity Disorder and Conduct Disorder

Chapter 53

Attention-Deficit Hyperactivity Disorder and Conduct Disorder

Introduction

Definition and Diagnosis

Attention-deficit hyperactivity disorder (ADHD) and conduct disorder (CD) are two important and common groups of childhood disorders, perhaps affecting as many as 7 percent of children and constituting the most common reasons for referral to psychiatric treatment (American Psychiatric Association 1987; Graham 1979; Taylor 1986; Trites and Laprade 1983). They each have significant morbidity. Although they are classified as distinct entities, they have similar associated problems: academic difficulties and underachievement, low self-esteem, mood lability, temper outbursts, low frustration tolerance, poor response to discipline, and impaired social functioning. They are both frequently associated with specific developmental disorders, especially developmental reading disorder. They often have a chronic course and may extend into adolescence and adulthood (Gittelman et al. 1985; Robins 1966; Rutter and Garmezy 1983; Sturge 1982; Weiss and Hechtman 1986).

Prior to the DSM-III-R designation (American Psychiatric Association 1987) of ADHD, this group of problems was referred to, among other labels, as minimal brain damage (Gesell and Amatruda 1949), minimal brain dysfunction (Clements 1966; Wender 1971), hyperactive child syndrome (Stewart et al. 1966), hyperkinetic reaction of childhood (DSM-II) (American Psychiatric Association 1968), and attention deficit disorder with or without hyperactivity (DSM-III) (American Psychiatric Association 1980).

As currently defined, it is characterized by varying degrees of developmentally inappropriate inattention, impulsivity, and hyperactivity, with an onset by age seven and a minimal duration of six months. Table 1 lists the DSM-III-R criteria for ADHD.

ADHD, as conceptualized in DSM-III-R, is an early-onset (often by age four) condition, three to nine times more common in boys than girls, and possibly more common in the first-degree relatives of those with ADHD. It is usually manifested to varying degrees in several situations, is associated with impaired school and social functioning (in addition to those features previously listed), and is sometimes diagnosed together with CD, oppositional defiant disorder (ODD), and specific developmental disorders. Its course is usually chronic throughout childhood. Approximately one-third of children with ADHD from clinic samples still continue to show signs of

Table 1. DSM-III-R Diagnostic Criteria for Attention-deficit Hyperactivity Disorder

Note: Consider a criterion met only if the behavior is considerably more frequent than that of most people of the same mental age.

A. A disturbance of at least six months during which at least eight of the following are present:

    (1) often fidgets with hands or feet or squirms in seat (in adolescents, may be limited to subjective feelings of restlessness)

    (2) has difficulty remaining seated when required to do so

    (3) is easily distracted by extraneous stimuli

    (4) has difficulty awaiting turn in games or group situations

    (5) often blurts out answers to questions before they have been completed

    (6) has difficulty following through on instructions from others (not due to oppositional behavior or failure of comprehension), e.g., fails to finish chores

    (7) has difficulty sustaining attention in tasks or play activities

    (8) often shifts from one uncompleted activity to another

    (9) has difficulty playing quietly

    (10) often talks excessively

    (11) often interrupts or intrudes on others, e.g., butts into other children's games

    (12) often does not seem to listen to what is being said to him or her

    (13) often loses things necessary for tasks or activities at school or at home (e.g., toys, pencils, books, assignments)

    (14) often engages in physically dangerous activities without considering possible consequences (not for the purpose of thrill-seeking), e.g., runs into street without looking

Note: The above items are listed in descending order of discriminating power based on data from a national field trial of the DSM-III-R criteria for Disruptive Behavior Disorders.

B. Onset before the age of seven.

C. Does not meet the criteria for a Pervasive Developmental Disorder.

Criteria for severity of Attention-deficit Hyperactivity Disorder:
Mild: Few, if any, symptoms in excess of those required to make the diagnosis **and** only minimal or no impairment in school and social functioning.

Moderate: Symptoms or functional impairment intermediate between "mild" and "severe."

Severe: Many symptoms in excess of those required to make the diagnosis **and** significant and pervasive impairment in functioning at home and school and with peers.

the disorder in adulthood. ODD and CD often develop in the course of ADHD, and a significant number of those with CD are later found to have adult antisocial personality disorder. Poorer prognosis is associated with the co-diagnosis of CD, low IQ, or severe mental disorder in the parents (American Psychiatric Association 1987; Gittelman et al. 1985; Weiss and Hechtman 1986). ADHD probably represents a heterogeneous group. There are no definitive tests for it. Etiologies are speculative and unknown at this time.

ADHD corresponds to the International Classification of Disease-9 (ICD-9) hyperkinetic syndrome (Rutter et al. 1979). However, the diagnosis is used relatively rarely in Europe and in the United Kingdom, where the broader concept of CD is preferred and where stimulant drugs are not frequently used (Rapoport 1987; Taylor 1986).

Early descriptions and definitions of ADHD stressed that it was a manifestation of "minimal brain dysfunction" or "brain damage." These ambiguous terms are now avoided because, as numerous authors (e.g., Klein et al. 1980; Rutter and Garmezy 1983; Taylor 1986) have summarized: 1) the terms are too general, and the type of damage is not specified; 2) there are no variables to quantify as minimal; and 3) there is no validation of a single syndrome.

The DSM-III definition reflected a belief that attention deficit is invariably present in this disorder (whereas motor restlessness is not), that the attentional problems are central to the other behaviors, and that stimulant drugs are effective primarily through their effects on attention (Douglas and Peters 1979). Subsequent studies have shown that inattention is not always present, that children with ADHD do not necessarily differ from controls on measures of sustained attention, and that "pure" attention-deficit disorder may be a distinct, although heterogeneous, group in itself. In addition, cognitive and behavioral effects of stimulants are not significantly correlated, and efficacy of stimulant treatment is mediated in part by direct motor effects (Gittelman 1975; Gittelman et al. 1985; Lahey et al. 1984; Maurer and Stewart 1980; Porrino et al. 1983a, 1983b; Rapoport 1987; Sargeant 1984). DSM-III-R has specified severity ratings and has eliminated the subdivisions, allowing more variety in the combination of symptoms. The core areas (i.e., inattention, impulsivity, hyperactivity) may be equally important; it is not clear how the three areas relate or whether any one of the areas is secondary to another. A new category of undifferentiated attention-deficit disorder, as yet unvalidated, has been added; disturbances previously included in the DSM-III category attention-deficit disorder without hyperactivity would be classified there.

Other unresolved issues in the diagnosis of ADHD include how to define better the concepts of inattention, impulsivity, and hyperactivity; how to distinguish validly between ADHD and CD; whether the grouping meets criteria as a true syndrome (i.e., distinctive grouping of characteristics and distinct etiology, biology, treatment response, course, or prognosis); and whether the disorder should be demonstrated across multiple situations (Achenbach and Edelbrock 1978; Ferguson and Rapoport 1983; Loney and Milich 1982; Rutter 1983a).

From a clinical point of view, the above issues mean that there may be difficulty in distinguishing between the normal and the developmentally inappropriate expressions of the core symptoms, that there is sometimes overlap between ADHD and CD, and that the diagnosis, which continues to change and to be refined, is ultimately made by considering a variety and pattern of variables.

Conduct disorder, like ADHD, is sometimes known as an externalizing disorder (Achenbach and Edelbrock 1978) or a disruptive behavior disorder (American Psychiatric Association 1987). CD is sometimes used synonymously with terms such as acting out, delinquency, sociopathy, and psychopathy (Rutter and Giller 1984). It is characterized by a repetitive and persistent pattern of misconduct, with violations of major age-appropriate societal rules or of the basic rights of others. Table 2 lists the DSM-III-R criteria for CD.

As defined in DSM-III-R, CD has prepubertal onset (although postpubertal onset does occur, more often for females), is about four times more common in boys than girls, and is more common in children of parents with antisocial personality disorder and alcohol dependence. It is associated with impaired school, social, familial, and community functioning; substance abuse; legal difficulties; high rates of personal physical injury; earlier than expected sexual behavior; and co-diagnosis with ADHD and specific developmental disorders (as well as the previously listed problems). The course is variable, with mild forms and the group type showing improvement and reasonably good adult adjustment, and severe forms being more chronic. Early-onset

> ### Table 2. DSM-III-R Diagnostic Criteria for Conduct Disorder
>
> A. A disturbance of conduct lasting at least six months, during which at least three of the following have been present:
>
> (1) has stolen without confrontation of a victim on more than one occasion (including forgery)
> (2) has run away from home overnight at least twice while living in parental or parental surrogate home (or once without returning)
> (3) often lies (other than to avoid physical or sexual abuse)
> (4) has deliberately engaged in fire-setting
> (5) is often truant from school (for older person, absent from work)
> (6) has broken into someone else's house, building, or car
> (7) has deliberately destroyed others' property (other than by fire-setting)
> (8) has been physically cruel to animals
> (9) has forced someone into sexual activity with him or her
> (10) has used a weapon in more than one fight
> (11) often initiates physical fights
> (12) has stolen with confrontation of a victim (e.g., mugging, purse-snatching, extortion, armed robbery)
> (13) has been physically cruel to people
>
> **Note:** The above items are listed in descending order of discriminating power based on data from a national field trial of the DSM-III-R criteria for Disruptive Behavior Disorders.
>
> B. If 18 or older, does not meet criteria for Antisocial Personality Disorder.
>
> **Criteria for severity of Conduct Disorder:**
>
> **Mild:** Few if any conduct problems in excess of those required to make the diagnosis, **and** conduct problems cause only minor harm to others.
>
> **Moderate:** Number of conduct problems and effect on others intermediate between "mild" and "severe."
>
> **Severe:** Many conduct problems in excess of those required to make the diagnosis, **or** conduct problems cause considerable harm to others, e.g., serious physical injury to victims, extensive vandalism or theft, prolonged absence from home.
>
> **Conduct Disorder Types**
>
> 1. group type
> 2. solitary aggressive type
> 3. undifferentiated type

CD has greater risk for adult antisocial personality disorder (American Psychiatric Association 1987; Robins 1966). In all likelihood, CD represents a heterogeneous grouping. It has unclear etiologies. CD corresponds to the ICD-9 disturbance of conduct. Antisocial personality disorder, the corresponding DSM-III-R adult disorder with a lifelong pattern, can be diagnosed after age 18.

Under CD, DSM-III-R has added severity criteria and eliminated the aggressive-unagressive and socialized-nonsocialized subtypes (which were not clearly substantiated or reliable), replacing them with three other types: group, solitary aggressive, and undifferentiated (Rapoport 1987; Robins 1984). The DSM-III-R symptom list is somewhat more explicit than that of previous editions and is ordered by discriminating power (as is the list for ADHD), based on results from a national field trial (American Psychiatric Association 1987).

A new classification of oppositional defiant disorder (ODD), corresponding to the DSM-III oppositional disorder, has been included under the DSM-III-R rubric of disruptive behavior disorders. The criteria, also ordered by discriminating power, are outlined in Table 3. ODD is sometimes conceptualized as being less severe on a continuum with CD or as being qualitatively distinct. The category of ODD exists in part because of a need to distinguish milder cases as well as to resolve the problems of classifying behavior of younger children. Many questions remain about the validity and diagnostic reliability of this category (e.g., Rutter and Shaffer 1980).

Major questions also exist about the diagnostic classification of CD. There is strong evidence that differentiating a category of internalizing emotional disorders (such as anxiety and depression) from a category of externalizing conduct disorders is valid, useful, reliable, and temporally stable, although mixed forms are known to exist (Jenkins 1973; Quay 1979a; Rutter and Garmezy 1983). In contrast, there are many problems with subdividing externalizing disorders, in terms of defining and measuring impulsivity, conduct, socialization, and aggression; validating subgroupings; distinguishing ADHD from CD; and confirming that CD meets "syndromal" criteria (Achenbach and Edelbrock 1978; Ferguson and Rapoport 1983; Loney and Milich 1982; Rutter 1983a).

Table 3. DSM-III-R Diagnostic Criteria for Oppositional Defiant Disorder

Note: Consider a criterion met only if the behavior is considerably more frequent than that of most people of the same mental age.

A. A disturbance of at least six months during which at least five of the following are present:

    (1) often loses temper
    (2) often argues with adults
    (3) often actively defies or refuses adult requests or rules, e.g., refuses to do chores at home
    (4) often deliberately does things that annoy other people, e.g., grabs other children's hats
    (5) often blames others for his or her own mistakes
    (6) is often touchy or easily annoyed by others
    (7) is often angry and resentful
    (8) is often spiteful or vindictive
    (9) often swears or uses obscene language

Note: The above items are listed in descending order of discriminating power based on data from a national field trial of the DSM-III-R criteria for Disruptive Behavior Disorders.

B. Does not meet the criteria for Conduct Disorder, and does not occur exclusively during the course of a psychotic disorder, Dysthymia, or a Major Depressive, Hypomanic, or Manic Episode.

Criteria for severity of Oppositional Defiant Disorder:
Mild: Few, if any, symptoms in excess of those required to make the diagnosis **and** only minimal or no impairment in school and social functioning.

Moderate: Symptoms or functional impairment intermediate between "mild" and "severe."

Severe: Many symptoms in excess of those required to make the diagnosis **and** significant and pervasive impairment in functioning at home and school and with other adults and peers.

Although there are theoretical and operational problems with the definitions of ADHD and CD, there are clinical sets of symptoms and difficulties that resemble each of these classifications and have long been described in the literature. Although flawed, the current definitions are experimentally and clinically helpful.

Ideally, diagnostic issues have implications for treatment. Clear definition of a diagnostic group should help to identify the population in need of treatment, as well as help define what is to be treated. The more precise the intervention goals, the more accurate the evaluation of treatment course and outcome. The prevalence, morbidity, and poor prognosis for a significant subgroup of ADHD and CD children make attempts at comprehensive and effective treatment imperative.

Research Issues

Research on the treatment of ADHD and CD is voluminous and has been characterized by many methodological difficulties that should be considered when examining the literature and evaluating the treatments. Problems include: poor sample definition; heterogeneity of diagnosis within a sample; changing diagnostic criteria; small sample size; single-subject case reporting; lack of placebo controls or untreated comparison groups; inadequate matching of control groups; nonrandom assignment to group; nonblind conditions; questionable validity, specificity, sensitivity, and/or standardization of measures; subject noncompliance with treatment; large numbers of drop-outs; inappropriate study duration; inattention to medication dosage and to timing of response; inappropriate statistical analysis; and lack of follow-up. Often missing are exact descriptions of treatment, cost-benefit analyses, and multidimensional, meaningful outcome assessments.

The treatment literature generally takes three approaches, describing the treatment of a group of children with roughly the same constellation of problems or the same diagnosis; the treatment of a particular symptom, such as aggression or inability to stay seated, without strict regard to population definition; or the application of a particular treatment to various problems or groups of children. The differences in approach, combined with methodological flaws and lack of detailed treatment descriptions, sometimes make it difficult to compare studies or make clinical applications. The practitioner, however, must design interventions and provide treatment. Despite shortcomings, there is a large body of knowledge with consistent research results to inform and guide the work of the clinician.

Clinical Issues

Research questions have progressed beyond asking if there are effective treatments for psychiatric problems to which treatments are effective for which children or which symptoms. There seems to be general agreement that for ADHD and for CD there is no one approach that would be comprehensively helpful, although some are better than others. Short-term efficacy of treatment has been very well documented for each of these disorders; long-term efficacy, although not extensively studied, does occur. No intervention has reliably been shown to be effective after its cessation or to alter substantially long-term (into early adulthood) prognosis. There are, however, promising leads for the treatment of ADHD and of CD (Kazdin 1985; Satterfield et al. 1987; Weiss and Hechtman 1986). Most experts in the field advocate multimodal management approaches. Emphasis is placed on a multisystem evaluation of the child, with recognition of diagnostic group; on high quality implementation of several interventions, usually aimed at a variety of symptoms or problems; and on careful assessment of treatment effects and outcome.

In this chapter major treatments of ADHD and CD are reviewed. The reference list is long, and there are no detailed descriptions on how to carry out the particular treatments. The chapter is best used as an adjunct to knowledge of and critical appraisal of the literature, as well as to current or previous supervised clinical training and experience.

Treatment of Attention Deficit Disorders

Treatment of ADHD, particularly drug treatment, may be one of the best researched topics in child psychiatry. Most studies focus primarily on prepubertal school-age boys of normal intelligence; the findings may be limited to that group. Since there is no one comprehensive therapy for children with ADHD, various treatments have been attempted, alone or together, and are often aimed at one or more of the various core symptoms (i.e., inattention, impulsivity, hyperactivity) as well as at presumed secondary symptoms (e.g., low self-esteem). Empirical data exist almost exclusively for medication treatment and for behavioral treatments.

Evaluation

A comprehensive initial (and then continued) evaluation of any child is important. Standard child psychiatric examinations are described in multiple sources (e.g., Chess and Hassibi 1986; Rutter and Hersov 1985; Shaffer et al. 1985; Simmons 1987). Those aspects significant for children with ADHD will be considered here. Table 4 outlines the basic work-up for children with ADHD and with CD.

Comprehensive assessment means evaluating the child's emotional functioning (e.g., presence of secondary symptoms such as dysphoria related to failure at school, poor self-image as a "bad" or "dumb" child), as well as functioning 1) at home (e.g., "no peace" in the evening at home because the child is constantly "on the go," "gets into everything," needs lots of attention and supervision, can't entertain him- or herself); 2) at school (e.g., the child is always out of the seat at school; blurts out answers and comments; doesn't wait to hear the teacher's instructions; rushes through the assignment or "doesn't seem to hear" the instructions because is "fiddling" with objects on the desk, looking out the window, watching classmates); 3) in the community (e.g., the child can't be taken to the supermarket or movies because the child "runs down the aisles," "won't stay put," frequently "gets up and down"); and 4) in social situations with children and adults (e.g., the child likes to be with other

Table 4. Basic Work-Up for Children with Attention-Deficit Hyperactivity Disorder and Conduct Disorders

- Comprehensive psychiatric examination
- Complete medical history and physical examination
- Vision, hearing, and speech screening
- Educational testing: IQ and achievement tests are helpful
- Medical laboratory tests: not necessary unless specific problem is suspected
- Electroencephalogram: not necessary unless neurologic disorder (e.g., a seizure disorder) is suspected

children but seems uncooperative because he/she can't wait for turns, "grabs for things"). Breadth of assessment is important because these children often have multiple difficulties and present with complicated clinical pictures. It also gives a sense of the child's strengths and weaknesses, which is helpful for treatment planning.

Parents or guardians, and the children themselves, sometimes spontaneously describe symptoms leading to a diagnosis of ADHD. However, if they do not, one must ask pertinent opening questions (e.g., how active or energetic is your child compared to other children the same age?), then continue down the criteria list, asking for examples and explanations to confirm the picture. Children are sometimes reluctant to describe their overt behaviors, but may describe what parents or teachers complain about to them (e.g., is your teacher always telling you to sit down, get back to your seat, or stop fiddling around?). In addition, they may be willing to reveal their feelings about such complaints.

A developmental approach to the history of the child's activity level or modulation, attentional skills, and self-control or impulsivity is used (e.g., younger children normally move more, are less attentive, and are more impulsive than older children). There are developmentally appropriate changes and age-related expectations in these core areas for normal children, which must be compared (e.g., a nine-year-old should be less impulsive and more capable of cooperative play, which includes waiting for turns, than a four-year-old). There are, also, some age-related changes in the presentation of ADHD symptoms (e.g., a decrease in gross motor activity with age, but continued fidgetiness or subjective feelings of restlessness). Questions should be geared to practical, everyday situations. All symptoms are explored extensively—with careful attention, within and across situations, to the core topics, cognitive skills, academic performance, aggression, difficulties in social interactions, conduct problems, oppositional behaviors, motor skills, ability to handle stress or frustration and to control temper, view of self, confidence, and mood.

Core signs and symptoms are rarely constant or present in every situation. They are more prominent in group situations and situations requiring sustained attention and self-paced work performance. Thus total consistency across time and place is not required. Diagnosis cannot be excluded on the basis of a one-to-one office interview or observation of the child in a novel setting because children often do not exhibit their symptoms under those circumstances.

One expects a history of variability, and thus possible variability of reports about the child's behavior. For those reasons, multiple observers (e.g., parents, teachers, grandparents, babysitters, in addition to the child) should give descriptions. There is some evidence that teachers are able to give more valid and systematic reports; therefore particular emphasis might be placed on teacher observations (Rapoport and Benoit 1975). Direct observations may be helpful.

In addition to pertinent inclusion criteria, one elicits pertinent exclusion criteria to exclude behavior inconsistent with the ADHD diagnosis or to make other diagnoses, such as mental retardation (IQ below 70); pervasive developmental disorder (which has much more pervasive and grossly abnormal cognitive and social development); bipolar affective disorder, manic state (which is episodic; may have family history of affective disorder; psychosis may be present; symptoms of elation, grandiosity, increased goal direction, pressured speech, or unusual energy may be more prominent) (Nieman and Delong 1987); and schizophrenia or other psychotic illnesses (psychosis, not secondary to drugs, is or has been present). In the above conditions, the symptoms of overactivity, inattention, and impulsivity may be present, but the particular syndromal pattern of ADHD is not.

Rating scales, usually completed by parents and teachers, may be useful in the assessment if the clinician wants a more structured and perhaps more consistent approach or a comparison with norms. There are general scales for rating a variety of child behaviors, for example, the Child Behavior Checklist (Achenbach and Edelbrock 1982), in addition to scales more specific for the problems of the ADHD population, for example Conners' Parent and Teacher Rating Scales (Rapoport et al. 1985). It should be noted that no scale can make a diagnosis or replace the rest of the clinical evaluation.

Of course as part of the assessment, one examines the child's living situation, which includes the individual functioning of significant adults, the functioning of the family unit, and the milieu of the school and community. The child is viewed both as an individual and as part of various systems.

Diagnosis of ADHD is sometimes difficult when the child has many other emotional and behavioral problems or comes from a chaotic home environment. It should be noted that presence of emotional difficulties doesn't preclude an ADHD diagnosis. There is no valid way to distinguish ADHD associated with emotional problems from any other type. When the home milieu is extremely disorganized, the clinician might compare the child with siblings, rely on reports of behavior in more structured settings outside the home (e.g., school), or settle on a tentative diagnosis while also attempting to modify the family environment.

A thorough medical history and physical exam are performed as a general screen for all children. There is nothing specific that would confirm an ADHD diagnosis, but other medical problems or relatively rare causes of hyperactive behavior (e.g., hyperthyroidism, lead poisoning) can be ruled out. One should ask about and observe for motor and vocal tics because ADHD and Tourette's syndrome can coexist, and treatment for each is different. As indicated in Table 4, no special medical tests are routinely required; an electroencephalogram need not be done unless indicated for other reasons (e.g., suspected seizure disorder).

ADHD is commonly associated with learning problems. Educational testing, mainly IQ and achievement testing, can provide helpful screening for academic functioning; these plus careful teacher observation of school performance might indicate need for more specialized tests. These form the basis for educational recommendations to the school.

Once the evaluation is completed, a problem list can be generated. The clinician then plans the treatment by exploring such aspects as 1) the child's, parent's, and school's ability to cope with problem behaviors (e.g., the teacher is willing to let the child fidget or get out of the seat as long as schoolwork is done) and to cooperate with treatment (e.g., the parents leave for work in the morning before the child gets up, but the school is willing to administer morning medication; the teacher feels there are too many children in the classroom to carry out an individualized behavior modification program); 2) their preferences and prejudices (e.g., the parent doesn't "believe in" medication); 3) the availability and costs of treatment (e.g., comparative costs in the community for dextroamphetamine and methylphenidate); and 4) the outcome of previous interventions (e.g., the parent states that stimulant medication given in the morning "didn't work" during the evening, not aware that duration of action is time limited) (for reviews, see Barkley 1981; Conners and Wells 1986; Kazdin 1984; Klein et al. 1980; Pelham 1982; Ross and Ross 1982; Taylor 1986; Whalen and Henker 1980).

Medication

Pharmacologic treatments for the behaviors included in ADHD have been well documented over the past 25 years. The major class of drugs indicated for ADHD is the central nervous system stimulants, mainly methylphenidate and dextroamphetamine and to a lesser extent magnesium pemoline. Tricyclic antidepressants (usually imipramine, desipramine, and amitriptyline) and clonidine are the second and third choices, respectively. Other antidepressants are being tested and may be helpful. Antipsychotic medications might be considered in exceptional circumstances.

Preparation for pharmacotherapy includes the medical history and physical examination, as well as baseline height, weight, blood pressure, heart rate, and perhaps blood or other medical tests, depending on the particular medication.

Stimulants have been shown to improve many ADHD behaviors: 1) performance on tasks of attention, vigilance, reaction time, impulsivity, rote-visual-verbal learning, short-term memory, performance IQ, and productivity or accuracy of classroom academic assignments; 2) on global impression, parent-, and teacher-rating scales; 3) on mother-child, teacher-child, and child-child interaction; and 4) on measures of hyperactivity (Barkley 1977; Brown et al. 1985b; Cantwell 1985; Cunningham and Barkley 1978; Firestone et al. 1981; Gadow 1983; Humphries et al. 1978; Porrino et al. 1983b; Varley 1985; Whalen et al. 1978, 1980a, 1980b). There is some indication that these improvements are clinically meaningful and substantial, so much so that behavior can sometimes be "normalized" and becomes almost indistinguishable from that of peers (Abikoff and Gittelman 1985a, 1985b).

Stimulant medications have been shown to improve academic performance; the issue as to whether they improve the acquisition of academic skills or lead to improved academic achievement is unresolved (Douglas et al. 1986· Gadow 1983; Pelham et al. 1985).

Also unresolved is the issue of whether several years of treatment with stimulants leads to better long-term prognosis. Some studies suggest that such treatment is associated with improved interpersonal relationships in adolescence and adulthood and more favorable memories of childhood (Weiss and Hechtman 1986).

Other areas of interest include 1) whether stimulants are associated with state-dependent learning effects; most studies have not substantiated this idea (Stenhausen and Kreuzer 1971; Swanson and Kinsbourne 1976; Weingartner et al. 1982) and 2) whether commonly used dosages, optimal for behavioral effects, lead to deleterious cognitive effects; many investigators have not found this to be true and have found linear dose-response curves for various cognitive tasks. It is likely that there is a complex interaction among dosage, timing, and particular responses (Conners and Wells 1986; Pelham et al. 1985; Sprague and Sleator 1977).

Stimulant effect on mood in children is a topic where research is needed. Stimulants have been thought not to induce euphoria, but there have been reports of both positive and negative mood changes, although usually of dysphoria and irritability (Barkley 1977; Office of Child Development 1971; Rapoport et al. 1978).

Of note is the fact that stimulant actions are not specific for children with ADHD; stimulants in acute doses have similar cognitive and behavioral effects on normal children and adults (Rapoport et al. 1978, 1980).

Dextroamphetamine and methylphenidate are equivalent in achieving the described effects. They are the drugs of choice. Magnesium pemoline appears to be similar, although there is much less research on its use.

Dosages for the stimulants are given in Table 5. They are well absorbed after oral administration and easily cross the blood-brain barrier. Dextroamphetamine achieves peak plasma levels in children in two to three hours and has a half-life of four to six hours (with large interindividual variation). Chronic use for six or more months yields a steady state half-life of about 10 hours. Methylphenidate reaches peak plasma levels in one to two hours and has a half-life of two to three hours (also with large interindividual and intraindividual variability). Magnesium pemoline reaches peak serum

Table 5. Dosage of Stimulant Medications*

Drug	Starting dose (mg)	Maximum dose (mg)	Daily dose range (mg)
Dextroamphetamine	5 qid or bid (ages 6 and older) 2.5 qid (ages 3–5)	40	0.3–1.0
Methylphenidate	5 bid	60	0.6–2.0
Pemoline	37.5 qd	112.5	0.5–2.0

*These are commonly used doses—they must be individualized for each child. Some children respond to lower doses; others may require higher amounts.

level in children in two to four hours; its half-life is 12 hours. Clinical improvement may take up to three or four weeks, although this may be an artifact of giving the drug at low doses and not increasing it as quickly as possible. (See Campbell et al. 1985; Cantwell and Carlson 1978; Donnelly and Rapoport 1975 for review and references.)

Stimulants are clinically effective with school-age children and adolescents. Use in preschoolers has not been routine, and effectiveness for that population has been less consistent (Barkley 1988; Cohen et al. 1981; Klorman et al. 1987; Schliefier et al. 1975; Varley 1985).

Contraindications to stimulant use are psychotic signs or symptoms. Relative contraindications are the presence of tics and any medical condition precluding use of sympathomimetics.

Stimulant treatment has several limitations: frequent failure to ameliorate all symptoms and associated problems, lack of adequate response in about 20 percent of children, possible rebound effects, and adverse side effects.

A drawback of treating only with stimulant medication is that substantial improvement in some symptoms might lead the practitioner to ignore other significant child, family, and school problems. The child, not just a symptom, should be treated.

The most common short-term adverse effects are anorexia and insomnia. Less common are weight loss, abdominal pain, and headache. These are generally short-lived, rarely require the stopping of medication, and usually can be managed with a decrease in drug dosage or a change in the time the drug is administered. Tics are also uncommon side effects (perhaps more common with pemoline). It is often recommended that medication be discontinued when tics appear, based in part on a belief that Tourette's syndrome can be induced or exacerbated; the latter belief is controversial (Comings and Comings 1984, 1987; Lowe et al. 1982; Price et al. 1985, 1986; Shapiro and Shapiro 1981). It seems reasonable to reduce, discontinue, or change medication if tics develop during treatment; exceptions might have to be made on a case-by-case basis, with consent of the parents, careful weighing of risks and benefits, and continued monitoring. Drowsiness, dizziness, mood changes, dyskinesias, and toxic psychosis are rare side effects. Idiosyncratic responses (such as blood dyscrasias) do occur. Relatively few side effects occur with dosages below 0.5 mg/kg of dextroamphetamine or 1.0 mg/kg of methylphenidate.

Suppression of height and weight has been found in short-term and chronic treatment with stimulants. There appears to be compensatory growth after medication is discontinued (Klein and Manuzza 1988; Klein et al. 1988; Mattes and Gittelman 1983; Safer et al. 1975).

Clinical use of stimulants is preceded by explanation and discussion with the parents, child, and school personnel. One starts with low doses, then increases the medication gradually, at minimum every three to five days (weekly for pemoline), until maximal therapeutic effect or adverse effects occur. One may want to begin with a slightly higher dose than the lowest starting dose if cooperation with treatment would be compromised by increasing too slowly; dosage could be decreased later. Dosage must be reevaluated as the child grows. Finding the optimal dose and timing is an individualized, systematic, often trial-and-error process.

Timing of doses is based on duration of action, which is relatively short for dextroamphetamine and methylphenidate and longer for pemoline. There are sustained release preparations of dextroamphetamine and methylphenidate, but no systematic studies have demonstrated their superiority. It is usual to give the medications two times per day. Some practitioners successfully use the short-acting preparations on a once-a-day regimen. One begins with a once-a-day morning dose to determine if and when a second dose should be given. Some clinicians attempt to avoid drug administration during school hours because children often do not want to be singled out by taking medication. This is often not practical for achieving maximal effects. However, one must attempt to decrease the possibility of stigmatization by making the situation as private and matter-of-fact as possible. Medication can also be given in the late afternoon, so that beneficial effects are seen during the evening hours. This regimen may be limited by resultant insomnia.

Lack of improvement after two weeks at maximum dosage of dextroamphetamine and methylphenidate or five weeks of pemoline is indication to stop. Dosage can usually be lowered for most side effects, although more severe adverse effects might require cessation of treatment.

Weekend "drug holidays" are common, since many children experience their significant problems at school, but exceptions must be made based on severity of difficulties outside of school. There is controversy over whether children should have "drug holidays" or should be given medication without frequent interruptions, in order to provide consistent benefits. Cessation of medication during the summer is also a common practice especially as a way to evaluate continued need and to provide for growth "catch-up." The drug should be discontinued at least once a year for a minimum of one to two weeks to assess continued need for treatment.

Tricyclic antidepressants have shown clinical efficacy for ADHD in multiple studies. Improvement is as rapid and sometimes as striking as with the stimulants, although effects may be short-lived (over months) and cognitive improvement may be less. Dosages are lower than those used for depression (less than 5 mg/kg/day; usually around 100 mg/day of imipramine or desipramine). Monitoring of cardiac effects (changes in heart rate, blood pressure, and electrocardiogram reading) is necessary. Other possible side effects include decreased appetite and anticholinergic effects, such as dry mouth (Donnelly et al. 1986; Garfinkel et al. 1983; Rapoport et al. 1974; Werry 1980).

Clonidine is another second-line medication for ADHD. Behavioral effects similar to those of stimulants have been reported, using oral doses of 5 μg/kg/day divided in four doses or equivalent dose in skin patch form (which can be worn for approximately five days). Blood pressure needs to be monitored. Sedation, sometimes short-lived, may be a side effect (Hunt 1986).

Several studies, using different classes of antipsychotics, have shown improvement in various symptoms of ADHD and additive effects with stimulants. However, overall clinical efficacy is not as striking. Associated side effects are anticholinergic effects (e.g., dry mouth, sedation), increased appetite, dystonic reactions, and withdrawal dyskinesias. Use of antipsychotics is limited because of possible adverse effects, such as impaired cognitive functioning and the development of tardive dyskinesia. Antipsychotics might be considered for short-term use when symptoms are severe and other treatments have failed.

The goal of pharmacologic treatment is, of course, to achieve maximal effects at the lowest possible drug dosage and with the minimum amount of side effects. It is not possible to predict who will respond to or will benefit from which drug. Children may respond to one but not the others. Therefore, the clinician must systematically go through the list of drugs before assuming lack of response to medication. There is little information on issues of compliance, but some studies suggest that this might be a significant problem with maintenance medication (Firestone 1982; Sleator 1982). More information and reviews are available elsewhere (Barkley 1977; Campbell et al. 1985; Cantwell and Carlson 1978; Donnelly and Rapoport 1985; Dulcan 1985; Klein et al. 1980).

Behavioral Treatment

Behavioral treatment is a modality that encompasses a variety of interventions and tactics, included under such terms as behavior modification, behavior management, parent management training, operant conditioning, and contingency-based reinforcement systems. Such treatments are implemented by parents, teachers, and/ or clinicians. They are the best researched nonpharmacologic treatment for ADHD. Studies, conducted mostly over the past 15 years, have commonly used single-case designs and, with groups, have not necessarily limited the sample to children with ADHD. To institute behavior therapy, the clinician makes a functional analysis of the child's difficulties, identifying the nature, frequency, context, and consequences of problem behaviors. Treatment is thus individually tailored. Generally, behavior therapy requires a combination of reinforcements and punishments, although the best balance of these for children with ADHD is unclear. Efforts should be aimed at generalizing effects and at setting goals that are clinically meaningful in the child's life.

Behavioral approaches have resulted in improvements in the behavior of children with ADHD: in social interactions (e.g., increased cooperation with peers and decreased disruptiveness or aggression); on various global, parent-, and teacher-rating scales; on specific "on task" behaviors; and on productivity, accuracy, and completion of academic assignments. These interventions are partially effective, in the short-term, for the particular behaviors and settings that have been targeted. Behavioral treatment, like pharmacotherapy, has not been shown to yield better long-term prognosis.

The overall clinical meaningfulness of behavioral treatment for some children has been questioned since often the ADHD behavior is not substantially changed. However, aggression, although not a core symptom, is common among children with ADHD and has been shown to decrease with a combination of behavioral approaches (Abikoff and Gittelman 1984). Indeed, behavior therapy has a stronger place in the treatment of conduct disorder, as discussed later in this chapter.

Some investigators feel that more substantial gains would occur if interventions were more comprehensive and intense, although such may not often be feasible.

In addition to those already mentioned, limitations of behavioral treatment include lack of response by a number of children, diminishment of improvement over time, lack of generalization, high cost in terms of time and money, and difficulty in gaining the active participation of parents and schools.

Behavior therapy is usually most helpful for children with ADHD when combined with pharmacotherapy (Abikoff and Gittelman 1984; Conners and Wells 1986; Gittelman-Klein et al. 1980; Hall et al. 1972; Klein et al. 1980; Madsen et al. 1979; Mash and Dalby 1979; O'Leary 1980; O'Leary et al. 1967, 1976; Pelham and Murphy 1986; Pelham et al. 1980; Ross and Ross 1982; Sprague 1983).

Cognitive Therapy

Cognitive therapy (or training) is a type of behavioral treatment that aims to instill children with more self-control and a more thoughtful approach to tasks and interactions. It was hoped that such techniques would change core deficits of ADHD, especially impulsivity and inattention. However, cognitive therapy alone and in combination with medication and other behavioral interactions has yet to be shown effective in improving ADHD behaviors or associated problems in that population. Age and cognitive developmental level may be important limiting variables, so that cognitive training strategies might have to take them into account. Modifications, such as adding self-reinforcement procedures and operant techniques to support generalization, have been suggested (Abikoff and Gittelman 1984, 1985a; Brown et al. 1985a; Douglas 1980; Kendall 1984; Meichenbaum 1981).

Social Skills Training

Children with ADHD often have poor relationships with peers and adults in addition to the basic deficits of the syndrome. Social skills training is a form of cognitive therapy that includes a broad array of techniques, such as modeling or operant training approaches, to improve social interactions. At present, studies of social skills training used as treatment have not demonstrated the expected improvement in peer interactions. However, there are some indications that when combined with operant behavioral procedures, social skills training may be more effective (Abikoff and Gittelman 1985a; Pelham and Bender 1982; Pellegrini and Urbain 1985; Urbain and Kendall 1980).

Psychotherapy

Psychotherapy techniques are diverse, and the difficulties in defining the method(s) and measuring the results are great. This probably leads to underrepresentation of psychotherapy in treatment research. The traditional psychotherapeutic techniques, which commonly focus on the therapeutic relationship as an agent for change, may be important for such goals as engaging a child and family in treatment, helping to implement other interventions (e.g., behavior management and pharmacotherapy), and aiding the child to identify, understand, and accept any limitations. They may also help with further child and family issues or in treating presumed secondary emotional problems. However, adequate studies have not tested these assumptions (Eisenberg et al. 1961, 1965; Satterfield et al. 1981, 1987).

Multimodal Treatment

Multimodal treatment refers to the simultaneous use of several interventions to maximize therapeutic effects. Strictly defined, it is the application of systematic specific treatments used in combination. With clinical practice, however, treatments are rarely given in pure form. In child psychiatry, treatment is often multimodal, in a loosely defined sense, because it is common to work with family members and school personnel in addition to the child. It is also common to use several treatment strategies when symptoms are varied and when no one treatment is comprehensive, as can be the case with ADHD.

Recommendations for multimodal treatment are common in the ADHD literature, even if they refer simply to supplementing pharmacotherapy with parent support and counseling and teacher consultation. Systematic studies of carefully defined and executed specific treatment combinations have been few and limited by methodological flaws, such as lack of no-treatment control groups. Precise details for multimodal treatment (e.g., which behavioral technique to use with which dose of which medicine at which time) have yet to be worked out.

There are suggestions that combined treatment can at times give better results than one treatment alone. This has been found for the addition of behavioral treatment to stimulant medication when improvement from stimulant alone is not maximal. It has also been suggested in one set of studies where stimulant medication was used with a varying combination of individual and family psychotherapy, behavioral treatment, and educational remediation. It is hoped that better designed research in the near future will help to clarify how to carry out multimodal therapy (Abikoff and Gittelman 1984; Brown et al. 1985a, 1985b; Cantwell 1985; Gittelman 1983; Gittelman-Klein et al. 1980; Klein et al. 1980; O'Leary 1980; Pelham and Murphy 1986; Pelham et al. 1980; Pellegrini and Urbain 1985; Rutter 1983b; Satterfield et al. 1981, 1987; Schmidt et al. 1984; Sprague 1983).

Other Treatments

There has been little written about the use of other common therapies specifically for children with ADHD. Many behavioral treatments are carried out within the format of a family or group (e.g., instruction of a family or school staff in the use of a contingency management program), but this is not, strictly speaking, family or group therapy.

A time-limited brief therapy does not seem appropriate because the problems of ADHD are chronic, and positive treatment effects have not been shown to extend much beyond termination of therapy.

Parent support groups might be beneficial, both therapeutically (for the children and family members) and politically (to help obtain resources). Descriptive literature and evaluation of such an intervention are lacking.

Although much attention has been given to dietary treatments, such as the Feingold diet (Feingold 1975) or other diets (which involve a reduction in sugar intake or elimination of food additives), they do not seem useful for the majority of children with ADHD. Controlled studies indicate that special diet is not as effective as previously described treatments, namely stimulants, and no better for most children than their accustomed diet (Barkley 1981; Conners 1980; Kavale and Forness 1983; Mattes 1983; NIH Consensus Development Conference 1982; Rimland 1983; Varley 1984). However, as long as more effective treatments are not withheld when indicated, it is certainly not harmful to pay attention to reports of improvement with dietary changes and to encourage whatever efforts seem helpful. In addition, many parent organizations have developed around concerns of dietary toxicity and may be effective support groups. Again, there are possible benefits of mutual support among parents and active parent participation.

Although it seems likely that special educational interventions might be needed for children with ADHD there is little systematic work on what specific techniques should be used. If the child is not performing commensurate with intellectual potential, tutoring and remediation are required. Structured classroom environments, as opposed to open classrooms, might be better for some youngsters with ADHD, although not necessarily so (Flynn and Rapoport 1976). Placement in special classes might be necessary if the child doesn't perform in the regular classroom with extra help (Klein et al. 1980; Sprague 1983).

Clinical Management

Clinical management of the child with ADHD is always an individualized process. The goals of treatment are to decrease problem behaviors, improve functioning, and promote normal development in multiple areas (e.g., emotional, behavioral, cognitive, social).

As previously reviewed, the clinician makes a multisystem evaluation, establishes a diagnosis, and assesses the feasibility of various interventions.

In general, the child, family, and often the school staff need education about ADHD, in addition to some support and counseling (e.g., that the child is not bad, that the parents and school staff are not incompetent or the cause). The treatment usually requires cooperation among various professionals—for instance, among a child psychologist who performs educational testing, a regular classroom teacher, a special education teacher, and a school nurse who administers medication. In addition, the therapist sometimes helps the parents advocate for the child in the educational and community service systems or helps the school staff evaluate the services available to a particular child.

The clinician prepares the child, family, and school for treatment by explaining as explicitly as possible such issues as the form of treatment (e.g., informing everyone that the child and family will have sessions weekly for the next three months); requirements of the participants (e.g., that the teacher will be asked to fill out behavioral ratings each week); particular expectations (e.g., that the stimulant medication should help the child to pay attention in the classroom, but won't prevent stealing, a problem that will be addressed in another way); eventual goals; and timing (e.g., that therapy may be chronic given the nature of the problems and that sessions may occur less frequently when things have improved).

Severity criteria, in addition to feasibility, guide the choice of initial interventions. When problems are mild, environmental manipulations, as well as education and counseling, can be beneficial. For example, the clinician may emphasize tolerance of the motor hyperactivity and recommend changing the child's seating arrangement in class, establishing a homework time and place after dinner in the home and helping a child to organize tasks by breaking them down into several steps. Other more structured interventions may then be added as needed.

When problems are moderate to severe, as is usually the case when a clinician is consulted, one uses medication and behavioral treatments, as needed, to achieve maximal results. The aim is to cover the broad range of problems usually seen in this population, institute treatment that is realistic for the particular family and school, and use medication in appropriate amounts to achieve the most benefit, but in the lowest dosage necessary and with the fewest side effects. Use of placebo medication, with informed cooperation of the family, may be a useful adjunct to pharmacotherapy.

Other problems, such as academic failure and enuresis, can be addressed concurrently. Improvement in these areas, although not focusing on the ADHD itself, may be helpful in fostering treatment for the ADHD and, of course, have significant meaning for the child's life.

Additional treatments, including psychotherapy for emotional problems or family therapy, may still be indicated if such difficulties are prominent or persist.

It is unusual for the child with ADHD to require hospitalization or institutional treatment. Such measures may sometimes be necessary for diagnostic clarification, treatment control and evaluation, presence of behavior that is dangerous to the child or others, or environmental conditions making outpatient therapy impossible. (See Institutional, Residential, and Day Treatment Programs for CD.)

It is necessary to assess the effects of treatment in a particular child across the multiple areas of functioning, including change in ADHD symptoms, conduct, academic performance, and social interactions. Initial evaluation delineates areas of dysfunction, which are then followed at regular intervals.

Data generated from behavioral interventions, such as number of points earned in a day for exhibiting certain behaviors or number of time-out periods required during the week, are an integral part of the treatment as well as the assessment. Charts and other coding systems encourage participation and are concrete indications of the treatment itself and of the changes.

Use of behavior rating scales also can be helpful in monitoring treatment changes. There are several available. The most common are the multiple versions of the Conners' teacher and parent rating scales, which vary according to who fills them out, length, and availability of norms. They are sensitive to practice effects so must be given at least twice at baseline before treatment. The abbreviated 10-item form is often the most practical for repeated use. See Rapoport et al. (1985) for a review of these and other scales, particularly for those sensitive to drug effects.

When medications are given, side effects evaluations, perhaps using scales such as the Subject Treatment Emergent Symptom Scale (STESS), should be performed prior to and regularly throughout treatment (Rapoport et al. 1985).

Finally, clinicians might try single-case research designs to assess treatment effects (Kazdin 1983).

Although it is not possible to predict how long it might take for a particular child to improve or to indicate how long therapy should last, there are some indications that treatment of three years or longer might be needed (Satterfield et al. 1987). In fact, since the condition may be chronic for some children, and treatments have unknown length of benefit after they are stopped, it is reasonable to continue some form of contact or follow-up for multiple years following the more active intervention(s).

Treatment of Conduct Disorder

Much has been written about the treatment of childhood conduct-disordered behaviors. However, major problems with definition, diagnosis, classification, and research methodology make this an area of great confusion. In all likelihood, the populations of children studied have been quite heterogeneous, making interpretation of results and translation to clinical treatment difficult. Most important are the differences in severity of the conduct problems—some studies have dealt with children who are disobedient in minor ways, whereas others have examined children who are incarcerated for serious crimes. Also, it is likely that many of the children in these studies would meet criteria for ADHD. It is not clear which variables are important for treatment outcome, although some characteristics—such as severity and kind (e.g., overt versus covert) of antisocial problems, age at onset, stealing, degree of aggressiveness, level of socialization, personality features, organicity, and family disorganization and discord—have been proposed. Most studies have dealt with boys in the adolescent age range. Many have included only children who have been convicted of crimes (often termed delinquent), creating a distinction between delinquent and nondelinquent groups. This is a legal, not clinical, distinction, which has unclear significance for therapy. Highly focused behavioral treatments, especially within a family context, have been the most well researched and have shown the most promise (Achenbach 1982; Kazdin 1985; Keith 1984; Patterson 1982; Rutter and Garmezy 1983; Rutter and Giller 1984).

Evaluation

Evaluation of the child with CD should be comprehensive. The basic workup is presented in Table 4; references for a standard child psychiatry assessment are given in the ADHD assessment section.

Children with CD have difficulties in numerous areas of functioning (e.g., emotional, interpersonal, cognitive) and in many settings (e.g., home, school, with friends, in the community). The particular symptoms and pattern will vary with the individual child. The clinician should probe all aspects specifically and in detail. It is helpful to obtain descriptions of real events and situations.

Overt conduct problems (e.g., aggressive acts, which are fairly easy to document) and evidence of covert problems (e.g., stealing) must both be assessed. The latter may be more difficult to establish and more difficult to treat. Of particular interest are rule-breaking behaviors, disobedience, substance abuse, aggressiveness, handling of anger, frustration tolerance, self-control, impulsivity, oppositionality, ability to relate to children and adults, social skills, response to discipline, motivating forces, sense of self and self-worth, mood, cognitive skills, and academic performance. One should also elicit information about the child's assets, strengths, and abilities. Time course of the difficulties is important; chronicity of at least six months is required. Otherwise, the clinician may be dealing with a reaction to some stressor(s), which must be identified.

A developmental perspective is used in the evaluation. Normal children also engage in aggressive, rule-breaking, disobedient behaviors. It is the timing (usually at an older than expected age); the greater quantity, frequency, and intensity of the problems; and sometimes the types of the behaviors (e.g., armed robbery) that differentiate the children with CD. For instance, oppositionality is common in youngsters of about 18 to 36 months of age; it then becomes less prominent. In general, this and all other aversive behaviors, such as aggressive acts, decrease with age. Older children, of course, are capable of carrying out more types of problem behaviors than younger ones. Covert acts, such as stealing, cheating, and truancy, are more frequent in the late school-age, early adolescent group. Prosocial skills increase with age. For example, most children by age five or six are aware that they shouldn't take others' possessions. In keeping with a developmental approach, the clinician also wants to know whether a child has ever developed skills, which are later not evident, or whether the child never attained them at all.

Rating scales, which can be completed by family members and school staff, may be helpful for cataloging the difficulties and comparing with norms. The Child Behavior Checklist (Achenbach and Edelbrock 1982), a more general scale, and the Parent Daily Report (Chamberlain and Patterson 1985), a list of conduct problems, are two such scales. Other scales are available (Chamberlain and Patterson 1985; Rapoport et al. 1985).

To get a well-rounded view of the child, one obtains information from as many sources as possible. Conduct problems are commonly the presenting complaints about the child from parents or others seeking consultation. Children, on the other hand, may not be forthcoming about their misconduct, although they are usually more informative about their thoughts and feelings. As previously stated, it is important to get information about strengths as well as weaknesses.

The setting of the evaluation may be a significant issue. Many children, and sometimes their parents or guardians, are forced to seek an assessment by legal or school authorities. Such issues must be handled directly and as soon as possible. The child and family must be informed about the extent and limits of confidentiality.

It is usually not difficult to identify a diagnosis of CD for a particular child. It is important, however, not to overlook coexisting problems, which may direct treatment or suggest variations in treatment. Since ADHD is frequently associated with CD, the clinician should carefully assess whether ADHD is present (as described previously in this chapter). Other symptoms, such as dysphoria and anxiety, are often evident; their presence does not preclude a diagnosis of CD, but they, too, must be addressed. Affective symptoms should be extensively explored, with special attention to the timing of symptom presentation. For instance, conduct problems may exist when a child has a major depressive or manic episode, but not at other times. On the other hand, a child with prior CD may become depressed; the depression, of course, requires treatment (Puig-Antich 1982).

Conduct problems may also be present in children with mental retardation, organic mental disorders, and post-traumatic stress disorders. A different pattern of difficulties, with some symptoms similar to those of CD, is seen with explosive disorder and partial complex seizures (e.g., the acts of aggression seem more impulsive, isolated, not planned). It is possible to have a seizure disorder and a CD, both of which should be treated. Children with psychotic disorders (such as schizophrenia) may, of course, exhibit conduct problems, but they have symptoms of psychosis (e.g., disorganized thought pattern, hallucinations, delusions) as well.

It is extemely important to perform an extensive family evaluation to identify possible risk factors and problems in addition to factors that might promote treatment. The clinician assesses psychopathology in family members (parents, siblings, and others) and pathology in the family system. The focus is on such issues as depression, alcoholism, criminal behavior, family size, level of household organization, marital or family discord, styles of interaction, methods of discipline, and particularly physical abuse and violent behavior. Presence of alcoholism and antisocial personality disorder in the father, parental psychopathology in general, large family size, marital discord, and family disorganization are associated with CD. Also correlated with CD are poor parental supervision of the children's behavior, harsh or erratic discipline, and cruel, passive, and neglecting attitudes on the part of the parents. Although such factors may or may not be causative, they are often considered contributory and targeted for treatment.

As in child psychiatry assessments for all children, the milieu of the school and the community are examined.

A thorough medical history and physical exam are performed. Again, as with a diagnosis of ADHD, there is nothing specific from these procedures that would confirm a CD diagnosis. However, other health problems might be discovered. This is especially important for children who have never received comprehensive health care. There are no special medical tests to be done; an electroencephalogram is not routine unless indicated for suspected seizure disorder or other reasons.

Since learning problems are prominent in the CD population, they must be carefully assessed. Reports of classroom academic performance, IQ testing, and achievement tests form the basic screens, from which further testing and other educational recommendations are made.

After completing the evaluation, the clinician outlines the difficulties and prepares for treatment by considering the same issues presented earlier for ADHD assessment. These include 1) how well the child, parents, and school cope with the difficulties (e.g., the mother is so upset that she is afraid she might "lose control" and become violent; the father, who is usually capable of setting limits with the child, has been getting drunk every day since he lost his job; the child threatens to kill himself and engages in self-destructive acts whenever punished); 2) whether they can cooperate with treatment (e.g., the teacher is able to give extra tutoring in subjects the child is failing; there is no one to babysit the three preschool siblings while parents attend sessions; the parent with schizophrenia is delusional, but refuses therapy); 3) whether they have preferences or prejudices about treatment (e.g., the parents feel that the child is at fault and don't understand why they have to attend therapy meetings); 4) the availability and costs for therapy (e.g., the family lives nearby and has transportation to the clinic; the family can afford only a limited number of sessions per year); and 5) the experience and outcome of previous interventions (e.g., the family attempted treatment but did not return after three sessions) (Chamberlain and Patterson 1985; Kazdin 1985; Klein et al. 1980; Lewis 1984, 1985; O'Donnell 1985; Robbins et al. 1983; Rutter 1985).

Behavioral Treatment

Behavioral treatments are the most extensively researched therapies for CD. A variety of behavioral techniques (e.g., contingency-based reinforcement, punishment, modeling, shaping) have been used in a variety of settings (i.e., individual, family, institutional, and community).

A social learning approach with families (termed parent management training) and in the classroom has been the most prominent, as well as the most promising. It involves mostly contact with one or both parents, in which parents are instructed in basic social learning principles and are taught to alter "coercive" interchanges with their children by using operant conditioning and other techniques. Use of this behavioral therapy has been shown to decrease deviant behaviors (e.g., aggression) and increase appropriate social behaviors at home and school, with concomitant improvement in the perception of the child's behavior by significant adults in the environment. Sometimes, there is improvement in the behavior of siblings and beneficial change for the parents (e.g., decreased depression) as well. Contingencies for school behavior must be included in the home system for behavior to change in the school setting without a particular program there, too. Parent management training is most effective when carried out by experienced therapists and perhaps when there is no limitation to the number of possible sessions. It is least effective in "high-risk" families (e.g., those with low socioeconomic status, parental psychopathology, lack of social supports for the parents, marital discord, absent fathers).

Behavioral family therapy, in which family interactions are modified with behavioral techniques, has not been extensively studied, but has led to improvements in the behavior of children with CD. The treatment attempts to increase negotiations, reciprocal interchanges, and positive reinforcement among family members.

Both of these types of family work probably have to be modified for high-risk families, as discussed under Family Therapy.

Social skills training, a cognitive-behavioral therapy, includes such procedures as instruction, modeling, practice, feedback, and reinforcement to foster the development of social skills. Few studies have specifically used children with CD, but efficacy has been shown. So far, it seems effective for specified behaviors in the particular treatment setting (usually an institution) itself.

In general, it seems that treatment goals should include improvement of social and academic skills rather than just suppression of deviant behavior to be effective and meaningful.

Limitations of behavioral interventions are similar to those described earlier under Behavioral Treatment for ADHD. Substantial improvement of behavior often does not occur; some children do not respond; improvement is difficult to maintain and does not generalize. Implementation requires much cooperation and certain skills or capabilities on the part of the family and school (Alexander et al. 1976; Bornstein et al. 1980; Chamberlain and Patterson 1985; Forehand and McMahon 1981; Frankel and Simmons 1981; Herbert 1982; Kazdin 1985; Kent and O'Leary 1976; Klein et al. 1980; Lewis 1985; Matson et al. 1980; McAuley 1982; Parsons and Alexander 1973; Patterson 1975, 1976, 1982; Pelham and Murphy 1986; Pellegrini and Urban 1985; Rutter and Garmezy 1983; Rutter and Giller 1984; WH Varley 1984; Weinrott et al. 1979; Wolff 1977).

Family Therapy

Therapy in a family context is a common treatment modality for children with CD, based on the consistent finding that families of these children are often disorganized and dysfunctional. There are two commonly used approaches. The first is to employ family members, usually the parents, in carrying out behavioral treatment plans, often in the form of parent management training (as discussed previously). It is clear that these families need more effective management techniques.

The second is to treat the family as a unit and to improve family functioning, which is often disordered in multiple areas, such as level of parental supervision or clarity, harmony, and consistency of communication. Therapy focuses on such aspects as quality of relationships and communication, coping skills, family power structure, and interpersonal and generational boundaries. Behavioral improvements have been found with the first approach. The latter modality has not been well tested as yet.

A combination of the two methods, or addition of other types of family work, in which there is consideration of various family problems beyond the CD of the child (e.g., the parent is depressed; the parent has no social supports; the family has very limited financial resources), is necessary for some families (especially high-risk families) (Chamberlain and Patterson 1985; Curry et al. 1984; Griest et al. 1982; Kazdin 1985; McAuley 1982; Parsons and Alexander 1973; Patterson 1974, 1975, 1982; Rutter and Giller 1984).

Institutional, Residential, and Day-Treatment Programs

The many types of institutions (e.g., hospitals, schools, residential treatment centers, group homes, jails), varied populations (e.g., delinquent, conduct-disordered, other psychiatrically ill), and differences in program philosophy (e.g., therapeutic with focus on treating problems with psychiatric techniques, correctional) make it difficult to summarize treatment results.

In general, studies have not consistently demonstrated that any of such settings are reliable in altering long-term outcome. However, the issue of which treatment in which institutional setting for how long has not been well tested.

It has been demonstrated that some positive behavioral changes do occur within various institutions. There seem to be certain attributes of a setting, such as firmness, warmth, harmony, good discipline, and high expectations, which are associated with improved behavior. Successful programs often have employed more behaviorally oriented approaches. However, the positive changes with institution treatment often do not generalize and are not maintained outside the particular setting.

At this time, choice of whether institutionalization is appropriate for a child with CD is usually made on clinical grounds of whether problems are too complicated (e.g., diagnostically unclear) or too severe, dangerous, or difficult to deal with at home and in the community. Children with CD need a structured setting with psychiatrically trained staff when they are suicidal or homicidal. They and/or others need to be protected, and treatment must be established. Sometimes children require an institutional setting when their behavior is not manageable (e.g., when they are aggressive or threatening; when they stay out all night and engage in potentially harmful activities). At times, problems in the home situation are severe (e.g., physical abuse, neglect, high levels of discord) and exacerbate the already existing problems of the child with CD. Placement in a structured program can provide safety, supervision, and an opportunity for families to reorganize and for individuals and families to establish more control. At other times, individual and family problems have not improved with outpatient interventions. Finally, certain diagnostic questions (e.g., whether a child is experiencing seizures or is psychotic) and treatment considerations (e.g., starting a medication with potentially harmful side effects; monitoring a medication response) might demand a specialized setting with professional expertise and opportunity for frequent and sophisticated observation.

It is clear that efforts must be made to provide a successful transition between the institution and the home and community and to provide follow-up services, coordinated with the institution, so that treatment gains might be maintained (Clarke 1985; Empey and Erickson 1972; Hersov and Bentovim 1977; Hobbs 1982; Jesness et al. 1975; Kazdin 1985; Kirigin et al. 1982; Lewis 1985; Marohn et al. 1980; Palmer 1971; Quay 1979b; Rutter and Giller 1984).

Psychotherapy and Counseling

Much of the literature does not support the position that, in themselves, traditional psychotherapy and counseling are effective for children with CD. Some data indicate that such interventions might be more helpful in certain subgroups of more anxious, introspective, and motivated patients, although other methods might be better. The addition of vocational counseling in older age groups may give somewhat better results. It should be noted that, in general, these approaches have not been adequately investigated (Kazdin 1985; Keith 1984; Rutter and Giller 1984; Shore and Massimo 1979; Sowles and Gill 1970; Truax et al. 1970).

Medication

There is a limited amount of literature on the pharmacotherapy of CD. In many instances, the sample populations are not well described or diagnosed. Most studies have been concerned with symptoms of aggression, "episodic dyscontrol," or delinquency, and mostly with adolescents. Several classes of drugs have been employed.

Stimulant medications have been useful in children with both ADHD and CD. Clinical drug management is the same as for children with ADHD alone. As yet, there are no major studies of stimulants with solely CD groups (although such studies are in progress).

Antipsychotic medications, particularly low dose haloperidol, have been effective in aggressive, undersocialized, often treatment-resistant children. Chlorpromazine (in doses of about 100–200 mg/day) and haloperidol (in doses of 0.025–0.20 mg/kg/day, range approximately 1–6 mg/day) have been used in both hospitalized and outpatient children with CD. Significant decreases in aggressive, negative, hostile behaviors have been demonstrated. Chlorpromazine is associated with excess sedation. Haloperidol is preferred, although the latter my result in mild cognitive impairments. These effects are dose dependent, so that haloperidol dosage should be kept as low as possible. All antipsychotics can have movement side effects (e.g., dystonic reactions, extrapyramidal symptoms, dyskinesias). Tardive dyskinesia is a serious possible adverse effect. Children's motor behavior (e.g., presence of tics, other abnormal movements, akinesia) should be carefully and frequently monitored before and during medication trials. There are several scales available for doing movement ratings (Rapoport et al. 1985).

Lithium has been effective in the CD population, with fewer side effects and similar benefits to those of haloperidol. Dosages are usually in the range of 1,200–2,000 mg/day, with blood lithium levels of 0.76–1.24 meq/l. Lithium seems to be the most promising of the pharmacologic treatments for CD. It has potential hematologic, thyroid, neuromuscular, and renal side effects, which must be monitored.

Antidepressant medications might be helpful in children with both CD and concurrent major depression. Puig-Antich et al. (1985) provide guidelines on antidepressant use in children and adolescents.

The place of anticonvulsant medications (e.g., carbamazepine, dilantin), aside from their utility in treating seizure disorders and some affective disorders, is unclear, although they generally have not produced satisfactory results. Propanolol has been used with a few children who exhibit periodic rage outbursts, most resembling episodic dyscontrol, but not in aggressive CD populations.

Since research with pharmacologic agents has not been extensive, medication for the treatment of CD may be helpful in carefully monitored selective instances, usually when other treatments are failing and when problems are severe. Medication alone without other interventions is not appropriate (Campbell et al. 1982, 1984a, 1984b, 1985; Greenhill et al. 1973; Klein et al. 1980; Leventhal 1984; O'Donnell 1985; Platt et al. 1984; Puig-Antich 1982; Sheard et al. 1976; Siassi 1984).

Multimodal Treatment

As previously indicated, treatment for children with serious disorders and multiple symptoms is most often multimodal, in a loosely defined sense. Academic deficiencies might require tutoring. Families need education. Medical problems must be addressed. Coexisting psychiatric disorders are treated in conjunction with the therapies for CD.

In a strict sense of multimodal treatment, however, there is little research on how to combine various specific therapies for children with CD. For youngsters with both ADHD and CD, combination of medication with other interventions (e.g., parent management training) is probably necessary. As previously stated, the clinician must often address a wide variety of family problems, of individual members, subunits (e.g., the marital couple), and the family unit, in addition to implementing specific behavioral programs. Also, there are some suggestions, as yet unproven in this population, that combining particular behavioral techniques (e.g., response contingencies with cognitive training) might yield better results than using one technique alone.

Work in this area is currently being pursued and is promising (Kazdin 1985; Klein et al. 1980; Pelham and Murphy 1986; Rutter 1983b, 1985; Rutter and Giller 1984).

Clinical Management

Children with CD are a diverse group. Therapy for a particular child is therefore an individualized process. As for all children in psychiatric treatment, the goals are to promote normal development, decrease problem behaviors, and improve functioning.

The first steps in treatment, as previously outlined, are making a multisystem evaluation (with special attention to family functioning) and establishing a diagnosis. It is especially important in this population to recognize other treatable problems or conditions (e.g., ADHD, depression, learning disabilities, enuresis), which can be addressed concurrently. Sometimes the CD problems are so dramatic or troublesome that other issues are unnecessarily overlooked.

Most children with CD, their families, and schools require some sort of support or counseling. When problems are mild, it may consist of providing reassurance that the situation is manageable. In other cases, it may be to provide necessary relief, to help reframe issues (e.g., away from a belief that the child is "bad"), and sometimes to ensure safety for the child and family (e.g., to intervene in violent behavior among family members). Much of the time these maneuvers will be part of more structured work with the families.

Cooperation among different professionals is generally required (e.g., among the child psychiatrist, the pediatrician who is treating the child's anemia, the special education teacher at school, and a worker from a community service or legal agency). The clinician will sometimes help the parents or guardians advocate for the child in various educational, community service, and legal systems.

Preparation for treatment is made by discussing as explicitly as possible the details of treatment (e.g., form, timing, short- and long-term goals). Requirements for the participants are explained (e.g., that the teacher will send home daily behavior reports; that both parents must attend family therapy sessions). Emphasis should be placed on the family as part of the solution, not the cause of problems.

The initial choice of interventions is guided by the type and severity of problems (e.g., the child is dependent on alcohol and needs detoxification in a hospital; the child is only disobedient or oppositional in the home and not at school, so that a behavioral program is not needed in the latter setting); the age and developmental level of the child (e.g., it is more difficult to monitor the details of an adolescent's behavior because adolescents are more independent); and feasibility for the family and school system (e.g., there are no family members available for treatment; the school has a vocational, in addition to its academic, program). Most important, of course, is the particular clinical picture, which is varied for this population of children.

Therapy will generally consist of at least a combination of behavioral treatments and family work. The setting will depend on where the child can be appropriately and safely managed. Institutional settings of some type may be necessary for those reasons elaborated earlier.

Changes in behavior during treatment should be carefully assessed. Included are all important areas of functioning, with symptoms and areas of dysfunction specifically targeted beforehand.

As previously discussed, data gathered from behavioral treatments can provide useful objective information for assessment. It is already an integral part of that therapy process. Behavior rating scales can be used for any type of treatment, however. Checklists specific for CD problems, such as the Parent Daily Report (Chamberlain and Patterson 1985), might be employed routinely, whereas more general or comprehensive behavior scales, such as the Child Behavioral Checklist (Achenbach and Edelbrock 1982) might be given at longer time intervals. If medication is administered, adverse and side effects ratings must be obtained before and during the pharmacotherapy. Rapoport et al. (1985) provide copies of several scales.

In addition, practitioners might try single case research designs to monitor treatment effects (Kazdin 1983).

As with the child with ADHD, and as might be expected with such a heterogeneous diagnostic group as CD, it is not possible to predict how long it might take for a particular child to improve or to indicate how long therapy should last. Since problems are chronic for a proportion of children, chronic intervention might be anticipated. It is reasonable to institute some form of contact or follow-up given the possible chronicity and unknown length of benefit once treatments have been discontinued.

Conclusion

Attention-deficit hyperactivity disorder and conduct disorder are evolving conceptual and diagnostic entities. Validation as separate syndromes, as well as clarification of subgroups, are major outstanding issues. Refinement of these categories will be important for treatment evaluation.

Both are common childhood disorders. They are often chronic, with significant morbidity (for family and child) and poor prognosis (in one-third to one-half of cases). Thus treatment is imperative.

Although much research is still needed, there are findings that can presently direct clinical interventions. There are no individual or comprehensive treatments for ADHD or CD. As yet, no particular treatments have consistently been shown to have major long-term benefits. For ADHD, medication and behavioral treatments are the most researched and most effective specific therapies. Combination of the two may yield better results for some children. For CD, behavioral treatments alone have the most empirical support. Children with ADHD and those with CD generally have multiple, complex problems, which must be addressed. Multimodal approaches are almost always necessary, especially if one regards parent counseling and modification of school milieu as such. Involvement of parents and school personnel in all or part of the treatment process is important. Precise ways to combine the more specific therapies have not been determined.

At this time, important treatment decisions are still made on clinical grounds, after consideration of research findings and the particular clinical situation.

References

Section 4
Attention–Deficit Hyperactivity Disorder and Conduct Disorder

Abikoff H, Gittelman R: Does behavior therapy normalize the classroom behavior of hyperactive children? Arch Gen Psychiatry 41:49–454, 1984

Abikoff H, Gittelman R: Hyperactive children treated with stimulants: is cognitive therapy a useful adjunct? Arch Gen Psychiatry 42:953–961, 1985a

Abikoff H, Gittelman R: The normalizing effects of methylphenidate on the classroom behavior of ADHD children. J Abnorm Child Psychol 13:33–44, 1985b

Achenbach TM: Developmental Psychopathology. John Wiley and Sons, New York, 1982

Achenbach TM, Edelbrock CS: The classification of child psychopathology: a review and analysis of empirical efforts. Psychol Bull 85:1275–1301, 1978

Achenbach TM, Edelbrock CS: Manual for the Child Behavior Checklist and Child Behavior Profile. Burlington, Vt, Child Psychiatry, University of Vermont, 1982

Alexander JF, Barton C, Schiavo RS, et al: Systems-behavioral intervention with families of delinquents: therapist characteristics, family behavior, and outcome. J Consult Clin Psychol 44:656–664, 1976

American Psychiatric Association: Diagnostic and Statistical Manual of Mental Disorders, 2nd ed. Washington, DC, American Psychiatric Association, 1968

American Psychiatric Association: Diagnostic and Statistical Manual of Mental Disorders, 3rd ed. Washington, DC, American Psychiatric Association, 1980

American Psychiatric Association: Diagnostic and Statistical Manual of Mental Disorders, 3rd ed. revised. Washington, DC, American Psychiatric Association, 1987

Barkley NA: The effects of methylphenidate on the interactions of preschool ADHD children with their mothers. J Am Acad Child Adolesc Psychiatry 27:336–341, 1988

Barkley RA: A review of stimulant drug research with hyperactive children. J Child Psychol Psychiatry 18:137–165, 1977

Barkley RA: Hyperactive Children: A Handbook for Diagnosis and Treatment. New York, Guilford Press, 1981

Bornstein M, Bellack AS, Hersen M: Social skills training for highly aggressive children: treatment in an inpatient setting. Behav Modif 4:173–186, 1980

Brown RT, Wynne ME, Medenis R: Methylphenidate and cognitive therapy: a comparison of treatment approaches with hyperactive boys. J Abnorm Child Psychol 13:69–87, 1985a

Brown RT, Borden KA, Clingerman SR: Pharmacotherapy in ADD adolescents. Psychopharmacol Bull 21:192–211, 1985b

Campbell M, Cohen IL, Small RM: Drugs in aggressive behavior. J Am Acad Child Psychiatry 21:107–117, 1982

Campbell M, Small AM, Green WH, et al: Behavioral efficacy of haloperidol and lithium carbonate. Arch Gen Psychiatry 41:650–656, 1984a

Campbell M, Perry R, Green WH: Use of Lithium in children and adolescents. Psychosomatics 25:95–106, 1984b

Campbell M, Green WH, Deutsch SI: Child and Adolescent Psychopharmacology. Beverly Hills, Calif, Sage Publications, 1985

Cantwell DP: Pharmacotherapy of ADD in adolescents: what do we know, where do we go, how should we do it. Psychopharmacol Bull 21:251–257, 1985

Cantwell DP, Carlson GA: Stimulants, in Pediatric Psychopharmacology: The Use of Behavior Modifying Drugs in Children. Edited by Werry JS. New York, Brunner/Mazel, 1978

Chamberlain P, Patterson GR: Aggressive behavior in middle childhood, in The Clinical Guide to Child Psychiatry. Edited by Schaffer D, Ehrhardt AA, Greenhill LL. New York, Free Press, 1985

Chess S, Hassibi M: Principles and Practice of Child Psychiatry, 2nd ed. New York, Plenum, 1986

Clarke RVG: Delinquency, environment, and intervention. J Child Psychology 26:505–523, 1985

Clements S: Minimal Brain Dysfunction in Children. NINDB Monograph No. 3. Washington, DC, US Public Health Service, 1966

Cohen NJ, Sullivan J, Minde K, et al: Evaluation of the Relative effectiveness of methylphenidate and cognitive behavior modification in the treatment of kindergarten-aged hyperactive children. J Abnorm Child Psychol 9:43–54, 1981

Comings DE, Comings BG: Tourette's syndrome and attention deficit with hyperactivity: are they genetically related? J Am Acad Child Psychiatry 23:138–146, 1984

Comings DE, Comings BG: A controlled study of Tourette syndrome. I. Attention-deficit disorder, learning disorders, and school problems. Am J Human Genetics 41:701–741, 1987

Conners CK: Food Additives for Hyperactive Children. New York, Plenum, 1980

Conners CK, Wells KC: Hyperkinetic Children: A Neuropsychosocial Approach. Beverly Hills, Calif, Sage Publications, 1986

Cunningham CE, Barkley RA: The interactions of hyperactive and normal children with their mothers in free play and structured tasks. Child Dev 50:214–217, 1978

Curry JF, Wiencort SI, Koehler F: Family therapy with aggressive and delinquent adolescents, in The Aggressive Adolescent, Clinical Perspectives. Edited by Keith CR. New York, Free Press, 1984

Donnelly M, Rapoport JL: Attention deficit disorders, in Diagnosis and Psychopharmacology of Childhood and Adolescent Disorders. Edited by Wiener JM. New York, John Wiley & Sons, 1985

Donnelly M, Zametkin AJ, Rapoport JL, et al: Treatment of childhood hyperactivity with desipramine: plasma drug concentration, cardiovasular effects, plasma and urinary catecholamine levels, and clinical response. Clin Pharmacol Ther 39:72–81, 1986

Douglas VI: Treatment and training approaches to hyperactivity: establishing internal or external control, in Hyperactive Children: The Social Ecology of Identification and Treatment. Edited by Whalen C, Henker B. New York, Academic Press, 1980

Douglas VI, Peters KG: Toward a clearer definition of the attentional deficit of hyperactive children, in Attention and Cognitive Development. Edited by Hale GA, Lewis M. New York, Plenum, 1979

Douglas, VI, Barr RG, O'Neill ME, et al: Short term effects of methylphenidate on the cognitive, learning and academic performance of children with attention deficit disorder in the laboratory and the classroom. J Child Psychol Psychiatry 27:191–211, 1986

Dulcan MK: The psychopharmacologic treatment of children and adolescents with attention deficit disorder. Psychiatric Annals 15:69–86, 1985

Eisenberg L, Gilbert A, Cytryn L, et al: The effectiveness of psychotherapy alone and in conjunction with perphenazine or placebo in the treatment of neurotic and hyperkinetic children. Am J Psychiatry 117:1088–1093, 1961

Eisenberg L, Conners CK, Sharpe L: A controlled study of the differential applications of outpatient psychiatry treatment for children. Japanese Journal of Child Psychiatry 6:125–132, 1965

Empey LT, Erickson ML: The Provo Experiment: Evaluating Community Control of Delinquency. Lexington, Mass, DC Heath & Co, 1972

Feingold BF: Why Your Child is Hyperactive. New York, Random House, 1975

Ferguson HB, Rapoport JL: Nosological issues and biological validation, in Developmental Neuropsychiatry. Edited by Rutter M. New York, Guilford Press, 1983

Firestone P: Factors associated with children's adherence to stimulant medication. Am J Orthopsychiatry 52:447–457, 1982

Firestone P, Kelly MJ, Goodman JT, et al: Differential effects of parent training and stimulant medication with hyperactives. J Am Acad Child Psychiatry 20:135–147, 1981

Flynn NM, Rapoport JL: Hyperactivity in open and traditional classroom environments. Journal of Special Education 10:285–290, 1976

Forehand R, McMahon RJ: Helping the Noncompliant Child: A Clinician's Guide to Parent Training. New York, Guilford Press, 1981

Frankel F, Simmons JQ: Behavioral treatment approaches to pathological unsocialized physical aggression in young children. J Am Acad Child Psychiatry 26:525–551, 1981

Gadow KD: Effects of stimulant drugs on academic performance in hyperactive and learning-disabled children. Journal of Learning Disabilities 16:290–299, 1983

Garfinkel BD, Wender PH, Sloman L, et al: Tricyclic antidepressant and methylphenidate treatment of attention deficit disorder in children. J Am Acad Child Psychiatry 22:343–348, 1983

Gesell A, Amatruda CS: Developmental Diagnosis, 2nd ed. New York, Hoeber Press, 1949

Gittelman R: Are behavioral and cognitive effects of stimulants correlated? International Journal of Mental Health 41:182–198, 1975

Gittelman R: Hyperkinetic syndrome: treatment issues and principles, in Developmental Neuropsychiatry. Edited by Rutter M. New York, Guilford Press, 1983

Gittelman R, Manuzza S, Sheker R, et al: Hyperactive boys almost grown up. Arch Gen Psychiatry 42:937–947, 1985

Gittelman-Klein R, Abikoff H, Pollack E, et al: A controlled trial of behavior modification and methylphenidate in hyperactive children, in Hyperactive Children: The Social Ecology of Identification and Treatment. Edited by Whalen C, Henker B. New York, Academic Press, 1980

Graham P: Epidemiologic studies, in Psychopathological Disorders of Childhood. Edited by Quay H, Werry J. New York, John Wiley & Sons, 1979

Greenhill LL, Rieder RO, Wender PH: Lithium carbonate in the treatment of hyperactive children. Arch Gen Psychiatry 28:636–640, 1973

Griest DL, Forehand R, Rogers T, et al: Effects of parent enhancement therapy on the treatment outcome and generalization of a parent program. Behavior Research and Therapy 20:429–436, 1982

Hall RV, Axelrod S, Foundopoulous M, et al: The effective use of punishment to modify behavior in the classroom, in Classroom Management: The Successful Use of Behavior Modification. Edited by O'Leary SG. New York, Pergamon Press, 1972

Herbert M: Conduct disorders, in Advances in Clinical Child Psychology. Edited by Lahey BB, Kazdin AE. New York, Plenum, 1982

Hersov L, Bentovim M: Inpatient units and day-hospitals, in Child Psychiatry, Modern Approaches. Edited by Rutter M, Hersov L. Oxford, Blackwell, 1977

Hobbs N: The Troubled and Troubling Child. San Francisco, Jossey-Bass, 1982

Humphries T, Kinsbourne M, Swanson J: Stimulant effects on cooperation and social interaction between hyperactive children and their mothers. J Child Psychol Psychiatry 19:13–22, 1978

Hunt R: Oral and skin patch administration of clonidine compared to methylphenidate in the treatment of attention deficit disorder with hyperactivity in children. Scientific Proceedings for the Annual Meeting, American Academy of Child and Adolescent Psychiatry 2:22, 1986

Jenkins RL: Behavioral Disorders of Childhood and Adolescence. Springfield, Ill, Charles C Thomas, 1973

Jesness CF, Allison R, McCormick P, et al: Cooperative Behavior Demonstration Project. Sacramento, California Youth Authority, 1975

Kavale KA, Forness SR: Hyperactivity and diet treatment: a meta-analysis of the Feingold hypothesis: Journal of Learning Disabilities 16:324–330, 1983

Kazdin AE: Single-case research designs in clinical child psychiatry. J Am Acad Child Psychiatry 22:423–432, 1983

Kazdin AE: Acceptability of aversive procedures and medication as treatment alternatives for deviant child behavior. J Abnorm Child Psychol 12:289–302, 1984

Kazdin AE: Treatment of Antisocial Behavior in Children and Adolescents. Homewood, Ill, Dorsey Press, 1985

Keith CR (ed): The Aggressive Adolescent, Clinical Perspectives. New York, Free Press, 1984

Kendall KC: Cognitive-behavioral self-control treatment for children. J Child Psychol Psychiatry 25:173–179, 1984

Kent RN, O'Leary KD: A controlled evaluation of behavior modification with conduct problem children. J Consult Clin Psychol 44:586–596, 1976

Kirigin KA, Braukmann CJ, Atwater JD, et al: An evaluation of teaching family (Achievement Place) group homes for juvenile offenders. J Appl Behav Anal 15:1–16, 1982

Klein DF, Gittelman R, Quitkin F, et al: Diagnosis and Drug Treatment of Psychiatric Disorders: Adults and Children. Baltimore, Williams & Wilkins Co, 1980

Klein RG, Manuzza S: Hyperactive boys almost grown up. III. Methylphenidate effects on ultimate height. Arch Gen Psychiatry 45:1131–1134, 1988

Klein RG, Landa B, Mattes JA, et al: Methylphenidate and growth in hyperactive children: A controlled withdrawal study. Arch Gen Psychiatry 45:1127–1130, 1988

Klorman R, Coons HW, Borgstedt AD: Effects of methylphenidate on adolescents with a childhood history of attention deficit disorder, I: clinical findings. J Am Acad Child Adolesc Psychiatry 26:363–367, 1987

Lahey B, Schaughnecy E, Strauss C, et al: Are attention deficit disorders with and without hyperactivity similar or dissimilar disorders? J Am Acad Child Psychiatry 23:302–309, 1984

Leventhal BL: The neuropharmacology of violent and aggressive behavior in children and adolescents, in The Aggressive Adolescent, Clinical Perspectives. Edited by Keith CR. New York, Free Press, 1984

Lewis DO: Conduct disorder and juvenile delinquency, in Comprehensive Textbook of Psychiatry, 4th ed, vol 2. Edited by Freedman AM, Kaplan HI, Sadock BJ. Baltimore, Williams & Wilkins Co, 1984

Lewis DO: Juvenile deliquency, in The Clinical Guide to Child Psychiatry. Edited by Shaffer D, Ehrhardt AA, Greenhill LL. New York, Free Press, 1985

Loney J, Milich R: Hyperactivity, inattention, and aggression in clinical practice, in

Advances in Behavioral Pediatrics, vol. 2. Edited by Wolraith M, Ruth DK. Greenwich, Conn, JAI PRESS, 1982

Lowe TL, Cohen DJ, Detlon J, et al: Stimulant medications precipitate Tourette's syndrome. JAMA 247:1729–1731, 1982

Madsen CH, Madsen CDK, Saudargas RA, et al: Classroom RAID (rules, approval, ignore, disapproval): a cooperative approach for professionals and volunteers. Journal of School Psychology 8:180–185, 1979

Marohn RC, Dalle-Molle D, McCarter E, et al: Juvenile Delinquents: Psychodynamic Assessment and Hospital Treatment. New York, Brunner/Mazel, 1980

Mash E, Dalby T: Behavioral interventions for hyperactivity, in Hyperactivity in Children: Etiology, Measures, and Treatment Implications. Edited by Trites R. Baltimore, University Park Press, 1979

Matson JL, Dazdin AE, Esveld-Dawson K: Training interpersonal skills among mentally retarded and socially dysfunctional children. Behav Res Ther 18:419–427, 1980

Mattes JA: The Feingold diet: a current reappraisal. Journal of Learning Disabilities 16:319–323, 1983

Mattes J, Gittelman R: Growth of hyperactive children on a maintenance regimen of methylphenidate. Arch Gen Psychiatry 40:317–321, 1983

Maurer R, Stewart M: Attention deficit disorder without hyperactivity in a child psychiatry clinic. J Clin Psychiatry 41:232–233, 1980

McAuley R: Training parents to modify conduct problems in their children. J Child Psychol Psychiatry 23:335–342, 1982

Meichenbaum D: Application of cognitive-behavior modification procedures to hyperactive children, in Strategic Interventions for Hyperactive Children. Edited by Gittelman G. New York, ME Sharpe, 1981

Nieman GW, Delong R: Use of the Personality Inventory for Children as an aid in differentiating children with mania from children with attention deficit disorder with hyperactivity. J Am Acad Child Adolesc Psychiatry 26:381–388, 1987

NIH Consensus Development Conference: Defined diet and childhood hyperactivity. Clin Pediatr (Phila) 21:627–630, 1982

O'Donnell DJ: Conduct disorders, in Diagnosis and Psychopharmacology of Childhood and Adolescent Disorders. Edited by Wiener JM. New York, John Wiley & Sons, 1985

Office of Child Development: Report of the Conference on the Use of Stimulant Drugs in the Treatment of Behaviorally Disturbed Young School Children. Washington, DC, US Department of Health, Education, and Welfare, 1971

O'Leary KD: Pills or skills for hyperactive children. J Appl Behav Anal 13:191–204, 1980

O'Leary KD, O'Leary S, Becker WC: Modification of a deviant sibling interaction in the home. Behav Res Ther 5:113–120, 1967

O'Leary KD, Pelham WE, Rosenbaum A, et al: Behavioral treatment of hyperkinetic children: an experimental evaluation of the usefulness. Clin Pediatr (Phila) 15:274–279, 1976

Palmer TB: California's community treatment program for delinquents. Journal of Research in Crime and Delinquency 8:74–92, 1971

Parsons BV, Alexander JF: Short-term family intervention: therapy outcome study. J Consult Clin Psychol 41:195–201, 1973

Patterson GR: Intervention for boys with conduct problems: multiple settings, treatments, and criteria. J Consult Clin Psychol 42:471–481, 1974

Patterson GR: Families: Application of Social Learning to Family Life. Champaign, Ill, Research Press, 1975

Patterson GR: Living with Children: New Methods for Parents and Teachers. Champaign, Ill, Research Press, 1976

Patterson GR: Coercive Family Process. Eugene, Oreg, Castalia, 1982

Pelham WE: Childhood hyperactivity: diagnosis, etiology, nature, and treatment, in Behavioral Medicine and Clinical Psychology: Overlapping Disciplines. Edited by Gatchel R, Baum A, Singer J. Hillsdale, NJ, Lawrence Erlbaum Associates, 1982

Pelham WE, Bender ME: Peer relationships in hyperactive children: description and treatment. Advances in Learning and Behavioral Disabilities 1:365–436, 1982

Pelham WE, Murphy HA: Attention deficit disorders and conduct disorders, in Psychopharmacology and Behavioral Treatment: An Integrated Approach. Edited by Hersen M. New York, John Wiley & Sons, 1986

Pelham WE, Schnedler RW, Bologna N, et al: Behavioral and stimulant treatment of hyperactive children: a therapy study with methylphenidate probes in a within subject design. J Appl Behav Anal 13:221–236, 1980

Pelham WE, Bender ME, Caddell J, et al: Methylphenidate and children with attention deficit disorder. Arch Gen Psychiatry 42:948–952, 1985

Pellegrini DS, Urbain ES: An evaluation of interpersonal cognitive problem-solving training with children. J Child Psychol Psychiatry 26:17–42, 1985

Platt JE, Campbell M, Green W, et al: Cognitive effects of lithium carbonate and haloperidol in treatment resistant aggressive children. Arch Gen Psychiatry 41:657–662, 1984

Porrino L, Rapoport J, Ismond D, et al: A naturalistic assessment of motor activity of hyperactive boys, I: comparison with normal controls. Arch Gen Psychiatry 40:681–687, 1983a

Porrino L, Rapoport J, Ismond D, et al: A naturalistic assessment of motor activity of hyperactive boys, II: stimulant drug effects. Arch Gen Psychiatry 40:688–693, 1983b

Price RA, Kidd KK, Cohen DJ, et al: A twin study of Tourette syndrome. Arch Gen Psychiatry 42:815–820, 1985

Price RA, Leckman JF, Pauls DL, et al: Gilles de la Tourette's syndrome and central nervous system stimulants in twins and nontwins. Neurology 36:232–237, 1986

Puig-Antich J: Major depression and conduct disorder in prepuberty. J Am Acad Child Psychiatry 21:118–128, 1982

Puig-Antich J, Ryan ND, Rakinovich H: Affective disorders in childhood and adolescence, in Diagnosis and Psychopharmacology of Childhood and Adolescent Disorders. Edited by Wrener JM. New York, John Wiley & Sons, 1985

Quay HC: Classification, in Psychopathological Disorders of Childhood, 2nd ed. Edited by Quay HC, Werry JS. New York, John Wiley & Sons, 1979a

Quay HC: Residential treatment, in Psychopathological Disorders of Childhood. Edited by Quay HC, Werry JS. New York, John Wiley & Sons, 1979b

Rapoport JL: DSM-III-Revised and child psychiatry, in Issues in Diagnostic Research. Edited by Last CG, Hersen M. New York, Plenum, 1987

Rapoport JL, Benoit M: The relation of direct home observations to the clinic evaluation of hyperactive school age boys. J Child Psychol Psychiatry 16:141–147, 1975

Rapoport JL, Conners CK, Reatig N (eds): Rating scales and assessment instruments for use in pediatric psychopharmacology research. Psychopharmacol Bull 21:4, 1985

Rapoport JL, Quinn PO, Bradbard G, et al: A double-blind comparison of imipramine and methylphenidate treatments of hyperactive boys. Arch Gen Psychiatry 30:789–793, 1974

Rapoport JL, Buchsbaum M, Zahn T, et al: Dextroamphetamine: cognitive and behavioral effects in normal prepubertal boys. Science 199:560–563, 1978

Rapoport JL, Buchsbaum M, Weingartner H, et al: Dextroamphetamine: cognitive and behavioral effects in normal and hyperactive boys and normal adult males. Arch Gen Psychiatry 37:933–946, 1980

Rimland B: The Feingold diet: an assessment of the reviews by Mattes, by Kavale and Forness, and others. Journal of Learning Disabilities 16:331–333, 1983

Robins LN: Deviant Children Grown Up. Baltimore, Williams & Wilkins Co, 1966

Robins LN: An Evaluation of the DSM-III Diagnosis of Conduct Disorder. Presented at the American Psychiatric Association Workshop on Attention Deficit Disorder and Conduct Disorder, 1984

Robbins DM, Beck JC, Pries R, et al: Learning disabilities and neurological impairment in adjudicated unincarcerated male delinquents. J Am Acad Child Psychiatry 22:40–46, 1983

Ross DM, Ross SA: Hyperactivity: Current Issues, Research and Theory, 2nd ed. New York, John Wiley & Sons, 1982

Rutter M: Behavioral studies: questions and findings on the concept of a distinctive syndrome, in Developmental Neuropsychiatry. Edited by Rutter M. New York, Guilford Press, 1983a

Rutter M: Psychological therapies: issues and prospects, in Childhood Psychopathology and Development. Edited by Guze SB, Earls FJ, Barrett JE. New York, Raven Press, 1983b

Rutter M: Family and school influences on behavioral development. J Child Psychol Psychiatry 26:349–368, 1985

Rutter M, Garmezy N: Developmental psychopathology, in Handbook of Child Psychology, 4th ed, vol 4. Edited by Mussen PH. New York, John Wiley & Sons, 1983

Rutter M, Giller H: Juvenile Delinquency, Trends and Perspectives. New York, Guilford Press, 1984

Rutter M, Hersov L (eds): Child and Adolescent Psychiatry, 2nd ed. Boston, Blackwell, 1985

Rutter M, Shaffer D: DSM-III, a step forward or backward in terms of the classification of childhood psychiatric disorders? J Am Acad Child Psychiatry 19:371–394, 1980

Rutter M, Shaffer D, Sturge C: A Guide to Multi-Axial Classification Scheme for Psychiatric Disorders in Childhood and Adolescence. London, Institute of Psychiatry, 1979

Safer D, Allen RP, Barr E: Growth rebound after termination of stimulant drugs. Pediatrics 86:113–116, 1975

Sargeant J: Cognitive Measures. Presented at the Annual Highpoint Hospital Symposium on Attention Deficit Disorder. Toronto, Canada, 1984

Satterfield JH, Satterfield BT, Cantwell D: Three-year multimodality treatment study of 100 hyperactive boys. J Pediatr 98:650–655, 1981

Satterfield JH, Satterfield BT, Schell AM: Therapeutic interventions to prevent delinquency in hyperactive boys. J Am Acad Child and Adolesc Psychiatry 26:56–64, 1987

Schleifer N, Weiss G, Cohen N, et al: Hyperactivity in preschoolers and the effect of methylphenidate. Am J Orthopsychiatry 45:38–50, 1975

Schmidt K, Solanto MV, Sanchez-Kappraff M, et al: The effect of stimulant medication on academic performance, in the context of multimodal treatment, in attention deficit disorder with hyperactivity: two case reports. J Clin Psychopharmacol 4:100–103, 1984

Shaffer D, Ehrhardt AE, Greenhill LL (eds): The Clinical Guide to Child Psychiatry. New York, Free Press, 1985

Shapiro AK, Shapiro E: Do stimulants provoke, cause or exacerbate tics and Tourette's syndrome? Compr Psychiatry 22:265–273, 1981

Sheard MH, Marini JL, Bridges CI: The effect of lithium on impulsive aggressive behavior in man. Am J Psychiatry 133:1409–1413, 1976

Shore MF, Massimo JL: Fifteen years after treatment: a follow-up study of comprehensive vocationally-oriented psychotherapy. Am J Orthopsychiatry 49:240–245, 1979

Siassi I: Lithium treatment of impulsive behavior in children. J Clin Psychiatry 43:482–484, 1984

Simmons JE: Psychiatric Examination of Children, 4th ed. Philadelphia, Lea & Febiger, 1987

Sleator E: How do hyperactive children feel about taking stimulants and will they tell the doctor? Clin Pediatr (Phila) 21:474–479, 1982

Sowles RC, Gill JH: Institutional and community adjustment of delinquents following counseling. J Consult Clin Psychol 34:398–402, 1970

Sprague RL: Behavior modification and educational techniques, in Developmental Neuropsychiatry. Edited by Rutter M. New York, Guilford Press, 1983

Sprague R, Sleator E: Methylphenidate in hyperkinetic children: differences in dose effects on learning and social behavior. Science 198:1274–1276, 1977

Stenhausen H, Kreuzer E: Learning in hyperactive children: are there stimulant-related and state-dependent effects? Psychopharmacology 74:384–390, 1971

Stewart M, Pitts F, Craig A, et al: The hyperactive child syndrome. Am J Orthopsychiatry 36:861–867, 1966

Sturge C: Reading retardation and antisocial behavior. J Child Psychol Psychiatry 23:21–31, 1982

Swanson J, Kinsbourne M: Stimulant-related state-dependent learning in hyperactive children. Science 192:1354–1357, 1976

Taylor EA (ed): The Overactive Child. Philadelphia, JB Lippincott Co, 1986

Trites RL, Laprade K: Evidence for an independent syndrome of hyperactivity. J Child Psychol Psychiatry 24:573–586, 1983

Truax CB, Warga MJ, Volksdorf FR: Antecedents to outcome in group counseling with institutionalized juvenile delinquents. J Abnorm Psychol 76:235–241, 1970

Urbain ES, Kendall PC: Review of social-cognitive problem-solving intervention with children. Psychol Bull 88:109–143, 1980

Varley CK: Diet and the behavior of children with attention deficit disorder. J Am Acad Child Psychiatry 23:182–185, 1984

Varley CK: A review of studies of drug treatment for attention deficit disorder with hyperactivity in adolescents. Psychopharmacol Bull 21:216–221, 1985

Varley WH: Behavior modification approaches to the aggressive adolescent, in The Aggressive Adolescent, Clinical Pespectives. Edited by Keith CR. New York, Free Press, 1984

Weingartner H, Langer D, Grice J, et al: Acquisition and retrieval of information in amphetamine treated hyperactive children. Psychiatry Res 6:21–29, 1982

Weinrott M, Bauske B, Patterson GR: Systematic replication of a social learning approach, in Trends in Behavior Therapy. Edited by Sjoden PO, Bates S, Dockens WS. New York, Academic Press, 1979

Weiss G, Hechtman LT: Hyperactive Children Grown Up. New York, Guilford Press, 1986

Wender P: Minimal Brain Dysfunction in Children. New York, Wiley-Interscience, 1971

Werry J: Imipramine and methylphenidate in hyperactive children. J Child Psychol Psychiatry 21:27–35, 1980

Whalen CK, Henker B (eds): Hyperactive Children: The Social Ecology of Identification and Treatment. New York, Academic Press, 1980

Whalen CK, Collins BE, Henker B, et al: Behavior observations of hyperactive children and methylphenidate effects in systematically structured classroom environments: now you see them, now you don't. J Pediatr Psychol 3:177–187, 1978

Whalen CK, Henker B, Finck D: Medication effects in the classroom: three naturalistic indicators. J Abnorm Child Psychol 9:419–433, 1980a

Whalen CK, Henker B, Dotemoto S: Methylphenidate and hyperactivity: effects on teacher behaviors. Science 208:1280–1282, 1980b

Wolff S: Nondelinquent disturbances of conduct, in Child Psychiatry, Modern Approaches. Edited by Rutter M, Hersov L. London, Blackwell Scientific Publications, 1977

Anxiety Disorders of Childhood or Adolescence

Chapter 54

Anxiety Disorders of Childhood or Adolescence

Fear and anxieties in children are common and are usually short lived (Barrios et al. 1981; Johnson and Melamed 1979), but may be long lasting and hard to define and trace. Many fears and anxieties tend to be age- or time-specific (e.g., developmental in their appearance). They begin with startle reactions to physical stimuli in infancy, and proceed to stranger and separation anxiety; to fears of monsters, ghosts, and animals; to fear of illness and death; and to socially determined anxiety in adolescence (Werry and Aman 1980).

When fears persist well beyond the ordinary age of appearance, we may call them anxiety disorders. Their natural history, however, is still hidden. Except for some connections between separation anxiety disorder in children and panic disorder in adults, the vast majority of adults with anxiety disorders do not appear to have had them as children (Barrios et al. 1981; Robins 1979). However, bridges between childhood and adulthood are beginning to emerge (Thyer et al. 1985).

At present, we are in a period of transition in the development of specificity of treatment approach for each condition. At this time, different methods are largely indistinguishable from one another in their efficacy (Bloch 1982; Werry 1979). They all have face validity but none have firmly established scientific validity. Therefore, it is especially important for the psychiatrist to be able to consider individual cases at multiple conceptual levels in designing the most appropriate treatment program.

That is the reason several different treatment approaches are used, separately or in combination, in clinical practice. This chapter examines four of these—behavioral, biologic, psychoanalytic, and family systems—treatment approaches for anxiety disorders in children and adolescents. It applies each of the four separate treatment approaches to three clinical cases that illustrate the three DSM-III-R (American Psychiatric Association 1987) categories of anxiety disorder in childhood or adolescence.

The aim is to present several treatment approaches for each of the anxiety disorders in children, not a single way. This is not simply to illustrate that several different paths can be taken to reach the same goal. Indeed there is overlap in modalities that were intended to be separate. Many of the techniques used in any given form of treatment are often used by clinicians when practicing other forms. For example, psychodynamic therapy may incorporate psychopharmacology, family therapy, and elements of behavioral therapy. For the sake of clarity, each form will be presented separately. But in actual clinical practice there is a combination, usually an integration.

The contemporary psychiatrist has a personal theoretical organizing framework with which to approach the treatment of patients. It may be based on one (or more) of the conceptual models presented here. But beyond this central model around which the work revolves, the psychiatrist should be familiar with a variety of conceptual models and therapeutic techniques and mold them into a personal amalgam to suit the needs of the individual patient situation. A technique is no substitute for knowledge of children and their families or for sound clinical judgment and skill. The best treatment plan is based on a systematized conceptualization of children and their functioning and the factors believed to be causing the anxiety disorder.

Diagnosis and Assessment

DSM-III-R proposes that anxiety in children and adolescents can be differentiated into three basic disorders: separation anxiety disorder, overanxious disorder, and avoidant disorder. Each has specific symptoms that point to the diagnosis. DSM-III-R further suggests that subsequent attempts to cope with continuing anxieties produces secondary reactions (e.g., phobic, obsessive-compulsive, dissociative, or somatoform reactions). It must be remembered, however, that anxiety is an organizing factor in personality development and that rapidly changing states are inherent in childhood development, both of which limit this method of diagnostic classification (Group for the Advancement of Psychiatry 1966). Childhood itself is stressful, and the developing personality may react to these stresses with transient or long-term anxiety symptoms. Therefore, there is not only an overlap between normal and abnormal anxiety in children, but there is often much overlapping in the various diagnostic categories as well (McDermott et al. 1987).

Assessment for Treatment Planning

In addition to a complete developmental history and physical examination, a good diagnostician pays special attention to the history of the anxiety disorder itself (i.e., the context in which the anxiety symptoms occurred and are maintained). What stimuli or events seem to produce the symptoms and how does the environment respond to them? This may be simple and obvious (e.g., fear of dogs after being frightened by one), but when anxiety is diffuse or complex, a careful search of the child's inner and outer world is needed to find the cause. This is often achieved by direct questioning (and observation) about when and where the anxiety is experienced, and the specific situations that elicit it. Indirect methods of assessment (e.g., play and drawings) also provide avenues to understand more complex and symbolic roots of anxiety symptoms.

Scales to identify and rate symptoms have been developed (or modified from adults) to provide a more complete picture of anxiety disorders in children and adolescents. Most identify such thoughts and feelings as panic, fright, worry, distractibility, fear, dread, and intrusive thoughts. The following instruments have been shown to possess good interrater or test-retest reliability: The State-Trait Anxiety Inventory for Children (Finch et al. 1974; Spielberger 1973), the Leyton Obsessional Inventory (Rapoport et al. 1980), Sarason's General Anxiety and Test Anxiety Scales (Sarason et al. 1960), the Teacher and Parent Separation Anxiety Rating Scales for Preschool Children (Doris et al. 1980), and the Child Behavior Checklist (Achenbach and Edelbrock 1979).

Finally, the clinician determines both which problems are the most serious and the best order and methods with which to approach them. Then the plan is explained to parents and child, including how progress is to be monitored.

Treatment

The four treatment approaches considered are behavior therapy, psychopharmacologic therapy, psychodynamic therapy, and family therapy. General principles of theory and practice will be presented separately for each approach, and then each will be applied independently to three clinical cases, modified from the *DSM-III Case Book* (Spitzer et al. 1981), which illustrates the three forms of anxiety disorder in childhood or adolescence described in DSM-III (American Psychiatric Press 1980).

Behavior Therapy

Theory

Behavioral theory assumes that there are certain naturally occurring, innate behaviors, evoked by simple stimuli, which form the foundation on which more complex behaviors are then built—learned or conditioned. Although behaviorists do not talk of personality, they have a somewhat equivalent concept (conditioning history or behavioral repertoire) in which different children must behave in a characteristic, individual way if the key stimulus to release such behavior is present.

Types of Learning or Conditioning

Respondent or Pavlovian. This concept is considered the primary way that anxiety is learned and is important in its treatment. The system involved in this form of learning is nearly always the autonomic nervous system, and the behavior reflexive, either life-saving or sustaining. Conditioned reflexes are built by pairing neutral stimuli (e.g., a bell) just before a natural (or unconditioned) stimulus (e.g., food) to the reflex behavior (e.g., salivation). After repeated experience, the bell evokes the salivation. Extinction of the conditioned reflex is obtained by repeatedly evoking it but not responding with the natural stimulus (food). When the stimulus or the response used is the opposite to that which is currently effective (e.g., silence for the bell, or the bell paired to drying in the mouth), counterconditioning is used.

Operant. In this form of learning, the organism is active rather than passive; the voluntary systems are involved; and the behavior is maintained by its consequences or contingencies. When a stimulus maintains or increases behavior, it is called a reinforcer. When a stimulus decreases the behavior, it is called punishment. Extinction is achieved by removal of reinforcers. Suppression is achieved by punishment.

Counterconditioning, in which an opposite response is attached to the eliciting stimulus (or vice versa), can also occur. Operant conditioning (or contingency management) is a common method used intuitively by parents of young children to shape their children's social behavior. Common examples are the use of rewards (e.g., praise, hugs) when a child performs well (e.g., cleans his plate) or punishment (e.g., scolding, spanking) when the behavior is unacceptable (e.g., temper tantrums).

Incidental (cognitive rehearsal). This type of learning is based on the fact that children learn complex sequences of behavior by watching important persons performing them. Modeling is one key process in incidental learning. One important feature of modeling is that it emphasizes the need for rapport between the child and the model for it to be effective. It depends on internal, unobservable processes that constitute a large part of human activity. Modeling probably accounts for a great deal of acquisition of social skills. For instance, younger children watch older ones at play and soon are found practicing what they have seen—in fumbling fashion at first, then more and more skillfully.

A final note: Since most fears in children are short lived, the question arises why some persist even in the clear absence of any danger to the child? The behavioral view is that they persist because the normal process of extinction is prevented. The child is unable to learn that the fear is unreasonable, excessive, unfounded, unlikely, or unrewarding. Fear and anxiety are seen as highly adaptive mechanisms. But so is extinction, the psychological equivalent of the development of immunity to infective organisms.

Practice

Usually children are brought for treatment because of fears that are judged abnormal in type or severity or when they are incapacitating. Such situations may arise: 1) when there has been an abnormal fear-provoking circumstance (e.g., child abuse), 2) when a child seems excessively easily conditioned to normal stimuli, and 3) when a normal fear has been exaggerated and sustained by desired consequences (secondary gain).

It follows from learning theory that, whatever the technique, the basic principle of behavioral treatment of anxiety is always the same: somehow the child has to experience the feared situation without the possibility of escape or reward for anxiety. That is, an anxiety-provoking stimulus that poses little risk must be endured.

Behavioral approaches are strongly ecologically oriented. Their principal axiom is that behavior is maintained by its environmental consequences, and that the easiest and most efficient way to change behavior is through changing the environment. This means that many treatment programs are designed to be carried out by parents and teachers (and less often by siblings and peers). As children get older, this changes to a more active involvement of the child in the treatment program.

We will now discuss the practice of five specific behavioral approaches.

Extinction. In this approach, the child is presented with the anxiety-inducing situation in which he or she will remain unharmed, rather than avoiding or escaping the situation. This is probably the most common way parents teach their children to overcome fears. It is common to present children with graduated degrees of intensity or duration with adult supervision and support. In the example of a dog phobia, extinction requires the child to be exposed to dogs in a graduated way (small dogs then big ones, first with, then without an adult present) until the fear is gone or manageable.

Although evidence in adults suggests that implosion or massive prolonged exposure (the equivalent of teaching a frightened child to swim by throwing the child in the deep end) may be more efficient than extinction, most of those who work with children consider this approach unsuitable for them (Johnson and Melamed 1979). Proper preparation and sufficient cooperation of child and parent are essential if the technique is to succeed.

When the anxiety has secondary gain or reinforcement attached to it, it must be neutralized. The most common source of these secondary gain contingencies to the child's behavior is attention from significant others in the child's environment (e.g., parents). This often occurs because of parental sympathy, identification with, or gain from the child's behavior.

Counterconditioning. This approach attaches an opposite or incompatible response (e.g., relaxation) to the anxiety-provoking stimulus. It is the basis of the well-established technique of reciprocal inhibition. In it, progressive muscle relaxation allows the patient to imagine increasing degrees of, or approximations to, the feared stimulus along a stimulus hierarchy. Such a technique requires considerable cooperation—ability to learn muscular relaxation and to imagine situations. Thus it is more suited to older children and adolescents (Richter 1984). In younger children, emotive imagery has been used. They are asked to imagine a pleasurable situation, and the therapist gradually introduces talk about the feared stimulus. Traditional play therapy techniques can even be considered a form of counterconditioning. But, as in adults, exposure in vivo is essential and greatly enhances imagined or simulated exposure (Ultee et al. 1982).

Operant procedures. This approach relies on providing the child with reinforcement for not avoiding or withdrawing from the fear-producing situation. The operant treatment of a dog phobia would prescribe praise for the child at each step along the way, and perhaps a special reward (e.g., a bicycle) when final success is achieved. Points and tokens that can be traded in later for "goodies" can also be used as a way of providing immediacy to the rewards.

In practice, it is difficult to separate this approach from extinction because liberal praise and reward are used in both. In theory, punishment can be used (and is often used by parents) to keep children in a feared situation. However, not only are there arguments for not using punishment with child patients, but practical ones as well. Punishment may make the stimulus more rather than less feared and thus aggravate the disorder.

Modeling. Timid children probably overcome many of their fears from models provided by other children or adults, who model the "brave" behavior. Models can also be presented in films and through puppet play in special situations, such as preparing children for surgery (Johnson and Melamed 1979).

Self-control. This approach involves such strategies as self-encouragement, instruction, or reward through methods such as "stopping," relaxation, and problem solving. There are (Karoly 1981) four necessary components of self-control techniques: 1) recognition of one's problem, 2) motivation to change, 3) availability of motor and/or cognitive skill necessary for self-guidance, and 4) awareness of what one should do (Barrios et al. 1981).

Psychopharmacologic Therapy

Theory

A working neurophysiologic-biochemical model of anxiety from animal studies likens it to an alarm system (Redmond 1985). Noxious stimuli are relayed to central structures, which in turn progressively activate structures known to influence the fight or flight response. If too great a stimulus load is introduced to the system, disturbance at various neurophysiologic points occurs, and pathologic anxiety results. The response rate of individual persons seems to be generally influenced by differences in catecholamine-related enzymes, receptor functions, and neurotransmitter release mechanisms.

A number of neurotransmitter systems seem directly or indirectly involved in the experience and expression of fear and anxiety (Charney and Redmond 1983; Costa 1982; Hoehn-Saric 1982; Redmond 1985; Stein et al. 1977; Usdin 1983). The gamma-aminobutyric acid (GABA)-ergic system appears to be the most important. GABA-ergic synapses are found throughout the central nervous system. They are involved with presynaptic and postsynaptic inhibition and are recognized as the most important inhibitory transmitters in the nervous system. Moreover, discovery of brain-specific benzodiazepine and noradrenergic receptors at or near synaptic receptor sites for GABA suggests an inherent anxiolytic regulatory mechanism within the mammalian central nervous system. They may mediate two separate forms of anxiety: 1) anticipatory or exogenous anxiety and 2) panic or endogenous anxiety (Insel et al. 1984).

The noradrenergic system and the serotonergic systems seem to be the most important in the psychobiology of anxiety disorders. The dopaminergic, peptide, histaminic, cholinergic, and adenosine systems are considered to play a less critical role (Hoehn-Saric 1982). Interactions of two or more neurotransmitters, even within the same cell, have been posited (Costa 1982; Hockfelt et al. 1980). However, the specific actions of antianxiety drugs are not yet fully understood.

Phenomenologically, separation anxiety in children has been related to the panic anxiety experienced by adult agoraphobic patients. Gittelman and Klein (1985) noted the presence of severe separation anxiety in the childhood histories of 50 percent of agoraphobic adult patients. They postulated a predilection for separation anxiety in adults with panic attacks and agoraphobia. Clinging, dependent behavior is learned, based "on the substrata of an innate biological control mechanism" (Klein 1981). The panic attacks of the agoraphobic have been shown to respond significantly to the tricyclic antidepressants and monoamine oxidase inhibitor antidepressants (Sheehan et al. 1980). On a behavioral biopsychosocial level, Klein (1981) suggested that these drugs raise the alarm threshold of panic attacks.

In further testing this hypothesis, a controlled investigation of separation anxiety disorder (school phobia) treated with tricyclic antidepressant medication (Gittelman-Klein and Klein 1973) showed significant improvement in imipramine-treated patients versus controls. The improvement was directly related to the separation anxiety, that is, venturing more freely without mother, less fear of going to school, less physical discomfort in attending school.

The autonomic nervous system symptoms of separation anxiety disorder provide a physiologic dimension that distinguishes it from other anxiety disorders and appears to be related to their effectiveness. The effective use of psychopharmacology as a therapeutic intervention requires measurable responses of the disorder. One of the critical dimensions for defining and measuring anxiety is visceral and somatic activation, and understanding its relation to childhood anxiety disorders is critical to comprehending psychopharmacologic treatment (Lang 1984). Somatic and visceral activation usually involves sympathetic arousal and results in the psychophysiologic symptoms described in the anxiety disorders. However, response patterns show individual variability. Anxious patients generally exhibit a disproportionate degree of central and autonomic arousal to the disturbing stimuli. Their ability to adapt is diminished. At rest, anxious patients often show increase in skin conductance (related to overproductive sweat glands), as well as increases in heart rate and blood pressure. Generalized muscle tension is also a frequent occurrence of separation anxiety disorder.

Practice

Drugs employed in the treatment of anxiety disorders fall into five major classes: anxiolytics, antihistaminics, antidepressants, neuroleptics, and beta-adrenergic blockers.

Anxiolytic agents.   The benzodiazepine group contains at least 12 generic drugs: those with a short half-life of four to 20 hours (e.g., oxazepam, lorazepam, alprazolam) and those with a longer half-life (e.g., chlordiazepoxide, diazepam, chlorazepate, flurazepam). The benzodiazepines are thought to normalize behavior responses suppressed by punishment or absence of reward (i.e., to cause "behavioral disinhibition"). Reduction of fear may be the mechanism of action in increasing behavioral responses that were formerly inhibited by punishment (Stein et al. 1977). Thus these agents may lead to an increase in behavioral response rather than a suppression of behavior. The sedation described in animal experiments is understood as a reduction in physiologic arousal to excessive stimuli and not a soporific effect (Haefely 1979).

The benzodiazepine group seems to be especially effective in anticipatory types of anxiety in adults (Klein et al. 1980; Redmond 1985; Rickels 1983). They have a high therapeutic index and have little deleterious effect on sleep (Usdin 1983).

There are few published reports of the effects of benzodiazepines on children treated for primary anxiety disorders other than reviews of the various case reports and uncontrolled studies (Gittelman-Klein 1978; Hlusko 1982; Jacobides 1980; Petti and Law 1982; Rapoport et al. 1978). Clinical experience suggests that while children seem to tolerate these agents without difficulty, stimulating and paradoxical effects may also occur because of disinhibition. Rapoport et al. (1978) suggested that benzodiazepines may be useful in sleep disorders, with acutely disturbed children, and in nonpsychotic anxiety.

The use of benzodiazepines in children is quite limited compared to their use in adults. However, prescribing patterns in adolescents approach those of adults (Coffey et al. 1983). While pharmacokinetics found in adolescents are similar to those found in adults, infants metabolize diazepam more rapidly (Coffey et al. 1983). In general, then, children appear to have an increased capacity to metabolize, but as their enzymes and excretory capacity mature, they become similar to adults.

Benzodiazepines have been suggested as potentially useful for children whose separation anxiety has cleared with tricyclic medications, but who are still hampered by anticipatory anxiety. In adolescents 5- to 10-mg doses of diazepam have been recommended to overcome inhibiting anticipatory anxiety.

Antihistaminic agents.   This group includes diphenhydramine, hydroxyzine, and promethazine. Blocking the central action of acetylcholine is their major mechanism of action, and they are considered to exert anxiolytic activity predominantly through their sedating properties. They have a relatively short half-life and may be used for inducing sleep in young children. The antihistamines have not been proven effective in the treatment of the anxiety disorders in children or adolescents (Gittelman-Klein 1978).

Antidepressants.　Two groups make up this category, the tricyclic antidepressants and the monoamine oxidase inhibitors. In the treatment of panic attacks accompanying agoraphobia in adults, both groups have been proven to be significantly more effective than placebo (Sheehan et al. 1983). They are effective in smaller doses and with a shorter time lag in anxiety states than in depression (Mavissakalian et al. 1984; Redmond 1985; Sheehan et al. 1983; Taylor et al. 1983).

The tricyclic antidepressants, particularly imipramine (Petti 1983), have been used effectively in anxiety disorders in children and adolescents. Major toxic effects include seizures (Preskorn et al. 1983) and changes in cardiac functioning. Deaths have been attributed to excessive dosage and overdosage of tricyclic antidepressants. Determination of plasma levels and pharmacokinetics are in process (Puig-Antich et al. 1987). Sixfold differences in dosage to reach the same plasma levels have been described (Weller et al. 1982). Doses up to 5mg/kg have been used with safety (Schroeder et al 1989). Dosages above 5 mg/kg/day are not recommended because of cardiotoxicity. If doses above 3.5 mg/kg are required, the patient should be followed with regular electrocardiograms (Klein 1986 personal communication; Petti 1986 personal communication).

Neuroleptics and beta-adrenergic blockers.　The neuroleptics (e.g., chlorpromazine, haloperidol, thioridazine) have been demonstrated to have some anxiolytic properties in adults. Controlled studies of their use in the anxiety disorders in children are lacking. Given their sedating effects and the potential for restricting cognitive functioning or of inducing tardive dyskinesia, their use for the anxiety disorders in children should be restricted except for the most severe anxiety.

The beta-adrenergic blockers are known to block the physiologic symptoms of anxiety. They may have both a peripheral and a central action on the physiologic mediators of anxiety. Their use in children and adolescents has been limited to the treatment of aggressive and rage-related behaviors (Williams et al. 1982). The kinetics related to behavioral effects are not available, but it is known that the serum half-life is short.

Psychodynamic Therapy

Theory

Psychoanalytic theory postulates that the anxiety disorders are caused by unconscious conflicts related to the basic drives of sex and aggression. The roots of these conflicts are found in earlier parent, child, and sibling interactions and are often Oedipal in nature (Group for the Advancement of Psychiatry 1966). Under certain pathogenic conditions these conflicts can no longer be successfully repressed, and the symptoms of overt anxiety erupt. Anxiety, then, is a symptom of internal conflict that can be manifested clinically as an anxiety disorder. In short, there are several levels of consciousness. Children may tell many of their thoughts and feelings to adults. Other thoughts and feelings are private or secret. Still others are stored away in the mind, not even to be told to themselves. But they may all be connected. For example, a boy who is afraid of dogs will tell others and ask for help. If, behind that fear, he is afraid of his father, he cannot admit that openly because it would compromise an important relationship in his life. At a further and deeper level, if he is afraid of his own angry and competitive impulses toward his father, he cannot admit that, even to himself. A later psychoanalytic theoretical underpinning for the anxiety disorders is a developmental one in which a number of childhood anxieties are related to losses at increasing chronological (developmental) age: loss of the womb with birth, loss of breast with weaning, loss of stool in toilet training, threatened loss of genitals in castration anxiety, loss of mother in hostile interactions with her, and loss of the mother object to the competitor (father) (Settlage 1983).

The theory of loss was given a further special focus, as the theory of separation anxiety, from direct observation of infants (Spitz 1965). This, in turn, led to a theory of separation-individuation (Mahler et al. 1975) based on direct longitudinal observations of children and their mothers. Unsuccessful mastery of the process of separation-individuation, it was postulated, could result in anxiety through two separate mechanisms: 1) fear of loss of mother by separation and the anxiety of not surviving without her or 2) fear of fusion with mother and the anxiety of not achieving a separate sense of identity and autonomy through separation and individuation. Further work on attachment behavior extended the psychological understanding of separation anxiety to include an interaction with biologic factors (Bowlby 1973), a relationship that had been postulated earlier (Greenacre 1941).

A current psychodynamic-developmental conceptual approach to anxiety disorders derived from psychoanalytic theory considers the anxieties in childhood to occur in a natural continuum, with emotional and cognitive growth. The first major event is stranger anxiety, ordinarily seen at four to six months of age when the infant has learned to differentiate mother from stranger. Next, separation anxiety is seen at about eight months, when the child becomes aware of being separate from mother on whom the child is dependent. This is heightened at 14 to 16 months of age, when the child becomes even more clearly aware of being separate, but also dependent, on mother for survival. The child feels helpless and vulnerable when her continuous availability is threatened.

Under normal conditions, with a good-enough life experience, these naturally occurring anxieties help stimulate the development of adaptive behaviors and increase the maturation of the internal psychic structure in the child. Between 18 and 36 months, the child achieves a state called object constancy—an internalized mental representation of a reliable external world (mother). From this experience, the child will develop a reliable representation of the self as well (self-constancy as well as object constancy). Under normal circumstances, as this basic personality structure is laid down, the child gradually becomes an individual who can cope with the challenges and master the problems of life, without being overwhelmed by the anxiety they arouse. If, however, these early stages of development are disrupted and remain unsolved, symptoms such as stranger anxiety and separation anxiety can continue or recur later in childhood, adolescence, or adulthood.

Psychoanalytic theory continues to track anxiety developmentally, from anxiety about harm (castration anxiety) during the Oedipal period, which is acute and overt, to post-Oedipal (superego anxiety), which is less overt and more subtle in its manifestations.

Practice

The goal of individual psychodynamic psychotherapy is an understanding and alteration of the underlying pathologic processes causing the symptoms of anxiety that interfere with the natural progression of growth and development.

The child's capacity to face and handle anxiety directly is not well developed. The child tends to see things in the here and now, and not tie the present with the past and future. Therefore, therapy with children must be done in a more indirect way. As described above, the several levels of consciousness are dealt with—the level of awareness of anxiety that the child talks about, but also the level the child wishes to keep secret, and the level the child keeps secret even from the self. It is the therapist's job to work at all three of these levels, the second and third often presenting in displacement to others, in drawings or in play.

Psychodynamic therapy with children is often carried out in such a way that the child is hardly consciously aware that treatment is going on. This is especially true with young children, where the therapy is done in play. In play therapy, most of the discussion of problems is done in the context of the "make believe" play world of the child. To relate these problems too quickly to the personal real world may be counterproductive. Only in the later stage of therapy is it advisable to relate the displacements in play directly to the real life of the child.

The three levels of conscious, preconscious, and unconscious often blend together. The child tells what is on his or her mind and the therapist reacts with interest, empathy, and curiosity so that the child expands on it further. Children may begin by relating a story or incident that happened to them, their friends, or family; an experience in school, on the playground, or at home; or a story they heard or something they saw on television. The therapist's task is to keep the material flowing and alive, focusing more and more on underlying fears and anxieties as they emerge in the extended story or play.

Defenses and resistances are exposed and addressed to uncover deeper underlying conflicts and issues that need to be understood and resolved. Strategies of confrontation, clarification, interpretation, and reconstruction are used to produce insight or self-understanding, which are translated into behavioral changes and lessening of anxiety. When transference elements appear, they are usually relatively simple current displacements from parents (Lewis 1980).

Principles of Psychodynamic Psychotherapy

A therapeutic alliance is essential.   The therapist focuses on understanding the child and the child's fears; in turn the child becomes an active partner in learning more about the inside self and its relation to the outside world.

Therapy proceeds from outside in.   In insight therapy with children, it is important to proceed from the level of overt behavior, to the affective or emotional level, to the level of defenses and resistances, before dealing with underlying conflicts and impulses. The focus is on what the child is doing before proceeding to define why the child is doing it. The child learns that self-reflection and self-understanding can lead to mastery and control of anxiety.

Therapy is more than insight.   Forces other than insight are involved in psychodynamic psychotherapy. These include suggestion, persuasion, identification, modeling, catharsis, and corrective emotional experiences. Maturational forces and the positive influences of teachers, family, and peers all contribute to therapeutic successes.

Education.   Education is judiciously used in the therapeutic process. However, psychodynamic therapy does not consider "lack of knowledge" about danger to be the root of anxiety in children. Emotional blocks must be removed before knowledge about real and imagined danger can be absorbed and understood.

Psychoanalysis may be indicated when the child's (or adolescent's) anxiety disorder is internalized and severe and chronic enough to warrant a more intensive form of psychotherapy. The aim in psychoanalysis is not only to obtain the relief of symptoms but to bring about a lasting fundamental change in the underlying personality structure.

Family Therapy

Theory

Anxiety disorders in children are seen as expressions of dysfunctional interpersonal sequences in the family. The child's symptom is first formulated as an individual problem, and then reformulated in terms of the family system (i.e., how the child's disorder coincides with the family style and behavior). After observing the child in the context of the family, the operations of the family are examined for patterns of reciprocity (e.g., triadic patterns reverberating between three or more members). Family theory conceptualizes the anxiety problem in interpersonal terms, using concepts such as triangulation, detouring, coalitions, go-between, and scapegoating. Anxiety interferes not only with the normal developmental process, with the child's schooling and peer relationships, but also the primary group, the family system. Thus this theory suggests that working with the family system is the most effective way to alleviate the discomfort experienced by the child and to restore appropriate developmental momentum.

Family-mediated stress has been related to physiologic anxiety in diabetic children (Minuchin et al. 1978), showing that, even at the biochemical level, family members are exquisitely responsive to one another. In other words, the formulation is expanded from the psychological and physiologic experience of the individual child to the relevent contexts, first the family system and then the extended family, school, and other social systems. While the child is the one with the anxiety, the sense of foreboding, the excessive worry, the increased pulse rate, and the diaphoresis, relate to the family experience, both as a consequence and as a cause, and thus is understood to be a part of a repetitive process. Breaking dysfunctional anxiety-producing repetitive patterns, and allowing the family to form new, more functional patterns, is the goal of family intervention.

Anxiety disorders of childhood that are mild may respond to simple changes invented and implemented by the family themselves. More complex or fixed problems require a family therapy program that integrates the expertise of the therapist with that of the family (and with that of any other relevant persons in the child's environment).

The conceptual framework of family therapy for anxiety disorders, then, is to disrupt the patterns that perpetuate family insecurity and help support the formation of secure activities. The search is for resources of family competence and ways to mobilize these in the treatment.

Practice

The family therapist's first explorations are into the actual experience of the problem by the family. What is going on in the family now? What was going on in the family when the problem developed? How have family members responded? How have they dealt with the school? Whom have they consulted, and what have they learned and felt about those consultations? With these questions, larger and larger circles are drawn around the child with the symptoms to include response patterns at wider levels: from child, to family, to school, to health care system. Extended family, neighbors, and other social networks (e.g., church) may also be included in these inquiries.

In raising these questions, the therapist is seeking information at a variety of levels. The first level is the factual answers given by the informants. The second level of information is difference. What may have been stated as a fact by one person is seen differently by another family member. The third level of information is behavior. What do the family members do with the anxiety? To elicit the data at this level, the therapist may request an enactment, asking simply, "Show me what you do." The therapist's understanding of the problem evolves from observations of the family's responses to this series of probes. The family members' understanding of themselves as an interacting system is brought into awareness by looking at themselves through the lens of this inquiry. The fourth level of information is pattern. At this level, the therapist is seeking to discover relevant, repetitive patterns of interpersonal activity that contain the problem. The symptom is understood to play a role in the repetition of these patterns. Again, they are seen in expanding areas of functioning—from the individual symptomatic child, to the interaction in the family, between the family and the child's school, and even in the intergenerational patterns of the parents' families of origin.

In children with anxiety disorders there is insufficient reassurance for the child from within the family system. It is also important to learn about the child's role in this pattern. A task is prescribed. For example, the therapist asks a parent to take charge of comforting a child. The parent may then show clumsiness at comfort, illustrating uncertainty with the youngster. The therapist may also observe the child shrugging the parent off, disqualifying the parent's efforts. This interaction—anxious child, parent offering support, child not receptive, child therefore continuing to be anxious—is a sequence that may represent a reverberating family problem whenever symptoms are experienced. They have now become part of a system of revolving family insecurities, one in which seeking reassurance leads to more insecurity, a system that may express its disturbance through the child's anxiety.

The general goal of family treatment is to disrupt the symptomatic reverberating pattern, to change the family relationship system, and to restore parental competence and confidence and age-appropriate child competence and confidence. This can be done through a variety of techniques. The family can reenact the experience around the anxiety symptom in such a way that the parents and child actually redo their behavior. Throughout this process, the therapist elicits parents' opinions about treatment, always acknowledging their greater familiarity and expertise with their child. The therapist searches for resources of family competence and, finding these, mobilizes them.

Treatment Cases

In the treatment of the cases that follow (modified from Spitzer et al. 1981), considerable license is taken. Each case is presented as if it had actually undergone the four separate treatment programs, and each is presented as a successful outcome. In actual practice, clinicians usually employ a combination or integration of several approaches. Naturally, outcome is not always successful.

Separation Anxiety Disorder

Michael, seven-and-a-half years old, was brought in by his mother, who had read an article in a local newspaper about a clinic that treated children with anxiety disorders. She believed that the description in the newspaper article of anxiety symptoms fit her child to a "T".

The presenting complaint was that Michael did not sleep in his own bed. He fell asleep in his parents' bed, was put in his own bed during the night in a room he shared with his five-year-old brother, Kevin, but was never found in his own bed in the morning. During the night he makes his way into his parents' bed. If they put him back in his room, they find him huddled by their door. This problem began at the age of two when he started having tantrums when put to bed.

Furthermore, Michael was developing physical symptoms, such as stomachaches and headaches. They occurred in the morning and were often accompanied by complaints that he was going to die and should be taken to the hospital. These never occurred on weekends or during the summer, but only on school days. He was now beginning to refuse to go to school because he got terrified at the idea of leaving home in the morning. His school performance in all subjects was considered at average or above-average level.

At the clinic, Michael separated easily from his mother but wanted to keep the office door open while being interviewed. He related well initially, laughing easily while talking about school, which he said he liked and in which he felt he was doing well. His affect changed markedly when the topic turned to his feelings. He became difficult to draw out and stated that he missed his mother in school, especially while staying with a baby-sitter after school until his mother came home from work. He constantly worried about whether his mother would pick him up from the baby-sitter's house or get into an auto accident and not be there when he was waiting for her. He said that at night he was plagued by scary dreams and thoughts about something happening to his parents. He reported "I'm afraid I'll never see them again." There was no family history of anxiety disorder.

A complete physical examination was reported as normal. He ranked in the 50th percentile for height and weight (48 inches, 50 pounds, 23 kg), had normal visual and auditory acuity, and showed no evidence of neuromaturational delay.

A Conners' Teacher Rating Scale (Conners 1969) showed slight elevation in factor 3 (tension and anxiety) and no elevation in factors relating to inattention or hyperactivity (factors 2 and 4). His score on the Bellevue Index of Depression was comparatively low.

Behavioral Therapy

Initial phase of treatment. Further history focused on exploring the context of Michael's entire day, looking particularly for other separation problems. It was found that Michael's mother (and to a lesser extent father) seldom if ever went out at night because Michael became so angry and upset at the prospect. This, and sheer exhaustion, had caused his mother to take the line of least resistance. On those rare occasions when she did go out, she had to specify exactly where she was going, what she was doing, and what time she would return. She had to call at hourly intervals until Michael fell asleep (often much later than when his parents were at home). His mother felt guilty about working and leaving him with a baby-sitter in the afternoon. She also resented his general bossiness and the way he tried to organize her life so that she was around him or in easy reach at all times.

In the course of the initial interviews, it was agreed by Michael and his parents that the problems most in need of help were 1) worry about seeing his parents again when he was away from them; and 2) being unable to sleep by himself, go to school easily, or let his parents go out at night. Bossing his mother around was also identified as a major problem.

The focus on current behavior was formulated according to the stimulus-response-reinforcement paradigm.

Stimulus: The stimulus was the absence or threatened absence of the mother. (Absence of the father seemed a much weaker stimulus and important only if the mother was also away.)

Response: The response had two aspects: (1) *emotional* (anxiety, anger, psychophysiologic symptoms), which acted as a further stimulus to (2) *behavioral* (refusing to go to school, getting into parents' bed, preventing mother from leaving, and physical complaints).

Reinforcement: The reinforcement (of operant behavior by anxiety relief), most of the time, resulted in reunion with the mother. The anxiety in school and at the baby-sitter's persisted because Michael was able to prevent separations for the rest of the day, and thus prevent extinction. Because of the physical symptoms, he was beginning to miss school and avoiding going to the baby-sitter's, thus further decreasing separation time (and the possibility of natural extinction of anxiety).

The key to treatment was seen in attempting to extinguish anxiety by increasing separation time. The problem was how to achieve this in such a way that both parents and child would cooperate. The choice of behavioral techniques was restricted by Michael's age because younger children are usually unable either to follow instructions in progressive muscular relaxation or are reluctant to perform the necessary practice sessions at home. In fact, these can easily become a new battleground between parent and child.

Since the basic treatment process was to be extinction of anxiety by experiencing it—not running away—the individual sessions with Michael focused on talk about Michael's wish to grow up and be independent. The therapist gradually introduced more and more challenging ideas of separation and praised him for success in discussing them. As part of these sessions, puppet play and role play with the therapist (switching roles) were used to prepare Michael for separation experiences. Michael looked forward to coming to the sessions and talking about separation situations with his mother, which soon ceased to evoke tearful behavior. The play facilitated lessening of the anxiety-producing power of separation.

After several sessions, Michael was brought to the clinic by his baby-sitter rather than his mother because it was believed that this would also aid the extinction of anxiety related to separation. Thus the first area of improvement was staying after school with his baby-sitter. This was facilitated by instruction to the baby-sitter on carrying out some of the desensitization activities that the therapist was using in the clinic.

As for school avoidance, it was decided that Michael would be taken to school by his father who was able to act more firmly and calmly in this arena than his mother. When Michael complained, he was to be reminded about "growing up," and distracted by talk about what he and his father would do on the weekend. If Michael resisted going on his own, he was gently but firmly taken to the car. His teacher was approached, apprised of the program, and asked to praise Michael on arrival and to give him some unobtrusive extra attention (e.g., occasionally putting her hand on his shoulder as she walked by and saying "good, Michael").

The two problems of Michael's mother not being able to go out in the evening and his inability to sleep in his own bed through the night were not approached at this stage. They were considered more difficult and less critical to address than Michael going to school and mother continuing her work.

Middle phase of treatment. As going to school and staying with the baby-sitter after school became minor problems, Michael was prepared in his individual therapy sessions to allow his mother to go out at night.

Initially, his mother simply went to the supermarket for an hour or so. She was instructed that the length of time away was to be highly variable and unpredictable. Michael was to be so told when he asked how long she would be away. She began with relatively short intervals, but was soon able to stay out longer than she needed to complete her shopping. During these absences, Michael was cared for by his father, but toward the end of this period, a carefully chosen baby-sitter whom Michael liked joined the father. The parents were now encouraged to go out together one evening per week and to leave Michael and Kevin in the care of the baby-sitter. The parents were instructed to be firm and calm and not to give in to pleas for exact time of return or for phone calls. Michael protested vigorously the first evening they went out, but the parents successfully carried it through. After that there was little difficulty.

Therapy sessions were now increasingly directed toward the problem of sleeping in his own bed. In role and doll play, Michael himself increasingly became more directive, apparently modeling his behavior on what his parents were doing. He forced the boy doll to stay in his own bed, carrying him back to the bed over and over.

At a family session, Michael, his parents, and the therapist decided on a plan to begin on a Friday night, because no one had to work the next day. First, Michael was to be put in his own bed. Then his mother (or father) would read him a simple story of his choosing. The parent would then leave the bedroom but stand in the doorway. If Michael protested, the parent would leave immediately and return to the doorway only when he was quiet again. If Michael left his bed, he was told to go back and, if necessary, carried. Once again, the parent left the room and returned to the doorway only when he was quiet again. The parents did not want to lock him in his room but agreed to carry him back to bed as many times as necessary. No attempt was yet to be made to deal with what happened after he fell asleep. If Michael could fall asleep in his own bed, he would receive praise and a special treat the next day.

The first Friday night was very difficult, and the father had to carry Michael back to his own bed many times. On Saturday night, it was necessary to carry him back only three times. By Sunday (after a bit of protest) he soon fell asleep. Coincidentally, there was a reduction in the frequency of his night waking and coming to his parents' bed. Again, after a family conference and rehearsal in therapy, it was decided that the next Friday night Michael's father would carry him back to his own bed as many times as necessary during the night. The father was to stay with him and stroke his head until he fell asleep. However, if he complained or cried, father was to leave and stand in the doorway, saying he would not come back until Michael was quiet. As on the previous weekend, Michael awoke several times on Friday night, but the problem was virtually resolved by Sunday night. (Had this not been successful, further treatment would have been postponed until the following Friday. Alternatively this plan could have been carried out during a vacation.)

Ending phase of treatment. By now Michael was more or less symptom free. There had been some difficulty getting him back to school after he had been out for a few days with the flu, but his parents dealt with this on their own, after a phone call to the therapist.

The problem now was that Michael was very attached to his therapist, and this separation had to be worked through. Interviews were shortened and the intervals between them lengthened. The therapist then began to phone Michael in lieu of visits. Finally, appointments were stopped, with the proviso that Michael could come back in the future if necessary. While this offer carried the risk of reinforcing symptomatic behavior, the therapist felt able to deal with it promptly and firmly should it emerge.

Thereafter Michael displayed intermittent signs of separation anxiety, particularly after illness kept him from school or when he or the family were undergoing other stresses. However, the parents, with an occasional phone call to the therapist, were now able to manage these quickly and prevent them from getting out of hand.

Psychopharmacologic Therapy

Initial phase of treatment. Further history revealed that a program consisting of forced attendance at school combined with a contract for remaining in school had not decreased Michael's dread of separation. He was sometimes able to complete a school day, but made frequent visits to the school nurse for headaches and other somatic symptoms.

In the interview, Michael said he wished that his sick feelings on school mornings would go away. He appeared sad when discussing school-related problems but neither his affect nor mood was depressed. He agreed that he would feel much better if he could get rid of his dread of going to school. Insight into his behavior was absent, and he was unable to recall the thoughts that preceded his feelings of distress. Michael was told that the psychiatrist had helped youngsters with problems very much like his and could help him if he really wanted to feel better. He responded with a mixture of hope and reserved pessimism.

The findings and a recommendation for treatment with imipramine were shared with the parents. They were told that imipramine should allow Michael to feel less anxious about going to school and less worried about them. The problems with stomachaches and headaches, and his scary feelings at night, should be expected to clear. The parents were advised that Michael might start expressing some anger and dissatisfaction about other family matters—worries and concerns not previously verbalized. Potential toxic side effects were described as follows:

> "Common side effects are dry mouth and constipation. Some children have fainting spells when they suddenly get up from lying down. We will increase the dosage slowly and do not expect this to occur. His recent physical examination suggests Michael's heart is normal and he is in good health. Some changes in the electrical activity of the heart have been reported, but we have not had this as a problem with the children we have treated. If there were any indication for it we would order an electrocardiogram to make certain that no problems exist to cause Michael difficulties with the way his heart works. If the dose needs to be increased beyond what we agree on today, we will certainly monitor it with cardiograms. Epileptic seizures have been reported in children on this medication. However, Michael shows neither evidence of a brain disorder nor previous seizures, which are usually found in children who have fits with this medication. Sometimes it is helpful to get blood levels, particularly at higher doses if there is no response. If that is the case, we will discuss this matter then. It is important once we start the medication not to stop suddenly. Responses of many children to abruptly terminating the medicine are having stomachaches, feeling tired and sleepy, getting agitated, and exhibiting flu-like symptoms. We may have some of those symptoms when we finally do stop the medication, but they should be minimal because of the gradual nature of the withdrawal phase."

In response to their questions, the parents were assured that the medication would be used for a limited period, probably less than three or four months, and that children rarely, if ever, develop an addiction to imipramine. Michael agreed to the use of medication. He, too, was given an explanation of how it worked and what to expect would happen, including the possibility of having a dry mouth, some constipation, and perhaps a fine tremor of the hand.

Michael's parents were asked to begin the medication, starting with 25 mg at bedtime for the first two days, then 25 mg in the morning and 50 mg at bedtime for the next three days, and finally 25 mg in the morning and 50 mg at bedtime until the next appointment. They were instructed to phone the therapist's office with any concern they might have about the medication. A phone call on the second day of medication revealed that Michael slept well and was actually feeling a little better. He still was apprehensive about going to school.

Prior to Michael's next appointment, the parents reported that he seemed brighter and less irritable but still apprehensive about going to school and staying with the baby-sitter after school. No side effects were reported.

In the next session, Michael reported feeling better, but was still afraid of going to school. However, it felt easier the past few days than it had been before. Stomachaches and a funny feeling in his heart didn't seem so bad. He was able to talk a little more about his worries that his mom would get in an accident on the way from work and that his dad might have something terrible happen to him on the job. He was asked to make a probability estimate of the actual occurrence. He said it was 50 to one. He was asked to keep that in mind and given verbal reinforcement for taking the medication and working hard at getting better. He and his parents agreed to an increased dose in two days if he was still bothered about going to school. If medication was to be increased, the cardiogram would be done to make certain no abnormalities developed.

Middle phase of treatment.   The parents called the office four days later to report that his symptoms had cleared and he was neutral about attending school. On the next visit, Michael was pleased that the stomachaches and the other autonomic symptoms of anxiety had cleared. His sleep had improved greatly, he felt better rested, and the scary dreams had ceased. Michael had not tried to sleep with his parents for the past week and a half. He still worried about something happening to them, but the intensity was markedly diminished. He was enjoying himself more while with a baby-sitter and feeling better overall. He asked whether the medication could be stopped now that his problems had cleared. In the meeting with Michael and his parents, it was agreed to maintain the present dosage of medication through the next six weeks. At that time, if everything continued to go well, the medicine could gradually be reduced, then stopped.

Michael and his parents were ready to resume addressing issues that had previously eluded them. Michael's improvement had allowed the therapist to move beyond concentration on school symptoms and into family issues. Contact with the school after Michael had been on the optimal dose for six weeks revealed perfect attendance. He was concentrating on his classwork, did not appear to be so preoccupied, and was more outgoing.

Ending phase of treatment.   The visit after eight weeks of the therapeutic dose of imipramine confirmed the continued improvement. Progress with sleep-related difficulties was maintained. The parents and Michael were worried about lowering the dose of medication. They were pleased with the results but fearful of relapse. They were visibly relieved when it was explained that almost all children who responded to imipramine continue to do well after cessation of the drug. It was agreed to decrease the dose by 25 mg/week starting the upcoming week.

Michael completed the trial of medication successfully. Signs of drug withdrawal were absent. However, he reported feeling apprehensive about recurrence of the physiologic symptoms as the dosage was lowered and stopped. He was pleased that he no longer required medication and that he had successfully overcome such a terrifying problem.

Follow-up indicated that Michael continued school without problems, with improved interactions with his peers and family. He was achieving at a higher level academically.

Psychodynamic Therapy

Initial phase of treatment. Further history from the parents revealed that Michael had been a good baby, and they had no trouble with him until his brother Kevin was born when he was two. Mother vividly recalled how Michael reacted with a startled look when they came home from the hospital and he first saw baby Kevin. Rather than running to her as she had expected, he turned to his grandmother who had been caring for him.

With the arrival of his brother Kevin, Michael's sleeping problem began. He cried and had temper tantrums if left to sleep by himself in his own bed. Mother, who had a close relationship with Michael, sensed his insecurity and started to let him fall asleep in her bed, hoping he would feel better with time. This pattern had persisted until the present, despite sporadic efforts to break him of the habit.

A history of the sibling relationship revealed that Michael tended to tease Kevin to tears, bringing the parents to Kevin's defense. Kevin tended to tattle on Michael to try to get him into trouble. They called each other "baby," Michael because Kevin cried when teased and Kevin because of Michael's sleeping problem.

Mother returned to work the year Kevin started school. Although Michael had some qualms about leaving for school last year, it was only in the past few weeks as school began for the new year that his problem had become increasingly more acute.

Michael's problem was considered to have several components.

1. A separation-individuation problem (loss), including
   a) loss of mother to brother,
   b) loss of mother to father (Oedipal) (original anxiety, reactivated by a), and
   c) loss of mother to work.
2. An Oedipal problem:
   a) Mother close to Michael (first born) and felt protective of him.
   b) Father critical of Michael (weak, a sissy, not like Kevin).
   c) Conflict between father and mother over Michael. Father felt mother was over-protective. Michael's wish to sleep with parents as a bed warmer and to break up parental relationship. Mother felt father was too harsh with Michael.
   d) Michael felt his father was critical (fear of father and fear of his own aggression toward father, brother, mother expressed as fear of monsters and worry about all of them being killed).
3. A School Problem. To uncover and deal with the dynamic issues behind the school refusal, it was felt that Michael must face the problem. (A school refusal is difficult to treat when school is out during the summer and the pressure is off.) The more school a child misses the harder it is to get the child back. There is a loss of academic grade level, as well as a loss of the socializing influence of school and

classmates. Getting to school, emphasizing coping and mastery rather than avoidance and regression, is a crucial practical issue to be faced at once.

In his first therapy session, Michael was hesitant to leave mother to enter the playroom with the therapist. After reassurance from both mother and therapist that she would be waiting for him all the time he was in the playroom, he was able to separate from mother.

In the playroom, he started to explore, finally ending up with plastic dinosaurs engaged in a fight. It seemed clear that he was identifying with the largest dinosaur and enjoyed it beating up the other dinosaurs. The therapist observed that it must feel good to be the biggest and strongest dinosaur so that you don't have to be afraid of anything. Michael agreed that it was much better than feeling scared. This led to a discussion of his fear of his mother leaving him when he came in the playroom, and of not picking him up at school. "She might get into an accident." Brother Kevin was not afraid and called him a baby for not sleeping in his own bed. The discussion of sleeping arrangements led to his nightmares and to his anger that Dad (as well as Kevin) called him a baby. Anger and fear were all mixed up in Michael, just as they were in his dreams and his play.

Michael acknowledged his fear of losing his mother, his hostility toward his brother, and his anger and fear of his father. There was establishment of a clear definition of his problem and a focus for treatment efforts.

In a session with Michael's mother, she talked about the very close relationship she had with Michael when he was a baby. When his sleeping problem began, she felt sorry for him. She knew it was because he felt displaced by the baby. She dealt with it by letting him fall asleep in their bed, expecting the problem to disappear with time. Now that the sleeping problem had persisted, she was becoming increasingly concerned, especially since her husband was getting much more impatient with the mother:

1. *Sleep problem*. It was important that Michael learn to sleep in his own bed. She and her husband should work out a united and concerted approach to resolve this problem.
2. *School problem*. The therapist stressed the importance of Michael's continued school attendance and his need to face this problem. The therapist reassured her about her feelings of anxiety and guilt about pushing him too much, encouraged her to be supportive and understanding, but to adopt a firm, consistent, and positive approach that Michael must attend school. She was to elicit the help of the school counselor to escort Michael to class in the morning.
3. *Sibling rivalry problem*. She was encouraged to work out with her husband how best to handle this issue. She thought they might start by her taking Michael to the library on Saturdays while Kevin spent the time with her husband.

In a session with the parents, Michael's father acknowledged that although he loved Michael, he had been increasingly annoyed at him for not sleeping in his own bed. It has interfered with the parents' sexual relationship. He felt his wife worried too much about Michael and tends to give in too easily to him. He has expressed the thought to his wife that Michael might be using his "fears" as a ploy to let him continue to sleep in their bed.

The father was raised to be strong and self-reliant. He is afraid that Michael's fears meant he would grow up to be a "sissy." He finds himself drawn more to Kevin because Kevin is "more of a boy." Yet this reaction makes him feel uncomfortable because he knows it is not fair. He finds himself getting too impatient and angry at Michael. His guilt and anger increase when his wife accuses him of being unfeeling and too harsh. Because of this, he has been leaving the care of Michael pretty much in her hands.

Both parents readily saw that their conflicts about Michael were not only contributing to his difficulties, but also interfering with their marital relationship and the relationship between the two boys.

Mother saw that she had overidentified with Michael and was overly concerned about upsetting him. Father saw that he was overly concerned about Michael being a sissy and that his angry outbursts and withdrawal were contributing to the problem. Father recalled having been called a sissy himself when he was growing up, and how much he hated it.

Both were able to see that the sleeping problem was not an isolated symptom but was affecting Michael's overall adjustment and must be resolved. It was decided that Michael would no longer be permitted to fall asleep in their bed. Instead, father would take over the bedtime routine by tucking both boys (first Kevin, then Michael half an hour later) in their beds after reading them a bedtime story. Michael was to be told in a firm, noncritical way that if he got upset at night he could call for his father, who would come to his bed to calm his fears. A nightlight would be left on in his room. He was to be praised when he could go through the night without any difficulties. Michael's mother readily agreed to let her husband take charge of the sleep issue and Michael's father was pleased to take over. By now he was beginning to see how he had seen himself in Michael and overreacted to his own concerns there.

Both agreed not to use Kevin as an example to humiliate Michael to change. They were also to discourage Kevin from teasing Michael.

Middle phase of treatment.   In one session, Michael mentioned that Kevin had a birthday party last week and had gotten a lot of presents. Michael took one of them and his mother made him give it back. She gets angry when he makes Kevin cry. Then, in the morning when he doesn't want to go to school, he gets even more worried that she will get in an accident. Expression of anger at Kevin and at his mother for siding with Kevin led to the relationship between anger and fear of losing his mother. These were explained and discussed with him.

Michael came to the next session tearful and reluctant to leave his mother. Michael's mother explained that she was caught in a traffic jam and was late picking Michael up at the baby-sitter's. He was fearful and wanted to go directly home rather than to the session. After much support and encouragement from both his mother and the therapist, he hesitantly went into the playroom. They were able to talk about his fear that the therapist would think him a cry baby, just like his Dad did. That's why he wanted to stay with his mother and go directly home.

Ending phase of treatment.   The parents had reported that Michael was no longer a problem at night and his separation problem was much improved. In therapy, Michael had given up his play with dinosaurs for more advanced games. He talked about Indian Guides, a club for boys and their fathers. He and his Dad were a team; they made totems together and were planning an overnight camp out.

He was proud of spending an overnight at a friend's house, just like an Indian Guide. A stuffed dog his mother gave him for his birthday helped him sleep in his own bed. They talked about termination and left the door open if worries should return. Michael's anger and fear had been split off from each other and resolved separately.

Family Therapy

Initial phase of treatment. Further history from the parents revealed that the sleep problem began around the time of the younger brother Kevin's birth. The parents' preoccupation with the new baby had led to sibling rivalry (i.e., a way for Michael to get some notice). The parents then attempted excessive indulgence, such as inviting him into bed with them, rather than setting reassuring limits about bedtime (maintaining consistency for him in the face of change in the family).

Mother went back to work when Kevin had begun school. There had been some conflict about this, with the father wanting her to stay home and Michael, in a coalition with dad, making mornings difficult for them. In any case, they didn't know what to do in the morning and couldn't agree. Should they send him to school with a stomachache or not?

In summary, Michael's parents were not in charge of bedtime or school time. Michael was, but unable to manage. This power in a small person results in anxiety and willfulness.

The whole family was invited in to the office, including younger brother Kevin. Kevin immediately found the toys and busied himself with them while Michael sat down between his parents, all three looking expectantly at the therapist.

The therapist probed: "Who can tell me the problem?" There was silence, then the father started, and the mother interrupted. She explained their concerns about Michael. She said he was upset, doesn't get enough sleep, and gets terrible stomachaches. She can't believe there isn't something physically wrong with him. The father said she was soft on him. He wondered why Michael doesn't have the stomachaches on the weekends. Michael says he doesn't know what's the matter. He says he gets scared at night, and his stomach hurts. Kevin volunteered that Michael could sleep with him because he's not scared. Michael scowled. Kevin went on to say that he loved school, but Michael has a mean teacher and a lot of hard work to do.

The therapist continued: "Tell me about bedtime for the boys. What time do they go to bed? Who puts them to bed? What routines are there?" The parents replied that the mother put the boys to bed at the same time. She reminded them about 15 minutes before bedtime, they took a quick bath, then into bed. They don't have a story because they like to watch television until the last minute.

The therapist asked, "Show me what goes on when you get up in the morning." (Kevin was asked to pretend he is Michael.) What time does it start? Who wakes up the boys? Kevin began with a dramatic groan, but the parents were slow to start. Who begins? Dad said, "Come on, Mike, get dressed and get all ready, get some breakfast into you, then you'll feel better." "Okay," said Kevin. "Is that what Mike does?" asked the therapist? "No," said Kevin. Kevin moaned some more. Mother said, "Try to get dressed now." "No-o-o-o-o!" moaned Kevin, who fell to the floor grasping his stomach. Everyone laughed, except Michael, who was angry and sullen. The therapist wanted to know what happened next. They said that Dad gets angry and Mom gets more concerned.

How does it end? Dad takes Kevin to school, while Mom soothes Michael, who does eventually get dressed, slowly. She then tries to take him to school, where he arrives late and without breakfast. She then goes on to work. She, too, is late. Otherwise, Michael just stays home.

To Michael, the therapist asked, "Did Kevin do a good job being you?" Michael answered, "No, I don't make that much noise." "You do, too," said Kevin.

The therapist asked the parents to decide whether to start with the sleep problem or the school problem. Mother wanted to start with the sleep problem because she thought lack of sleep gave him stomachaches. Father wanted to start with the school problem because it upset everyone's day. The therapist asked them to decide between themselves. They had a brief discussion, and Dad gave in to Mom even though he didn't agree with her. The therapist commended them on a decision, repeated their description of the problem, and reviewed their description of the bedtime routine. The session ended with a task for the parents to assess what changes they could make in the bedtime routine. It was suggested that nothing be done to change the morning routine until the sleep problem was under control.

In summary, Michael did not have a good relationship with his brother and was not differentiated as a child from his parents. He was much too involved with his parents. This was seen in Kevin's early ability to occupy himself, and his objective "playing" of the Michael role versus Michael's attachment to the parents and the therapist.

The parents have differences that they cannot resolve. They argue and experience continued failure in solving their family problems. The strategy was to have the parents make decisions mutually. This had already begun in the first session when they agreed to begin with the sleep problem.

Middle phase of treatment.   Next, the concept of differentiation was introduced. Michael was the older brother. In this way, he needed to find his own place in the sibling relationship. Should he have a different bedtime? Should he go with one parent while the other is with Kevin? Should he have a different story? The parents were asked to think of the feasibility of these ideas for their family. They decide something; Michael complains, and they back off. The therapist encouraged them to pursue their decision.

A similar process will be implemented over the stomachaches, although it was felt they may abate when the parents change their attitudes about managing the children and about dealing with each other. When the pattern of parent-child interaction shifts around bedtime, it may change around stomachaches and school, too.

Ending phase of treatment.   After the family members expressed their satisfaction with bedtime—the parents with pleasure, Michael with sheepish acknowledgment, and Kevin with boisterous support of his brother—the therapist asked if they were ready to work on the school and stomachache problems. Michael volunteered, "I don't have stomachaches anymore." The therapist was incredulous, "Not even one a week? Not even a little twinge—you know what a twinge is, don't you?" Michael insisted, no more stomachaches. The therapist turned helplessly to the parents. "This is serious. I'm concerned that Michael has given up all of his symptoms so quickly. He may be relieving you of the job of negotiating with each other about how to take care of him. For this reason, I am going to ask you to pretend that Michael has a stomachache in the morning, and to consider the problems you had when he really did have a stomachache. That means you have to have a discussion about whether he should get dressed or not, whether he should eat breakfast, and whether he will be ready to leave for school when he is supposed to. I don't for a minute want you to think that being agreeable parents is easy. And, Michael, if you could just pretend to have a stomachache one or two mornings this week, I think that will really help your parents to do their job, okay?"

Everyone thought this was silly. The therapist asked Michael to demonstrate how he would act if he has a stomachache. He was not nearly as reticent as in the first session, and did a fine performance. Kevin was delighted and offered to pretend he had a stomachache, too. "That's a great idea,' said the therapist. "That way your parents will really have a job trying to figure out what to do." The parents enjoyed their boys' game and promised to be really mean the next time they complained of a stomachache. "But, remember," warned the therapist, "Michael really does have stomachaches. He didn't just make them up, although I hope he will make up a few in the next week or so, so you won't get out of practice."

By "restraining" the family from too rapid change, the therapist attempted to deal with the phenomenon of a "flight into health." In this case, it was related to Michael's accommodation to his parents in a way that looks as if things are better, but in which no real change has taken place. Usually the family does carry out the task and has a hilarious tale to tell about their experiences. The old pattern of the stomachache and the troubles they had getting Michael to school becomes a much loved family story, to be told and retold over and over. "Remember when you and daddy used to fight about whether I should go to school?" queries Michael.

Follow-up reveals that Michael was going to school, sleeping in his own bed, and starting Little League. Kevin was acting up and complained about Michael's privileges. The therapist asked the parents, "You know how to handle that?" "Yes," they replied.

Treatment Failures with Separation Anxiety Disorder

The most common cause of treatment failure with separation anxiety disorder lies in the inability of the parents to carry the program through. This is particularly so when the child lives with a single parent who is socially isolated and highly dependent on the child. It is also a problem when the key parent has unresolved separation anxiety problems of their own that make them powerless to stand outside the child's problems. The other major difficulty is when the child is older and actively dislikes school or is quite unsuccessful at it. Brief hospitalization is sometimes needed in treatment failures, particularly when the parent is unable to get the child to school; this can then be carried out by the staff of the psychiatric unit. The ultimate aim with older children is to get them to school on their own initiative.

Overanxious Disorder

Nancy, a 12-year-old, pubertal, only child, came for a consultation because of a one-year history of "nervousness." About a year before the consultation, her parents had separated. Their marriage had been apparently stable and outwardly satisfactory up until that time, and their child-rearing practices were unremarkable. Following her parents' separation, Nancy developed several fears and a relatively persistent state of anxiety. She began to bite her nails and to worry about her school performance; she became afraid of the dark and unable to fall asleep. She appeared to live in a relatively constant state of apprehension. Her worries were mostly realistic, but greatly exaggerated. She worried about her father getting lung cancer because of his smoking; if a hurricane was predicted for the area she was sure it would hit her house; after a minor laceration Nancy would worry for days about "blood poisoning." She reported relatively constant feelings of nervousness and anxiety, which seemed to be exacerbated by almost any event in her life. She experienced no panic attacks and no specific fears on separation from her parents, although she was occasionally worried about their safety without good reason.

Nancy was always a shy girl who often had difficulty making friends, although she had developed lasting and close relationships with several peers. Her only outside activity was weekly piano lessons. Her menstrual periods had begun the year before and were normal. School records described a good student, an overly sensitive child who had never been a behavior problem. Her tendency to strive for perfection and to require above-average amounts of teacher approval dated back to third grade. The teacher commented on the form that Nancy never seemed to be satisfied with her efforts and that she was actually an overachiever.

During the interview, her palms were sweating, it was hard for her to look at the examiner, and she was rather inhibited and tense. She denied persistent feelings of sadness or lack of interest in her environment, and she said she was able to enjoy things except for the times when her anxiety peaked. Nancy freely talked about her worries, and justified them with logical explanations (e.g., the incidence of lung cancer in men). When asked about guilt, she reported with difficulty that sometimes she felt that somehow she was responsible for her parents' separation or divorce, although she really couldn't say how. The Conners Teacher Rating Scale revealed an elevated factor 3 scale (tension, anxiety). Relevant endorsed items were as follows: overly sensitive (2); overly serious or sad (2); submissive (2); shy (3); fearful (1); excessive demand for teacher's attention (1); and overly anxious to please (3). Physical examination findings were unremarkable. Specifically, she had no goiter or exophthalmos, and thyroid indices were within normal limits. Neurologic findings were unremarkable except for a mild tremor of extended hands during the examination, but this did not interfere with fine motor skills.

Behavioral Therapy

Beginning phase of treatment.   Further history revealed that while anxiety had gotten worse since her parents' separation, worrying had been a way of life for Nancy as long as she could remember. Her father, an easygoing man, had usually been able to josh her out of it. On the other hand, her mother was a worrier, too. Since the parents' separation, the situation had deteriorated markedly without the father's buffering influence.

In the interview, Nancy talked freely and seemed mature for her age. She was relieved to have a neutral adult to talk to. She defined her problem as "worrying too much" but said "I just can't help it!"

A stimulus-response-reinforcement formulation of the problem was as follows:

Stimulus: Practically any thought, even slightly anxiogenic, seemed to trigger Nancy into worrying. While some stimuli, such as the death of her father or sickness in herself, were considerably more powerful, there was no great specificity to stimuli. (This stands in sharp contrast to separation anxiety, in which all the situations are united by the common stimulus of separation from the most important attachment figure.)

Response: The response was primarily emotional (anxiety) rather than behavioral or operant (as in separation anxiety disorder).

Reinforcement: Nancy's way of trying to relieve her anxiety was to try to think it through and search for solutions. Thus the key to prevent her father from dying of cancer was to persuade him to stop smoking. Sometimes these thoughts and induction of a plan relieved the anxiety (this is characteristic of "normal" experience). However, in Nancy's case, it led to further problems, that is, she knew her father would never give up smoking because she had been after him in the past to do so. This then became another anxiogenic stimulus and the cycle was repeated, until distraction, exhaustion, or habituation stopped the cycle of thinking. (In obsessive compulsive disorders, this obsessional type of thinking leads to an attempt to relieve anxiety by a motor act or compulsion.)

Organismic factors: Nancy had noticed that when she was stressed in certain ways (e.g., by impending examinations, or fights between her parents and worrying by her mother), she became much worse. (This illustrates that if the general level of arousal or anxiety is raised, the probability of the cycling effect occurring is greatly increased.)

The treatment plan consisted of a general reduction of Nancy's anxiety level. Anything to achieve this was likely to reduce the prospect of the obsessional cycling. Total extinction of anxiety was considered unrealistic as it was an essential part of her temperament. But it seemed that some toughening up or "inoculation" of Nancy against anxiety should be possible. This would be done first by teaching her ways of reducing anxiety, and then dosing her in individual practice sessions with fantasies of increasingly anxiogenic situations along a stimulus hierarchy. Implosion techniques, although often highly effective in this kind of problem, were felt to be too traumatic for a child of this age. But they could be considered later if all went well and if a high level of rapport and trust developed between Nancy and her therapist. "Thought stopping" and distraction, to interrupt the worrying cycle, were considered the most useful techniques she could learn to carry out in her everyday life outside therapeutic sessions. But operant procedures were considered to be crucial in rewarding Nancy for not worrying. These rewards could be both parent- and self-administered.

Since reduction of Nancy's overall level of anxiety seemed to be the critical first step, exploratory sessions were carried out, first with her mother and then her father. Both were instructed in ways to minimize feedback into Nancy's anxiety. Nancy's life was scrutinized closely to see if there were any unnecessary sources of stress. These were dealt with by environmental manipulation or discussion with Nancy herself. For example, piano lessons (which she hated, involved an hour's traveling, and interfered with possible peer group activities) were discontinued.

Nancy was then taught progressive muscular relaxation. This proved difficult at first because she worried about whether she was doing it "right." Strong suggestion helped overcome this. A stimulus hierarchy of least to most anxiogenic thoughts was constructed. Thought stopping was also taught by asking her to think about a neutral topic, then interrupt it by the therapist shouting "stop," then repeating "stop" herself, and finally just saying "stop" quietly to herself. As she learned to relax, the key words for thought stopping were "stop and relax." She would then attempt to follow the thought stopping with active relaxation. Next, thought stopping was extended to mildly anxiogenic thoughts, and, gradually, on up the hierarchy. This technique was quite successful at lower levels of anxiety, but less so at the top of the hierarchy, especially in thoughts of death and injury to herself and/or her parents.

Nancy was instructed to practice relaxation and thought stopping in the evening in bed. This ultimately cured the difficulty of falling asleep, which had been a problem.

Each parent was instructed to ignore her "assurance-seeking" questions because these prevented natural extinction by escape-avoidance. Rather, they were to provide attention and affection whenever she appeared unworried. Her mother found greater difficulty in doing this than did her father because Nancy's anxiety fed into her mother's. Nancy was helped to construct a work plan of steps in her treatment program, and also to work out ways of rewarding herself for achieving particular targets. She worked on a point system and when she had acquired a certain number of points, she was able to exchange them for special events and purchases.

Middle phase of treatment.   As treatment moved along, Nancy was able to turn off mild worries and prevent them from growing. She was able to mitigate moderate worries. Overall she felt much better. The general procedures had considerably reduced her overall level of anxiety.

Next, to deal with the most severe worries, she was taught to distract herself if the thought stopping did not work. This was done by thinking about something pleasurable (e.g., an upcoming holiday, or picturing herself as a character in her favorite television soap opera). This helped reduce the level of frequency and severity and, although they did not disappear, she felt they were manageable.

Ending phase of treatment.   Therapy sessions were decreased in frequency, although from time to time Nancy would need check-up sessions for reinforcement. After several months, she was greatly improved but still something of a worrier. She had become very dependent on her therapist and had a tendency to phone him at the office and at home when worries got out of hand. The therapist did not object to this because, with an occasional reinforcement session, he was able to reinforce Nancy's own thought stopping and relaxation techniques. Ultimately these telephone calls ceased.

However, whenever Nancy encountered a life crisis, she would recontact her therapist and receive further short courses of treatment, much of which were simply talking through the situation and reinforcing the thought stopping and relaxation techniques.

Psychopharmacologic Therapy

Beginning phase of treatment.   Further history revealed that several weeks before, Nancy's family doctor had prescribed trial of diphenhydramine (25 mg hs) for sleep. The hope was to decrease the morning fatigue that was interfering with her schoolwork. This and a subsequent increase to 50 mg hs had little effect. When increased to 25 mg tid and 50 mg hs, it produced a minimal decrease in symptoms, and drowsiness and fatigue became worse. The reported symptoms of anxiety persisted even after discontinuation and during a trial of hydroxyzine 25 mg qid. Reassurance that her somatic symptoms were a normal reaction to her parents' separating and would soon improve reduced neither their intensity nor severity. In fact, she reported resentment that the doctor did not appreciate her anguish and that she resented the need for pills to make her better. Nancy's family doctor had decided that her anxiety was developing into an ingrained pattern and referral to a psychiatrist was indicated. Nancy was appropriately prepared for the consultation and enthusiastic about having the chance to talk with someone about her problems.

Nancy reported falling asleep as a major problem, sometimes taking as long as one to two hours. Difficulty concentrating in school, daydreaming, and poor memory were described as significant problems for the past four months. Her mother reported that Nancy had always been on the "nervous, high-strung side" and a barometer of family tensions. Her mother was concerned about Nancy's long-standing need to approach tasks compulsively and to resent silently situations that she could not control. Nancy and her mother agreed to see the therapist two more times for assessment and then to discuss a plan of action. The hydroxyzine was to be discontinued over two weeks because it did not appear to be beneficial.

In the psychiatric interviews, Nancy described her resentment over taking a pill to control her behavior and considered it an unacceptable form of external control. She said her mother also disapproved of the idea of pill taking. Her dad seemed disappointed in her and had become even less available since she had started taking the medication. Nancy recalled similar fears and worries dating back to second grade when she began to ruminate about her grades. Intermittent, nonmigraine headaches had persisted since that time and seemed to correlate with school examination periods.

She also reported discomfort about the "lump in my throat and butterflies in my stomach when I have to write or give a report" dating from that same period.

The findings were discussed with both parents and Nancy. In the interpretive interview, the father was asked and agreed to be more consistent in scheduled visitation with Nancy, even though he was in the process of moving. The mother was asked and agreed to provide positive reinforcement for age-appropriate achievements and to make a concentrated effort to minimize excessive demands. Given the development of a nearly incapacitating level of symptoms, a trial of anxiolytic medication was proposed.

Use of medication was placed in the structure of a vicious cycle or self-fulfilling prophecy. Nancy had developed a habit of experiencing anxiety whenever faced with a situation that would test her competence. The expectations she had set for herself were unrealistically high and therefore not achievable. She feared disapproval of her parents and teacher if she did not achieve at a given level and was equally fearful of disappointment and rejection.

Nancy's actual achievement fell below the level of her goals and hence her concerns were confirmed. Diazepam was expected to block the anticipatory anxiety of frustration and failure, to allow her to relearn how it felt to succeed at realistic levels of expectation, and hence to assist her in feeling in control of herself and her emotions. The goal was to interrupt the negative cycle of anticipatory anxiety and failure to allow her to benefit more fully from the improved family relationships toward which the parents had agreed to work.

Although both parents were concerned about the use of medication because of their fear of potential addiction, they agreed to a monitored short-term trial with diazepam and extended exploration of Nancy's problem.

The diazepam would be used for a maximum of eight weeks, followed by a two-week tapering period. It would be accompanied by weekly working sessions devoted to grading the severity of the anxiety to targeted situations, with Nancy following her own progress.

In this and similar situations, issues related to the psychodynamics of pill taking and their potential impact on the outcome of psychotropic treatment in children and adolescents may be considered (Petti and Sallee 1986; Shapiro 1977; Whalen and Henker 1976). Factors to be considered are the child's positive or negative orientation to taking (or being forced to take) a pill; the parents' responses (e.g., positive, negative, conflicted, or overdetermined), all of which can be overt or covert; the effect of the teacher's attitudes; and the contribution of the "laying on of hands" or "placebo" effect (Petti and Sallee 1986).

The critical importance of the parents' combined acceptance and support of the use of medication in their very sensitive daughter was discussed as well as the nature of their concerns about medication (i.e., "drugs") and their fears of addiction. Then they were cautioned about a possible increase in aggressive behavior, anger, and hostility as part of the disinhibiting effect of the medication (Petti and Conners 1983). Discussion focused on how such behaviors might realistically be handled.

Work with Nancy around the issue of medication was similar to that with the parents. However, over the next two sessions her concerns about medications were explored more fully and the possibility raised that medication could help her reassert control over her life and emotions. She overcame her major reservations by assuming the role of participant observer in the monitoring process with mutually agreed on concrete operational criteria in this "experiment."

Other cognitive and behavioral techniques (e.g., probability estimations of harm to her parents, charts of progress, logs) were employed. The initial focus was on the frequency and severity of the more severe anxiety symptoms (psychophysiologic) as well as the frequency and duration of "happy feelings." Brief telephone contacts to monitor the program were held the day after the sessions to address any difficulties with the monitoring.

Middle phase of treatment. Diazepam was begun at 2 mg hs and gradually increased over three weeks to 2 mg tid. Nancy conscientiously followed the program and did her "homework." She became more verbal in the sessions, expressing increased anger and ambivalence toward both parents, especially her father. She was able to fall asleep within half an hour and was less bothered by problems concentrating and excessive worrying. She continued to experience psychophysiologic symptoms prior to test or performance situations, but the intensity was less severe and easily controlled. Feelings of contentment and pleasure occurred with increasing frequency, and she asked that her dosage not be increased. Her worries about her parents had also decreased in frequency and severity.

After the fourth week of medication, the teacher documented a decrease in oversensitivity, seriousness, and need to please. The parents noted that she appeared less anxious, was talking more, and not biting her nails as often. They reaffirmed their commitment to the treatment plan and expressed relief at having something constructive to do in helping Nancy.

By the end of week seven of drug treatment, the mother expressed the opinion that Nancy had returned to her "old self." She did seem more positive and self-confident than before, but still had self-doubt and concern about getting things just right. Nancy's mother was apprehensive about discontinuation of medication and about possible problems when Nancy visited her dad during the summer.

Ending phase of treatment. Nancy expressed similar concerns but was appropriately anxious to discontinue the medication. During the last week of full dose and during the two weeks of tapering off medication, the monitoring process revealed minor increases in frequency and intensity of anxiety symptoms related to anticipation of stress-related events. The sleep problems and exaggerated worries did not recur. The mother reported an absence of symptom escalation. A follow-up Teacher Rating Scale showed a decrease in factor 3 scale but a continued elevation above normal levels: shy (3); submissive (2); anxious to please (2); overly sensitive (1); and overly serious (1).

A final session, two weeks after the diazepam was discontinued, summarized the results of therapy. Nancy's father called to say that he wanted to do whatever necessary to prevent a recurrence of the acute symptomatology. Nancy agreed that medication would no longer be required but she would like to change some of the things that had distressed her for so long. She appeared ready for psychotherapy, if indicated.

Psychodynamic Therapy

Beginning Phase of Treatment. Further history revealed that Nancy had always been a rather shy and inhibited youngster. Her mother attributed this to the fact that Nancy, as an only child, had no siblings with whom to learn give-and-take. Nancy's worrisome nature became full-blown when her father left home the year before to live with his secretary, a young woman named Vicky. He now wanted a divorce to marry her. Nancy's mother refused to agree, hoping that he would get over this "infatuation."

Nancy's father had always spent a good deal of time at work and left the care of Nancy to his wife. Now he was supposed to see Nancy on Saturdays for visitation, but often canceled visits for business and social reasons. He tried to make up for it by buying Nancy presents and by taking her to expensive restaurants.

Nancy's mother resented the fact that she was the only one to discipline Nancy and to see that she carried out her daily routines. Nancy tended to procrastinate in her chores and in practicing the piano. Nancy complained that her mother was a nag. The father, before leaving home, often sided with Nancy and accused his wife of being "too compulsive."

Her mother was especially annoyed when Nancy complained that life at home was boring, and how much fun it was with her father. The mother knew she should not react negatively to this, but at times she burst out with critical remarks about Nancy's father and accused Nancy of being ungrateful to her.

The mother saw the father's girlfriend Vicky as the cause of her marital problems and believed it was morally wrong for them to be living together. Although she wanted Nancy to spend time with her father, she did not like the fact that much of the time Nancy spent with her father was also with Vicky.

Nancy agreed that her "nervous" condition seemed to coincide with the separation of her parents. She didn't like it but she claimed she had learned to accept it. After all, she was not the only one in school whose parents were separated or divorced. She could not see any direct connection between the separation and her symptoms. She rationalized her worries (e.g., fear of her father getting lung cancer) by quoting statistics about the frequency of lung cancer in men who smoke. But she agreed that the symptom was interfering with her life, and she was willing to come in for therapy if it could help.

In the early sessions, Nancy avoided talking about emotionally disturbing material and preferred talking about what she watched on television. A favorite program was a series about a close family. She spoke admiringly of her own father and complained about her mother getting after her to practice piano lessons when she didn't like the piano. Nancy's mother liked the piano and was good at it.

The data so far suggested a strong unresolved Oedipal problem: admiration of father and rejection of mother. It appeared that Nancy's overanxious disorder was significantly related to the parental separation. Her feelings and fantasies about it would be explored in individual psychotherapy. The mother also needed to be seen, with the focus on her relationship with Nancy.

After several sessions, Nancy talked about the parents of a friend who had just separated and how much it hurt her friend. Thereafter, she was able to talk about how upset she was about the separation of her own parents. She enjoyed seeing her father, yet felt guilty because she knew her mother was deeply hurt by her father's move from home. She got angry at her mother for the critical remarks about her father, then felt guilty because she knew how much her mother missed her father. She liked her father, but was also angry with him for "deserting" them. She knew her father wanted her to like Vicky. When she tried to like Vicky, however, she felt disloyal to her mother. Like her mother, Nancy saw Vicky as the temptress who had broken up their home. All these concerns had made her very nervous. "Yes," she said to the therapist, "It's like a hurricane hitting our house."

When asked whether the separation had some bearing on her fears, she related it to the worsening of her fear of lung cancer in her father. Her father was a heavy smoker; her mother was a nonsmoker, trying to help her husband cut down. At present, however, her father was smoking more than ever, and Vicky was no help because she was a smoker, too.

Nancy still hoped that her father would give up Vicky and return home. When questioned about whether she felt she had contributed to the separation, she recalled arguments between her mother and father in the past. She and mother had battled about piano practice. When her father was around, he told his wife it was not important to practice that much. This led to a bigger argument, with her mother accusing her father of not being around enough to help raise Nancy. Nancy sometimes wondered whether these arguments might have contributed to the separation.

Several sessions later, Nancy came in obviously looking "down." She said it was "that time of the month." She and the therapist talked about puberty and how some girls were proud of their breast development. Nancy hated her breasts. She was flat-chested like her mother. Vicky was sexy and that's how she got the father.

The issue of sex was brought out in the open. Nancy's feelings of inadequacy about her physical development were related to her feeling she could not compete with Vicky (for her father).

Middle phase of treatment. Nancy was preoccupied with an attractive woman patient who came to the therapist's office. Good-looking women get all the attention. Her conclusion that her father chose Vicky over her was refocused as a problem between the mother and the father. It didn't mean he didn't love Nancy. But a few sessions later, her father missed a planned visit because of a date with Vicky. Nancy began to see him as imperfect, and the need for her to look for friends and other people in her life became important. Disappointed by her father, Nancy gained a more realistic appraisal of him and with it, a willingness to give him up.

A session with the father revealed that his relationship with Vicky was not an infatuation. He felt much more in common with her than with his wife, (e.g., their mutual interest in business). He wanted a divorce to marry Vicky. He loved Nancy and was very interested in her welfare. He would try his best not to let other things interfere with his visits with Nancy and not put Nancy in the position of having to choose between him and his wife.

In a subsequent session, Nancy again mentioned the problems her friend Jill, whose parents were divorced, was having over her mother dating men again. Jill liked to see her mother going out and having a good time, but she also felt neglected when her mother went out and left her at home. In addition, the men her mother was dating were not the type Jill liked. Nancy said she would not need to worry about her mother dating again because she was too "old." As the discussion went on, she began to realize her mother was not too old to date. In fact, Nancy realized she had brought up Jill's problem because she, too, was worrying about her own mother dating. If her mother was to remarry, how would she get along with a new stepfather?

Later, a session with the mother revealed that she had decided to give up on her husband and begin to expand her own social life. That would make it easier for Nancy to escape being caught in the middle of the parental conflicts. The mother and Nancy were getting along better, and visits with her father were working out better as well.

Ending phase of treatment. Nancy was developing a life of her own. She canceled a weekend visit with her father because of a slumber party. She was talking excitedly about friends, including boys, and wanted to stop treatment. Nancy was proud of her mother's new independence and happy her mother had a boyfriend. Her worries were once again in the background, and the sessions became less frequent.

The mother had given up her husband and was working out her own new life. Nancy was no longer so caught in conflicts about her parents. She was becoming independent and autonomous, looking forward to growing up.

Family Therapy

Beginning phase of treatment.   For further history, the family was seen together. The parents were more than willing despite the fact that they were separated because they both cared about their daughter. Nancy sat between them, looking very uncomfortable.

The therapist asked what the problem was. They started to talk; the therapist focused on Nancy. She couldn't talk, and looked frozen, like a frightened rabbit. The therapist asked if she moved from between her parents and sat across from them, would her parents be all right? She laughed a little, looked at them, and said, "I guess so." She didn't move. "Will you give it a try?" asked the therapist. She moved.

The therapist then addressed the parents. "Tell me about the problem." They gave concurrent versions. The mother told the story; the father concurred.

The therapist asked the father to tell about how the marriage came apart. Nancy protested: "That's not about me. I thought this was to help me." The therapist continued to address the parents, asking if it was something they would rather discuss in private. They indicated they would. The therapist asked Nancy to leave and asked her if she thought they would be all right. She said "Yes, but I don't know what it has to do with me." The therapist said, "Maybe nothing. But you did tell me that the symptoms began with the separation, so I thought it might have something to do with that." Nancy left.

The parents told their story. The father began. The mother and Nancy had been very close since Nancy's birth. He never felt involved. When he tried to help with the baby, the mother would criticize and take her away from him. He got more involved with work, stayed away more, and became involved in an affair with his secretary, Vicky.

The mother complained that he never seemed to have enough time for her and Nancy. They didn't fight or argue; they just drifted apart. Nancy felt, according to the mother, that the father betrayed her with his affair but begged her mother to forgive him.

The therapist urged the parents to express their own feelings about the marriage. The father was angry and hurt at having been shut out. The mother was hurt and angry about his affair.

At the end of the session, the therapist noted that Nancy had not been a part of the conversation. "She needs your assurance that you are all right. But the content of the discussion is between the two of you and me. She doesn't need to be involved in it."

In summary, it appeared the parents had not been able to speak about their own pain, or to "take their own sides" (Bozsormenyi-Nagy and Spark 1973). Thus the girl had become a confidant of the mother and a manager of parental affairs. She had been "parentified." This was too great a task to assign a 12-year-old: to worry excessively about her parents and hold herself responsible for their well-being.

A formulation of the problem was as follows:

1. The parents did not acknowledge their differences with each other to themselves. The parents worried about Nancy's worrying, but didn't take her worries seriously.

Thus they didn't help her stop her worrying, especially in areas it is not her place to assume responsibility (e.g., the father's smoking).

2. The covert conflict between the parents had gone on a long time. Nancy had been a great comfort to both of them. This was a big responsibility for her and interfered with her own social development.

3. Nancy's schoolwork was a source of neutral conversation for everyone in the family.

Middle phase of treatment.   The focus, then, was to get Nancy out of the parental subsystem by: 1) having the parents take charge of their own grievances with each other (i.e., "to take their own sides") so that Nancy didn't have to do this for them; 2) limiting their discussions with Nancy about their personal affairs (i.e., "deparentifying" Nancy); and 3) increasing the father's competent involvement with Nancy, with the mother's approval, as the custodial parent.

Some sessions would be spent with all three together, some sessions with the parents alone. With the three together, the content focused on what was going on with Nancy, in her social life, and in school. When any one of the three changed the subject, (e.g., to a concern with the father's smoking or the mother's unhappiness since the separation), the therapist redirected the conversation back to "Nancy issues" and reassured them that these concerns would be taken up later.

When the parents were without Nancy in therapy, they were asked to take "I" positions. For example, if the father worried about the mother's loneliness, the therapist asked the mother to tell how she felt, and what she was going to do about it. The therapist would also ask the father to talk about whether he was lonely or not. Similarly, if either parent brought Nancy into the conversation (e.g., "Nancy thinks I should go out more"), the therapist directed that parent to express his or her own wants and leave Nancy out of it.

Nancy moped and worried more, thus forcing the parents to talk about her instead of themselves. When this happened, it provided an opportunity for the father to take an active role with her, with the mother's coaching. He visited her school, talked with her teachers, and took a special interest in her academic life. His involvement (with the mother staying less involved) at this time let Nancy know that they, the parents, were functioning more effectively as a subsystem and were placing the focus on important areas of her functioning as a 12-year-old child.

In one session, Nancy wanted to go downtown by herself with a girlfriend. In this instance, Nancy stressed the changes in the family system by testing her mother's readiness to let her be more independent. When the mother found herself in a quandary about what to do, she consulted the father. Again, this let Nancy know that she was being taken care of by both parents.

Ending phase of treatment.   As the therapy came to an end, Nancy was more independent and less anxious, but the mother continued individual sessions to work on her own relationships, especially with other adults, on professional commitments, and general issues of self-esteem. Work with the mother continued with periodic inclusions of Nancy when there were mother-daughter struggles to be addressed. The father was in touch with the therapist about his daughter, but basically the relationship between them became a good one. This was a credit to the mother's progress as well.

Treatment Failures in Overanxious Disorders

Success in every treatment program is dependent on active participation by the patient. It is also greatly influenced by the actual severity and pervasiveness of the anxiety. True obsessional thinking of a stereotyped nature is much more difficult to manage than worries that change from day to day.

Avoidant Disorder

Betty, a 15-year-old, the youngest of four siblings of an immigrant family, was referred for consultation by a school counselor who felt she was shy and inhibited and lacked self-confidence. In school, it was noted that she kept to herself, had no friends, and avoided extracurricular activities. Although her written work was good, her teachers remarked that she had a very difficult time speaking in front of her classmates, sometimes becoming tearful when called on.

In the interview, Betty avoided looking directly at the examiner, was tense and anxious, and found it difficult to speak. It took some time to make her feel at ease, but she was finally able to relax enough to express herself. She stated that although she had been always shy in social situations (her mother told her she had been afraid of strangers even as a baby), she did much better in her old school where she had some friends and felt much more accepted. This was her first year in a new school (ninth grade) where she felt the youngsters were cliquish. Betty felt the other girls were more stylishly dressed and socially sophisticated than she was and felt out of place with them. She wanted to make friends but became embarrassed and frightened when talking to new classmates. She had made no friends and went directly home as soon as school was out. Schoolwork was not difficult for her except for her oral presentations, when she became very self-conscious and anxious. She said she was afraid others would be critical of her.

She spoke about her family in a warm and animated way but was embarrassed by them as well because they spoke broken English. Betty considered her mother her best friend, the only one she could do things with and confide in. She spent her weekends with an older married sister and played well with her little nieces and nephews. Betty would like to marry and have children as her older sister had but was pessimistic about getting a boy to accept her because she felt she was not pretty enough. She insisted she wanted to be more outgoing like the other girls at school but was afraid of rejection and making a fool of herself.

Her teacher rated most group participation items on the Teachers Rating Scale (TRS) as being often true (3) (e.g., isolative behavior, nonacceptance by group, lacking leadership, not getting along with the same or opposite sex). Behaviors also rated as severe were overly sensitive, overly serious or sad, cries often and easily, and shy and fearful.

Behavioral Therapy

Beginning phase of treatment. Further history revealed that Betty saw her problem as long-standing shyness and lack of self-confidence. However, in keeping with her style of interpersonal relationships, she rapidly relaxed after the first interview and warmed to the therapist (who was about the same age as her parents).

A stimulus-response-reinforcement formulation of the problem revealed the following:

Stimulus: Unlike overanxious disorder but like separation anxiety disorder, the anxiogenic stimuli all belonged in a narrow class (i.e., social situations) where the person or persons present were not close friends or intimates of Betty.

Response (behavioral and emotional): The response was anxiety and its psychophysiologic concomitants.

Reinforcement: Betty's tendency to avoid social situations and to withdraw from them as rapidly as possible (e.g., coming home straight after school) served to relieve her social anxiety and so reinforce this avoidance behavior and prevent the natural extinction of the anxiety. If she was unable to escape her high level of situational anxiety, she experienced psychophysiologic symptoms, which further interfered with her functioning (i.e., "punished her" for attempting to perform in a social situation). Thus in the end, they became even more aversive and she even more lacking in self-confidence. A classic vicious cycle was set up, in which anxiety led to failure and further avoidance.

The treatment plan had two main foci: 1) preventing social withdrawal to extinguish both social anxiety and feelings of inadequacy and 2) minimizing psychophysiologic effects of anxiety to prevent some of the vicious cycling effect.

To prevent social withdrawal, Betty was taught some skills in conversing with and responding to peers. This was role played with her therapist and in a group therapy program. She was also taught muscle relaxation to deal with the psychophysiologic symptoms and was systematically desensitized to public speaking and social situations. This was done partly in individual therapy using fantasy along a stimulus hierarchy and classical reciprocal inhibition. But most of it occurred in an adolescent therapy group. The emphasis in the group was on role playing real-life situations and on discussing how one felt about it afterward. For example, speaking up in class or in public was dealt with by the group arranging the room to look like a classroom. Betty stood up several times in each session and spoke, first just a phrase, then 30 seconds longer each time. When she could do this easily, one member of the group was told to interrupt her and then to make critical comments. After each group session, the therapist would, in individual sessions, review the experience and rehearse in fantasy (with relaxation) any especially traumatic incidents that had occurred until they ceased to evoke anxiety.

Middle phase of treatment. In the therapeutic group, Betty developed a close friendship with another shy girl, Ann. They began to plan things together after school and on weekends. Unfortunately, Ann did not attend the same school as Nancy. The school counselor was approached and asked two classmates to help Betty get to know the other youngsters and generally to "steer her around." These classmates encouraged her and were able to get her to join selected extracurricular activities that appealed to her.

After about two months, Betty had a few close friends and spent an increasing amount of time away from home. However, she still spent time in warm, confiding relationships with her mother and sister. She was still shy and easily flustered, but her friends kept her socially involved. Although she continued to spend more time with her family than most of her peers, it was now more by choice than by default. Her friends ultimately arranged a date for Betty and took her to a school dance, over her protests. Fortunately, the date selected was rather shy himself, so that to her surprise, Betty found herself comfortable and taking the initiative. She still considered herself less attractive and less "with it" than her peers, but it worried her much less.

Ending phase of treatment Betty was reluctant to leave the therapist after several months of treatment. Leaving the group presented less difficulty, as her outside friendship patterns developed. She continued to drop in, call, or occasionally write from time to time and soon regarded the therapist more as a friend than a therapist.

When the time came to go to college, Betty consulted her therapist about what she should do. The therapist advised her to choose a local college where her friends were going, rather than the more distant one her parents preferred.

Psychopharmacologic Therapy

Beginning phase of treatment. Further history in an interview with Betty revealed that she wished she were "normal," but was unable to elaborate. Attempts to elicit further wishes failed. Betty produced tears instead and blushed when asked about interest in boys. She nodded yes to questions related to feeling miserable about the problems she was experiencing and her inability to say more than a few words at a time. The latter occurred even when she had lots more to say.

Betty agreed to the listing of a number of target behaviors that would allow her to feel better and to become more sociable. These included the following: 1) not blushing when answering a question, 2) not tensing muscles when talking to peers, 3) speaking in sentences of more than five words, 4) answering questions without getting scared, 5) answering questions without crying, 6) asking a classmate to visit her at home, and 7) initiating conversation at least once every three opportunities.

Past history from the parents confirmed the avoidant nature of Betty's behavior across all situations outside the home. The inhibited behavior was especially prominent at school. She had been close to a neighborhood girl at her old school but "chummy" behavior was never noted. Descriptions of her were: "loner," "nice but quiet," and "very sensitive." The parents each completed a Child Behavior Checklist (CBCL) (Achenbach and Edelbrock 1979), which was strongly positive for items related to fearfulness and shyness.

Betty and her family were told that of the options available for treatment, the use of an anxiolytic agent appeared to be a good one. Although other individual and family interventions might be indicated, they would be more effectively used after Betty was able to overcome major barriers to verbalizing thoughts and feelings to others and to remove the block to an expanded social life.

They discussed using diazepam, a drug that should decrease Betty's tension when confronted with social situations. They talked about Betty's avoidance as a bad habit that was being reinforced by her fear and worries. The therapist explained that the drug should help interrupt such maladaptive behavior by freeing Betty to do things and not just to relieve her anxiety. Betty liked the explanation that there were two parts to her personality: an old witch who kept her finger on the no button and a princess who wanted Betty to fulfill all her positive wishes. The medicine would slowly take away power from the witch and place it in the hands of the princess. Ultimately, Betty would need neither of these characters to direct her life.

The expected procedures using the diazepam were described as follows. The program would start off with a low dose to be taken at bedtime. Prior to falling asleep, she should imagine successfully performing all the tasks she had listed. In the morning she would rehearse all the target behaviors once again and decide which one she would try to achieve that day in school on school days, and in the neighborhood or at church on the weekend. At the end of the day, she was to rate how well she had done and record it in her log. The range of ratings was: 1) did not try at all; 2) tried but could not find the words; 3) tried and was partially successful; 4) tried and was very successful; 5) tried, did it, and felt great! The log was to be shared with the psychiatrist at each visit. He said:

We will move from once a day for one behavior to several times a day for two or more targeted goals. We may need to select when you need to take the pills. The medicine stays in your system for a while, so you won't need to use it every time you try to work on acting and feeling better. Mom and dad have the job of being certain you are able to get here to see me and to be certain you have the medicine when needed.

You and your parents will agree on rewards to be earned for completing your goals at the end of each day, week, and month. I'll help if you need assistance. For example, for day one, if you accomplish your goal to speak in a sentence of at least five words, mom's job is to brush your hair. If you accomplish your goals for five of the seven days, then you can pick a schoolmate or neighbor to go with you and your older sister to the movies.

Middle phase of treatment. Betty and her parents agreed to the plan, although her father and Betty felt it was childish. Diazepam was begun at 2 mg hs; the dosage increased once a week. Her parents were to complete the CBCL every other week and the school counselor and homeroom teacher were to complete the TRS weekly. Sleepiness, trouble getting up in the morning, and feeling a trifle unsteady were the predominant effects reported during the first week. Betty was able to think more easily about achieving her goals but still feared trying her exercises. The TRS reflected a decrease in severity for the anxiety items (sensitivity, sadness, shy, fearful) and for crying easily. The parents noted that she was less demanding of their attention and was more verbal about happenings at school. The dosage was increased to 1 mg in the A.M. and 2 mg hs.

On the increased dosage, Betty complained of a sluggish feeling. She reported that she was able to complete one goal in three of the seven days and was proud of her accomplishment. On the CBCL, the parents again ranked as "somewhat true" the items related to fears, fears school, and feels persecuted, and "very true" the items related to nervous, anxious, self-conscious, worrying, shy-timid, and needs to be perfect. The dosage was then increased to 2 mg in the A.M. and 2 mg hs.

At the next session, Betty proudly announced that she had accomplished one task per day for the past week. Her parents were providing the rewards, although she felt they were no longer needed. She had invited a classmate to the movies with her older sister and all had a great time. Her affect was much improved, and she verbalized to a much greater extent. The TRS revealed improvement in all items, but those related to nonparticipation in groups were still elevated. Betty said she was feeling better but still nervous about trying to accomplish her tasks. The dosage was increased to 4 mg in the A.M. and hs.

Ending phase of treatment. Prior to the next session, the parents called to express their delight. Their daughter was engaging more actively with neighbors (adults and younger children) and had fewer positive items on the CBCL. The TRS showed continued improvement. In the session, her increased sharing of school and neighborhood matters suggested that Betty had really improved. She was still somewhat apprehensive about speaking up in class and meeting new people but had acclimated herself to her new school and was feeling comfortable with her classmates. Betty was maintained on this dosage for four more weeks, then slowly tapered, and finally the medication was discontinued. Betty's log, the TRS, and the CBCL all indicated continued improvement. Individual symptoms, however, were still present at a lesser level of frequency and severity.

Withdrawal symptoms were mild and consisted mainly of anxious feelings and difficulty sleeping. The recommendation was made for some psychotherapy, depending on how she felt after the medication had ceased.

Psychodynamic Therapy

Beginning phase of treatment. Further history from the parents revealed they were older, had been born in Poland, and spoke English with an accent. Both had little formal education and lived in a Polish-speaking enclave. Both worked long hours running a small store. It was clear that they cared very much for Betty, but they did not quite understand why they were being seen and what was wrong with her.

They reported that Betty was their baby. They had three other children in their 30s, all married. Only the older daughter lived nearby. Compared to their other children, Betty had always been shy around strangers but they thought she would outgrow it. They attributed this to her being the youngest; they had babied her the most.

They also reported that they themselves were not very sociable. Except for a few church activities, their lives revolved around their work and their family.

It appeared that, raised by older and foreign-born parents, Betty had been infantilized so the parents would not have an "empty nest" as they grew older. Betty had not had the social experience to face and deal with the outside world in adolescence because of this block in her development. More personal experience behind this, however, needed to be uncovered.

Initially, Betty was painfully shy and inhibited in therapy. However, she desperately wanted help to change, which made her come regularly. There were long silences in the early sessions, and the therapist tried to be active to keep the conversation going. Gradually she became more comfortable relating to the therapist and began to explain the origin and meaning of her symptoms.

In one session she recalled how her symptoms first began in school. Because her parents spoke Polish in the home, she began school not fluent in English. She vividly remembered the day she was asked a question by her teacher in class and answered in Polish. To her acute embarrassment, the children laughed. To this day, she feels extremely anxious when asked to recite in class.

Another memory that made her self-conscious was the way she was dressed as a child. Her mother did not particularly care about style, as long as the clothes were clean and warm. Betty felt this made her look different from the other children.

During the course of later sessions, Betty commented about the people living in her neighborhood. The therapist picked up a derisive tone to her comments and asked her to expand. She talked of her strong feelings of shame for her parents' immigrant background. This was generalized into being ashamed of being Polish. To her, being Polish meant being different (and inferior) from others. She found it hard to be comfortable around non-Polish people. Because she was not proud of her Polish heritage, however, she also refused to participate in the activities of the Polish community.

She talked about how upset she felt when she heard people tell Polish jokes. She recalled a Father's Night at school. All the students were supposed to bring their fathers. She never told her father about it because she was afraid she would be too embarrassed.

The therapist asked whether there was any relationship between her feelings about her father and the therapist. She said she was sure the therapist's children would have no qualms about taking him to a Father's Night program: "Because you are not like my father—you are educated, you speak well, you are a doctor, your children can be proud of you."

The therapist replied he could appreciate how sensitive she felt about her Polish background. He wondered, however, whether her experience in the first grade (speaking Polish in class and the children laughing) had a lot to do with being ashamed of her father's foreign background. He asked what others thought of her father. She said that people liked him. He was respected as hard working, generous, and honest with others. The therapist said these were admirable traits, and perhaps some day, when she had more confidence in herself, she would not be so ashamed of her father and of being Polish.

In summary, Betty devaluated her father and idealized the therapist. (The therapist had noted she was showing increasingly positive feelings toward him.) He chose to approach this by helping her to see that her devaluation of her father was more related to a past traumatic experience and her own insecurity than to current reality.

Several sessions later, Betty casually mentioned that the night before, her sister's family had visited them. This had prompted her father to bring out his mandolin and play it for family singing. She spoke enthusiastically about how this often happened when her family got together and how much she liked singing. In fact, this was the one activity she enjoyed, even in school. Music was her favorite class. The therapist asked her what kind of songs her family sang. She said they were lively Polish songs her father had taught them.

The therapist capitalized on this. Perhaps singing could provide the socializing experience and success she needed in school. Betty mentioned that they had a girls chorus group in school and she would not mind joining. Her school counselor was contacted and was glad to help her get into the group.

Middle phase of treatment.   Several sessions later, Betty seemed depressed. She mentioned that a boy in her class had asked her about a math problem. She knew the answer, but got so flustered, she became tongue-tied. She felt so stupid. The discussion developed her current new interest in boys and how anxious and insecure she felt with them. An intensification of her avoidant symptoms was increased by the emergence of heterosexual feelings and the anxiety around them.

Betty said her favorite books were romantic novels. After some hesitation, she revealed her fantasy about being a popular girl, courted by many boys. In the privacy of her bedroom she practiced dance steps after watching television shows. In reality, however, it was the opposite. She felt so awkward around boys that she could hardly talk. She had never been to a dance or even had a dance lesson. She envied other girls with comfortable relationships with boys. She desperately wanted a boyfriend.

In summary, an exhibitionistic fantasy lay behind Betty's extreme self-consciousness and inhibition with boys. Strong heterosexual feelings and anxiety compounded the avoidant disorder.

In subsequent sessions, she talked about how she was treated like a princess at home. She was the center of attention and pretty much got whatever she wanted from her parents. For example, she got her father to buy her a videocassette recorder and cassettes of her favorite performing stars. Her older siblings said she was spoiled because she got so much from her parents. (In a later session with the parents, they agreed that they may have given too much to Betty. It was because she is the youngest and the only one at home they could buy things for. They felt sorry for her because of her problem with shyness in school. It was to make up for the fact that they spent so much time in the store, leaving Betty alone at home.)

At the next session, the therapist pointed out to Betty that there was a connection between her being the center of attention at home and her shyness in school. At home she was treated like a princess. At school, where she wanted to be the center of attention so desperately, she hadn't learned how to compete with other youngsters for ordinary attention. To be sure, she deserved attention. But she not only had to learn how to compete for it. If she didn't expect so much to be the center of attention, it would be much easier to compete for and get normal attention away from home.

Ending phase of treatment. Betty had shown steady improvement in her avoidant behavior. She was able to work through feelings of being ashamed of her parents' foreign background and replaced that by developing a more positive appreciation of them and her own Polish heritage.

Through her sister, she got to know another girl who was active in a Polish-American youth group. With the support of the therapist, Betty started to attend their activities. Although still shy, she found the chance in this group to learn to relate to other teenagers (both males and females) on a give-and-take basis. She learned how to dance and began to enjoy going to the socials. This real experience with boys greatly lessened her need to escape into a world of fantasy.

Her participation in the girls chorus had also worked out well. It strengthened her self-confidence and interpersonal skills. She invited her parents to attend the spring recital of her choral group.

Along with several others from her group, she had gotten a summer job in a local drive-in frequented by teenagers. Now she learned to earn her own spending money rather than depending on her parents to give her things. Because of the steady improvement in her condition and her summer job (and the continued support of her social network), the therapist and Betty decided that therapy could be terminated at the end of the school year.

At the termination of treatment, she was much more comfortable with herself, her ethnic heritage, and relating to others. She would come back for checkups after school began again in the fall.

Family Therapy

Beginning phase of treatment. Further history from the parents revealed that Betty was their "change of life" baby. Since their oldest child was now in her mid-30s, their married life had been consumed with raising children. The family was close and intensely loyal. Sunday dinners and holidays had always been important family events.

The problems with Betty were not new, but had intensified with the beginning of high school when the student body increased, and she no longer had the familiar group in homeroom.

Next, Betty was seen with her parents, her older sister who lived nearby, the brother-in-law, and her nieces and nephews. The adults and Betty sat in chairs while the younger children explored the room. The therapist began by socializing with the young kids. Betty was very active with them. She told the therapist about them, teased them, and got them to perform and sing their ABCs. The therapist commented to Betty that she was very good with kids, and to the sister and brother-in-law: "Such a good helper. You're really lucky. Does she baby-sit?" When they replied, "Only on weekends," Betty's spirits seemed to drop. She became serious and awkward. The parents talked about what a good student Betty was. The little children had found something to play with and ignored the adults. The adults began to talk among themselves about Betty's problem, how she shouldn't be shy, how some nice boy would eventually come along, but he'd better be the right kind. Betty sank deeper.

The therapist called "time-out." He said, "Wait a minute. Everyone is talking at once. Everyone is talking about Betty. I don't even know what Betty thinks." Everyone became quiet, waiting for Betty, who began to cry. The father was encouraging and tried to hug her, but she pulled away. He gave up rather sheepishly. The mother whispered to him to leave Betty alone, "I told you, just let her alone when she gets like this."

The therapist asked Betty if there was anyone who understood her. Betty shook her head no. "Not your brother-in-law or your sister or your nieces or nephews?" She shook her head again. How about a girlfriend or a boyfriend? No. Well, that's not a very good state of affairs.

The therapist took a history of the family, allowing Betty to participate or not, as she wished, but not pushing her. The family revealed its closeness, and the older sister described how hard it was for her to get through high school because she felt different from the other children. "You see," she says, "my parents believe that family is all you need . . . more important than education or friends." The therapist asked, "So how did you get out?" "My new husband was invited in," she laughed. He laughed, too, and added that he felt the parents did overprotect Betty, that she always seemed to be more relaxed when she was staying over on the weekends baby-sitting. The therapist said to Betty that it seemed she wasn't the only one to have had these troubles, that her sister seemed to have moved on, and maybe she could give her some help. Betty was silent.

The therapist asked the parents what they thought. They acknowledged their older daughter's points. They also expressed their concerns about "teenagers today," to which the younger couple reacted in a teasing manner, calling them "old-fashioned." The therapist asked the parents if they could think of some ways they would feel safe about Betty doing more things away from home. They could think of nothing. The brother-in-law laughingly suggested that she baby-sit during the week so he could see more of his wife. The therapist asked the parents: "Would that be all right with you?" They replied yes, if she could get her schoolwork done. "What about it, Betty?" She agreed, unenthusiastically.

In summary, the parents in this close family saw the outside teenage world as dangerous for their daughter. But their older daughter was more comfortable. She and her husband represented a safe transition from the parents' generation to Betty's.

Betty's identity as a member of this close family is represented in her shyness with outsiders and in her area of manifest competence—with the children of her sister.

Inviting extended family members to the first sessions allowed the therapist to see an area of Betty's competence and to hear from the older sister about how the family worked.

Middle phase of treatment.   The therapist continued to involve Betty's sister's family as "go-betweens," to help encourage the parents to let Betty go. In general, Betty and her parents were seen in therapy sessions, but Betty was told that if she felt stuck with her mom and dad, she should ask her sister to come. At first Betty didn't want to inconvenience her sister. The therapist called the sister on a loud-speaker phone during one session so she could participate. Although they were all pleased with this idea, the sister said she'd rather be there in person to see the expressions on mom and dad's faces. Betty agreed to ask her to come the next time she needed her.

The therapist encouraged Betty to go out, to get away from the parental home, whenever reasonable: at first baby-sitting for her sister, progressing to baby-sitting for others in the neighborhood, and finally to a job working with youngsters after school. Progress was reported in the therapy sessions, but the therapist had to continue to "stretch" the family by asking, "What next?" Once Betty's father reported that one of the children she was sitting for got a bad cut and needed stitches. He started to describe how she managed. He was very proud of her. The therapist gently interrupted him, and asked Betty to tell the story herself. Betty demurred, saying that her father could tell it better. "I know you are very proud of her," said the therapist, "and I guess you must be proud of yourselves that you taught her to be so level-headed in a crisis." Then, turning to Betty, he asked her to tell him about the excitement. Betty described how she called the police to take her and the child to the emergency room, then called her mother to take care of the other kids while she was gone. She said she couldn't reach the kids' parents because they were at a movie. Then Betty burst out that she thought she would like to be a nurse. Her parents were shocked and protested, "Darling, you said you would get married and give us more grandchildren." Betty said she wanted to look into nursing schools.

In each session, the therapist blocked other family members from speaking for Betty, but also tried to avoid painful silence when the pressure on Betty to express herself might seem like disloyalty to her parents.

Ending phase of treatment   Problems came up when the mother discovered the drug culture in Betty's school. Special work was devoted to her learning how her daughter was beginning to socialize with her classmates without becoming involved in drugs. The same problems arose over dates, sex, and driving.

If the parents didn't bring up these issues of growing up, the therapist raised them. Betty was still a reserved young lady. She now had one good girlfriend and had gone to a few carefully screened parties. She baby-sat in the neighborhood and had a regular after school job with a family down the street. She was planning to take a mother's helper job with a family at a nearby lake the next summer. She was studying harder to get into nursing school.

Betty's sister was supportive of Betty's moves and was a model for her parents. She was planning to move to a city several hundred miles away because her husband had a job opportunity there.

Treatment Failures in Avoidant Disorder

Lack of success with avoidant disorder is very much dependent on the ability of the environment to provide suitable opportunities for the patient to experience social relationships and to overcome shyness or anxiety. Successful treatment also depends on the patient having personal assets (e.g., athletic talent is the factor most often related to popularity with peers). The motivation and actual involvement in peer-related activities is essential for a favorable outcome.

Conclusion

Four major treatment approaches have been presented for each of the three DSM-III-R anxiety disorders in childhood and adolescence. The principal differences among the approaches can be seen in the context of the problem. The context of the illness can be viewed from a day in the life of the patient or from a continuum of life events over the years or from the child's experience with others. (Indeed, each approach utilizes other persons in the child's milieu in the diagnostic formulation and treatment, but the selection and degree of involvement varies.)

While the specific approaches are presented to sharpen their differences, in reality there is considerable overlap or blurring of distinctions between them. They had seven features in common. First, each therapist took a more detailed history of the symptoms beyond that given. Second, each spent considerable time building rapport and a therapeutic alliance with the child and family. Since the treatment would cause discomfort, the child's confidence and motivation had to be developed before a specific plan could be fully implemented. Third, all four therapists viewed themselves as coexplorers with the child into the world of anxiety. They entered the child's life by direct discussion of the anxiety, or through play and role play, to repair the damage. Fourth, each worked toward a change in attitude, thinking, and feeling about the self and the illness, with increased autonomy as common goals. Fifth, each used significant others in the child's environment as part of the treatment. Sixth, each was sensitive to the separation of the child from treatment, the need for gradual decrease of therapist assistance, and re-discovery of the outside world. Seventh, while problem solving, encouragement, education, and reward were common elements, exposure to the feared situation was an essential ingredient of all four approaches. In some cases, it was reexperienced; in others, reconstructed or simulated at a distance. In others, it was simply experienced anew with a new psychologic or physiologic threshold.

In summary, specific features differentiate certain techniques from each other, but flexibility of therapist response (i.e., ability to combine and integrate them into a comprehensive treatment plan) is as important as knowledge of specific therapies for specific conditions. A universal component of all is some degree of therapeutically designed, graduated exposure to the feared situation, which is necessary to produce relief of anxiety and decreasing avoidance of the feared situation. This exposure can be actual, imaginary, or symbolic. In all cases, however, understanding the problem was translated into change in behavior.

It would appear that until specificity of treatment technique for the anxiety disorder is developed under a unifying theoretical framework, the clinician must be able to think about a symptom at multiple conceptual levels to find the best "fit" with the needs of the individual patient. This goes beyond the pursuit of different pathways to achieve the same goal. It involves the use of a multimodal treatment program. It means that the knowledge and skill to combine and integrate various therapeutic strategies is necessary in a contemporary psychiatrist who undertakes the treatment of anxiety disorders in children. The ability to assess biological factors (e.g., autonomic symptoms) is critical in developing the treatment approach, as is the assessment of the contribution of psychosocial stresses (e.g., divorce). The final common pathway for choosing or combining the various therapeutic techniques to mold a personal therapeutic amalgam is sound clinical judgment.

References

Section 5
Anxiety Disorders of Childhood or Adolescence

Achenbach TM, Edelbrock CS: The child behavior profile, II: boys aged 12–16 and girls aged 6–11 and 12–16. J Consult Clin Psychol 47:2, 1979

American Psychiatric Association: Diagnostic and Statistical Manual of Mental Disorders, 3rd ed. Washington, DC, American Psychiatric Association, 1980

American Psychiatric Association: Diagnostic and Statistical Manual of Mental Disorders, 3rd ed, revised. Washington, DC, American Psychiatric Association, 1987

Barrios BA, Hartman DP, Shigetomi C: Fears and anxieties in children, in Behavioral Assessment of Childhood Disorders. Edited by Mash EJ, Terdal LG. New York, Guilford Press, 1981

Bloch S: Psychotherapy, in Recent Advances in Clinical Psychiatry, vol 4. Edited by Granville-Grossman K. Edinburgh, Churchill Livingstone, 1982

Bozsormenyi-Nagy I, Spark G: Invisible Loyalties. New York, Harper & Row, 1973

Bowlby J: Attachment and Loss, Vol 2: Separation, Anxiety and Anger. London, Hogarth Press, 1973

Charney DS, Redmond DE: Neurobiological mechanisms in human anxiety. Neuropharmacology 22:1531–1536, 1983

Coffey B, Shader Rl, Greenblatt DJ: Pharmacokinetics of benzodiazepines and psychostimulants in children. J Clin Psychopharmacol 3:217–225, 1983

Conners CK: A teacher rating scale for use in drug studies with children. Am J Psychiatry 126:884–888, 1969

Costa E: Coexistence of putative neuromodulators in the same axon: pharmacological consequences at receptors, in Co-Transmission. Edited by Cuello AC. London, Macmillan, 1982

Doris J, McIntrye A, Tamaroff M: Separation anxiety in preschool children, in Handbook on Stress and Anxiety. Edited by Kutash IL, Schlesinger LB, et al. San Francisco: Jossey-Bass, 1980

Finch AJ, Montgomery LE, Deardorf PA: Reliability of state-trait anxiety with emotionally disturbed children. J Am Acad Child Psychiatry 2:67–69, 1974

Gittelman R, Klein DF: Childhood separation anxiety and adult agoraphobia, in Anxiety and the Anxiety Disorders. Edited by Tuma AH, Maser JD. Hillsdale, NJ, Lawrence Erlbaum Associates, 1985

Gittelman-Klein R: Psychopharmacological treatment of anxiety disorders, mood disorders, and Tourette's disorder in children, in Psychopharmacology: A Generation of Progress. Edited by Lipton MA, MiMascio A, Killam KF, New York, Raven Press, 1978

Gittelman-Klein R, Klein DF: School phobia: diagnostic considerations in the light of the imipramine effects. J Nerv Ment Dis 150:199–215, 1973

Greenacre P: The predisposition to anxiety. Psychoanal Q 10:66–94, 1941

Group for the Advancement of Psychiatry: Psychopathological Disorders in Childhood: Theoretical Considerations and a Proposed Classification (report 62). New York, Group for the Advancement of Psychiatry, 1966

Haefely WE: Biological basis of the therapeutic effects of benzodiazepines, in Benzodiazepines Today and Tomorrow: Proceedings of the First International Symposium on Benzodiazepine in Rio de Janeiro. Edited by Priest RG, Filho UV, Amrein R et al. Baltimore, University Park Press, 1979

Hlusko P: Benzodiazepines and children. International Drug Therapy Newsletter 17:7, 1982

Hockfelt T, Lundbert JM, Schultzberg M, et al: Coexistence of peptides and putative transmitters in neurons. Adv Biochem Psychopharmacol 22:1–23, 1980

Hoehn-Saric R: Neurotransmitters in anxiety. Arch Gen Psychiatry 39:635–642, 1982

Insel TR, Ninan PT, Aloi J, et al: A benzodiazepine receptor mediated model of anxiety. Arch Gen Psychiatry 41:741–750, 1984

Jacobides GM: Some salient clinical findings from the use of benzodiazepines in childhood and adolescence, in Benzodiazepines: Today and Tomorrow. Edited by Priest EG, Filho UV, Amrein R, et al. Baltimore, University Park Press, 1980

Johnson SB, Melamed BG: The assessment and treatment of children's fears, in Advances in Clinical Child Psychology, vol 2. Edited by Lahey BB, Kazdin AE. New York, Plenum, 1979

Karoly P: Self management problems in children, in Behavioral Assessment of Childhood Disorders. Edited by Mash EJ, Terdal LG. New York, Guilford Press, 1981

Klein DF: Anxiety reconceptualized, in Anxiety: New Research and Changing Concepts. Edited by Klein DF, Rabkin JG. New York, Raven Press, 1981

Klein DF, Gittelman R, Quitkin F, et al: Diagnosis and Drug Treatment of Psychiatric Disorders: Adults and Children. Baltimore, Williams & Wilkins Co, 1980

Lang PJ: In state of the art conference reviews new developments in characterizing, treatment anxiety. Hosp Community Psychiatry 35:9–10, 1984

Lewis M: Principles of intensive individual psychoanalytic psychotherapy with children, in Anxiety Disorders of Childhood. Edited by Gittelman R, 1980

Mahler MS, Pine F, Bergman A: The Psychological Birth of the Human Infant: Symbiosis and Individuation. New York, Basic Books, 1975

Mavissakalian M, Perel JM, Michelson L: The relationship of plasma imipramine and N-desmethylimipramine to improvement in agoraphobia. J Clin Psychopharmacol 4:36–40, 1984

McDermott JF, Werry JS, Petti TA, et al: Anxiety disorders, in Psychiatry. Edited by Cavenar J, Michels R. New York, JB Lippincott Co, 1987

Minuchin S, Baker L, Rosman BL: Psychosomatic Families. Cambridge, Harvard University Press, 1978

Petti TA: Imipramine in the treatment of depressed children, in Affective Disorders in Childhood and Adolescence. Edited by Cantwell DP, Carlson GA. New York, Spectrum Publications, 1983

Petti TA, Conners CK: Changes in behavioral ratings of depressed children treated with imipramine. J Am Acad Child Psychiatry 22:355–360, 1983

Petti TA, Law W: Imipramine treatment of depressed children: a double-blind pilot study. J Clin Psychopharmacol 2:107–110, 1982

Petti TA, Sallee FR: Issues in childhood and adolescent psychopharmacology, in Advances in Learning and Behavioral Disabilities. Edited by Gadow KD, Poling AD. Greenwich, Conn, JAI Press, 1986

Preskorn SH, Weller EB, Weller RA, et al: Plasma levels of imipramine and adverse effects in children. Am J Psychiatry 140:1332–1335, 1983

Puig-Antich J, Perel J, Lupatkin W, et al: Imipramine in prepubertal major depressive disorders. Arch Gen Psychiatry 44:81–89, 1987

Rapoport JL, Mikkelsen EJ, Werry JS: Antimanic, antianxiety, hallucinogenic and miscellaneous drugs, in Pediatric Psychopharmacology. Edited by Werry JS, New York, Brunner/Mazel, 1978

Rapoport J, Elkins R, Mikkelsen E, et al: Clinical controlled trial of chlorimipramine in adolescents with obsessive-compulsive disorder. Psychopharmacol Bull 16:61–63, 1980

Redmond DE: Neurochemical basis for anxiety and anxiety disorders: evidence from drugs which decrease human fear or anxiety, in Anxiety and the Anxiety Disorders. Edited by Tuma AH, Maser J. Hillsdale, NJ, Lawrence Erlbaum Associates, 1985

Richter NC: Efficacy of relaxation training with children. J Abnorm Child Psychol 12:319–344, 1984

Rickels K: Benzodiazepines in the treatment of anxiety: North American experiences, in The Benzodiazepines from Molecular Biology to Clinical Practice. Edited by Costa E. New York, Raven Press, 1983

Robins LN: Follow-up studies, in Psychopathological Disorders of Childhood, 2nd ed. Edited by Quay HC, Werry JS. New York, John Wiley & Sons, 1979

Sarason SB, Davidson KS, Lighthall FF, et al: Anxiety in Elementary School Children. New York, John Wiley & Sons, 1960

Schroeder JS, Mullin AV, Elliott GR, et al: Cardiovascular effects of desipramine in children with eating disorders or ADD. J Am Acad Child and Adolescent Psychiatry (in press, May 1989 vol. 28, no. 3)

Settlage CF: Pathogenesis in the Separation-Individuation Process of a Three-Year-Old. Presented at the Annual Meeting of the American Academy of Child Psychiatry. San Francisco, October 28, 1983

Shapiro T: Developmental considerations in psychopharmacology, in Psychopharmacology in Childhood and Adolescence. Edited by Wiener JM. New York, Basic Books, 1977

Sheehan DV, Ballenger J, Jacobson G: Treatment of endogeneous anxiety with phobic, hysterical and hypochondriacal symptoms. Arch Gen Psychiatry 37:51–59, 1980

Sheehan DV, Davidson J, Manschreck T, et al: Lack of efficacy of a new antidepressant (Bupropion) in the treatment of panic disorders with phobias. J Clin Psychopharmacol 3:28–31, 1983

Spielberger CD: Preliminary manual for the state-trait anxiety inventory for children ("How I Feel Questionnaire"). Palo Alto, Calif, Consulting Psychologists Press, 1973

Spitz R: The First Year of Life. New York, International Universities Press, 1965

Spitzer RL, Skodol AE, Gibbon M, et al: DSM-III Case Book, 1st ed. Washington DC, American Psychiatric Association, 1981

Stein L, Beluzzi JD, Wise D: Benzodiazepines: behavioral or neurochemical mechanisms. Am J Psychiatry 134:665–669, 1977

Taylor DP, Riblet LA, Stanton HC: Dopamine and anxiolytics, in Anxiolytics: Neurochemical, Behavioral and Clinical Perspectives. Edited by Malic JB, Enna SJ, Yamamura HI. New York, Raven Press, 1983

Thyer BA, Parrish RT, Curtis GC, et al: Ages of onset of DSM-III anxiety disorders. Compr Psychiatry 26:113–122, 1985

Ultee CA, Griffisen D, Schellenkens J: The reduction of anxiety in children: a comparison of the effects of systematic desensitization in vitro and systematic desensitization in vivo. Behav Res Ther 20:61–67, 1982

Usdin E: Anxiolytics: an overview, in Anxiolytics: Neurochemical, Behavioral and Clinical Perspectives. Edited by Malick JB, Enna SJ, Yamamura HL. New York, Raven Press, 1983

Weller EB, Weller RA, Preskorn SH, et al: Steady-state plasma levels in prepubertal depressed children. Am J Psychiatry 139:506–508, 1982

Werry JS: Family therapy: behavioral approaches. J Am Acad Child Psychiatry 18:91–102, 1979

Werry JS, Aman MG: Anxiety in children, in Handbook of Studies on Anxiety. Edited by Burrows GD, Davies B. Amsterdam, Elsevier/North Holland, 1980

Whalen CK, Henker B: Psychostimulants in children: a review and analysis. Psychol Bull 3:1113–1130, 1976

Williams DT, Mehl R, Yudofsky S, et al: The effect of propranolol on uncontrolled rage outbursts in children and adolescents with organic brain dysfunction. J Am Acad Child Psychiatry 2:129–135, 1982.

Eating Disorders

Chapter 55

Introduction

Anorexia nervosa, bulimia, pica, rumination disorder, and atypical eating disorders are disturbances in eating behavior that have been studied comprehensively and with systematic methodologies only recently. These eating behavior conditions are entities and not diseases with a common cause, common course, and common pathology. The eating disorders are best conceptualized as syndromes and therefore must be classified on the basis of the cluster of symptoms that are present. Since the DSM-III (American Psychiatric Association 1980) was published, information from current investigations made many of us realize that the criteria for anorexia nervosa and bulimia ought to be revised. The current recommendations from the DSM-III-R (American Psychiatric Association 1987) for criteria for anorexia nervosa and bulimia nervosa are listed in Table 1.

The changes in some of the criteria for anorexia nervosa and bulimia nervosa do not affect the treatment approaches for these disorders. Since this volume discusses the treatment of these disorders, it is not appropriate to have a lengthy discourse on the rationale for criterion changes. A discussion of the problems with the DSM-III-R classification for these disorders can be found elsewhere (Halmi 1985).

Treatment of an eating disorder allows one to indulge in the use of a variety of therapeutic skills. Although there are very few controlled treatment studies of the eating disorders, accumulated clinical experience has led to the development of multifaceted treatment programs. The necessity of having to use a variety of treatment modalities is emphasized in most of the specific treatment chapters that follow. An effort has been made to be as objective and critical as possible in lieu of the sparse experimental proof of efficacy of any particular modality.

Continued refinement of diagnostic classification and treatment techniques for the eating disorders is necessary. We need longitudinal studies on normal weight bulimics to compare their long-term outcome with the outcomes of exclusively dieting anorectics and bulimic-anorectics to determine if separate classifications are justified for these disorders. Perhaps we will find that subtypes of classifications will be necessary. There is a need for controlled studies of treatment efficacy in the eating disorders. Even careful follow-up studies of a particular type of treatment approach would be useful. The question of whether one should immediately hospitalize an anorectic for medical treatment or try to accomplish weight gain in outpatient treatment needs to be answered. Which technique is best for long-term outcome? What can we do to prevent relapses in both anorexia nervosa and bulimia nervosa? How long should bulimic patients be maintained on antidepressant medication? The clinician who wishes to refer an eating disorder patient for treatment should use good critical judgment in evaluating the available choice of treatment programs. The chap-

---

Table 1. DSM-III-R Diagnostic Criteria for Eating Disorders

307.10 Anorexia Nervosa

A. Refusal to maintain body weight over a minimal normal weight for age and height, e.g., weight loss leading to maintenance of body weight 15% below that expected; or failure to make expected weight gain during period of growth, leading to body weight 15% below that expected.

B. Intense fear of gaining weight or becoming fat, even though underweight.

C. Disturbance in the way in which one's body weight, size, or shape is experienced, e.g., the person claims to "feel fat" even when emaciated, believes that one area of the body is "too fat" even when obviously underweight.

D. In females, absence of at least three consecutive menstrual cycles when otherwise expected to occur (primary or secondary amenorrhea). (A woman is considered to have amenorrhea if her periods occur only following hormone, e.g., estrogen, administration.)

307.51 Bulimia Nervosa

A. Recurrent episodes of binge eating (rapid consumption of a large amount of food in a discrete period of time).

B. A feeling of lack of control over eating behavior during the eating binges.

C. The person regularly engages in either self-induced vomiting, use of laxatives or diuretics, strict dieting or fasting, or vigorous exercise in order to prevent weight gain.

D. A minimum average of two binge eating episodes a week for at least three months.

E. Persistent overconcern with body shape and weight.

307.50 Eating Disorder Not Otherwise Specified

Disorders of eating that do not meet the criteria for a specific eating disorder.

Examples:

1. a person of average weight who does not have binge eating episodes, but frequently engages in self-induced vomiting for fear of gaining weight
2. all of the features of anorexia nervosa in a female except absence of menses
3. all of the features of bulimia nervosa except the frequency of binge eating episodes.

---

ters in this volume should provide the information necessary for a thorough critical assessment of eating disorder treatment programs.

Chapter 56

Medical Evaluation and Management

Assessment of Medical Status

The medical assessment of the patient with anorexia nervosa must begin with a physical examination. The profound emaciation in these patients is often the most striking finding to the examining physician. The patient's height and weight should be measured and compared with figures from charts matching the patient's age, height, and frame size. Thus the physician may get an estimate of the degree of emaciation.

Skin changes such as dryness, scaliness, and poor tone reflect the patient's state of malnutrition and dehydration. Lanugo, or fine soft hair, may cover the skin surfaces. In the oral cavity, dental caries and mucosal changes may be present secondary to poor nutrition or, more frequently, to chronic self-induced vomiting (Hellstrom 1977). Enlarged salivary glands are associated with vomiting behavior (Hasler 1982). Hand lesions (Russell's sign) may be evident in the form of calluses, sometimes crusted or ulcerated, over the knuckles of patients who self-induce vomiting (Russell 1979).

Changes in cardiac status are also commonly present. The most common are bradycardia and hypotension. Arrhythmias and other changes may be present in the electrocardiogram (EKG), which should be done on all patients. EKG changes are especially prevalent in the patient who has a history of purging behavior, (i.e, laxative or diuretic abuse or self-induced vomiting), where EKG changes may be reflective of electrolyte imbalance (Thurston and Marks 1974). However, a study employing Holter monitor EKG indicated that potentially fatal arrhythmias may arise without evidence of hypokalemia in patients who binge and purge, whether they be emaciated or within a normal weight range (Zucker 1984).

Laboratory Tests

Many of the physiologic changes seen in anorexia nervosa are reflected in abnormal laboratory values. Most of the changes described below are a result of starvation or of purging behavior. The metabolic aberrations due to starvation return to normal with nutritional rehabilitation.

451

Hematology.   The hematologic profile of the patient with anorexia nervosa often reveals a severe leukopenia with relative lymphocytosis. Some studies have shown bone marrow hypoplasia in anorexia nervosa. However, all studies indicate a return to normal bone marrow morphology after refeeding (Carryer et al. 1959; Lampert and Lau 1976).

Whether the leukopenia places the anorectic patient at an increased risk of infection has been studied by several investigators. Peripheral blood leukocytes show a reduced in vitro bactericidal capacity, which is reversed by weight restoration. Despite frequent and often severe leukopenia, patients with anorexia nervosa appear to have no more infections than normal controls (Bowers and Eckert 1978). However, due to the reduced bactericidal capacity, the morbidity risk may be significantly greater in those anorectic patients that do develop infections.

A low erythrocyte sedimentation rate is commonly seen in emaciated anorectics (Anyan 1974). The low rate may be helpful in distinguishing the patient with anorexia nervosa from a patient presenting with weight loss due to an occult malignancy, hyperthyroidism, Crohn's disease, or chronic infection.

When evaluating the anorectic patients' red cell indices, one must keep in mind that the values may be elevated secondary to dehydration. Anemias secondary to malnutrition states should thus be evaluated on rehydration. As with the other indices, the anemic states are correctable by nutritional rehabilitation.

Bleeding and clotting studies, including bleeding time, prothrombin time, partial thromboplastin time, clot retraction, and platelet counts, are typically within normal limits in patients with anorexia nervosa.

Serum electrolytes.   Many patients with anorexia nervosa and with bulimia nervosa engage in self-induced vomiting and/or abuse laxatives and diuretics. These patients are susceptible to developing hypokalemic alkalosis and present with an elevated serum bicarbonate, hypochloremia, and hypokalemia. One may see a metabolic acidosis with a low serum bicarbonate in laxative abusers. In addition to direct loss of potassium by vomiting, fasting and subsequent dehydration may cause an indirect loss of potassium through renal mechanisms (Mitchell et al. 1983). Symptoms of electrolyte imbalance include weakness, lethargy, and in some cases disturbances of cardiac rhythm.

Blood glucose.   During the emaciated state, anorectic patients show a low fasting blood glucose. These values return toward normal with refeeding. Low fasting serum glucose levels are observed in most emaciated states.

Enzymes.   Elevations of enzymes in the serum are not uncommon in anorexia nervosa. Serum glutamic-oxalacetic transaminase (SGOT), lactate dehydrogenase (LDH), and alkaline phosphatase are the enzymes most frequently elevated. It is worth noting that these enzyme levels may actually increase over the course of refeeding, perhaps reflecting some fatty degeneration of the liver. An elevated alkaline phosphatase may represent changes in bone metabolism in anorexia nervosa patients. It is known that osteoporosis may develop in anorexic patients, especially in those who have a history of chronic vomiting. In some cases, symptoms of pain led to appropriate X rays, which showed rib fractures, hip fracture, and compression fractures of the vertebra (Halmi and Falk 1981; McArney 1983). One should bear in mind that radiographic changes indicative of osteoporosis are evident only after marked calcium loss has already occurred.

Serum bilirubin, total protein, and serum albumin levels are usually within the normal range and remain so throughout the course of treatment (Halmi and Falk 1981).

Serum amylase. Serum amylase levels, especially salivary and sometimes pancreatic, are commonly elevated in those patients who self-induce vomiting (Mitchell et al. 1983). These values return to normal with cessation of the vomiting behavior. Thus serum amylase values may serve as a useful indicator of the patient's progress in treatment.

Cases have been reported of refeeding pancreatitis in patients who have been refed too rapidly. Thus a gradual approach to refeeding and prompt investigation of pancreatic enzymes for complaints of abdominal pain are recommended.

Blood urea nitrogen and serum creatinine. Blood urea nitrogen values may vary widely and reflect the hydration state of the patient. Serum creatinine levels are generally within the normal range and remain so throughout treatment.

Serum carotene. Carotenemia is sometimes present in anorexia nervosa and may represent an acquired but reversible error of metabolism of β-carotene and vitamin A precursors in anorexia nervosa (Robboy et al. 1974).

Serum cholesterol. Serum cholesterol and triglyceride levels vary widely in anorexia nervosa. Elevations in serum cholesterol levels may reflect a diminished cholesterol turnover secondary to a delayed low-density lipoprotein metabolism (Mordasini et al. 1978).

Endocrine Assessment

Amenorrhea is a major diagnostic symptom of anorexia nervosa. The loss of menses in these patients may precede actual weight loss. The return of the menstrual cycle lags behind the return of normal body weight after treatment and the timing of its return is associated with marked psychological improvement (Falk and Halmi 1982). Urinary secretion and plasma levels of gonadotropins are decreased in anorexia nervosa. Current evidence suggests that the age-inappropriate luteinizing hormone secretion pattern seen in anorexia nervosa is multidetermined and not solely based on weight loss (Weiner 1983).

A lower than normal value of triiodothyronine and a normal thyrotropin reserve reflect the hypometabolic state associated with anorexia nervosa and are not unique to the disorder. Thyrotropin-stimulating hormone response to thyrotropin-releasing hormone may be delayed in a majority of patients with anorexia nervosa.

The incomplete suppression of adrenocorticotropic hormone and cortisol levels by dexamethasone and the reduced metabolic clearance rate of cortisol are seen in protein calorie malnutrition as well as in anorexia nervosa. The adrenal secretory activity returns to normal with weight recovery (Halmi and Sherman 1979).

It has been estimated that about one-third of patients with anorexia nervosa have elevated levels of growth hormone. Although increased levels of growth hormone are seen in protein calorie malnutrition, there are additional aberrations of growth hormone regulation in anorexia nervosa. Anorectics, both in the emaciated and weight-recovered state, have an impaired growth hormone response to L-dopa, apomorphine, and insulin. This abnormality is also present in some patients with depression (Halmi and Sherman 1979).

Electroencephalogram

Electroencephalogram (EEG) abnormalities such as epileptiform dysrhythmias, 6/sec spike and wave, and 6 to 14/sec spikes have been described in both anorexia nervosa and in association with bingeing and purging behavior irrespective of weight status. The clinical significance of these findings is unclear but abnormalities on EEG were greatest in those patients who were engaged in purging behaviors (Crisp et al. 1968; Shimoda and Kitagawa 1973).

Computed Tomography Scans

The routine use of computed tomography (CT) in anorexia nervosa and bulimia nervosa patients is not indicated. CT scans should be saved for those patients who present with unusual signs or symptoms or who are particularly intractable to treatment. While some studies have reported abnormalities in cranial CT scans in some patients with anorexia nervosa, these abnormalities often revert to normal with adequate nutritional rehabilitation. The abnormalities present do not suggest any specific treatment approach (Heinz et al. 1977).

Medical Treatment

Treatment of anorexia nervosa must begin with a return of the patient to a medically sound weight. This should be accomplished by a slow gradual weight gain. Attempts at too rapid weight restoration may result in acute gastric dilatation, signs of congestive heart failure, or refeeding pancreatitis (Schoette 1979). If the anorectic is only 15 to 20 percent below a normal weight range and is not vomiting or abusing laxatives, an outpatient program with behavior contingencies is likely to be effective for inducing weight gain. Due to the severity of the illness and the difficulty in treatment of these patients, refeeding can often best be accomplished in the hospital. Liquid dietary formulas, such as Sustacal and Ensure, have treatment advantages in the nutritional rehabilitation. The formulas are nutritionally balanced, easily tolerated, and often easier for the emaciated anorectic to accept. A safe rate of weight gain is 1/4 lb/day. Refeeding with these formulas also aids in rehydration of the patient and obviates the need for intravenous fluids to correct electrolyte imbalances in most cases. These liquid formulas also offer adequate vitamin and iron supplementation for the patient. Patients may be kept on the dietary formulas until they reach a normal weight range. They are then ready for the next step in nutritional rehabilitation: the transition to nutritionally balanced trays of food of sufficient calories to maintain their weight. Once comfortable with eating from the prepared trays of food, the patient makes the transition to choosing his or her own diet freely. The use of behavioral therapy techniques, such as having the patient observed after meals, and the use of commodes that the patient has the responsibility for cleaning is often quite successful in eliminating vomiting behavior. The structured setting of the inpatient unit prevents the use of laxatives. Often patients on liquid formulas, particularly those with a previous history of laxative abuse or those who are placed on medications with anticholinergic properties, may benefit from the use of stool softeners such as docusate sodium. These can usually be discontinued once the patients resume a normal diet. The risks associated with hyperalimentation are considerable and alternative methods of weight gain should be considered (see Chapter 60).

With refeeding, most laboratory values return to normal as the patient approaches to a healthy weight. During the active refeeding phase, values of SGOT, LDH, and alkaline phosphatase may increase.

Most cases of metabolic alkalosis will respond to a refeeding program as outlined above. In severe cases, hospitalization on a medical ward for correction of acid-base imbalance is indicated. In such severe cases, changes in the cardiac conduction system must also be monitored closely. For complicated cardiac problems, of course, a cardiologist should be consulted.

The time that the patient will experience a return of her menstrual period cannot be predicted as weight gain alone does not ensure its return. The resumption of menstruation is correlated with psychological improvement in the weight-restored patient. Estrogen-progesterone combinations should not be used to induce menses unless the patient has maintained a normal weight for at least six months without bingeing and purging and has shown psychological improvement.

Chapter 57

Hospital Treatment

Sir William Gull (1874) laid the foundation for modern knowledge of both the clinical course and inpatient treatment of anorexia nervosa. Although much information has been gained since then about anorexia nervosa, its fundamental cause remains unknown, and Gull's principles of treatment remain valid. This disorder is often a serious and prolonged one, with a death rate reported in the past to be as high as 15 percent. Among the significant therapeutic challenges posed by anorexia nervosa to clinicians, the most common are: 1) increasing the weight of the emaciated patient, 2) treating the individual's multiple psychological symptoms, 3) treating the distressed family, and 4) providing long-term maintenance of inpatient improvement.

The landmark papers of Gull (1874) and Lasegue (1873) serve as models of astute approaches to treatment. Gull advocated sequential stages of treatment, proceeding from intensive nutritional rehabilitation to dealing with the psychological dysfunction of the patient. Lasegue richly described the pitfalls the physicians face in underestimating the intensity of the anorectic illness and described in comprehensive fashion the complex interaction between patients and their families. More recently, Lucas (1981) reviewed changing concepts of the origin of anorexia nervosa. An important point that should be drawn from his article, and from the history of medicine in general, is that one's beliefs about the origin of illness often guide the kind of practice chosen. These etiologic assumptions need to be carefully examined because they serve to generate treatment methods.

The Problem of Low Weight and Starvation

Tables 1 through 4 summarize methods used to increase weight in starved anorectic patients. Each category of treatment is described in terms of the underlying beliefs, the practice methods, the advantages and disadvantages, and specific examples.

Nutritional rehabilitation by nursing staff. Gull (1874), Russell (1973), and Andersen (1985) advocated a nursing-supervised refeeding. This method is historically validated and begins by removing the patient from the family situation to an inpatient setting. Refeeding takes place by encouraging patients to eat in an atmosphere that is supportive but carefully supervised. The assumption is that patients are too ill to choose appropriate kinds and quantities of food but that these choices may be gradually returned to them as weight is regained. Gull summarized his approach as follows: "The patients should be fed at regular intervals, and surrounded by persons who would have more control over them, relations and friends being generally the worst attendants." Russell continued this approach: "Nowadays the principles enumerated by Gull . . . are best applied by means of skilled nursing care" (Table 1).

Behavioral treatment. Systematic behavioral modification programs for weight gain were initially described in the 1970s by several investigators (e.g, Garfinkel et al. 1977; Stunkard 1972) and then later refined (Halmi 1984b). These treatments induced weight gain by using principles of operant conditioning. This method rewards healthy behavior by the gaining of privileges, by praise, and by decreasing aversive situations such as restriction of mobility. Some principles of a behavioral treatment plan are implicit in virtually all programs (Table 2). Behavioral modification methods differ from these general programs by systematically structuring the method of weight gain with specification of the exact weight that must be gained to achieve progressive privileges. This approach can be carried out in general medical or pediatric units as well as in psychiatric facilities (see Chapter 60).

Medication. Table 3 summarizes some principles associated with the use of medication to increase weight (see Chapter 59).

Table 1. Methods of Weight Gain in Anorexia Nervosa: Nursing-Supervised Refeeding

Underlying beliefs:	Patient assumed to be temporarily unable to choose necessary food because of medical and psychological dysfunction. Decision about food and weight initially given to staff.
Practice methods:	Nurses sit with patients during and after meals for support and supervision. Decisions about eating gradually returned to patient. Intermediate in rate of weight gain.
Advantages:	Safe. Effective for most patients. Few medical complications. Patients learn to eat normally.
Disadvantages:	Requires large, well-trained staff. Occasional near-terminal patient may be unsuitable.
Examples:	Gull (1874) Russell (1973) Andersen (1985)

Table 2.   Methods of Weight Gain in Anorexia Nervosa: Behavioral Reinforcement of Weight Gain

Underlying beliefs:	Abnormal feeding behavior and low weight may be corrected by positively reinforcing weight gain. Assumes weight loss is learned behavior.
Practice methods:	Required daily or weekly weight gain rewarded and reinforced by acquiring privileges. Negative reinforcement may be used for lack of weight gain.
Advantages:	Smaller staff required. May be accomplished in psychiatric or medical setting. Weight gain substantial in many patients. Often combined with other methods of treatment.
Disadvantages:	Patients may learn tricks to fake weight gain, and sometimes "eat their way" out of hospital. May be very impersonal, if used as the sole treatment modality.
Examples:	Stunkard (1972) Halmi (1984a) Garfinkel et al. (1977)

Table 3.   Methods of Weight Gain in Anorexia Nervosa: Medication to Induce or Assist Weight Gain

Underlying beliefs:	1) Weight loss due to subtle neurologic dysfunction in hypothalamus; or 2) medication may empirically produce weight gain; or 3) depressive illness underlies anorectic symptoms.
Practice methods:	Medications prescribed with monitoring of therapeutic levels.
Advantages:	Small staff required. Medical-pediatric wards may be used. Often combined with other methods.
Disadvantages:	Does not deal with psychological issues and cannot be used as the sole treatment modality because it does not teach normal pattern of eating. May induce compensatory behaviors to avoid weight gain (e.g., overexercising, self-induced vomiting).
Examples:	See Chapter 59

Hyperalimentation and nasogastric feeding.   Peripheral or central hyperalimentation or nasogastric feedings have also been employed to induce weight gain (Table 4). Pertschuk et al. (1981) described a program utilizing parenteral nutrition, which resulted in many medical complications. Parenteral feedings should be given only to patients who are severely medically ill and should be terminated as soon as possible. If a patient is completely noncompliant for nutritional intake, it is much safer to use nasogastric feedings than hyperalimentation.

Common problems faced by staff.   Table 5 lists some of the common problems facing the inpatient staff who treat anorexia nervosa. Relatively few research papers have examined the factors that increase or decrease the effectiveness of staff who are the conveyers of the variously described treatment programs. Suggestions are made later about what constitutes an ideal inpatient treatment program from the viewpoint of the staff as well as the patient.

Table 4. Methods of Weight Gain in Anorexia Nervosa: Hyperalimentation or Nasogastric Feeding

Underlying beliefs:	Medical distress of patient requires prompt, intensive nutritional intervention not dependent on patient compliance.
Practice methods:	Balanced, high-calorie refeeding by nasogastric feeding; some restriction of maximum calories and protein intake with hyperalimentation.
Advantages:	Prompt weight gain. Effective in near-comatose, debilitated patients. Does not require psychiatric facilities.
Disadvantages:	Hyperalimentation may have severe medical-metabolic complications. It does not address psychological aspects or teach normal eating and should be used only in desperate medical conditions. Nasogastric feeding is much safer, more cost-efficient, and more practical than hyperalimentation in severely medically ill anorectics.
Examples:	Pertschuk et al. (1981)

Table 5. Common Problems Facing Staff Treating Inpatients with Anorexia Nervosa

1. Lack of comprehensive knowledge about illness.
2. Lack of team orientation to treatment.
3. Noncompliance of patient with weight-gaining programs.
4. Exhaustion from inadequate staffing, unacknowledged countertransference issues, unrealistic expectations.
5. Staff splitting.
6. Weight gain by staff treating anorexia nervosa.
7. Past or present eating disorders in staff.
8. Inadequate facilities.

Treatment of Individual Psychopathology

Most descriptions of inpatient treatments have recognized that nutritional rehabilitation is only part of the treatment and that a change in the psychological status of the patient is of paramount importance. Gull (1874), Lasegue (1873), and virtually all the other historically sound literature have linked methods to produce weight gain with some approach to the treatment of the psychopathology of anorexia nervosa.

Table 6 summarizes the multiple factors contributng to the global psychopathology of patients with anorexia nervosa. The psychological status of an individual admitted to an inpatient unit for treatment of anorexia nervosa derives from multiple sources. Starvation itself has a profound effect, as noted by Keys et al. (1950) in their classic study of experimental starvation. Low weight causes a restriction of affect, preoccupation with thoughts of food, decreased social consciousness, and an immaturity and caricaturing of personality features. If the psychopathology of anorexia nervosa were solely due to starvation, then medical treatments alone would produce enduring improvement. This is not the case, however. Psychological conflicts underly the starvation. Bruch (1978) and Crisp (1980), for example, described somewhat similar approaches to conceptualizing a central dynamic conflict leading to anorexia nervosa.

Table 6. Factors Contributing to Psychopathology of Patients with Anorexia Nervosa

1. Psychological consequences of starvation: anhedonia, restricted affect, preoccupation with thoughts of food, accentuation of obsessional personality features, decreased mental concentration.
2. Central dynamic conflict: the purpose anorexia nervosa serves in the individual's life.
3. Specific symptoms of anorexia nervosa: fear of fatness, pursuit of thinness, severe perceptual distortion (if present).
4. Predisposing personality features: obsessional, histrionic, borderline.
5. Consequences of chronic illness: prolonged dependence; immaturity; change, or lack or progression, in social role.
6. Associated psychiatric syndromes: depressive illness, obsessive-compulsive disorders, anxiety syndromes.
7. Learned misbeliefs from family, peers, or society about the value of thinness.

In addition to this psychodynamic contribution, there are specific psychopathologic symptoms of anorexia nervosa that need to be treated, such as the fear of fatness, the pursuit of thinness, and a distortion of perception. A major contributing factor to the global psychopathology of anorexia nervosa is the predisposing personality of the patient (King 1963). Improvement in the psychopathology of anorexia nervosa must be coupled with a change in the patient's chronic adaptation to illness. Prolonged dependency, immaturity, and lack of progression in social-role development may not improve without specific treatments, even though progress is made in other areas of psychological dysfunction. Occasionally, individuals, in addition to their anorectic symptoms, will meet criteria even after nutritional rehabilitation for a major depressive illness or an obsessive-compulsive disorder. These syndromes must then be treated. Finally, woven in among the multiple factors contributing to the psychopathology of patients with anorexia nervosa are learned misbeliefs from family, peers, and society about the value of thinness, which may need specific treatment. (See specific chapters for strategies taken for the treatment of these multiple psychological aspects of anorexia nervosa found in inpatients.)

One of the biggest changes in the inpatient treatment of psychological aspects of anorexia nervosa in the last decade has been the uniform assertion that psychotherapy must take place along with or after substantial weight gain. Prior to weight gain, psychotherapy is relatively ineffective. The complexity of the mood state of severely ill anorectic patients has been clarified by Eckert et al. (1982) and others who have increased our appreciation of the multiple contributions to the depressed mood of these individuals. A single explanation for the psychological symptoms of patients with anorexia nervosa is no longer tenable.

Families are always involved in the precipitation or maintenance and certainly in the consequences of anorexia nervosa. Many theoretical assumptions exist concerning the role of the family (see Chapter 62). In practice, families generally are exhausted, demoralized, and feel an unnecessary burden of guilt by the time their daughter or son is admitted for treatment. Hedblom et al. (1981) described the need of families for information, support, relief of guilt, problem solving, and preparation for the reintroduction of the anorectic patient after treatment.

Only a long-term follow-up can confirm or refute the benefits of a seemingly effective short-term program for anorexia nervosa. Morgan and Russell (1975) followed 41 patients for an average of four years and described unfavorable predictors as including a relatively late age of onset, chronicity of illness, previous psychiatric treatment on an inpatient service, abnormal relationships within the family, and the presence of a personality disorder. Hsu (1980) criticized many programs for their lack of multiple methods of evaluation and for lack of long-term outcome studies. Steinhausen and Glanville (1983) reviewed follow-up studies of anorexia nervosa treatments and noted the difficulties in evaluation that occur when even a single factor, such as rate of dropouts from treatment, varies from 11 to 77 percent.

Several comprehensive studies of inpatient treatment should be noted. Pierloot et al. (1982) described 145 patients who were treated in two phases, a "symptom-directed" phase and a "problem-oriented" phase, employing a combination of methods for weight gain and psychotherapy of the individual and the family. Lucas et al. (1976) described an integrated program of treatment on an inpatient service. These and other large, experienced programs generally assume a multifactorial origin for anorexia nervosa and employ a multidisciplinary team treatment.

Criteria for Inpatient Treatment

Table 7 summarizes some of the most common reasons for referring anorectic patients for inpatient treatment. Patients with severe weight loss generally require an initial hospital treatment phase. The absolute weight is probably not as important as the level of functioning and the capacity of the individual to benefit from outpatient treatment. As a result of the relentless force of the psychopathology of anorexia nervosa, agreements made during outpatient treatment often cannot be carried out without more structure than is present in the lives of anorectic individuals. There may be agreement about what needs to be done between therapy sessions, but the will to carry out these agreements plummets when the patient is faced with the same circumstances within the self and the everyday environment that have promoted the disorder.

Significant metabolic problems independent of the weight (e.g., hypokalemic alkalosis) may need to be treated on an inpatient basis. These abnormalities may be life threatening. Depressive symptomatology is not as common in the classic food-restricting anorectic as in the anorectic with bulimic complications. Anorectic patients with bulimic complications have truly lost control of their eating in contrast to food restricters (who fear but do not experience the loss of control), and they suffer great psychological distress as a result. Thoughts about suicide and suicide attempts are not uncommon; where present, they should be treated on an inpatient service. At times there may be no single criterion that requires inpatient treatment, but the lack of effective functioning in the life of the patient or the family or the lack of response to outpatient treatment may justify a referral to the inpatient service.

Table 7.   Criteria for Inpatient Treatment of Anorexia Nervosa

1. Low weight.
2. Metabolic abnormalities from illness, especially hypokalemic alkalosis from bulimic complications.
3. Depressed mood; thoughts or intents of suicide.
4. Nonresponsiveness to outpatient treatment.
5. Demoralized, poorly functioning family or hostile, nonsupportive environment.

Inpatient Treatment Program

Since the fundamental causes of anorexia nervosa are not known, confidence regarding ideal treatment must be tempered by reality. Despite this lack of absolute knowledge, however, a pragmatically ideal approach to treatment can be described by synthesizing the results from experienced programs with demonstrated long-term results. It is clear that inpatient treatment has become more and more effective. The death rate has been lowered to close to zero in some programs, even for the most seriously ill patients. Contributing to our understanding of what would constitute an ideal program today are studies such as those by Vandereycken and Pierloot (1983), who identified reasons for dropouts from treatment.

An ideal program should effectively and safely restore weight in an anorectic patient within a few months of admission. The two methods that currently have best demonstrated effectiveness and safety are nutritional rehabilitation by nursing-supervised refeeding or a thoughtfully designed behavioral therapy program. At this writing there is no demonstrated psychopharmacologic agent that reliably increases weight to a clinically significant extent. Some medications may be used as an adjunct to weight-gaining treatment but should not be used alone as the entire method of producing weight gain.

An ideal program recognizes that multiple factors contribute to the complex psychological status of an inpatient and employs appropriate methods to deal with the psychopathology of the patient comprehensively. Psychotherapy should initially be supportive, helping the patient to accept weight gain without excessive fear. An intermediate phase of cognitive therapy may reduce the effects of irrational ideas. The psychotherapy should gradually become more dynamic and attempt to deal with understanding and meeting in other ways the purpose the anorexia nervosa serves in the individual's life. The goal is not to take away anorexia nervosa but to make it unnecessary. Psychotherapy should be nonblaming and flexible, varying with the age, sophistication, and psychological-mindedness of the individual. Psychotherapy needs to be continued after discharge from the hospital.

An ideal program recognizes the importance of the family in the precipitation and maintenance of anorexia nervosa. Such a program includes the family from the very beginning, first in evaluation and then in treatment.

Ideal programs will have multiple goals and use multiple methods of evaluation of outcome. The treatment of patients with anorexia nervosa can be a challenging boost to the morale of the staff or a source of exhaustion and demoralization. The effect of treatment efforts on the part of staff may be related to knowledge about and beliefs about anorexia nervosa. Often staff believe in advance that these patients are unresponsive to treatment and prone to relapse. In fact, there is virtually no aspect of anorexia nervosa that is not potentially responsive to treatment, and the potential for improvement must be emphasized. An intimate knowledge of the natural history of the disorder will lead staff to anticipate problems and see them as symptoms rather than as a frustration of their efforts.

It is vital that team treatment be a reality and not a slogan. Daily rounds that include psychiatrists, psychologists, nursing staff, social worker, occupational therapist, and dietician are essential. Information from individual and family therapy must be coordinated. Anorectic patients have much energy, time, and motivation to resist weight gain because of the fears springing from their illness. Effectively countering these fears requires a coordinated staff. The anorectic symptoms should be the motivation for a therapeutic alliance between patient and staff rather than a source of frustration. Most patients have a sufficient intellectual awareness to recognize that their symptoms are injurious to their long-term health. If they can be given practical reassurance that they will not be made overweight and that whatever purpose the anorexia serves in their life will be met by healthier, more adaptive methods, then they often will engage in treatment. Tinker and Ramer (1983) discussed staff subversion of therapy.

Special Situations

Holmgren et al. (1984) evolved an optimistic but realistic approach toward chronically ill patients. One should distinguish between chronically ill but formerly treated patients and chronically ill individuals who simply never have had the chance for adequate treatment.In some cases, the anorexia nervosa may not have been recognized or treatment facilities may not have existed within the geographic area of the patient. The rehabilitation of chronically ill patients can be very rewarding. The most productive attitude for staff to take toward chronically ill patients is that these are human beings who suffer from potentially treatable symptoms rather than that they have an untreatable disease. Staff, despite psychiatric training, may suffer from the belief that former lack of response by these patients is an indication of the "willfulness" of the patient and that there is a large element of volition in the continuation of chronic anorexia nervosa. Such an unfortunate attitude is not common toward patients with other chronic diseases and should not be taken toward chronic anorectic patients.

Anorectic patients with bulimic complications, as described by Garfinkel et al. (1980), require an integration of techniques that deal with the problems previously mentioned as well as the urge to binge and vomit or to use weight-lowering medication. Staff should recognize not only the overt symptomatology but appreciate differences in the underlying psychopathology of patients with bulimic complications in contrast to the food-restricting anorectic. They often have more histrionic or borderline personality features. It should be remembered that a substantial percentage of patients with anorexia nervosa will go on to develop bulimic complications, although this figure may vary from report to report.

Chapter 58

Outpatient Treatment

Although outpatient treatment is virtually always part of the comprehensive management of patients with anorexia nervosa, there are few descriptions of outpatient programs. The principles of individual psychotherapy with anorectics have been described by Bruch (1973), Crisp (1980), Dally (1969), Garfinkel and Garner (1982), and others, but these descriptions usually do not include specific guidelines for managing outpatients. Family therapists, on the other hand, often manage the patient and the family as outpatients, Minuchin et al. (1978), in particular, managed young, less ill anorectics exclusively as outpatients.

The mainstay of outpatient treatment is often individual psychotherapy. Traditional insight-oriented psychotherapy has been found to be ineffective in anorexia nervosa and modifications have been proposed by Hilda Bruch (1973). She posited that there are two types of behavior in a child: those that are self-initiated and those in response to the expectations of others. The potential anorectic grows up in a family that rarely responds to child-initiated cues, and the youngster grows up responding to the needs and expectations of others, unaware of his or her own thoughts, feelings, and wishes. The psychotherapeutic approach that Bruch thinks is most effective is one that combines reeducative techniques with nurturance of the sense of identity that emerges during therapy. This approach requires that the therapist be willing to educate the patient about psychotherapy and to correct misconceptions while simultaneously encouraging the patient to recognize and identify his or her own thoughts and feelings.

In a similar vein, Selvini-Palazzoli (1978) identified a maldevelopment in early object relations that results in a mind-body split in the anorectic patient. The anorectic comes to equate the body with the bad incorporated object (usually the mother), which is conceptualized and felt as a negative overpowering force. Unconsciously, the emerging anorectic concludes it is better to oppose this force (the body) and separate it from the mind (the ego). According to this theory, the body becomes a symbol for all the drives experienced by the person. From this formulation, it follows that individual psychotherapy must include measures that serve simultaneously to reunite the mind-body dichotomy while improving object relations. Like Bruch (1973), Selvini-Palazzoli (1978a) recommended reeducative techniques that actively enlist the patient's cooperation and correct the misconceptions that result in the mind-body split.

Although Gull (1868) initially proposed isolation from the family and "parentectomy" has recently been suggested for certain patients (Harper 1983), family therapy in the management of anorexia nervosa is often crucial. In fact, it was disappointment with the results of individual psychotherapy that resulted in Selvini-Palazzoli's (1978) interest in family structure and functioning. Minuchin et al. (1978) described five characteristics of families with an anorectic member: enmeshment, overprotection, rigidity, lack of conflict resolution, and involvement of the anorectic in the regulation of family conflict. Enmeshment refers to a transactional style in which the boundaries between members are inappropriately blurred or diffuse. Hoffman (1975) has described an enmeshed system as one that is "too richly cross-joined." The family therapists contend that removing one member from an enmeshed family is not only met with marked resistance, but, even if successful, may be devastating to the anorectic who is incapable of functioning outside the family. Furthermore, even in those patients in whom a sense of self is nurtured through individual psychotherapy, failure to attend to family issues may be disastrous since the intensity of the family's influence is much more powerful than generally recognized. The newly emancipated but fragile anorectic may return to the same enmeshed family. Although initial claims for success with family therapy for anorexia nervosa were overenthusiastic and the methods recommended often flamboyant, occasionally with underlying rigid conflicts about family functioning, current family theorists and practitioners have provided flexible practical guidelines for the assessment of families and utilization of their strengths in promoting recovery (Miller 1984). Attention to family issues in the context of individual psychotherapy when the family is unable or unwilling actually to be in the room has also been proposed to improve outcome (Chabot 1983).

Although there is much disagreement about the treatment of anorexia nervosa, authorities agree that it is crucial to restore weight to normal for the psychological or etiologic issues to be successfully addressed. Since, by definition, anorectics resist weight restoration, outpatient treatment can be quite difficult. Crisp (1980) stated that the anorectic patient's weight must be restored to normal before the patient can begin to grapple with adolescent conflicts, the fear of which precipitated the weight loss. Garfinkel and Garner (1982) reemphasized the psychological consequences of semi-starvation that were initially described by Keys et al. (1950). These include obsessions, compulsive handling of food, irritability, and egocentricity. Since all of these symptoms may decrease with weight gain, prompt weight restoration is crucial.

Evaluation Phase

Initial evaluation as an outpatient includes a thorough psychiatric and medical history, family evaluation, mental status examination, evaluation of body image, anthropometric measures, physical examination, selected psychological testing, and laboratory evaluation. The initial evaluation can be facilitated by collecting demographic and symptom information by questionnaire. This information can include demographic data, diagnostic information, and data on weight, binge-eating, and purging behavior. During the initial interview, a complete psychiatric history is obtained, including the individual, family, and cultural factors that facilitated weight loss and those factors that promote its maintenance. Some patients who present symptoms of eating disorders have other psychiatric disorders that are primary; these need to be identified. Schizophrenia, depression, and conversion disorders are the most common. Occasionally, anorexia may coexist with another psychiatric disorder. A complete history of possible organic causes of weight loss (e.g., malignancies, gastrointestinal conditions, certain endocrinopathies) and the consequences of weight loss and abnormal eating and purging behavior need to be obtained.

A mental status examination should be a routine part of the initial interview in which the examiner looks particularly for mood disturbances, thought disorders, delusions, misperceptions (including misperceptions about body size), and certain cognitive distortions.

Garner and Bemis (1982) identified common cognitive distortions in anorexia nervosa (see Chapter 61). In terms of treatment, identification of these cognitive disturbances is important. Some of the distorted beliefs about food and some of the egocentric interpretations of events may be due to the state of semi-starvation. Other of the disturbed cognitions may represent an arrest in the development of abstract thinking. Piaget (1952) described four stages in the development of abstract thinking: sensorimotor, preoperational, concrete operational, and formal operational. Bruch (1973) stated that the anorectic is at the concrete operational state in which theories cannot be constructed nor logical deductions made without reference to direct experience, in part because the development of self-initiated thinking has been stifled. In any case, the cognitive distortions may offer the therapist an opportunity to begin the reeducative process by correcting these misconceptions.

The physical examination is performed to detect the unusual organic causes of weight loss that may mimic anorexia nervosa (e.g., a supracellar tumor resulting in weight loss and bitemporal hemianopsia) as well as the common consequences of semi-starvation. Anthropometric measures, including height, weight, and various fatfold measures are a necessary part of the examination. Unusual eating habits, purging behavior, and overexercising may also produce signs. Signs of semi-starvation include orthostatic hypotension, bradycardia, and decreased muscle and fat mass. Parotid gland enlargement can be a sign of binge eating and arrhythmias or buccal erosions may signify vomiting.

Laboratory testing need not be extensive but should include a complete blood count, SMA-18, urinalysis, electrocardiogram (EKG), and chest X ray. Results of the physical examination and laboratory evaluation can be used to facilitate the reeducative process aimed at reuniting the patient's mind-body dichotomy. Characteristically, during the initial evaluation, patients (and often their families) deny any problems; tactful confrontation with the symptoms, signs, and laboratory data may allow the denial to be partially relinquished. The following case illustrates the point:

> Amy is a 17-year-old who was 5 feet 6 inches (168 cm) and 80 pounds (36 kg) and who had been exercising up to six hours/day. Although her physician-mother noted her thinness and her cyanosis after swimming 60 laps, no evaluation was sought for many months. In the initial interview, Amy claimed she felt wonderful and kept up a bright, cheerful, somewhat superficial conversation with the examiner. On physical examination, she had a pulse of 40 beats per minute, acrocyanosis, and orthostatic hypotension. The EKG revealed U waves, bradycardia, and an occasional premature ventricular beat. She had a potassium of 2.5 meq/l. These findings were presented to the family along with an explanation of some of the cardiac hazards known to occur with anorexia nervosa. Her mother was shocked and encouraged her daughter to go to the hospital.

Psychological testing at the initial evaluation need not be extensive. At a minimum, it should include some test to detect the presence or absence of body-image disturbances. There are many tests available, none of which are ideal; these have been reviewed by Garner and Garfinkel (1981).

The criteria for selecting outpatient care rather than inpatient care have not been clearly established, although recommendations have been made by several authors. Anyan and Schowalter (1983) listed six criteria to determine if outpatient treatment is suitable. The first criterion is a weight score; the patient's current weight is multiplied by 100 and the product is divided by the expected lean body mass as derived by a method described by Forbes (1972). If the patient's weight score is below 90, the patient is likely to have signs of malnutrition, including fatigue, functional hypothyroidism, and bradycardia, and hospitalization is recommended. A simpler version of this criterion is that patients more than 20 to 25 percent below ideal body weight require hospitalization. The second criterion for outpatient care is the patient's own recognition of the problem and need of treatment. The third requirement is that the patient believe he or she can improve as an outpatient. The final three items one should evaluate are family factors: 1) relative marital harmony; 2) realization on the part of the parents that treatment is necessary and the capacity to unite in supporting the patient's efforts toward health; and 3) absence of significant parental anger or anxiety. These factors suggest outpatient treatment will be effective. Halmi's (1984a) criteria are similar but exclude chronic patients from outpatient treatment. She stated that patients who have been ill less than six months, who have had no previous failed treatment efforts, who have not lost significant amounts of weight, who are not bingeing and purging, who do not have the major physiologic sequelae of semi-starvation or purging, and who have intact families willing and able to participate in treatment are candidates for outpatient care.

Patients Who Refuse Hospitalization

Some patients who do not meet the guidelines for outpatient treatment none-theless refuse hospitalization. This problem has been addressed by several authors. Crisp (1984), who evaluates patients with a known well-established diagnosis of anorexia nervosa, spends an initial three-hour evaluation enlisting family and patient commitment to inpatient hospitalization. He offers a reevaluation in nine months to those who refuse hospitalization. Garfinkel and Garner (1982) use a different strategy for patients who refuse recommended hospitalization. They proposed an experimental period during which the patient attempts to gain weight as an outpatient; if unsuc-cessful after a specified period, they ask the patient to agree to hospitalization. Usually the trial period lasts four to eight weeks, with a slow gradual weight gain of about one pound (.45 kg) per week expected.

Outpatient Treatment: Primary Modality

Weight Restoration

For patients who meet the criteria for outpatient treatment, the psychological and physiologic issues must be addressed simultaneously. Dally (1969) commented: "In any discussion of treatment it is essential to remember that anorexia nervosa involves psychological and physical factors and to treat one and neglect the other is illogical" (p. 47). Weight gain must begin early and binge eating and purging must be relinquished.

Several methods have been used to assist the patient to accomplish weight gain; most include elements of behavior modification. Essentially, there are four steps in an operant conditioning weight restoration program. First, eating and exercise be-havior is carefully documented, usually in a diary. Second, stimuli that precede eating and exercise are identified. Third, techniques are developed to increase the likelihood of consuming more calories. Fourth, the consequences of eating more and exercising less are altered.

Various techniques are available for implementing operant conditioning programs but positive reinforcement techniques have been most commonly used. One example is as follows. A patient may be asked to keep a diary of her food intake and instructed in the calorie intake necessary to result in a slow gradual weight gain. She can then set certain weight goals and choose either daily rewards for herself for consuming the requisite number of calories or weekly rewards for achieving a planned weight gain. The situations that promote cessation of eating, such as feeling guilty or feeling full after consuming small portions are identified. Techniques for altering the act of eating or feeling sated are devised. For example, patients who feel full after consuming small amounts may have a physiologic explanation for this sensation. Holt et al. (1981) noted that gastric contractions decrease, especially in chronically ill patients. Meto-clopramide (Reglan), which promotes gastric contractions, may decrease the full sen-sation and result in increased consumption (Moldofsky et al. 1977). Another method for increasing intake is to teach the patient to consume compact calories; patients who have been eating large quantities of salads, for example, may substitute juices with more calories and less bulk. Some patients can consume supplemental formula drinks (such as Sustacal); it is sometimes easier to think of these formulas as medi-cations rather than foods. Another useful technique is to have the patient use a larger plate so that the quantity eaten seems somewhat less. Keeping a diary and identifying the situations that result in less eating or more exercise may be quite easy for the patient, but choosing rewards may be very difficult. Often this relates to the lack of self-awareness and the patient's inability to choose. Some patients can choose more easily given a list of possible positive consequences; others are able to learn to choose when this difficulty is identified in individual psychotherapy as part of the underlying problem of "paralyzing ineffectiveness" (Bruch 1973).

Using Garfinkel and Garner's (1982) "trial period" is essentially a form of behavior therapy. If the patient eats and gains weight (behavior), the patient is congratulated on the accomplishment (a positive reinforcement). The possibility of hospitalization is removed (this is a negative reinforcement in which an aversive stimulus—the threat of hospitalization—is removed). The patient who fails to gain weight is no longer allowed to be an outpatient (i.e., there is a removal of a positive consequence) and hospitalization occurs (an aversive stimulus).

Management of Binge Eating and Purging Behavior

Although most anorectics who binge eat and purge require hospitalization, certain behavioral techniques have been used with outpatients. Patients who binge eat may be asked to record the food they eat and the situations in which they eat and may contract to eat at certain times and in certain situations. Strategies are devised to reduce the availability of food. The technique of exposure and response prevention has also been used with patients who binge eat and purge (Rosen and Leitenberg 1982). In this technique, the patient consumes the food characteristic of a binge and remains with the therapist, who encourages the patient to focus on the discomfort until the urge to vomit decreases. Other patients who vomit can be asked to remain with a friend or family member after each meal.

Marlatt and Gordon (1983) described relapse prevention techniques for the management of alcoholics. This technique has been used with patients who binge or purge. Essentially, it is a detailed conceptualization of the chain of factors that initially elicit certain behavior and the cognitive consequences that serve to increase the behavior once it has occurred the first time. The patient learns to identify high-risk situations (i.e., those situations that elicit overeating or purging) and learns to identify the cognitions that follow the lapse. Commonly, after a "slip" when the taboo behavior occurs, it is followed with all-or-none thinking or rationalizations. For example, a person who has just binge eaten might say: "You've blown it now, you're certain to be fat" and decide to follow a rigid fast that is in itself a high-risk situation (since fasting results in hunger, which predisposes to binge eating). Rationalization might occur following vomiting: the patient may say "I'll just vomit this once to correct for any weight I've gained today."

Identification of the high-risk situations and alternative coping techniques can be useful. Also, substitution of matter-of-fact statements for all-or-none thinking or rationalizations may interrupt the binge-purge cycle. For example, the patient who overeats might say "If I decrease my food intake slightly during the next 24 hours, I will not gain over my target weight for the week."

Individual Psychotherapy

For many patients for whom outpatient treatment is the primary modality, individual psychotherapy plays a pivitol role. Some patients may need both individual therapy and family therapy, and close collaboration between therapists will be needed. The various types of psychotherapies are described in Chapter 64 but general principles applicable to a wide variety of theoretical orientations will be reviewed here. First, any attempt at individual psychotherapy must occur simultaneously with a weight-restoration program. Although it is true that some of the psychological symptoms (e.g., obsessions, poor concentration) may decrease with weight gain, it is very unwise to implement a weight-restoration program without concomitant psychotherapy. Separating the treatment of the physical and psychological aspects of the condition may intensify the mind-body dichotomy, which must be resolved for full recovery to occur. Whatever theoretical orientation the therapist has, the initial focus must be reeducative. This reeducation includes teaching the patient the relationship between certain signs and symptoms and their state of semi-starvation and the correction of the cognitive distortions. Early in treatment, it is often necessary to explain the purpose of psychotherapy and to take a more active role than in traditional psychotherapy. It may be necessary to allow the patient to know more about the therapist than is customary. Jourard (1971) used the term *transparency* to mean that the therapist's emotions are apparent to an observer; if the therapist becomes "transparent" rather than a nondisclosing blank screen, therapy may be facilitated. Another complicating factor, which rarely occurs in traditional psychotherapy, is that the therapist may have to take certain actions. For example, it may be necessary to weigh the patient or to order blood tests or to hospitalize the patient. These actions may need to be taken at a time when individual and family psychodynamics are poorly understood.

Another general principle of psychotherapy with anorectics is to avoid premature interpretations. Some patients believe "mother knows best" and it is wise to avoid replaying this as "therapist knows best." Interpretations are often experienced as confrontations by these patients and should usually be avoided initially. If interpretations are offered, it is helpful to start with the least threatening level of interpretation or limit oneself to clarification.

Part of the reeducative process includes teaching the patient that the abnormal eating behaviors are usually a smokescreen for certain unresolved psychological conflicts. These include grief, family conflict, lack of preparation for tasks of adolescence and adulthood (Crisp's theory), lack of a sense of self and autonomy (Bruch's primary anorexia nervosa), and a borderline personality organization (Masterson 1977). Treatment of grief utilizes the principles of Lindemann (1944). Patients for whom the primary precipitant is family conflict usually require family therapy as the primary modality of treatment. Patients unprepared for the tasks of adolescence or who lack a coherent sense of self usually require lengthy therapy. Patients with a borderline personality organization may benefit form the treatment described by Masterson: behavior is circumscribed (a weight-restoration program is implemented); the patient is taught the relationship between feelings and behavior (reeducative psychotherapy); and intensive insight-oriented psychotherapy begins.

The treatment of anorexia nervosa is challenging, and countertransference problems are common. Some of these stem from failure to recognize the severity of certain implacable cognitive distortions. Some arise from the need for multiple therapists to interact with one patient or family. These patients are usually adept at detecting covert conflict within the treatment team, and their symptoms may worsen if the team is not communicating well. Splitting is a common defense mechanism, especially among patients with a borderline personality, and the patient may relate to one therapist as all good and another as all bad, thereby promoting dissension within the team.

Drug Therapy

Although many anorectics have symptoms characteristic of depression, including sleep disturbance, fatigue, weight loss, irritability, sad mood, and poor concentration, these may be due to the state of semi-starvation. Thus use of antidepressants prior to weight restoration is unnecessary and may be hazardous in those patients who have a low potassium or cardiac arrhythmias. Occasionally, an anorectic whose weight is near normal may still have signs of depression, and a cautious trial of amitriptyline (Halmi et al. 1983) can be used. Antidepressants have not improved weight gain in double-blind studies. Small doses of chlorpromazine may be helpful for severely obsessive-compulsive patients (Crisp 1965; Halmi 1984b). Cyproheptadine, an antihistaminic drug, has been shown to increase weight gain significantly in hospitalized patients but its role in the treatment of outpatients is not established (Halmi et al. 1983). Metoclopramide may have a place in relieving the symptom of fullness in patients attempting to gain weight (Moldofsky et al. 1977). Other drugs have not been found effective in the management of outpatients (see Chapter 59).

Family Therapy

Patients still in their nuclear family or for whom family conflict was a major precipitating factor usually benefit from family therapy (see Chapter 62). For married patients, intervention with the spouse is nearly always required. Married anorectics have a poorer prognosis, perhaps because they are older or perhaps because their spouse reinforces the factors that maintain the disorder. Marital therapy or individual therapy for the spouse is often necessary; many husbands claim the only problem is their wife's eating behavior and deny any other problems in the relationship. The therapeutic strategies that are useful in working with resistant parents are often useful with reluctant spouses.

Aftercare Program

For patients who have been hospitalized, the outpatient therapist should be the person with the best relationship with either the patient or family while the patient was hospitalized. The direction of the outpatient program depends on the inpatient course. Certain patients will benefit from intensive psychotherapy; others will need structured monitoring of weight and eating behavior; others will need family therapy; and some will need all three. Nutritional counseling is often an integral part of this phase of treatment as the patient moves from the hospital (where one is sedentary) to a more active life-style.

Most inpatient programs now aim for the patient to reach a normal weight before discharge. Behavioral techniques can be used with outpatients to facilitate weight maintenance. For example, a patient may be weighed weekly by the school nurse and only allowed to participate in physical education that week if she has maintained her weight. The behavior (normal eating) results in increased activity (a positive reinforcement). Similarly, weight loss can result in the removal of an enjoyed activity. For example, one college student was required to remain at home rather than return to her sorority house for a week if she lost weight.

The outpatient therapist must be alert to signs that indicate the need for rehospitalization. Significant weight loss or incapacity to correct a weight loss, onset or worsening of binge eating or purging, rapid uncontrolled weight gain, or the onset of significant depressive symptoms may signal the need for rehospitalization.

Treatment Team

Usually several professionals are needed for an optimal outpatient program. More than one professional may work with one patient. A method called "dual transference" therapy has been proposed in which one therapist monitors weight gain and another provides individual psychotherapy (Solomon and Morrison 1972). This is probably more useful for inpatients (Powers and Powers 1984), but may have application early in treatment with some outpatients.

Nutritional counseling is a useful adjunct to psychotherapy. Despite seeming knowledgeable in nutrition, many anorectics actually know little or nothing about the value of carbohydrates or fats and operate on the assumption that "protein is good" and the only essential nutrient. The role of the nutritionist is well outlined by Eubanks (1984) and includes analyzing current intake, calculating the needed nutrients, and incorporating this change smoothly into the patient's life-style. Occasionally the nutritionist can monitor the weight-restoration program. Individual or family therapy can be with any well-trained clinician familiar with the special problems posed by these patients. Nursing personnel can determine accurate weights and need to be aware of the potential for deception (e.g., one patient sewed weights into her underwear). The physiologic consequences of semi-starvation and binge eating and purging must be closely monitored by a physician (often the psychiatrist providing the individual or family therapy).

Ideally, there is close communication among team members. Frequent scheduled meetings including all involved professionals help avoid the possibility of intense countertransference problems by providing a support network for the therapist treating these difficult patients.

Goals

Probably most patients require inpatient hospitalization at some point in their management. Certain patients (those with the good prognostic signs enumerated earlier) can be completely managed as outpatients; in our treatment center about 10 percent can be so managed. Perhaps more importantly, however, an effective aftercare program may promote weight maintenance and improved psychosocial functioning, which can obviate relapse and the need for rehospitalization.

Ideally, when outpatient treatment concludes, the patient is at normal weight and comfortable at that weight with no body-image disturbance or preoccupation with weight, food, or size. Also, ideally, the patient has satisfying relationships at work and at home and can reach his or her intellectual and interpersonal relationship capacity. Unfortunately , these goals are often unrealistic. Some patients are never able to have meaningful interpersonal relationships. It is perhaps more reasonable to anticipate normal weight, but on the low side of the height-weight tables, with remaining disturbances in body image and occasional preoccupations with food and weight. Patients who have had bulimic anorexia may be slightly overweight. The recovered anorectic will probably be able to function occupationally. Some may be married, but often in a rather mechanical relationship, frequently without children.

Chapter 59

Drug Therapy

The medical severity inherent in the syndrome of anorexia nervosa and the often refractory nature of the syndrome have prompted trials of a wide variety of therapies. Virtually every form of somatic treatment known to psychiatry has been employed in this illness and at some point described as being useful. Application of rigorous scientific methods, primarily double-blind placebo-controlled trials, has begun to provide some clarity concerning the utility of medications for this syndrome. However, it should be emphasized that, at present, medications play at most a secondary role in the treatment of anorexia nervosa as one component of a comprehensive treatment approach.

Antipsychotic Agents

The first well-described pharmacologic intervention in anorexia nervosa was the use of chlorpromazine. Dally and Sargant (1960) described a treatment approach using chlorpromazine in doses of 150 to 1,000 mg/day, combined with subcutaneous insulin sufficient to produce hypoglycemia and hopefully to stimulate appetite. Dally and Sargant (1966) reviewed their experience in 48 women with anorexia nervosa treated with these medications in combination with hospitalization and bed rest. They compared them with 48 patients treated in the preceding 20 years without the use of chlorpromazine and insulin. They found that the patients treated with chlorpromazine and insulin gained weight twice as rapidly and were discharged from hospital significantly sooner than the historical control group. However, the follow-up data on the two groups did not show any substantial benefit for the chlorpromazine-treated patients. In each group, 30 percent were readmitted within two years, and bulimia occurred in 45 percent of the group treated with chlorpromazine compared to 12 percent of the nonpharmacologically treated patients. While the authors felt that the chlorpromazine was particularly effective because it "lessens the patient's fear of and resistence to eating" (p. 794), there was no suggestion that the medication in any definitive or lasting manner altered the patients' psychological disturbances. The chlorpromazine was given in relatively high doses and was associated with grand mal seizures in five of the 48 patients. The authors subsequently eliminated insulin from the treatment program and have become less enthusiastic about the usefulness of chlorpromazine in anorexia nervosa (Dally 1981).

Vandereycken and Pierloot (1982) reported a double-blind placebo-controlled crossover study of the antipsychotic drug pimozide. Eighteen women with anorexia nervosa were treated as inpatients with a behavior modification program and also received medication for six weeks. For three weeks each patient received pimozide (4 or 6 mg/day, probably equivalent to 400 to 600 mg of chlorpromazine) and for three weeks they received placebo. The assignment of patients to the placebo-pimozide or pimozide-placebo sequence was random, and the investigators were blind to drug assignment. The patients who were assigned to begin treatment with pimozide gained weight faster than those patients who initially received placebo, but this difference persisted after the crossover to the alternate medication. Overall, there was a trend favoring an effect of pimozide on weight gain but it was not statistically significant. Further, the staff's rating of patients' attitudes did not reflect any clear advantage for pimozide. A trial of similar design using another dopamine antagonist, sulpiride, also failed to demonstrate significant advantage for drug over placebo (Vandereycken 1984).

Antipsychotic agents may be of use in the treatment of some particularly difficult patients with anorexia nervosa in whom supportive hospitalization and behavior modification regimes are ineffective. However, because of the potentially serious side effects inherent in the use of such drugs (e.g, tardive dyskinesia, seizures, hypotension), antipsychotic medications have a limited place in the treatment of patients with anorexia nervosa.

Cyproheptadine

Cyproheptadine is a serotonin and histamine antagonist that is licensed in this country for the treatment of a variety of allergic conditions. It was observed that patients treated with cyproheptadine for these inflammatory syndromes frequently gained weight, and clinicians wondered if this effect might be useful in the treatment of patients with anorexia nervosa. Vigersky and Loriaux (1977) reported a double-blind placebo-controlled trial of cyproheptadine in 24 patients with anorexia nervosa. Patients were treated on an outpatient basis; additional forms of therapy received by the patients were not specified. Patients received cyproheptadine (12 mg/day) or placebo for eight weeks. Four patients in the drug-treatment group gained weight compared to only two on placebo, a difference that was not statistically significant.

Goldberg et al. (1979) reported on a multicenter trial of cyproheptadine in patients hospitalized for anorexia nervosa. Patients were randomly assigned to receive either cyproheptadine or placebo and either behavior modification treatment or no behavior modification. Cyproheptadine was given in doses of 12 to 32 mg/day for 35 days. The average weight gain in the cyproheptadine-treated group was slightly but not statistically significantly higher than the average weight gain in the placebo-treated group. However, a post hoc analysis suggested that cyproheptadine was more effective in patients with histories of birth complications, severe weight loss, and prior treatment failures as outpatients. Although this finding was unexpected, it led the authors to wonder if cyproheptadine might be useful in a more severe subgroup of patients with anorexia nervosa.

Halmi et al. (1985) completed a double-blind study comparing cyproheptadine (32 mg/day) to amitriptyline and placebo in 72 hospitalized patients with anorexia nervosa. Cyproheptadine was slightly more effective in inducing weight gain and in relieving depression than placebo. However, the overall magnitude of the effects was small. There was a differential drug effect present in the bulimic subgroup, with cyproheptadine significantly increasing treatment efficiency in the nonbulimic patients and impairing treatment efficiency in bulimic patients.

In summary, there are indications that, in combination with an inpatient program, cyproheptadine may both promote weight gain and relieve depression in some patients with anorexia nervosa. However, the overall magnitude of these effects appears modest, and it is not yet clear whether there is a subgroup of patients with anorexia nervosa who derive particular benefit from cyproheptadine. It should be noted that even in the relatively large doses used (32 mg/day), cyproheptadine has not been associated with serious side effects, a major advantage in treating medically ill patients with anorexia nervosa.

Antidepressant Medication

The presence of significant depressive symptomatology among patients with anorexia nervosa has prompted clinicians to employ antidepressant drugs in their treatment approach. While several reports have described impressive therapeutic results (Hudson et al. 1985; Needleman and Waber 1976), other clinicians have been skeptical about the utility of antidepressant drugs in this illness (Mills 1976).

There are three reports of double-blind placebo-controlled trials of antidepressant medication in anorexia nervosa. Lacey and Crisp (1980) reported a trial of clomipramine in 16 women hospitalized with anorexia nervosa. Clomipramine is a tricyclic antidepressant drug, widely used in Europe, which appears to have both antidepressant and antiobsessive properties that potentially might make it particularly useful in patients with anorexia nervosa. However, the dose of drug used in the study was quite low (50 mg/day) even allowing for the low weights of the patients being treated. No difference was found between the drug- and placebo-treated groups.

The two other controlled trials have studied amitriptyline. Biederman et al. (1985), in a small study using both inpatients and outpatients at two centers, found no advantage for amitriptyline over placebo. The above-mentioned study of Halmi et al. (1985) comparing amitriptyline, cyproheptadine, and placebo was larger and methodologically more refined, but detected only a marginal advantage for amitriptyline (160 mg/day) over placebo.

Although there are theoretical grounds for believing such an approach might have merit, there is, at present, no convincing evidence of antidepressant efficacy in the treatment of patients with anorexia nervosa. On the other hand, the placebo-controlled trials of antidepressants in this illness have used only tricyclic antidepressants, sometimes in low dose and usually without the benefit of plasma levels of drug. Thus the status of antidepressant medication in anorexia nervosa remains somewhat uncertain.

Other Agents

Although anxiety is at times a prominent symptom in patients with anorexia nervosa, the use of antianxiety medication has received no systematic study. Some experienced clinicians believe that the judicious use of antianxiety agents, such as short-acting benzodiazepines, may be of use in helping some patients deal with the distress that often accompanies meals during weight restoration (Andersen 1987). The psychiatrist should be alert to the fact that some patients, particularly those with bulimia, may be predisposed to abuse antianxiety medication.

The successful use of lithium carbonate in anorexia nervosa has been described in several case reports (Barcai 1977; Stein et al. 1982). Using a double-blind placebo-controlled design, Gross et al. (1981) evaluated the utility of lithium carbonate in addition to a behavior modification program in 16 women hospitalized for anorexia nervosa. The lithium-treated group gained more weight than the placebo-treated group but, because of the small sample size, the short duration of the trial, and baseline differences between the two groups, and because both groups did improve significantly, it is difficult to determine from this study whether there is any role for lithium in the treatment of patients with anorexia nervosa. Therefore, except for the rare patient who has both bipolar affective illness and anorexia nervosa, there is currently no clear indication for the use of lithium in this syndrome.

Patients with anorexia nervosa frequently complain of feeling bloated for prolonged periods of time after meals. Studies of gastric emptying have, in fact, revealed that food exits from the stomach at a substantially reduced rate in patients with anorexia nervosa compared to normal controls (Dubois et al. 1981). Several authors have reported that gastric emptying can be increased in patients with anorexia nervosa by the administration of drugs such as metoclopramide, bethanecol, and domperidone, which increase the rate of gastric emptying (Dubois et al. 1981; Moldofsky et al. 1977; Saleh and Lebwohl 1980). While in these small trials patients have had fewer complaints of bloating after meals, the overall therapeutic utility of such drugs was not clear. Furthermore, the use of metoclopramide was associated with depression and with endocrine changes (Moldofsky et al. 1977).

Because of the appetite-enhancing effects of marijuana, Gross et al. (1983) undertook a double-blind study of the active ingredient of marijuana—delta-9-tetrahydrocannabinol (THC)—in 11 patients. Patients received THC for two weeks and diazepam for two weeks in randomly assigned sequence. Weight gain during treatment with THC was no greater than weight gain during placebo treatment; three patients dropped out of the study while receiving THC because of severe dysphoric reactions. Thus THC is of no therapeutic benefit and of possible psychological harm in patients with anorexia nervosa.

Finally, a number of other drugs, including glycerol, phenoxybensamine, L-dopa, and anabolic steroids, have, on the basis of single case reports, been described as being useful in the treatment of patients with anorexia nervosa (Caplin et al. 1973; Johanson and Knorr 1977; Redmond et al. 1976; Tec 1974). None of these drugs has been evaluated by double-blind placebo-controlled study, and there is little evidence for their utility in patients with anorexia nervosa.

In summary, anorexia nervosa remains a psychiatric syndrome in which medication, at the moment, can play no more than an ancillary role. Antianxiety medication may be of help in relieving the severe anxiety that sometimes occurs at mealtime; antipsychotic medication may be useful for an occasional very difficult patient. There is recent evidence that some patients may derive modest benefit from cyproheptadine and possibly from some antidepressants.

Chapter 60

Behavior Therapy

Most if not all effective treatment programs for anorexia nervosa have incorporated behavioral methods. Often these techniques are not identified as behavioral. For example, the mere act of hospitalization is incorporating a behavioral contingency. It is probably not possible to treat anorexia nervosa without using subtle, behavioral techniques. For this reason, it is difficult to design behavior therapy efficacy studies that have a "pure" no-behavior treatment control.

Theoretical Basis and Literature Review

Both respondent and operant principles of learning have been used to explain the development, maintenance, and treatment of anorexia nervosa. Respondent conditioning deals with stimuli that evoke responses. The stimuli can be unconditioned or conditioned. Theorists who espouse the respondent model view anorexia nervosa as a conditioned fear or anxiety (Brady and Rieger 1972; Crisp 1970). Regardless of the initial stimulus for dieting, eating and weight gain begin to generate anxiety, while not eating and weight loss serve to avoid anxiety. Behaviors such as taking laxatives and self-induced vomiting further reduce anxiety by preventing weight gain. In time, these food and weight-related behaviors come to dominate the anorectic's life and usually begin to function autonomously from the original motivation for weight loss. Therefore, these behaviors should be addressed specifically, and behavioral methods appear useful for this purpose.

Based on the respondent model for anorexia nervosa, the behavioral techniques of systematic desensitization and exposure with response prevention have been employed. Systematic desensitization involves counterconditioning the anxiety associated with eating and weight gain by substituting a relaxation response for the anxiety. This is accomplished using relaxation coupled with visual imagery for a graded hierarchy of situations associated with eating and weight gain. Only a few reports on the use of systematic desensitization for the treatment of anorexia nervosa have appeared (Hallsten 1965; Lang 1965), and these do not indicate a compelling efficacy for this technique.

Exposure and response prevention entails exposure to and not allowing escape from the anxiety-producing situation. Application of this technique to anorexia nervosa requires exposure to the twin fears of eating and weight gain. An extension of the technique involves using response prevention to treat anorectic rituals, which have an anxiety-reducing function. These rituals include vomiting after meals, use of laxatives, compulsive exercising, and weighing frequently. Response prevention entails forced avoidance of these rituals (e.g., not allowing access to laxatives, monitoring after meals to prevent vomiting). Reports using exposure and response-prevention techniques for the treatment of anorexia nervosa are emerging (Cinciripini et al. 1983; Mavissakalian 1982).

The anorectic disorder has been compared to obsessive-compulsive disorder (Solyom et al., 1982) or phobic disorder (Crisp 1970). It has been shown (Steketee et al. 1982) that a helpful treatment for obsessive-compulsive disorder involves exposure to the anxiety-producing stimuli and preventing the compulsive rituals (response prevention). In phobic disorders, the essential therapeutic requirement is thought to be exposure to the phobic object (Klein et al. 1983). However, there is some controversy concerning how precisely anorexia nervosa can be regarded as a phobic illness. Salkind et al. (1980) argued against a precise association because they have found minimal skin conductance changes in anorectic patients to the presentation of a series of food and weight-related stimuli.

In operant conditioning, behavior is increased or decreased by its consequences. The consequence is considered reinforcement if it increases the behavior. Reinforcement can be a presentation of a favorable event, a positive reinforcer. Reinforcement can also be a removal of an aversive event, a negative reinforcer. Based on principles of the operant model, anorexia nervosa is said to develop or be maintained because of the reinforcing consequences. There are ways that anorectic behavior could be positively reinforced, such as by our culture's value of thinness (Dally 1969). Food-rejecting behavior may eventually be reinforced by the attention it produces from other (Ayllon et al. 1964). Anorectic behavior can be negatively reinforced by painful psychological issues, including the responsibility and demands that accompany biologic maturity (Crisp 1970). In this instance the anorectic behaviors allow the patient to avoid painful events. The patient may be facilitating the avoidance of family conflict by maintaining the anorectic symptoms (Liebman et al. 1974). Operant conditioning treatment of anorexia nervosa has received considerable attention, primarily as a means to gain weight. Systematic studies have used selective positive reinforcements consisting of increased physical activity, visiting privileges, and social activities contingent on weight gain, and powerful negative reinforcements such as bed rest, isolation, or tube feeding for failure to gain weight (Azerrad and Stafford 1969; Bachrach et al. 1965; Brady and Rieger 1972; Garfinkel et al. 1973; Halmi et al. 1975).

Paradoxical intention is a behavioral technique that has been described as helpful for some chronic anorectic patients who have proven their resistance to standard treatment regimens and who are in a power struggle with helping professionals over weight gain or control of anorectic behaviors (Hsu and Liebman 1982). Patients are told that it is better for them to keep their anorexia nervosa because previous attempts to treat them have resulted in only temporary remission of the illness. The "benefits" of the illness, as they are understood, are explained to the patients. The authors noted that, paradoxically, this reduces the anorectic's need to maintain such rigid and dangerous control and allows some patients to change their oppositional stance and improve. The authors suggested caution in use of this technique.

Agras et al. (1974), using applied behavioral analysis in single case experiments, isolated four important variables contributing to control of weight gain in anorectic patients. Patients ate in order to leave the hospital, an example of negative reinforcement. Positive reinforcement for weight gain was important but was maximally effective only when informational feedback to patients about weight and calorie intake was used in conjunction. Another variable was the amount of food served; the larger the amount served, the greater the ingestion. A combination of these variables appeared most effective.

Only one randomized control study tested the efficacy of behavioral therapy, specifically operant therapy (Eckert et al. 1979). This study, a large multicenter project, found no difference in weight gain between standard milieu treatment and the combination of standard milieu treatment and reinforcement of small increments of weight gain. However, evidence indicated that the particular behavioral program used in this study was not maximally effective. The limited length of study time of 35 days may have been insufficient to demonstrate a significant treatment difference. The program did not use individualized reinforcements. Individual reinforcements may be more effective than constant reinforcers used in all patients. The schedule of reinforcements may be a significant factor. The program reinforced weight gain every five days rather than daily. One study has shown, by using both daily and delayed reinforcement programs consecutively in individual patients, that daily reinforcement is more effective for weight gain than delayed reinforcement (Eckert 1983). General principle dictates that the more immediate the reinforcement, the greater the effectiveness of the reinforcer. The previously discussed multicenter study also did not clearly separate the significant behavioral treatment variables. Informational feedback, caloric manipulation, and the negative reinforcement value of hospitalization to goal weight were utilized in both treatment groups. The only difference in the two treatment groups was the use of a limited operant reinforcement schedule to increase weight, and this was not powerful enough to exert a significant effect.

Agras and Werne (1978) addressed the effectiveness of behavioral treatment compared to more traditional therapies by looking at long-term outcome. Utilizing as a data base 21 nonbehavioral and five behavioral studies for which enough data were published to allow comparative conclusions between studies, no overall long-term outcome differences emerged. The authors pointed out that the similar outcome data may be attributable to the overlapping techniques employed in both so-called behavioral and nonbehavioral approaches.

Recently, behavior therapists have recognized the importance of cognitive factors in the conceptualization and modification of behavior. Anorectics have cognitive distortions that maintain their maladaptive behavior. Unless these distortions are modified, techniques to modify the behavior will be ineffective. Although operant techniques may induce a patient to gain weight, relapse is likely to occur unless cognitive distortions are altered. Cognitive behavioral therapy shows promise as an important addition to behavioral treatment programs (Garner and Bemis 1982).

In addition, many behavior therapists believe that deficits in coping skills must be addressed and that it is essential to teach skills that will foster more adaptive ways of functioning, such as assertiveness, social skills, and problem-solving skills. Many anorectic patients have major interpersonal problems, compounded perhaps by the disruption of normal social development. Pillay and Crisp (1981) tested the efficiency of incorporating social skills training within an in-hospital treatment program. Twenty-four patients were randomly allocated to a placebo social contact or 12 sessions of social skills training. Four weeks after restoration of normal weight, no significant changes in social skills were found in either group, but the social skills group was significantly less anxious and depressed. At one-year follow-up, the fear of negative evaluation was significantly lowered only in the group given social skills training. Overall, social skills training was thought to have a weak effect on strengthening social skills in this study.

A Behaviorally Based Treatment Program for Anorexia Nervosa

There are four general treatment goals for anorectic patients: 1) to resume physical health by gaining and maintaining weight; 2) to resume normal eating habits; 3) to assess and treat relevant psychological issues in the patient; and 4) to educate families about the disorder by assessing the family's impact on maintaining the disorder and assisting them in developing methods to promote normal functioning in the patient. Restoring physical health should have primary emphasis initially, with increased attention to the other goals as the patient's improved medical condition provides more energy and allows better concentration on other issues. The goals are the same for hospitalized patients as well as outpatients.

Hospitalization is considered if weight is more than 15 percent below a normal standard and is urged if weight is more than 25 percent below normal. No firm rule for mandatory hospitalization can be set because the urgency will depend on a variety of indicators, including rapidity of weight loss, medical instability, overriding psychiatric problems (e.g., depression or thoughts of suicide), or other severe starvation symptoms. It is wise to hospitalize patients with persistent vomiting and laxative abuse. Hospitalization should be considered for outpatient treatment failure defined as approximately 12 to 16 weeks of ongoing regular outpatient treatment with no significant improvement or with deterioration. In the opinion of some clinicians, beginning with outpatient therapy may be successful in anorectics who are motivated to improve, have had anorexia nervosa for less than four months, have no binge eating and vomiting behavior, and have parents who are likely to cooperate and participate effectively in family therapy.

Outpatient Behavioral Treatment of Anorexia Nervosa

Outpatient behavioral treatment of anorexia nervosa has received little or no attention in the literature. With the current emphasis on cost-effectiveness, it is imperative that behaviorally based outpatient and perhaps day-hospital treatment programs involving family, group, and individual therapy be developed. Behavioral techniques applicable in this situation include implementation of a structured eating program, informational feedback, graded exposure to normal eating and weight gain, and operant reinforcement of adaptive eating habits and weight control.

A contract, usually written, involving the patient and the family is important. The terms of the contract will depend on individual need. For example, for a patient who is continuing to lose weight, the contract may specify that no further weight loss be allowed and that the patient must now maintain current weight. The patient may agree to this far more readily than to gain weight. The contract should specify a reinforcement system such as rehospitalization or loss of privileges if the patient loses weight, and positive reinforcement agreed on by the individual and the family if the weight is maintained. If this contract is successful, later contracts can be directed toward weight gain.

A dietician may help in designing a structured meal plan to aid the patient. If the contract calls for weight maintenance, the dietician can help the patient design a diet using an exchange meal planning system. The specifics of the diet to be followed should be arrived at by active collaboration between the patient and the dietician because without the patient's agreement, this diet will certainly not be followed. Although a balanced diet with all types of food is recommended, patients are initially often unable to follow such a diet because they fear certain foods. In this situation, a diet utilizing foods that cause little anxiety is helpful. Feared foodstuffs can be reintroduced later into the diet, according to the behavioral principle of graded exposure. A structured monitoring sheet on which the patient can self-monitor meals and problem behaviors such as binge eating, vomiting, and laxative abuse may be used. Such informational feedback devices can help patients feel better able to control their behavior.

Patients are advised not to weigh themselves at home. Normal variations of weight may trigger intolerable anxiety and interfere with the normalization of weight and eating patterns. However, they are weighed weekly in the clinic to assess progress.

No matter what behavioral techniques are utilized, it is well to involve the family in treatment. Family members need to be aware of their own misperceptions about the illness and need to be educated. Furthermore, behaviors by family members that maintain or reinforce the eating behavior need to be explored and changed. For example, discussions of the patient's anorectic behavior at mealtime often increases the patient's anxiety and may reinforce the illness. Attempts should be made to deemphasize the family's attention to the anorectic behavior. Although generally the family should have little direct involvement in correcting anorectic behaviors except to support constructive efforts, there are exceptions. For example, after failing to gain weight on her own, one 14-year-old patient agreed to eat a specified diet only if her mother would serve it. Having the mother serve was an acceptable initial step because weight gain was the first priority. It also accomplished necessary exposure to normal eating. Later, of course, the patient had to manage her own meals. Consistency, not rigidity, is emphasized to help relieve the confusion and anxiety around eating. Limits on anorectic behavior within the family are warranted. Families must not let the anorectic illness dictate dietary habits or otherwise dominate the family life. For example, a special low-calorie diet offered in an attempt to stimulate food intake seldom gets the anorectic to eat. Such measures only reinforce the illness. Limits may be placed on binge eating and vomiting by required payment for missing food and requiring that the bathroom be cleaned after vomiting.

Behavioral Treatment of Hospitalized Anorectics

For hospitalized anorectic patients, the treatment can be divided into three phases: medical stabilization, weight gain, and weight maintenance. The medical stabilization phase usually lasts several days, and the expectation is that the patient will at least maintain current weight. A structured eating program for weight maintenance is implemented. This usually means starting on a balanced diet of 1,500 calories/day in divided meals that the patient will be required to finish. This may include feared foods that the patient has systematically deleted form the diet, only foods not associated with extreme anxiety, or a nutritionally balanced liquid diet. A liquid diet is useful because some patients feel less anxious drinking their calories than eating them. It also allows them to avoid making decisions about which foods to eat. However, it is imperative that feared foods are soon systematically added because exposure to them is important. Not to do so would be to condone maintenance of anorectic behavior. If the patient does not finish the food provided within a prescribed length of time, specific contingencies follow. For example, the next meal may be liquid, or other individualized negative reinforcers may be put into effect. Given clear guidelines and strict application of the treatment plan, tube feeding is rarely needed.

The anorectic behaviors needing correction with behavioral techniques are defined through observation and discussion with the patient. If binge eating and vomiting occur, they are addressed using response prevention techniques such as mealtime monitoring by nursing staff to prevent binge eating, the hoarding of foods, and vomiting. This monitoring may be necessary for one to two hours after meals, including accompanying patients to the bathroom to prevent vomiting.

During the weight gain phase of treatment, a goal weight is decided on; this should not be lower than the weight that will assure regaining menses (Frisch and McArthur 1974) and is usually the lowest normal standard weight for age and height.

No negotiation is allowed on this. The behavior to be reinforced is determined: weight gain, mouthfuls eaten, or meals eaten in a restricted period of time. Usually, it is most practical to reinforce weight gain alone. Reinforcement of food eaten may result in vomiting because the anorectic does not wish to gain weight. If weight gain is the reinforced behavior, a realistic and safe rate of gain for most patients is 1/2 lb/day. The reinforcement procedure must be determined. Positive reinforcements for weight gain are preferred. These usually consist of a combination of individualized daily reinforcers, including access to visitors, phone calls, and physical activities, plus delayed reinforcements involving a gradual expansion of off-ward privileges as predetermined weight levels are achieved. If positive reinforcement alone fails, negative reinforcement (e.g., the requirement that a patient remain isolated in her room for 24 hours if she fails to make the expected weight) may be added. Such a program involving isolation is very effective in promoting weight gain in most patients. There are occasional patients who are socially withdrawn and prefer to isolate themselves in their rooms. For these patients, it would be better to make access to the rooms contingent on weight gain.

A structured eating program during this phase is not always necessary but often helpful. The calorie content of provided food gradually increases to approximately 3,500 kcals/day in six divided feedings. The food provided serves as a guide to gain the required weight. Measures to prevent vomiting and binge eating are used. It is important to give informational feedback to the patient about other abnormal eating habits. Staff should identify these abnormal habits, including picking at food and swirling the food around the plate. A patient may then be asked to keep a frequency count of these behaviors and later to decrease their frequency gradually. Often just recording the occurrence of these behaviors is sufficient to eliminate them. Otherwise, improvement in eating habits may be specifically reinforced.

Patients are usually weighed every morning in a hospital gown after voiding and told what they weigh. Weight scales are never available for patients during the day. Patients are asked to keep a daily weight graph. The graph serves as important informational feedback. Some patients should be weighed less frequently because they will be more likely to maintain a steady dietary intake.

As patients approach their goal weight, their anxiety may again increase at the prospect of being unable either to regulate or maintain weight. A period of weight maintenance lasting two to four weeks at "normal weight" prior to discharge may assure the patient that he or she will not keep gaining and get "fat." This maintenance period may also help to correct body-image distortion, to solidify psychiatric gains, and to allow time for physiologic changes to stabilize. It is best to change the goal to a range of weights once goal weight is attained. This range is usually 4 or 5 lb. Since some weight fluctuation is inevitable, keeping weight within a range is a more realistic goal, thus protecting against anxiety. Operant contingencies for weight maintenance may continue during this phase. A structured eating program may be very useful at this time to teach the patient about weight maintenance requirements. It may be more important during this phase to present the patient with three balanced meals per day calculated to maintain weight and to provide reinforcement for finishing these meals than to reinforce weight maintenance. Emphasis on maintaining a regular schedule of food intake will improve weight stability, which in turn will do much to decrease anxiety. It is important that external controls such as structured diets and operant contingency programs be removed before the patient is discharged and that the patient resume complete control, usually with a graded stepwise procedure, over eating and weight. To discharge a patient before this has been accomplished is an open invitation to relapse.

The maintenance period is intended to provide gradual transition to outpatient status. When it is clear that the patient is maintaining weight, passes home are encouraged. This is useful because problems involved with transition to the home environment can be identified and addressed before discharge. The patient is also asked to compile a list of potentially difficult situations that may threaten maintenance of weight and normal eating behaviors. If eating in various situations such as restaurants or the school cafeteria are potential problems, the patient may benefit from practice sessions. For example, staff may accompany the patient the first time at an outing to a restaurant. Later, the patient may practice eating in situations alone or with others.

As part of the outpatient follow-up plan, it may be helpful to negotiate a behavioral contract involving the patient and the family. If this is done, the guidelines outlined previously should be followed. The contract will be maximally effective if there is active collaboration between the patient, family, and staff about the problems to be addressed and the approach taken. It is helpful if the patient is asked to discuss signs of relapse with his or her family and to negotiate a plan with them to prevent relapse.

Treating Other Psychological Problems

A complete behavioral treatment program for anorectics utilizes a balanced approach between changing abnormal eating and weight and attending to other psychological issues. While weight is low and eating behaviors are very disordered, therapy should mainly support efforts to modify eating behavior and gain weight. This involves educating patients about the effects of starvation and the physiologic and psychological changes that can be expected as weight is gained, correcting illogical thinking and reassuring them by maintaining a realistic optimism.

Once weight gain has occurred and eating problems are under control, significant psychotherapeutic issues may become evident. Each patient has a unique set of problems, but there are common and recurring themes. These are 1) a distorted sense of reality, 2) problems with separation and autonomy, 3) poor psychosocial skills, 4) a negative self-concept, and 5) defective recognition and expression of certain affective states. Through a problem-oriented reeducative therapy, patients are taught skills needed to facilitate normal thinking and functioning. The distorted sense of reality, including body-image distortion and cognitive errors of thinking are addressed by labeling them and teaching methods of cognitive correction (definition, challenge, and substitution of erroneous assumptions and attitudes). Feedback techniques such as videotaping are useful for some patients to help correct body-image distortion. It is important to differentiate depression requiring antidepressant medications from negative self-concept. An assessment of how the patient handles affective expressions is made. Techniques to label feelings (e.g., keeping a written journal to identify feelings) and to encourage appropriate expression of these feelings (e.g., giving practice assignments) can be utilized. Assertiveness training, role-playing, modeling, and practical behavioral assignments may be helpful for increasing social interactional skills and self-esteem. Independence-seeking is promoted. Patients are helped to separate their needs from the expectations of others. Problem-solving techniques are taught to deal more effectively with difficult areas and to foster responsibility.

Chapter 61

Cognitive Therapy

Distorted attitudes about food, weight, and the body are consistently recognized as characteristic of anorexia nervosa. Moreover, it is frequently observed that maladaptive thinking in anorexia nervosa extends beyond food and weight to other areas of experience (Bruch 1973, 1978).

The cognitive-behavioral treatment principles are aimed at the broad range of misconceptions that appear to maintain the syndrome (Garner and Bemis 1982; Garner et al. 1982b). The cognitive principles are derived from the model described by Beck and his colleagues (Beck 1976; Beck et al. 1979) as well as the methods advocated by other cognitive theorists (Ellis 1962; Goldfried 1971; Mahoney 1974; Meichenbaum 1974). However, the form and content of cognitive therapy for anorexia nervosa have had to be adapted to this disorder, and new clinical strategies have been created to meet the special needs of these patients. The cognitive strategies proposed for anorexia nervosa are also applicable for non-emaciated patients with bulimia. Similar cognitive and behavioral methods have been recommended for both disorders (Fairburn 1981, 1984; Garner and Bemis 1982, 1984; Loro 1984; Orleans and Barnett 1984).

The Cognitive Model

Anorexia nervosa has been conceptualized from a range of different theoretical vantage points. Explanations have been offered that emphasize early developmental events, faulty interactional patterns, fears of psychosexual maturity, specific personality traits, behavioral contingencies, biologic determinants, and the social context of the disorder (Garfinkel and Garner 1982; Garner and Garfinkel 1984). Each of these formulations may be relevant to a subset of patients. Thus anorexia nervosa is probably best understood as a final common pathway that may be entered through the interaction of various psychological, familial, and social predisposing factors (Garfinkel and Garner 1982).

The cognitive approach to understanding anorexia nervosa emphasizes how the symptom pattern logically derives from the faulty assumption world of the patient. The apparently bizarre eating patterns and the resolute refusal of adequate nourishment become plausible given the anorectic patient's conviction that thinness is absolutely essential for happiness or well-being. The surplus meaning that has become attached to thinness also provides a window into the patient's broader system of self-evaluation. One advantage of a cognitive approach to anorexia nervosa is that it is not necessarily incompatible with other models that view the origin of the disorder from a wide variety of conceptual perspectives. Some of these formulations emphasize events that are remote in time from the expression of symptoms; others concentrate on events more proximal to the development of the disorder. Several authors have accounted for the development and maintenance of anorexia nervosa by an analysis of functional relationships between antecedent events, positive reinforcers, and negative reinforcers (Bemis 1983; Garner and Bemis 1982, 1984; Garner et al. 1982b; Slade 1982). Much of the speculation regarding the pathogenesis of the disorder conforms to a paradigm that presumes that behavior is maintained by its ability to reduce aversive consequences (i.e., a conditioned avoidance model). A number of theories have been advanced that explain the anorectic patient's behavior as an adaptive avoidance response to real or perceived fears associated with separation, sexuality, and performance expectations. Crisp (1965, 1980) fully developed this viewpoint in his conceptualization of anorexia nervosa as a "weight-phobia" whereby dieting becomes the mechanism by which threatening aspects of psychosexual maturity may be avoided or reversed. It is well recognized that avoidance behavior is resistant to extinction because it insulates the individual from recognizing when the aversive contingencies are no longer operating. However, it has been noted that the anorectic patient's behavior is motivated not simply by a fear of body weight and all that it might imply, but also by a "drive to be thinner" (Bruch 1962, 1978). The relentless dietary restraint displayed by the anorectic is fueled by the gratification and sense of mastery it provides. The tangible success at weight loss or simply the hope of rewards with anticipated weight reduction provide pleasure and a sense of supreme accomplishment. This explains the patient's reluctance to part with certain symptoms of the disorder. As Slade (1982) indicated, these feelings are particularly potent when the individual experiences extreme dissatisfaction in other areas of his or her life. Noting that perfectionistic tendencies have also been associated with anorexia nervosa, Slade postulated that the combination of perfectionism and general dissatisfaction are setting conditions for the disorder. They optimize the likelihood that the potential anorectic will turn to self-control in general and control over one's body in particular as means of consolation. The anorectic's relentless dieting is maintained by cognitive self-reinforcement from the sense of mastery, virtue, and self-control it provides (Garner and Bemis 1982, 1984; Garner et al. 1982b). It is not difficult to understand why an adolescent who is struggling with extreme feelings of ineffectiveness might embrace the idea that a thinner shape might lead to a greater sense of adequacy. The message that thinness is an assured pathway to beauty, success, and social competence is a consistent theme transmitted through the fashion and dieting industries (Garner et al. 1983a, 1984; Wooley and Wooley 1982; Wooley et al. 1978).

Thus the simultaneous operations of positive and negative reinforcement contingencies may distinguish anorexia nervosa from the phobic or depressive disorders and may also account for its recalcitrance. What is important for the purpose here is that these contingencies may be covert or cognitive events that are often maintained by distorted beliefs and faulty reasoning.

While there are significant differences in theoretical derivation, it is reassuring that there are remarkable similarities in the clinical strategies that have evolved independently on the basis of experience. Cognitive therapy offers a variety of powerful clinical strategies that may be applied to distorted beliefs associated with eating and body shape as well as a range of developmental, interpersonal, and self-attributional themes. On at least some level, most psychological theories focus on beliefs, meaning, misperceptions, and misattributions.

Drawing from other writers, Garner and Bemis (1984) delineated a number of features that characterize the practice of cognitive therapy: 1) reliance on conscious and preconscious experience rather than unconscious motivation, 2) explicit emphasis on meaning and cognitions as mediating variables accounting for maladaptive feelings or emotions, 3) use of questioning as a major therapeutic device, 4) active and directive involvement on the part of the therapist, and 5) methodological allegiance to psychology in which theory is continually shaped by empirical findings. This involves a commitment to clear specification of treatment methods and objective assessment of changes in target behaviors.

Conventional cognitive therapy must be adapted in consideration of the particular features and needs of the anorexia nervosa patient: 1) idiosyncratic beliefs related to food and weight, 2) the interaction between physical and psychological components of the disorder, 3) the patient's desire to retain certain focal symptoms, 4) the development of motivation for treatment with emphasis on the gradual evolution of a trusting therapeutic relationship, 5) the prominence of fundamental self-concept deficits related to self-esteem and trust in internal state, and 6) a long duration of therapy because of the time required to reverse the patient's deteriorated physical state and because of the nature of the focal symptoms.

Throughout the course of therapy, the therapist may adhere to a conscious two-track approach to treatment. The first track pertains to the patient's current eating behavior and physical condition. The therapist must be aware of these at all times and plan specific cognitive and behavioral interventions aimed at their normalization. The second track involves the more complex task of assessing and modifying misconceptions reflected in self-concept deficiencies, perfectionism, separation or autonomy fears, and disturbed family or other interpersonal relationships. Often these issues are directly tied to beliefs about weight; other times they appear to be relatively independent. Since themes on both tracks are characterized by reasoning errors, faulty beliefs, and distorted underlying assumptions, they may be addressed using cognitive therapy prinicples. A disproportionate emphasis on the first track is required early in the course of therapy because other contributing factors may not be meaningfully assessed until starvation symptoms and chaotic eating patterns are brought under control. It is essential for the therapist to begin with a thorough understanding of methods for normalizing eating and weight. Starvation, severe dieting, or electrolyte disturbances resulting from vomiting and purgative abuse all may have a dramatic effect on mood, thinking, and personality (Garfinkel and Garner 1982). A first step in this process involves motivating the patient to gain weight and to discontinue potentially dangerous weight control practices.

Developing Motivation for Treatment

The circumstances surrounding the initiation of treatment and the manner in which the therapist deals with these are particularly important in anorexia nervosa. It is not uncommon for the anorexic patient to arrive for an initial consultation with opposition or at least ambivalence toward treatment. Agreeing to a consultation may have been a reluctant compromise under pressure from family or friends. In these cases, the patient is resolutely poised to resist an assault on the "ego-syntonic" symptoms. Standard cognitive therapy has been developed for less reluctant depressed and anxious patients who voluntarily seek help because of their psychological discomfort. With anorexia nervosa, formal cognitive therapy methods must be introduced more gradually once the patient has begun to express a desire to change.

During the initial phase of therapy, there must be a gradual evolution of trust and openness. Rather than exclusively focusing on weight, the goal of therapy should be defined as understanding the patient's emotional distress, which has led to weight loss. If distress is denied, the point should not be pressed and greater attention should be focused on describing the effects of starvation and conveying information about anorexia nervosa. The actual format of the initial interview as well as other recommendations for eliciting motivation for therapy have been presented in detail elsewhere (Casper 1982; Garner and Bemis 1982, 1984; Garner et al. 1982b).

In general, the patient must be helped to recognize that although the symptoms are functional in the sense that they provide short-term pleasure or relief from pressures, they have disastrous long-term consequences. For most patients, anorexia nervosa is a misdirected attempt to achieve mastery and personal well-being. Some patients become genuinely motivated for recovery once they recognize that the effort required to maintain the disorder as well as its emotional consequences virtually preclude sustaining interpersonal and vocational goals.

The sequence of events in psychotherapy is crucial. Most patients share the traditional psychotherapeutic view that eating and weight-related symptoms will naturally disappear once the underlying unhappiness has been resolved. This sequence of events rarely applies in anorexia nervosa because of the self-perpetuating nature of the syndrome.

Weight gain and normal eating elicit intense anxiety for the patient with anorexia nervosa. Since therapy requires the patient to experiment gradually with discarding the symptoms and actually feel worse on the road to recovery, motivation must be elicited repeatedly during the course of treatment. Stringent dieting, retaining a suboptimal weight, avoiding fattening foods, and vomiting must be repeatedly redefined as inconsistent with the ultimate goal of recovery. The therapist may assist by helping the patient redefine the short-term goal of therapy as amelioration of the starvation symptoms rather than simply weight gain. The patient must be encouraged to examine the long-term consequences of anorectic behavior on a daily basis. A key ingredient in the patient's willingness to exchange the positive experience of control over eating and weight for the promise of ultimate improvement is a trusting therapeutic relationship.

Various systems of psychotherapy have acknowledged the role of the therapeutic relationship in promoting change (Frank 1973; Marmor 1976) and recent elaborations of cognitive therapy are no exception (Beck et al. 1979; Guidano and Liotti 1983; Mahoney 1974). In adapting the cognitive approach to anorexia nervosa, several authors have maintained that a strong therapeutic alliance is a prerequisite for effective psychotherapy (Garner and Bemis 1982, 1984; Guidano and Liotti 1983). As mentioned earlier, the quality of the relationship plays a vital role in motivation for recovery. A trusting relationship is necessary in cognitive therapy because this approach places a premium on assessment of cognition, affect, and behavior through self-reported, introspective data. Moreover, the relationship provides a conduit for examining distortions and misperceptions that the patient applies to his or her interpersonal world. When the patient's reactions to the therapist are viewed within the context of other current or past relationships, data that may illuminate salient beliefs, assumptions, and attitudes are provided.

Psychoeducational Material

Psychoeducational material related to starvation effects, physical complications, the biology of weight regulation, consequences of dieting, nutrition, obesity, self-monitoring, and the social context of eating disorders has become an integral component of a growing number of treatment approaches to anorexia nervosa and bulimia (Fairburn 1984; Garner and Bemis 1982, 1984; Johnson et al. 1983; Long and Cordle 1982; Mitchell et al. 1984; Wooley and Wooley 1984). Didactic instruction in therapy meetings may be supplemented by selected written material (Garner et al. 1984). Not only is psychoeducational material helpful in enlisting motivation for change, but because it focuses on attitude change, it is complementary to other cognitive strategies.

Reasoning Errors

Based on Beck's (1976) taxonomy of logical errors in the thinking of depressed and phobic patients, faulty thinking patterns that may be clinically observed in anorexia nervosa have been described (Garner and Bemis 1982; Garner et al. 1982b). The following is a synopsis of the more common reasoning errors. The order of presentation does not reflect their relative prominence or sequence of appearance in psychotherapy.

Dichotomous Reasoning

This thinking style involves thinking in extreme, absolute, or all-or-none terms. This type of thinking is typically applied to food, eating, and weight. The patient insists in dividing foods into good (calorie sparing) and bad (fattening) categories. A 1-lb weight gain may be equated with incipient obesity. Breaking a rigid eating routine produces panic because it means a complete loss of control. In anorexia nervosa, rigid attitudes and behaviors are not restricted to food and weight but extend to the pursuit of sports, careers, and school. It is most evident in the area of self-evaluation. Patients usually evaluate themselves harshly and in extreme terms, despite the fact that they may view others more realistically. The anorectic often believes that such personal attributes as self-control, independence, self-confidence, and social ability must be completely and continually maintained. This leads to idealized and unattainable notions of happiness, contentment, and success.

Personalization and Self-Reference

This involves the egocentric interpretations of impersonal events or the overinterpretation of events related to the self. The anorectic patient frequently displays the conviction that strangers or casual friends would notice if a pound was gained or if a previously forbidden food was eaten. This style of thinking extends to other interpersonal situations in which the patient is unusually sensitive to disapproval from others.

Superstitious Thinking

This error in reasoning is reflected in the belief in cause-and-effect relationships of noncontingent events. It is often reflected in magical thinking, which is applied in the maintenance of eating or exercise rituals. Eating a small amount of a forbidden food may precipitate taking laxatives despite the knowledge that they do not result in malabsorption. Extreme anxiety is often experienced following a minute deviation from exercise rituals because of the belief that some vague punishment will accrue. This is often unrelated to the calorie-burning effect of exercise because patients will display great reluctance to perform even one less of a particular calisthenic after a standard has been set.

Magnification

Magnification involves overestimation of the significance of undesirable consequent events. For the anorectic patient, the significance of small increases in weight are reliably overinterpreted. Moreover, momentary lapses in willpower are viewed as a precedent for consistent poor self-discipline. In a manner similar to that observed in depressed patients, the anorectic magnifies poor performances and minimizes accomplishments in self-evaluation.

Selective Abstraction

This error in thinking is characterized by basing a conclusion on isolated details while ignoring contradictory or more salient evidence. This style of thinking is illustrated by the belief that thinness is the sole frame of reference for inferring self-worth. It is also represented by the reciprocal belief that fatness is a clear indication of incompetence. These beliefs persist in defiance of examples to the contrary.

Overgeneralization

Overgeneralization involves extracting a rule on the basis of one event and applying it to other dissimilar situations. Overgeneralization is evident in the inferences drawn about thinness. For example, a patient may conclude that weight loss would be the secret to competence because someone that she knows who is competent is also thin. Similarly, she may assume that because she was unhappy at a normal weight, weight gain will produce unhappiness. Overgeneralization is also evident in self-evaluations. A patient may infer that if she fails in one area, she is an abject failure as a person. Similarly, rejection from one person is viewed as a sign of social incompetence.

Underlying Assumptions

Beck et al. (1979) described underlying or silent assumptions that organize and determine much of the depressed person's disturbed thinking. These may be distinguished from simple faulty beliefs in that underlying assumptions may not be readily identified or verbalized by the patient. The ideas that "shape is a valid frame of reference for inferring self-worth" or that "family members are infallible" are underlying assumptions that are typical in anorexia nervosa. These assumptions are often central to the anorectic patient's personal identity. Directly challenging them is usually not advisable because this may be interpreted as a personal attack and may elicit despair or rage, which could otherwise seriously damage the therapeutic relationship. A particular class of underlying assumptions is relevant to self-concept deficits common in anorexia nervosa.

Self-Concept Deficits

There are two components of self-concept: self-esteem and self-awareness. Whereas self-esteem relates to attribution of one's own value or worth, self-awareness has been defined as the ability to identify and accurately respond to inner experiences (Garner and Bemis 1984). Deficits in self-esteem and self-awareness have formed the cornerstone of the etiologic speculations of many prominent theorists (Andersen 1983; Bruch 1973, 1978; Casper 1982; Crisp 1980; Goodsitt 1984; Lucas et al. 1976; Russell

1979; Selvini-Palazzoli 1978; Slade 1982). Modification of what may be defined as cognitive aspects of self-concept is a complex task that must be distinguished from changing simple beliefs and attitudes. Although some cognitive theorists may be reluctant to consider such global aspects of personality as amenable to cognitive restructuring because they seem so far removed from traditional behaviorism, there is a growing interest in applying cognitive methods to more complex problems (Guidano and Liotti 1983; Mahoney 1974).

Guidelines for modifying the anorectic patient's low self-esteem involve gradually assisting the patient in challenging the tendency to construe self-worth from external frames of reference. In therapy, more emphasis is placed on self-validation through the pursuit of self-defined goals and the experience of pleasure rather than exclusive reliance on external performance standards. This is an idea that is completely foreign to most patients. They are exceptionally outcome-oriented and rarely experience pleasure from the process of engaging in an activity. Many are terrified or feel guilty at the prospect of hedonic experience. This is often concealed by a supercilious facade of disinterest but almost invariably reflects a genuine incapacity in this area. An essential aspect of psychotherapy is the gradual modification of the cognitive appraisal systems and underlying assumptions related to self-esteem.

The deficits in self-awareness have been best captured by Bruch (1973), who has provided valuable clinical examples of patients' sense of "not knowing how they feel" (p. 338). This inner confusion is often related to distorted beliefs or assumptions about feelings or sensations arising in the body (Garner and Bemis 1984). They may relate to physiological needs or emotional states, and may represent a conflict between the inner experience and the belief about its appropriateness, acceptability, justification, or legitimacy. The general principles for facilitating the development of self-awareness are similar to those for improving self-esteem and may be broken down into interrelated steps as follows:

1. identification of emotions, sensations, and thoughts,
2. identification of distorted attitudes about these experiences,
3. gradual correction of these erroneous convictions by cognitive methods (which will be outlined later),
4. practice in responding to previously avoided experiences, and
5. reinforcement of the patient's independent expression of previously avoided emotions, sensations, and thoughts.

The misperceptions, faulty reasoning, and erroneous beliefs that anorectic patients have about their body must be identified and labeled as such without undermining their confidence that they possess the ability to think for themselves. Thus the treatment must proceed very gradually in correcting distortions and confirming authentic expressions of inner state.

Basic Cognitive Techniques

I will now describe specific interventions that have been derived from Beck and other cognitive theorists but adapted to anorexia nervosa (Garner and Bemis 1982, 1984; Garner et al. 1982b). The order of presentation of the basic cognitive techniques does not reflect a particular sequence of application; cognitive methods may be interwoven and applied as errors in thinking emerge in therapy.

Articulation of Beliefs

The mere articulation of beliefs may lead to belief change. One anorectic patient reported that hearing herself repeatedly verbalize her negative stereotype of obesity was an important factor in belief change because it was so inconsistent with her attitudes toward other minority groups.

Operationalizing Beliefs

The precise or explicit definition of a construct that may have idiosyncratic meaning to the patient may lead to more realistic thinking. A patient's repeated observation that he or she automatically defines a wide range of favorable attributes (e.g., achievement, fulfillment, popularity, competence) in terms of weight status may lead gradually to questioning the validity of these inferences.

Decentering

Evaluating a particular belief from a different perspective may lead to the development of more realistic attitudes. Despite "feeling fat," patients often evaluate others of a similar weight as "too thin." This recognition along with other convergent observations over many months may lead to the gradual erosion of the unrealistic beliefs attached to one's own weight. Through other examples of decentering over the course of therapy, patients often are able to appreciate that the standards for performance that they expect of themselves are far more stringent and unforgiving than those that are applied to others. The use of analogies and similes may provide another means of distancing patients from their own distorted frame of reference. For example, a patient who feared weight gain because it meant losing her "identity as an anorectic" found that it was helpful to think of relinquishing her disorder as analogous to surrendering a treasure of counterfeit money.

Decatastrophizing

Originally proposed by Ellis (1962), this technique may be used to challenge anxiety resulting from the arbitrary definition of negative consequences as intolerable despite evidence to the contrary. For example, the implicit assumption that performing one less sit-up would have disastrous consequences may be explored by the question, "what would be the worst thing that could really happen?"

Challenging the "Shoulds"

The extreme thinking indicated by dichotomous reasoning, magnification, and overgeneralization is often reflected by the "moralistic" use of the words should, must, or ought (Beck 1976; Ellis 1962; Horney 1950). Many of the anorectic's internal imperatives about food, weight, and performance in general are framed by these words, and detailed analysis usually reveals the errors in reasoning.

Challenging Beliefs Through Behavioral Exercises

The interdependence between cognitive and behavioral change is so fundamental that it is somewhat misleading to consider them separately. Particularly in the areas of food and weight, behavior change is an important vehicle for modifying both attitudes and emotions. Patients must recognize that, for the same reason that it is fruitless to expect the elevator phobic to make progress by simply talking in the therapist's office, it is unrealistic to assume that food and weight fears can be overcome without approaching these "phobic objects." Interweaving specific graded behavioral exercises with cognitive methods is a fundamental part of therapy with anorexia nervosa.

Prospective Hypothesis Testing

This technique is particularly well suited for use with behavioral exercises because it involves generating specific predictors that may be tested through behavioral experiments. For example, a patient may assume that reduced exercise will have a major impact on weight. The consequences of a moratorium on exercise may be evaluated objectively and can be used to disconfirm the fear. If a client is self-conscious about eating a dessert because she assumes others will view her as gluttonous, she might be encouraged to conduct an informal poll to determine people's attitudes about dessert. However, if experiments involve obtaining feedback from others, the patient must be prepared in advance to interpret potential negative results in a nondestructive manner.

Reattribution Techniques

Patients with anorexia nervosa often misperceive amounts of food eaten, hunger versus satiety, and their body size. They then make self-defeating decisions based on their erroneous judgments. Rather than directly modifying these refractory misperceptions, one may assist patients in altering their interpretations of these experiences (Garner and Garfinkel 1981).

Since misperceptions in these areas are characteristic of anorexia nervosa, it is helpful to attribute them to the disorder, with the recognition that subjective experience is unreliable in these cases. This approach is opposite to the general therapeutic goal of promoting trust in the validity and reliability of internal experiences. However, these patients are so confused about body shape and eating that perceptions in these areas must be temporarily replaced by "non-self-defeating" rules for conduct.

The actual process of cognitive therapy closely conforms to that outlined by Beck and his colleagues (Beck 1976; Beck et al. 1979). Although the process is not simple or linear, it may be summarized by the following steps:

1. Patients are taught to monitor their own thinking or to heighten awareness of their own thinking. This involves extracting the essential or core aspects of particular dysfunctional beliefs. Beliefs must be articulated, clarified, and operationalized to determine their consequences.
2. The patient is helped to recognize the connection between certain dysfunctional thoughts and maladaptive behaviors and emotions.
3. Together, the patient and therapist examine the evidence for the validity of particular beliefs. The implications of certain attitudes or assumptions should be followed to their logical conclusion.
4. The patient is taught gradually to substitute more realistic and appropriate interpretations based on the evidence.
5. The ultimate goal is the modification of underlying assumptions that are fundamental determinants of specific dysfunctional beliefs.

Course and Duration of Therapy

The treatment of anorexia nervosa must extend beyond the task of weight restoration, which may be "relatively simple and usually successful" (Hsu 1980). Even behavior therapists recognize the need for posthospital management over several years to prevent relapse (Geller 1975; Hauserman and Lavin 1977). Disturbed eating patterns, bulimia, vomiting, laxative abuse, and distorted attitudes or beliefs about weight frequently persist in patients at follow-up (Dally and Gomez 1979; Hsu 1980; Steinhausen and Glanville 1983; Theander 1970). Even in clinically recovered patients, there may be a vulnerability to these symptoms under stressful conditions. Dally (1967) observed that fear of eating and food fads persist in almost one-third of "recovered" patients. The prominence of dysfunctional attitudes related to food and weight as well as disturbed thinking patterns in other areas has led to the proposal of cognitive-behavioral treatment principles directly aimed at these symptoms. Although cognitive-behavioral methods are typically applied in a time-limited manner (Beck et al. 1979), this may be unrealistic for anorexia nervosa where the treatment process may be protracted. Considerable time may be required to reverse the patient's deteriorated physical state, to elicit motivation, to vitiate the positive meaning ascribed to certain focal symptoms, and to resolve psychosocial conflicts that emerge with weight gain.

Chapter 62

Family Therapy

Family therapy for the eating disorders, anorexia nervosa and bulimia, has attracted considerable clinical interest and activity. In this chapter, I will set forth many of the underlying assumptions and treatment strategies relevant to family therapy for both of these disorders. In the present chapter on the family treatment of anorexia nervosa, I will detail these issues; Chapter 71 (on the family treatment of bulimia nervosa) will be briefer and rely heavily on material presented here.

In many ways anorexia nervosa is a relatively inviting disorder for family therapists to study and to treat. First, the disorder occurs at a time in life when the child or adolescent is still quite involved with the family of origin, and when virtually all members of the family are reasonably verbal. Second, the families tend, perhaps more than many other families with major psychiatric disorders, to be intact. Third, given that a sizeable number of these patients come from upper middle-class homes, many of these families have both the financial means and sufficient awareness of psychological issues for them to consider that family issues may contribute to the problems and that ongoing family therapy may help.

Given that anorexia nervosa is a model biopsychosocial problem for psychiatry, the question for most clinicians who have a comprehensive perspective is not whether to involve the family in treatment but rather how, when, and in what ways to combine family interventions with the rest of a comprehensive treatment plan.

A Rationale for Family Therapy

Several observations combine to provide a rationale for a family approach to the treatment of anorexia nervosa. These include the fact that eating disorders are transmitted in families to a greater extent than they appear in the general population. While biologic vulnerability may contribute in this regard, transmission through modeling, social learning, and transactional inducement of the psychological anlage for anorexia nervosa are probably of at least equally great importance. Family systems have been implicated both in initiating and sustaining symptoms, and particular family features appear to be related to the prognosis of the individual patient. Finally, stress responses occur among family members as they are impacted by the devastation of anorexia nervosa, and this turmoil invites intervention at the family level.

Family Transmission of Eating Disorders

The transmission of eating disorders in families has been documented in a large number of studies. Gershon et al. (1983) found that eating disorders occurred in 6.4 percent of the first-degree relatives of anorexia nervosa patients as compared to 1.3 percent of control relatives; bulimia was more common than anorexia nervosa. Strober (1981) also found eating disorders to aggregate more in the relatives of eating disorder probands than among affective disorder probands. Studies by Crisp et al. (1980) and Kalucy et al. (1977) found histories of significantly low adolescent weight, anorexia nervosa, or weight phobias in a high percentage of first-degree relatives. In all, the estimated prevalence of anorexia nervosa among mothers and sisters of anorexia nervosa patients ranges between 3 to 10 percent in various studies (Beaumont et al. 1978; Dally and Gomez 1979; Garfinkel et al. 1980; Morgan and Russell 1975; Theander 1970). About half of the reported monozygotic twin pairs with anorexia nervosa are concordant for the disorders, a higher percentage than among dizygotic twins, but this still may suggest that both nature and nurture play a role (Nowlin 1983; Vandereycken and Pierloot 1981). Crisp's (1980) reported case of anorexia nervosa occurring in the adopted daughter of a man with anorexia nervosa informs us that psychological issues in the family are likely to be important. In addition to eating disorders, other psychiatric disorders have been reported to be more prevalent among relatives of patients with anorexia nervosa. In particular, unipolar depression and bipolar disorders have been found to be more common (Cantwell et al. 1977; Hudson et al. 1983; Kalucy et al. 1977; Strober 1983; Winokur et al. 1980). Alcoholism has also been reported to be more prevalent, particularly among fathers of patients with anorexia nervosa (Garfinkel et al. 1980; Hudson et al. 1983a; Pyle et al. 1981; Strober et al. 1982; Yager et al. 1983).

Family Systems as Initiating and Sustaining Symptoms

A wide variety of personality types has been described among the parents of patients with anorexia nervosa (Yager 1982). Different percentages of mothers and fathers have been found to be obsessional, rigid, compulsive, forceful, weak, remote, tense, neurotic, dominant, and passive. There is great diversity.

With regard to family systems, "typical" patterns have also been described, none of which are pathognomonic for anorexia nervosa. These patterns, however, are thought to be characteristic of "psychosomatic" families, that is, families in which the child or adolescent's symptoms are sustained by emotional overinvolvement and maladaptive communication patterns in the family (Minuchin et al. 1978). Goldstein (1981) described that the parents of anorexia nervosa patients demonstrated far more dependency and insecurity compared to the parents of other disturbed adolescents.

Strober (1981) administered the Moos Family Environment Scale and a Lock Wallace Short Marital Adjustment Scale to parents of children with anorexia nervosa. Considerable marital disharmony was evident in these parents. These findings are supported by studies of Garfinkel et al. (1983) and Garner et al. (1983), using the Family Assessment Measure, which obtains perceptions of family functioning in various areas (e.g., task accomplishment, role performance, communication and affective expression). Families of anorexia nervosa patients reported more difficulty in all of these subscales than did controls. The difficulties that were reported are not specific to anorexia nervosa but are found in other families with chronic dysfunction as well.

To summarize, it would seem that emotionally troubled families, particularly those with eating disorder, depression, and alcoholism, provide fertile ground for the development of eating disorders in the offspring. Kalucy et al. (1977) attempted to explain some of the specificity by suggesting that anorexia nervosa develops in troubled families where concerns about eating, body shape, and weight are major content areas around which the family communicates.

Family Factors in Prognosis

Similar to work in other areas of psychopathology, data are accumulating to demonstrate that family attitudes are of prognostic import in anorexia nervosa. Several authors have related parental conflict and rejecting, hostile parents to poor outcome (Crisp 1980; Dally and Gomez 1979; Morgan et al. 1983). Szmukler (1983) suggested that high negative expressed emotion will predict poor outcome in the family of the anorexia nervosa patient as in schizophrenia.

Family Stress Reactions

In the wake of major insults such as intractable anorexia nervosa, families experience adjustment responses and demonstrate disturbed behavior that may not be typical for them. The threat confronted by parents at virtually every meal is that of a seemingly willfully starving child. Given the etiologic ambiguity, it is virtually certain that every parent will experience guilt or denial and projection of guilt. Frustrated in that none of their positive or negative, entreating, begging, or threatening behaviors seem to make any difference in aborting the child's self-destructive trajectory, parents feel increasingly frantic, impotent, and alienated toward one another. According to the predominant cognitive style of each family member, from denial through hypervigilance, various arrays of maladaptive disorganization may appear. Dally (1969) described five different types of mother-daughter interactions for anorexia nervosa, which essentially exaggerate all possible patterns of the ordinary adolescent-parent conflicts, ranging from cooperation to hostile confrontation to meek acquiescence of either mother or daughter. The shifting appearances of the family through the course of these adjustments have not been adequately studied, so that it is uncertain to what extent therapeutic intervention can claim credit for the improvements in family relationships and communication patterns that sometimes occur over time. These changes may, indeed, represent primarily the natural resolution of adjustment responses in the family. Similarly, negative and maladaptive patterns that seem to unfold may not have been present in the same way prior to the onset of the anorexia nervosa, but may in part represent the family's version of a post traumatic chronic stress response.

Given these various levels of family involvement with anorexia nervosa, the rationale and directions for family therapy are evident. The therapist will attempt to assess features in the family that may be sustaining anorexia nervosa and that may be contributing adversely to prognosis. By attending to the other distressed members of the family and helping them to resolve their own emotional reactions to the patient's problems, the therapist hopes to create an environment in which healing can best occur.

Assessment of the Family

Concepts relevant to the assessment of the family have been provided by many clinicians and theoreticians, and a large number of potentially salient dimensions of family systems have been suggested. The variety of dimensions available for characterizing families provide the therapist with tools—cognitive grappling hooks—that may be useful as the therapist starts to work with a family. Otherwise elusive phenomena may be more easily recognized and comprehended through such dimensions. It behooves the therapist to be familiar with as many of these concepts as possible because it is never clear at the start which features of a family will emerge as most salient.

Most familiar to clinicians who work with eating disorders are those concepts derived from a psychoanalytic perspective and from a systems point of view (most notably, Haley 1976; Minuchin et al. 1978; Selvini-Palazzoli 1978). Other concepts that have not as yet been extensively applied to anorexia nervosa families include the living systems theory (Miller and Miller 1983), the expressed emotion of families (Szmukler 1983), and additional structural and process typologies that permit a far more differentiated conceptualization of families than has hitherto been available (e.g., Beavers and Voller 1983; Kantor and Lehr 1975; Kog et al. 1983; Olson et al. 1983; Riess 1981; Wertheim 1973). Each of these frameworks can offer the clinician working with the anorexia nervosa family some useful perspectives on organization and dynamics of the family.

From a systems view, the family is seen as a supra-individual organism, a living system that is constantly reorganizing and attempting to evolve and develop while maintaining its integrity. This is not a homeostatic entity, except perhaps in the short run. Families maintain their internal structure by means of subtle but definite rules that regulate communication, the expression of affect, the distribution of power and roles, and their openness versus impermeability to the outside world. The family serves as a transmitter, interpreter, and filter of various cultural pressures coming from the outside, and as a powerful shaper and reinforcer of the beliefs, attitudes, and perceptions of the individuals within the family (i.e., the "subsystems"). The habits, miscommunication patterns, and transactional "dances" that occur within a family seem to achieve a life of their own, larger than any one member. In this view, families may be seen as having a natural tendency to be resilient if the family is allowed to free itself and become "unstuck" from pathologic and maladaptive ruts.

It is also important to recognize that serious, rate-limiting constraints are built into family systems by the rigidities and limitations of the individuals who comprise them. For example, the most perfect of therapies won't enable a damaged child to spring back to perfect health unless the necessary prerequisites for health (e.g., neurologic integrity) are there to start. A patient whose hypertension and serious cerebral vascular accident are blamed on family stresses may still not be able to regain full mental functioning following the stroke even if those family stresses are subsequently resolved. This same sense of potential limitation must be appreciated in the treatment of severe chronic anorexia nervosa: although the more resilient and healthy anorexia nervosa patient can certainly be aided significantly by appropriate family intervention, there are still patients for whom all of our best efforts produce little tangible gain.

In this regard, it is useful to conceive of an interplay of various individual vulnerabilities with various family problems in the pathogenesis of anorexia nervosa. Perhaps extemely problematic families can provoke anorexia nervosa in relatively healthy individuals who reside within the family. Conversely, the individual with a strong disposition for anorexia nervosa may develop the disorder even in a relatively benign family. Therefore, assessment of the family system must attend adequately to the individual strengths and weaknesses of each member of the family as well as the family as a whole system.

According to Minuchin et al. (1978), there are four characteristics of families in which anorexia nervosa is found. First, enmeshment occurs when family members are overinvolved with one another, may answer for one another, and intrude on each other's thoughts and feelings. Second, overprotectiveness occurs when parents and children attempt to cushion one another from life's assaults in an infantilizing manner. Third, rigidity includes the need to maintain conventional social roles often at the expense of both honest expression of feelings and of autonomous fulfillment of each individual's needs. The fourth characteristic is a tendency to avoid overt conflicts within the family, resulting in lack of clear resolution of those issues that might stir up dissent. These features, further elaborated below, have been observed by others; Selvini-Palazzoli (1978) used slightly different words to described essentially the same concepts.

The assessment of the family should take place in sessions in which the family is seen as a whole group as well as in sessions in which family members are seen alone and in relevant diads and triads, the subunits of the family system. Minuchin et al. (1978) creatively conducted assessment during a "family lunch session," observing the attempts of family members to get their child with anorexia nervosa to eat with them (Liebman et al. 1983).

Sometimes certain members of the family may not be identified as being critically important initially (e.g., an absent sibling or grandparent). Whenever the therapist realizes that an absent member is very important to an understanding of the patient in the family, that person should be interviewed whenever feasible and be invited to participate in the assessment and, if necessary, in the treatment. Seeing individual family members alone provides an opportunity for them to discuss perspectives or secrets that they might not feel comfortable bringing up with the others present. Such information, which may constitute missing pieces to a puzzle, might not otherwise be available to the therapist.

The goals of assessment are to permit the therapist to determine the extents to which: 1) maladaptive communications, rules, and rituals in the family have contributed to the onset and maintenance of the patient's illness; 2) the patient's illness is maintained because it stabilizes other maladaptive aspects of a family system (e.g., keeping potentially divorcing parents together); 3) manifest psychological disturbance seen in various family members may be adjustment responses secondary to the impact of the devastating illness; 4) specific family-based themes and conflicts may be important in the individual psychotherapy of the anorexia nervosa patient; 5) the family's criticism and high negative expressed emotion may serve to undermine progress and promise a poor prognosis; 6) the family evidences strengths and support that may be of use to the patient in recovery; and 7) various members of the family are to be included in ongoing treatment of the anorexia nervosa.

It may be useful to formulate the assessment according to the family's past, present, and future, as presented below. In practice, it is often most instructive to start with a family's perspectives about its future because this may provide the most immediately relevant information regarding goal setting, tactics, and strategies for the therapy. Once goals are in mind, the pertinent past and present information necessary for helping the clinician more clearly delineate and achieve those goals can be obtained. Of course, goals may be modified during the course of therapy, and they may differ greatly from case to case.

For clarity of presentation, these areas will be described in historical sequence. In practice, however, the assessment of various dimensions usually takes place concurrently, as relevant clinical leads are followed as they come up.

Assessing the Past

The genogram.   The genogram consists of a genetic family tree, with extensions beyond the nuclear family to include at least three generations. Information obtained includes history of medical and psychiatric illnesses; meaningful psychological relationships; shared "mythic," constitutional, or temperamental characteristics between and among individuals; and ages of major events such as deaths, divorces, separations, and illnesses.

Family myths, loyalties, scripts, and implied contracts.   These provide the often unspoken assumptions that channel lives in various directions. They are constructed from the collective and individual expectations of family members as to destiny, roles that various family members should serve for one another, and the values and "glue" that bind family members to certain obligations to one another.

Secrets.   Secrets limit communication and create gaps in otherwise potentially trusting and loving relationships. They may absorb the energy of the secret keeper and further distance him or her from others in the family. Extensive rationales may be elaborated as to the importance of maintaining secrets and about the terribly destructive effects that revelation might provoke. Common secrets include those regarding adoptions, incest or abuse, perversions, extramarital affairs, and illegal behaviors.

Historical typology.   Several family typologies have been suggested (e.g., Beavers and Voeller 1983; Lewis et al. 1976; Lidz 1976; Riess 1981). To illustrate, over long periods of time, a couple's relationship may be viewed as symmetrical or complementary. In a symmetrical relationship, there is mutual interdependence and exchange of important roles. In a complementary relationship, one parent is more powerful than the other and usually makes most of the important decisions, whereas the other takes a back seat and is more dependent on the primary person. These relationships also vary in their stability and satisfactoriness. In many clinicians' experience, the marital relationships of parents of anorexia nervosa (and bulimia) patients are usually complementary rather than symmetrical.

Assessing the Present

Structure. Family structure includes the boundaries of the nuclear family system in relation to the parental families (families of origin), and the parent-to-parent, parent-to-child, and child-to-child subsystem boundaries as they form various coalitions and alliances. The boundary of the nuclear family is considered to be stable and secure when the relationships between the parents, for example, are stronger than those between either parent and a grandparent. Under normal conditions, the parental coalition is stronger and more influential than any of the coalitions between a parent and a child. Triangles are formed involving parents and a child, or two children and a parent. Some may exist as perverse triangles in which are played out continuous, maladaptive "games without end," scapegoating, detouring, and other triangulation phenomena. The roles that each family member plays and the potential for role reversals are examined here. Examples of roles include parenting support, nurturant problem solving, and financial provider. The stability of these roles needs attention. For example, a parent may be able to sustain an important parental role only some of the time, at other times leaving gaps that the children are expected to either fill for themselves or fill through other influential adults outside the nuclear family. Other structural dimensions have been suggested by Miller in his writing on living systems theory, structures that can be identified in every living system from cell to community. A preliminary application of these concepts has been attempted with families with anorexia nervosa (Miller and Miller 1983), but further work is necessary to determine their ultimate clinical utility.

Process. Processes that can be assessed in families include communications styles, defensive operations, transactional patterns, tendencies to bind or disperse, and tendencies to grow or stagnate.

Communications styles contain affective and behavioral components. The verbal and nonverbal (paralexical and body language) patterns of communication act as strong behavioral prompts and reinforcers, from both classical and operant conditioning perspectives. From an individual psychoanalytic point of view, defense mechanisms and defensive operations can be seen at work in the various family members (e.g., projective identification or using the other as a self-object, other familiar defensive distortions). As these are used in relation to other family members, reciprocal induction of behaviors may occur. On an interpersonal level, chronically maladaptive transactions such as the games described by transactional analysts can be seen.

Some families have internal authoritarian communication patterns, whereas others operate more by consensus of family members. Some tend toward morphostasis (remaining the same), whereas others demonstrate morphogenesis (evolution). Some families are adaptable, whereas others are rigid. Some are enmeshed, whereas others are differentiated. Some are overprotective, whereas others encourage autonomy. Some tend toward cohesion within the family, whereas other families are more likely to disperse. Some are centripetal, whereas others are centrifugal. Some families are primarily concerned about maintaining internal consensus, whereas others are more sensitive to outsiders, and still others distance themselves from outsiders and from one another.

Another aspect of process concerns the family's stage in its own family life cycle. The parents may still be dealing with issues of individuation and of becoming autonomous from their own parents. They may be dealing with early, middle, or late parenthood, with the decline of their parents' health or their own, and so on.

Experiential aspects.   Family members will each have unique understandings and sets of beliefs about the nature and causes of the eating disorder, and will vary in the extent to which they are concerned about and upset by the impact of the disorder on themselves separately and collectively. The individual and family self-concepts, cognitive and coping styles, and attitudes and values will all differ. Of particular importance is each person's sense of blame and guilt concerning the disorder, and how separate from or loyal to the family each feels.

Assessing the Future

Expectations regarding the eating disorder.   Of importance are various family members' concepts of expected and "appropriate" treatment, prognosis, and the impact that the future course of the illness and its treatment will have on each individual and on the family as a whole.

Degree of commitment to the patient and to one another.   By the time some families present for treatment, one of the family members has decided to leave the rest of the family for self-protection without having explicitly announced it. At times, bringing the identified patient to treatment at a specific time is a prelude to the hidden agenda of separating from the patient, or abandonment. By placing the patient in professional care, some family members hope to diminish the burden of guilt they will bear by extricating themselves from further responsibilities.

Capacity of various individuals and of the family system as a whole for change. Included here are the interest and accessibility of family members for therapy or other outside interventions. For example, it has been suggested that those families willing to engage in family therapy may be more likely to have a better prognosis (or at least make better use of the therapy) than are those families who at the start are unwilling or unable to engage. The possibility of change may also be related to the tenacity of the family myths and scripts, and how much they continue to form the family's framework for the future.

Indications for Family Therapy in Anorexia Nervosa

No family is perfect, and few are without their share of difficulties. From a systems perspective, no patient can fail to benefit from some form of family intervention, including family education and counseling. But more intensive family therapies are indicated only when there are specific findings in the family system that seem to be promoting or sustaining the anorexia nervosa. These include the following:

1. *Communications problems.* Extensive communications problems such as lack of clarity, failure to deal directly with affectively charged issues, lack of explicit com-

mitment, and chronic, demeaning hostility may be present and detrimental to the patient's recovery and well-being.

2. *Structural problems involving the parental pair and the patient.* Pathologic triangulations (e.g., detouring, scapegoating) that reinforce and support the patient's eating disorder are indications for therapy. In some cases, excessively intrusive grandparents and inadequate capacity of the parents to maintain their boundaries with respect to the grandparents contribute to the chaos sustaining the disorder.

3. *Hostile relations among siblings.* Parents are sometimes overwhelmed and ineffective in their attempts to abort or diminish intense hositility or competitiveness between close siblings. When several siblings are hypersensitive, or when several are striving for inadequate parental attention, their interactions may fuel and sustain an ongoing eating disorder.

4. *Parental paralysis or burnout.* After months of dealing ineffectively with an anorexia nervosa patient, a parent may feel incapable of making further decisions or of coping adequately, essentially displaying "learned helplessness." At such times, family therapy may facilitate the parent's rehabilitation, with the therapists temporarily assuming some of the critical parental roles until the parent can regroup and recover.

5. *Threatened family dissolution.* If the family is in the anticipatory stages or actual throes of separation or divorce, outspoken or unspoken tensions may contribute to sustaining the disorder.

6. *Family violence.* Intervention is indicated whenever there is overt violence among family members (e.g., when a parent passes beyond the threshold of contained exasperation). Of interest, family violence seems less common among families with anorexia nervosa patients than in many other troubled families.

7. *Excessive separation anxiety.* When either the child or a parent experiences excessive anxiety about threatened separation, family therapy is indicated. Often parents of older teenage or young adult anorexia nervosa patients feel put upon when their overly anxious children, who "should" be leaving the parental home, make no effort to do so and, in fact, appear to be burrowing in. In other cases, overly anxious parents are very reluctant to give up their children who are making attempts, even feeble ones, to separate. In the accumulated experiences of many clinicians, when a therapist simply engages in a premature tug of war with parents in an attempt to pull the patient with anorexia nervosa away, the therapist and the patient end up losing because the patient's ties to the parents are usually much stronger than they are to the therapist. For some families, the fear of the patient's death, as the ultimate separation, is preoccupying and requires attention.

8. *Excessive family guilt and blame.* Family belief systems that focus on guilt and blame tie and bind the family members together in maladaptive ways, while leaving the various parties feeling hurt, angry, and generally impotent. Blame, toward the child for being ill or toward the parents for causing the disorder, serves little therapeutic purpose. In the context of high negative expressed emotion, constant blaming of the patient contributes to poor outcome. The identification of such a system suggests the need for family therapy.

9. *Concerns of children whose mothers have anorexia nervosa.* There are women with anorexia nervosa who have children of their own, some of whom are in latency and adolescence. The needs of these children should be recognized. For example, in one clinic, daughters of anorexia nervosa patients became mildly to moderately obese. These daughters told their mothers that they ate excessively so that they wouldn't get anorexia nervosa. As with other major parental illnesses, attention

should be given to the experiences and concerns of the children who are living with its effects and uncertain implications for their futures.

Therapy

Guidelines for the family component of treatment must fall within an overall perspective on the nature of anorexia nervosa and a comprehensive treatment plan.

1. Anorexia nervosa consists of a heterogeneous group of syndromes. Furthermore, the families are heterogeneous as well.
2. Pathogenesis among different patients is variably related to biologic, psychological, family, and cultural influences. Each of these levels contains its own set of constraints that limit possibilities for successful therapeutic interventions at the various levels.
3. Effective treatment plans for anorexia nervosa rarely consist of single modalities in an either-or fashion, but usually include a combination of and-and treatment options.
4. Given what we know about the natural history of anorexia nervosa, cure is not always possible and should not necessarily be the goal in every case.
5. In devising an intervention algorithm, one should start with those most likely to be effective and least harmful, and only later add those with greater "costs" as they seem necessary if the initial efforts are not adequate.
6. The clinician must be pragmatic, use what works, and creatively design a therapy plan to fit the specific case. It is essential to achieve a comprehensive perspective on the biologic, individual, and family levels, analogous to being able to peer through the microscope at high, medium, and low power to perceive all potentially relevant treatment openings.

It is clear that while the individual's psychological and biologic issues must always be taken into account, the family perspective cannot be excluded.

Given the need to at least think about family aspects of anorexia nervosa, the clinician must consider several questions: When is family evaluation indicated? In this view, almost always. To what extent should family therapy be part of the treatment plan? This depends on the extent to which the assessment reveals indications as described above that would suggest real therapeutic potential from a family therapy approach.

Who in the family should be involved? There are no strict rules. One cannot categorically state that everyone needs to be involved, nor that anyone in particular should be excluded. It is usually fruitless to require an intransigently paranoid, rigid, hostile family member to participate in family sessions on an ongoing basis. Family therapy may occur in combinations of diads, triads, and larger groupings within the nuclear family, and should sometimes include members from the extended intergenerational family as well.

Should family therapy ever be used without individual therapy, or vice versa? In most clinicians' experiences, both are indicated, usually concurrently.

Determining the Goals and Strategies

The strategies to be used depend on the therapeutic goals for the family. The first order of business is to define these goals, with the patient and family contributing their views as explicitly as possible. Very often, helping the family to clarify its own treatment goals, to be more precise than the obvious "getting better," is an important initial task. The therapist will, of course, have his or her own views about what the goals should (or could) be, and should present these to the family as clearly as possible, with a rationale and statement as to how achieveable they are. Such goals may be couched in aspirations for the physical and emotional well-being of various members of the family, for better communication between A and B, more effective problem solving about C and D, and so on.

The goals for therapy may depend in part on the stage of the family in its life cycle. The younger patient who will be staying with the family for at least several years requires a strategy that will allow the family to live together more comfortably. The older adolescent or young adult may need help to leave, or the parents may need help in getting the patient to leave home or in accepting the patient's inability to do so.

As preliminary goals, the therapist should attempt to settle the chaos in the family, reduce destructive interaction, and return some parenting authority and semblance of control to the parents (in the case of the younger patient). The goals of family therapy will shift with the phase of the illness and with the evolution of its course. Survival issues are paramount in the acutely hospitalized young patient, whereas during the resolution phase, once their concerns about their child's immediate safety are settled, parents may spend more time in assessing their own relationship.

The ambivalences of family members regarding commitments to maintain supportive emotional and economic relationships are often issues in setting goals. Helping family members deal with these ambivalences may initially take precedence before other goals can be set.

Therapeutic strategies to be employed will depend on the skills of the therapist, on the family's beliefs and willingness to participate in various forms of therapy, and on some of the specific characteristics of the family. For example, Will (1983) described different treatments for the overanxious family and for the family with a low level of anxiety. With the overanxious family, he suggested explicitly dealing with feared imagined consequences of change, with feared imagined powers attributed to the therapist, and with fears that family secrets may be revealed. He gives assurances that secrets will not be revealed unless there is consent, and he holds a tactical individual session with the most highly anxious member to learn more about what is provoking the anxiety. When secrets exist, he obtains a therapeutic mandate about what can be openly talked about. With the low anxiety family, Will uses authoritarian techniques and others designed to generate a sense of crisis. This, he feels, is necessary to get the family involved in treatment. He particularly attempts to prevent family members from projecting their anxiety onto staff members or one another, and he attempts to get each person to take additional responsibility for the patient's outcome.

The Hospital Phase

In many cases, hospitalization is one of the earlier events in the long-term treatment of this disorder. At this time, a very thorough assessment of the family should take place. As with many other issues in the therapy of anorexia nervosa, controversy exists regarding how much the involvement and interaction should be permitted between families and patients during the hospital phase. Some authorities (e.g., Minuchin et al. 1978) keep hospitalization to a minimum and actively involve the family in therapy with the patient from the very beginning, continuing active family therapy through the hospital and discharge periods. Others advocate a modified "parentectomy" during hospitalization, separating the patient from the family and encouraging active family involvement only toward the latter part of the hospital stay and in follow-up (Harper 1983; Vandereycken and Meerman 1984). The rationale for parentectomy has several arguments. First, exhausted parents may need a prescribed period of "rest and relaxation" from the child, and they cannot do this guilt free unless ordered to do so in an authoritarian manner by the treating staff. Second, to the extent that the family's hostile criticism persists and sustains anorexia nervosa symptoms, putting distance between those criticisms and the patient may help recuperation. Third, constant overinvolvement on the part of the parents and splitting of the parents and staff by the patients may serve to heighten commotion on the inpatient unit and to sustain maladaptive anorectic behavior. For example, an overinvolved mother may become so distressed by her daughter's pleas to rescue her from "being tortured by a terrible hospital staff" that expects her to eat, that the mother may wittingly or unwittingly undermine the staff's treatment plan. Fourth, absence of the parents may force the patient to relate to and rely on the staff rather than on the parents. This may interrupt old illness-sustaining patterns in the family, and heighten for the patient the ideas that the self-destructive anorectic patterns are being taken very seriously and that they should be modified.

Should the family be seen by a different therapist than the one who sees the patient individually? Some programs have found it practical to divide therapy (e.g., having a social worker see the family while a psychiatrist sees the patient). If this is the case, close interaction of the various involved therapists is essential to prevent splitting and taking of sides. Often one therapist can work effectively with both the individual patient and the family. This must be decided on the capacity of the patient to trust that the therapist will not become an agent of the family to the patient's detriment. Sometimes having a second therapist in family sessions is useful, but not required.

A Prudent Approach to Family Therapy

Family therapists ordinarily interact with families in a myriad of complex ways that are not easily captured by any one set of descriptions. The therapist simultaneously acts as a member of the family, advocate, clarifier, interpreter, prompter, reinforcer, coach, model, surrogate, persuader, coercer, and irritant. The therapist may provide nurturance or permission to act to any and all members, and serve as a general coping device for the family. The therapist's verbal and nonverbal behaviors are all influential. In addition to the actual content of what the therapist says, the therapist's gaze, body language, steadiness, and those qualities that may be subsumed under charisma determine the extent to which family members allow themselves to be influenced by what transpires.

With this in mind, and with the basic assumptions about therapy listed above as background, we can set forth a prudent approach to family therapy:

1. Start with a thorough assessment of the family. The past, present, and future dimensions described above can be evaluated.
2. Formulate the case at a family level. Here, the task is to differentiate how the family has, and has not, contributed to the appearance of the syndrome, how anorexia nervosa impacts on the family, and how the syndrome may be sustained by the family system.
3. Assess indications for family therapy as described above.
4. Determine therapeutic goals with the family. Pick achievable goals. These may be

relatively modest. Unachievable grandiosity on the part of the therapist or the family can be counterproductive, and ultimately undermine belief in the value of therapy. If there is little of underlying ego strength, the therapist is probably best served by not pushing too hard for unrealistic and unachievable change. Fundamental transcendent changes in family systems that may require forceful interventions, some of which are described below, may simply not be achievable in many instances.

5. Generate a treatment algorithm, staging the family intervention and integrating it with the other individual, psychological, behavioral, and/or medication treatments that are to be employed. Estimate expectations about how long each intervention might take, and plan alternatives if these expectations are not met within a reasonable period of time (e.g., several weeks to months).

6. Start by focusing on issues that concern the family most. Therapy should address those incidents and behaviors that are most problematic and uppermost in everyone's minds. The focus should be problems, not persons. By starting with the explicitly stated central problems defined by the family, the therapist can obtain needed orientation and not get lost in the morass of other readily identified but potentially less relevant issues. Crisis-generated problem-solving sessions, even if held only intermittently, may serve as a prelude for more intensive or regularly scheduled family work. This approach may be a necessary first step to engage treatment-reluctant families.

7. Sequence interventions. A prudent approach begins with education and interpretative-clarification techniques and proceeds as necessary through directive-prescriptive techniques to the occasional use of paradoxical interventions.

Therapeutic Interventions

Psychoeducation. The family is educated about anorexia nervosa in general and about the patient's specific condition. A comprehensive biopsychosocial (including family) formulation is provided, using perspectives that family members may use to understand, deal with, and help the patient. The family should be told what is known about prognostic indicators and outcomes for anorexia nervosa. The therapist must often help the family to understand behaviors in the patient they attribute solely to spitefulness and willfulness. Providing a family with the perspective that the pathogenesis of anorexia nervosa remains obscure, and that biologic as well as psychological causes may exist, can help reduce guilt and blame.

Interpretive-clarifying and communication techniques. The therapist facilitates communication—exploring, clarifying, interpreting, and extracting clear statements from those confused, vague, or diffuse messages that have obfuscated meanings and intentions. In family sessions, the therapist will often restate in clear declarative sentences what he or she thinks has been said, and will request clarification and confirmation from family members. The connotations and the nonverbal communications surrounding the words are not ignored, but are dealt with explicitly. For example, by absorbing the snide remarks and caustic asides that accompany various statements, the therapist acts as a capacitor, buffer, and modulator. Content and process issues at multiple levels are identified, distilled, reformulated, and examined.

Clarifications include helping the family to decide exactly who is responsible for which feelings, intentions, tasks, and symptoms. Each member is encouraged to accept appropriate personal responsibility rather than project onto others or hold others accountable for all the problems. The experiences and concerns of each of the family members, patient included, are validated in their own right, but validation of experience should not give any single member a license to blame or wrong another person.

Explorations may concern those long-standing family myths and loyalties that appear to sustain symptoms, the family's values concerning performance and appearance, the extent to which individuals are encouraged to be autonomous, pockets of unresolved or anticipated grief (including those concerning poor outcome for the patient), potential sources of secondary gain for the illness, and resistance to recovery. For example, the therapist may explore with the patient and other family members exactly how things would change for all concerned if the patient, in fact, fully recovered.

It is most important in interpretive and clarifying work for the therapist to maintain and contain a constructive emotional tone in the family session. For example, while honest uncovering of previously unexpressed feelings is encouraged, it is counterproductive simply to allow venomous and unchecked yelling and screaming on the part of the patient or other family members. The therapist needs to recognize when a family has passed the productive threshold for communication and work, and may find it necessary to call for a time-out, permitting overheated emotions to abate before the sessions continue. It is counterproductive to invite the family to "let it all hang out," in which no holds barred, dirty fighting, and mean, provocative, and hurtful displays are supported as "therapeutic." Such sessions create problems; they don't solve any.

In this regard, a perspective of the family as a "non-zero sum game" is often useful. In this view, either everyone in the family wins or everyone loses. Some family members may believe that one person can gain something only if another one loses (i.e., a zero sum game). The therapist attempts to help everyone to do well, not to "cure" one person at the expense of another, although realistically this isn't always feasible. A very dependent family member may find that as others emancipate or focus more on satisfying their own previously ignored needs, they may be less willing to sacrifice themselves altruistically for the dependent person. But even here the therapist will still try to find ways to support the dependent individual until such time as that person may be able to assume more autonomous responsibility.

Directive-prescriptive techniques. Family interventions subsumed under this label include structural (Minuchin et al. 1978), strategic (Haley 1976), and systematic therapies (Selvini-Palazzoli 1978), and other direct and behavioral types of interventions. Various authors have constructed contrasting theoretical superstructures, but the extent to which their practices actually differ from one another in clinically meaningful ways is not clear.

Structural and systemic theories see maladaptive families as caught up in pathologic family games that never end, but go on and on repetitively. As an example of such a recursive self-sustaining maladaptive pattern of interaction, consider the following situation: Father acts cold, aloof and withdrawn. As a consequence, mother becomes tearful and depressed and overinvolves herself with daughter. As a consequence, daughter withdraws into herself and becomes more preoccupied with her anorectic behavior. As a consequence, the parents draw together and both come to the daughter's aid. At this point, mother cuddles and rocks daughter to comfort her. As a consequence, the father becomes more aloof and withdrawn because he thinks the mother is too lenient and feels angry toward her. Such families are thought to be particularly vulnerable to individual or collective emotional breakdown at times of external stress and change.

The theorists suggest that by injecting new tasks and constraints into the family system at critical points in this cycle, these recursive constants will destabilize and the old family patterns will break up. In the illustration, for example, father may be asked to rock the patient to comfort her. Such unexpected and discontinuous shifts in behavior are thought to be able to effect meaningful and sustained changes in the family's equilibrium. In family systems parlance so-called first-order changes are those that occur as various family members extend or diminish in a continuous straight-line fashion those ordinary behaviors in which they already engage. In some cases, first-order changes are all that are needed to improve the family's situation (e.g., more attention, more limits, less criticism). However, with very recalcitrant families, those that are firmly entrenched in maladaptive games, it has been postulated that discontinuous changes in the system may have to be provoked, that is, total reorganizations of certain family patterns, major transformations that are predicted to follow a major assault on the family's ordinary modes of operating. This has been called second-order change.

The new tasks or constancies injected into the family system to provoke second-order change may take the form of unusual or novel prescribed behaviors for one of the family members, new family rituals, seemingly paradoxical behavioral prescriptions that generate oppositional behavior, positive rewards, and actual or threatened negative consequences such as shame or humiliation if changes aren't forthcoming.

The parents may be essentially co-opted and enlisted as "paratherapists" by being given new ways to act with the patient. To illustrate, whereas previously the parents may have routinely screamed at or pleaded with the child to eat, for a while they may be asked to only keep detailed records of what the patient eats, but not to do more. This concept of training is used in a variety of behavioral interventions. Parents might be required to respond in new, carefully scripted ways to the patient's requests and provocations, to spend time in prescribed and unfamiliar interactions or settings with the patient, and so on. Specific instructions may be offered to get the family to reduce hostile angry criticisms. Time-outs during the week, during which family members stay away from one another if excessive closeness unfailingly generates conflict, may be established.

Many of the prescriptions are designed to strengthen structural alliances within the family. In particular, the parental bond is strengthened where possible, attempts are made to interfere with perverse triangles by explicitly encouraging or prohibiting certain dyadic interactions, and reliance on grandparents or others in the extended family is reduced.

On occasion, symptoms themselves are redirected, with the goal of bringing certain symptoms under voluntary control by prescribing the conditions under which they occur (e.g., regarding the time, place, and content of eating binges, family arguments, discussions concerning food).

In cases where communication problems are paramount, where vague communications or unremitting fury prevent messages from being adequately communicated and received, family members may be asked to communicate by letter, with explicit requests and responses written out. This technique is sometimes useful in getting families to focus on the tasks at hand and prevent them from getting constantly sidetracked.

Asking the family to tape-record its conversations and arguments at home is also useful. Family members are asked to collect "field data" as if they were anthropologists, and all members have permission to turn on the tape recorder whenever they want to. This procedure produces several effects. First, the tape recorder often inhibits arguments because many family members are reluctant to allow their seemingly immature rantings to be recorded for the therapist. Second, hearing the playback often has a powerful impact. Although family members can usually describe their relatives' outbursts accurately, they often are less aware of what they themselves are like during outbursts. Listening to the tapes can strengthen their "observing egos."

The therapeutic mealtime is another device. On an ongoing basis, the therapist may join the family members in their home or a restaurant for regular meals, commenting on and directing interactions around food among family members.

Before attempting to bring about major family system changes through direct or paradoxical interventions, the therapist must assess the extent to which the family is capable of containing the considerable emotional arousal sometimes generated during these maneuvers. It is also important for the therapist to use all available means to channel the family's changes in the desired direction and to prevent upheavals from leading to unanticipated and deleterious shifts. Second-order changes are intended to induce a spring toward health rather than provoke family dissolution, suicide, or other untoward negative consequences.

Paradoxical techniques. Paradoxical techniques are those that would seem, at first, designed to promote or strengthen the symptoms, but that in theory result in positive change. It has been suggested that of all the family therapy techniques, paradoxical techniques are most likely to produce second-order changes. Several dramatic case histories have been described in which paradoxical techniques have been credited with bringing about major upheavals, reorganizations, and long-standing health-sustaining changes. However, it is not known how often such attempts at change simply fall flat or how often such interventions are counterproductive, perhaps resulting in a termination of therapy or even in iatrogenically induced disasters.

Familiar paradoxical techniques include encouraging the patient to maintain or even increase the symptoms and ordering family members to maintain a certain maladaptive pattern. Presumably, such techniques capitalize on the assumed tendencies among family members to be oppositional; these techniques work along the lines of "negative psychology." That is, it is assumed that if the therapist tries to "take control" of the symptom, the patient or family will rebel and behave differently. The extent to which this actually occurs is a matter for future research.

Another paradoxical technique has the therapist asking someone other than the patient, usually a well-behaved sibling or a martyr-like parent, to "make trouble" for awhile, to create distraction and a new stress with which the family must contend. Again, the idea of destabilizing a maladaptive equilibrium is central.

In reading the descriptions and watching some of the well-known family therapists using paradox, one is often struck by the theatrical flare and overacting in which they sometimes engage. Must effective family therapy require such showmanship? Probably not, although some charisma never hurts. A sympathetic and compassionate appreciation for the struggles of the family must always be maintained. Even when the family is offered a formulation and set of prescriptions designed to induce second-order change, it is never necessary for the therapist to be duplicitous or ingenuine.

When confronted with ingenuineness, families may quickly surmise what the therapist is attempting to do and, regardless of the outcome, may lose trust in the therapist and, by extension, in other therapists. Some family therapists who use provocative paradoxical techniques often find that they have engendered the animosity of the families, even when the families may get better. In an alternative strategy, the therapist may provide the family with a full description of what seems to be going on together with suggested changes, including the idea that paradoxical behaviors may be able to shake up a nonfunctioning but entrenched system. To illustrate the difference between these two approaches, in a classic paradoxical intervention, a straight-faced therapist might say to an anorectic daughter: "Clearly you are being a good daughter to your mother by not eating. Therefore I want you to continue to not eat so that your mother can have something to worry about and feel needed." In the alternative approach, the therapist would say: "Let me describe your family. As you can see, one could almost describe what's happening in your family in the following way. As ridiculous as it sounds, it's almost as if you're helping your mother by not eating. . . . Do you really want to help her in that way? One way to interrupt this pattern would be for you to help your mother to feel needed by doing so and so. . . . If you don't believe me, try it. In fact, if you aren't able to improve your eating on your own in a week or two, I'd like you to try what I just suggested and see what happens."

Here, the mother's and daughter's secondary gains that presumably sustain the anorexia nervosa are exposed to the family. In some instances this revelation may be sufficiently provocative and embarrassing to induce change.

Difficulties, Resistances, and Problems in Family Therapy

A myriad of difficulties can occur in family therapy, and many treatments do not follow the "textbook." Difficulties may originate with the patient, the family, or the therapist.

With regard to the patient, major psychopathology, particularly regressive behavior with psychotic-like thinking, impulsivity, and rage, may test the best family and the best family therapist. The substantial psychological regression that occurs in the severely starving patient also limits the extent to which patients may profitably participate in active family therapy. The therapist must decide at any given stage whether the patient is ready for such work.

Problems emanating from the family are severalfold. In some families, one of the major figures may refuse to participate, in which case the therapist must make the best of it with those family members who will participate. At times the family may seem to wish to protect another vulnerable member (e.g., a mother or father), even at the expense of the patient, afraid that active family sessions may uncover or generate even more trying problems for the family. Particular problems of the severely overanxious and underanxious families have been previously described. Some families present with an unassailable family myth (e.g., a folie en familie, a hyperreligious explanation for the anorexia nervosa, or some other immutable belief).

Therapist problems include those countertransference and structural traps into which therapists may unwittingly fall. If a therapist needs excessively to ally with the parent (who is paying the bills), some of the interests of the child may be sacrificed. Some therapists are too timid to confront a family adequately, whereas others are excessively bold, without adequately thinking through the impact of forceful interventions. The therapist may be countertherapeutically and unintentionally put in the position of paranoid object for the family, or be seduced into acting as the patient's resentful mouthpiece vis-a-vis the parents.

When difficulties such as these limit the extent to which the intervention is effective, ongoing supervision and cotherapy are extremely useful to help the therapist rethink the goals and tactics for the case.

Evaluation of Family Therapy

Unfortunately, available data permit only a modest statement about the usefulness of family therapy in the treatment of anorexia nervosa. Russell et al. (1987) described a controlled trial that compared family therapy with individual supportive therapy in a group of 80 patients with anorexia nervosa or bulimia nervosa who were treated following discharge from a hospital weight-restoration program and reassessed after a year of therapy. For patients with anorexia nervosa whose illness was not chronic and had begun before age 19, family therapy was found to be more effective than individual supportive therapy. More tentatively, there was a trend for older patients to benefit more greatly from individual therapy. Overall, a relatively small proportion of the patients had recovered from either anorexia nervosa or bulimia nervosa. Of further note, this study examined only family therapy versus individual supportive therapy. It did not consider the effects of combining the two, a common event in clinical practice. There are virtually no other controlled studies of family therapy.

Crisp et al. (1980) suggested that the receptivity of certain patients or families for therapy may have prognostic import, but it may be that the family characteristics here are more important prognostically than is the treatment itself. In the most extensive report of family therapy cases thus far published, Minuchin et al. (1978) suggested that for relatively young anorexia nervosa patients whose families accept therapy, the prognosis may be better than for other groups of patients with anorexia nervosa. However, family therapy per se cannot be uncritically credited with these results because, in other series, younger patients have done comparably well even without such therapy. Furthermore, it has yet to be demonstrated that structural family therapy interventions have, in fact, brought about changes in the family's communication and structural patterns that would be suggested by the theory.

Studies are currently underway to see if interventions with families characterized by high negative expressed emotion will make a difference in outcome (Szmukler 1983). For the future, a comparison among different forms of family intervention (e.g., education and support compared to structural intervention) would be worthwhile. Also still needed are detailed naturalistic descriptions that will produce more sophisticated hypotheses as to which particular individual and family characteristics respond best to which types of combinations of interventions, so that empirically based treatment algorithms can evolve.

Chapter 63

Group Therapy

Although group therapy has been incorporated into several anorexia nervosa treatment programs, group therapy for anorectics has received little attention in the medical literature, and the utility of the group approach for these patients has not been tested experimentally. However, clinical experience indicates that a group approach can be helpful as a strategy to address some of the problems seen in patients with anorexia nervosa when the group is used as an adjunctive component in a more comprehensive treatment program. A group approach should not be considered the primary, sole treatment for this disorder.

There are several general considerations regarding the use of groups in treating anorexia nervosa patients. The first concerns the treatment setting. Clinical experience suggests that groups can be employed with success in both outpatient and inpatient settings. A second consideration involves group membership. Patients with anorexia nervosa vary considerably as to their ages and level of maturity, and the group tasks will vary depending on the admixture of patients involved. It is important to avoid forming a group where one or two individuals are quite different from the other group members on such variables. A third consideration involves the role of the therapist in the group. Patients with anorexia nervosa frequently are not very verbal, insightful, or spontaneous early in the course of a group. Most are not accustomed to emotional expressivity, particularly in front of a group. Group members often turn to the therapist for a parent-authority figure. This situation provides a special challenge for the therapist. The therapist often needs to assume responsibility for the group process and structure while at the same time avoiding too much control.

Group Strategies

A variety of group therapy strategies may be employed with patients with anorexia nervosa. Some groups find it useful to shift between different approaches. For example, a group may begin primarily as an educational unit and advance to a format that encourages more openness and interpersonal learning. Regardless of the eventual progression, these groups usually begin slowly. One of the first tasks of the therapist is to engage the group as collaborators. This involves communicating to the patients an understanding of their individual problems and a genuine concern for their welfare.

The direction the group eventually takes will depend on a variety of variables, one of which is the treatment context of the group. In situations where patients are also receiving individual and/or family therapy, the group may focus specifically on peer interpersonal issues. In other situations, where concurrent psychotherapy is not part of the treatment plan, more time may be devoted to family and individual psychodynamics.

One facet of the treatment of anorexia nervosa where a group approach is particularly useful is as the educational component. A group format allows a great deal of information to be presented to several patients simultaneously and is thereby cost-effective. A good example of such an educational function is nutritional counseling, an important part of anorexia nervosa treatment (Huse and Lucas 1983). Patients with anorexia nervosa can be counseled in a group setting as to proper dietary habits, meal planning, and food choices. In addition to being desirable in terms of the dietician's time, this strategy permits patients to observe and discuss each other's irrational ideas concerning food and eating.

A group approach also offers a unique opportunity for patients with anorexia nervosa to observe the illness in others. Anorexia nervosa patients frequently have considerable insight into the attitudes and behaviors of other patients. The group can be used to illustrate and discuss such common issues as perfectionism and rigidity, self-criticism, and the need for control. The group approach also offers an opportunity for interpersonal learning. This can be particularly helpful for patients who have been withdrawn and unable to maintain appropriate relationships with peers. They can develop socialization skills, observe and experiment with emotional expression, engage in imitative behavior as other group members make advances, and experience a sense of group cohesiveness and support. The group may also provide the role models of other patients who are improving in terms of both weight and attitude. Such models may be very useful for patients who are convinced that they will become overweight and more depressed if they gain weight.

There are several potential problem areas in conducting group therapy for anorexia nervosa patients that should be considered. The problem of therapist control has already been discussed. Another problem is medical instability. Patients who are quite low in weight may evidence cognitive impairment and may function poorly in a group. An additional potential problem concerns subgroups of anorectics. In a group composed primarily of fairly nonverbal, withdrawn, depressed young girls, one or two verbally aggressive group members may be dominant and overly threatening to other group members. The therapist must be alert to this possibility.

The use of a parents' group for parents of anorexia nervosa patients has been described (Rose and Garfinkel 1980). The group was specifically designed for a series of parents where family therapy was thought to be inappropriate or had been refused. The results were perceived as positive by both the therapists and a majority of the parents at follow-up.

Although group therapy is commonly employed in treating patients with anorexia nervosa, no outcome studies that specifically examine the utility of groups or compare specific group strategies have been reported (see Chapter 72).

Chapter 64

Psychodynamic Individual Psychotherapy

The recognition of anorexia nervosa as a nosologic entity coincided with the ascent of psychoanalysis. As a result, psychodynamic explanations of anorexia nervosa have closely reflected the history of ideas in psychoanalysis.

Early on, Freud (1905/1913) considered anorexia nervosa the equivalent of melancholia in the sexually immature organism. This formulation preceded the libido theory and was based on the assumption that anorexia nervosa was associated with real loss of appetite, observed in melancholia.

Subsequent psychological explanations focused more on the symptom of food refusal. Jones (1911/1938) saw not eating as the rejection of the "the incorporated penis," whereas Abraham (1924/1953) proposed that disgust about oral incorporative fantasies and guilt over cannibalistic wishes to possess the father's penis contributed to the rejection. Alexander (1935) interpreted anorexia nervosa as a gastric neurosis, related to conflicts over the genital localization of pregnancy. In the 1940s, conflicts over oral aggression and the denial of oral sadistic fantasies were believed to be involved in the food refusal (Masserman 1941).

The first de novo analytic formulation was suggested by Benedek (1936), who noted that the desire for thinness was motivated by a fear of the adult mature feminine body, related to fears of becoming (like) the mother. Benedek's contribution went further in that she recognized and described a pathologic cognitive structure in anorexia nervosa, the system of dominant regulatory ideas "not to have a woman's body" and not to eat certain foods, which drive the patient's feelings and actions toward starving her body. However, Benedek's article at the time received little or no attention. Instead the publication by Waller et al. (1940) on the central role of conflictual oral impregnation fantasies leading to anorexia overshadowed all other dynamic explanations for several decades.

Looking back, one might say that each of these theories represents single ideas over conflicts with impulse expression, condensed fantasies, and fears of sexuality that seem ubiquitous. For example, the thought that impregnation occurs orally is common in childhood as is the notion that babies grow in the stomach; such fears may persist into adolescence but rarely, if ever, are revealed as the main determinant of anorexia nervosa. There is currently no evidence that these dynamics play a more important role in anorexia nervosa than they would in any other developmental disorder of female adolescence or young adulthood. Besides, the notion that a single fantasy can be pathogenic unless, as in Benedek's (1936) proposal, it subsumes a complete array of other ideas, strikes us nowadays as simplistic.

The tenacity with which these theories were kept alive in the analytic community (Bliss and Branch 1960; Eissler 1943; Masserman 1941), despite the fact that their therapeutic application did not improve the patient's condition, reflects the strength of an ideological structure disregarding clinical facts. Thus it was left to Bruch (1973) to become a pioneer in the field by studying the clinical manifestations of anorexia nervosa anew. She found little supporting evidence for existing theories to explain the illness, which enabled her to move on to new formulations. Bruch, based on her studies of early infant-mother interactions in obesity, considered anorexia nervosa as the outcome of faulty transactional experiences early in life. The parents' failure to transmit an adequate sense of self-value and competence to their children left them poorly prepared for the challenges of adolescence. Anorexia nervosa patients, she noted, withdraw to their bodies and use starvation "in their search for self-hood and self-directed identity." Bruch explicitly noted that although fear of sexuality and aggression exist in these patients, this should not be considered the dynamic explanation of the illness but rather a result of early maldevelopment.

Many of the dynamics described for anorexia nervosa were applied to the syndrome of bulimia, which until recently was considered a variant of anorexia nervosa. Too few cases existed before 1960 to be studied in their own right, such as the case of Ellen West (Binswanger 1958), until the recent dramatic increase in the incidence of bulimia nervosa. Several studies (Beaumont et al. 1976; Casper et al. 1980; Garfinkel et al. 1980; Strober 1981) have shown that the fasting form of anorexia nervosa and the bulimic form represent two distinct nosologic entities. They might be placed along a continuum, with fasting anorexia nervosa at one end and normal weight bulimia at the other, and close to the latter the bulimic form of anorexia nervosa. Psychodynamic theories tend to think in antonyms; for example, abstention from food tends to be considered as the expression of a repressed wish to devour. However, it has been experimentally confirmed that bulimia nervosa is not simply the opposite of anorexia nervosa because different psychological structures seem to characterize each type. In consistently fasting patients, the ability to maintain control over food extends into the personality, cognitive function, emotionality, and relationships. Vice versa, the intermittent loss of control over food in bulimia nervosa is associated with impulsivity, cognitive disorganization, and affective lability. Abstaining anorexia nervosa patients tend to be emotionally inhibited (this includes sexual feelings), to experience moderate anxiety and depression, and to be introverted and sometimes withdrawn. In contrast, patients who binge eat and vomit or use laxatives to undo the surfeit tend to experience feelings strongly. They can be highly anxious, profoundly depressed, and more extroverted; show sexual interest and impulsive behavior such as kleptomania and alcohol abuse; and often enter into volatile stormy relationships. Thus the dynamic issues in the treatment of each disorder would be expected to be different.

Dynamic Psychotherapy

At first sight anorexia nervosa and bulimia nervosa patients appear to be poor candidates for psychotherapy based on psychodynamic principles. Freud (1905/1913) advised against using psychoanalysis: "Psychoanalysis should not be attempted, when the speedy removal of dangerous symptoms is required as, for example, in a case of hysterical anorexia."

For example, the pursuit of thinness defended in anorexia nervosa is rarely, if ever, surrendered on the interpretation that fear of fatness may reflect fear of the feminine body and perhaps pregnancy. Similarly, the irresistible urge to eat and overeat does not easily yield to interpretations of oral greed. The sense of loss of control over the starvation process, albeit denied in anorexia nervosa, and the sense of loss of control over binge eating, painfully acknowledged in bulimia, suggest mechanisms recalcitrant to psychological influence. Bulimia nervosa patients themselves comment on the addictive nature of the binge eating, implying physiologic dependence.

Thus before we look at some of the psychodynamics, we want to stress that the main purpose of psychodynamic psychotherapy is the reorganization of the sick personality through individual and family therapy. Dynamic psychotherapy cannot replace the steps that need to be taken to nourish the patient or bring the binge eating under control (Casper 1982). It can, however, deal with the feelings and reactions that occur as a result of those interventions. The malnourished, starving patient and the binge eating, vomiting patient cannot benefit from psychotherapy alone. The starvation process must be brought under control through physical support with a refeeding regime. The worst case of chaotic binge eating-vomiting requires the same kind of close attentive supervision and regular feeding regime in a hospital. Whereas in anorexia nervosa weight gain can generally be achieved without additional medication, bulimia treated on an outpatient basis, especially in individuals who suffer from depression, may require antidepressant medication. The physical decompensation needs to be addressed for another reason, and this is a dynamic one. Starvation and binge eating psychologically constitute defensive maneuvers. Unless these defenses are interfered with, psychotherapy cannot make any progress.

Psychotherapy requires sincerity and honesty on the patient's part. Trust and honesty, however, are rarely present in patients with eating disorders. Their presence suggests a good prognosis. As a rule, denial of the emaciation and indifference toward the starvation signs characterize anorexia nervosa patients, who cling to their skinny bodies as their most treasured possession, unwilling and resistive to change. Any treatment intervention is experienced by the anorexia nervosa patient as an overpowering attack and coercion. Under the self-endorsed motto of the supreme value of thinness, the anorexia nervosa patient cheats and manipulates the environment.

How then is it possible to build a therapeutic alliance under such adverse circumstances? In anorexia nervosa, the family, by bringing the patient in for treatment, becomes an important part of the therapeutic alliance. In the fasting anorexic patient, psychotherapy consists of minute attempts to build the therapeutic alliance as the patient gains weight. If that alliance can be achieved while the patient is reaching a normal weight, the patient can be said to have recovered from anorexia nervosa even if individual and interpersonal problems require further treatment.

Concepts of Anorexia Nervosa

Which dynamic issues are addressed depends on the conceptualization of the illness. I will briefly summarize certain points that are necessary for comprehending elementary dynamic issues specific to anorexia nervosa. The writings of Benedek (1936), Selvini-Palazzoli (1978), and Bruch (1973) have decisively contributed to this formulation.

Personality Problems

As Bruch (1977) noted, individuals who later develop anorexia nervosa suffer from personality maldevelopment. We consider the ultimate severity of the illness a function of the personality disorder. Cocooned in a symbiotic tie to the mother, catering to the mother's needs, these individuals seem to have failed to take the progressive steps toward individuation since early childhood. Their core personality remains undifferentiated, and they tend to feel overcontrolled and inadequate. This lack of sense of self is remembered as timidity and being different from others in early relationships. By adolescence, issues of identity and separation cannot be avoided any longer and must be addressed in one way or another. If these patients are then confronted with having to function independently, their personal selves feel impoverished, inadequate, and of little value to themselves. With little self-confidence and ill-equipped emotionally to struggle themselves free within the realm of interpersonal relationships, patients arrive at a spurious solution and individuate by withdrawing into their bodies (Casper 1983b).

The Pathologic Process

Once patients discover the body as the instrument in their struggle for autonomy, once patients realize that, unlike relationships, they can successfully control their body and lose weight, they employ this power over their body weight to become (pseudo) independent from outside influences as well as from internal urges and needs. Gradually they create a world of good and bad of their own. Desirable and undesirable aspects of the self are attributed to the body. Loss of control as well as unacceptable anger or aggressive feelings become associated with "fatness"; successful control over these feelings and impulses becomes valued as thinness. This internal reorganization in anorexia nervosa occurs gradually, supported by starvation, and represents a profound psychological regression in association with the physical regression. The ultimate outcome of this regression is anorexia nervosa as a syndrome, as a new psychological and physical structure. In it patients are firmly identified with their thin bodies, so much so that they are unaware that their lives are endangered. Consequently they ignore the secondary signs of starvation. We cannot easily explain what it is that enables patients to disregard so completely their wasted bodies except that disavowal seems to play a role in the process. Patients feel, often for the first time, truly free and autonomous because, as a result of their emotional withdrawal into their bodies, people or relationships do not hold as much power over them as before. In the chronic case of anorexia nervosa, this regression seems permanent and irreversible. In this instance, I believe anorexia nervosa could be considered a somatopsychosis, in the form of a paranoia somatica.

Dynamic Issues in Acute Anorexia Nervosa

Following the described formulation, the dynamic issues specific to anorexia nervosa can be said to belong to the phase between the symbiotic stage and the cognitive differentiation of self and object, which is largely preverbal, with communication being confined to motor activity, facial expression (including eyes), and, of course, all kinds of vocalizations. The dynamics become apparent to anyone who attempts to treat such patients, and manifest themselves less through words and more as abnormal behavior. Because abnormal behavior can best be observed in the interaction with the human environment, especially in family interactions, family therapy becomes of utmost importance in anorexia nervosa.

By definition, dynamic psychotherapy cannot be described in separation from the process. For instance, dynamic issues are identifiable in each relationship, including any (certainly the patient-doctor) interaction. They are at the heart of those interactional manifestations that fall under the general category of transference. What turns psychotherapy into dynamic psychotherapy is the training and knowledge of the therapist who recognizes the kind of dynamic at work, its significance to the patient, how and when to interpret it, and how to respond to the patient's reaction to the interpretation. Depending on the kind of patient, the illness severity, the stage of illness, the patient's age and personality, and the parents' pathology, the same dynamic issue can have a vastly different meaning and requires different handling. For this reason, it seems virtually impossible to advise on how to address particular dynamic issues in each case.

Nevertheless, there seem to be certain dynamics germane to anorexia nervosa that are reproduced in virtually every case in one form or another during the early phases. Without appreciation of these early interactions, many of the more traditional later problems cannot be worked through and integrated. Most seem to be an offspring of experiences in the preverbal stage; that is, they cannot be articulated in words but instead are expressed through behavior and in actions. Anorectic patients do not talk about their feelings as much as they let them be known through their behavior. In general, one might say that treatment recreates an early struggle for individual survival in a symbiotic relationship. Anyone who has attempted to treat anorexia nervosa patients is well familiar with the patient's struggle for control. The patient resists change and wants to maintain the status quo. The institution of a refeeding program puts the therapist in one way or another in the position of becoming the overwhelming and dangerous mother, ignoring the patient's wishes because health and survival are put before individuality. The patient deeply resents this pressure and rarely forgets it. Having another person administer the feedings does not mute the issue but tends to promote the patient's tendency toward splitting into good and bad objects, making it more difficult to integrate later acceptable and unacceptable aspects of the self. At a later point during treatment, the therapist needs to explore the patient's experiences and feeling states during this phase, verbalize them, and help the patient understand the dynamic significance so that they can be integrated.

To the experienced therapist, the patient's struggle for control has all the elements of a struggle against feeling controlled by others. The struggle hides the patient's feeling of powerlessness, helplessness, and ineffectiveness. If this knowledge can be shared with the patient and if the fear of being overwhelmed and being annihilated can be understood as underlying a struggle for control, then the patient may be able to relinquish some control in the hope that someone has understood and will understand the suffering. Similarly, the negativism and stubbornness often cover up despair over being inadequate in relationships and unable to influence others. The negativism is much in contrast to the patient's compliance, which has been described as a character trait (Bruch 1973). This tendency to give in to others seems not to be based on the knowing acceptance of someone else's wishes but seems to represent submissive defeat and to hide persistent anger at the other person for the humiliation of having to yield to someone else's wishes. The issue of compliance is more noticeable in some patients than in others; however, it is present in all. It often covers up a fear of losing the other person's love. Unless compliance is correctly understood and unless the patients can develop alternate ways to respond to expectations, pressure, and the attitudes of others, little personality change will occur. For example, some patients comply smoothly with the refeeding program. Secretly they go along in the expectation that this will enable them to leave the hospital. Such patients often relapse after discharge.

The issues of control, with the negativism and compliance, then seem to be variations of the same theme: the patient's emotional confusion, poor self-concept, and lack of differentiation from others. They constitute the main defenses available to patients who feel equally helpless and passive under the influence of their inner feelings and impulses and who view the bodily changes in puberty as under the influence of outside forces. Another early issue is denial of anything abnormal or pathologic, be it the seriousness of the starvation or the emotional problems. We have shown (Casper et al. 1981) that acutely sick patients are fully aware of their precarious emotional state, moodiness, loneliness, and poor self-concept. The denial is not accessible to interpretation without adducing evidence in support of it from the patient's history. Patients are often extremely skillful, especially if they are gaining weight, in denying any emotional or interpersonal problems. The denial thus presents another situation in which there is danger of overpowering the patient by insisting on the existence of emotional difficulties. Minute evidence, most often in family therapy, needs to be collected to have patients and the family become aware of dysfunctioning areas as a first step toward eventual change.

Summary

Dynamic psychotherapy during the early phase seeks to address two interrelated areas. The first relates to the patient's lack of differentiation and poorly developed sense of self, a result of a developmental arrest at the symbiotic stage. The goal here is to help patients change their self- and self-object representations by separating emotionally and cognitively from their mothers and sometimes from their fathers. This step toward independent dependence is most effectively accomplished through family therapy in conjunction with individual therapy. The second move, which often cannot occur until these basic changes through the family have been accomplished, addresses particular aspects of the dysfunctioning personality. Psychotherapy at this later point helps patients, through the transference and through interpretations, accept themselves, recognize their conflicted feelings, and reconcile their weaknesses and deficiencies without having to resort to an artificial structure—a thin body—as a better self.

Chapter 65

Medical Evaluation and Management

Although the physical signs of bulimia nervosa are less striking than the obvious low weight and emaciation seen in anorexia nervosa, the medical complications can be just as serious and potentially life threatening. The presence of physical signs may serve as a clue in making the diagnosis in those patients reluctant to disclose to a therapist their binge and purge behaviors.

Physical Signs

Russell first described the sign of abrasions and calluses on the dorsum of the hand. This "Russell's sign" is the result of scraping the hand against the teeth during attempts at self-induced vomiting (Russell 1979). Changes in the teeth and gums frequently result in the patient's dentist being the first person to make the diagnosis of bulimia nervosa. Erosion of the teeth can be severe, causing pathologic pulp exposures and gum irritations and resulting in diminished masticatory ability as well as an unaesthetic appearance (Stege 1982).

Another telltale mark of bulimia is bilateral swelling of the parotid glands. This enlargement may be intermittent, occurring one to two days following a binge-vomiting episode. The physiologic mechanism for the swelling is unknown as biopsies have revealed normal glandular tissue (Hasler 1982).

Medical Emergencies

Acute gastric dilatation, previously reported in anorexia nervosa patients during refeeding, has recently been reported in normal weight patients with bulimia (Mitchell et al. 1982). Severe abdominal pain in a patient with bulimia should alert the physician to the possibility of gastric dilatation and the need for nasogastric suction, X rays and surgical consultation, thereby avoiding the potentially fatal complications of gastric rupture (Mitikainen 1979).

Esophageal tears can occur in those patients who chronically or vigorously induce vomiting. Such an esophageal tear could result in serious blood loss and shock. Reports by patients of upper gastrointestinal bleeding should be thoroughly investigated. Patients with chronic bulimia may also evidence reflux esophagitis, with its concomitant symptoms of heartburn and discomfort on lying flat.

Serum Electrolyte Abnormalities

A metabolic alkalosis or a hypokalemic alkalosis can result from purging behaviors such as self-induced vomiting or abuse of laxatives or diuretics. In one study (Mitchell and Bantle 1983), 49 percent of bulimic patients demonstrated electrolyte abnormalities, which included elevated serum bicarbonate, hypochloremia, and hypokalemia. A few cases, particularly in laxative abusers, showed a low serum bicarbonate, indicating a metabolic acidosis. It is important to remember that fasting can promote dehydration: the resulting volume depletion induces the production of aldosterone, which promotes potassium excretion from the kidneys. Thus there can be an indirect renal loss of potassium as well as a direct loss through self-induced vomiting. Electrolyte disturbances in these patients can present as complaints of weakness and lethargy and may induce episodes of cardiac arrhythmia and the danger of cardiac arrest. Normal weight bulimic patients may be at risk for severe cardiac rhythm disturbances despite normal serum electrolytes (Zucker 1984).

Serum Enzyme Abnormalities

Almost one-third of bulimic patients in one study demonstrated elevated serum amylase levels. The frequency of elevated amylase values was significantly higher in those patients reporting more frequent binge eating and more frequent vomiting (Mitchell et al. 1983). Serum amylase may be an effective way to monitor bingeing and vomiting behavior in bulimic patients. It is possible to fractionate the serum amylase into pancreatic and salivary components, the latter being the fraction commonly elevated in bulimic patients. An elevated pancreatic fraction that does not return to normal with the cessation of bingeing and vomiting may indicate a chronic pancreatitis.

While it is not unusual for serum enzymes reflecting liver function to be elevated in anorexia nervosa, elevation in bulimia is less likely. Elevation of the enzymes serum glutamic-oxalacetic transaminase, lactic dehydrogenase, and alkaline phosphatase likely reflects fatty degeneration of the liver (Mitchell et al. 1983).

The periodic episodes of fasting with binge eating may bring about a disturbed bone metabolism in bulimia patients. An increase in alkaline phosphatase could be a sensitive measure for detecting changes in bone metabolism and should be assessed in those patients with long-standing bulimia. Since the fractures in osteoporosis have been associated mainly in anorectics who engage in self-induced vomiting, it is important to be alert to these problems in bulimics who have been purging for years.

Endocrine Abnormalities

Bulimic patients, despite their abnormal eating patterns, have normal fasting blood glucose levels and a normal glucose tolerance curve (Mitchell et al. 1983). Examination of the response of thyroid-stimulating hormone (TSH) to thyrotropin-releasing hormone (TRH) has yielded contradictory results. While one study indicated a normal TSH response (Mitchell and Bantle 1983), another revealed a blunting of the response to TRH (Gwirtsman et al. 1983).

While basal levels of growth hormone are normal in patients with bulimia, challenges by TRH administration and oral glucose yield abnormal results (Mitchell and Bantle 1983). These findings may be related to the bulimic's aberrant eating pattern or may represent a nonspecific manifestation of stress or illness.

Dexamethasone nonsuppression is present in about one-half to two-thirds of the normal weight bulimic patients tested, indicating an abnormality of cortisol suppression (Gwirtsman et al. 1983; Hudson et al. 1983b). The meaning of these physiologic findings is not clear but may reflect acute changes in weight from the fasting to the bingeing state. Neither study associated the existence of depression or the existence of a diagnosis of major depressive disorder with response to dexamethasone in the bulimic patients.

Any conclusions as to the intactness of the hypothalamic-pituitary-ovarian axis in bulimia is not possible at this time because careful, systematic studies of follicle-stimulating hormone (FSH) and leutinizing hormone (LH) have not been conducted in these patients. Sporadic menstrual irregularities with low FSH and LH levels have been reported in bulimic patients (Weiner 1983).

It is important to look for and suspect alcohol, drug, and ipecac abuse in bulimics. Stimulant drugs such as amphetamines and their analogs, caffeine, and nicotine are often used to excess for weight control. Alcohol and cocaine are used for anxiety reduction. Ipecac is used to induce vomiting and may cause cardiac failure and death by an irreversible cardiomyopathy. The onset is sudden and can be considered a medical emergency with symptoms of precardial pain, dyspnea, and generalized muscle weakness. Electrocardiogram (EKG) will show inversion of T waves in all leads and prolongation of QT intervals.

The initial medical evaluation of a bulimic patient should include serum electrolytes and enzymes, an EKG, and a dental examination. The severity of the bingeing and purging will determine the frequency for which serum electrolytes and serum amylase are obtained. Serum amylase is an excellent way to follow purging behavior since elevation of this enzyme is positively correlated with severity of self-induced vomiting.

The medical problems in bulimia appear to be directly related to the bingeing and purging behavior. Although many clinicians are treating hypokalemia in bulimics with supplemental potassium, this treatment is more beneficial to the clinicians than the patients. The best way to treat hypokalemia is to stop purging behavior. If the serum potassium falls below 2.5 meq/l, the patient should be hospitalized to have serum electrolytes restored to normal range. This may have to be done intravenously if the purging cannot be controlled in a structured setting. Dehydration, metabolic alkalosis, or acidosis can always be corrected with appropriate intravenous fluids, but often oral fluids are sufficient if the purging behavior can be controlled.

Bingeing and purging behaviors are most effectively reduced immediately with behavior techniques and antidepressant medications.

Chapter 66

Hospital Treatment

Indications for Hospitalization

For some patients with bulimia nervosa, hospitalization is indicated. Purging activities such as frequent vomiting and abuse of laxatives and diuretics can create serious electrolyte imbalances and dehydration that may require hospitalization (Mitchell et al. 1983). These patients may present with complaints of weakness and lethargy and are at risk for developing cardiac arrhythmias. Inpatient treatment is often the only way to stabilize the patient's medical status and break the binge-purge cycle.

There are other situations that can present as a medical emergency and require hospitalization. These include acute gastric distension due to binge eating and esophageal tears due to self-induced vomiting (Mitchell et al. 1982; Mitikainen 1979). Cardiac arrhythmias also require emergency treatment.

Another indication for inpatient treatment of bulimia is severe depression. Often bulimic patients will experience symptoms of major depression and frequently report suicidal ideation. The patient's ability to function may be seriously compromised. Patients with severe bulimia may spend every waking moment planning binges, buying food, and then bingeing and purging. These patients are no longer able to function at school or work and their social relationships markedly deteriorate. Inpatient treatment is also indicated for the patient with a history of previous treatment failures.

Aims of the Hospital Treatment Program

The aims of a hospital treatment program for bulimia nervosa are multiple. The first objective is to stop the binge-purge behavior. This must be achieved if the patient is to make real progress in treatment. The goal with regard to the bulimic behaviors is one of total abstinence. With the interruption of the binge-purge cycle, reestablishment of normal eating behavior can take place. This is a very important objective in patients who may have alternately fasted and binged for years before coming into the hospital.

Treatment of depression is another aspect of the treatment program. Often the interruption of the binge-purge cycle alone restores a sense of well-being and a lessening of hopelessness. In addition to individual and group therapies, antidepressant medications may be helpful in alleviating depression as well as in aiding in the patient's control of the urge to binge and purge (Pope et al. 1983) (see Chapter 68).

Identification and treatment of psychological problems is a major goal of the psychotherapeutic approach to the bulimic patient. Commonly these patients present with a markedly low sense of self-esteem coupled with a pervasive feeling of personal ineffectiveness. Often there are dependency issues that the patients have not resolved with their families or significant others. The presence of a body-conceptualization disturbance often exacerbates the aberrant eating behavior. Despite maintaining a normal body weight, most female bulimics express dissatisfaction with their bodies. The frequent vacillation between fasting and binge eating speaks to the importance of control for the bulimic patient. Personal control, which is often seen in terms of self-deprivation, particularly in diet, is one goal bulimics feel they can strive to achieve; other goals such as a career or satisfactory interpersonal relationships may be viewed as unobtainable.

Invariably, the bulimic patient experiences a number of interpersonal difficulties. An important aim of the treatment program is to identify these interpersonal problem areas for therapy. Since bulimia by its nature is a secretive disorder, patients may no longer feel comfortable in social situations, a result of self-imposed isolation. Many of these patients benefit from a social skills training program.

An important aspect of the treatment of bulimic individuals is a family assessment, especially for those patients living at home. Parents and siblings need help in understanding the illness and direction from the therapist as to how best to deal with the troubled family member. The form or type of family therapy should be one clinically appropriate and feasible for that family (see Chapter 71).

At the time bulimic patients seek treatment, they may be unemployed or pursuing a career that is not particularly suitable or feasible for them. For this reason, vocational assessment and training is a very valuable component in the patients' rehabilitation.

The Hospital Treatment Program

Phase I

The major aim of the initial phase of treatment is to stop the binge-purge behavior. The opportunity to binge must be removed. Patients receive balanced meals of sufficient calories to maintain their weight. Access to food must be restricted to mealtimes and supervised snacks. Patients should be observed during meals and for at least several hours after meals. Access to bathrooms must be restricted and supervised to prevent surreptitious vomiting. Stool examinations are necessary to monitor laxative abuse.

The assessment of the patient's medical condition must begin on admission. Such an assessment should include a physical exam, chest X ray, hematology profile, and blood chemistries with particular attention to serum electrolytes and enzymes. Elevations of serum amylase are usually indicative of vomiting behavior (Mitchell et al. 1983).

The patient should also be assessed for the signs and symptoms of depression. Affective signs that do not improve with the cessation of the binge-purge cycle and maintenance of a normal weight may indicate the need for a trial of antidepressant medication. A number of medications have been used in the treatment of bulimia. Among these are the tricyclic antidepressant imipramine, the monoamine oxidase inhibitor phenelzine, and the antiseizure medications phenytoin and carbamazepine. Recent studies have suggested the value of antidepressant medications in reducing the frequency of binge-purge behaviors in addition to having antidepressant effects (Pope et al. 1983) (see Chapter 68).

Behavioral principles play an important role in the treatment of bulimia nervosa. The response prevention technique does not allow the patient to binge or to vomit after eating when conditions would ordinarily suggest this to the patient. The initial isolatory restrictions of the hospital program are negative reinforcements from which patients may work their way out with continued appropriate behavior (see Chapter 69).

Phase 2

During the middle phase of hospitalization, patients learn or relearn patterns of normal eating behavior. Patient progress from prepared trays of food to choosing freely their own diet while maintaining their weight within a medically sound range. Caloric intake should be sufficient to maintain the target weight plus a 30 percent increment for physical activity.

Also important in this phase of the hospitalization is the increased focus on interpersonal relationships and the development of social skills. Many of these patients have isolated themselves from their family and friends for such a long period of time that they must relearn how to interact with others. Group therapy and therapeutic activities are especially helpful in this process (see Chapter 72).

While stereotyping of patients or families is not possible in eating disorders, some common themes include an inability to express anger, issues of dependency and control, and a perfectionistic, overly critical attitude toward the self with an inability to give to oneself. These themes may emerge in the individual or family therapy. It is often during the family therapy that the factors that perpetuate the disorder become elucidated. It is important to assess how these or other issues are acted out in terms of the symptom choice and what possible meaning this may have for the patient.

Patients with bulimia often come to the hospital with no structure to their lives except for the bulimia itself. Jobs may be in jeopardy or school performance seriously deteriorating. Vocational assessment and training, if appropriate, are an important part of the hospital treatment program in phase 2.

Phase 3

The criteria for discharge from the hospital involves the achievement of a number of goals. The patient should have achieved a complete cessation of the binge-purge behavior. A stable pattern of normal eating behavior should have resumed. The patient must also have demonstrated an ability to maintain the gains made in the hospital in a variety of situations. Along with the changes in behavior, the patient will have also made significant psychological improvement by the time of discharge.

Preparing for discharge is the most critical task of the inpatient treatment. One goal to be accomplished is becoming comfortable eating outside the hospital setting. The period prior to discharge is often a stressful and frightening time for patients as they confront their feelings and fears on leaving the perceived safety of the hospital. Passes out of the hospital with family and with peers become an important laboratory for patients to test out newly learned techniques while returning to situations in which they had binged and purged in the past. Sometimes these first attempts are not successful and the therapy staff must work with the patient in understanding what emotions the situation evoked and which alternative behaviors would have been helpful in handling the situation differently.

Arrangements must be made for where patients will live after they leave the hospital. Therapy has helped the patients and their families understand more about the illness and where the conflicts lie in their relationships to one another. It may be recommended that the patient not return home but to a more independent living situation. Often patients are not ready for living on their own, and a placement in a structured living situation such as a half-way house can be an effective transition to an independent living arrangement. The structure provided by such a setting is also very helpful in continuing the gradual increases in responsibilities that began in the hospital. This stepwise transition back into life outside the hospital is often reassuring to the patient and may be helpful in avoiding a quick return of symptoms in the newly discharged patient.

The patient's return to work must also be discussed and planned during this last phase of the hospital treatment. The discharged patient is easily overwhelmed and should be advised to resume responsibilites cautiously and slowly. For the patient with a severe and chronic history of bulimia, a period of day hospitalization may be indicated following the inpatient stay.

Prior to the patient's discharge, arrangements must be made for the patient's outpatient therapy. Individual therapy, incorporating the principles of cognitive therapy and behavioral modification, provides the patient with the opportunity to continue the gains in self-understanding that began in the hospital and also serves as a significant source of support following discharge (Garner and Bemis 1982). A referral to group therapy is often indicated; a bulimic group, if well run, may be very helpful. Depending on the patient and situation, family therapy may be indicated following the inpatient stay.

Plans must be made for the patient to be followed on any medications that are to be continued on discharge. The question of when to discontinue medications in the treatment of bulimia remains an open one. However, for the more severely ill patient, medication should be continued for a period of at least four to six months after discharge from the hospital. Because of the dangerous medical complications that can go along with bulimia, it is advisable that a physician be involved in the patient's treatment. Periodic monitoring of the patient's weight, EKG, serum electrolytes, and serum amylase levels are indicated in the medical aftercare of the patient.

Chapter 67

Outpatient Treatment

Several reports suggest considerable interest in the use of outpatient treatment approaches for bulimia nervosa (Fairburn 1981; Lacy 1983; Mitchell et al. in press). While little outcome research has been reported to date, available reports do suggest that outpatient treatment can be both safe and effective.

Before discussing various outpatient approaches, it is important first to define the population of patients who can be effectively treated in the outpatient setting. The term *bulimia*, when interpreted broadly, may be used to identify several different groups of patients rather than one homogeneous group. One such group of patients who engage in bulimic behaviors, although they do not meet DSM-III-R (American Psychiatric Association 1987) criteria for bulimia nervosa, may be the bulimic subgroup of patients with anorexia nervosa. Such patients require a treatment approach that focuses on weight as well as eating pattern. Therefore these patients usually require programming, which is different from that used to treat patients of normal weight with bulimia. A third group, who may meet DSM-III-R criteria for bulimia nervosa, are actually overweight or obese individuals who binge eat but do not self-induce vomiting or abuse laxatives. They also constitute a distinct group that may not be effectively treated in programs designed for normal weight bulimic patients. In this chapter I will focus on the treatment of individuals who are of approximately normal weight who have bulimia characterized by binge eating and usually self-induce vomiting and/or laxative abuse as part of the syndrome.

Components

Several specific components need to be considered in each treatment program. The elements can be integrated into a single treatment approach, such as a group that shifts focus to encompass these elements, or can be offered as separate units in which patients can participate. These components will be discussed separately.

Nutritional Rehabilitation

Bulimia is not just a disorder of binge eating but is a disorder characterized by a variety of abnormal eating-related behaviors. Patients with bulimia rarely eat normal meals whether or not they are binge eating and frequently present with idiosyncratic ideas about food and weight. Therefore, proper nutritional instruction is an important part of any treatment program. In some treatment settings, the area of nutritional instruction is augmented by the use of structured meal planning techniques. Patients who are to go into outpatient treatment programs all attend a meal-planning clinic where they are taught meal-planning techniques and are given a diet that will allow flexibility as to food choice while ensuring adequate caloric intake to maintain a normal body weight. Such an approach allows for a careful assessment of each patient's attitudes and knowledge about food and eating and provides a structured setting where patients can have their questions answered by individuals knowledgeable about nutritional issues. Regardless of the format to be utilized, the emphasis needs to be on the practice of regular, planned, healthy meals. Patients are frequently quite resistant to developing such patterns, but a firm, consistent emphasis on the importance of these behavioral changes will usually be effective. Patients need to begin eating regular meals to break the binge eating-vomiting-fasting cycle.

Nutritional rehabilitation also should emphasize proper weight management. Patients with bulimia frequently need to stabilize their weight if they wish to overcome bulimic behaviors. If they are attempting to diet and lose weight, as most are when they first come for treatment, it will be difficult if not impossible for them to cease binge eating. When dieting, these patients will markedly restrict their food intake, become hungry, and then be likely to binge eat again. It is generally best to encourage weight maintenance or a very gradual weight reduction and to discourage any attempt at rapid weight loss early in therapy.

Pharmacotherapy

Depression is a very common symptom in the bulimia syndrome. Growing literature attests to the utility of antidepressant drug therapy in the treatment of these patients (Pope et al. 1984). Antidepressants have been shown to be quite effective in alleviating the depressive symptoms seen in these patients and also appear to improve eating behavior. Whether the effect on eating behavior is a separate effect or secondary to the improvement in depression is, at this point, unclear. Although it is not yet established that antidepressant therapy is best for all patients with bulimia, or even a majority of such patients, drug therapy should be available for bulimic patients whose depressive symptoms fail to resolve with normalization of eating pattern or where the clinical history is highly suggestive of a primary affective disorder (see Chapter 68).

Medical Evaluation and Follow-Up

Medical problems can either mimic bulimia or complicate the course of the disorder. For these reasons, patients with bulimia need to be carefully screened medically when seen for evaluation. This screening should include a complete medical history, physical examination, and screening laboratory work. On physical examination, special attention should be focused on the state of hydration, oral hygiene, and vital signs. Some of the medical problems that may be seen in association with bulimia are fluid and electrolyte abnormalities, gastric dilatation, and severe erosion of the dental enamel. The electrolyte problems and the gastric dilatation can be serious, even life threatening.

Outpatient treatment programs should also have the capacity for medical follow-up. Some patients will require periodic monitoring of metabolic dysfunction and may require hospitalization if they become medically unstable or if outpatient treatment is unsuccessful.

Psychotherapy

The mainstay of the treatment of bulimia is the psychotherapeutic component. Different psychotherapeutic approaches have been described in the literature using varying formats and theoretical systems. Many of those that have been described have relied on behavioral techniques, some using individual and some group formats.

Individual approaches have been described (Grinc 1982; Long and Cordle 1982; Mizes and Lohr 1983; Rosen and Leitenburg 1982). Fairburn (1981) described in detail an outpatient individual approach that uses cognitive behavioral techniques. This approach is divided into two parts. During the first part, patients are seen frequently, usually two or three times a week, to interrupt the behavior. Education about bulimia, the use of self-monitoring techniques, the development of alternative behaviors, and the use of goal setting are all employed. This phase rarely continues beyond eight weeks. During the second part of therapy, the therapist attempts to help the patient to develop better coping skills, use problem-solving techniques, and examine irrational concerns. Patients are encouraged to reintegrate feared foods into their diets.

Several group approaches have also been described. These include two outpatient group approaches that focused on cultural biases involved in the disorder (White and Boskind-White 1981), a time-limited group approach using behavioral techniques and insight-oriented discussion (Dixon and Kiecolt-Glaser 1981), a short-term program combining group and individual therapy (Lacey 1983), a structured three-phase program (Johnson et al. 1983), and a two-month intensive program (Mitchell et al. in press).

Before turning to the common themes in these different therapies, there are several points that should be examined concerning the theory and practice of therapy of bulimia. The first concern is the focus of therapy. Put in dichotomous terms, should the focus of the therapy be on the disordered eating behavior itself or on the psychological and interpersonal problems that accompany the disorder? Fortunately, the choice does not have to be between these two extremes, and most authors seem to have chosen a path that tries to address both of these models. For example, some programs tend to focus on eating behavior during the early stages of therapy, with a gradual shift in focus to a more psychological-interpersonal approach (Fairburn 1981; Johnson et al. 1983; Mitchell et al. in press). However, in all of the reports published to date, one assumption that comes through clearly is that part of the therapy must address the eating behavior. The therapist cannot assume that the eating behavior will automatically normalize if the patient develops psychological insight. This position reflects the understanding that whatever causes bulimia may be very different from what perpetuates it. Put simply, bulimia becomes a habit for many patients, a habit that has to be interrupted.

Another consideration is the intensity of treatment. Several authors have found it useful to meet with patients more frequently than once a week, particularly early in treatment (Fairburn 1981; Johnson et al. 1983; Mitchell et al. in press; White and Boskind-White 1981). These clinicians have found that more intensive therapy is often necessary to provide the patient with the support needed to bring the behavior under control. The intensity of the therapy can then be decreased over time.

General Principles of Outpatient Treatment

The outpatient treatment programs that have been described have certain similarities, suggesting considerable overlap in approach. Techniques commonly used by several different programs include the following:

Patient education. Many authors stress the importance of the educational component, particularly early in treatment. Education as to what is known about bulimia, the medical consequeces of the behavior, and the specific behavioral techniques that can be helpful in treatment may all be covered as part of this educational process (Johnson et al. 1983; Lacey 1983; Mitchell et al. in press; Rosen and Leitenburg 1982). Many patients derive a sense of hope and encouragement from the knowledge that much is known about the diagnosis and treatment of their disorder.

Self-monitoring techniques. Self-monitoring has proved to be a very useful strategy as a means to increase each patients' awareness of their eating behaviors as well as to gather baseline data to evaluate subsequent change (Boskind-Lodahl and White 1978; Fairburn 1981; Johnson et al. 1983; Mizes and Lohr 1983; Rosen and Leitenburg 1982). A variety of techniques have been employed, ranging from food diaries to the use of instruments designed to record abnormal eating-related behavior (Mitchell et al. 1981).

Contracting and goal setting. This can involve either group contracting or individual contracting (Johnson et al. 1983; Lacey 1983; Long and Cordle 1982; White and Boskind-White 1981). The potential target goals include a reduction in the frequency of specific bulimic behaviors or the maintenance of weight within a certain range.

An examination of behavioral antecedents. Certain antecedents can precipitate bulimic behaviors. These may include situational factors (e.g., being in a grocery store, coming home from school), emotional factors (e.g., depression, anger), social factions (e.g., an argument with a parent, a dinner party), cognitive factors (e.g., feeling fat, feeling unimportant), and physiologic factors (e.g., hunger). Several authors have found it useful to have patients examine these behavioral antecedents (Fairburn 1981; Grinc 1982; Mitchell et al. in press).

Manipulation of behavioral antecedents. As suggested by the previous technique, if patients learn to recognize behavioral antecedents then they can begin to change them or at least to respond to them differently. This may involve avoiding certain situations, changing jobs, and changing relationships with other people (Fairburn 1981; Johnson et al. 1983). Patients can also be taught response delay as a management technique to avoid abnormal eating-related behaviors in response to certain environmental stimuli.

The development of alternative or competing behaviors. It is well-known clinically that patients with bulimia often can avoid a binge-eating episode if they plan alternative behaviors (e.g., seeing a friend or going for a walk), behaviors that are incompatible with bulimic behaviors. Such plans can be made well in advance (e.g., deciding how to spend the evening) or can be developed as last-minute alternatives (e.g., deciding to walk around the block rather than binge eat). Several programs specifically incorporate the development of alternative behaviors into their treatment programs (Fairburn 1981; Mitchell et al. in press).

Manipulation of the consequences of the behavior. Patients can be taught to reinforce adaptive eating behavior using a variety of rewards, including monetary, cognitive, and social rewards (Mitchell et al. 1983). For example, patients can save the money they would have spent binge eating and spend it instead on clothing.

Adaptive skills. Several different types of adaptive skills training have been incorporated into different treatment programs, including behavioral problem-solving (Fairburn 1981), assertiveness training (Boskind-Lodahl and White 1978; Dixon and Kiecolt-Glaser 1981; White and Boskind-White 1981), and relaxation training (Johnson et al. 1983; Mizes and Lohr 1983).

Cognitive restructuring. Different authors have advocated different techniques or theoretical models; however, most seem to agree that some effort at cognitive restructuring should be part of every treatment program. This usually involves an examination of the patients' ideas or beliefs about their own bodies, their sense of self-worth, their relationships with other people, and the role of food in their lives (Fairburn 1981; Grinc 1982; Long and Cordle 1982).

Cultural perspective. Bulimia is predominantly a disorder of women. Some authors have stressed the necessity of examining possible cultural determinants of bulimia, particularly as they relate to the roles of women in our culture and expectations for slimness (Boskind-Lodahl and White 1978; White and Boskind-White 1981).

Relapse prevention.   Available data indicate quite clearly that patients are at risk for relapse to active bulimic behavior for at least several months following successful treatment. Most patients who come for treatment indicate that they have had periods of weeks or months when they were able to control their eating behavior but have always fallen back into their previous patterns. For this reason, it is important for patients to plan what they will do if signs of relapse develop and, most importantly, to learn not to overreact to isolated episodes of bulimic behavior. Unfortunately, some patients use a single binge eating or vomiting episode as an excuse to return to their previous pattern.

Family and friends.   Consideration should be given to involving family or interested friends in the treatment. Some programs specifically incorporate informational elements for family and friends as a way to improve their knowledge about the disorder and to encourage healthy responses on the part of relatives and friends to recovering patients (Fairburn 1981). This also serves as a way to break the isolation that many patients feel.

Most authorities seem to agree that, in the treatment of bulimia, the specific eating patterns need to be addressed directly. However, normalization of the eating pattern is rarely sufficient. At some point in the therapy, the myriad of psychosocial problems that accompany the disordered eating must also be addressed. To accomplish this latter task, techniques and skills developed in other types of psychotherapy can then be utilized.

Chapter 68

Drug Therapy

Pharmacologic approaches to the treatment of bulimia have been based primarily on two conceptualizations of this syndrome. Several reports in the mid-1970s noted similarities between bulimia and seizure disorders and described impressive responses to anti-convulsant medication. In the early 1980s a number of investigators proposed that bulimia is in some way linked to affective illness and began to explore the usefulness of antidepressant agents.

In a series of articles between 1974 and 1979, Green and Rau described compulsive eating in patients of below normal, normal, and above normal body weights (Green and Rau 1974, 1977; Rau and Green 1975; Rau et al. 1979). Because in some patients these eating binges appeared unpredictably, were perceived by the patients as being beyond their own control, and were sometimes preceded by an aura and associated with other ego-dystonic behaviors, these authors proposed that "compulsive eaters have a primary neurologic disorder similar to epilepsy" (Rau and Green 1975, p. 228). In support of this hypothesis, they described a high frequency of mildly abnormal electroencephalograms (EEGs) in patients with "true" compulsive eating. On the basis of this formulation, they openly treated 47 patients with phenytoin and described impressive results in 57 percent (Rau et al. 1979).

Wermuth et al. (1977) conducted a double-blind crossover trial of phenytoin in 20 patients with binge eating. Ten patients were of normal body weight, nine were overweight, and one had anorexia nervosa. Patients were randomly assigned to receive six weeks of phenytoin (300 mg/day) followed by six weeks of placebo or the opposite sequence. In the 10 patients who received phenytoin first, there was a significant decline in binge frequency when the drug was initiated. However, contrary to the authors' expectations, this symptomatic improvement persisted through the placebo period. Thus, in this group, there was no difference between phenytoin and placebo. In the group that received placebo first, there was no change in binge frequency during the first six weeks, but the patients did improve when they were switched to phenytoin. Overall, six of the 19 patients who completed the trial were felt to have improved markedly on phenytoin, but only one patient ceased bingeing entirely. Four of these six markedly improved patients continued phenytoin beyond the study period and two of the four relapsed during follow-up, while on the medication. EEGs were obtained on all 20 patients; definite EEG abnormalities were found in only three. The patients' drug responses were not correlated with their pretreatment EEG findings or with their plasma levels of phenytoin.

Greenway et al. (1977) reported on a very small series of obese women who probably had bulimia. None of the 7 women had EEG abnormalities. In a double-blind crossover study of phenytoin versus placebo, there was no indication of benefit from phenytoin.

The studies of Wermuth et al. (1977) and Greenway et al. (1977) are the only controlled trials of phenytoin in bulimia at this writing. While their implications are limited by their selection criteria, crossover design, and small sample size, they do indicate that the initial reports of Green and Rau were overly optimistic. Clearly, conventional anticonvulsant activity does not explain what therapeutic effects phenytoin has in binge eating; unlike its effects on seizures, phenytoin's effects on bulimia are related neither to the patient's EEG abnormalities nor to the plasma level of the drug. Furthermore, dramatic improvement on phenytoin appears to be unusual and difficult to sustain.

Antidepressant Treatment of Bulimia

The last several years have witnessed a dramatic increase in interest in the treatment of bulimia with antidepressant medication. As clinicians began to see more patients with bulimia, they became increasingly aware that mood disturbances, particularly major depressive episodes or dysthmia, were frequently present in bulimic patients. Patients typically described a chronic depression of mild to moderate severity, with a reactive mood and high levels of anxiety. Because of the prominence of these affective symptoms, clinicians began to explore the utility of medications used to treat depression. As of this writing, information is available from the treatment of several hundred patients with bulimia with antidepressant drugs, including 11 double-blind placebo-controlled trials.

There have been isolated case reports of successful treatment of bulimia with antidepressant medication at least since 1978 (Rich 1978). The first series of patients treated with antidepressants were described by Pope and Hudson (1982), who used tricyclic antidepressants, and by Walsh et al. (1982), who used monoamine oxidase inhibitors. Since the appearance of these reports, 11 double-blind placebo-controlled trials of antidepressants have been conducted, and several more are currently underway. These trials (Table 1) focused on the treatment of normal weight women who met DSM-III (American Psychiatric Association 1980) or DSM-III-R (American Psychiatric Association 1987) criteria for bulimia and who were treated as outpatients. Patients were usually seen every one or two weeks for the duration of the studies. In addition to the medication, they were given only supportive therapy and limited behavioral interventions (e.g., being asked to keep an eating diary).

Seven of the 11 controlled trials used tricyclic antidepressants (imipramine, desipramine, and amitriptyline), two used monoamine oxidase inhibitors (phenelzine and isocarboxazid), and two used novel antidepressants not currently available in the United States (mianserin and bupropion). Nine of the 11 trials found that use of the antidepressant was associated with a significantly greater improvement in eating behavior than was use of the placebo. These data leave little question that, within the limitations noted below, antidepressant medication is superior to placebo in the short-term treatment of patients of normal weight with bulimia. The magnitude of improvement varies substantially among the trials, but, on average, about 75 percent of patients treated with an antidepressant reduce their binge frequency by 50 percent or more, and about 25 percent cease binge eating entirely.

Despite these promising results, a number of questions about the role of antidepressant medication in the treatment of bulimia remain unanswered. The patients in the double-blind placebo-controlled trials have been selected according to a variety of criteria, and the results of these trials may not be extended automatically to the treatment of other bulimic patients. For example, since these studies were offering treatment with antidepressants, they may have attracted patients who tended to be depressed and may therefore have been more likely to respond to such treatment. Patients in these studies were compliant in taking medication. Drug compliance is certainly not a feature that characterizes the entire bulimia population. The placebo-controlled trials that have found a significant advantage for the active drug have treated patients with moderate to severe and chronic bulimia for relatively short periods of time. Whether antidepressants are more effective than placebo in the

Table 1. Controlled Trials of Antidepressants in Bulimia

Reference	Drug	No. completing trial	Duration of trial/wks	Drug versus placebo ($p <$)
Sabine et al. (1983)	Mianserin	36	8	NS
Pope et al. (1983)	Imipramine	19	6	.01
Mitchell and Groat (1984)	Amitriptyline	32	8	NS
Hughes et al. (1986)	Desipramine	22	6	.01
Agras et al. (1987)	Imipramine	22	16	.05*
Kaplan et al. (1987)	Imipramine	11	6	.01
Walsh et al. (1988)	Phenelzine	50	6	.001
Kennedy et al. (in press)	Isocarboxazid	18	6	.02
Barlow et al. (in press)	Desipramine	24	6	.01
Blouin et al. (in press)	Desipramine	10	6	.05
Horne et al. (in press)	Bupropion	49	8	.01

*One-tailed t-test.

treatment of milder and less chronic forms of this syndrome is unknown. It is also unknown how long patients who respond to antidepressant medication need to remain on the medication and how they fare after the drug is discontinued.

It is also unclear how to distinguish patients who are likely to respond to medication from those who are not. The major impetus for using antidepressants in bulimia was the association between bulimia and mood disturbance, and it seemed reasonable that depressed bulimic patients would be particularly likely to respond to antidepressant medication. In fact, several of the controlled trials indicate that bulimic patients with minimal symptoms of depression may respond to antidepressants.

An additional unanswered question is whether and when medication should be combined with other forms of treatment. As is discussed in other chapters, promising forms of psychotherapy for bulimia have also been developed in recent years, and it is currently unclear how to choose a particular form of treatment for a particular patient and whether combinations of treatments produce better results.

Several guidelines can be offered concerning the use of antidepressant medications in bulimia. It is critically important to assess and elicit the patient's compliance with a pharmacologic approach. The antidepressant medications that appear to be useful in the treatment of bulimia are lethal in overdose and, because of the propensity of patients with bulimia to be depressed and to be impulsive, the risk of suicide must be carefully evaluated. Some clinicians working in this area have the impression that monoamine oxidase inhibitors may be the single most effective type of antidepressants for the treatment of bulimia. However, monoamine oxidase inhibitors are substantially more difficult to use because of a higher frequency of side effects and because of the necessity for the patient to remain on a strict tyramine-free diet. Therefore, treatment is probably best initiated with a tricyclic antidepressant drug. It may be particularly advantageous to use imipramine, desipramine, or nortriptyline because the plasma levels required for antidepressant efficacy of these drugs are reasonably well established and the psychiatrist can assess the adequacy of the trial through the use of plasma level measurements (Glassman et al. 1985). If tricyclic antidepressant treatment is unsatisfactory, a trial of monoamine oxidase inhibitors should be considered for appropriate patients.

Other Agents

One report described a single patient successfully treated with carbamazapine in a double-blind crossover protocol (Kaplan et al. 1983). Carbamazepine is a drug widely used in the treatment of seizure disorders. It has a chemical structure similar to that of the tricyclic antidepressants and has been shown to be effective in the treatment of bipolar affective illness. Its utility in the treatment of bulimia awaits further investigation.

Hsu (1984) described good responses in 12 of 14 bulimic patients treated with lithium carbonate. Because of the increased danger of lithium intoxication in patients who are inducing vomiting or purging, careful monitoring is mandatory. As in the case of carbamazepine, lithium's effectiveness in the treatment of bulimia needs to be investigated in a controlled study.

Chapter 69

Behavior Therapy

Most of the psychotherapeutic approaches to the treatment of bulimia have relied heavily on behavioral techniques. Behavioral similarities between individuals with bulimia and individuals with alcohol and drug abuse problems have been described (Hatsukami et al. 1982). These behaviors include excessive self-administration of a substance, a sense of loss of control, and maintenance of the behavior despite negative consequences. Because of these similarities, behavioral techniques used with addictive or excessive behaviors (e.g., alcoholism, smoking, obesity) have been applied to individuals with bulimia (Mahoney and Mahoney 1976; Miller 1976; Pomerleau and Pomerleau 1977).

Theoretical Basis and Literature Review

According to the respondent model of learning, bulimia is viewed as an anxiety-based disorder similar to anorexia nervosa. As in anorexia nervosa, there is a morbid fear of weight gain. Eating, particularly binge eating, elicits anxiety; vomiting reduces it. Once an individual has learned that vomiting following food intake leads to anxiety reduction, rational fears no longer inhibit overeating, and binge eating may become more severe and frequent. Thus the driving force of this disorder may be vomiting, not binge eating. Binge eating may not occur if the person could not vomit afterward.

Vomiting may serve an anxiety-reducing function similar to compulsive rituals in obsessive-compulsive neurosis. Accordingly, in line with behavioral treatment of obsessive-compulsive neurosis, exposure and response prevention techniques should be effective (Rosen and Leitenberg 1982). This entails exposure to and not allowing escape from the anxiety-producing situation. Leitenberg et al. (1984), using an exposure and response treatment paradigm in bulimic patients, found that anxiety and the urge to vomit decreased and normal food consumption increased with treatment. By the end of treatment, four of five subjects had either substantially reduced or completely stopped vomiting and binge eating, even though the focus of the treatment sessions was primarily on vomiting rather than on binge eating. Improvement on self-report measures of eating attitudes, depression, and self-esteem was also observed.

Based on principles of the operant model of learning, bulimia is said to be maintained because of its reinforcing consequences. Some positive reinforcing consequences of binge eating are eating experienced as a pleasant event and stress relief. Vomiting acts as a negative reinforcer because of anxiety reduction associated with vomiting. Consequences of bulimic behavior also include punishments that should decrease binge eating. Punishments include self-disgust, physical problems (e.g., weakness and electrolyte abnormalities), and financial problems because of the cost of food. It is known that the strength of a reinforcer diminishes the farther it is removed from the actual behavior (Rimm and Masters 1979). Therefore, binge eating continues because the immediate reinforcing consequences outweigh the later maladaptive consequences. Operant treatment techniques include manipulating the consequences, such as rewarding of abstinence from binge eating and vomiting and punishment of mental images of binge eating or vomiting by the use of a small electroshock (Kenny and Solyom 1985).

Antecedent events can also control the occurrence of bulimic behavior. Antecedent events may be situational (e.g., being alone in the house with binge-foods readily available, stressful interpersonal conflicts), physical (e.g., fatigue, hunger), emotional (e.g., anger, depression, anxiety, boredom), or cognitive (e.g., negative self-reliance thoughts). Binge eating is thought to be precipitated by negative feelings and by interpersonal stress (Abraham and Beaumont 1982). Binge eating momentarily decreases the stress and, in time, develops into an all-purpose maladaptive coping mechanism.

Manipulating the antecedents involves breaking the relationship between the precipitating antecedent events and binge eating and thereby decreasing the probability of binge eating. Such measures include stimulus control techniques and practicing alternative behavior. Stimulus control involves minimizing the cues related to binge eating by control of amount and type of food present in the environment or avoiding situations most frequently associated with binge eating. Such stimulus control methods have also been used to help obese patients adhere to prescribed eating patterns (Mahoney and Mahoney 1976). Use of competing alternative behaviors involves scheduling pleasurable activities at times that are associated with a high frequency of binge eating.

Another treatment strategy, which involves manipulating the antecedent, is teaching problem-solving and adaptive skills. As mentioned, some people binge eat because they cannot handle interpersonal stress. Learning skills such as assertiveness and effective communication may help the patient resist binge eating.

The cognitive-behavioral treatment described by Fairburn (1981) combines cognitive treatment with behavioral strategies. It follows primarily an antecedent stimuli model of learning. The patient is helped to resist binge eating at times of stress and to practice other stress-reducing behaviors instead. Three stages of treatment may be distinguished. In the first stage, establishing control over eating is emphasized, and the techniques used are primarily behavioral (use of self-monitoring techniques, prescription of a pattern of regular eating, stimulus control methods, and the development of alternative behaviors). The second stage of treatment is more cognitively oriented. Emphasis is placed on the examination of irrational concerns but also on development of improved coping skills and the use of problem-solving techniques. Patients are also encouraged to reintroduce feared foods into their diet (exposure). In the final stage, the focus is on maintenance of changes and relapse prevention.

Johnson and Brief (1983) described an "energy balance" model of bulimia. According to this view, bulimia develops because of a deficit in knowledge or skills about normal weight maintenance through appropriate regulation of food intake and activity. The disorder begins with attempts to lose weight by following increasingly unrealistic diets. Binge eating develops in a rebound fashion following semi-starvation (Wardle and Beinart 1981). Continued inability to control eating leads to the binge-purge cycle, which eventually becomes a necessary strategy for regulating energy balance. According to this model, treatment involves helping the individual resist urges to binge and to establish realistic eating and exercise habits similar to those employed with obesity. Components of treatment include scheduled eating, a balanced diet, increased aerobic exercise, stimulus control techniques, cognitive restructuring, and self-reward.

Outcome data for individual and group treatment studies incorporating behavioral techniques are encouraging. Binge eating and vomiting episodes are significantly reduced with treatment and at follow-up in several uncontrolled studies (Fairburn 1981; Johnson et al. 1983; Long and Cordle 1982; Mitchell et al. 1985; Mizes and Lohr 1983; Schneider and Agras 1985). Schneider and Agras described a group treatment of bulimia adapting Fairburn's cognitive-behavioral approach. Along with a significant reduction in binge eating and vomiting during 16 weeks of treatment and a six-month follow-up period, significant psychological improvement over treatment time was demonstrated on measures of depression, eating attitudes, and assertiveness.

Several controlled studies have demonstrated that treatments involving behavioral or cognitive-behavioral techniques are more efficacious than control treatments in reducing bulimic behavior. Lacey (1983) reported a controlled study utilizing weekly treatment sessions involving individual and group meetings. Treatment combined behavioral, cognitive, and psychodynamic approaches. This 10-week study involving 30 bulimics resulted in an impressive outcome, with complete cessation or greatly reduced frequency of bulimic behavior in all patients. There was no improvement in 15 patients serving as waiting list controls. A two-year follow-up indicated maintenance of improvement.

Ordman and Kirschenbaum (1985) reported a controlled study involving 20 bulimic women randomly assigned to primarily cognitive-behavioral individual therapy or a brief-intervention waiting list and treated over five months. Those treated with cognitive-behavioral therapy, relative to the waiting list controls, substantially reduced the frequency of binge eating and vomiting, improved their psychological adjustment, and improved their attitudes about food, dieting, and their bodies. There was a dramatic reduction in the urge to vomit and level of discomfort in the actual eating situation.

Kirkley et al. (1985) reported a controlled study comparing cognitive-behavioral group treatment, which emphasized control of eating and vomiting behavior, with a nondirective group treatment, which gave no instructions about altering eating behaviors. In the nondirective group, emphasis was placed on self-discovery, understanding one's bulimia and self-disclosure. Both groups met weekly for 16 weeks and self-monitored bulimic behavior. The cognitive-behavioral treatment group had fewer dropouts and yielded a significantly greater decrease in binge eating and vomiting than did the nondirective treatment group. At three months' follow-up, 38 percent of the cognitive-behavioral and 11 percent of the nondirective group participants continued to abstain from binge eating and vomiting, but these differences were not statistically significant.

A Behaviorally Based Treatment Program for Bulimia

One goal of therapy is to help the patient resume normal eating behavior and to disrupt the bulimic behaviors, which include binge eating, vomiting, and laxative abuse. Another goal is to identify factors maintaining the disorder and to teach patients to cope more effectively with the circumstances or thoughts that result in bulimic behavior. Binge eating is usually the behavior targeted for intervention rather than vomiting, on the premise that cessation of binge eating will stop the vomiting. Patients may be expected to cease bulimic behavior abruptly or gradually. No data are available to support one approach over the other. Treatment can be on an outpatient or in-hospital basis in either group or individual format. In outpatient treatment, control of the behavior remains completely with the patient, and treatment outcome depends a great deal on the patient's commitment to change. In the treatment of hospitalized patients, external controls are typically applied by the treatment staff during the initial treatment phase to ensure that the patient eats normally and does not exhibit bulimic behavior. Control of eating is then gradually transferred back to the patient. Most bulimic patients respond to outpatient treatment and do not need hospitalization.

The initial task in outpatient treatment is for the patient to self-monitor eating behavior. Patients are often reluctant to do this because they are ashamed of the extent of their abnormal behavior. This reluctance is anticipated and discussed. They are told that monitoring the abnormal behavior and thereby confronting it is the first step in overcoming it. Typically, patients are asked to record the amount, type, and frequency of food intake and any bulimic behavior, as well as the circumstances and feelings associated with binge eating, vomiting, or laxative abuse. Self-monitoring of eating behavior usually continues throughout treatment.

Self-monitoring helps both patient and therapist analyze eating habits and their antecedents, the circumstances in which problems arise. This analysis helps determine treatment intervention. For example, if the patient frequently binge eats for relief of stress, teaching stress management may be a helpful intervention. Analysis and exploration of the adverse consequences of bulimic behavior is also important. The patient may have become socially withdrawn, depleted his or her savings, and missed days at work. Confrontation with these factors may enhance motivation for treatment. Positive consequences of bulimic behavior are explored as well. For example, bulimic behavior may increase attention by family members. The patient may be reluctant to give up this attention. Treatment may involve teaching the patient more appropriate ways to obtain attention.

Education concerning the nature and complications of bulimia and associated aspects occurs early in treatment. Patients are informed about the physical complications of bulimia, such as electrolyte disturbance and dehydration, which may cause weakness, lethargy, and cardiac arrhythmias. They are also informed about the effects of starvation and restrictive dieting. Dieting and starvation can cause binge eating as well as irritability, depression, and sleep disturbance. Maintaining weight in a normal range is therefore preferable. Although bulimics often desire to lose weight, they are advised to maintain their weight at onset of treatment because dietary restraint only encourages overeating and interferes with efforts to control eating behavior. Patients are advised that vomiting and laxative and diuretic abuse are relatively ineffective in controlling weight. Vomiting does not usually retrieve everything eaten, and it encourages overeating. Laxatives have a minimal effect on decreasing caloric absorption. Laxatives and diuretics primarily influence fluid balance.

Most bulimics are overconcerned about their weight and weigh frequently, often several times a day. Normal variations in weight and the apparent variation due to shifting fluid balance lead to anxiety and interfere with establishing a normal eating pattern. Patients are advised to weigh only weekly, preferably in the morning before breakfast.

A structured food plan is implemented. The patient is asked to restrict eating to three planned meals (and perhaps one snack) spread throughout the day. No skipping of meals is allowed. Regular eating will decrease the tendency to binge eat. Nutritional counseling, best done by a dietician knowledgeable about bulimia, is important. Bulimics attempt to limit their diet severely because of misperceptions about the effects of certain types of food on their bodies. For example, they believe that small amounts of sweets or fat-containing foods will markedly increase their weight. Although a balanced, varied diet is preferable, patients may at first limit the types of food eaten to foods that are not likely to trigger binge eating or vomiting. Patients should be actively discouraged from counting calories. Emphasis should be on portions instead of calories. Therefore, instruction in the use of food exchanges, similar to the system used in diabetics, is practical. Since sensations of appetite, "fullness," and hunger are initially disturbed in bulimics, they are advised to ignore these feelings and adhere to the prescribed food plan.

Self-control strategies help patients adhere to the prescribed eating pattern by manipulating the antecedents to bulimic behavior. Such methods include making binge foods unavailable, preparing a shopping list before going to the grocery, and avoiding shopping when hungry or when overeating is likely. Bulimic patients often eat rapidly while focusing attention on nonfood-related activities such as watching television. They are taught to keep eating a "pure" experience by eating only in a prescribed place such as the dining room, eating slowly, and pausing frequently, including putting down utensils between mouthfuls. Patients are taught to use competing or alternate behaviors instead of binge eating. They are asked to construct a list of pleasurable activities such as exercise, telephoning a friend, or taking a bath. Such activities are used to occupy time between meals and to cope in times of increased risk of binge eating.

The patient is rewarded for adhering to the prescribed food plan and abstaining from bulimic behavior. Therapists should praise each small step toward improvement. The patient should devise a system of self-reward, which may be material or mental. For example, a patient may save money previously spent on binge eating and use it to buy something special after attaining a certain goal. The patient is taught to make positive self-statements for successfully completed tasks.

Once the bulimic behavior is under control, the task is to stabilize the eating by treating problems associated with the eating disorder and preparing for the future by addressing relapse prevention. Earlier analysis of the antecedents to bulimic behavior provided a list of problems that led to bulimic behavior. Typically, these problems include low self-esteem, poor communication and interpersonal skills, and poor stress management. Patients are taught adaptive skills to cope with these problems. These may include relaxation and stress management, assertiveness, and communication and social skills. It is wise to examine patients for depressive symptoms at this time. Most patients show some depressive symptoms at the onset of treatment. Often depressive symptoms resolve when the bulimic behavior is brought under control. However, some patients will continue to show depressive symptoms after treatment is underway despite improvement in eating behavior. These patients may require antidepressant medication to help prevent relapse.

Bulimic patients have many irrational thoughts and beliefs that may lead to binge eating. These may be related to food, weight, body shape, or other things. For example, the patient may have the following thought: "I've gained two pounds. I have no alternative but to binge eat and vomit." Patients are taught to identify, evaluate, challenge, and replace these maladaptive thoughts, using cognitive restructuring techniques (Beck 1976).

An important aspect of relapse prevention involves exposure to foods and situations that are at high risk of leading to binge eating. The patient is first asked to complete a hierarchical list of foods and situations that lead to binge eating. Although initially controlling eating behavior while avoiding foods that lead to binge eating, the patient is now encouraged to introduce gradually but systematically these high-risk foods into the diet, beginning with foods least likely to lead to a binge. Continued avoidance of high-risk foods increases the chances of binge eating on these foods because they are typically foods the patient enjoys. Likewise, patients should practice eating in situations that previously led to binge eating.

Although eating behavior is usually in control by the time treatment ends, episodes of bulimic behavior may occur in the future, especially during times of stress. Patients should prepare, discuss with their therapists, and write out a plan of action to use when there is danger of recurrence of bulimic behavior.

Chapter 70

Cognitive Therapy

In an excellent historical review, Casper (1983) documented that bulimia appeared to be a rare symptom in anorexia nervosa throughout the past century but since about 1940 it has become more common. She postulated that the gradual emergence of bulimia as a syndrome may be linked to the appearance of a desire for thinness as a pervasive cultural motive. In the past several years, there has been a growing recognition that bulimia is a common symptom not only affecting patients with anorexia nervosa (Garfinkel and Garner 1982), but also those who present at a normal weight (Cooper and Fairburn 1983; Fairburn and Cooper 1984; Halmi et al. 1981; Pyle et al. 1983), and with obesity (Edelman 1981; Gormally et al. 1982; Loro and Orleans 1981). Some (e.g., Lacey 1982) have argued that patients with bulimia occurring without a history of emaciation may be clearly distinguished from those with the bulimic subtype of anorexia nervosa (American Psychiatric Association 1980).

In the short time since its recognition as a clinical entity, bulimia has been conceptualized from a range of different theoretical vantage points. Explanations have been offered that emphasize early developmental traits, behavioral contingencies, biologic determinants, and the social context of the disorder. Most of these formulations acknowledge the presence of distorted attitudes toward food, eating, weight, and the body. On standardized psychometric measures, bulimic patients report attitudes toward eating and body shape that are at least as aberrant as those observed in the restricting subtype of anorexia nervosa (Garner et al. 1982a, 1983b). Particularly salient beliefs that characterize both the bulimic and anorexic patients are a "morbid fear of fatness" (Russell 1979), dissatisfaction with body shape, and the inexorable conviction that strict control over body weight or thinness is necessary for happiness or well-being. Fairburn (1981, 1983, 1984) clearly articulated the details of a cognitive-behavioral treatment program for bulimia that is derived from methods used with obesity (Mahoney and Mahoney 1976). Three stages are distinguished in the treatment process (Fairburn 1983, 1984). Stage one lasts between four and six weeks and focuses on self-monitoring, a prescribed meal plan, information about sequelae, and self-control techniques. Conjoint interviews with family or friends are also advised. Stage two lasts approximately two months and involves the introduction of avoided foods, training in problem solving, and cognitive restructuring. Stage three consists of three or four meetings at two-week intervals at which earlier gains are consolidated. Cognitive-behavioral methods have been employed in several recent case studies with bulimic patients. Grinc (1982) reported the successful treatment of a patient with a 10-year history of bulimia using self-monitoring, stimulus control, and cognitive restructuring. Long and Cordle (1982) described successful treatment of two bulimic patients using cognitive restructuring combined with self-monitoring, behavioral self-control procedures, dietary education, and resocialization. A positive outcome was also reported by Linden (1980) in a similar multicomponent approach using cognitive methods. In an uncontrolled outcome study of 11 bulimic patients, Fairburn (1981) reported a marked reduction of bingeing and vomiting following cognitive-behavioral intervention. Several other authors have advocated cognitive-behavioral interventions as part of broad-based programs combining approaches from various orientations (White and Boskind-White 1981; Johnson et al. 1983; Loro 1984; Mitchell et al. 1984; Orleans and Barnett 1984; Roy-Bryne et al. 1984). Loro (1984) identified a number of cognitive distortions and dysfunctional attitudes that have been observed clinically in bulimia patients.

The Vicious Cycle of Bulimia

Factors that cause and then maintain the bulimic symptom pattern do not appear to be uniform across all individuals. Although many exhibit psychological disturbances that have been identified in anorexia nervosa, some cases of bulimia appear to be relatively free of primary psychopathology (Fairburn 1982; Lacey 1982; Russell 1979). Russell originally conceptualized bulimia as a self-perpetuating cycle involving an interaction between psychological and physiologic mechanisms. Because of their relevance to cognitive and behavioral treatment principles, an adapted and abbreviated version of Russell's model will be reviewed. First, shape dissatisfaction, usually (but not necessarily) accompanied by low self-esteem and in some cases by more severe personality disturbance, leads to an organized system of beliefs aimed at strict dieting and weight loss. Second, weight loss and a sustained "sub-optimal" weight produce physiologic responses reflected by increased hunger, food preoccupations, and bouts of overeating, all of which are designed to return the organism to a "health weight" (Russell 1979) or to a constitutionally determined "set point" for body weight. Third, cognitive and/or emotional factors determine whether binge eating will be "triggered" or prevented. For example, even the slightest transgression from rigidly prescribed dieting leads to the conclusion that one might as well give in to the urge to eat since perfect self-control has been "blown" (Fairburn 1984; Garner et al. 1982; Mahoney and Mahoney 1976; Orleans and Barnett 1984; Polivy et al. 1984). Emotional distress may interfere with the cognitive self-control processes required to sustain dieting in the presence of intense hunger. Fourth, the reliance on self-induced vomiting perpetuates the disorder by keeping weight at a reduced level and by diminishing anxiety associated with consuming foods perceived as fattening (Garner et al. 1982; Johnson and Brief 1983; Rosen and Leitenberg 1982, 1984; Russell 1979). Occasionally, self-induced vomiting may be maintained by positive contingencies such as attention from family members or by pleasurable sensations (Garner et al. 1982; Stoller 1982).

These four sets of interacting mechanisms do not constitute the only factors contributing to this heterogeneous syndrome. They do not explain why some individuals who successfully manage to suppress their weight (restricting anorexia nervosa patients being the quintessential example) fail to develop bulimia. Moreover, for some individuals, bulimia may be linked to an affective or neurologic disorder (Hudson et al. 1983b; Rau and Green 1984; Walsh et al. 1982). However, it is proposed that the above mechanisms account for the majority of cases, and they form the basis of the cognitive-behavioral treatment principles recommended for its management.

The Cognitive Model

The cognitive approach to understanding bulimia emphasizes how the symptom pattern logically derives from the faulty assumptive world of the patient. The apparently bizarre eating patterns and the resolute refusal of adequate nourishment become plausible given the bulimic patient's conviction that dieting and weight control are absolutely essential for happiness or well-being. The surplus meaning that has become attached to weight control also may provide a window into the patient's broader conceptual system, which is characterized by low self-esteem, depressive thinking, poor impulse control, perfectionism, and interpersonal fears. One advantage of a cognitive approach to bulimia is that it is not necessarily incompatible with other models that view the origin of the disorder from a wide variety of conceptual perspectives (Garner and Garfinkel 1984). Some of these formulations emphasize events that are remote in time from the expression of symptoms. Others concentrate on events more proximal to the development of the disorder. Recently, several authors have accounted for the development and maintenance of bulimia by an analysis of functional relationships between antecedent events, positive reinforcers, and negative reinforcers (Hawkins et al. 1984; Slade 1982). As with anorexia nervosa, much of the speculation regarding the pathogenesis of the bulimic symptom pattern conforms to a paradigm that presumes that behavior is maintained by reducing aversive consequences (i.e., a conditioned avoidance model).

Dieting is sustained by its presumed efficacy in avoiding fatness. Vomiting and purgative abuse serve a similar role, but also allow avoidance of the negative consequences of consuming large quantities of food. It is well recognized that avoidance behavior is resistant to extinction because it insulates the individual from recognizing when the aversive contingencies are no longer operating. However, the bulimic patient's behavior is motivated not simply by a fear of fatness and all that it might imply, but also by cognitive self-reinforcement. The dietary restraint is often fueled by the gratification and sense of control or mastery that it provides. The tangible success at weight loss or simply the anticipation of rewards for weight reduction become powerful determinants of the bulimic's behavior. This same form of cognitive self-reinforcement has been credited with a major role in maintaining anorexia nervosa (Garner and Bemis 1982, 1984; Slade 1982). Unpleasant sensations usually associated with hunger take on new meaning for the bulimic because they connote success at the much valued goal of weight control. Gastric emptiness becomes associated with virtue and mastery, while eating or fullness indicates weakness or lack of self-discipline. Encouraging the bulimic patient to discard this powerful system of cognitive self-reinforcement is one of the major obstacles in therapy. It has become deeply ingrained and is central to the patient's self-evaluation. In many cases, it may be the singular or predominant frame of reference for bolstering an abysmal self-esteem. As Slade indicated, these feelings are particularly potent when the individual experiences extreme dissatisfaction in other areas of his or her life. Noting that perfectionistic tendencies have also been associated with bulimia and anorexia nervosa, Slade postulated that the combination of perfectionism and general dissatisfaction are setting conditions for both disorders. They optimize the likelihood that the potential patient will turn to self-control in general and control over his or her body in particular as a means of consolation. It is not difficult to understand why an adolescent who is struggling with extreme feelings of ineffectiveness might embrace the idea that a thinner shape might lead to a greater sense of adequacy. The message that thinness is an assured pathway to beauty, success, and social competence is a consistent theme transmitted through the fashion and dieting industries (Garner et al. 1983a; Wooley et al. 1979).

Thus the simultaneous operations of positive and negative contingencies may account for bulimia's recalcitrance. What is important for the purposes here is that these contingencies may be covert or cognitive events. Cognitive therapy offers a variety of powerful clinical strategies that may be applied to distorted beliefs associated with eating and body shape as well as a range of developmental, interpersonal, and self-attributional themes. The distinctions between cognitive therapy and other approaches recommended for bulimia are the same as those described within the context of anorexia nervosa.

Conventional cognitive therapy must be adapted in consideration of the following specific features of bulimia: 1) idiosyncratic beliefs related to food and weight, 2) the interaction between physical and psychological aspects of the disorder, 3) the patient's desire to retain certain focal symptoms, and 4) the prominence of fundamental self-concept deficits related to self-esteem and trust of internal state.

Two-Track Approach to Treatment

The first track pertains to the patient's current eating behavior and physical condition. The second track involves the more complex task of modifying misconceptions reflected in self-concept deficiencies, perfectionism, poor impulse regulation, depression, and disturbed family or other interpersonal relationships. Since themes on both tracks are characterized by reasoning errors, dysfunctional beliefs, and distorted underlying assumptions, they may be addressed using cognitive-behavioral therapy principles. A disproportionate emphasis on the first track is required early in the course of therapy; other contributing factors may not be meaningfully assessed until the bulimic symptom pattern is brought under control. It is essential for the therapist to begin with a thorough understanding of methods for normalizing eating and weight. A first step in this process involves motivating the patient to discontinue potentially dangerous or ineffective weight control practice.

Developing Motivation for Treatment

Several authors have suggested that bulimic patients' motivation to receive treatment may be contrasted with the resistance and denial typical of anorexia nervosa patients (Fairburn 1983; Fairburn and Cooper 1982; Lacey 1982). However, the bulimic's motivation may quickly fade with the recognition that the goals of treatment go beyond control of the distressing symptoms of bingeing and vomiting. Bulimic patients are often as intransigent as their restricting anorectic counterparts in relinquishing "ego-syntonic" symptoms such as dieting and, in many cases, the steadfast pursuit of a suboptimal weight (Russell 1979). Some patients are so resolved in their commitment to maintaining a suboptimal body weight that they admit that they would rather continue to struggle with bulimia, vomiting, and all of their pernicious consequences than to gain weight. Although it is not articulated as such, a minority of bulimic patients essentially request to be converted to what could be characterized as the restricting subtype of anorexia nervosa (i.e., submenstrual weight and rigidly controlled eating). The patient must gradually recognize that although the dieting behavior is functional in the sense that it provides short-term pleasure or a reliable means of self-rating, it has disastrous long-term consequences. Eating a wider range of foods and inhibiting the urge to vomit elicit intense anxiety for the patient with bulimia. Since therapy requires the patient to engage gradually in these behaviors and actually feel worse on the road to recovery, motivation must be elicited repeatedly during the course of treatment. Stringent dieting, retaining a suboptimal weight, avoiding fattening foods, and vomiting must be repeatedly redefined as inconsistent with the ultimate goal of recovery. Patients must be taught to examine the long-term implications of their behavior on a daily basis. A key ingredient in the patient's willingness to exchange the positive experiences of dietary and weight control for the promise of ultimate improvement is a trusting therapeutic relationship.

Normalization of Eating and Weight

The process of psychotherapy is seriously influenced by chaotic eating patterns, vomiting, and rigorous dieting in that the physiologic consequences of these behaviors exert a profound effect on cognitive and emotional functioning. Although specific strategies for dealing with distorted attitudes about eating and weight will be described later, there are a number of practical considerations in these areas that may be outlined.

Psychoeducational Material

Providing the patient with advice regarding the physical consequences of bulimia, the biology of weight regulation, the consequences of dieting, and the social arguments against weight suppression is often helpful in enlisting motivation for change. Didactic instruction, which may be supplemented by written material, has become an integral component of a growing number of approaches to bulimia (Fairburn 1984; Garner et al. 1984; Johnson et al. 1983; Mitchell et al. 1984; Wooley and Wooley 1984). Since it is directly aimed at attitude change, educational material is complementary to other cognitive strategies for modifying misconceptions about dieting, weight regulation, and nutrition.

While dealing with eating and weight in therapy may seem like a mundane, "nonpsychological" task, it is vital for reasons beyond the obvious physical implications. It emphasizes the interdependence between physical and psychological aspects of the disorder, it is the area of immediate concern to the bulimic patient, and it allows evaluation of dysfunctional attitudes that may be modified using cognitive therapy principles.

Stimulus Control

It is widely recognized that binge eating may be triggered by certain stressful circumstances, relationship conflicts, or negative feeling states (Abraham and Beaumont 1982; Edeleman 1981; Fairburn 1981, 1983, 1984; Grinc 1982; Hawkins and Clement 1984; Johnson and Larson 1982; Lacey 1982; Loro and Orleans 1981; Orleans and Barnett 1984; Stunkard 1959). Various methods have been proposed for helping patients identify cues that elicit bingeing and then either avoid them or develop more adaptive means of coping (Fairburn 1981, 1984; Grinc 1982; Orleans and Barnett 1984). Behavioral techniques may be supplemented by cognitive stimulus control methods such as thought stopping, guided imagery, delay, and distraction (Orleans and Barnett 1984; Wilson 1984). Although emotional or situational factors may trigger bingeing or vomiting, this must be understood within the context of dieting or weight suppression. It could be predicted that bulimia would be an unlikely response among stressed or emotionally disturbed individuals who have not been dieting.

Tables 1 and 2 are the outlines for the specific techniques that are described in Chapter 61.

Course and Duration of Treatment

Fairburn's (1981, 1983) approach tends to be time-limited, lasting between four and six months with a different focus in the three stages. However, Fairburn (1983) indicated that the duration of treatment must be tailored to the individual needs of the patient, with some requiring a more lengthy course. There is a remarkable variability in the course and duration of treatment across patients with bulimia. Thus it is difficult to specify uniform stages to the treatment process. For some patients, treatment is quite straightforward and largely limited to "track one" issues outlined earlier. Control of bingeing and vomiting is achieved with behavioral methods aimed at interpreting the process of dieting. The educational aspects of treatment are effective in discouraging vomiting and purgative abuse. The cognitive component is primarily restricted to modifying unrealistic attitudes about shape, with a major emphasis on challenging cultural values that have led to dieting. For these patients, treatment may be brief and highly successful. For others, many of whom have had a long history of anorexia nervosa, multiple treatment failures, and extremely chaotic eating patterns, their disorder may be complicated by profound psychosocial disturbances. Norman and Herzog (1984) reported on a sample of bulimia patients, who demonstrate a greater level of persistent social maladjustment than normal, alcoholic, and schizophrenic women. These patients may at some point require brief hospitalization, and the course of cognitive therapy is quite variable. Track one principles may have to be persistently applied over many months or reinstituted when eating patterns periodically deteri-

Table 1. Reasoning errors

1. Dichotomous reasoning	4. Magnification
2. Personalization and self-reference	5. Selective abstraction
3. Superstitious thinking	6. Overgeneralization

Table 2. Basic cognitive techniques

1. Articulation of beliefs	5. Challenging the "shoulds"
2. Operationalizing beliefs	6. Challenging beliefs through behavioral
3. Decentering	exercises
4. Decatastrophizing	7. Perspective hypothesis testing
	8. Reattribution techniques

orate. Cognitive therapy must focus not only on intransigent assumptions related to eating and shape but also on self-concept deficits, depressive thinking, poor impulse control, and pervasive interpersonal fears. Although brief therapy should be the aim, some patients require cognitive therapy of longer duration.

Thus differences in patient populations may be a major factor accounting for conflicting opinions about treatment course and duration. As Long and Cordle (1982) observed, optimistic reports have been largely based on college samples, where severe psychological disturbance may be less typical (Boskind-Lodahl and White 1978; Coffman 1984; Linden 1980; Mizes and Lohr 1983; Rosen and Leitenberg 1982). Some treatment programs admit only patients who, in advance, agree to comply with the treatment protocol (Lacey 1982), including abstinence from vomiting (Mitchell et al. 1984). In contrast, less auspicious reports have come from centers that have developed a reputation in the professional community for treating bulimic patients with anorexia nervosa (Crisp 1980; Lucas et al. 1976; Russell 1979).

The attitude change is a prerequisite for complete recovery for most patients with bulimia and cognitive-behavioral treatment is a valuable method for achieving this end. Preliminary reports have been encouraging and must be followed by more systematic evaluation of the active components in treatment, predictors of outcome, and durability of change.

Chapter 71

Family Therapy

Bulimia nervosa is a heterogenous disorder and consists of a variety of behavioral and psychological components in a variety of personality types, which are themselves embedded in a variety of different biological makeups. Proper treatment of the bulimic person requires careful assessment at each of these levels. Given the diversity and complexity of the syndrome, a single treatment approach for all patients with bulimic problems cannot be supported. As with the other therapies described in this section, family therapy may be useful in some, but not necessarily in all, cases. In this chapter, I will discuss the family in varieties of normal weight bulimic syndromes, a rationale for family intervention in some cases, indications for treatment, and a discussion of the potential contributions that family therapy can offer in relation to other forms of intervention. For extended discussions concerning family assessment and specific strategies for intervention, the reader is referred to Chapter 62. Given that the literature specifically pertaining to family assessment and treatment of normal weight bulimia is sparse in comparison to that concerning anorexia nervosa, this chapter will necessarily be far more impressionistic.

As yet, very few systematic studies or even extended clinical series of patients with bulimia nervosa have been reported who have been treated primarily with family therapy (Russell et al. 1987; Schwartz et al. 1985), nor have series of cases been reported in which family therapy was systematically employed as a major adjunctive component of treatment.

Among persons with normal weight and bulimic eating patterns, a number of subgroups can be identified. Although these subgroups require systematic empirical validation, they may ultimately be shown to differ with respect to optimum treatment and prognosis.

Experimental, "trendy" bulimia.   A large number of women in college sororities, certain high school cliques, and related social groupings will occasionally or even routinely vomit as a form of weight reduction. In certain sororities, the percentages of women who engage in repeated vomiting and who could meet criteria for bulimia on survey checklists are high. Whether these women all deserve a psychiatric diagnosis is debatable. For many, the bulimic pattern has been short lived, several months to a year, and very often these behaviors will abate once the woman is removed from the facilitating social situation. Such women are often helped by education, group therapy, and cognitive-behavioral interventions and do not ordinarily require family therapy.

Bulimia as an alternative to morbid obesity.   There are a number of patients who were morbidly obese at earlier ages who later developed bulimic patterns (including purging) as the only way short of surgery to keep their weights down. While such patients are theoretically interested in giving up their bulimic patterns, they usually much prefer remaining bulimic to returning to severe obesity. Many of these patients have been married, and the marital relationship may contribute to, sustain, or inevitably be impacted by the bulimic behavior patterns. In these cases, family assessment is usually indicated, but intensive family therapy may or may not be necessary.

Bulimia nervosa with affective disturbance.   Bulimia often occurs concurrently with affective disturbance or in patients with a past history of affective disturbance. In such cases it may be difficult to tease apart the extent to which the bulimic syndrome precedes or follows the onset of affective symptoms, and a family assessment may help clarify these issues. In a large majority of bulimic patients one sees at least secondary dysphoria, with the affective disturbance representing the patient's unhappy, disappointed response to feeling out of control in relation to the eating symptoms. In cases of primary depression, bulimic behaviors may be one symptomatic manifestation of the depression. As will be described below, a high prevalence of depression and alcoholism has been reported in families of bulimic patients, so that disturbed family relationships often appear.

Bulimia nervosa in impulse-ridden character disturbance.   A sizeable percentage of bulimic patients are self-destructively impulsive in a variety of areas. They may have difficulty in tolerating frustration and in regulating themselves in such areas as eating, sleeping, emotionality, time management, sexuality, and relationships. Many may have atypical depression, rejection-sensitive dysphoria, and/or borderline personality disorganization; for them bulimic behavior is simply one further manifestation of distress. Gorging behavior may serve as one mechanism for alleviating primitive tensions, counterbalanced in these patients by cultural forces to be thin, which lead to compensatory purging. Many patients in this group also have problems with alcohol and street drugs. Family dynamics and family patterns in such patients are very similar to those described for the bulimic (as opposed to restricter) anorexia nervosa patient, and the normal weight bulimia and bulimic anorexia nervosa may be points along a continuum rather than categorically distinct.

Normal weight bulimic patients with nervosa who have had anorexia nervosa. While DSM-III (American Psychiatric Press 1980) defined bulimia as separate from anorexia nervosa, DSM-III-R (American Psychiatric Press 1987) has corrected this misunderstanding. In practice, large numbers of patients are seen who may have had an episode of frank anorexia nervosa earlier in life, but who regained weight at the expense of developing bulimic patterns. Problems with impulsivity described above are common in this group, and anorectic psychological attitudes in the patients often persist following weight gain. In both the normal weight impulse-ridden character disturbance group and in the normal weight bulimic former anorexia nervosa patients, family assessment is indicated, and family therapy is often necessary. These families are usually in turmoil, frequently manifest a high degree of negative expressed emotion, and often reveal the bulimic patient to be enmeshed with one of the parents, most often the mother.

A Rationale for Family Therapy

The rationale for conducting family therapy with some bulimic patients parallels that for anorexia nervosa: family systems appear to play a role in initiating and maintaining the symptoms, and the symptoms themselves cause a great deal of distress among and provoke negative responses from other family members, destructive for themselves and for the patient.

A high prevalence of affective disturbance and alcoholism in families of patients with normal weight bulimia has now been documented by several studies (Hudson et al. 1983a; Pyle et al. 1981; Yager et al. 1983). In addition, the large number of normal weight bulimics report obesity and binge eating in parents, and they also report a much higher than expected prevalence of parental anorexia nervosa (Yager et al. 1983). Although this study was limited by the self-report methodology of the subjects, it was noteworthy that in only 12 percent of respondents were both parents described as free of either an emotional or eating disturbance. The implication here is that bulimia is most likely to find fertile grounds for development in the family in which there is an eating disturbance or emotional disturbance (e.g., depression or alcoholism).

In numerous families of normal weight bulimic patients, the classically described family dynamics for anorexia nervosa families may be evident: enmeshment, rigidity, overprotectiveness, one overinvolved and one aloof parent, and complementary rather than symmetrical parental relationships. While it must be stressed that these family dynamic patterns are far from ubiquitous and cannot at this point even be said to exist for the majority of patients with bulimia, in those cases where they are found they are virtually identical to those described in the so-called psychosomatic families (Minuchin et al. 1978).

Finally, in those families of origin (i.e., the bulimic patient and the patient's parental family) and families of insertion (i.e., ordinarily the patient and the patient's spouse) where family members are aware of the patient's bulimia, the bulimic behaviors often generate a great deal of familial turmoil. However, among the more disturbed, impulse-ridden normal weight bulimics, the bulimia per se, while disturbing, is only one among the many concerns, points of contention, and difficulties, and not necessarily the most worrisome either for the bulimic or the rest of the family. The identified patient is often the subject of intense blaming, criticism, and attention. The parents may triangulate and use the patient's problems as a focus and excuse by which to avoid dealing with their own marital difficulties. Often, the family tensions experienced by the bulimic patient build dramatically and need to be discharged. Given that the patient lacks more direct and effective ways of addressing the interpersonal problems, bingeing and purging serve as a form of displacement behavior in an ethological sense. In this regard, the bulimic behaviors may well be less self-destructive than other self-destructive impulsive alternatives available to the patient.

Consequently, several rationales emerge for the use of family therapy in some cases of bulimia nervosa. First, as with anorexia nervosa, it is important to identify the extent to which unresolved conflicts in the family may contribute to the appearance and maintenance of the bulimic symptoms. If, for example, constant tension-generating issues and processes in the family can be identified that are potentially more effectively resolved through direct negotiation than through the existing indirect perverse communication patterns, therapy aimed at dealing with these matters may reduce the tension and, in turn, the bulimic episodes triggered by it. Second, since bulimia nervosa is so often a secretive disorder, the fact that the patient is able to share and receive some caring support from the rest of the family may in itself yield nonspecific therapeutic advantage, reducing the isolation and demoralization of the bulimic person. Third, in those situations where a "toxic family" with unremitting high negative expressed emotion is identified, the bulimic patient may be validated in his or her perception of the family, some changes may be attempted, or the patient may gain support for efforts to leave the family. Given that most of the bulimic patients we have seen are in their early 20s, the expectation to leave home is realistic for many. Fourth, in some families the development of specific behavioral programs to deal with bulimic episodes, utilizing positive and/or negative contingency programs, requires family cooperation.

Indications for Family Assessment

Several issues to help the clinician decide whether to conduct a family assessment have already been mentioned above. For the clinician who is receptive to hearing it, patients will very often provide indications that an assessment of the family is in order. Of particular note are those patients whose bulimic symptoms are exacerbated by visits, telephone conversations, or other contacts with their families, or who explicitly describe tension-filled, overinvolved, or toxic families. Every married patient should be questioned regarding the spouse's general level of support or lack of support, current knowledge about the symptoms, specific attitudes regarding the symptoms, expectations when they were first married (i.e., was the spouse knowingly marrying a "sick" person), and capacity to accept clear-cut improvements in the patient.

Indications for Family Therapy

Many have been implied in the foregoing discussion. Generally speaking, for "uncomplicated" bulimia in a young woman who is not living with her family and who is not overly distressed by her interactions with them (e.g., the patient with experimental or trendy bulimia), family therapy is usually not necessary. However, when there are clear concerns regarding the transmission, incitement, and maintenance of the bulimic symptoms in the family setting, and where changes in family expectations and behaviors might make it easier for the patient to give up the bulimic symptoms, as with anorexia nervosa, family therapy can be beneficial and may be essential in some cases. In couples with disturbed marital relationships, where secretiveness about the symptoms interferes with intimacy, therapy is potentially very beneficial.

Goals of Family Therapy

There are several worthwhile goals for family therapy. Informing the family about the nature of bulimia nervosa, factors that may be helpful in treatment, and how serious or not so serious it may be from a medical viewpoint can alleviate worry and concern in some instances or appropriately generate concern in others. In those cases where specific family systems disturbances in communication, structure, and process have been uncovered, interventions aimed at correcting those specific problems should be formulated and offered to the family, as with the anorexia nervosa population.

Strategies for Family Intervention in Bulimia

Strategies include all of those described in the chapter on family treatment for anorexia nervosa. The family and couples groups may be used to good advantage. These may consist of six to 12 structured one-and-one-half-hour weekly sessions in which bulimic patients and their parents, or spouses, are all included. Four such groups have been completed (Slagerman et al. unpublished). The groups usually begin in a highly structured manner, with the group leaders providing didactic information about bulimia—its causes, consequences, and treatment options. The "lecture" portion of any session never takes more than half the meeting. At the start of each sequence of meetings, the most useful format for patients and their families has been the question-and-answer session, largely didactic. In every instance, the family groups have quickly moved on to an exchange of experiences and information among the families and patients. This sharing and the recognition that they are not unique in their tribulations are reassuring and helpful to families. The family groups ordinarily develop a high degree of openness very quickly. Subsequent meetings in these series usually evoke more personally revealing material and reflectiveness. Acceptance of these group meetings has been very high among those who have participated, and their demands for additional contact resulted in the formation of a monthly booster group after the scheduled weekly sessions ended. Of course, only the motivated families elect to participate. A number of families who have been invited to join these groups have declined. Some have opted out of the family groups for a variety of excuses after only one or two sessions.

Individualized family therapy is usually offered to those families who at assessment are found to be particularly troubled or troubling to the patient. Some of the families, particularly those with impulse-ridden members, may be so chaotic that it might be virtually impossible to keep them in treatment or to do productive work. Some families may start in individualized family therapy only after having gone through a family group, when they have found that looking at the problems from a family perspective is useful for them. Many of the patients and families learn more adaptive specific strategies for dealing with one another, and reformulate their relationships. Concurrent individual or group therapy often helps the patients make better use of the family sessions.

One particularly useful event that the UCLA clinic sponsored was a "town council." They invited all the patients who were at that point participating in the clinic and their families to spend a three- to four-hour evening with the entire clinic staff for a freewheeling question-and-answer session. About 90 patients and family members attended. The information exchange per se was only one of the many benefits. The involvement and concern of the family members, and their desires to be involved, led to the demand for additional family therapy services.

Evaluation of Family Therapy for Bulimia Nervosa

At present little systematically collected information exists concerning the contribution that family therapy can make for the treatment of bulimia nervosa.

Russell et al. (1987) compared the effects of family therapy versus individual supportive therapy in 23 patients with bulimia nervosa treated after discharge from a hospital program for weight gain and reassessed after a year of therapy. An unspecified number also received antidepressant medication. With 19 patients completing the trial, no differences were seen in outcome in relation to the type of psychotherapy.

Describing their experiences with 30 consecutively treated cases of bulimic patients and their families, Schwartz et al. (1985) found family therapy to be of considerable benefits for at least two-thirds of patients. But, it should be noted, these patients were referred to family therapy in the first place.

The overall experience suggests that for some patients it is virtually impossible to do meaningful therapeutic work without some involvement of the family because ignoring the family will result in undoing, sabotaging, or premature termination of therapy. In these instances, simply respecting and acknowledging the family's presence, interest, concern, and power are important in permitting the patient to improve, or even to engage in other types of treatment (e.g., individual psychotherapy, the use of medication). For example, families often have extremely strong feelings one way or the other about medications, usually negative ones. Without their involvement in some discussion as to the benefits of any of the alternative therapies, some family members may guarantee that no therapy will get done. If for no other reason than to promote their support of any therapy, in such cases attention to the family is important.

Chapter 72

Group Therapy

The treatment literature on bulimia nervosa has focused on the use of group psychotherapy techniques. Beginning with the report by Boskind-Lodahl and White (1978), many group approaches have been described. Although most of these reports have been descriptive, since 1983 10 controlled trials comparing some form of group psychotherapy to either a waiting list control or a comparison treatment have been reported at this writing. These studies suggest quite clearly that group psychotherapy can be a very useful treatment approach to bulimia nervosa. The experiences of the investigators in these studies suggest specific techniques that can be employed in a group context. The controlled group psychotherapy studies have focused almost exclusively on behavioral, particularly cognitive-behavioral techniques. Many other therapeutic strategies, which on theoretical grounds might be useful in the care of these patients and may eventually be found to be effective, have not yet been rigorously evaluated.

Before turning to a discussion of the published studies, there are some important theoretical questions concerning the treatment of bulimia nervosa that should be mentioned. First is the issues of self-help versus structured treatment. Over the last decade there has been a marked increase in the number of self-help groups available in the community for people with this disorder. Some of these groups have evolved from chemical dependency treatment programs. Some have been developed from structured mental health or eating disorder programs to provide aftercare for patients. Some have been developed by former bulimic patients. Overeaters Anonymous has also been a resource for many people with bulimia nervosa. Very little is known about the effectiveness of self-help groups in the treatment of this disorder because, by their very nature, self-help approaches are difficult to evaluate. Based on clinical experience, however, a few suggestions regarding self-help groups can be made. First, such groups should not be regarded as uniformly helpful for individuals with bulimia nervosa. Some groups, particularly those in which many or all of the participants are actively bulimic, may actually perpetuate the symptoms. Therefore, it is useful to encourage patients who are seeking involvement in self-help groups to find groups in which the majority of the members are free of the symptoms and can serve as models for recovery. Second, the theoretical orientations of some self-help groups may reinforce certain negative beliefs in bulimic individuals. For example, some groups use the model "once a bulimic—always a bulimic," which is clearly not true. Some groups suggest that certain foods are "bad" and need to be avoided indefinitely. These notions are not helpful for most bulimic individuals. We know that most bulimics who make a good recovery find that they can reintroduce most or all foods into their diet, and that many individuals can recover from this disorder and do not need to see themselves as "recovering" indefinitely.

A second theoretical point regarding bulimia nervosa treatment is the amount of emphasis placed on abstinence from bulimic symptoms during treatment. Some programs have adopted a model analogous to a chemical dependency model, requiring that patients need to interrupt their bulimic symptoms early in the course of treatment. In some programs recurrences of bulimic symptoms are potential grounds for termination from the group. As discussed by Bemis (1985), strict adherence to such a model may reinforce the dichotomous thinking that is already problematic in these patients and may unnecessarily burden them with a sense of shame and guilt. Although some degree of emphasis on the interruption of bulimic behaviors is useful for many patients, therapists must take great care to keep this a positive goal and not to create an atmosphere in which patients experience recurrences of problem behavior as evidence of failure, which may drive the patient from treatment and worsen the situation.

Controlled Trials

Information on the controlled group treatment trials is summarized in Table 1. Several of the trials have compared two forms of groups or compared a group to a waiting list control (Connors et al. 1984; Kirkley et al. 1985; Lee and Rush 1986; Wilson et al. 1986; Yates and Sambrailo 1984). Three of the trials involved mixed approaches, either individual combined with group therapy (Lacey 1983; Wolchick et al. 1986) or a comparison of group and individual approaches (Freeman et al. 1988). Two employed individual psychotherapy only (Fairburn et al. 1986; Ordman and Kirschenbaum 1985). As can be seen in Table 1, the durations of therapy have varied, but most of these studies have used time-limited, structured therapeutic approaches.

The number of subjects entered into each protocol, the number who completed treatment, and the short-term outcome results for the group components are summarized in Table 2. Sample sizes in most of these protocols have been fairly small, with the largest study being that by Freeman et al. (1988). Dropout or premature termination rates have varied, but the available data do suggest a problem with dropouts in psychotherapy interventions. The treatment outcome results in terms of percentage of reduction in binge eating behavior, pretreatment to posttreatment, are

Table 1. Treatments Used in Controlled Group Psychotherapy Trials

Reference	Group	Comparison	Duration (weeks)
Lacey (1983)	Group + Individual	Waiting List	10
Connors et al. (1984)	Psychoeducational	Waiting List	10
Yates and Sambrailo (1984)	CBT + Behavioral	CBT Alone	6
Kirkley et al. (1985)	CBT	Group Nondirective	16
Ordman and Kirschenbaum (1985)	Full	Group Brief	Variable
Fairburn et al. (1986)	Individual CBT	Short-term Focal	18
Freeman et al. (1988)	Group	Individual CBT, Individual Behavior Therapy, Waiting List	15
Lee and Rush (1986)	CBT	Waiting List	6
Wilson et al. (1986)	Cognitive Restructuring/ERP	Group Cognitive Restructuring	16
Wolchik et al. (1986)	Psychoeducational	Waiting List	7

Note. CBT = cognitive behavioral therapy; ERP = exposure and response prevention.

Table 2.   Completion and Outcome Data for Subjects in Active Group Treatment

Reference	Started treatment	Completed treatment N	%	Reduction binge-eating (%)	Abstinent last week of treatment (%)
Lacey (1983)	30	30	100	95	80
Connors et al. (1984)	26	20	77	70	62
Yates and Sambrailo (1984)	24	16	67		6
Kirkley et al. (1985)	14	13	93	97	
Ordman and Kirschenbaum (1985)	10	10	100	79	20
Fairburn et al. (1986)	24	22	92	85	32
Freeman et al. (1988)	92	65	71	84	
Lee and Rush (1986)	15	11	73	70	29
Wilson et al. (1986)	17	12	71	67	54
Wolchik et al. (1986)	13	11	85	58	9

also summarized in Table 2. As can be seen, percentage of reduction in target behaviors such as binge eating frequency have been quite dramatic, with considerable evidence for improvement in these studies. However, data are also given on the percentage of subjects free of bulimic behaviors during the last week of treatment. As can be seen, most patients in the majority of these studies are still evidencing some bulimic behaviors, albeit at a markedly reduced frequency, at the end of treatment. The significance of this is unclear. Is this the logical process of improvement, or do persistent symptoms suggest the possibility of relapse at a later date? The long-term follow-up results from these studies are quite limited, but the data do suggest that many patients seem to maintain their improvement at follow-up. However, we need considerably more information about long-term outcome.

What can we conclude from these reports? Active treatments employing mixtures of behavioral and cognitive-behavioral techniques appear to have a significant advantage over minimal intervention, unstructured, or waiting list comparisons. What can clinicians learn from these studies? Several of the important component variables included in these programs are outlined in Table 3. Many programs emphasize two basic areas—meal planning and nutritional counseling techniques and behavioral and cognitive-behavioral techniques. The packages are clearly different, but many of the same elements, as summarized, are present in most programs. The specific nutritional counseling techniques used vary widely, but all at minimum include the strong directive to modify eating patterns, not just by controlling binge eating and vomiting but in eating regular balanced meals. One program specifically mentions the advisability of encouraging patients to reintroduce feared foods that have been excluded from their diet.

All of the programs use self-monitoring techniques, owing in part to the fact that these are research studies where the eating pattern is an important outcome variable. However, most clinicians working in this area have a strong belief that self-monitoring is in itself therapeutic. All programs also include some mention of cognitive restructuring, similar to the techniques used in cognitive-behavioral therapy of depression (Beck et al. 1979). Some programs discuss cue restriction, particularly early in treatment, such as avoiding access to binge foods or situations associated with binge eating. Many programs have patients develop lists of alternative behaviors that they can engage in, such as calling a friend or taking a bath when faced with the urge to binge eat. Three programs also specifically include exposure and response prevention,

Table 3. Treatment Components Mentioned in Active Group Treatments

Reference	Nutritional				Behavioral					
	Modify Eating Pattern	Edu-cation	Meal Plan	Reintro-duce Feared Foods	Self-Monitor	Cognitive Restruc-turing	Cue Restricting	Alter-native Behaviors	Delay Vomit	ERP
Lacey (1983)	+		+		+	+				
Connors et al. (1984)	+				+	+	+	+		
Yates and Sambrailo (1984)	+				+	+		+	+	
Kirkley et al. (1985)	+	+	+	+	+	+	+	+	+	
Ordman and Kirschenbaum (1985)	+		+		+	+			+	+
Fairburn et al. (1986)	+	+		+	+	+	+	+		
Freeman et al. (1988)	+				+	+				
Lee and Rush (1986)	+		+		+	+		+		
Wilson et al. (1986)	+				+	+				+
Wolchik et al. (1986)	+	+	+		+	+	+	+		

Note. ERP = exposure and response prevention.

whereby individuals are encouraged to eat or overeat but then prevented from the vomiting response. This technique, advocated by Rosen and Leitenberg (1982), can be administered in various forms.

There is a related literature, some of it more theoretical, that has strongly influenced the design of most of these trials and that summarizes the treatment experiences and recommendations of several clinician researchers. These individuals working at different centers, including Garner, Fairburn, Bemis, and their collaborators, have written elegantly and persuasively about the treatment of this disorder; their work has strongly influenced the discussion that follows (e.g., Fairburn 1981, 1983, 1985; Fairburn et al. 1986; Garner 1986; Garner and Bemis 1982, 1985; Garner et al. 1985).

Logistics of the Therapy

Therapists who work with bulimic patients need to be active and at times directive, as well as supportive. It is useful for patients to regard the therapist as an expert on the disorder. This will give the patient a sense of confidence that they can be helped and lend credence to the educational component of the therapy. However, it also should be made clear early in the course of therapy that the locus of responsibility for change must reside with the patient.

It is difficult to stipulate optimal duration and frequency of visits using a group technique. It is safe to assume that most patients will require, at minimum, 12 weeks of therapy. There are considerable advantages to seeing patients several times a week, particularly early in treatment, when they are attempting to gain control of their eating behavior. An extreme example of this would be an intensive program used at the University of Minnesota wherein during the first phase of treatment patients come to the clinic five evenings a week for three hours each evening.

Treatment Components

The following is a suggested list of components that might be included in a group treatment program, and most have been included in some form in the published research studies.

A. *Psychoeducational Component.* Many authors emphasize the need for careful patient education early in therapy. This educational component may include the following elements:
   1. Information about the prevalence of bulimia nervosa.
   2. Careful delineation of the associated symptoms (e.g., binge eating, vomiting, laxatives, diuretics) and associated problems (e.g., depression, substance abuse, social isolation, job or school problems) that patients may have encountered.
   3. Discussion of medical complications, with emphasis on the fact that most medical complications resolve quickly when eating symptoms improve.
   4. Discussion about weight regulation and set-point theory. It is important for patients with bulimia nervosa to understand that they may be choosing an unrealistic body weight and that recurrent dieting to achieve this body weight may have adverse metabolic consequences.
   5. Discussion of the glamourization of eating disorders by the media.
   6. Discussion about the ineffectiveness of the weight control techniques practiced by many bulimic individuals, including the ineffectiveness of laxatives and diuretics, because these behaviors result in dehydration and not in loss of body fat.
B. *Eating Pattern.* As mentioned previously, there should be an early clear emphasis that patients need to establish a pattern of regular, adequate food intake. The sophistication with which this information is imparted will vary a great deal among programs.

It is important to confront patients' irrational ideas about food. Many bulimic patients indicate that they are quite knowledgeable about nutrition, but on careful questioning will have irrational beliefs, frequently around issues of good versus bad foods, presumed food allergies, or their belief that they are "different" and "can't eat breakfast." Also patients should monitor their eating behavior; these records need to be reviewed.

It is often unclear what the optimal caloric intake for each patient should be early in treatment. In general, we recommend that patients who are within 10 percent of ideal body weight be placed on a weight maintenance diet. Overweight individuals are placed on a weight-maintenance diet for an ideal body weight range, which will allow them to lose weight very gradually. However, we discourage much weight loss early in treatment because if patients are actively dieting, it will be very difficult for them to cease binge eating.

There are some foods that serve as "trigger" foods for some patients in that they are associated with binge eating episodes. Some patients will do better if these foods are excluded from their diet early in the course of treatment. However, most of the foods that patients prefer to exclude are not really trigger foods but feared foods—foods the patients think are bad, such as foods containing fat—

and it is best to encourage patients strongly to include these foods in their diet. Excluded foods should be reintroduced by the end of treatment.

C. *Self-Monitoring*. Early in the course of treatment, patients should be taught a system for self-monitoring eating behavior, including binge eating, vomiting, laxative abuse, and diuretic abuse. These records should be reviewed regularly.

D. *Antecedents, Behaviors, and Consequences*. It is useful to have patients begin to understand the antecedents or cues (both internal and external) that precede binge eating episodes, to develop alternative behaviors to bulimic behaviors and to manipulate the conseqeunces of food-related behaviors.

Several different methods can be used to examine antecedents. One simple way is to have patients write down the chain of events that transpired during the day prior to a binge eating episode. This may help them to identify specific cues (e.g., an argument with their boss, shopping for clothes and feeling fat) that precede binge eating episodes. If they understand their pattern, it can then be modified. Some cues need to be dealt with through cognitive restructuring. However, certain antecedents can be manipulated early in treatment before there is any significant insight. For example, if a patient tends to binge eat at work by buying candy from a candy machine, she can take money only for lunch and transportation and not have extra money at work for candy, which may decrease the likelihood of binge eating. Another example would be a patient who stops at the bakery on the way home from work. She could devise a different way of getting home, such as taking a bus rather than driving her car, or she could take an alternative path to avoid seeing the bakery.

Patients should also discuss and list behavioral alternatives to binge eating. For example, when faced with the urge to binge eat, they can practice delay, whereby they contract not to binge eat for a period of time after the urge. Also they can have a list of alternative behaviors in which they can engage when faced with an urge to binge eat (e.g., take a walk, brush their teeth) or activities that they can plan in advance when they are more likely to binge eat (e.g., making plans for Saturday evening if this is a time when they usually binge eat).

An attempt can also be made to manipulate the consequences of the eating behavior. For example, have the patient save the money that would have been spent on binge eating episodes each week and instead spend the money on something positively reinforcing (e.g., clothes, or books).

E. *Cognitive Restructuring*. The basic assumption behind these techniques is that patients with bulimia nervosa have reasoning errors whereby they are at times illogical in their thinking. Several particular reasoning errors have been suggested in the literature. The work of Garner, Fairburn, and Bemis, previously cited, has been particularly influential here.

1. Dichotomous Thinking. Patients with bulimia nervosa tend to see many issues in either good or bad terms. This is particularly true concerning shape and weight. To be thin is good; to be overweight (even slightly overweight) is bad. To eat only a markedly restricted diet, avoiding all feared foods, is good; to overeat or, for most of these patients, to eat what one wants to eat, is bad.

2. Egocentricity. Patients with bulimia nervosa tend to be egocentric in their thinking in that they tend to misperceive feedback from their environment. For example, they may believe that other people will notice if they gained a pound of weight or if they are eating forbidden foods.

3. Superstitious-Ritualistic Thinking. Many patients with bulimia nervosa develop fairly elaborate rituals regarding their eating behavior, and develop the illogical

belief that they can control their weight if they avoid certain foods and only eat a small amount of food (unless they are planning on vomiting).

4. Selective Abstraction. Many patients with bulimia nervosa demonstrate a style of thinking in which they base conclusions on inadequate information and ignore evidence to the contrary.

5. Magnification. Patients with bulimia will overevaluate the importance of certain events. For example, a weight gain of a pound may be regarded as an overwhelming catastrophe.

F. *Reintroduction of Risk Foods.* It is important for patients to be able to eat all of the foods that they are likely to encounter. To continue to avoid certain foods may increase the likelihood of relapse.

G. *Relapse Prevention.* Toward the end of treatment, it is very useful to focus on issues of relapse and, in particular, techniques for dealing with lapses. Patients should understand the difference between slips or lapses, wherein minor recurrences of the problem behaviors appear, and relapses. Lapses are quite common in the course of recovery of patients who do quite well long-term.

H. *Other Elements.* Other specific elements can be included, depending on the needs of the patients in the group, including assertiveness training, behavioral problem solving, and relaxation training. It is also useful to include some information on exercise.

In summary, a group treatment of bulimia nervosa has received considerable attention by researchers in this field. The literature in this area, which has expanded dramatically in the last few years, suggests that such treatment can be quite effective for these patients, but many questions remain concerning what elements constitute an optimal group program.

Chapter 73

Psychodynamic Individual Psychotherapy

Excessive and uncontrollable eating or bulimia occurs as a symptom in a variety of conditions (Casper 1983a). Currently bulimia is most often observed in association with weight dysregulation (e.g., in anorexia nervosa) in patients who are overweight and most often in patients who have a normal body weight but who deliberately try to lose weight. The term *bulimia nervosa* refers to the dieting bulimic patient in whom certain other psychopathologic features are associated with the eating disorder. Bulimia nervosa seems to be a heterogeneous disorder. Its course can be deteriorating, at times marked by sudden improvements. It can continue for decades, or stop at any stage and lead to full recovery with or without treatment. It seems important to recognize that bulimia nervosa exists in varying degrees and shadings on the entire scale from pathologic to normal.

Historically the voracity that characterizes the eating behavior of bulimic patients, their uninhibited devouring of food, has been linked to animal behavior. The Greek term *kynorexia*, and the Latin expression *fames canina* referred to repeated episodes of intolerable hunger followed by overeating and vomiting; whereas *bulimia* or *fames bovina* designated initially attacks of uncontrollable hunger only (Ziolko 1982). Pleasure in eating and the discriminating enjoyment of food are lacking.

Patients' reports have taught us that besides the sight, smell, or availability of food, sensations other than hunger (e.g., inner tension, self-recrimination, psychic pain, boredom) can trigger the bulimic cycle. Psychologically, bulimic behavior seems to serve a reparative and, albeit temporary, stabilizing function in the patients' emotional life (Casper 1981).

Dynamic Explanations

Most contemporary dynamic explanations share the notion that the bulimic behavior (i.e., the binge-vomiting cycle) is a reenactment of attempts on the patient's part to come to terms with internalized self-object representations that disrupt self-consonance. Sours (1980) viewed bingeing as a way to deal with helplessness by recreating the fantasy of union with an idealized mother. However, he also noted that eating brings about erotic excitement, with eventual buildup in the abdomen and pelvis, the so-called alimentary orgasm. Casper (1983b) suggested that the bulimic symptomatology serves a defensive purpose against intolerable tension and self-disintegration through employing food perversely as a self-object (Kohut 1977). In bulimia nervosa, food loses its primary function of nourishment and becomes an intermediary or self-object that, considering the symptomatology, is experienced as simultaneously comforting and intolerably overwhelming. The act of chewing or eating seems temporarily to suspend the cognitive and emotional overload and thereby to consolidate the self. Food becomes an accessible object presence. Once ingested, not necessarily in excessive amounts, the connotation changes and food is felt as something alien, dangerous, and oppressive, threatening self-fragmentation. Only through getting rid of it, does the patient regain some control over the self and the environment. Sugarman and Kurash's (1982) view is similar: a failure at the separation-individuation subphase (Mahler et al. 1975) in bulimic patients has led to a narcissistic fixation on the body and its use as a transitional object. In this model, food symbolizes the mother, which is accepted or rejected in the process of bingeing and vomiting. The authors stressed the act of eating as representative of the fleeting union with the mother or the maternal object.

Even though these dynamic explanations are intuitively persuasive, they are hard to verify because the patient seems altogether unaware of the mental context of these connections either during the disorder or following recovery. This makes the psychological meaning of the bulimic behavior per se inaccessible to interpretation. The sense of loss of self-control and the intense distress caused by a host of feelings seem to preclude any thinking or remembering. In bulimia nervosa, interpersonal relationships seem never to be abandoned to the same extent as in anorexia nervosa because personal relationships continue to coexist along with the struggle over food.

On Table 1, the severity of illness assignment of a particular case proceeds horizontally. The top represents the mildest form and the bottom the profoundest disturbance, with the analogue scale (from 1 to 10) permitting some measure about the frequency.

According to this classification, a patient who does not eat regular meals and who reports binge eating varying amounts of food (from small to excessive) three times daily and vomiting after each eating binge would be expected to have fairly severe trouble in keeping her personal life organized and to have marked difficulty in her personal relationships. This patient would not be as profoundly disturbed, however, as a patient in the last category, who frequently binge eats and uses vomiting and purgative drugs to regain self-control.

The obstacles to psychotherapy are not unlike those encountered in anorexia nervosa, where distrust and fear over the anticipated power of the therapist open a gulf that needs first to be bridged. Bulimic patients suffer and hence admit more easily to their abnormal behavior and maintain a relatedness, albeit a volatile and distorted one.

Unfortunately, patients most often seek symptom removal, instead of wanting psychotherapy with its implications for personal as well as time commitment and financial sacrifice. They want to normalize their eating habits, yet may not be willing to give up their goal for an unrealistically low body weight. Initially, most patients are unaware of character problems. This is understandable because character is the result of unconscious or preconscious determinants. Any suggestion to change meets with denial and resistance. Furthermore, the tendency and insistence among eating disorder patients, on viewing the thin body as the solution to a disparaging self-image, preclude searching for inner sources of the self-dissatisfaction. The therapeutic relationship is viewed with suspicion, not only because of its potential for closeness and intimacy, which would mobilize old fears over being hurt, mislead, abused, and disappointed, but also old defenses (e.g., denial, resistance, distancing), which would surface as patients sense the danger of regression in a dependent relationship. Patients fight psychotherapy in a number of ways. Either knowingly or unconsciously, they

Table 1. The Differential Diagnosis and Measurement of Bulimia

Body mass index ($=\text{kg/m}^2$)		Eating	Scale	AMOUNT		FREQUENCY	SEVERITY
	> 20	Overeating	1			■	
		Eating binges	2	▲		F	S
N	20	Binge eating with vomiting	3	A		R	E
O	R		4	M		E	V
	A	Binge eating with vomiting	5	O	+	Q	E
R	N			U		U	R
M	G	Binge eating with laxative and/or diuretic abuse	6	N		E	I
A	E		7	T		N	T
L	17	Binge eating with vomiting and laxative and/or diuretic abuse	8			C	Y
	<17		9			Y	
			10				

withhold information that they believe could be considered incriminating, a maneuver that often leaves little of a personal nature for communication to the therapist. Their strong need to be accepted and to appear in a favorable light to the therapist makes patients consciously and unconsciously select what they say.

In mild cases, brief goal-directed psychotherapy can often help patients to reorganize internally and to abandon the abnormal eating. As a result, patients restructure their own lives and relationships. Much more often, however, we encounter severe cases of bulimia. We have to keep in mind that because changes in traditional exploratory psychotherapy come about slowly, it may be supplemented by personal contact, hospitalization, cognitive therapy, pharmacotherapy, and family therapy.

If we follow the proposition that bulimia serves as a regulator of disorganizing affective states resulting from unstable, contradictory, and unintegrated internal self and object representations, then personal contact alone within a structured benevolent situation should provide stability enough to improve the patient's condition. This is actually so; bulimic patients rarely experience bulimic impulses during a session. Unfortunately, the effects of the therapeutic contact do not last. Patients require either constant contact or long periods of psychotherapy before they begin to internalize aspects of the therapeutic relationship. On the other hand, bulimic patients are often on the brink of decompensation and thus require swift help. In this situation, there are several treatment options. Either continuous contact and structured supervision is provided through hospitalization, or patients are treated through family therapy with the parents so that the conflictual parental representations can be experienced as less noxious and more benign through a direct corrective emotional experience. Another option is cognitive therapy (Fairburn 1984; Lacey 1983), which calls for structured participation and calls on the patient's resources through self-regulatory devices; it also offers a supportive relationship. Antidepressant pharmacotherapy can tone down depressive feelings and the emotional intensity (Lacey 1983; Mitchell and Groat 1984; Walsh et al. 1984) and might block the disinhibition involved in the binge eating.

The psychotherapeutic approach needs to be informed and eclectic. If psychotherapy is to be helpful in bulimia, it needs to respond to the total dilemma so that psychotherapy can be integrated in the overall treatment plan. If psychotherapy turns out to be successful, it will change the patient's self-concept and ability to relate to others. By self-concept, we shall mean the totality of the individual's thoughts and feelings having self-reference. The manifest goal in the case that will be presented was to explore the internal and external contributions to the patient's self-depreciation to change her self-critical attitude enough so that she could accept herself and become free from her misdirected fixation on her body size. These goals, which are by no means modest (Rosenberg 1979), were formulated on the basis of an assessment of the patient and her position within the family. In this case, individual psychotherapy was the guiding spirit in a comprehensive treatment approach, which included hospitalization, supervised meals, and family therapy.

The first goal in the treatment of bulimia is to bring the disordered eating pattern under control and to restore a sense of self-control. This approach opens up the possibility to explore what contributed to the need for an often unrealistically low body weight and to understand more about the process that led to the internal disorganization, self-medicated by overeating.

Because most patients do not have psychotherapy in mind when they apply for treatment, education about the purpose and limitations of psychotherapy is important. It is wise to attempt a prognosis because each case imports its own constraints. Each assessment varies. Typical issues that need consideration, however, are similar:

1. The person's premorbid functioning, the presence of other symptoms and/or major psychiatric illnesses prior to the onset of the bulimic syndrome.
2. The duration and severity of the bulimia.
3. Personal motivation for change.
4. Previous psychiatric treatment; the kind of treatment attempted and its effectiveness or failure.
5. The overall functioning and health of the family; the quality of the person's relationship to each parent; each parent's potential and willingness for supporting and helping the child, and each parent's potential and willingness for change; the quality of the parental relationship to each other and the health of other children in the family.
6. Reality considerations (e.g., insurance, financial support, distance).

Case Vignette

The first contact in this case was made by the patient's mother, who phoned in late spring to inquire whether her 20-year-old daughter attending a university 450 miles away could be hospitalized for an eating disorder between the end of her spring term and before going to camp as a camp counselor in the summer. An initial assessment over the telephone, as it turned out with the father present (he later joined the discussion), revealed that the patient had had a manifest eating problem in the form of eating binges for about four years starting in her junior year of high school. Over the past two years the patient had increasingly lost control over her eating and suffered uncontrollable eating binges, with an increase in weight to 185 lb at a height of 5 feet, 8 inches. In between, the patient had briefly regained some control through dieting and fasting. She had always managed to lose weight at summer camp, where the environment was highly structured. The patient did not vomit or abuse laxatives. She had been in treatment at the university for about two years with a female psychiatrist in individual and group therapy. Despite treatment, her bingeing and chronic feelings of worthlessness and moodiness had persisted.

The disturbed eating and repeated bingeing were experienced as humiliating by the patient and had isolated her from her girlfriends. Consequently she called home frequently asking for help, which upset and frustrated her parents. The father complained that his daughter had become a spendthrift. He said she barely managed to finish her course work and dreaded being at school and equally dreaded coming home.

The patient herself, who also was interviewed over the telephone, reported feeling depressed and despondent about her overweight and her inability to lose weight. She reported chronic feeling of worthlessness and said she felt ashamed of her impulsive eating and painfully different from other girls at school. Despite a diet of vegetables and fruits, she had been unable to lose weight and ended up bingeing several times daily. The patient reported difficulty sleeping, particularly after bingeing, when she tended to remain in bed in the morning. She reported having thought about suicide but said she knew she would never go through with it. The only relevant fact in the medical history was a "high fever" at age nine that lasted three weeks and led to hospitalization without a diagnosis being made. The patient had never received psychotropic drugs and was not taking any medication, except aspirin once in a while.

A family evaluation was scheduled following the patient's return home from school. The patient was a tall, pleasant, shy, 20-year-old markedly overweight yet attractive and well-groomed young woman. She related how desperate she felt about her eating binges and her inability to lose weight and how much she was afraid to be home because all she could think about was what to eat. She had never dated and felt intimidated by boys and thought of herself as an ugly duckling. She denied sexual fantasies. Her father's position as an executive had led to frequent moves of the family during her childhood, which prevented her from retaining close friends. She thought she had a good personality and was trustworthy and usually was involved with a group of friends but rarely kept a close friend for long. The parents had strongly encouraged her and her brother's athletic activities. Throughout high school the patient excelled in volleyball. Volleyball practice after school, however, had isolated her from other girls. During her junior year, the volleyball coach increased his demands as younger ambitious team members surpassed her. The competition led her to give up volleyball altogether. Subsequently, a profound depression set in. She began to eat excessively at home out of boredom and frustration and gained weight fairly fast because of her inactivity. Contrary to her, her brother, who was four years younger, had an outgoing and gregarious nature like her mother and was popular in school. The patient's mother, a 46-year-old strikingly attractive tall, slender woman, appeared cheerful and articulate. The patient's father, a tall, heavy-set, reserved but friendly man, announced that he was an alcoholic who had recovered through Alcoholics Anonymous five years ago. He said his father and an uncle had also been alcoholics. When the family's eagerness and optimism regarding treatment and their determination that everything could be achieved in six weeks of hospitalization was discussed, the family showed some willingness to remain flexible concerning the time limits.

This family was considered to have many strengths and a potential for change. Given the patient's good premorbid functioning, the clear precipitant related to competition (which initiated the binge eating), the brother's good adjustment, the father's ability to overcome his alcoholism, and the mother's emotional presence and nurturance, and the lack of open conflict between the parents, a decision was made to go along with a six-week hospitalization trial. The treatment plan, which centered on individual psychotherapy five times a week in conjunction with family therapy once a week, was discussed with the patient and her parents beforehand. The patient reluctantly agreed to participate in family therapy. Her superficially strongly dependent relationship covered a strong sense of alienation and antagonism toward her parents.

Keeping the time constraints in mind, psychotherapy was conceived along certain priority issues for which family therapy seemed essential. The first issue was related to the patient's personality: her passivity and quiet reserve, which seemed reinforced by a lack of self-confidence. The second was linked to the first, a deep-seated conviction that her opinion and her feelings were not worthy of attention or consideration. Furthermore, it was expected that an exploration of the circumstances that led the patient to give up on volleyball and be preoccupied with food would shed some light on the underlying dynamics. Because time was short and follow-up not assured, a clear purpose of psychotherapy was to reintegrate the patient into her family so that she could continue to grow up with her parents' support and help.

In the hospital, the patient was placed on supervised regular meals, which were slightly below the maintenance requirement in calories to permit gradual weight loss. She was also encouraged to take regular walks of at least one hour daily. Protected by hospitalization and regular meals, the patient's desire to overeat lessened substantially. Her depressive feelings lifted and returned only intermittently when she felt she was losing weight at too slow a pace. The same therapist conducted individual psychotherapy and family therapy and therefore was able to address related issues.

The family sessions were also attended by a social worker experienced in psychotherapy, who received family therapy training. On the hospital ward, the patient appeared pleasant and compliant. She got along well with others but kept a distance from peers and nursing staff, arguing that her stay would not be long enough to make it worthwhile to get closely involved. Since this issue was an apparent reenactment of a pattern of her past, this issue and some of its ramifications were discussed in psychotherapy. As so many other themes, however, this one could not be pursued and fully understood due to time constraints. The patient had trouble motivating herself initially to take walks and required much coaxing by staff. Similarly in psychotherapy, the patient spoke little spontaneously. Her silence was not withholding or an angry distance, but rather as if she was waiting in the expectation to be spoken to. The idea that she could talk about herself seemed quite alien to her. When this was explored, she explained that in the company of people she could rarely think of anything of a personal nature to say. When she felt the expectation to talk, she froze up and felt empty and awkward. Knowing her cheerful and talkative mother, it was not difficult to gather that this was a defensive attitude that suited the patient's temperament, an attitude she had assumed so she could keep in contact with her mother, without disappointing her or getting overwhelmed by her. When this was suggested to her, the patient revealed that her silence made her feel like a graceless and deficient child in comparison to her articulate and lively mother, but she felt her mother had no ill intent and was genuinely concerned, except she thought the mother did not really understand why the patient was so different and so unhappy. This attitude and dynamic, being locked into being the mother's passive extension, seemed to have prevented the patient from differentiating, which would also have meant to voice her feelings of envy and resentment toward this mother to whom, she felt, everything had come easy, or to express her jealousy toward her brother, who was as carefree and successful as her mother. In appearance and bodily build, the patient resembled her father, who was dark-haired; her brother was slender and light-haired as was the mother.

The patient's mother came from an upper-class southern family, who had considered her marriage to the father much below her class. Despite the father's drinking problem, the mother had loyally stayed with him and helped him overcome it. The patient was aware of her outward resemblance to the father, but despised herself for it. In her associations, her physical resemblance reflected other similarities (i.e., emotional trouble, being overweight and dependent, and staying forever in the background). The father expressedly stated early in treatment that he believed his daughter resembled him, arguing that she had as much difficulty being spontaneous and open and seemed as critical and perfectionistic as he was. The patient's fateful resemblance and partial identification with her father, her unspoken rejection of him, and her yearning to be like her mother turned out to be another impediment to developing an identity of her own. This second dynamic became another recurrent theme in both individual and family treatment.

The patient was fearful that if the parents knew about any of these feelings, in addition to her already existing problem, she would be considered bad and would be rejected and abandoned. It required a great deal of work in individual psychotherapy before the patient mustered the courage to let her parents know about these feelings. When she decided to talk about her feelings, she spoke of herself in relation to her father as a failure and of her anger toward herself for being like him. The father felt attacked and was visibly hurt about this revelation, but instead of attacking in turn he was able to reach out to her and get her to understand that he knew how painful these feelings were because he had gone through them himself and had been able to change. The father then spoke about the hardships of his own childhood, not in a preaching manner but more to explain where he came from.

The gradual rapprochement between father and daughter that followed became the third theme. The father talked more about himself and how much he had missed out on a close relationship with his daughter because of his drinking and extensive traveling during her childhood. The mother needed support to refrain from interfering too much in this father-daughter dialogue.

Not until the patient had made these disclosures to her father did she feel secure enough to let her mother know about feeling cheated and about her envy, which made it seem that her mother had everything desirable, everything the patient lacked. The mother initially tended to dismiss the patient's statements as inaccurate, insisting that the daughter had everything in her childhood she had had and wondered why could she not simply be like her, charming and outgoing? Even with a good deal of exploration and explanation, the mother had difficulty adjusting to the idea that her daughter was not merely a replica of herself but different, not only in appearance and in her manner of relating, but with a quiet charm of her own that needed to be developed. The father saw the situation more clearly and supported his daughter. Ultimately, the mother was able to respond to her daughter with understanding and to listen to her, only to discover that she had hardly known her. The mother revealed that she had been at a loss to comprehend what had gone wrong between herself and her daughter because she considered herself equally devoted to both her children, but had always felt her daughter's distance.

The family sessions thus provided some of the material for individual psychotherapy, where the patient reworked memories of feeling clumsy in the presence of her graceful mother and of being compared to her and expected to be like her by her grandparents, all of crucial importance for her self-perception. The patient also remembered feeling displaced on the volleyball team by a new younger team member—a sophomore who was slender, tall, attractive, and popular and with whom she felt competition was out of the question. She became aware of the connection to her mother and her brother and how much her defeatism was related to her resentment for having everything come easy to her mother whereas everything had come the hard way for herself. The camp experience, which appeared so important early on, turned out to be connected to the same dynamic; in camp the patient had made a place for herself as a camp counselor and had felt liked and respected in her own right, not because of being her mother's daughter.

These then were principal dynamics, which were worked through in many variations in psychotherapy and family therapy. Every family member appeared to make some changes during these weeks. For instance, the father reported an incident where he had called on his staff to help resolve a difficult situation that had upset him, and how encouraging he had found the comments he had received about this approach. The patient's mother became more thoughtful, spoke less, and listened more to what her daughter had to say, accepting the daughter's fears or her discouragement instead of talking her out of it. The patient's quiet composure did not change because this was her nature. However, she spoke more freely in company and, when she spoke, it was not merely to give in to the pressure of having to respond but because she had something to say. She regained her old self-confidence. Her changing self-perception was noticeable in her behavior. She approached people more often instead of waiting to be approached. She became more cheerful, and her posture became more upright and almost proud.

Several trial home passes before discharge went well. Yet the fact that the patient awoke on an overnight pass from a nightmare, in which she found herself uncontrollably bingeing, indicated that the changes were not consolidated. Her apprehension and the risk of relapse were extensively discussed with the patient and the family. Despite her fears, the patient wished to try discharge. She accepted the fact that she had lost no more than 8 lb in six weeks, acknowledging that the changes in her self-perception and in relation to her family counted more than weight. She was confident she would be able to lose more while she was in camp, as she had done before. On the day of discharge, as she took leave and expressed her gratitude, she presented the therapist with a picnic basket filled with miniature food, food she liked but could not have in the hospital due to her reduction diet. Through this gift she revealed a great deal about her feelings toward the therapist, a largely admiring and idealizing transference tinged with envy and a sense of deprivation. The father gave the social worker a practical present from company products.

In the follow-up, the patient and her parents have kept in touch. She has done well for more than two years and is about to graduate from college. She has kept her weight around 135 to 145 lb and is involved in a close relationship with a young man.

That so much could be achieved in this case in such a short time was the result of several favorable circumstances. The primary factor among them was the parents' genuine wish to understand and help their daughter, even if it meant to reveal their own shortcomings and to tolerate not always comfortable internal changes. Secondly, although the parents' relationship was by no means without conflict, they were committed to and able to support each other. Thirdly, the patient's personal strength contributed much to her recovery; despite feeling bad, depressed, and angry, she retained a sense of self and could tolerate these feelings.

In this brief period, the patient began to work through what would be called adolescent conflicts. Actually it would be more accurate to say that the patient began the process of working through, and that psychotherapy provided her with her own tools and reintroduced (through family therapy) the parents as co-actors. The binge eating had been symptomatic of a developmental impasse. As the patient became more able to take command of her life and as her relationships became more satisfactory, the symptom was no longer necessary.

Most patients with a full-blown bulimia nervosa syndrome are more disturbed than the case described. The relative ineffectiveness of dynamic psychotherapy in these instances is the result of the depth of the pathology that has led to fixation in a defensive position and to internal immobility. To put it more succinctly, in the severely bulimic patient, the internalized interpersonal conflicts and affective states do not easily and not for a long time become part of the transference. Such dynamics, of course, make these patients relatively easy to manage, except that their condition does not change. This inhibition to develop a negative transference is one of the principal features that distinguishes patients with bulimia nervosa from borderline patients (Casper et al. 1982), who develop massive negative affective transferences early on. The kind of transference resistance in bulimia suggests that, in this disorder as well, the trauma suffered occurred prior to verbalization and self-object differentiation (Gedo and Goldberg 1973). Other dynamic issues, such as guilt over sexual conflicts, are strongly determined by the early developmental matrix. The therapist must be prepared to work with primitive defenses such as displacement, dissociation, projective identification, denial, overideational circumstantial thinking, and deviant reasoning. A few patients can reintegrate and heal sufficiently with a kind of empathic psychotherapy without explicitly working through particular issues eventually to abandon the bulimic defense, except that their progress is not so much due to verbal interpretation (Nemiah 1978) as to the accepting, empathic, and knowledgeable presence of the therapist.

Chapter 74

Rumination

Rumination, an uncommon disorder occurring from infancy throughout adulthood, is derived from the Latin *ruminare*, meaning "to chew the cud." Merycism, derived from the Helenic, is the act of postingestive regurgitation of food from the stomach, back into the mouth, followed by chewing and reswallowing (Brown 1968). Rumination is associated with medical complications such as aspiration pneumonia, electrolyte abnormalities, and dehydration (Herbst 1983), and is considered in the differential diagnosis of vomiting (Fleischer 1979b) and failure to thrive (Sheagran et al. 1980) in infants and young children. From latency through adulthood, rumination frequently has a benign course (Levine et al. 1983). Recently rumination has been associated with bulimia (Blinder 1983; Fairburn and Cooper 1984b), anorexia nervosa, and depression (Levine et al. 1983). Past studies have reported a lack of reciprocity and attunement between mother and child, stemming primarily from maternal depression and anxiety (Gaddini and Gaddini 1959; Lourie 1954; Richmond et al. 1958). Medical disorders such as gastroesophageal reflux and hiatal hernia have also been reported (Gryboski 1983; Herbst et al. 1971). Applications of formal behavior contingencies in treatment have led to viewing ruminatory activity as a habit disorder (Halmi 1980; Lang and Melamed 1969).

In DSM-III-R (American Psychiatric Association 1987), rumination is designated as a disorder of infancy (307.53). The infant shows "a characteristic position of straining and arching the back . . . and sucking movements of the tongue and . . . the impression of the gaining of satisfaction with the activity" (p. 70). Diagnostic criteria included repeated regurgitation without apparent nausea or associated gastrointestinal illness for at least one month following a period of normal functioning. There may be weight loss or failure to make expected weight gain. Irritability is noted between regurgitations and the presence of hunger inferred. Although the disorder occurs most often after three months of age, it has been reported in a three-week-old infant (Hollowell and Gardner 1965) and in the neonatal intensive care unit (Sheagran et al. 1980). Resultant failure to thrive with malnutrition may produce severe developmental delays (Halmi 1980). Rumination has been described in families spanning four generations, and learning to ruminate by imitation has been suggested (Brockbank 1907).

Rumination may be underreported, with only severe cases (malnutrition, electrolyte disturbances, hiatus hernia) referred to a gastroenterologist and minor cases treated by a parent or primary physician. Rumination in adolescents and adults is embarrassing, leading patients to conceal the problem when giving a medical history. Furthermore, primary physicians are often unacquainted with the disorder. Rumination in anorexia nervosa and bulimia nervosa may be underreported due to omission in the systematic medical history and reluctance of patients to volunteer specific clinical information (Blinder 1986).

The course of rumination may depend on the severity of complications and the age of the patient. Mortality has been as high as 25 to 40 percent in infants (Kanner

1957). Although the infant may show manifest hyperphagia, postingestive regurgitation leads to progressive malnutrition (i.e., a sham eating status). In the adolescent, bulimia and affective disorder may be present (Fairburn and Cooper 1984b). Rumination in adults has been reported in association with gastric carcinoma (Long 1929) and anemia (Djaldetti et al. 1962; Geffen 1966). More frequent medical complications occur in the retarded (Danford and Huber 1981), with a mortality rate of 12 to 20 percent (Rast et al. 1981).

Extended posttreatment evaluation of patients with rumination is rare. Investigators most often report one- or two-year follow-up (Fleisher 1979a; Sheagran et al. 1980). Kanner (1957) stated that long-term follow-up of ruminating patients revealed a notable subsequent incidence of psychiatric disorder.

Presentation at Different States of Development and Special Conditions

Infancy and Early Childhood

The classic description of rumination in infancy was contributed by Cameron (1925):

> After taking the meal the infant lies quiet for a time, then begins certain purposive movements, by which the abdominal muscles are thrown into a series of violent contractions—the head is held back, the mouth is opened, while the tongue projects a little and is curved from side to side so as to form a spoonshaped concavity on its dorsal surface. After a varying time of persistent effort, sometimes punctuated by grunting or whimpering sounds, expressive of irritation at the failure to achieve the expected results . . . a successful contraction ejects a great quantity of milk forward into the mouth. The infant lies with an expression of supreme satisfaction upon its face, sensing the regurgitated milk and subjecting it to innumerable sucking and chewing movements. It is very evident that achievement of this purpose produces a sense of beatitude, while failure results in nervous unrest and irritation. The power to ruminate successfully is not suddenly acquired. In the earliest stages, before dexterity has been achieved, the act differs relatively little from vomiting. In its earlier development, therefore, rumination is very apt to be mistaken for habitual vomiting due to other causes, and it may require careful observation to make the distinction evident. Nor are such babies easy to observe. It is characteristic of the ruminating child that if it sins it sins only in secret. To watch it openly is to put a stop to the whole procedure. Only when the child is alone and in a drowsy, vacant state does the act take place. (p. 875)

Rumination has been reported in infants, with a tendency toward vomiting and reflux associated with reflux esophagitis (Herbst 1983), hiatal hernia (Chatoor et al. 1984b; Gryboski 1983; Herbst et al. 1971), necrotizing enterocolitis with malabsorption and malnutrition, prematurity, severe bronchopulmonary dysplasia (Sheagran et al. 1980), growth failure (Hollowell and Gardner 1965), autism (Chatoor and Dickson 1984a), tuberous sclerosis (Marholin et al. 1980), heroin withdrawal (Vadapalli and Williams, personal communication), barbiturate withdrawal (Chatoor et al. 1984b), labile autonomic nervous system (Chatoor et al. 1984a), object loss (Griffin 1977; Lourie 1954), and infection (Brockbank 1907; Chatoor et al. 1984b).

Infants with rumination have been described as passive and sensitive to rejection. Rumination seems to relieve inner tension in an infant distressed from rejection or overstimulation (Lourie 1954).

Rumination, considered as a habit disorder, has been observed in children with repetitive self-stimulatory behavior (e.g., head banging, body rocking, genital and fecal play, finger and thumb sucking) (Richmond et al. 1958). This self-reinforcing habit becomes so potent that the infant may become unavailable and resistant to mother's attempt to interrupt, preferring soothing through rumination (Chatoor et al. 1984b).

Latency

Rumination in latency-age children who are not retarded is rarely reported. Brockbank (1907) discussed a three-year-old girl and a six-year-old boy who imitated a ruminant housekeeper and a 7-year-old boy who imitated his ruminant foster mother. Griffin (1977) reported that a seven-year-old boy with no gastrointestinal abnormality developed rumination after the loss of his caretaker grandmother.

Adolescence

Except for reports of mentally retarded individuals, there is virtually no mention of rumination in adolescence. Brockbank (1907) may have described the first adolescent with rumination and a restrictive eating disorder when he reported a 15-year-old female who "ate but little" (p. 425). Blinder (1983) documented rumination in adolescents with bulimia nervosa. Levine et al. (1983) described three adolescent ruminators referred for halitosis: a 15-year-old female, a 13-year-old female, and a 15-year-old male. They had no associated gastrointestinal complaints; barium studies were normal. The two females had rumination since birth, the 15-year-old male for four years. Family history was negative for rumination in each case.

Geffen (1966) described a 17-year-old male with iron deficiency anemia secondary to bleeding from esophagitis, whose involuntary lifelong rumination was associated with "nervousness and tension." Rumination with belching produced marked embarrassment.

Adulthood

Adult rumination is a chronic disorder (Levine et al. 1983), except when associated with bulimia (Fairburn and Cooper 1984b). The individual episode is postprandial, without nausea, effortless, and predominantly involuntary. It may occur after a hastily eaten meal, causing embarrassment, or may appear seemingly voluntary and pleasurable (Brown 1968; Levine et al. 1983; Long 1929). The symptomatic presence of active ruminatory behavior varies from as little as six months to a lifetime (Brockbank 1907; Levine et al. 1983). Patients may complain of food returning to the mouth, belching, precordial distress (possibly due to esophagitis), indigestion, halitosis, and excessive dental difficulties.

Special Conditions

Long (1929) described two men who exhibitionistically exploited their rumination capacity in theatrical presentations, alleging willful selection of ingested food to be brought up. Long also described two interesting uses of rumination: 1) as a sham-eating technique and 2) as a way to eat and dispose of foods contraindicated medically (e.g., fatty foods, meat) yet having strong palatability and preference for the patient.

The presence of specific psychiatric disorder in rumination is undefined. Associated psychopathology noted in prior reports include the following:

1. Neurasthenia (Brockbank 1907).
2. Performance anxiety with somatic delusions of fatal illness (Long 1929).
3. Emotional irritability, immaturity, and passivity.
4. Schizophrenia with hysterical traits (Brown 1968).
5. Atypical personality (Pope, personal communication).
6. Affective disturbance (Levine et al. 1983).
7. Eating disorder—bulimia (Fairburn and Cooper 1984b) and anorexia nervosa (Levine et al. 1983).

There were no structured psychiatric evaluations or uniformity of diagnostic criteria noted in the literature until Levine et al. (1983) evaluated nine patients with both a psychiatric interview and a questionnaire. Interviews revealed a family psychiatric history or disturbed family relationships in four of the patients. Three patients had psychiatric histories (overdose, anorexia nervosa, brief reactive depression). Seven patients had personalities that were anxious, five were obsessional, and six were sensitive. Four of five adult patients had psychosexual and marital problems. However, on current formal mental status exam, only one (anxiety state) of the nine patients had current psychiatric symptoms.

The results of questionnaires revealed that mild traits of anxiety, hysteria, and neuroticism were present. In only one patient did symptoms interfere with psychosocial functioning, and the group revealed no evidence of a current psychiatric illness. The authors concluded that there was absence of substantive psychiatric disorder in this group of patients. However, the findings are suggestive of affective spectrum disorder (depression, anorexia nervosa, overdose) in three of five adults and significant family history of psychiatric disorder in four of eight patients whose family history was accessible. An instrument such as the Schedule for Affective Disorders and Schizophrenia (Spitzer and Endicott 1978) might have been a more significant diagnostic tool for detecting psychiatric disorder in the adult ruminator group studies. The designation of rumination as a "benign" (Levine et al. 1983) disorder is questionable (Blinder 1986).

Fairburn and Cooper (1984b) reported rumination with a duration of at least 12 months in seven of 35 female patients with bulimia nervosa. Three patients had postprandial effortless regurgitation on a daily basis. Food was reswallowed or regurgitated. The patients complained of loss of control of eating, with an attitude of shame about their rumination. All patients had disturbed eating habits, abnormal attitudes toward body and shape, and high psychiatric co-morbidities. In the subgroup of bulimic ruminators, as compared to the bulimic nonruminators, a prior history of both anorexia nervosa and psychiatric treatment for an eating disorder was more prevalent. The ruminating habit itself was difficult to interrupt, but successful treatment of the bulimia led to cessation of the rumination. Blinder (1983) reported a subgroup of normal weight bulimic patients with primary ruminatory behavior antedating bulimic symptoms. The patients were more likely to be polyphagic during binge episodes rather than demonstrating the more usual specific carbohydrate preference. Ruminatory behavior shifted to regurgitation during adolescence to promote weight loss. The patients may not show the pattern of impulsive behavior, affective disturbance, or family history of alcoholism seen in other patients diagnosed as bulimic.

There may be two adult subgroups of ruminators. One has minimal psychiatric problems and the second has either associated eating disorder (e.g., anorexia nervosa or bulimia) or associated anxiety, affective, or marital and familial psychiatric disturbances. Since patients are reticent about their illness, a diagnosis of psychiatric disturbance may be underreported.

At times, rumination is associated both with central nervous system disorders and mental retardation. The frequency of eating disorders associated with the institutionalized retarded includes pica 25 percent, anorexia 7 percent, and rumination 2.7 percent. Individuals with pica frequently also exhibit rumination (Danford 1982). Rast et al. (1981) reported an incidence of rumination of 8 percent and a mortality rate of 12 to 20 percent in mentally retarded ruminators. Postingestive gastroesophageal reflux has been associated with mental retardation, central nervous lesions such as cerebritis, dilated ventricles, cerebral palsy, sudden infant death syndrome infants with apnea, and laryngospasms. Rumination has also been associated with tuberous sclerosis (Marholin et al. 1980), hypsarrythmia (Renuart, personal communication), infantile spasms, and grand mal seizures.

Danford and Huber (1981) summarized several clinical features in the retarded associated with the presence of rumination. These included male predominance, self-abuse, other food-related behaviors (e.g., pica, hyperphagia, anorexia), and medical complication.

Rumination in the retarded appears to be a self-stimulating behavior that relieves internal tension states that are blocked from social release due to marked communication deficit and inability to seek external stimulation (Woolston, personal communication). Although several reports of behavioral treatment of retarded ruminants have appeared using aversive conditioning, such as localized electroshock (Lang and Melamed 1969) and lemon juice (Sajwaj et al. 1974), there is little discussion of environmental changes that could have precipitated the rumination. A retarded child may suffer significant object losses both when taken from the family to an institution and when staff changes occur within the institution (Menolascino 1972). Prompt social stimulation and reinforcement may abort or terminate the ruminatory disorder related to institution adjustments.

Theories of Rumination

Developmental and Psychodynamic

The concept of understimulation and overstimulation proposed by Lourie (1954) will be illustrated. He reported a five-month-old as overstimulated due to the tense and fearful mother who was inappropriately "constantly doing something with the baby." The baby was cued to the mother's tension. However, despite the presence of mild esophageal dilation as an organic factor, substitute care by a nurse was effective in abolishing rumination.

Infants with rumination described on a neonatal intensive care unit (Sheagran et al. 1980) may be both overstimulated due to high noise levels and multiple procedures, and understimulated due to a lack of a consistent nurturing figure.

Lourie (1954) felt that ruminating infants lacked basic trust in their maternal objects. This caused a failure of appropriate attachment and fulfillment of the infant's dependency needs (Bowlby and Mostyn 1969). The infant's immature ego was overwhelmed due to external and internal conditions, and a regression from a previous level of object relations occurred (Fenichel 1945). Lourie felt that infants used the defense of denial of the overwhelming reality situation and, while ruminating, might substitute hallucinatory wish fulfillment of the inadequately available maternal object

(Ferenczi 1950). Thus the infant reacts to the overwhelming environmental overstimulation or understimulation by literally voluntarily feeding him- or herself. The infant reexperiences, by the rumination, a self-directed, pleasurable habit replacing the inadequate maternal infant relationship (Gaddini 1969). Thus ruminating in infants can be conceptualized as a defensive habit pattern that, once started for whatever reason, becomes a self-reinforcing behavior that is difficult to arrest (Chatoor and Dickson 1984a). Erotization of the esophagus is proposed; in many reports, the ecstatic pleasurable feeling during rumination followed by marked diminished tension has been described (Richmond et al. 1958).

Stress and pain exceeding a protective tolerance threshold, as in hiatal hernia, may be associated with rumination in a child. Lourie (1954) described an infant with irritability, crying, and a hiatal hernia.

Reciprocity between mother and infant implies sensitivity and attunement of the mother to her child's individuality, rhythm, communications, and reciprocal ability to initiate and maintain communication needs. This mutual "fitting together" of mother and infant is critical for reciprocity. A temperamental mismatch due to the baby's heightened sensitivities (to sound, touch, or noise) and mother's impatience may occur (Bergman and Escalona 1949). Failure of reciprocity may occur in rumination. Disturbed mothers may be emotionally unavailable to develop reciprocity with their child (Gaddini 1969; Gaddini and Gaddini 1959; Lourie 1954; Richmond et al. 1958).

Many authors have commented on the presence of maternal psychopathology in association with rumination in the infant (Gaddini and Gaddini 1959; Hollowell and Gardner 1965; Lourie 1954; Menking et al. 1969; Richmond et al. 1958). Richmond et al. (1958) noted the mother's inability to relate and "emotionally give of herself" to her child. A mother's fears that the baby might die and her rejection when the child vomits have been described (Gaddini and Gaddini 1959). Gaddini (1969) also noted that mothers were generally rejecting, irritated, and ambivalent toward their unplanned children; the mothers were characterized as "immature, inadequate personalities who are anxious and had disturbed object relations."

Behavioral

Since 1968, there have been many reports documenting behavioral treatment of rumination (Winton and Singh 1983). Behaviorists report effective treatments that diminish rumination usually within two weeks (Lavigne and Burns 1981).

Behavioral theory is used to explain rumination as a habit pattern. Reinforcement enhances and maintains a specific behavior that is temporally linked to its consequences. A positive reinforcement such as food increases the frequency of antecedent behavior. The reduction or removal of an undesirable event, such as electroshock (negative reinforcement), also increases the likelihood of an antecedent behavior. Maternal attention, especially to a child who is receiving inadequate nurturing is a very powerful, positive reinforcement; mother's attention following vomiting associated with rumination may be a reinforcer contributing to its maintenance. Behavior theories focus on the events that maintain rumination (Winton and Singh 1983). Lavigne and Burns (1981) believe that rumination is an operant behavior maintained by its consequence and that it is a learned habit that can be extinguished.

Lourie (1954) regarded rumination as a pleasurable self-stimulating behavior in an understimulated child who gained a degree of mastery over a chronic tension state. Rumination allowed the child to obtain increased attention in the form of medical treatment. Wright and Thalassinos (1973) considered rumination as a "learned illness behavior." Remission of chronic ruminative vomiting occurs through a reversal of social contingencies.

The idea of a habitual mode of response as a characteristic of rumination is suggested by a seeming voluntary quality, frequent waxing and waning with environmental stress, and extinction response to aversive stimuli.

Association with Affective Disturbance

There are four lines of evidence linking rumination and affective disorders.

1. Infants and children with rumination have been described as appearing sad and withdrawn (Chatoor et al. 1984b; Gaddini and Gaddini 1959; Lourie 1954). Lourie described a ruminating child who developed features of an anaclitic depression due to the absence of a satisfactory love object. A seven-month-old with rumination and hiatal hernia (Lourie 1954), was described as being withdrawn, expressionless, crying a great deal, irritable, and sleepless. Both cases demonstrate a passive (affective) reaction to helplessness in the face of psychic or physical pain. Several reports (Gaddini and Gaddini 1959; Hollowell and Gardner 1965; Lourie 1954; Richmond et al. 1958) described the emotional unavailability of a mother to her child due both to feelings of rejection toward an unwanted infant and to maternal depression. The child suffers a significant object loss (perceived or imagined) of the primary caretaker. This conceptualization also related to Lourie's notion of understimulation in infants with ruminatory disorder.

   Lourie (1954) noted passivity and diminished affective expression of needs in infants with rumination. Such behavior could foster parental confusion in responding to the child's immediate needs and leads to frustration, helplessness, and depressive affect. Lourie also noted these children to be markedly rejection sensitive, a trait observed in atypical depression (Leibowitz and Quitkin 1984).
2. There is a subgroup of children for whom object loss is a manifest onset condition for the appearance of ruminatory behavior (Flanagan 1977). Review of the literature reveals that object loss is the most frequent psychosocial onset event associated with rumination.

   A pleasurable self-stimulating component of ruminatory behavior may serve as a defense against the pain of object loss (Hoffer 1949, 1950; Kris 1951). Protest, despair, and withdrawal, which are associated with object loss (Bowlby and Mostyn 1969), may also be developmentally specific clinical features in the symptom context of rumination following loss.
3. Observations link ruminatory behavior in adults with depressive symptoms, anorexia nervosa, and bulimia (Blinder 1983; Fairburn and Cooper 1984a; Levine et al. 1983).
4. Maternal affective disorder may lead both to a genetic factor in the infant and to deprivation consequences to nurturance, contributing to increased risk to the infant for both mood vulnerability and ruminatory disorder.

There may be a subgroup of infants and children with rumination who have an affective disturbance, rejection sensitivity, passivity, and increased incidence of psychiatric disorder (Leibowitz and Quitkin 1984).

Biologic Determinants

Reflux Subtypes

Proponents of a biologic etiology of rumination equate rumination with gastro-esophageal reflux. Winter (personal communication) found abnormal gastroesophageal acid reflux, esophagitis, and normal or diminished lower esophageal sphincter pressure (LESP) in infant and child ruminators. It is unclear why children with gastro-esophageal reflux develop rumination, although the psychological context is considered important. Conversely, other gastroenterologists (Berquist, personal communication; Fleischer 1979a) evaluating ruminators have uncovered no significant gastrointestinal structural or motility disturbances. There may be two subgroups of ruminators: one with significant gastrointestinal problems such as reflux or hiatus hernia and another with no significant gastrointestinal problems.

As many as 20 percent of children who spit up food or vomit during the first year of life have gastroesophageal reflux defined as "a failure of the sphincter mechanism at the junction of the esophagus and stomach that allows acidic gastric material to flow into the esophagus" (Herbst 1983, p. 75).

Reflux of acidic gastric material can cause peptic esophagitis with associated chronic blood loss, iron deficiency anemia, and possibly hematemesis. Esophagitis may diminish LESP and further increase reflux.

Reflux may be associated with vomiting and failure to thrive. Rumination is considered in the differential diagnosis of psychogenic vomiting and nonorganic failure to thrive. Complications of gastroesophageal reflux (e.g., aspiration pneumonia) and esophageal stricture are often treated by surgery (Herbst 1983).

Reflux has also been associated with Sandifer's syndrome (Herbst et al. 1976). This disorder is of special interest to psychiatrists because the patient who displays head cocking, abnormal movements of the head and neck, and unusual postures may be misdiagnosed as having a tic or dystonic disorder. These abnormal postures occur during gastroesophageal reflux in the child with hiatus hernia. Surgical repair of the hernia abolishes the reflux, terminating the abnormal movements within several days.

Jolley et al. (1979) noted three patterns of gastroesophageal reflux. The type I occurs in patients who have continuous postcibal reflux and large hiatal hernias, which frequently require antireflux surgical procedure. A functional motility disorder suggesting delayed gastric emptying appeared to be important in infants with discontinuous reflux (type II) (Bitar et al. 1982; Byrne et al. 1981). These infants had frequent gastroesophageal reflux for two hours postcibally, antral pylorospasm (Byrne et al. 1981), increased lower esophageal sphincter pressures, high incidence of pulmonary symptoms, and nonspecific watery diarrhea. The mixed (type III) pattern of gastroesophageal reflux occurred in a small number of infants who exhibited features of both type I and II patterns. Dodds et al. (1982) noted the association in adults of gastroesophageal reflux with 1) continuous lower esophageal sphincter pressure; 2) normal pressure, with momentary drop in pressure; or 3) increased abdominal pressure.

Geffen (1966) posited that rumination occurs due to an increased pleutoperitoneal gradient across the diaphragm, with simultaneous relaxation of the cricopharyngeal and lower esophageal sphincters. Rapid gastric peristalsis with a contraction of the abdominal musculature, which is unconscious in certain patients (Dodds, personal communication), further increases this pressure gradient. Incompetence of the lower esophageal sphincter, secondary to hiatus hernia, exacerbates this process. Herbst et al. (1971) discussed the mechanism of rumination observed during fluoroscopy in a six-year-old. The esophagus distended with barium in the superior esophageal sphincter. When the child made sucking movements of the mouth and tongue, the superior esophageal sphincter opened, and barium flowed into the mouth. Normal deglutition followed and initiated a peristaltic wave, which emptied the esophagus (Herbst et al. 1971). The mechanism of rumination may not differ greatly from that of gaseous eructation (Geffen 1966).

Levine et al. (1983) speculated that there is an unconscious postprandial intraabdominal pressure that occurs with coordinated relaxation of the upper and lower esophageal sphincter. Of the nine cases they reported, one patient had a large postprandial pressure wave, starting first in her stomach and then spreading to the esophagus. They also posited that rumination was a benign habit disorder.

Esophageal motor dysfunction has been associated with reflux and rumination. A progressive esophageal peristaltic wave is normally present after the swallowing of food. In rumination, uncontrolled peristaltic movements are seen (Herbst, personal communication). Esophageal contraction abnormalities (e.g., increase in mean wave amplitude, increase in mean wave duration, increased frequency of motor responses and triple peak waves) (Clouse and Lustman 1983) producing reflux are seen in children as well as adults (Clouse, personal communication). Therefore, emotional stress in the infant or child may produce esophageal contraction abnormalities leading to reflux and rumination (Leitch and Escalona 1949). Fleischer (personal communication) found a strong association between emotional stress, dyadic mother-infant disturbance, and upper gastrointestinal dysfunction (Kulka et al. 1966).

Herbst et al. (1971) discussed three cases of hiatus hernia associated with rumination. Herbst et al. (1976) suggested that the abnormal findings associated with rumination should be viewed as parts of an extended syndrome of a presentation of gastroesophageal reflux.

A second type of gastrointestinal pathology, in which the passage of food through the stomach to the duodenum is impaired, is termed delayed gastric emptying (DGE) and is associated with reflux. DGE, which is associated with antral dysmotility (Byrne et al. 1981), pylorospasm, short segment pylorospasm (Swischuk et al. 1981), and pyloric stenosis, has not been reported in association with rumination.

In two cases of adult rumination (Blinder et al. 1986a), no delay was noted in gastric emptying time as measured by radionuclide gastrography. The time course of gastric emptying did, however, affect the frequency and intensity of the ruminations. As gastric emptying progressed, rumination frequency diminished. Levine et al. (1983) also noted no delay in gastric emptying.

Case studies of rumination in adults associated with a range of gastrointestinal pathophysiology and medical consequences (microcytic and macrocytic anemia) have been reported by several authors.

Increased pleuroperitoneal pressure gradient with incompetence or other abnormality of the lower esophageal sphincter may play a role in rumination with some adults. Rumination may lead to chronic esophageal irritation, with the possibility of the induction of metaplasia (Barrets esophagus) or frank neoplasia. A case of long-standing rumination reported with gastric carcinoma suggested that chronic irritation may have contributed to this malignancy (Long 1929).

Rumination associated with esophagitis (Herbst, personal communication) causes chronic bleeding, resulting in microcytic anemia.

Gastrointestinal Neurohormonal Substrate (Neuropeptides)

The role of neuropeptides (including opioids) in rumination remains to be precisely defined. Effects of upper gastrointestinal tract functions pertinent to postingestive rumination will be reviewed. The neuropeptides that elevate LESP are gastrin and motilin. Neuropeptides that decrease LESP are glucagon secretin, cholecystokinin, and vasoactive intestinal peptide (VIP). VIP is considered the primary inhibitory gut neurotransmitter. VIP-containing nerve fibers, originating in the myenteric plexis of the lower esophagus sphincter, diminish LESP. VIP also promotes gastric mucle relaxation, which decreases both LESP and gastric emptying. In the stomach, VIP inhibits gastrin release. Increased acetylecholine relase from vagal stimulation is accompanied by increased VIP (Table 1). Esophageal distention in animals increases VIP. Circulation clearance of VIP occurs within one minute of its release, suggesting its role as a neurotransmitter. It may have a paracrine function effecting relaxation of circular muscle cells immediately adjacent to the neurofibers of origin.

Opioid Containing Sphincter

Dynorphin exhibits preferential agonist effects at kappa receptors; metenkephalin is agonistic at delta receptors. Mu and kappa receptor stimulation produce lower esophageal sphincter (LES) relaxation; delta and sigma receptor stimulation produce LES contraction (Goyal, personal communication). Opioids diminish acetylcholine release, produce transient smooth circular muscle contraction, and block inhibitory transmission in circular muscle.

Blinder et al. (1986) have shown that an opioid agonist (paregoric) totally inhibited postingestive rumination in both a 33-year-old woman with a lifetime rumination

Table 1. Some Agents Influencing Human Lower Esophageal Sphincter Pressure

Agent	Raise	Lower	No change

Neuropeptide hormones	Gastrin
	Motilin
	Prostaglandin
		Estrogen and
		  progesterone
		Glucagon
		Secretin
		Cholecystokinin
		Prostaglandin
		Vasoactive intestinal
		  peptide
			Prolactin,
			  somatostatin

Pharmacologic agents	Sodium pentobarbital Metoclopramide Bethanechol Histamine Edrophonium Indomethacin Antacids	Atropine Theophylline Meperidine	Diazepam
Other (nutrition, substance use)	Protein in diet Coffee	Smoking Fat in diet Alcohol	

history and a 23-year-old woman with rumination and bulimia. Naloxone administered intravenously inhibited this opioid agonist effect.

Premeal administration of both intravenous metoclopramide (50 mg) and oral haloperidol (3 mg) also abolished rumination. This effect was blocked by intravenous naloxone. Since dopamine receptor blocking agents (haloperidol and metoclopramide) increase endogenous opioid neurotransmission, their effective inhibition by naloxone suggests a central or peripheral opioid mechanism in rumination characterized by opioid receptor insensitivity or reduction in endorphinergic neruotransmission. Studies in sheep have demonstrated opioid inhibitory and stimulating control of ruminant stomach motility in the central nervous system involving mu, delta (inhibition), and kappa (stimulus) receptors (Ruckebusch and Bardon 1984).

Chatoor et al. (1984b)—acknowledging the foregoing finding and noting the hypothesis of Panksepp (Herman and Panksepp 1978) suggesting that attachment behavior is mediated by endogenous opioids—hypothesized that deficiency of attachment and the occurrence of separation may diminish endogenous opioid activity, thereby provoking rumination behavior in infancy. Subsequently, the ruminating activity may act as a compensatory mechanism, increasing endogenous opiod levels and creating a type of self-stimulating addiction. Adjunctive autoerotic behaviors in infancy that persist after loss and detachment may entail a like mechanism (Kris 1951).

Rumination and vomiting have been reported during the postnatal withdrawal phase in infants born of narcotically addicted mothers (Davis, personal communication; Mirin and Weiss 1983; Vadapalli, personal communication). Rumination has been noted in an infant born to a heroin-addicted mother. The child was small for a premature gestational age. Understimulation due to maternal deprivation and a hearing loss may have contributed to the ruminatory disorder, along with the narcotic withdrawal (Blinder et al. 1986; Davis, personal communication). Two infants in the intensive care unit with multiple medical and surgical problems did not terminate rumination in response to paregoric (Sheagran et al. 1980).

Treatment

Treatment in Infants and Children

Since rumination in infants and young children may be life threatening, a multidisciplinary approach is mandatory. The primary physician must decide whether hospitalization is indicated. The decision may be based on the chronicity of the rumination or the presence of significant medical complications (e.g., failure to thrive, dehydration, electrolyte abnormalities) or gastrointestinal disturbances (e.g., hiatal hernia). Hospitalization may also be indicated when the primary caretaker's ability is severely compromised. Since rumination often occurs in multiproblem families, careful evaluation of the child's psychosocial situation is mandatory.

Although many authors have stressed deficient mother-infant interactions (Gaddini and Gaddini 1959; Lourie 1954; Richmond et al. 1958), more recent reports (Chatoor et al. 1984b; Lavigne and Burns 1981) have noted a positive relationship between the mother and the infant. Rumination without severe weight loss or other physiologic alterations, in the context of a supportive family, may respond to outpatient treatment.

Hospitalization of the child is often a negative experience for the mother. (Gaddini and Gaddini 1959). She may feel guilty, inadequate, and responsible for her infant's problem. She should be given permission to ventilate her fears and frustration that her child is not getting well immediately and to know that there are medical and psychological reasons for the rumination. A description of reflux may be helpful.

Documentation of the staff's observations of the temperaments of mother and child and the degree of reciprocity should be recorded. A structured interview with the mother, father of the child, or other primary caretaker is crucial. The mother's own developmental and personal psychiatric history may often contain determinants of current conflictual attitudes and behavior toward the infant.

Dickson (personal communication) emphasized minimizing the mother's guilt. Rumination can be attributed to a baby who has a problem with homeostasis and withdrawing into a maladaptive habit. The mother should be told she is both an expert with her child and an important colleague in the treatment process. Her fantasies about the child's rumination, the associated failure to thrive, what techniques have been helpful in reducing the rumination, and what events seem to have precipitated the rumination should be explored. The mother's fragile self-esteem and her feelings of incompetence should be acknowledged and countered by designating her an important colleague in the child's treatment.

In the hospital, the baby should be placed near the nursing station to increase the child's visual and auditory stimulation. There should be a specific nurse on each shift that will give primary care to the child. Frequently, a social worker who is involved will be able to pick an empathetic nurse who will be emotionally available during an eight-hour shift to spend much of the time with the child.

A nurse acts as a substitute (surrogate) mother with whom the baby can develop an attachment (Lourie 1954). Where there is a failure of attachment, substitution of primary care may be critical. As this attachment develops, the child restores a stable object relationship. Later, the mother will become more involved with feeding. The child will transfer its attachment and thus develop a restorative object relationship with the mother. The next therapeutic task will be interruption of the rumination. The child's unique ruminative pattern should be recorded, for example, occurring when the baby is alone or occurring when the mother pushes the baby away (Dixon, personal communication). The nurse who is aware of this pattern should be present to interrupt the possible anxiety-producing situation or frustration that may precipitate rumination. Another therapeutic task focuses on the relinquishing of maladaptive ruminative and self-stimulatory patterns.

Lourie (1954) reported that a number of ruminators have hypersensitivity to touch and sound (Bergman and Escalona 1949). Placing the child on a pillow with minimal touching, but with visual or auditory stimulation, would be helpful. In one child who was not interested in people, a relationship was started by a nurse who interested him with bright-colored clothing and jewelry. These auditory and visual stimuli, combined with the crib rocking, initiated the attachment process. In another infant who withdrew from any social contact, placement in a crib with another baby was helpful in starting an object attachment. Later holding both children on a nurse's knee was helpful in reinforcing the attachment process.

Hospital Milieu

Sheagran et al. (1980) discussed a multisensory stimulation approach (Table 2). They noted that in their three cases using a limited number of nurses and placing the child in an open crib, children started to gain weight, developed a social smile, and had improved interaction with their caretakers.

The use of videotape may aid in analysis of the dyadic mother-child interactions,

Table 2. Suggested Activities for a Sensory Stimulation Program

Visual

- Place the infant in face-to-face contact with caretaker, inside and outside of crib, particularly during feeding, diapering, and so on.
- Place brightly colored mobiles about 7 to 12 inches above the infant's face.
- Place face patterns on the side of the Isolette or crib.

Tactile

- Skin-to-skin contact while being held.
- Gentle stroking to back, legs, and arms.
- Gentle patting on the infant's back.

Auditory

- Frequent exposure to the human voice, particularly during routine care, and concomitant with eye contact with infant.
- Soft music from music box, placed in Isolette or crib during alert periods.

Kinesthetic-Vestibular

- Gentle rocking while cradled in caretaker's arms.
- Frequent changes in infant's body position (e.g., sitting in infant seat, lying prone, lying on side).
- Carrying infant around room in various positions (e.g., on shoulder, cradled in arms).

---

emphasizing tension states and separation-withdrawal in the mother and infant and their link to ruminatory behavior.

Mother will need to recognize her child's strivings for autonomy, and the baby needs to be a stimulated and active participant in the feeding process, as many ruminant babies are quite passive. Feeding should terminate when the child is finished; rigid schedules should be abandoned. The mother may need to stimulate the infant by increasing her eye contact, vocalizing, and smiling during feeding. She may have to work through her uncomfortable feelings, which have been present during the feeding process (Levy 1981).

A number of reports of maternal depression have been described (Chatoor and Dickson 1984a; Gaddini and Gaddini 1959; Lourie 1954; Richmond et al. 1958). Therefore, a long-term goal may include individual treatment for a depressed mother. If the child continues to ruminate, placement outside the home may be necessary. As a part of discharge planning, home visits and increased support from the mother's friends and family are advised. The mother should be seen after discharge both individually as indicated, with the child at least once per week for psychological management, and at least once a week by the pediatrician.

Since rumination in young children can result in death, the resistent mother may have to be confronted about the poor prognosis if the mother's emotional state and environmental conditions are not modified.

Medical-Surgical and Pharmacotherapy

Herbst (1983) stated that many cases of rumination are primarily related to excessive reflux. Thus the management of rumination is essentially the same as the medical management of reflux (Gryboski 1983). The initial treatment includes elevation of the infant to the position of a 30- to 45-degree angle, avoidance of juices, and small, frequent, thickened feedings.

A six-week medical course is usually instituted (Gryboski 1983; Herbst, personal communication). After each meal, aluminum hydroxide, an antacid, can be alternated with magnesium hydroxide. If symptoms persist (Gryboski 1983) in an infant over one year of age, cimetidine, which blocks H-2 receptors, diminishing gastric acid production, is given at the dose of 20 to 30 mg/kg/day in four divided doses (tid and bedtime). Bethanechol, 8.7 mg/m of body surface, two to three times daily, may also be given. In older children, administering a dopamine antagonist such as metoclopramide (acting centrally and peripherally) or the investigational drug domperidone (acting peripherally) increases LES pressure, gastric tone, and peristalisis, and improves gastric emptying (Brogden et al. 1982). Side effects (e.g., extrapyramidal reactions) may occur with metoclopramide but rarely with domperidone (Sol et al. 1980). If a six-week trial of medical treatment is ineffective, surgery may be indicated (Gryboski 1983).

Winter (personal communication) evaluated five cases of rumination in infants and young children who displayed pathologic gastroesophageal acid with clearance. Reflux and esophagitis, both treated by positional therapy, antacids, and cimetidine, abolishing rumination, suggested evidence for a medical etiology. Nasogastric tube feeding may be utilized in severe reflux to prevent dehydration and electrolyte abnormalities (Chatoor et al. 1984b).

Criteria for surgery are: persistent vomiting after vigorous medical management, failure to thrive with nutritional depletion, gastroesophageal bleeding from esophagitis, aspiration pneumonia, and esophageal stricture (Herbst, personal communication). The surgical procedure of choice is the Nissen fundoplication.

Treatment in Adults

Treatment of adult rumination presents a different context from that of the child. Family physicians may not recognize adult rumination as a discrete phenomenon. Often patients are confused by explanations of the behavior that allude to stress or emotional disorder. They become guilty about their problem and need reassurance. Pope's (personal communication) technique is to discuss gastroesophageal reflux, using a diagram of the stomach and esophagus. Pictorial illustrations may be helpful. By explaining the mechanism of reflux to the patient, this problem is appropriately recognized, and the patient feels reassured and relieved (Levine et al. 1983; Pope, personal communication).

Medical treatment with antispasmodics has been ineffective (Brown 1968). Since the esophageal, contractile abnormalities producing reflux may be secondary to an agitated depression or anxiety disorder (Clouse and Lustman 1983, and personal communication), some patients with rumination may have features of a specific psychiatric disorder.

An experimental treatment utilizing an opioid agonist (paregoric) and medications that enhance endogenous opioid transmission (metoclopramide, haloperidol) has been effective in diminishing rumination behavior in two adult patients (Blinder et al. 1986). Preprandial hypnosis has been successful in an adult with chronic rumination (Kahn, personal communication).

Behavioral Treatment

Behavioral treatment of rumination was first reported in 1968. Mild electroshock, an aversive stimulus to the finger, was employed in a severely dehydrated child who did not respond to psychological management (Lang and Melamed 1969).

Winton and Singh (1983) concluded that electroshock should be used only in life-threatening cases that have proved refractory to other forms of therapy and that its use should always be paired with positive reinforcement of appropriate behavior.

Tart and bitter substances, such as lemon juices (Sajwej et al. 1974) and pepper sauce (Murray et al. 1976), have been squirted into the mouth to stop rumination. Singh (1979) found pepper sauce was more effective than lemon juice, which can dissolve tooth enamel. Both substances, however, were difficult to apply effectively.

Duker and Seys (1977) used overcorrection, requiring the patient to clean up after each vomiting episode. Negative punishment is a technique that deletes or delays a desirable event following rumination. Usually, food or staff attention is removed for a specific period of time. The efficacy depends on the potency of the reinforcement that has been removed. This technique was slower and produced less reduction than more aversive punishment.

Wolf et al. (1970) used extinction where a reinforcer specific for a child was discontinued to abolish any favorable social consequence of rumination.

Newer techniques have deemphasized aversive stimuli, which often lead to staff resistance. Satiation techniques have been reported. A subject is allowed to eat as much food as is desired; this can result in a supression of rumination. A beneficial side effect is an increase of weight for a malnourished patient (Rast et al. 1981). Foxx et al. (1979) followed vomiting with a mouth-cleansing punishment combined with satiation. Singh et al. (1982) suppressed rumination with oral hygiene alone.

Winton and Singh (1983) stated that the "mother substitute" psychodynamic approach is based on selective attention to more appropriate behaviors while ignoring the rumination. An effective social aversive technique is to state the word *no* as the child appears to ruminate and to avoid physical and eye contact for five minutes (Chatoor et al. 1984b).

Positive side effects of behavioral treatment are improved feeding skills, increased general motor activity and play, increased cognitive function, and decreased tantrum crying and stereotyped behavior. Negative side effects reported by Becker et al. (1978) included head slapping, rocking and weaving, self-mutilitation, hair pulling, and masturbation.

Winton and Singh (1983) concluded that rumination could be eliminated or effectively reduced by varied positive reinforcers such as attention and social interaction and changing stressful antecedent conditions associated with eating that may be effective in reducing vomiting. There is concern about the design of behavioral treatment studies and efficacy in producing long-term suppression of rumination. In most reports, patients were in institutions or understimulated and were moderately to severely retarded.

Barmann (1980) employed a technique with a six-year-old retarded boy utilizing positive reinforcers such as verbal praise and vibratory stimulation (from a vibrator worn on a special vest) for having dry hands after eating. Since institutional staffs are reluctant to offer aversive reinforcement, this technique may be a useful variant.

Biopsychosocial Synthesis

The etiology of rumination is unclear. Physiologic, psychodynamic, and behavioral theories have been discussed. Rumination is a psychobiologic disorder in which psychological and physiologic abnormalities combine in various degress to produce the ruminatory behavior.

Rumination may be on a continuum wherein a patient might have maximal gastrointestinal pathophysiology (e.g., severe reflux and hiatus hernia) and minimal psychological concomitants, or the converse where a patient could have minimal gastrointestinal pathophysiology but severe psychopathology or psychosocial stress. Proponents of the biologic theories believe that psychological factors definitely influence rumination. Herbst (personal communication) evaluated 20 ruminators with significant reflux, with 50 percent requiring surgery. No apparent psychopathology in the infant or mother was found.

Multiple stresses in children can produce similar symptomatic behaviors (Greenspan, personal communication). For the child, irritability and discomfort may result in feeling overwhelmed, anxious, or depressed, or may be manifest as severe reflux with esophagitis. Inferred reflux esophagitis treated either medically or surgically may result in a feeling of well-being and a termination of rumination (Herbst, personal communication).

Psychodynamically oriented therapy, using a substitute care giver, may reduce rumination for two reasons. First, the child receives increased stimulation, which aids in trust and attachment. Second, this additional care is effective since the child is held upright during the period of stimulation, diminishing both reflux and esophagitis. The esophagitis, which subsides, augments lower esophageal sphincter pressure, further diminishing reflux. Diminished esophagitis results in a reduced psychological tension, promoting a feeling of well-being in both mother and infant.

Maternal anxiety may promote secondary physiologic changes in a child. For example, a mother feeling overwhelmed by a stressful situation or feeling anxious secondary to her child's persistent vomiting and weight loss may exhibit increased muscle tension. This is transmitted to the child, who becomes tense and develops a more rapid heart rate (Kulka et al. 1966). The increased autonomic response might release acetylcholine and VIP, producing lower esophageal sphincter relaxation and increased reflux. Thus the tendency of the child to ruminate may be increased by an anxious mother. Psychiatric disorder has been associated with reflux and esophageal contractility abnormalities (Clouse and Lustman 1983). Transmitted maternal stress could result in infant gastroesophageal contractile dysfunction, promoting reflux and rumination. Finally, association of ruminatory disorder with object loss and depressed affect and evidence of a possible opioid regulatory mechanism with links to attachment (Blinder et al. 1986; Chatoor et al. 1984b) suggest an underlying neuroendocrine relationship to mood disorder.

Chapter 75

Pica

Pica is defined as a pathologic craving for either a single food item or its constituents or for substances not commonly regarded as food (Danford and Huber 1982). DSM-III-R (American Psychiatric Association 1987) emphasizes repeated nonnutritive ingestion as a habitual mode of response for a designated period of time (at least one month).

A broader perspective of determinants of pica would include age level, physiologic state, and level of cognitive and intellectual development. Sociocultural and historical patterns may also determine the idiosyncratic and ritualistic food selections of a people or a region (Koptagel and Reimann 1973; Singh et al. 1981). Animal studies suggest that pica may be a result of specific nutrient deficiencies or a form of nutrient-specific appetite (Danford et al. 1982). A similar pattern has been inferred in humans (Jollie 1963). Nutrient deficiencies and medical consequences such as iron deficiency, lead intoxication, growth and cognitive impairment, and intestinal obstruction are frequently associated with peculiar dietary habits that accompany pica.

Pica has been reported in certain schizophrenic patients (Fishbain and Rotondo 1983) and is frequently observed in the mentally retarded (Danford and Huber 1981). It has been attributed to delusional beliefs (Fishbain and Rotondo 1983), a behavioral lag (Danford and Huber 1981), and the developmental chaos of autistic children (Cohen et al. 1976).

Etiology

Much of the early work is based on superstition and folklore. Early case studies are conspicuously absent. Many investigators deal primarily with pica in pregnant women, although references to its occurrence in both sexes appear. Recommendations for dietary alterations and the empirical use of iron preparations as treatment appeared before iron deficiency was proposed as a factor in the development of pica. Indeed, the empirical treatments most often deemed beneficial involved nutritional fortification. Moral weakness, perverted instinct, and psychological factors were implicated, although several lines of rational investigation have emerged. Ambiguity found in the early clinical descriptions continues to the modern era.

Current efforts to define and explain the phenomenom of pica include 1) developmental studies (vestigal instinct); 2) psychodynamic theories (deprivation, conflict); 3) need-state hypotheses that propose nutritional deficit and homeostatic compensation; 4) sociocultural determinants that involve ethnic group traditions and beliefs related to rites of passage, health, and fertility; 5) consequences of erratic reinforcement in a chaotic unstructured environment (adjustive behavior model); and 6) neurobiologic basis of food selection and ingestive behavior in animal investigations (iron deficiency leading to pago phagia, labrythine stimulation and pica; iron deficiency and decreased dopamine neurotransmission as an etiologic factor in spontaneous pica) (Blinder et al. 1986).

Psychodynamic studies describe childhood pica as resulting from either maternal and/or paternal deprivation and a maternal fostering of oral defenses against anxiety (Singhi et al. 1981) or resulting from excess oral stimulation followed by aggression toward the mother after the introduction of solid food. A mother may foster oral defenses against anxiety by late weaning, using the bottle as a pacifier, displaying pica behavior herself, or seducing her child into eating nonnutritive substances (Millican 1968).

In a study of 95 children with pica, Millican (1968) found 31.2 percent had a positive history of maternal facilitation of pica and the concurrence of paternal deprivation. In contrast, the later clinical features were found in 21.4 percent of a psychiatric group and 3.7 percent of a normal comparison group. Millican emphasized that the critical factor for determining the choice of pica as a symptom is the "shunting" of the child to oral satisfaction. Pueschel (1977) confirmed these findings in a group of lead-poisoned children with a constellation of inadequate mother-child interaction, paternal deprivation, culturally dependent maternal oral interests, and significant stress factors leading to pica. The behavioral manifestations of oral drives may increase in intensity and be exaggerated when there are "extra pressures" promoting them and "inadequate patterns of control" (Lourie et al. 1963). Alternatively, oral deprivation may lead to developmental and psychostructural deficits that are predominantly nonoral in nature (Blinder 1980).

Along with poor parental supervision and oral overstimulation, maternal pica (63 percent in Millican's 1968 pica group) and cultural acceptance of pica (especially common in families with African lineage and in Southern communities) may represent the additional factors that allow pica to become manifest in a child prone to intense oral focus of drive satisfaction. Singhi et al. (1981) studied a group of children with iron deficiency anemias subdivided according to the presence or absence of pica and found that certain psychosocial stressors were significantly associated with pica: maternal deprivation, parental neglect, child beating, impoverished parent-child interaction, and disorganized family structure.

Psychological stress and external conflict situations were present in a group of children with pica compared to matched controls (Koptagel and Reimann 1973). There were no significant differences between the pica group and nonpica controls in education, socioeconomic level, internalized psychological conflict, and intelligence. Children in both pica and control groups displayed hypochromic anemia. Psychological stress and environmental disturbance were more significant than anemia in contributing to the development of pica.

Lourie's (1977) contention that pica is a predictor of later addiction behavior is supported by a longitudinal study, which showed that a significant number of children with pica developed alcoholism in adulthood. Mitchell et al. (1977a) reported similar findings and proposed visceral conditioning as the critical mechanism in both pica and alcoholism.

Implications of Animal Models of Pica

Rats exhibit pica in response to gastrointestinal distress in the same way as other animals respond with emesis. Mitchell et al. (1977a) paired saccharin with cyclophosphamide (which induces pica in rats), after which pica was elicited by the presentation of saccharin alone. A visceral conditioning process was evidenced by the presence of loose stools in geophagic rats receiving cyclophosphamide and geophagic rats receiving saccharin alone. That this effect is separate from a substance-induced toxic response was shown by the development of geophagia in rats in response to rotational stimulation. A physiologic basis for geophagia has been implicated, namely gastrointestinal malaise, which persists by conditioning after the original stress has been removed (Mitchell et al. 1977).

There are reports of pica induced in rats by iron deficiency, a low-calcium diet, various toxins, and stress (Mitchell 1976). In the albino rat made iron deficient by venopuncture, a preference for ice eating (pagophagia) over water intake occurs. Following iron repletion, pagophagia disappears (Woods and Weisinger 1970). Rats fed a low-calcium diet voluntarily ingested greater proportions of lead acetate solutions than did iron-deficient or control rats. Thus calcium deficiency promoted lead pica in rats ingesting a low-calcium diet. These rats showed an increased toxicity to lead exposure manifested by increased body lead (Snowden and Sanderson 1974).

Burchfield et al. (1977) reported that rats stressed by Freund's adjuvant injection producing arthritis had increased kaolin (clay) consumption. This finding suggested that geophagia may occur in response to nonspecific homeostatic alteration or stress. Geophagia may be communicated to naive rats from stressed cage mates.

Furthermore, Mitchell (1976) reported that when rats were poisoned with lithium chloride, red squill, or cyclophosphamide, they preferred kaolin to food, again indicating toxic stress-induced pica. Studies of rats engaging in amylophagia (starch eating) revealed lower fertility rates. Extreme lack of interest or concern for the offspring exhibited by the starch-eating mother resulted in total 24-hour motality of the litters (Keith et al. 1979).

The foregoing models of animal pica suggest etiologies that may pertain to humans and deserve further experimental verification and replication.

The theory that the eating of nonnutritive substances is a need-determined behavior is supported by studies of food selection in young infants. Of special interest is a child with rickets who selectively drank milk laced with cod liver oil until his blood calcium and phosphorus were normal and roentgenographic evidence of his rickets had disappeared (Davis 1928). Richter (1942/1943) demonstrated the ability of adrenalectomized rats to drink enough salt solution to remain symptom-free. This self-regulatory behavior was abolished by sectioning of the taste nerves, indicating the presumptive role of taste in dietary selection. In a later study, Richter (1943) proposed that taste thresholds vary with internal needs, as adrenalectomized rats can distinguish far more dilute (1:33,000) solutions of salt than normals (1:2,000). Rolls' (1988) studies of food selection suggested two adaptive mechanisms in the control of eating. The first, sensory-specific satiety, is when a person's perception of a specific food eaten as pleasant changes as a function of time since last eaten. This may be a cognitive parallel to Richter's concept of changing taste thresholds. The second, neophobia, is the avoidance of food not in a person's current food repertoire. Both mechanisms have an adaptive value. Sensory-specific satiety leads to increased variety. Neophobia ensures against eating possibly dangerous or nonnutritive foods. Perhaps both mechanisms may be impaired or inoperative in pica.

Numerous writers have observed that the pica associated with iron-deficiency anemia ceases after treatment with iron (Lanzkowsky 1959). In contrast, several authors have argued that the pica causes the iron deficiency (Cavdar 1983; Leming et al. 1981). Gutelius (1963) proposed two types of pica that are recognizable syndromes: 1) children with severe anemia in whom the pica is terminated by treatment of the anemia and 2) an anemic group with pica that persists after iron therapy. The existence of the latter group suggests the presence of a conditioned response similar to that in animal studies (Mitchell et al. 1977a).

The significance of iron deficiency in pica has been long debated. Lanzkowsky (1959) found cessation of pica after iron replacement in anemic dirt eaters. Jollie (1963) suggested that a rise in serum iron was sufficient to remove the cravings found in pica. Libnoch (1984) described a woman with erythrocytosis who developed pica with normal hemoglobin values but low tissue iron stores resulting from repeated therapeutic phlebotomy. On administration of oral iron, her serum ferritin, mean corpuscular volume, and serum iron returned to normal, and the pica ceased. The foregoing suggests a relationship between tissue iron depletion and pica. McGehee and Buchanan (1980) also supported the role of iron therapy for relief of pica in anemic subjects.

On occasion, pica may be a cause of iron deficiency where the nonnutritive substance (e.g., clay, starch) interferes with dietary intake or absorption of iron (Cavdar and Arcasoy 1972; Leming et al. 1981). However, iron deficit as a cause, rather than the result, of pica is most clearly seen in patients with pagophagia (ice eating). Ice displaces no known nutrients and does not alter the absorption of iron (Coltman 1969, 1971; Crosby 1971).

Olynyk and Sharpe (1982) and Youdim and Holzbauer (1976) suggested iron-dependent appetite regulation. The studies by Youdim (1980) indicated that systemic iron deficiency results in decreased activity of iron-dependent enzymes and changes in catechol neurotransmitter metabolites in the central nervous system (CNS). Youdim (1982) linked decreased brain iron specifically to decreased dopamine D_2 receptors and consequent reduction of CNS dopamine-driven behaviors. Further research in this area is clearly desirable.

Studies that cast doubt on iron deficiency in the etiology of pica include those by Gutelius (1962). Gutelius utilized a double-blind approach with well-matched, anemic controls and found that although pica decreased with iron replacement, hemoglobin levels rose in both the treated and nontreated subjects. Furthermore, relapses of pica behavior were not associated with a drop in hemoglobin levels. Gutelius noted "the cure of pica, like the cause seems to be a complicated problem involving multiple factors in varying degrees" and "iron medication is not a specific therapy for pica." The attention shown the families during treatment and an increased awareness of the pica behavior and its antecedents may account for part of the ambiguity. The increase in hemoglobin levels in the nontreated subjects suggests that partaking in a study made the mothers in both groups more conscious of nutrition despite the lack of any specific evidence on the matter.

The Incidence and Prevalence of Pica

The incidence and prevalence of pica is difficult to establish due to variations in definition and reluctance of patients to admit to abnormal cravings and ingestion.

More than half of pregnant women describe cravings for specific foods (Danford and Huber 1982). Other studies reveal a 33 percent incidence of amylophagia (starch eating) in pregnancy (Danford et al. 1982). Bruhn and Pangborn (1971) reported that 38 percent of pregnant women experience pica. Past studies have reported that up to half of all Southern black women engaged in starch and clay eating (Danford and Huber 1982).

In children ages one-and-a-half to three years, pica is considered normative, with an incidence greater than 50 percent. However, persistence of excessive hand-to-mouth movements found in pica is abnormal in children older than three years of age (Lourie et al. 1963). The incidence of pica is 30 percent in black children ages one through six in contrast to 10 to 18 percent of Caucasian children matched on age and social class. The incidence of pica is highest in psychotic non-Caucasian children, reaching 50 percent (Danford and Huber 1982). Baltrop (1966) felt pica decreased with age, reporting that approximately 10 percent of children beyond age 12 engaged in pica.

Lead poisoning found in children one through five years of age is frequently associated with pica. One-third of children with pica have lead poisoning. In a group of children with lead poisoning, 79 percent ingested paint chips as the source of intoxication (Danford 1982).

In the institutionalized retarded, Danford and Huber (1981) reported the prevalence of pica to be 26 percent. In contrast, Macalpine and Singh (1986) reported a prevalence of only 8.4 percent in the same population. While both groups of investigators found the highest occurrence of pica at ages 10 through 19, Danford and

Huber noticed an increase in pica beyond 70, whereas Macalpine and Singh noted no occurrence of pica after age 45.

Ethnic differences occur in pica. The majority of cases of lead poisoning in New York were of Puerto Rican heritage. The incidence increases in summer, when vitamin D elevation by sunlight synthesis may promote an increased lead absorption (Jacobs 1982).

Pica is endemic among sedentary Australian aborigines. As diet and eating customs changed with colonization and monotonous foods replaced the once varied diet, there was a wish in the people to return to the traditional folkways and customs. For example, clay was readopted to be eaten as a fertility food (Bateson and Leboy 1978; Eastwell 1979). In Turkey, pregnant young women were encouraged to eat clay to enhance their fertility (Cavdar 1983). Traditional beliefs originating in black cultures encouraged pregnant females, both in Africa and later in the United States, to eat various types of clay to enhance childbearing (Cooper 1957).

Demographic information on incidence reveals that pica has been associated with diets low in iron, zinc, and calcium compared to a controlled diet (Edwards 1959). Four percent of pregnant women had iron-poor diets.

In the mentally retarded, there are differing occurrence rates of pica, depending on age, IQ, medication, and manifestations of behavior and appetite. The majority of patients with pica are moderately underweight. Pica is more prevalent in patients with lower IQs. An increased incidence of pica occurred in patients with CNS congenital abnormalities and associated medical problems (e.g., diabetes, deafness, seizures). The occurrence of pica was also increased in patients taking neuroleptics (Danford and Huber 1981). Decreased dopaminergic neurotransmission in this patient subgroup may be akin to the D_2 receptor diminution demonstrated in iron deficiency (Blinder et al. 1986b; Youdim 1981), suggesting a common dopaminergic pathway for the occurrence of spontaneous pica in selected clinical populations.

Behavioral problems associated with pica in the retarded include stereotypic behavior (52 percent), hyperactivity (39 percent), self-abuse (39 percent), and food-related abnormal behaviors including eating off the floor (73 percent) and chewing of nonfoods (73 percent). Pica may co-occur with rumination (53 percent), hyperphagia (47 percent), and anorexia. There were no significant racial or sexual differences for pica in the mentally retarded group (Danford and Huber 1981).

Medical Complications

Clinical Description

There are numerous specific types of nonnutritive ingestion reported in the literature in different age groups and social and cultural contexts. Geography, sociocultural factors, and developmental considerations have all been significant in determining the type of pica.

Special forms of pica and their medical complications include the following. Paper pica may lead to mercury poisoning. Olynyk and Sharpe (1982) reported a patient with paper pica who was found to have decreased serum iron and terminated the pica after iron therapy. There are numerous clinical cases described in the literature in which the appearance of pica was associated with occult iron deficiency, which resulted in the spontaneous appearance of nonnutritive and unconventional ingestion of objects such as match heads (cautopyreiophagia) (Libnoch 1984) and raw potatoes (geomelophagia) (Perry 1977). Arcasoy et al. (1978) have shown both decreased serum iron and zinc in association with geophagia in Turkish children. The latter syndrome may also be associated with hepatasplenomegaly, hypogonadism, and dwarfism in Iranian children (Prasad et al. 1961).

The term *Bezoar* derives from the Persian word signifying antidote. These were concretions from the alimentary canal of animals and were thought to have both medicinal and magical properties. Clinically, Bezoars can be characterized as tricho (hair), phyto (plants), and gastroliths (mineral or chemical substances). Tricho and phyto Bezoars account for more than 90 percent of reported clinical cases (Allan and Woodruff 1983; DeBakey and Ochsner 1938). Certain occupational situations (e.g., asphalt workers, painters who swallow shellac), medical procedures and treatments (e.g., radiography, bismouth), and medically prescribed special diets may predispose to Bezoar formation.

Graham (1978) described a giant trichlobezoar in a 17-year-old female with normal intelligence. The hair ball took up the entire stomach and gastrostomy was required for its removal. Singh and Winton (1984) described severe fecal impaction in two school-age children resulting from sand eating.

Additional medical complications reported from nonnutritive eating have included intestinal perforation, dental complications, hyperkalemia associated with geophagia (Gelfan et al. 1975), hypokalemia and anemia (Mengel et al. 1964), and parasitosis (Marcus and Stambler 1979). Nine of 23 children with toxocariasis had a history of pica (Stagno 1980).

Patients with pica should be screened for parasitism and other orally transmitted diseases. Foreign body ingestion may be seen in delusional schizophrenic patients who may ingest glass, pins, or other nonnutritive items. Parotid hypertrophy may be seen in starch eating. Ulcerative colitis and iron deficiency have been described in an eight-year-old who ingested masonary (DiCagno et al. 1974). An interesting syndrome of nicotinism and myocardial infarction was described by Neil et al. (1977) in a psychotic delusional patient who ate tobacco. Neil et al. noted that Kraepelin was the first to document an extraordinary array of inedible materials consumed by psychotic patients and felt that this behavior might be a vegetative sign of psychosis: "perversion of the appetite."

Pica and Iron Deficiency

Numerous authors reported pica associated with iron deficiency (Ansell and Wheby 1972; Lanzkowsky 1959; Reynolds 1968). Gutelius (1962) concluded in a double-blind study that intramuscular iron was no more effective than saline injection in reducing pica. However, patients in this study were evaluated at two-month intervals. Since iron generally abolishes pica in less than seven days (Lanzkowsky 1959; Reynolds 1968), the preferential effect of iron in abolishing pica might not be apparent. Also, the educative approach over the relatively long period of the study may have facilitated the mother's prohibitions against pica and may have improved mother-child interactions, diminishing stress promotion of pica. The most compelling argument for the association of pica and iron deficiency is suggested by the studies of Reynolds (1968) and Coltman (1969) on pagophagia (the obligatory urge to eat at least one tray of ice daily for at least two months). Ice eating does not reduce iron levels and is not a culturally determined pica. Reynolds (1968) found pagophagia associated with a serum iron level of less than 70 µg/100 ml. Iron repletion, which increased serum iron prior to correction of the anemia, abolished pagophagia. Coltman (1969) reported cessation of pagophagia in 19 of 25 women with iron deficiency after iron supplementation for five days with intramuscular injection and 11 days with oral iron administration.

Ambiguity in the sequence of pica and iron deficiency is in part due to the situation of geophagia (clay eating). In geophagia of Turkish clays (Cavdar 1983), a culturally determined behavior, adsorption of both iron and zinc occurs, producing iron and zinc deficiency. Although the Turkish diet is both low in protein and contains phytate, which binds iron and zinc, it is unclear if the patient is iron and/or zinc deficient prior to the geophagia (Cavdar 1983).

The mechanisms of the association or iron deficiency in pica is unclear. Coltman (1969) proposed that iron-dependent peripheral tissue enzymes such as catalase or cytochrome-C were deficient in iron deficiency. However, he could not explain why the changes in these enzymes would promote pica. Using rats made iron deficient, Youdim (1981) reported a specific reduction of CNS dopamine (D_2) receptor binding sites (50 percent), leading to a down regulation of dopaminergic activity similar to that found in neuroleptic-treated animals. There was a decreased behavioral response to both pre- and postsynaptic dopamine-acting drugs.

Another form of pica, amylophagia (starch eating), has been associated with iron deficiency. Thomas et al. (1976) found that starch inhibited mucosal iron uptake. Keith et al. (1970) found more severe iron deficiency in pregnant women who engaged in amylophagia.

Table 1 illustrates a number of clinical situations of iron deficiency in conjunction with various types of pica. There are reports of eating match heads or ashes in patients who became iron deficient as a result of colonic carcinoma (Libnoch 1984; Moss et al. 1974). Thus pica may be a presenting symptom that can alert the clinician to anticipate iron deficiency and pursue a careful differential diagnosis. Pica frequently ceases after a few days of iron repletion, suggesting a role for iron loss in initiating and promoting this disorder.

Treatment Approaches

Behavioral Treatment

Several behavioral techniques have been utilized to diminish pica behavior exhibited by mentally retarded patients in a residential setting. One method is a time-out procedure to interrupt pica. A verbal reprimand was given to a 14-year-old male patient who ate food wrappers, erasers, and string, resulting in intestinal obstruction that required surgical correction. A paradigm consisting of verbal reprimand, response interruption, setting generalization, and reward resulted in discrimination training (Ausman et al. 1974). Overcorrection as a procedure was employed by Foxx and Martin (1975). A patient was forced to spit out the pica item immediately followed by administration of oral hygiene consisting of mouth flush, tooth brushing, and wiping of the lips. This procedure was effective in decreasing the occurrence of parasitosis in pica-eating patients.

There are conceptual differences in the definition of pica limited to ingesting nonfood items in contrast to eating food on the floor. The use of experimental tactics such as baiting the patient and the absence of data about generalization and maintenance of improvement make comparative evaluation of different treatment techniques difficult. Furthermore primary developmental factors, particularly the perpetuation of a finger-feeding stage interfering with the use of utensils in retarded patients, may be related to the persistence of pica.

Table 1. Pica and Iron Deficiency: Clinical Features and Response to Treatment

Patient	Type of pica	Associated clinical features	Response to treatment	Source
46-year-old female	Pagophagia	Ingested 20 to 40 ice cubes daily, anemia from uterine blood loss	Iron abolished pica in four days	Sacks (1971)
25 females	Pagophagia	Ingested at least one tray ice cubes daily; severe hypermenorrhea except for three patients	Completely resolved by treatment with iron insufficient in amount to correct either the anemia or iron lack	Coltman (1969)
35-year-old female	Pagophagia	Ingested six to eight trays of ice cubes daily for five months	Oral iron begun on sixth day of study; on 50th day refused all ice	Coltman (1971)
42-year-old female	Olive craving	Ate approximately five to seven jars green olives weekly for four months; menorrhagia	Treated oral ferrous sulfate 300 mg 3× day. In one week, craving diminished; in two weeks down to one jar per week; after one week discharge from hospital; stopped eating olives	Chandra and Rosner (1973)
44-year-old female	Lettuce craving	Ingested four to five heads of lettuce daily for several months	Oral iron therapy in one month; hemoglobin 14.0; no craving for lettuce	Marks (1973)
26-year-old female	Ice-cold raw potatoes or peanuts	Symptomatic erythrocytosis requiring phlebotomy every other month; menorrhagia	Oral iron; returned to normal including no pica within one month	Libnoch (1984)
76-year-old female	Magnesium carbonate	Microcytic hyperchromic anemia; consuming 60 to 80 g/d three years prior to hospital admission	Repeat admissions about each month; given oral and parenteral iron; no blood loss site found; only improved in hospital	Leming et al. (1981)
78-year-old female	Pagophagia to lectophagia	Hematocrit 27; enzyme changes consistent with myocardial infarction; at discharge began to consume three trays of ice cubes daily; cut to two cups per day; began to eat many heads of lettuce per day; found on BE apple core lesion colon	Responded to two units of packed cells, gave total remission of signs and symptoms	Moss et al. (1974)
39-year-old male	Pagophagia	Gastrointestinal bleeding, Billroth II procedure; increased ice consumption	Oral iron gave total relief; no longer wanted ice	Coltman (1971)

In a series of studies on response-contingent physical restraint (Singh and Winton 1984; Singh et al. 1981), it was demonstrated that the physical restraint technique alone can control pica. A duration of 10 seconds of physical restraint appeared more effective than either 30-second or three-second restraint. Physical restraint was easy to use, required minimal staff training time, and no specific equipment. It was pointed out that it is important to initiate treatment in a number of different settings to promote generalization. Singh and Winton (1984) showed that physical restraint was more efficacious than overcorrection for the treatment of pica. Since institutions are often understaffed, an easily employable brief treatment is desirable.

Another aversive response interruption involves blindfolding or facial screening immediately following pica behavior. Improvement in the pica is also accompanied by reduction of other disruptive behaviors (Singh and Winton 1984).

Often the control of pica in mentally retarded adults with complicated histories represents a clinical problem that must be approached through individualized design and the presence of aversive consequences. Friedin and Johnson (1979) described the treatment of copraphagia by linking it to aversive consequences (viz., delay of a shower).

Behavioral treatment approaches in pica involve careful observational analyses and the application of consistent contingent responses by a trained, compassionate staff.

Nutrient Approaches

Nutrient treatment of pica has been reported for almost 1,000 years. Avicenna in the 10th century added iron to wine as a treatment for earth eating (Danford and Huber 1981). There are numerous case reports (Lanzkowsky 1958; Reynolds 1968) indicating that iron treatment will abolish pica. Cavdar (1983), reviewing a geophagia syndrome (iron-deficiency anemia, hepatosplenomegaly, hypogonadism, and dwarfism found in Turkey), reported that in iron-treated anemia the addition of zinc was necessary for linear growth and pubertal advance. There are also a number of reports of zinc deficiency associated with pica. Hambridge and Silverman (1973) reported a 10-year-old boy with sickle cell disease who ingested kitchen cleanser. With oral zinc 225 mg twice daily, serum zinc increased from 27 µg/ml to 100 µg/ml and pica was terminated.

A critical review (Youdim 1982) of clinical reports reveals that the majority of authors verify the efficacy of iron repletion in abolishing both food and nonfood pica associated with iron-deficiency states for different etiology. This suggests a possible common pathway such as mediation by decreased CNS dopamine neurotransmission reported to result from iron-deficiency states.

Pharmacologic Treatment of Pica

There have been no specific pharmacologic treatment studies of pica. Although Jakab (1984) reported thioridazine reduced pica as well as a number of other problematic behaviors (e.g., aggression in hospitalized mentally retarded patients), Danford and Huber (1981) noted an increased pica incidence (39 percent) in a subgroup of institutionalized retarded patients receiving neuroleptic medication in contrast to a 25 percent incidence of picas in a medication-free group. Does diminished dopaminergic neurotransmission promote pica? In animal studies, Youdim (1985) reported a 50 percent diminution of CNS dopamine (D_2) receptors with iron depletion. Decreased dopamine transmission resulting from both iron deficiency and administration of neuroleptics may be a critical determinant in the appearance and maintenance of pica. A pharmacologic approach that increases dopaminergic transmission (e.g., bromocriptine, ritalin) may be worthy of investigation in a subgroup of patients in whom pica is both refractory and hazardous.

Psychosocial Treatment

Lourie (1977) recommended a psychoeducational treatment approach. Mothers would be instructed about the danger of pica, which could result in lead poisoning. Social workers would provide a social support system for mothers who may be depressed, meet their dependency needs, and help mothers be more available to their children. Strategies of prohibiting pica would be taught to mothers so that they would spend more time with their children and interrupt pica behavior. Lourie et al. (1963) suggested that identifying families at high risk for pica could aid in primary prevention.

Chapter 76

Atypical Eating Disorders

Atypical eating disorders are defined by DSM-III (American Psychiatric Association 1980) as "a residual category for eating disorders that cannot be adequately classified in any of the previous categories." In this chapter, I will examine the historical use of the term *atypical eating disorders*, present data on a series of atypical patients, propose an expanded definition of the term, and discuss implications of this diagnostic category for practice and theory.

King (1963) noted the heterogeneity of "secondary" anorexia nervosa patients, a term he used for patients who suffered weight loss in the course of other psychiatric syndromes such as depressive illness. Bruch (1973) discussed her concept of the differences between primary and atypical anorexia nervosa. Primary anorexia nervosa required a disturbance in body image and inaccurately perceived stimuli from within. Primary anorexia nervosa patients manifested a pervasive sense of ineffectiveness, pursued thinness, and took pride in weight loss. "Atypical anorexia nervosa" patients "do not want to stay thin, or value it only secondarily as a means of coercing others" (Bruch 1973). They did not pursue thinness. Some of her cases illustrating this concept of atypical anorexia nervosa suffered from depressive illness, personality disorders, or a schizophrenic-like illness, making her use of the term *atypical* functionally similar to King's secondary anorexia nervosa.

In the psychiatric literature since that time, the term *atypical anorexia nervosa* has been used in a variety of ways, usually for patients who differ from the common presentation of a young female who loses substantial weight. McFarlane et al. (1982) employed atypical anorexia nervosa for a male patient. Button and Whitehouse (1981) found that 5 percent of postpubertal females developed a "subclinical" form of anorexia nervosa. This is probably the most common current use of the term *atypical anorexia nervosa*: to describe a mild version of anorexia nervosa, not meeting full diagnostic criteria. Halmi (1983) critically examined the classification of eating disorders, noting controversies and problems.

The existence of an atypical category of eating disorder implies the presence of typical patients. Since the definition of a typical patient has varied over the years, the atypical group has varied along with these changes. Andersen (1977) described various categories of atypical anorexia nervosa patients based on their relationship to the Feighner criteria. With the introduction of the DSM-III criteria for eating disorders, the atypical category, therefore, has had to be redefined.

The definitions used in this chapter are as follows: primary anorexia nervosa and primary bulimia refer to patients who meet DSM-III criteria. Atypical anorexia nervosa or atypical bulimia describe patients with essential similarity to the primary patients who fail to fulfill all diagnostic criteria. For example, a patient who meets DSM-III criteria for anorexia nervosa but has lost only 14 percent of body weight is atypical. Secondary anorexia nervosa or bulimia describe patients with weight loss or binge eating due to a clearly defined underlying psychiatric or medical condition other than anorexia nervosa or bulimia. For example, weight loss from a depressive illness is due to secondary anorexia, implying a true loss of appetite.

Of the 241 consecutive referrals to the Eating and Weight Disorders Clinic of Johns Hopkins Hospital, 181 (75 percent) met DSM-III criteria for anorexia nervosa or bulimia and 22 (9 percent) were classified as having an atypical eating disorder.

When the demographic features of the atypical patients were contrasted with classic anorexia nervosa, restricting type, there were no significant differences. There was also no difference regarding duration of illness or past treatment experience. Interestingly, no male patients were classified as having an atypical eating disorder. They either had typical cases or another disorder.

Patients with atypical eating disorders reached a minimum of 81 percent of their ideal body weight, whereas classic patients reached a low of 72 percent, a statistically significant difference. Atypical patients were much more likely (40 percent) to have regular menstrual periods present at the time of referral than were classic patients (10 percent). Significantly fewer atypical patients (5 percent) were referred for inpatient hospitalization after consultation (5 percent) versus classic patients (32 percent).

Most of the patients in this series classified as having atypical eating disorders suffered from a mild case of anorexia nervosa. A few experienced occasional bulimic symptoms. The common psychopathologic features of all of these patients were fear of fatness, pursuit of thinness, and preoccupation with body weight and the caloric content of foods. Their weight loss was not sufficient to qualify for a diagnosis of anorexia nervosa. They all experienced distress from intrusive thoughts about food, feared fatness, and suffered uncomfortable physical symptoms, most often feeling cold or weak.

It may be worth considering why any diagnostic category should be proposed for these atypical patients. Individuals with atypical eating disorders have a higher than average risk for developing a classic eating disorder. Early identification of a vulnerable person with a mild version of the disease may prevent this occurrence. There is a similarity of symptomatology in these atypical patients. They live lives preoccupied with concern about weight, and they manifest abnormal eating behaviors. In short, they have symptoms of an illness.

On the one hand, patients with atypical eating disorders differ from the weight-preoccupied individuals so prevalent in our society (Garner et al. 1984). Atypical patients go beyond conventional overconcern with weight. Many suffer from physiologic abnormalities consequent to weight loss (e.g., absent or irregular menstrual periods). Their mental lives alternate between adequate self-esteem when weight is lost and self-criticism when weight increases or binges occur.

On the other hand, there are reasons for not grouping these patients together with those having the full syndrome of anorexia nervosa or bulimia nervosa. A number of these individuals with early or mild signs of illness may soon return to normal. A person's sense of identity as well as practical concerns for job and schooling may be improved by not having ever received a diagnosis of anorexia nervosa or bulimia nervosa.

Table 1 describes a suggested classification for atypical eating disorders. The common features of this category are a fear of fatness, pursuit of thinness, preoccupation with body size and shape, and abnormal behavior toward food. By following a group of atypical patients separately from those meeting DSM-III criteria for anorexia nervosa or bulimia, we may better understand their prognosis.

There are a number of implications for clinical practice growing out of a diagnostic category of atypical eating disorders. Ideally, all vulnerable individuals in the future will be identified in the early "atypical" states of their eating disorders so they would never go on to meet the full criteria. The category of atypical patients summarizes a combination of mild chronic subclinical cases, partially recovered former classic patients, and early diagnosed individuals that are recognized before severe illness is established.

Table 1. Proposed Atypical Eating Disorders Classification

General Criteria for categories 307.50–307.56:
1. Fear of fatness on mental state examination.
2. Mental preoccupation with pursuit of thinness.
3. Abnormal behavior toward food.
4. Significant dissatisfaction with body size and shape.

307.50 Mild symptoms of anorexia nervosa, without a past episode, but not meeting full criteria. For example:
    a. Insufficient weight loss or after-dieting weight above average.
    b. Menses still present in a female.
    c. Episode less than three months in duration.

307.51 Mild symptoms of anorexia nervosa, with history of anorexia nervosa (residual, chronic anorexia nervosa).

307.52 Bulimia nervosa symptoms, not meeting full criteria. For example, less frequent episodes, and/or persisting for fewer months than stated in criteria.

307.53 Bulimia nervosa symptoms, not meeting full criteria, with past history of bulimia (residual, chronic bulimia).

307.54 Rumination after childhood, associated with fear of fatness.

307.55 Compulsive repetitive dieting or severe preoccupation with fear of weight gain, without substantial weight loss or binge eating.

307.56 Other eating disorders, not meeting above criteria or for anorexia nervosa, bulimia, pica, or rumination disorder of infancy.

These patients are not distinguishable in advance by predieting weight or degree of weight loss desired.

Treatment Focus

Treatment of atypical eating disorders should be carried out using appropriate modifications of techniques for patients meeting full criteria for anorexia nervosa or bulimia. Necessary treatment modifications grow out of the milder nature of these disorders (e.g., the lack of severe lowering of weight). The treatment of the underlying common psychopathologic themes of fear of fatness and pursuit of thinness will be much the same, however, with a balance maintained between the psychodynamic, cognitive, behavioral, and nutritional aspects of therapy.

Most patients with atypical eating disorders will be treated on an outpatient basis with techniques similar to those for outpatients with classic anorexia nervosa or bulimia. The outpatient setting is less structured than an inpatient milieu. Much more, therefore, depends on the patient's motivation and ability to structure the self and the environment in a fully controlled in-hospital setting. On the positive side, however, this means that treatments can be successfully learned in a realistic, everyday setting, and the transition between an inpatient service and an outpatient world never needs to be made. The treatment begins with a focus on nutritional rehabilitation and interruption of any binge-purge behavior. It then proceeds to a logical sequence of psychotherapeutic methods, with some attention to behavioral programs and psychopharmacology as needed. Some relapses and plateaus are common and should not be taken as a source of discouragement for either patient or therapist.

Nutritional rehabilitation means essentially the development of a normal weight, normal patterns of eating, and normal kinds of food eaten. Good record keeping is essential for outpatient treatment. Patients are asked to record on a 3 × 5 card the following items surrounding each meal or ingestion of food: time, location, food eaten, events (including binge or purge behavior), and feelings. Each outpatient session begins by looking at these cards. The purpose is not to provoke guilt or criticism but rather to look at how well the patient was able to carry out the agreements made in the previous session. Here the psychotherapeutic emphasis is on support and on psychoeducation. By looking at this record keeping with the therapist, patients often become aware of patterns that they previously had not seen (e.g., the linking of anxiety about an upcoming test with food restriction or a binge episode). Where weight is under a healthy point, a weight gain of 1 to 2 lb/week is realistic. The hospital nutritionist or a nutritional consultant can prescribe for the patient a set number of calories of well-balanced food groups to meet these nutritional goals. Vegetarian patterns of eating are not allowed, although a moderate number of individual preferences are respected. Assurance is given that the patient will not be allowed to become overweight.

With younger patients especially, the family occupies a larger role in food preparation and supervision of eating than with an adult. The family is seen at the beginning of treatment and, depending on the age of the patient, may be seen for a small part of each session and occasionally as a family unit once a month or so. Sessions generally take place once a week but at times of stress or crisis may be two or three times a week.

The term *weight restoration* is used rather than *weight gain* because, in fact, the emphasis is not on gaining weight, which in our society usually means becoming overweight, but on restoring what has been lost. The psychotherapeutic work that begins with support and education gradually shifts to resolution of alexithymia and cognitive therapy principles. Many individuals with atypical eating disorders are intellectualized and find it hard to identify specific feeling states. They come to learn that by identifying these specific feelings, fear of fatness will diminish because this global term of dysphoria serves as a nonspecific indicator of any kind of emotional distress. The "reward" for a specific identification of dysphoric mood states is that they can do something about anxiety, anger, or boredom that will lead to relief. Patients come to understand irrational kinds of thinking and their own particular faulty defenses such as intellectualization, all-or-none reasoning, and projection.

Finally, as treatment enters the three- to six-month phase, the emphasis often shifts to a more psychodynamic one. The focus on feelings and cognitive therapy principles gradually leads to a mutual understanding of the purpose the illness serves. Effective treatment always involves an attempt to understand a central dynamic formulation for the illness. By this is meant a comprehensive integrating view of the purpose the illness serves. Patients come to understand that the goal is not to take away the illness but to make it unnecessary.

No single psychopharmacologic agent has been found to be generally useful for the treatment of mild cases of anorexia nervosa. A major mistake in treatment occurs when clinicians assume that these eating disorders involve fundamental problems in appetite instead of recognizing the central issues of fear of development and fear of loss of control. There is developing interest in the possibility of using tricyclic antidepressants. Several convincing studies have been done showing consistent improvement with an integration of behavioral and cognitive psychotherapeutic techniques for bulimia nervosa. At the present time, clinicians would be well advised to treat patients on an individual basis, emphasizing psychotherapeutic and behavioral aspects and selectively employing antidepressants. Newer medications such as fluoxetine may be of special benefit.

Another area of developing interest is the interrelationship between mood disorders and eating disorders. There is a large overrepresentation of mood disorders in the families of patients with mild or severe cases of eating disorders. There are complex, multiple interactional effects between mood disorders and eating disorders. The best indication for antidepressants is in eating disorder patients who have diagnosable major depressive illness despite restoration of weight and normalization of binge-purge behavior.

A positive prognostic outlook is warranted in the treatment of atypical eating disorders. Many of these illnesses represent episodes of attempting to cope with crises in development, with uncomfortable mood states, and with intrapsychic conflicts. The therapy of these patients has behind it the knowledge that, in general, these are young people with good futures ahead of them.

A balance must be struck between symptom reduction and the enhancement of growth and development. The real goal of treatment of symptoms is to help individuals resume their stages of development. Successful resolution of an atypical eating disorder may leave a person in a state of greater preparation for successful living.

The best form of treatment is often a preventative approach, and efforts are being made in elementary and high school populations to prevent these disorders. Educators must be taught to recognize early cases of eating disorders and refer them to appropriate facilities. At the same time, students must be encouraged to develop self-esteem based on an appreciation of their human qualities rather than on the achievement of excess slimness.

There are implications for the theoretical understanding of eating disorders resulting from treatment efforts of this category. The need for this kind of category reflects the lack of fundamental understanding of the nature of eating disorders. The conceptualization of atypical eating disorders varies pari passu with the definition of typical eating disorders. Long-term follow-up may help increase our understanding of the spectrum nature of eating disorders (Andersen 1983).

References

Section 6
Eating Disorders

Abraham K: A Short Study of the Development of the Libido Viewed in the Light of Mental Disorders (1924): Selected Papers. New York, Basic Books, 1953

Abraham SF, Beaumont PJV: How patients describe bulimia or binge-eating. Psychol Med 12:625–635, 1982

Agras WS, Werne J: Behavior therapy in anorexia nervosa: a data-based approach to the question, in Controversy in Psychiatry. Edited by Brady JP, Brodie HKH. New York, WB Saunders Co, 1978

Agras WS, Barlow DH, Chaplin NH, et al: Behavior modification of anorexia nervosa. Arch Gen Psychiatry 30:279–286, 1974

Agras WS, Dorian B, Kirkley BG, et al: Imipramine in the treatment of bulimia: a double-blind controlled study. International Journal of Eating Disorders 1:29–38, 1987

Alexander F: Über den Einfluss psychischer Faktoren auf gastrointestinale Störungen. Int Z ärztl Psychoanal 21:188–219, 1935

Allan JD, Woodruff J: Starch gastrolith: report of a case of obstruction. N Engl J Med 268:776–778, 1983

American Psychiatric Association: Diagnostic and Statistical Manual of Mental Disorders, 3rd ed. Washington, DC, American Psychiatric Association, 1980

American Psychiatric Association: Diagnostic and Statistical Manual of Mental Disorders, 3rd ed, revised. Washington, DC, American Psychiatric Association, 1987

Andersen AE: Atypical anorexia nervosa, in Anorexia Nervosa. Edited by Vigersky RA. New York, Raven Press, 1977, pp 11–19

Andersen A: Anorexia nervosa and bulimia: a spectrum of eating disorders. J Adolesc Health Care 4:15–21, 1983

Andersen AE: Practical Comprehensive Treatment of Anorexia Nervosa and Bulimia. Baltimore, Johns Hopkins University Press, 1985

Andersen AE: Uses and potential misuses of antianxiety agents in the treatment of anorexia nervosa and bulimia nervosa, in The Role of Drug Treatments for Eating Disorders. Edited by Garfinkel PE, Garner DM. New York, Brunner/Mazel, 1987, pp 59–74

Ansell JE, Wheby MS: Pica: its relation to iron deficiency: a review of the recent literature. Virginia Medical Monthly 99:951–954, 1972

Anyan WR: Changes in erythrocyte sedimentation rate and fibrinogen during anorexia nervosa. J Pediatr 85:525–527, 1974

Anyan WR, Schowalter JE: A comprehensive approach to anorexia nervosa. J Am Acad Child Psychiatry 22:122–127, 1983

Arcasoy A, Cavdar AP, Babcan E: Decreased iron and zinc absorption in Turkish children with iron deficiency and geophagia. Acta Haematol (Basel) 60:76–84, 1978

Ausman J, Ball TS, Alexander D: Behavior therapy of pica with a profoundly retarded adolescent. Ment Retard 12:16–18, 1974

Ayllon T, Haughton MA, Osmond HO: Chronic anorexia nervosa: a behaviour problem. Canadian Psychiatric Association Journal 9:147–154, 1964

Azerrad J, Stafford RL: Restoration of eating behavior in anorexia nervosa through operant conditioning and environmental manipulation. Behav Res Ther 7:165–171, 1969

Bachrach AJ, Erwin WJ, Mohr JP: The control of eating behavior in an anorexic by operant conditioning techniques, in Case Studies in Behavior Modification. Edited by Ullman LP, Krasner I. New York, Holt, Rinehart & Winston, 1965

Baltrop D: The prevalence of pica. Am J Dis Child 112:116–123, 1966

Barcai A: Lithium in adult anorexia nervosa: a pilot report on two patients. Acta Psychiatr Scand 55:97–101, 1977

Barlow J, Blouin J, Blouin A, et al: Treatment of bulimia with desipramine: a double-blind crossover study. Can J Psychiatry in press

Barmann BC: Use of contingent vibration in the treatment of self-stimulatory hand-mouthing and ruminative vomiting behavior. J Behav Ther Exp Psychiatry 11:307–311, 1980

Bateson EM, Leboy T: Clay eating by aboriginals of the Northern Territory. Med J Aust 1:1–3, 1978

Beaumont PJV, Abraham SF, Argall WJ, et al: The onset of anorexia nervosa. Aust NZ J Psychiatry 12:145–149, 1978

Beavers WR, Voeller MN: Family models: comparing and contrasting the Olson Circumplex Model with the Beavers System Model. Fam Process 22:85–97, 1983

Beck AT: Cognitive Therapy and the Emotional Disorders. New York, International Universities Press, 1976

Beck AT, Rush AJ, Shaw BF, et al: Cognitive Therapy of Depression: A Treatment Manual. New York: Guilford, 1979

Becker JV, Turner SM, Sajwaj TE: Multiple behavioral effects of the use of lemon juice with a ruminating toddler-age child. Behavior Mod 2:267–278, 1978

Bemis KM: A comparison of functional relationships in anorexia nervosa and phobia, in Anorexia Nervosa: Recent Developments. Edited by Darby PL, Garfinkel PE, Garner DM, et al. New York, Alan R Liss, 1983

Bemis KM: "Abstinence" and "non-abstinence" models for the treatment of bulimia. International Journal of Eating Disorders 4:407–437, 1985

Benedek T: Dominant ideas and their relation to morbid cravings. Int J Psychoanal 17:40–56, 1936

Bergman P, Escalona SK: Unusual sensitivities in very young children. Psychoanal Study Child 3/4:333–352, 1949

Beumont PJV, George GCW, Smart DE: 'Dieters' and 'vomiters and purgers' in anorexia nervosa. Psychol Med 6:617–622, 1976

Biederman J, Herzog DB, Rivinus TM, et al: Amitriptyline in the treatment of anorexia nervosa: a double-blind, placebo-controlled study. J Clin Psychopharmacol 5:10–16, 1985

Binswanger L: The case of Ellen West, in Existence. Edited by May R, Angel E, Ellenberger H. New York, Basic Books, 1958

Bitar KN, Saffouri B, Makhlouf GM: Cholinergic and peptidergic receptors on isolated human antral smooth muscle cells. Gastroenterology 82:832–837, 1982

Blinder BJ: Developmental antecedants of the eating disorders: a reconsideration. Psychiatr Clin North Am 3:579–592, 1980

Blinder BJ: In Bulimia: The Binge Purge Compulsion. Edited by Cauwels JM. New York, Doubleday & Co, 1983, pp 77–79

Blinder BJ: Rumination: a benign disorder? International Journal of Eating Disorders 5:385–386, 1986

Blinder BJ, Bain N, Simpson R: Evidence for an opioid neurotransmission mechanism in adult rumination. Am J Psychiatry 143:254, 1986a

Blinder BJ, Youdim M, Goodman S: Iron, dopamine receptors and tardive dyskinesia. Am J Psychiatry 143:277–278, 1986b

Bliss EL, Branch CHH: Anorexia Nervosa: Its History, Psychology and Biology. New York, Paul Hoeber, 1960

Blouin AG, Blouin JA, Perez EL, et al: Treatment of bulimia with fenfluramine and desipramine. J Clin Psychopharmacol in press

Boskind-Lodahl M, White WC: The definition and treatment of bulimarexia in college women: A pilot study. Journal of the American College Health Association 27:84–97, 1978

Bowers TK, Eckert E: Leukopenia in anorexia nervosa: lack of increased risk of infection. Arch Intern Med 138:1520–1523, 1978

Bowlby E, Mostyn J: Attachment and Loss. New York, Basic Books, 1969

Brady JP, Rieger W: Behavioral treatment of anorexia nervosa, in Proceedings of the International Symposium on Behavior Modification. New York, Appleton-Century-Crofts, 1972

Brockbank EM: Merycism or rumination in man. Br Med J 1:421–427, 1907

Brogden RN, Carmine AA, Heel RC, et al: Domper idone. Drugs 24:360–400, 1982

Brown WR: Rumination in the adult: a study of two cases. Gastroenterology 54:933–939, 1968

Bruch H: Perceptual and conceptual disturbances in anorexia nervosa. Psychosom Med 24:187–194, 1962

Bruch H: Eating Disorders: Obesity, Anorexia Nervosa and the Person Within. New York, Basic Books, 1973

Bruch H: Psychological Antecedents of Anorexia Nervosa. Edited by Vigersky RA. New York, Raven Press, 1977

Bruch H: The Golden Cage: The Enigma of Anorexia Nervosa. Cambridge, Harvard University Press, 1978

Bruhn CM, Pangborn RM: Reported incidence of pica among migrant families. J Am Diet Assoc 58:417–20, 1971

Burchfield SR, Elich MS, Woods SC: Geophagia in response to stress and arthritis. Physical Behav 19:265–267, 1977

Button EJ, Whitehouse A: Subclinical anorexia nervosa. Psychol Med 11:509–516, 1981

Byrne WJ, Kangarloo H, Ament ME, et al: Antral dysmotility: an unrecognized cause of chronic vomiting during infancy. Ann Surg 193:521–525, 1981

Cameron JC: Lumeian lectures: on some forms of vomiting in infancy. Br Med J 1:872, 1925

Cantwell D, Sturnzenberger S, Burroughs J, et al: Anorexia nervosa: an affective disorder? Arch Gen Psychiatry 34:1087–1093, 1977

Caplin H, Ginsburg J, Beaconsfield P: Glycerol and treatment of anorexia. Lancet 1:319, 1973

Carryer HM, et al: Relative lymphocytosis in anorexia nervosa. Staff Meetings of the Mayo Clinic 34:426–429, 1959.

Casper RC: Treatment principles in anorexia nervosa. Adolesc Psychiatry 10:431–454, 1982

Casper RC: On the emergence of bulimia nervosa as a syndrome: a historical view. International Journal of Eating Disorders 2:3–16, 1983a

Casper RC: Some provisional ideas concerning the psychologic structure in anorexia nervosa and bulimia, in Anorexia Nervosa: Recent Developments in Research. Edited by Darby PL, Garfinkel PE, Garner DM, et al. New York, Alan R Liss, 1983b

Casper RC, Eckert EE, Halmi KA, et al: Bulimia: its incidence and clinical significance in patients with anorexia nervosa. Arch Gen Psychiatry 37:1030–1035, 1980

Casper RC, Offer D, Ostrof E: The self-image of adolescents with acute anorexia nervosa. J Pediatr 98:656–661, 1981

Casper RC, Halmi KA, Goldberg SC, et al: Anorexia nervosa and bulimia. Arch Gen Psychiatry 39:488–489, 1982

Cavdar AO, Arcasoy A: Hematologic and biochemical studies of Turkish children with pica. Clin Pediatr (Phila) 11:215–223, 1972

Cavdar AO: Geophagia in Turkey: iron and zinc deficiency, iron and zinc absorption studies and response to treatment with zinc in geophagia cases. Prog Clin Biol Res 129:71–79, 1983

Chabot DR: Historical perspective on working with the individual in family therapy. The Family 10:76–85, 1983

Chandra P, Rosner F: Olive craving in iron deficiency anemia. Ann Intern Med 78:973–974, 1973

Chatoor I, Dickson L: Rumination: a maladaptive attempt at self-regulation in infants and children. Clin Proc CHNMC 40:107–116, 1984a

Chatoor I, Dickson L, Einhorn A: Rumination: etiology and treatment. Pediatr Ann 13:924–929, 1984b

Chatoor I, Dickson L, Schaefer S, et al: Nonorganic failure to thrive: a developmental perspective. Pediatr Am 13:829–835, 38, 840–842, 1984c

Chatoor I, Schafer S, Dickson L, et al: Observational scales for the interactions between mothers and their infants or toddlers during feeding. Unpublished manuscript, 1985

Cinciripini PM, Kornblich SJ, Turner SM, et al: A behavioral program for the management of anorexia and bulimia. J Nerv Ment Dis 171:186–189, 1983

Clouse RE, Lustman PJ: Psychiatric illness and contraction abnormalities of the esophagus. N Engl J Med 309:1337–1342, 1983

Coffman DA: A clinically derived treatment model for the binge-purge syndrome, in The Binge-Purge Syndrome: Diagnosis, Treatment and Research. Edited by Hawkins RC, Fremouw WJ, Clement PG. New York, Springer, 1984

Cohen DF, Johnson WT, Caparulo BK: Pica and elevated blood lead level in autistic and atypical children. Am J Dis Child 130:47–48, 1976

Coltman CA Jr: Pagophagia and iron lack. JAMA 207:513–516, 1969

Coltman CA Jr: Pagophagia. Arch Intern Med 128:472–473, 1971

Connors ME, Johnson CL, Stuckey MK: Treatment of bulimia with brief psychoeducational group therapy. Am J Psychiatry 141:1512–1516, 1984

Cooper M: Pica. Springfield, Ill, Charles C Thomas, 1957

Cooper PJ, Fairburn CG: Binge-eating and self-induced vomiting in the community: a preliminary study. Br J Psychiatry 142:139–144, 1983

Crisp AH: Clinical and therapeutic aspects of anorexia nervosa: a study of 30 cases. J Psychosom Res 9:67–78, 1965

Crisp AH: A treatment regimen for anorexia nervosa. Br J Psychiatry 11:505–512, 1965

Crisp AH: Anorexia nervosa: 'feeding disorder,' 'nervous malnutrition,' or 'weight phobia'? World Review of Nutrition & Diet 12:452–504, 1970

Crisp AH: Anorexia Nervosa: Let Me Be. New York, Grune & Stratton, 1980

Crisp AH: Overview of the Eating Disorders. Presented at Second Annual Advances in Psychosomatic Medicine. Tampa, University of South Florida, 1984

Crisp AH, Fenton GW, Scotton L, et al: A controlled study of EEG in anorexia nervosa. Br J Psychiatry 128:549–556, 1968

Crisp AH, Hsu LKG, Harding B, et al: Clinical features of anorexia nervosa. J Psychosom Res 24:179–191, 1980

Crosby WH: Food pica and iron deficiency. Arch Intern Med 127:960–961, 1971

Dally PJ: Anorexia nervosa: long-term follow-up and effects of treatment. J Psychosom Res 11:151–155, 1967

Dally PJ: Anorexia Nervosa. New York, Grune & Stratton, 1969

Dally PJ: Treatment of anorexia nervosa. Br J Hosp Med 25:434, 437–438, 440, 1981

Dally PJ, Gomez J: Anorexia Nervosa. London: William Heinemann Medical Books, 1979

Dally PJ, Sargant W: A new treatment of anorexia nervosa. Br Med J 1:1770–1773, 1960

Dally P, Sargant W: Treatment and outcome of anorexia nervosa. Br Med J 2:793–795, 1966

Danford DE: Pica and nutrition. Annu Rev Nutr 2:303–322, 1982

Danford DE, Huber AM: Eating dysfunctions in an institutionalized mentally retarded population. Journal of Intake Research 2:281–292, 1981

Danford DE, Huber AM: Pica among mentally retarded adults. Am J Ment Defic 87:141–146, 1982

Danford DE, Smith JC Jr, Huber AM: Pica and mineral status in the mentally retarded. Am J Clin Nutr 35:958–967, 1982

Davis CM: Self selection of diet by newly weaned infants. Am J Dis Child 36:651–679, 1928

DeBakey M, Ochsner: Bezoars and concretions. Surgery 4:934–964, 1938

DiCagno L, Castello D, Savio MT: Un casodi colite ulcerosa assoc a pica. Minerva Pediatr 26:1768–1777, 1974

Dixon KN, Kiecolt-Glaser J: Group Therapy for Bulimia. Presented at the American Psychiatric Association Meeting. New Orleans, May 15, 1981

Djaldetti M, Pinkhas J, deVries A: Rumination and cardioesophageal relaxation associated with pernicious anemia. Gastroenterology 43:685–688, 1962

Dodds WJ, Dent J, Hogan WJ, et al: Mechanisms of gastroesophageal reflux in patients with reflux esophagitis. N Engl J Med 307:1547–52, 1982

Dubois A, Gross HA, Richter JE, et al: Effect of bethanecol on gastric functions in primary anorexia nervosa. Dig Dis Sci 26:598–600, 1981

Duker PC, Seys DM: Elimination of vomiting in a retarded female using restitutional overcorrection. Behav Ther 8:255–257, 1977

Eastwell HD: A pica epidemic: a price for sedentarism among Australian ex-hunter-gatherers. Psychiatry 42:264–273, 1979

Eckert ED: Behavior modification in anorexia nervosa: a comparison of two reinforcement schedules, in Anorexia Nervosa: Recent Developments in Research. Edited by Darby PL, Garfinkel PE, Garner DM, et al. New York, Alan R Liss, 1983

Eckert ED, Goldberg SC, Halmi KA, et al: Behavior therapy in anorexia nervosa. Br J Psychiatry 134:55–59, 1979

Eckert ED, Halmi KA, Casper R, et al: Depression in anorexia nervosa. Psychol Med 12:115–122, 1982

Edeleman B: Binge-eating in normal weight and overweight individuals. Psychol Reports 49:739–746, 1981

Edwards CH: Clay and cornstarch eating women. J Am Diet Assoc 35:810–815, 1959

Eissler KR: Some psychiatric aspects of anorexia nervosa. Psychoanal Rev 30:121–145, 1943

Ellis A: Reason and Emotion in Psychotherapy. New York, Stuart, 1962

Eubanks R: Role of the nutritionist, in Current Treatment of Anorexia Nervosa and Bulimia. Edited by Powers PS, Fernandez RC. New York, Karger, 1984, pp 180–107

Fairburn CG: A cognitive behavioral approach to the treatment of bulimia. Psychol Med 11:707–711, 1981

Fairburn CG: Binge-eating and bulimia nervosa. London, Smith, Koine & French Publications, 1982

Fairburn CG: The place of a cognitive-behavioral approach to the management of bulimia, in Anorexia Nervosa: Recent Developments. Edited by Darby PL, Garfinkel PE, Garner DM, et al. New York, Alan R Liss, 1983

Fairburn CG: Bulimia: its epidemiology and management, in Eating and Its Disorders. Edited by Stunkard AJ, Stellar E. New York, Raven Press, 1984, pp 235–258

Fairburn CG: Cognitive-behavioral treatment for bulimia, in A Handbook of Psychotherapy for Anorexia Nervosa and Bulimia. Edited by Garner DM, Garfinkel PE. New York, Guilford Press, 1984

Fairburn CG: Cognitive-behavioral treatment for bulimia, in Handbook of Psychotherapy for Anorexia Nervosa. Edited by Garner DM, Garfinkel PE. New York, Guilford Press, 1985

Fairburn CG, Cooper PJ: Self-induced vomiting and bulimia nervosa: an undetected problem. Br Med J 284:1153–1155, 1982

Fairburn CG, Cooper PJ: The clinical features of bulimia nervosa. Br J Psychiatry 144:238–246, 1984a

Fairburn CG, Cooper PJ: Rumination in bulimia nervosa. Br Med J 288:826–827, 1984b

Fairburn CG, Cooper PJ, Kirk J, et al: A comparison of two psychological treatments for bulimia nervosa. Behav Res Ther 24:629–643, 1986

Falk JR, Halmi KA: Amenorrhea in anorexia nervosa: examination of the critical body hypothesis. Journal of Biological Psychiatry 17:799–806, 1982

Fenichel O: Psychoanalytic Theory of Neurosis. New York, WW Norton & Co, 1945

Ferenczi S: Stages in the development of the sense of reality, in Sex and Psychology. New York, Basic Books, 1950

Fishbain D, Rotondo D: Single case study: foreign body ingestion associated with delusional beliefs. J Nerv Ment Dis 171:321–322, 1983

Flanagan CH: Rumination in infancy past and present. J Am Acad Child Psychiatry 16:140–149, 1977

Fleischer DR: Infant rumination syndrome. Am J Dis Child 133:266–269, 1979a

Fleischer DR: Nervous Vomiting in Infancy. Presented at the American Academy of Pediatrics, 1979b

Forbes GB: Relation of lean body mass to height in children and adolescents. Journal of Pediatric Research 6:32–37, 1972

Foxx RM, Martin ED: Treatment of scavenging behavior (coprophagy and pica) by overcorrection. Behav Res Ther 13:153–162, 1975

Fox RM, Snyder MS, Schroeder F: A food satiation and oral hygiene punishment program to suppress chronic rumination by retarded persons. J Autism Dev Disord 9:399–412, 1979

Frank JD: Persuasion and Healing, Baltimore, Johns Hopkins University Press, 1973

Freeman C, Barry F, Dunkeld-Turnbull J, et al: Controlled trial of psychotherapy for bulimia nervosa. Br Med J 296:521–525, 1988

Freud S: On Psychotherapy (1905). London, Hogarth Press, 1913

Friedin BD, Johnson HK: Treatment of a retarded child's feces smearing and coprophagic behavior. J Ment Defic Res 23:55–61, 1979

Frisch RE, McArthur JW: Menstrual cycles: fatness of a determinant of minimum weight for height necessary for their maintenance or onset. Science 185:949–951, 1974

Gaddini E: On imitation. Int J Psychoanal 50:475–484, 1969

Gaddini RD, Gaddini E: Rumination in infancy, in Dynamic Psychopathology in Childhood. Edited by Jessner L, Opavenstedt E. New York, Grune & Stratton, 1959

Garfinkel PE, Garner DM: Anorexia Nervosa: A Multidimensional Perspective. New York, Brunner/Mazel, 1982

Garfinkel PE, Kline SA, Stancer HC: Treatment of anorexia nervosa using operant conditioning techniques. J Nerv Ment Dis 157:428–433, 1973

Garfinkel PE, Garner DM, Moldofsky H: The role of behavior modification in the treatment of anorexia nervosa. J Pediatr Psychol 2:113–121, 1977

Garfinkel PE, Moldofsky H, Garner DM: The heterogeneity of anorexia nervosa: bulimia as a distinct subgroup. Arch Gen Psychiatry 37:1036–1040, 1980

Garfinkel PE, Garner DM, Rose J, et al: A comparison of characteristics in families of patients with anorexia nervosa and normal controls. Psychol Med 13:821–828, 1983

Garner DM: Cognitive therapy for bulimia nervosa. Adolesc Psychiatry 13:358–390, 1986

Garner DM, Bemis KM: A cognitive-behavioral approach to anorexia nervosa. Cognitive Therapy and Research 6:123–150, 1982

Garner DM, Bemis KM: Cognitive therapy for anorexia nervosa, in A Handbook of Psychotherapy for Anorexia Nervosa and Bulimia. Edited by Garner DM, Garfinkel PE. New York, Guilford Press, 1984

Garner DM, Garfinkel PE: Body image in anorexia nervosa: measurement, theory and clinical implications. Int J Psychiatry Med 11:263–284, 1981

Garner DM, Garfinkel PE: in A Handbook of Psychotherapy for Anorexia Nervosa and Bulimia. Edited by Garner DM, Garfinkel PE. New York, Guilford Press, 1984

Garner DM, Olmsted MP, Bohr Y, et al: The Eating Attitudes Test: psychometric features and clinical correlates. Psychol Med 12:871–878, 1982a

Garner DM, Garfinkel PE, Bemis KM: A multidimensional psychotherapy for anorexia nervosa. International Journal of Eating Disorders 1:3–46, 1982b

Garner DM, Garfinkel PE, O'Shaughnessy M: Clinical and psychometric comparison between bulimia in anorexia nervosa and bulimia in normal weight women, in Understanding Anorexia Nervosa and Bulimia. Editied by Ross Laboratories. Columbus, Ohio, Ross Laboratories, 1983

Garner DM, Garfinkel PE, Olmsted MP: An overview of the socio-cultural factors in the development of anorexia nervosa, in Anorexia Nervosa: Recent Development. Edited by Darby PL, Garfinkel PE, Garner DM, et al. New York, Alan R Liss, 1983a

Garner DM, Olmsted MP, Polivy J: Development and validation of a multidimensional eating disorder inventory for anorexia nervosa and bulimia. International Journal of Eating Disorders 2:15–34, 1983b

Garner DM, Olmsted MP, Polivy J, et al: Comparison between weight-preoccupied women and anorexia nervosa. Psychosom Med 46:255–266, 1984

Garner DM, Rockert W, Olmsted MP, et al: Psychoeducational principles in the treatment of bulimia and anorexia nervosa, in Handbook of Psychotherapy for Anorexia Nervosa and Bulimia. Edited by Garner DM, Garfinkel PE. New York, Guilford Press, 1985

Gedo JE, Goldberg A: Models of the Mind: A Psychoanalytic Theory. Chicago, University of Chicago Press, 1973

Geffen N: Rumination in man. American Journal of Digestive Disorders 11:963–972, 1966

Gelfan MC, Zarate A, Knepshield JH: Geophagia: a cause of life-threatening hyperkalemia in patients with chronic renal failure. JAMA 234:738–740, 1975

Geller JL: Treatment of anorexia nervosa by the integration of behavior therapy and psychotherapy. Psychother Psychosom 26:167–179, 1975

Gershon ES, Hamorit JR, Schreiber JL, et al: Anorexia nervosa and major affective disorders associated in families: a preliminary report, in Childhood Psychopathology and Development. Edited by Guze SB, Earls FJ, Barret JE. New York, Raven Press, 1983

Glassman AH, Schildkraut JJ, Orsulak PJ, et al: Tricyclic antidepressants: blood level measurements and clinical outcome: an APA task force report. Am J Psychiatry 142:155–162, 1985

Goldberg SC, Halmi KA, Eckert ED, et al: Cyproheptadine in anorexia nervosa. Br J Psychiatry 134:67–70, 1979

Goldfried MR: Systematic desensitization as training in self-control. J Consult Clin Psychol 37:228–234, 1971

Goldstein M: Family factors associated with schizophrenia and anorexia nervosa. Journal of Youth and Adolescence 10:385–405, 1981

Goodsitt A: Self-psychology and the treatment of anorexia nervosa, in A Handbook of Psychotherapy for Anorexia Nervosa and Bulimia. Edited by Garner DM, Garfinkel PE. New York, Guilford Press, 1984

Gormally J, Black S, Daston S, et al: Assessment of binge eating severity among obese persons. Addict Behav 7:47–55, 1982

Graham DM: Caffeine: its identity, dietary sources, intake and biological effects. Nutr Rev 36:97–101, 1978

Green RS, Rau JH: Treatment of compulsive eating disturbances with anticonvulsant medication. Am J Psychiatry 131:428–432, 1974

Green RS, Rau JH: The use of diphenylhydantoin in compulsive eating disorders: further studies, in Anorexia Nervosa. Edited by Vigersky RA. New York, Raven Press, 1977, pp 377–382

Greenway FL, Dahms WT, Bray GA: Phenytoin as a treatment of obesity associated with compulsive eating. Current Therapy Research 21:338–342, 1977

Griffin JB Jr: Rumination in a 7-year old child. South Med J 70:243–245, 1977

Grinc GA: A cognitive-behavioral model for the treatment of chronic vomiting. J Behav Med 5:135–141, 1982

Gross HA, Ebert MH, Faden VB, et al: A double-blind controlled trial of lithium carbonate in primary anorexia nervosa. J Clin Psychopharmacol 1:376–381, 1981

Gross H, Ebert MH, Faden VB, et al: A double-blind trial of delta-9-tetrohydrocannabinol in primary anorexia nervosa. J Clin Psychopharmacol 3:165–171, 1983

Gryboski JD: Fatroesophageal reglux, in Gastrointestinal Problems in the Infant, 2nd ed. Edited by Gryboski JD, Walker WA. Philadelphia, WB Saunders & Co, 1983

Guidano VF, Liotti G: Cognitive Processes and Emotional Disorders: A Structural Approach to Psychotherapy. New York, Guilford Press, 1983

Gull WW: Address in medicine delivered before annual meeting of the British Medical Association at Oxford. Lancet 2:171, 1868

Gull WW: Anorexia nervosa (apepsia hysterica, anorexia hysterica). Transactions of the Clinic of the Society of London 7:22–28, 1874

Gutelius MF: Children with pica: treatment of pica with iron given intramuscularly. Pediatrics 29:1018–1023, 1962

Gutelius MF: Treatment of pica with a vitamin and mineral supplement. Am J Clin Nutr 12:388–393, 1963

Gwirtsman HE, Roy-Byrne P, Yager J, et al: Neuroendocrine abnormalities in bulimia. Am J Psychiatry 140:559–563, 1983

Haley J: Problem Solving Therapy. San Francisco, Jossey-Bass, 1976

Hallsten EA Jr: Adolescent anorexia nervosa treated by desensitization. Behav Res Ther 3:87–91, 1965

Halmi KA: Eating disorders, in Comprehensive Textbook of Psychiatry, 3rd ed, vol 3. Edited by Freeman AM, Kaplan HI, Sadock BJ. Baltimore, Williams & Wilkins Co, 1980, pp 2603–2604, 3354

Halmi KA: Behavioral management of anorexia nervosa, in Treatment of Anorexia Nervosa and Bulimia. Edited by Garner DM, Garfinkel PE. New York, Guilford Press, 1984a, pp 147–160

Halmi KA: Somatic and behavioral treatment of anorexia nervosa, in Current Treatment of Anorexia Nervosa and Bulimia. Edited by Powers PS, Fernandez RC. New York, Karger, 1984b, pp 48–62

Halmi KA: Classification of the eating disorders. J Psychiatr Res 19:113–119, 1985

Halmi KA, Falk JR: Common physiological changes in anorexia nervosa. International Journal of Eating Disorders 1:16–27, 1981

Halmi KA, Sherman EN: Prediction of treatment response in anorexia nervosa, in Biological Psychiatry Today. Edited by Obiols, Ballus, et al. New York, Elsevier/North Holland, 1979, pp 609–614

Halmi KA, Powers P, Cunningham S: Treatment of anorexia nervosa with behavior modification. Arch Gen Psychiatry 32:93–96, 1975

Halmi KA, Falk JR, Schwartz E: Binge-eating and vomiting: a survey of a college population. Psychol Med 11:697–706, 1981

Halmi K, Eckert E, Falk J: Cyproheptadine: an antidepressant and weight-inducing drug for anorexia nervosa. Psychopharmacol Bull 1:103–105, 1983

Halmi KA, Eckert E, LaDu TJ, et al: Anorexia nervosa: treatment efficacy of cyproheptadine and amitriptyline. Arch Gen Psychiatry 2:177–181, 1986

Hambridge KM, Silverman A: Pica with rapid improvement with dietary zinc supplementation. Short Reports 567–568, 1973

Harper G: Varieties of parenting failure in anorexia nervosa: protection and parentectomy, revisited. Am Acad Child Psychiatry 22:134–139, 1983

Hasler JF: Parotid enlargement: a presenting sign of anorexia nervosa. Oral Medicine 6:567–573, 1982

Hatsukami D, Owen P, Pyle R, et al: Similarities and differences on the MMPI between women with bulimia and women with alcohol or drug abuse problems. Addict Behav 7:435–439, 1982

Hauserman N, Lavin P: Post-hospitalization continuation treatment of anorexia nervosa. J Behav Ther Exp Psychiatry 8:309–313, 1977

Hawkins RC, Clement PF: Binge eating: measurment problems and a conceptual model, in The Binge-Purge Syndrome: Diagnosis, Treatment and Research. Edited by Hawkins RC, Fremouw WJ, Clement PF. New York, Springer, 1984

Hawkins RC, Fremouw WJ, Clement PF: The Binge-Purge Syndrome: Diagnosis, Treatment and Research. New York, Springer, 1984

Hedblom JE, Hubbard FA, Andersen AE: Anorexia nervosa: a multidisciplinary treatment program for patient and family. Soc Work Health Care 7:67–86, 1981

Heinz ER, Martinez J, Haenggeli A: Reversability of cerebral atrophy in anorexia nervosa and Cushing's syndrome. J Comput Assist Tomogr 1:415–418, 1977

Hellstrom I: Oral complications in anorexia nervosa. Scand J Dent Res 85:71–76, 1977

Herbst JJ: Diagnosis and treatment of gastroesophageal reflux in children. Pediatric Review 5:75–79, 1983

Herbst JJ, Friedland GW, Zboralske FF: Hiatal hernia and rumination in infants and children. J Pediatr 78:261–265, 1971

Herbst JJ, Johnson DG, Oliveros FF: Gastroesophageal reflux with protein-losing enteropathy and finger clubbing. Am J Dis Child 130:1256–1258, 1976

Herman BH, Panksepp J: Effects of morphine and naloxone on separation distress and approach attachment: evidence for opiate mediation of social affect. Pharmacol, Biochem Behav 9:213–220, 1978

Hoffer W: Mouth, hand, and ego integration. Psychoanal Study Child 3/4:4955, 1949

Hoffer W: Development of the body ego. Psychoanal Study Child 5:18–23, 1950

Hoffman L: Enmeshment and the too richly cross-joined system. Fam Process 14:451–468, 1975

Hollowell JG, Gardner LI: Rumination and growth failure in male fraternal twin: association with disturbed family environment. Pediatrics 36:565–567, 1965

Holmgren S, et al: Phase 1 treatment for the chronic and previously treated anorexia bulimia nervosa patient. International Journal of Eating Disorders 3:17–36, 1984

Holt S, Form M, Grant S, et al: Abnormal gastric emptying in primary anorexia nervosa. Br J Psychiatry 139:550–552, 1981

Horne RL, Ferguson JM, Pope HG, et al: Treatment of bulimia with bupropion: a multi-center controlled trial. J Clin Psychiatry in press

Horney K: Neurosis and Human Growth: The Struggle Towards Self-realization. New York, WW Norton & Co, 1950

Hsu LKG: Outcome of anorexia nervosa: a review of the literature (1954–1978). Arch Gen Psychiatry 37:1041–1046, 1980

Hsu LKG: Treatment of bulimia with lithium. Am J Psychiatry 141:1260–1262, 1984

Hsu LK, Lieberman S: Paradoxical intention in the treatment of chronic anorexia nervosa. Am J Psychiatry 139:650–653, 1982

Hudson JI, Pope HG Jr, Jonas JM, et al: Family history study of anorexia nervosa and bulimia. Br J Psychiatry 142:133–138, 1983a

Hudson JI, Pope HG, Jonas JM, et al: Hypothalamic-pituitary-adrenal-axis hyperactivity in bulimia. Psychiatry Res 8:111–117, 1983b

Hudson JI, Pope HG, Jonas JM, et al: Treatment of anorexia nervosa with antidepressants. J Clin Psychopharmacol 5:17–23, 1985

Hughes PL, Wells LA, Cunningham CJ, et al: Treating bulimia with desipramine. Arch Gen Psychiatry 43:182–186, 1986

Huse DM, Lucas AR: Dietary treatment of anorexia nervosa. J Am Diet Assoc 83:687–690, 1983

Jacobs A: Non-haemotological efforts of iron deficiency. Clin Haematol 11:353–364, 1982

Jakab I: Short term effect of thioridazine tables versus suspension on emotionally disturbed retarded children. J Clin Psychopharmacol 4:210–215, 1984

Johanson AJ, Knorr NJ: L-dopa as treatment for anorexia nervosa, in Anorexia Nervosa. Edited by Vigersky RA. New York, Raven Press, 1977, pp 363–372

Johnson CL, Larson R: Bulimia: an analysis of moods and behavior. Psychosom Med 44:333–345, 1982

Johnson CL, Conners M, Stuckey M: Short-term group treatment for bulimia. International Journal of Eating Disorders 2:199–208, 1983

Johnson WG, Brief DJ: Bulimia. Behavioral Medical Update 4:16–21, 1983

Jolley SG, Herbst JJ, Johnson DG, et al: Patterns of postcibal gastroesophageal reflux in symptomatic infants. Am J Surg 138:946–949, 1979

Jollie H: Adv Pediatr 191:417–425, 1963

Jones E: Papers on Psychoanalysis (1911). Baltimore, William Wood & Co, 1938

Jourard S: The Transparent Self. New York, Van Nostrand, 1971

Kalucy RS, Crisp AH, Harding B: A study of 56 families with anorexia nervosa. Br J Med Psychol 50:381–395, 1977

Kanner L: Rumination, in Child Psychiatry, 3rd ed. Springfield, Ill. Charles C Thomas, 1957, pp 484–487

Kantor D, Lehr W: Inside the Family. San Francisco, Jossey-Bass, 1975

Kaplan AS, Garfinkel PE, Darby PL, et al: Carbamazepine in the treatment of bulimia. Am J Psychiatry 140:1225–1226, 1983

Kaplan AS, Garfinkel PE, Garner DM: Bulimia Treated with Carbamazepine and Imipramine: New Research. Presented at the 140th Annual Meeting of the American Psychiatric Association. Chicago, 1987

Keith L, Brown ER, Rosenberg C: Pica: The unfinished story background: correlations with anemia and pregnancy. Perspect Biol Med Summer 626–632, 1970

Keith L, Bartizal F, Brown E: Controlled amylophagia in female mice. Experientia 27:847–849, 1979

Kennedy SH, Piran N, Warsh JJ, et al: A trial of isocarboxazid in the treatment of bulimia. J Clin Psychopharmacol in press

Kenny FT, Solyom L: The treatment of compulsive vomiting through faradic disruption of mental images. Can Med Assoc J 105:43–48, 1985

Keys A, Brozek J, Henscel A, et al: The Biology of Human Starvation, vol 2. Minneapolis, University of Minnesota Press, 1950

King A: Primary and secondary anorexia nervosa syndromes. Br J Psychiatry 109:470–479, 1963

Kirkley BG, Schneider JA, Agras WS, et al: Comparison of two group treatments for bulimia. J Consult Clin Psychol 53:43–48, 1985

Klein DF, Zitrin CM, Woerner MG, et al: Treatment of phobias, II: behavior therapy and supportive psychotherapy: are there any specific ingredients? Arch Gen Psychiatry 40:139–145, 1983

Kog E, Pierloot R, Vandereycken W: Methodological considerations of family research in anorexia nervosa. International Journal of Eating Disorders 2:79–84, 1983

Kohut H: The Restoration of the Self. New York, International Universities Press, 1977

Koptagel G, Reimann F: An investigative on the psychopathology of pica and hypochromic anemia: 9th European Conference on Psychosomatic Research, Vienna 1972: Psychother Psychosom 22:351–358, 1973

Kris E: Some comments and observations on early autoerotic activities. Psychoanal Study Child 6:95–116, 1951

Kulka AM, Water RD, Fry CP: Mother-infant interaction as measured by simultaneous recording of physiological processes. J Am Acad Child Psychiatry 5:496–503, 1966

Lacey JH: The bulimic syndrome at normal body weight: reflections on pathogenesis and clinical features. International Journal of Eating Disorders 2:59–62, 1982

Lacey JH: Bulimia nervosa, binge-eating and psychogenic vomiting: a controlled treatment study and long-term outcome. Br Med J 286:1609–1613, 1983

Lacey JH, Crisp AH: Hunger, food intake and weight: the impact of clomipramine on a refeeding anorexia nervosa population. Postgrad Med J 56(suppl):79–85, 1980

Lampert F, Lau B: Bone marrow hypoplasia in anorexia nervosa. Eur J Pediatr 124:65–71, 1976

Lang PJ: Behavior therapy with a case of anorexia nervosa, in Case Studies in Behavior Modification. Edited by Ullman LP, Krasner L. New York, Holt, Rinehart & Winston, 1965

Lang PJ, Melamed BG: Case report: avoidance conditioning therapy of an infant with chronic ruminative vomiting. J Abnorm Psychol 74:1–8, 1969

Lanzkowsky P: Investigation into the etiology and treatment of pica. Arch Dis Chldhd 34:140–148, 1959

Lasegue C: De l'anorexie hysterique. Arch Gen de Med 385:1873

Lavigne JV, Burns WJ: Rumination in infancy: recent behavioral approaches. International Journal of Eating Disorders 1:7082, 1981

Lee NF, Rush AJ: Cognitive-behavioral group therapy for bulimia. International Journal of Eating Disorders 5:599–615, 1986

Leibowitz MR, Quitkin FM: Psychopharmacologic validation of atypical depression. J Clin Psychiatry 45:22–25, 1984

Leitch M, Escalona S: The reaction of infants to stress. Psychoanal Study Child 3/4:121–125, 1949

Leitenberg H, Gross J, Peterson J, et al: Analysis of an anxiety model and the process of change during exposure plus response prevention treatment of bulimia nervosa. Behavior Therapy 15:3–20, 1984

Leming PD, Reed DC, Martelo OJ: Magnesium carbonate pica: an unusual case of iron deficiency. Ann Intern Med 94:660, 1981

Levine DF, Wingate DL, Pfeffer JM: Habitual rumination: a benign disorder. Br Med J 287:255–256, 1983

Levy R: Mother-infant relations in the feeding situation, in Textbook of Gastroenterology and Nutrition in Infancy. Edited by Lebanthal E. New York, Raven Press, 1981

Lewis JM, Beavers WR, Gossett JT, et al: No Single Thread: Psychological Health in Family Systems. New York, Brunner/Mazel, 1976

Libnoch JA: Geophagia: an unusual pica in iron-deficience anemia. Am J Med 76:A69, 1984

Lidz T: The Family and Human Adaptation. London, Hogarth Press, 1976

Liebman R, Minuchin S, Baker L: An integrated treatment program for anorexia nervosa. Am J Psychiatry 131:432–436, 1974

Liebman R, Sargent J, Silver M: A family systems orientation to the treatment of anorexia nervosa. J Am Acad Child Psychiatry 22:128–133, 1983

Lindemann E: Symptomatology and management of acute grief. Am J Psychiatry 101:141–148, 1944

Linden W: Multicomponent behavior therapy in a case of compulsive binge-eating followed by vomiting. J Behav Ther Exp Psychiatry 11:297–300, 1980

Long CF: Rumination in man. Am J Med Sci 178:814–822, 1929

Long CG, Cordle CJ: Psychological treatment of binge-eating and self-induced vomiting. Journal of Medical Psychology 55:139, 1982

Loro A: Binge eating: a cognitive-behavioral treatment approach, in The Binge-Purge Syndrome: Diagnosis, Treatment and Research. Edited by Hawkins RC, Fremouw WJ, Clement PF. New York, Springer, 1984

Loro A, Orleans CS: Binge eating in obesity: preliminary findings and guidelines for behavioral analysis and treatment. Addict Behav 6:155–166, 1981

Lourie RS: Experience with therapy of psychosomatic problems in infants, in Psychopathology of Childhood. Edited by Hoch PH, Zubin J. New York, Grune & Stratton, 1954

Lourie RS: Pica and poisoning. Am J Orthopsychiatry 41:697–699, 1977

Lourie RS, Layman EM, Millican FK: Why children eat things that are not food. Children 10:143–146, 1963

Lucas AR: Toward the understanding of anorexia nervosa as a disease entity. Mayo Clin Proc 56:254–264, 1981

Lucas AR, Duncan JW, Piens V: The treatment of anorexia nervosa. Am J Psychiatry 133:1034–1038, 1976

Macalpine C, Singh NN: Pica in institutionalized mentally retarded persons. J Ment Defic Res 30:171–178, 1986

Mahler MS, Pine T, Bergman A: The Psychological Birth of the Human Infant. New York, Basic Books, 1975

Mahoney MJ: Cognitive and Behavior Modification. Cambridge, Ballinger, 1974

Mahoney MJ, Mahoney K: Permanent Weight Control. New York, WW Norton & Co, 1976

Marcus LC, Stambler M: Visceral larva migraines and eosinophilia in an emotionally disturbed child. J Clin Psychiatry 40:139–140, 1979

Marholin D II, Luiselli JK, Robinson M, et al: Response contingent taste-aversion in treating chronic ruminative vomiting of institutionalized profoundly retarded children. J Ment Defic Res 24:47–56, 1980

Marks JW: Lettuce craving and iron deficiency. Ann Intern Med 79:612, 1973

Marlatt G, Gordon J: Relapse Prevention. New York, Guilford Press, 1983

Marmor J: Common operational factors in diverse approaches to behavior change, in What Makes Behavior Change Possible. Edited by Burton A. New York, Brunner/Mazel, 1976

Masserman JH: Psychodynamisms in anorexia nervosa and neurotic vomiting. Psychoanal Q 10:211–242, 1941

Masterson J: Primary anorexia nervosa in the borderline adolescent: an object-relations review, in Borderline Personality Disorders: The Concept, the Syndrome, the Patient. Edited by Hartocollis P. New York, International Universities Press, 1977, pp 475–494

Mavissakalian M: Anorexia nervosa treated with response prevention and prolonged exposure. Behav Res Ther 20:27–31, 1982

McArney ER: Rib fractures in anorexia nervosa. J Adolesc Health Care 4:40–43, 1983

McFarlane AH, Bellissimo A, Upton E: "Atypical" anorexia nervosa: treatment and management on a behavioral medicine unit. Psychiatr J Univ Ottawa 7:158–162, 1982

McGehee FT Jr, Buchanan GR: Trichophagia and trichobenzoar: etiologic role of iron deficiency. J Pediatr 946–948, 1980

Meichenbaum D: Therapist Manual for Cognitive Behavior Modification. Waterloo, Ont, University of Waterloo Press, 1974

Mengel CE, Carter WA, Horton ES: Geophagia with iron deficiency and hypokalemia. Arch Intern Med 114:470–474, 1964

Menking M, Wagnitz JG, Burton JJ, et al: Rumination: a near fatal psychiatric disease of infancy. N Engl J Med 280:802–804, 1969

Menolascino FJ: Primitive, atypical and abnormal-psychotic behavior in institutionalized mentally retarded children. J Autism Child Schizophr 3:49–64, 1972

Miller JG, Miller JL: General living systems theory and small groups, in Comprehensive Group Psychotherapy, 2nd ed. Edited by Kaplan HI, Sadock BJ. Baltimore, Williams & Wilkins Co, 1983

Miller PM: Behavioral Treatment of Alcoholism. New York, Pergamon Press, 1976

Miller S: Family therapy of the eating disorders, in Current Treatment of Anorexia Nervosa and Bulimia. Edited by Powers PS, Fernandez RC. New York, Karger, 1984, pp 92–112

Millican FK: Study of an oral fixation: pica. J Am Acad Child Psychiatry 7:79–107, 1968

Mills IH: Amitriptyline therapy in anorexia nervosa (letter). Lancet 1:687, 1976

Minuchin S, Rosman BL, Baker L: Psychosomatic Families: Anorexia Nervosa in Context. Cambridge, Harvard University Press, 1978

Mirin SM, Weiss RD: Abuse of opiate drugs, in Practitioners Guide to Psychoactive Drugs. Edited by Bassuk EL, Schoonover SE, Galenburg AJ. New York, Plenum Press, 1983

Mitchell D: Poison induced pica in rats. Physiol Behav 17:691–697, 1976

Mitchell D, Winter W, Morsiaki C: Conditioned taste aversions accompanied by geophagia: evidence for the occurrence of psychological factors in the etiology of pica. Psychosom Med 39:402–411, 1977a

Mitchell D, Laycock JD, Stephens WF: Motion sickness induced pica in the rat. Am J Clin Nutr 30:147–150, 1977b

Mitchell JE, Groat R: A placebo-controlled double blind trial of amytriptylene in bulimia. J Clin Psychopharmacol 4:186–193, 1984

Mitchell JE, Bantle JP: Metabolic and endocrine investigations in women of normal weight with the bulimia syndrome. Biol Psychiatry 18:355–365, 1983

Mitchell JE, Pyle RL, Eckert ED: Frequency and duration of binge-eating episodes in patients with bulimia. Am J Psychiatry 138:835–836, 1981

Mitchell JE, Pyle RL, Miner RA: Gastric dilatation as a complication of bulimia. Psychosomatics 23:96–98, 1982

Mitchell JE, Pyle RL, Eckert ED, et al: Electrolyte and other physiological abnormalities in patients with bulimia. Psychol Med 13:273–278, 1983

Mitchell JE, Hatsukami D, Goff G, et al: Intensive outpatient group treatment for bulimia, in A Handbook of Psychotherapy for Anorexia Nervosa and Bulimia. Edited by Garner DM, Garfinkel PE. New York, Guilford Press, 1984

Mitchell JE, Hatsukami D, Goff G, et al: An intensive outpatient group treatment program for patients with bulimia, in Handbook of Psychotherapy of Anorexia Nervosa and Bulimia. Edited by Garner DM, Garfinkel PE. New York, Guilford Press, in press

Mitikainen N: Spontaneous rupture of the stomach. Am J Surg 138:451–452, 1979

Mizes JS, Lohr JM: The treatment of bulimia (binge eating and self-induced vomiting): a quasi-experimental investigation of the effects of stimulus narrowing, self-reinforcement and self-control relaxation. International Journal of Eating Disorders 2:59–65, 1983

Moldofsky H, Jeuniewic N, Garfinkel PE: Preliminary report on metoclopramide in anorexia nervosa, in Anorexia Nervosa. Edited by Vigersky RA. New York, Raven Press, 1977, pp 373–376

Mordasini R, Klose G, Greten H: Secondary type II hyperlipoproteinemia in patients with anorexia nervosa. Metabolism 27:71–79, 1978

Morgan HG, Russell GFM: Value of family background and clinical features as predictors of long term outcome in anorexia nervosa: four year follow-up study of 41 patients. Psychol Med 5:355–371, 1975

Morgan HG, Purolog J, Welbourne J: Management and outcome in anorexia nervosa: a standardized prognostic study. Br J Psychiatry 143:282–287, 1983

Moss, J, Nissenblatt MJ, Inui TS: Successive picas. Ann Intern Med 80:425, 1974

Murray ME, Keele DK, McCarver JW: Behavioral treatment of rumination. Clin Pediatr (Phila) 15:591–596, 1976

Needleman HL, Waber D: Amitriptyline therapy in patients with anorexia nervosa (letter). Lancet 2:580, 1976

Neil JF, Horn TL, Himmelhoch JM: Psychotic pica, nicotinism, and complicated myocardial infarction. Diseases of the Nervous System 38:724–726, 1977

Nemiah JC: Alexithymia and psychosomatic illness. Journal of Continuing Education in Psychiatry 39:25–37, 1978

Norman DK, Herzog DB: Persistent social maladjustment in bulimia: a one-year follow-up. Am J Psychiatry 143:444–446, 1984

Nowlin NS: Anorexia nervosa in twins: case report and review. J Clin Psychiatry 44:101–105, 1983

Olson DH, Russell CS, Sprenkle DH: Circumplex model of marital and family systems, VI: theoretical update. Fam Process 22:69–83, 1983

Olynyk F, Sharpe DH: Mercury poisoning in paper pica. N Engl J Med 306:1056–1057, 1982

Ordman AM, Kirschenbaum DS: Cognitive-behavioral therapy for bulimia: an initial outcome study. J Consult Clin Psychol 53:305–313, 1985

Orleans CT, Barnett LR: Bulimarexia: guidelines for behavioral assessment and treatment, in The Binge-Purge Syndrome: Diagnosis, Treatment and Research. Edited by Hawkins RC, Fremouw WJ, Clement PF. New York, Springer, 1984

Perry MC: Cautopyreiophagia (letter). N Engl J Med 296:824, 1977

Pertschuk MJ, Forster J, Buzby G, et al: The treatment of anorexia nervosa with total parenteral nutrition. Biol Psychiatry 16:539–550, 1981

Piaget J: The Origins of Intelligence in Children. New York, International Universities Press, 1952

Pierloot R, Vandereycken W, Verhaest S: An inpatient treatment program for anorexia nervosa patients. Acta Psychiatr Scand 66:1–8, 1982

Pillay M, Crisp AH: The impact of social skills training within an established inpatient treatment programme for anorexia nervosa. Br J Psychiatry 139:533–539, 1981

Polivy J, Herman CP, Olmsted MP, et al: Restraint and binge eating, in The Binge-Purge Syndrome: Diagnosis, Treatment and Research. Edited by Hawkins RC, Fremouw WJ, Clement PF. New York, Springer, 1984

Pomerleau OF, Pomerleau CS: Break the Smoking Habit: A Behavioral Program for Giving up Cigarettes. Champaign, Ill, Research Press, 1977

Pope HG, Hudson JI: Treatment of bulimia with antidepressants. Psychopharmacology 78:176–179, 1982

Pope HG, Hudson JI, Jonas JM, et al: Bulimia treated with imipramine: a placebo-controlled, double-blind study. Am J Psychiatry 140:554–558, 1983

Pope HG, Hudson JI, Jonas JM: Antidepressant treatment of bulimia: preliminary experience and practical recommendations. J Clin Psychopharmacol 3:274–281, 1984

Powers PS, Powers HP: Inpatient treatment of anorexia nervosa. Psychosomatics 25:512–523, 1984

Prasad AS, Halstead JA, Nadim M: Syndrome of iron deficiency anemia. Am J Med 31:532–546, 1961

Pueschel SM: Pathogenetic considerations of pica in lead poisoning. Int J Psychiatry Med 8:13–24, 1977

Pyle RL, Mitchell JE, Eckert ED: Bulimia: a report of 34 cases. J Clin Psychiatry 42:60–64, 1981

Pyle RL, Mitchell JE, Eckert ED, et al: The incidence of bulimia in freshman college students. International Journal of Eating Disorders 2:75–85, 1983

Rast J, Johnston JM, Drum C, et al: The relation of food quantity to rumination behavior. J Appl Behav Anal 14:121–130, 1981

Rau JH, Green RS: Compulsive eating: a neuropsychologic approach to certain eating disorders. Compr Psychiatry 16:223–231, 1975

Rau JH, Green RS: Neurological factors affecting binge eating: body over mind, in The Binge-Purge Syndrome: Diagnosis, Treatment and Research. Edited by Hawkins RC, Fremouw WJ, Clement PF. New York, Springer, 1984

Rau JH, Struve FA, Green RS: Electroencephalographic correlated of compulsive eating. Clin Electroencephalography 10:180–189, 1979

Redmond DE, Swann A, Heninger GR: Phenoxybenzamine in anorexia nervosa. Lancet 2:307, 1976

Reynolds RD: Pagophagia and iron deficiency anemia. Ann Intern Med 69:435–440, 1968

Rich CL: Self-induced vomiting: psychiatric consideration. JAMA 239:2688–2689, 1978

Richmond JB, Eddy E, Green M: Rumination: a psychosomatic syndrome of infancy. Pediatrics 22:49–55, 1958

Richter CP: Total self-regulatory functions in animals and human beings. The Harvey Lecture Series 38:63–103, 1942/1943

Richter CP: Self-Selection of Diets: Essays in Biology. University of California Press, 1943

Riess D: The Family's Construction of Reality. Cambridge, Harvard University Press, 1981

Rimm DC, Masters JC: Behavioral Therapy. New York, Academic Press, 1979

Robboy MS, et al: The hypercarotenemia in anorexia nervosa: a comparison of vitamin

A and carotene levels in various forms of menstrual dysfunction protexia. Am J Clin Nutr 27:326–327, 1974

Robischon P: Pica practice and other hand-mouth behavior and children's developmental level. Nurs Res 20:4–16, 1971

Rolls BR: Palatability and preference: basic studies, in The Eating Disorders: Medical and Psychological Basis of Diagnosis and Treatment. Edited by Blinder BJ, Charlin BF, Goldstein RS. New York, PMA Press, 1988, pp 101–120

Rose JC, Garfinkel PE: A parents' group in the management of anorexia nervosa. Can J Psychiatry 25:228–233, 1980

Rosen J, Leitenberg H: Bulimia nervosa: treatment with exposure and response prevention. Behavior Therapy 13:117–124, 1982

Rosen J, Leitenberg H: Exposure plus response prevention treatment of bulimia, in A Handbook of Psychotherapy for Anorexia Nervosa and Bulimia. Edited by Garner DM, Garfinkel PE. New York, Guilford Press, 1984

Rosenberg M: Conceiving the Self. New York, Basic Books, 1979

Roy-Bryne P, Brenner K, Yager J: Group treatment for bulimia: a year's experience. International Journal of Eating Disorders 3:97–116, 1984

Ruckebusch Y, Bardon TH, Pairet M: Opioid control of the ruminant stomach motility: functional importance of mu, kappa and delta receptors. Life Sci 35:1731–1738, 1984

Russell GFM: The management of anorexia nervosa, in Symposium: Anorexia Nervosa and Obesity. Edited by Robertson RF. Edinburgh, Royal College of Physicians of Edinburgh, 1973, pp 44–62

Russell GFM: Bulimia nervosa: an ominous variant of anorexia nervosa. Psychol Med 9:429–448, 1979

Russell GFM, Szmukler GI, Dare C, et al: An evaluation of family therapy in anorexia nervosa and bulimia nervosa. Arch Gen Psychiatry 44:1047–1056, 1987

Sabine EJ, Yonace A, Farrington AJ, et al: Bulimia nervosa: a placebo-controlled double-blind therapeutic trial of mianserin. Br J Clin Pharmacol 15:195S–202S, 1983

Sacks S: Perversion of appetite (pica) a universal symptom of sideropenia. Revista Medica de Child 99:848–851, 1971

Sajwej T, Libet J, Agras S: Lemon-juice therapy: the control of life-threatening rumination in a six-month old infant. J Appl Behav Anal 7:557–563, 1974

Saleh JW, Lebwohl P: Metoclopramide-induced gastric emptying in patients with anorexia nervosa. Am J Gastroenterol 74:127–132, 1980

Salkind MR, Fincham J, Silverstone T: Is anorexia nervosa a phobic disorder? A psychophysiological enquiry. Biol Psychiatry 15:803–808, 1980

Schneider JA, Agras WS: A cognitive behavioral group treatment of bulimia. Br J Psychiatry 146:66–69, 1985

Schoettle UC: Pancreatitis. Am Acad Child Psychiatry 38:384–390, 1979

Schwartz RC, Barrett MJ, Saba G: Family therapy for bulimia, in Handbook of Psychotherapy for Anorexia Nervosa and Bulimia. Edited by Garner DM, Garfinkel PE. New York, Guilford Press, 1985

Selvini-Palazzoli M: Self-Starvation: From the Intrapsychic to the Transpersonal Approach to Anorexia Nervosa. New York, Aronson, 1978a

Selvini-Palazzoli M: Self-Starvation: From Individual to Family Therapy in the Treatment of Anorexia Nervosa. New York, Jason Aronson, 1978b

Sheagran TG, Mangurten HH, Brea F, et al: Rumination a new complication of neonatal intensive care. Pediatrics 66:551–555, 1980

Shimoda Y, Kitagawa T: Clinical and EEG studies on emaciation. Journal of Neural Transmission 34:195–204, 1973

Singh NN: Aversive control of rumination in the mentally retarded. Journal of Practical Approach to the Developmentally Handicapped 3:2–6, 1979

Singh NN, Manning PJ, Angell MJ: Effects of an oral hygiene punishment procedure on chronic rumination and collateral behaviors in monosygous twins. J Appl Behav Anal 15:309–314, 1982

Singh NN, Winton AS: Effects of a screening procedure on pica and collateral behaviors. J Behav Ther Exp Psychiatry 15:59–65, 1984

Singhi S, Singhi P, Adwani GB: Role of psychosocial stress in the cause of pica. Clin Pediatr (Phila) Peds 20:783–785, 1981

Slade PD: Towards a functional analysis of anorexia nervosa and bulimia nervosa. Br J Clin Psychol 21:167–179, 1982

Snowden CT, Sanderson BA: Lead pica produced in rats. Science 183:92–94, 1974

Sol P, Pelet B, Guignard JP: Extrapyramidal reactions due to domperidone. Lancet 2:802, 1980

Solomon A, Morrison D: Anorexia nervosa: dual transference therapy. Am J Psychother 26:480–489, 1972

Solyom L, Freeman RJ, Miles JE: A comparative psychiatric study of anorexia nervosa and obsessive neurosis. Can J Psychiatry 27:282–286, 1982

Sours JA: Starving to Death in a Sea of Objects. New York, Aronson, 1980

Spitzer R, Endicott J: Schedule for Affective Disorders and Schizophrenia. New York, New York Psychiatric Institute, 1978

Stagno S: An outbreak of taxoplasmosis linked to cats. Pediatrics 65:706–712, 1980

Stege P: Anorexia nervosa: review including oral and dental manifestations. J Am Dent Assoc 104:648–652, 1982

Stein GS, Hartshorn S, Jones J, et al: Lithium in a case of severe anorexia nervosa. Br J Psychiatry 140:526–528, 1982

Steinhausen HC, Glanville K: Follow-up studies of anorexia nervosa: a review of research findings. Psychol Med 13:239–249, 1983

Steketee G, Foa EG, Grayson JB: Recent advances in the behavioral treatment of obsessive-compulsive disorder. Arch Gen Psychiatry 39:1365–1371, 1982

Stoller J: Erotic vomiting. Arch Sex Behav 11:361—365, 1982

Strober M: The significance of bulimia in juvenile anorexia nervosa: an exploration of possible etiological factors. International Journal of Eating Disorders 1:28–32, 1981

Strober M, Salkin B, Burroughs J, et al: Validity of the bulimia restrictor distinction in anorexia nervosa: parental personality characteristics and family psychiatric morbidity. J Nerv Ment Dis 170:345–351, 1982

Stunkard A: New therapies for the eating disorders. Arch Gen Psychiatry 26:391–398, 1972

Sugarman A, Kurash C: The body as a transitional object in bulimia. International Journal of Eating Disorders 1:57–67, 1982

Swischuk LE, Hayden CK Jr, Tyson KR: Short segment pyloric narrowing: pylorospasm or pyloric stenosis? Pediatr Radiol 10:201–205, 1981

Szmukler GI: A study of family therapy in anorexia nervosa: some methodological issues, in Anorexia Nervosa: Recent Developments in Research. Edited by Darby PL, Garfinkel PE, Garner DM, et al. New York, Alan R Liss, 1983

Tec L: Nandrolone in anorexia nervosa (letter). JAMA 229:1423, 1974

Theander S: Anorexia nervosa: a psychiatric investigation of 94 female patients. Acta Psychiatr Scand [Suppl] 214:38–51, 1970

Thomas CW, Rising JL, Moore JK: Blood lead concentrations of children and dogs from 83 Illinois families. J Am Vet Med Assoc 169:1237–1240, 1976

Thurston J, Marks P: Electrocardiographic abnormality in patients with anorexia nervosa. Br Heart J 36:719–723, 1974

Tinker DE, Ramer JC: Anorexia nervosa: staff subversion of therapy. J Adolesc Health Care 4:35–39, 1983

Vandereycken W: Neuroleptics in the short-term treatment of anorexia nervosa: a double-blind, placebo-controlled, study with sulpiride. Br J Psychiatry 144:288–292, 1984

Vandereycken W, Meerman R: Has the family to be treated? in Anorexia Nervosa: A Clinician's Guide to Treatment. Edited by Vandereycken W, Meerman R. Berlin, Walter de Gruyter-Aldine, 1984

Vandereycken W, Pierloot R: Anorexia nervosa in twins. Psychother Psychosom 35:55–63, 1981

Vandereycken W, Pierloot R: Pimozide combinged with behavior therapy in the short-term treatment of anorexia nervosa: A double-blind, placebo-controlled, cross-over study. Acta Psychiatr Scand 66:445–450, 1982

Vandereycken W, Pierloot R: Drop-out during inpatient treatment of anorexia nervosa: a clinical study of 133 patients. Br J Med Psychol 56:145–156, 1983

Vigersky RA, Loriaux DL: The effect of cyproheptadine in anorexia nervosa: a double-blind trial, in Anorexia Nervosa. Edited by Vigersky RA. New York, Raven Press, 1977, pp 349–356

Waller JV, Kaufman RM, Deutsch F: Anorexia nervosa: a psychosomatic entity. Psychosom Med 2:3–16, 1940

Walsh BT, Stewart JW, Wright L, et al: Treatment of bulimia with monoamine oxidase inhibitors. Am J Psychiatry 139:1629–1630, 1982

Walsh BT, Stewart JT, Roose SP, et al: Treatment of bulimia with phenelzine. Arch Gen Psychiatry 41:1105–1109, 1984

Walsh BT, Gladis M, Roose SP, et al: Phenelzine vs. placebo in 50 patients with bulimia. Arch Gen Psychiatry 45:471–475, 1988

Wardle J, Beinart H: Binge-eating: a theoretical review. Br J Clin Psychol 20:97–109, 1981

Weiner H: Hypothalamic-pituitary-ovarian axis in anorexia and bulimia nervosa. International Journal of Eating Disorders 2:109–116, 1983

Wermuth BM, Davis KL, Hollister LE, et al: Phenytoin treatment of the binge-eating syndrome. Am J Psychiatry 134:1249–1253, 1977

Wertheim E: Family unit therapy and the science and typology of family systems. Fam Process 12:343–376, 1973

White WC, Boskind-White M: An experiental-behavioral approach to the treatment of bulimarexia. Psychotherapy: Theory, Research and Practice 18:501–507, 1981

Will D: Some techniques for working with resistant families of adolescents. J Adolesc 6:13–26, 1983

Wilson GT: Toward the understanding and treatment of binge eating, in The Binge-Purge Syndrome: Diagnosis, Treatment and Research. Edited by Hawkins RC, Fremouw WJ, Clement PF. New York, Springer, 1984

Wilson GT, Rossiter E, Kleifeld EI, et al: Cognitive-behavioral treatment of bulimia nervosa: a controlled evaluation. Behav Res Ther 24:277–288, 1986

Winokur A, March V, Mendels J: Primary affective disorder in relatives of patients with anorexia nervosa. Am J Psychiatry 137:695–698, 1980

Winton AS, Singh NN: Rumination in pediatric populations: a behavioral analysis. J Amer Acad Child Psychiatry 22:269–275, 1983

Wolchik SA, Weiss L, Katzman MA: An empirically validated, short-term psycho-educational group treatment program for bulimia. International Journal of Eating Disorders 5:21–34, 1986

Wolf MM, Birmbrauer J, Lawler, et al: The operant extinction, reinstatement and re-extinction of vomiting behavior in a retarded child, in Control of Human Behavior from Cure to Prevention, vol 2. Edited by Ulrich R, Statnik T, Mabry J. Glenview, Ill, 1970

Woods SC, Weisinger RS: Pagophagia in the albino rat. Science 169:1334–1336, 1970

Wooley OW, Wooley SC: The Beverly Hills eating disorder: the mass marketing of anorexia nervosa (editorial). International Journal of Eating Disorders 1:57–69, 1982

Wooley OW, Wooley SC, Dyrenforth SR: Obesity and women, II: a neglected feminist topic. Women's Studies International Quarterly 2:81–92, 1979

Wooley SC, Wooley OW: Intensive outpatient and residential treatment for bulimia, in A Handbook of Psychotherapy for Anorexia Nervosa and Bulimia. Edited by Garner DM, Garfinkel PE. New York, Guilford Press, 1984

Wright L, Thalassinos PA: Success with electric shock in habitual vomiting. Clin Pediatr (Phila) 12:594–597, 1973

Yager J: Family issues in the pathogenesis of anorexia nervosa. Psychosom Med 44:43–60, 1982

Yager J, Landsverk J, Lee-Benner K, et al: Bulimia Spectrum Disorder: The Glamour Survey. Presented at the American Psychiatric Association meeting. New York, 1983

Yates AJ, Sambrailo F: Bulimia nervosa: a descriptive and therapeutic study. Behav Res Ther 5:503–517, 1984

Youdim MBH: The effects of iron deficiency on brain biogenic monoamine biochemistry and function in the rat. Neuropharmacology 159:259–267, 1980

Youdim MBH: Iron deficiency-induced circadian rhythm reversal of dopaminergic-mediated behaviors and the thermoregulation in rats. Eur J Pharmacol 74:295–302, 1981

Youdim MBH: Brain iron and dopamine receptor function molecular pharmacology, in CNS Receptors from Molecular Pharmacology to Behavior. Edited by Mandel P, DeFeudis FV. New York, Raven Press, 1982

Youdim MBH: Brain iron metabolism: biochemical aspects in relationship to dopaminergic neurotransmission, in Handbook of Neurochemistry, vol 10: Pathological Chemistry. Edited by Lajitha A. New York, Plenum Press, 1985

Youdim MBH, Holzbauer M: Physiological Aspects of Oxidative Deamination of Monoamines: Monoamine Oxidase and Its Inhibition: Ciba Foundation Symposium 39 (New Series). Amsterdam, Elsevier, 1976

Ziolko HU: Hyperphage Esstoerungen. Munch. med. Wschr, 124:685–688, 1982

Zucker S: Disturbances in Cardiac Rhythm in Bulimia. Presented at the First International Conference on Eating Disorders. New York, April 8–9, 1984

1

Paraphilias and Gender Identity Disorders

Chapter 77

Pedophilia

The pedophilics illustrate, perhaps better than any other group, the danger of making any broad generalizations about sex offenders. . . . [T]here is probably no group of criminal offenders with which the court can get more help in arriving at proper disposition through a complete psychiatric evaluation than the pedophilics. (Guttmacher and Weihofen 1952, p. 115)

Traditionally it has been asserted that men engaging minors in sexual behavior are shy, passive, and unable to relate to adult women. The "passivity" of pedophiles has been assumed in clinical practice, although we do know some of them are sadistic and even kill their victims. Recent research suggests that violence may be a more common and integral part of the lives and sexual behavior of some pedophiles than previously believed (Langevin 1983, p. 135).

The essential feature of *pedophilia*—literally love of children—is the act or fantasy of engaging in sexual activity with prepubertal children as a repeatedly preferred or exclusive method of achieving sexual excitement (Table 1).

If the individual is an adult, the prepubertal children are at least 10 years younger than the individual. If the individual is a late adolescent, no precise age difference is required, and clinical judgment must take into account the age difference as well as the sexual maturity of the child (American Psychiatric Association 1980, pp. 271–272; 1987 pp. 284–285).

Pedophilia is a sustained erotic preference for the body shape of children (under age 11) as opposed to that of pubescence (ages 11–14 in females and 11–16 in males) and physically mature persons. In pedohebephilia there is an approximately equal

Table 1. Features of Pedophilia

Essential features	Associated features	Other features
• Identification with and narcissistic investment in immature sexual objects compensate for early deprivation	• The central and preemptive fantasy focuses on children as sexual objects	• Sexual activity with children is preferential and may occur repeatedly
• Control, domination, and seduction of the child compensate for early powerlessness		• The object choice may be homosexual or heterosexual, but it is almost always exclusively one or the other

Note.   Reproduced with permission from Kaplan and Sadock (1981, p. 558).

erotic attraction to the body shape of children and pubescence (Freund et al. 1984, p. 194).

> [P]edophilia is essentially a state in which an individual is predisposed to children for his or her sexual gratification. . . . We define pedophilia as occurring when an adult has a conscious sexual interest in children. (Arajii and Finkelhor 1986, p. 90)

Phenomenology

The primary phenomenological factors in the concept of pedophilia are the choice of the object (victim) and the nature of the act. These factors define the agent (offender) so that his personal and social characteristics can be studied (Mohr et al. 1964). The interaction of the three factors permits inferences on the natural history of the deviation and its consequences. As Langevin stated,

> [T]o understand the phenomenon it is necessary to define the preferences and perhaps first study men who have an obvious attraction for immature partners, that is, attraction to those with no pubic or axillary hair, smaller genitals, and lack of swelled breasts in females or lack of chest hair and beard in males. Then the more subtle differences in preferences for emerging adults could be studied. It is also important to distinguish heterosexual from homosexual pedophiles before attempting to define common features. This had not been done in practice so that theories and data combine both groups. (Langevin 1983, p. 264)

The Object (Victim)

The sexual object in pedophilia is a child. The sex of the child determines whether the act is heterosexual, homosexual, or undifferentiated (bisexual).

Most victims in heterosexual pedophilia are between the ages of 6 and 11 years, with the majority between 8 and 10 years. In homosexual pedophilia most victims are between 12 and 15, coinciding with puberty.

Pedophilic deviation requires a significant age difference between the offender and his object. A five-year difference is an absolute minimum in addition to the prepuberty-postpuberty dividing line.

The victim is seldom a total stranger to the offender. In most heterosexual cases the offender belongs to the close environment of the child. Most victims have known the offender prior to the sexual act. The degree of relationship tends to be closer in heterosexual cases than in homosexual offenses, at least in cases that come before the courts. Since offenders known to the child are more easily detected, they may be overrepresented in court samples. On the other hand, parents are less likely to charge family members and friends than strangers. Children may be more likely to report advances by strangers than by those closely associated with home. (See also The California Study 1953, 1954; and The Cambridge Study 1957)

The Act

Two things determine the nature of the sexual act, the act itself and the intention or direction of the act.

There is a wide range of sexual acts of pedophiles. Penetration and intravaginal coitus are among sexual acts with prepubertal children. The sexual acts in heterosexual pedophilia consist of exhibiting, voyeurism, and molesting. The nature of the act corresponds to the maturity of the victim rather than to that of the offender. The intent is erotic gratification.

Abel et al. found that

> Most (84.9 percent) had a hands-on experience (usually fondling, oral sex or less frequently, vaginal or anal intercourse); 13.4 percent expose themselves to children; 0.9 percent are attracted to particular parts of the child such as a fetish for boy's feet; 0.4 percent are voyeurs of children and 0.4 percent first have contact with a child during a sadistic attack upon a child. (Abel et al., unpublished manuscript, p. 5)

Sexual acts in male homosexual pedophilia are deviant by the choice of a male object. Homosexual acts, although more aggressive and orgasmic in nature, also are common among prepubertal and pubescent boys as part of adult-child exploration.

In heterosexual pedophilia the age of the victim and the nature of the offense provide a basis for diagnosis and classification of the deviant offender. The differentiation is less clear in homosexual pedophilia, where the acts appear much the same as for adult partners.

Homosexual pedophilia has a recidivism rate from 13 to 28 percent, second only to exhibitionism among the paraphilias. Persons committing heterosexual offenses against children have about half this recidivism rate. Recidivism increases from about 10 percent for first offenders to 33 percent for those with previous sexual convictions and 50 percent for those with previous sexual and nonsexual convictions (Mohr et al. 1964).

Christie et al., as quoted by Langevin (1985, p. 139), reported the incidence of violence used in sexual acts by pedophiles as 58 percent. This sample was from prison settings.

The Agent (Offender)

Data on the agent (offender) show most pedophilic behavior occurs in three distinct age groups with peaks at puberty, the mid to late thirties, and the mid to late fifties. According to the three age groups in which pedophilia occurs, we can classify the deviations as adolescent pedophilia, middle-age pedophilia, and senescent pedophilia. It was once assumed that senescent pedophilia was either the only or the predominant form of this deviation. The middle-age group consistently emerges as the largest one. However, the real peak of adolescent pedophilia may occur in a juvenile age group and will be reported. Most of the data come from institutions, and the young offender usually gets special treatment by the courts and escapes institutionalization.

The following classification of pedophiles is suggested by Tasto (1980, p. 816):

> Type I pedophiles are unable to interact socially with women because of anxiety or social deficits, or both. These individuals are sexually aroused by both normal objects and children.
>
> Type II pedophiles can interact socially with adult women but are unable to become sexually aroused by them. They are sexually aroused only by children.
>
> Type III pedophiles cannot interact socially with women and are unable to become sexually aroused by them. They are sexually aroused only by children.

The Site

Data on the site of the offense further emphasize the situational component of pedophilic acts, especially the heterosexual ones (Table 2). As the victim-offender relationship tends to be established before the sexual act, the place of the act is usually one commonly frequented by the victim.

The Adolescent Pedophile

This patient generally shows a retarded maturation resulting in impaired social relationships, functioning, and judgment. Parents and others are seen as either gratifying or not gratifying the patient's strong dependency needs. Relationships with the parents must be assessed in regard to these distortions and their potential for correction.

In their prison study, Christie (1978) found that 31 percent of pedophiles had received frequent violent beatings.

Barnard found that 40 percent of pedophiles had been physically abused by their parents, and 56 percent had been sexually abused as children by relatives. These findings suggest the victim to victimizer modeling of behavior (Barnard et al. 1985).

Childhood sexual victimization through sex ring activities is discussed by Burgess (Burgess 1984).

Berlin and Krout (1986) quote Groth: [M]any men who experience pedophilic erotic urges as adults were sexually involved with adults when they were children. Thus, in treating the pedophile one is in point of fact often treating a former 'victim.' " They continue to say that "Money proposed that excessive prohibition of early sexual expression may also put one at risk of developing pedophilic sexual desires. He has reported that many men with sexual disorders have come from homes where even the slightest expression of sexuality, including masturbation, was severely chastised" (Berlin, 1983, p. 17).

Table 2. Place of Offense

Place	Total (N = 55)	Heterosexual pedophile (N = 27)	Homosexual pedophile (N = 23)	Preference-undetermined pedophile (N = 5)
Home of offender	15	9	6	0
Home of offender and victim	9	6	2	1
Home of victim	1	1	0	0
Total	25 (45%)	16 (59%)	8 (35%)	1
Place of work	2	2	0	0
Car of offender	9	3	5	1
Public building (theater, etc.)	3	1	1	1
Public place (street, park)	9	4	3	2
Total	23 (42%)	10 (37%)	9 (39%)	4
Not known	7	1	6	0

Note.   Reproduced with permission from Mohr et al. (1964, p. 31).

The adjustment of the adolescent to school or work must be assessed. Relationships with male peers, if any, tend to be loose, and relationships with females are virtually absent. In the heterosexual group, an improvement in sexual aim usually occurs with improvement in general maturation, but improvement in the homosexual pedophile must be measured by assessing the relative strengths of homosexual and heterosexual strivings. This complication is one factor in the poorer prognosis of this group in a legal and social climate that does not accept homosexuality.

These factors accent the importance of social learning and are indicators for group therapy. Resolution of childhood sexual victimization is critical.

The Middle-Aged Pedophile

Since the patients in this group may be married, an assessment of marital and family relationships is of primary importance. Family relationships usually have deteriorated, producing conflicts among family members. Complicating social factors may be dissatisfaction with work and alcoholism. The wife may attempt to sabotage the patient's progress unless closely involved in the treatment. The patient's possible involvement in teaching and youth work often constitutes an attempt to have access to children. The patient's contacts with children should be examined. Many pedophilic acts occur because the pedophile seeks out children. He may need to be removed from access to children. This may be achieved by a court order prohibiting access to children or locations frequented by children, for example, a school.

The Senescent Pedophile

The predominant social factors for this group are loneliness and isolation. Excluding the chronic group and those with specific clinical symptoms of aging, most patients show a psychologically intact personality, but lack outlets for their emotions. This calls for attention to personal and social contacts in the environment.

The developmental pattern of pedophiles may be characterized by a singular degree of closeness and attachment to the mother and a relative lack of fathering.

Incidence

The Canadian National Population Survey (Badgley 1984, p. 193) refers to victims under 21—not all offenders are pedophiles:

1. About one in two females and one in three males had been victims of sexual offenses.
2. Children and youths constitute a majority of the victims. About four in five of the victims were under age 21 when the offenses were first committed against them. Fewer than one in five persons was victimized for the first time when he or she was an adult.
3. A high proportion of persons in all parts of the country reported having been victims of these offenses.
4. On the basis of offenses reported by adults of all ages, it appears that there has not been a sharp increase recently in the incidence of sexual offenses.
5. Most sexually abused victims did not seek the assistance of public services, and when they did, physicians and the police were the groups most frequently con-

tacted. Sexual offenses are committed so frequently and against so many persons that there is an evident and urgent need for better preventive measures. The Canadian Committee's mandate was "to determine the adequacy of the laws and other means used by the community in providing protection for children against sexual offenses and to make recommendations for improving their protection."

They found the following:

At sometime during their lives, about one in two females and one in three males have been victims of one or more unwanted sexual acts. These acts include being exposed to, being sexually threatened, being touched on a sexual part of the body, and attempts to assault or being sexually assaulted.

Two in 100 young persons have experienced attempts to actual acts of unwanted anal penetration by a penis, or by means of objects or fingers.

Acts of exposure constituted the largest single category of sexual offenses committed against children. Cases were documented where such acts were followed by sexual assault.

Few young victims were physically injured; substantially more suffered emotional harms.

About one in four assailants is a family member or a person in a position of trust; about half are friends or acquaintances; and about one in six is a stranger.

Virtually all assailants are males; one in 100 is a female.

A majority of victims or their families do not seek assistance from public services. When they do, they turn most often to the police and doctors. (Badgley 1984, pp. 1–2)

In the Canadian survey, the following information was obtained from 703 convicted child sexual offenders:

1. One in three had no prior criminal record. One in four was a sexual recidivist (previous sexual offense conviction) and the remainder had previous convictions for nonsexual offenses.
2. One in five was the victim's father (natural, step, foster, adoptive, common law). One in four was a stranger (Table 3).
3. One in six had been hospitalized for mental illness at least once prior to his current conviction.

In comparison to sexual recidivists, those who had previously committed non-

Table 3.   Relationship Between Victim and Offender

Type of association between victim and suspected assailants	National population survey (%)
Incest relationship	9.9
Other blood relative	8.4
Guardianship position	3.0
Other family member	2.5
Position of trust	1.0
Friend or acquaintance	48.0
Other person (known)	9.4
Stranger	17.8
Total	100.0

Note.   Reproduced with permission from Badgley (1984, p. 217).

sexual offenses had more often injured victims and had committed more serious sexual offenses. The findings suggest there is a progression from minor to more serious sexual acts by sexual recidivists.

There is a prevalent belief that most pedophiles are male. Badgley stated that "virtually all assailants are males; one in 100 is female."

Treatment

West (1980), at the Cropwood Conference in 1979, stated the following:

1. One of the problems of therapeutic work within the context of criminal justice is that the system selects the clients by legal processes that do not necessarily turn up those most in need of help.
2. To cater to all the needs described would require a range of facilities that no one service, prison, probation, or national health agency, could reasonably be expected to provide.
3. There are many instances in which, if treatment is possible at all, it will take the form of training in self-restraint and social responsibility, rather than being directed specifically to sexual matters.
4. The use of groups and the concept of a therapeutic community in which everyday interactions can be observed and discussed by peers as well as therapists have added considerably to the realism and general applicability of the psychotherapeutic approach. Psychotherapists have moved away from exclusive preoccupation with the past, utilizing more and more the analytic scrutiny of current behavior and exploiting the power of a group of offenders to confront the subterfuges with which one of their members may try to deny or deceive himself as to his true feelings and conduct. In this wider context psychotherapy, especially group psychotherapy, has won increasing acceptance as the method of choice for treating most sex offenders.
5. One of the obstacles to the establishment of new treatment programs is the difficulty of obtaining conclusive evidence from follow-up research that the known forms of treatment are effective.
6. There are strong indications of need for various kinds of help for a substantial number of sex offenders. This calls for a coordinated program with which all relevant agencies can cooperate and that would provide appropriate aid from the earliest stages, when minor problems first come to light, through to the more serious offenders for whom residential treatment for a substantial period is necessary. (West 1980, pp. 141–148)

Treatment approaches to pedophilia were divided into three groups by Tasto (1980):

1. Physiologic techniques are based on the fact that the sexual drive can be reduced by castration or by administering hormones. These treatment techniques, although not generally used in the United States, have been employed in The Netherlands and in some Scandinavian countries. Hormonal treatment in conjunction with psychological treatment has been used to temporarily reduce the sexual drive.
2. Traditional psychotherapy (individual and group), supplemented by recreational therapy, occupational therapy, sex education, and other activities, is used in some

treatment facilities. However, reports are mixed on the effectiveness of traditional psychotherapy with pedophiles. Some researchers suggest that traditional psychotherapy may be helpful when combined with behavioral techniques. Others question whether "insights" achieved by pedophiles in therapy actually change their behavior or if they merely give pedophiles different justifications for their deviant behavior.

3. Behavioral approaches in treating pedophiles are used to 1) increase or facilitate adequate social interaction with adult women, 2) increase sexual arousal to women, and 3) decrease sexual arousal to children, reduce sexual fantasies and thoughts involving children, and decrease urges to engage in sexual activities with children. (Tasto 1980, p. 821)

Some offenders are conformist in all but sexual habits. Frustrated by shyness or ineptitude, these inhibited men may turn to deviant outlets with children because it is less threatening rather than because it represents their true preference. The presence of nondeviant sexual interests must be considered in the assessment since it may point to a need for social skills training rather than for sexual reorientation. Both will be needed in some cases.

There is no major contraindication between psychotherapy and behavior modification (Gelder 1979). Although psychotherapy may be necessary for many offenders to be brought to recognize their sexual pathology and decide they want to do something about it, it alone may not suffice. Conditioning techniques for modifying erotic responses have progressed considerably since the days of simple aversion. (West 1980, p. 144). Positive "shaping" of masturbation fantasies by changing a deviant stimulus into a more appropriate subject as the moment of orgasm approaches, aversion by satiation (continued masturbation to a deviant stimulus beyond the point of orgasm), and aversion by forced verbalization of deviant sexual routines to a critical audience are among the promising methods now being used. Combined with penile plethysmography, these methods have the advantage that their immediate effects can be demonstrated objectively, thereby giving encouragement to patient and therapist. Some of these methods (e.g., covert sensitization) have the additional convenience of availability to the patient outside the therapeutic sessions.

Treatments for the diverse problems of sex offenders ideally should cover every stage at which these individuals come to notice, the earlier stages being the most important from the point of view of prevention (West 1980). General practitioners, marriage counselors, walk-in clinics, voluntary agencies, social workers dealing with children, and police at the stage where discretion can be exercised might make use of specialist treatment centers where individuals at risk of offending, or reoffending, could be referred.

For those who are prosecuted, the existence of active treatment units under supervision of a mental health specialist would provide the courts with a constructive disposition, namely, probation with required treatment. These orders can last up to three years and have the built-in safeguard of incarceration if the offender fails to cooperate. Probation may appear lenient for serious offenders, but this would not be true if the treatment were sufficiently intensive and prolonged and if breaches were prosecuted with speed and firmness. Ethical problems caused by coercing unwilling offenders into treatment are partly overcome by the fact that the offender must give informed consent to the proposal.

It is very difficult also for therapists to be sure the pedophile is not abusing children when not under supervision or in a residential setting.

Release of sex offenders from prison presents difficulties (West 1980). Therapy cannot be successfully completed in a closed and largely one-sex establishment, since the offender's reactions to a normal environment cannot be tested. The offender most needs the support of the therapist when he reenters society and faces its temptations and stresses. Therapy that ceases when the man is discharged is futile. The patient can be referred to a clinic or therapist with this mandated by the parole terms, but a change of therapist at this critical time is not ideal.

Cox says of the treatment of sexual offenders in a hospital-prison setting:

> I regard the task of enabling the patient to recover lost self-esteem, or enabling the patient who has usually had impoverished relationships from his early life to establish a measure of self-esteem which hitherto he has never had, as one of the major therapeutic tasks. Self-esteem regulation is a core therapeutic task in most instances. (Cox 1980, p. 183)

Cox continues:

> [D]ynamic psychotherapy is the process in which a professional relationship enables a patient to do for himself what he cannot do on his own. . . . An eclectic approach is essential because no single etiology underlies all sex offenses. Therefore each therapeutic policy must be subjected to constant reappraisal, though maintaining the patient's self-esteem at an optimal level is an ubiquitous and perennial task. (Cox 1980, pp. 185, 188)

The history of the treatments of sexual offenders is notable for the way it has reflected the changing attitudes of society and medicine (Hawton 1983, p. 248). The range of behavioral techniques recently has broadened with the introduction of cognitive forms of treatment and a change in emphasis away from suppression of deviant sexual behavior and toward the positive development of socially appropriate behavior. A more flexible approach to management has developed with greater emphasis on designing treatment for each patient's needs.

Three approaches have been used in the management of deviant sexuality. First, there are procedures to produce a decrease in deviant sexual interest and behavior. Second, there are techniques to increase nondeviant sexual interest and behavior. These include measures to improve social and interpersonal adjustment. Finally, there are procedures for individuals who do not wish to abandon their deviant sexuality but want to adjust to it.

Fay Knopp (1984) states that the goal of treatment is to teach the sex offender to control his sexually abrasive or assaultive behaviors. She describes eight residential treatment programs. One example is the Adult Diagnostic and Treatment Center in New Jersey, the only independent prison facility in the United States designed to evaluate and treat committed sex offenders. They are treated by group therapy, individual psychotherapy, marital-couples therapy, behavioral therapy, and sex education. The Center is increasing its emphasis on socioeducational skills and assertiveness training. Relaxation groups develop skill in coping with emotional stress.

Another is the Fort Steilacom, Washington, program based on intensive, guided self-help philosophy and a graduated release procedure. This program is divided into four phases: evaluation, inpatient treatment, work release, and outpatient care. On admission the offender completes a 22-page biographical data sheet and writes an autobiography. Psychological tests are administered. The therapy group evaluates the offender. If the offender meets the definition of a sexual psychopath and is amenable to treatment, he will be in the program for a minimum of two years of inpatient treatment (Knopp 1984; Wachtel and Lawton-Speert 1983).

The WSH Orientation Manual states that treatment is learning that irresponsible sexual behavior is learned from childhood. Treatment is a relearning process mainly concerned with stopping the deviant sexual acting out; teaching the man to understand his behavior and to learn the appropriate controls for it; and helping him to develop a positive self-concept and a lifestyle that will reinforce his new concepts while retaining other positive behaviors. The core of the treatment is peer-group therapy with offenders treating offenders under the guidance of a professional supervisor. Each offender spends a minimum of 25 hours a week in peer-group therapy.

During the period of work release the offender must work or attend school in the community 40 hours a week, returning to the hospital each night. He attends the evening inpatient meetings and weekly outpatient meetings of his therapy group. After discharge, the offender is required to attend outpatient meetings of his group at Western State Hospital. The first six to eight months of outpatient living are crucial in assisting the offender to readjust to community life (Knopp 1984). The reoffense rate from December 1965 to November 1982 was 23.3 percent (Knopp 1984).

Abel and Becker (1984) investigated the relative effectiveness of six treatment modalities after the completion of a 30-week outpatient treatment program. Eighty-seven voluntary offenders were in the study. The treatment elements consisted of the following:

1. Satiation, which reduced arousal by satiating or boring the patient with his own deviant sexual fantasies.
2. Covert sensitization, which teaches the patient to disrupt fantasies of young children by replacing them with aversive images.
3. Cognitive restructuring attacks faulty attitudes or beliefs by feedback from others regarding the individual's faulty cognitions.
4. Basics of sex education.
5. Social skills training to interact more effectively with adult partners, including conversation.
6. Assertive skills training in expressing feelings and emotions toward others.

This study determined the most effective sequence of treatment modalities. Abel and Becker (1984) found that covert sensitization and satiation should be provided first, followed by social skills, assertiveness training, cognitive restructuring, and sex education. The optimal group size was 14. Less than 6.6 hours of therapist time per patient was required. The success rate (i.e., those who did not molest) after 6 to 12 months was 97.2 percent.

Groth (1983) believes that whatever the degree of risk a pedophile poses to the community, ultimately the best protection for society is some form of treatment:

> The crime is a symptom; the offense may be punished, but the condition must be treated. The offender must be held responsible for his behavior, but he also has to be helped to change that behavior if we want our community to be a safer one. Otherwise, we are simply recycling him back into the community at the same risk he was prior to incarceration. Incarcerating him is only a temporary solution. (Knopp 1984, p. 16)

Berlin also emphasizes there is no evidence punishment works, and theoretically there is no reason to expect it to do so:

> There is nothing about going to jail that makes it any easier for you to resist temptation if what you are tempted to do is have sex with little boys. There is nothing about being punished that diminishes your sexual appetite or your sexual hunger for little boys. We hear over and over again about people who have been in jail for a number of years—they are out on work release for about three months and they are back into their old

offending behaviors. It is because their unconventional sex drive is still with them and it is very, very hard for many of them not to respond to that when temptation presents itself. (Berlin 1982, quoted in Knopp 1984, p. 16)

The Massachusetts Treatment Centre at Bridgewater is described by Prentkey et al. (1985). This is a residential treatment center rather than incarceration, but the clinician must be satisfied that the sexual aggression can be controlled by the offender before release.

Most sex-offender treatment specialists believe that many sex offenders can be treated successfully—if evaluation is competent, if placement is appropriate, if the treatment meets the needs of the client, and if the offender wants to change.

West et al. (1978) believe that understanding the offender's mind may promote safer methods of control than years of unconstructive detention leading eventually to the release of men more embittered and antisocial.

According to Abel and Becker, "Covert sensitization, masturbatory satiation, sex education, sex therapy, training in assertiveness, and cognitive therapy are the components of their treatment approach. . . . This approach can prevent victimization or interrupt it before large numbers of offenses have been committed, but confidentiality must be guaranteed" (Abel and Becker 1984, p. 19).

Langevin (1983) states that two assessment tools are most valuable in working out erotic preferences patterns; phallometry or measurement of penile reactions and a standardized sex history questionnaire. To date, penile reactions are the most valid index of erotic behavior in a cooperating individual.

With regards to phallometry, Barlow and others developed the strain gauge and Freund developed the volumetric transducer. The phallometer has clear application in sex research and can be a valuable tool in assessment and treatment. It can serve to establish an index of the patient's erotic preferences and provide him and his therapist with new information.

To understand the phenomenon it is necessary to define the preferences and to study men who have an obvious attraction for immature partners, that is, to those with no pubic or axillary hair, small genitals, and lack of swelled breasts in females or lack of chest hair and beard in males. Then the more subtle differences in preferences for emerging adults could be studied. It is also important to distinguish heterosexual from homosexual pedophiles before attempting to define common features.

Multiple Treatment Approaches

The advantage of the multiple treatment approach is that patients usually have many problems requiring more than one method of treatment (Table 4). Aversive conditioning can be used to reduce the frequency of a pedophile's urges toward children, but he may have difficulty relating to women so that assertive therapy or reciprocal inhibition may be useful.

Marshall (1973) used avoidance conditioning with orgasmic reconditioning in a mixed group of patients with sexual deviations that included two heterosexual pedophiles, two homosexual pedophiles, and one bisexual pedophile. The unique feature of his study was the pre- and posttreatment assessment of penile circumference changes. Reactions to children generally decreased, whereas those to adults increased. One homosexual pedophile relapsed but the others were successful after 3 to 16 months.

Table 4. Summary of Treatment Effectiveness for Pedophilia

Method	Results
Aversion therapies	Success comparable to other anomalies; unknown whether erotic preference for children has been changed and in fact it is not usually assessed systematically; no controlled study available
Multiple behavior	Positive in case studies; same therapy problems of multiple treatment as in other anomalies: what are effective ingredients?
Positive methods: assertion therapy, systematic desensitization, Masters and Johnson method	Case studies positive; one unique treatment adapted homosexual pedophile to androphilia
Group therapy	Poorly evaluated, mixed programs in general; outcome ambiguous
Psychotherapy	Only a few case reports; some positive outcomes
Antiandrogens	Generally positive results but patient usually on high doses of drugs; physical risks become problem of concern; no controlled study
Castration	Outcome positive but no controlled study of pedophilia per se; only a few cases may have been treated

Note. Reproduced with permission from Langevin (1983, p. 295).

Positive Behavior Therapy Procedures

Too few studies have been reported to allow a definite conclusion on the effectiveness of positive conditioning procedures for pedophilia. They can be as effective as aversion therapy in other sexual offenders, and since they are more humane and less dangerous, they should be tried more often on pedophiles.

Aversion Therapy

Quinsey reviewed methodological issues in evaluating aversion therapy and concluded that "the success rate of aversion therapy is not high enough to permit confidence in deciding whether an individual should be released into the community" (Quinsey 1973, p. 286).

He also compared response-contingent shock (operant conditioning) and biofeedback (Quinsey et al., 1980). Repeated offenders showed larger penile reactions to children after treatment than first offenders. The data are preliminary and the sample is small, but the diagnostic significance of the results is promising.

Most published reports on aversion therapy include pedophiles as part of a larger heterogeneous group of offenders. This is unfortunate because pedophiles will not uniformly respond to the same treatment (Quinsey 1977, p. 214).

There is only one behavioral treatment study of pedophiles in which successes and failures have been compared at follow-up. Steffy and Gauther (see Langevin 1983) compared 11 persons who had committed or were suspected of committing further sexual offenses with 12 (out of 32) treated child molesters who were nonrepeaters. Pre- and posttreatment ratings of sexual attraction and GSRs (galvanic skin response) to slides of persons varying in age and sex were obtained from each inmate. An avoidance procedure similar to that of MacCulloch et al. (1971) was used in treatment. Failures showed little difference in their GSR to either their preferred-sex child or adult or to whether the persons were nude, partially dressed, or dressed, whereas successes showed differences in their GSRs according to the state of dress of the preferred-sex child or adult. These differences occurred before and after treatment.

These studies appear to indicate that aversion therapy can modify inappropriate sexual preferences, although the magnitude of these effects is not large, and followup data are inadequate.

A more serious difficulty with the treatment programs described above is they are not based on a detailed analysis of the individual patient's problems. There have been few attempts at designing separate treatments for different types of child molesters, particularly as the problems extend to sexual behaviors with adult partners.

Castration

Castration is an irreversible and controversial solution. The sexual drive of the patient is reduced dramatically and recidivism for sexual offenses has been reduced by castration to under 10 percent. It is an unproven method, and penile arousal is still possible after castration.

Pharmacotherapy

Hucker (1985), Freund (1976), Berlin (1983), Berlin and Meincecke (1981), Spodak et al. (1977), Laschet (1973), and Langevin (1983) describe the effectiveness of cyproterone acetate (Androcur) and medroxyprogesterone acetate (Provera). The use of progesterone is noted by Freund (1976). It is possible to reduce sex drive in males considerably by cyproterone medication. Cyproterone has been available in Europe for years under the name of Androcur (Schering) and is now available in Canada. Medroxyprogesterone acetate is also used. Both drugs are believed to compete with the male sex hormone on cell receptors of the brain tissues involved in sexual arousal. The aim of the medication is to keep the drive low enough to prevent recidivism yet high enough, particuarly in married patients, to avoid erectile difficulties. Patients make daily notes on sexual urges and outlets as a base for regulation of drug dose.

According to Hucker, medroxyprogesterone acetate has antigonadotrophic properties and effectively lowers the testosterone level.

> Anecdotal evidence and uncontrolled studies indicate that Provera can be very useful in dealing with some patients whose behavior is difficult to control by other means. . . . Oral dosage can begin with 100 to 200 mg daily. Some patients seem to need as much as 400 mg daily, though it is clearly undesirable to use such high doses of a steroid hormone without very compelling reasons. With Depo-Provera, a dose of 200 to 400 mg intramuscularly every seven to ten days is usually required. A careful physical examination is highly recommended with monitoring of full blood count, liver function test, serum testosterone, FSH, LH, and blood sugar. (Hucker 1985, p. 153)

The drugs present dangers—testicular atrophy, liver damage, diabetes, feminization, weight gain, increased sleep requirements, fatigue, and mood disturbance—

but since they have not been used in large number of patients, few serious side effects have been reported.

Langevin (1983) notes that the drugs affect only arousal, and the man will not change his erotic preference. A pedophile will continue to prefer children but will have a reduced sexual drive while on the drugs. He believes the drugs are a useful treatment for sex offenders who do not respond to other methods, but the drugs can be used only for a short term. They are not a treatment for sexual deviations per se, but only an adjunct to other treatments.

Spodak (1977) and his colleagues reported seven cases treated with medroxyprogesterone acetate (Depo-Provera) up to a maximum of 500 mg per week. Five cases were pedophilic: four homosexual and one heterosexual. No treatment time or follow-up was given, but two homosexual pedophiles were arrested again. The heterosexual patient was able to have sex with his wife, but the two homosexual patients appear to have had no sexual contacts. Knopp (1984) describes the medroxyprogesterone acetate treatment by Berlin, who administers approximately 500 mg of the drug to about 80 sex offenders weekly. Most of the men are on probation or parole, and about one dozen are incarcerated in the Maryland State Penitentiary. All are voluntary candidates for medroxyprogesterone acetate therapy. Berlin contends that the weekly injections aid compulsive offenders to curb their sexual drive and fantasies through the suppression of testosterone. The drug has been used primarily with the most compulsive paraphiliacs, namely, exhibitionists and homosexual male pedophiles.

Before medroxyprogesterone acetate is administered, Berlin and his staff screen the sex offender to determine whether the behavior is treatable without the drug, or whether the behavior is so ingrained and compulsive that it eludes other modalities. Procedures usually consist of: 1) preadmission screening (outpatient); 2) inpatient admission for a period of 20 or 30 days while further assessment and treatment are planned and the effects of the drug are monitored; and 3) outpatient treatment and follow-up.

Knopp (1984) outlines the controversies over the use of medroxyprogesterone acetate:

1. Its short-range negative effects.
2. Its potential for more harmful long-range effects.
3. Its potential for use under conditions that are involuntary, unmonitored, and indiscriminately punitive rather than remedial.
4. Its efficacy in controlling sexually aggressive behaviors.

This drug requires careful medical monitoring. Opponents of its use fear it may be carcinogenic. Medroxyprogesterone acetate has been approved by the Food and Drug Administration (FDA) for treating inoperable cancer of the endometrium and kidney but not for the treatment of sex offenders. The ethics of antiandrogen therapy are discussed in an editorial in the *American Journal of Psychiatry* by Halleck (1981).

Many clinicians treating pedophiles recommend the combination of antiandrogen therapy with psychotherapy.

Bradford and Paulak (1987) demonstrated the effects of antiandrogen treatment on a sadistic homosexual pedophile.

Individual Psychotherapy

Mohr et al. (1964) stated that psychoanalytic treatment of pedophilia was reported by Hadley (1926), one case; Cassity (1927), five cases; Karpman (1950), one case; and Socarides (1959), one case. The studies concentrated on psychodynamic factors and their relation to the pedophilic symptom. Outcome is reported only by Karpman (1950), in whose case (an adolescent heterosexual pedophile with pubic hair phobia) a lasting cure was achieved. Socarides (1959) reported remission of symptoms in a chronic homosexual pedophile while under treatment.

Conn (1949) reports excellent results with brief psychotherapy with which he successfully treated seven of eight heterosexual pedophiles and three homosexual pedophiles. None of the pedophiles referred to him refused treatment.

Crown raised basic issues in the psychotherapy of sexual deviation:

> Moral and ethical considerations are involved in all areas of sexual deviation but most obviously in the more emotion-laden and controversial. Pedophilia is perhaps the best example in that, with our current understanding of it, it may be fixed and unalterable pattern of feeling and behavior, a subject of fear and stigma, unlikely ever to be sanctioned by the law and within larger society.
>
> The psychotherapeutic assessment of sexual deviation broadly follows the standard plan of history-taking, examination of the mental state, psychodynamic assessment and assessment and assigning to the appropriate treatment or treatment combination. These may include more than one psychotherapeutic modality (e.g., individual plus behavioral or cognitive) and may, if relevant, include psychotropic medication.
>
> A helpful general method is to make the sexual deviation itself the central focus and to diversify questioning from this to encompass other aspects, e.g., the family history; personal history; possible complications of the sexual deviation; professional stigma; and suicide attempts. (Crown 1983, pp. 243–245)

Psychodynamic factors should be assessed. These include the factors in the patient likely to lead to success (e.g., psychological-mindedness and motivation of psychological exploration) and negative forces (e.g., attachment to a given way of life with little personal motivation for change). The psychodynamic assessment should reveal the patient's strengths and weaknesses and the structure and efficacy of his defenses (e.g. Does he take responsibility for himself and his predicament or does he project it on to the outside world? Is he paranoid? How effective is he in life generally, especially work?). The quality of emotional and other relationships to men and women is particularly important, and so is the attitude of relevant outside persons toward the patient.

Psychodynamic approaches attend to social inadequacy and deviant eroticism. It is assumed that the fault lies in learning processes and that offenders have the potential for relearning. It is assumed that the fault is not a mere lack of opportunity, but a positive emotional block to learning created by fears and conflicts arising in infancy. Irrational anxieties and aversions need to be ventilated and explored. The psychodynamic model suggests a link between faulty sexual learning, as in sexual victimization, and faulty personality development, since both are presumed to stem from emotional complexes established through mishandling of the child's instinctual sexual and aggressive impulses. Thus, sex offenders are likely to appear aberrant in many ways, such as unsocialized aggression, inability to sustain close emotional ties, and hostile or paranoid attitudes toward members of the opposite sex.

Group Psychotherapy

Hartman established an outpatient group in 1960 in Toronto "aimed at exploring the dynamics of pedophilia, and to test the treatment techniques in a context of long-term psychotherapy with the sexual deviate" (Hartman 1965, p. 283). The members of this group were all chronic cases considered refractory to treatment. Some had a 15-year history of pedophilia. All were heterosexual and between the ages of 20 and

30 and, with one exception, were married and had small children. They attended weekly 90-minute sessions for four years. Common characteristics of the men were the chronicity and the intensity of the pedophilic urges and the acting out. All had an unhealthy attachment to the mother in their formative years, while the father had been physically or psychologically absent. Attempts to motivate were seen as a major part of the treatment process. The immediate therapeutic task was to strengthen the basic ego function of impulse control. Their pedophilic acts occurred after real or perceived frustrations in object relationships; therefore, therapeutic efforts were directed mainly toward enhancing the capacity to form object relationships without their customary fears and apprehensions and to enable them to rely on their own strengths.

All seven group members experienced more or less distinctive character changes. Six were considered recovered, or at least as having reached a degree of improvement that allowed them to control their infrequent mild pedophilic urges.

Outcome

In Radcinowicz's (1957) study of 1,985 sex offenders with a four-year follow-up 13 percent of the heterosexual pedophiles and 27 percent of the homosexual pedophiles were reconvicted (Gribbens 1983).

Fitch (1962) studied 139 men. Homosexual offenders were twice as likely to be reconvicted upon release from prison.

Quinsey (1985) quotes the study by Frisbie: "Of 617 offenders released, 15 percent were convicted of a new sex offense within 3.5 years" (Frisbie 1969, p. 42). Frisbie concluded on the basis of the follow-up interviews that economic stress, overcrowding and lack of privacy, unsatisfactory familial relationships, difficulties in occupational or social situations, health problems, and aging were all unrelated to recidivism. The following variables were found important: alcohol abuse, unorthodox ethical values, problems in establishing meaningful relationships with adult females, and the desire for physically immature females as sexual objects.

As stated by Quinsey (1985),

[B]ecause of our incomplete knowledge concerning the etiology of child molesting and the historically nonempirical approach to intervention, it is perhaps not surprising that the treatment of such offenders has been marked by confusion and failure. . . . There are, however, signs that the situation is improving rapidly. The more recent literature on the treatment of child molesters is more empirical in nature, much more humble in its claims, and attempts to tailor the treatments to theoretically relevant aspects of the offenders' behaviours . . . given the variety of treatments which have been used for sex offenders, it is almost as important to demonstrate unambiguously that something does not work as it is to demonstrate efficacy. (Quinsey 1985, pp. 84–85)

The consensus of numerous reviews of correctional treatment programs for convicted sexual offenders suggests there is insufficient evidence available to warrant the conclusion "that nothing works" or the optimism that certain programs have been "demonstrably successful" (Badgley 1984, p. 880).

No system has succeeded fully in reconciling the needs of treatment with those of justice and security. Justice demands fixed terms of detention as a punishment for past crimes. Penal authorities are charged with a responsibility to protect the public from criminals for the duration of their sentence. They cannot risk relaxation of security, or permit trial periods of freedom, for offenders whose criminal history suggests that they are potentially dangerous. The medical treatment model, on the other hand, calls for some flexibility in the time spent in custody according to the offenders' progress towards emotional re-orientation. Even more important, a realistic treatment program concentrates on read-justment to the community rather than adjustment to artificial institutional life. The most critical phase of treatment starts when the offender begins to face life outside once again. That moment is the testing time for treatment gains made during incarceration. It is also the moment when emotional conflicts are liable to be reawakened and help is most needed and most likely to be effective. In concrete, practical terms, the psychiatric approach calls for release by easy stages while the offender is still under supervision and still an active participant in a treatment program. Without this essential provision, treatment schemes are not being given a fair chance and should not be blamed if they fail to prevent recidivism. (Badgley 1984, p. 880)

Chapter 78

Fetishism and Transvestism

The paraphilias occupy a curious position in psychiatric nosology. Due to the variety of sexual fantasies in "normative" populations, there is some question if paraphilias are psychiatric disorders (Kendall 1984). The paraphilic fantasy or behavior in the DSM-III-R definition denotes an obligate and repetitive focus for sexual excitement, thus differentiating the behavior from a normal variant (American Psychiatric Association 1987). The paraphilias become categorical syndromes since they can be demarcated from normal sexual excitement; having a lifelong course; and are operationally defined by the nature of a specific stimulus (Clare 1979). Crepault and Couture (1980) have noted the heterogeneity of male erotic fantasies but document that the paraphilic fantasies are unusual and deviate from the norm. The male erotically aroused by a pornographic picture of a seminude woman in a lace negligee would not be a fetishist unless the imagery or clothing were mandatory for sexual arousal and orgasm. Paraphilia literally means "attraction to that which is beyond normal." The essential characteristic is that unusual or bizarre fantasies or behavior become the preferred and necessary focus for sexual excitement (American Psychiatric Association 1980). These behaviors and fantasies are preferred as a noninterpersonal means of sexual arousal in a repetitive, involuntary manner. Fetishism and transvestism are conditions defined by their focus on preferred use of nonhuman objects or human part objects for sexual arousal.

Kendall (1984) has discussed the semantic difficulty in defining such behaviors as mental disorders. Although the DSM-III-R has described a mental disorder as a "clinically significant behavioral or psychological syndrome" that may be associated with distress or disability, many individuals who practice either of these fetishes experience minimal psychological or behavioral distress when viewed superficially. Kendall thus urges that more thought be given to how major mental disorders can be clearly defined, especially when categorizing such conditions. Culver and Gert (1982) state that paraphilias are best defined as sexual "maladies." They argue that such paraphilic behaviors often involve fantasies more than overt behaviors and may be ego syntonic since no "evil" is suffered as the individual is caused no distress. They state that transvestism should be considered an ego syntonic sexual deviance in fantasy or behavior and is best not considered a mental disorder. They demarcate sexual behaviors that cause harm to an individual or others from those that do not.

Paraphilias, however, clearly depart from normality whether normality is viewed as a utopian idea, a statistical norm, or a transactional outcome of various systems such as interpersonal social systems or cultural norms. Careful examination, however, of paraphilic individuals reveal them to be limited in their capability of interacting with others; i.e., they have flawed object relations. This requires a dynamic perspective that is more difficult to objectively quantify. Meyer has described the interpersonal limitations due to the borderline personality organization that the paraphilic possesses (Meyer 1980). Although the overt clinical description of either the fetishist or transvestite may not clearly demonstrate the distress or disability typically found in a mental disorder, Meyer feels that paraphilics, when viewed from a psychodynamic perspective, have impairment in gender and reality sense that obscure flaws in their sense of bodily integrity. Their characteristically borderline personality organization may limit paraphilic individuals from a full interpersonal relationship. Thus, the clinician is not making a value judgement that a man who enjoys wearing women's clothes in private as a form of sexual release is disordered, but is focusing upon his whole range of interpersonal behaviors and ability to fully engage in a loving relationship. Measurement of such interpersonal relationships is difficult and presently defies good quantitative measurement. Careful clinical observation will document the presence of various psychopathological defenses, which limits fully developed, mature adult object relationships.

Data regarding fetishists and transvestites are limited since clinicians see only those individuals who seek treatment. Relatively few fetishists have been described in the psychiatric literature and there are no good epidemiologic studies to suggest the incidence in a general population. One may infer, however, that both fetishism and transvestism are common if one views the frequency of both paraphilic pornography and accouterments in stores catering to such individuals.

Etiologic Considerations

Lazare (1973) emphasizes that various models—such as sociocultural, biologic, learned, or psychological—help explain psychiatric phenomena. Sociocultural issues have been noted by Stoller (1979). Most cultures utilize accouterments to enhance sexual excitement. Even when nudity is common, other attributes such as the nape of the neck in Japan produce sexual excitement. Thus paraphilic behavior may be molded by sociocultural factors so that body parts may be erotic in one culture but not in another. There is little to suggest that sociocultural factors cause paraphilias, but Gebhard (1969) speculates that literate and industrialized civilizations may promote fetishism by the lack of tolerance of childhood sex play and early knowledge of coitus. He hypothesizes that fetishism develops in literate societies where there is greater use of and dependence upon written and verbal symbols. He bases this speculation on his impression that fetishistic behavior is not found in preliterate societies.

Sociologists and anthropologists explain transvestism in terms of role. They suggest that transvestism allows certain males to avoid the harsh tasks of food gathering and fighting (Munroe and Munroe 1977). Buhrich (1977b) has reviewed the role of transvestism throughout history. Early Hebrew law forbade individuals to wear garments worn by the opposite sex. Greek mythology portrays Hercules as cross-dressing. The French female novelist George Sand lived for many years cross-dressed as a male. The difficulty within the anthropologic, sociologic, and historical literature is the vague definition of transvestism. These reports assume all cross-dressing is homogeneous, but adoption of the opposite gender role is done for many reasons.

Biologic explanations of fetishism and transvestism are also hypothetical, but are based on observations of fetishism in individuals with structural brain damage. At present there is no evidence for a biologic basis of either fetishism or transvestism. Only Benjamin, using ambiguous definitions, has suggested that endocrinologic factors are important (Benjamin 1954). Buhrich et al. (1979) found no differences in plasma testosterone, serum follicle-stimulating hormone, and serum luteinizing hormone between a group of transvestite and controls. Family studies of transvestism may suggest constitutional causes or the mechanism of identification in the genesis of this condition. Buhrich (1977) reported a case of a father and son who were well-defined fetishistic cross-dressers. The son denied knowledge of his father's cross-dressing. The mother's role in her son's deviation is unknown, but she knew of her husband's activities. Krueger (1978) reported a father and three sons who were heterosexual fetishistic cross-dressers. He discusses a dynamic etiology within the family and discusses the role of identification with the father as an explanation of this behavior in family units.

Psychoanalytic theory has focused much attention on the paraphilias. It must be understood that psychoanalytic theory is an evolving series of constructs that have been shaped by clinical material that is generally restricted to single case reports and retrospective personal histories. With these caveats in mind, psychoanalytic theory has provided a rich source of hypotheses to explain fetishism and transvestism. The fundamental basis from which psychoanalysts have evolved their explanations has been Freud's concept of bisexuality elucidated in "Three Essays on Sexuality" (Freud 1905, reprinted 1954). Although Freud intended this to be a biologic theory, psychological analogs of masculine and feminine identifications remain as a heritage to the early theory (Stoller 1972).

The relationship of paraphilic behavior to normal sexuality from a psychoanalytic perspective is best understood by reviewing Stoller's work on sexual excitement (Stoller 1979). Utilizing a naturalistic research strategy of investigating themes found in pornography, Stoller describes elements that contribute to both normal and deviant sexual arousal. These include adornments of clothes, cosmetics, body styles, language, fantasy, and autoerotic experiences. For Stoller, sexual excitement is composed of a series of events that includes both overt genital stimulation and covert fantasies (Stoller 1976). Normal sexual excitement finds a series of fantasies that appear to be driven by hostility, overt in the perverse while sublimated in the normal, that generates such erotic drive. This hostility attempts to undo childhood traumas and frustrations. In paraphilics, issues of such hostility are not resolved and find their expression in the core fantasy or behavior of the paraphilic. Stoller generalizes from the part object fear of castration to the whole individual and hypothesizes that the fetishist represents a more general process of dehumanization of the total human object, generally a feared and hated object, who has humiliated the man in the past (Stoller 1975b).

Money explains paraphilic behavior via learning theory. He hypothesizes that an individual's "love map" is developed by childhood identification and rehearsal from older figures (Money 1984). This behavioral identification normally develops into a heterosexual mode. Once the learned behavior is distorted, the individual's erotic fantasies and corresponding practices are subverted and a paraphilia results. Marks (1972) also suggests that fetishism may be a learned phenomenon that is reinforced by periods of increasing androgen levels in the developing male adolescent. Both psychodynamic and behavioral explanations emphasize developmental traumas or subversions that may sidetrack the normal sequence of events due to unfolding anatomic and hormonal changes in puberty that complement developing sexual fantasies. This ontologic sequence gets subverted into preferred and obligate modes of deviant sexual excitement in the paraphilic.

The treatments reported for transvestism and fetishism depend primarily on each therapist's theoretical orientation. Organic treatments are used when the therapist views the dysfunction as a treatable brain disorder. The behaviorist treats the overt symptom as a learned process. The psychoanalyst attempts to investigate the multiple determinants that form the fetishistic symptom, which is viewed as a compromise formation due to an underlying conflict.

The following sections will describe clinical features and treatments for fetishism and transvestic fetishism. The studies are severely limited by the flaws in most psychotherapy outcome research (Karasu et al. 1984). The studies rarely are controlled, the clinical description of patients frequently is limited, and the therapy, except in specific behavioral therapies, often is vague. Finally, patients who seek treatment may present biased samples.

Fetishism

Definition

The term "fetish" was used in 1760, when Charles Brosses, a French anthropologist, reviewed the role of carved wooden figures and small stone objects imbued with magical powers by natives in West Africa (Nagler 1957). It is derived from the Portuguese "feitico," which means "an object made both by art and skillfully conceived to symbolize a larger object" (Greenacre 1979). Within this definition are the components of the sexual deviation labeled fetishism (American Psychiatric Association 1980). Fetishism is defined operationally as the repeated, preferred, or exclusive method of achieving sexual excitement via the use of nonliving objects or part objects. This behavior was catalogued by early sexologists such as Krafft-Ebing and comprehensively reviewed by the French psychologist Alfred Binet in 1887. The behaviors were explained as the outcome of a learned occurrence in constitutionally vulnerable individuals (Krafft-Ebing 1886, reprinted 1967). Over the past century, a variety of theories have attempted to explain this sexual deviation. This review will discuss theoretical considerations as they determine treatment approaches.

Clinical Characteristics

The essential feature of the fetishist is the necessity of an inanimate or part object to maintain sexual arousal. There is the repeated and obligate need for the fetishistic article or fantasy for sexual arousal and for maintenance of potency and orgasm. It differs from transvestism where full female apparel is used in cross-dressing for sexual arousal, and from behaviors that episodically augment sexual response, such as use of vibrator. There are limited data about the clinical characteristics of fetishists since those who seek treatment may not be representative of a behavior that rarely causes personal distress. Psychoanalysts hypothesize that the external anatomy of the male promotes castration fear and the psychological economics of male development makes fetishistic symptomatology primarily in the male (Segal 1966). Nevertheless, women have been noted to have fetishistic behavior (Zavitzianos 1971).

Chalkley and Powell (1983) reviewed the clinical characteristics of 48 fetishists, 98 percent of whom were male. Twenty-two percent were homosexual. Thirty-five percent reported only one fetish, but the remainder described a number of inanimate objects used to promote sexual arousal. The fetishistic objects could be divided into those of media i.e., hard or soft, and form, i.e., shoes, lingerie, or limbs. Hard textures, such as rubber items, were used by 23 percent and leather by 10.5 percent. Sixty percent of the respondents reported soft-textured fabrics to be arousing, whereas the remaining 14.6 percent found human skin to be the arousing medium. Fetish as a form often involved shoes, lingerie, and parts of the body such as amputated limbs or feet. The behavior to promote sexual arousal included viewing the object, stealing the item, or masturbating when in direct contact with the fetish.

Concurrent psychiatric disorders in this sample included depression and personality disorders. Only 3 of the 48 were psychotic. Other authors have noted a variety of psychiatric disorders to coexist with fetishism such as sadomasochism in individuals with hard media or leather fetishism. Prince and Bentler's (1972) survey of self-designated transvestites reported that 13 percent also utilized fetishistic behaviors. Kleptomania and other impulsive disorders have been associated with fetishism. Recent investigators comment upon the fetishists' borderline personality organization (Meyer 1980).

Treatment Approaches

At present, no single treatment is considered entirely effective. Most clinical reports suffer from methodologic flaws that create problems in evaluating treatment responses. Imprecise labeling vitiates certain clinical reports' general applicability. Greenacre (1968) discusses a case of fetishism that does not meet the DSM-III-R diagnostic criteria. Other problems, as noted by Kilmann et al. (1982) include lack of control groups; multiple treatments without isolation of the effects of a specific treatment; heterogenous paraphilias, such as fetishists who are also masochistic; patients coerced into treatment by the law; and problems with follow-up. Social desirability factors make self-report follow-ups suspect, especially with subjects who fear legal difficulties.

Biologic Therapy

Krafft-Ebing (1886, reprinted 1967) first noted a relationship between epilepsy and fetishism. Mitchell et al. (1954) successfully treated a patient with a safety pin fetish by a temporal lobectomy. Epstein (1960) reported similar patients and suggests treatment by seizure control. Ball (1968) reported a haircutting fetishist who had a left temporal tumor. Anticonvulsant medication and neuroleptics dramatically decreased his fetishistic activity. Anticonvulsant medication, in particular carbamazepine, may be useful when fetishistic behavior appears as episodic dyscontrol and epileptic phenomena, but the incidence of EEG abnormalities in individuals with fetishes is unknown. There are no data to indicate the usefulness of anticonvulsants in individuals without evidence of a seizure disorder. The most recent biologic approach, reserved for hypersexual individuals whose fetishistic behavior is of the compulsive, unremitting fashion, is antiandrogenic medication, such as medroxy-progesterone acetate (Depo-Provera) (Berlin and Meinecke 1981; Cooper et al. 1972). See the section on management of gender dysphoric transvestite (below) for full discussion of medroxyprogesterone acetate administration.

Psychodynamic Therapy

As Freud noted, individuals rarely seek treatment for their fetish, and the absence of a motivating affect, whether shame, anxiety, or guilt, limits the wish to change (Freud 1927, reprinted 1959).

Nagler's comprehensive discussion mentions diminution in his patient's foot fetish following analytic investigation and understanding of the etiologic roots (Nagler 1957). Zavitzianos (1971) discusses the treatment of a woman with episodic fetishistic behaviors but makes no mention of treatment response. Difficulties in treating fetishists can be characterized by a detailed self-report of a fetishist whose behavior was so compelling and gratifying that there was no motivation for change (Boots 1957).

Utilizing Stoller's conceptualization of the developmental roots of a fetish, the psychodynamic therapist may attempt treatment if the genetic roots of the fetish are understood as a repetitive, obligate focus to revive a traumatic event generally incurred from a parental figure. Stoller notes that the fetish develops when an individual undergoes a sequence of events: 1) the individual who originally traumatized the patient will be harmed in fantasy by the repetitive fetishistic act. 2) To do this, the originally offending individual is stripped of humanity and transformed into a part object, i.e., the fetish. Stoller's conceptualization may provide a guide for psychodynamic treatment of patients truly motivated to change, but the prognosis is guarded (Stoller 1975d).

Kernberg (1975) notes that individuals with sexual deviations and underlying borderline personality organization who also use predominantly perverse, masturbatory fantasies have limited ability to change. Meyer (1980) states that dynamic psychotherapy may be the most appropriate treatment to help individuals cope with other life stresses and free them from preoccupation and chaos due to the perversion. Such treatments are difficult, as patients often will flee therapy or manifest the variety of problems seen in treating borderline personality disorders. Kernberg (1975) has outlined difficulties that include conscious withholding of materials, consistent devaluation of the therapist, and focusing on the meaninglessness of the therapy. Severe regressive phenomena and promiscuous acting-out within the transference can occur. Fetishistic patients often have associated psychopathologic phenomena that include chronic demoralization and other impulsive disorders such as kleptomania (frequent in fetishism). Such individuals may be conceptualized as the borderline personalities described by Kernberg but may not have the total borderline personality disorder described in DSM-III-R. Malitz (1960) reported that brief dynamic psychotherapy that investigated a fetishistic patient's view of his parents and his anger and repressed aggression appeared to modify a diaper fetish. He notes that the patient was coerced into therapy by legal difficulties and may have reported improvement for this reason. The use of peer support should be mentioned. There are organized groups of cross-dressers, many of whom would be defined as transvestites. Some of these groups support the behaviors and put on fashion shows and provide a small social system for cross-dressers. Referral to such organizations is dangerous, as Person and Oversey have noted, since many transvestites become terrified by the group members, many of whom are gender dysphoric or transsexuals (Person and Oversey 1978).

In summary, psychoanalytic investigations have offered much in providing developmental hypotheses that contribute to fetishism, but therapists using this modality must understand the nuances of treating individuals with borderline personality organization and watch for the regression and fragmenting that may occur.

Behavior Therapy

Behavioral treatment of fetishistic behaviors is based upon the learned acquisition of deviant sexual stimuli. Rachman and Hodgson (1968) empirically demonstrated a classical conditioning paradigm to condition erectile response in young men without paraphilic behaviors to the stimulus of high-heeled boots. They demonstrated that heterosexual men could be sexually conditioned to various classes of erotic stimuli (Rachman and Hodgson 1968). By rapidly alternating slides of nude females with slides of fur-lined boots, they were able to demonstrate that heterosexual men could develop erections in response to the pictures of the boots. Three of the seven subjects generalized their erection response to other pictures of shoes. Since learned behavior may be facilitated at certain periods of development, various behavioral approaches have been developed. These treatments include behavioral analysis of the paraphilia to document discrete sexual stimuli. Therapists must use a detailed personal history to note other contributing problems such as depression or other deviant practices. Careful baseline measures are developed utilizing paraphilic and nonparaphilic stimuli via videotape and slides and normal heterosexual stimuli and fantasy production. Response is measured by self-report and penile plethysmography. Following the baseline measurement, aversive conditioning is used to condition backward the deviant behavior (Marks 1976). By using aversive stimuli, which can be electrical shock, apomorphine injections to induce nausea, or covert fantasy production of anxiety and disgust, deviant cues are coupled with the negative states. Some behavioral treatment models will pair heterosexual stimuli to shape and model normative sexual behavior and use instruction in masturbation with heterosexual fantasies or stimuli. Finally, patients often are instructed to regulate deviant impulses by coupling fetishistic fantasies with the use of smelling salts, a noxious stimulus, to inhibit such thoughts.

Utilizing combinations of the above treatments, the behavioral literature contains clinical descriptions and outcome measures for the treatment of fetishists. Kilmann et al. (1982) have reviewed single cases and larger studies. The interpretation of results is questionable since many patients were in legal difficulties and the follow-up relied often upon self-report. The course and nature of the treatment setting and the unreliable follow-ups mitigate the generally successful results reported.

Other Approaches

There are no data on family or group treatment. Hypnosis was reported to modify fetishistic behavior in one case to a limited degree at a three-year follow-up (McSweeney 1972). Although the fetishist views his behavior without much anxiety, there clearly is shame in publicly expressing and discussing his behaviors. Frances and Clarkin (1981) have discussed "treatment of no choice" as one approach to borderline patients. They note that patients who previously have had severe transference difficulties, masochistic individuals, and patients who enter treatment only to justify financial compensation may best be managed by a prescription of no treatment. This would be appropriate only for a patient who had tried unsuccessfully psychological and behavioral techniques and who was brought to treatment by outside pressure.

Problematic areas in the treatment of fetishism.   First, there is the basic ethical issue of treating a behavior that a patient views as enjoyable and that does not hurt others. One may rationalize that the behavior limits the individual's ability to relate fully to others, but if the fetishist does not seek treatment voluntarily, the therapist is at a disadvantage in forming a treatment alliance. Aversive conditioning techniques that inflict pain and discomfort produce difficulties. Only a noncoerced, voluntary patient would be appropriate for such treatments. Since fetishists often have other difficulties such as depression, kleptomania, pervasive loneliness, and more aggressive sexual behaviors like pedophilia, a variety of symptoms must be treated.

The problem of symptom substitution is vexing. The behavioral literature does not report this, but the development of depression, masochistic behaviors, and other sexual dysfunctions such as impotence have been reported in more detailed psychoanalytic investigations. Khan (1979) reported the amelioration of a foreskin fetish in a homosexual male who later developed masochistic and self-destructive behavior. Whether this could be considered a symptom substitution or just another expression of a borderline personality organization needs to be better defined.

Transvestic Fetishism

Transvestic fetishism overlaps with fetishism in that 13 percent of the transvestites sampled also practiced fetishistic behavior, yet the difference between the disorders is more than one of degree. Although the fetishist uses the inanimate object as a "sexual prop," the transvestite assumes a "total" image (Prince and Bentler 1972). This charade can merge into the wish to become a woman so that some individuals eventually become gender dysphoric and request sexual reassignment. This has not been reported in fetishism.

Definition

Stoller (1971) has discussed the problems of definition and defined the transvestite as a fetishistic cross-dresser who is heterosexual in orientation and initially experiences genital arousal from wearing women's clothes. This definition has been refined in DSM-III, wherein transvestism is operationally defined as: 1) recurrent and persistent cross-dressing by a heterosexual male, 2) initial sexual arousal concurrent with the cross-dressing, 3) intense frustration if the cross-dressing is prohibited, and 4) the lack of fulfillment of the criteria for transsexualism (American Psychiatric Association 1980). The conditions to be considered in the DSM-III differential diagnosis include transsexualism and male homosexuality. The DSM-III-R has changed this diagnostic label to *transvestic fetishism*. An additional criterion is a six-month time duration of recurrent preoccupation with intense sexual urges and sexually arousing fantasies involving cross-dressing (American Psychiatric Association 1987).

The course of transvestism may lead to gender dysphoria, producing difficulties with a cross-sectional approach to labeling (Meyer 1974). The criteria for transsexualism may be retrospectively distorted by an individual who demands sexual reassignment. The full life history must be considered in categorizing a male who wears women's clothes. This includes the nature of prior sexual object choices, character of past gender identification, and the presence of prior fetishistic arousal (Blanchard 1985). The transvestite must be differentiated from the transsexual, effeminate homosexual, and latent psychotic with borderline phenomenology. The gender dysphoric transvestite must be differentiated from other clinical variants who may be gender dysphoric and may seek sexual reassignment (Wise and Meyer 1980a). The transsexual has an underlying lifelong history of being unhappy with his assigned biologic sex. He rarely has strong masculine identifications and frequently has had little sexual experience with either sex. The effeminate homosexual, on the other hand, values his penis as a source of sexual stimulation and has been very active in the homosexual culture (Stoller 1971). Finally, there are psychotic individuals with gender ambiguity. They have an atypical psychosis with reality testing so impaired that classification of a sexual disorder is not appropriate.

Clinical Characteristics

Transvestism was initially described by Magnus Hirschfeld, a physician who established an institute for sexual research in Berlin (Hoenig 1977). The descriptive information on transvestism has been most comprehensively studied from two separate sources. Prince studied 504 subscribers to a transvestite journal (Prince and Bentler 1972). They described themselves as predominantly heterosexual with self-characterized split personalities. Seventy-four percent had fathered children. Seventy-eight percent felt they were different personalities when dressed. Twenty-seven percent preferred to cross-dress while having intercourse and 85 percent had cross-dressed publicly. Seventy-five percent had never seen a psychiatrist and of those who had sought treatment, only 47 percent felt the treatment helped. Almost three-quarters of the sample wanted to expand their cross-dressing. Although the sample may have included some effeminate homosexuals, the data demonstrate that few practicing transvestites seek help. Bentler and Prince (1970) utilized an "unpublished MMPI-type inventory" and found no differences between a control population and the transvestite population. Studies using depth psychology disagree; they find transvestites to have severe characterologic problems.

The second source, a series of phenomenologic studies by Buhrich and McConaghy, further elucidated clinical characteristics of transvestites (Buhrich 1978). They interviewed members of a transvestite social club and found transvestite behavior represented a continuum from the nuclear transvestite, to the marginal transvestite, to the nuclear transsexual. The nuclear transvestite has a clear heterosexual interest with the history of fetishistic arousal when cross-dressing. Motivations for cross-dressing were relaxation, comfort, and relief from stress. Feelings of sensuality, elegance, and beauty were common self-reports. Sexual arousal during cross-dressing was prominent during adolescence but less so in adulthood. Transvestite subjects required more time to dress and make up, spent more time looking at themselves in mirrors, and possessed more photographs of themselves when cross-dressed than individuals seeking sexual reassignment in a gender dysphoria clinic. Transvestites rarely report homosexual interest and only feel they possess a feminine identity when cross-dressed. They see this as a split aspect of their personality in contradistinction to transsexuals who are convinced that they are totally feminine.

Transvestites, but not transsexuals, have fetishistic arousal from cross-dressing. The transvestite group rarely sat down to urinate or took female hormones. Transvestites more commonly were aroused by sadomasochistic and bondage fantasies than were those seen at a gender dysphoria clinic. The phenomenology of transvestism merges with transsexualism when gender identity is a symptom. Reports such as Newman and Stoller's (1973) and Buhrich and McConaghy's (1976) discussion of fetishistic behavior in transsexuals and episodic reports of heterosexual individuals who become gender dysphoric make sense when these individuals are seen as transvestites who have regressed. Their symptomatology is that of gender dysphoria. The psychotic process that Golosow and Weitzman (1968) described in a man labeled as a transsexual becomes understandable when viewed as a psychotic illness in a transvestite. In contrast to the above, Lukianowicz (1959) concluded that transvestites are no more prone to psychotic or neurotic illness than others.

It is important to emphasize the gender dysphoric transvestite because of the serious morbidity and mortality that can ensue from mismanagement. A recent review of individuals requesting sexual reassignment documented that those best labeled as transvestites were the most common. The transvestite who becomes gender dysphoric is a clinical category that clinicians must recognize and learn to manage properly. They have been categorized previously as marginal transvestites or atypical transsexuals. Wise and Meyer (1980a) reviewed the clinical characteristics of transvestites who became gender dysphoric. They found histories of fetishistic cross-dressing but not of homosexuality. The transvestites may have had fleeting homosexual experiences, but their basic sexual orientation was heterosexual.

Stresses that lead to gender dysphoria include forced intimacy in marriage, oedipal flowering of children in which sons revive early childhood traumas, physical illness or separation through illness, and bereavement. An important element in management is recognition that the individual has had a long-standing history of transvestism. Careful evaluation will reveal no evidence of early unhappiness with the individual's assigned sex. There may be a history of depression or a sense of emptiness, but not of gender dysphoria. In the dramatic request for sexual reassignment, there may be retrospective distortion with recounting of lifelong histories of gender dysphoria. The data are compounded by depression and unhappiness and the fact that many have read about gender dysphoric individuals and transsexuals and have learned the right answers. These individuals tend to have borderline personality organizations with their masculine and feminine identifications and self-images split during their more functional periods. When stresses challenge the defensive splitting, the result is gender dysphoria.

Childhood observations of boys who cross-dress have been hampered by imprecise definitions. Young boys who have worn women's clothes and appeared feminine have been labeled transvestite. Transvestism necessitates genital arousal so these studies are misleading and describe boys with difficulty in consolidating their gender identity. Green (1975) has discussed the significance of feminine behavior in young boys. The outcome of such boys may be homosexuality, heterosexuality, or transexualism in adulthood, but not necessarily transvestism (Davenport 1986; Green 1986). Treatment directed toward the effeminate behavior is essential. The conclusions of Friend et al. (1954) regarding transvestism are vitiated due to their labeling childhood cross-dressing as transvestism. Transvestism by DSM-III-R criteria is confined to males, but Stoller (1982) has reported three cases of female fetishistic cross-dressers. The classification of such individuals is problematic and raises questions about the nature of fetishism in women.

Treatment Approaches

A literature review of the treatments of transvestic fetishism reveals two basic problems. First, as with fetishism, imprecise labeling has led to reports of treatments of individuals who could not be reliably classified as transvestites. Subjects labeled transvestites are often effeminate homosexuals or transsexuals. Second, there is rarely a reliable measure of success. Most treatments rely upon self-report and Person and Oversey (1978) suggest that reported successes are often temporary and that the patient has deceived the therapist. Rosen and Kopel (1977) reported that the behavioral treatment of a transvestite was successful, but later concluded that the subject consciously deceived the therapist. He continued to have persistent wishes to cross-dress, but pressures from his wife and expectations from the therapists led him to false reporting (Rosen and Kopel 1977). Third, fetishistic cross-dressing is generally ego syntonic and gratifying to the subject. Individuals tend to seek treatment for reasons other than their transvestism, such as depression, coercion from spouse, or gender dysphoria (Croughan et al. 1981). This makes it necessary to develop a clear set of goals and expectations for these patients. Brierley (1979) comprehensively discussed the treatment and management of the transvestite. He partitions efforts to modify or cure fetishistic cross-dressing from management of complicating problems such as discovery by the family. The clinician must separate these elements.

Biological Therapy

Electroconvulsive therapy has modified cross-dressing in individuals who did not strictly meet criteria for transvestism but who had acute psychotic episodes (Liebman 1944). Stilbestrol has been used to diminish the drive to cross-dress, but since the natural course of transvestism is a reduction of the erotic sensations from cross-dressing over time, the utility of such treatment is not clear (Jones 1960).

Psychodynamic Therapy

Transvestite behavior is seen as a developmental defense against guilt from incestuous feelings towards the mother and a method of reducing castration anxiety due to the father's wrath. The behavior avoids anxiety and guilt directed toward the object, i.e., the father, in the oedipal triangle. Psychoanalysts view the defense of splitting as a primary mechanism in transvestite behavior. Freud (1938, reprinted 1950) alluded to the role of splitting to maintain reality perception despite perverse behavior. Current psychoanalytic theorists emphasize pregenital factors (Socarides 1960). Bak (1953) sees the pregenital fixations of transvestism as pathologic identification with an active figure. This supports Freud's earlier observations that transvestism was a fantasized reaffirmation of the phallic mother. Sperber (1973) views transvestism as a method of "limitation" of the mother with less emotional attachments than other psychoanalysts would suggest. Greenacre (1971) builds upon this theory and involves flawed body-image development in the early life of transvestites and fetishists. Difficulties in the first 18 months of life, such as severe mother-child conflicts or constitutional problems such as malnutrition or early illness, give rise to sensory disturbances and result in flawed body images. Environmental traumas, such as witnessing accidents, deaths, or sibling births, may intensify this early body ego defect, resulting in castration anxiety. Meyer (1980) notes that transvestites possess borderline personality organizations that are maintained as long as the splitting is effective.

Stoller (1974) uses patient material and transvestite pornography to support his theory that transvestites have often been dressed in feminine clothes at an early age and that transvestism is the hostile mastery of this early trauma of humiliation and shame. He thinks pornography is "the manifest content of perversion" and views the genesis of transvestite behavior as the hostile retaliation of the adult who was forced to wear women's clothes as a child. Stoller sees the transvestite having powerful feminine identifications while maintaining a sense of maleness. The transvestites he describes frequently have been cross-dressed as a child. The act itself is "the ultimate triumph of maleness: his penis is orgasm . . . the little boy . . . recapitulates the details of the childhood trauma and has preserved his maleness and his sexual capacity." Use of transvestite pornography to build an etiologic theory is controversial. Buhrich and McConaghy (1976) have reviewed transvestite fiction and found the transvestites' actual experience at variance with the fantasies portrayed in the pornography. Instead of hostility, Person and Oversey (1978) feel anxiety is the central affect causing transvestism. This anxiety comes from flawed early development wherein the sense of self is incomplete. They see the genesis of transvestism as not "the invention of the mother," but conflict within the child due to environmental vicissitudes.

The women who marry transvestites have received surprisingly little attention in the literature. Stoller (1967) describes them as women who need to care for defective men or "malicious male haters who resolve their hostility by marrying men with this behavior." Wise et al. (1985) supported this and noted the "moral masochism" of such women. These characteristics of transvestites' wives make premature advice for separation inadvisable as the paraphilia may reward the spouse's characterological conflicts (Wise 1985).

In summary, psychodynamic contributions are limited by imprecise definitions and single case studies. Psychoanalytic theories see transvestism as rooted in early development that inhibited the individual's ability to have full object relations without resorting to cross-dressing. Only Segal (1966) addresses why certain men adopt transvestism as a sexual release while others use full cross-dressing. Segal sees transvestism closer to homosexuality than fetishism. Single case reports of insight-oriented therapy are hampered by poor follow-up and lack of validation. Wise (1979) reported the ongoing psychotherapy of a transvestite who initially sought treatment for gender dysphoria but through insight-oriented treatment relinquished cross-dressing behavior.

Behavioral Therapy

Learning theory has been proposed by Money (1967) to explain transvestism. He conceptualizes it as a product of "postnatal programming." He suggests that gender role is developed by "identification" with the same sex individuals. The behavior is positively or negatively reinforced by "complementary" action of the opposite-sex parental figure. Transvestism evolves from disturbances of these early identification and faulty reinforcement phenomena. Behavioral therapy has been utilized with several specific paradigms to modify arousal from cross-dressing. The treatment models have used overt sensitization with faradic or chemical aversion or covert sensitization with subject fantasies. Social skills training, orgasmic reconditioning, and thought-stopping have been used. Although outcome measures frequently have been positive, validation remains a problem, even when measured by careful baseline parameters, as in the Rosen and Kopel (1977) report where the patient consciously deceived the therapists. Hypnosis also has been reported to modify transvestite urges (Wise and Meyer 1980b).

In summary biologic, psychodynamic, and behavioral treatments have been disappointing in ablating the wish to cross-dress, but several aspects of management should be considered. The therapist should identify feasible goals related to the specific request of the patient (Brierley 1979). Some individuals seek consultation due to rapidly escalating pressure to cross-dress accompanied by frequent masturbatory behavior. If a hypomanic or manic disorder is not present, the use of antiandrogenic drugs may reduce libidinal drive (Brantley and Wise 1985). A second situation is the individual who wishes to reduce, but not stop, cross-dressing. As cross-dressing is often used for anxiety reduction, insight-oriented psychotherapy may help the transvestite cope with the dysphoric affects and thereby reduce the pressure to cross-dress. Unfortunately, total cessation of cross-dressing is rare, and psychotherapy must also deal with the depression that the transvestite often experiences. The inability to control the behavior rather than the behavior itself is usually the conscious source of distress. Behavior modification should be considered if the patient wishes to stop cross-dressing and does not have the capacity or desire for insight-directed treatment.

The transvestite frequently seeks treatment because of family pressure. The transvestite and spouse come with the request that the patient stop his cross-dressing. The transvestite often will want the therapist to convince his partner that the behavior is acceptable, whereas the wife will want it stopped. It is useful to understand that many transvestite partners have masochistic character disorders often characterized by early developmental losses (Wise et al. 1985). They have sought relationships with a transvestite as a compromise in the prevention of more pain. Little is known about conjoint couples treatment except that the therapist must be aware of the covert wishes of each partner and not be manipulated. The value judgment that transvestism behavior is wrong or harmless must be avoided until the neurotic and characterologic flaws of each member become apparent (Wise 1985).

Management of the Gender Dysphoric Transvestite

Gender dysphoria in the transvestite is an episodic condition occurring at times of stress. It is essential to diagnose the condition properly and avoid irreversible surgery. A history of previous masculine identifications and eroticized cross-dressing is critical in diagnosing the transvestite. Careful management of the patient will include ways to monitor the patient's gender dysphoria and lead to a decline of the urges for sexual reassignment. Even when the dysphoria abates, the clinician must recognize that exacerbations can occur with future stresses. The therapist should understand the psychotherapeutic elements of treatment of borderline patients (Kernberg 1982).

The therapy of the gender dysphoric transvestite should include an initial period for the development of a therapeutic alliance (Wise 1979). This should begin with delineation of gender identity criteria as noted above. Referral to a gender identity clinic may be helpful as it allows the therapist to concentrate on the roots of the behavior and manage the depression. Although this may seem coercive, it will provide a stable format to allow the therapist and patient to look at the stresses that may have provoked the regression. After the therapeutic alliance has been tentatively established, the aging transvestite may experience a depression as he begins to face the stresses that have promoted the gender dysphoria. This mood disorder may lead to acute suicidal ideation or autocastration. Supportive therapy, family support, antidepressant medication, or hospitalization may be needed. The final phase of therapy is continued support as the gender dysphoria wanes.

In hypersexual gender dysphoria, demonstrated by intense and frequent masturbatory activity, antiandrogen medication such as medroxyprogesterone acetate (Depo-Provera) may be tried (Berlin and Meinecke 1981). Medroxyprogesterone acetate can be administered once or twice per week intramuscularly to reduce circulating levels of testosterone. It does not cause feminization of appearance. The dosage varies widely but is generally from 100 to 800 mg/week, usually given in 100 mg/ml concentrations. Lowered testosterone levels indicate compliance. Normal for an adult male is 575 plus or minus 105 ng/dl. The goal is suppression of the serum testosterone to 125 ng/dl while following the patient's behavior. Side effects include weight gain, mild sedation, occasional leg cramping, cold sweats, and hyperglycemia. The clinical signs to follow are the repetitive urge to masturbate or fetishistically cross-dress. The medication can be titrated to allow some ability for erection and ejaculation. The treatment is experimental and not appropriate for the transvestite who is not hypersexual. When administering antiandrogens, close collaboration with an endocrinologist is important. In summary, gender dysphoria in transvestites is a clinically serious condition that demands constant attention to the possible emergency of self-destructive behaviors.

Summary

Fetishism and transvestic fetishism infrequently lead to psychiatric consultation due to the gratification the individual receives from the behavior. Shame and anxiety are infrequent when inanimate objects or cross-dressing are used to achieve sexual arousal and release. The ethical considerations are complex. Halleck (1974) has voiced concern about the potentials of behavioral control, especially when the patient has given consent under duress or is nonconsenting. Bancroft (1981) has discussed the specific ethical issues of aversive conditioning and feels that fully informed consent is possible once a therapeutic alliance has developed. Coercion from family and spouse may limit the patient's freedom of choice. This is a problem that must be judged on an individual basis but that can never be ignored by therapists.

Until a specific treatment can be developed for these paraphilias, efforts to better classify them and to study them in relationship to the normal population are needed. Valid investigation of treatment responses also is essential. Uncritical acceptance of such behaviors is different from supportive empathy and recognizing that these behaviors limit lifestyles. Encouragement of active pathological behavior by therapists is never warranted, even with the limitations of treatment.

This discussion has reviewed the clinical course and approaches to the treatment and management of fetishists and transvestites. Although paraphilic behaviors are difficult to modify, continued research into the etiology and treatment methods of these behaviors is needed.

Chapter 79

Sexual Sadism and Sexual Masochism

Definitions

The DSM-III describes the essential feature of masochism as "recurrent, intense, sexual urges and sexually arousing fantasies, of at least six months duration, involving the act (real, not simulated) of being humiliated, beaten, bound, or otherwise made to suffer. The person has acted on these urges, or is markedly distressed by them" (American Psychiatric Association 1987, p. 286). The essential feature of sadism is "recurrent, intense, sexual urges and sexually arousing fantasies, of at least six months duration, involving acts (real, not simulated) in which the psychological or physical suffering (including humiliation) of the victim is sexually exciting. The person has acted on these urges or is markedly distressed by them" (American Psychiatric Association 1987, p. 287).

These definitions are broad and do not account for or explain the characteristics of these paraphilias. According to DSM-III-R, paraphilias are characterized by "recurrent, intense sexual urges and sexually arousing fantasies generally involving either (1) non-human objects, (2) the suffering or humiliation of one's self or one's partner (not merely simulated), or (3) children or other non-consenting persons" (American Psychiatric Association 1987, p. 279).

Clinically, a rapist whose activity was to force submission on the victim regardless of the intent to harm or abuse would qualify for the diagnosis of sadism. The difficulty with the definitions is they are nonspecific and do not address clinical problems encountered in everyday practice. Each clinician is aware of sadistic and masochistic relationships that do not qualify for the diagnosis of sexual sadomasochism because they exclude sexual activity as an overt aim of the aggressive or hostile interchange. The frequency of sadomasochistic fantasy in many cultures further confuses the clinician who treats individuals with sadomasochistic practices.

Debate

Marmor believes that most human beings in our society violate rigid conventional standards of proper sexual behavior in one way or another (Marmor 1978a, 1978b). Nevertheless, certain more widespread sexual deviant patterns fall outside the range of "normal sexual behavior." These behaviors are not discrete phenomena. Deviant individuals seen by clinicians usually are unable to achieve satisfactory sexual relationships with an adult partner unless a specified set of behaviors or activities takes place. The male's ubiquitous use of fantasy containing sadistic and masochistic themes has been debated in articles by Marmor (1978a, 1978b) and Stoller (1975). The use of sadomasochistic fantasies preserves and controls primitive fears of children much the same as physical punishment or the fear of losing love, and the fears are seen as represented in the activities called sadism and masochism. (Marmor 1978). On the other hand, Stoller (1975) defines perversion as the overt or covert expression of hostility directed at another person, whereas aberration is defined as a variant of sexual activity. An aberration is an erotic technique that has as its goal achievement of sexual excitement with activity designed to lead to complete sexual activity. The goal of perversions is direction of hostility toward another person. Stoller further states that perversions are fantasies usually expressed as actions rather than as daydreams. The criteria that Stoller (1975) used suggest the following:

1. Gender identity disorders such as effeminacy are central to perversion. He believes gender disorders are present most of the time independent of sexual excitement and may be found in perverse and nonperverse men.
2. Whether an aberration is variant or perverse is determined by one's attitude toward the object.
3. Each time the perverse act is performed with others or privately, a triumph is celebrated.
4. The trauma of childhood mentioned in the definition actually occurred and is memorialized in the details of the perversion.

Stoller believes that precocious excitement contributes to perversion; however, when too much stimulation and too little discharge of guilt result, a traumatic event must be redone or reworked as a successful venture. Stoller states that aberration, on the other hand, can occur as a result of excessive stimulation at a young age with much gratification and little guilt. He sees perversion as a necessary channeling of intrafamilial hostility into less destructive sexual expression acted out repetitively in a manner that preserves the family structure and reduces the level of hostility, which could threaten the family unit. Others have argued that elements of sexual sadism and masochism are widespread in many cultures and that lovemaking and sexual activity between members of the culture carry with them intense forms of aggression and physical infliction of pain (Ford and Beach 1951). In a movie, *The Emerald Forest*, a tribal marriage is humorously depicted when the female has to teach the young male courting her how to be aggressive and do it "the right way," such as hitting her on the head and carrying her away from her village. Such signs of aggression, power, dominance, and submission are present in all cultures studied by Ford and Beach (1951). It is Marmor's (1978a) opinion that such stimulation, particularly during sexual activity or coitus, may reflect inherent biologic capacity for increased sexual excitement as a result of inflicting or experiencing some form of pain.

Sexual fantasies, sadistic and masochistic, are common in many cultures and may be imbedded in the entire framework of sexual mores. The frequency of sadomasochistic practices in our culture is unknown, even though the fantasies are common in both sexes. In the less restrictive and more permissive societies, pornography and perversion appear to be less attractive.

Discovery

The detection of sadomasochistic behavior is difficult since clinicians only incidentally learn of it after an injury or some threat to the relationship.

Most persons engaging in sadomasochistic behaviors appear to be males. Its infrequent occurrence in females is unexplained. Some psychoanalytic explanations (Greenson 1968; Stoller 1966, 1975) indicate that castration anxiety is at the root of perversion. That a theory such as castration anxiety is used to explain all perversion makes it suspect (Marmor 1978b). The fact that individuals with similar family histories may or may not engage in perversion or adopt variant sexual fantasies as an attempt to repair early developmental wounds challenges such a universal theory. That males must go through a more complex process of turning from feminine identity during the oedipal stage is hypothesized as a primary cause of increased perversion in males (Stoller 1966).

It seems more likely that differences in brain dimorphism plus circulating androgen levels during adolescence play a strong role in sexual fantasies of males and females. Males have a longer history of adolescent sexual excitation and behavior when the culture forbids sexual expression (Kinsey et al. 1948). This contributes to the different patterns of erotic fantasies and behaviors in males and females. Marmor (1978a) believes that always to attribute castration anxiety to guilt over incestuous impulses becomes a ritualistic formula that explains nothing primarily because it is used to explain everything. Gebhard et al. (1965) state that primitive forces are operative in the meaning of the behavior of individuals engaging in sadomasochistic practices. Primarily, the masochist is acting out a fantasy in which there is excessive guilt for engaging in sexual activity promulgated by an early developmental crisis. The individual may act this out by taking charge of what happens to him, thereby converting humiliation into triumph through alternative expressions of sexual interests coupled with punishment. The simple idea of receiving punishment for obtaining pleasure is seen as the basic core of the masochistic act. Sadism, on the other hand, is an outlet for hostility and aggression and can be explained as a sense of overwhelming anger acted out as triumphant power and control over another individual. In Gebhard et al.'s studies (1965) the majority of people engaging in sadomasochism were masochistic and very few were pure sadists. Another dichotomy between males and females is that females engage in masochistic fantasies (Gebhard et al. 1965; Kinsey et al. 1948), but the female sadist usually acts out fantasies directed by a masochistic partner in charge of the relationship.

Summary of Theoretical Issues

Basic theoretical issues have centered about the following:

1. The sexual activity is a triumph, converting an original childhood trauma into success and mastery.
2. The reason for the overrepresentation of sexual sadomasochism by males is undetermined.
3. That similar dynamics and family structures are factors in some people's behavior, but not in all, illustrates the inadequacy of retrospective case studies.
4. One unexplored theory is that risk taking may promote a high degree of autonomic nervous system stimulation required by individuals with a predilection for perverse activities.

Persons with these disorders may require higher levels of parasympathetic and sympathetic arousal for sexual functioning. Exposure to danger may produce the sympathetic stimulation necessary for orgasm. Clinical evidence suggests that persons with delayed ejaculation have repressed hostility and require increased stimulation or use of fantasy to switch from parasympathetic to sympathetic stimulation to trigger orgasm. I propose the following subdivisions of sadomasochistic disorders based on developmental factors.

Primary disorders arise from an intense developmental problem in the earliest stages of individuation and separation from family of origin. They are the most difficult to treat and require intensive long-term involvement, but under the best of circumstances, the prognosis is poor.

Secondary sadomasochistic disorders arise from a later stage in development after some degree of separation and individuation of self has been attained. A failure to attain and hold meaningful relationships other than of a fleeting, intensive nature is the hallmark. Treatment of secondary sadomasochistic disorders requires intensive involvement and produces variable results.

Tertiary sadomasochistic disorders are characterized by the development of more stable and mature relationships with a love object over time. The best results are obtained with this group.

Primary Sadomasochism

Primary sadomasochism stems from difficulties in the early phases of development. Its hallmarks are difficulties in separation and individuation from the family of origin. The failure to form significant primary attachments to others stands out in the clinical history. The patients tend to resist change and stubbornly hold to isolation from others. They exhibit a fear of closeness and, if placed in such positions, develop intense autonomic responses. They fear rejection, change, or interpersonal risk taking and have a strong need to continue acting out the conflict.

Strong masochistic fantasies may be acted out during the male's late adolescence with significant danger to self and others. The self-bondage fantasies during masturbation may lead to heightened sexual arousal, but may be hazardous. Examples of self-bondage with stimulation suggest that this is a behavior usually limited to adolescence when a partner is not available.

Case 1

David was the only son of an extemely caring mother who was overenmeshed with her son and a passive father who had focused many of his own inadequacies and concerns on his son. David, 27 years old when first seen, had suffered from regional enteritis from age nine. There had been frequent hospitalizations for surgical procedures, steroids, and other medical treatments throughout his formative years. He first began by masturbating with fantasies of females defecating or passing gas. The connection between his sexual excitation and sounds of bathroom activities became driven and repetitive. David would spend hours driving about searching for a bathroom used by both males and females. His ritual was to linger outside a male/female restroom waiting for a particularly attractive female to use it. He then would enter the restroom and search the area for pubic hairs or other signs of the woman's presence. If he found a pubic hair, he swallowed it and then masturbated, leaving a few drops of semen visible on the toilet seat or on the floor. This had become an oft-repeated ritual. Frequently he would lick the toilet seat and imagine himself sexually involved with the woman who had used the bathroom. He first came to clinical attention when he became so ashamed and disturbed by his behavior that he confessed to his parents, who sought psychiatric attention.

David was not psychotic but had strong elements of concrete thinking. He gave a history of overcompliance with his parents' wishes in an attempt to please them, alternating with periods of explosive rage toward them. His parents were frightened of conflict with him and would go to great lengths to avoid it, even giving him money to quiet his outbursts.

David's sexual activity and onset of puberty were delayed until age 17 when he first began to masturbate with erotic fantasies of eliminative functions. Although he was 27 and an employed college graduate when he sought help, he remained at home, intensely overprotected by his parents. The episodes of anger toward his mother usually occurred after they had discussed his sexual interests and his desire for a relationship with a woman. His interests centered solely on the physical attractiveness of a woman.

David previously had been treated unsuccessfully as an outpatient with low-dose antidepressants and antianxiety agents. During hospitalization, he was treated with individual and group psychotherapy with particular attention to the origin of developmental conflicts and the meaning of his intense fears of relationships with others. He tended to avoid all interpersonal relationships with women and pretended to be aloof and detached from them to protect himself from feelings of shame and embarrassment. Family therapy focused on separation from his parents, their overenmeshment with him, and their need to rescue and placate him.

Outpatient treatment using behaviorally oriented group and individual psychotherapy focused on the development of dating behaviors. David became able to ask a woman out, but he later cancelled the date and treatment. One year later he returned unchanged except for increasingly aggressive behavior toward his family. A similar course of treatment failed to produce significant change. All attempts at intervention failed to substitute for the gratification he obtained by acting out his sexual impulses.

David's history demonstrates six difficulties of primary sadomasochism: failure to individuate from family, failure to form primary attachments, resistance to change, intense fear of rejection, repetitive acting out of the conflict, and resistance to treatment.

Case 2

Ralph, a 30-year-old male, first sought treatment after marriage. All his life he had had extreme autonomic fear responses in the presence of women. He would blush, have many symptoms of panic disorder, and feel an intense fear of being rejected. He entered treatment because his bride had become angry over their unconsummated marriage. He had had no previous sexual activity, and his primary sexual fantasy involved women who would force him to have sex. He had married after a four-month courtship devoid of *any* sexual behavior. On the first evening of their honeymoon, he had difficulty with erection and was unable to have contact with his wife, even of a tender or touching nature. She was 32 years old and had no sexual experience. She became very upset and berated Ralph for being "dumb, stupid, inept and horrible." He attempted many times to initiate sex without success. He thought of suicide and became so enraged he had murderous impulses toward her. After three or four nights, she left him. He was sad, helpless, and hopeless, especially after his wife annulled their marriage.

Ralph was the only child of an extemely overenmeshed mother who doted on him and controlled his every act. His father was passive and played a peripheral role in his development. Following graduation from high school, he moved west for one year to "travel" and had his first experience with street drugs, primarily marijuana, and alcohol. After returning home, he obtained a steady job, which gave him a sense of self-esteem and respect from his co-workers.

Combined individual treatment and group therapy focused on his masochistic fantasies and intense shame, attempted behavioral management of his anxiety, and discussed his fear of women. He continued to act out this fear by failing to address those issues even in the safe and supportive environment of group therapy. He attended for six months but failed to follow through on even the small behavioral changes recommended. He was unable to speak to a woman outside the group. After six months he dropped treatment and returned to the recreational use of marijuana and alcohol. Two years later he was essentially unchanged.

These cases illustrate the principles of primary sadomasochism. Each patient had a poor sense of self as differentiated from the family of origin. Second, each had intense, unrealistic attachments to females that existed largely in fantasy. Third, repetitive themes of humiliation, degradation, or revenge were a hallmark of their sexual fantasies but never were acted out. Fourth, each showed a profound resistance to intervention, including 1) chemical, 2) individual psychotherapy focused on behavioral change, 3) use of erotic material to shape sexual arousal, and 4) involvement in group and family therapy.

Secondary Sadomasochism

Secondary sadomasochism is characterized by a greater differentiation of self from family than found among primary sadomasochists. The men usually have moved from the family of origin and led an independent existence. They have formed attachments to other people, although usually fleeting in nature, and have shown less dependence on their partners. Unlike primary sadomasochists, they use their genitalia in relationships to carry out sadomasochistic fantasies. Secondary sadomasochists act out primarily because of the lack of attachment to the partners. There is danger to the individual or his partners because of the transitory nature of the relationships. Finally, there is a tendency for the severity of the masochistic or sadistic behaviors to increase over time.

Case 1

Dale, the youngest child of three, perceived himself as unwanted from birth. He was born with a wolf snout and cleft palate and had multiple surgical procedures throughout childhood. He began talking late and described himself as the object of much ridicule in school. In adolescence he turned toward inanimate objects and pets as his primary objects of trust and affection. He developed an interest in horticulture and animals and was distrustful of peers and others, particularly family members. There was intense anger at the exposure of his body to ridicule within his family and during his multiple surgical procedures. When he first started to self-stimulate, his sexual fantasies were focused on the development of power over and humiliation of others. There were some "normal" heterosexual relationships, but sadomasochistic fantasies continued to accompany masturbation. He began to have casual sexual activities with males in his early 20s. This involved fleeting contacts in which he was in control of the sexual activity. Bondage, "water sport" (enemas), and dominance over others always produced satisfaction in masturbatory fantasies and sexual activity with others. Anger was a principal focus of most of his relationships. He came to clinical attention only incidentally; he denied a need for treatment and was committed to his lifestyle.

Case 2

This case illustrates secondary and tertiary sadomasochistic disorders. Harvey, like many tertiary sadomasochists, developed a long-standing relationship, but as with secondary sadomasochists, he maintained intense, dangerous, fleeting sexual contacts outside marriage.

Harvey, an executive president with a large corporation, sought treatment for difficulty with erection and a low sexual desire. His wife had been sexually assaulted before she met Harvey, and throughout their 12 years of marriage, she had avoided sexual contacts. She had been one of his students when he was a professor at a midwestern university.

They were seen conjointly, but as a psychosexual history was obtained, it became clear that the primary difficulty existed apart from the marital relationship. Before and during marriage, Harvey had had sadistic sexual fantasies toward women and had carried out activities such as voyeurism and obscene calls, for which he had been arrested two times. His sexual fantasies, accompanied by themes of force and power, continued throughout college. He had picked up hitchhikers many times and, using a weapon, forced them to fellate him.

Harvey, the only male child of four children, described his mother as extemely controlling and guilt inducing. His father had died when he was approximately six years of age, and he had been estranged from his mother for most of his memory.

Treatment began with an attempt to improve communication in the marriage, including sexual activity. Harvey had never throught of using pornography with his wife, but he had no difficulty in using it away from home. After some couple's work and some separate sessions with his wife, she became increasingly assertive regarding their sexual activity and the couple separated. Initial individual treatment involved substitution of a more appropriate sexual outlet for masturbation by the use of an erotic telephone answering service. He quickly adjusted to this and began to confine his sexual activity to phone calls only. He also was seen psychoanalytically to explore his early background and begin to sort out his conflicted view of women. He began to date and to be sexually active. Although he developed good relationships with several partners, he was never able to achieve real intimacy.

His treatment was designed 1) to interrupt the behavioral pattern previously reinforced by sexual gratification, 2) to provide substitute sexual satisfaction through self-stimulation with erotica, and 3) to masturbate to satiation. In the latter, the patient masturbates to orgasm, then continues to masturbate using fantasies associated with his previous dangerous behavior. Fading techniques are designed to decrease the power of previously arousing sexual stimuli. While arousal was high, he was asked to use more socially appropriate sexual stimuli prior to and during orgasm. He remained in treatment for 1½ years and at termination was sexually active with no aggressive activity outside his primary relationship.

Each of these secondary sadomasochists had strong, intense, negative relations with women. Each had incorporated the anger, bitterness, and fear into sexual activity carried out in a repetitive fashion. Only the patient in Case 2 sought treatment, at the request of his wife, and was able to modify his activities.

Tertiary Sadomasochism

Tertiary sadomasochism is characterized by a higher level of developmental attainment. Its primary features are 1) a history of a sexual relationship that has been adequate at one time or another; 2) a history of frequent sexual dysfunction; 3) presence of sadistic or hostile behaviors usually surrounding sexual activity; 4) evidence of extremely rigid, self-punitive ideas with excessive guilt; and 5) destructive behavior usually threatening the relationship, especially when the sadomasochism surfaces. Threats of separation with blame of the partner for unusual, different, or perverse acts are prominent. These patients are easier to treat, demonstrate corrective behavioral changes more rapidly, remain in treatment longer, and respond to both education and social relearning.

Case 1

This is an unusual case, as it involves a woman. She was a 32-year-old graduate student married to a white collar professional. She told of early trauma by a brutal father who was very strict and liberal in handing out corporal punishment. He frequently used ridicule and humiliation as methods of shaping behavior. She described her mother as long-suffering and the object of abuse by the father's tirades. During courtship with her future husband, Ms. G. frequently provoked attacks by bitterly berating him about his attributes and actions. He eventually would become enraged and once pushed her out of a moving automobile. She sustained only minor injuries. He was apologetic, and as soon as he had helped her back in the car, they had sexual intercourse.

Throughout early marriage she was aversive to everything sexual, even unable to change her own tampons. She would ask her husband to do this and to help her in all genital hygiene. Her sexual fantasies were of domination and submission to a powerful male. They frequently would enact humiliation and bondage scenes with her being bound and forced to fellate her husband. Polaroid snapshots of their activities were treasured for later use in self-stimulation. She continued to be aversive to sex, and during the course of graduate school, this became a threat to the marriage. He considered leaving her, so she entered treatment. A major concern was what would become of the photographs that had been taken during the course of their five-year marriage.

Individual sessions began with a thorough exploration of her history, followed by behaviorally focused couple's sexual work designed to increase the variety of sexual behaviors in which they engaged. They did well, and she was referred for long-term psychotherapy aimed at working through the hostility and fear that had been grafted onto her sexual activity. At the end of one year of treatment, the couple was enjoying sexual activity with little hostility, domination, or control evident. She had been able to switch much of her fantasy material to nonmasochistic themes.

Case 2

Dr. R. consulted a psychiatrist because of increasing sexual impotence. His impotence was sporadic, but erection necessitated fantasies of hostility directed toward a female. The fantasies included seducing an older woman who was married to a man of position and prominence. The woman in his fantasies was reticent to engage in sexual activity, but would become increasingly aroused by Dr. R.'s persistent sexual overtures.

He previously had been treated conjointly with his wife for several years without change. His wife of seven years was 12 years his senior. She appeared very angry, distrustful, and hostile toward Dr. R. during an assessment of the marriage. She was a rigid, critical, and controlling woman formerly married to a man who was unfaithful and eventually left her after a long, hostile, dependent relationship. She had fallen in love with her present husband, Dr. R., who was a junior associate of the first husband, during her separation. They were followed during courtship by a detective and involved in a bitter divorce action. Throughout marriage there were episodes of physical violence in which expressions of distrust, fear, and anger always preceded their lovemaking attempts.

The initial treatment attempts were futile since Mrs. R.'s primary focus was repeatedly insisting that Dr. R. was the problem. Each attempt to explore her contribution to the problem was met with rigid resistance. She bitterly denounced him and insisted upon his absolute fidelity and loyalty to include constantly keeping her apprised of his whereabouts on a 24-hour basis. Individual treatment was recommended for Mrs. R. with another therapist.

Dr. R. was one of six children born to a rigid mother who insisted on strict adherence to Roman Catholic dogma. Although Dr. R. could recall his parents' bitter arguments in early childhood, his father changed dramatically when Dr. R. was approximately six years of age and became passive, dutiful, and compliant to his wife. Dr. R. idealized his father as a stable and exceptionally child-centered father. He had much affection for his father, but he greatly feared disapproval from his mother.

Psychotherapy aimed to increase his awareness of his strong attachment to and overcompliance to his mother and wife. Dr. R. began to identify a general pattern of overcompliance, yet increasingly hostile fantasies accompanied all sexual arousal. He became aware of ambivalence about leaving his wife and gained insight into the remarkable similarities between his wife and his mother. Despite escalation of bitter arguments that usually occurred at night and involved much physical abuse, the patient remained committed to "being a family man." Each violent episode usually ended in lovemaking while he continued to fantasize extramarital sexual activity. Dr. R. finally established a separate residence, but he continued to expose himself to abuse by frequently attempting to renew the relationship with his wife. After several months, his sexual impotence disappeared and he began to form a close and equal relationship with a female. The frequency of his hostile interchanges with his wife gradually diminished even though she continued to harass him at his office and home. In his sexual fantasies he now began to be more in charge of the relationships. At the end of one year of treatment, he had formed an excellent relationship in which he no longer felt the need to control or be controlled by the female. His sexual fantasies became much more centered on the realistic interrelationship between males and females and were no longer necessary for erections.

Chapter 80

Transsexualism

The treatment of transsexualism is one of the more controversial and, in many ways, one of the more disappointing areas in psychiatry today. When the concept of trans-sexualism—and the possibility of its treatment by surgical remodeling—first came to public attention in 1953 with the worldwide publicity given to the Christine Jorgenson case, two major preoccupations were set in motion. For thousands—perhaps tens of thousands—of people who were uncomfortable or unhappy with their gender in varying degrees, the possibility of a definitive "solution" to their problems was raised in the form of what came to be known as the "sex change operation." For psychiatry and the rest of medicine, a new dilemma was created: i.e., how to respond to the growing numbers of people who now defined themselves as transsexuals and who argued, often insistently, that the only treatment they would consider acceptable was gender reassignment by surgery.

Psychiatry, which usually devoted its knowledge and skills to helping people cope with and adapt to the finite real world, including such "givens" of life as one's body and gender, was now faced with a sizable number of people who wanted to change their bodies and gender in a direct physical way, with hormones, electrolysis, the amputation of devalued organs, and the reconstruction, as much as possible, of new organs. The initial and understandable response of most psychiatrists faced with this dilemma was to define such patients as seriously disturbed, with diagnoses ranging from the neurotic (e.g., obsessional neurosis) to the psychotic (e.g., delusional behavior). At a practical level, psychiatrists tried to help their patients become more comfortable with, or less conflicted about, their masculinity or femininity, but for the most part this approach failed, basically for two reasons. First, those individuals who had already concluded that they were transsexual and had decided that they wanted gender change surgery usually did not want to participate in psychotherapy, which they perceived as an obstacle rather than as an opportunity. Second, those who agreed, albeit reluctantly, to try psychotherapy rarely found it helpful in creating gender comfort where long-term and profound discomfort had been the rule. Patients often turned to surgeons, who were more willing to remake the body and less insistent on trying to remake the mind. In a number of medical centers, interdisciplinary teams, including urologists, surgeons, endocrinologists, psychiatrists, and psychologists, formed gender identity boards to try to evaluate and sort out the often bewildering array of complaints, claims, and problems brought to their attention. They offered a range of treatments and services, from simple counseling to hormonal treatment and reconstructive surgery. A "black market" developed, both foreign and domestic, where anyone who insisted upon surgical reassignment and wished to avoid a pro-longed evaluation could get the definitive surgery if willing to pay for it.

Out of these clinical and treatment experiences some clarity began to emerge. Clinical and developmental research contributed to an understanding of the nature of gender identity, its development, and its vicissitudes (Money and Ehrhardt 1972). The concept of core gender identity, launched in the early months of life and well established by age 2½ or 3, was established. Recognition grew that individuals experienced varying degrees of comfort or discomfort with their gender, and a spectrum of gender dysphoria was described, ranging from mild and occasional discomfort to full-blown transsexualism. It was found useful to differentiate the transsexual syndrome into two constellations: *primary transsexualism*, starting in the earliest years when gender behavior first appears and remaining constant throughout life, and *secondary transsexualism*, characterized by intense discomfort in the defined biological sexual role coupled with a desire to undergo gender reassignment, but starting later in life and not necessarily constant (Person and Oversey 1974a, 1974b). Secondary transsexualism so defined usually seemed to be a defense against or reaction to life's problems rather than a core identity problem.

In either case, the common denominator in this area is the individual who asserts that he has always felt trapped in a male body (or, for a woman, in a female body) and that he (or she) wants the medical profession to assist in achieving as much gender reassignment as possible. (The phrase "as much as possible" is used because it is obvious to everyone that true gender change is a biological impossibility.) Since physicians are the only people in society who can safely provide the reconstructive surgery that such procedures entail, it becomes necessary for the person who wants such gender reassignment to enlist the aid of the medical profession. Physicians, especially psychiatrists, are therefore placed, and place themselves, in the role of gatekeepers as well as therapists, deciding on who shall be "transformed" and assisting in the transformation when they concur with the patient's belief in the reality of his or her condition and the necessity for treatment. Thus, the most effective way a person wanting gender reassignment can convince a physician to "let him or her through the gate" is to convince that physician that he or she has a condition, transsexualism, that requires such treatment, or that he or she is transsexual in the sense that one is diabetic, epileptic, or hypertensive.

Evaluation for Treatment

For all these reasons, evaluation for treatment is a key and complex process in the treatment of transsexualism. Such an evaluation must assess the following:

1. What degree of gender dysphoria is present?
2. What are the biological, psychological, and social factors contributing to this dysphoria?
3. Does the dysphoria reach the extent characteristic of transsexualism?
4. If so, is the pattern the lifelong and constant pattern characteristic of primary transsexualism, or is it more consistent with secondary transsexualism?
5. If more characteristic of secondary transsexualism, what other problems or issues are being reacted to or defended against?
6. What are the patient's ego strengths and assets?
7. What are the patient's ego weaknesses and liabilities; is there vulnerability to psychosis or substantial suicide risk?
8. Has the patient given sufficient time and thought to these issues?
9. What are the patient's relationships and responsibilities to other people, including family?
10. What type of treatment would be most helpful to the patient? What would be most acceptable? What would be the least disruptive or irrevocable? What is available?

This type of treatment evaluation is usually best conducted by a team or inter-disciplinary group who can investigate these issues fully with the patient and coordinate the treatment. Such a team usually consists of a psychiatrist, clinical psychologist, internist-endocrinologist, and general surgeon or urologist, preferably all with experience in assessing transsexual patients. The treatment evaluation should include a full medical workup, endocrinological evaluation, and psychological testing, including an evaluation of gender identity and dysphoria, personality organization, ego strengths and vulnerabilities, and psychological stability. Chromosomal typing can be helpful and occasionally will pick up unexpected abnormalities. Although very experienced clinicians may be able to abbreviate, curtail, or combine some of these steps, most often a comprehensive workup is indicated, particularly if major gender reassignment is contemplated.

Treatment of Primary Transsexualism

Since the primary transsexual is, by definition, an individual who has felt miscast in his or her body from early childhood on and has exhibited gender behavior characteristic of the opposite sex from the time of the formation of core gender identity, it is unlikely that psychotherapy will succeed in making such an individual comfortable with his or her biological gender. Only one case has been reported in which an adult male primary transsexual has become comfortable with his masculinity through psychotherapy. (Should such a patient genuinely want to try, however, an attempt at a definitive therapy might be made, as long as the patient realizes that he or she and the therapist are sailing in relatively uncharted waters.) Most primary transsexuals come to medical or psychiatric attention because they are dissatisfied with merely playing the role of the desired opposite sex; cross-dressing is no longer sufficient. What almost all such patients want is definitive gender reassignment, concluding with hormone treatment, electrolysis, the removal of the penis and testes, and construction of an artificial but functional vagina in the case of male primary transsexuals, and the removal of breasts and female organs of reproduction and the construction of an artificial penis on the part of female primary transsexuals.

The following protocol can serve as a guide for the treatment of the primary transsexual:

1. Full treatment evaluation, as outlined previously.
2. Upon completion of evaluation, a full discussion with the psychiatrist or therapist of the options for treatment and their consequences. This step could take several sessions or several months depending on the patient's needs.
3. Reaching a decision mutually agreeable to the patient and his physicians.

If the decision is to prepare for sex reassignment, the following should then occur:

4. The patient should be asked to live in the role of the opposite sex for at least one year and demonstrate to himself or herself and to the treatment team that he or she can do this successfully. While living in that role as fully as possible, other aspects of the treatment can continue. (It may be that the patient has already spent one or more years in the desired gender role; if so and if the patient can demonstrate the competencies needed, then "credit" should be given for the experience rather than requiring the patient to spend another year waiting.)

5. The patient should continue in a counseling or therapeutic relationship during this period to further discuss, evaluate, and integrate his or her experiences and prepare for the likelihood of surgery and full gender reassignment. Reconsideration is still possible.
6. Appropriate hormonal treatment should be instituted or continued under the supervision of the internist-endocrinologist. The patient must be apprised of the slight but real increased risk of cancer associated with long-term hormonal treatment, as well as other side effects.
7. Ancillary cosmetic support, such as electrolysis when indicated, should be performed during this transitional period.
8. If all the above are positive and the patient is still certain and firm in the resolve to continue with surgical reassignment, the patient's doctors must decide if they concur and are prepared to proceed.
9. A thorough, thoughtful, formal *informed consent session* is necessary, in which the patient is apprised of all of the risks, physical, psychological, and emotional, to which he or she will or might be exposed. These should be described in a language easily understood. In addition, the central point that the surgical procedures are *truly irreversible* must be made as clear and definite as possible. For everyone's protection the consent session should be witnessed and a written record—or even a tape recording—of it should be kept. There are few situations in medicine or psychiatry where fully informed consent is more essential.
10. During the initial postoperative period, the patient should continue to have full access to the key doctors involved; he or she will have been through major surgery and will need much support.
11. For at least two to three months after surgery, follow-up visits with both the surgeon and the psychiatrist are recommended. Subsequent follow-up on a periodic basis is also helpful. For the male transsexual, this period is often critical for maintaining the patency of the artificial vagina. It is also often a time of adjustment even for those who had extensive experience living in the role of the preferred sex, and discussing these experiences is usually helpful. The therapist can be alert for postsurgical anxiety or depression and respond accordingly.
12. Longer team follow-up or supportive psychotherapy is sometimes indicated and should be decided on a case-by-case basis.

Although the vast majority of primary transsexuals will opt for gender reassignment, some will not be able or willing to go through with surgery for a variety of reasons. Such reasons may include medical or psychiatric problems that preclude surgery, substantial financial constraints, the unavailability of the procedure locally, or personal and/or family obligations that make gender reassignment awkward or impossible. In all these cases, supportive therapy or counseling should be aimed at helping the patient make the best of the situation—perhaps by finding some comfort in substitute activities, such as transvestic behavior, or sexually ambiguous or androgynous behavior.

Treatment of Secondary Transsexualism

It is useful to remember that many—although not all—secondary transsexuals give a history of substantial periods of time during which they have been able to function comfortably and successfully in their natural gender roles and even have enjoyed their bodily equipment. They look to a transsexual solution to life problems that threaten to overwhelm them, such as unhappy marriages, job failures, overwhelming responsibilities, and so forth. Some male transsexuals may be effeminate homosexuals, others are transvestites, still others are bisexual, and some are effeminate men who are ambivalent, confused, and conflicted about their sexuality. The belief that they are transsexual may be transient, and it is a mistake to rush into surgical reassignment for what may be a neurotic defense. Hence the importance of a thorough evaluation. Indeed, the evaluation and treatment of the secondary transsexual is harder and more problematic than that of the primary transsexual, since the underlying problems, even when identified, do not always admit of easy solution, and the patient is often clamoring for a quick, dramatic, and "magical" solution through surgery.

Most secondary transsexuals have concluded that they are transsexual at a later point in life than the classic primary transsexual, but they adhere to this view of themselves with the same sincerity, intensity, consistency, and steadfastness as do the primary transsexuals. Like some religious converts, these patients bring an intensity of commitment to their cause that is awesome and unshakable. However, it would appear that some of these patients who have undergone gender reassignment seem to have done as well as the primary transsexuals who have undergone the same procedures.

Given the heterogeneous backgrounds, motivations, and psychologies of the secondary transsexual, an equally thorough evaluation for treatment must be done, with special attention paid to stresses, losses, failures, and disappointments that might have led to conviction that what is wrong is that one has been sexually misassigned. If it becomes clear that a patient's belief in his or her gender misidentification is secondary to some stress, loss, or failure, then every attempt should be made to help the patient cope with that stress or loss as well as regain comfort with his or her natural gender. Fortunately, some patients have used psychotherapy to work through such stresses and losses and have rediscovered pleasure and pride in their natural gender. Others have used therapy to discover a wider range of acceptable behaviors and tastes within a given gender designation—for example, the discovery that a male can enjoy art, music, or cooking and still be male; or that a female can enjoy sports, strength, and physical activity and still be female.

Unfortunately, therapy may reduce stress or assuage loss without reversing a patient's conviction that he or she is misidentified. Some patients are unwilling to engage in sustained psychotherapy, sensing that they and their therapists are working at cross-purposes. At this point the question of permanent sex reassignment again rears its head and must be taken seriously. The protocol previously described for the primary transsexual can then be followed, if the physicians concur that it is indicated. If the physicians do not agree that gender reassignment is appropriate, they should so advise the patient and explain their reasons.

For the physician who participates in gender reassignment, the moral and professional issues are even more complex than the technical, surgical issues. The most compelling moral justification for the physician's participation in gender transformation is the belief that the patient is suffering in his or her current state, that the suffering is intense, and that it can best be alleviated by gender transformation. The suffering argument is a powerful—but not totally definitive—argument in favor of such action. Certainly there is little doubt that the individual who feels intense discomfort with his current gender is suffering. What is sometimes in doubt is whether surgical sex reassignment is the best and most effective way of alleviating that suffering.

Guidelines for Action

As noted above, the issues involving sex reassignment are extremely complex and go far beyond the usual definitions of condition and treatment.

What, then, might serve as a guideline for action? Perhaps only that patient and physician must search their souls before embarking on so major a joint enterprise. The patient must seriously consider the reasons that brought him or her to this present situation, the possible alternatives, the possible consequences of action for himself and others, and the risks involved. The patient must be prepared to take full personal responsibility for his or her decision. The physician must fully apprise himself or herself of the patient's desire for change and the reasons behind it and should encourage the patient to consider less radical solutions if possible. The physician should be convinced that he or she is helping rather than harming and that gender reassignment is the only way of relieving substantial suffering. As Robert Stoller has wisely written, "In dealing with such patients there are two truths. The first is biological and is the scientist's concern. The second is psychological and is of crucial concern to the patient. When the two truths lead to incompatibility, e.g., the chromosomes are male but the identity is fixed in femininity with a sense of femaleness, then the identity truth should prevail. Decisions about sex reassignment must be based on the patient's sense of self" (Stoller 1985, p. 1041).

The physician also must decide if he or she feels that the patient's reasons are sufficiently compelling to lend his or her skills to this enterprise. The physician should be free to participate or not, based on his or her own values and understanding. As with abortion, the physician may or may not choose to lend his or her skills to the task. Just as the patient who is refused abortion by one physician may find another who will do it, the individual who wants gender reassignment should be free to find someone else if he or she wishes. In a situation of this complexity, the freedom to act—or refrain from action—must be available to both parties.

Chapter 81

Gender Identity Disorder of Childhood

Clinical attention to children with gender identity disorder has been influenced by the recognition of the adult syndrome of transsexualism (Benjamin 1966; Green 1974; Stoller 1968). When asked to recall their childhood sex-typed interests and gender identity, many adult transsexuals described behavioral patterns that correspond closely to what are now the descriptive features of the gender identity disorder of childhood. Accordingly, some of the efforts to alter the behavior of children with this disorder have been motivated by the hope of preventing transsexualism and the complex of cooccurring emotional difficulties during adolescence and adulthood. An association between extensive childhood cross-gender behavior and subsequent homoeroticism has also been recognized; however, there is currently much less consensus than there was in the past as to whether the prevention of homosexuality per se need be (or should be) part of the rationale for treatment during childhood.

Conceptually, the clinical characteristics of childhood gender disturbance may be partitioned into two components: gender identity and gender role. A child's sense of gender identity can be understood as having both cognitive and affective features. In very young children, this is manifested as the recognition that one is a boy or a girl and an emotional valuing of that recognition. In children with gender identity disorder, the deviation takes one of two forms. In one form, a very young child literally misclassifies his or her gender, as judged by self-labeling and reference to sexual anatomy. The more common form, however, involves correct self-labeling as a boy or a girl but a persistent desire to be of the other sex. In addition, there may be a sense of discomfort about one's sexual anatomy. Clinically, therefore, it is important to realize that children with this disorder almost invariably know their assigned sex (Zucker et al. 1980); it is their discontent with that assignment that requires therapeutic attention. However, it is also important to realize that young children often cannot separate their behavior from their identity (Kohlberg 1966); thus, in unstructured situations, such as play therapy or projective testing, instances of gender identity confusion may be observed.

Gender role refers to the vast array of behaviors, attitudes, and personality characteristics that a culture designates as masculine or feminine. Children with gender identity disorder manifest deviations in gender role behavior in a number of ways, including peer, toy, dress-up, and role preferences. In the case of boys, for example, this would involve affiliation with female peers, play with female-type dolls (e.g., Barbie dolls) and other culturally typical feminine toys, simulated or actual cross-dressing in women's or girls' clothing, the use of makeup, emulation of females in role play (mother, Wonder Woman, etc.), and the presence of feminine sex-type mannerisms. In addition, there is an aversion to rough-and-tumble play, particularly in the domain of competitive group sports, and other stereotypical masculine behaviors and activities (Green 1974, 1976).

Perhaps the most important point to consider in diagnosing gender identity disorder in a particular child is its extensiveness, as judged by the frequency, intensity, and duration of the behaviors. In short, it is the degree to which a child is cross-gender identified that is probably of greatest concern for the clinician in making treatment decisions (Zucker 1982, 1985). Stoller (1968, 1975, 1985) has probably made the most extreme case for this point, in that he argues that boys who are profoundly feminine not only differ in etiology from less feminine boys but will also respond differently to treatment. Before proceeding, we will offer clinical vignettes of children who either meet the criteria of the gender identity disorder of childhood or else fall within the spectrum of the phenomenology under consideration. Detailed clinical descriptions of these children may be found elsewhere (Green 1974; Green and Money 1960; Stoller 1968; Zuger 1966).

Clinical Vignettes

Case 1

This vignette illustrates an apparent misclassification of one's gender and disavowal of one's sexual anatomy. Ellen is a four-year-old girl who is emotionally immature, though of average intelligence (IQ = 104). According to her parents, she has claimed "for some time now" that she is a boy. She doesn't mind being referred to as Ellen, apparently because she does not recognize that this is a culturally stereotyped girl's name. Ellen has told her parents that she will be a daddy when she grows up. Since the age of two, she has claimed to have a penis, or that she will have one. A few weeks prior to assessment, she employed a darning needle to simulate a penis. She attempts to urinate standing up and insists on using public washrooms for boys. In the course of clinical assessment, she had the following discussion with one of the examiners:

Interviewer (I): Remember before I [asked] are you a boy or a girl? What did you say?
Child (C): A boy . . .
I: Now, your name is Ellen, right?
C: Yeah.
I: Are you a girl or a boy?
C: A boy.
I: Tell me, how do you know that you're a boy?
C: I can't (unintelligible). I know I have a bum-bum. . . . (After acknowledging that her brother has a penis:) I have a penis! (Points to her crotch.) That's my penis.
I: (After further discussion.) If I said that Ellen is really a girl, what would you say?
C: I . . . I would say I'm a boy, boy, boy, boy, boy.

Case 2

This vignette represents a typical case of cross-gender identification. Ed is a four-year-old boy (IQ = 104) who since the age of two has shown a marked preference for culturally stereotypical feminine activities. Currently, he plays exclusively with girls and is described by his day-care staff as quite involved in "little girl fantasies" such as "playing at getting married" or "the handsome captain is going to marry me." He enjoys cross-dressing and loves to watch his mother dress, wanting to "slip on" her dresses. He plays with Barbie dolls to the extent of it being considered a "fixation." His fantasy hero is Wonder Woman. He avoids rough-and-tumble play with other boys for fear of getting hurt. According to his parents, Ed sometimes talks about wanting to be a girl. Recently, he has mentioned wanting his penis to change into a vagina; however, he does stand to urinate.

Case 3

This last vignette is of a child who manifests a variety of cross-gender behaviors; however, he does not profess the strong desire to be of the opposite sex, which precludes giving the diagnosis of gender identity disorder. Research and clinical studies show that there is an age-related reduction in the expression of cross-sex wishes (Green 1975; Zucker et al. 1984); it is not yet clear whether this reflects a qualitative shift in the nature of cross-gender identification or is simply a social desirability maneuver. Bill, age 10 (IQ = 109), was referred by school authorities because of their concern about his preference for female playmates and feminine activities. The precipitant was Bill's dressing as a girl for the school's Halloween party. Apparently, he was so convincing that some of the other children became concerned that he really was a girl. At the time of the assessment, Bill preferred to play with girls and participate in feminine activities. He had a history of extensive cross-dressing, but this was now limited to occasional wearing of his mother's shoes "because they feel different." His motoric movements during the assessment were notably feminine or effeminate. He claimed that Wonder Woman was his hero. When asked whether he wanted to be a girl, he became tearful and stated that sometimes he wished he "could be a girl, because then they [the boys] would not know who I am and would not tease me." His parents denied any knowledge of cross-sex yearnings in Bill. Although he was somewhat involved in contact sports, he would back off if the sport became rough. He is teased by his peers for being "effeminate," and his older sister is teased that her brother is a "transsexual."

Treatment Approaches

Behavior Therapy

Twelve single case reports in the literature have employed behavior therapy with gender-disturbed children, the majority of these by Rekers and his associates (Dowrick 1983; Dupont 1968; Hay et al. 1981; Myrick 1970; Rekers 1979; Rekers and Lovaas 1974; Rekers and Mead 1979; Rekers and Varni 1977a, 1977b; Rekers et al. 1974, 1976, 1977). The most common forms of intervention have been differential social attention, self-regulation, and token economy. The targets of these interventions involved a variety of cross-gender role behaviors, including toy and dress-up play, peer affiliation, and mannerisms. Treatment of these behaviors has been conducted in the clinic, the home, and the school. None of these case reports have focused specifically on the child's verbal statements or fantasies about wanting to be of the opposite sex. In a narrow sense, then, the aim of these interventions has been to modify specific patterns of overt sex-typed behavior. With regard to play, for example, Rekers and Lovaas (1974) stated that the therapeutic goal (for boys) was to "extinguish feminine behavior and to develop masculine behavior" (p. 179). Despite the focus on specific sex-typed behaviors, the therapists do appear to consider the child's general sense of well-being as a boy or a girl in evaluating the effectiveness of the intervention.

Social attention procedures have been directed primarily to the child's sex-typed play within a clinic setting. The basic strategy is to have an adult (e.g., the mother) attend to the child's same-sex play (e.g., by verbal praise, visual regard, and smiling) and to ignore cross-sex play. A number of studies have shown the effectiveness of this intervention in reducing the amount of cross-sex play (Rekers 1979; Rekers and Lovaas 1974; Rekers et al. 1976; Rekers and Varni 1977a, 1977b). However, two main limitations of the treatment have been noted. First, the child tends to revert to cross-sex play patterns in the adult's absence or in other environments, such as the home (a problem of "stimulus specificity"); second, there is little evidence of generalization to other (nontreated) cross-sex behaviors (a problem of "response specificity"). Similar limitations have been noted with the use of token economy systems, in which the child is given "points" for engaging in a same-sex behavior or penalized points for engaging in a cross-sex behavior (Rekers and Lovaas 1974). Thus, it has generally been necessary to apply these procedures separately to each to-be-treated behavior, both within and across settings.

The problems of stimulus and response specificity have led behavior therapists to consider more effective strategies of promoting generalization. Self-regulation techniques have been one such strategy (see Blount and Stokes 1984; Meador and Ollendick 1984; O'Leary and Dubey 1979). The basic idea is to have the child reinforce him- or herself when engaging in a sex-typical behavior. This eliminates the necessity of providing external reinforcement (e.g., social praise), which may not always be feasible. As Blount and Stokes note (1984), by allowing the child to control his or her own behavior the "problems of generalization from one setting to another and from the presence to the absence of external behavior change agents may be avoided" (p. 196). Rekers and Varni (1977b), for example, employed a self-regulation strategy with a four-year-old boy and found some evidence for greater generalization than that resulting from a social attention intervention. Treatment occurred initially in a clinic setting. The child wore a wrist counter and was told that he should press the counter only when playing with "boys' toys." This behavior was initially facilitated by behavioral cuing, in which the child wore a "bug-in-the-ear" device and was told periodically when to press the counter. This self-monitoring procedure resulted in a substantial decrease in cross-sex play and showed moderate evidence of generalization. The child was subsequently treated in his nursery school setting, in which a self-reinforcement procedure was superimposed upon the self-monitoring technique: the child was given candy if he accrued a sufficient number of points on the wrist counter. Similar evidence of behavioral change was reported.

Covert modeling, a technique similar to self-regulation, was employed by Hay et al. (1981) in treating a 10-year-old boy's feminine mannerisms and gestures. With the aid of the therapist, the child practiced a series of behaviors that were to be part of the covert modeling procedure. The main aspect of the technique was to have the child use his imagination "whenever he wanted to remind himself how to perform one of the target behaviors in a masculine way" (p. 390). It was hoped that the use of covert modeling would facilitate generalization, since the child was instructed "to practice in imagination . . . the . . . target behaviors in a variety of environmental settings" (p. 389). Hay et al. reported that the treatment was not only effective in the clinic setting, but was generalized to the home setting and to nontreated cross-sex behaviors (e.g., play) as well. As noted by Zucker (1985), continued research by behavior therapists will be required to determine the relative superiority of these varied treatment techniques. Nevertheless, the covert modeling technique may have particular merit, especially with older children, whose cross-gender symptomatology may have greater "internally based" cognitions and fantasies that are less susceptible to external modification.

Psychotherapy

Analytic and analytically oriented treatment reports of gender-disturbed boys have appeared periodically in the literature since the 1950s (Bleiberg et al. 1986; Charatan and Galef 1965; Fischhoff 1964; Francis 1965; Friend et al. 1954; Gilpin et al. 1979; Greenson 1966; Herman 1983; Lee 1985; Loeb and Shane 1982; Lothstein 1988; Meyer and Dupkin 1985; Pruett and Dahl 1982; Sack 1985; Sackin 1983; Schultz 1979; Sperling 1964; Thacher 1985; Zaphiriou 1978). Very little has been written about gender-disturbed girls, perhaps because they are less often brought to the attention of the psychiatric profession than gender-disturbed boys, at least during childhood (for exceptions, see Holder 1982; Hopkins 1984; Meyer and Dupkin 1985). Over the years, analytic reports on gender-disturbed boys have paid increased attention to "preoedipal" rather than "oedipal" factors, both with regard to etiology and treatment, a shift that reflects general changes in psychoanalytic accounts of gender identity development (Fast 1984; Kleeman 1976; Mendell 1982; Roiphe and Galenson 1981; Stoller 1965, 1968, 1974, 1976, 1985; Wong 1982). Although oedipal issues, such as castration anxiety, are given varied emphasis in these reports, there has been a general recognition that such factors do not tell the whole story, given that so much cross-gender symptomatology appears prior to the emergence of this phase-dominant developmental conflict (Green 1974).

General principles of analytic and analytically oriented therapy with children will not be considered here; rather, the focus will be on some of the particular issues that have received prominence in the treatment of gender-disturbed children. Essentially, these treatment issues revolve around both interpersonal experience, especially with parents, and intrapsychic representations of such experience. The extent to which the intrapsychic representations correspond with actual experience varies from case to case, contingent, at least in part, on the child's general ego functioning or level of ego development.

A number of interpersonal factors have been considered crucial. Perhaps the most prominent factor has been the parents' attitudes toward masculinity and femininity and how these influence the child. A number of reports, for example, have noted that the mothers devalue masculinity and are envious of and angry toward men, and that these attitudes are sensed by the young boy. In some cases, the mother actively encourages feminine behaviors in her son; in other cases, she simply tolerates such behavior as it emerges. The fathers in these cases typically receive attention only by default, in that they are viewed as unable psychologically to counteract the mother's femininizing influence. Stoller (1968, 1975), among others, has alluded to the presence of what might be called "subclinical" gender conflicts in the childhood of mothers of very feminine boys. Less attention has been given to the possibility of childhood gender conflicts in the fathers; rather, their weak sense of self and peripheral familial involvement have been emphasized by some authors (e.g., Stoller 1979). Although it would be an error to assume that all mothers of gender-disturbed boys suffer from distortions in both feeling and attitude toward gender identity issues, it appears (at least among clinical referrals) that attention to this factor is warranted in a substantial number of cases. In fact, it has been noted in a number of reports that the ability of parents to shift their attitudes and expectations about gender identity issues is correlated with clinical improvement in the child (e.g., Green et al. 1972).

Another characteristic of the parents that has received increased attention is their general personality functioning. There has been a growing interest in the possible connection between certain forms of personality disturbance (e.g., the borderline and narcissistic conditions) and affective states (e.g., depression) in the parents, especially the mother, and gender disturbance in the child (Bradley 1985; Marantz 1984; Stoller 1975). A common impression is that the mothers turn to their sons for nurturance, an experience missing in their own childhood and in their relations with their husbands. In some way, then, by being feminine, such a son provides his mother with the "mothering" that she felt was missing in her own childhood. Another conjecture, noted by Marantz (1984), is that "in need of narcissistic mirroring" the mother "is able to respond to her son's expression of interest and affirmation in her femininity when she is able to respond to little else" (p. 93).

At least two child characteristics have received regular attention in analytic reports. The first concerns the general ego functioning of the child. Stoller's (1968, p. 25) early claim that "it is possible for children to be severely damaged in the development of their gender identity and still remain quite intact in other aspects of identity development and ego functions" has not received substantial support from the subsequent literature. There is an emerging consensus that gender-disturbed children, on average, show at least moderate levels of psychopathology (Coates and Person 1985; Zucker 1985), ranging from minimal to severe in individual cases. Although the connection between general psychopathology and gender disturbance has not yet been worked out, the child's general ego functioning will, no doubt, be a factor in treatment.

The other characteristic has concerned the breadth of the preoedipal issues involved in the gender disturbance. Difficulty in individuating from the mother (for whatever reason) has been one of the more prominent explanations of boyhood femininity by psychoanalysts. Included under this general factor would be femininity induced by maternal overcloseness, separation anxiety (actual or perceived), and identification with a mother who is experienced as omnipotent and overwhelming.

Stoller (1966, 1975) has probably described the clearest illustrations of femininity induced by maternal overcloseness. With regard to separation anxiety, the essential notion is that the boy's feminine interests represent "symbols" of the lost object and presumably function as anxiety reducers. In this case, the femininity is viewed as resulting from severe disruptions in attachment relations, not overcloseness. Gilpin et al. (1979), for example, reported a case in which the boy's feminine symptoms apparently began subsequent to the departure of his "nanny" (see also Bleiberg et al. 1986). In less severe instances, the feminine objects are viewed as serving a transitional function, which helps the boy tolerate separation from the mother.

Boyhood femininity induced by a felt sense of powerlessness vis-a-vis the mother was reported in a case of a four-year-old boy by Fischhoff (1964). After the birth of a younger brother, the boy began to think that his mother did not like him, which left him feeling angry and helpless: "To him, she seemed an overwhelmingly powerful figure whom he was dependent upon and yet feared. He wanted to be as powerful as she and, to him, this meant being a woman" (p. 280). In some respects, the mechanism appears to involve an identification with the "aggressor."

Two aspects of analytic treatment will be described here: the behavior of the therapist and the involvement of the parents. The stereotypical descriptor of the child analyst as relatively passive does not seem to characterize the behavior of most of the therapists in the above-noted reports. In fact, many of the therapists appeared to actively address the "symptoms" of cross-gender identification. Greenson (1966), for example, argued that the central problem of a five-year-old boy was a "gender symbiosis," in which there was a virtual absence of boundaries between the boy and his mother. In his play, the boy often referred to a Barbie doll as "I" or "we." A main part of the treatment involved trying to move the boy away from his overclose relationship with his mother by pointing out the difference between liking and being another person. Much of this entailed discussing gender issues quite actively with the child. Many other treatment reports have also emphasized gender symbiosis, though there is considerable debate regarding how "conflictual" the mother-son relationship is.

Because parental factors have been viewed as central to the genesis of gender disturbance, parents have often been involved in treatment. To the extent that parental factors continue to contribute to the child's gender difficulties, some would argue that treating the parents is essential (Stoller 1970, 1978). The analytically oriented therapist should, therefore, carefully consider the likelihood of treating the child successfully without involving the parents. As a rule of thumb based on the literature to date, the greater the inter- and intrapersonal difficulties of the parents, the less successful treatment of the child alone is likely to be.

Green and his colleagues have reported a more eclectic or multimodal approach to the treatment of cross-gender-identified boys (Green et al. 1972; Green and Newman 1973; Kosky 1987; Lim and Bottomley 1983; Metcalf and Williams 1977; Newman 1976; Wrate and Gulens 1986). Green et al. described four objectives of the intervention: 1) to develop a relationship of "trust and affection" between the boy and a male therapist; 2) to heighten parental concern regarding the boy's femininity so that they begin to disapprove of it; 3) to increase the father's involvement in the boy's life; and 4) to sensitize the parents to the dynamics of their own relationship, so that the mother-son "overcloseness" and the father's peripheral role in the family can be altered. Typically, this approach has involved working with the child and parents separately. In the child's therapy, following the establishment of a therapeutic alliance, the therapist quite explicitly began to convey to the child that his feminine behavior was "not right" and should be given up; of course, this message was conveyed in a manner appropriate to the child's developmental level. In therapy, approval was given for "any signs of masculinity" in either overt behavior or fantasy. Green et al. (1972) reported reductions in much of the boys' extreme cross-gender behaviors, though they concluded that the therapy was least successful in those cases in which intervention with the parents was most difficult.

An aspect of this general therapeutic strategy that has been reevaluated over the years concerns the sex of the therapist, an issue that is commonly raised by practitioners seeing a gender-disturbed child for the first time. In the case of some feminine boys, it is felt that a male therapist would be particularly valuable, given that most of the child's close relationships have been with women. Moreover, it has been argued that a same-sex therapist makes the task of same-sex identification less complicated. Although these points have merit, it may also be argued that an opposite-sex therapist has the potential to "correct" distortions (e.g., that to be valued means to be feminine) that have developed in the child's relationship with his opposite-sex parent. Schultz (1979) has provided what is probably the clearest example of this point to date. Thus, it is probably not crucial that the therapist be of the same sex as the child. What is perhaps more important is the therapist's ability and sense of comfort in dealing with the child's cross-gender identification.

For various reasons, therapeutic work with the parents, especially with respect to gender issues, is particularly important during the early period of the child's treatment. In this connection, the following summarizes some of the more salient issues that we have dealt with in our experience.

1. It is not uncommon for the parents to have vacillated for a number of years as to whether there is reason to be concerned about their child's gender identity development. The reasons for this vary. Some of the relevant intra- and interpersonal factors have been alluded to earlier. In some instances, the uncertainty has been reinforced by professionals who, when consulted by the parents, indicated that the behavior was only a phase. In other instances, the parents may have been uncertain about where to draw the line, given the purported cultural changes in what is considered sex-appropriate behavior. Thus, once the clinician determines that the child does have a gender identity conflict, he or she has to deal with the parental uncertainty that has preceded the consultation. Many parents will respond with a sense of relief when informed that their child is experiencing conflict, but that there are ways of resolving it.

2. In the typical cases, part of the therapy involves limiting the child's extreme cross-

gender behavior during day-to-day life. In the case of a boy, for example, this might involve prohibiting cross-dressing, discouraging feminine role playing and toy play, attempting to include boys as part of his peer group, and pointing out the merits of his sexual anatomy. During this period, many parents rely quite strongly on the therapist for support and feedback. This is a particularly good time to deal with parental resistance in implementing change, as the motivations that underlie the parents' behavior become clear. Two main dangers in this period have been observed. One is that some parents, especially fathers, can be somewhat authoritarian in limiting their child's behavior. It is important at this juncture to help the parents to be both systematic and sensitive in their dealings with the child. The other danger is that the parents will attempt to alter the child's behavior but will overlook the overall therapeutic aim. In this regard, K.J.Z. in particular has found it useful to frame the desired changes in the context of trying to make the child feel more comfortable about his or her gender identity, pointing out that permitting extensive cross-gender behavior to continue probably perpetuates the child's fantasies about wanting to be of the opposite sex.

3. Newman (1976) has pointed out that some parents believe that the child's long-term psychosexual identity is a fait accompli (i.e., that the child is "doomed" to be either transsexual or homosexual). A number of strategies can be used to deal with this belief. For example, it can be pointed out that while the available evidence does indicate that the child has a greater than average chance of becoming transsexual or homosexual in later life (Green 1985, 1987; Zucker 1985), prediction of outcome in individual cases is not warranted. Moreover, it can be noted that there is little benefit in focusing on what will happen years later. On the other hand, considerable benefit may be derived from concentrating on changing the child's current behavior, given the evidence that doing so appears to result in a reduction of childhood gender dysphoria (which, presumably, lessens the probability of a transsexual outcome). Parental feelings toward homosexuality can then be dealt with separately, as appropriate.

Zucker et al. (1985) have provided some empirical evidence of the merit of working with the parents. They found that the number of parent therapy sessions correlated more strongly than the number of child therapy sessions with reductions in cross-gender behavior between the time of assessment and a one-year follow-up in a sample of 44 gender-disturbed children.

As noted earlier, very few therapy reports have described treatment strategies with gender-disturbed girls. In principle, none of the therapeutic approaches employed with boys would require substantive modification with girls; for example, behavior therapists would not assume that the mechanisms of acquisition of cross-gender behavior would differ between the sexes (cf. Rekers and Mead 1979). Similarly, Green (1982) has suggested that his therapeutic strategy with feminine boys can also be employed with masculine girls. From a psychoanalytic perspective, there is evidence that cross-gender behavior in girls emerges during the preoedipal years (see Green et al. 1982), as it does in boys. However, the dynamics that might underlie cross-gender identification are probably different for the sexes. For example, it would be difficult to account for masculine behavior in girls that is the result of separation difficulties from the mother, since this problem in boys is linked with increased femininity. Stoller (1975) has argued that adult female-to-male transsexualism results, in part, from an extremely distant mother-daughter relationship and a compensatory identification with the father. Unfortunately, the relevance of such processes for girls with gender identity disorder is not known.

Summary

The above-described treatment strategies represent the most common forms of intervention available to the practitioner. At present, the clinical evidence suggests that these varied therapeutic strategies all have some success in reducing the child's cross-gender identification. To date, however, no controlled studies comparing the relative efficacy of these forms of intervention have been undertaken. In addition, information is still lacking with regard to long-term treatment effects. Nevertheless, the more limited therapeutic aim of reducing childhood gender identity conflict appears to be attainable by these current techniques, a result that is probably in the best interests of the individual child.

Chapter 82

Exhibitionism and Voyeurism

Exhibitionism and voyeurism may be viewed as opposite sides of the same coin—to see or to be seen. The two conditions were described by Krafft-Ebing in 1886 (reprinted 1965) and Lasegue in 1887. Krafft-Ebing saw it as having a close parallel with sado-masochism in that sexual excitement was obtained in the setting of a heightened emotional state of fear and apprehension. He noted that both exhibitionists and voyeurs began their practices at or soon after puberty and described them as sensitive, usually shy, and rarely a threat to their victims. In his day, as today, exhibitionists are the most common sexual offenders to come before the court. Voyeurs, according to Johnson (1973), are rarely caught and much less information is available about them. Voyeurs generally are more furtive by virtue of the nature of their particular paraphilia, enabling them to escape notice even by the victim and still less so by the authorities. Although the two conditions are related and sometimes occur in the same individual, there are some distinct differences that may involve the assessment of risk and, therefore, the restrictions needed and the therapy to be utilized.

Incidence

Both conditions are common, but there are no exact figures on incidence. Some recent studies of potential victims have shown that in several locations in Great Britain (Gittleson et al. 1978), the United States (Cox and McMahon 1978), Hong Kong (Cox et al. 1982), and Guatemala (Rhoads and Padilla-Borjes 1981) approximately half the young women had been the object of exhibitionism. Court figures and incidence estimates from psychiatrists are largely useless—indicating only those who are caught and brought to trial and those who are caught and referred by the legal system. Since most exhibitionists and voyeurs do not consider themselves to be ill, they almost never come to treatment without outside pressure.

Clinical Definition

Exhibitionism and voyeurism may occur concurrently in the same individual. Either may be combined with other personality or paraphilic disorders. Krafft-Ebing and Lasegue defined exhibitionists as not sexually aggressive. DSM-III-R defines exhibitionism as "recurrent, intense sexual urges and sexually arousing fantasies, of at least six months' duration, involving the exposure of one's genitals to a stranger" (American Psychiatric Association 1987, p. 282). If limited to such a definition, then exhibitionists (and voyeurs) are indeed not harmful.

Hackett (1975) concluded that most voyeurs and exhibitionists are more a nuisance than a menace. Rooth (1973) studied a group of 30 persistent exhibitionists and reached the conclusion that sexual violence was exceptional among them. However, his conclusion seems not to agree with his data, as among his exhibitionists, there were five voyeurs, three hebephilics, two incestuous pedophilics, eight involved in repeated frottage, two involved in sexual assaults, and four in "indecent assault convictions." From his report, it is not clear which of these involved overlaps. Most of his subjects had been arrested, often repetitively, and therefore may have constituted a hard core. Abel et al. (1977), Gebhard et al. (1965), and Holmstrom and Burgess (1980) present data indicating that many rapists and other dangerous sex offenders may also be involved in acts of voyeurism or exhibitionism. Gray and Mohr (1965) note that the recidivism rate for exhibitionism is extremely high, reaching 71 percent for those with a history of previous sexual and nonsexual offenses.

Smith and Meyer (1965), commenting on the combining of paraphilias, state that exhibitionists may be derived from different personality types: 1) neurotics, 2) neurotic inadequate, 3) unaware (secondary to somatic disorders), and 4) characterological. They add, "Though the fourth group is apparently small in terms of percentage, it does pose a small threat of aggression to the victim; and because of the high absolute number of exhibitionists, some social concern is warranted." Most studies indicate that the majority of voyeurs and exhibitionists are harmless nuisances, often a joke to the general public (as witness the frequent cartoons of flashers). However, all do not fit the benign aspect assigned them by DSM-III-R, and this behavior may be just one facet of a potentially dangerous sex offender (Abel et al. 1977). Both conditions occur in males (whether they occur in females is open to controversy) (Hollender et al. 1977).

Smith (1983) advocates a broader definition of the disorder based on the fact that individual cases are quite varied and need individualized formulation. He notes that theories regarding the disorders are broadly divided into behavioral and psychodynamic. The behavioral view, he states, provides a basis for treatment that is relatively effective, while inattentive to the origins of the disorder; whereas the psychodynamic view offers an explanation for the problem, though offering less in terms of treatment results. He tends to agree with Rickles (1942) that the phenomenon has a marked compulsive quality to it. He also notes that it can be a presenting symptom of somatic disease, including such conditions as hypoglycemia, cerebral arteriosclerosis, or brain tumor. The specific acts usually follow some sudden drop in self-esteem that produces a rising titer of anxiety (Allen 1980; Mathis and Collins 1970; Sperling 1947). The action aims to restore self-esteem to tolerable levels by reassuring the men of masculinity and by allowing the expressions of hostility to women through the particular paraphilia (Stoller 1975). The fact that voyeurs and exhibitionists have such fragile self-esteem regulatory mechanisms and so much denial of illness may account for the high frequency of acts, many times per week in some individuals.

The conditions vary greatly in intensity from man to man. One many may exhibit several times per week under moderate to mild stress, whereas another averages less than one time per month, and then only under extreme stress. One voyeur may be cautious and never be apprehended, whereas another takes ridiculous risks and courts arrest.

Treatment

Years of experience have established that moral suasion, punishment, and legal threats are virtually worthless as treatments. Almost all intervention, even being apprehended by the law, produces only a temporary reduction of the aberrant urge. Unfortunately, this lasts a few weeks or months at most. With rare exceptions, psychoanalysis, and probably traditional psychodynamic therapies, have limited usefulness (Allen 1980; Fensterheim 1974). As Marmor (1978) has pointed out, removing a man's principal means of sexual expression leaves a void and, until this is filled, the actions are apt to continue. Even though hostility more than sex appears to be the driving force for these conditions, the same principle appears to hold.

The literature indicates that the most time- and cost-effective treatments for controlling the behaviors are various forms of aversive conditioning (Evans 1967; Marmor 1978; Maletzky 1974; Serber 1970; Wickramasekera 1980). However, the recurrence rate continues to be high. It appears that Marmor's concept holds here, as it does with alcoholics and addicts, so that unless some ego assets are added to the individual's makeup, he is apt to slip. In this respect, group therapy (Mathis and Collins 1970) and/or various behavioral techniques (as advocated by Brownell et al. 1977; Brownell 1980; and D'Alessio 1968) such as assertive training, social training, and so forth would appear to make the maximum contribution. Daitzman and Cox (1980) present an extended case report listing 19 treatment sessions in which they utilized assisted covert sensitization, aversive imagery scenes, and marital therapy.

It is difficult to set a definite length of time for treatment. The aversive treatments generally can be carried out in a dozen or so visits over a month or two, but the ego-building techniques may extend for as long as a year or more with weekly visits. The length of time depends on the degree of control achieved by the aversive conditioning and on the motivation of the individual for self-improvement and his ability to develop newer, more adaptive, and more socially acceptable techniques for self-expression. Particular attention must be paid to the appropriate expression of hostility.

Evans's (1967) electrical aversion trials averaged 13.6 sessions over 4.8 weeks. He quotes others whose trials varied from three to 22 with variable booster periods. Maletzky's (1974) treatment involved 35 sessions of varying lengths over three to four months with booster sessions at 3-, 6-, and 12-month intervals following active treatment. Brownell (1980) reports 19 sessions of covert sensitization after an evaluation period.

Mathis's group therapy involved the use of male and female cotherapists for weekly meetings with six months' mandatory attendance. They revised this period to one year, as both they and group members agreed that six months was insufficient to eradicate denial (Mathis 1969). Sperling's psychoanalytic case (1947) and one by Rhoads (1983) averaged three years, although both these cases included therapy of characterological problems over and above the exhibitionism.

Most of those attempting therapy of exhibitionists today agree that a multimodal therapeutic approach is warranted, usually initiated and backed by a court order. Such therapy may involve not only one or several types of behavioral treatment, but may also be combined with group therapy or with individual psychodynamic therapy of either a supportive or insight-oriented type.

In the above context, Evans (1980) issues a number of cautions about electrical aversion therapy, and he believes it should be only part of a comprehensive treatment approach. He quotes Bancroft (1975), who lists four objectives for treatment: 1) the establishment of a rewarding sexual relationship, 2) improvement of sexual functioning, 3) control of unwanted behavior, and 4) possibly adaptation to a deviant sexual role. To this end, Evans adds a crucial fifth objective, "the development of socially acceptable alternative behaviors." Thus, if exhibitionism occurs in response to tension-inducing situations, the therapist may utilize systematic desensitization in addition to electrical aversion, as well as positive stimuli aimed at improving function. The theoretical rationale for electrical aversion therapy involves the pairing of some representation of the exhibitionist's behavior with electric shock, with the goal of alleviating the deviant behavior. The deviant behavior can be performed, represented in pictoral form, imagined, or represented by a combination of these methods.

Cautela's (1967) method of covert sensitization has been utilized by a number of therapists, including Wickramasekera (1972), Brownell and Barlow (1976), and Maletzky (1974). These methods involve taking a detailed history of the favored manner of deviation and the construction of an in vivo or imaginal aversion scene or image. This behavioral approach may be augmented by such techniques as assertive training, social training, or group therapy stressing social interactions.

Summary

In summary, exhibitionism and voyeurism are not the same in all individuals. Even if one eliminates the rare physical causes, such as dementias, psychotic states, temporal lobe disorders, and deliriums, and limits the consideration of exhibitionism and voyeurism to the DSM-III-R criteria, the patients are not a homogeneous group (Allen 1962). Given this, Rooth (1980) has declared that therapists must have different treatment approaches available. These should include some form of behavioral management for quick control of the symptoms and some type of treatment that addresses the ego deficits and immaturities of the patient. Finally, one must recognize the inherent difficulty of treating these patients, many of whom are poorly motivated, seen under duress (court order or threat of legal action), and in whom the condition is ego syntonic.

References

Section 7
Paraphilias and Gender Identity Disorders

Abel GG, Becker J: Child molesting: more prevalent than once believed. Psychiatric News, October 5, 1984

Abel GG, Barlow DH, Blanchard EB, et al: The components of rapists' sexual arousal. Arch Gen Psychiatry 34:895–903, 1977

Abel GG, Blanchard EB, Barkin DH: Measurement of sexual arousal in several paraphilias: the effects of stimulus modality, instructional set and stimulus content on the objective. Behav Res Ther 19:25–33, 1981

Abel GG, Mittelman MS, Becker JV: Sexual offenders: results of assessment and recommendations for treatment. New York, undated (unpublished manuscript)

Abraham K: Remarks on the psychoanalysis of a case of foot and corset fetishism, in Selected Papers on Psychoanalysis. London, Hogarth Press, 1948

Allen C: A Textbook of Psychosexual Disorders. Oxford, Oxford University Press, 1962

Allen DW: A psychoanalytic view, in Exhibitionism: Description, Assessment and Treatment. Edited by Cox DJ, Daitzman RJ. New York, Garland STPM Press, 1980

American Psychiatric Association: Diagnostic and Statistical Manual of Mental Disorders, 3rd ed. Washington, DC, American Psychiatric Association, 1980

American Psychiatric Association: Diagnostic and Statistical Manual of Mental Disorders, 3rd ed., revised. Washington, DC, American Psychiatric Association, 1987

Anonymous: Nature and management of transvestism. Lancet 919–921, 1974

Arajii S, Finkelhor D: Chapter 3, in A Sourcebook on Child Sexual Abuse. Edited by Finkelhor D, et al. Beverly Hills, Calif, Sage Publications, 1986

Badgley RF: Sexual Offences Against Children: Report of the Committee of Sexual Offences Against Children and Youth Appointed by the Minister of Justice and Attorney General of Canada and the Minister of National Health and Welfare, vol I. Robin F. Badgley, Chairman. Ottawa, Minister of Supply and Services, 1984

Bak RC: Fetishism. J Am Psychoanal Assoc 1:285–298, 1953

Bak RC: Ten phallic women, in Psychoanalytic Study of the Child, vol 23. New York, International Universities Press, 1968

Ball JRB: A case of hair fetishism, transvestism, and organic cerebral disorder. Acta Psychiatr Scand 44:249–254, 1968

Bancroft J: The behavioural approach to sexual disorders, in Psychosexual Problems. Edited by Milne H, Hardy SJ. Baltimore, University Park Press, 1975

Bancroft V: Ethical aspects of sexuality and sex therapy, in Psychiatric Ethics. Edited by Bloch S, Chodoff P. New York, Oxford University Press, 1981

Barnard JW, Robbins L, Newman G, et al: Differences found between rapists, child molestors. Psychiatric News 20:34–35, 1985

Benjamin H: Transsexualism and transvestism as psycho-somatic and somato-psychic syndromes. Am J Psychother 8:219–230, 1954

Bentler PM, Prince C: Psychiatric symptomatology in transvestites. J Clin Psychol 26:434–435, 1970

Berlin FS: Sex offenders: a biomedical perspective and a status report on biomedical treatment, in The Sexual Aggressor: Current Perspectives on Treatment. Edited by Greer JG, Steward IR. New York, Van Nostrad Reinhold, 1983

Berlin FS, Meinecke CF: Treatment of sex offenders with antiandrogenic medication: conceptualization, review of treatment modalities, and preliminary findings. American Psychiatry 135:601–607, 1981

Binet A: Fetishisme dans l'amour. Revue Philosophique 24:143–167, 252–274, 1887

Blanchard R: Typology of male-to-female transsexualism. Arch Sex Behav 14:247–261, 1985

Bleiberg E, Jackson L, Ross JL: Gender identity disorder and object loss. J Am Acad Child Psychiatry 25:58–67, 1986

Blount RL, Stokes TF: Self-reinforcement by children, in Progress in Behavior Modification, vol 18. Edited by Hersen M, Eisler RM, Miller PM. New York, Academic Press, 1984

Boots: The feelings of a fetishist. Psychiatric Quarterly 31:742–758, 1957

Bradford JMcDW, Paulak A: Sadistic homosexual pedophilia: treatment with cyproterone acetate: a single case study. Can J Psychiatry 32:22–30, 1987

Bradley SJ: Gender disorders in childhood: a formulation, in Gender Dysphoria: Development, Research, Management. Edited by Steiner BW. New York, Plenum Press, 1985

Brantley JT, Wise TN: Antiandrogenic treatment of a gender-dysphoric transvestite. J Sex Marital Ther 11:109–112, 1985

Brierley H: Transvestism: A Handbook with Case Studies for Psychologists, Psychiatrists and Counselors. New York, Pergamon, 1979

Brownell KD: Multifaceted behavior therapy, in Exhibitionism: Description, Assessment, and Treatment. Edited by Cox DJ, Daitzman RJ. New York, Garland STPM Press, 1980

Brownell KD, Barlow DH: Measurement and treatment of two sexual deviations in one person. J Behav Ther Exp Psychiatry 7:349–354, 1976

Brownell KD, Haynes, SC, Barlow DH: Patterns of appropriate and deviate sexual arousal: the behavioral treatment of multiple sexual deviances. J Consult Clin Psychol 451:144–155, 1977

Buhrich N: A case of familial heterosexual transvestism. Acta Psychiatr Scand 55:199–201, 1977

Buhrich N: Transvestism in history. J Nerv Ment Dis 165:64–66, 1977b

Buhrich N: Motivation for cross-dressing in heterosexual transvestism. Acta Psychiatr Scand 57:145–152, 1978

Buhrich N, McConaghy N: Can fetishism occur in transsexuals? Arch Sex Behav 6:223–235, 1976

Buhrich N, McConaghy N: Clinical comparison of transvestism and transsexualism: an overview. Aust NZ J Psychiatry 11:83–86, 1977a

Buhrich N, McConaghy N: The discrete syndromes of transvestism and transsexualism. Arch Sex Behav 6:483–495, 1977b

Buhrich N, McConaghy N: Parental relationships during childhood in homosexuality, transvestism and transsexualism. Aust NZ J Psychiatry 12:103–108, 1978

Buhrich N, Theile H, Yaw A, et al: Plasma testosterone, serum FSH, and serum LH levels in transvestism. Arch Sex Behav 8:49–53, 1979

Burgess AW, Hartman CR, McCauslend MP, et al: Response patterns in children and adolescents exploited true sex rings and pornography. Am J Psych 141:656–662, 1984

The California Study: California sexual deviation research. State of California, Department of Mental Hygiene, January 1953

The California Study: California sexual deviation research. State of California, Department of Mental Hygiene, March 1954

Cassity JH: Psychological considerations of pedophilia. Psychoanal Rev 14:189–199, 1927

Cautela JR: Covert sensitization. Psychol Rep 20:459–468, 1967

Chalkley AJ, Powell G: The clinical description of forty-eight cases of sexual fetishism. Br J Psychiatry 142:292–295, 1983

Charatan FB, Galef H: A case of transvestism in a six-year-old boy. Journal of the Hillside Hospital 14:160–177, 1965

Christie M, Marshall W, Lanthier R: A descriptive study of incarcerated rapists and pedophiles, unpublished manuscript. Canadian Penit Services, Kingston, Ontario, 1978

Clare A: The disease concept in psychiatry, in Essentials of Postgraduate Psychiatry. Edited by Hill P, Murray R, Thorley A. New York, Grune and Stratton, 1979

Clark DF: Fetishism treated by negative conditioning. Br J Psychiatry 109:404–407, 1963

Coates S, Person ES: Extreme boyhood femininity: isolated behavior or pervasive disorder? J Am Acad Child Psychiatry 24:702–709, 1985

Conn JH: Brief psychotherapy of the sex offender. Journal of Clinical Psychopathology 10:347–372, 1949

Cooper AJ, Ismail AA, Phanjoo AL, et al: Antiandrogen (cyproterone acetate) therapy in deviant hypersexuality. Br J Psychiatry 120:59–63, 1972

Cox DJ, McMahon D: Incidence of male exhibitionism in the United States as reported by victimized female college students. Int J Law Psychiatry 1:453–457, 1978

Cox DJ, Sang K, Lee A: A cross-cultural comparison of the incidence and nature of male exhibitionism among female college students. Victimology 7, 1982

Cox M: Personal reflections upon 3,000 hours in therapeutic groups with sex offenders, in Sex Offenders in the Criminal Justice System. Papers presented to the 12th Cropwood Round Table Conference, December 1979. Edited by West DJ. Cambridge, Cropwood Conference Series no. 12, 1980

Crepault C, Couture M: Men's erotic fantasies. Arch Sex Behavior 9:565–581, 1980

Croughan JL, Saghir M, Cohen R, et al: A comparison of treated and untreated male cross-dressers. Arch Sex Behav 10:515–528, 1981

Crown S: Psychotherapy of sexual deviation. Br J Psychiatry 143:242–247, 1983

Culver CG, Gert B: Philosophy in Medicine. New York, Oxford, 1982

Daitzman RJ, Cox DJ: An extended case report: the nuts and bolts of treating an exhibitionist, in Exhibitionism: Description, Assessment, and Treatment. Edited by Cox DJ, Daitzman RJ. New York, Garland STPM Press, 1980

D'Alessio GR: The concurrent use of behavior modification and psychotherapy. Psychotherapy: Theory, Research, and Practice, 154–159, 1968

Davenport CW: A follow-up study of 10 feminine boys. Arch Sex Behav 15:511–518, 1986

Dowrick PW: Video training of alternatives to cross-gender identity behaviors in a 4-year-old boy. Child and Family Behavioral Therapy 5:59–65, 1983

Dupont H: Social learning theory and the treatment of transvestite behavior in an eight year old boy. Psychother Theory Research Practice 5:44–45, 1968

Epstein AW: Fetishism: a study of its psychopathology with particular reference to a proposed disorder in brain mechanism as an etiologic factor. J Nerv Ment Dis 130:107–119, 1960

Evans DR: An exploratory study into the treatment of exhibitionism by means of emotive imagery and aversive conditioning. Canadian Psychologist 8:162, 1967

Evans DR: Electrical aversion therapy, in Exhibitionism: Description, Assessment, and Treatment. Edited by Cox DJ, Daitzman RJ. New York, Garland STPM Press, 1980

Fast I: Gender Identity: A Differentiation Model. Hillsdale, NJ, Erlbaum, 1984

Fischhoff J: Preoedipal influences in a boy's determination to be "feminine" during the oedipal period. J Am Acad Child Psychiatry 3:273–286, 1964

Fitch JH: Men convicted of sexual offenses against children: a descriptive follow-up study. British Journal of Criminology 3:18–37, 1962

Ford CS, Beach FA: Patterns of Sexual Behavior. New York, Harper Bros, 1951

Frances A, Clarkin J: Differential therapeutics: a guide to treatment selection. Hosp Community Psychiatry 32:537–546, 1981

Francis JJ: Passivity and homosexual predisposition in latency boys. Bulletin of the Philadelphia Association of Psychoanalysts 15:160–174, 1965

Freud S: Splitting of the ego in the defensive process (1938), in Collected Papers, vol 5. London, Hogarth Press, 1950

Freud S: Three Essays on the Theory of Sexuality (1905). New York, Basic Books, 1954

Freud S: Fetishism (1927), in Collected Papers, vol 5. Edited by Strachey J. New York, Basic Books, 1959

Freund K: Diagnosis and treatment of forensically significant anomalous erotic preferences. Canadian Journal of Criminology and Corrections 18:181–189, 1976

Freund K, Heasman G, Racansky IG, et al: Pedophilia and heterosexuality vs. homosexuality. Journal Sex Marital Ther 10:193–200, 1984

Friend MR, Schiddel L, Klein B, Bunaeff D: Observations on the development of transvestism in boys. Am J Orthopsychiatry 24:563–575, 1954

Frisbie LV: Another look at sex offenders in California. California Mental Health Research Monograph no. 12. State of California, Department of Mental Hygiene, 1969

Gebhard PH: Fetishism and sadomasochism. Science and Psychoanalysis 15:71–80, 1969

Gebhard PH, Gagnon JH, Pomeroy WB, et al: Sex Offenders. New York, Harper and Row, 1965

Gelder M: Behaviour therapy for sexual deviations, in Sexual Deviation. Edited by Rosen I. London, Oxford University Press, 1979

Gilpin DC, Raza S, Gilpin D: Transsexual symptoms in a male child treated by a female therapist. Am J Psychother 33:453–463. 1979

Gittelson NL, Earott ST, Mehta BM: Victims and indecent exposure. Br J Psychiatry 132:61–66, 1978

Golosow N, Weitzman EL: Psychosexual and ego repression in the male transsexual. J Nerv Ment Dis 149:328–336, 1968

Gray KG, Mohr FW: Follow-up of male sexual offenders, in Sexual Behavior and the Law. Edited by Slovenko R. Springfield, Ill, Charles C Thomas, 1965

Green R: The significance of feminine behavior in boys. J Child Psychol Psychiatry 16:341–344, 1975

Green R: One-hundred ten feminine and masculine boys: behavioral contrasts and demographic similarities. Arch Sex Behav 5:425–446, 1976

Green R: Gender identity disorders and transvestism, in Treatment of Mental Disorders. Edited by Greist JH, Jefferson JW, Spitzer RL. New York, Oxford University Press, 1982

Green R: Gender identity in childhood and later sexual orientation: follow-up of 78 males. Am J Psychiatry 142:339–341, 1985

Green R: The Sissy Syndrome and the Development of Homosexuality. New Haven, Yale University Press, 1986

Greenacre P: Perversions: general considerations regarding their genetic and dynamic background, in Psychoanalytic Study of the Child, vol. 23. New York, International Universities Press, 1968

Greenacre P: Certain relationships between fetishism and the faulty development of the body image, in Emotional Growth. New York, International Universities Press, 1971

Greenacre P: Fetishism, in Sexual Deviation. Edited by Rosen I. New York, Oxford Press, 1979

Greenson RR: A transvestite boy and a hypothesis. Inter J Psychoanalysis 47:396–403, 1966

Greenson RR: Disidentifying from mother. Inter J Psychoanal 49:370–374, 1968

Gribbins: Soothill Way, 1983

Groth AN: Treatment of the sexual offender in a correctional institution, in The Sexual Aggressor: Current Perspectives on Treatment. Edited by Greer JG, Steward FR. New York, Van Nostrand Reinhold, 1983

Guttmacher MS, Weihofen H: Psychiatry and the Law. New York, W.W. Norton and Company, 1952

Hadley E: Comments on pedophilia. Medical Record 124:157–166, 1926

Halleck SL: Legal and ethical aspects of behavioral control. Am J Psychiatry 131:381–385, 1974

Halleck SL: The ethics of antiandrogen therapy. Am J Psychiatry 138:642–643, 1981

Hartman V: Notes on group psychotherapy with pedophiles. Canadian Psychiatric Association Journal 10:283–389, 1965

Hawton K: Behavioural approaches to the management of sexual deviation. Br J Psychiatry 143:248–255, 1983

Hay WM, Barlow DH, Hay LR: Treatment of stereotypic cross-gender motor behavior using covert modeling in a boy with gender identity confusion. J Consult Clin Psychol 49:388–394, 1981

Herman SP: Gender identity disorder in a five-year-old boy. Yale J Biol Med 56:15–22, 1983

Hoenig J: Magnus Hirschfeld, 1868–1935, in Handbook of Sexology. Edited by Money J, Musaph H. Amsterdam: Excerpta Medica, 1977

Holder E: A latency girl's struggle towards femininity. Bulletin of the Hampstead Clinic 5:55–70, 1982

Hollender MH, Brown CW, Roback HB: Genital exhibitionism in women. Am J Psychiatry 134:436–438, 1977

Holmstrom LL, Burgess AW: Sexual behavior of assailants during reported rapes. Arch Sex Behav 9:427–439, 1980

Hopkins J: The probable role of trauma in a case of foot and shoe fetishism: aspects of the psychotherapy of a 6-year-old girl. Int Rev Psychoanal 11:79–91, 1984

Hucker SJ: Management of anomalous sexual behaviour with drugs. Modern Medicine of Canada 40:150–153, 1985

Johnson J: Psychopathia sexualis. Br J Psychiatry 112:211–218, 1973

Jones K: The effect of stilboestrol in two cases of male transvestism. Journal of Mental Sciences 106:1080–1084, 1960

Kaplan HI, Sadock BJ: Modern Synopsis of Comprehensive Textbook on Psychiatry, 3rd ed. Baltimore, Williams & Wilkins, 1981

Karasu TB, Conte HR, Plutchk R: Psychotherapy outcome research, in The Psychiatric Therapies. Edited by Karasu T. Washington, DC, American Psychiatric Association, 1984

Karpman B: A case of pedophilia (legally rape) cured by psychoanalysis. Psychoanal Rev 37:235–276, 1950

Kendell RE: Reflections on psychiatric classification for the architects of DSM-4 and ICD 10. Integrative Psychiatry 2:43–47, 1984

Kernberg O: Borderline Conditions and Pathologic Narcissism. New York, Aaronson, 1975

Kernberg OF: Supportive psychotherapy with borderline conditions, in Critical Problems in Psychiatry. Edited by Cavanar JO, Brodie HKH. Philadelphia, Lippincott, 1982

Khan MMR: Alienation in Perversions. New York, International Universities Press, 1979

Kilmann PR, Sabalis RF, Gearling ML, et al: The treatment of sexual paraphilias: a review of outcome research. J Sex Res 18:193–252, 1982

Kinsey AC, Pomeroy WB, Martin CE: Sexual Behavior in the Human Male. Philadelphia, W. B. Saunders, 1948

Kleeman J: Freud's views on early female sexuality in the light of direct child observation. J Am Psychoanal Assoc 24:3–27, 1976

Knopp FH: Retraining Adult Sex Offenders: Methods and Models. Vermont, 1984

Kohlberg L: A cognitive-developmental analysis of children's sex role concepts and attitudes, in The Development of Sex Differences. Edited by Maccoby EE. Stanford, Stanford University Press, 1966

Kosky RJ: Gender-disordered children: does inpatient treatment help? Med J Australia 146:565–569, 1987

Krafft-Ebing R von: Psychopathia Sexualis (1886). New York, G.P. Putnam's Sons, 1965

Krueger DW: Symptom passing in a transvestite father and three sons. Am J Psychiatry 135:6, 1978

Langevin R: Sexual Strands. Understanding and Treating Sexual Anomalies in Men. Hillsdale, NJ, Lawrence Erlbaum Associates, 1983

Langevin R: Erotic Preference, Gender Identity, and Aggression in Men: New Research Studies. Hillsdale, NJ, Lawrence Erlbaum Associates, 1985

Laschet U: Antiandrogen in the treatment of sex offenders: mode of action and therapeutic outcome, in Contemporary Sexual Behaviour: Critical Issues in the 1970's. Baltimore, Johns Hopkins University Press, 1973

Lasegue C: Les exhibitionistes. L Union Medicale 23:709–714, 1877

Lazare A: Hidden conceptual models in clinical psychiatry. N Engl J Med 288:345–351, 1973

Lee AC: Normal and pathological gender-role development in children, in From Research to Clinical Practice—The Implications of Social and Developmental Research for Psychotherapy. Edited by Stricker G, Keisner RH. New York, Plenum Press, 1985

Liebman S: Homosexuality, transvestism and psychosis—study of a case treated with electroshock. J Nerv Ment Dis 99:945–948, 1944

Lim MH, Bottomley V: A combined approach to the treatment of effeminate behaviour in a boy: a case study. J Child Psychol Psychiatry 24:469–479, 1983

Loeb L, Shane M: The resolution of a transsexual wish in a five-year-old boy. J Am Psychoanal Assoc 10:419–434, 1982

Lothstein LM: Self-object failure and gender identity, in Frontiers in Self Psychology, vol III. Edited by Goldberg A. Hillsdale, NJ, Analytic Press, 1988

Lukianowicz N: Transvestism and psychosis. Psychiatry Neurol (Basel) 138:64–78, 1959

MacCullough MJ, Birtles CJ, Feldman MP: Anticipatory avoidance learning for the treatment of homosexuality: recent developments and an automated aversion therapy session. Behavior Therapy 2:151–169, 1971

Maletzky BM: "Assisted" covert sensitization in the treatment of exhibitionism. J Consult Clin Psychol 42:34–40, 1974

Malitz S: Another report on the wearing of diapers and rubber pants by an adult male. Am J Psychiatry 122:1435–1437, 1966

Marantz SA: Mothers of extremely feminine boys: psychopathology and childrearing patterns (unpublished doctoral dissertation). New York, New York University, 1984

Marks IM: Phylogenesis and learning in the acquisition of fetishism. Danish Med Bull 19:307–310, 1972

Marks IM: Management of sexual disorders, in Handbook of Behavior Modification and Behavior. Edited by Leitenberg H. New Jersey, Prentice-Hall, 1976

Marks IM, Gelder MG: Transvestism and fetishism: clinical and psychological changes during faradic aversion. Br J Psychiatry 113:711–729, 1967

Marmor JMD: Sexual deviancy: Part I. Journal of Continuing Education in Psychiatry 39:23–31, 1978a

Marmor JMD: Sexual deviancy: Part II. Journal of Continuing Education in Psychiatry 39:21–30, 1978b

Marshall WL: The modification of sexual fantasies: a combined treatment approach to the reduction of deviant sexual behavior. Behav Res Ther 11:557–564, 1973

Mathis JL: The exhibitionist. Medical Aspects of Human Sexuality 3:89–101, 1969

Mathis JL, Collins M: Mandatory group therapy for exhibitionists. Am J Psychiatry 126:1162–1167, 1970

McSweeney AJ: Fingernail fetishism: a report of a case treated with hypnosis. Am J Clin Hypn 15:139–143, 1972

Meador A, Ollendick TH: Cognitive behavior therapy with children: an evaluation of its efficacy and clinical utility. Child and Family Behavioral Therapy 6:25–44, 1984

Mendell D (ed): Early Female Development: Current Psychoanalytic Views. New York, Spectrum Publications, 1982

Metcalf S, Williams W: A case of male childhood transsexualism and its management. Aust NZ J Psychiatry 11:53–59, 1977

Meyer JK: Clinical variants among sex reassignment applicants. Arch Sex Behav 3:527–558, 1974

Meyer JK: Psychotherapy in sexual dysfunction, in Specialized Techniques in Individual Psychotherapy. Edited by Karasu T, Bellak T. New York, Brunner-Mazel, 1980

Meyer JK, Dupkin C: Gender disturbance in children: an interim clinical report. Bull Menninger Clinic 49:236–269, 1985

Mitchell W, Falconer MA, Hill D: Epilepsy with fetishism relieved by temporal lobectomy. Lancet ii, 626–630, 1954

Mohr JW, Turner RE, Jerry MB: Pedophilia and Exhibitionism. Toronto, University of Toronto Press, 1964

Money J: Paraphilias, in Handbook of Sexology. Edited by Money J, Musaph H. Amsterdam, Excerpta Medica, 1967

Money J: Two names, two wardrobes, two personalities. J Homosex 1:65–70, 1974

Money J: Paraphilias: phenomenology and classification. Am J Psychother 38:164–179, 1984

Money J, Ehrhardt A: Man and Woman, Boy and Girl. Baltimore, Johns Hopkins Press, 1972

Munroe RL, Munroe RH: Male transvestism and subsistence economy. J Soc Psychol 103:307–308, 1977

Myrick RD: The counselor-consultant and the effeminate boy. Personal Guidance Journal 48:355–361, 1970

Nagler S: Fetishism: a review and case study. Psychiatric Q 10:713–741, 1957

Newman LE: Treatment for the parents of feminine boys. Am J Psychiatry 133:683–687, 1976

Newman LE, Stoller R: Nontranssexual men who seek sex reassignment. Am J Psychiatry 131:437–441, 1973

O'Leary SG, Dubey DR: Applications of self-control procedures by children: a review. Journal Applied Behavioral Analysis 12:449–465, 1979

Person E, Ovesey L: Transvestism: new perspectives. J Am Acad Psychoanal 6:301–323, 1978

Prentky R, Cohen M, Seghorn T: Development of a rational taxonomy for the classification of rapists: the Massachusetts Treatment Center system. Bull Am Acad Psychiatry Law 13:39–70, 1985

Prince V, Bentler PM: Survey of 504 cases of transvestism. Psychol Rep 31:903–917, 1972

Pruett KD, Dahl EK: Psychotherapy of gender identity conflict in young boys. J Am Acad Child Psychiatry 21:65–70, 1982

Quinsey VL: Methodological issues in evaluating the effectiveness of aversion therapies for institutionalized child molesters. The Canadian Psychologist 14:350–361, 1973

Quinsey VL: The assessment and treatment of child molesters: a review. Canadian Psychological Review 18:204–220, 1977

Quinsey VL: Men who have sex with children, in Law and Mental Health: International Perspective, vol 2. Edited by Weisstub D. New York, Pergamon, 1985

Quinsey VL, Chaplin TC, Carnigan WF: Biofeedback and signaled punishment in the modification of inappropriate sexual age preferences. Behavior Therapy 11:567–571, 1980

Rachman S, Hodgson RJ: Experimentally-induced "sexual fetishism" replication and development. Psychological Record 18:25–27, 1968

Radcinowicz L: Sexual Offences: A Report of the Cambridge Department of Criminal Science. Toronto, Macmillan, 1957

Rekers GA: Sex-role behavior change: intrasubject studies of boyhood gender disturbance. J Psychol 103:255–269, 1979

Rekers GA, Lovaas OI: Behavioral treatment of deviant sex-role behaviors in a male child. Journal Applied Behavioral Analysis 7:173–190, 1974

Rekers GA, Mead S: Early intervention for female sexual identity disturbance: self-monitoring of play behavior. J Abnorm Child Psychol 7:405–423, 1979

Rekers GA, Varni JW: Self-monitoring and self-reinforcement in a pre-transsexual boy. Behav Res Ther 15:177–180, 1977a

Rekers GA, Varni JW: Self-regulation of gender-role behaviors: a case study. J Behav Ther Exp Psychiatry 8:427–432, 1977b

Rekers GA, Lovaas OI, Low BP: The behavioral treatment of a "transsexual" preadolescent boy. J Abnorm Child Psychol 2:99–116, 1974

Rekers GA, Yates CE, Willis TJ, et al: Childhood gender identity change: operant control over sex-typed play and mannerisms. J Behav Ther Exp Psychiatry 7:51–57, 1976

Rekers GA, Willis TJ, Yates CE, et al: Assessment of childhood gender behavior change. J Child Psychol Psychiatry 18:53–65, 1977

Rhoads JM: The psychoanalysis of an exhibitionist. Case presentation, N.C. Psychoanalytic Society, April 7, 1983

Rhoads JM, Padilla-Borjes E: The incidence of exhibitionism in Guatemala and the United States. Br J Psychiatry 139:242–244, 1981

Rickles NK: Exhibitionism. J Nerv Ment Dis 19:11–17, 1942

Roiphe H, Galenson E: Infantile Origins of Sexual Identity. New York, International Universities Press, 1981

Rooth G: Exhibitionism, sexual violence, and paedophilia. Br J Psychiatry 122:705–710, 1973

Rosen RC, Kopel SA: Penile plethysmography and biofeedback in the treatment of a transvestite-exhibitionist. J Consult Clin Psychol 45:908–916, 1977

Sack WH: Gender identity conflict in young boys following divorce. Journal of Divorce 9:47–59, 1985

Sackin HD: Cross-dressing and fetishism in childhood: the analysis of a five-year-old magician (unpublished manuscript). Toronto, Hospital for Sick Children, 1983

Schultz NM: Severe gender identity confusion in an eight-year-old boy (unpublished doctoral dissertation). New York, Yeshiva University, 1979

Segal MM: Transvestism as an impulse and as a defense. Int J Psychoanal 46:209–217, 1966

Serber M: Shame aversion therapy. J Behav Ther Exp Psychiatry 1:213–215, 1970

Smith P: Exhibitionism: a clinical conundrum, in Symposium of Sexual Deviation. Br J Psychiatry 143:231–235, 1983

Smith SR, Meyer RG: Workings between the legal system and the therapist, in Exhibitionism: Description, Assessment, and Treatment. Edited by Cox DJ, Daitzman RJ. New York, Garland STPM Press, 1980

Socarides CW: Meaning and content of pedophiliac perversion. J Am Psychoanal Assoc 7:784–794, 1959

Socarides CW: The development of a fetishistic perversion—the contribution of preoedipal phase conflict. J Am Psychoanal Assoc 8:281–311, 1960

Sperber MA: The "as if" personality and transvestism. Psychoanal Rev 60:605–612, 1973

Sperling M: Fetishism in children. Psychoanal Quart 32:374–392, 1964

Spodak MK, Falck A, Rappeport JR: The hormonal treatment of sexual aggressives with depo-provera. TSA News 1:2, 1977

Stoller RJ: The sense of maleness. Psychoanal Q 34:207–218, 1965

Stoller RJ: The mother's contribution to infantile transvestic behavior. Int J Psychoanal 47:384–395, 1966

Stoller RJ: Transvestites' women. Am J Psychiatry 124:333–339, 1967

Stoller RJ: Sex and Gender, vol. I. The Development of Masculinity and Femininity. New York, Aronson, 1968

Stoller RJ: Psychotherapy of extremely feminine boys. Int J Psychiatry 9:278–281, 1970

Stoller RJ: The term "transvestism." Arch Gen Psychiatry 24:230–237, 1971

Stoller RJ: The "bedrock" of masculinity and femininity: bisexuality. Arch Gen Psychiatry 26:207–212, 1972

Stoller RJ: Symbiosis anxiety and the development of masculinity. Arch Gen Psychiatry 30:164–172, 1974a

Stoller RJ: Sex and Gender, vol I. The Development of Masculinity and Femininity. New York, Aronson, 1974b

Stoller RJ: Sex and Gender, vol II. The Transsexual Experiment. New York, Aronson, 1975a

Stoller RJ: Perversion, the Erotic Form of Hatred. New York, Partheon, 1975b

Stoller RJ: Sex and Gender, vol 22. New York, Aronson, 1975c

Stoller RJ: Sex and Gender, vol II. The Transsexual Experiment. London, Hogarth Press, 1975d

Stoller RJ: Sexual excitement. Arch Gen Psychiatry 33:899–909, 1976a

Stoller RJ: Primary femininity. J Am Psychoanal Assoc 24:59–78, 1976b

Stoller RJ: Boyhood gender aberrations: treatment issues. J Am Psychoanal Assoc 26:541–558, 1978

Stoller RJ: Fathers of transsexual children. J Am Psychoanal Assoc 27:837–866, 1979a

Stoller RJ: Sexual Excitement, Dynamics of Erotic Life. New York, Touchstone, 1979b

Stoller RJ: Transvestism in women. Arch Sex Behav 11:99–115, 1982

Stoller RJ: Gender identity disorders in children and adults, in Comprehensive Textbook of Psychiatry, 4th ed., vol. 1. Edited by Kaplan H, Sadock B. Baltimore, Williams and Wilkins, 1985a

Stoller RJ: Presentations of Gender. New Haven, Yale University Press, 1985b

Tasto DL: Pedophilia, in Modern Legal Medicine Psychiatry and Forensic Science. Edited by Curran WJ, McGarry AL, Petty CS. F.A. Davis, Philadelphia, 1980

Thacher B: A mother's role in the evolution of gender dysphoria: the initial phase of joint treatment in the psychotherapy of a 4-year-old boy who wanted to be a girl. Paper presented at the meeting of the Division of Psychoanalysis, American Psychological Association, New York, 1985

Wachtel A, Lawton-Speert S: Child sexual abuse: descriptions of nine program approaches to treatment. Child Sexual Abuse Project, Working Paper Three. Vancouver, B.C., Canada, United Way of the Lower Mainland, October 1983

West DJ: Treatment in theory and practice, in Sex Offenders in the Criminal Justice System. Papers presented to the 12th Cropwood Round Table Conference, December 1979. Edited by West DJ. Cambridge, Cropwood Conference Series no. 12, 1980, pp 141–148

West DJ, Roy C, Nichols FL: Understanding Sexual Attacks. London, Heinemann Education Books, 1978

WSH [Western State Hospital] Orientation Manual. Fort Steilacoom, Wash, South Group Philosophies

Wickramasekera I: A technique for controlling a certain type of sexual exhibitionism. Psychotherapy: Theory, Research, and Practice 9:207–210, 1972

Wickramasekera I: Aversive behavior rehearsal: a cognitive-behavioral procedure in exhibitionism, in Exhibitionism: Description, Assessment, and Treatment. New York, Garland STPM Press, 1980

Wise TN: Psychotherapy of an aging transvestite. J Sex Marital Ther 5:368–374, 1979

Wise TN, Meyer JK: The border area between transvestism and gender dysphoria: transvestitic applicants for sex reassignment. Arch Sex Behav 9:327–342, 1980a

Wise, TN, Meyer JK: Transvestism: previous findings and new areas for inquiry. J Sex Marital Ther 6:116–128, 1980b

Wise TN, Dupkin C, Meyer JK: Partners of distressed transvestites. Am J Psychiatry 138:1221–1224, 1985

Wong MR: Psychoanalytic-developmental theory and the development of male gender identity: a review, in Men in Transition: Theory and Therapy. Edited by Solomon K, Levy NB. New York, Plenum Press, 1982

Wrate RM, Gulens V: A systems approach to child effeminacy and the prevention of adolescent transsexualism. Journal of Adolescence 9:215–229, 1986

Zaphiriou M: David: the analysis of a latency boy with poor physical endowment. Bulletin of the Hampstead Clinic 1:17–30, 1978

Zavitzianos G: Fetishism and exhibitionism in the female and their relationship to psychopathy and kleptomania. Int J Psychoanal 52:297–305, 1971

Zucker KJ: Childhood gender disturbance: diagnostic issues. J Am Acad Child Psychiatry 21:274–280, 1982

Zucker KJ: Cross-gender-identified children, in Gender Dysphoria: Development, Research, Management. Edited by Steiner BW. New York, Plenum Press, 1985

Zucker KJ, Doering RW, Bradley SJ, et al: Gender constancy judgments in gender-disturbed children: a comparison to sibling and psychiatric controls. Paper presented at Child Psychiatry Day, Hospital for Sick Children, Toronto, 1980

Zucker KJ, Finegan JK, Doering RW, et al: Two subgroups of gender-problem children. Arch Sex Behav 13:27–39, 1984

Zucker KJ, Bradley SJ, Doering RW, et al: Sex-typed behavior in cross-gender-identified children: stability and change at a one-year follow-up. J Am Acad Child Psychiatry 24:710–719, 1985

Zuger B: Effeminate behavior present in boys from early childhood, I: The clinical syndrome and follow-up studies. J Pediatr 69:1098–1107, 1966

SECTION 8

Tic Disorders

Chapter 83

Tic Disorders

Phenomenology, Diagnosis, and Assessment

Tourette's syndrome (TS) is a complex neuropsychiatric disorder first described more than 100 years ago (Gilles de la Tourette 1885). Although Gilles de la Tourette identified a core constellation of severe symptoms including incoordination (tics), echolalia, and coprolalia, TS is currently understood to encompass a broad range of involuntary motor movements and phonic productions with an onset usually before late adolescence. Traditionally, these motor and phonic tics have been further divided, though at times arbitrarily and ambiguously, into simple and complex phenomena. Simple tics are abrupt movements, usually restricted to one or a few isolated muscle groups, resulting in nonpurposive short-lived actions. Complex tics involve many groups and may be carried out in longer sequences. Complex tics bear close resemblance to ordinary actions except for their intensity, repetitiveness, or incongruence in the given context. Examples of each category of simple or complex, motor or phonic tics are given in Table 1. As can be readily seen, tics can reproduce any motion or sound within the body's repertoire of voluntary behaviors.

Several characteristic tic features, some of which were identified by Tourette himself, enable one to differentiate tics from other neurological disorders. These features include abruptness, suppressibility, variability, and diminution during sleep (Fahn 1982).

In contrast to most abnormal movements, tics may be suppressed for brief periods, especially when of mild to moderate severity. Clinicians experienced in the evaluation of TS symptoms frequently see patients who can remain very still or quiet in the consultation room, much to the bemusement and frustration of the teachers and parents who observe constant tics in their respective settings. However, symptoms are rarely suppressible for more than hours and severer symptoms may not be suppressible at all.

Unlike dystonic, ballismic, choreiform, or athetoid movements of other disorders, simple tic movements are brief. Detailed analyses of tic movements suggest that they can occur singly, but usually occur in bursts that have an average duration of one to three seconds. This feature of abruptness does permit some differentiation, although it may still be quite difficult to separate symptoms of certain disorders from complex tics.

Tics display features of variability across several dimensions: anatomical location, development, duration, frequency, intensity, situation, and time (Fahn 1982). Anatomical variability refers to the distribution of movements over time, usually beginning

Table 1.   Examples of Tourette's Syndrome Symptoms

Simple motor

eyeblinks, grimacing, tongue thrusting, eye widening, jaw jerks, head jerks, nodding, head turning, shoulder jerks, arm movements, finger movements, stomach jerks, kicking or leg movements, tensing parts of the body

Complex motor

holding funny expressions, squinting, grooming hair, cracking joints, repeated touching of parts of the body, tapping, hopping, stomping, picking at things (self, clothes), pushing on eyes, hitting self, slamming things, copropraxia (giving the finger, etc.)

Simple phonic

coughing, hawking, squeaking, "aaaaaaa," "tttttttuh," throat clearing, "uh,uh,uh," blowing across upper lip, popping, snorting, gnashing teeth

Complex phonic

"uh huh," "you bet," "all right," "yeah, yeah," palilalia (repeating sentences after one's self), echolalia (repeating sentences after others), swearing, obscene language, obscene noises, racial slurs, colloquial insults.

with eyes, face, and head and subsequently progressing to include arms, torso, abdomen, legs, and feet. This pattern of distribution is not so universal as to constitute a rule, but symptom progression is common (Jagger et al. 1982). Variability of duration, frequency, amplitude, and intensity are characteristic of tics when compared to other disordered movements. They are inconstant events with an unpredictable character and, over brief periods of time, stereotypical form.

Variability with situation has been alluded to above and occurs across emotional climates for many patients. During periods of increased arousal, anticipation, or anxiety many persons observe increases or decreases in symptoms. For some persons tics increase at the peak of emotional arousal (e.g., while opening Christmas presents), whereas for others the greatest intensity is observed following the peaks (e.g., in the hours or days following an oral classroom presentation).

Variability may also be observed over time. For each patient, certain times of the day or seasons of the year may affect tic frequency and intensity. Developmental variability is also common. One pattern is for symptoms to decrease following puberty, although increases may be seen periodically thereafter. For a small portion of TS patients, continuous, severe symptoms are seen throughout development.

Tourette reported an inconsistent finding that tics disappeared during sleep. His premise has been revised and currently it appears that often during sleep, especially during REM stages, tics are observed, but at reduced frequency (Glaze et al. 1983).

Associated Behaviors, Cognitions, and Perceptions

Two additional behaviors have been consistently demonstrated in large cohorts of TS patients: attention deficit hyperactivity disorder (ADHD) and obsessive-compulsive disorder (OCD) (Jagger et al. 1982; Stefl 1983). ADHD manifest by inability to concentrate, difficulties with focusing attention, high levels of distractibility, impulsivity, and excessive motor activity has been reported in as many as 50 percent of TS sufferers. When compared to the general population frequency of 10–15 percent of children, the higher frequency in TS suggests a possible shared etiology.

However, several observations leave this conclusion open to question. First is that the constellation of ADHD is ambiguous and the thresholds for diagnosis are arbitrary. Diagnosis often depends on teacher and parent observations and many of the symptoms are difficult to delineate from the movements of TS. Second, some genetic studies have suggested that even when such a delineation can be made, there appears to be a separate inheritance of ADHD even in families with TS. This has led some investigators to hypothesize that the increased association may be a result of a variety of referral bias, first described by Berkson (1946), in which a combination of disorders, such as TS plus ADHD, is more likely to bring patients to medical attention.

Obsessions and compulsions occur in 50–60 percent of TS patients. Classically, obsessions are defined as thoughts, images, or impulses that invade the consciousness of the sufferer, are involuntary, are seen as excessive or silly, arouse distress, and cannot be dismissed despite vigorous efforts. Similarly, compulsions are usually seen as behaviors arising in response to obsessions either as the executions of obsessive urges or to ward off obsessional thoughts. They also are perceived as being silly or excessive, cause distress, and cannot be dismissed even with great effort. Yet clinicians have regularly observed symptoms in TS patients that are not so neatly categorized as either obsessions-compulsions or tic phenomena. Examples of these ambiguous symptoms are repetitive touching, self-injurious behaviors, needs for symmetry, needs to carry out tasks until they "feel" right, and mental urges to move in the absence of movements. The obsessions and compulsions in persons with TS can also assume the presentation of typical compulsive phenomena such as washing and checking. The distinctions between highly complex motor tics and compulsions can be difficult to define, as seen, for example, in repetitive touching a certain number of times. Some investigators believe that the experience of obsessions and compulsions is different in persons with TS than in those with OCD but without TS. Some have hypothesized that TS patients with obsessive-compulsive symptoms do not experience the dread described by OCD patients, or that the degree of resistance or interference is less in TS. As a result, some investigators have questioned whether the thoughts or behaviors in TS patients meet the classic criteria for OCD, as described in DSM-III-R (American Psychiatric Association 1987) especially with regard to the severity of impairment and degree of resistance (that is, how much of an effort a patient makes to stop his thoughts or actions). One useful way to think about these phenomena is based on their content or temporal relationship to tics. Examples of "tic-related" experiences reported by TS patients include repetitive thoughts preceding or following tics, ritualized movements substituted to ward off tics, magical arrangements of items to control movements, and an involuntary, consuming, elaborate, psychological scheme for balancing mental and physical intensity. Symptoms unrelated to tics have included the more traditional behaviors of washing, cleaning, checking, and counting rituals. How fruitful these distinctions are for predicting genetic risk, natural history, treatment response, and prognosis will be determined by further investigation. Whatever findings are produced from studies of phenomenology, the clinical impact is clear. It can be readily seen that many TS patients experience some decrease in functioning as a result of obsessive-compulsive symptoms; for some the disability resulting from these symptoms can be incapacitating and surpass the impairment caused by their tics.

The conclusion that there is a shared etiology for TS and some OCD rests on findings of dramatically increased prevalences of obsessive-compulsive symptoms in TS patients when compared to the general population prevalence of 1–2 percent.

Furthermore, there appears to be a dramatically increased prevalence of obsessive-compulsive symptoms in first degree relatives of TS patients (23 percent) even in the absence of obsessive-compulsive symptoms in the probands (Pauls et al. 1986). Based on the data from a family-genetic study of TS, estimates of penetrance using the combination of TS, chronic multiple tics, and obsessions and compulsions as alternative expressions of the same gene gave the best results and were consistent with a single gene hypothesis with an autosomal dominant mode of transmission (Pauls and Leckman 1986). This suggests that some OCD may be an alternative expression of the same gene that results in TS (Pauls and Leckman 1986).

Etiology and Pathophysiology

The causes and pathophysiology of TS have not been fully elucidated. Most investigators agree that TS is likely to be an etiologically heterogeneous disorder in which genetic factors play an important role. Evidence from investigations relying on current concepts and technologies of family-genetic studies and pedigree analysis strongly suggests that some forms of TS arise from a single genetic vulnerability, perhaps via a Mendelian autosomal dominant mode of transmission with variable penetrance (Pauls and Leckman 1986). Twin studies comparing concordance among monozygotic and dizygotic twin pairs also support these findings (Price et al. 1985). Investigations under way drawing on restriction fragment length polymorphisms and recombinant DNA technology have the potential to demonstrate a major genetic locus (or loci) in the near future, especially with the availability for study of large families with several generations of individuals with TS.

However, for any individual, genetic hypotheses do not completely explain the appearance or specific manifestations, such as severity. There remains the possibility that environmental or nongenetic contributions exert important modifying or precipitating effects. These include processes or events at different developmental periods, prenatal (e.g., fetal compromise), perinatal, or early in life (e.g., stress, exposure to stimulants). Findings from one study in which decreased birth weights were observed in the affected cotwins of discordant monozygotic pairs further support this possibility (Leckman et al. 1987). The relationship between genetic vulnerability and environmental factors in shaping the nature of the final disorder has both research and clinical importance.

Neurophysiologic evidence points to a major role of the catecholamine neurotransmitter dopamine in the pathophysiology of TS. A portion of the evidence stems from the clinical efficacy, in TS sufferers, of pharmacologic agents demonstrating powerful in vitro and in vivo inhibition of central nervous system dopaminergic neurons, such as the neuroleptic medications haloperidol, penfluridol, pimozide, and fluphenazine. This hypothesis is strongly supported by findings of tic inhibition by α-methyl tyrosine, a substance inhibiting dopamine synthesis, and by tetrabenazine, which inhibits the accumulation of dopamine in presynaptic storage vesicles. Also several substances known to facilitate dopaminergic transmission, such as L-dopa, and stimulants (e.g., methylphenidate, dextroamphetamine, pemoline) increase symptoms in TS patients. Direct measurement of dopamine in the brain is not possible, but levels of the major central nervous system metabolite of dopamine, homovanillic acid, has been found to be decreased in TS patients during baseline measures of cerebrospinal fluid (CSF) and following probenecid loading. This has suggested to some investigators that TS may result from a hypersensitivity in postsynaptic dopamine receptors (Cohen et al. 1978; Butler et al. 1979). These findings and the dopamine hypothesis would predict increased numbers of dopaminergic receptors, yet this increase has not been seen in positron emission tomography studies (Chase et al. 1984). In addition, the response to dopaminergic blocking agents is not universal. Taken as a whole, the evidence favors a role for dopaminergic dysfunction underlying some component of the syndrome, but further study will be required to explain these inconsistent findings.

Disturbances in other central neurotransmitter and neuromodulator systems (norepinephrine, dopamine, serotonin, GABA, neuropeptides, and others) may also contribute to the development of TS. What little work has been done on GABAergic and cholinergic mechanisms has not produced convincing results (Leckman et al. 1988). Trials of medication employing cholinergic agonists have shown few positive responders (Stahl and Berger 1982), and CSF levels of acetylcholinesterase and butyrylcholinesterase have been found to be normal in TS sufferers.

Evidence from investigation of the GABAergic system, though difficult to interpret, does suggest that closer study is warranted. The neuroanatomical proximity and connections between GABA and dopamine systems support some interrelationship and responses to the GABAergic agent clonazepam have been positive in some TS patients (Gonce and Barbeau 1977). Yet other equally potent GABAergic agents, such as diazepam, have yielded negligible responses (Connell et al. 1967), leading some to speculate that the effects of clonazepam result from some other mechanism. Furthermore, CSF and whole blood GABA were the same in TS patients and normal subjects in studies by van Woert et al. (1982).

Since systems relying on serotonin neurotransmitters send projections to the substantia nigra and the striatum, they could have an important role in the pathophysiology of TS. CSF levels of the major serotonin metabolite in the central nervous system, 5-hydroxyindolacetic acid, may be reduced in TS (Cohen et al. 1979). However, medications affecting this system have inconsistent effects on tics.

Interest in norepinephrine (NE) stems from the efficacy of clonidine, which inhibits NE via presynaptic α_2-adrenergic agonistic activity. Although there is little direct support for hypotheses positing downstream effects by NE on dopamine activity directly, there may be indirect effects via serotonin (Leckman et al. 1986). Studies comparing CSF, plasma, and urine levels of either NE or its primary central nervous system metabolite, 3-methoxy-4-hydroxyphenylethylene glycol (MHPG), in normal subjects and TS patients have not found differences.

Application of pharmacologic probes with specific activity sites, like clonidine or yohimbine, have not differentiated TS patients from normal subjects. As better methods, such as debrisoquin loading, are used to obtain activity measures of central dopamine and other transmitters, the role of catecholamine physiology may be clarified (Riddle et al. 1986). The application of neuroimaging techniques, such as magnetic resonance and positron emission tomography, may identify influential anatomical regions and clarify physiologic relationships. These techniques may increase our understanding of the pathophysiology in TS of pathways communicating via dopamine transmitters and of the manner in which noradrenergic and serotonergic activity may modulate symptoms.

Differential Diagnosis

In addition to TS, tics may occur subsequent to brain injury (e.g., trauma, infection, carbon monoxide intoxication), with drug toxicity, and in degenerative disorders. The spectrum from chronic single tics to chronic multiple tics to TS probably represents an etiologic continuum (Pauls and Leckman 1986), whereas the relationship of transient tics of childhood to these other tic disorders is more obscure.

The differential diagnosis of tics includes tremors, myoclonus, chorea, ballism, athetosis, dystonia, paroxysmal dyskinesias, akathisia, hyperekplexias, tardive dyskinesia, and tics (Fahn 1982; Fahn and Erenberg 1988). The differentiation between these disorders is a clinical task for which no laboratory test is currently available. Although differentiation can usually be accomplished by relying on several features common to tics (Fahn and Erenberg 1988), in some cases it may be difficult. This is especially true and important for distinguishing between tardive dyskinesia and TS when patients have been treated for prolonged periods with neuroleptic medication.

The presence of ocular movements is rare in other disorders but is a common tic symptom. Variability, abruptness, brevity, and suppressibility can be seen individually in other movement disorders, but do not commonly occur together. A further distinguishing feature, inconsistently reported among TS patients, is the presence of an urge or mental sensation to carry out a tic. This is rarely reported for other disorders, with the possible exception of akathisia and the restless leg syndrome. Although the diagnosis of TS does not usually require an elaborate medical evaluation, the presenting symptoms can be complex, closely mimicking other disorders in some patients. For these individuals referral to a neurologist for confirmation is desirable.

Assessment of Tic Disorders

The difficulties experienced by TS patients are not confined to the diffuse movements and production of sounds but may influence virtually every segment of their lives. The consequence is that a narrow, somatic perspective is not adequate for a complete assessment. In fact, several features of TS force the clinician to go beyond the assessment of the severity of tics: the presence of effects, at times profound, on familial, educational, and social functioning; the emergence of symptoms relatively early in development; and the reciprocal relationship between environment and course of symptoms. For these reasons, the complete assessment of a TS patient requires understanding at many levels. One must begin to understand the person in terms of self-esteem, mood regulation, defensive capacities, and sense of self. Beyond a patient's current neurological status, an appreciation of past history, functioning at school (or work), in the family, and with their peer group is needed.

Several areas of inquiry assume a larger import in the evaluation of TS patients than with other disorders. A detailed history in which the clinician catalogues the onset, course, frequency, disturbance, and response to intervention of movements and sounds is valuable. The strong genetic predisposition places greater demands on the clinician to obtain a careful pedigree looking with extra care for tics, obsessive-compulsive symptoms, and the hyperactivity, distractibility, inattention, impulsivity, and school difficulties of ADHD.

The physical examination also includes a detailed description of the movements and nonlocalizing neurological "soft signs" such as synkinesias, clumsiness, and mixed dominance. Potentially helpful laboratory investigations include EEG and blood chemistries such as calcium, ceruloplasmin, liver function studies, and, if pharmacotherapy is anticipated, complete blood count with differential and ECG. EEGs may be abnormal in as many as 40 percent of patients but findings are not epileptiform and appear to be nonspecific.

The essential characteristics of tics add to the difficulty in assessing TS severity. Among the most troublesome is the situational, chronological, developmental, and anatomical variability of symptoms. Variability increases the difficulty in evaluating severity by simply following specific tic movements and rating their exacerbation or remission.

A second problem derives from the multidimensional character of tics. One patient may have very frequent mild tics and another infrequent loud bizarre sounds. What is the suitable metric for comparison, frequency or intrusiveness? When prospectively observing the course of illness in an individual patient, one usually is forced into making these kinds of comparisons and selecting some dimension(s).

Tics are polymorphous and this also undermines assessment strategies. They may present as rapid, solitary motions, in bursts, as orchestrated acts, or in dysynchronous montages. When considering those actions that are not merely single twitches, there are no conventions governing how the events are to be regarded, whether as multiple single acts strung together or as single, highly complex movement units.

When effects on social and academic (or occupational) functioning occur, the patient may not be fully aware of the impact of his symptoms. The clinician needs to obtain accurate data from multiple sources. Subjective reports may not cover sufficiently the variety of symptoms and effects. Formal measures are often necessary in addition to the observations in the consulting room, the parents' or family's reports, and whatever written or verbal reports are available from teachers, employers, or organization leaders. A list of instruments, parent- or self-rated and clinician-rated, is given in Table 2.

These ratings introduce two further problems, however. When using formal measures, the accuracy of ratings conducted by lay persons, many of whom often have little experience with TS, can be questionable. Biases introduced by lay raters can be enormous and result in unintentional distortions that hinder qualitative assessment. For example, for the parent whose child has just been diagnosed with TS,

---

Table 2.   Instruments for Assessment of Tourette's Syndrome

I **Self-rated instruments**
  Data bases

  - Tourette's Syndrome Questionnaire (TSQ)

  Tourette's syndrome symptoms

  - Tourette's Syndrome Symptom List (TSSL)

  Associated disorders

  - Conners' Parents' Questionnaire (attention deficit hyperactivity disorder)
  - Leyton Obsessional Inventory (Adult Version) (obsessive-compulsive disorder)

II **Clinician-rated or clinician-assisted instruments**
  Data bases

  - Tourette's Syndrome and other Behavioral Disorders Questionnaire (TSOBDQ)

  Tourette's syndrome symptoms

  - Tourette's Syndrome Global Scale (TSGS)
  - Tourette's Syndrome Severity Scale (TSSS)
  - Tanner, Goetz and Klawans Protocol

  Associated disorders

  - TSOBDQ
  - Conners' Teacher's Questionnaire
  - Leyton Obsessional Inventory (Child Version) (obsessive-compulsive disorder)

  Global assessment

  - Global Assessment Scale (GAS) (Child or Adult)

---

the severity rating of mild multiple motor movements, such as frequent grimacing and eyeblinks, may range from "severe" to "absent." Also the clinician may be frustrated in his or her efforts to arrive at a meaningful conclusion when combining ratings by multiple raters, each of whom makes their observations under different conditions. It is common to see children present with, for example, one parent and several teachers seeing many movements and hearing noises constantly, whereas health professionals, other teachers, and the other parent perceive few worrisome symptoms.

The accuracy of self- or parent-rated instruments is highly dependent on the rater's understanding of and capacity for objective observation. Careful explanations about the nature of tics and the frequency of movements are critical. One caveat deserving emphasis is that, in some highly anxious families, tic ratings may have undesirable effects. When parents or other relatives begin to turn constant, meticulous attention to a patient's every movement, the mounting anxiety and stress experienced by the family and the patient may lead to an increase in family distress and changes in symptoms.

Two self-rated scales have been developed for use in TS, and two other adjunctive scales, the Conners' Parents' Questionnaire (Conners 1973) and Leyton Obsessional Inventory, may be of value in rating associated symptoms. The Tourette's Syndrome Questionnaire is a self-administered historical data base focusing on basic family and personal data, previous evaluations, onset and severity of symptoms, and developmental history. It has been most commonly used in genetic or epidemiologic studies but is also useful in clinical settings to screen for positive findings in the family and individual history and to open the way toward further exploration during the initial interview.

The Tourette's Syndrome Symptom List is a self-rating instrument that has been successfully used to assess severity throughout one week. It identifies current symptoms and asks the respondent to rate current severity of each symptom daily over one week. Standard anchor points for frequency are suggested.

The Conners' Parents' Questionnaire (Conners 1973) is an established diagnostic screening device for ADHD and associated problems. It offers common symptoms seen in childhood, loaded for ADHD, and asks parents to rate whether these occur never, a little, a lot, or always.

The Leyton Obsessional Inventory (adult version) is a commonly used, though methodologically limited, screening device for OCD (Cooper 1970). Thoughts or habits are posed, and the respondent is asked whether these are true of themselves and then, if so, to assess how much they are resisted and how much interference they create. The original inventory was developed as a card-sorting task requiring an examiner who would offer minor assistance and observe the respondent during its administration. Subsequent work has shown that it may be equally valid when conducted as a pencil and paper task. In the childhood version this original card-sorting technique was retained, but the topics queried, the number of questions, and their wording were modified (Berg et al. 1986).

Clinician-rated scales may rely either on evaluations made following direct face-to-face observation of the patient or while viewing videotapes. Each has its advantages, but in general, the rating following interviews is the more common, cheaper, easier, and more versatile. For prospective longitudinal observations and under proper conditions, video recordings are highly desirable since they place less reliance on the memory of the observer, permit review at a subsequent time, and leave the data largely unaltered (Tanner et al. 1982).

There are two clinician-rated scales, the TS Global Scale (TSGS) and TS Severity

Scale (TSSS). The TSGS assesses severity of symptoms. This assessment is based on scores from two domains: tics and social function. The tic domain examines the frequency and disruption, each with a dimensional range from 0 to 5, of each of the four categories of tics: simple and complex, motor and phonic. The social function domain assesses impairment in general behavior, school or occupational function, and motor restlessness on scales dimensionally ranging from 0 to 25. The scores on these domains are calculated so that a total score will fall between 0 (no impairment) and 100 (most severe impairment) (Harcherick et al. 1984).

The TSSS draws from five probes (tics noticeable to others, tics elicit curiosity, patient considered odd or bizarre, tics interfere with functioning, patient homebound or hospitalized) to ascertain the severity of impairment from TS. Each probe has a different range on an ordinal scale, although half-step ratings are permitted. Originally designed for assessment of severity during treatment with pimozide in a double-blind drug trial, this scale has been used to monitor severity over time (Shapiro and Shapiro 1984).

Both the TSGS and TSSS need further development. The TSGS has two problems. For one, small deviations in category scores can result in large differences in the total score owing to the formula for calculation of the total score. Another is that the total score is weighted unevenly toward the social function domain. Neither scale permits a rating of the complexity and intensity of movements, which may be as important as their frequency or degree of disruption. The anchor points of the TSSS are ambiguous, and raters may not understand what information is being requested.

The development of clinician-rated measures for assessment of ADHD remains a research challenge. At the present time no quick, reliable, and accurate cross-sectional scales have been generally adopted. The closest approximation is information from teachers in school reports using the Conners' Teacher's Questionnaire (Conners 1973).

Overall functioning has been reliably assessed using the Global Assessment Scale (Endicott et al. 1976), or its analogue for children (Shaffer et al. 1983). The advantage of these measures is that a condensed, single rating is available for later comparison. The measure is simple, highly reliable, and useful for comparisons across disorders, conditions, and over time.

Summary

The assessment of a patient with TS calls upon a variety of skills from one or more health providers. At one level of expertise it requires a general knowledge of the presentation of tic movements, from the simplest to the most complex, an ability to appreciate the differential diagnosis, and an ability to interpret diagnostic tests for phenocopies. But it also requires, at another level, the ability to assess the degree of impairment not defined solely by the severity of tics, but derived from an understanding of the individual's progression along the dimensions of psychological development, work or academic performance, personal coping strategies, and intimate and peer relationships. It should be noted that TS is a lifelong condition and that remissions are common. This is a significant consideration in evaluating treatment.

The task is not eased by any established algorithm. The limitations of standard assessment tools and techniques force the clinician to evaluate information of diverse quality and variable accuracy. At times the clinician must participate as a health provider, educator, school liaison, social service worker, and family confidant.

On the brighter side, the great majority of cases are not severe; the information gained through careful research has generated compelling evidence concerning many aspects of the disorder including genetic factors and natural history; improved assessment devices have been developed; and effective treatments are available that are capable of benefiting many patients.

TS is a model neuropsychiatric disorder of childhood from which we may learn a great deal about the relationships between genetic vulnerability, environmental stressors, and the risk and protective factors influencing development.

General Considerations for Treatment

A proposed preliminary etiologic model of TS drawn from the current evidence would include genetic determinants, environmental stressors, and psychological components that combine to yield neurophysiologic changes that subsequently produce movements and sounds. This combined model is supported by the contributions of neurochemistry, neuropharmacology, and neurophysiology, as elucidated by responses to pharmacologic probes and treatment agents (Ang et al. 1982; Leckman et al. 1983, 1984; Riddle et al. 1986), and human genetics, as suggested by results from twin and family studies (Pauls and Leckman 1986). The model also reflects clinical experience, which suggests that the patient's response, typology, and experience of the disorder are modified and shaped by such psychological components as psychological distress, defense and coping mechanisms, and self-esteem. How an individual's constitutional vulnerability to TS interacts with mental upset to produce an exacerbation of symptoms has yet to be understood.

Historically, a perspective on TS in which psychological factors were primary in the etiology was consistent with the prevailing Zeitgeist of the 1930s and 1940s. When clinicians were faced with an idiopathic condition and symptoms that were socially dramatic and sometimes scatological or sexual, patients would be routinely referred for psychological treatment. A few clinicians proposed that the etiology of TS was best explained as a psychological disturbance, as described below, whereas others did not see a central role for the psychological dimension. Currently, we know that a middle course between these extremes provides the most complete explanation for what is observed and reported. Psychological components, such as the meaning of symptoms to the patient, the effects of these chronic, socially unacceptable symptoms on psychological development, the psychological impairment of symptoms, and the emotional cost of treatment maneuvers, have become helpful considerations in making decisions about the goals and efficacy of treatment. Psychological functions can have an important effect on TS symptoms and, reciprocally, like any chronic illness, TS can have powerful psychological effects.

The purpose of this chapter is to describe the educational, family, and psychotherapeutic approaches to the treatment of TS. Many of these interventions should precede the use of medication. The premise of this chapter is that treatment should reflect what we have learned about the disorder and provide TS patients and their families with optimal care. To do this, clinicians need to consider the patient's internal experience of the disorder and the reactions to his movements and sounds of those around him.

School and Occupational Intervention

In children, any chronic disorder can affect learning. TS, by virtue of several unusual characteristics, can have a significant impact on a child's education stemming both from the primary disorder, such as specific neuropsychological deficits and the outright physical impairment of involuntary movements, and secondary consequences of the disorder, such as social isolation, being regarded as an object of contempt, impairment of self-esteem, and so on. When it has been determined that a child's educational capacity is not being met as a result of TS, offering assistance by providing a school with an understanding of the disorder and their pupils' educational needs can be a critical, far-reaching intervention.

Recent research on cognitive or learning functions in TS suggests that specific learning deficits may be a part of the syndrome. Work reported by Incagnoli and Kane (1982) and Hagin and Kugler (1988) has suggested that TS patients may perform especially poorly on the coding and subtest of the Wechsler Intelligence Scales for Children. This confirms findings by Golden (1984), who reviewed 12 studies of neuropsychological function in TS patients and reported that impairment in motor control, a major factor affecting performance on the coding subtest, was evident in eight of them. Yet although the coding subtest places demands on visual-motor functions, not all visual-motor tasks are impaired in TS patients. Therefore, the interpretation of the specific deficits on the coding subtest cannot be generalized. In a similar vein, data from Hagin and others (Dykens 1987) have suggested that TS patients may exhibit a specific weakness in mathematics.

As discussed in the section on phenomenology, there is continuing debate about whether ADHD is intrinsic to TS. The presence of ADHD has implications for the interpretation of poor performance on mathematics and coding subtests. Since many of the cognitive studies in TS patients have not stratified samples according to the presence of ADHD, it is difficult to determine whether the identified neuropsychologic deficits may be attributed to ADHD as a comorbid condition. Some evidence suggests that the results may be specific to TS and not attributable to ADHD (Dykens 1987).

The adverse effects on learning that result from pharmacologic treatments comprise an iatrogenic consequence of TS. Although some investigators believe there are intrinsic drug side effects that impair learning, others do not. Patients on haloperidol and pimozide have been observed to have deficits in memory, concentration, and motivation by experienced clinicians. Neuroleptic medications and clonidine can cause severe sedation and subsequently hamper learning. More subtle emotional effects on academic functioning such as the appearance of dysphoria (Bruun 1982; Caine and Polinsky 1979) and school phobia (Linet 1985; Mikkelson et al. 1981) also occur in children treated with haloperidol and pimozide.

The secondary consequences of TS are diverse. As internal dynamics and social events affect one another, complex cycles can develop. Frightening or frustrating social experiences (such as isolation from or being teased by peers, being held up to public ridicule by adults, or being viewed as willfully oppositional by persons of authority) fuel inner vulnerabilities of low self-esteem, poor frustration tolerance, lack of motivation, hopelessness, and anxiety. The loop is completed when these internal feelings lead to behaviors that increase negative social experiences. Since school is a vital social, as well as educational, environment for children most of these negative experiences occur there. The assistance of caring, informed professionals is needed to break these cycles by intervening with the school and the child. Without help children commonly generalize their negative feelings toward particular individuals to include an entire setting, and they develop intense feelings of fear and anger about "the whole school." Anxiety, avoidance, or opposition are common behavioral consequences.

Specific interventions at school can improve a child's social and educational adjustment. Hagin and Kugler's (1988) survey of school modifications that worked successfully for TS patients suggests that a compassionate, positive, supportive attitude from teachers and efforts to reduce classroom stress can often be useful. These efforts to reduce stress included classroom structure, one-to-one assistance, setting reasonable goals divided into small segments, sensitivity to and flexibility with time pressures, and offering specific assistance with instructions. Many children with TS also benefit from being freed from any time constraints on their examinations. Typewriters can be an immense relief when handwriting becomes hindered by severe movements or compulsions. Hagin and Kugler (1988) stress that, when their symptoms are frequent, many children benefit from time and a place away from class where they can be alone. Subjects' responses also suggested that a moderate amount of structure was most appropriate, although some students benefited from programs that were at one or the other extreme. Not every child will need all of these aids, but most will need some of them. Teachers, like clinicians, have found that it is most helpful to view the child as a whole person, develop a broad view of a pupil's overall academic and social functioning at school, and avoid the temptation to fix upon target symptoms.

For adults in the workplace similar modifications can be useful. Many adult patients with TS are capable of working in any environment and require no modifications of their tasks. However, more severely affected individuals do benefit from the availability of structured tasks that can be broken into discrete pieces, flexibility with regard to time deadlines, specific assistance with instructions, and the ability to structure time so that they may take time away from clients and co-workers to be alone. Some have specifically requested and benefited from working in noisy locations. Experienced clinicians also have observed a high degree of variability in symptoms on the job. Although logically an employer might assume that certain tasks, such as detailed drawings, high-pressured sales positions, technical presentations, or public performances, would be beyond an employee with TS—especially those who are severely affected—paradoxically, many are able to complete these assignments with skill. Such work may be beyond some persons with TS, or may be impossible for some at certain times, but the characteristic waxing and waning of symptoms makes an ultimate determination almost impossible. The complexity of this problem can be reduced by obtaining the assistance of the person with TS in making decisions about assignments. In addition, an expert's explanation and recommendations to employers, occupational medical staff, and job supervisors can be of significant benefit by broadening their understanding of TS in general and their employee specifically. As a result, flexibility, compassion, and productivity can be increased for symptomatic patients in their workplace.

Family Intervention

As stressed in the chapter on evaluation, TS affects patients physically and socially. It affects others around them—their families and peer group most of all. Although TS is not "caused" by pathological family relationships, it is obvious that the reciprocal dynamics that develop with family members in response to symptoms form an integral part of a patient's experience of the disorder. For many patients these dynamics may be the most troubling consequence of their symptoms and can be the most impaired dimension of their lives. This may be as true for the adult with TS who lives with his or her own spouse and children as for the child with TS who lives with his or her family of origin. Cohen et al. (1988) have described how the assessment of these relationships draws on an understanding of two or three components. From the patient's side there are the relationships with the family, the internal understanding of the role the patient plays in the family, and family members' responses to him or her. From the parents' or spouse's perspective, there is their view of the child or spouse as a person, the meaning of their child or spouse to them, their expectations of and fantasies about him or her, and their understanding of the causes and consequences of his or her symptoms. When there are siblings at home, their view(s) of their family member and his symptoms and their responses to the potential encroachments by their affected family member on the sibling's view of himself, the family's life together, and social relationships are also important. The compilation of such an assessment cannot occur in a single visit or even within a brief series of meetings. Usually it is derived from a clinical relationship with a patient and his family, from information reported and observations made of the process over an extended time. During this time a sensitive, trained clinician can come to know many features of the family such as communication and alliances between family members, the family's management of privacy and revelation, the mechanisms by which members satisfy others and achieve satisfaction of their own needs, their capacity for shielding from and permitting exploration of the "outside world," the balance of hatred and love, and the accessibility to and protection from the wider family network. Throughout this process, the clinician is required to be a careful observer and form an understanding from his or her own experience of being "part of the family." He or she must also consider the meaning and impact of his or her interest on the family.

The boundary between treatment and assessment of the family can become blurred owing to the duration and intensity of this process. Results of the evaluation may suggest a need for specific family therapy techniques, and referral specifically for family treatment can be a useful intervention. Nevertheless, the opportunity to discuss the disappointments, painful secrets, fears, and frustrations of living with TS in the presence of an informed, warm, accepting professional can have an immensely calming, salutary effect. It is easier to describe the goals than the techniques of family intervention for most families presenting with a member with TS. These goals are consonant with the ones described earlier. In children they include the promotion of developmental progress with respect to feelings of self-esteem and competency; the capacity to explore and draw from one's peer group; to be challenged by and persevere in work or school; to tolerate frustration, disappointments, and losses; and to develop satisfying, intimate attachments. The goals for adults are similar and include a kind of flexibility so that family members do not assume guilt for exacerbations of symptoms, realistically recognize their relative's needs for assistance, and can assist in offering alternatives. Many of the same conflicts about work, relationships, and intimate attachments, tolerance of frustration, and loss of control also pertain.

Family intervention begins with the perspective that a patient's family is always a component in his life, including his illness. In this way TS can be understood as a familial disorder on many levels. Invariably, the TS patient presents himself and his family when he comes for treatment or evaluation; the family's genetics, current dynamics, and influences on personality and self-image each make contributions to the presentation of the whole person.

Psychodynamic Psychotherapy with TS Patients

TS has a powerful impact on the inner life of a patient. For TS patients the aim of psychodynamic treatment is not to abolish symptoms. The primary goal is to help patients understand and cope with their illness, to treat conflicts occurring at a psychological level that affect or result from symptoms, and to alleviate other psychological problems that are revealed during the evaluation. Patients are assisted to recognize those circumstances that are regularly associated with exacerbation, to understand how such circumstances arise, and to work toward ways of diffusing or avoiding them. In some cases this may include the explanation and interpretation of behaviors or feelings of which the patient may not be fully aware. There is a difference, however, between employing psychodynamic perspectives and methods on the one hand and presuming a primary psychodynamic etiology on the other. A psychodynamic perspective is especially useful in understanding the patient's full experience and is not inconsistent with a biological approach to etiology (Abraham 1953; Fenichel 1945). When psychodynamic observations are added to the current understanding obtained from children with other chronic illnesses, such as diabetes, asthma, or colitis, the role of psychotherapeutic intervention can be placed in some perspective. Clinicians have appreciated the immediate and enduring therapeutic value of assisting in the management of anxiety; sustaining a patient's progress on his optimal developmental path; assessing and reducing impediments to self-esteem; improving the patient's relationship to health care providers; and promoting the capacity to observe, understand, and respond to internal, familial, and social pressures that derive from and contribute to chronic illness. Without the appreciation and assessment of a patient's inner life, the question of how much psychological work needs to be done cannot be fully answered.

Although every TS patient is unique, several psychological reactions are commonly reported in response to TS symptoms. The losses of impulse control, in thought as well as in body, yield psychological reactions well described by Mahler and Rangell (1943), Ascher (1948), and Silver (1988). These reactions are an understandable consequence of the dilemma of the TS patient who cannot help doing what he wishes not to do and who causes humiliation or shock when what he wishes is to pass unnoticed. The conflict for these patients was characterized in the classical literature as between two different wills: one conscious and appropriately controlled and the other only partially conscious, involuntarily propelled into action, and arousing considerable embarrassment. Accompanying the experience of feeling overwhelmed by unacceptable thoughts or urges, patients frequently describe anxiety, anger, and the cognitive features, frequently seen in depression, of guilt, hopelessness, helplessness, and worthlessness. The appearance of obsessional defenses in the face of the loss of control in TS is understandable, although in some patients these defenses can become hypertropied resulting in obsessional symptoms or compulsive personality disorders. Although these phenomena may actually represent an alternative expression of the underlying etiology that relentlessly gives rise to tics, a great deal remains to learned about the psychological defensive function of milder obsessional phenomena in TS sufferers.

Another reaction to the loss of control in a person with TS may be to relinquish any efforts to modulate impulses, resulting in more generalized, overt, physical and verbal aggression and heightened impulsivity. When this happens, the aggression may become syntonic with the person's character. When patients with TS exhibit aggressive behaviors, often others are left with the task of trying to answer the impossible: are the behaviors voluntary or involuntary? Faced with the kind of impulsivity described by TS patients, this sort of dichotomy is meaningless. A more constructive line of inquiry focuses on the extent to which and the circumstances under which these behaviors are controllable. If the behaviors are not completely syntonic, several legitimate foci of psychodynamic exploration may arise from them, such as their meaning to the patient, identification of the affects preceding and generated by this disinhibition, and the defenses employed to contain them. An appreciation of these dynamics may assist in increasing compliance with educational and medical resources and favorably affect the outcome of whichever treatments are applied.

The decision to employ psychodynamic treatment in TS is based on the presence of impairment in function with these findings: dysfunctional defenses employed against the experience of the disorder, lagging psychological development for a period following the appearance of TS, impairment in self-esteem arising from the reaction of family and social contacts to the symptoms of the disorder, and impairment in occupational or school role performance over and above physical disruption caused by symptoms. The complete evaluation of the TS patient demands an account of these features. In addition, the adjunctive value of psychodynamic treatment may be more strongly considered in patients who have had only marginal responses to pharmacotherapy and in patients whose families develop pathological dynamics related to the disorder.

Persons with TS have at least an equal, if not a greater, lifetime risk as the general population for other psychiatric disorders. The stress of their chronic illness may actually confer a greater risk for depression and anxiety disorders. Psychodynamic treatment may deserve stronger consideration in those with prominent neurotic dysfunction such as the anxiety disorders, in those with dysthymic disturbances, and when psychological defensive functions operate in an exaggerated and subsequently maladaptive manner.

Behavioral Treatments

The essential quality of suppressibility of tics has broad implications for treatment. Prior to seeking professional consultation, some TS patients will experiment with behavioral techniques to control their movements or sounds on their own. The success of these efforts suggests that control of symptoms can sometimes be favorably influenced by behavioral intervention. It is therefore useful to elicit information about these efforts in the initial evaluation of a TS patient.

Several techniques for controlling tics that capitalize on behavioral principles have also been applied with success by behaviorally oriented clinicians. These include massed negative practice, contingency management, relaxation training, self-monitoring, and habit reversal (Azrin and Peterson 1988). Massed negative practice refers to the technique of self-imposed, forceful, repeated execution of a tic for a specified period, perhaps half an hour, with regular brief rest periods of minutes. Over time the subject becomes fatigued and the frequency theoretically decreases. Results from studies of observational cohorts are equivocal in the demonstration of efficacy, although clearly some patients appear to respond.

Contingency management applies, in combination or alone, the familiar principles of positive or negative reinforcement to tic behaviors. Rewards can include parental praise, special gifts, money, or other desired items, whereas negative punishments have ranged from noise to social isolation to the controversial extreme of physical pain. It is virtually impossible to imagine a treatment paradigm that does not include some version of these principles, since whatever kind of treatment is applied, praise from clinicians, parents, teachers, and peers is a nearly universal response when symptoms decrease. Systematic study of these methods is hindered by the difficulty of adequately and ethically applying a control maneuver.

Self-monitoring may be a corollary maneuver to reinforcement. Essentially, it formalizes and records the results of an activity that many TS patients do spontaneously. Self-observation of tics and recording of tic counts during specified periods of the day promotes an increased awareness of movements and may promote efforts to extinguish movements. Efforts to understand the mechanisms underlying the success of this method are underway.

Habit reversal is described as a combination of the behavioral techniques listed above with the addition of isometric muscle tensing to oppose motor tics (Azrin and Nunn 1973). It resembles mass negative practice to the extent that opposing action is required for every tic movement, self-monitoring is required to oppose movements, and punishers are brought into play when subjects interrupt their activity and exert themselves forcefully. Investigations to date have employed only a few patients but suggest some success (Azrin and Peterson 1988).

Patients frequently try relaxation training, which employs tensing followed by relaxation, imagery, or deep breathing. For some these methods can be temporarily helpful. However, for prolonged control these maneuvers usually lose effectiveness and are often abandoned. Future investigations of relaxation training would benefit from rigorous methodology employing carefully selected samples, avoidance of co-maneuvers, clearer descriptions of methods used, control maneuvers, blinded raters, and more objective, sophisticated measures of efficacy (Azrin and Peterson 1988; Rosen and Wesner 1979).

As with other interventions, the successful application of behavioral treatment requires a familiarity with the techniques, adequate methods of assessment, persistence, and a committed client. Further study of these techniques may provide useful alternatives for the treatment of this disorder.

Social Issues

As with other persons suffering from chronic illnesses, general social policies can have a specific impact on persons with TS. Public policies on discrimination and the availability of public resources are especially relevant. This is generally a realm into which few clinicians travel or about which they have much information. For this reason, clinicians corresponding with local and federal agencies on behalf of TS patients need assistance in order to maximize the help these agencies offer. Meyers (1988) has underscored the fact that many of these agencies have not had much experience with cases involving TS and that clinicians can be immensely helpful by offering more than diagnostic labels when asked to explain a patient's needs. In governmental administration TS in particular suffers from a categorical inconsistency in which it is viewed as a "mental illness" by some agencies and not others. TS patients frequently experience discrimination in education or vocational rehabilitation, employment, life and health insurance, housing, and disability reimbursement. Findings from the Ohio TS study of 114 adults in that state (Stefl 1983) suggest that among persons with TS, unemployment was four times the state average and did not necessarily correlate with the degree of disability. Forty percent had reported suffering job discrimination. Similarly, finding and keeping adequate housing for patients with prominent vocal tics can be impossible. As a result of the categorical ambiguity about TS, patients are denied certain protections and access to some resources such as specific supervised care facilities. Since the needs for each case are so specific, it is recommended that clinicians develop a relationship with their local or national Tourette's Syndrome Association (TSA). The TSA is capable of providing general information, instructions for corresponding with local and federal agencies for insurance and disability benefits, and lists of programs and insurance companies with more experience with TS. (The address of the national TSA is Tourette Syndrome Association, Inc., 42-40 Bell Boulevard, Bayside, NY 11361, (718) 224-2999.) For clinicians treating the most severely affected TS patients, this type of intervention—including such elements as finding shelter, public assistance, and vocational rehabilitation—is the most basic, complex, and difficult of all. Assistance from the TSA is especially important for these patients.

Pharmacologic Treatment

Subsequent to supportive and educational or occupational intervention, pharmacologic interventions are among the most widely used treatments for TS and assume increasing importance as symptom severity increases. In a recent survey of TS subjects in the Ohio Tourette's Syndrome Association, 70 percent reported a history of medication treatment (Stefl 1983). Although for the individual patient and his clinician the most burning questions have to do with whether any relief is available from a medication and what side effects he or she may be required to endure, the observed effects of pharmacologic agents are also heuristically important and have led to several provocative hypotheses about the pathophysiologic mechanisms of TS.

There is general agreement among those treating TS about the efficacy and limitations of many currently available agents. What disagreements exist appear to stem from which ones are preferred and how the medications are to be administered. The purpose of this section is not to provide a comprehensive review of all agents ever used in the treatment of TS or to advocate a single method of pharmacologic intervention. Instead, the focus will be on a few of the more widely administered agents and the guidelines for their use in TS.

The Context for Pharmacotherapy

Before initiating pharmacologic interventions, several general therapeutic strategies are important to consider. The aim of treatment, whatever the modality, is to place the patient back on his or her optimal developmental path. This will encompass self-esteem, family and peer relationships, and academic or occupational functioning. Decisions about intervention must address the benefits and impingements in each of these arenas.

Subsequent to the decision to intervene, a consistent method of monitoring a patient's course is critical to the treatment process. For patients with mild symptoms, supportive counseling and observation may be the only longitudinal interventions necessary. As reviewed in the section entitled "Phenomenology, Diagnosis, and Assessment," standardized assessment instruments or videotape records, or both, can be extremely useful, objective tools for following the course and severity of symptoms. Such tools are particularly helpful when deciding to change or institute medication.

The value of family interventions including education, reassurance, supportive listening, and, on occasion, dynamic therapy can be immense. The escalating spiral of family stress derived from ignorance, fear, disappointment, frustration, and helplessness may have definite detrimental effects on the patient's course. Assisting the family to disengage from guilt and responsibility for symptoms, sustain appropriate expectations, remain active in their own advocacy, and respond compassionately to the patient's difficulties are essential components to the success of treatment.

Most teachers, principals, and school administrators have little experience educating TS patients. Their inexperience may yield attitudes, classroom responses, and school programming that hinder a patient's optimal academic performance. These fuel the cycle of increasing stress and increasing symptoms that may lead to school failure and further social isolation. For these reasons, the clinician often needs to meet with school officials and teachers to explain the causes and unique deficits of TS patients and break patterns of reciprocal blame and frustration. Some TS patients may need contained classrooms and designation as special education students. Psychological and educational testing that will clarify specific areas of weakness can also be of considerable assistance.

There is also a place for psychological treatments, group or individual, in the total care of some patients with TS. The decision to use psychological treatments is usually based upon the patient's current functioning (not merely tic severity), his or her level of self-esteem, and the responsiveness of the environmental systems to the other interventions. A method of phasic intervention, in which a clinician will have periods of intensive involvement, perhaps lasting months, alternating with long quiescent periods, may be especially well suited for TS patients.

Basic Principles of Pharmacotherapy in TS

The basic principles governing pharmacotherapy of any neuropsychiatric disorder are equally applicable to the treatment of TS. These principles are listed in Table 3.

In general, it is useful to start patients on the smallest doses of medication possible and make any increases (or decreases) gradually. This practice usually results in fewer and milder side effects, especially with the dopaminergic blocking agents or clonidine. It also appears to improve subsequent compliance.

Assuring an adequate duration of a drug trial using sufficient doses increases the clinician's chances of learning whether a patient is responsive to a particular agent. Physicians not accustomed to TS may terminate drug trials prematurely, either because the patient fails to improve or if side effects are observed. Consequently, it becomes difficult to determine whether another agent should be tried. When the patient, the patient's family, or school are clamoring for rapid relief of symptoms, it can be especially difficult to permit a sufficient time to elapse for an agent to demonstrate its potential and to find the optimal dose.

Maintaining the lowest effective doses is a prudent course. This is especially imperative with the dopaminergic blocking agents, since the clinician is obligated to consider the risks of subsequent tardive dyskinesia. Often this may mean finding an effective dose and then, when the time is appropriate, gradually tapering downward. For patients who have been locked into a cycle of continually escalating doses and symptoms, this sometimes means enduring a considerable increase in symptoms during a rebound period before striking the new equilibrium where a lower dose is equally effective. For patients who have developed tardive dyskinesia subsequent to treatment for TS, this can be even more challenging.

Polypharmacy, the use of more than one medication simultaneously in the treatment of a disorder, is usually considered when single agents have only partially

Table 3.   Basic Principles of Pharmacotherapy of Tourette's Syndrome

- Start patients on the lowest doses of medication possible
- Increment upward slowly
- Assure an adequate duration of a drug trial
- Use sufficient doses
- Maintain the lowest effective dose
- Avoid polypharmacy
- Make changes in regimens as sequences of single steps

ameliorated symptoms, or when complex combinations of symptoms are observed, such as TS with attention deficit disorder or obsessive-compulsive disorder. Too often, however, polypharmacy is not a last resort, and as the regimen grows the untoward effects that result from drug-drug interactions, toxicity, and side effects can become impossible to decipher. It is unknown whether combinations of agents are more effective than single drug schedules. As a result, clinicians are often uncertain about which agents they should use and when to use them.

A corollary of this principle about polypharmacy is that changes in regimens are usually most instructively made as a sequence of single steps. For example, if one reduces the dose of one medication while adding another, whatever course the patient's illness takes, it can be confusing. It may not be possible to discern whether improvement or exacerbation resulted from the new drug, a synergy of both agents, or the reduction of the old one. This also implies a need for washout periods. When a patient is switched from a drug with a long serum half-life and the potential to cause a rebound of symptoms as levels decrease to a different drug, adequate washout periods are crucial for appreciating the efficacy of the second agent.

Pharmacotherapy in the Treatment of TS

A clinician who decides to use medication for the treatment of TS should be skilled in the use of these medications and recognize that pharmacotherapy is a potentially harmful, serious, major intervention strategy. A clinician unfamiliar with these agents is advised to work in close collaboration with a more experienced clinician until he acquires a first-hand understanding of the range of possible positive and untoward effects.

At this point in the United States there are only four established pharmacologic interventions based upon evidence from large trials: haloperidol, clonidine, pimozide, and fluphenazine.

Haloperidol. The most widely investigated agent for the treatment of TS is haloperidol, a butyrophenone. All the butyrophenones bear a distant physical resemblance to the phenothiazines and share the property of primarily blocking dopaminergic receptor sites, although direct effects are noted at noradrenergic and serotonergic loci as well. Roughly 70 percent of patients with TS will improve moderately or more when treated with haloperidol (Nee et al. 1980; Wassman et al. 1978). Its efficacy in decreasing tics is cited as the strongest evidence favoring a dopaminergic mechanism in the pathophysiology of TS. Investigations with haloperidol have produced evidence suggesting that a drug's affinity for inducing dopaminergic blockade at the D_2 receptor site (dopamine receptors that are noncoupled or negatively coupled to adenylate cyclase) appears to correlate best with efficacy in inhibiting tics. Haloperidol also has the desirable properties of being less sedating and less anticholinergic than many other dopaminergic blocking agents.

Ordinarily it is recommended that the lowest possible doses of haloperidol be given when beginning pharmacotherapy. In general 0.5 mg is given before sleep or upon arising. Increments in 0.5 mg-steps at weekly intervals are given if symptoms remain severe. Maximum doses vary among clinicians and situations. In children without other serious difficulties, doses of 2–4 mg/day are commonly required with occasional patients benefiting from less or more. In adults or among children with serious behavioral or attentional difficulties as much as 15 mg/day may be offered. Usually medication is given in a single dose although some clinicians prefer twice-daily dosing.

Side effects are a major problem in maintaining patients on haloperidol. Roughly 60 percent of patients treated with haloperidol will discontinue it because of side effects. In general these include parkinsonian side effects, sedation, weight gain, decreased concentration, decreased memory, anergia, dysphoria, akathisia, personality changes, loss of libido, sexual dysfunction, anxiety reactions resembling phobias or panic, and, after chronic use, tardive dyskinesia. Controversy surrounds the timing of instituting anti-parkinsonian medication. Some clinicians will use medication beginning with the first dose of haloperidol. Others prefer to wait until haloperidol doses reach 2–3 mg/day before beginning. A third group prefers to wait until parkinsonian side effects arise before prescribing anti-parkinsonian medication.

The risk of tardive dyskinesia deserves discussion with the patient. Warning about tardive dyskinesia and annual assessments for dyskinetic movements are advisable, although in general tardive dyskinesia is an infrequent side effect in TS patients. When tardive dyskinesia develops in patients with TS, the diagnosis can be a difficult one (Riddle et al. 1987). The natural history of tardive dyskinesia demands that the patient be carefully informed of subsequent consequences of further neuroleptic treatment before proceeding. It should also be stressed that tardive dyskinesia should be distinguished from withdrawal emergent side effects and that the diagnosis of tardive dyskinesia should be deferred until a patient has been off all medication for several months. Given the severity of potential side effects associated with haloperidol and the other neuroleptics, many clinicians will reserve its use for subjects with moderate to severe symptoms.

Other neuroleptics.   Alternatives to these agents are other phenothiazine compounds. The most investigated and effective agent in this category is fluphenazine. Its side effect profile is roughly identical to that of haloperidol, but some patients report fewer side effects and tolerate them better. In general, dose ranges similar to those recommended for haloperidol, up to 5 mg/day for the low-dose responders and up to 12 mg/day for the higher dose responders, are employed. Beginning at lower doses, such as 1.0 mg per day, is advised.

Clonidine.   An alternative agent in the treatment of TS is clonidine, an imidazoline compound with α-adrenergic agonist activity. Although clonidine exerts both post- and presynaptic activity, it acts preferentially at the presynaptic site. In low doses clonidine "down-regulates" α-adrenergic neurons in the locus ceruleus, decreasing the release of central norepinephrine. Clonidine has several other direct central effects including inhibition of ACTH, stimulating growth hormone release, and stimulating central H_2 histamine receptors. Indirect effects on dopamine and serotonin have also been proposed (Bunney and DeRiemer 1982).

In TS it appears that clonidine may be effective for a smaller portion of patients, perhaps 40 to 60 percent (Cohen et al. 1980). However, in the opinion of some clinicians, although there may be a reduced response rate, the occurrence of fewer side effects offsets this and on the balance favors use of clonidine when it is effective. Efforts to draw conclusions about the efficacy of clonidine have been hampered by problems in sample size and by making comparisons between studies with wide disparities with regard to comorbid conditions, baseline severity, average age, and assessments of symptom severity.

Variables considered in the administration of clonidine include the maximum doses, rate of increasing doses, and latency of action. Most clinicians have used low doses, less than 0.25 mg per day, while others have used doses as high as 0.90 mg per day. Also, the experience of some clinicians suggests that the rate of increasing doses is irrelevant and that patients may be started and move up quickly. Others have advocated that a slow, gradual progression is desirable for maximum effect with a minimum of side effects. Lastly, there are reports that suggest that clonidine response may have a very long latency time, as long as 12 weeks, whereas others have suggested that 6-week trials are adequate.

Although clonidine may have a lower response rate, some clinicians will begin with it when pharmacotherapy is indicated because no known indications or constellations of symptoms predict response. Low-dose treatment usually begins with 0.05 mg daily and increases by 0.05 mg in weekly intervals. The medication is increased by increasing the dosing frequency (0.05 mg twice daily, three times daily, etc.) to a maximum of four times daily. In other patients doses as high as 0.6 mg/day may be needed. In general, if patients do respond, the compliance with clonidine therapy is greater because fewer or less disturbing side effects are experienced. The most commonly observed side effects are sedation and dry mouth (xerostomia). Rarely, increased symptoms and manic episodes have been reported. In higher doses hypotension becomes more likely.

Pimozide.   Recently, pimozide was approved for the treatment of TS and it now is in relatively common use. Neither a butyrophenone nor a phenothiazine, it is a diphenyl-butylpiperidine with potent dopaminergic blocking properties and, putatively, relative D_2 receptor selectivity. As with haloperidol, roughly 70 to 80 percent of TS patients will respond to pimozide (Moldofsky and Sandor 1988; Shapiro and Shapiro 1984). However, somewhat more than half of these patients, perhaps 60 percent, will tolerate side effects well and remain on the medication.

The side effects that have been identified, especially akathisia, extrapyramidal effects, and sedation, are similar to, but probably less severe than, those found with haloperidol. These also include the more unusual side effects such as phobias, depression, and galactorrhea (Linet 1985; Shapiro and Shapiro 1984). Studies suggest that, when compared with haloperidol, pimozide causes side effects in fewer patients. This may also be true for the development of tardive dyskinesia (Chouinard and Steinberg 1982). Reports of ECG and cardiac problems, U waves and inverted T waves, in early studies led to concern about cardiotoxicity. Further investigations with larger numbers of patients have failed to support these concerns (Moldofsky and Sandor 1988). Nevertheless, routine ECG studies at monthly or bimonthly intervals are recommended.

In general doses begin at 1 mg and increase slowly to 3 mg/day with a majority of patients responding to this dose over a six-week trial. Some patients may require as much as 8 mg/day for maintenance. Maximum recommended doses are 10 mg/day for children and 20 mg/day for adults. The half-life of the drug permits single daily dosing, or divided doses may be given twice each day to diminish sedation.

Combinations of medications.   Some clinicians have proposed using combinations of medications when a single agent is only partially effective. There is clinical experience suggesting that haloperidol plus clonidine or pimozide plus clonidine may act synergistically. Careful steps to ensure adequate doses for a sufficient duration are vital prerequisites to the use of combination approaches. It should be noted that there have been no larger scale published trials of these combinations.

The Dilemma of Stimulant Medication

It is clear that tic symptoms, usually dose related and transient, have developed in children with ADHD who were under treatment with stimulant medication (Denkla et al. 1976; Golden 1977; Lowe et al. 1982). It is also true that as many as 50 percent of children with TS will experience an increase in symptoms when treated with stimulant medication. Therefore, a consistent common problem arises when patients previously responsive to stimulant medication develop tics, when patients with ADHD also have a strong family history for tic disorders, or when patients with moderate to severe impairment resulting from ADHD and TS present for pharmacologic treatment. Recent evidence has been interpreted to suggest that stimulant medication may unleash TS in vulnerable individuals, exacerbate TS in patients who already have the disorder, or, some believe, may cause TS in previously unsusceptible individuals. Currently available data are difficult to interpret, and there may be important individual differences. More remains to be learned before the relationship between tics and stimulants will be understood.

At the present time there are no generally agreed upon guidelines for the combined treatment of tic disorders and ADHD (Golden 1988). Some clinicians will use stimulants in any patient with ADHD and simply observe the patient closely. Others will optimize environmental interventions and then use clonidine or antidepressant medication, setting aside stimulants. The middle of the road has been to discontinue stimulants in ADHD patients who develop tics while on stimulant medication and, if educational and therapeutic interventions have been optimal, to start clonidine or antidepressants. When patients without tics present with ADHD and have a positive family history for tic disorders, then a cautious trial of stimulant medication may be employed.

There is a diversity of opinion about the treatment of patients with TS and ADHD. Some clinicians will begin with stimulants and, if they prove helpful, discontinue them only if tic symptoms increase. Others avoid stimulants altogether in this group and prefer starting with clonidine or antidepressants. Another approach to the problem is the combined administration of haloperidol and stimulants (Commings and Commings 1984; Shapiro and Shapiro, 1988). Prescribing the lowest possible effective dose of stimulants, clinicians using this regimen maintain that tics are not exacerbated by the combination, and that the complementary interactions may offer significant relief to seriously impaired children. This combination has also been applied to combat the side effect of akinesia that results from haloperidol administration (Shapiro and Shapiro 1988). Although transient increases in tics have been observed, they are reportedly short lived and easily managed. Careful investigations on larger populations of patients with tics and ADHD are obviously necessary before a clear approach can be defined.

Obsessions and Compulsions in TS

In descriptive investigations of TS as many as 50 percent of patients have obsessions or compulsions, or both, including symptoms such as rituals, repetitive touching, "evening up," self-injurious behavior, and mental urges. "Classic" compulsive symptoms of washing and checking and obsessions such as horrific images, dreaded thoughts, and doubting are also reported. Like movements and sounds, these symptoms wax and wane, although the severity of obsessive-compulsive symptoms may not correlate with the severity of other symptoms. Often obsessive-compulsive symptoms are observed after movements and sounds have been present for several years, and for some patients, the obsessive-compulsive symptoms may be the most disabling and distressing ones of all. Results from drug trials in obsessive-compulsive disorder suggest that tricyclic antidepressants, such as imipramine or clomipramine, monoamine oxidase inhibitors, or newer heterocyclic antidepressants, such as fluoxetine, may be useful in ameliorating symptoms in some patients (Towbin et al. 1987). Yet these trials were designed for OCD patients and their findings cannot be generalized to TS patients without caution. In response to recent studies, TS patients are now routinely evaluated for OCD, and we anticipate the availability of more data on the response of these symptoms to standard agents for tics, such as haloperidol, pimozide, and clonidine. There are anecdotal reports of patients developing worsening tics when treated with tricyclics and monoamine oxidase inhibitors (Caine et al. 1979; Fras and Karlavage 1977) although no systematic trials have been conducted in TS patients to treat OCD.

Patients with serious impairments resulting from obsessions or compulsions, or both, warrant consideration of treatment with imipramine or investigational agents such as clomipramine or fluoxetine (Towbin 1988). Certainly the determination of safety and efficacy of these investigational agents in TS patients will have to await specific controlled trials, but OCD patients' response to these agents offers some hope to the most seriously disabled patients with TS and OCD. In addition, the benefits and hazards of drug combinations, such as tricyclic or heterocyclic antidepressants plus clonidine, pimozide, or haloperidol deserve further study.

Maintenance and Discontinuation

One possible outcome of pharmacologic treatment is the return to appropriate development and minimized symptoms. It should be stressed that when development is proceeding smoothly and symptoms are in some control, it is reasonable to gradually discontinue pharmacologic treatment. On the other hand, there is no formula for predicting the optimum duration of drug treatment. The majority of patients who respond to a medication may remain on it for several years or more. Rating scales and videotapes may help document the new baseline for future reference. It can be useful to remind patients that, should symptoms return, the same agents may be employed. It does not appear that responders convert to nonresponders, although experience is scanty.

Gradual reductions are recommended for discontinuation of any of these agents. When clonidine is rapidly discontinued rebound hypertension often follows and exacerbation of tics lasting as long as six or eight weeks has been reported (Leckman et al. 1986). When abrupt reductions in haloperidol are attempted, withdrawal dyskinesias may be observed over a duration of two to three months and can be confused with exacerbation of tics. Even when reductions in neuroleptics are carried out gradually, dyskinetic movements, perhaps previously masked by the neuroleptic, may be seen. These movements tend to be less intense and more variable in duration than those caused by abrupt discontinuation (Shapiro and Shapiro 1988).

Another possibility is that patients will continue to have disturbed development with severe symptoms. In persons who are unresponsive to medication it is even more important to review nonpharmacologic interventions. This can assure that the patient's immediate and future living environment and academic or vocational development are optimal. Sometimes clinicians are tempted to prescribe larger and larger doses of medication with the hope that more medication will yield better control. However, especially where the dopaminergic blocking agents are concerned, the benefits do not appear and increasing side effects and risks of tardive dyskinesia appear to outweigh any symptom amelioration. In the case of clonidine, higher doses usually result in hypotension and sedation. For the patient with severe symptoms who does not respond to medication, nonpharmacologic interventions and education, as discussed previously, assume an even more central position.

Future Directions in Treatment

There are several reasons to feel optimistic about the treatment of TS in the future despite the current inability to fully control symptoms without side effects. Among these are the increasingly rapid pace of discovery about the underlying mechanisms in TS, especially in regard to genetic risk and mechanisms of transmission. This raises the possibility of discovering the biological pathways leading to symptoms in the next decade. As a result, more effective treatments could be available. In addition, it is important to recognize that currently many persons with TS achieve as much in life as persons without the disorder. TS does not generally lead to serious social and occupational debility, as some dramatic portrayals would suggest. Furthermore, clinicians are developing increasing familiarity with TS and its treatment. Information about TS is more readily available at all levels (Cohen et al. 1988; Shapiro et al. 1988). In the community, educators and the general public are also acquiring a greater understanding of TS, permitting patients to lead more normal lives and receive the information, compassion, and care they need.

References

Section 8
Tic Disorders

Abraham K: Selected Papers on Psychoanalysis. New York, Basic Books, 1953

American Psychiatric Association: Diagnostic and Statistical Manual of Mental Disorders, 3rd ed, revised. Washington, DC, American Psychiatric Association, 1987

Ang L, Borison R, Dysken M, et al: Reduced excretion of MHPG in Tourette's syndrome, in Advances in Neurology: Gilles de la Tourette Syndrome, vol 35. Edited by Friedhoff AJ, Chase TN. New York, Raven Press, 1982, pp 171–177

Ascher E: Psychodynamic considerations in Gilles de la Tourette disease (Maladie des Tics). Am J Psychiatry 105:267–276, 1948

Azrin NH, Nunn RG: Habit reversal: a method of eliminating nervous habits and tics. Behav Res Ther 11:619–628, 1973

Azrin NH, Peterson AL: Behavior therapy for Tourette's syndrome and tic disorders, in Tourette's Syndrome and Tic Disorders: Clinical Understanding and Treatment. Edited by Cohen DJ, Bruun RD, Leckman JF. New York, Wiley, 1988, pp 237–257

Berg C, Rapoport JL, Flament M: The Leyton Obsessional Inventory—child version. J Am Acac Child Psychiatr 25:84–91, 1986

Berkson J: Limitations of the application of fourfold table analysis to hospital data. Biometrics 2:47–50, 1946

Bruun RD: Dysphoric phenomena associated with haloperidol treatment of Tourette syndrome, in Advances in Neurology: Gilles de la Tourette Syndrome, vol 35. Edited by Friedhoff AJ, Chase TN. New York, Raven Press, 1982, pp 433–436

Bunney BS, DeRiemer SA: Effects of clonidine on dopaminergic neuron activity in the substantia nigra: possible mediation by noradrenergic regulation of serotonergic raphe system, in Advances in Neurology: Gilles de la Tourette Syndrome, vol 35. Edited by Friedhoff AJ, Chase TN. New York, Raven Press, 1982, pp 99–104

Butler IJ, Koslow SH, Seifert WE Jr et al: Biogenic amine metabolism in Tourette syndrome. Ann Neurol 6:37–39, 1979

Caine ED, Polinsky RJ: Haloperidol induced dysphoria in patients with Tourette syndrome. Am J Psychiatry 136:1216–1217, 1979

Caine ED, Polinsky RJ, Ebert MH, et al: Trial of clorimipramine and desipramine for Gilles de la Tourette syndrome. Ann Neurol 5:305–306, 1979

Chase TM, Foster NL, Fedro P, et al: Gilles de la Tourette syndrome: studies with the fluorine-18 labeled fluorodeoxyglucose positron emission tomographic method. Ann Neurol 15(suppl):175, 1984

Chouinard G, Steinberg S: Type I tardive dyskinesia induced by anticholinergic drugs, dopamine agonists and neuroleptics. Prog Neuropsychopharmacol Biol Psychiatry 6:571–578, 1982

Cohen DJ, Shaywitz BA, Caparulo BK, et al: Chronic multiple tics of Gilles de la Tourette's disease: CSF acid monoamine metabolites after probenecid administration. Arch Gen Psychiatry 35:245–250, 1978

Cohen DJ, Shaywitz BA, Young JG, et al: Central biogenic amine metabolism in children with the syndrome of chronic multiple tics of Gilles de la Tourette: norepinephrine, seratonin and dopamine. J Am Acad Child Psychiatry 18:320–341, 1979

Cohen DJ, Detlor J, Young JG, et al: Clonidine ameliorates Gilles de la Tourette syndrome. Arch Gen Psychiatry 37:1350–1357, 1980

Cohen DJ, Ort SI, Leckman JF, et al: Family functioning and Tourette syndrome, in Tourette's Syndrome and Tic Disorders: Clinical Understanding and Treatment. Edited by Cohen DJ, Bruun RD, Leckman JF. New York, Wiley, 1988, pp. 179–196

Commings DE, Commings BG: Tourette's syndrome and attention deficit disorder with hyperactivity: are they related? J Am Acad Child Psychiatry 23:138–146, 1984

Connell PH, Corbett JA, Horne DJ, et al: Drug treatment of adolescent ticquers: a double blind trial of diazepam and haloperidol. Br J Psychiatry 113:375–381, 1967

Conners CK: Rating Scales. Psychopharmacology Bulletin: Special Issue on Pharmacotherapy of Children. Washington, DC, NIMH, U.S. Government Printing Office, 1973, pp. 35–42, 55–60

Cooper J: The Leyton obsessional inventory. Psychol Med 1:48–64, 1970

Denkla M, Bemporad J, Mackay M: Tics following methylphenidate administration: a report of 20 cases. JAMA 235:1349–1351, 1976

Dykens E: Intellectual and Adaptive functioning of Tourette's Syndrome children with and without ADHD. Poster presented at the Annual Meeting of the American Academy of Child and Adolescent Psychiatry, Washington, DC, 1987

Endicott J, Spitzer RL, Fliess JL, et al: The clinical global scale: a procedure for measuring overall severity of psychiatric disturbance. Arch Gen Psychiatry 33:766–771, 1976

Fahn S: The clinical spectrum of motor tics, in Advances in Neurology: Gilles de la Tourette Syndrome, vol 35. Edited by Friedhoff AJ, Chase TN. New York, Raven Press, 1982, pp 341–344

Fahn S, Erenberg G: Differential diagnosis of tic phenomena: a neurologic perspective, in Tourette's Syndrome and Tic Disorders: Clinical Understanding and Treatment. Edited by Cohen DJ, Bruun RD, Leckman JF. New York, Wiley, 1988, pp 41–55

Fenichel O: The psychoanalytic theory of neurosis. New York, WW Norton, 1945, pp 317–322

Fras I, Karlavage J: The use of methylphenidate and imipramine in Gilles de la Tourette disease in children. Am J Psychiatry 134:195–197, 1977

Gilles de la Tourette G: Study of a neurologic condition characterized by motor incoordination accompanied by echolalia and coprolalia (1885). Translated by Goetz CG, Klawans HI. In Advances in Neurology: Gilles de la Tourette Syndrome, vol 35. Edited by Friedhoff AJ, Chase TN. New York, Raven Press, 1982, pp 1–16

Glaze DG, Frost JD, Jankovic J: Gilles de la Tourette's syndrome: disorder of arousal. Neurology 33:586–592, 1983

Golden GS: The effect of central nervous system stimulants on Tourette syndrome. Ann Neurol 2:69–70, 1977

Golden GS: Psychologic and neuropsychologic aspects of Tourette's syndrome. Neurol Clin North Am 2:91–102, 1984

Golden GS: The use of stimulants and Tourette's syndrome, in Tourette's Syndrome and Tic Disorders: Clinical Understanding and Treatment. Edited by Cohen DJ, Bruun RD, Leckman JF. New York, Wiley, 1988, pp 317–329

Gonce M, Barbeau A: Seven cases of Gilles de la Tourette's syndrome: partial relief with clonazepam. Can J Neurol Sci 75:225–241, 1977

Hagin RA, Kugler J: School problems associated with Tourette's syndrome, in Tourette's Syndrome and Tic Disorders: Clinical Understanding and Treatment. Edited by Cohen DJ, Bruun RD, Leckman JF. New York, Wiley, 1988, pp 223–237

Harcherick DF, Leckman JF, Detlor J, et al: A new instrument for clinical studies of Tourette's syndrome. J Am Acad Child Psychiatry 23:153–160, 1984

Incagnoli T, Kane R: Neuropsychological functioning in Tourette syndrome, in Advances in Neurology: Gilles de la Tourette Syndrome, vol 35. Edited by Friedhoff AJ, Chase TN. New York, Raven Press, 1982, pp 305–309

Jagger J, Prusoff BA, Cohen DJ, et al: The epidemiology of Tourette's syndrome. Schizophr Bull 8:267–278, 1982

Leckman JF, Detlor J, Harcherick DF, et al: Acute and chronic clonidine treatment in Tourette's syndrome: a preliminary report on clinical response and effect on plasma and urinary catecholamine metabolites, growth hormone and blood pressure. J Am Acad Child Psychiatry 22:433–440, 1983

Leckman JF, Cohen DJ, Gertner JM, et al: Growth hormone response to clonidine in children ages 4–17: Tourette's syndrome vs. children with short stature. J Am Acad Child Psychiatry 23:174–181, 1984

Leckman JF, Ort SI, Cohen DJ, et al: Rebound phenomena in Tourette's syndrome after abrupt withdrawal of clonidine: behavioral cardiovascular and neurochemical effects. Arch Gen Psychiatry 43:1168–1176, 1986

Leckman JF, Price RA, Walkup JT, et al: Nongenetic factors in Gilles de la Tourette's syndrome. Arch Gen Psychiatry 44:100, 1987

Leckman JF, Riddle MA, Cohen DJ: Pathobiology of Tourette's syndrome, in Tourette's Syndrome and Tic Disorders: Clinical Understanding and Treatment. Edited by Cohen DJ, Bruun RD, Leckman JF. New York, Wiley, 1988, pp 103–119

Linet LS: Tourette syndrome, pimozide and school phobia: the neuroleptic separation anxiety syndrome. Am J Psychiatry 142:613–615, 1985

Lowe TL, Cohen DJ, Detlor J, et al: Stimulant medications precipitate Tourette's syndrome. JAMA 247:1729–1731, 1982

Mahler MS, Rangell L: A psychosomatic study of Maladie des tics (Gilles de la Tourette's disease). Psychiatr Q 17:519–605, 1943

Meyers AS: Social issues of Tourette syndrome, in Tourette's Syndrome and Tic Disorders: Clinical Understanding and Treatment. Edited by Cohen DJ, Bruun RD, Leckman JF. New York, Wiley, 1988, pp 257–267

Mikkelson EJ, Detlor J, Cohen DJ: School avoidance and social phobia triggered by haloperidol in patients with Tourette's disorder. Am J Psychiatry 138:1572–1575, 1981

Moldofsky H, Sandor P: Pimozide in the treatment of Gilles de la Tourette, in Tourette's Syndrome and Tic Disorders: Clinical Understanding and Treatment. Edited by Cohen DJ, Bruun RD, Leckman JF. New York, Wiley, 1988, pp 281–291

Nee LE, Caine ED, Polinsky RJ, et al: Gilles de la Tourette syndrome: clinical and family study of 50 cases. Ann Neurol 7:41–49, 1980

Pauls DL, Leckman JF: The inheritance of Gilles de la Tourette's syndrome and associated behaviors: evidence for autosomal dominant transmission. N Engl Med 315:993–997, 1986

Pauls DL, Towbin KE, Leckman JF, et al: Evidence supporting a genetic relationship between Gilles de la Tourette's syndrome and obsessive-compulsive disorder. Arch Gen Psychiatry 43:1180–1182, 1986

Price RA, Kidd KK, Cohen DJ, et al: A twin study of Tourette's syndrome. Arch Gen Psychiatry 42:815–820, 1985

Riddle MA, Shaywitz BA, Leckman JF, et al: Brief debrisoquin administration to assess central dopaminergic function in children. Life Sci 38:1041–1048, 1986

Riddle MA, Hardin MT, Towbin KE, et al: Tardive dyskinesia following haloperidol treatment in Tourette's syndrome. Arch Gen Psychiatry 44:98–99, 1987

Rosen M, Wesner C: A behavioral approach to Tourette's syndrome. J Can Clin Psychol 41:303–312, 1979

Shaffer D, Gould MS, Brasic J, et al: A children's global assessment scale. Arch Gen Psychiatr 40:1228–1231, 1983

Shapiro AK, Shapiro E: Controlled study of pimozide vs. placebo in Tourette's syndrome. J Am Acad Child Psychiatry 23:161–173, 1984

Shapiro AK, Shapiro E: Treatment of tic disorders with haloperidol, in Tourette's Syndrome and Tic Disorders: Clinical Understanding and Treatment. Edited by Cohen DJ, Bruun RD, Leckman JF. New York, Wiley, 1988, pp 267–281

Shapiro AK, Shapiro ES, Young JG, et al: Gilles de la Tourette Syndrome. NY, Raven Press, 1988

Silver AA: Intrapsychic processes and adjustment in Tourette syndrome, in Tourette's Syndrome and Tic Disorders: Clinical Understanding and Treatment. Edited by Cohen DJ, Bruun RD, Leckman JE. New York, Wiley, 1988, pp. 197–207

Stahl SM, Berger PA: Cholinergic and dopaminergic mechanisms in Tourette's syndrome, in Advances in Neurology: Gilles de la Tourette Syndrome, vol 35. Edited by Friedhoff AJ, Chase TN. New York, Raven Press, 1982

Stefl ME: The Ohio Tourette study. Cincinnati, Oh, School of Planning, University of Cincinnati, 1983

Tanner CM, Goetz CG, Klawans HL: Cholinergic mechanisms in Tourette's syndrome. Neurology 32:1315–1317, 1982

Towbin KE: Obsessive-compulsive symptoms in Tourette's syndrome, in Tourette's Syndrome and Tic Disorders: Clinical Understanding and Treatment. Edited by Cohen DJ, Bruun RD, Leckman JF. New York, Wiley, 1988, pp. 137–151

Towbin KE, Leckman JF, Cohen DJ: Drug treatment of obsessive-compulsive disorder: a review of findings in the light of diagnostic and metric limitations. Psychiatr Dev 5:25–50, 1987

van Woert MH, Rosenbaum D, Enna SJ: Overview of pharmacological approaches to therapy for Tourette's syndrome, in Advances in Neurology: Gilles de la Tourette syndrome, vol 35. Edited by Friedhoff AJ, Chase TN. New York, Raven Press, 1982, pp. 369–375

Wassman ER, Eldridge R, Abbuzahab F, et al: Gilles de la Tourette syndrome: clinical and genetic studies in a Midwestern city. Neurology 28:304–307, 1978

Elimination Disorders

Chapter 84

Elimination Disorders

Functional Enuresis

History

Functional enuresis is primarily a childhood problem that has concerned children, parents, and physicians since biblical times. The earliest recorded treatment (circa 1550 B.C.) employed a combination of juniper berries, cypress, and beer (Glicklich 1951). Enuresis first became viewed as an economic and social problem during the nineteenth century. Many of the treatments recommended then persist in current practice: limiting fluid intake and emptying the bladder prior to bedtime and waking the child to avoid deep sleep. At the same time, medications were prescribed including chloral hydrate, strychnine, and belladonna. In 1830, the first prototype of the bed alarm was invented by Nye. It was modified a century later by the Mowrers, who replaced the electric shock with ringing of a bell to awaken the patient. The development of psychoanalytic theory during the twentieth century facilitated increased understanding of emotional factors involved in enuresis. Contemporary approaches to enuresis have been the subject of recent reviews (Gross and Dornbusch 1983; Shaffer 1985).

Definition

The term *enuresis*, derived from the Greek *enouein*, means "to void urine." The frequency and the time of day of wetting are usually included in the definition of enuresis, but no standardized clinical definition exists in the medical literature. A diagnosis of *functional* enuresis is given in the absence of a demonstrable organic cause. The DSM-III-R diagnostic criteria for functional enuresis are: 1) repeated voiding of urine during the day or night into bed or clothes, whether voluntary or involuntary; 2) at least two such events per month for children between the ages of five and six, and at least one event per month for older children; 3) chronologic age at least five, and mental age at least four; 4) and not due to a physical disorder, such as diabetes, bladder infection, or a seizure disorder (American Psychiatric Association 1987).

Enuresis may be classified as *primary* if the child has never achieved urinary continence and *secondary* if continence was achieved for at least one year and subsequently lost. *Nocturnal*, the most common type of enuresis, refers to passage of urine during sleep only; *diurnal* enuresis refers to passage of urine during waking hours.

Subclassification

Attempts to subclassify children with functional enuresis have been unsuccessful. Based on clinical experience, Anders and Freeman (1979) proposed a subclassification of functional enuresis into five categories: sociocultural (resulting from unsatisfactory toilet training); separation-individuation (associated with power struggles between the child and parent); regressive (developing in response to stressful events); with "masked" depression; and adolescent (perhaps associated with severe psychopathology). Variables selected for determining the subclasses included age, sex, primary versus secondary enuresis, time of wetting, family history, and associated behavioral and psychiatric symptoms. To test the validity of the proposed subclassification scheme, Fritz and Anders (1979) studied 116 enuretic children, aged 4 to 14 years, identified in various outpatient settings. Based on this study, the authors concluded that none of the "categories of organic or functional enuresis were found to be valid clinic subgroups. Furthermore, no other organization of the variables produced meaningful or statistically significant subgroups within the enuretic population" (Fritz and Anders 1979, p. 110).

Shaffer and colleagues (1984) studied 126 enuretic children to test the hypothesis that "there may be psychiatrically disturbed enuretic children who have no biological evidence of bladder dysfunction whose prior experiences might reasonably be held to have led to both enuresis and psychiatric disorder, and another group who have disturbed bladder function but no significant psychiatric problems" (Shaffer et al. 1984, p. 781). The authors concluded: "Our findings do not indicate that there are distinct groups of enuretics with either behavior or bladder disturbance, at least as indicated by low FBV [functional bladder-volume]. Rather there is a close association between bladder dysfunction and deviant behavior" (Shaffer et al. 1984, p. 787).

Prevalence

Reported estimates of prevalence of functional enuresis vary widely throughout the world, perhaps reflecting differences in definition (Hallgren 1956; Rutter et al. 1973). The most comprehensive epidemiological studies of enuresis in the United States were carried out in the 1960s (National Center for Health Statistics 1967, 1969; Oppel et al. 1968). The major findings of these studies are: 1) primary nocturnal enuresis is the most prevalent form of wetting, 2) the prevalence of bed-wetting declines with age, and 3) bed-wetting prevalence is generally higher among boys than girls. The authors of DSM-III-R suggest that the prevalence of functional enuresis is "at age 5, 7% for boys and 3% for girls; at age 10, 3% for boys and 2% for girls; and at age 18, 1% for boys and almost nonexistent for girls" (American Psychiatric Association 1987).

Etiology

Commonly, the cause of functional enuresis cannot be found in an individual child. Genetic, physical, social, and psychological factors may all play a role.

Genetic factors.   Several lines of evidence implicate genetic factors in the etiology of functional enuresis. The observation that enuresis occurs more frequently in the parents and siblings of enuretic patients was first made over 50 years ago (Frary 1935) and has been replicated by several investigators (Bakwin 1961; Cho 1984; Hallgren 1957; Stockwell and Smith 1940). Twin studies indicate that concordance for enuresis is significantly greater in monozygotic then dizygotic twins (Hallgren 1960; 68 percent versus 36 percent, Bakwin 1973). Although there have been no studies on twins reared apart, Kaffman and Elizur (1977) investigated young children living on an Israeli kibbutz, where toilet training usually occurs away from the parents. Sixty-seven percent of enuretic children had enuretic siblings compared to 22 percent of dry children. Neither the mode of transmission nor the specific genetic mechanisms underlying functional enuresis has been identified.

Physical factors.   Possible physical causes of functional enuresis—urinary tract outflow obstruction, limited functional bladder capacity, sleep disturbance, EEG abnormalities, and maturational delay—have been proposed.

Among reports of an association between marginal obstruction of the urinary outflow tract and enuresis, perhaps the most influential was that by Mahoney (1971), who concluded that 96 percent of boys and 97 percent of girls with enuresis showed evidence on intravenous pyelogram and voiding cystourethrography of an "obvious or potentially obstructive lesion of the vesical outflow system" (p. 951). However, because of methodological problems, none of these urological studies have presented convincing evidence that outflow obstruction plays a role in the etiology or pathogenesis of functional enuresis. Recently, in a study of excretory urograms of 216 primary enuretic adult males, aged 18 to 20 years, no patient was found to have evidence of obstruction (Libson et al. 1986).

It has been observed that most enuretic children void more frequently during the day than comparable nonenuretics, but that they do not void larger total volumes of urine. Pompeius (1971) found that 30 percent of enuretics had a low functional bladder volume. Shaffer et al. (1984) reported that 55 percent of enuretic children had a functional bladder volume one standard deviation below that which would be expected. However, there is considerable overlap in bladder capacity between enuretic and nonenuretic children (Starfield 1967; Troup and Hodgson 1971). Thus, it cannot be determined whether limited functional bladder capacity is a causal factor or secondary phenomenon in the enuretic child.

Although the earliest studies involving EEG measurement during sleep suggested that enuretic events occurred during deep sleep, enuresis has been observed during all sleep stages, occurring most commonly in delta or slow-wave sleep (stages 3 and 4). Based on the results of EEG studies, Broughton (1968) proposed that enuresis is a disorder of arousal and suggested that enuretic episodes originate during slow-wave sleep, being preceded by brief "arousal" events manifested by lightening of sleep. In a large study, Mikkelsen et al. (1980) showed that children with enuresis have a larger component of slow-wave sleep than nonenuretic children. However, enuretic events occurred in all stages of sleep and were not associated with a particular sleep stage. In a study of seven enuretic children who had suprapubic catheters inserted to measure bladder pressure during sleep, "preliminary investigations have shown that the pelvic floor and the bladder show silence for a couple of hours [following the onset of sleep], then a sudden increase in bladder pressure occurs without forewarning. By examining the cerebral activity [EEG], the preliminary results show no evidence of alteration in sleep stage during enuretic episodes" (Norgaard et al. 1985, p. 319).

The concept of enuresis as an "epileptic equivalent" emerged following studies that reported a high rate of paroxysmal phenomena in the EEGs of children with enuresis. However, these studies failed to control for factors that might affect the rate of EEG abnormalities. In a more carefully designed study, Poussaint et al. (1967) found that the rate of EEG abnormalities was not higher in children with enuresis than in a group of carefully selected normal children studied in Scandinavia (Eeg-Oloffson 1971; Eeg-Oloffson et al. 1971; Peterson and Eeg-Oloffson 1970).

Large survey studies in both Great Britain (Essen and Peckham 1976) and the United States (Gross and Dornbusch 1983; National Center for Health Statistics 1967, 1969) have shown that, as a group, children with enuresis show small but significant signs of developmental delay, such as delayed motor and language milestones, bone age, and sexual maturation.

In summary, although limited functional bladder capacity and minimal delays in physical development have been observed in children with enuresis as a group, no specific physical etiologies have been identified.

Social factors. Numerous studies have examined the role of toilet training in the development of enuresis. These studies have been reviewed by Shaffer (1985, p. 470), who concludes that "intensive and well-timed toilet training with an emphasis on praise and rewards for contingency, but some disapproval for incontinence, is likely to be most helpful. Some cases of enuresis may be a consequence of poor training."

Douglas (1973) has examined the relationship between certain stressful life events at age three to four years and subsequent enuresis. A child who had experienced substantial stress, such as family breakup through death or divorce, temporary separation from mother for at least a month, birth of a younger sibling, moving to a new home, admission to a hospital, accident, or surgical procedure, was twice as likely to become enuretic.

An association between lower social class and higher rate of enuresis has been observed in several countries; this association is usually greater for boys than for girls. The different social factors that increase the prevalence of enuresis—chronic disadvantage, stressful life events, and inadequate toilet training—commonly occur together.

Psychological factors. The early psychoanalytic literature contains several psychological explanations for enuresis, including enuresis as an exhibitionistic defense against castration anxiety (Angel 1935) and wetting as satisfying a repressed hostile or sexual drive (Michaels 1961). Enuresis has also been viewed as a manifestation of anxiety, an indirect expression of aggression, and an immature form of gratification.

Both population surveys (Essen and Peckham 1976; Rutter et al. 1973) and studies of children referred for treatment (Cho 1984; Couchells et al. 1981) have shown an association between enuresis and emotional-behavioral disturbance. Some evidence suggests that children with enuresis are less confident and more retiring and acquiescent than nonenuretic peers (Lovibond 1964; McHale 1967; Stein and Susser 1965).

Attempting to assess these putative psychological factors, Achenbach and Lewis (1971) reviewed edited chart notes of boys referred to a psychiatric clinic for enuresis, encopresis, or learning disorders. Surprisingly, enuretics were less passive and less likely to "relinquish the care" of their bodies than the other groups. Enuretics did not differ significantly from the other groups in their tendency to express aggression indirectly.

Although clinical experience suggests that secondary enuresis is more likely to be associated with psychiatric disorders or stressful life events than primary enuresis, several research studies have failed to find such an association (Cho 1984; Fritz and Anders 1979; Rutter et al. 1973; Shaffer et al. 1984).

In summary, most children with functional enuresis do not have a discrete psychiatric disorder or prototypical "psychological profile." About 50 percent of children with functional enuresis have an identifiable behavioral or emotional disturbance, but a causal relationship is difficult to establish.

Diagnosis and Assessment

Assessment of a child with enuresis often occurs in a multidisciplinary setting. Frequently the parents have consulted a pediatrician or urologist before the child is referred to a child psychiatrist. Demonstrable medical causes of wetting, such as urinary tract infection or diabetes mellitus, can be ruled out before a diagnosis of functional enuresis is made.

The child and family will benefit most if they feel that their story has been heard by a clinician who appreciates the potential inconvenience, embarrassment, and shame that can result from repeated wetting. A clear understanding of the circumstances surrounding the wetting behavior—time, place, frequency, the child's feelings, and parental feelings and response—will facilitate development with the family of an appropriate treatment strategy. It is helpful to obtain a baseline recording of the child's enuretic behavior for several weeks against which the effects of therapeutic intervention can be compared. Reviewing the family history of enuresis, if it is positive, can provide useful information regarding parental and sibling attitudes and prior experience with evaluation and treatment.

Treatment

Only a third of enuretic children have seen a physician about the condition (Foxman et al. 1986; Miller 1973), and only 60 percent of those seen have received treatment (Foxman et al. 1986). On the one hand this is surprising, since the majority of children and parents report that they are distressed by the wetting (Foxman et al. 1986); on the other hand, it is not unexpected given the self-limiting nature of enuresis (the annual spontaneous cure rate is about 15 percent; Forsythe and Redmond 1974).

Education and support, behavioral-conditioning therapy, psychotherapy, and pharmacotherapy are all accepted treatments for functional enuresis (Schmitt 1982). Although some urologists continue to advocate surgical interventions such as urethral dilation, meatotomy, or procedures to enlarge the bladder, no controlled studies documenting their efficacy are available, and many child psychiatrists would consider such procedures not without harm.

Education and support.　Education and reassurance about the high prevalence rate of functional enuresis, the absence of identifiable physical causes, the high spontaneous cure rate, and the availability of effective treatments can reduce the child's (and parents') anxiety and guilt. The combination of reassurance and practical suggestions—positive reinforcement for dry nights, avoidance of negative comments or punishment, avoiding excessive fluid intake and caffeine-containing drinks before bedtime, and toileting before going to bed—may be sufficient to reduce or ameliorate the wetting. It is helpful to inform parents of interventions that have not been shown to be effective—fluid restriction, waking the child to void, elimination of certain foods from the diet, and urine retention training (see below).

Behavioral-conditioning therapy.　Successful behavioral treatment of functional enuresis requires that the child take responsibility for the symptom. The simplest behavioral intervention that facilitates involvement of the child in his own treatment is the keeping of a calendar in which the child credits himself for each dry night. All members of the family may be encouraged to praise the child each morning after a dry night. Intrafamilial conflict can be reduced if a plan is agreed upon regarding responsibility for stripping the wet bed and washing soiled sheets. Most children who awaken wet during the night can change to dry pajamas, cover the wet area with a dry towel, and return to bed without awakening their parents.

Retention control training—instructing the child to delay micturition by increments of two to three minutes per day for several weeks, sometimes in conjunction with rewards—has been advocated by many clinicians. However, a well-designed study by Fielding (1980) showed that the bell and pad technique (see below) was superior to retention control training followed by the bell and pad. Because retention control training is time consuming (working parents may not be available during the day) and can lead to further frustration and failure for the child and parents, it appears to have no place in the treatment of functional enuresis.

By far the most effective treatment for nocturnal enuresis involves use of an alarm to awaken the child when wetting is initiated (Schmitt 1982). Surprisingly, results of a recent epidemiological study indicate that only 3 percent of American children who receive treatment for their enuresis from a physician are prescribed the bed alarm (Foxman et al. 1986). Perhaps this low prescription rate is due to problems with the older model alarm system, the bell and pad, which is relatively expensive, rather complicated to set up, and requires passage of 10 ml or more of urine to be triggered. Two newer enuresis alarms are inexpensive (about $40), simple to set up, and are triggered by only a few drops of urine. When urine completes a circuit between two small electrodes attached to the front of the underwear, a buzzer sounds awakening the child. These devices are thought to work by causing the child to contract his external bladder sphincter upon sudden awakening. After repeated buzzer-induced awakenings, the child presumably develops increased sensitivity to nocturnal bladder contractions and either learns to inhibit the micturition reflex until arising the next morning or develops a habit of awakening at night to urinate into the toilet. Generally, several weeks of treatment are required before dry nights occur. Continued use of the alarm during three weeks of consecutive dry nights reduces the likelihood of relapse. Approximately 70 percent of children treated with the newer alarms attain long-term cure (Schmitt 1982). The chances of cure can be increased by selecting children who express an interest in trying the alarm and who can understand the basic idea underlying this technique.

Psychotherapy. Most children with functional enuresis will respond to the treatment strategies described above. For the child with associated behavioral or emotional problems or the child whose self-esteem has been affected by his wetting or the family's or peers' responses to it, or both (probably the majority of enuretic children referred to child psychiatrists), psychodynamically oriented psychotherapy may be indicated. In general, the conflicts and concerns that emerge during the therapy may have more to do with associated symptoms than the enuresis itself. In order for the therapist to maintain a nondirective stance, it may be useful to have the child's pediatrician manage some or all of the behavioral treatment targeted at the enuresis.

If the family is unable to comply with a behavioral treatment plan or if intrafamilial conflict is interfering with effective treatment of the child's symptoms, family therapy may be indicated.

Pharmacotherapy. When other treatments have failed and the child continues to be distressed by his symptoms, a trial of medication is indicated.

Imipramine is the only medication that has been shown effective in the treatment of functional enuresis in repeated double-blind studies (Rapoport et al. 1980). The mechanism by which imipramine reduces wetting is unknown. Titrating the proper dosage to maximize effect and minimize side effects must be done with each patient. The usual starting dose is 25 mg at bedtime. Dosage may be increased by 25 mg every two to three days until the wetting is reduced or side effects emerge. Rapoport et al. (1980) found a low but significant correlation between clinical effect and plasma concentration of drug. However, there was no threshold blood level that corresponded with clinical effect. Plasma blood levels may be useful in evaluating the child who is not responding on relatively high doses of medication or who is experiencing side effects on low doses.

Most enuretic children are partial responders to imipramine; few become completely dry (Rapoport et al. 1980). The response to imipramine usually occurs within one week. Tolerance to the antienuretic effect of imipramine develops in some children. Commonly, relapse occurs when medication is withdrawn.

The most common side effect of imipramine is dry mouth. Other side effects include abdominal cramps, increased or decreased appetite, weight gain, dizziness, and drowsiness. Dosage reduction often ameliorates these side effects. Cardiovascular side effects can be minimized by monitoring the child's EKG.

Although imipramine has been studied more intensively, its metabolite desipramine appears to be equally effective (Rapoport et al. 1980). If a child fails to respond to imipramine or desipramine, a trial of a second medication is indicated. Oxybutynin, an antispasmodic agent that reduces uninhibited detrusor muscle contractions, is effective in many patients who are nonresponsive to imipramine (Thompson and Lauvetz 1976). Initial studies suggest that the vasopeptide DDAVP (desamino-D-arginine vasopressin) also has antienuretic effects (Aladjem et al. 1982).

Functional Encopresis

History and Definition

Uncontrolled fecal soiling was first described as a condition in the 1880s by clinicians who recognized the importance of psychological stress in the pathogenesis of this disturbing childhood disorder (Fowler 1882). The term "encopresis" was proposed in the 1920s as a parallel to enuresis (Pototsky 1925). During the 1950s, Richmond et al. (1954), in a classic study differentiating encopresis from aganglionic megacolon (Hirschsprung's disease), proposed the term "psychogenic megacolon" because in many children with encopresis the bowel or colon is functionally dilated.

DSM-III-R diagnostic criteria for functional encopresis are: 1) repeated passage of feces into places not appropriate for that purpose (e.g., clothing, floor), whether voluntary or involuntary (the disorder may be overflow incontinence secondary to functional fecal retention); 2) at least one such event a month for at least six months; 3) chronological and mental age at least four years; and 4) not due to a physical disorder, such as aganglionic megacolon (American Psychiatric Association 1987).

Encopresis can be classified as primary or secondary. In primary encopresis the child never has completed bowel training; in secondary encopresis bowel training was completed and the child subsequently became incontinent. Retentive encopresis refers to the child who leaks fecal material around an impaction; nonretentive encopresis refers to the child who simply passes formed bowel movements. The frequency and severity of encopretic episodes may wax and wane over time. In addition, the same child may manifest either retentive or nonretentive encopresis at different times.

Epidemiology

Reported estimates of prevalence of functional encopresis range from 1.5 percent of 7-year-olds (Bellman 1966) to about 1.0 percent of 10- to 12-year-olds (Rutter et al. 1970, reprinted 1981). The prevalence of encopresis declines with age. Boys are more commonly affected than girls by a ratio of 4–6:1. There does not appear to be a relationship between social class and prevalence of encopresis. Multiple studies have shown a high association between enuresis and encopresis.

Etiology

Commonly, the cause of functional encopresis is difficult to determine in an individual child. Clinical experience suggests that fecal soiling develops following the interplay of multiple physical, social, and psychological factors (Levine 1982).

Genetic factors.   There is no clear evidence implicating a genetic etiology of encopresis. Although Bellman (1966) found a history of encopresis in 15 percent of biological fathers of encopretic children, this familial transmission could have social as well as genetic origins.

Physical factors.   Accumulating evidence from studies by pediatric gastroenterologists suggests that anorectal physiological dysfunction plays a role in the pathogenesis of functional encopresis in some children. Proposed scientific abnormalities include increased thresholds of conscious sensation of rectal distension (Loening-Baucke 1984; Meunier et al. 1979, 1984; Molnar et al. 1983); weakness of the internal anal sphincter (Loening-Bauke 1984; Loening-Baucke and Younoszai 1984); and active contractions of the anal sphincters during defecation attempts (Holschneider 1983; Loening-Baucke and Cruikshank 1986; Robinson and Gibbons 1976; Wald et al. 1986). However, not all studies agree. For example, in a study of carefully selected children with functional encopresis, Wald et al. (1986) failed to find abnormalities of sensation threshold or internal anal sphincter strength. Unfortunately, it is not possible to determine whether the physical abnormalities described above caused the chronic constipation and soiling or resulted from it.

Social factors.   Since Huschka (1942) introduced the concept of coercive training almost half a century ago, inadequate or inappropriate toilet training has been identified as a cause of encopresis (Anthony 1957; Bellman 1966; Prugh 1954). Various problems during toilet training—excessive coercion, premature or inadequate involvement by the mother, or excessive demands for perfection—play a role in the development of subsequent toileting problems in selected children. However, not all children who are inappropriately trained develop encopresis, and many children with bowel dysfunction did not experience abnormal training.

The onset of secondary encopresis has been associated with a stressful event— the start of or difficulty at school, separation from mother, or birth of a sibling—in over 50 percent of secondary encopretics (Bellman 1966).

Psychological factors. Two recent studies using parental reports and self-reports have provided preliminary behavioral and psychological data about children with encopresis. In a study of children with encopresis evaluated in pediatric clinics or private practice, numerous behavioral problems were reported by parents (Gabel et al. 1986). The overall severity of the problems, however, was less than that found in children referred for mental health services. No specific psychological profile or symptomatic pattern could be identified.

In another study of locus of control and self-esteem in children with encopresis referred to a pediatric specialty clinic, these children "tended to feel less in control of positive life events, had lower self-worth, and were more apt to want to change and be different than children with other chronic symptoms" (Landman et al. 1986).

For many children with encopresis, the emotional and behavioral problems they experience—social isolation, anxiety, depression—are secondary to the chronic soiling. For a few, psychogenic factors may play an important etiological role, but no specific psychogenic profile has been identified.

Assessment

Prior to referral to a child psychiatrist, most children with encopresis will have received a comprehensive physical examination and pediatric evaluation to rule out organic etiologies such as aganglionic megacolon, hypothyroidism, hypercalcemia, and medical or neurological disorders of the lower gastrointestinal tract.

The encopretic child may be reluctant to tell his story. Reassurance that soiling is a common problem for which there are effective treatments may facilitate the history taking. Only the child may know the circumstances surrounding the soiling behavior—time of day, frequency, place, and so forth—since embarrassment and shame about the symptom may have led to secretive behavior. It is important to obtain a baseline recording of the child's current encopretic behavior against which the effects of therapeutic intervention can be compared.

Evaluation of possible psychosocial mechanisms responsible for the development and maintenance of the encopresis necessitates a careful review of toilet training, the onset of the first bowel-related symptoms, and the reactions of family members and peers to the symptoms. The child or parents can sometimes identify conditions in the environment that are promoting or aggravating the symptom. The child and family may have acquired secondary adaptive strategies—most commonly social isolation—to cope with the social consequences of fecal odor or visible staining. Both the child and parents will have ideas about the underlying cause of the soiling that may not have been previously expressed.

Management

Perhaps two-thirds of children with encopresis improve dramatically following treatment approaches that combine education, supportive therapy, and positive reinforcement (Berg and Jones 1964; Berg et al. 1983; Hein and Beerends 1978; Levine and Bakow 1976; Taitz et al. 1986). Generally, three months or more of active treatment are necessary.

Although some pediatricians recommend initial, vigorous bowel clean-out using repeated enemas and laxatives followed by maintenance with daily mineral oil treatments (Levine 1982; Levine and Bakow 1976), a recent placebo-controlled trial employing a senna laxative (Senokot) resulted in equal response rates in the group receiving active medication and the group receiving placebo (Berg et al. 1983). All subjects in this study received education, supportive therapy, and positive reinforcement in addition to the medication.

Factors associated with treatment failure include social disadvantage and emotional problems within the family (Taitz et al. 1986) and external locus of control (Rappaport et al. 1986).

Child psychiatrists are most likely to see those children who have not responded to straightforward educational and behavioral treatment approaches. These children are most likely to have individual or familial emotional or behavioral difficulties that require a more intensive psychotherapeutic approach. As with the enuretic child, the concerns and conflicts that emerge during therapy may have more to do with associated symptoms than with the encopresis itself. Treatment of the associated conflicts often leads to an improvement in the encopretic symptoms. In order for the therapist to maintain a nondirective stance, it may be useful to have the child's pediatrician manage the behavioral treatment targeted at the encopresis.

If the family is unable to comply with a behavioral treatment plan or if intrafamilial conflict is interfering with effective treatment of the child's symptoms, family therapy may be indicated.

References

Section 9
Elimination Disorders

Achenbach T, Lewis M: A proposed model for clinical research and its application to encopresis and enuresis. J Am Acad Child Psychiatry 10:535–554, 1971

Aladjem M, Wohl R, Boichis H, et al: Desmopressin in nocturnal enuresis. Arch Dis Child 57:137–140, 1982

American Psychiatric Association: Diagnostic and Statistical Manual of Mental Disorders, 3rd ed, revised. Washington, DC, American Psychiatric Association, 1987

Anders TF, Freeman ED: Enuresis, in Basic Handbook of Child Psychiatry, vol II. Edited by Noshpitz JD. New York, Basic Books, 1979, pp 546–555

Angel A: From the analysis of a bedwetter. Psychoanal Q 4:120–134, 1935

Anthony EJ: An experimental approach to the psychopathology of childhood: encopresis. Br J Med Psychol 30:146–175, 1957

Bakwin H: Enuresis in children. J Pediatr 58:806–819, 1961

Bakwin H: The genetics of bedwetting, in Bladder Control and Enuresis. Edited by Kolvin I, MacKeith R, Meadows RS. Clinics in Developmental Medicine, no. 48/49. London, Heinemann/Spastics International Medical Publications, 1973, pp 73–77

Bellman M: Studies on encopresis. Acta Paediatr Scand [Suppl] 170:1–151, 1966

Berg I, Jones KV: Functional fecal incontinence in children. Arch Dis Child 39:465–472, 1964

Berg I, Forsythe I, Holt P, et al: A controlled trial of 'Senokot' in faecal soiling treated by behavioral methods. J Child Psychol Psychiatry 23:543–549, 1983

Broughton RF: Sleep disorders: disorders of arousal? Science 159:1070–1078, 1968

Cho, SC: Clinical study on childhood enuresis. Seoul Journal of Medicine 25:599–608, 1984

Couchells S, Johnson S, Carter R, et al: Behavioral and environmental characteristics of treated and untreated enuretic children and watched non-enuretic controls. J Pediatr 9:812–816, 1981

Douglas JWB: Early disturbing events and later enuresis, in Bladder Control and Enuresis. Edited by Kolvin I, MacKeith RC, Meadows SR. Clinics in Developmental Medicine, no. 48/49. London, Heinemann/Spastics International Medical Publications, 1973, pp 48–49

Eeg-Oloffson O: The development of the EEG from the age of 1 through 15 years— positive spike phenomena 14 and GHz. Neuropaediatrie 2:405–427, 1971

Eeg-Oloffson O, Petersen S, Sellden V: The development of the EEG in normal children from the age of 1 through 15 years. Neuropaediatrie 2:375–404, 1971

Essen J, Peckham C: Nocturnal enuresis in children. Dev Med Child Neurol 18:577–589, 1976

Fielding D: The response of day and night wetting children and children who wet only at night to retention-control training and the enuresis alarm. Behav Res Ther 18:305–317, 1980

Forsythe WI, Redmond A: Enuresis and spontaneous cure rate: a study of 1129 enuretics. Arch Dis Child 49:259–263, 1974

Fowler GB: Incontinence of faeces in children. American Journal of Obstetric Diseases in Women and Children 15:984, 1882

Foxman B, Valdez RB, Brook RH: Childhood enuresis: prevalence, perceived impact and prescribed treatments. Pediatrics 77:482–487, 1986

Frary LG: Enuresis: a genetic study. Am J Dis Child 49:557, 1935

Fritz GK, Anders TF: Enuresis: the clinical application of an etiologically-based classification system. Child Psychiatry Hum Dev 10:103–113, 1979

Gabel S, Hegedus AM, Wald A, et al: Prevalence of behavioral problems and mental health utilization among encopretic children: implications for behavioral pediatrics. Dev Behav Pediatr 7:293–297, 1986

Glicklich LB: A historical account of enuresis. Pediatrics 8:859–876, 1951

Gross RT, Dornbusch SM: Enuresis, in Developmental-Behavioral Pediatrics. Edited by Levine M, Cary W, Crocker AC, et al. Philadelphia, W.B. Saunders, 1983, pp 573–586

Hallgren B: Enuresis: a study with reference to certain physical, mental and social factors possibly associated with enuresis. Acta Psychiatr Neurol Scand 31:405–436, 1956

Hallgren B: Enuresis: a clinical and genetic study. Acta Psychiatr Neurol Scand 32 (suppl 114):1, 1957

Hallgren B: Nocturnal enuresis in twins. Acta Psychiatr Neurol Scand 35:73–90, 1960

Hein HA, Beerends JJ: Who should accept primary responsibility on the encopretic child? Clin Pediatr (Phila) 17:67–70, 1978

Holschneider A: Elektromanometrie des Enddarmes: Diagnostik und Therapie der Inkontinenz und der chronischen, in Obstipation, 2nd ed. Munich, Urban and Schwarzenberg, 1983, pp 110, 126

Huschka M: The child's response to coercive bowel training. Psychosom Med 4:301–308, 1942

Kaffman M, Elizur E: Infants who become enuretics: a longitudinal study of 161 kibbutz children. Monogr Soc Res Child Dev 42:170, 1977

Landman GB, Rappaport L, Fenton T, et al: Locus of control and self-esteem in children with encopresis. Dev Behav Pediatr 7:111–113, 1986

Levine MD: Encopresis: its potentiation, evaluation, and alleviation. Pediatr Clin North Am 29:315–330, 1982

Levine MD, Bakow H: Children with encopresis: a study of treatment outcome. Pediatrics 58:845–852, 1976

Libson E, Bloom RA, Dinari G: Evaluation of the excretory urogram in adult enuresis. Clin Radiol 37:287–288, 1986

Loening-Baucke VA: Sensitivity of the sigmoid colon and rectum in children treated for chronic constipation. J Pediatr Gastroenterol Nutr 3:454, 1984

Loening-Baucke VA, Cruikshank BM: Abnormal defecation dynamics in chronically constipated children with encopresis. J Pediatr 108:562–556, 1986

Loening-Baucke VA, Younozai MK: Abnormal anal sphincter response in chronically constipated children. J Pediatr 100:213–218, 1982

Lovibond SH: Conditioning and Enuresis. Oxford, Pergamon, 1964

Mahoney DT: Studies on enuresis, I: incidence of obstructive lesions and pathophysiology of enuresis. J Urol 106:951–958, 1971

McHale A: An investigation of personality attributes of stammering, enuretic and school-phobic children. Br J Educ Psychol 37:400–403, 1967

Meunier P, Merechal JM, Jaubert de Beaujeu M: Rectoanal pressures and rectal sensitivity studies in chronic childhood constipation. Gastroenterology 77:330, 1979

Meunier P, Louis D, Jaubert de Beaujeu M: Physiologic investigation of primary chronic constipation in children: comparison with the barium enema study. Gastroenterology 87:1351, 1984

Michaels JJ: Enuresis in murderous aggressive children and adolescents. Arch Gen Psychiatry 5:490–493, 1961

Mikkelsen EJ, Rapoport JL, Nee L: Childhood enuresis, I: sleep patterns and psychopathology. Arch Gen Psychiatry 37:1139–1144, 1980

Miller PM: An experimental analysis in retention-control training in the treatment of nocturnal enuresis in two institutionalized adolescents. Behavior Therapy 4:288–294, 1973

Molnar D, Taitz TS, Urwin OM: Anorectal manometry results in defecation disorders. Arch Dis Child 58:257–261, 1983

National Center for Health Statistics: Plan, Operation and Response Results of a Program of Children's Examinations. Public Health Service publication 1000, series 1, no. 5. Washington, DC, US Department of Helath, Education, and Welfare, 1967

National Center for Health Statistics: Plan and Operation of a Health Examination Survey of U.S. Youths 12–17 Years of Age. Public Health Service publication 1000, series 1, no. 8. Washington, DC, US Department of Health, Education, and Welfare, 1969

Norgaard JP, Hansen JH, Bugge Nielsen J, et al: Simultaneous registration of sleep-stages and bladder activity in enuresis. Urology 26:316–319, 1985

Oppel WC, Harper PA, Rider RV: Social, psychological and neurological factors associated with nocturnal enuresis. Pediatrics 42:627–641, 1968

Petersen RA, Eeg-Oloffson O: The development of the EEG in normal children from the age of 1 through 15 years: non-paroxysmal activity. Neuropaediatrie 2:247–304, 1970

Pompeius R: Cystometry in pediatric enuresis. Scand J Urol Nephrol 5:222–228, 1971

Pototsky C: Die enkopresis, in Psychogenese und Psychotherapie Korperlicher Symptome. Edited by Schwartz O. Berlin, Springer, 1925

Poussaint AF, Koegler RR, Riehl JL: Enuresis, epilepsy and the EEG. Am J Psychiatry 123:1294–1295, 1967

Prugh DG: Childhood experience and colonic disorder. Ann NY Acad Sci 58:355–376, 1954

Rapoport JL, Mikkelsen EJ, Zavardil A: Childhood enuresis II. Psychopathology, tricyclic concentration in plasma, and antienuretic effect. Arch Gen Psychiatry 37:1146–1152, 1980

Rappaport L, Landman G, Fenton T, et al: Locus of control as predictor of compliance and outcome in treatment of encopresis. Behav Pediatr 109:1061–1064, 1986

Richmond JB, Eddy JE, Garrard SD: The syndrome of fecal soiling and megacolon. Am J Orthopsychiatry 24:391–401, 1954

Robinson BA, Gibbons ISE: Paradoxical external anal sphincter function in fecal retention with soiling, and its control by operant conditioning. Gastroenterology 70:930A, 1976

Rutter ML, Yule W, Graham PJ: Enuresis and behavioral deviance: some epidemiological considerations, in Bladder Control and Enuresis. Edited by Kolvin I, MacKeith R, Meadows SR. Clinics in Developmental Medicine, no. 48/49, London, Heinemann/Spastics International Medical Publications, 1973, pp 139–147

Rutter M, Tizard J, Whitmore K (eds): Education, Health and Behavior. London, Longman, 1970

Schmitt B: Nocturnal enuresis: an update on treatment. Pediatr Clin North Am 29:21–36, 1982

Shaffer D: Enuresis, in Child and Adolescent Psychiatry: Modern Approaches. Edited by Rutter M, Hersov L. Oxford, Blackwell Scientific Publications, 1985, pp 465–481

Shaffer D, Gardner A, Hedge B: Behavior and bladder disturbance in enuretic children: the rational classification of a common disorder. Dev Med Child Neurol 26:781–795, 1984

Starfield B: Functional bladder capacity in enuretic and nonenuretic children. J Pediatr 70:777–781, 1967

Stein ZA, Susser MW: Sociomedical study of enuresis among delinquent boys. Br J Prev Soc Med 19:174–181, 1965

Stockwell L, Smith CK: Enuresis: a study of causes, types and therapeutic results. Am J Dis Child 59:1013, 1940

Taitz LS, Wales JKH, Urwin OM, et al: Factors associated with outcome in management of defecation disorders. Arch Dis Child 61:472–477, 1986

Thompson IM, Lauvetz RQ: Oxybutynin in bladder spasm, neurogenic bladder and enuresis. Urology 8:452–454, 1976

Troup CW, Hodgson NB: Nocturnal functional capacity in enuretic children. Pediatric Urology 105:129–132, 1971

Wald A, Chandra R, Chiponis D, et al: Anorectal function and continence mechanisms in childhood encopresis. J Pediatr Gastroenterol Nutr 5:346–351, 1986

Other Disorders of Infancy, Childhood, or Adolescence

Chapter 85

Introduction

When in perusing a nosologic scheme, one comes on a category that starts with "Other," one can assume that the category is for those titles or syndromes that don't quite fit anywhere else in the scheme of things. That is the case here. Other sections are composed of syndromes that have much in common. These disorders have few common threads. One is restricted to babies and another is restricted to adolescents. A third has to do with language and motoric functions. Two of them are much concerned with behavioral manifestations and border on characterologic problems. Indeed, in DSM-III-R (American Psychiatric Association 1987), there remain five disorders in the "other" category, but only three of them are included in this section. One (schizoid disorder) has been dropped. One (oppositional disorder) has been moved out to a new family and given a new middle name. Two (stereotypy/habit disorder and undifferentiated attention-deficit disorder) have been moved in with slightly changed names and descriptions. They remain the other disorders of childhood with a relationship similar to foster-siblings in a group home (from a developmental point of view).

The reader will find that the chapters do not all carry equal emphasis on a particular mode of therapy. In one there may be a detailed description of the process of dynamic psychotherapy and in another will be found details of the course of behavior therapy.

There is an extensive review of the literature on reactive attachment disorder of infancy (chapter 86) because so much has been written about this disorder and over so long a period of time, beginning with Spitz's pioneering studies 40 years ago. A discussion of the relationship between early maternal-infant bonding and this disorder helps clarify the issues. Much of the review deals with etiology, an understanding of which is so essential in planning treatment for this disorder.

The reader will also find that one chapter argues against using the diagnosis of personality disorder in work with children, while another is in favor of such use. This is the state of the art. The first argument points out the difficulties in diagnosis because of the fine distinction between schizoid disorder and avoidant disorder and follows with a discussion of the differential diagnosis of this syndrome (chapter 87). This chapter also picks up some of the debates preceding the revision of DSM-III (American Psychiatric Association 1980), focusing on the continuing need for a category of schizoid disorder.

The second argument makes an interesting expostulation for a new look at some of the personality disorders (passive-aggressive, narcissistic, and dependent) included on Axis II of DSM-III and DSM-III-R, generally not to be used in diagnosing children or young adolescents (chapter 89). It would have a new category of immature personality disorders of children and adolescents, which would include four subtypes. Whether the reader agrees with this notion of applying personality disorders to younger children or prefers to consider these subtypes of oppositional disorder, the concept is worth thinking about and the distinctions are useful in treatment planning.

Chapter 88 takes issue with the idea that elective mutism has a benign course. That impression is probably derived from studying young children who are showing a developmentally normal reluctance to talk in new situations, rather than true elective mutism. Children with this syndrome are more often treated with behavioral techniques than any of the other groups (except perhaps oppositional disorder). Behavioral approaches, therefore, receive more elaboration in this chapter than in others. The chapter does not, however, ignore the importance of psychodynamics in the etiology and treatment of this affliction.

In understanding and planning treatment of identity disorder (chapter 90), developmental considerations are of paramount importance; this syndrome reflects a derailment of normal developmental processes. (So do the other syndromes but probably less so.) Identity disorder was recognized only in 1980 with the publication of DSM-III, making it a fairly recent diagnostic category.

Chapter 86

Reactive Attachment Disorder of Infancy

The pioneering work of Spitz (1946, 1947a, 1947b) on hospitalism and anaclitic depression drew attention to the serious consequences for the infant if the caretaking environment interfered with the normal attachment behavior of infancy. Although his observations were in an institution, it was soon recognized that infants reared at home could also show the signs of disorders of attachment.

Bowlby (1973a, 1973b, 1980, 1982) for over 40 years continued to study attachment and its disorders. He reported that the early signs of disturbances in attachment were anxiety and anger, and later signs, when loss occurred, were sadness and depression. First the infant protested; then, if there was no intervention, the signs of despair occurred and eventually detachment. If intervention does not occur, the infant has frequent illnesses, continues to lose weight, and may eventually die. Or, if the infant receives adequate nutrition, stimulation, and affectionate care, the process is halted and reversed. With Bowlby, some view attachment as a special class of behavior with its own dynamics distinct from feeding or sex. The biologic function attributed to it is that of protection. It has been stated that it is probably the best supported theory of social-emotional development yet available. There is a difference of opinion whether the enduring attachment bond is confined to a few. There are also varying opinions as to whether disorders of attachment make the individual more vulnerable to later stressful experiences and whether they are more likely to meet with further difficulties in the future. It is possible that because of impairment in the capacity to relate, if the disorder of attachment is prolonged, when these infants grow and become parents many years later, they will have difficulties caring for their infants. However, there are no studies that confirm or fail to confirm this hypothesis.

Helfer and Kempe (1976), in their pioneering work with parents who abused or neglected their children, did not specifically express an opinion as to whether the parents sustained attachment disorders or had been subjected to deprivation. However, they were of the opinion that the parents were subjected to a variety of abnormal emotional or physical experiences by their parents. As adults, they felt isolated, alienated, deprived, and had low self-esteem.

Rutter (1972, 1979, 1981) critically reviewed the literature on maternal deprivation several times. He stated that it is thought to be the cause of mental subnormality, delinquency, depression, dwarfism, acute distress, and affectionless psychopathy. It is his opinion that the experiences covered by maternal deprivation are diverse and complex and that distortion or lack of adequate caretaking experience is more frequent than loss. Rutter classified the reported studies into five groups:

1. Children in hospitals and their immediate reactions to acute distress.
2. Developmental retardation in poor quality institutions, which results in intellectual impairment with long-term institutionalism.
3. The association between delinquency and broken homes.
4. Affectionless psychopathy in association with multiple separations and institutional care.
5. Psychosocial dwarfism in rejecting and affectionless homes.

The issue of parent-infant bonding is relevant to the question of reactive attachment disorder of infancy. Klaus and Kennell (1982) pioneered in the study of parent-infant bonding and wrote that there is a two- to fourfold increase in incidents of nonorganic failure to thrive and child abuse among infants who, because of prematurity or early neonatal illness, were separated from mothers. The studies of Klein and Stern (1971) and Fanaroff (1970) are representative of a number of studies in the 1970s that concluded that a high proportion of children who were abused or failed to thrive were premature, born by cesarean section, or hospitalized for other reasons in the first weeks of life. Their attachments were distorted, diminished, or blunted.

Chess and Thomas (1982), Herbert and Sluckin (1982), and Rutter (1972, 1979, 1981) published extensive critical reviews, taking issue with the position that there is a sensitive period in the first few minutes and hours after an infant's birth that is optimal for the parent-infant attachment. They ask if infants are doomed to less than optimal development if mothers are unavoidably unable to have immediate skin-to-skin contact with their newborns, either because of illness in the baby or mother or because of inflexible hospital routines. Rutter (1981) concluded:

> The . . . proposition is that the first or main attachment differs in time from all other subsequent ones. Most research findings suggest that this is not the case. The balance of evidence suggests that separation of mother and child in the neonatal period may have

effects on maternal behavior which lasts a few months but that it is unusual for effects to persist for longer than that.

Egeland and Vaughn (1981) compared 32 infants identified as not receiving adequate maternal care in the first year of life with a matched group of 33 infants receiving good maternal care. They found no significant differences between the two groups in the perinatal factors making for mother-child separation after birth: prematurity, delivery complications, and medical problems requiring separation from the mother. Svejda et al. (1980) compared 15 mothers having extended immediate postnatal contact with their infants with 15 mothers following the usual postnatal routine and found, using 28 meaures, no differences in maternal behavior between the two groups. They suggested that other studies with different findings did not control sufficiently for other variables. Minde et al. (1980) observed the interactions of 32 mothers and their infants with very low birth weight during visits to the premature nursery and during the infants' first three months at home. They found no association between the type of contact the mother had with her baby initially and her later activity pattern. Egeland and Vaughn believe that when parent-child bonds break down, as in cases of abuse and neglect, researchers should look for multiple causes rather than pinpointing some very early event as the predisposing single trauma.

DeChateau (1980), Jones et al. (1980), and Robson and Kuman (1980) are representative of investigators who concluded that a mother's attachment to her infant has to do with a variety of factors other than short-duration postpartum contact. Among these factors are that mothers over 19 years of age demonstrated greater responsiveness toward their infants. Mothers were less responsive to their infants if they had a forewater amniotomy and also had a particularly painful and unpleasant labor or had been given analgesics. Robson and Kuman found that three months after giving birth "a mother was more likely to express feelings of dislike or indifference towards her baby if she was clinically depressed at the time." In an extensive review of the literature, Herbert and Sluckin (1982) remarked that practitioners overlook the fact that measures of mother-infant interaction described in the literature referred to mother-infant relationship and not specifically to either mother or infant behavior. They conclude the usage of the term *bonding* is often misleading because of a tendency to reify and simplify attachment phenomena. It is apparent that the issue of a sensitive or critical period in humans and its relevance for bonding has not been resolved.

Kotelchuck and Newberger (1984) conducted a controlled study of family characteristics with infants who failed to thrive. They found that three factors distinguished these families from the controls: "They had a more sickly child, were more isolated from neighbors and family support, and had a larger discrepancy in parents' education." The demographic factors, pregnancy, poverty, and contemporaneous stress were not significant. However, the investigators stated that their study was limited in its ability to assert that maternal psychopathology in interactional behavior is or is not the cause of failure to thrive. In contrast to Kotelchuck and Newberger's study, a number of other investigations reported significant positive findings in the home environment, mother-infant interaction, psychosocial environment, and mother's personality (e.g., Casey et al. 1984; Evans et al. 1972; Fischhoff et al. 1971; Pollitt et al. 1975; Whitten et al. 1969). The results of these studies are summarized below. Whitten et al. observed the feeding practices of mothers whose infants failed to thrive. Mothers were observed feeding their children in the hospital and in the home. Initially there was no intervention, and the infants did not gain weight. When they were fed by others over a period of time, infants gained weight. They concluded that the growth failure from deprivation was secondary to undereating and not due to depression in the infants. Casey et al. (1984) found that the mothers of failure-to-thrive infants were generally less responsive, provided less vocal stimulation to the infants, and were less accepting of their infants. The homes of the children were more disorganized. They emphasized that assessing parent-infant interaction is essential and assessing parent and infant separately may miss the cause of the failure to thrive. Relying on nonspecific sociodemographic data (e.g., education level or family income) is not helpful.

Assessment of the mother's childhood often revealed that she had a psychiatrically ill, alcoholic, or addicted parent; that there was separation or divorce; or that she was raised by others in foster care. Mothers were often dissatisfied with the maternal role. During pregnancy they were emotionally disturbed, with symptomatic behavior such as suicide gestures, drinking, and acting out, at times accompanied by the use of drugs. The mothers appeared less involved in caring for objects, including property or pets. They responded less frequently to their children's approaches. They often felt upset in relating to and caring for their infant. There was less expression of maternal affection in verbal and nonverbal ways.

Evans et al. (1972) constructed profiles of three groups of mothers. A mother in the first group gave good physical care to the child but her affect was one of extreme depression. The mother-child interaction was strained and unsure, and the mother perceived the child as ill or retarded. She usually had a severe object loss or severe emotional stress within four months of the child's hospitalization. With this group of infants, the prognosis was good if the mother received psychotherapy. The second group of mothers were in very deprived living conditions. The physical care of the infant was poor. The mothers' affect was that of depression. Again, the mother-child interaction was strained or unsure. Mothers frequently perceived the infant or child as retarded. In their pasts, they had many losses. The prognosis for this group of infants was guarded unless there was a dramatic change in the home environment. Frequently the mother did not respond to treatment, and the infant was placed in foster care. In the third group, the living conditions were good but the mother was neglectful of the child. The mother-child relationship was an angry, hostile one, and interaction was overtly angry. The mother perceived the child as "bad." She also had chronic losses. In this group, the prognosis was poor unless the child was placed in a foster home.

Fischhoff et al. (1971) conducted a psychiatric study of mothers whose infants experienced deprivation and reactive attachment disorder. The majority of mothers were found to exhibit inappropriate affect, evidence of depression, few fantasies of hope for themselves, a predisposition to acting out, behavior of initial contact indicative of psychopathology, an abnormal past history, concrete thinking patterns, poor self-image, poor performance in day-to-day activities, poor object relationships, and significant use of isolation and denial as defense mechanisms. Roberts (1984) confirmed a number of these characteristics on the Minnesota Multiphasic Personality Inventory with an experimental and control group of mothers.

Etiology

For the sake of brevity, the term *mother* is used for mother, other primary caretakers including father, grandmother, other relatives, foster parents, and any other individual who is the infant's significant caretaker. In the majority of cases of reactive attachment disorder, the primary caretaker is the natural or birth mother.

Winnicott (1958), writing from a psychoanalytic view, believed that a healthy mother goes through a period of

> Primary Maternal Preoccupation. . . . It gradually develops and becomes a state of heightened sensitivity during, and especially towards the end of pregnancy. The memory mothers have of this state tends to become repressed. Only if a mother is sensitive in the way I am describing, can she feel herself in her infant's place, and so meet the infant's demands.

In another context, Winnicott (1957) wrote:

> I think that an important thing about a young mother's experience of early contact with her baby is the reassurance that it gives her that the baby is normal . . . because she has had all sorts of ideas of giving birth to something awful, something certainly not so perfect as a baby. It is as if human beings find it very difficult to believe that they are good enough to create within themselves something that is quite good. I doubt whether any mother really and fully believes in her child at the beginning.

Since the time Winnicott (1957, 1958) theorized about the intrapsychic changes a healthy woman undergoes during pregnancy, many studies have focused on the forces that contribute to the development of the syndrome of attachment disorder. The etiologic factors in reactive attachment disorder in infancy are multiple and include the mother's early life experiences and the unconscious determinants of her present behavior, her present status (including emotional, physical, and environmental factors), her perception of the infant and the infant's physical status, and the mother-infant interaction.

Barbero (1982) described these and other factors as follows:

1. Past events: Early parental life deprivations, loss of parent figures early in the life of the parent, illness during parent's childhood, death or illness in prior children.
2. Pregnancy events: Protracted emotional or physical illness, deaths or major illness of key family figures.
3. Perinatal events: Complication of parturition, acute illness in mother or infant, prematurity, congenital defects, diseases, iatrogenic or institutional disruptions.
4. Current life events: Marital strains, mental illness, medical illness, alcoholism, drugs, financial crisis.

Barbero's multifactorial etiology is representative of the pediatric literature, but psychiatric studies and my own findings indicate that the mother's psychiatric condition is the primary cause of reactive attachment disorder in infancy in the majority of cases. In fact, Starr et al. (1982, 1984) did not find that children contributed to their own abuse, nor did children with handicapping conditions have an increased frequency of abuse or neglect.

Diagnosis

The DSM-III-R (American Psychiatric Association 1987) diagnostic criteria for reactive attachment disorder in infancy are shown in Table 1. The infant's developmental level can also be assessed by means of the Bayley or Brazelton developmental scales. Diagnosis and treatment of the infant, the mother-infant distorted interaction, and the mother are concurrent procedures. Observation of the mother-infant interaction

---

Table 1.   DSM-III-R Diagnostic Criteria for Reactive Attachment Disorder of Infancy or Early Childhood

A. Markedly disturbed social relatedness in most contexts, beginning before the age of five, as evidenced by either (1) or (2):

  (1) persistent failure to initiate or respond to most social interactions (e.g., in infants, absence of visual tracking and reciprocal play, lack of vocal imitation or playfulness, apathy, little or no spontaneity; at later ages, lack of or little curiosity and social interest)

  (2) indiscriminate sociability, e.g., excessive familiarity with relative strangers by making requests and displaying affection

B. The disturbance in A is not a symptom of either Mental Retardation or a Pervasive Developmental Disorder, such as Autistic Disorder.

C. Grossly pathogenic care, as evidenced by at least one of the following:

  (1) persistent disregard of the child's basic emotional needs for comfort, stimulation, and affection. *Examples*: overly harsh punishment by caregiver; consistent neglect by caregiver.

  (2) persistent disregard of the child's basic physical needs, including nutrition, adequate housing, and protection from physical danger and assault (including sexual abuse)

  (3) repeated change of primary caregiver so that stable attachments are not possible, e.g., frequent changes in foster parents

D. There is a presumption that the care described in C is responsible for the disturbed behavior in A; this presumption is warranted if the disturbance in A began following the pathogenic care in C.

Note: If failure to thrive is present, code it on Axis III.

---

is an important procedure in determining whether the mother is responding appropriately to her infant. The therapist observes the interaction for insufficiency of interaction, distorted interactions, and discontinuity of relationships. Direct observation is essential because, in general, the histories given by the mothers are unreliable. The majority believe that they are interacting appropriately and attribute the infant's difficulty to something within the infant. However, direct observation of the mother-infant interaction reveals that the mother infrequently holds the infant in the enface position, so there is diminished eye contact between infant and mother. The mother may hold the child on her lap with the infant facing away from her. When holding the infant and speaking to another adult, the mother for long periods of time does not respond to any cues or signals given by the infant when the cues involve the need to be soothed, comforted, or relieved from some distress. The infant also may be left for long periods of time in the crib without stimulation. The mother does not respond, or responds inconsistently, to the infant's vocalizations. This leads to diminished or no vocalization on the part of the infant. She does not read appropriately the infant's signals or cues. For instance, while feeding the infant, she may believe the infant is satiated if the infant stops for a rest or to burp. Then, if the infant cries, she is not aware that the infant is still hungry, and not just irritable and unable to be satisfied.

When feeding their infants, some mothers push the bottle in and out of the infant's mouth at frequent intervals and are not sensitive to the infant's rhythm. They do not understand why the infant then becomes irritable. Other mothers overfeed their infants. During this process, the infant becomes extremely quiet, only to vomit soon after the feeding process terminates. This leads the mother to believe the infant has some type of gastrointestinal disorder. If there are other infants or children present, the mothers often ignore their infants. A large proportion of these mothers do not believe that they are interacting insufficiently or in a distorted manner with their infants; in fact, they frequently say that they are competent in their roles as mothers (Fischhoff et al. 1971; Whitten et al. 1969). When the attachment disorder is serious and the infant is failing to thrive, hospitalization is indicated for the infant because the infant can eventually develop serious infectious diseases or may eventually die of starvation. A very small percentage of the mothers have a serious mental illness (e.g., schizophrenia or bipolar affective disorder) or are substance abusers. It may be necessary to remove the infant from the home if the mother's disorder seriously interferes with the ability to care for the infant. This decision is based on how well the mother functions with the infant, and not on her psychiatric diagnosis. There are some mothers who have sustained stressful events and who respond to reassurance, education, and supportive or (if necessary) uncovering psychotherapy rather well.

Mothers in the largest group have a history of many years' duration of low self-esteem, isolation, alienation, and deprivation. Their early life histories include parental deprivation, loss of parent figures early in life, emotional or physical abuse, and a history of poor adaptation and coping of many years' duration (Casey et al. 1984; Evans et al. 1972; Fischhoff et al. 1971; Pollitt et al. 1975; Whitten et al. 1969). Often they left school early and had their first pregnancy at a young age, although the infant with the reactive attachment disorder may not be the first pregnancy. The infant's attachment disorder is one more sign of the mother's chronic maladaption. Married or not, the mothers' relationships with men are poor. Their men have personalities similar to theirs. These mothers and fathers have relationships based on need gratification primarily. Since they have low self-esteem and a minimal sense of trust, they are extremely vulnerable to small slights and hurts. Their tolerance for frustration is low. Their impaired capacity for object relationships and empathy makes it difficult for them to be aware of and care for the infant's needs. Direct treatment of such parents is indicated and involves various types of intervention. If there is a man in the home, both parents are involved with the treatment. It is not uncommon for such a parent to have seen physicians for multiple physical and emotional complaints, for which they were given neuroleptics, anxiolytics, or antidepressants. The medication may or may not have been appropriate, depending on the diagnosis of the parent. The medication should be assessed for its appropriateness. It may be correct or it may serve to foster their dependent needs and direct their attention away from the significant emotional and marital problems.

The focus has been on the mothers since, in the majority of the studies of reactive attachment disorders of infancy, the mothers have been the primary caretakers; the literature on fathers and other caretakers is sparse and anecdotal.

Treatment Approaches

Direct treatment of the infant can occur at home or in the hospital. If the infant's attachment disorder is serious enough to involve hospitalization because of failure to thrive, treatment begins in the hospital. If the disorder is minimal or moderate, treatment of the infant can occur through the mother with the help of allied health personnel, while simultaneously helping the mother in treatment to understand her contribution to the infant's condition. Whether treatment begins in the hospital or home, the mother is immediately involved in the process with the infant. She is helped to interact with and appropriately stimulate the infant. She is encouraged to spend hours each day with her infant, with instruction and encouragement from the staff in the caretaking process. Concurrently, she is also engaged in individual, family, or group therapy as indicated. In-hospital treatment of the infant, in a general pediatric unit, can last from two to several weeks, depending on the infant's and mother's response.

Videotapes of mother-infant interaction provide baseline data and are useful in treatment. They allow the mother to see her interaction with her infant and offer the therapist an opportunity to suggest alternative ways to improve this interaction. Teaching tapes of appropriate mother-infant interaction are also helpful. Some mothers accept being videotaped and others do not, so preparation of the use of tapes and an explanation of their potential benefit is necessary.

Group therapy consisting of psychotherapy, parent education, and guidance is helpful in diminishing the mother's sense of isolation, alienation, and deprivation.

> Seventeen-year-old Donna brought her four-month-old daughter, Jane, to the doctor because she had a fever and diarrhea. On examination, Jane was lethargic and her weight was that of a two-month-old infant. Jane was hospitalized and her fever and diarrhea responded quickly to treatment. No organic cause was found for her low weight. However, she was nonresponsive to her mother and the medical staff. She did not smile, lacked interest in the environment, and uttered few sounds. The ward staff reported that when Donna visited, she held Jane but spent most of the time watching television. She rarely initiated interaction with Jane, and responded to Jane's cues for care only when they were strong.
>
> The pediatrician told Donna that nothing organic was found to account for Jane's low weight and asked her to speak with the psychiatrist. Donna agreed without much interest or enthusiasm. Donna told the psychiatrist that she had wanted to become pregnant. Several of her friends, who were a year younger or older than Donna, had babies or were pregnant. Donna had been sexually active since age 13. Her mother worked full-time, expected Donna to do most of the household chores and be responsible for her younger brother. Her mother had high expectations for Donna but emphasized her "faults" and not her successes. Donna said she was unhappy with her mother's treatment but her mother "worked hard for us and is tired when she comes home. I have never had a father and my mother raised us." Donna's mother was angry with her when she became pregnant and said she was too young to have a baby. She wanted her to have an abortion. Donna wanted a baby because she would be less lonely and would enjoy playing with the baby. After Jane's birth, Donna felt that even more demands were being made of her because "a baby takes so much care," and her mother was critical of how she cared for Jane. Although Donna continued in high school and a neighbor cared for Jane while Donna was in school, she felt that caring for Jane after school was a chore in addition to the others she had. Her loneliness and depression increased. The warmth, closeness, and pleasure she daydreamed about during her pregnancy did not materialize after Jane's birth.
>
> Donna's mother was anxious to speak with the psychiatrist. She told him that Donna had always been a "good girl and a good student." However, for the past two years she was "more and more stubborn." Donna's mother wanted much more for her children than she had had when she was a child. She did not know her father. Her mother neglected her but she was determined to "make something of myself." When she became pregnant with Donna, her live-in partner left her. She delivered Donna and continued to work. Sometime later "I made the same mistake again," meaning that she thought the father of Donna's brother would marry her but he did not. While the psychiatrist continued to have sessions with Donna and her mother, the nursing staff engaged Jane in stimulating encounters to which she responded, and she began to gain weight. Concurrently, the nursing staff and social work staff showed Donna that they were interested in her and encouraged her to care for Jane as they did. Donna consented to being

videotaped with Jane. She learned from the sessions and instruction tapes that she was not interacting with Jane as she thought she was. Donna responded to the staff's concern and encouragement, and Jane became an alert baby who ate well. After Jane's discharge, the psychiatrist continued individual sessions with Donna and conjoint sessions with her and her mother in which their feelings of mutual disappointment, anger, and frustration were slowly resolved and verbal communication improved. Treatment was terminated after a year with the understanding that they could contact him if and when necessary.

It is very possible that another daughter and her mother could not resolve their difficulties and the infant would be at risk after discharge from the hospital. The recommendation then perhaps would be for the daughter and infant to live out of the grandmother's home. The daughter would continue in therapy and continued efforts would be made to resolve the difficulties between mother and daughter. However, during this time, the risk for the infant would be minimized.

For failure-to-thrive infants with attachment disorder, although adequate caloric intake is provided, the infant often does not gain weight rapidly in the early stages of treatment. As Barbero (1982) observed, social and behavioral improvement occurs before physical improvement. The treatment program includes visual, tactile, kinesthetic, and auditory stimulation. These forms of stimulation are necessary because the infant frequently has been exposed to environmental deprivation, which makes the infant appear physically and neurologically handicapped. Visual stimulation consists of hanging brightly colored mobiles over the crib and carrying the infant around to various rooms where individuals can be seen and objects observed.

Some infants exhibit a frozen stare or an adversive action when approached. For these infants, the initial contact is best made by not looking at the infant directly but by allowing the infant to reach out and touch a part of the therapist's body (e.g., the hand or arm that is still) or by offering an inanimate object to the infant while not looking at him or her. When the infant has made an attachment to the "safe" inanimate object, the examiner then can gradually turn toward the infant, and attachment can form between the infant and therapist through the inanimate object. Tactile stimulation by soothing and stroking the infant is carried out during feeding and other times. It is not enough to do it only when the infant is being fed. Kinesthetic stimulation occurs while carrying the infant or sitting with the infant in a rocking chair and, whenever possible, creating eye contact with the infant. Auditory stimulation occurs during feeding, and at other times by talking and singing to the infant. Many infants with attachment disorder have delayed vocalization because of the environmental deprivation they have experienced. Preterm infants (Leib et al. 1980) have also responded to this type of program when modified to suit their development status.

The nutritional requirements are calculated on what would be the caloric intake for the infant's chronological age and ideal weight. The goal cannot be attained immediately, but it is possible in a few days to a few weeks. Vitamin supplements are given routinely and antibiotics when indicated. The use of psychoactive medications is not indicated or necessary. Both the irritable and lethargic infant will respond to appropriate nutritional, sensory, and psychosocial interventions without the use of psychoactive medication.

The infant with an attachment disorder may be allowed to stay at home, with care being provided by the mother if she shows the potential to respond to professional support, therapy, education, and instruction in how to stimulate her infant. The instruction can be carried out by the clinic staff or visiting nurses in a community agency. The therapist visits the home once a week to instruct and support the mother. Mother and infant have pediatric clinic visits every two weeks to monitor progress.

Diane and Mary were treated in a home care program. Diane, who was 20 years old, brought Mary, her three-month-old, to the pediatrician for an examination because she was not eating. On examination, Mary was in the 20th percentile for height and weight, did not follow eyes and faces, did not smile, and had poor muscle tone and a weak cry. No physical cause was found for Mary's illness. Diane was afraid that Mary had a serious physical illness and might die. She said she loved Mary very much and Mary was all she "had in the world." Diane's history was that her mother was neglectful and Diane and her siblings were placed in an institution and then in separate foster homes. She was in permanent foster care in several homes until she was 17 years old, and then placed in independent living status with social service funds. Diane received vocational training in food service and had a position in a restaurant. She was financially independent and had lived alone. Diane was aware that she had been "lonely" for years. Many times she attempted to establish a relationship with her mother, who rejected all attempts and told Diane she would "never amount to anything." A few months before she conceived Mary, she met a man who said he cared for her, but when she became pregnant, he said he was not ready to settle down and left her. Diane did not want to terminate the pregnancy because she wanted a baby very much.

An intervention program was outlined for Diane and Mary. An experienced nurse visited her once a week and demonstrated how to relate to and care for Mary. The nurse also was supportive and encouraging and became Diane's confidant. Diane was given the nurse's phone number and could call her when necessary. Diane expressed her feelings of low self-esteem, loneliness, and depression, especially related to her abandonment by her boyfriend. She also attended a weekly group meeting for mothers with similar problems. Diane was responsive to instructions about feeding and stimulating Mary, who responded rapidly in attaining developmental norms in the social and behavioral areas, and more slowly but definitely in weight and physical development. Mary was a healthy infant in three months. Diane continued in group therapy for a year because she recognized that she was feeling better about herself, she could share her problems with others, and her feelings of loneliness and depression diminished. Diane also realized that her recent depression was only one aspect of her years of feeling she was not capable, and that this was related to her belief that she was defective in some way to have been given up by her mother. She became aware of her repressed anger at her mother for having done so. Diane began to take positive steps in making friends. With assistance, she arranged for appropriate care for Mary when she was at work. Antidepressant medication was considered in the diagnostic phase of treatment, but because Diane's overt symptoms decreased rather rapidly, medication was not necessary.

Fraiberg et al. (1975) described in detail the vicissitudes of treating the mothers. Progress can be slow and crises many as the mother gradually resolves her past conflicts. At times, court intervention may be for the infant's benefit. If court intervention occurred before a referral for therapy, the resistance to therapy is often great. It may be months before the mother sees the therapist as an individual who wants to help her. During the process of therapy, the therapist must be careful not to exhibit too great an interest in the infant because the mother will think the therapist is interested only in the infant and not in her, thus leaving her with the feeling that nobody cares for her and confirming her past experience. Many of the mothers have had dependent, yet angry and hating relationships with their own mothers, and it is inevitable that the initial transference relationship will be very fragile and very ambivalent. Marital therapy is also indicated if the mother is not a single parent.

Linda and John were in their late 20s and had three children: seven-year-old Alan, five-year-old June, and seven-month-old Robert. Robert weighed 4 lb 11 oz at birth, with a moderate right club foot but no other complications. The deformity was responding to conservative treatment. Robert's pediatrician noted that at the monthly visits Robert was not gaining weight as expected, even taking into account his mild prematurity. His mother was very anxious at each visit, asked numerous detailed questions, worried that Robert had a serious illness that was not diagnosed, and appeared depressed. The pediatrician, after he determined that Robert had no physical illness, referred the family to a child psychiatrist.

The psychiatrist observed on the initial visit with Robert and his parents that Robert did not smile or respond to voices and lacked spontaneity and interest in the environment. His parents said Robert slept excessively and seemed weak. Linda appeared anxious and depressed. John was anxious and continued to raise the question of an organic cause for Robert's condition. He said that as parents they had raised two children and were experienced parents. He was willing to accept the psychiatrist's observation that Linda appeared depressed and anxious and asked Linda what was wrong. With tears she said she was afraid that Robert was fragile because he was premature and although she was anxious with Alan and June, they were born healthy. Also, over the years, John was devoting more and more time to his work, and she felt he was becoming disinterested in her and the children. John expressed surprise at what Linda said. This was the beginning of marital and family therapy that continued for several months. Family sessions were initiated because Linda felt John was too demanding of Alan and June. In these sessions, Alan especially complained that his father spent little time with him and only seemed interested in how he was doing in school. In marital sessions, the parents became freer in their ability to relate to each other and not suffer in silent frustration and anger. Robert, who initially was the identified patient, responded to his parents' modified manner in relating to him soon after the first visit and ceased to be the subject of the sessions. Linda became aware that she was raised to meet her parents' high expectations and, being less than perfect, was not good enough. Robert's birth was a sign of her failure. John felt he had to present the image of a successful professional to the world and, sensing Linda's anxiety, rarely allowed himself to confide in her for fear of upsetting her. Marital therapy enabled them to be "more human," as John said, and develop a sense of closeness and trust that they had not experienced before. Linda said that they ceased being "good" and were able to say they were frustrated and angry without fear of disapproval and rejection.

Ounsted et al. (1974) have written about inpatient treatment of families in a setting that fosters regression. All the members of the family are cared for, housed, and made to feel safe. In this safe, trusting environment, psychodynamic distortions and distortions in communication are resolved and maturation occurs. Facilities for this type of treatment are not readily available, however. Outpatient psychotherapy for the group of mothers who suffer from isolation, alienation, and deprivation, if successful, generally lasts from one to two years.

Legal Intervention

Involvement by legally mandated authorities may be necessary when the diagnosis of reactive attachment disorder is made. This step can occur at any of several points. The parents of an infant who is hospitalized in poor physical condition may be resistant to becoming involved in treatment and, although the infant improves, the infant will be at risk if discharged to the parents. A family in outpatient treatment with an infant who has not required hospitalization may not respond to treatment. If treatment is not going to be successful, the therapist can determine this in a few months and recommend to protective services and the court that the infant who was initially identified as the patient and perhaps other children in the family are at risk for prolonged neglect and possible physical abuse and should be placed out of the home with a relative or in foster care. Neglect and abuse can occur simultaneously, a circumstance the therapist should always keep in mind. In all jurisdictions, reporting suspected abuse and neglect has priority over confidentiality. The therapist should inform the parents that, out of concern for the infant and family, a report must be filed with the protective services division of the department of social services and that this is required by law. As mentioned earlier, this procedure may alter the therapeutic relationship but the serious risk to the infant of prolonged exposure to deprivation, neglect, physical injury, or possible death takes precedence over all other considerations. The following case illustrates this point.

Alice, who was 23 years old and unmarried, had a three-year-old daughter, and Kevin, six months old. Alice began using heroin in mid-adolescence and was in methadone programs intermittently without success. Her childhood was marked by neglect and abuse. In adolescence she engaged in delinquent behavior and was made a ward of the court and placed in a residential center. She was angry, mistrustful, and assaultive. Her response to treatment was minimal. When she was discharged after two years, she became a drug user. Alice was never employed but engaged in illicit activities to obtain money in addition to the general assistance funds she received for support.

Alice was known to protective services because she had neglected her three-year-old daughter. Social services provided minimal intervention then. When she became pregnant with Kevin, she was asked to attend the clinic for high-risk pregnancies because she abused heroin, but she attended the clinic sporadically. After Kevin's birth, Alice did not bring him for monthly clinic appointments, although outreach services were provided. Finally, at the insistence of social services, she brought Kevin to the clinic. Kevin, at six months of age, was below the third percentile for height and weight and was hospitalized. He had no interest in his environment, was hypotonic, and had poor muscle tone. He lacked alerting and turning toward adult's voices, had no vocal reciprocity, lacked spontaneous reaching, and did not participate in playful games.

Alice visited Kevin sporadically during his hospitalization. When she did, she showed little interest in relating to him. She also resented any approaches by the staff to help her in relating to Kevin. She was angry when a suspected child abuse and neglect report was filed and she was instructed to bring her three-year-old daughter for a medical examination. The daughter was found to be physically and developmentally delayed without an organic cause, as was Kevin. Alice was angry with what she saw as interference by authorities and maintained that she knew how to raise her children. She resisted all efforts to involve her in an intervention program. The two children were made wards of the court and placed in the home of a relative. For several years Alice visited the children sporadically. She insisted that she wanted the children to be with her, but resisted any help for herself. The court did not terminate Alice's parental rights, and the children continued to live in the relative's home, where they were developing normally.

Prognosis

Prognosis in a case is dependent on the response of the infant and mother to treatment. The infant demonstrates a positive response to treatment by somatic growth, an increased repertoire of affective responses (e.g., smiling, laughing, crying, anger), decreased apathy and lethargy, improved coordination, diminished developmental lags, appropriate responses to caretakers, and improvement on developmental testing as measured by standardized tests. The mother's improvement is indicated by her decreased sense of isolation, alienation, deprivation, and hopelessness. Her self-esteem will increase as will her initiative in daily activities and interactions. She will develop the capacity to utilize community resources for her child and herself. Positive improvement in mother-infant interaction is observed when the mother responds appropriately to the infant's behaviors (e.g., movements, vocalizations, and affect such as pleasure and distress, laughing and crying). She also reaches out and initiates interactions: talking, singing, using age-appropriate toys, soothing when indicated, and exhibiting normal concern, pleasure, or contentment in reaction to her infant's responses.

Prevention

The Parent-Infant Growth Program (Rowe 1984) is a preventive program that has demonstrated success utilizing trained volunteers to work with at-risk mothers or families from the time the mother is seven months pregnant until the infant is one year old. The volunteer serves as a supportive friend and teacher. The mother has one individual to whom she can relate for emotional support. The volunteer teaches the mother how to observe, interpret, and respond to her infant's behavior. The volunteer sees the mother weekly or more often. In addition to helping her relate to her infant, the volunteer listens to her concerns about herself, her marriage, family, and lack of finances or resources, and provides helpful information. When she encounters difficulties beyond the limits of her role, she turns to the professional supervisory staff for guidance. Some European countries have a home health visitor system for families who have been identified as having special needs while the mother and infant are still in the hospital.

Others have addressed the issue of prevention of reactive attachment disorder of infancy (Kemp 1976; O'Connor et al. 1980; Sugarman 1977; Williams 1980). A number of areas have been investigated, assessed, and discussed: family life education in the schools to diminish sexual ignorance and unwanted pregnancies, the contribution of adolescent childbearing with its higher risk of physical impairment in the infant and lack of the adolescent mother's ability to care for the infant, the reduced incidence of parenting inadequacy following rooming-in, greater management and control of the birthing process, avoidance of high technology and artificial obstetric intervention, and early discharge for normal newborns and mothers with follow-up at home. These discussions and techniques deserve serious consideration because a number of factors that lead to reactive attachment disorder of infancy can be identified and possibly prevented.

Chapter 87

Schizoid Disorder of Childhood or Adolescence

Historical Background

As psychiatric disorders were classified with increasing exactness in the early 1900s, many investigators described individuals with traits of shyness, inability to make friends, and difficulty in establishing emotional closeness with others. Kraepelin described these traits, which, when found in children, predisposed to later development of dementia praecox. The term *schizoid* was applied by Bleuler to people who were "shut-in, suspicious, uncomfortably dull, sensitive, and pursuers of vague purposes" (Wolff and Chick 1980, p. 85). The relationship between schizoid disorder and schizophrenia became a matter of considerable debate. Opinions ranged from the position that schizoid individuals have a mild form of schizophrenia to the position that the schizoid disorder was a distinct entity qualitatively different from schizophrenia. Researchers in general confirmed the early impression that persons with schizoid characteristics were predisposed to later development of schizophrenia. However, it was also noted that many schizoid individuals never showed overt schizophrenia. Almost from the beginning, it was observed that schizoid characteristics typically occurred as a lifelong pattern. In 1944 Asperger described a group of children whom he had identified as having "autistic psychopathy of childhood." These children showed characteristics that closely resembled later descriptions of children with schizoid characteristics (Asperger 1944 in Wolf and Chick 1980). Various names have been applied to children who showed schizoid traits. In DSM-II (American Psychiatric Association 1968), these children were categorized as having "withdrawing reaction of childhood (or adolescence)." The withdrawing reaction of childhood (or adolescence) was described as "characterized by seclusiveness, detachment, sensitivity, shyness, timidity, and general inability to form close interpersonal relationships." In the DSM-II classification, it was stated that "this diagnosis should be reserved for those who cannot be classified as having schizophrenia and whose tendencies toward withdrawal have not yet stabilized enough to justify the diagnosis of schizoid personality."

Despite the controversies concerning its usefulness, the term *schizoid* has persisted in the psychiatric literature. Its application to children has been significantly clarified by the inclusion of "schizoid disorder of childhood or adolescence" in DSM-III (American Psychiatric Association 1980). The DSM-III exposition of diagnostic criteria for this disorder provides a more consistent basis for the diagnosis of this condition than has been available in the past.

It should be noted that the term *Asperger's syndrome* is widely used in Europe to apply to many children with symptomatology that would be diagnosed in the United

States as schizoid disorder of childhood or adolescence. While admitting that Asperger's syndrome can be classified as a form of schizoid personality, Wing (1981) feels that such a classification has no useful implications; the term *Asperger's syndrome* is more specific and has the advantage of avoiding the adjective *schizoid*, which for some may imply the assumption of a clearly defined link with schizophrenia. As mentioned above, the original term applied by Asperger was *autistic psychopathy of childhood*. Wing pointed out that use of the term *Asperger's syndrome* is also preferable to Asperger's original nomenclature because of its avoidance of confusion resulting from the fact that psychopathy is, at times, equated with sociopathic behavior (Wing 1981). Asperger's syndrome includes the following characteristics that were not specifically addressed by the DSM-III criteria for schizoid disorder of childhood or adolescence:

1. Abnormalities of speech, particularly involving content that tends to be pedantic and frequently consists of long discourses on favorite topics. Vocal intonation is often monotonous and at times exaggerated.
2. Abnormalities of nonverbal communication, including decreased facial expression except during strong emotion such as sadness or anger. Comprehension of the expressions and gestures of other people is poor.
3. Attachment to repetitive activities and resistance to change.
4. Abnormalities in motor coordination with gross motor movements, which are clumsy and poorly coordinated.
5. A tendency to develop intense interest in certain subjects or skills to virtual exclusion of other activities.
6. Difficulties at school with a tendency to follow their own interests, whether or not these coincide with the teachers' instructions. Their social eccentricities frequently result in their being perceived as peculiar and frequently bullied by other children. Asperger's syndrome also includes the difficulties in social interaction, which are basically the same as those described in the DSM-III criteria for schizoid disorder (Wing 1981, pp. 116–117).

Autistic psychopathy as viewed by Asperger can be considered as "hypertrophy of intellect at the expense of feeling" (Van Krevelan 1971, p. 85). The possible linkage between early infantile autism as described by Kanner and Asperger's syndrome has been discussed by many authors. Most researchers agree with Van Krevelan that these two syndromes are distinct from each other.

Overall it appears that schizoid disorder of childhood or adolescence is broader than Asperger's syndrome in that patients described as having Asperger's syndrome could also be diagnosed as having schizoid disorder. However, a considerable number of patients who meet DSM-III criteria for schizoid disorder may not meet all the criteria for Asperger's syndrome. There is thus considerable overlap but not complete congruence between these two patient groups.

Criteria for Diagnosis

Schizoid disorder of childhood or adolescence is described in DSM-III as follows: The essential feature is a defect in the capacity to form relationships that is not due to any other mental disorder, such as pervasive developmental disorder; conduct disorder, undersocialized, nonaggressive; or any psychotic disorder, such as schizophrenia.

Children with this disorder have no close friends of similar age other than a relative or a similarly socially isolated child. They do not appear distressed by their isolation, show little desire for social involvement, and prefer to be "loners," although they may be attached to a parent or other adult. When placed in social situations, they are uncomfortable, inept, and awkward. They have no interest in activities that involve other children, such as team sports and clubs. They often appear aloof, reserved, withdrawn, and seclusive. The duration of the disturbance is at least three months. If 18 or older, the individual does not meet the criteria for schizoid personality disorder.

These children may be belligerent and irritable, especially when demands for social performance are made. They are erratically sensitive to criticism, displaying occasional outbursts of aggressive behavior. They are frequently scapegoated by their peers. These children often are vague about their goals, indecisive, absentminded, and detached from their environment ("not with it" or "in a fog"). They often appear self-absorbed and engage in excessive daydreaming. They tend to pursue solitary interests and hobbies and are often preoccupied with esoteric topics, such as violence or supernatural phenomena. However, they show no loss of reality testing.

The DSM-III criteria for schizoid disorder of childhood or adolescence suffer from the same problems of low diagnostic reliability among raters as are seen in the personality disorders. Frances (1980) has described two inherent reasons for the problems in reliability with the personality disorders as follows. First, most of the personality disorders are probably no more than the severe variance of normally occurring personality traits that are distributed continuously and without clear boundaries to indicate pathology. Second, personality assessment is inevitably confounded by intercurrent state and role factors.

Differential Diagnosis

The distinction between schizoid disorder of childhood or adolescence and avoidant disorder of childhood or adolescence is based on whether the patient is interested in social participation or not. In schizoid disorder of childhood or adolescence, the patient has no apparent interest in social participation; in avoidant disorder of childhood or adolescence, the individual desires social participation but is inhibited from this by the severe anxiety experienced in the desired social setting. This is a fine distinction and must be based on the judgment of the clinician. The situation is complicated by the fact that many patients with schizoid disorder of childhood or adolescence, if asked directly whether they desire social interaction, will reply affirmatively. However, the patients with schizoid disorder of childhood or adolescence, in fact, make little or no effort toward increased social interaction and appear in general content with an isolated existence. The differentiation between schizoid disorder of childhood or adolescence and schizoid personality disorder is basically a determination made by age. If the symptoms of schizoid disorder of childhood or adolescence persist beyond the age of 18, as is often the case, the diagnosis is changed to schizoid personality disorder.

Patients with schizoid disorder are often vague about their goals in life and, in this area, overlap the category of identity disorder. However, patients with an identity disorder are much more involved with other people than are patients with schizoid disorder. Many of the interpersonal relationships for patients with an identity disorder are conflictual but intense; in contrast, the patient with schizoid disorder is isolated and has very few relationships with other people.

The distinction between schizoid disorders and borderline conditions has frequently been blurred in the psychiatric literature. Diagnostic categories classified within the borderline continuum may include pseudoschizophrenia, psychotic character, borderline personality, schizoid personality, the false-self organization, the as-if personality, and even identity diffusion (Meissner 1982/1983).

The pattern of unstable and intense interpersonal relationships characteristic of the borderline personality is not the pattern typical of adolescents and children with schizoid disorder who withdraw from such relationships. Individuals with borderline personality disorder are usually intolerant of being alone, whereas children and adolescents with schizoid disorder often appear most comfortable when they are involved in solitary pursuits. The impulsivity and self-injurious behavior often seen in borderline individuals is much less frequent in patients with schizoid disorder.

Schizophrenia and pervasive developmental disorders in childhood and adolescence can be differentiated from schizoid disorder by the presence of psychotic symptoms or major defects in many areas of functioning. Although children with conduct disorder, undersocialized, nonaggressive experience difficulty in establishing emotional bonding with others, the number of social relationships in which they are involved is usually much greater than that of the child or adolescent with schizoid disorder. In addition, children with conduct disorders show many antisocial activities not characteristic of children with schizoid disorder.

Although there is some overlap between the diagnostic criteria for schizotypal personality disorder and those for schizoid disorder of childhood or adolescence, there are also important differences. Both have social isolation and may show undue anxiety in social situations. However, the magical thinking, ideas of reference, and recurrent illusions seen in the schizotypal personality disorder are not characteristic of the schizoid disorder.

Current Problems in Diagnosis

There were some difficulties with the DSM-III criteria for the diagnosis of schizoid disorder. The wording expressed an absoluteness that is rarely seen in the clinical setting. The wording, if taken literally, would have meant that a child with schizoid disorder could never express an interest in making friends nor have any pleasure from interactions with peers. Wording that would be much more applicable to what is seen clinically would be "little or no apparent interest in making friends" and "and little or no pleasure from usual peer interactions."

In formulating DSM-III-R, the question of whether to continue the category of schizoid disorder of childhood or adolescence was debated. It was argued that the major distinction between schizoid personality disorder and schizoid disorder of childhood or adolescence is simply one of age and that it would make sense to apply the term *schizoid personality disorder* to children or adolescents rather than to have a separate category. There were also arguments against this course of action. Child psychiatrists have consistently been reluctant to make personality diagnoses during childhood and adolescence because of the wide range of developmental fluctuations seen during these years. Furthermore, there are insufficient data regarding the ultimate outcome of patients with schizoid disorder of childhood or adolescence. While it is undoubtedly true that most of these individuals have schizoid traits as adults, there is good evidence to suggest that they may have a variety of outcomes later in life, including schizophrenia, schizotypal personality disorder, or, in a few cases, no mental disorder. The category of schizoid disorders of childhood or adolescence allows the clinician to make a diagnosis that may have less long-term implications than is the case when a diagnosis of personality disorder is made.

Clinical Course

Precise figures regarding the prevalence of this disorder are not available. It is felt to be rare. Wolff and Barlow (1979) found that between 3 and 4 percent of new referrals to a general child psychiatry department presented with a clinical picture fitting the category of schizoid personality disorder. The disorder occurs more frequently in boys than in girls. In the Wolff and Barlow series, the ratio of boys to girls was nine to one. This disorder typically begins during childhood, although the symptoms may not become severe enough to bring the individual for treatment until the teenage years. The diagnosis is rarely made prior to the age of five years. Careful examination of the histories of these children will ordinarily elicit evidence of difficulties occurring even earlier than five years, although these problems are not usually sufficient to bring the child for psychiatric treatment.

There is a considerable variation in the amount of disability in patients with this disorder. Some degree of impairment in academic or work performance is frequent. In some cases, this impairment may be quite severe. Some of the children with this disorder will become highly resistant to attending school, but they do not show the excessive anxiety about separation from major attachment figures that is characteristic of the separation anxiety disorder. Many of the children appear to do best in school when they are able to "blend into the woodwork." They do not seem bothered by lack of attention from their peers. They will, of course, become anxious and distressed if made the object of ridicule by their peers.

The prognosis for these individuals may depend ultimately on the amount of life stress they encounter. Many authors have reported that schizophrenia may develop as an outcome of this disorder. As has already been mentioned, the most likely outcome is schizoid personality disorder during the adult years. Varying degrees of depression often occur in children and adolescents with schizoid disorder. This may be pronounced in some patients. It is quite possible that some patients diagnosed as having schizoid disorder may develop a major affective disorder in adulthood, but definitive data on this outcome are not currently available.

Although precise figures are also not available regarding the frequency with which transition to normality occurs, it is clear that a significant number of these patients may achieve a life adaptation good enough to avoid their being identified as having a mental disorder later in life. These individuals usually continue to be withdrawn and often are regarded as somewhat eccentric by others. This outcome probably occurs more frequently in females than in males. However, it is important to avoid the misconception that patients with schizoid disorder are inevitably disliked and in conflict with those around them. Patients with schizoid disorder are often intelligent, shy, passive, unaggressive, noncompetitive, and nonthreatening. In certain circumstances, such as occupations that allow them to work in considerable isolation, they may be regarded with acceptance and approval. Some females, particularly if they are physically attractive, may be able to accept the advances of male partners and eventually marry. It is not unusual for males with this disorder to remain single throughout their lives.

The prevalence of schizoid personality as opposed to schizoid personality disorder in the adult population is not known. Cull et al. (1984) expressed the opinion that there is a high probability of there being many schizoid children in the community whose symptomatology is mild enough that they do not come in for treatment. Persons with a schizoid personality may show many behavioral characteristics that are similar to but less severe than those seen in patients who have a schizoid personality disorder. Many individuals who have a schizoid personality are self-supporting and lead quiet but productive lives. The following case history illustrates such a life adaptation:

> Mr. C was an elderly man who had been withdrawn and isolated throughout his life. During adolescence he left home to enter college but stayed only a few weeks before suddenly returning home. His only explanation for why he returned home was that his college roommate had been borrowing his clothes without asking his permission. Mr. C never returned to college, but entered the family business where he worked as bookkeeper. Within the family he was quiet, shy, and unassertive. He rarely engaged in conversation except when the conversation was directed into one of his areas of particular interest. He always seemed content to be alone. After the death of his parents, Mr. C inherited a considerable amount of money, which made him self-sustaining without the need for regular work. He bought a house where he lived alone. He became active in a small church and supported a number of benevolent enterprises. He never married and continued his solitary existence until the time of his death.

Many of the individuals who have schizoid personality without sufficient disability to qualify as a disorder have mastered the technique of maintaining distance from others without bringing ridicule on themselves. This technique of successful withdrawal may be maintained throughout life.

Etiology

Although many theories have been advanced to explain why schizoid disorder develops, the etiology of this condition remains unknown. Psychodynamic explanations have been prominent among the various theories. Pine's (1974) studies of borderline disorders in children have indicated the presence of developmental arrest or aberrant development. The aberrant development occurs principally in the area of ego function and object relationship. Those children with schizoid personality in childhood tended to be preoccupied with peculiar thoughts and were emotionally distant from other persons while maintaining enough ego function to permit satisfactory work in school. Many of the children had an extremely active fantasy life that served a defensive function. Pine stated: "They simultaneously function in the real world and hold themselves aloof from it emotionally while relating mainly to their odd (but not delusional) thought processes" (p. 361).

In some cases family psychodynamics appear to contribute significantly to the development of the schizoid disorder in childhood. Some of the parents experience great difficulty in letting go of their children. Many of the mothers who have major difficulty in this area have schizoid or borderline personalities themselves. These mothers receive much gratification from the dependency of their children. In many subtle ways they undermine the self-confidence of their children and reward the children for remaining in a dependent state. Whether these tendencies on the part of the mother are sufficient in themselves to create a schizoid disorder in the child is not clear. Certainly clinicians are well aware that many families support, sometimes quite strongly, the tendencies toward withdrawal seen in schizoid disorder of childhood or adolescence.

Little information is available regarding familial patterns in schizoid disorder of childhood or adolescence. In those patients who later develop schizophrenia, it seems apparent that there is a relationship between the schizoid disorder and schizophrenia. In many cases it appears that whether schizoid disorder develops into schizophrenia depends on how much emotional stress the individual experiences. Schizoid patients who experience repeatedly the situation that Gregory Bateson has described as a "double bind" or other prolonged emotionally stressful conflicts are particularly prone to develop schizophrenia.

Some genetic studies of schizophrenia have also suggested a relationship between schizoid disorder and schizophrenia. In a study of 16 pairs of identical twins of whom one was a schizophrenic, Tienari found no schizophrenic co-twins but 12 co-twins with schizoid traits (Tienari in Wolff and Chick 1980). Such studies raise the possibility that a biologic factor may be operating in patients with the schizoid disorder.

In many ways, the criteria for schizoid disorder of childhood or adolescence describe the temperament or behavioral style of those who fit this diagnosis. Carey (1985) aptly pointed out that research on temperament has demonstrated some evidence for stability in temperament and some for change. However, increasing stability of behavioral style appears to occur as children get older.

Patients with schizoid disorder have difficulty picking up cues to the feelings of other people. The nuances of nonverbal behavior often escape them. Objective demonstration of some of these difficulties in nonverbal communication was reported in a study by Scott (1985), which tested the ability of patients with Asperger's syndrome to recognize and produce nonverbal aspects of facial and spoken communication through the use of photographs, audiotapes, and videotapes.

Even when careful histories are taken in cases of schizoid disorder, it is often difficult to date the onset precisely. In some cases, it appears that these children were different from the norm even in infancy. Although at this point definitive proof is lacking, it seems quite possible that those who develop schizoid disorder during childhood have some predisposition to this disorder at birth. It should be noted that these children ordinarily do not show an increased incidence of neurologic abnormalities, specific developmental disorders, nor attention-deficit disorders.

Environmental factors may play a significant part in the development of this disorder. Frequently one or both parents are socially isolated, detached individuals who have difficulty teaching social skills to their children. Some children with schizoid disorder come from deprived backgrounds in which there has been neglect or abuse. Such children often have had multiple caretakers and constant uncertainties in their lives. In some of these cases, the development of schizoid disorder appears to be a defensive reaction to the overwhelming stress that these children face.

In other cases children with schizoid disorder appear to have made an identification with a parent who has either a schizoid personality disorder, schizophrenia, or a schizotypal personality disorder. As they learn the same reaction of withdrawal that their parents use, they tend to become overly dependent on the parent. This may result in significant arrest in the separation-individuation phase of development.

Schizoid disorder may also be viewed within a behavioral framework as the result of defective patterns of reinforcement. Within such a framework, these children may be seen as having developing response patterns of withdrawal and isolation. These patterns may develop either as the result of unusual stimuli or pathologic patterns of reinforcement.

Treatment

Evaluation of the various treatment modalities used for schizoid disorder of childhood or adolescence has been difficult. With the more specific diagnostic criteria as outlined in the DSM-III-R, it may be possible to compare various treatment modalities more accurately than has been the case in the past. This problem is complicated by the small numbers of patients with this disorder as compared to many of the other psychiatric disorders in children and adolescents. Although there has not yet been a demonstration that a particular treatment can completely change the basic underlying personality characteristics of patients who have schizoid disorder of childhood or adolescence, appropriate management can greatly diminish or in some cases remove the handicaps resulting from this condition. The present discussion will focus on the most frequently used forms of treatment.

Play Therapy

Some form of play therapy is commonly utilized with children with schizoid disorder who are less than 12 years of age. Play therapy is also often appropriate for schizoid individuals in the early adolescent years because these patients are in many ways often emotionally younger than their chronological age. When these children come to therapy, they have a very strong tendency to externalize their conflicts. They are often uncomfortable about these conflicts and may present with anxiety, depression, or both. Their perception of their difficulties tends to be that they are being harassed by external forces beyond their control. Many become anxious and unhappy when forced into social interactions, such as those at school, and will try in various ways to avoid these situations by withdrawing. In general, however, they do not see their shyness or their tendency to withdraw as a problem for them. Rather, they see the problem as being that they are not allowed to avoid the situation that causes them emotional pain. Thus, as is characteristic of the personality disorders in adults, the children may have anxiety, but the anxiety is not about their personality characteristics. In treatment the children often make it quickly clear that they see nothing basically wrong with themselves but just wish that "everyone would leave me alone."

This desire to be left alone quickly extends to the therapist. Such children will not infrequently plaintively complain that they do not want to talk about their difficulties because it makes them "feel bad." Typically they have a conviction that talking will not change anything. When therapy begins, they are quiet, shy, and reticent but usually polite. They will answer questions but are quick to reply "I don't know" to any questions that are emotionally revealing. They rarely volunteer information.

Long periods of silence are rarely fruitful with schizoid children. The therapist who attempts to use silence as a way of breaking through their defenses has little chance of success. The children are very adept at withdrawing into their own fantasies and may sit for long periods preoccupied with their own thoughts. A frequent result of such periods of silence will be that the child will extend the withdrawal tendency to becoming actively resistant to being brought to the treatment sessions.

Play therapy gives a technique for obviating many of these problems. When the schizoid child is allowed to engage in some activity that he or she enjoys with a warm, concerned, nonthreatening therapist, the child then sees a reason for coming to treatment. Play therapy techniques allow the therapist to discuss emotional issues with the child in much less threatening ways than through direct inquiry. However, these children are so guarded that initially play therapy may have to be started with structured activities such as crafts or games designed primarily to build rapport and establish a sense of comfort in the therapeutic situation. Gradually, drawing, painting, puppet play, and storytelling techniques can be used to explore the autistic fantasies of the child. The therapist must provide steady support for the child as increased openness in the therapeutic situation is developed. The therapist must be very cautious, bearing constantly in mind the extreme sensitivity of these children. For example, a humorous remark may be taken the wrong way by the child and result in instant withdrawal. Clarifications, confrontations, and interpretations must be made gently and at a rate that will not trigger withdrawal.

Within the play setting, the therapist often can accomplish significant gains. The child learns that increased openness with the therapist does not produce pain but rather produces an emotionally gratifying sense of closeness. Within this protective relationship, the child is often able to discuss a variety of relationships that are unsatisfactory, such as interactions with peers, teachers, and family members.

Play therapy does not result in a total change in the basic personality structure of these children. However, the improvement produced is often sufficient to allow these children to function much better than before therapy. Children who have consistently been experiencing ridicule and bullying from peers may learn to interact in ways that call less attention to themselves. Thus, although they continue to be withdrawn, they may be able to attend school without major conflict. Many of these children have the capacity to learn which aspects of their behavior create major negative reactions in other people. Once they have been able to identify these characteristics, they frequently can modify them enough to participate successfully on the fringe of the group in activities such as those at school, church, or scouting.

Play therapy with children who have schizoid disorder can afford a nonthreatening situation in which these children gradually examine problem areas in their lives. They can learn in the play setting how to relate in much more appropriate ways with peers and adults. Issues that are dealt with in play therapy tend primarily to involve present problems that the schizoid child is confronting and is thus primarily supportive in character. However, some reparative work is also possible in which the child evaluates areas of strength and weakness realistically. For example, these children may learn to modify their shyness to the point that they are not regarded as markedly different by their peers.

Psychodynamic Psychotherapy with Adolescents

Psychodynamic psychotherapy with adolescents who have schizoid disorder also involves emphasis in the early stages on making the adolescent feel comfortable in the therapy setting. Early in therapy considerable portions of each interview may be taken up with discussions of areas of special interest for the patient. These adolescents are often strongly invested in viewing their problems as being the result of the actions of other people. For example, they often blame their resistance to participating in group activities as being due to hostility on the part of their peers. When their avoidance also includes resistance to attending school, the ensuing conflict often brings them to therapy. Since schizoid adolescents are often quite dependent on their families, clinicians must be careful to avoid the mistake of thinking that they are dealing with a separation anxiety disorder when in fact they are dealing with the withdrawal tendencies of a schizoid adolescent.

Schizoid adolescents are very rigid and have a meager repertoire of adaptive responses. Consequently, they are much more dependent on the circumstances of their external environment than the usual adolescent. If resistance to attending school is an important part of the reason for coming to treatment, the clinician should examine very closely the circumstances of the school. Whereas changing schools is rarely effective for children or adolescents with a separation anxiety disorder, a change of schools may be appropriate for patients with schizoid disorder. A highly structured school with small classes and strong discipline often permits the authority figures to intervene quickly when an adolescent begins to be subjected to physical or verbal abuse. Schizoid youngsters may fit in much better in such an environment than they can in school settings where adult supervision is less available.

In some schizoid adolescents, a positive transference to the therapist may develop. However, this is characteristically much weaker than is seen in most other therapy situations. As this transference develops, the adolescent often asks for increasing direction from the therapist. The therapist is frequently confronted by questions such as "What do you think I should do?" The therapist should avoid making decisions for the schizoid adolescent but should not do this so rigidly that power struggles develop. The schizoid adolescent will rarely engage in an overt power struggle with the therapist but rather will use passive-aggressive maneuvers and withdrawal. In exploring emotional issues with adolescents who have schizoid disorder, it is advisable to avoid pursuing the adolescent's feelings so vigorously that the adolescent becomes quiet and begins responding repeatedly, "I don't know."

Long-term psychotherapy with adolescents who have schizoid disorder will eventually involve not only discussion of problems that exist in the present but also identity issues. Schizoid adolescents often are very vague about their motivations and future life directions. Therapy can be of great help to them in exploring various possibilities for their lives. The therapist should carefully evaluate the talents and capabilities of these adolescents so that an adequate data base for realistic vocational choices can be obtained. Termination of therapy with schizoid adolescents may be somewhat indefinite. When regular therapy is completed, it is often advisable to continue occasional visits once every six to 12 months for several years to provide a continuing contact that will make it easy for the adolescent to return to therapy when trouble develops. Although some adolescent patients may never need to return for further therapy, the eccentricities and rigidities that adolescents with schizoid disorder have often result in later periods of emotional difficulty.

In the treatment of both children and adolescents with schizoid disorder, adjunctive work with the family is of great importance. Not infrequently, one or both parents have emotional difficulties. Some of the parents themselves have schizoid personalities. It is always important to address the emotional pathology of the parents when it is present. Some parents feel gratification from the withdrawal of the schizoid child or adolescent. They may feel needed because the child or adolescent turns to the family for most emotional needs. If the parent responds to the emotional enticement of this situation, there is a strong tendency to keep the child or adolescent in an immature, dependent state. When this develops, the parents will often unconsciously thwart the therapist's efforts to develop better socialization skills in the child until their unconscious desires to keep the child in a dependent state are explored and interpreted.

In the case of healthier parents who do not have needs of their own that are met by the child's schizoid tendencies, the therapist's task is easier. Such parents genuinely wish to promote independence and better social adjustment for their children but are perplexed and confused about how to do this. The therapist can be of great help in carefully selecting areas of new interaction that will be tried by the child or adolescent. Extended family members may be of considerable assistance in the initial efforts to move the child into activities outside the nuclear family. Such family members often are privy to the difficulties that the child is experiencing and may provide major support during times when the patient visits them. For example, a schizoid adolescent girl who would never visit overnight with peers was persuaded to begin visiting the warm, accepting family of some cousins who lived in another town a short distance away. After successfully completing visits with these cousins and other relatives, she was then able to begin social activities outside the extended family. Over several years, she began limited dating and eventually married.

Timing is very important in work with schizoid adolescents. They respond much better to steady encouragement than to pressure. If they are pushed too hard or too rapidly, they immediately withdraw, and it may take weeks to return to the same level in therapy.

Family Therapy

Family therapy is a form of psychotherapy in which the major focus is on working with the family as a unit. It assumes that the interactions between family members significantly determine their behavior, and it emphasizes the importance of understanding the organization and structure of the family. An important tenet of family therapy is that families cannot be understood simply by studying the way the members function as individuals. Heavy emphasis in family therapy sessions is placed on improvement of communication skills within the family and developing changes in behavior by use of specific intervention techniques. Specific models of family therapy have been developed and are often associated with the names of major contributors to this field, such as Nathan Ackerman, Carl Whittaker, Virginia Satir, Jay Haley, Don Jackson, and Salvador Minuchin (Simon 1985). It is beyond the scope of this chapter to compare the various models of family therapy in their application to patients with schizoid disorder of childhood or adolescence. Rather, in the discussion that follows, some basic principles of family therapy that have application to all or most models will be stressed. It goes almost without saying that family therapy requires specific training and should only be attempted by therapists who have adequately developed their skills in this technique.

Since the major area of difficulty for patients with schizoid disorder involves social interaction and the most consistent involvement of these patients socially is with their families, it appears logical that family therapy would constitute a major modality for the treatment of these patients. Surprisingly, there is a great paucity of articles describing the use of family therapy with patients who have schizoid disorder. In contrast, McFarlane (1983) and many others have written extensively about the use of family therapy in schizophrenia.

At the beginning of family therapy with patients who have schizoid disorder, it is important that the therapist establish emotional contact with each family member emphasizing that, in the family therapy sessions, the family functions as a group in which the therapist acts as facilitator and leader. The family may be coming for treatment in part because they are disorganized, isolated from on another, and in conflict, but within the family therapy sessions they need to understand that all are participants. The therapist must remain accessible to all and should give each member a feeling that he or she is respected and understood. In the process of making certain that every member of the family is recognized as a participant, the therapist also begins the process of contracting with the family. The therapist establishes a contract with the patients in more or less formal terms that outline the goals, process, rules, and structure for family therapy. Before the process of introduction of significant change into the life of the family is begun, it is important for the therapist to have collected a careful history of the family members. Even young children can rather quickly be brought to an understanding that the family therapy group is directed toward problem solving. Problems within the family in their relationships with each other are addressed, and problems in the relationships of the family with neighbors, schools, and other groups outside the family are explored.

Patients with schizoid disorder have difficulty communicating emotionally with family members just as they do with other individuals. Parents and other family members often complain that the member with schizoid disorder does not let them know what he or she is really thinking. They also may express the feeling that when they communicate their thoughts to the child or adolescent with schizoid disorder, they are either ignored or misunderstood. In family therapy sessions it is particularly useful to teach all the family members to be open and explicit in their communications.

The vulnerabilities of the patient with schizoid disorder often result in anxiety about functioning outside the family. This is frequently compounded by the fact that many parents of these children and adolescents have themselves failed to resolve adequately conflicts around separation-individuation. When this is the case, the parents readily accept the child's or adolescent's reluctance to venture outside the family. Family therapy sessions offer an excellent opportunity for elucidating these tendencies and moving the family into a more productive life position (Berkowitz 1981).

The problem of enmeshment is a frequent one in families with one or more members with schizoid disorder. These families tend to turn inward on themselves and become isolated from the social community. The family members can become so dependent on each other for their emotional needs that even children in the family who do not have schizoid disorder may find it very difficult to establish normal participation in groups outside the family. In such families the members can, in family therapy sessions, frequently be brought to an understanding of the problems created by their enmeshment and gradually be led to try options for more extrafamily social interaction (Goldstein and Dyche 1983).

Scapegoating is frequently a significant problem in families of patients with schizoid disorder. These individuals are often different from other family members, occupy positions of relative isolation in the family, and have major difficulties in communicating. All of these characteristics make them particularly vulnerable to being used as a scapegoat in the family. The patient with schizoid disorder may be labeled as the sick member and may become the focus of family psychopathology. Such families may use the problems of the child or adolescent with schizoid disorder as a way of avoiding dealing with other family psychopathology. The family therapist can help the family understand scapegoating and then move them toward assumption of a coherent family organization in which roles are clearly defined and appropriate. Some of the ways in which family therapy can be of benefit are illustrated by the following case history:

> A 15-year-old boy with schizoid disorder of childhood was brought for treatment because of failing grades in school despite a high IQ, depression, and conflicts with his parents. He had two friends, both of whom were also very isolated adolescents. He spent many hours playing Dungeons and Dragons with his friends.
>
> His parents, both of whom were quite outgoing, expressed frustration at their inability to understand him. He was careless about chores and responsibilities at home but was not overtly rebellious. He became silent when his parents would reprimand him. He would not answer them nor speak to them for hours and sometimes a day or so after they reprimanded him. When his silence infuriated them to the point that they instituted punishment, he simply withdrew further.
>
> Eventually, the parents were able to understand that his refusal to communicate with them when they became angry was not entirely stubbornness but also carried a strong component of not knowing how to react when faced by their strong emotions.
>
> As the parents learned that they were overwhelming him, they began to relate to him more calmly and found to their surprise and pleasure that he could gradually com-

municate with them better. It also become apparent that putting heavy pressure on him to perform in school created such anxiety and anger that he performed less well rather than better. The parents became much more encouraging and supportive and agreed to allow him to attend a different school, with the result that his grades improved to average levels even though not to levels as high as those he seemed capable of.

Family therapy may be very useful in aiding all members of the family to understand the problems of the schizoid individual. Siblings who begin to view the schizoid patient as having emotional limitations rather than as being stubborn, difficult, or selfish can be of great help in bringing about improvement. Siblings as well as parents often become much more supportive as they begin to understand that the behavior of the schizoid child or adolescent is not entirely under voluntary control.

Group Therapy

Since difficulty in socialization is a major part of the schizoid disorder pattern, group therapy can be a very useful treatment if carefully conducted. In a group setting, the schizoid individual can observe the emotional reactions of others and develop a feeling that he or she has problems that are not totally different from those experienced by others. The interaction within the group often diminishes the sense of isolation felt by the schizoid individual. In group therapy, the schizoid individual is typically silent and hesitant to join in the group interaction. The group leader must be very supportive of the schizoid individual and must be able to intervene firmly if other group members begin to attack the schizoid person because of his or her silence. If gentle inquiries are made of the schizoid individual in a nonthreatening way, gradual participation in the group often occurs. Groups present immediate feedback to the patient with schizoid disorder regarding the way in which he or she is perceived by others. Sharing of their feelings in a group situation and learning experientially that they are not, in fact, harmed by their self-revelations can develop an increased capacity for openness. With group therapy, as with other modalities, the outcome is not usually a person who is radically open as compared to the condition before therapy but rather a person who can, with certain people and under particular circumstances, be open about some feelings. Although still reserved and shy, these individuals will have achieved major gains if they can share their feelings with even a few people since in the past they were closed emotionally to almost everyone.

Behavior Therapy

Behavior therapy has been used to develop a systematic plan for reinforcing desirable behavior and eliminating undersirable behavior. Difficulties in behavior are viewed as learned responses that can be corrected by new learning experiences. In respondent conditioning, the behavior therapist seeks to change the circumstances leading up to a particular behavior. Systematic desensitization is an example of respondent conditioning. Operant conditioning alters the circumstances following a behavior through carefully planned manipulation of the consequences that appear to control the behavior (Barker 1983). Schizoid children and adolescents at times respond well to these programs in part because such programs do not entail as much self-revelation as is the case with psychotherapy. In addition, schizoid individuals often see this approach as logical, although they may be resistant to admitting that some of the behaviors that are to be reinforced are actually desirable. Assertive responses are almost always introduced and reinforced. Relaxation techniques may be useful in helping children and adolescents deal with the high anxiety that they experience as they begin to be more assertive and attempt increased social interactions. Modeling techniques may also be used to promote desired responses.

Success of behavior therapy is often limited unless the child's environment—both intra- and extra-family—steadily reinforces new patterns of behavior (LaVietes 1980, p. 2613).

Many patients with schoizoid disorder have physical complaints during times of stress. Some patients within this group develop psychosomatic disorders. Marked difficulty in putting feelings into words (i.e., alexithymia) is often present. As is true with other alexithymic patients, behavioral techniques are often particularly useful in this group (Nemiah and Sifneos 1970; Sifneos et al. 1977).

Pharmacologic Treatment

Use of medications with patients who have schizoid disorder has little effect on the basic nature of the disorder. However, during times of stress, use of medications may be of help in returning the patient to an adaptative equilibrium. Many patients with schizoid disorder have periods when they manifest symptoms or characteristics of major depressive disorder. When these symptoms occur, treatment with an antidepressant such as imipramine in standard dosages is often quite helpful. Patients with schizoid disorder sometimes suffer periods of anxiety that may be incapacitating. These periods of anxiety may also need to be treated at times with medication. Although many schizoid patients respond well to low doses of neuroleptic medications such as thioridazine or haloperidol, other antianxiety agents are generally preferable because of the potential for serious side effects (e.g., tardive dyskinesia) with neuroleptic drugs. Children and adolescents with schizoid disorder who are acutely anxious often respond to short-term treatment with minor tranquilizers such as diazepam. Treatment with medications should not be carried out longer than absolutely necessary for reestablishment of the psychological equilibrium since the therapist obviously does not want to create a state of psychological or, in the case of the minor tranquilizers, physical dependence on drugs.

Environmental Manipulation

As has been mentioned previously, children and adolescents with schizoid disorder of childhood are acutely sensitive to their environment because they have such a limited repertoire of adaptive responses. Consequently, it is important for the therapist to examine the environment of the schizoid patient minutely to ascertain areas of stress. Teachers should be flexible and willing to find a compromise between allowing the child to follow his or her own inclinations completely on the one hand, or insisting that the child follow all the rules on the other. The therapist should encourage the patient to explore alternatives to stressful situations. The therapist's effort in doing this is directed toward helping the schizoid patient find environmental alternatives that are productive, rather than continuing the usual pattern of withdrawing into solitude and nonproductivity. The patient can be encouraged to reflect on which situations in the past have been good ones and which ones have caused unhappiness, thus beginning a process of developing guidelines that can be used in making personal choices. Schizoid patients often struggle with feelings that they must either behave exactly like their peers or avoid their peers. Gradually in therapy many of them are able to perceive that they can fit into society in a useful way while still maintaining a life pattern that is relatively free of those social interactions that create stress for them. Therapists should be creative in helping patients explore various environmental possibilities. For example, many schizoid patients have a strong tendency to pursue certain activities in great depth. These interests may involve hobbies (e.g., collecting books or antiques). Some of these activities may have the potential to become full-time occupational endeavors. Others may remain avocations but bring the schizoid child or adolescent into contact with a supportive group. Such groups, whose members are united by a single major interest, are often very tolerant of the behavioral eccentricities shown by schizoid individuals.

Patients with schizoid disorder do best when they have sufficient social contacts that allow them to feel that they are a useful part of society and are not weird or odd. When they pull back into a highly solitary existence, they almost always do this as a defensive maneuver rather than their choice of what they would like to have in terms of social interaction.

In children whose schizoid disorder appears to be either the result of a defensive reaction to overwhelming stress, with identification with a parent who has a schizoid personality disorder, schizophrenia, or schizotypal personality disorder, or the result of defective patterns of reinforcement, improvement is likely to occur much faster with environmental manipulation than in schizoid disorders of childhood that may have other etiologies.

Hospitalization and Residential Care

Hospitalization is necessary for only a small percentage of patients with schizoid disorder. When hospitalization does become necessary, it is usually because of a crisis, such as the development of an acute psychotic episode. Some patients with schizoid disorder become involved in drug abuse and, unless containment can be provided, may be very resistant to treatment. As Zinn (1979) pointed out, there are times when none of the interventions of outpatient practice or medication can interrupt the gratifications of an entrenched regressive pattern of behavior. For such patients, long-term residential care in a drug treatment facility is often necessary. Short-term hospitalization for detoxification frequently precedes such residential care.

Although residential care might be of great value in teaching socialization skills to most patients with schizoid disorder, in actual practice it is rarely used except for the circumstances just mentioned. One reason for this is that the parents of these patients do not regard their behavioral abnormalities as being sufficiently severe for as dramatic a step as residential care.

Case History

The following case history is illustrative of the manner in which several modalities of treatment are often used with patients with schizoid disorder.

> Leslie was seen at the age of 14 years because of anxiety, depression, and resistance to attending school. She had been seen six years previously with a school phobia that responded well to play therapy. Leslie was a bright, moderately attractive girl who was very isolated. She had no close friends and seemed content to focus her activities within her family. She was interested in reading and other solitary pursuits.
>
> Because of the severity of her depression, she was treated with antidepressants, and psychotherapy was begun. Her anxiety and depression improved greatly but her resistance to school continued for many months. When she reached the age of 16, she dropped out of school. She eventually enrolled in a correspondence high school course and obtained a high school diploma. She discussed many of her fears of social relationships

during therapy and gradually became able to engage in a wider spectrum of activities outside the family. At the age of 21, she was still living with her family and did not date. However, she was actively pursuing employment and eventually began work as a sales clerk in a local store, where she performed her job quite well.

Future Directions

Although patients showing the characteristics of schizoid disorder of childhood or adolescence have been reported for many years, this diagnostic category has only recently been described in behavioral terms that are generally applied. There now exist criteria that will make possible an increasing number of scientific studies of individuals who show this pattern. There is a great need for longitudinal studies to give hard data regarding outcome for children and adolescents who have schizoid disorder. This is a relatively rare condition, and it is likely that multicenter studies will be needed to elaborate the most effective treatment modalities for these patients.

While the diagnostic entity has been officially dropped from DSM-III-R, at least for now, the symptom complex remains with us and is very debilitating to the group of children and adolescents afflicted. With better understanding of the treatment of these young people, some of the disabling complications of the condition may be prevented.

Chapter 88

Treatment of Elective Mutism

Definition

Children who manifest elective mutism characteristically refuse to speak in school and to strangers. However, they can and do speak to specific people, usually one or both parents. Sometimes they speak to peers or to certain peers, and they nearly always speak to siblings. Although they tend to be shy and somewhat withdrawn, many of these children function effectively on a nonverbal level and may communicate extensively by using pantomine, nodding or shaking the head, or occasionally short verbal utterances. Some of the children have normal language skills, others have delay in language development or speech problems such as articulatory defects. Other disorders that may cause mutism (e.g., hearing loss, schizophrenia, hysterical aphonia and aphasia) should be differentiated from elective mutism. The onset is usually before the age of five, but the disorder is frequently not identified until the child enters school. This fact has led to some disputes regarding the frequency of this disorder in school-age children. A number of authors have pointed out that young children are frequently shy and reticent around strangers and that it is not uncommon for the preschool child to fall silent when spoken to by a stranger. This reticence persists in many children up to the time they enter school. It is not uncommon for kindergarten and first-grade teachers to relate that they have had children in their classes who were mute the first few days of school and who began to speak only after they became accustomed to the teachers and other children. Elective mutes, however, are those children who do not spontaneously abandon this behavior (Kolvin and Fundudis 1981; Laybourne 1979). Immigrant children seem to be particularly prone to be shy and reticent on entry into school; some of them do not spontaneously recover (Bradley and Sloman 1975; Brown and Lloyd 1975).

While elective mutism does not seem to be a disorder of adults, there are rare cases in the literature that indicate that it may persist well into early adolescence. Wergeland (1979) reported a case of an adult elective mute who spoke normally in a town where she was not known to have been mute, but she continued to be silent in her hometown when she returned for weekend visits.

The above findings are important considerations regarding the decision to treat or not treat any specific child. Obviously there are pitfalls at both ends of the spectrum. If a child is six years old and mute in school, the child has a statistically good chance of spontaneously recovering without treatment. On the other hand, it is incorrect to assume that elective mutes will "outgrow" the disorder in approximately two years.

Etiologic Considerations

The disorder of elective mutism has been conceptualized in many different ways by many different authors. Some therapists consider the pathology basically or exclusively within the child and focus their attention on the individual psychopathology of the child; they attempt to treat it with an analytic approach utilizing primarily play therapy and interpretation to resolve the conflict and remove the symptom (Chethik 1980). Another way of viewing the disorder is more systems oriented, that is, the disorder may be seen as a result of individual pathology within the mother, father, and child, and its interaction to produce the symptom (Browne et al. 1963). Learning theory has developed a number of approaches that seem to be successful in removing the symptom, but do not necessarily explain why the symptom developed in the first place. Some authors advocate the utilization of both behavior and family therapy techniques because they feel the behavioral therapy is effective in removing the symptom but the pathologic processes within the family need to be dealt with in order for the behavioral techniques to work. There are a number of observations that lend support to all of these formulations. There has been a tendency to combine several forms of therapeutic approach in the treatment of elective mutism. The eclectic form of therapy has the advantage that it can attack the disorder at a number of different levels simultaneously. The problems of evaluating any therapy for elective mutism are multiple. Many of the case reports are single cases. Some of the children have been treated previously by other therapists and other techniques. Some of the therapeutic interventions are carried on over a period of several years. Other life events occur, which could affect the symptomatology but are ignored by the author; there are no studies using control groups. Despite all these limitations, there is a body of information concerning well-documented approaches to these children, and it is possible to derive a logical treatment approach based on a careful evaluation of what seemed to be the important variables. Furthermore, over the last 25 years, there has been a tendency to recognize that a child is a biologic, psychological, and social being. As a result of this, there is more willingness on the part of various therapeutic schools to utilize approaches from other treatment modalities. Reed (1963) proposed that the syndrome of elective mutism be split into two categories on the basis of function and symptom, which he feels can represent 1) a normal learned behavior used as an attention-getting mechanism or 2) a fear-reducing device. The latter formulation is that proposed by most authors and presumably applies to the majority of cases. Clinical experience does confirm, however, that some of the children are not particularly sensitive and shy and rather enjoy the attention that their behavior attracts.

Treatment Procedures

Psychoanalytically Oriented Psychotherapy

In the early literature, a number of authors reported treatment of these children by the use of psychoanalytically oriented psychotherapy. Pustrom and Speers (1964) conceptualized the symptom as an expression of family conflict. The mothers were actively involved with the therapy and seen frequently. The fathers were seen occasionally but were less involved in the treatment. Direct therapy with the child was classic play therapy. The child was encouraged to use projective methods such as drawing, finger painting, and using a typewriter to communicate made up stories. The child was not pressed early or directly to talk. Instead, interpretations were offered, which focused on the aggressive aspects of talking and the child's demand for dependency relationships with the mother. In all three of the cases, the child eventually talked to everyone but the therapist.

Chethik (1980) reported in detail the intensive treatment of an elective mute, Amy. At the time he first saw her, she was six-and-a-half years old and presented the usual characteristics that elective mutes demonstrate. She was stubborn, passive, and had a withdrawing quality not only in her speech difficulty but in many areas of life. She began showing disturbances in her development as early as 16 months, when her brother was born. She had feeding difficulties and subsequently became overtly hostile toward the new baby. Toilet training was extremely difficult, and Amy had many accidents between the ages of two and three. During her third year, she scratched herself and inflicted many lesions on her skin. Chethik worked intensively in play therapy with Amy for approximately two years, during which time they worked on oral, anal, and phallic striving at various points in the treatment. He felt that the primary vehicle for therapeutic work was through the transference. Amy did recover from her mutism and did talk to everyone except the therapist.

The mother was seen on a regular basis through much of the time that Amy was in treatment. She became pregnant, however, and the father brought Amy during the later months of pregnancy. The mother was utilized basically as an informant regarding what had been happening to Amy between interviews, but there was some discussion of her attitudes about therapy and some of the reality problems the family was facing.

In contrast to this, Brown et al. (1963) described conjoint therapy of parents and child. The therapy was conceptualized as being directed toward helping the mother and father to clarify their relationship with each other as well as with the child. They stated that "the child needs to be helped to resolve his anxious hostile relationship toward his parents and adults in general and give up his neurotic mechanisms in order to mature psychologically." The following case illustrates these points:

Billy seemed to develop normally in the early months of his life. He said words at eight months and simple sentences at 18 months, but never used personal pronouns. Temper tantrums appeared at 16 months. The parents reacted differently to these, the father becoming angry and the mother trying to reason with the child. A maid who came in twice a week seemed best able to deal with Billy and his angry outbursts. At the age of 16 months, Billy developed urticaria that was present during the day, but disappeared during the night. At 22 months, he was hospitalized for four days with acute urticaria, which was generalized and severe. Billy cried for 18 hours without resting after being taken to the hospital. He wanted to turn the lights off and on constantly and to drink from the water fountain. No one was able to quiet him until, finally, the maid was called to the hospital and Billy stopped crying. The following day, when his mother appeared, Billy immediately began screaming and became upset. At the age of three, Billy stopped talking to the nurse on visits to the doctor's office. At the age of three-and-a-half, when the mother was in the hospital for the birth of the younger sister, Billy refused to talk to the aunt who cared for him. From that time, he became more selective of people to whom he would talk, eventually narrowing it to his immediate family, his two grandfathers, and neighborhood children, but only with the latter if they played without adult supervision. He would talk on the telephone to some adults to whom he would not talk in person. At the age of three-and-a-half, Billy became identified with Roy Rogers, and his sentences changed from "Billy wants" to "Roy wants." He would answer only to this name and had a cowboy hat from which he was inseparable. The parents felt he carried the pretense too far, seeming to live in a world of his own. At the age of four, his previously good toilet training broke down and he became enuretic at night. At the age of five, he was evaluated by the speech department. They found he was intellectually within normal limits and that he suffered from no speech pathology other than his mutism. Prior to coming to child psychiatry at the age of six, he was seen by a psychiatrist in private practice who tried working with Billy by also being mute. This was discontinued as Billy began screaming from the time they stopped at the doctor's office and had to be forced into the interview. Billy did not speak in class or on the playground during his kindergarten year, but asked his mother for a magic toy to make him talk at school. It is interesting that she seriously considered giving him a toy.

Billy was treated on an outpatient basis while he remained in his own home and in public school classes. He was seen for 27 months with a total of 125 treatment hours. For the first 13 months of treatment, there was difficulty in separating the boy from his mother. It appeared that the mother clung to him as much as he clung to her. Initially the therapist assured Billy he would not be pressured to talk. The first eight hours were characterized by passive, immature, and disorganized play. Always he came with his pockets full of bits of paper and string, which he began to show to the therapist after about 10 hours of therapy. By then he felt secure enough to begin hammering with his fists on the steel cabinets and on the screen and the window. The therapist permitted this behavior, but interpreted the angry feelings revealed. Billy became more aggressive with this and began throwing the ball at the therapist. Then he used the ball in many ways (e.g., to masturbate, to get bodily contact with the therapist, to show her where to go for the hour). At this point, it was necessary for her to prevent Billy from smearing paint or glue on her. The earliest communications with the therapist were animal sounds and "yes" and "no" sounds, which Billy made with his head in the wastebasket. Later, written notes were passed back and forth in the playhouses under the table. Next, he moved out to the blackboard. As his play became more integrated, he showed distinct regressive behavior with his therapist. He wanted more bodily contact. He would cling to her back or legs, would find opportunities to explore the therapist sexually, the latter behavior being limited repeatedly. He began to lie flat on the floor and close his eyes; next, he moved to lie across the legs of the therapist. After seven months of treatment, he urinated in the playroom. Three weeks later, while allowing himself to be held in the therapist's arms for the first time, he soiled. Following this, he wanted to be pushed around the playroom on a roller chair, while he held his head back against the therapist.

It was much like pushing a baby in the buggy. After nine months of no verbal communication other than that described above, the therapist began to feel angry and frustrated with Billy and told him so. He then began a limited speech in a falsetto voice. At the end of the year, he was building with bricks and beginning to make crude models with the train tracks and cars. He no longer fought limitations. He had stopped wetting the bed. After 13 months (80 hours), a decision to attempt to reenact the traumatic hospital experience was decided on. The playroom was set up for a hospital scene. A doll was placed in the crib, and an intravenous set was obtained with a hypodermic needle attached. He reacted to this by treating the doll with injections and sugar pills. Fascinated, he continued this play for the next three hours. Following the second hour, he broke out in giant urticaria, which lasted for the rest of the day. This was the first time he had experienced urticaria since he was in the hospital at the age of 22 months. The change following this spectacular physiologic regression was marked. In the third hour, Billy began talking freely in a normal voice. Once he had begun talking, he manifested resistance to coming to therapy. He told the therapist that his house had burned down and that he was moving away. The resistance lasted for the next five weeks. Then he began playing out some of the problems related to his home. His father had no car license, he had to go to jail, he had no money, etc. The ball had been neglected for the previous several months. He began playing with it again, but it was no longer used for bodily contact. He no longer behaved like a baby during his therapeutic hour.

In the last seven months, Billy worked through such things as cheating in play. He began talking to the children in school and reading in a very low voice. He had one recurrence of bed-wetting after three canceled appointments that had not been explained to him by his parents. During his therapy hours, he began to verbalize his feelings. The last six months, he went outside of the playroom for part of each hour. When he first began going outside of the playroom, he would not talk; then he began talking if there were no others around. Later he would speak while in the coffee shop when there were no strangers around. Later he talked with the therapist in the waiting room. Next there was a three-way conversation including his mother. His behavior improved markedly in all spheres. He became a leader with the children and did average or above average work in school. He included all relatives in his conversation. The teacher reported Billy began talking in the halls and in line, both places where speech was forbidden.

The mother was seen twice weekly for the first six months and then was seen once weekly for the last year and a half. In the early sessions, separation of the mother and child for the therapeutic hours was marked by extreme difficulty. She was tense and anxious and complained that she could not remember details about anything. It was difficult for her to express and clarify her feelings. The only emotion she could clearly identify was the intense anger that she experienced at certain times when she would lose control. This was dealt with and worked through during many therapeutic sessions with support, clarification, and interpretation. The mother became free enough to discuss her real feelings about her relationship with her husband and her own personal conflicts. She had a deep resentment toward her husband, which she was unable to express verbally in any constructive way and which came out in periodic explosive outbursts.

Because of her frustration with her husband, the mother had developed a symbiotic-like relationship to Billy. In the past she had sobbed and clung to him in an attempt to deal with her feeling of disappointment in her husband. Billy and his mother seemed to team up against the father in their anger. At times Billy was muted and closed up when in the presence of his father. There was a seductive quality in the mother's behavior with Billy, which she probably could not resolve until a more satisfactory relationship with the father was developed.

The mother was helped to allow Billy to establish independence in areas where he seemed competent and to recognize those instances where his need was for her to be more giving and supporting. Separation became less of a problem as she was able to recognize her own feelings of wanting and needing the child to cling to her. Firmness and consistency were hard for the mother to develop, but as she worked at it, she began to experience results, and Billy began to show a gradually increasing maturity.

During the early hours of the father's therapy, he attempted to keep the relationships superficial. He limited discussions to the problems with his son; deeper material was not dealt with. We knew from work with the mother that the father was acting out his conflicts; he was writing bad checks and was seriously in debt, thus threatening the financial integrity of the family. Since we felt it was undesirable to cross-communicate this material, we decided to deal with the acting-out by confronting the father with the fact that he was not paying his clinic bill and that he needed to pay this following each therapeutic session. He responded to this confrontation by continuing to "forget" to pay his bill and, when it was discussed with him, there was always an excuse. It became necessary for the therapist to remind the father in each session that he must pay the bill. It later became necessary for her to accompany him while he paid the bill. Even then, there were repeated attempts to escape by not having the correct change, trying to cash a bad check, and so on. Following the confrontation of the father around the failure to pay the bill, he began to work during his therapeutic hours. It became clear that he equated love and money and most of his acting-out had been centered around this conflict. He was able to talk about his discovery, at the age of 14, that his father was not really his father but his stepfather. Until that time he had always been industrious and hard working, but he suddenly changed and began to spend his stepfather's money recklessly and became a "playboy." Following his discussion of this episode, he began to handle his money better. It was not the end of his acting-out, however, regarding the clinic bill. He wrote a bogus check to the clinic from a bank where his wife had an account but he did not. It was decided that we would deal with this by means of a family conference, attended by both parents and their therapist, the child's therapist, and the clinic director. The mother was unaware of the fact that he had written a bad check to the clinic but on many previous occasions had either picked up his bad checks herself or had persuaded her husband's father to do so. In the conference, the self-destructive quality of the father's behavior and the mother's contribution to it was discussed with them.

Following the conference, the father began to pay his bill on a regular basis. In the therapeutic hours, he began to verbalize his feelings and developed considerable insight into his lifelong behavior disorder. He began working regularly as an insurance salesman and paying on the numerous bills he had incurred. He asked for a joint interview with his wife to discuss their mutual problems.

There would appear to be a direct correlation between the improvement in the father and the improvement in the child. It was apparent from the work with the child that he was aware of his father's financial difficulties and dishonesty. He verbalized it very clearly in the play sessions. When his father began to meet his responsibilities in a more mature way, the boy became more relaxed, and therapy with him progressed much more rapidly.

Behavioral Approaches

Behavior Modification

Laybourne (1979) reported in the earlier behavioral literature that "behaviorists conceptualize the symptom as a basic problem and do not hesitate to attack it directly, utilizing various degrees of coercion if necessary." Halpern et al. (1971) presented two cases of behavior modification. In the first case, the child was given a choice. When he had completed a test, he could either communicate verbally or tap his teacher's hand. Once this was accomplished, he was required to say "go" before leaving the room with his classmates. He was informed of this contingency in the class and received much praise from the teacher and classmates when, with some difficulty, he was able to comply. From this point on, his speech production spread to other areas, and his shy, withdrawn behavior improved markedly. Halpern also reported a case of electively mute twins who were successfully treated by behavior modification.

More recent reviews of the behavioral literature reflect a much more imaginative approach to the problem. The earlier attempts at treating elective mutism emphasized contingent, positive reinforcement for language imitation (Lovaas et al. 1966). Basically this is an approach where mouth movement, sounds, and word imitations are reinforced in hopes that this will eventually lead to speech. Apparently the problem with this approach is that the child experiences it as a direct assault on the mutism and tends to become resistant (Laybourne 1979).

Stimulus Fading

Another description of therapeutic approach involves the child talking to the parent as he or she is approached by nonfamily members. This theme is repeated in a number of papers, as the following study by Conrad et al. (1974) illustrates:

> An 11-year-old American Indian child who had never spoken a word in the reservation classroom during the entire five years of her schooling was treated by behavioral therapy that employed stimulus fading procedures. The theoretical approach was to place the child in a situation where the child readily responded verbally. This was done by first having the therapist go to the home where the mother was present and having the mother ask the child to respond to flash cards presented by the therapist. The therapist then reinforced the child with candy when she responded to flash cards. Gradually they left the home with the therapist and went to the psychology clinic with the patient and classmate, who was a friend of the patient. Again the patient was given arithmetic and spelling flash cards and reinforced for responses. Then the teacher was brought to the mental health clinic with the classmate friend and the mental health technician present. Finally the teacher instead of the mental health workers presented the flash cards. When responses were firmly established, the teacher moved to the classroom with the patient and five classmates and then finally with the entire class present. The patient was reinforced for responding. Follow-up a year later indicated that the child spoke when spoken to in a routine class situation but rarely spontaneously verbalized or initiated conversation. Verbal behavior was no longer considered a problem by school officials.

Relaxation Technique

Croghan and Cravan (1982) presented a case of elective mutism extending over five years. They at first treated the child by placing her in a resource room with two other children and a teacher and rewarding verbal responses. This was disappointing in its results so they changed the paradigm because they realized that the basic problem seemed to be anxiety rather than attention seeking. With the help of a therapist, the child developed a hierarchy ranging from the mildest to the severest anxiety. A therapist introduced the technique of relaxation to her, and she was assigned home exercises involving systematic desensitization to the hierarchy of anxiety-producing events. This approach led to her talking in school and in all situations, and she apparently made a complete recovery. The authors indicated, however, that they probably would have had better and quicker results had they used the technique of stimulus fading by having people with whom the child was accustomed to speaking (e.g., mother, father, siblings, or familiar peers).

Combination Approaches

Paraverbal therapy. Heimlich (1981) described a therapeutic technique called paraverbal therapy in which she uses another patient as an assistant therapist in working with the children.

> She utilized a nine-year-old boy with a conduct disturbance and poor self-control to work with her in helping a nine-year-old girl with depression and elective mutism. Her

therapy took place in a hospital setting. Apparently stimulus fading had been utilized because the patient talked freely to her family at school, but she communicated with her teacher and fellow students only by using a toy telephone. The therapist encouraged both children to use musical instruments for communication. The boy used symbols to express his feelings, and the patient followed suit rather feebly. The therapist then introduced a folk song with lyrics that allowed the children to insert words that had to do with their feelings. The girl chose the word "crying" and began to communicate in a sentence that she felt like someone had gone off on a trip and left her alone. The boy was able to express his feelings of anger toward his parents and admit that he hit the other children when they teased him because his parents did not visit him. He was encouraged by the therapist to say something that would make him feel better but yet not get him into trouble. He finally yelled the word "shit." The patient was encouraged to imitate him and was able to express her own angry feelings by using the same word. The children were then encouraged to engage in other activities with play materials that would express their feelings. This treatment format is reminiscent of stimulus fading in that it introduces a peer with whom the new child is presumably acquainted and specific instruments are used to encourage speech. It also uses techniques reminiscent of Norman and Broman (1970), who used visual feedback from a volume level meter of a tape recorder to induce sounds and raise volume in an electively mute boy. The third factor in therapy is a psychodynamically oriented one in that the children are both encouraged to express their feelings regarding experiences with their parents.

Family therapy.   There have been several observations that support the use of family therapy: the symbiotic aspects of the family system (Browne et al. 1963; Mora et al. 1962); suspiciousness of the outside world and fear of strangers (Browne et al. 1963; Goll 1979); language difficulties, particularly in children of immigrants (Bradley and Sloman 1975); and marital disharmony (Browne et al. 1963; Meijer 1979). Mothers of elective mutes have been described as being resentful of fathers and pleased when children do not talk to the fathers (Browne et al. 1963; Meijer 1979). Modeling of mutism has also been described (Browne et al. 1963; Goll 1979).

Meyer (1984) described a case of elective mutism treated with a family system approach. She used Goll's formulation of the family of elective mutes. The participants in the family were divided into the elective mute model and a family member that did not talk when angry or afraid, a symbiotic partner that was a family member closely tied to and dependent on the identified patient, and a ghetto leader, a person or persons who distrust society and its official representatives. She pointed out that the child of an immigrant family is confronted with frightening strangers when starting kindergarten. Oftentimes the nuclear family speaks the language of their native country while the child is expected to talk to strangers in an unfamiliar language not spoken at home. If the above model is used to explain elective mutism, then obviously a family systems framework would be needed to successfully treat a case of elective mutism. Meyer (1984) reported the case of a five-year-old Chinese-American girl identified as the patient.

Her mother was her mute model since she learned from her to be silent as a way of dealing with anxiety and manipulating others' behavior. The mother and daughter were "symbiotic partners who needed others to survive." The seven-year-old brother was the sibling partner and the target of her anger and hostility. The father was identified as the ghetto leader through whom all communication in the family went. She stated that the family was characterized by extreme shyness and suspiciousness of the outside world, with language difficulties, marital disharmony, and strong tensions. As has been so often described in immigrant families, the mother and daughter symbiotic relationship seems to be the result in part of an unsatisfactory relationship between the mother and father. Therapy was directed toward working on and improving the marital relationship, which in turn weakened the symbiotic relationship between the mother and child without being a direct threat to the child. The child in turn developed a therapeutic relationship with the therapist, which reduced her need to depend on her mother. The child's silence was conceived as representing, at least in part, an intense loyalty to her traditional Chinese family. The silence protected her from revealing any family secrets in the perceived unfriendly environment of a diverse American society. The patient was not only treated in classic family therapy sessions with the child and the entire family together, but she was also seen in play therapy at her home and in the therapist's office. The author did not state how long therapy lasted, but did say that following therapy she had three follow-up visits over a span of four years. In that time, the child became verbal and her mother was functioning as an independent women with a voice in the family. The father, who had trouble with headaches, became headache-free and the brother who had asthma became free of asthma. The author did not describe any specific verbal interchanges between herself and the parents or the patient, nor did she describe any verbal interactions among the family members during family sessions. Consequently the reader has no clear idea of exactly how the therapeutic interventions were brought about.

Combined family therapy and behavior therapy approach.   It is not surprising that a combination of family therapy and behavioral therapy has evolved in the treatment of these children. The literature repeatedly reflects the fact that many of these children live in families that foster continuation of the symptom. It would seem logical not only to intervene with behavioral techniques to eliminate the symptom of mutism, but also to intervene with family therapy to restructure the family dynamics. Rosenberg and Lindblad (1978) took what they called a two-pronged approach. They felt that no attempt should be made to coerce the child to speak. This in turn should eliminate the struggle between the child to maintain the mutism and the family, teachers, and therapists who may have tried to get the child to speak. The only reference to mutism that is made to the child in the family setting is that the child will begin speaking when he or she feels that things are going better in the family. It is the goal of starting with family therapy to remove the pressure from the child and to examine the family system that has been dysfunctional. They conceptualized that a behavioral paradigm "gives the child an out so that he can begin to speak." They stated:

> As the child begins to speak in the family setting the therapist can state matter of factly that the mutism is no longer the problem since the child is now speaking. The clinician can proceed from there and continue to work on family interactional problems.

They presented the case of a six-and-a-half-year-old boy who did not speak in kindergarten and was in the first grade at the time treatment began. They divided the report into two sections, stating that a thorough evaluation involving all family members was done and then treatment began:

> For 15 sessions, three times a week, the patient, his sister, and his mother were seen. By applying reinforcement theory, counterconditioning, and progressive approximations, they were able to reduce the patient's behavioral constriction with the therapist as well as getting his speech to generalize within his family and to people outside the family. Nevertheless, he was not talking at school. It was at this point that the therapist arranged to make home visits because the father was confined to the home, recuperating from a foot injury. There were a total of four family sessions. Tony and his mother sat together whispering to each other while his father complained that he couldn't hear what was being said. It was at this time that the father spoke of a childhood accident that had left him deaf for about four years, and it was during this time that the children at school teased him by always whispering. The therapist identified the father, not the mother, as the person who found Tony's not talking in school intolerable. In subsequent sessions, it became clear that there was a coalition between the mother and child, which the mother

used as a way of retaliating against the father for his lack of involvement with the children. At the same time, she contributed to his distance by attempting to persuade him that he was too sick to come down from his bedroom to participate in the family sessions. As a result of these interventions, the husband-and-wife relationship improved, which left the patient no longer triangulated by his parents. He began speaking spontaneously at school shortly after this. Six-year follow-up indicated that the patient had made a satisfactory adjustment on entering junior high school.

Pharmacologic Approaches

A search of the literature failed to reveal any reports of the use of drug therapy to treat elective mutism. There is a group of children who literally seem to be afraid of the sound of their own voice; if they hear their own voice on a recording, they will respond with rapid heartbeat, shallow breathing, sweating, and tremor, and frequently bolt from the room (Hayden 1980).

Work with phobic adults and adolescents had demonstrated the efficacy of a combination of tricyclic antidepressants and benzodiazapine. Treatment with these drugs reduces anticipatory anxiety and panic attacks to a level that is manageable by the patient so that he or she can learn more appropriate responses to the situation. It would seem logical that speech-phobic children would respond in a similar manner. This hypothesis remains to be tested.

Comment

In view of the fact that electively mute children make up such a heterogenous group, it is not surprising that various therapeutic techniques have evolved. A review of the literature reflecting the current state of the art would seem to encourage an eclectic approach, with one or more different techniques being utilized. While stimulus fading seems to be a successful technique in many of the cases reported, it is unlikely that stimulus fading would be successful in treating a child who was severely enmeshed in a family struggle between the mother and father or who was a member of an immigrant group.

Children in enmeshed families and children of immigrant groups probably need family therapy intervention as well as behavior modification. Children with a background of severe abuse may not respond to treatment in their home unless therapeutic intervention is able to protect them from further abuse. Although most follow-up studies indicate that the children do well once they have given up the symptom of elective mutism, there are studies that indicate that the disappearance of a symptom of mutism is not necessarily related to good future adjustment. This fact should be kept in mind when dealing with this group of children.

Chapter 89

Oppositional and Other Immature Personality Disorders of Childhood

The DSM-III-R classifications of children with interpersonal behavior problems are as oppositional or conduct disorders (American Psychiatric Association 1987). The diagnoses of passive-aggressive, dependent, and narcissistic personality disorders are limited to adolescence and adulthood. Whether or not they should be applied to children is controversial. Excluding children is based on the belief that children do not have fixed personality traits as do adults. It also reflects an effort to avoid imposing clinical concepts of adults on children and a reluctance to assign the unfavorable prognosis associated with adult personality disorders to children.

While these considerations are valid, there is empirical research and clinical evidence that the oppositional and conduct disorder categories do not apply to large numbers of children with immature personality traits that interfere with their interpersonal relationships and academic performance (Achenback 1980; Westman 1989). Although manipulating authority figures and failing to meet adult expectations, these children are not overtly disobedient and defiant nor do they violate the rights of others or societal standards. They do show repetitive behavioral patterns, often evident for years. These children fit the criteria for the adult personality disorders formerly regarded as immaturity reactions. Moreover, the correspondence between their manifestations in childhood and adulthood derives from their common origins in characterologic arrests at early developmental stages.

Because they all are expressed through immature personality traits, the oppositional, passive-aggressive, narcissistic, and dependent personality disorders will be discussed in this chapter. Our understanding of these disorders, however, is hampered by their lack of specific symptoms (e.g., phobias, elective mutism) that would facilitate diagnostic consensus and follow-up studies.

Character Structures and Personality Traits

First of all a discussion of what is meant by personality is appropriate because of the varied usages of the term. A useful distinction can be made between personality traits and character structures. The word *character* is derived from roots that mean engraved essential qualities; the term *personality* derives from roots that mean the external presentation of a person as in the persona, or mask, of an actor. Thus personality traits can be defined as external behavior manifestations of the internal operations of character structures, which include temperamental, cognitive, and thinking styles in addition to impulse control, values, and self-concepts. Examples of personality traits are negativism, forgetfulness, stubbornness, and shyness.

The classic personality disorders, such as the schizoid, antisocial, and borderline types, are the result of defects in character structures. In accordance with the preceding distinction between character and personality, the term *character disorder* is more appropriate for them and for the conduct disorders of childhood. The term *immature personality disorder* can be used when character structures are intact but operate at levels with personality traits characteristic of earlier stages of development. The evidence suggests that childhood character defects are more likely than immature personality traits to persist into adulthood (Robins 1966)

The development of character structures is influenced by genes, cultural values, conflicts between drives and the external world, and family relationships. Through families, the social order reproduces itself in the character structures of children. In this sense, one's character structures are the biologic crystallizations of cultural and sociological processes of a given epoch, so that their reflection in personality traits varies with the times.

In addition to their sociocultural origins, character structures also can bind anxiety in the same sense as do neurotic symptoms. Psychoanalytic formulations of pathologic character development provide a useful conceptual framework for psychotherapy with children who have personality disorders. Reich's (1949) classic work called attention to a model of the way in which character structures can form as armory against the expression of unconscious drives.

The body armoring of oral eroticism may be expressed through personality traits based on characterologic passivity and expecting entitlement to personal gratification. The armoring of anal eroticism may produce an exaggerated external locus of control and lead to personality traits involving struggles for power with others. The armoring of urethral eroticism may inhibit focused aggressiveness and lead to personality traits that avoid competitiveness.

Character structures also are formed in the crucible of family relationships, and resulting personality traits evoke responses in others to actualize unconscious fantasies (Sandler 1981). These fantasies associated with repressed drives hover beneath conscious awareness like phantoms and shape behavior that reenacts infantile relationships in current situations and evokes corresponding responses from other people. The resulting personality traits are compromises between underlying wishes and the fear of expressing them. Like neurotic symptoms, these personality traits permit the disguised appearance of forbidden unconscious wishes. Unlike neurotic symptoms, discomfort is not directly experienced by the child but results from clashes and misunderstandings with other people.

Thus immature personality disorders are habitual patterns of reacting based on degrees of fixation of character structures at earlier stages of development. Their behavioral manifestations are persistent caricatures of behavior seen at a particular earlier stage of development.

In the immature personality disorders, behavioral traits predominate in interpersonal manipulative patterns without prominent subjective symptoms. These disorders prevent the age-appropriate sublimation of drives and inhibit character development. The children engage in maladaptive patterns of behavior that are self-defeating even though they achieve pyrrhic victories in the manipulations of other persons. Furthermore, their capacities for empathy are impaired by interpersonal maneuvers in which other persons are regarded as objects to be manipulated rather than as collaborators in life. Discomfort is experienced by parents and teachers more than by the children, whose motivation for change usually is low. Accordingly, treatment must rely initially on family and behavioral methods. Still, a psychotherapeutic focus on the children's intrapsychic issues is needed to promote the maturing of character structures.

General Principles of Treatment

The trend toward outgrowing immaturity and the behavioral expressions of immature personality disorders in interpersonal relationships and schoolwork cloud the objective evaluation of the effectiveness of specific treatment methods. Because they reflect immaturity, the immature personality disorders would appear to offer a more favorable prognosis with treatment during childhood than during adulthood. Because of their personal, familial, and social roots, optimal treatment should involve several levels (Group for the Advancement of Psychiatry 1982). Therefore, a clinical-family-educational team approach based on a psychiatric diagnostic formulation is important. These children require a combination of family and individual psychiatric and specialized educational techniques over extended periods of time because of the need for changes in their family, teacher, and peer relationships and academic achievement.

The first stage of treatment should focus on disentangling family members from pathologic interactions. The treatment of parents and siblings in family therapy, and sometimes in marital couple and individual psychotherapy, is necessary. The progress of family psychotherapy can be enhanced by communication between the parents and school through establishing a regular reporting system that defines expectations of the child and brings out how responsibility is being handled by the child.

At the same time, only gradual improvement in the child's motivation and responsiveness to rational interventions can be anticipated. Thus the timing and nature of educational interventions are important. When specific educational disabilities exist, the focus should be on helping the child and parents understand their nature and obtaining tutoring designed to remediate them. The child's response to tutoring can be used in family psychotherapy as a source of information about a child's conflicts. At the same time, strengthening the child's academic skills relieves anxiety and embarrassment in school. When available, group therapeutic techniques in the school can be helpful in reversing peer rejection and isolation.

As family therapy progresses, a variety of options can be pursued, depending on the needs of each child and family. Marital couple therapy may be needed to address marital tensions and to strengthen the parental relationship. Parent educational materials can be useful in handling discipline and in promoting autonomy of children through behavioral management techniques (Patterson 1976). Intensive individual psychotherapy can be employed to expose and resolve intrapsychic conflicts that underlie developmental arrests. Imaging techniques can help family members become more sensitive to their inner lives. Desensitization techniques can be useful in overcoming phobic symptoms that may emerge in the child. Education in communication and problem-solving strategies can be helpful in family administrative matters. Because psychotherapy inevitably touches sensitive parental and marital issues and because the children lack motivation to change, resistances to treatment from both parents and children can be anticipated.

Specific Treatment Considerations

The immature personality disorders share the common elements of fixation at early developmental stages, incomplete assuming of responsibilities for one's actions, self-defeating life-styles, frustrating interpersonal relationships, and varying degrees of underachievement in schoolwork. These children fall short of assuming age-appropriate responsibility for their lives.

The specific classification of these immature, self-defeating children is warranted because certain personal characteristics and family patterns have different treatment implications. Although clear-cut distinctions are not always possible, the following children can be identified in clinical populations: 1) the oppositional child, who openly resists adult influence; 2) the passive-aggressive child, who overtly complies while covertly sabotaging adult authority; 3) the narcissistic child, who feels entitled to complete effortless gratification; and 4) the dependent child, who helplessly clings to adults. The treatment strategies and issues for each disorder are summarized in Table 1. The format and duration of the treatment depend on the psychopathology of the child and of other family members.

Oppositional Personality Disorder

The essential feature of the oppositional personality disorder is a pattern after the third year of life of excessively disobedient, negativistic, and provocative opposition to authority figures, especially parents and teachers (Gilpin and Maltz 1980). It has

Table 1. Treatment Strategies for Immature Personality Disorders

Treatment Strategy	Oppositional Personality Disorder	Passive-Aggressive Personality Disorder	Narcissistic Personality Disorder	Dependent Personality Disorder
Aim	Individuation as autonomous person	Sublimation of aggressive drives	Empathic reciprocal relationships	Independent self-responsibility
Core targets	Contrary defiance; power-seeking control	Martyred superhero; revenge-seeking saboteur	Selfishness, omniscience and omnipotence; attention-seeking entitlement	Infantile care seeking; magical avoidance of growing up
Family therapy focus	Parental ambivalence	Parental suppression of aggression	Parental indulgence and adulation	Parental overprotection; parent-child triangulation
Behavior therapy focus	Defuse parental battle through extinguishing; child chooses from options; framing expectations	Foster personal successes; sublimating athletic and musical activities	Limit setting; building frustration tolerance; fostering reciprocal empathy	Desensitization of phobic fears; reward personal responsibility
Child psychotherapy focus	Define self-boundaries; expose self-doubt, indecisiveness	Insight for self-defeating behavior; expose hostility	Expose painful vulnerability, low self-respect, projection, denial	Expose fear of aggressiveness

been regarded as a precursor of the passive-aggressive personality, although it is seen in its characteristic form throughout childhood (Group for the Advancement of Psychiatry 1966).

These children display an oppositional attitude even when contrary to their interests and well-being. If a suggestion is made, they are against it; if asked to do something, they refuse or become argumentative; and if asked to refrain from an act, they feel obliged to carry it out. When thwarted, they have temper tantrums. They do not regard themselves as oppositional but see others as making unreasonable demands on them.

During the first year of life, developmental oppositional behavior in response to painful situations protects an infant through recoiling from noxious influence and gaining time for recovery, such as in passive resistance to being awakened and active resistance to being fed. In the process of later individuation, the capacity to resist external influence enables a child to develop his or her own inner resources. Thus developmental oppositional behavior prior to the third year of life actually is not hostile, but is protective and self-defining (Levy 1955).

When one's personality traits are oriented around opposition, however, a child negativistically defines oneself in terms of what one is against rather than what one is for. Negativism spawns contrariness, rigidity, and social isolation in the child rather than independent self-control and self-esteem. Consequently, interpersonal relationships for these children revolve around issues of control.

The principal aim of treatment for the oppositional child is achieving individuation as an autonomous person. The therapeutic targets are the child's power-seeking contrariness and defiance. Through family therapy, the parents can be helped to identify their own ambivalence, which embroils them in fruitless power struggles with the child. The parent-child struggles can be defused through behavioral techniques that place responsibility on the child for decision making. This can be done through giving the child options from which to choose and extinguishing confrontations over issues of authority. Ignoring oppositional behavior and rewarding cooperative behavior also are helpful in defusing interpersonal conflicts (Strain et al. 1982), as are framing statements that provide rationales and consequences for behavioral expectations. Psychotherapy with the child can focus on the development of self-boundaries and exposure of the child's indecisiveness and self-doubting, which reflect an underlying fear of assuming responsibility.

Case Example

A seven-year-old boy was referred because of failing grades in school, uncooperativeness, negativism, and fighting with peers. At home he was argumentative and defiant. As a young child he showed excessive separation reactions from his parents but habitually opposed their authority.

After the initiation of family therapy, a long-standing pattern of parental arguments was disclosed. It became evident that the parents were generally critical of their son, constantly correcting and attempting to change him. After several months of family therapy focused on parent-child relationships, the parents could see that they were reacting to the unacceptable parts of themselves reflected in their son. By monitoring each other, they then altered their approach to him from one of making demands to one of providing options from which he could choose. They also were helped to frame their expectations of him so that the rationale for his compliance would be clear to him.

The format of treatment then shifted to marital couple therapy and individual psychotherapy for the boy. Over the next year, the parents worked on resolving their own tendencies to project their unacceptable self-concepts on each other. In his psychotherapy, the boy revealed his own indecisiveness and lack of individuation from his mother. He divulged his fear that he would lose a battle of wills, and his own identity, if he submitted to her. As he acknowledged his appropriate dependency on the therapist in the transference, he more appropriately accepted the influence of his parents and teachers. The overall course of treatment was two years, including a gradual termination phase. At that time, he achieved at grade level in school. The family style of disagreement continued at a tolerable level consistent with the skepticism of his scientist parents.

Passive-Aggressive Personality Disorder

The essential feature of the passive-aggressive personality disorder is indirect resistance to adult expectations of adequate performance in school and social functioning. In contrast with oppositional children, these children are compliant while sabotaging adult expectations. This occurs most clearly in schoolwork, in which their aim is to fail, a subtle but effective expression of their resentment toward adults.

These children react to the expectations of others by automatic negative inner responses with obsessional neurotic qualities (Mallinger 1982). They tend to magnify the coercive aspect of situations and are preoccupied with a paranoid sense of being endangered by external demands. When they perceive an external expectation that they do something, conscious reluctance is experienced. Usually there is initial outward compliance, while progressive inner resentment grows. Leaving something undone, then, represents a refusal to yield completely to a perceived demand. Boredom, fatigue, loss of interest, resentment, and fantasies of the quality of martyred superheroes often are experienced.

These children feel unfairly treated and resent expected schoolwork and resist indirectly through such maneuvers as procrastination, dawdling, stubbornness, intentional inefficiency, and forgetfulness. They are late for classes, do not keep promises, forget to bring schoolwork, and do not complete tasks. They claim self-sufficiency but lack independent self-reliance. Their grades in school progressively slip downward.

Passive-aggressive behavior is self-defeating because it impairs productivity and interpersonal relationships. It is accompanied by a lack of a sense of ownership of one's endeavors, culminating in a feeling of estrangement from running one's own life and a loss of a sense of volition (Perry and Flannery 1982). Life, then, is experienced as a perpetual exertion of false autonomy through undercutting others (Mallinger 1982).

These children may have been confused by their own parents' sabotage of their performance through lack of confidence in them (McIntyre 1964). As children, they may have been subjected to a barrage of prohibitions, warnings of danger, cautions, discouragement of risk taking, and suppression of self-expression. In that atmosphere, their own acceptability depended on adhering to parental prohibitions and expectations. Thus their passive-aggressive behavior may have been the only safe way to express resentment within a suppressive hierarchical family (Parsons and Wicks 1983).

The overall aim in treating the passive-aggressive child is achieving sublimated channels for the expression of aggressive drives. The principal therapeutic targets are the child's revenge-seeking behaviors that express underlying martyr and superhero fantasies. When the parents have been able to recognize and manage their own suppressive tendencies with their child in family therapy, they can employ behavioral techniques that award progressively increasing responsibility to the child. They specifically can foster personal successes for the child and sublimate aggressiveness through supporting the child in personally attractive activities (e.g., athletics, music). Psychotherapy with the child aims to expose underlying hostility and to promote insight regarding the self-defeating nature of the child's sabotage of adult authority.

Case Example

A 10-year-old boy was referred because of underachievement; he did not work in school or at home. His forgetfulness, stubbornness, procrastination, and carelessness frustrated his parents and teachers, who knew he could obtain high grades if he only would try to do so. As a young child, toilet training was prolonged, and he showed little interest in playing with other children.

Family therapy over the course of six months disclosed that the parents had held high expectations for their son and criticized his shortcomings from the time of school entry. His father had been a poor student in school and wanted his son to excel. Parental efforts to punish their son were unsuccessful and only resulted in further deterioration in school performance. When the parents could see that their son was sabotaging their goals for him, they shifted their emphasis to realistic rewards for his achievements. Then family therapy sessions were held at monthly intervals, and a reporting system was implemented in which the boy carried feedback between his teachers and parents on a day-by-day, subject-by-subject basis. This permitted recognition of achievements and more detailed knowledge of the aspects of schoolwork that were difficult, so that the parents became aware of the frustrations in their son's daily life, including those with peers.

During a subsequent 12-month course of psychotherapy, including several family meetings, the boy revealed his paranoid stance in which he felt that others were against him, thereby justifying his vengeance. As he felt the support of his parents and teachers, he could acknowledge that he had fallen behind in academic skills and accept tutoring with the school's resource teacher to remedy them. He ultimately obtained passing grades in school and devoted himself to athletics.

Narcissistic Personality Disorder

Narcissism can be defined as an affectively laden fantasy of perfection with the conception of oneself as omniscient and omnipotent (Rothstein 1980, 1983). As such, it is not pathologic when a reflection of the egocentricity of early life.

Preadolescent children show narcissism in the form of cognitive conceit as they gradually relinquish the omniscience of earlier life and prefer their own views over those held by adults. A much more intense investment in the veracity of their own ideas, however, is seen in children with narcissistic personality disorders. They may have failed as toddlers to realize that their parents were imperfect separate individuals with their own interests and to relinquish gradually the illusion of their own grandiosity.

The immature state of narcissistic children's character development is reflected in their persistent syncretic merging of ideas, emotions, and actions. If their ideas do not prevail through action, they experience painful insult. They feel entitled to the adulation of others and to have their wishes granted. Because they believe that they are omnipotent and omniscient, they deny their weaknesses and lack of knowledge. They cannot bear to make mistakes, are intolerant of frustration, and are enraged by criticism. School may have little to offer them because they "know it all." Through the defense of projection, responsibility for their personal failures or unhappiness is attributed to others.

Older narcissistic children are conceited, self-centered, vain, and admiration seeking. At the same time, they paradoxically lack self-respect. Actually, because love tends to overestimate the loved one, love and respect are different. One can love another person but not respect that person. The same applies to love of oneself. Narcissistic children may love, and consequently overestimate, themselves; however, they lack self-respect and seek the adulation of others. When they do obtain the attention of others, they find that their own self-respect is not enhanced and feel that they have "fooled another one."

The grandiose lives of these children are on a collision course with the people around them. They pursue self-destructive life courses based on guilt stimulated by their murderous rage at frustrating persons whom they also depend on. Angry demandingness, prolonged screaming, and occasional violence mark them as exceptional from their earliest years (Noshpitz 1984). Narcissistic children can tolerate neither their own defects nor the less than ideal nature of others, of whom they are hypercritical. They feel entitled to the presence of ideal persons. Consequently, they are easily slighted and attack others as deficient or unfair. They show hostile behavior in school, where they react to authority with defiance, temper outbursts, and testing of limits. In addition to academic underachievement because of their uncooperative attitude, they may be feared by teachers and other children when they lose control of their emotions.

The overall aim of treatment is the narcissistic child's achievement of awareness of the reciprocity of human relationships so that empathy becomes possible. The specific targets of treatment are the child's omnipotence, omniscience, sense of entitlement, and attention seeking. Family therapy can help the parents recognize their own use of the child, such as for exalting their own narcissism. Behavioral interventions can be employed to set limits, teach frustration tolerance, and sensitize the child to the consequences of one's behavior on others. This can be accompanied by efforts to help the child accept the realistic limitations of oneself and others. Individual psychotherapy with the child can be employed to expose the painful vulnerability and helplessness that underlie the defenses of denial and projection.

Case Example

A nine-year-old boy was initially referred because of underachievement in school, temper tantrums, and arrogant behavior. He refused to do schoolwork, which he regarded as boring. His parents viewed him as a gifted child and blamed the school for failing to stimulate him. He dominated two younger siblings.

In this case, the treatment strategy initially emphasized three months of family therapy, which exposed the parental idolization of their son and subtle support of his arrogance with teachers and peers. When they finally were able to recognize the way in which their attitudes were backfiring and that their son actually was lagging in reading skills because he had not applied himself in earlier reading instruction, the parents began to set firm limits and penalize failure to perform schoolwork and arranged for reading tutoring.

In individual psychotherapy, the boy gradually (over the course of a year) came to grips with his intolerance of making mistakes and exposing his vulnerability.

Repeated gentle confrontations by his therapist helped him to recognize the impact of his behavior, first on the therapist and then on others. He discovered that his own behavior impeded fulfillment of his own selfish interests. His growing ability to acknowledge his lack of knowledge and skill made it possible for him to assume the role of student in school and to accept the assistance of teachers and peers in reaching his goals. The course of treatment concluded with several family meetings in which the recognition of his realistic role as an older brother permitted him to relinquish exercising illegitimate power over his younger siblings.

Dependent Personality Disorder

The essential feature of the dependent personality disorder is passively allowing others to assume responsibility for major areas of one's life. These children subordinate their own needs to those of others on whom they depend to avoid having to be self-reliant. Such children behave immaturely and resort to whiny, clinging behavior that demands the attention of adults. They abdicate responsibility for making decisions about how to dress, what to eat, what to do, and with whom to associate. They are consciously fearful of initiative and assuming responsibility.

These children show a conspicuous absence of sustained activity with a sense of deliberateness and intention. They lead unplanned lives and drift with the prevailing current (Shapiro 1965). For them, knowing facts signifies independence and thinking for themselves signifies growing up with responsibility for themselves. Both of these are perceived as dangers, which stimulate anxiety and block the learning process.

The dependent personality has been described in the literature as "pseudoimbecility," "pseudobackwardness," "pseudostupidity," and "learning impotence." The children manifesting this syndrome conceal knowledge through ineptitude in schoolwork but appear to be indifferent to their failures and actually wield power over adults through their passive-dependent behavior (Westman and Bennett 1985). These children depend on others for direction. For example, one boy had to be reminded to get up in the morning, get dressed, catch the bus, take out his pencil in class, work on his lesson, take books home, do his homework, take a shower, and go to bed. None of these things would be done without prompting. Despite all this, he failed in school. These children wish to return to a former age when the satisfaction of their needs was the responsibility of parents. At the core of the child's clinical picture is a vivid fantasy life, epitomized by the Peter Pan theme, which enables the child to resolve internal and external conflicts through imagined magical powers.

In the typical family pattern of boys with dependent personality disorder, the mother exercises covert power in the family and rewards the child's failure in controlling, seductive, and unwittingly ways (Peck and Stackhouse 1973). The father does not participate in growth-producing experiences with his child and depreciates the child's abilities. Although appearing dominant, he typically lacks self-confidence and is easily manipulated by his wife and children. The boys are in competition with their father for their mother's attention. The sons submit helplessly to their mothers and sacrifice themselves to their fathers through appearing nonthreatening, but they covertly achieve an "Oedipal victory" through shaming their fathers. A reverse family pattern of an "Electra victory" is seen with girls. The girls are in competition with their mothers, whom they shame, for their father's attention, which they seek through helplessness.

The aim of treatment with the dependent child is achieving independent responsibility for oneself. This usually is a difficult therapeutic task because of the unconscious family dynamics. The principal target is the infantile magical hero fantasy, which permits the child smugly to expect the care of others. In addition to family therapy, marital couple therapy may be necessary to unravel the parental dynamics that contribute to the child's Oedipal or Electra victory. When the parents relinquish their overprotectiveness and reduce the rewards for helplessness, behavioral techniques that desensitize the child to the fear of age-appropriate responsibilities and provide rewards for assuming personal responsibility can be used. A useful aphorism is that to become responsible as an adult at 21, a child should be one-third responsible at age seven and two-thirds responsible at age 14 (Finch and Green 1979). Psychotherapy can focus on exposing the child's fears of aggressive impulses and of growing up.

Case Example

An eight-year-old girl in the third grade was referred because of her failure to turn in schoolwork, forgetfulness, tardiness, general ineptitude, and enuresis. Although she was of high average intelligence, her teachers thought that she performed academically as though she were mildly mentally retarded.

The overall course of treatment encompassed two years and involved family therapy, marital couple therapy, and individual psychotherapy with the girl. Family therapy disclosed a pattern in which the child literally had to be reminded to carry out each routine of daily living. Her parents believed that if they did not prod her and at times do things for her, she would be incapable of doing anything. They believed that she was brain damaged because of febrile seizures during infancy. Her father dominated the household and pampered his daughter, and her mother curried his favor while overprotecting her daughter.

After six months of family therapy, an intervening four-month course of marital couple therapy was necessary to shift the parents' displacement of their own marital problems on their daughter. They were helped to see how her Electra victory resulted from their permitting her to immobilize her mother and gain her father's attention through helplessness. Family therapy then could deal with the self-fulfilling prophesy in which the child was realizing her parents' picture of her as helpless and ineffective. The parents began to permit their daughter to experience the consequences of their relinquishing control over her life. She kept her own record of achievements, at first at the level of simply dressing and toileting. Bell-and-pad biofeedback training eliminated her enuresis. As her daughter improved, her mother became depressed, and marital couple therapy was resumed.

In individual psychotherapy, the girl revealed her wish to remain a young child because she feared growing up and assuming responsibility for herself. As she gradually overcame her fear of success, she began to experience satisfaction in personal mastery and achievement in school. By the fifth grade, she was able to perform at a superior level in school.

Summary

Although the use of personality disorder diagnoses with children has been questioned, defining a group of immature personality disorders has value because of their prevalence in clinical populations and their treatment implications.

The immature personality disorders are defined by their manipulative interpersonal manifestations rather than by neurotic symptoms, bizarre behaviors, or basic character defects. They reflect the persistence of immature behavior patterns. Complaints are registered by parents, teachers, siblings, and peers about these children rather than by the children themselves. Because of their personal, family, and social roots, the treatment of personality disorders usually involves individual, family, and educational system levels. The parents are central figures in the treatment process.

Children with immature personality disorders fall short of assuming age-appropriate responsibility for their lives. The oppositional child automatically resists adult influence and needs to achieve individuation as an autonomous person. The passive-aggressive child sabotages adult influence and needs to develop channels for sublimating aggressive impulses. The narcissistic child feels entitled to complete effortless gratification and needs to develop the capacity for empathy in reciprocal human relationships. The dependent child clings to caretaking by adults and needs to achieve independent responsibility for oneself.

The general treatment approach for children with immature personality disorders is to devise a strategy that focuses on target traits and fantasies in the child and pathologic interactions in their families. In so doing, the techniques of family, behavioral, and child psychotherapy are employed over extended periods of time. Because these children frequently underachieve in school, coordination with school personnel of psychiatric treatment and identification and remediation of coexisting educational disabilities is essential to their successful treatment.

Chapter 90

Identity Disorder

The syndrome designated as identity disorder takes its origin from the seminal writings of Erik Erikson (1950, 1956, 1968), who developed the concept of identity formation as the central task of adolescence. He described this elusive concept in the following manner:

> The wholeness to be achieved at this stage I have called a sense of inner identity. The young person, in order to experience wholeness, must feel a progressive continuity between that which he has come to be during the long years of childhood and that which he promises to become in the anticipated future; between that which he conceives himself to be and that which he perceives others to see in him and to expect of him . . . . Identity is a unique product, which now meets a crisis to be solved only in new identifications with age mates and with leader figures outside the family. (Erikson 1968, p. 87)

If a failure of identity formation should occur, the young person may experience an acute identity diffusion. Signs of such a crisis include a loss of time perspective, isolation, paralyzing self-doubt, work inhibition, role fixation, and sexual identity confusion.

There is a large conceptual leap from identity diffusion as explicated by Erikson to that of identity disorder, as described by DSM-III-R (American Psychiatric Association 1987). Clinicians have found Erikson's formulations to be extraordinarily helpful in understanding both normal adolescent processes and psychopathology. In essence, the inclusion of identity disorder in DSM-III (American Psychiatric Association 1980) signified an attempt to transform Erikson's dynamic conceptualizations of a commonly seen state of adolescent disturbance, acute identity diffusion, into a psychiatric syndrome definable by objective descriptive characteristics. How successful this attempt has been is not yet clear.

It must be remembered that identity disorder was designated as a distinct diagnostic entity only in 1980 with the publication of DSM-III, and therefore systematic, empirical study of this disorder is virtually nonexistent. One study suggested that it is a fairly common disorder: Stangler and Printz (1980) found a prevalence of 3.8 percent among a college sample of 500 students. They noted that it was twice as common in females as in males.

Normal Development

The clinical syndrome identity disorder is closely related to the normal developmental processes of mid- and late-adolescence and cannot be understood separately from them. There appear to be two major tasks during this phase of the life cycle. One task is to accelerate markedly the process of separation-individuation from parents: although this has been a continuous unfolding since infancy, it takes on new immediacy in adolescence (Blos 1975). The other task is the consolidation of a separate, distinct ego identity, the core of which involves a reorganization of the self-system and its internal self- and object-representations.

A confluence of forces joins at adolescence that demands that there be a major structural realignment of the self, the successful completion of which is epitomized by the emergence of a distinct individual identity prepared for the challenges of young adulthood and beyond. The striking physical and sexual changes that the adolescent experiences hardly need to be remarked on. Suffice it to say that such changes alone would require an important restructuring of the self, particularly in the domains of self and body image and impulse control. Other changes, more subtle and not as visibly arresting to the observer, also exert an impact of major proportions. For instance, only in adolescence do individuals become capable of formal operations in the Piagetian sense. This maturational step allows abstract thinking to arise for the first time: the young person can now reflect deeply about the self and significant others and his or her potential future. As a corollary of this cognitive gain, moral principles are now open to reconsideration and a shift from the law-and-order mentality of childhood to that of transcendent moral values as the ultimate determinate of actions becomes possible. Compounding the entire process, the adolescent is required to undergo these transformations within the context of our ever-changing society in which a multitude of competing value systems, behaviors, and lifestyles are offered for emulation. Moreover, too little is given in the way of support and direction.

In normal development, the passage from childhood into adolescence and young adulthood will require a significant revision of the self-system. Blos (1984) pointed out the need of the adolescent to rework or discard faulty childhood internalizations while retaining healthy, adaptive identifications and idealizations. In addition, new self-structures based on present positive experiences have to be elaborated, whether derived from an awareness of one's own developing competencies, valued perceptions of sympathetic age mates, or the idealization of worthy adult figures. Dashef (1984) called these emergent, adult-adaptive self-structures that form the building blocks of identity, as it were, "recombinant identifications," signifying their roots in the past of childhood, the present of adolescence, and a hoped-for future adulthood.

Certain pivotal structures of the self will particularly be in need of major overhaul. For instance, the childhood superego is categorical and restrictive in comparison to the adult superego. It is not a reliable guide in the healthy expression of impulse life, whether directly or in a sublimated fashion, nor does it aid in the setting of realistic self-expectations and goals. In other words, control must be wrested from the superego and placed at the disposal of the restructuring, reality-based ego; as gratifications move from superego to ego control, there is a growth in the capacity to regulate self-esteem internally (Josselson 1980).

Ego integration occurs with the reworking of inadequate parental identifications and idealizations that hinder the young person in meeting the tasks of adolescence. The goal of this sifting and restructuring is to gain some distance from the internalized parents (i.e., to transcend infantile object ties) (Josselson 1980). Because of the advent of formal operations, the adolescent is now able to objectify and rework the inner object world. As the ego is freed from its childhood origins, it grows in its synthetic power and exhibits a new capacity to resolve opposing feelings, thoughts, and identifications (Dashef 1984). In concert with this ego restructuring, there will be the slow emergence of higher level defensive operations (e.g., anticipation, altruism, sublimation, suppression) that, on balance, are less concerned with warding off unbidden mental contents and more directed at coping with external reality.

The work of Kohut (1971, 1977) alerted clinicians to the need for early narcissistic structures such as the grandiose self-image and idealized parental image to be similarly transformed at adolescence. With the success of this process, childish grandiosity yields to realistic ambition, and the need to idealize others is ultimately transfigured into sustaining values and ideals.

In the majority of adolescents, the restructuring of the self and the emergence of a cohesive identity takes place slowly over time in a silent, piecemeal process. Why then do some adolescents experience identity diffusion and others do not? A convincing answer to this question is supplied by the signal research of Offer and Offer (1975), who studied the developmental course of modal adolescents from their high school years into young adulthood. It appears that a tumultuous course is one of three identifiable normal routes through adolescence. Their research suggests that a tumultuous route, in contrast to a smooth or continuous route, is largely a function of an unfavorable genetic and environmental background. For instance, the tumultuous group demonstrated the following characteristics: history of mental illness in the family; overt, long-standing marital conflict; major traumatic events in childhood such as death, illnesses, separations, and parental divorce; poor parent-adolescent relationships; and a sense that previous developmental stages had not been adequately mastered. In contrast, the continuous group had been blessed. They showed a pattern of intact nuclear families, good parent-child relationships, an absence of stressful or upsetting life events in their history, and a strong identification with their parents' values and ideals.

A cautionary note needs to be made with respect to the temptation to equate the tumultuous growth group of Offer and Offer (1975) with a frankly identity-disordered clinical population. There are similarities and differences. Subjects were selected for inclusion in the Offers' longitudinal study on the basis of modal adjustment at age 14; a conscious attempt was made to exclude those who demonstrated extraordinarily good or poor adjustment. However, with the passage of time, the tumultuous group was noted to traverse adolescence with much distress and the development of overt behavioral problems at home and school. Thus, while it would be imprudent on the part of clinicians simply to equate the two groups, it would not seem unreasonable to suppose that the tumultuous group is at risk to develop identity disorder. Clearly, there is a pressing need to study identity-disordered populations systemically in their own right.

In summary, what is being suggested is that identity disorder is a behavioral-symptomatic referent for the critical failure to reorganize the self-system, a normative task of adolescence. Because of previous adverse life experiences that result in faulty and distorted internalizations, some adolescents are handicapped in this process and at risk to become identity disordered. However, adolescence per se does provide an unparalleled opportunity to reorder the self-system, and, in so doing, to formulate a coherent identity on which succeeding life phases can be built.

Clinical Presentation

Table 1 lists the DSM-III-R diagnostic criteria for identity disorder. The central feature is the inability to reconcile diverse aspects of the self into a relatively integrated and acceptable sense of self. Because of the inability to achieve a coherent self, these young people suffer significant subjective distress and/or impairment in social or occupational functioning. The patient seems to be plaintively asking the questions "Who am I?" and "What should I do with my life?"

DSM-III-R does not mention the importance of pressing environmental factors in precipitating identity disorder. Erikson (1956) noted that acute identity diffusion usually becomes manifest in response to environmental challenges for greater physical

---

Table 1. DSM-III-R Diagnostic Criteria for Identity Disorder

A. Severe subjective distress regarding uncertainty about a variety of issues relating to identity, including three or more of the following:

    (1) long-term goals
    (2) career choice
    (3) friendship patterns
    (4) sexual orientation and behavior
    (5) religious identification
    (6) moral value systems
    (7) group loyalties

B. Impairment in social or occupational (including academic) functioning as a result of the symptoms in A.

C. Duration of the disturbance of at least three months.

D. Occurrence not exclusively during the course of a Mood Disorder or of a psychotic disorder, such as Schizophrenia.

E. The disturbance is not sufficiently pervasive and persistent to warrant the diagnosis of Borderline Personality Disorder.

intimacy, decisive occupational choice, vigorous competition with peers, and greater psychosocial self-definition. Therefore, any number of life events and challenges will initiate the disorder: moving away from home, parental divorce, stiff academic competition, entry into an intimate relationship, graduation and the choice of the first "real" job, and so on. Obviously, the single, uniting thread is that the person is faced with a serious psychosocial challenge, a challenge that will demand a new level of adaptation on his or her part if it is to be successfully met. The majority of young people are able to negotiate such challenges without experiencing an identity diffusion. Others, who have not been so favored by constitution, family circumstances, or life experiences, will succumb to an identity breakdown.

Two case vignettes will be employed to illustrate the presentation of identity disorder at initial clinical assessment.

Case 1

Gerri, a 21-year-old white, single female, sought help at a university health service during her senior year. She complained of feeling "depressed and alienated." Gerri had spent the previous summer overseas. While she had found travel to be a carefree and stimulating experience, her return to campus was accompanied by a growing sense of confusion and self-doubt. Her approaching graduation was bearing down heavily on her; she had been unable to formulate any postcommencement plan that seemed remotely satisfactory to her. She was intensely ambivalent about her boyfriend, Tom, whom she had dated steadily since her freshman year. She was quite unclear as to whether the relationship should continue. Although Gerri had a wide social circle at school, a growing sense of alienation characterized her friendships. She felt that a number of "close" friends had repeatedly taken advantage of her during college. Her growing cynicism frightened Gerri, who was a highly affiliative person.

Gerri's academic performance had been stellar; as a result, she had a wide variety of options available to her postgraduation, but she was unable to decide on one or the other. She considered entering graduate school, or working in her hometown or a far distant city, or traveling in Europe and spending the next year "on the loose." A quandary of the same magnitude surrounded her relationship with Tom. At the first interview, she spontaneously expressed her sense that she felt emotionally trapped by him much as she did in her nuclear family during high school. On the one hand, she feared making a deeper commitment lest she should curtail her freedom; on the other hand, she doubted that she could bear the aloneness if she were to end the relationship. Undeniably compounding her confusion were the strikingly different cultural and religious backgrounds that they brought to the relationship. Her parents had tacitly disapproved of her dating Tom, hoping that it represented a phase. To the interviewer, she seemed neither able to comply happily with nor to defy successfully her parents.

Gerri's family history was, of course, extremely helpful in understanding her present dilemma. Her family was an American success story: her grandparents were born into poverty in Northern Italy, and her father had transformed a small family business into a large corporate enterprise. In the process of rapid "Americanization," the inevitable conflicts around values, loyalties, and religious identifications had been felt by Gerri and her family. It was a family group in flux on many levels and contradictory imperatives had taken their toll on the parents' marriage, which Gerri described as rocky. The mother was an emotional person who had tried to mold Gerri to suit her own unfulfilled wishes. She had high expectations for her daughter and had pushed her toward conventionally defined success in a number of areas. Gerri had grudgingly complied but derived little satisfaction from her efforts. The father was described as a passive and detached man preoccupied with work throughout her childhood. Gerri had been habitually caught in a triangular situation: the father acting as her supporter and the mother as her critic.

A course of psychotherapy was recommended. It was clear that Gerri needed help in defining whom she was and what she wanted. Another important focus of work was the reworking of her harsh superego. There was a strong internal constraint against taking the initiative and directly asserting herself. Such a prospect filled her with doubt and guilt. This was one of the several important factors that contributed to her paralysis in coming to grips with the important decisions facing her.

Case 2

Gordon, a 17-year-old high school student, asked to see a psychiatrist on the first anniversary of his parents' separation. By his account he had never recovered from this experience. He complained of depression, alienation from his family, uncertainty about his future, and periodic abuse of alcohol and marijuana. His family appeared to be a collection of volatile, intense individuals, and his parents' marriage had been far from tranquil. Still, the preeminent value that the parents had espoused over the years was one of loyalty: that the family stayed together no matter what their differences. Thus, when the unexpected breakup occurred, Gordon experienced it as a severe traumatic disillusionment. He said, "When the illusion of family unit crumbled, I did too." His own internal life reflected his perplexity about whether to identify or disidentify with characteristics of his parents. For example, a few months after the separation, he precipitately ended a relationship with a girlfriend who had a personality similar to his mother's. In relation to his college plans, Gordon was obsessed with whether to pursue a course of study in engineering (his father's profession) or in the fine arts (his mother's interest). His own sense of consistency and continuity had been shattered by the parental separation. He complained forthrightly that there seemed to be no way he could reconcile his past and present into a workable, rewarding future.

Differential Diagnosis

Differential diagnosis is important in determining if a given clinical picture is actually an identity disorder or one of a number of conditions that resemble it in one aspect or another. Feinstein (1980) contended that diagnostic reassessment is required if an identity disorder lasts longer than a year because the natural course of this condition is usually a matter of months, not years. His statement highlights the importance of diagnostic assessment both at presentation and on a continuing basis during the course of treatment.

According to DSM-III-R, identity disorder must be distinguished from normal conflicts associated with maturing, such as "midlife crisis" or "adolescent turmoil." By definition, normal developmental conflicts are not associated with severe subjective distress or significant impairment in occupational and social functioning as is required for the diagnosis of identity disorder. Identity disorder must also be differentiated from disturbances on the schizophrenic spectrum (i.e., schizophrenia, schizoaffective disorder, and schizophreniform disorder). Although all the schizophrenic conditions manifest pronounced perplexity about the self, they are set apart from identity disorder by severe disturbance in the content and form of thought and the breakdown of reality testing. Identity-disordered patients often display mild anxiety and depression, but these features are not of sufficient severity or duration to meet criteria for an affective or anxiety disorder. Of course, some patients will warrant concurrent identity disorder and other psychiatric diagnoses.

In practice, the most difficult distinctions are faced when attempting to sort out identity disorder from borderline personality disorder and adjustment reactions. Disturbance of identity is central to both identity disorder and borderline personality disorder, but in borderline conditions identity confusion is only one of several major areas of disturbance. Borderline patients invariably show such associated features as tense and unstable interpersonal relationships, which are often ended by traumatic disruptions, unpredictable and impulsive behaviors, extreme mood instability, angry outbursts, and chronic feelings of loneliness, emptiness, and boredom. In short, although identity perplexity is common to both conditions, extreme, brittle instability in a variety of realms—interpersonal, mood, affect, and behavior—is indicative of borderline disorder. The cardinal feature of adjustment reaction is a maladaptive reaction to an identifiable psychosocial stressor that occurs within three months of the onset of the stressor. In an adjustment reaction, there are minor disturbances noted in feeling, mood, conduct, or work productivity. Many cases of identity disorder share these characteristics, but major identity issues such as goals, values, loyalties, friendship patterns, and career choice are not at stake in adjustment disorders. Questions as "Who am I?" and "What do I want?" are not prominent in adjustment disorder; they are always present in identity disorder.

Of course, the severity of disturbance in identity disorder presents as a spectrum phenomena; there are mild, moderate, and severe cases. Milder cases most strongly resemble adolescent turmoil and adjustment reactions; severe cases are closely related to borderline personality disorder. A clear distinction between the two disorders may be impossible.

Treatment

Since identity disorder represents a failure in the normal adolescent task of restructuring the childhood self, treatment must be directed at facilitating the completion of this stalled process. Thus psychotherapy, which entails the influencing of the patient toward healthier modes of adaptation, is the treatment of choice. Most of the discussion will be given over to individual psychotherapy because this is the most widely employed treatment approach for identity disorder. A number of other modalities will be briefly touched on.

Individual Psychotherapy

It is generally accepted that a substantial percentage of identity disorders can be successfully treated in a brief therapy format. More extensive treatment is indicated in some cases, especially when serious character pathology or poor premorbid adjustment is a complicating factor. Feinstein (1980) stated that the natural course of identity disorder is, in general, rather benign and that it responds surprisingly well to simple support and acceptance. He stated that treatment should be aimed at the resolution of conflict rather than characterologic reconstruction. Implicit in his view is the assumption that the psychotherapist has an important ally: the natural developmental thrust of the adolescent toward identity formation. Therefore, the primary goal of therapy is to help overcome the internal obstacles that have resulted in a developmental derailment. Once the adolescent is "back on track," he or she may feel little need to continue treatment, its purpose having been served.

Psychotherapy is a clinical art informed by an accrued body of knowledge about human behavior and motivation. Although each psychotherapy is unique in its own right, it is possible to provide an overall orientation to the process and to delineate guiding principles. As a point of departure, it is useful to approach the psychotherapy of identity disorder from three orienting perspectives: what the therapist should bring to therapy, what the patient should bring, and what has to occur in the therapist-patient interaction for change to occur.

What should the therapist bring to the psychotherapeutic encounter? Naturally, there are a number of characteristics (e.g., caring, empathy, knowledge, perseverance, the capacity to set limits) that the therapist should bring to bear no matter what the disorder or the age of the patient. However, working with adolescents requires additional inclinations and skills. First and foremost, a therapist for this age group must genuinely like youth and feel the need to foster their growth. This wish to help and care for the next generation is an example of what Erikson (1950) called "generativity." Knowledge of the normal developmental processes that adolescents and youth undergo is also of vital importance. By having an age-specific model or norms in hand, it is possible to determine the degree of deviation; when a clear deviation is present, it will guide therapeutic interventions (Blos 1984). Therapists need to have an awareness of their own adolescence and to have worked through a healthy resolution of their own adolescent conflicts. In comparison to working with an adult-age group, there is general agreement that the therapist has to engage with the younger patient actively. Adolescents do not easily tolerate passivity or excessive silence on the part of the therapist.

Besides distress and dysfunction, patients should bring certain features that will allow the work to proceed. Meeks (1979) cited two patient characteristics that are paramount. First, the patients should be genuinely concerned and troubled about some aspect of their psychological function. They should also sense that the source of their trouble is at least partially internal. Adolescents who rely heavily on externalization as a key characterologic defense will prove to be difficult therapy cases. Second, patients should have some capacity to observe themselves and to report honestly their conscious feelings and thoughts. In a nutshell, the patients should be motivated to look into their internal world and to share it with the therapist to the best of their ability.

As Meeks (1971, 1979) so well stated, the cornerstone of a successful adolescent-therapist interaction is the emergence of a working or therapeutic alliance. Nicholi (1978) defined the therapeutic alliance as "those aspects of the therapist-patient relationship based on the patient's conscious and unconscious desire to cooperate with the therapist's efforts to help him" (p. 7). The establishment of such a relationship with the therapist is not an easy task. To do so means to enter into a dependent relationship with an adult when one of the major aims of adolescence is to become independent of such figures. Another potential impediment to the therapeutic alliance is the issue of physician allegiance. The adolescent may feel that the therapist ultimately works for the parents, not him or her, because they have chosen the therapist and are paying for the treatment. If there is indication of such an attitude, it should be brought into the open and the confidentiality of the sessions emphasized. Fortunately, these contradictions are not insurmountable but they do demand exquisite sensitivity and tact on the part of the therapist.

The therapeutic alliance furnishes a safe environment in which the necessary objectification of the inner object world can unfold. Furthermore, the alliance will allow the patient to use the therapist as a new object, at least for a sufficient period of time to permit the reorganization of the self-system. It will act as a supporting buttress to the patient during the often painful process of disidentification and de-idealization: a process that leaves the adolescent open to feelings of emptiness and estrangement until a new identity coalesces (Blos 1984). The best approach to the securing of a therapeutic alliance is the empathic, nonthreatening clarification of affective and ideational states in the here and now of treatment (Meeks 1979). This fosters the sense that the patient will be understood but not intruded on or manipulated by the therapist. As the therapist repeatedly makes accurate and empathic clarifications, the adolescent feels drawn to participation, and the necessary depth of relationship is achieved.

As the therapeutic alliance builds, the reworking of the self-structure and the formation of recombinant identifications on which the new identity will rest can begin. Naturally, the self-structure is a largely unconscious, silent entity. The issue then becomes how to raise the self-structure to the level of consciousness so that the doctor and patient can collaboratively approach it. A classic route is through the investigation of symptoms. For example, identity-disordered patients often suffer from an oppressive superego that leaves them paralyzed in relationship to self-initiated activity and mildly depressed. The therapist can then point out to the patient that the depression is a reflection of how hard and self-negating the patient is and that this surely must be explainable on the basis of childhood experience. When the patient has had the chance to objectify this negative, self-accusatory identification, the door is open to relinquishing or modifying it eventually.

Another route to gaining access to the self is through the investigation of peer relationships. At no other time in the life cycle do individuals relate so intensely to peers. It provides a fertile ground for psychotherapeutic work as early self- and object representations are dramatically played out in relationship to age mates. For instance, a young woman who finds herself, much to her dismay, pleading with her boyfriend to let her share in his emotional life, realizes that this is a reenactment of a pattern earlier established with her distant father.

The analysis of transference is another means of uncovering the self-system. However, such an ambitious effort is obviously precluded within the context of a brief therapeutic approach. There is also general pessimism about the value of focusing heavily on the analysis of the transference, particularly its genetic reconstruction, in the adolescent age group. Adatto (1966) spoke for many when he contended that the narcissistic adsorption of this period is so great that it is difficult to get a fully actualized transference. Moreover, too avid attention to transference manifestations in the treatment of identity disorder may be construed by the adolescent as a threatening, highly disruptive experience, with the result a flight from treatment. To make an important distinction, it almost always enhances the therapy to investigate feelings and thoughts about the therapist as they emerge in the here and now, but caution has to be exerted with respect to tying them repeatedly and insistently to distorted childhood experiences as the primary focus of work.

The management of resistance has not been previously mentioned. Of course, before the therapist can assist in the restructuring of the self, resistance to the demonstration, clarification, and working through of the inner object world must be dealt with. This will not be such a difficult undertaking if the resistance consists of relatively mobile defensive operations of a basically strong ego. The ego can be enlisted in the analysis of the defenses that often represent identifications with early objects. The situation is made vastly more complex when the ego is relatively weak and has fortified itself with a rigid, deeply ingrained character armor. The focus of work must then switch to the analysis of character in its transference and extra-transference manifestations. This will very much lengthen the course of treatment. A characterologic reorganization will have to occur hand in hand with restructuring of the self.

Other Treatment Approaches

Hospitalization is rarely warranted in the case of identity disorder. If a deteriorating course or disabling symptomatology should require a hospital setting, the patient needs to be reassessed from a diagnostic point of view. In such circumstances, there is likely a concurrent psychiatric disorder (e.g., major depressive episode, drug and alcohol abuse, borderline personality) that accounts for the clinical deterioration. If this is so, the treatment plan needs to be shifted to manage the more serious, overriding disorder immediately. Medication plays a minor role, at most, in the treatment of this condition. However, it can be useful in alleviating associated symptomatology (e.g., anxiety, sleep disturbance) that arises during periods of acute stress. Behavior therapy has little to offer in identity disorder because the essential feature of the disturbance (i.e., the inability to reconcile diverse aspects of the self into a coherent whole) is not amenable to behavioral techniques.

In contrast, family and group psychotherapies have a clear-cut place in the treatment of identity-disordered adolescents and young adults. While the primary locus of work in family therapy is ongoing relational difficulties, the effect is similar to what occurs in individual therapy: the young person experiences differentiation from his or her parents, and the process of identity formation is enhanced. In many cases, individual and family therapy can be profitably combined. As Brockbank (1980) noted, group therapy depends on the inherent proclivity of youth to act out important internal conflicts in relationship to peers; the resourceful therapist then acts to turn this predisposition to the processes of growth.

Whatever the psychotherapeutic approach, what are some indications that the goals of treatment have been reached? First among many are signs that the young person is more able to sustain commitment to others and to self-chosen values and ideals. For instance, adolescents may enter into a new heterosexual relationship that is conspicuous by its lack of tumultuous interactions, or they may find the energy and direction to undertake new educational or occupational challenges. They will not be plagued by the paralyzing self-doubt so typical of identity disorder. Associated symptoms such as anxiety and depression will have been alleviated, or at least markedly diminished. Supported by a more cohesive identity, they will be prepared to join their peers in searching out interpersonal and occupational niches for themselves in the adult world.

References

Section 10
Other Disorders of Infancy, Childhood, or Adolescence

Achenback TM: DSM-III in light of empirical research on the classifications of child psychopathology. J Am Acad Child Psychiatry 19:395–412, 1980

Adatto C: On the metamorphosis from adolescence into adulthood. J Am Psychoanal Assoc 14:485–509, 1966

Ambrosino SV, Alessi M: Elective mutism: fixation and the double bind. Am J Psychoanalysis 39:3, 251–256, 1979

American Psychiatric Association: Diagnostic and Statistical Manual of Mental Disorders, 2nd ed. Washington, DC, American Psychiatric Association, 1968

American Psychiatric Association: Diagnostic and Statistical Manual of Mental Disorders, 3rd ed. Washington, DC, American Psychiatric Association, 1980

American Psychiatric Association: Diagnostic and Statistical Manual of Mental Disorders (3rd ed.-revised). Washington, DC, American Psychiatric Association, 1987

Asperger H: Die Autitsischen Psychopathe in Kindesalter. Arch Psychiat Nervhranth 117:76–137, 1944

Barbero G: Failure to Thrive in Maternal Attachment and Mothering Disorders. Pediatric Round Table: 1, 2nd ed. Edited by Klaus M, Leger T, Trause M. New Brunswick, NJ, Johnson & Johnson, 1982

Barker P: Basic Child Psychiatry, 4th ed. Baltimore, University Park Press, 1983, pp. 252–255

Berkowitz DA: The borderline adolescent and the family, in Family Therapy and Major Psychopathology. Edited by Lansky MR. New York, 1981, pp 183–201

Blos P: The second individuation process of adolescence, in The Psychology of Adolescence. Edited by Esman A. New York, International Universities Press, 1975

Blos P: The contribution of psychoanalysis to the psychotherapy of adolescents, in Adolescent Psychiatry, vol 11. Edited by Sugar M. Chicago, University of Chicago Press, 1984

Bowlby J: Attachment and Loss, vol 1: Attachment. New York, Basic Books, 1973a

Bowlby J: Attachment and Loss, vol 2: Separation—Anxiety and Anger. New York, Basic Books, 1973b

Bowlby J: Attachment and Loss, vol 3: Loss—Sadness and Depression. New York, Basic Books, 1980

Bowlby J: Attachment and loss: retrospect and prospect. Am J Orthopsychiatry 52:664–677, 1982

Bradley S, Sloman L: Elective mutism in immigrant families. J Am Acad Child Psychiatry 14:510–514, 1975

Brockbank R: Adolescent psychodynamics and the therapy group, in Adolescent Psychiatry, vol 8. Edited by Feinstein S, Giovacchini P, Looney J, et al. Chicago, University of Chicago Press, 1980

Brown JB, Lloyd L: A controlled study of children not speaking at school. Journal of the Association of Workers of Maladjusted Children, pp 49–63, 1975

Browne E, Wilson V, Laybourne PC: Diagnosis and treatment of elective mutism in children. J Am Acad Child Psychiatry 2:605–617, 1963

Carey W: Some Pitfalls in Infant Temperament Research: Annual Progress in Child Psychiatry and Child Development. New York, Brunner/Mazel, 1985

Casey PJ, Bradley R, Wortham B: Social and nonsocial home environments of infants with nonorganic failure-thrive. Pediatrics 73:348–353, 1984

Chess, S, Thomas A: Infant bonding: mystique and reality. Am J Orthopsychiatry 52:48–62, 1982

Chethik M: Amy: the intensive treatment of an elective mute. J Am Acad Child Psychiatry 12:482–498, 1980

Conrad RD, Delk JL, Williams C: Use of stimulus fading procedures in the treatment of situation specific mutism: a case study. Behavior Therapy and Experimental Psychiatry 5:99–100, 1974

Croghan LM, Craven R: Elective mutism: learning from the analysis of a successful case history. J Pediatr Psychol 7:85–93, 1982

Cull A, Chick J, Wolff S: A consensual validation of schizoid personality in childhood and adult life. Br J Psychiatry 144:646–648, 1984

Dashef SS: Aspects of identification and growth during late adolescence and young adulthood. Am J Psychother 38:239–247, 1984

DeChateau P: Parent-neonatal interaction and its long term effects, in Early Experiences and Early Behavior. Edited by Simmel EC. New York, Academic Press, 1980

Egeland B, Vaughn B: Failure of "bond formation" as a cause of abuse, neglect and maltreatment. Am J Orthopsychiatry 51:78–84, 1981

Erikson EH: Childhood and Society. New York, WW Norton & Co, 1950

Erikson EH: The problem of ego identity. J Am Psychoanal Assoc 4:56–121, 1956

Erikson EH: Identity: Youth and Crisis. New York, WW Norton & Co, 1968

Evans SL, Reinhart JB, Succop RA: Failure-to-thrive: a study of 45 children and their families. J Am Acad Child Psychiatry 11:440–457, 1972

Fanaroff A: Followup of low birth weight infants: the predictive value of maternal visiting patterns. Pediatrics 49:288–290, 1970

Feinstein SC: Identity and adjustment disorders of adolescence, in Comprehensive Textbook of Psychiatry, 3rd ed, vol 3. Edited by Kaplan HI, Freedman AM, Sadock BJ. Baltimore, Williams & Wilkins Co, 1980

Finch SM, Green JM: Personality disorders, in Basic Handbook of Child Psychiatry. Edited by Noshpitz JD. New York, Basic Books, 1979

Fischhoff J, Whitten CF, Pettit M: A psychiatric study of mothers of infants with growth failure secondary to maternal deprivation. J Pediatr 79:209–215, 1971

Fraiberg S, Adelson E, Shapiro V: Ghosts in the nursery: a psychoanalytic approach to the problems of impaired infant-mother relationships. J Am Acad Child Psychiatry 14:387–421, 1975

Frances A: The DSM-III personality disorders section: a commentary. Am J Psychiatry 137:9, 1980

Gilpin DC, Maltz P: The oppositional personality in childhood. Child Psychiatry Hum Devel 11:79–86, 1980

Goldstein SJ, Dyche L: Family of the schizophrenic poor, in Family Therapy in Schizophrenia. Edited by McFarlane WR. New York, Guilford Press, 1983, pp 289–307

Goll K: Role structure and subculture in families of elective mutists. Fam Process 18:55–68, 1979

Group for the Advancement of Psychiatry: Psychopathological Disorders in Childhood: Theoretical Considerations and a Proposed Classification. New York, Group for Advancement of Psychiatry, 1966

Group for the Advancement of Psychiatry: The Process of Child Therapy. New York, Group for the Advancement of Psychiatry, 1982

Halpern WI, Hammond J, Cohen R: A therapeutic approach to speech phobic elective mutism reexamined. J Am Acad Child Psychiatry 10:95–105, 1971

Hayden TL: Classification of elective mutism. J Am Acad Child Psychiatry 19:118–133, 1980

Heimlich EP: Patient as assistant therapist in paraverbal therapy with children. Am J Psychother 35:262–267, 1981

Helfer RE, Kempe CH: Child Abuse and Neglect: The Family and the Community. Cambridge, Mass, Ballinger, 1976

Herbert M, Sluckin W: Mother-to-infant "bonding." J Child Psychol Psychiatry 23:205–221, 1982

Jones FA, Green V, Krauss DR: Maternal reponsiveness of primi-parous mothers during the postpartum period: age differences. Pediatrics 65:579–584, 1980

Josselson R: Ego development in adolescence, in Handbook of Adolescent Psychology. Edited by Adelson J. New York, John Wiley & Sons, 1980

Kemp CH: Approaches to preventing child abuse: the health visitor concept. Am J Dis Child 130:941–947, 1976

Klaus M, Kennell J: Parent-infant bonding, 2nd ed. St. Louis, CV Mosby Co, 1982

Klein M, Stern L: Low birth weight and the battered child syndrome. Am J Dis Child 122:15–18, 1971

Kohut H: The Analysis of the Self. New York, International Universities Press, 1971

Kohut H: The Restoration of the Self. New York, International Universities Press, 1977

Kolvin I, Fundudis T: Elective mute children: psychological development and background factors. J Child Psychol Psychiatry 22:219–232, 1981

Kotelchuck M, Newberger E: Failure to thrive: a controlled study of familial characteristics. J Am Acad Child Psychiatry 22:322–353, 1984

LaVietes RL: Schizoid Disorder, in Comprehensive Textbook of Psychiatry, 3rd ed, vol 3. Edited by Kaplan HI, Freedman AM, Sadock BJ. Baltimore, Williams & Wilkins, 1980

Laybourne PC: Elective mutism, in Basic Handbook of Child Psychiatry. Edited by Nosphitz JD. New York, Basic Books, 1979, p. 475

Leib SA, Benfield DG, Grudubaldi J: Effects of early intervention and stimulation on the preterm infant. Pediatrics 66:83–90, 1980

Levy D: Oppositional syndromes and oppositional behavior, in Psychopathology of Childhood. Edited by Hoch PH, Zubin J. New York, Grune & Stratton, 1955

Lovaas OI, Berberich JP, Perloff BG, et al: Acquisition of imitative speech by schizophrenic children. Science 151:705–707, 1966

Mallinger AE: Demand sensitive obsessionals. J Am Acad Psychoanal 10:406–426, 1982

McFarlane WR: Multiple family therapy in schizophrenia, in Family Therapy in Schizophrenia. Edited by McFarlane WR. New York, Guilford Press, 1983, pp 141–172

McIntyre PM: Dynamics and treatment of the passive-aggressive underachiever. Am J Psychother 28:95–108, 1964

Meeks JE: The Fragile Alliance. Baltimore: Williams & Wilkins Co, 1971

Meeks JE: The therapeutic alliance in the psychotherapy of adolescents, in The Short Course of Adolescent Psychiatry. Edited by Novello J. New York, Brunner/Mazel, 1979

Meijer A: Elective mutism in children. Israel Annals of Psychiatry and Related Disciplines 17:93–100, 1979

Meissner SJ: Notes on the potential differentiation of borderline conditions. Int J Psychoanal Psychother 83:3–49, 1982/1983

Meyer SV: Elective mutism in children: a family systems approach. American Journal of Family Therapy 12:39–45, 1984

Minde K, Morton P, Manning D, et al.: Some determinants of mother-infant interaction in the premature nursery. J Am Acad Child Psychiatry 19:1–21, 1980

Mora G, Devault S, Schopler E: Dynamics and psychotherapy of identical twins with elective mutism. J Child Psychoanal Psychiatry 3:41–52, 1962

Nemiah JC, Sifneos P: Psychosomatic illness: a problem in communication. Psychother Psychosom 18:154–160, 1970

Nicholi AM: The therapist-patient relationship, in Harvard Guide to Modern Psychiatry. Edited by Nicholi AM. Cambridge, Mass, Belknap Harvard, 1978

Norman A, Broman HJ: Volume feedback and generalization techniques in shaping speech of an electively mute boy: a case study. Percept Mot Skills 31:463–470, 1970

Noshpitz JD: Narcissism and aggression. Am J Psychother 38:17–34, 1984

O'Connor S, Vietze PM, Sherrod KB, et al: Reduced incidence of parenting inadequacy following rooming-in. Pediatrics 66:176–182, 1980

Offer D, Offer JB: From Teenage to Young Manhood: A Psychological Study. New York, Basic Books, 1975

Ounsted C, Oppenheimer R, Lindsay J: Aspects of bonding failure: the psychopathology and psychotherapeutic treatment of families of battered children. Dev Med Child Neurol 16:447–456, 1974

Parsons RD, Wicks RJ (eds): Passive-Aggressiveness: Theory and Practice. New York, Brunner/Mazel, 1983

Patterson GR: Families: Applications of Social Learning to Family Life. Champaign, Ill, Research Press, 1976

Peck BB, Stackhouse TU: Reading problems and family dynamics. Journal of Learning Disorders 6:43–48, 1973

Perry JC, Flannery RB: Passive-aggressive personality disorder. J Nerv Ment Dis 170:164–173, 1982

Pine F: On the concept "borderline" in children: a clinical essay. Psychoanal Study Child 341–368, 1974

Pollitt E, Eichler AW, Chan C: Psychosocial development and behavior of mothers of failure-to-thrive children. Am J Orthopsychiatry 4:525–537, 1975

Pustrom E, Speers RW: Elective mutism in children. J Am Acad Child Psychiatry 3:287, 1964

Reed CF: Elective mutism in children: a reappraisal. J Child Psychol Psychiatry 4:99–107, 1963

Reich W: Character Analysis. New York, Noonday Press, 1949

Roberts B: Nonorganic failure to thrive: an analysis of mothers personalities and a measure of loss. Unpublished manuscript, dissertation research. Michigan State University, 1984

Robins LN: Deviant Children Grown Up. Baltimore, Williams & Wilkins, 1966

Robson KM, Kuman R: Delayed onset of maternal affection after childbirth. Br J Psychiatry 136:247–353, 1980

Rosenberg JB, Lindblad MB: Behavior therapy in a family context: treating elective mutism. Fam Process 17:77–82, 1978

Rothstein A: The Narcissistic Pursuit of Perfection. New York, International Universities Press, 1980

Rothstein A: The Structural Hypothesis: An Evolutionary Perspective. New York, International Universities Press, 1983

Rowe B: The Parent-Infant Growth Program: Annual Report. Pontiac, Mich, Family and Children Services of Oakland County, 1984

Rutter M: Maternal deprivation reconsidered. J Psychosom Res 16:241–250, 1972

Rutter M: Maternal deprivation, 1972–78: New findings, new concepts, new approaches. Child Dev 50:283–305, 1979

Rutter M: Maternal Deprivation Reassessed, 2nd ed. Middlesex, England, Penguin Books, 1981

Sandler J: Character traits and object relationships. Psychoanal Q 50:694–708, 1981

Scott DW: Asperger's syndrome and non-verbal communication: a pilot study. Psychol Med 15:683–687, 1985

Shapiro D: Neurotic Styles. New York, Basic Books, 1965

Simon R: Family therapy, in Comprehensive Textbook of Psychiatry, 4th ed. Edited by Kaplan HI, Sadock BJ. Baltimore, Williams & Wilkins, 1985

Spitz R: Hospitalization: an inquiry into the genesis of psychiatric conditions in early childhood. Psychoanal Study Child 1:53–74, 1946

Spitz R: Anaclictic depression. Psychoanal Study Child 2:313–342, 1947a

Spitz R: Hospitalism: a followup report. Psychoanal Study Child 2:113–117, 1947b

Stangler RS, Printz A: DSM-III: psychiatric diagnosis in a university population. Am J Psychiatry 137:937–940, 1980

Starr R, Dietrich KN, Fischhoff J: The contribution of children to their own abuse. Presented at the Society for Research in Child Development. Boston, April 1982

Starr R, Dietrich KN, Fischhoff J, et al: The contribution of handicapping conditions to child abuse. Topics in Early Childhood Special Education 4:55–70, 1984

Strain PS, Steele P, Ellis T, et al: Long-term effects of oppositional child treatment with mothers as therapists and therapist trainers. J Appl Behav Anal 15:163–169, 1982

Sugarman M: Parental influences on maternal-infant attachment. Am J Orthopsychiatry 47:407–421, 1977

Svejda M, Campos J, Ende R: Mother-infant "bonding": failure to generalize. Child Dev 51:775–779, 1980

Van Krevelan DA: Early infantile autism and autistic psychopathy. J Autism Child Schizophr 1:82–86, 1971

Wergeland H: Elective mutism. Acta Psychiatr Scand 59:218–228, 1979

Westman JC: Handbook of Learning Disabilities. New York, Gardner Press, 1989

Westman JC, Bennett TM: Learning impotence and the Peter Pan fantasy. Journal of Child Psychiatry and Human Development 15:153–166, 1985

Whitten CF, Pettit M, Fischhoff J: Evidence that growth failure from maternal deprivation is secondary to undereating. JAMA 209:1675–1682, 1969

Williams GF: Toward the eradication of child abuse and neglect at home, in Traumatic Abuse and Neglect of Children at Home. Edited by Williams GF, Money J. Baltimore, Johns Hopkins University Press, 1980

Wing L: Asperger's syndrome: a clinical account. Psychol Med 11:115–129, 1981

Winnicott DW: The Child, the Family and the Outside World. London, Tavistock Publications, 1957

Winnicott DW: Collected Papers: Through Pediatrics to Psychoanalysis. New York, Basic Books, 1958

Wolff S, Barlow A: Schizoid personality in childhood: a comparative study of schizoid, autistic and normal children. J Child Psychol Psychiatry 20:29–46, 1979

Wolff S, Chick J: Schizoid personality in childhood: a controlled follow-up study. Psychol Med 19:85–100, 1980

Zinn D: Hospital treatment of the adolescent, in Basic Handbook of Psychiatry. Edited by Noshspitz JD. New York, Basic Books, 1979, pp 263–288